WIT

D0426226

STALIN

THE MAN AND HIS ERA

Adam B. Ulam

Beacon Press   Boston

Beacon Press
25 Beacon Street
Boston, Massachusetts 02108–2800

Beacon Press books
are published under the auspices of
the Unitarian Universalist Association of Congregations.

05 04 03 02 01   9 8 7 6 5 4

Title page drawing by Robert W. Arnold

Library of Congress Cataloging-in-Publication Data
Ulam, Adam Bruno
Stalin: the man and his era.
Reprint. Originally published: New York: Viking Press,
1973.
Includes index.
1. Stalin, Joseph, 1879–1953.   2. Heads of state—
Soviet Union—Biography.   3. Revolutionists—Soviet
Union—Biography.   4. Soviet Union—History—1925–1953.
I. Title.
DK268.S8U4   1987   947.084′2′0924 [B]   89–42586
ISBN 0-8070-7005-X (pbk.)

Contents

Preface

"Like a dread spirit he hovered over us, to others we paid no heed," wrote a Soviet poet in 1960, referring to the man whose name until 1953 was synonymous with Soviet Russia and Communism. Even in his death Stalin hovers over contemporary Soviet reality. His memory is both a burden and a challenge to his successors and to the people over whom he reigned for more than a generation. What was the secret of his power, more absolute than that recorded of any ruler in history; of the unparalleled sufferings he was able to inflict upon his own society; of the unprecedented triumphs achieved by the Soviet Union under his leadership? And within the larger mystery there are special puzzles: why were countless innocent people sent, at his orders, to their doom; what is the explanation of the apparently mysterious events which preceded and followed his death?

Answers must be sought not only in the character and life of Stalin himself, but in the history of the movement and society in which his fantastic career unfolded and which he then succeeded in molding in his own image.

I want to acknowledge helpful hints I received from Professor Leonard Schapiro, of London, and Professor Edward Keenan, of Harvard. And I must also thank those who helped with my study: my research assistants Messrs. Sanford Lieberman and Christopher Jones, my secretaries Miss Mary Towle and Miss Elizabeth Mead. Elisabeth Sifton has been a rigorous and uncommonly patient editor.

Adam B. Ulam

The Russian Research Center
Harvard University
March 1973

Introduction to the Expanded Edition

It is not just a question of historical interpretation. As of this writing there is no political issue of greater importance in the Soviet Union than the significance of the man who has been dead for thirty-six years and the legacy he left to the people he ruled so masterfully and cruelly. With *perestroika*, Gorbachev and his partisans have attempted to undo the political and economic structure Joseph Stalin had erected over Soviet society, and which until very recently resisted all efforts at a basic reform. For the average Soviet citizen, if not for high Party dignitaries, *glasnost* has brought a veritable deluge of horrifying revelations about Stalinism.

And yet the problem of J. V. Stalin has not been laid to rest. Far from it. Every Soviet regime since 1953 has grappled with this problem (though none as resolutely as Gorbachev's). The first wave of de-Stalinization, under Khrushchev, dealt a definite blow to the legend, but it was far from successful in eliminating the dead despot's posthumous influence. Witness the poem by Yevtushenko printed in *Pravda* on October 21, 1962, "On Stalin's Heirs." Awful poetry, but a significant admission by Russia's most political rhymester: "No, Stalin has not given up. We threw him out of the Mausoleum, but how to root Stalin out of the minds of his heirs . . . who condemn Stalin from the platform, but at night pine for the old days. Evidently, not without reason do Stalin's heirs nowadays suffer heart attacks."

Stalin's ghost even helped defeat a live politician, when Nikita Khrushchev was overthrown in October 1964, one of the reasons being undoubtedly his excessive garrulity (as his Politburo colleagues saw it) about his one-time boss. De-Stalinization was muted (though not, as many had feared, reversed) during the "period of stagnation," as the present rulers refer to the Brezhnev reign. It was then resumed with great vigor under Gorbachev. The ending of a recent play by Michael Shatrov can be seen as symbolic of the dilemma which still faces Soviet society in connection with its longtime ruler and oppressor. Author of several theatrical productions designed to expose both Stalin and the Stalinist version of Soviet history, Shatrov, in *On . . . and on . . . and on,* evokes Lenin and the main figures of the October Revolution in a tribute to its maker and a strong condemnation of his successor. And, yet, witness the play's last moments:

> The personages leave the stage one after another in the same order they entered. Only Lenin, deep in reflection, stands in the center, looks at the hall, and is about to say something. All have left except for Stalin. Lenin waits . . . Stalin does not leave. And when the situation becomes really tense, Stalin cannot stand it anymore and breaks the silence.
> STALIN: I would like to talk with you, explain.
> LENIN (severely): There is nothing to talk about between us. (To the audience:) We must go on . . . and on . . . and on.
> (And so they remain at quite a distance from each other. One wishes Stalin would leave, but as yet he remains on the stage.)
> Curtain.[1]

"He remains on the stage. . . ." And along with him remain many questions about this fabulously unusual figure, unmatched in modern world history in terms of both the extent of the power he exercised and the character of his rule over his country and the entire Communist world. Most of the "revelations" about Stalin released within the last three years in the U.S.S.R. concern matters that were already known to Western observers and students of the Stalin era. And they will not come as a surprise to the readers of this book.

The political importance of the anti-Stalin campaign launched under *glasnost*, however, renders it of great interest to us as well as to the Soviets. Let us recall that not long prior to Gorbachev's assumption of power the regime occasionally tolerated attempts at a resuscitation (on a much more modest scale, to be sure, than before 1953) of the Stalin cult. A popular writer, Ivan Stadnyuk, included a fulsome eulogy of the tyrant in his book *War,* published in the 1970s. In general, as critical treatments of the pre-1953 era receded, positive ones, especially when it came to assessing Stalin's role during World War II, appeared more frequently. As time went on, one had the distinct impression that many in the Party's highest circles longed to shut and nail down

---

[1] *Znamya* (The banner) (Moscow), January 1988, pp. 1–54.

the Pandora's box so precipitously thrown open by Khrushchev. In 1984, Vyacheslav Molotov, probably the most important of Stalin's servants and accomplices, was restored to the Communist Party membership of which he had been stripped in 1961. This gesture could not be interpreted merely as one of forgiveness for an aged sinner (the former chairman of the Council of Commissars and foreign minister was ninety-four); it had to be understood as a conscious repudiation of Khrushchev's indictment of the tyrant and his main henchmen.

In March 1985, what could be called the era of invalids (Brezhnev visibly enfeebled during his last few years, Andropov and Chernenko clearly ailing already at their election as General Secretary) came to an end when Michael Gorbachev was elected head of the Party by the Politburo. Apart from his age, nothing could have suggested that the new leader would resume Khrushchev's struggle with Stalin's ghost, or otherwise try to shake up the Soviet establishment. He had been Party Secretary since 1978 and a full Politburo member since 1980. Why should he want to rock the boat?

It is still not clear what persuaded the General Secretary to launch his campaign of reform, or whether in 1985 he had a clear idea of how far he would go, or be driven within the next three years. To be sure, having been born in 1931, he had to have a perspective on Stalinism different from most of his Politburo colleagues, septuagenarians who had benefited from the purges in the 1930s by becoming important officials while still relatively young. In any case, Gorbachev soon associated himself with a group of reform-minded officials who had resented the *immobilisme* and corruption of the Brezhnev era. By 1986 *restructuring*, *openness*, and *acceleration* (in the economy) were the slogans of the new Kremlin team. *Perestroika*—restructuring—was first applied to the faltering Soviet economy, but it soon became evident to the leadership that the political structure had to be overhauled as well.

Essential to *perestroika* was the recognition that, even with Stalin gone and with all the efforts under Khrushchev, the institutional framework of Soviet society in 1985 was still Stalinist. Absolute rule by the Party, repression of dissent at home, expansion—by military means if need be—abroad, to mention only some of the most important facets of the Soviet regime, were a clear legacy from the Stalin era (even if, in some ways, as the reader will note later, they were influenced by developments under Lenin). On the economic side strict centralization of industrial planning and administration and, above all, collectivization of Soviet agriculture both went back to Stalin's time. By 1985, both of these practices, and especially the latter, were recognized as the main reason for the precarious state of the Soviet economy.

At the same time it would be churlish to ascribe the new Gorbachev course simply to political and economic calculations. If not Gorbachev himself, then some of his counsellors must have recognized that the economic slowdown, inefficiency, bureaucratic torpor, and corruption afflicting the Soviet system were symptoms of a deeper malaise. And in order to counteract that malaise and heal society the regime had to grant greater freedom and initiative to its citizens. That in turn required greater frankness about the past and a more resolute attack at Stalinism than under Khrushchev.

Gorbachev advanced quite warily in his campaign against Stalin's ghost. In May 1985, celebrating the fortieth anniversary of the victory in Europe, he still found it fitting to emphasize that this victory was achieved under the leadership of Joseph Stalin. By the end of 1986, the General Secretary telephoned the exiled academician Sakharov, offering him full freedom. In the context of Soviet reality, this was a clarion call for an end to the repression of dissidents and a harbinger of the coming campaign for democratization (not democracy) in the Soviet Union. And the main victim of this campaign was to be Stalin. The painstaking attempt by the regime following Khrushchev's fall to restore respectability to the dead tyrant, to portray him, no longer as a divinity, to be sure, but as a great statesman who "committed some errors," was now given up. There ensued a flood of memoirs, literary productions, historical appraisals, all painting a lurid picture of life in the U.S.S.R. under the rule of the "genius-like leader of all progressive mankind."

By the end of 1987, however, the official voice of the regime was not as yet unambiguous. Witness Gorbachev's keynote address at the celebrations of the seventieth anniversary of the October Revolution: "It is obvious that it was the absence of a proper degree of democratization of Soviet society that made possible the cult of personality and violations of the law, arbitrariness and repressions of the 1930s. To speak without euphemisms, those were transgressions arising out of an abuse of power."[2]

The reader of this book will be able to decide whether such a characterization of what went on in the 1930s is adequate. But then the General Secretary tackled more directly the subject of his dread predecessor: "There is now much discussion about the role of Stalin in our history. There were contradictory strains in his personality. . . . We must accept as *irrefutable* Stalin's contribution to the struggle for socialism and in defense of its achievements, just as we see the gross political errors and arbitrariness exhibited by him and his entourage for which our people paid so dearly. . . . Sometimes it is argued that

[2] Quoted in *Izvestia*, November 3, 1987.

xii

Stalin did not know about the violations of the laws. The documents which we have testify that he did. Stalin's guilt, as well as that of those close to him, is enormous and unpardonable, the guilt before the Party and the people for the mass repressions and lawlessness. Let it be a lesson for all generations."[3]

Stalin's "irrefutable contribution. . . ." Later on, Gorbachev was more specific: "Stalin played a great role. In the achievement of victory [in World War II]. Through his enormous political decisiveness, sense of purpose and persistence, through his gift to direct and *discipline* people. . . ."[4]

Gorbachev promised further investigation of the crimes and other phenomena of the era of the "cult of personality": "The process of restoring justice was not complete, and in fact was arrested in the middle of the 1960s. Now, in accordance with the decision of the October '86 Plenum of the Central Committee, we shall resume the investigations. The Politburo has appointed a commission which is to conduct an exhaustive study of new, as well as already known facts and documents bearing on those questions. . . . We shall draw appropriate conclusions from the commission's findings."[5]

Apart from his leadership in the war, Stalin's most significant and contentious achievement was the collectivization of agriculture—stupendous in its extent and human cost. Here again, Gorbachev's assessment of that fateful feat of social engineering, possibly as important in the lives of the Soviet people as World War II, was not clear cut. On the one hand, "today it is clear there were departures from Lenin's policy toward the peasants in that enormous reform which affected the fate of the majority of the population. The whole transformation involving that complex social problem, where so much depended on local circumstances, was carried out by mainly administrative methods. . . . There were gross violations of the principle of [voluntary] collectivization. . . . There were also some excesses in the struggle against the *kulaks*. . . ."[6]

As I shall show in the chapter on collectivization, "administrative methods" is a rather feeble euphemism for acts of violence and what was in fact the enslavement of an entire class, in the process of which millions lost their lives. And Gorbachev felt constrained to qualify even that mild criticism with a positive assessment: "But, comrades, if one has to estimate the overall role of collectivization in the strengthening of socialism in the countryside, then in the final analysis it is a

[3] *Ibid*. My italics.
[4] *Ibid*. My italics.
[5] *Ibid*.
[6] *Ibid*. My italics.

most important turning point. Collectivization meant a basic restructuring of the entire life of the mass of the population, placing it on a socialist basis. It created a social foundation for the modernization of the agrarian sector . . . made possible an increase in the productivity of labor."[7]

Yet, before those words were spoken, the General Secretary and his collaborators had already been working out plans to free Soviet agriculture at least partially from the deadening effects of state ownership and management which collectivization involved, plans that included licensing family farming, long-term leases to individual peasants, and other measures to restore private initiative and incentives in the countryside. Under *glasnost*, some prominent economists have even felt uninhibited enough to pronounce Stalin's entire rapid collectivization and industrialization campaign to have been a catastrophe which, quite apart from exacting millions of victims, was a colossal error, its disastrous results still seen in today's plight of Russia's agrarian economy.

Gorbachev's verbal calisthenics concerning Stalin's role reflected most likely a politician's caution: at the end of 1987 there were still some in the highest Party circles for whom an unqualified condemnation of the tyrant was unacceptable, not because of any sentimental concern for his reputation, but simply because complete frankness threatened to undermine still further the prestige of Communism.[8] But with *glasnost*, some writers now felt uninhibited by such considerations. Stalin's faults recouped by his wartime role? A well-known military commentator, V. Anfilov, addressed a subject much discussed in the West, but until recently rarely mentioned in Soviet historiography: why the German attack in June 1941 found the Soviets so unprepared. "The main cause of our debacles in the beginning of the war was Stalin's most disastrous miscalculation when it came to evaluation of the military-strategic situation and the timing of the attack by the enemy."[9] Stalin disregarded all warnings about the imminence of the German attack. Another military commentator, Colonel General D. Volkogonov, has been more lenient in his views of Stalin. Perhaps one cannot.expect a high-ranking officer to be a fervent believer in *glasnost*, but even Volkogonov reminds the Soviet reader that, through his purges of the officer corps between 1937 and 1939, the dictator not only deprived the Red Army of its most capable com-

[7] *Ibid.*

[8] In the current official terminology, the period of Stalin's rule (1925–53) is branded as one of the "cult of personality," that of Brezhnev's (1964–82) as one of "stagnation." Thus forty-six of the seventy years of the Communist era are exposed as having been vitiated by bad if not criminal leadership.

[9] V. Anfilov in *Sovyetskaya Rossiya* (Soviet Russia), June 19, 1988.

manders, but literally decimated the officer corps. "Our earthly divinities err occasionally, and the price others have to pay for their mistakes can be fantastically great."[10]

If two such already pre-1985 establishment figures can criticize Stalin so scathingly, then it is no wonder that others, long constrained to remain silent, have erupted under the impulse of *glasnost* with revelations and assessments of Stalin that go far beyond Gorbachev's still somewhat temperate verdict of November 3, 1987. Under the new dispensation, the hitherto monolithic tone of the Soviet press and media in general[11] has taken on varying political colorings. Journals such as *Ogonyok* (Little fire), *Literaturnaya Gazeta* (Literary journal), and *Znamya* (The banner) have been the vanguard of *glasnost*. It is in them that one finds the most severe and revealing accounts and judgments of the Stalinist past. There, incidents from the hecatombs in the thirties to the sinister developments of Stalin's last years are described without any euphemisms, with no extenuating circumstances being adduced for what at times are referred to in those journals as mass murders.

But the current debate about Stalin is far from being one-sided. Defenders of the tyrant's reputation are found not only in the high Party circles and among the dwindling band of aged former officials for whom the purges of the thirties and late forties offered opportunities for rapid advancement. To some in Soviet society, that now distant era is still seen through the prism of the heroic struggle to build socialism and preserve it from the class enemy, to defend the Fatherland from the Nazi invader, and finally to outwit the American imperialists who would have denied the U.S.S.R. the fruits of victory in World War II, and sought to blackmail the Soviets with their monopoly of the A-bomb. In all those struggles it was Joseph Stalin who defied and confounded the schemes of domestic and foreign enemies of Communism and of the Fatherland. By contrast, *perestroika* appears to its die-hard critics to depart from the salutary principles of Lenin and Stalin; *glasnost* has given license to irresponsible intellectuals to desecrate the past; law and order in Soviet society are breaking down; things unimaginable a few years ago, such as claims for autonomy or even secession of the non-Russian parts of the U.S.S.R., are voiced openly and with impunity; Soviet youth is aping Western ways, listening to the unspeakable rock and roll, etc., etc. And of course the root cause of all that mischief is the campaign to denigrate Stalin!

[10] D. Volkogonov, "On the Eve of the War," *Pravda*, June 20, 1988.

[11] To be fair, there were before 1985 occasional dissonances in the Soviet journals. Thus *Novyi Mir* (New World), when edited by Tvardovsky in the Krushchev era, departed at times from the official orthodoxy.

Such views are not infrequently encountered in the columns of the Soviet press. Repression? As one reader writes, "Since that time we had in our country the fifth column (that horde of spies and wreckers from all over the world running into the tens of thousands) and as the war with Germany was unavoidable, Stalin had only one choice: to use severe measures."[12] Another reader objects to an article condemning Stalin's ways of dealing with dissidents. "As this doctor of social sciences should know, the Trotskyites, Zinovievites, etc., became a counterrevolutionary opposition . . . that indulged in anti-Party and anti-Soviet activities . . . not all the enemies of the Party and of the people were crushed. Many survived, and afterwards they revenged themselves on those who supposedly slandered them. . . . Now their consequences are blamed on Stalin. Yes, he was guilty: he failed to finish off all the enemies of the people."[13]

Stalin's name is identified by his partisans with law, order, and decorum. Anti-Stalinism, by the same token, leads to unworthy breast-beating and anarchy. "During *perestroika*, we need more than ever before a patriotic impulses, spiritual divinity, and revolutionary strivings. But instead, we all beat our breasts. Enough of *Repentance*, of *Children of the Arbat*, of *On . . . and on . . . and on . . .*[14] Those productions will not contribute to our enlightenment."[15]

How can the dead tyrant still attract sympathy from some Soviet people? A number of observers, both inside and outside the U.S.S.R., attribute it to the fact that *glasnost*, while received enthusiastically by the intelligentsia, has met with but a lukewarm reception from the masses. For the man and woman in the street, greater freedom of speech and other measures of liberalization are, allegedly, of little importance in comparison to their material situation, which until now *perestroika* has failed to improve. But, as we shall see, there may be other reasons for that lingering sympathy for a man who, whatever his other qualities, presided over the most tyrannous system the modern world has known. And, as the editor of a journal in the forefront of the struggle for *glasnost* has said, "Stalinism is not just something in the past, it is in the present. It lives amongst us and we meet it every day."[16]

---

[12] From a letter to the editor, *Sovyetskaya Kultura* (Soviet culture) (Moscow), August 30, 1988.

[13] *Ibid.*

[14] *Repentance* is a strongly anti-Stalinist movie; *Children of the Arbat*, by Rybakov, a novel with the same theme.

[15] *Ibid.*

[16] Quoted from Georgi Baklanov in the *New York Times*, January 29, 1989.

The most basic argument put forward by the defenders of Stalin's reputation links his name with the very existence of the Soviet Union and the greatness of the socialist Fatherland. This argument was advanced in a letter published on March 13, 1988 in *Sovietskaya Rossiya* (*Soviet Russia*), which threw fear into the hearts of the believers of *perestroika*. The lengthy letter was signed by a Leningrad chemistry instructor, Nina Andreyeva, but its form and content suggest very strongly that it was inspired and at least partly written by someone else, possibly a high intra-Party opponent of Gorbachev's. "Take the question about the role of J. V. Stalin in the history of our country. . . . [His] era is one of an unexampled rise of a whole generation of Soviet people who only now are gradually leaving the social and political arena. The formula of the 'cult of personality' is supposed to describe [those achievements] of industrialization, collectivization and cultural revolution that brought our country the status of a superpower. All that is being questioned. We've reached the point where the 'Stalinists' (a very flexible term) are insistently required to repent publicly." Ms. Andreyeva admits that the mass repressions of the thirties and forties were indeed reprehensible and regrettable, "but common sense argues against painting all those complex times and problems with the same brush as is being done in some of our journals." The guilt for those repressions the writer lays at the feet of the then "Party-government" leadership. But if Stalin was somewhat guilty in that connection, it must not be forgotten that Peter the Great could also be hard on his contemporaries. But he did make Russia a great power. "And the flowers which are constantly deposited on his [Peter's] sarcophagus . . . testify to the respect and gratitude [he had earned] from our contemporaries. . . ."

In conclusion, the writer reminds readers how V. I. Lenin dealt with scholars and authors who criticized the Party line in the early twenties: they were thrown out of the country. (In fact, as Ms. Andreyeva neglected to add but as many of her readers must have remembered, quite a few of them were dealt with more severely.)

Andreyeva's letter aroused considerable apprehension among the Soviet intelligentsia. Rumors credited the inspiration, if not the authorship, of the letter to Politburo member Yegor Ligachev, who was well known for his conservative and anti-*glasnost* views. And indeed, the long delay in the appearance of an answer to Andreyeva's outburst suggests considerable hesitation, perhaps a clash, on the Soviet Olympus about how to deal with this manifestation of neo-Stalinism. Finally, on April 5, *Pravda* published a lengthy rebuttal.

The answer was carefully phrased. Without denying Ms. Andreyeva the right to her opinions, the author (more likely, authors) castigated her defense of Stalin in terms almost identical to those used by Gorbachev in his November 1987 speech: "One still hears it said that Stalin did not know about the acts of lawlessness. Not only did he know, but he organized and directed them. By now it has been proved to be a fact. And Stalin's guilt, just like that of those closest to him, the guilt before the Party and the people for all the mass repressions and lawlessness, is very great and unforgivable."[17] No, the rebuttal continues, to expose Stalin does not mean to minimize the achievements of the Soviet people during those years. But how much more could have been achieved without those crimes and sufferings!

Proponents of *glasnost* could breathe more freely after *Pravda*'s piece. The prevailing view within the Party leadership had reaffirmed the anathema of Stalin. But, to repeat, it would be hugely premature to conclude that the Stalin question has been resolved. As Shatrov says, many in the U.S.S.R. wish that "Stalin would leave," but "he remains on the stage." The problem of Stalinism remains in the political arena as well. Of course, it is unlikely Stalin could be rehabilitated. But should Gorbachev or any putative successor of his decide to tighten the reins over *glasnost* and *perestroika*, it is quite possible that the debate about Stalin would be severely constrained. In many ways, the debate touches on the very basis of the Communist system. Implicit in the painful examination of the Stalinist past is an unspoken question, Did we err in 1917, and, if not then, at what point? And the immediate corollary to this question is, What of Lenin? Does he carry any share of the responsibility for the phenomenon of Stalinism taking root in Soviet soil? The Nineteenth Party Conference in May 1988 directed that a memorial should be erected to the victims of the repressions. The idea is not new. It had been broached by Khrushchev but had never been acted upon. But now there is increasing pressure for a monument that would commemorate those who, largely at the instigation of one individual, perished at the hands of their fellow countrymen. But if there is to be a visual tribute to the memory of all those innocent men and women, how could it coexist with the memorials to the people who were responsible for their ordeal? Or will the ashes of Stalin and some of his most culpable associates be relocated from their current places of honor in the Kremlin Wall? As with more substantive issues, this question sharply outlines the dilemmas of the Soviet system when it comes to the man who for thirty years loomed over it "like a dread spirit."

[17] *Pravda*, April 5, 1988.

Rehabilitation of Stalin's victims began in earnest under Khrushchev. The great majority of notables—Party, government, and military leaders whose names were then cleared of the opprobrious charges— had died, whether at the hand of the executioner or in one of the camps. Among those restored to full honor as patriotic citizens and talented commanders were the military figures savaged in the *pogroms* of the Red Army between 1937 and 1939; they ranged from marshals of the Soviet Union to the rank and file of the officer corps. But on the Party and government side the job of rehabilitation was far from complete. Nothing was done to erase the charges and verdicts under which Zinoviev, Bukharin, and many other members of the Old Bolshevik guard were sent to their deaths in the Moscow trials of 1936– 38. Nothing was done officially to clear the name of the man who had organized the Red Army from the ludicrous and infamous accusation that he had been a traitor and Nazi agent. Nor were the full circumstances of Leon Trotsky's death truthfully presented to the Soviet public. Rehabilitation of other victims, whether high officials or simple citizens caught in the whirlpool of terror during those terrible years, went on even during the Brezhnev era, but in most cases it was done quietly and without attracting public attention.

Stalin had tied up the Soviet system in knots: to denounce the Moscow trials for what they really were—travesties of justice—would have been an indictment of the whole system of socialist justice as it existed not only under Stalin but before and after as well. In 1956 Khrushchev had already mentioned the cases where the secret police had used torture to exact false confessions, but until now the regime had been fearful about the possible effect of revelations that it was widespread torture and the infliction of even more hideous psychological ordeals that accounted for the confessions of those accused in the trials. To lift the absurd charges made against Trotsky would have been to destroy one of the most persistent legends of Stalinism: Trotsky as the evil spirit of Communism, practically from its inception. As with other aspects of the unpleasant past, the post-Khrushchev regime seemed to act as if the passage of time would make people forget about the Moscow trials. And so between Khrushchev's fall and Gorbachev's ascendance the charges and sentences against the fallen greats of Communism were not featured in the official literature and press, but neither were they quashed. Of course, instead of alleviating the problem, this head-in-the-sand attitude compounded the regime's predicament. The victims of the judicial murders had relatives and friends who kept petitioning for the restitution of their good names, and besides, how could any Communist "forget" that Trotsky, Bukharin,

Zinoviev, and others had been among the makers of the Revolution and the Communist state?

It is understandable that the Gorbachev team has treated the problem of rehabilitation gingerly, and that its resolution of it, while more honorable than that tried by its predecessors, is still awkward. Political rehabilitation came first: under *glasnost* various writers (e.g., Shatrov) and the media argued the absurdity of trying to charge Lenin's closest companions with heinous crimes, and laid the blame for the slander and crime on Stalin's servitors, with a clear implication that he himself authorized the outrage. Many of the accused and condemned were hailed as exemplary Communists. In fact, something resembling a "cult of personality" was woven around the figure of Bukharin. Some Soviet publicists now claim that, in the late twenties, Bukharin offered Communism an alternative path to that taken subsequently by Stalin, and that, unfortunately, Stalin bested him through intrigues and villainy. With Bukharin at its helm, the argument continues, the U.S.S.R. would have avoided the violence of forcible collectivization and the purges—it would have arrived at "socialism with a human face."

Judicial rehabilitation came in 1988. The Supreme Court of the U.S.S.R. reviewed the cases of those tried and condemned in the three great Moscow trials—1936, 1937, and 1938—and declared their confessions and sentences to have been secured by impermissible methods and fraudulent testimony, and pronounced them innocent. The awkwardness of the whole procedure is underlined by one exception to the rehabilitation. Henryk Yagoda, who was tried and condemned in 1938, was not rehabilitated because, allegedly, no one petitioned for a reversal of his verdict. Yagoda, as the reader of this book can conclude from an account of the trials, was without doubt a scoundrel, and probably deserved his fate, but certainly not for what he was charged with at the trial—the accusation against him was as false as the ones against Bukharin and the others.

More recently the Central Committee of the Communist Party appealed to (i.e., ordered) the government organs to annul wholesale the verdicts of the special courts which, during the terror, "judged" and, usually in a matter of minutes, condemned thousands upon thousands of Soviet citizens. No verdict on Stalin's times could be more devastating than this avowal that there was no need to research or review individual cases, that there is virtual certainty that all those— thousands or even millions—were innocent, whether of "Trotskyism," "wrecking," or of being "people's enemies," "agents of German intelligence," and so on. "Society, relatives, and those close to the victims await full rehabilitation of all innocently repressed and the perpetuation of their memory," the Central Committee announced.[18]

And so the replaying of Soviet history continues. Yet the need to rehabilitate publicly the victims of Stalinism may not be what keeps the process going. Ever since Khrushchev's revelations, few Soviet citizens could have believed that those who had perished or been sent to the camps were really guilty. Rather, one feels, it is the regime that is trying to rehabilitate itself and restore the good name of Communism.

But we must not become preoccupied exclusively with the political dimensions of the debate about Stalin and Stalinism. And since we don't need further convincing (although some in the U.S.S.R. still do) of the evil the man wrought, one grows a bit weary of the continuing recitations of Stalin's transgressions, which by now have become almost as monotonous and ritualistic as the chorus of praise during his lifetime. What we do need, especially from the point of view of students of Soviet history, whether in Russia or in the West, is to learn more about the man and his times. Has *glasnost* added substantively to our knowledge?

Unfortunately, up to now, it has not added very much. To a large extent the Party has preempted the field of study of those tragic times. A high-ranking Politburo commission, currently headed by Alexander Yakovlev, has been charged with investigating the Stalin era. And while it is no longer unthinkable for a Soviet historian to try to anticipate the findings of an official commission, not many have tried, and one must assume that those who have do not find it easy to gain access to the archives or Politburo minutes (if many from those years are still extant) that contain materials that could enrich our knowledge of that extraordinary man and his times.

One of the key events in the history of those grim years was the assassination of Kirov. Foreign students of the Soviet scene have long concluded that, one way or another, Stalin secretly instigated the murder because he had come to fear Kirov's popularity within the Party. Recent Soviet sources have come close to insinuating the same thing. But, as I suggest in this book, we still lack definitive proof or an outright statement from the regime that it was Stalin who was behind the drama of December 1, 1934 in the Smolny Institute in Leningrad. On the fifty-fourth anniversary of the momentous assassination, the local newspaper printed an excerpt from unpublished memoirs of an eye witness to the deed who had lived until 1985 (and who had been

[18] *New York Times*, January 6, 1989.

in a forced labor camp from 1935 to 1956; it was often assumed that no one close to Kirov had survived him by more than two or three years). The author, once fairly close to the dead leader, would have, one assumes, arrived at a definite conclusion as to the reasons for the crime. Indeed, he cites some new facts: "S. M. Kirov was hit by one bullet, but we (nearby) heard two shots." He also records that the actual assassin, Nikolayev, was found lying, revolver in hand, by the side of his victim. But, after recounting other details, the writer lamely concludes, "And thus the investigation took place so hurriedly and far from established the truth. Publicly there were expressions of love and gratitude to Kirov, in fact what happened was a mockery of paying its due to the sacred memory of a true Leninist. The murder was done by Nikolayev. [But] who was behind and manipulated him?"[19] In all, the account adds but little to what Khrushchev had said about the murder in 1956 and what is recorded in this book.

This failure to dot the i is found in other accounts of sensitive episodes of the Stalin era. Thus we get a truthful and fairly detailed account of Trotsky's assassination, one vastly different from what the Soviet press wrote at the time of the deed.[20] The author recounts in a straightforward fashion the plot against Trotsky's life that was organized by the Soviet secret police, and states that the assassin, after his release from jail, spent the remaining years of his life in Castro's Cuba, Prague, and Moscow. Stalin's hatred of his brilliant rival is clearly delineated, and the Soviet reader could have few doubts as to who ultimately ordered the assassination. "Having reached the conclusion that he had no further use for Trotsky, [Stalin] either decided himself, or let it be known in his entourage that it was high time to finish off Trotsky."[21] But, again, the account, while undoubtedly startling to many in the U.S.S.R., does not add one iota to what has long been known and written in the West. Incidentally, while Trotsky is cleared of the absurd charges levied against him in the 1930s, the author, in line with the present official position, expresses a very negative view about his personality and politics: "Under the pretense of struggle against Stalin, Trotsky tried to exchange one 'ism' [Stalinism] for another 'ism' equally hostile to Leninism [i.e., Trotskyism]." But he

[19] *Leningrad Pravda*, December 1, 1988, from an unpublished manuscript by M. V. Roslyakov.

[20] On August 24, 1940, *Pravda* concluded its reprehensible description with: "He [Trotsky] was killed by his own followers. He was done in by the same terrorists whom he taught to practice clandestine terrorism, treason and other crimes against the Land of the Soviets."

[21] N. Vasetsky, "The Liquidation: Who Killed Trotsky and Why?" (testimonies and different versions in *Literaturnaya Gazeta* [Literary gazette]), January 4, 1989.

approves of Trotsky's characterization of Stalin as "perfidious and vengeful."

The serialization, so to speak, of the story of Stalin's crimes obviously reflects fears among the progressive circles of the Soviet intelligentsia that the present course of *glasnost* might be arrested or ever reversed. Hence the eagerness to carry out the destruction of the Stalin myth beyond any possibility of even partial restoration. "At times we are asked: why summon the ghosts, why disturb the past? There is this simple answer: we must know about the past. So that, among other things, the future should be finally free from the past."[22] A Western observer might find such fears quite irrational. How do you restore the reputation of a man whose dark deeds have been so strenuously publicized; a man who most recently has been accused in the press of being ultimately responsible for causing upward of twenty million deaths among his fellow countrymen?[23] But to one who has been immersed in the Soviet history of the last fifty or so years, nothing appears impossible. *That man* cast a veritable spell over the Soviet people, and over many outside the U.S.S.R. as well. Is it entirely incredible that there should be a revival of Stalinism? "Impossible" is not a word to be applied to any future contingency in Russia, if one keeps in mind what has gone on there during the last seventy years.

Two areas of Stalin's activity have until recently been relatively exempt from the wholesale attack: his leadership during World War II and his guidance of Soviet foreign policy after it. But by now Stalin, the generalissimo and the statesman, is also under attack. Marshal Zhukov's daughter claims to have found among her dead father's writings some which he had not been allowed to include in the several versions of his autobiography published in his lifetime. It is no surprise that the new material contains a shattering evaluation of Stalin as a war leader: he was not really competent as commander-in-chief; his main concern was to claim credit for the victories scored by others; he tried constantly to instigate quarrels and mutual distrust among his most prestigious marshals and generals.[24] And, as we know from other sources, such was Stalin's envy and apprehension of the Soviet Union's most outstanding war commander that, following the war, Marshal Zhukov was sent to a provincial command, and evidently very narrowly avoided a much worse fate.

But, surely, if you are a patriotic Russian, you must draw the line at attacking Stalin for his foreign policy. Of course it can be criticized

[22] Serge Mikoyan, "His Servant," in *Komsomolskaya Pravda* (Komsomol Pravda), February 21, 1988.

[23] Reported in the *New York Times*, February 4, 1989.

[24] G. K. Zhukov, "Briefly about Stalin," *Pravda*, January 20, 1988.

from the ethical point of view, but what great power's policy is free from reservations on that count? And didn't Stalin run circles around people as astute as Churchill and Roosevelt? Did he not contribute mightily to raise the Soviet Union, bloodied and exhausted at the end of the war, to a superpower, and that in the face of the enormous industrial might of the United States and its monopoly of the A-bomb? No, the "new thinking" does not spare Stalin on that count, and some writings in this vein are disarmingly critical of the overall thrust of Moscow's foreign policy. "During Stalin's rule Lenin's principles were seriously distorted, not only insofar as domestic, but also insofar as foreign policy was concerned. In its essence, foreign policy as practiced by Stalin and his closest entourage was based on the ultra-left ideas of Blanqui and Trotsky[25] that are alien to socialism. He forcibly disseminated, especially following World War II, the Stalinist type of socialism wherever it was possible, and regardless of the special circumstances of the given country. Concentration of power in domestic policy inevitably led to hegemonism and great power arrogance in foreign relations. One of the obvious examples was the ejection of Yugoslavia from the socialist camp in 1948. Simply because it refused to submit to Stalin and to obey his orders, Yugoslavia's leadership was then accused of all sorts of mortal sins. Later on came the breaks with China and Albania, caused by mistakes also on our part. Conflicts and dissensions would also arise with other socialist countries."[26] Well, Stalin would protest that the break with China and Albania came some time after his death, and that, indeed, during his rule, no one in the Communist world, with the single exception of Yugoslavia, dared to defy him. But the author is not really wrong in his assessment of what was wrong with Soviet policy, even if he does not quite spell it out. Stalin subordinated the whole Communist world to the interests of the Soviet Union as he saw them, i.e., to his wishes, and that pattern could not endure. Thus, for all the apparent and glittering successes of his diplomacy, the tyrant's legacy in foreign policy has also turned out to be unfortunate. His insistence on the Kremlin's absolute domination of Communist parties everywhere was bound eventually to split the movement. China certainly could not be expected to remain a docile satellite of the U.S.S.R. And how troublesome for the present Moscow leadership has been Stalin's imposition of Communist regimes in East Europe. Never accepted as legitimate by the majority of their population, almost all are currently on the verge of economic bankruptcy, and are tottering politically. Gorbachev and Co. must see the

[25] *Sic!*

[26] Article by Vyacheslav Dashichev, "East-West: The Search for a New [Type] of Relations," *Literaturnaya Gazeta* (Literary gazette), May 18, 1988.

regimes in Poland, Czechoslovakia, and so on as a source of continuous concern rather than as reliable allies.

And so as of the beginning of 1989, J. V. Stalin stands, as far as the progressive part of the Soviet media is concerned, condemned on all counts. And the official Party assessment of the man, while not as far-reaching and explicit in its condemnation, is still devastating.

And yet, in the playwright's words, Stalin refuses to go away. Is the reason, perhaps, that while we have heard a great deal in the last three years in the way of condemnations, we have had but little that is new in the way of explanation? Questions that have been raised in this book still remain unresolved in view of scant new information, even under *glasnost*. Things about which people in the Soviet Union just whispered a few years ago are now being openly discussed. Foreign sovietologists' reconstructions of events in Stalin's time, which once were branded by their colleagues (even the ones who were far from sympathizing with Communism on the Soviet Union) as inspired by anti-Russian sentiments, have now been confirmed, sometimes in even more horrifying detail by the Soviet press. But in many cases the historian still does not have an answer to the questions that must be asked: What really happened? And why? What is the full story of Kirov's assassination? What really went on in the last weeks of Stalin's life? Were the events such as the Nineteenth Party Congress and the announcement of the "doctors plot" really a prelude to another purge of the top leadership?

There are many other such questions on which definitive information is still lacking. Perhaps because of the long-standing aversion in the U.S.S.R. to anything that smacks of the psychoanalytical school (something partly explicable by Marxism and its insistence on social and economic determinants of behavior), few writers there have attempted anything approaching a psychological analysis of Stalin. Granted, this approach, when it comes to historical figures, has often been overused and misused. Still, one would like to know more about the dictator's personal life. In the West, the word "paranoid" has occasionally been used to describe his actions. But isn't inordinate suspiciousness a professional ailment of tyrants? And couldn't he have resorted to mass terror cynically, from a hideous rational calculation, rather than because of morbid apprehensions?

And so the quest for the facts and for further explanations of what made Stalin and his rule possible continues.

Introduction

Joseph Stalin was to be buried on March 9, 1953. Though he had been stricken with a brain hemorrhage on the night of March 1–2, the news was announced to Soviet citizens only on March 4, when his condition was already deemed hopeless. Furious bargaining and maneuvers began virtually at the bedside of the sick and unconscious man for shares of that vast, unlimited power which he had held for more than a quarter of a century. On March 6 the expected, inevitable sequence: announcement by the governing bodies of the Party and the state that as of the preceding evening, at 9:50, Stalin was dead. The man whose power could be but most inadequately summarized by his main titles—Secretary of the Central Committee, Chairman of the Council of Ministers, Generalissimo of the Armed Forces—was no more.

In his life Stalin had been praised so constantly and extravagantly that now the Soviet media could not find an appropriate language of eulogy. On March 5 and 6 the front pages of *Pravda* and *Izvestia* carried the mournful communiqués, but the back pages were still filled with routine and banal stories: elections to the legislature in Communist China, worldwide discussion of Stalin's book on economy published the year before, the usual stuff to which readers had become accustomed in the gray years since the war. The front-page news, though, was numbing, and the average Russian could not tell at first whether he felt fear or relief. In the old times the death of a Muscovite ruler, even a cruel one, would be greeted by the populace with alarm: there was the danger of anarchy added to oppression; the nobles would ravage the country while struggling for power. But these historical precedents appeared faint and were of little help in the moments after the death of a man who not only had accumulated unprecedented power but also in a strange way had entered the life of each of his subjects, regardless of whether the latter was a victim of persecution, a beneficiary of Stalin's rule, or both. In this case political power had been transmuted into something much more vast and elemental, something that could not be expressed by any

3

set of figures—be they statistics of the great industrial growth of the U.S.S.R.; or the total number of victims of the purges, wars, and collectivization; or the quantity of lands and peoples conquered by Communism since the then little-known Djugashvili-Stalin acceded to supreme power in his still backward and devastated country. Stalinism could not be described as an ideology, a system of government, or even a religious cult. For a Russian before March 6, 1953, it had been all that and something more: it was a destiny one endured because there could be no other. A religious or political allegiance can be discarded or changed; even under a tyranny one can preserve one's internal freedom. But during Stalin's rule the most indomitable and skeptical spirit among the huge numbers of citizens of the U.S.S.R. could not have remained unaffected by Stalin and what he represented.

And now this distant and fearsome deity was dead. He had ruled Russia in a conspiratorial manner, and a large part of the awe surrounding him had proceeded from the average Russian's (not to speak of the foreigner's) ignorance of how and where decisions affecting his life, decisions of war and peace, were reached. And this conspiratorial air colored the circumstances of Stalin's death. The belated communiqué announcing his stroke was emphatic that it had occurred in his quarters in the Kremlin. Yet it was to his country villa, his favorite residence of the last twenty years, that his daughter Svetlana was summoned on March 2 to be by his deathbed. Unless we accept the fantastic supposition that the dying man was spirited out of the Kremlin and transported some thirty miles, we must conclude that the original communiqué was blatantly false in at least one detail. He was stricken away from Moscow. We shall see later what reasons prompted Stalin's successors to begin their reign with this seemingly pointless lie. ☆☆☆

SVETLANA ALLILUYEVA'S account of her father's last days describes the Politburo members at the deathwatch as grief-stricken, with tears in their eyes. Some of them may have had an accurate idea of their fate had the "genius leader of mankind" been vouchsafed a few more months: a new and great purge was evidently in the offing, and most of Stalin's older collaborators were to incur the fate that so many Old Bolsheviks had suffered in the 1930s. Yet it is credible and human that they were in tears: there are, as the Roman poet said, *lacrimae rerum*—tears of events. Those unpleasant and power-greedy men in their middle and late middle age still must have reflected, if momentarily, on the long past which the dying man represented, on what they had once been and what they had become.

4

In yet another way the oligarchs who would grasp and contend for supreme power paid their tribute to Stalin. For the moment the whole edifice of the Soviet state and society, built with so much work, so many sacrifices and sufferings, was shaken and vulnerable because one seventy-three-year-old man was first incapacitated and then dead. His oldest subordinates, trained in conspiracy and dissimulation, feared him and hated each other, but now they could not conceal a new fear: of the people. The official announcement on March 7 beseeched the public to avoid any kind of "disorder and panic." Not many days were to pass before Stalin's successors felt constrained to promulgate a widespread amnesty. Amnesties had traditionally been proclaimed on such occasions of official rejoicing as the Tsar's coronation or the birth of an heir to the throne, and, after 1917, on major anniversaries of the Revolution. But this amnesty was an expression not of joy—the shock of Stalin's passing was still too strong for the relief to set in—but of the recognition that with him gone, no one could or would govern Russia in the same manner. To the tragedy of a great and obsessed man who had stamped his resolution and his criminal obsessions upon an entire society, there would now succeed the drama of oligarchs struggling for his inheritance and for the credit of removing the blight of his ways from Russia and Communism. Hence the haste to change and moderate the phantasmagorical system of penalties which in the past had men imprisoned for years and exiled to Siberia for such crimes as being late to work, becoming through no fault of their own prisoners of war, or of being related to people condemned on mere suspicion. The official reason given for this hurried reform was that "law observance and socialist order have grown stronger. . . ."

The unconscious irony of the statement reflects another characteristic of the era that was drawing to an end: it was preposterous. Had a nation's as well as millions of individuals' tragedies not been compounded in it, the outward manifestations would have made a wonderfully humorous tale. The period during which Stalin ruled Russia abounded with ridiculous rituals in the worship of one man which were so excessive as to be grotesque, so pervasive that they could have been caused not merely by one man's vanity but by something much deeper. Now Stalin's successors, or rather contenders for succession, and professional eulogists were striving for new superlatives. The funeral plans called for Stalin's body to join Lenin's in the Mausoleum, the temple of the Revolution containing the mummy of its maker, but this was to be but a provisional form of immortalization, for the Mausoleum itself was deemed not impressive enough to have the remains of the *two* supreme geniuses of all history. In its first outburst of extravagance the post-Stalin regime pledged to replace it by a vaster structure, the Revolutionary Pantheon, where Stalin and Lenin would repose, surrounded by lesser divinities, those revolutionaries and Bolsheviks who having died in good standing were buried in the Kremlin Wall. The Pantheon was never to be built. But neither was that monument promised by Khrushchev in 1961, when Stalin's own remains were banished from the Mausoleum: a memorial to the countless victims of the "cult of personality."

The last rites of that cult took place during those March days in 1953. From the moment of the announcement of Stalin's death the center of Moscow was surrounded by security troops, as if the rulers were afraid that in their shock and liberation the people might throw themselves upon the Kremlin to overthrow Stalin's whole fantastic network of power and oppression. But he had also killed the great revolutionary tradition of the Russians. People congregated not to demonstrate but to parade past Stalin's bier. From March 9 his body lay in state in the House of the Unions, where some of the most spectacular purge trials had taken place. In the great Hall of Columns, Muscovites could view the leader whom for many years they had seen only at a distance, standing on the top of Lenin's Mausoleum on state and Party celebrations. He lay there, not in the worker's blouse which he had affected throughout most of his reign, but in the uniform of the last phase, that of Generalissimo of the Soviet Union. One of the bards of the "cult of personality," Alexei Surkov, commented how white was "his familiar, so infinitely dear face" against the red silk covering of the bier. There was an effusion of bad poetry. "Death closed those eyes which had looked so far into the future," wrote Surkov. Tributes came from writers who in a few years would present startlingly realistic pictures of the cruelty of Stalin and the horrors of his era. Konstantin Simonov could find "no words to render how insufferable our loss . . . how we grieve you, Comrade Stalin." Alexander Tvardovsky was later to describe Stalin as a vengeful deity looking from afar and above on his suffering people, but on this March day he also could not "find words to express our nation's sorrow." But there were dirges from those whose emotional involvement with the legend of the dead leader was more genuine and tragic. Fadeyev, Stalin's satrap for literature, was not feigning when he spoke: "We are children of the Stalin era. We have the right to say that all Soviet people live with Stalin in their heart." And when the Party began to disclose the truth about the past, its child Fadeyev took his own life. Some reached for the obvious precedent and model for expressing national sorrow. On Lenin's death a poet had sung, "Lenin lives. . . . Lenin is more alive than the actually living." And so Gribachev, "Stalin is dead. Stalin eternally with us, Stalin—life." Unfortunately for the Soviet people and the world, this was to prove to be not just a poetic hyperbole.

At 10:05 A.M. on March 9 the eight senior members of the Presidium of the Central Committee of the Communist Party lifted the coffin of their leader and placed it on an artillery carriage. They had just completed their first public defiance of Stalin's will and had provisionally adjudicated their own claims for succession: in a hurried reshuffle most of the newcomers to the Presidium—their putative successors after the planned purge—had been ejected and their own power restored. The man who held primacy, shakily as it turned out, Georgi Malenkov, was the chief mourner. Behind him came Lavrenti Beria, whom Stalin's death saved but only for a few months from certain removal but who now renewed his ascendancy over the government's chief instrument of terror, the Secret Police. Then the only prominent Old Bolshevik in the group, Vyacheslav Molotov, the only one likewise with whom Stalin was on terms of personal intimacy, his oldest and closest servant, but a slighted one and probably marked to be discarded. After Molotov came the men who had ranked closest to Stalin during his tempestuous ascent to power in the 1920s and during the nation's ordeal of the 1930s, Klementi Voroshilov and Lazar Kaganovich. Then Anastas Mikoyan who, though close to the summit, still had escaped the danger and notoriety of undue prominence. Of the eight only he would retire in good standing, survive Stalinism, de-Stalinization, and its reversal unscathed (though his family had suffered). Finally the two more recently recruited satraps: Nikita Khrushchev and Nikolai Bulganin. Each of the eight, for all the panoply of powers, offices, and privileges they enjoyed, had reasons to fear their deceased leader, all of them had been servile instruments of his will until his last moments, conscious that their individual or even collective eminence could not save them from his wrath or whim.

Among the many foreign Communist dignitaries one was accorded ostentatious precedence over all but the first three of Stalin's Soviet lieutenants, and this was an event as symbolic as the funeral itself. It was Chou En-lai, the representative of what had been since 1949 the largest Communist-controlled nation in the world. China's supreme head did not deign to attend the obsequies in person, and never again would the head of the U.S.S.R. be an undisputed leader of world Communism. The Soviet leaders' nervousness over their bereavement and over that too complete victory of the Chinese Communists was revealed by a naïve and transparent deception. Alongside the photographs of the funeral scenes which the press was to print on March 10 there appeared a picture of Malenkov alone with Stalin and Mao. This hint at Malenkov's legitimate succession and its blessing by the leader of the "Great Chinese people" was in fact a crudely executed composograph of a photograph taken at the signing of the Sino-Soviet alliance barely three years earlier, when the three gentlemen in question were standing amidst a number of other dignitaries and officials. To many who recalled the original picture this must have been a revelation of the new regime's insecurity, perhaps more telling and ominous than those thousands of security troops who had ringed Moscow.

Thus the funeral reflected not only the past but also, in a kaleidoscopic fashion, apprehensions of the present and problems of the future.

The artillery carriage on which the casket reposed, and the Generalissimo's uniform, suggested a military funeral rather than a revolutionary's. With the coffin placed before the Mausoleum flags were paraded and dipped before it, saluting "the greatest military leader of all times and all nations." This was a fantastic exaggeration but also a recognition of one indisputable achievement of Stalin's reign: from the weak third-rate industrial and military country which she had been in 1924, Russia had become one of the world's two superpowers. Power was what Stalin sought for himself and his country, and literally everything else had been sacrificed in its pursuit. The provisional triumvirate—Malenkov, Beria, Molotov—delivered orations banal and predictable in their content: it was an irreparable loss, but let no one mistake the Soviet people's sorrow for a sign of weakness or confusion; the Party and the whole people were united and determined to follow the path indicated by Lenin and Stalin. The only speech with a shadow of personal feeling, and the only one to dwell at some length on the dead man's revolutionary past, was Molotov's—this faithful servant was at one point close to breaking down. In his last years Stalin had tried rather pathetically to add the reputation of a great theorist to his claims on history. As if still trying to flatter his terrible master, Molotov's speech proclaimed Stalin's commonplace outpourings on economics and linguistics as "new and most important discoveries of Marxist-Leninist science." Then the same eight lifted the coffin and carried it inside the Mausoleum. At noon an artillery salute and factory whistles throughout Russia announced conclusion of the ceremonies.

Stalin was entombed, and his successors could turn their minds to the everyday business of politics and intrigue. An era in history had passed. But Stalinism proved hardier and longer-lived than the man. His successors could not and would not rule the Soviet Union in his manner. For a while the collective leadership strove to let the passage of time perform the task of creating oblivion. With the worst excesses and irrationalities of the pre-1953 era abolished or tempered, people would gradually tend to forget their former anguish and awe and in their gratitude for a tolerable present would not ask questions about the past. But Khrushchev's more direct tackling of the problem in 1956, when in his "secret" speech to the Twentieth Party Congress he lifted the official curtain on some of the issues and tragedies of the Stalinist past, was prompted not only by personal political calculations but by the realization that these tactics were unavailing. Tension had been built up which had to be released, and a reform of the Soviet system, which he genuinely though inconsistently sought, was impossible without telling some part of the truth. The subsequent eight years present a bizarre drama: the struggle between a dead dictator and his living successor. The contest was to prove unequal. The machine, in fact the society, over which Khrushchev ruled was the product of Stalinism. When after intermittent hesitations and retreats Khrushchev in 1961 opened a full-fledged attack upon the dead man, he faltered, then fell. His colleagues and successors realized that Stalin was too much a part of Soviet reality to be torn from it without endangering the whole. It was unavailing to remove Stalin from the Mausoleum and rebury him in the Kremlin Wall. The Mausoleum is still the symbol of Stalin's "cult of personality," though again its only occupant is Lenin.

In fact, that term itself expresses the dilemma and the deception. On its surface "cult of personality" was a useful euphemism, a skillful slogan intended to convey what went wrong with the Soviet Union and Communism between the 1920s and 1953. One man had distorted and debased the noble heritage of the Revolution; through his vanity and crimes had harmed, though he could not destroy, the humane and liberating ideals and message of scientific socialism. One man bore the weight of guilt, and he and a handful of accomplices represented an excrescence on an otherwise healthy and noble organism. That this view and the term itself gained such a wide currency is another example of how one can through sheer repetition become convincing, and of the skill with which the Communist regime projected its self-image. And yet how unreasonable such a perspective on Stalin and Stalinism! We shall be dealing with a man who operated as a conspirator throughout much of his life, even when dictator. But at critical points in his rise to power his advancement was made possible by the good opinion in which he was held and by the support he received from others—from Lenin, from his colleagues on the Central Committee after Lenin's death, and at one time from a majority of the members of the Communist Party of the U.S.S.R. Can his success in procuring this support be explained merely by his guile and ability to deceive? He was at times a superb politician, but he exhibited throughout his life a streak of irritability which often made him tactless and coarse and, by the same token, incapable of being a toady or a mere popularity-seeker.[1] Once at the summit could Stalin's personal power—even vaster and more absolute than that enjoyed at any point by Hitler—be explained by the machinery of terror at his disposal? To a large extent yes. But can an entire nation's submission to,

---

[1] An incidental and unintended result of some of the revelations of the Khrushchev era was that they showed Stalin as being quite independent and at times rude to Lenin when his career was in the latter's hands.

9

numb acceptance of, collective oppression and countless acts of cruelty over individuals be explained only by intimidation? The worship of Stalin was not confined to the territorial limits of the U.S.S.R. and the Communist empire. Foreign Communists who had seen their closest friends or relatives destroyed in Russia continued in obedience to the despot. The spell cast by Stalin in his lifetime outside the borders of his empire cannot be explained by naïveté or by simple loyalty to Communism as such. Certainly no such worship surrounded Lenin in his lifetime. And it would be preposterous to begin to compare any of his successors with Stalin on this count.

Following the defeat of the first Russian Revolution of 1905–6, a variety of heresies—or to give them their technical name, deviations—struck the dispirited Bolsheviks. One of them, frantically combated by Lenin, became known as God-building. One of its exponents wrote, "You seek God? God is mankind. Build up God by joining with the leading elements in society." These sophomoric outpourings were soon decreed as incompatible with scientific socialism, and "God-building" appears if at all only as a footnote in histories of Communism. And yet in a strange way "God-building," or "God-seeking" as it is sometimes called, has been one of the outstanding characteristics of the twentieth-century movement, which itself claims continuity with the nineteenth-century radical tradition with its device "neither God nor master." Without it, Communism becomes a gray business of bureaucracies, production statistics, and police. We can see it plainly in post-Stalin Russia—where the dethronement of one deity had to be compensated for by a more intense cult of the other, Lenin. We can see it in a country with an entirely different cultural and historical tradition from Russia, where the cult of Mao is obviously an imitation and (even granting the preposterous features of the original) recalls Hegel's saying that history repeats itself by tragedy being reenacted as comedy.

What is behind this God-building propensity in Communism? Here again "cult of personality" hides the real answer. Already after Lenin's death, when such tributes were not yet manufactured on command, the poet of the Revolution, Mayakovsky, wrote, "When we say Lenin, we mean Party, when we say Party, we mean Lenin." "Cult of the Party" rather than "cult of personality" explains and constitutes the essence of Stalinism. The Party *was* Stalin, even when at his orders the human beings who constituted it were being decimated. How then was it possible for a convinced Communist to contemplate striking at Stalin if in so doing he would be striking at the Party?[2]

---

[2] In a novel by Simonov an army officer is arrested during the Great Purge and sentenced on a trumped-up charge. His foster son denounces him publicly and changes his name; his wife is deprived of their apartment, which in Moscow of the

We must go even deeper and pose the question to what extent the cult of the Party was prepared and facilitated by the belief in alleged forces of history which at times (most of the time, it turns out) require and justify sacrifice of human lives and freedom. Since the Party is the instrument of progress and liberation, in going against it one challenges history itself. "Subjectively" the Party may authorize cruel and inhuman acts, it may do absolutely irrational things, yet "objectively" it never ceases to advance the grandiose task of human freedom and dignity. The people with whose lives we shall be concerned, including our main figure, learned to forget that words like "class," "revolution," "Party" were but abstractions standing for a mass of human beings and their activities, learned to attribute to them powers and properties transcending human needs, errors, and sufferings. It is not so much that the end came to justify the means, but that both the end and the means became abstract and somehow unreal. Life had to take its revenge and abstractions become clothed with real men, but since they were not only human beings but forces of history they had to be seen as having superhuman stature. There is no place in the socialist movement for an infallible pope, the Russian Marxists used to repeat, but the flowering of scientific socialism is unalterably associated with names like Lenin, Stalin, and Mao. The doctrine allows but a subordinate place for the individual, history is made by social classes, they, in turn, by economic forces. And yet Communism tells its story in terms of heroes and villains, saints and heretics. By not allotting any share in history to accident, inertia, human fallibility, or whim, the most prosaic political and economic development is seen as resulting from miracle-making or treason. Communism has often been inhumane, precisely because it has not applied a human scale to human beings who make history. This was the tragedy of Russian socialism, which began with genuine compassion for the mass of the people and which found its culmination in Stalinism. How it came about must be a large part of our story.

The major part is about Stalin himself. Having just objected to mechanical concepts distorting a true sense of history, we should not make the error of seeing Stalin as an *inevitable* result of his ideology, his era, or his society. But all of them in varying ways contributed to enabling this extraordinary man to become an unprecedentedly powerful and cruel master of a vast country and a worldwide movement. One smiles at Secretary of State Cordell Hull's comment after meeting the dictator: "I thought to myself that any American having Stalin's per-

---

1930s meant being thrown into the streets. Still our hero when in a forced labor camp beats up a fellow prisoner, a "Trotskyite" whom he overheard "slandering" the Party and accusing it of degeneracy. Similar incidents, judging from real-life accounts we have about the camps, were not infrequent.

sonality and approach might well reach high public office in my own country."[3] But the remark reflects not only Stalin's capacity to dissimulate but also his genuine ability. He did have gifts valuable to a statesman of any culture: tenacity of purpose, a sense of timing, a ruthless approach to power. But it was the system that he inherited, and to be sure developed, which enabled this ruthlessness to assume the form of criminal cruelty and one man's obsessions to become a nation's tragedy. Those obsessions grew and were nourished by years of conspiracy required when in the underground, but they continued when Stalin was in power. One may see the seed of obsession in nineteen-year-old Joseph Djugashvili making his first steps as a rebel, infuriated by his teachers' spying on his private reading, but they become part and parcel of the aged despot's personality. Mme. Alliluyeva describes her father's reaction to the discovery of her rather innocent first romance. Most fathers would be angry on learning of a daughter's secret meetings with a man considerably her senior, and some, one dares say, would readily consign him to a forced labor camp were it in their power. But this rather normal solicitude and rage was accompanied by a reaction as abnormal as it was evidently genuinely felt and spontaneous: the man's dossier revealed him as once having had some drinks with British newspapermen (this was in wartime); he was therefore punished not only a would-be seducer but as a British spy!

If years of conspiracy, with its suspicions and betrayals, were to leave an indelible print on Stalin's personality, so did the notion of historical forces so deeply ingrained in Marxism-Leninism. Addressing his people after the German invasion on July 3, 1941, at the most desperate moment in the history of Soviet Russia, Stalin affected to be just one of them. "Brothers, sisters. . . . I speak to you, my friends." But he also called upon the nations of the Soviet Union to unite around "the Party of Lenin and Stalin." There have been many accounts in Soviet literature, laudatory or critical depending on the period when they were written, of this famous speech, but none of them finds it extraordinary or even vain. Enormous as Stalin's vanity was in his latter years, and recognized as such by most who in July 1941 were fighting for their country and not because of any ideology, the Communist Party was to everyone the "Party of Lenin and Stalin," and so it remains as of this writing.

A biography must strive to understand the man as well as his legend. We are dealing with social and political developments but also with the development of one man's personality. To repeat: much of the Russia of the 1930s and 1940s is explained by Joseph Djugashvili's personality, but not all. We may find in Stalin's personality some clue as to why he

[3] *The Memoirs of Cordell Hull* (New York, 1948), II, 1311.

dealt with his closest friends and associates in the way he did, but not why he was served unquestioningly by men whose brothers had been tortured and executed, whose wives had been exiled, whose sons were imprisoned, all at his orders, and why none of them felt he could express his anguish by raising his hand or his voice against the dictator. No incident in Stalin's childhood, no personality trait of his can explain such behavior on the part of Orjonikidze, Molotov, or Mikoyan. When it comes to Stalin himself, one must beware of falling into a trap prepared both by Soviet historiography and by much that passes for psychological wisdom in the West: not to allow for the rhythm of the man's development. If one follows Soviet sources, Lenin's life exhibits a uniform pattern of virtue and wisdom while Trotsky's that of villainy and betrayal. And so with Stalin: one must resist the temptation to read into the personality of the young Georgian socialist and agitator all and already fully developed characteristics of the dictator. But if one studies Stalin's life dispassionately (admittedly not an easy task) one sees how it was affected not only by the natural rhythm of human existence, but by the politics of the time and the movement. It is the latter which allowed seemingly minor characteristics of the youth to become passions of a middle-aged dictator and then obsessions of an old man. The secret of Stalin does not lie in some clandestine past incident, but mostly in the question of why the people who surrounded him came to believe the things they did, and why his age found politics not just the means to let the ordinary business of life go on, but the all-encompassing expression of human passions. Goethe's "Gray is all dogma but ever green is the tree of life" was one of Lenin's favorite quotations. But for Russian Marxists dogma became life, and that is why a Georgian shoemaker's son could become the most absolute and ruthless ruler in modern history.

Twenty years after Napoleon's death his reputation and the character of Bonapartism were a matter of contention only in his adopted country. Possibly some eccentric or madman might at some future time try to revive the cult of Hitler, but Nazism's and Hitler's destructive and self-destructive character is too clearly recognized for such ventures to achieve any significance. But Stalin's reputation, and Stalinism, remain issues of current and great importance in the Soviet Union and will remain so as long as the system endures. Nor is this limited to Russia. Hundreds of millions of Chinese live under a government which for all its national and nationalistic trappings would be inconceivable without the example and lessons of what went on in Russia between 1924 and 1953. Elsewhere in the Communist world the worship of one leader may at the time be impractical or out of fashion, but many of its aspects remain an everyday reality for Czechs, Poles, and others, even in countries where Communism is not in power.

Only the most fatuous moralist will deny that Stalinism is an example of an oppressive social system which in terms of its own premises worked. Some of the most horrifying tales of Stalin's time bear witness to that uncomfortable truth. There is no political opposition or alienation in Ivan Denisovich's camp: indeed it would have been grotesquely unrealistic for the writer to introduce them there. Nadezhda Mandelstam's gripping book about her poet husband, martyred for writing a few irreverent verses about Stalin (which he read just to a few closest friends, at least one of whom denounced him) was seen by an American reviewer as a testimony to how art triumphs over tyranny and injustice. But the writings of Osip Mandelstam, who died, probably demented, in a forced labor camp in 1938 or 1939 (the exact time and circumstances cannot be ascertained), are still proscribed in the Soviet Union, and any criticism of Joseph Stalin must again be temperate and balanced by recognition of his great services to the Party and state. Any critique of Stalin's system that enumerates its cruelties—and it could never be complete or vivid enough—encounters an obvious rebuttal: Why, then, could such a society not only survive, but defeat a powerful foreign enemy, create a mighty industrial base, and become an object of worldwide emulation and of the loyalties of millions living in countries where no such atrocities were being perpetrated? To see the essence of Stalinism in its terror leads inevitably to the question whether there was something about Communism that enabled it to survive and thrive despite the terror (or perhaps because of it), even to outdistance other social systems despite the fact (or perhaps because) the latter did not require such a price in human sacrifice. And of the man himself: What elements of greatness enabled Stalin to overcome the effects of his own crimes and obsessions and die in old age worshiped and feared by so many?

There is another dimension of the problem. Clandestine literature in the Soviet Union has turned to another, at first glance much less dramatic and damning aspect of the period when Stalin ruled. That literature tells how in many ways, in general as well as specifically, Stalinism was just preposterous. Pompous slogans, grotesque rituals, doctored production figures, literature and art and scholarship harnessed by senseless formulas, the whole style of the period one of contrived vulgarity as well as of contrived unctuousness, an all-pervasive bureaucracy that was at once the most meddlesome and the most frightened of any in history—these are also important aspects of Soviet reality in Stalin's day. For reasons that do not require elaboration but do credit to his successors' understanding of politics and the training they received under their leader, the post-Stalin leaders have been more sensitive to and more afraid of those tales of the ridiculous than they have of accounts of the tragic. Hence the logic of approving for publication Alexander Solzhenitsyn's *One Day in the Life of Ivan Denisovich* (to be sure, it began to disappear from libraries after Khrushchev's fall) while imprisoning Yuli Daniel and Andrei Sinyavsky and sending Zhores Medvedev to a mental institution. The question is not only what enabled and impelled one man to impose so much suffering as well as to evoke so much heroism from his people, but also why he exacted and they endured so much that was merely preposterous.

Such, then, are the diverse strains of the legacy and challenge of the era that ended with Joseph Stalin's death.

~1~

A PEASANT FROM THE PROVINCE OF TIFLIS

Few men, even among those born into royalty, have their paths of life determined so much by the accident of their birth and the circumstances of their early existence as Joseph Djugashvili. He was born to a peasant couple on December 9, 1879, in the small Georgian town of Gori. His class origins were no different from those of the large majority of inhabitants of the Russian Empire of his day, and yet they were to be of great importance at a crucial point in his future career. Betwen 1910 and 1912 the Bolshevik faction of the Russian Socialist Party was in disarray and the whole revolutionary movement at a low ebb; some of the Bolsheviks' most prominent leaders quarreled with Lenin or retired from politics. Lenin searched for new blood to staff his organization and to revive the somewhat moribund underground movement in Russia. He was in one of his rather frequent moods of irritation with the middle-class intellectuals who had traditionally led the Party, and on the look-out for somebody who had come "from the people." Yet, preferably, he should be not just a worker or a peasant, but someone with education. There were not many available who could meet such criteria, but one whose credentials were impeccable on both counts was a Caucasian revolutionary of hitherto only regional reputation, Joseph "Koba" Djugashvili. In 1912 he was coopted to become one of ten members of the Bolshevik Central Committee. And so after the February 1917 revolution, Joseph Stalin would return not to Baku or Tiflis but to Petrograd, not a committeeman of an organization of a few hundred members, but one of the highest officials of a movement that would soon have hundreds of thousands of followers and in eight months would seize power.

Fortune also decreed that the Georgian origin of our hero would be of great significance in his first steps on the stage of world history. Lenin, always aware of the great importance to the revolutionary cause of the nationality problem, was looking for somebody to expound the correct (i.e., his own) Marxist view of the subject in a treatise. He felt it politic that it be written by a member of one of the oppressed nationalities of the empire, rather than by a Russian like himself. But which one? A Pole or a Jew was bound to one or another extreme point of view, both thought by Lenin to be incorrect, i.e., harmful to the revolutionary struggle. He would plead for national separatism and independence or, if culturally Russified, and for obvious psychological reasons, he would argue that the national problem was wholly irrelevant to the Marxist movement, the founder of which had declared that "the workers have no country." Hence preferably the author should be a member of another national group—a Georgian, say. Also, one suspects, Lenin looked for someone who was not so heavily endowed with theoretical erudition and facility of exposition that he would take amiss some editorial hints and directions. And thus in Vienna—one of the founts of Marxist knowledge, where he had been dispatched to study the views on the subject (largely incorrect!) of the Austrian Social Democrats—Koba-Stalin completed in January 1913 his *Marxism and the National Question*. The short treatise was subsequently published, perfectly legally, in Tsarist Russia. The Caucasian revolutionary was now, as behooved a candidate for a leading position in a Marxist party, a "theorist." That he should have been the author of an authoritative Bolshevik exposition of this very important question was to affect decisively his future and that of Russia. After the October Revolution and the Bolsheviks' seizure of power some fellow Caucasians of equal standing in the Party (such as his friend, political ally, and finally victim, Gregory Orjonikidze) were sent on missions to or near their native regions. Stalin stayed at the center; he was the obvious choice for the Commissar of Nationalities in the first Bolshevik government.

When in the 1920s some Communist notables were asked to provide autobiographical data for publication, Stalin was one of the few who did not have to strain to present his childhood as one of poverty and deprivation.[1] Both his parents, Vissarion and Catherine (Geladze), were

---

[1] A record of some sort in this respect is held by the poet Demyan Byedny, whose propaganda doggerel was once popular in the Party circles: in detail and rather enthusiastically he described how his mother was by temperament as well as profession a prostitute, and his father a drunkard. Finally mother with the help of her lovers dispatched father to the other world, which did not keep the dutiful son from supporting her when he became a kind of Bolshevik poet-laureate and, as he writes

born serfs before the emancipation of peasants which took place in Georgia in the 1860s, somewhat later than in the rest of the Empire. His father then made an effort at modest social advancement, migrated to the small town of Gori, and set himself up as a shoemaker. His enterprise, which if successful would have made him according to Marxian categories a petty bourgeois, failed, and he regressed into the proletariat, hiring himself out as a worker in a shoe factory in Tiflis. Vissarion must remain a shadowy figure. He was, as various stories of Stalin's childhood suggest and his daughter confirms, a drinking man and he met his end in a drunken brawl sometime around 1890. The mother had to support young Soso, her only child (two other children died in infancy), which she did by taking in laundry, working as a seamstress, etc. It was her labor that enabled her son to go on to the Tiflis Theological Seminary after finishing the parochial school, for the scholarship he obtained, three rubles per month, obviously would not have been sufficient. Catherine lived to see her son become the ruler of Russia and world Communism. She never left Georgia and was literate only in her native language. There are appropriate stories of her dressing in her old age always in black, even on a hot day. To do otherwise, she held, would not be fitting in view of her son's position. All the same, she remained, according to her granddaughter, religious to the very end and regretted that her Soso had not become a priest. There is another story: in the 1930s the old lady had an apartment in the building housing the offices of the Georgian Council of Commissars. At the beginning of the purges the security guards were strengthened, and ministers inquired of their deputy chairman, Budu Mdivani, of the reasons for the new precautions. Those were orders from Moscow, replied the irrepressible Mdivani, one of the very few then capable of joking in public on the subject: Catherine Djugashvili had to be watched so she would not give birth to another Stalin.

Efforts to probe into Stalin's ancestry founder because of the paucity of evidence. Since his personality conforms but little, to put it mildly, to the stereotype of the Georgian national character, with its alleged mercurial gaiety and chivalry, rumor has made him of Ossete descent.[2] But it is useless to speculate. Georgian was his native tongue; to the end he spoke Russian with an accent. Though he retained some native habits, his self-identification with Russians progressed very rapidly. One

---

modestly, famous all over Russia. *The Encyclopedia Dictionary*, XLI, *Part I* (Moscow, 1926), 110–18.

[2] Ossetes, who speak a language unrelated to Georgian, form one of the numerous minority groups in what is now the Georgian Soviet Socialist Republic. A Georgian with his pride in his nation's ancient culture would not take kindly to being identified with a tribe so recently primitive, and Mandelstam compounded his crime when in his fatal poem he called Stalin an Ossete.

day his little daughter would be puzzled when her brother Vassily excitedly announced to her a new discovery: Father *used* to be a Georgian.

Since the process of Russification began well before Stalin became the ruler of all the Russias it must be traced to his social position. On this count Joseph Djugashvili's identity papers—that internal passport which had to be carried by every inhabitant of the Tsar's empire, a document abolished by the Revolution but restored by Stalin—classified his social rank uncompromisingly as "peasant from the Gori District of Tiflis Province." That description alternated in the police documents with one referring to the social status he achieved by gaining, through the Tiflis Theological Seminary, an equivalent of intermediate and part of higher education: *"intelligent."*[3]

The classification "peasant" stamped on Joseph Djugashvili's official documents differentiated him from most of his early associates, friends as well as enemies, in political work. Almost all of them came from a higher social, not to mention economic, station in life, certainly from a more cultured family background. That it should have been so was due not only to the peculiarity of the Russian revolutionary movement of the time, but to specifically Georgian conditions. This small country had probably a higher proportion of its population inscribed on the rolls of nobility than any other area of the Empire. Many Georgian nobles were of course impoverished, such as Gregory Orjonikidze's father, whose life was essentially that of a peasant and whose son had to seek the career of a *feldsher* (medical assistant)—hardly an aristocratic occupation. But there was no denying a difference. The closest associates and contemporaries of Soso Djugashvili in his earliest political activity in Tiflis were Lado Ketskhoveli, son of a priest who himself had come from petty gentry, and a genuine (to be sure a Georgian) prince, Alexander Tsulukidze. To the son of barely literate serfs, the cultural and historical traditions of his small nation could not have the same meaning as they did to those who were "gentlemen" by birth.

The poverty and harshness of Stalin's early life left other indelible

---

[3] I shall repeat here the definition of the intelligentsia I offered in my biography of Lenin: ". . . the stratum occupied by the officials, members of the free professions and the like. . . . In the narrower sense of the term, membership of the intelligentsia came to denote a certain political attitude, one which but inadequately can be described as progressive or liberal. . . . The preceding sentences cry for warnings and qualifications. Was a police official or an army officer a member of the intelligentsia? No, but his son might be in the broader sense of the word, if he became a lawyer, and in the narrower sense if he took to reading J. S. Mill and criticizing the autocracy. On the other hand, Prince Troubetskoy, who became a university professor and a leader of the Constitutional Democrats, has to be classified as an *intelligent* despite his ancient title and his lands. The reader may come to share, though for different reasons, the sentiments of Nicholas II, who wanted to eliminate 'intelligentsia' from the Russian language." *The Bolsheviks* (New York, 1965), pp. 6–7.

imprints. It must have been conducive to his unsentimental view of the life of the lower classes and also to his retention of so many of its characteristics and crudities. In the small world of Gori the talented son of a drunken father and a laundress could not have escaped the childish cruelties of classmates and contemporaries. In an interview he gave in his later years he rejected the imputation that he had been treated particularly badly by his parents. But Svetlana Alliluyeva passes on the family tradition (i.e., what she heard from her mother's sister) that young Soso was frequently beaten and that he had to witness many a scene between his parents. Following Vissarion's departure for Tiflis in 1883, from which he would occasionally return, the mother and son moved from a little two-room combination of residence-workshop to a priest's house, where Catherine was evidently a domestic servant.[4] Childhood ailments left their permanent traces; smallpox pockmarked his face, and an infection or accident led to stiffness in his left arm which kept him from being drafted into the Russian army in 1916.

Soviet accounts of the leader's early years are of little value. That he was bright and a good student is confirmed from other sources, but that he excelled at games, and that in view of his gaiety and spirit was acknowledged by other boys as their leader, is not. He was an excellent swimmer, we are told, but Alliluyeva is quite emphatic that her father never learned to swim.[5] In 1939, on his sixtieth birthday, several of Stalin's old pals from the church school and seminary published their reminiscences, appropriately enough in the *Enemy of Religion*, a journal devoted to combating religious superstitions. Those are in the main what might be expected of such recollections at such a time, but there are a few details which sound genuine. Soso, one recalls, was very diligent in performing his religious duties while in the school, but by the time he left Gori to go to the seminary he was already inclined toward atheism. Another childhood friend reports how in 1892 they watched an unusual event in the life of a small town: the public hanging of three criminals convicted of innumerable armed robberies. (This might well have been the same execution Maxim Gorky witnessed in the Caucasus that year, and he describes how he was struck by the condemned men's fearless demeanor and exchange of jokes [!] with the viewers.) The boys fell into a typical adolescent argument: Were the criminals to suffer also beyond the grave? No, held Soso, then evidently still in his religious phase: they had paid for their sins in this world and it would

---

[4] Yuri Shukov Gori-Tiflis in *New World* (Moscow), December 1939, p. 144. The original dwelling was turned into a museum, the local Soviet authorities enclosing it in a mantle of marble, glass, and steel, not a bad if unconscious symbolism.

[5] Svetlana Alliluyeva, *Twenty Letters to a Friend* (in Russian; New York, 1967), p. 31.

not be fair to punish them in the next.[6] Young Djugashvili may have already read in some Russian history book how Tsar Ivan the Terrible used to dispatch letters to monasteries, enumerating his past and intended victims and asking for prayers for their souls.

His illnesses and the need for special tutoring in Russian meant that the future Stalin completed his church school only in 1894. For somebody in his circumstances the only path to higher education and social advancement had to lead through either a teachers' or a theological seminary. There was no university in the Caucasus, and it was inconceivable that without some well-to-do patron he could afford the expenses of a gymnasium (the regular high school) and of a university in European Russia. That her son should become a priest was obviously his mother's preference, and an important consideration was also the small scholarship he would receive, because no doubt of his mother's connection with the local priest. At first glance the prospects of a theological career must have appeared uninviting to an ambitious youngster, even if he had not, as suggested, already lost his faith. All that one could hope for at the end of six years' strenuous training was the career of a parish priest. The road to higher preferments in the Orthodox Church was barred to the ordinary married clergy, for bishops and other dignitaries were selected from the "black" (i.e., monastic) clergy. But it must have been clear to Stalin, if not to his mother, that many boys went through the seminary just to obtain the best education available to the poor (it was superior in this respect to a teachers' school) and without the slightest intention of becoming priests.[7] Besides, as a career of a somewhat older but already notorious schoolmate from Gori had already suggested, there could be all sorts of exciting things one could do while at the seminary.

Djugashvili would return to Gori early in his revolutionary career to hide from the police, but later on, when he became better known, a town of about six thousand could not offer much security in this respect. His mother and other relatives there remained simple people, and they did not provide that spiritual base and support which many other revolutionaries (such as Lenin) drew from their more cultivated families, where almost everybody was involved in political work or sympathized with the cause. Stalin was to seek such support through both of his marriages, which connected him with families of Party comrades. Nor did his youth endow him with that passion for country life which

---

[6] *The Enemy of Religion* (Moscow, December 1939), p. 20.

[7] Two of the worthies who recalled young Stalin recorded proudly in 1939 how they went into other professions on graduation from the seminary and yielded to the clerical calling only in 1914 when being a priest exempted one from the military service in the war.

so many Bolsheviks from the gentry and intelligentsia displayed when power gave them the opportunity to indulge it. He hunted and fished of necessity when in exile in Siberia, but not in his later life. His occasional diversion of shooting at hares illuminated by automobile headlights would horrify a good sportsman and interest a psychologist. The numerous country residences and villas he acquired or had erected in his years of power—none of them entirely satisfactory or to his taste for long— suggest that he sought but never could find relaxation. ☆☆☆

THE Tiflis Theological Seminary to which Joseph Djugashvili repaired at the age of fourteen was a very unusual school of divinity. Its recent history was largely the result of the Tsarist government's refusal to open a university in the Transcaucasia. Universities, the bureaucrats held—and who today could quarrel with the acuteness of that perception?—were the breeding places of all sorts of political troubles. Didn't they spawn the revolutionary troubles of the 1860s and 1870s? The students were the main carriers of those subversive ideas which finally matured in revolutionary Populism and its fatal fruit, the terroristic People's Will organization which on March 1, 1881, culminated its war upon the autocracy with the assassination of Alexander II. To establish a university amid the welter of nationalities which was the Caucasus was to ask for trouble, to strengthen the already considerable anti-Russian and antiautocracy stirrings among the Georgians, Armenians, and even the Tatars.[8] More affluent members of those nationalities could always go to the Russian universities, where, it was hoped, their dangerous proclivities would be diluted by cultural Russification, while the ambitious among the lower orders would have to be content with becoming priests, teachers, *feldshers*, and the like. But as in so many other cases an apparent premise was to lead to unfortunate consequences. The theological school became the main surrogate for higher education for the whole area and as such drew into its student body many young men from whose minds the pursuit of the quiet and beneficial life as parish priests was remote. In a real university their unquiet spirits might have been tempered by the seductions of learning and the prospects of a distinguished career. Cooped up in a theological school, exposed to the rigors of old-fashioned doctrinal training, at a time of life which even

[8] Contemporary documents and sources refer thus to the Azeiri Turks, who constitute today the majority group in Soviet Azerbaijan, where the oil center of Baku is located, and this nomenclature will be followed here.

22

for the most conformist person is one of questioning and rebellion, many of them progressed during their seminary years from being recalcitrant students to professional revolutionaries. The roll of alumni of the Tiflis school reads like a *Who's Who* of the revolutionary movement in Georgia before World War I. Its history for some twenty years before Djugashvili's enrollment was one of intermittent disturbances and scandals: student strikes, mass expulsions, assaults upon officials. (The most drastic case was in 1886: the knifing of the rector of the school by a seminarian.) The most recent trouble had taken place in 1893, when a student strike led to a temporary closing of the school and expulsion of eighty-seven students, twenty-three of whom were forbidden for a time to live in Tiflis. One of the leaders of the turbulence was Vladimir (Lado) Ketskhoveli, three years Djugashvili's senior and a fellow pupil at Gori. The students' complaints echoing through the troubled history of the school centered about the repressive discipline, the teachers' spying on the students and searching of their rooms for forbidden books, the condescending if not outright insulting attitude among the Russian teachers toward Georgia and her culture. There are also hints that some of the pedagogues suffered from a tendency not unusual in a boarding school and not alone in Georgia and which, the Russian folk tradition indelicately hints, is widespread among monks and Orientals.

In an interview given some forty years later Stalin did not seek to enhance the reputation of his alma mater: the atmosphere there was "jesuitical" and the student subject to constant petty chicaneries and espionage. As to being "jesuitical," the term is surely inappropriate: Jesuit schools were renowned for their *effective* discipline and indoctrination, and for imparting to their graduates a certain urbanity; on both counts the Tiflis seminary was sadly deficient. If the discipline there, and for that matter in an average Russian high school of the period, was repressive, it ought still to be kept in mind that in some respects it compared favorably with, say, British boarding schools of the same period. Thus corporal punishment was unheard of and unimaginable.

The seminary's administration was not entirely insensitive to the students' demands and some reforms were inaugurated in the wake of the students' protests of 1890 and 1894; among other things, Georgian history and literature were added to the curriculum. Students who could afford it, such as the future leader of Georgian Marxism, Noah Jordania, who went there a decade before Stalin, could board outside. Considering that this was the Russian Empire at a period of the deepest reaction, it must be granted that even the most unruly students were treated with a certain indulgence. Philip Makharadze, a future Bolshevik notable, led the student strike of 1890 but was still allowed to graduate. Even Ketskhoveli was issued appropriate documents so that though expelled he could enroll in a seminary in Kiev. The school authorities tolerated some of its students' renting of premises in town where they kept a library and discussed literary and political subjects (one version has the seminary paying for them). The charge that the pupils' schedule was strictly and tyrannically regulated is sufficiently refuted by the very fact that some of them found time and opportunity to participate in the workers' and other outsiders' radical discussion circles. We will not be mistaken if we see in the seminary regimen a blend of brutality, indulgence, and inefficiency that is characteristic of so many features of Russian life at the time. And of course it is such a mixture which provides the most fertile soil for revolution.

There was also, of course, education. Writers who, like Trotsky, portray Stalin as being but one step above illiterate ignore the fact that the seminary furnished him with a not negligible fund of knowledge: one had to study Latin, Greek, and Church Slavonic, as well as Russian history and literature. The most glaring deficiency of the curriculum was the absence of modern foreign languages and of training in sciences. On both counts the then regular Russian high school was greatly superior. Stalin was never to achieve that command of German thought in his revolutionary apprenticeship to be a vital requirement for a would-be Marxist leader.[9] And lack of training in what constitutes the scientific method and in mathematics undoubtedly contributed to his obscurantism in this respect and that scorn for pure research, both of which were to do such horrendous harm to Soviet science and scientists.

As to other elements of his education, the contribution, or lack of it, of the Tiflis seminary is more difficult to assess. The theological bent of his studies is asserted to have contributed to the hackneyed figures of speech which Stalin's style imparted to general Soviet parlance. Even today editorials and official speeches repeat inordinately "as is well known" (which usually is not), and Party members and Soviet citizens are urged to defend something or other like "the pupil of one's eye." But those might well be features of the didactic style he purposefully cultivated while at the summit, rather than a legacy of his ecclesiastical training. Where this training is clearly discernible is in the repeated question-and-answer form characteristic of his oratory ("Can it be said that National-Socialists are nationalists? No. . . ."), and in a litany-like repetition and invocation of the same theme or person ("In leaving us, Comrade Lenin. . . . We swear to you, Comrade Lenin."). The Russian of his earliest articles is certainly stilted and forced, confused and inept where it touches on anything theoretical. But by the time he wrote his treatise on nationality and especially in his polemics after the Revolution, one

[9] According to Svetlana Alliluyeva he could, with the help of a dictionary, work his way through a few pages of German.

discerns clarity of exposition and a certain crude but effective eloquence. All of which testifies to a considerable effort at self-instruction and to the absence of a talented teacher who could have imparted real feeling for the Russian prose and literary style.

"Manners makyth man." Already in the 1860s, writing of the generation of radicals which succeeded his own, which had been rooted in the Russian gentry with links to the European Enlightenment of the eighteenth century, Alexander Herzen criticized their manners and mentality. They displayed, he wrote, rather indelicately for a Populist, the traits of their background in "the servants' rooms, the theological seminary, and the barracks." The seminary was an enlarging experience compared with a small church school, Tiflis a veritable metropolis in relation to Gori. But in the nature of things it offered little or no opportunity of contacts with families of classmates of a more cultured background. Most of the students were Georgians, with some Russians and Armenians of similar impoverished gentry or peasant antecedents. One had no opportunity to meet and form friendships with an occasional Jew or Catholic, to broaden one's perspective beyond the struggle for advancement and against oppression, to learn tolerance not because of an injunction of political philosophy but as a human experience. The seminary, one need hardly add, could not endow a village boy with refined manners or with the taste for and ease in mixed company. Indeed, to those who think in such terms, the Russian Orthodox Church and the semi-Oriental character of Georgia must appear permeated with the spirit of male chauvinism. Stalin's favorite relaxation of his later years—those rather ghastly nocturnal banquets with their exclusively male company, their gross character and jokes and frequently obscene language—bear witness to the enduring character of the taste, or rather lack of it, acquired in his adolescence. The Russian radical movement inscribed women's emancipation among its principal goals, and all the Russian revolutionary parties boasted some very prominent female members. But nothing in Stalin's career suggests that he had a very high regard for women's intellectual accomplishments or potentialities. That it was so was perhaps fortunate for some female Old Bolsheviks when the purges came in the 1930s and 1940s. They were to claim a horrifying number of women, but in most cases these suffered because of the real or alleged transgressions of their menfolk—husbands, sons, fathers, lovers—rather than on their own account. The tyrant's wrath was vented also against women in his own family and circle, those whom he suspected had turned his wife against him. But some of the prominent female veterans of the movement who in the past had been his political opponents, such as Alexandra Kollontay, or in possession of derogatory information about him, as in the case of Lenin's principal secretary, Lydia Fotyeva, were allowed to live out their old age. One can hardly attribute this to an oversight or to any sense of chivalry in a man who did not spare the wives and children of his victims.

But what of the young Joseph Djugashvili, as yet many light-years distant from such grandeur and atrocity? Even taking into account his clandestine activities and the fact that he was to leave before completing the required six years' course, his career in the seminary did not stamp him as unusual among his classmates. He was a good but not outstanding student. He evidently wrote some poetry in Georgian which appeared under a pseudonym in a Tiflis journal, but though his authorship was affirmed, the verses were not included in his collected works, which began appearing at a time when he was loath to overemphasize his Georgian roots. The scraps of recollections one has about those years suggest a sensitive and irascible youth. Classmates returning from vacation would greet each other with an embrace and kiss on both cheeks, then a common practice among schoolboys in Russia. Djugashvili refused to extend this conventional greeting to boys with whom he was on less than a friendly footing. He could not take a joke, but reacted with blows even to good-natured taunts, something his contemporaries could not understand in a Georgian.

The boy's sensitivity and vile temper, and the consequent temptation for others to "pick on" him, reappear in the young revolutionary and exile, and are attested to in a middle-aged Soviet leader. His colleagues in the Tiflis underground in 1901 found him overbearing and suggested he transfer to another locality. A police record from the time of his first arrest and exile branded him "rude, insolent, disrespectful toward authorities."[10] Returning in 1917 from exile to Petrograd and the Revolution, Stalin was barred at first from full participation in the Bolshevik Central Committee of which he was a member, and the official reason given, even granted the blunt temper of the times, reads like a slap in the face: ". . . on account of certain personal characteristics of his" the Bureau proposed to allow him just a consultative vote.[11] On March 14, 1921, the already powerful Politburo member and commissar was cited before the Party Control Commission for being rude and abusive to a Moscow stationmaster.[12] That he was sinned against as well as sinning is apparent from another incident. As we shall see, Stalin was just one Bolshevik and by no means the most prominent of those involved in armed robberies carried out after the Revolution of

[10] *Hard Labor and Exile* (Moscow), xxII (1926), 285. This does not suggest what the Soviet publication intended: merely indomitable behavior when under arrest. Political prisoners were expected to and usually did display condescending courtesy toward their jailors, and the latter were not accustomed to such rudeness from an *intelligent.*

[11] Quoted in M. Moskalev, *The Bureau of the Central Committee of the Social Democratic Party in Russia, August 1903–March 1917* (Moscow, 1964), p. 284.

[12] *Pravda,* March 15, 1921.

1905 to secure funds for the Party. But in 1918, when there was still some opposition press in Soviet Russia, the Mensheviks chose to attack him for an expropriation carried out in Baku in 1907. Another Bolshevik would have shrugged off the charge, since it was correct in essence and hardly shocking in the context of the times, but Stalin exploded. It was a "despicable lie," he claimed, and demanded that its perpetrator, Martov, be tried before the Revolutionary Tribunal for defaming a Soviet official![13] The Revolutionary Tribunal refused to grant Stalin full satisfaction though it reprimanded Martov. Evidently many Bolshevik notables were not too displeased about this digging up of old scandals connected with a man they did not like. We shall encounter other episodes in which Stalin was singled out for censure or ridicule even though his behavior was by no means unique. And often and for long his reaction to such charges and taunts bore little of that steel-like equanimity which his assumed name would imply, but he would lash out at those guilty or suspected. Lenin's "Stalin is too rude . . . ," which he would hear repeated by others to his face, came to him as a culmination of charges and characterizations which he had earned and had had to endure since his boyhood.

There had to be an obverse, however; a boy with such a disposition, if he is also spirited and enterprising, will have not only enemies but followers, those who are impressed by nonconformist "tough" demeanor and who see in it defiance of oppressive authorities and convention. And thus Soso Djugashvili was drawn and invited into the clandestine circles which had become as much a part of seminary life as the divinity lessons. Such circles anywhere else but in Russia of that time would have been considered ordinary discussion groups in which the students sought to supplement their dry and formal education. And the "forbidden literature" which they discussed would seem the object of natural curiosity: novels with adult themes, popularizations of materialistic and scientific philosophies then very en vogue, nothing very subversive or even political but appropriate reading matter for a future priest. But having tasted such forbidden fruit, many seminarians felt drawn toward more specifically political circles. ☆☆☆

THOUGH the majority of its 150,000 citizens were no longer Georgian but of Armenian or Russian extraction, Tiflis had been the ancient capital of independent Georgia and was now the center of

13 The incident was recalled in the March 31, 1939, *Socialist Herald*, a Menshevik paper then published in Russian in Paris.

Georgian cultural and political revival. The little country's independence had been forfeited early in the nineteenth century, and its absorption into the Russian Empire was the conclusion of some centuries-long process of Russian imperial expansion and of various Georgian rulers' seeking of support and protection from a fellow Christian state against the encroaching Muslim empires, Persia and Turkey. National opposition to Russian rule and, conversely, the official effort at Russification never had the intensity shown in such non-Russian parts of the Empire as Poland. Georgia's small size, the fact that most Georgians were, like the Russians, also of the Orthodox persuasion, and finally the presence of sizable non-Georgian minorities were among the reasons. But the latter half of the nineteenth century was a period of national awakening all over Europe and Asia.[14] And so national consciousness, the awareness of the ancient cultural heritage going back to the beginnings of Christianity in Georgia (allegedly in the fourth century A.D.), began to percolate from the aristocracy and intelligentsia to the peasant masses. This nationalism appeared, as elsewhere, not in an undiluted form but in conjunction with the ideologies currently fashionable in the West and in Russia proper. There were three waves or generations of political and intellectual activism in Georgia. The first one reflected Western liberalism and corresponded to the ideas which inspired the great reforms of the 1860s in the Empire, such as the emancipation of peasants, the institution of a modern judicial system, and rudimentary local self-government. Russian Populism also found some Georgian adherents, though the heroics and terrorism of the Land and Freedom group and of the People's Will did not spread to the Caucasus. And in the 1890s a new light from the West, Marxism, inspired a group of Georgian intellectuals who became known as *Mesame Dasi*—the Third Group. Within a decade in this largely peasant country, with but a small proportion of its population urbanized and a negligible number of industrial workers, the Marxist Socialist Party had more popular support than in any other part of the Empire, more, one may add without exaggeration, than in any other country in contemporary Europe.

The primary credit for this remarkable achievement belonged to a handful of intellectuals, most of them graduates of the Tiflis seminary, who, instead of engaging in pastoral duties, seemingly discovered a most incongruous other vocation and enrolled in the Warsaw Veterinary Institute. None of them is on record as having practiced this useful science either, but Warsaw in the 1880s and early 1890s was a place with a pleasingly anti-Russian atmosphere where Marxist ideas had already gained some footing among the intelligentsia, unlike St. Petersburg or

[14] Whether Transcaucasia is part of Europe or of Asia and whether Stalin is thus to be considered an Asian is left to those who delight in such subjects.

Moscow, where echoes of Populism still dominated radical and student circles. Returning to their native land, the ex-seminarians and veterinary students propagated their gospel of nationalism and Marxism, and the most fertile ground for this missionary work was of course their old school. It was the "Warsaw group" which was behind the 1893 seminary strike. As was the case with a small circle of socialist intellectuals already active in St. Petersburg in the same year (one of whose members was a twenty-three-year-old lawyer, Vladimir Ulyanov, the future Lenin), Marxism came to its young neophytes not merely as an economic theory and philosophy of history but as a new faith showing the road to salvation for the individual and the nation. The new creed not only urged the need for revolution, but taught that it was inevitable, that it would come not as Populism had willed as a consequence of individual heroics and assassinations, but as the result of education of the masses, through the growth of class consciousness among the workers and the oppressed. It is no mere metaphor that the writings of Marx, Engels, and Lasalle were a revelation for those young Georgians; their discussion of the intricacies of the system had all the characteristics of a theological exegesis. One of them, Chkheidze, chairman of the Petrograd Soviet after the February 1917 Revolution and then among the most important politicians in all of Russia, referred to the Master so repeatedly that he became universally known as Karl Marx Chkheidze, and not a few books list his first name as Karl rather than Nicholas.

Thirteen of these zealots, meeting in the small town of Kvirili on December 25, 1892, founded the Third Group.[15] Its program was formulated by Noah Jordania under the suggestive title *What Is to Be Done?*[16] Its Marxian gist was simply expressed by another early star of Georgian Marxism, Sylvester Djibladze, when, at a speech at a comrade's funeral,[17] he said, "our life shows us two hostile classes, one the representatives of physical and mental labor, the other the bourgeois and capitalists."[18] Well, not *exactly* Marx's concept of the class struggle, but then the corpus of his works was still imperfectly known to his Georgian disciples, though what was available of Marx was voraciously read and assiduously quoted. In all of Tiflis's libraries of the time

[15] Gregory Uratadze, *Reminiscences of a Georgian Social Democrat* (in Russian; Stanford, Calif., 1968), p. 12.

[16] In reference to the great event (definitely not a great book) in the history of the Russian revolutionary movement, Chernyshevsky's 1860s Utopian socialist novel of the same title. The most famous *What Is to Be Done?* is, of course, Lenin's treatise of 1902, setting the organizational and ideological foundation of Bolshevism.

[17] Speeches and demonstrations at funerals of prominent figures played an important part in the Georgian as well as in the Russian revolutionary ritual. Uratadze, p. 12.

[18] *Ibid.*, p. 14.

(1894) one could find but one copy of the Russian translation of his *Capital*, Volume I.

As early as 1895 or 1896 Soso Djugashvili began to attend Marxist circles at the seminary. This could not yet be construed as *revolutionary* activity. Marxism at first was viewed by the Tsarist authorities as unlikely to shake the foundation of the Empire. The first Russian translation of the first volume of *Capital* in 1872 was passed by the censor, undoubtedly on the same grounds that a British minister in the eighteenth century licensed the publication of an anarchist tract: a thick theoretical book costing a guinea could not do much harm.[19] It was felt that these revolutionaries who believed in reading and expounding dull books instead of throwing bombs could not be dangerous. "Such a small group," said an indulgent police chief of St. Petersburg when members of Lenin's Petersburg circle were arrested in 1895, "perhaps in fifty years something might come out of it." In Tiflis the police authorities were even more indulgent or, what is likelier, more ignorant. The local Marxists acquired in 1898 a Georgian weekly, *Kvali* (*The Furrow*), in which cautiously but openly they expounded the ideas that in nineteen years were to become the ruling creed of Georgia and Russia. By participating in a Marxist circle, Djugashvili did not risk much beyond expulsion from the seminary.

Not so with his next step in political apprenticeship. One day in 1898 Sylvester Djibladze brought the young initiate from Gori into a little clandestine group which he ran and which included not only intellectuals and students but also workers. Stalin thus stepped over the line which in the eyes of the authorities separated mere discussion of "dangerous ideas" from subversion. This was agitation, stirring up the workers, explaining to them that their poverty was not accidental or caused by the greed of the particular employer, but the inevitable result of the whole economic and political system headed by the Tsar.

Djibladze, as Stalin had the candor to acknowledge in 1926, long after he had broken with him and a few years after he died from the effect of his exertions against *Communist* rule in Georgia, was his first real political mentor, the man who introduced him to revolutionary work. It was Djibladze who more than ten years earlier had slapped the rector of the Tiflis seminary because of his insulting words about Georgia and who by now had become one of the leading propagandists of the Third Group. It was his patronage which enabled Stalin, despite those "personal characteristics of his," to play an active part in the socialist circles in Tiflis during the next three years. He was not, as the silly exaggeration of Communist propaganda was to claim after 1930, the leader of Marx-

---

[19] Alexander Tsulukidze acquired *Capital* for twenty-five rubles, a worker's monthly wages and a considerable strain even for his princely pocket.

ist activity in Tiflis. Rather he was sort of an aide-de-camp of one of the actual leaders, Djibladze, as well as instructor of some workers' circles, each containing ten to fifteen members.

In 1899 Djugashvili was excluded from the seminary, not because of being caught red-handed in revolutionary work, as it is sometimes presented, but simply because he failed to take examinations. His mother's recollection that it was she who insisted on his quitting because his health was being undermined suggests that he felt constrained to mollify her by alleging that his health was the reason for disappointing her hopes. But the truth was that his studies, in which he had lost real interest some time before, were interfering with his political activities. He would now scratch out his living by giving private lessons or being a bookkeeper, but he would be in a better position to indulge his taste for politics and conspiracy.

Suddenly, it seemed, in the late 1890s, in Georgia as in the rest of Russia, illegal political activity broke out of its previous bounds of occasional student riots and sedate reading and discussion circles into political conspiracy. The life of conspiracy in which Joseph Stalin was to spend the rest of his days in a strange way always retained a certain atmosphere of adolescence.

The world of revolution was at first a world of youth. All the branches of the revolutionary movement, and not only those socialists who one day would call themselves Communists, lived by a different time scale than that of ordinary mortals. In joining the conspiracy at the age of nineteen or twenty, Soso Djugashvili was far from being young in the sense that revolution understood the word. For an initiate to be young was to be fourteen or fifteen, the age at which characters as diverse as Ilya Ehrenburg and Vyacheslav Scriabin (later Molotov) joined the Bolsheviks. In one's late teens and early twenties one was expected to be a mature revolutionary, a veteran of imprisonment or exile. In his middle twenties the revolutionary was deemed ripe for leadership, for central committees, and, if a Marxist, for authorship of a theoretical treatise or at least some articles. The thirties were old age.

In 1905 the Third Congress of the Russian Socialist Party was opened, as custom dictated, by its oldest delegate, Caucasian Bolshevik Michael Tshakaya. This venerable patriarch was then all of thirty-nine years old. Following this moment of glory Tshakaya, we are told in all seriousness by an author, became senile and never again played a very active role in the Bolshevik movement.[20] For all the exaggeration inherent in such comments, it is true that many devoted revolutionaries simply "could not take it" after they reached the age of thirty or thirty-

[20] He was to die in good standing in Georgia at eighty-six; perhaps his "senility" enabled him to survive the purges.

five. It was not simply the matter of police harassments, imprisonments, and exiles, but the whole feverish, emotional pitch of the revolutionary's existence amid intraparty squabbles, violent personal feuds, and the like. Some settled abroad. Others, from being "practitioners" (and we shall see how important was this term and what it meant to convey for Stalin), became mere sympathizers of the cause, resumed their real identity, devoted themselves mainly to their families and professions, and occasionally would provide shelter and financial help to their illegal comrades. Many simply turned their backs upon the movement and repudiated their earlier enthusiasms and obsessions. The handful who carried their clandestine activities into their middle age would in turn be subject to attrition through deaths from ailments contracted in or aggravated by prison or Siberia, and from nervous breakdowns and suicides.

But apart from the numerical preponderance of the young, not uncommon in other radical movements and in other societies, Russian revolutionary socialism bore a peculiarly adolescent imprint. The themes of betrayal and suspicion continually appeared—in connection with the Secret Police's penetration of the movement, and in the fear (only too often substantiated) that one's closest comrade might be a spy. Equally grueling were the intraparty and intrafaction struggles, constant charges and countercharges of betrayal of Marxism, of lapsing into this or that deviation, personal rivalry and envy compounded by ideology—for leadership was to be the reward not only for individual bravery and organizational skill but also for intellectual attainments. Youthful theatricality blended with the serious side of conspiracy and politics: at times, much of the secrecy surrounding the activities of the Bolshevik Party was not only superfluous but harmful. The pathos and exalted oratory—"Onward to a bloody struggle, March forward, O working people, To the just and sacred fight"—as the most famous Russian revolutionary song urged, clashed with the more prosaic analyses and predictions of Marxism. It claimed after all to be *scientific* socialism. Inevitably a certain ambivalence was bound to affect mental processes of even the most idealistic revolutionary: there was impassioned oratory to stir up the masses, there was the sober and unromantic awareness of what the future might bring.

What, then, set young men like Joseph Djugashvili on the road so beset with danger, prompted them to assail the autocracy which to many in 1898 still seemed unassailable? Here one must avoid two opposite but equally misleading stereotypes. The young Marxists were for the most part not just hotheads who impulsively felt the vocation for glory and martyrdom. They were gradually drawn, rather than suddenly thrust, into the revolutionary profession. Unlike the previous generation of revolutionaries who were ready to risk the gallows so that their sacrifice *might* stir up the people, the Russian Marxist at the turn of the century entered his struggle with the firm conviction that it was the Tsar's government, and eventually capitalism, that faced unequal odds. History proved that *he* would be on the winning side: patience as well as conspiratorial skills were the revolutionary's necessary equipment.

On the other hand we must not too glibly identify the young revolutionary's motivations and impulses with cynicism and craving for power or, by analogy with our own times, see him as acting out of "alienation" as it is currently understood, out of revolt against parental authority—those by now platitudinous terms which the bewildered middle-aged offer to the young in explanation of their boredom and rage. Whatever the psychological machinery behind his motivation, wherever it would lead him in the future, the Russian revolutionary acted from a perfectly rational premise that the system he was fighting was oppressive and anachronistic. Almost unique in Europe of 1898 in these respects, Russia did not have a parliament, its laws did not protect from arbitrary arrest nor provide for workers' unions. To himself and to others, Soso Djugashvili was a recruit to the cause of liberation, a word which in Russia of 1898 required no quotation marks or psychoanalytic elaboration.

From that same year, 1898, Stalin was to date his accession to Russian socialism or, to give it the formal name, the Russian Social Democratic Workers Party. There was no such *party* at the time. To be sure, in the same year *nine* delegates of various Marxist circles met in the distant Byelorussian town of Minsk and held what is grandiloquently described as its First Congress. But there was no party in the usually accepted sense of the word—i.e., with specific membership, central organs, rules, etc.—until the Second Congress, held in 1903 in London. In dating his accession from 1898, Stalin in fact showed a certain restraint; others gave even earlier dates, e.g., Krasin, 1890, Lenin, 1893—those were years in which they joined Marxist discussion circles. And some socialist veterans were even less inhibited. Thus from the very beginning the story of the movement is recounted in half history and half fiction. Many a future historian and biographer spent so much time bewailing and decrying the palpable untruths that little was left for ascertaining the facts.

And so in the case of our hero. Though tempted, we must not fall into a peevish dispute with the official Soviet version of Stalin's life, which sees Djugashvili from 1898 to 1901 leading the left, activist wing of the Third Group and the Tiflis Social Democrats, confounding his "opportunist" elders, the future Mensheviks Jordania and Djibladze; nor on the other hand with the survivors among his political enemies, who allege his utter insignificance at that time. In fact, he was one of the most active members of the small group which carried on propaganda among the Tiflis workers. We must visualize an evening meeting in some workers' quarters on the periphery of Tiflis: a group of ten or twelve surrounding a young *intelligent* expounding the ABCs of Marxism. The workers hardly need to be told of their poverty or the relative luxury in which "they"—their mostly Russian and Armenian bosses and officials—live. But they listen eagerly, if somewhat incredulously, to their instructor's tales of how in other countries the workers are organized, how through strikes they can force the capitalist to increase their wages, and how in the West they have their own holiday—the first of May—when they demonstrate and publicly voice their demands, with the police not daring to do anything about it. To those workers who are literate, the propagandist distributes some of the few tracts available in Georgian, such as the translation of *By What Do Different Classes Live?* by the Polish socialist Samuel Dickstein, then very much used for this purpose, and urges them to pass it on and discuss it with their fellow workers. Finally the conspirators (for such they would be considered by the police) cautiously, one by one, disperse into the night.

Djugashvili's horizons soon expanded beyond this elementary type of propaganda.[21] He sought to be enrolled among the collaborators of *Kvali*, in which socialist ideas were being publicly purveyed in a somewhat veiled form. But its moving spirit, Noah Jordania, thought him not quite ready for this more advanced, literary work. Perhaps this was a factor in Stalin's siding with Bolsheviks when the Georgian Marxists split in 1903–4 and Jordania led most of them into the Menshevik faction. Around 1900 he began to have contacts with some of the more sophisticated among the Tiflis workers. These were for the most part Russians employed in the city's few factories but mainly in the railway yards, Tiflis being not only the principal communications center in the Caucasus but also the locus of important railway shops. Some of them had already had experience with the workers' political circles and the police in Russia proper. Railway workers tended, not surprisingly, to be among the most politically advanced of all. While the Georgian- and Russian-speaking socialist circles were at first separate, in the late 1890s they began to draw closer. The first encounters took place through joint celebrations of May 1, when a group held a picnic somewhere in the rural environs of Tiflis. A watch was posted to warn of the police or any suspicious passerby, and the holidaymakers listened to speeches, unfurled the red flag, and sang some appropriate songs.

It was in such bucolic circumstances that in 1898 a railway worker named Sergei Alliluyev met Djibladze and Jordania. The circle of his Georgian socialist acquaintances then expanded, and in 1900 he en-

---

[21] Strictly speaking, this was agitation, propaganda in the Marxian lexicon being reserved for "higher" theoretical discussions.

countered the man with whom his connection was to bring his family so much tragedy. Stalin's future father-in-law was then in his middle thirties. Of peasant origin and practically without any formal training, his native acumen had enabled him to acquire several skills, and he worked intermittently as locksmith, engine driver, and master electrician. It is easy to see why early in life he had been drawn to revolutionary associations: Alliluyev by his own accounts had a quick temper and a need to defy authority. This repeatedly led to his being fired because of quarrels with foremen and fellow employees, even when, as in one case, his boss was a fellow socialist. His contacts and devoted revolutionary work brought him in touch with the leaders of the socialist movement, but because of his working background he was never to be one. In the evening of his life the old revolutionary occasionally visited his son-in-law's Kremlin quarters, waiting meekly for a chance to speak with him but then hurriedly taking his leave when Stalin arrived for supper surrounded by Politburo potentates. It is a measure of Russia during the 1930s that this man of fierce temperament and strong loyalties could not or would not dare to intercede on behalf of threatened members of his own family or of his old comrades.[22]

When Alliluyev recorded his memories for the first time, in 1922, Stalin figured in them but dimly. Yet the article[23] remains a valuable testimony concerning the increased intercourse between Russian and Georgian socialists in Tiflis at the turn of the century. The Third Group became the Georgian component of the Russian socialist movement, and in fact the name was not used after that time. The main credit for that development belonged to two remarkable men, contemporaries of Djugashvili and his associates in the Tiflis circle: Alexander Tsulukidze and Vladimir Ketskhoveli.

The socialist prince Tsulukidze had become a member of the seminarians' clandestine group in 1895–96 although, as befitted his station in life, his education was much more elaborate. He finished a classical high-school course and then attended the jurisprudence faculty of Moscow University. He was an early contributor to *Kvali* and also wrote, beginning in 1896, for the much more prestigious periodical with a progressive orientation, *Iberia*.[24] Tsulukidze was the first in Tiflis to expound in Georgian and in writing the more theoretical side of Marxism. As one

[22] His granddaughter ascribes it to his delicacy. Alliluyeva, pp. 45–46.

[23] Sergei Alliluyev, in *The Red Chronicle* (Moscow), No. 5 (1922).

[24] *Iberia* was edited by Prince Ilya Chavchavadze, then considered the national poet and man of letters of Georgia. Chavchavadze, a veteran of an earlier nationalist and liberal orientation, was at first sympathetic to the new Marxist ideas. But gradually he became antagonistic, and when printers' strikes began to interfere with the publication of his journal, he referred to the socialist agitators as swine. The aged writer was assassinated in 1908, and the crime and motives behind it were never solved.

of the two Georgian socialists in those early days who actually had read *Capital*,[25] his writings on economics show a certain flair, and but for his untimely end he might have developed into a leading theoretician of the Communist movement. But he was frail and consumptive, and political passions and agitation aggravated his condition. Some years later Tsulukidze, long under police surveillance, was arrested but after a few weeks released on account of his health. It was the revolutionary spring of 1905, and also the time of intrasocialist factional disputes between the Mensheviks and Bolsheviks. Tsulukidze had taken Lenin's side, and at a political meeting a Menshevik berated him with an obvious if unfair thrust: here you have a prince, the son of a landowner, preaching about exploitation and inequality! The audience could not have been much impressed: because of peculiarly Georgian conditions there were noblemen in all revolutionary parties. But the sick man was deeply affronted, we are told, and it probably brought on his subsequent hemorrhage. He died on June 8, 1905. His funeral in his ancestral seat turned into a public demonstration in which all branches of the Georgian revolutionary movement participated, Joseph Djugashvili being one of the speakers.

The fate of Ketskhoveli was tragic in a different way. This fellow alumnus of the Gori and Tiflis schools was the most striking personality in the seminarians' revolutionary circle in the 1890s and the one most instrumental in merging the Georgian revolutionary movement with the broader stream of Russian Marxism. Writing in 1922, Alliluyev was constrained to admit that "David" (Ketskhoveli's Party pseudonym) was the most important member in the circle to which Stalin then belonged. While the latter was still giving his lessons in elementary Marxism, Ketskhoveli in 1899 organized a strike of the employees of the Tiflis horse-drawn tramcars. Soon thereafter he conceived an idea that was to have great consequences for the socialist movement, not only in Georgia, but in the whole Empire as well.

The idea was to set up an illegal printing press which would be big and efficient enough to print a clandestine revolutionary journal in Georgian, even big enough to become one of the central producers of illegal literature for all of Russia. To us this might seem not very original. But in the context of the Russian revolutionary movement it was bold and far-reaching. Illegal literature was the very lifeblood of the revolutionary movement. The Marxist journals and theoretical works which were published openly, such as *Kvali*, had to be restrained in their tone and were not designed for mass audiences. Dispersed and uncoordinated, the clandestine circles could exist for decades before making an impact on the mass of workers. Thus really revolutionary literature

[25] The other one was, of course, Nicholas "Karl Marx" Chkheidze.

36

had to be smuggled from abroad or published on small hand presses. And indeed, in 1900 an event occurred that was much more pregnant with consequences for the future of Russian revolutionary socialism than the "congress" of 1898: *Iskra* (*The Spark*) began to appear abroad, published by a band which included the father of Russian Marxism, George Plekhanov, and the thirty-year-old Vladimir Ilyich Ulyanov. But the smuggling into Russia of this first central organ of Russian Marxism was cumbersome and dangerous; many copies were confiscated, lost in passage, or undistributed.

Ketskhoveli, with his indefatigable energy, managed to procure first the money and then up-to-date printing equipment capable of speedy and accurate reproduction of thousands of copies of journals and pamphlets, and finally found an ideal conspiratorial location for the press in the Muslim sector of the Caucasian oil center of Baku.[26] Thus, in the summer of 1901 in the house officially belonging to a certain Ali Baba,[27] there began functioning a clandestine press which was for five years, to the befuddlement of the police, the source of a massive flow of revolutionary literature in Georgian as well as in Armenian and Russian. The establishment—*Nina*, as it became known in the conspiratorial code—soon provided a partial solution to the difficulties experienced in the propagation of *Iskra*. Mats of the journal were dispatched from Western Europe on a long journey to northern Persia, whence, by sea or on horses, they were delivered to Baku, there to be set and printed in large quantities by *Nina*. What customs official would look for revolutionary literature entering from *Persia?* The Tsarist bureaucrats and police officials were confounded by this underground press, just as seventy years later their infinitely more powerful and efficient Communist successors are still perplexed as to what to do about *samizdat*, that increasingly large body of illegal literature circulating in Soviet Russia.

Nina functioned in strictest secrecy. Sought avidly by the police, its location was changed several times. In fact the secrecy surrounding the operations of the press was so thorough that several well-informed accounts of the history of socialism in the Caucasus state that it ceased operating in 1902, while some others confuse it with the Tiflis press, *Nadya*, set up in 1903. *Nina*'s crew, its first boss tells us, were forbidden to leave their conspiratorial premises except at night.[28] But within the

26 Baku, for reasons which will be dealt with later, was preferable to and safer than Tiflis. In order to purchase a large press, one had to have a government permit. Ketskhoveli procured an official form and signed it with a governor's name.

27 A Muslim's home was less likely to be searched casually by the police because of the Muslims' feelings about the privacy of their womenfolk and the usually explosive situation in Baku's Casbah.

28 Abel Yenukidze, "History of the Organization and Work of Illegal Socialist Presses in the Caucasus, 1900–1906," in *The Proletarian Revolution* (Moscow), No.

socialist world Ketskhoveli was now famous. From distant London and Geneva, Lenin and other editors of *Iskra* inquired anxiously about *"Nina's* father," as he was now known in the coded correspondence. Krasin, then the chief socialist figure in Baku and about whom we shall have a lot to say, often referred to Ketskhoveli as an organizational genius. Djugashvili was also to attest his admiration and friendship for his fellow alumnus who gave him his start as publicist by inviting him to write for *Brdzola (The Struggle)*, the revolutionary journal in Georgian which *Nina* began to print in 1901.

Only some thirty years later was Stalin to demonstrate that his admiration must have been tinged with envy. By that time Lado Ketskhoveli was long dead, killed by a prison guard's bullet on August 17, 1903. Most accounts attribute his murder to an unprovoked and premeditated savagery of the prison administration. But while murder it was, its circumstances were much more complex.

In his makeup, Ketskhoveli suggests more a revolutionary of the previous generation—that of the People's Will, with its sacrificial, often suicidal impulses—than the usually level-headed and prudent new breed of Russian socialists. In 1901–2 a wave of arrests hit Caucasian socialists. Among the arrested was a local agent of *Iskra*, Sophia Ginsburg, a dentist by profession,[29] on whom the police found a number of names and addresses. Though he was not at first detained, arrests of his associates deeply depressed Ketskhoveli, who then actually precipitated his own arrest by volunteering his true identity during a police search of an associate's apartment; though he was armed, he did not try to resist. Imprisoned in the Tiflis jail, the ancient citadel of Metekh, his spirits at first improved, but then another incident thrust him into utter despondency. He tried to smuggle out a note to a comrade, it was intercepted, and the addressee, Abel Yenukidze, was arrested in turn. Alliluyev, who was in the jail at the same time, makes it clear that Ketskhoveli decided to goad the guards into killing him.[30] Day after day he would stand in the embrasure of his cell window and in a stentorian voice shout to other prisoners and passersby. His fellow political prisoners' pleadings and the guards' threats were unavailing. The unhappy man, helped by a trigger-happy guard, finally met his desired end.

The untimely demise of his two closest associates and contemporaries, one a victim of physical, the other of psychic ailments, sets off Djugashvili's good fortune in these respects. Short in stature (about five

13 (1922), p. 149. By 1935 his account was deemed injurious to the Stalin legend and contributed to Yenukidze's meeting the grim fate of an "enemy of the people."
29 This may come as a surprise to an American or British reader, but in some respects turn-of-the-century Russia was amazingly modern. In fact there were *two* female dentists named Ginsburg in the ranks of the revolutionary movement.
30 Alliluyev, p. 17.

foot five) but with a vigorous constitution that would enable him to endure the rigors of the Siberian winter, he was certainly not of a disposition to grow despondent over a fellow prisoner's arrest. And only time would show what complexes lurked behind the restlessness and irascibility of this alleged man of steel. ☆☆☆

FROM the end of 1899 Stalin had a cover for his illegal work: he was employed as a clerk in the Tiflis Geophysical Observatory and lived on its premises. By 1900 we have evidence that he was already more than a rank-and-file revolutionary worker. When Abel Yenukidze came from Baku to obtain the Tiflis comrades' financial assistance for setting up the *Nina* printing press, he met in a tavern with Sylvester Djibladze, then known all over Georgia, and a young and taciturn companion, Soso Djugashvili. But the three Georgians could not agree. The Tiflis representatives would help only if the press were located in their own city.

If this testified to a certain residual parochialism on the part of the local Marxists, the events of 1900 were soon to dissipate it. Contacts between Georgian and Russian socialists multiplied. Among the latter whom Djugashvili met was Victor Kurnatovsky, a chemical engineer and early convert to the cause. From him he must have heard about Vladimir Ilyich Ulyanov, whom Kurnatovsky had met while exiled in the same district in Siberia between 1897 and 1900. It is of course unlikely that the name of the future Lenin meant much to the Georgian socialists. For he was merely one of a group of six who were then setting up *Iskra* in Western Europe. Soso and the others were no doubt much more assiduous in their inquiries about Plekhanov, whom Kurnatovsky met while in the West, and about those other veterans now also lending their hands and prestige to the journalistic enterprise, Vera Zasulich and Paul Axelrod.

In July–August, Tiflis's first major strike broke out along the railway depot and shop workers, organized and led by Russians, among whom were Alliluyev and the future President of the Soviet Union, Michael Kalinin. The authorities now took serious notice of the contacts between the Georgian intellectuals and the workers. Alliluyev, who was arrested and detained for some months, was questioned about his acquaintances among the ex-seminarians. Socialist activity in Tiflis was entering a new, more advanced phase, just as all over the Empire there were signs of revolutionary stirrings, student disorders, demands for constitutional liberties, portents of the new age.

Shortly after his accession to the throne in 1894 Nicholas II was presented with a petition by a group of liberal nobility expressing hope for constitutional reforms. The prepared text of his answer referred to such notions as "ideas without any foundation" but the ill-fated monarch instead blurted out "senseless dreams." This now became the sardonic battle cry among the liberal elements pressing for a parliament. And around 1900 another future rival of the Russian Social Democrats was founded, the Socialist Revolutionary Party, which believed in individual terror as a political weapon, stressed the peasant rather than the industrial worker, and was thus closer to old Populism than to Marxism.

In March 1901 a number of Tiflis socialists were arrested. On March 21 Djugashvili's room at the Observatory was searched by the police. All biographical and historical accounts, whether Soviet or Western, friendly or hostile, declare this date to be the beginning of Stalin's clandestine existence.[31] Why this should be so is a mystery, for he went on working at the Observatory for another week after the search.[32] Instead of Djugashvili vanishing suddenly into the long night of the underground we must picture him one week later prosaically collecting his pay and things. The search had not turned up anything incriminating, but it was advisable to move elsewhere, possibly to go to Gori, until the heat was off. Nor did he even then go "illegal," to live under a false name and with forged papers. When arrested in Batum one year later, he was still operating under his real name. The Tsarist police were sometimes devious, but more often lackadaisical, as far as suspects of no great importance were concerned.

The arrest of many prominent Tiflis socialists did make Djugashvili more important on the local scene, however. He was instrumental in arranging the first open socialist demonstration on May Day of 1901. On April 22[33] about two thousand workers marched through the center of town singing revolutionary songs such as the famous "Varshavianka" and carrying banners with radical slogans. The police were constrained to call on the Cossacks—the mark of a real revolutionary event—to disperse the demonstration. Some of them were injured, many more arrested. All in all it was a great propaganda success, which put Tiflis on

31 E.g., "After the search Comrade Stalin went 'underground.' " Lavrenti Beria, *On the History of the Bolshevik Organization in Transcaucasia* (trans. from the 4th Russian ed.; London, 1940), p. 23. "He had to shed his identity. . . . Now he was descending into the actual underground from which he was to emerge finally only in 1917, shortly before he became a member of the first Soviet Cabinet." Isaac Deutscher, *Stalin: A Political Biography* (New York, 1967), p. 37.

32 "March 21, J. V. Stalin's quarters in the Observatory searched. . . . March 28, J. V. Stalin leaves work in the Physical Laboratory. . . ." From the chronology in Stalin, *Collected Works* (Moscow, 1946–52), I, 417–18.

33 Because of the difference in the two calendars, the Western May 1 corresponded to April 19 in Russia, and sometimes this would be varied by holding the celebration on the closest Sunday.

the map of Russian socialism, and it was noted as such from afar by *Iskra*.

According to much later accounts, Djugashvili around this time began to intrigue against Djibladze, was brought before a Party court, and then toward the end of the year eased out of Tiflis. This is undoubtedly an exaggeration. Personal squabbles were a common occurrence among the young radicals, and Soso was already acquiring a reputation in this respect. But he remained a revolutionary in good standing.

That summer he became a contributor to *Brdzola*. Stalin's *Collected Works* claim for him authorship of the editorial in the first issue of September 1901.[34] As late as 1941 Soviet sources were still unaware that Comrade Stalin was the author of that historic document.[35] And it is more likely, as Deutscher concludes, that it was a joint effort, with Stalin lending a hand.[36] The editorial gave reasons why a legal newspaper which is subject to censorship cannot speak for socialism. Some commentators have seen this as a confirmation of the Soviet thesis that Djugashvili, Ketskhoveli, and Tsulukidze were struggling against Jordania et al.—the group publishing *Kvali*—but it is more likely a typical conspiratorial mystification designed to throw the police off the scent of *Kvali*, the offices of which had been repeatedly raided. A similar motivation accounts for the editorial's pretense that *Brdzola* was being published abroad: "We who live far from our country cannot follow the revolutionary developments in Georgia. . . ."[37]

The other literary production claimed for Stalin for 1901 is a lengthy article in the next issue of *Brdzola* for March–December 1902 entitled "The Russian Social Democratic Party and Its Tasks at Hand." It is also unsigned, and though the style is reminiscent of the later Stalin some suspicions about its authorship must remain, since even the faithful Beria did not credit it to the Leader but merely talked about Stalin sending materials and articles to Baku, where Ketskhoveli would edit them for the paper. And so this also is most likely a product of joint authorship. The article gives a standard exposition of the ideology and tactics of Russian Social Democracy as then propagated by *Iskra* and condemns various heresies then sprouting up in Western and in Russian Marxism. It castigates the Revisionism then advocated by the German

---

[34] Stalin's *Collected Works* began to appear only in 1946, after he had been master of Russia for nearly twenty years. This uncharacteristic restraint was due to his realistic recognition that his literary output, certainly before 1917, was not very impressive in quantity and quality and that the comparison with Lenin's *Collected Works* could not be very flattering. In the introduction to the first edition it was claimed that many of his works from 1901 to 1907 still had not been located.

[35] See J. Djaparidze, *The Proletarian Revolution* (Moscow), No. 1 (1941), pp. 162–63.

[36] Deutscher, p. 38.

[37] Stalin, I, 10.

socialist Eduard Bernstein, who argued that certain parts of Marx's canon had now become obsolete and that socialism should shift its emphasis from revolution to parliamentarism and the fight for democratic rights. And it assails the Economists, that handful of Russian Marxists publishing the illegal *Workers' Thought* in St. Petersburg who wanted the workers to concentrate on the economic struggle, for higher pay, unions, shorter working hours. On the contrary, argues *The Struggle*, what is needed is emphasis on the political struggle and a strong Party organization. Clashes with the authorities, those demonstrations which bring forth the charging Cossacks and leave behind numerous casualties, are useful because they enhance the class consciousness of the workers. The piece *does* have that mixture so characteristic of the mature Stalin of stylistic awkwardness and repetitiousness with occasional eloquence. After commenting on student disorders, the article says, "It is the working class which should take up the Russian banner from the weak hands of the students and, having inscribed on it 'Down with the Autocracy, Long Live a Democratic Constitution,' lead the Russian people to freedom."[38]

Whatever his share in writing for *Brdzola* it could not obviously fill all the time of an energetic and restless man, and Djugashvili was now also without a job. In November 1901 twenty-five Tiflis Marxists met and elected a committee of nine to guide the party organization; Djugashvili was one of the nine. It is concerning the composition of the committee that we have the first reliable notice of his squabbling with others. An account of the socialist movement in the Caucasus first written in 1907 and 1908 and published abroad in 1910 mentions a "young, energetic comrade" who argued that there were no workers suitable for committee functions. "Is there among you a single man suitable for committee work? Tell the truth with your hand on the heart." How could conspiracy be preserved with workers on the committee? Won't the police catch on when they see a house frequented by both intellectuals, with their coats and ties, and workers in their overalls and blouses?[39] The real reason for these objections may have been not so much intellectual snobbery, though it was quite prevalent in the socialist circles, as fear that the proletarian members would infect the committee with "economism," push it in the direction of prosaic eco-

[38] Stalin, I, 25. In his very last public speech, on October 14, 1952, Stalin said to the representatives of foreign Communists in Moscow for the Nineteenth Party Congress, "The banner of democratic freedom has been cast overboard by the bourgeoisie. . . . It is up to you, representatives of Communist and democratic parties, to lift this banner and carry it forward if you wish to gather the people around you."

[39] The argument was not entirely puerile. An experienced detective, or a janitor functioning as an informer, could usually spot a middle-class person masquerading as a worker.

nomic demands rather than glorious revolutionary struggle. But three workers were elected, and the disgruntled young *intelligent* began to look for another place where he could satisfy his "personal whim and tendency to seek power."[40]

This delicate situation was resolved by Djugashvili's being delegated to carry out socialist propaganda in Batum. This Black Sea port of some 35,000 inhabitants became in 1900 the outlet of an oil pipeline from Baku. It had several oil refineries, a bottling plant, and two tobacco factories. But its 11,000 workers were, even by comparison with those in Tiflis, politically backward. They were for the most part Georgian peasants, many of them using their wretchedly paid industrial work as a means to save a few rubles and then go back to their villages. Unlike Baku and Tiflis, there were no government factory inspectors in Batum, and the workers were often mistreated by their managers and foremen. On the surface it was an ideal situation for socialist propaganda. But Russian Marxists were for the most part still hesitant about associating themselves with the workers' "narrow" economic grievances, and the Batum workers were too primitive to establish a connection between their deprivations and the political system under which they lived. Noah Jordania recounts in his memoirs how hard it was at first to propagandize the Georgian peasants, how after one pedagogical session at which he talked about such marvels of modern scientific inventions as electricity one village worthy exclaimed, "Glory be to the Lord! What will our Tsar think of next!"

To try to instruct such people in the intricacies of Marxism, the evils of revisionism and economism, was to beat one's head against the wall. Fortunately for the cause of socialism, if not for the Batum workers, the economic situation soon enabled them to receive a practical lesson in the meaning of class struggle. ☆☆☆

O N February 26, 1902, the administration of an oil refinery owned by the Rothschilds[41] gave, because of decline in demand, two weeks' notice to three hundred eighty-nine of its workers. Thereupon all of its roughly nine-hundred-man crew struck. The provincial governor warned the workers that if they persisted, they would be forcibly returned to their villages—something which gives a good idea of the

[40] S. T. Arkomed, *The Workers' Movement and Social Democracy in the Caucasus, 1880–1903* (Moscow, 1923), pp. 84, 87.

[41] They, as well as the Nobel brothers, were among the most substantial owners of oil fields and plants in the area.

rights of the worker and of the idiocy of the local administration, for what better way of spreading radicalism among the hitherto backward and placid peasantry? When the warnings did not bring results, thirty-two of the strike leaders were imprisoned to await compulsory repatriation.

Up to this point the workers' movement had been entirely spontaneous. But now it was natural for them to seek a man with "education" to advise them what to do next. One of the few workers with some socialist training, Konstantin Kandelaki, had been host to such a man, Soso Djugashvili. As behooved a man with knowledge of the world, Soso did have an ingenious idea: let the workers march on the jail and demand the freeing of their comrades or, if not, that they all be imprisoned. The demonstration took place on March 8, but the commander of the troops now summoned to Baku foiled the stratagem by accommodating the workers and arresting all four hundred or so of the demonstrators. Now the facilities of the local prison were strained and it was obvious to experienced revolutionary strategists that a much larger crowd presenting the same demand would make the officials retreat in discomfiture. Djugashvili pooh-poohed the possibility that there might be serious trouble: the soldiers would not dare to shoot. And so on March 9 an "enormous crowd," according to the official account, some three thousand people according to others, approached the transit prison, which was guarded by a platoon of soldiers. More troops were summoned and the commander demanded that the demonstrators disperse. Their leaders repeated their demands, and when they were refused, stones and bricks began to be thrown to shouts of, "Beat them! Grab their arms! They cannot shoot!" A warning salvo in the air had no effect, and the soldiers then were ordered to shoot into the crowd. Fourteen of the demonstrators were killed, more than fifty wounded.

The above description comes from the official Soviet account of the event, published in 1937.[42] From it—and this shows how one can glean the uncomfortable truth even from documents published at the height of Stalin adulation—one can discover such facts as that Djugashvili did not participate directly in the workers' activities but communicated his counsels through Kandelaki[43] and that some of the survivors of the demonstration, if arrested, were ready to place all the blame on the emissary from Tiflis. He certainly was not among the leaders of the crowd that surged forth on March 9, though a policeman claimed to have seen him in it.

In any case, on April 5, Joseph Djugashvili, "of no specific occupation

[42] *The Batum Demonstration of 1902*, with an introduction by Lavrenti Beria (Moscow, 1937), p. 156.
[43] *Ibid.*, p. 181.

and unknown residence," was arrested in the environs of Batum—testimony, to give him his due, to the young man's courage or even foolhardiness in staying on in the small town where he had every reason to expect he might be denounced and traced. Another incident three days later reminds us that this already somewhat Machiavellian revolutionary was still only a boy of twenty-two with disarmingly naïve ideas on how the police could be fooled. A note which he tried to smuggle out of jail, intercepted by the guards, asked its would-be recipient to go to Gori to tell his mother, his uncle, and his friend the local schoolteacher Iremashvili, that if asked by the police, they were to say that he, Soso, had spent all the previous summer and winter in Gori and did not leave till March 15.

Leo Tolstoy, in one of those majestic inconsistencies expected of a genius, stated that no one who has not been in jail knows what the state is. (He, of course, had never been in one himself, yet was very sure he knew that the state was evil.) Soso Djugashvili now had a prolonged opportunity to find out. He was in Batum jail until April 19, when he was transferred to one in the provincial center of Kutais; then in the fall he was returned to Batum prior to being sent to Siberia. Tsarist jails were not a bad epitome of Tsarist society, sometimes brutal (witness Ketskhoveli's fate), often indulgent, but almost always sloppy, irritating, and irrational. To the political prisoner, the jail was the place where he finished his education: he was allowed serious literature, could talk and dispute with other prisoners of his and different political persuasions, and at least for a period before 1906–7 was not barred from contacts with sympathizers on the outside. Lev Bronstein became world famous as Leon Trotsky, the name he took after a friendly jailer. Krasin was to confess that the only real rest he got in the tumultuous days after the Revolution of 1905–6 was the month he spent in prison. There are to be sure other tales: of sadistic guards, chains, humiliations, and prisoners' hunger strikes.

The government soon instituted proceedings against the alleged leaders of the Batum riot. Djugashvili's and Kandelaki's names were not joined in the act—for obvious reasons: in the Russian autocracy the judiciary stood out as an enclave of professional probity, and the courts were not likely to convict anybody on hearsay evidence. The result of the trial justified the government's apprehensions. Most of the accused workers, defended by Russia's leading liberal lawyers, who refused fees and came down from St. Petersburg and Moscow at their own expense, were found innocent. The ones about whose guilt there could be no doubt were given nominal sentences, which they were held to have fulfilled through their pretrial detention, the judges finding extenuating circumstances in "general ignorance and low social background" of the accused. The judgment was generally and correctly held to imply a censure of the officials' actions, and the workers of Batum bade a tumultuous farewell to the departing judges and advocates.

But the other side of Russian justice was evident in the fact that since there was no nonsense about *habeas corpus*, political prisoners could be dealt with without any bother about courts, trials, etc. And so it pleased His Imperial Majesty on July 9, 1903, to approve the Minister of Justice's "most humble submission that peasant Joseph Vissarionovich Djugashvili, guilty of crimes against the state, be sent into exile to eastern Siberia, there to be under open police surveillance for three years."

~2~

AMONG
THE
BOLSHEVIKS

Sometime during his first incarceration Soso Djugashvili became Koba, which was, until 1914, his most often used Party name. The length of his imprisonment was connected with the fact that the authorities were investigating in a rather leisurely fashion the affair of Georgian socialism as a whole.[1] The same rescript which assigned Koba to Siberia also prescribed exile for a number of Tiflis Marxists, including Kurnatovsky and Djibladze.

Administrative exile was a relic of the once widespread European punishment system of transportation—the getting rid of criminals and troublemakers by sending them to distant places—the system that contributed to the history of the American Georgia, and Australia, French Guiana, and New Caledonia. By the time Koba became acquainted with it many of the horrors connected with Siberian exile had been abolished or moderated. Prisoners no longer made their way to distant places on foot and in chains. In some cases, such as that of Lenin in 1897, the exile was allowed to repair to his destination on his own and unguarded. But more often they were sent under guard and by "stages," i.e., the whole party was detained (sometimes for a long period) in various jails on the way before being sent on by railway, horse, or boat. Having arrived at the last stage, usually a minor administrative seat, prisoners were then distributed throughout the vast area of the assigned Siberian province, some in the few towns where there might be fellow

---

[1] A police document dated February 9, 1903, seems to imply that Djugashvili was then free in Batum, though under special police surveillance, but the date is probably wrong and should be 1902. *The Batum Demonstration of 1902* (Moscow, 1937), p. 190.

47

political exiles, others to small villages and settlements inhabited by primitive natives and where the only Russian and "authority" would be the village constable. Here one usually rented a hut or a room from a native (the government gave exiles a small allowance, but one needed help from friends or relatives for such luxuries as tobacco and hunting equipment). There was no interference with one's life, though too frequent and suspicious correspondence might bring a police search party. One could hunt, fish, read and write, visit "neighboring" comrades (sometimes hundreds of miles away), or, if so inclined, pursue one's anthropological and ethnographic studies. For a young, healthy, and self-reliant man it was not an intolerable existence, certainly preferable to an ordinary jail, not to mention such notorious ones as the fortress of SS. Peter and Paul or Schlüsselburg. For others, the rigors of the Siberian winter and most of all the loneliness proved unbearable and precipitated physical collapse or suicide.

In reading the biographies of several men who endured these Siberian exiles, one must conclude that escape was not too difficult. There were already opportunities en route. The exiles' party might be too large for a local jail and the "politicals" would be quartered in private homes, required only to report regularly to the police. If the travel arrangements were atypically efficient and the prisoners delivered promptly to the final destination, there was still hope, even in the Godforsaken settlements in the midst of the snowy wastes. The local constable was often friendly— the exile was after all the only other "cultured" resident—and was frequently drunk for days on end. For a few rubles the natives would furnish a carriage or sleigh and horses for a trip to the nearest railway station or river junction. Here there were usually other exiles to help with money or false identity papers; if not, the local *intelligent*, doctor, or schoolteacher (himself a former exile or descendant of one) would feel bound to help the fighter for freedom even if he was of a different political persuasion. And government authorities in Siberia were often more liberal than those in Russia proper. During his exile in 1911–12 in the Narim region, Jacob Sverdlov, a future Soviet dignitary, tried repeatedly to flee. He was recaptured four times but instead of being punished or incarcerated was simply returned to his previous location. On the fifth attempt he was successful. In fact one might well wonder why so many others never tried to escape. But circumstances varied. Some exiles would not or could not risk the lengthy trip back to Russia and the exposure to terrible winter storms. Others, like Lenin in 1897– 1900, were not yet committed to living illegally under false names or migrating abroad, and those were the alternatives if one fled.

The official story of Koba's trip has him traveling through the Black Sea area—Novorossiysk, Rostov, Tsaritsyn (which one day would bear his name as Stalingrad), Samara (later, Kuibyshev); then the long trip to Irkutsk, along with a usual exile party which contained criminals as well as "politicals." On November 27, 1902, we are told, he reached his destination, the village of New Uda, in the Balagan region of the province of Irkutsk, whence on January 5, 1904, he fled, arriving in the Caucasus in February. There is nothing implausible about that chronology, but there must remain some doubts about it, and about whether he in fact ever reached Siberia, for one fairly authoritative source contradicts these assertions. A collection of biographical materials about prominent socialists collected in Russia in 1922, i.e., before he had assumed power, states flatly that he fled not from New Uda but from a transit prison.[2] There are some obvious inaccuracies in this source, but what lends weight to this version of the escape is that it is based on a police circular from the year 1904.

The reason for doctoring the story is also at hand, for it would fit in with one palpable falsification in Stalin's biography. Shortly after Lenin's death Stalin was to claim that in December 1903, while in New Uda, he received a note from Lenin, then in Geneva. There is no evidence to support the claim and there could be none: if by any chance Lenin in 1903 had heard of Djugashvili, which is unlikely, he had no reason to write him a letter. But if the story was to have any faint air of probability, Koba *had* to be in his destined location in Siberia—for otherwise how would Lenin have sent the letter: "To the Batum jail for the state criminal Joseph Djugashvili. Please forward if necessary"? But even though the two men did not communicate in 1903, that was the year in which their destinies became interwoven with fateful results for their country and the world. ☆☆☆

O N July 30[3] fifty delegates of various Russian socialist circles and organizations at home and abroad assembled in Brussels. When they adjourned on August 23 in London (where the Congress had to transfer because of the Belgian authorities' request), the Russian Social Democratic Workers Party had been born, this time a real organization and no longer just a name, as it still had been in 1898, after the First Congress. The Second Congress not only adopted the Party program and several resolutions, elected governing organs, etc., but was at

[2] V. I. Nevsky, *Materials for a Biographical Dictionary of the Social Democrats* (Moscow, 1923), p. 238.
[3] Dates of events in the West are given according to the Western calendar.

the origin of the momentous split in the movement between Bolsheviks and Mensheviks.

Those names, which now resound through the pages of history, were the simple consequence of a vote on one of many issues before the meeting on which the Bolsheviks—"men of the majority"—obtained more votes than the Mensheviks—"men of the minority." And the question was whether the editorial board of *Iskra* should have three or six members![4]

Were the Bolsheviks "hard" and the Mensheviks "soft"? Did the former believe in violence and revolution, the latter in democracy and parliament? It can be stated categorically that until April 1917 there were no major ideological differences between the two factions, and whatever minor ones arose were temporary and unstable—i.e., at one point the Bolsheviks would be more militant and the Mensheviks more cautious, at another vice versa. The almost universal belief that the two factions represented two different breeds of men is the result of a vast outpouring of literature which began at the very moment of the split and increased manifold with the Russian Revolution. The victors then gloated over their enemies' un-Marxist and unrevolutionary hesitation and scruples. The vanquished bewailed their oppressor's undemocratic and unsocialist inclination to violence and deception. But while such stereotypes have *some* validity for 1917–18, they are grossly misleading when projected back to the years before 1917.

Prior to that date, the difference between the two sometimes warring, sometimes cooperating, factions can be summarized and delimited in one word: Lenin. It was one man's resolution and personality which kept the Party divided, first on the issue of people who should run it, then on tactics. But Lenin changed his mind as frequently as his opponents did—now proposing armed struggle, then decrying it and arguing that the socialists should work through legal institutions, but always holding that the opposing or even slightly different view was a betrayal of Marxism and Revolution. His personality gradually imprinted itself on his faction, but until the moment of victory many Bolsheviks could not quite understand why they followed this man, so unreasonable at times, so capable of being irascible and explosive over trivia. In the end he also mesmerized many of his opponents: many Mensheviks came almost to believe that, yes, they had been "opportunists," "liquidators" (people who faintheartedly believed in advancing the Revolution through legal means). He who excuses himself too much ends by incriminating himself, says the French proverb, and indeed under the

[4] Votes did not necessarily mean individual adherents, since some delegates had two votes and others were there in an advisory capacity. On the *Iskra* vote, the Bolsheviks got nineteen votes (or twenty-two, according to another ballot) against the Mensheviks' seventeen.

whiplash of Lenin's childlike repetition "yes, you are . . . ," and then with the trumpeting of thousands of Soviet books and pamphlets, the remnants of the defeated faction came to contribute to the myth.

The Mensheviks had no single leader. Even the leading group fluctuated, with Plekhanov and Trotsky sometimes in, sometimes standing aside. The more "stable" leaders, such as Lenin's erstwhile closest friend Martov, or Dan, never sought or were able to dominate the faction as Lenin did his.

Yet as one looks at the two branches of Russian Marxism until the fateful days of 1917, one finds a striking similarity of views and, for the most part, of tactics. Both believed in the eventual coming of socialism, the dictatorship of the proletariat. Intellectually as well, the Bolsheviks and Mensheviks followed the Marxian conclusion that Russia was not ready for socialism, that following the bourgeois-democratic revolution there would be a period when a parliamentary republic would allow capitalism to function until the economy and society were ready for the next phase. But *temperamentally* most Russian Marxists could not really acquiesce in the imperative of their theory, could not visualize that the glorious struggle for freedom should conclude, even if temporarily, in the rule of capitalists and bourgeoisie, in those parliamentary games which they observed and so detested in contemporary France or Germany. With very few exceptions Russian revolutionary Marxists of all persuasions, often men of compassion as well as dedication, lacked those two qualities so fundamental to civilized political life: tolerance and patience. ☆☆☆

VLADIMIR Ilyich Ulyanov, who went by the name of Lenin, was at the time of the birth of Bolshevism thirty-three years old. From then until October 1917 his activity reminds one of a story Tolstoy tells: he saw at a distance a man whose motions suggested that he was mad; coming closer, he realized that in fact the man was sharpening a knife. The charge that Lenin was mad was made repeatedly until October 1917 and not always as a figure of speech. Yet he did sharpen the knife, the Party, which, under improbable and fantastic conditions of Russia in 1917, would seize power, then hold it against equally fantastic odds.

Lenin's background, temperament, and mode of activity, were in drastic contrast to his successor's. He was by birth and training an *intelligent*. In appearance as well as habits a middle-class Russian from the Volga region, there remained about Lenin to the very end a certain parochialism which made him feel ill at ease even in Petersburg and

Moscow, not to mention London or Paris. Though he lived abroad so much and had an excellent command of the major European languages he was in a way *more* parochial than the Georgian peasant who succeeded him. Lenin was little interested in or understanding of, even though thoroughly conversant with, the West, with its institutions and thought. It is almost impossible to imagine him in a familiar conversation impressing Churchill, Roosevelt, or De Gaulle. All that he was interested in and passionately sought in the West was Marxism, its development there, its revolutionary opportunities. So his fervent though unconscious Russian nationalism was strikingly different from Stalin's. He loved rural and small-town Russia, with its quaint customs and passivity, much as the Marxist in him saw that as backwardness. "Our Russians are too mild," he was wont to say, and for the tough Party tasks he would often prefer Jews, Poles, Caucasians. The assimilated Georgian, on the other hand, came to admire the rapacious side of the Russian tradition, its greatness and expansiveness, figures like Peter the Great and Ivan the Terrible.

Lenin was not, certainly not until well after the Revolution, a dictator or what is described as a charismatic leader, and perhaps he never sought to be one. The key to his ascendancy was self-assurance and endurance in argument: where he stood, Marxism and Revolution were; everywhere else was error or opportunism. This self-assurance freed him from personal vindictiveness but also from humanitarian scruples. Once they admitted the errors of their way and came back to work, the "Judases," "traitors," and "scoundrels" of his oratory were again valuable collaborators. But there was to be no generosity when his acknowledged teacher, Plekhanov, was dying in destitution and under harassment from the Red Guards. He *remained* a political enemy.

Lenin's ideas on the organization of the revolutionary socialist party were laid down in his *What Is to Be Done?*, written in 1902. He sought a centralized party structure, which in view of the Russian conditions of the day had to be conspiratorial and which would be capable of infusing the growing Russian working class with Marxism and revolutionary zeal. One year later he sought to implement those ideas at the Brussels Congress. He fought the idea that Russian Social Democracy could be a loose confederation of various organizations such as was being prepared by the Jewish socialist group, the *Bund*. He wanted the Party statutes to emphasize that it was a party of activists, propagandists, and political workers, and not just a collection of people who sympathized with the ideas of Marxism and the overthrow of the autocracy.[5] But above all he fought to secure control of *Iskra*.

[5] His motion on that count was defeated in favor of Martov's looser definition of membership, and many were mistakenly to believe that this was the issue on which the Bolsheviks and Mensheviks split.

To a large extent *Iskra* had been the Party between 1900 and 1903. Now Lenin proposed that its board, the directing group of Russian Marxism, be composed of just three: himself, Plekhanov, and Martov. To others, this was an undeserved slight of three former co-editors, veterans of the revolutionary movement. But some, like Martov and twenty-three-year-old Leon Trotsky (very active at the Congress), were sure that they discerned something else behind this not wholly unreasonable attempt to get rid of three less active editors. They saw it as an attempt by one man to impose his will on the Party. Martov was to write many years later, "I was *never* to notice any element of personal vanity in Lenin's character."[6] But to a Russian Marxist, Lenin's insistence (and his frenzy on discovering that Martov, his closest friend, would not go along with him) betrayed something worse than personal vanity: a self-deluding conviction that *he* knew what was right for the Party at this precise moment and that no scruples, comradely comity, or votes would keep him from pursuing his goal. This was the Russian Social *Democratic* Workers Party, and it would never put up with anybody's claim to infallibility.

The man who was going to disprove decisively that assumption was at the time in Kutais jail, but he was referred to obliquely at the Congress. Among the reports of various socialist groups from Russia to the Congress there is one from Batum which mentions "a propagandist Social Democrat who with the assistance of some leading Tiflis workers organized a circle which spread social democratic ideas among the workers."[7] But the Batum organization was not represented, and it is doubtful that except for the three delegates from other Caucasian groups anyone at the Congress knew the man referred to in such a conspiratorially vague way.

On his voyage to exile Koba may have heard rumors of the dissension at the Congress, for such news spread very rapidly and the recent prisoners who joined the convoy may have heard something. But it is unlikely that at the time anyone really could tell what it was all about: it is difficult enough now even when one reads the protocols. Following the Congress the intraparty situation got even more entangled. Martov would not serve on the new three-man editorial board, Plekhanov shifted his position away from Lenin's, and the old editorial team of six was reinstated. Then Lenin resigned and the Mensheviks triumphantly "seized *Iskra*." How could anyone even in the West, not to mention a Samara or Irkutsk jail, make any sense of this mishmash?

Geneva, then the center of the Russian socialist migration, became a

---

[6] *Notes of a Social Democrat* (in Russian; Berlin, 1922), p. 268.
[7] *The Second Congress of the Russian Social Democratic Workers Party, Protocols* (Moscow, 1959), p. 681.

beehive of political intrigues and feuds, some of which assumed an extremely petty form. The Mensheviks' temporary recovery was due to the accession of—or, in Lenin's language, betrayal by—Plekhanov. This venerable patriarch of Russian Marxism (all of forty-seven years old) was as sensitive as he was erudite. He was all too conscious of his role as the only Russian socialist with an international reputation and as the living link with the old revolutionary tradition of the People's Will. Confronted by an impudent young man who would not bow to his legendary authority, Plekhanov would intone: "You were not even born when I was walking in the shadow of the gallows." The Bolsheviks rather delightedly stuck pins in this idol. One of Lenin's lieutenants, Lepeshinsky, who ran an eatery where the Mensheviks and Bolsheviks met and quarreled, was on the side a talented caricaturist. He now made some anti-Menshevik sketches that alluded indelicately to the fact that one of Plekhanov's brothers was a police chief in Russia! The infuriated Plekhanov recalled that he had been a student at a military academy and threatened to challenge Lepeshinsky to a duel![8]

Lenin himself, after recuperating from nervous prostration, plunged feverishly into the struggle to recapture the Party. He and his secretary-wife, Nadezhda Krupskaya, bombarded their contacts in Russia with letters decrying the Mensheviks' perfidy and anarchistic behavior in refusing to submit to the "majority." For a time he was without a paper and funds, but in the course of 1904 the latter miraculously appeared (probably, as we shall see, from Krasin in Baku), and beginning with December 1904 Lenin had his own paper, *Vperyod* (*Forward*), where repeatedly and monotonously he denounced the Mensheviks and *Iskra*: they were not real proletarians but a bunch of intellectuals and littérateurs; everybody knows, and massive correspondence from Russia confirms, that the mass of class-conscious proletarians sternly demands that these unruly intellectuals submit to the will of the majority; etc.

The initial bewilderment in Russia gradually sorted itself out as the local socialists with a sigh ranged themselves behind either Lenin or the Mensheviks. Again it is important to realize, despite everything that has been written since 1917, that the lines of demarcation remained fluid and that nobody thought of the two factions as becoming one day two separate parties, two philosophies, and two worlds. This was an intra-family quarrel aggravated by the conditions of émigré life, in which

---

[8] Mme. Lepeshinskaya was to achieve fame on her own. Though at the time engaged in cooking and dishwashing, she was actually a doctor. In the post–World War II period, when the achievements, real and fictitious, of Soviet science were being triumphantly paraded to confound the "cosmopolites," this now aged woman was awarded the Stalin Prize for her sensational discovery that bathing in soda water prolonged life.

people don't have to dodge the police and hence can allow themselves the luxury of getting excited over trivia. In Russia, especially in the Caucasus, it was obvious that there were more important things on the agenda: important events, perhaps a revolution, loomed on the horizon.

In 1904 Noah Jordania returned from abroad. He had been at the Second Congress and now threw his great prestige among the Georgian socialists behind the Mensheviks. Though both factions believed in a centralized Socialist Party rather than a loose coalition of national groups as advocated by the *Bund,* Jordania perceived, correctly, that Lenin's personality implied a more authoritarian direction for his faction. Jordania's authority then made sure that most of the Georgian socialists would follow him into the Menshevik camp.

What persuaded Koba to join the Bolsheviks? In the beginning, undoubtedly, ambition. In 1904-5 to be a Menshevik in Georgia meant to follow such acknowledged leaders as Jordania and Djibladze. To be a Bolshevik gave one, to put it crudely, a much better chance of a speedy promotion, of being not lost in a crowd but attracting attention beyond the frontiers of Georgia. Later on, Koba fell under the spell of Lenin's personality, though his admiration for his leader was from the first tinged with some resentment.

This resentment was originally due not to envy or impatience with being subordinate but to something else. Koba was now an "illegal," living under an assumed name and subject to arrest, and while this existence for the most part was neither so hazardous nor so dramatic as it is sometimes pictured, it was bound to breed resentment of people who were *writing* about revolution in the safe havens of Geneva or Paris. In the 1946 foreword to his *Collected Works,* Stalin contrasts some of Lenin's views with those held by "us practitioners of Bolshevism." On another occasion he was to refer to a number of his defeated enemies, not yet physically liquidated, such as Zinoviev, Trotsky, and Kamenev, as "littérateurs," people who conducted their revolutionary activities in cafés in various Western capitals. This characterization was hardly fair: they all had experienced arrests and exiles. But unlike them, Koba was in the underground or imprisoned or exiled almost continuously from the foundation of the Party until the February Revolution.

Beginning in February 1904 the work of a "practitioner" of revolution took Koba first to Tiflis, then to Batum. In neither place was he welcomed with great enthusiasm. The memories of the brash young agitator who through his lighthearted advice had contributed to the tragedies of March 9, 1902, in Batum were still fresh. He presumably spent time in Gori. Some biographers have read sinister implications in his returning to such familiar surroundings after an escape. Thus Trotsky: "Fugitives who were in the least conspicuous seldom returned to their native haunts where they could too easily be observed by the ever vigilant police."[9] But Trotsky does not or chooses not to remember: the Tsarist police were seldom "ever vigilant," certainly not at that time. A Georgian Menshevik recalls how after escaping from a prison convoy in the Urals, he traveled *without any identity papers* and without any trouble back to the Caucasus and his home town. There he felt safe. Georgian countrymen did not take kindly to an informer or a local constable who would denounce one of his own.

But the same year Koba's revolutionary career took a decisive turn, and he advanced beyond the narrow confines of Georgian socialism. On March 20, 1903, the Caucasian Union Committee of the Russian Socialist Party had been organized to supervise Party activities in all of the Caucasus (i.e., in the area now covered by the Soviet republics of Georgia, Armenia, and Azerbaijan). Official historians made Djugashvili, then in jail, an original member of that body. Actually he was coopted only in 1904 alongside the man who was to become his rival for the leadership of Caucasian Bolshevism, Stephen Shaumyan.

Shaumyan was a year older and had had the advantage of better education, having studied engineering in Riga and philosophy in Germany. From his early attachment to Armenian nationalism he shifted—possibly under the direct influence of Lenin, whom he had encountered abroad—to Marxism. The Georgian and the Armenian were to become not only rivals for political leadership but bitter personal enemies. Shaumyan was to refer to Koba as "the viper," and he made sure that Koba's critical remarks about Lenin became known to the great man. At one time Stalin was widely believed, though as we shall see wrongly, to have denounced his fellow Bolshevik to the police. In 1918 the rivalry of the two men was finally resolved. Shaumyan headed the pro-Communist regime in Baku. Under internal pressure and threatened by the Turkish army, the Baku Bolsheviks yielded power to a conglomeration of other parties. Shaumyan and some Communist notables tried to flee but were caught and executed—to pass into Communist martyrology as the "twenty-six Baku commissars shot by the British."[10] Stalin's verdict was singularly unsentimental: "Without any need for it, our Baku comrades bowed out of the political arena, leaving the field of battle to our enemies."[11]

To return to the summer of 1904, the intraparty struggle at that time

[9] Cited in Trotsky's *Stalin, An Appraisal of the Man and His Influence*, ed. Charles Malamuth (London, 1968), p. 43.

[10] There is a grain of truth in this tale, insofar as the British liaison officer with the Baku regime did not exert himself to save the men. The story has one of the condemned shout to the commander of the firing squad: "Scoundrels! You will pay for this, your turn will come!" The reply would please a believer in the existence of the Russian soul: "We know it, brother, but what can we do?"

[11] Stalin, *Collected Works* (Moscow, 1946–52), IV, 254.

finally erupted all over the Caucasus. Ever since February the Empire had been at war with Japan; revolutionary rumblings were audible, especially in Georgia's countryside. But at the political meetings now held almost openly, Bolshevik and Menshevik orators, after denouncing the autocracy and gloating over its discomfitures in the war with a small Asian power, would pounce upon each other and regale the uncomprehending audience with dark tales of intrigue and un-Marxist behavior by the other side. Koba, according to all accounts, was acquiring a name as the most indefatigable Bolshevik propagandist, and was enhancing his reputation for rudeness. For all their animation intraparty arguments were still supposed to adhere to comradely convention; he often, it was said, transgressed such bounds.

Meanwhile his literary production was scant. The Caucasian Union Committee produced an illegal sheet in Georgian and Armenian, *The Proletariat's Struggle*; Koba wrote for the September issue an article on the nationality problem as seen by the Social Democrats. It is a frequently muddled, occasionally incisive polemic against the views of other parties and on the need for a single party to unite socialists of all nationalities.

Lenin's instructions to his followers at home urged them to write letters abroad denouncing the Mensheviks and thus creating the impression of mass support in Russia for his position as against that of the intriguers who, in addition to *Iskra*, "seized" other central organs of the Party. He set a rather high standard of vituperation. In a letter to Caucasian Bolsheviks, he wrote of his Party comrades: "You are far from full knowledge of the reptilian villainy of the Party Council and the Central Committee." Koba fell in readily with two letters from Kutais to a Georgian then in Germany; he shows no inhibition in denouncing the highest authorities of Marxism currently on the Menshevik side: "When it comes to *new problems* I think that Plekhanov just does not understand them."[12] As for other veterans of the Russian revolutionary movement and the chief ideologue of German Marxism, Karl Kautsky, whom Marxists everywhere considered heir to the Master himself, but who was then on the pro-Menshevik side: as old friends they scratch each other's backs! This is the only explanation for their unprincipled behavior! It is quite daring for a twenty-four-year-old to write in such terms of inhabitants of the Marxian Olympus, but the letters, when shown to Lenin, must have made him take notice of Koba.

At home such impudence toward the Marxist divinities was bringing no results: Jordania and Djibladze were firmly entrenched, and Georgian Menshevism was acquiring that mass support which it was to preserve for twenty years, until the national rising against Soviet rule in

[12] Stalin, I, 57.

1924 was drowned in blood. So, without as yet severing his ties with his homeland, Koba transfered more and more of his activities to Baku.

Most Americans would be surprised to learn that this onetime Tatar village was, in 1904, the greatest oil center in the world. Oil fields around Baku accounted for 95 per cent of Russia's production, which in turn was more than half of the world total. From a population of about 14,000 in 1860, it had jumped to 265,000: local Tatars (i.e., Azeiri Turks) as well as those from northern Persia, and Russians, Armenians, Georgians. Much of the oil industry was owned by foreign capital, but there were also local entrepreneurs and millionaires. Their luxury dwellings in the city proper contrasted with the squalor of the Balakhan and Bibi-Eibat suburbs, where the workers lived in company-owned compounds, often in conditions that even government inspectors found unfit for human habitation.

Baku was a city of fantastic contrasts, not unlike the American West in some ways. Visitors were struck by its atmosphere of violence and lawlessness, unusual even for the Caucasus. Assassinations were common, their perpetrators rarely apprehended. Local men of substance would seldom venture abroad unaccompanied by hired gunmen or bodyguards. Sporadically an incident would spark a racial or, more properly speaking, national riot (usually between the Tatars and Armenians) which would envelop the city in slaughter and arson.

At the same time there was a kind of progressive atmosphere about turn-of-the-century Baku. Many of the local magnates were self-made men who, in view of the helplessness of the local administration to cope with the problems arising from Baku's rapid growth, provided the city with the necessary utilities, additional policemen, etc. (Even so, the water supply was inadequate, and in the Oriental manner drinking water was sold in the street by itinerant salesmen.) Some were men of advanced political views, and as we shall see, many a reform and even revolutionary group owed its financial survival to the help of the Baku capitalists.

In brief, while one's life and property were probably less safe in Baku than anywhere else in the Empire, it was by the same token not a bad place for a revolutionary seeking a relatively safe haven from the long arm of the Okhrana.[13] ☆☆☆

---

[13] The Tsarist political police. The Okhrana and its Soviet successors, the Cheka, GPU, MGB, etc., are usually called secret police—a term somewhat illogical in view of the fact that though having secret collaborators they have operated in the open, with distinctive uniforms, etc.

I N 1900 a man came to Baku who deserves the recognition which he has not received as having been a co-founder of the Bolshevik movement, Leonid Borisovich Krasin. The career of this extraordinary man brings into vivid relief some of the most important and neglected facts about revolutionary Russia, Bolshevism, Lenin, and Stalin. It is also an enticing tale—one which should have attracted Hollywood in preference to those endless ones about Rasputins, Nicholases and Alexandras, et al.

Krasin—"Nikitich," "Winter," to mention some of his conspiratorial names—could boast that his revolutionary activity preceded Lenin's. His Party membership dated from 1890, when as a student in the St. Petersburg Polytechnic he joined and led a socialist circle. He was an effective propagandist, especially among young ladies, who while not yet accepted as full students were free auditors in university courses. His masculine charm and romantic proclivities persisted throughout his hazardous life—even in his fifties, when he was the chief Soviet diplomat and trade negotiator with the West, Party circles were scandalized to hear of Krasin's intrigue, to give it an appropriately Edwardian term, with an adventuress. But Krasin's charm captivated men as well as women, dissolved political enmities, loosened capitalist pursestrings, mollified reactionary bureaucrats. When he broke with Lenin, the latter, who was singularly unrestrained and vituperative on such occasions, could only sigh, and after the Revolution he implored Krasin strenuously and repeatedly to rejoin the Bolsheviks.

There was, to be sure, an air of self-imposed theatricality and mystery about him. "I am a man who has no shadow," he used to repeat to his friend Gorky.[14] On his deathbed in 1926 Krasin astounded his English doctor by sitting up and delivering, in German, Hamlet's soliloquy. But there was also real mystery about the man who moved simultaneously and with apparent ease in the diverse worlds of terrorists and industrial managers, of the clandestine Party hierarchy and high society.

Arrested and sent into exile, Krasin spent his time not too unpleasantly working as a draftsman on the construction of the Siberian railway. Then back to the Polytechnic Institute to finish his education, this time in Kharkov. There he persisted in his revolutionary activities, but the rector of the institution could never bring himself to include Krasin's name in the list of troublemakers transmitted to the police, and so he received his engineer's diploma.

---

[14] Referring to the famous tale by the German romantic Chamisso.

Where in 1900 could a revolutionary banned from the main cities of European Russia aspire to go to work but Baku? And who should be the director of the Baku Electric Works but an old comrade from the socialist circle in St. Petersburg, Klason![15]

The Baku power station soon became the shelter for socialists from all over the Caucasus and even farther afield. Alliluyev, who worked there for a while, testifies how even the workers complained that Klason and chief engineer Krasin protected their fellow socialists, while being prompt to fire or fine those with other political views. But Krasin now began to operate on a much wider scale. He helped, as we have seen, to set up Ketskhoveli's press. Through his contacts he was able to secure funds for the *Iskra* group, and by 1903 he was in Lenin's words the finance minister of the Bolshevik movement. Among the contributors were not only local industrialists but literary and theatrical figures passing through Baku who struck up an acquaintance with the young engineer at some reception given by local society. Gorky, who became his lifelong admirer, gave him the proceeds of the Caucasian performances of *The Lower Depths*. A famous actress recalled that after a recital her admirers (including the local police chief) presented her with a tastefully arranged bouquet of hundred-ruble notes and that a single rendezvous with Krasin persuaded her that the money should be given to the Cause.

In 1904 Krasin departed from Baku. At different times he was to give different reasons for this step: the term of his exclusion from the main cities of European Russia had ended; Baku's wretched climate and polluted air were bad for his health; he was needed for Party work at the center. The latter probably comes close to the truth, but there was also a strike of the workers at the power station, and the Socialist Revolutionaries among them threatened their Social Democratic bosses Klason and Krasin. Intrarevolutionary squabbles in Baku were not infrequently settled with the gun, and the two Marxist managers hurriedly departed.

Krasin then became the chief engineer for the enterprises of Savva Morozov, the scion of a famous capitalist family and a generous contributor to radical causes. According to Gorky, a friend of both, their relationship was one of mutual admiration and respect. But the "great proletarian writer" sometimes substituted fiction for history, and for once Krasin left a shadow in describing his true relationship with this unfortunate captain of industry: ". . . Savva was a thorough coward. . . . [He] was a bit uneasy when meeting me alone. Perhaps he was afraid of some far-reaching demands, perhaps he was embarrassed by his opportunistic liberal behavior when seeing before him a real revolution-

---

[15] Richard Edwardowich Klason deserves a footnote for having instigated the most famous revolutionary union of all. It was in his Petersburg apartment that Nadezhda Krupskaya first met the young lawyer and socialist Vladimir Ulyanov.

ary who any day might go to jail, Siberia."[16] Morozov sought an escape and cure for his nerves abroad. Leaving a handsome legacy to the Bolsheviks, he shot himself in Vichy two days after being visited by Krasin. His suicide, according to his mercurial "friend," was due to his fear of being denounced to the authorities by his wife. One wonders.

Krasin's activities during the years of the Revolution of 1905–6 defy imagination. He had a full-time job as an industrial manager, first in Moscow, then in St. Petersburg. He was also "the main organizer and leader of all our underground activities, of the guerrilla activities of our Party, one of the chief leaders of the uprisings during our first revolution."[17] More than ever before he was the finance minister of the movement, squeezing money not only out of the Morozovs and their like, but even from people of liberal and antisocialist sympathies. His methods were ingenious. There were heiresses with socialist sympathies but alas under legal age: to dispose of their estates Krasin would arrange marriages with trusted Bolsheviks so the Party could get its hands on the inheritance. Maxim Gorky was dispatched to America on a lecture tour to collect money for the cause. Krasin wanted Litvinov to chaperone him, since Gorky, though then a Bolshevik, could not be entirely trusted. But Litvinov refused and was instead sent to buy arms in Belgium. (He would see the United States only in 1933, as Commissar for Foreign Affairs and guest of President Roosevelt.) Instead of Litvinov, Gorky went with the actress Maria Andreyeva, and sure enough there was a scandal when his puritanic hosts realized that the famous Russian fighter for freedom was traveling in sin.

But Krasin's favorite occupation in those years was terror. He and a chemist, Tikhvinsky, ran a laboratory where explosives were manufactured and revolutionaries of all political persuasions trained in their use. (Unlike Lenin, Krasin got along famously with revolutionaries of different political parties.) It was in this laboratory that the bombs used in the attempt to blow up Prime Minister Peter Stolypin's villa were made. And it was in Krasin's office that plans for many of the "expropriations"—i.e., armed robberies of state treasuries and banks, the proceeds of which (but not always *all* of them) went to the Party coffers—were hatched. Some of his ideas were a madcap combination of terrorism and schoolboy prank. Who else would devise ways to steal a cannon from a marine regiment's armory and then secret it near the Winter Palace to start its bombardment at the appropriate moment. "Ah, those years were full of fun," Krasin used to recall when he was a sedate diplomat and commissar.

Krasin was constantly on the move; traveling to Party meetings (after

---

[16] As cited in M. N. Lyadov and S. M. Posner, *Leonid Borisovich Krasin* (Moscow, 1928), p. 218.
[17] *Ibid.*, p. 5.

1905 he was a member of the Central Committee), to various places in Russia and abroad to pursue his fantastically varied activities. He found time to start raising a family when an erstwhile disciple from the young ladies' socialist circle returned to her first love, fifteen years and two husbands later.

Krasin's career on several occasions crisscrossed Stalin's. He was not among Stalin's favorites and would not have fared well in the 1930s. But his case also throws some circumstantial light on a problem that has beguiled some of Stalin's biographers and led others to dark suspicions or worse: How was Koba able to avoid arrest while in the underground and, when arrested, repeatedly to escape from exile? What is interesting is that the Okhrana's negligent inefficiency concerning Koba, until 1912 a revolutionary of only regional importance, pales in comparison with its record in regard to Krasin, between 1905 and 1908 one of the main manipulators of the entire Russian revolutionary movement. His role *must* have been known to *someone* in the Secret Police, for it had an agent within the Bolshevik organization in Germany who furnished fairly accurate information concerning the Bolshevik high command and its members' whereabouts. Yet Krasin, living under his own name, managed to stay free.

His record and behavior must inevitably arouse suspicions. He seemed excellently informed about Okhrana moves and about its agents provocateurs. In 1905 the police broke in on a conspiratorial meeting of the Bolshevik Central Committee members and arrested them all—except Krasin. He had happened to notice suspicious activities around the house in question, and had not come in.

He also warned his comrades about "Mother" Serebriakova, the celebrated supporter of radical causes, who indeed was unmasked as an agent provocateur some years later. And on at least one occasion he ordered the liquidation of a secret collaborator of the Okhrana. In 1907 he was arrested but released with apologies after seventeen days. In March 1908 his luck appeared to have run out: he was detained in Finland, and the prosecutor told him they had the goods on him, he might not be able to escape "Stolypin's necktie" (as the gallows being set up all over Russia were called, after the iron-handed Prime Minister). But Finnish law provided that evidence be produced within a month or the suspect be freed. Though only a few hours' travel separated St. Petersburg from Krasin's place of detention, the evidence against him was not forthcoming. And so, with a perfectly legal passport, Krasin and his family left for Germany. In 1912 came the crowning touch. Krasin, who for all his cosmopolitan habits missed his homeland terribly, was allowed after some discreet negotiations with the Ministry of the Interior to return. The chief instigator of countless bombings, expropriations, and assassinations returned to become the director of the Siemens-Schuster enterprises in Russia.

In 1910, we are told in the recollections of a high political police official, a prominent member of the Bolshevik Central Committee was tried by the Party court on charges of complicity with the Okhrana. He was completely exonerated, with the help of the official in question. The Tsarist administration, its police included, contained individuals who were sympathetic to the revolutionary cause. Krasin had unusual "pull," but many subordinate Party officials, such as Stalin and, even more, Shaumyan during his Baku period, could not have carried on their activities without somebody in authority looking through his fingers or, at appropriate times, giving helpful hints. People who faced the firing squads or endured hard imprisonment at the height of the Revolution of 1905–6 and during the reaction that followed it were for the most part rank-and-file revolutionaries. But no one in the revolutionary movement of those years could escape the atmosphere of distrust and suspicion, the gnawing feeling that one's worst enemy might be found not in the ranks of the police but right at one's elbow. One looked constantly for signs of betrayal. Once imprisoned or even bested in a Party squabble, one anxiously reviewed the evidence and analyzed comrades' behavior and views. People who lived at the Party heights, or for the most part abroad, as Lenin did, tended to minimize these problems. How could a mass movement whose eventual success was ordained by history be harmed by the activity of a handful of spies and provocateurs? For others, the "practitioners," such an Olympian attitude was impossible. The conspirator's exhilaration in the revolutionary struggle and hostility to open enemies were submerged in implacable hatred of those who had been Party comrades but who had betrayed, slandered, or suspected him. ☆☆☆

AT this time Koba-Djugashvili was still in the early stages of the career that would ineradicably imbue him with such feelings. His role in the Party was modest. In June 1904 he intervened in an intra-party squabble. Along with another Bolshevik, A. M. Stopani, he was sent to Baku to "straighten out" the local committee, which was mostly Menshevik in its complexion. Acting under the authority of the All-Caucasian Union Committee of the Social Democratic Party (which at the time had a Bolshevik majority), Stopani with Koba's assistance (in the Soviet literature, it is hardly necessary to say, this order is usually reversed) installed a pro-Bolshevik group, which in turn immediately became torn by dissension. In November Koba was back in Baku. But his contribution to the important events which gripped the city during the next few weeks was not great.

He did not have then nor would he ever acquire any significant ability to impress a large crowd, to guide a mass movement through oratory and on the strength of his personality. One day Stalin emerged as a most effective political speaker, but to an audience of Party functionaries. Until then, his main strength was as a tactician and organizer, preferably working behind the scenes. Whatever minor oratorical successes he scored were among the people whose psychology he knew: Georgian peasants and Party members. But in a multinational proletarian setting, such as Baku, neither homely country similes nor examples of Marxian erudition carried one very far.[18] As a matter of fact, until the feverish days of 1917 most Russian Marxists of whatever faction were somewhat ill at ease and fumbling when it came to dealing with those "masses" of workers of which they spoke so frequently, and whose leadership, they assumed, belonged to them by right.

It was a great scandal to all orthodox Marxists that the great 1904 strike in Baku was initiated neither by Bolsheviks nor by Mensheviks but by rank outsiders. These were the famous—or, in the parlance of Soviet historians, notorious—Shendrikovs. When the four of them appeared on the Baku scene, they managed within a few months to set up something which the Bolsheviks and Mensheviks, preoccupied with fighting each other, had been incapable of organizing: a labor union with mass following. Ilya, the leader, was, the Bolsheviks regretfully conceded, a gifted demagogue, which in the language of the time meant a speaker with a bellowing voice capable of outlasting and outvituperating any opponent in a debate. Even the most grass-roots movement required the ministrations of an *intelligent*, and that necessary ingredient was provided by brother Lev, a former student and the brains of the family. Ilya's wife, Claudia, astounded the largely Muslim audiences and infuriated the Bolsheviks by her eloquent denunciations of their condescending attitude toward real workers. The third brother, Gleb, a shadowy figure, was assigned tasks of lesser importance. This was a formidable quartet, and the Shendrikovs soon outraged the local Marxists (with whom Lev initially had some connection) by steering their union in the direction of the workers' "narrow" economic demands rather than the class struggle. Instead of promoting those mass

---

[18] One Marxist recalls how he regaled his proletarian audience to some of the most heartrending passages from *Capital*, Volume i, in which Marx describes how industrial work under capitalism leads inevitably to the worker's physical degeneracy. There was an uproar in the hall and some listeners of Herculean proportions advanced on the speaker: Were *they* anemic and degenerate?

demonstrations with subversive slogans that were bound to bring the charging Cossacks and thus enhance class consciousness, the Shendrikovs pushed for a general strike to force the bosses to negotiate and to grant higher pay, sick pay, and various other fringe benefits.[19] Having tried in vain to stop it, the local Bolshevik committee got on the bandwagon and supported the strike, which began on December 13, but not without sulking about its "anarchist" rather than socialist character and trying to smuggle in political as well as economic slogans. The strike ended on December 30 with the first collective agreement between workers and employers in the history of the Russian Empire. The oil workers won most of their demands. The Shendrikovs scored an impressive victory but not as far as the official Soviet history is concerned. Every Soviet schoolboy has learned from his textbook that it was the Bolshevik city committee which led the strike to its victorious conclusion despite all the efforts of the Shendrikovs to sabotage it. Furthermore, between 1930 and 1961 he would also have learned that Comrade Stalin himself was in direct command of the struggle to secure the Baku workers' rights.

In fact, Stalin's role was so small that even the more reliable Soviet sources do not credit him with any significant share in this momentous event in the history of the Russian labor movement. One Bolshevik who did play an important part in the strike was the twenty-four-year-old Prokofiy (Alyosha) Djaparidze. During the next two years he would be mainly responsible for the Bolsheviks' relentless and eventually successful drive to discredit the Shendrikovs and destroy their union.

After their success the Shendrikovs sought support and obtained a sort of affiliation with the Mensheviks, thus redoubling the Bolsheviks' fury. The Shendrikovs, bewailed Djaparidze in 1905 at the Third Bolshevik Party Congress, were acting like gangsters rather than Social Democrats: they got payoffs from the industrialists by threatening them with murder and arson. There was, to be sure, some substance in these charges, but the Baku Bolsheviks themselves were not above assassinations and blackmail. Djaparidze personally disposed of a police official—one of the very rare instances when an important Bolshevik or Menshevik lent his hand to such an act rather than ordering it. If in this case the alleged reason was political,[20] there were on the Bolsheviks' own testimony plenty of instances of what can only be called plain blackmail, when employers were threatened with arson and dynamite unless they

[19] Edward Keenan, "Some Remarks on the History of the Revolutionary Movement in Baku, the General Strike of December 1904," *Studies in the History of the Russian and Soviet World*, III, No. 2 (April–June 1962), 244.

[20] The official in question was accused by the Tatars of stirring up the pogrom against the Armenians in February 1905. About the same time and on the same charge, the Governor of Baku, Prince Nakashidze, was murdered by an Armenian nationalist.

gave money to the Party. Decrying the subventions the Shendrikovs were getting from the industrialists, a Soviet author thus relates coolly how he obtained 40,000 rubles from the same source for the Bolshevik-sponsored union of unemployed. And for all of the Marxian condemnation of individual terror, the Bolshevik city committee ordered assassinations of recalcitrant industrialists.[21]

As in many other cases the Bolsheviks were finally able, through sheer persistence, to get to the Shendrikovs. In 1906 Lev went before the Party court (the Bolsheviks and Mensheviks were currently reunited) on the charge of obtaining money from the bosses for his own use. Djaparidze was the prosecutor; the defender was a young lawyer of Polish extraction, Andrei Vishinsky. In Stalin's Russia he was to reverse his roles, be a Bolshevik and a prosecutor, and his "Shoot them like the mad dogs that they are" resounded as the refrain of the Great Purge trials. But this time his efforts were unavailing for the same reason they were to be so brilliantly successful in the 1930s: the court was "fixed." Lev was excluded. In 1907 he died, and the Shendrikov organization collapsed. It was then that Koba and Shaumyan made Baku the base for Bolshevik activities throughout the Caucasus.

But in 1905 it was still an uphill fight against the Shendrikovs and the Mensheviks. Events of the year dwarfed, though they did not entirely end, the Party intrigues in the Caucasus and elsewhere. Russia was in the throes of a revolution. ☆☆☆

A S was to be true in February 1917, the Revolution of 1905 was triggered by an organization that owed its origin to the government. Some years before, S. V. Zubatov, a Moscow police official, had had an ingenious idea for beating the revolutionaries at their own game: the police would organize labor unions. These unions would vigorously pursue the workers' economic demands, but they would shun politics or, rather, preach loyalty to the established authorities. Zubatov, a onetime radical (who was also largely responsible for seeding the revolutionary parties with agents provocateurs), was not a cynical manipulator but a man who believed in what might be called a populist version of autocracy. The workers would realize that the Tsar was their father and protector, and would reject the noxious intellectuals who tried to stir

---

[21] See A. Rogov, "Revolutionary Work in Baku," *Hard Labor and Exile* (Moscow), xxxv (1927), 103, and A. Sukhov, "How I Spent Three Months Working with the Shendrikovs," *The Proletarian Revolution* (Moscow), No. 45 (October 1925), 120.

them up for their own purposes. His ideas succeeded, in fact too well. For when in 1903 a wave of strikes conducted by those police unions broke out, the ingenious police chief became the target of attacks and denunciations: foreign and domestic capitalists expostulated with the government, envious bureaucrats intrigued against their—as we would say today—innovative colleague, the reactionary press dubbed him "servant of the Jews" (he had also organized unions among the Jewish workers in the Ukraine). And so Zubatov, like a true revolutionary, was sent into administrative exile.

But Zubatov's work of police socialism, as it was dubbed, had some continuators, the most prominent of whom was a young Orthodox priest, George Gapon. The Little Father (the common appellation for a parish priest) shared some characteristics of his contemporary Gregory Rasputin (who, popular legend notwithstanding, was neither priest nor monk but what we might call an unlicensed guru), such as love of liquor, personal magnetism, and a passion for politics. With the appropriate background as chaplain of St. Petersburg jail, he was felt by the police to be just the man to organize the Union of Russian Factory Workers, which began functioning in February 1904. The Union was guaranteed against subversive infiltration: its members had to be Russians by nationality and Christians by religion. With such precautions, it was hoped, the members would, in the police chief's words, "spend their free time wisely, and *soberly*"[22] in various forms of self-improvement: concerts, literary evenings, listening to lectures on the general theme of the blessings of the autocracy, etc. Members of the directorate of the Union (carefully vetted by the police), "intelligent persons of priestly and secular vocations," began their activity by requesting that the Minister of the Interior "lay at the feet of His Imperial Majesty their most humble assurances of love and loyalty," which the Minister, Von Plehve, did, shortly before being blown up by a terrorist's bomb. His Majesty deigned to express His Most Gracious Thanks.

The Union of Russian Factory Workers grew by leaps and bounds, and the police chief could congratulate himself on finding "a firm barrier against the spread of subversive socialist teachings among the workers." The impression of the organization's complete reliability was conveyed to him not only "from the reports by the Okhrana sources, but also from personal discussions with the priest Gapon, who regularly reported to him in person." All the greater the surprise when Gapon, this model of loyalty, following a wave of strikes which seized St. Petersburg at the end of the year, announced suddenly that he would lead the working people of the capital in a mass procession to the Winter Palace to lay at the feet of His Majesty, but this time in person, a petition to remedy

---

[22] My italics. Even the police chief should have known better.

their grievances and misery. Within a few months Gapon had become an idol of St. Petersburg workers, and the unfortunate police chief had to confess that to put into effect the order for his arrest would lead to an uprising.

And so on January 9, 1905, an enormous crowd from all parts of the capital began a march on the palace. The police and troops tried to bar their way and, when they pressed on, opened fire. One hundred and forty persons were killed, according to the government, a thousand or so according to other sources. Gapon, who had begun the day's proceedings by celebrating a mass for God's blessing on the Imperial Family, was slightly wounded. He was hidden by the workers and then fled the country, leaving behind a proclamation cursing Nicholas II as the hangman of his people and urging his overthrow. This was the Bloody Sunday of January 9, 1905, which ushered in the Revolution. ☆☆☆

DEFEAT in war, strikes and uprisings throughout the country, mutinies in army and naval units—all these elements were present in the Revolution of 1905–6. Paradoxically, the Revolution was in a sense more elemental than the successful one of February 1917. The Bolshevik Revolution was centralized, the events and institutions in the capital dominated and set the tone for all of Russia. In 1905 St. Petersburg provided the spark, but the flame of the Revolution burned more brightly in other areas. And the Revolution lacked a central organ and focus, such as was provided in 1917 by the Petrograd Soviet of Workers and Soldiers Deputies. In 1905 soviets, ad-hoc elected councils of workers' representatives, spread all over the Empire, in places wresting governmental functions from the paralyzed Tsarist bureaucracy, but they were entirely uncoordinated. The wall that had protected the autocracy had been breached by a defeat in war, by the blow rendered to the Tsar's personal prestige by the events of January 9. Through the breach now flowered torrents of hitherto repressed aspirations: the middle classes' for parliamentary institutions and freedoms such as in the West; the non-Russians' for their national rights; the peasants' for more land; the workers' for the alleviation of their economic grievances. At times the radical parties themselves seemed to be swamped by the flood of the Revolution, as the governmental authorities were. Here and there they bobbed to the surface to lead this or that uprising, to provide guidance to a soviet or a rural revolutionary movement, but in most cases they could not hold any position and when the flood receded they were swept back to where they had been before.

Georgia provides an exception to this picture. Here one branch of the revolutionary movement became so firmly implanted that even the subsequent years of reaction would be unable to uproot it and destroy its hold on the large masses of the population. Ironically, one of the beneficiaries of the Mensheviks' success was the man who in the long run was to destroy them, Joseph Koba-Djugashvili.

The Caucasus had been stirring for a year before Bloody Sunday. Indeed, it was the Baku workers' success in obtaining a collective agreement that may have inspired the St. Petersburg unionists to advance similar demands to their employers on the eve of their momentous demonstration. But with the news of the massacre spreading through the Empire it was the Georgian countryside that erupted into open rebellion. By March 1905 the central authorities were being bombarded with news of incredible goings-on in this backward and, it was assumed, politically safe region. In the district of Dushet, reported the Vice-Governor of Tiflis, governmental authority had completely collapsed. Local officials were presented with a list of demands by the peasants, to be met within seven days. Some reflected the land hunger then more acute in Georgia than anywhere else in the Empire: the government's and large landowners' properties were to be distributed free to the peasants. Some testified to the movement's spontaneous anarchic character: villages were to have the fullest possible autonomy; excise taxes were to be abolished; army recruits were not to be stationed or serve outside the Caucasus; schools were to be run by the local communities. But a number of slogans and demands testified to the effectiveness of propaganda work carried on in the villages by the Social Democrats, mostly Mensheviks. "Why do our men have to go abroad, what do we have to do with the Japanese?" Those mostly illiterate peasants also demanded abolition of censorship of the press and free public libraries.[23]

In Guria, the hinterland of Batum, the Revolution was at its most intense. There the government reaped the fruits of its imbecility over the years in returning troublesome workers to their native villages. These men now constituted the revolutionary cadre of the movement which turned the once placid area into the "Guria Republic." In the first four months of 1905 there were 111 attempts at assassination of local officials. Survivors fled to the garrison towns, leaving the countryside in the hands of elected committees. The change in the power structure was recognized by some priests who in their services now omitted the customary prayer for the Emperor and his family, invoking instead God's blessing on His servants, the local committee of the Social Democratic Party.[24]

[23] S. Maglekiladze and A. Yavidze, *The Revolution of 1905–7 in Georgia* (Tiflis, 1956), pp. 141–42.
[24] *Ibid.*, p. 231.

Where was Koba-Djugashvili during this historical upheaval in his native land? He was doggedly pursuing the work of an itinerant Bolshevik propagandist and organizer. Not even his official chronology can ascribe to him actual leadership of any major revolutionary enterprise. To be quite fair, most socialist leaders in the Caucasus, Mensheviks and Bolsheviks alike, remained in the background rather than leading the insurrectionary activities in person. The only current and future notable named in the long list of people apprehended by the police for such activities in 1905–6 was the nineteen-year-old Gregory (Sergo) Orjonikidze, caught conveying arms to the rebels.

As a participant in the joint socialist revolutionary enterprise, Koba, like others, exulted in the defeat of the Empire by Japan: "Once again the senile decrepitude of the Autocracy has been exposed—the Tsar's battalions are decimated, the Tsar's fleet destroyed, Port Arthur has shamefully surrendered,"[25] he wrote in January 1905. In 1946, when this celebration of his country's defeat appeared in Russian, some of the most gleeful passages had to be omitted, for readers must have remembered how on September 2, 1945, announcing Japan's capitulations, Generalissimo Stalin recalled how "we of the older generation" had waited all too long for this historic retribution of Japan's perfidious attack on and defeat of Russia in 1904–5.

While pursuing such all-Party all-revolutionary themes, Koba was earning his marks as a Bolshevik by vigorously campaigning against his Menshevik comrades. One would have thought the Revolution should have led to a union of all revolutionary forces against the common foe of Tsarism, not to mention socialists of all factions, and most revolutionaries in Russia in fact regarded with a certain distaste those hardly comprehensible intrigues and counterintrigues of the Martovs and Lenins. Not so Koba. He stood out among the Georgian Bolsheviks for his continuing readiness to pursue the polemic, to assail the Martovs and Plekhanovs, almost as if they were Tsarist governors, or those liberal lawyers and professors attempting to turn the Revolution into "respectable" nonviolent channels. The leaders of the Mensheviks, he wrote in his pamphlet, "Briefly[26] About Intra-Party Differences," "refused to submit their 'I' to the sacred cause, they gave themselves to decrepit whimpering when they were outvoted at the Second Congress. . . . After the Congress they bewailed the loss of their leading positions, and because of that loss they provoked the Party split."[27] The Mensheviks represented intelligentsialike looseness and discipline; the Bolsheviks stood for proletarian firmness. There is a certain primitiveness and

25 Stalin, I, 74.
26 Forty-two pages of small print!
27 Stalin, I, 129.

fanaticism about the argument that stayed with Stalin to the end of his days. An obscure Soviet textbook writer in 1952 would use a phrase he did not like, and the all-powerful dictator would explode against this insignificant and servile creature as if he were Trotsky or Bukharin assailing him before a Party Congress. Disagreement was not a matter of opinion, not even of possible error: it was a crime, a treason against the sacred cause. A fortuitous majority of two or three votes became for Koba a line between those in darkness and those in light. The Georgian Mensheviks—representing a by now mass movement in his native land—are "submissive slaves" of the minority. They are, he says, groping for a vituperative metaphor but finding one that makes no sense in the context of his argument, like a pickpocket who cries "Stop thief!" Stalin was able, as we shall see, during his long ascent to power to temper his passion for vituperation and denunciation, at one point gaining a reputation for tolerance, but impatience and intolerance always smoldered beneath the surface, and when he no longer felt constrained, it erupted with savage intensity.

It can be imagined what reputation Koba was earning among the Mensheviks. But his didactic, choleric partisanship attracted Lenin's favorable attention. In his pamphlet Koba quoted Lenin ad nauseam, and there is no question that this was partly calculated. But there was also an element of genuine attachment and imitation. Lenin's heavy sarcasm was more in his style than Martov's or Plekhanov's urbane irony. Lenin's self-assurance was a model. He undoubtedly believed his argument that an ideological and psychological gap separated the two factions, but no impartial observer looking at Russia in 1905 could allege that the Bolsheviks were hard or the Mensheviks soft. Koba had only to look around Georgia to see how unfair such imputations were. But he wore partisan blinkers. He could not see that it was the Bolsheviks if anyone who had exhibited distaste for and suspicion of innovations like the soviets and armed uprisings in the countryside. They smacked of spontaneous action by the masses, and did not Lenin condemn spontaneity in his *What Is to Be Done?*

Abroad the Party potentates were in fact in a considerable quandary about the Revolution. In April–May Lenin assembled thirty-three Bolsheviks in London and proclaimed the gathering to be the Third Congress of the Social Democratic Workers Party. According to Party statutes this was illegal, but as Vladimir Ilyich, himself a lawyer, soothingly explained, "To be sure according to the *strict letter* of the statute it can be considered illegal, but we should be guilty of a grotesque formalism if we should interpret the statute that way."[28] The Menshe-

---

[28] *The Third Congress of the Russian Social Democratic Workers Party, Protocols* (Moscow, 1959), p. 46.

viks, with lesser gall, called *their* meeting a conference. On both sides there was considerable uncertainty about what kind of revolution this was. According to the Marxian canon, Russia was not ready for a socialist revolution; this had to be a bourgeois-democratic revolution. But if so, did it mean that the socialists should lead the masses in their heroic struggle, only to hand power over to bankers and professors, who would set up their parliaments and other features of rotten liberalism? Koba, like most other Marxists at the time, admitted that, yes, the issue of the Revolution had to be a democratic republic as ordained by the Constituent Assembly, and full socialism lay far in the future. But again he used a brochure on the subject mainly to attack the Mensheviks. They, unlike the Bolsheviks, argued that if Tsarism collapsed, socialists should not enter the Provisional Revolutionary Government, seemingly a more radical position. But as Engels proved (he had been dead ten years), exclaimed Koba, such a position had nothing to do with socialism and played right into the hands of the capitalists, who would monopolize power and oppress the workers.

As yet there was no such government on the horizon, one of the reasons being that each revolutionary party was split, and the situation was not much better among the Kadets (the Constitutional Democrats). Paul Axelrod, a veteran Social Democrat, made what was on the surface an eminently rational suggestion: for the moment all revolutionary parties should unite in a workers' party. But the majority of Menshevik and Bolshevik leaders greeted the suggestion with horror. Another would-be unifier of revolutionary forces appeared in the person of George Gapon. Just as once he had dreamed of being summoned by the Tsar to be Prime Minister, his fantasy now put him at the head of the Revolution. It says something about the leaders of the various revolutionary factions that though they had no doubts about the Little Father's character and background as police agent, they now competed to lure him into their particular group. Lenin at the Third Congress referred to this deranged man as "comrade" and tried to capture him for the Bolsheviks. But he would have to bone up on Marxism! Gapon was not a bookish type and preferred the more pragmatic revolutionary ways of the Socialist Revolutionaries. With their blessing he returned to Russia, only to fall into his old habits and to start negotiations with the police. Instead of denouncing Gapon, as the revolutionary code prescribed in such cases (since he had not yet delivered anybody to the police), the Central Committee of the Socialist Revolutionaries ordered his death. Gapon was lured into a trap by a man he had every reason to believe was his friend and garroted. The Socialist Revolutionaries compounded this sordid act by publicly denying their responsibility for it. Some years later it turned out that the chief of their fighting organization, Yevno Azev, had all along been a double agent who had betrayed many revolutionaries to the police. *He* was allowed to get away. ☆☆☆

THE Revolution surged ahead, in spite of the revolutionaries' squabbles. In August 1905 peace with Japan was purchased by the recognition of Russia's defeat and minor territorial concessions—a further blow to the prestige of tottering Tsarism. This brought the Revolution to its crescendo. Strikes, armed uprisings, and mutinies became the order of the day. Already in June the most famous incident of the Revolution (certainly for a non-Russian), the mutiny on the battleship *Potemkin*, immortalized in Sergei Eisenstein's film, had taken place. Here was another harbinger of 1917: sailors in the vanguard of the Revolution. The Bolsheviks, who except for Krasin viewed with suspicion such insurrectionary eruptions (that spontaneity again), found added discomfiture in the fact that the few politically literate sailors in the *Potemkin* crew were Mensheviks. Koba's article on the subject of armed uprisings shows him something of a bad sport, and from the revolutionary point of view rather unduly cautious in the presence of exhilarating views. He does not refer to the *Potemkin* by name but only to a "mutiny in the Black Sea fleet" and is against jumping into the stream of insurrection without first carefully testing the water. One must meticulously plan ahead, learn the topography of the city in question, the most vulnerable governmental institutions, etc., "and under no circumstances should we tolerate such measures as indiscriminate arming of the population."[29] The Party should have its own guerrilla and fighting units, carefully controlled by its central authorities. Had such caution been with the Bolsheviks in 1917, it is probable that they rather than their enemies would have spent the subsequent years in bitter exile. Even at the time the advice seemed fainthearted. All over the Empire, especially in the Caucasus and there especially in Georgia, peasants and workers were arming themselves and engaging in what now could be called guerrilla attacks. And here was a revolutionary arguing in effect that the people should desist from such activities until the socialists had trained their own fighting units, worked out a central plan of action, assessed the regime's weakness, and launched an attack. Objectively the caution might well have been justified—uncoordinated uprisings such as the one in Moscow in December 1905 were to lead to nothing but a needless sacrifice of lives—but it throws light on subsequent charges by

[29] Stalin, I, 135.

73

Bolshevik and Soviet historians that the armed uprising collapsed because of the Mensheviks' cowardice and their unwillingness to arm the people.

Intermittently the government sought to repress and to appease the Revolution. Fortunately in 1905, unlike in 1917, the rulers of the Empire had two capable statesmen, one of whom through concessions was able to slow the Revolution's momentum, and the other through a combination of reforms and repressions to break its spine.

The first was the man who signed the peace with Japan, Count Sergei Witte. It was he who persuaded the bewildered Emperor and the panic-stricken Imperial Family and bureaucrats (Nicholas II lacked the intelligence to become panicky even in these cataclysmic circumstances) that a policy of sheer repression must be unavailing[30] and that Russia must become a constitutional state.

In the Caucasus the policy of concession to popular aspirations was meant to be symbolized by the appointment of a new Viceroy, Count Vorontsov-Dashkov. This elderly nobleman had once been a member of the liberal circle around Alexander II and enjoyed a fairly progressive reputation. He did, in fact, attempt to combine what today in America one might call a law-and-order approach with a "dialogue" with the rebels. A high official, Sultan Krim Girey, considered suitable for the job on account of both his non-Russian descent and connections and his opinions, was dispatched to appease the Georgia countryside. What he heard during his discussions with the village elders and other representatives of the aroused peasantry could not have been particularly comforting: the peasants' demands amounted to a virtual dissolution of imperial authority.

On October 17 came the Tsar's Manifesto, promising constitutional freedoms and an elected parliament (Duma) to pass on all the laws. At first this seemed only to add fuel to the revolutionary fire. For the liberals the step was a belated one, and revolutionaries of all hues were temperamentally if not intellectually averse to playing the parliamentary game. The Manifesto at first was taken as a sign of capitulation by the authorities. The soviet form of revolutionary self-government which had been spreading since the summer invaded the capital. St. Petersburg was now virtually ruled by the council of workers, its guiding spirit young Leon Trotsky, who in advance of other socialist eminences hurried back to Russia and the Revolution and now at twenty-six jumped into the limelight as an unmatched revolutionary orator and organizer. In places crowds stormed jails and released prisoners. A railway strike paralyzed the country's communications.

---

[30] This policy was epitomized by the governor of St. Petersburg, Trepov, with his famous order to the troops on the occasion of a riot: "Blanks are not to be issued. Real bullets are not to be spared."

In the Caucasus the "days of freedom," as the first weeks after the Manifesto became known, were especially bizarre. From the local policeman to the viceroy, officialdom was panicking. Some time before, an emissary of the Bolshevik Central Committee had been arrested in Baku with members of the local committee. It did not take much to persuade the jail superintendent to allow the gentlemen in question to change places with some workers (who when unmasked were given but a two weeks' sentence). The free committeeman set out for Moscow only to have the train stop because of the strike. But a fellow traveler, a retired general with liberal convictions, turned out to be an amateur engine driver, and with the general at the wheel and the Bolshevik as the stoker, the train carrying messengers of revolution sped toward Moscow. Alliluyev was in a prisoners' party in the fortress of Kars when the great news came. The governor of the fortress opened negotiations with the political prisoners as to their wishes and, cheered by the remaining populace of Kars, they embarked to go back to Tiflis. Here the Viceroy was carrying on anxious negotiations with the local Menshevik leaders as to how to restore order. The general excitement—and, if the socialists are to be believed, the reactionaries' plots—led to a new crisis between the Armenians and the Tatars, and a bloodbath was threatening.

Now the local Bolsheviks turned into envious social reporters. The Menshevik leader Isidor Ramishvili was attending teas at the viceregal palace, they sneered. And, like many other noble ladies at the time, Countess Vorontsov-Dashkov was impressed by the revolutionary, this snide report went on: "he has such honest eyes," she is alleged to have told her husband. Whether or not this was a decisive consideration the Viceroy authorized the issuance of five hundred rifles to the workers' militia which patrolled the city, and tried not very effectively to curb the riot. The Bolsheviks were full of carping criticism. Why did the Mensheviks indulge in such unsocialist opportunistic dealings with the Tsar's satrap? Why hadn't they gotten more rifles? The ones they did get were mostly defective, and after the emergency passed they opportunistically returned them to the government's armory. The other critical party was the Emperor, who jotted on the margin of a report, "incomprehensible action by Count Vorontsov-Dashkov." (When the news of the February Revolution reached him, he noted in his diary: "some trouble in Petrograd. The weather is cold.")

The Viceroy's action was understandable in view of the utter demoralization of the police and of many regular army units. In the petition of Batum policemen of December 1905 there are elements familiar to anyone who has lived in the United States in the 1960s: the cops complain that because of society's hostility toward them they cannot perform their functions. Further, they demanded that they be freed of the task of pursuing *political* crimes, that supervision of police units be placed in the hands of the municipal authorities, that the policeman's status be upgraded by requiring entrants into the service to have intermediate education.[31]

This disarray was not peculiar to the Caucasus. But nowhere else did the government go so far in trying to appease rebels as to appoint a radical as governor. This was Vladimir Staroselski, an agronomist by profession who gained great renown and popularity in Georgia, where wine producing and drinking are as important as in France, for devising effective measures to restore the local viniculture, hurt by a plant disease. And now amid all the turbulence this scholarly man was appointed governor of Kutais, a startling contrast to the usual general or veteran bureaucrat. Staroselski, a typical contemporary *intelligent*, declined any police or military escort and traveled in his province guarded by the rebels' militia. He found it in a state of complete anarchy. Officials had fled, army units confined to their barracks were being attacked by the rebels, officers kidnaped, several government treasuries "expropriated"— which puts aright the Mensheviks' future charges that only the Bolsheviks engaged in armed robberies and similar un-Marxist activities. In his speeches the governor, copiously quoting from Marx, tried to persuade his peasant listeners to turn their dissent into constructive nonviolent channels. Russia was going to have a parliament. *He* understood their feelings and actions, but now the time had come to change tactics. Anyone who read Marx would easily understand that Russia was not ready for a *socialist* revolution. Though Staroselski was greeted courteously, his speeches had the same effect as such speeches always have on similar occasions.

Meanwhile the authorities recovered their nerve. The Viceroy yielded to the scandalized expostulations from St. Petersburg and the military. Staroselski was dismissed, which is understandable, but also arrested, which is less so. The new governor's very name and title suggested the difference from his predecessor—General Alikhan-Avarsky. In the manner of his distant ancestors he dealt with dissent by turning the rebellious villages and towns to fire and sword.[32] The atrocities committed, especially by Cossacks angered by earlier chicanery at the hands of the natives, were so pronounced that they brought protests even from the landowners who had been despoiled of their properties by the rebels.

The end of 1905 and the beginning of 1906 marked a partial turning

---

[31] G. Isakyan, *Central Papers of the Russian Social Democratic Workers Party About the Caucasus* (Erivan, 1965), p. 224.

[32] Alikhan-Avarsky was subsequently shot by a terrorist. Staroselski worked his way abroad, where he hobnobbed with Bolsheviks and was addressed by Lenin as "Comrade Governor." He died one year before the Revolution of 1917 and thus missed an almost certain career in the Kerensky regime, which was composed largely of men of his type.

of the tide. The Revolution went on, but the government under Witte's intelligent leadership regained its self-confidence. The St. Petersburg soviet was liquidated in December, and to Trotsky belongs the credit (which needless to say he has not received in Soviet accounts) for having persuaded its members to surrender peacefully, thus avoiding the street fighting like that which took place in the same month in Moscow.

The Manifesto was accompanied by a wide amnesty for past political crimes. This meant that émigré revolutionary leaders could now come back to Russia in relative safety. Martov and Lenin, among others, took advantage of this opportunity, and returned to the country they had left five years earlier as members of an insignificant revolutionary sect and which now resounded with their radical slogans.

The relaxation of censorship also meant an opportunity for legal publication of socialist journals and literature. The Bolshevik press ranged from St. Petersburg's *New Life*—for which the indefatigable Krasin had enlisted the financial help of Andreyeva, its nominal publisher, and her friend Gorky, and which had not only Lenin but various stars of the contemporary artistic and literary world as collaborators—to the cumbersomely named *Caucasian Workers' News Sheet*, edited in Tiflis by Koba and Shaumyan. The one brief article Djugashvili wrote for this short-lived journal in November 1905 has several points of interest. It is the first sample of his writing in Russian that we have, and it shows that when he did not have to wander into theory or the convolutions of intraparty debates, he could write simply and effectively. For an article in a journal appearing quite legally, the piece is amazingly inflammatory, speaking openly about the need to overthrow the autocracy and to build on its ruins a free democratic republic. For a man who had just argued for the socialists' participation in a provisional regime, Koba here shows himself uncompromisingly hostile to the liberals, the bourgeoisie, and any participation by the socialists in the parliament-Duma.

All branches of the Russian revolutionary movement displayed considerable distaste for the forthcoming parliament. Traditionally, reaction and revolution in Russia detested parliamentary institutions: according to the reactionaries, they would only separate the Tsar from his people, and according to the radicals they were democratic tomfoolery designed to conceal from the people that they were being governed by and for the bourgeoisie. In addition there was a fear, somewhat excessive judging by the subsequent events but in principle well grounded, that neither the Mensheviks nor the Bolsheviks could do brilliantly in free elections. The Socialist Revolutionaries were quite popular among the peasants (even though their leadership, like that of the Social Democrats, was almost entirely composed of middle-class intellectuals), but the socialists could appeal only to the militant element among the industrial workers, still a small minority of the population. Only the *Georgian* Mensheviks were confident of wide popular support and they were going into the elections despite the disapproval of their Russian brethren.

To work out their strategy the Bolsheviks arranged a conference, this time inside Russia or, more precisely, in the Finnish town of Tammerfors. Finnish officials as a rule were not eager to help their Russian colleagues, and Tammerfors could not be safer. Its police chief was a friend of Krasin's and a socialist sympathizer. Koba, a delegate from the Caucasus, for the first time traveled outside his native regions as a free man. And in Tammerfors he first met Lenin.

He was to describe his recollections of the great man almost twenty years later, after Lenin's death. "I expected to see a veritable mountain eagle of our Party, a great man not only politically but, if you please, also physically."[33] He was disappointed to find a small insignificant-looking man, in surroundings completely lacking in pomp and circumstance, and acting just as if he were an ordinary delegate. The famous passage has been declared by some biographers—whether indulgent, like Isaac Deutscher, or outright hostile, like Boris Souvarine—to smack of vulgarity and to indicate Koba's crude parochial outlook. But this misses the point. His recollection comes from a public lecture delivered to the students of the Kremlin Military School on January 28, 1924, and at the time it was a shrewd psychological thrust to discuss Lenin in this way. Stalin was of even smaller stature than the deceased leader, and his listeners and readers must have reflected how Stalin's *own* unpretentious manner and easy comradely ways contrasted with the revolutionary heroics surrounding the Trotskys and Zinovievs.

At the conference Lenin was inclined to have the Bolsheviks participate in the elections to the Duma, but the majority were against it. And he—in a preview of the reasonable, statesmanlike Lenin of 1917-21—submitted with a smile and retreated, as he said, "in good order." Both the international socialist movement, as represented by the Second International, and the activists in Russia called for the Social Democrats to reunite; the Bolsheviks pledged to work for unity and for a new, this time joint Party Congress.

There now began the incongruous spectacle of an electoral campaign in the midst of a revolution. All over the Empire, Party members took time out from expropriations, insurrections, and manifestations to foregather and listen to Menshevik and Bolshevik spokesmen extol their respective points of view and ask for votes. The meetings were virtually open, though undoubtedly chaperoned by police agents. The leaders could move around fairly freely, their previous sentences having been quashed by the October amnesty, and the government still would not

[33] Stalin, VI, 54.

risk offending society by arresting prominent revolutionaries unless they were caught in the act of armed rebellion. But the conspiratorial habits persisted. Lenin moved around St. Petersburg in a bourgeois disguise, wearing a derby and glasses, though he must have been aware that the police knew who and where he was. There was no reason for Koba not to resume his real name and "legal" existence, but he does not seem to have done so.

When the results of the elections were in, their results were not comforting to the Bolsheviks. They were now in a minority, the "minoritarians" in a majority. The situation was particularly depressing in the Caucasus: of the twelve mandates in Georgia, only one was held by a Bolshevik—Koba; the Mensheviks loudly protested that his election was fraudulent, since there were hardly any Party members in the district that allegedly had delegated him. Another well-known Bolshevik was elected in Baku, Peter Montin, very popular among the workers. But one evening while walking with his fiancée on a crowded boulevard, this gay and mercurial Ukrainian was set upon and, before he could reach for his gun, shot to death. It was never discovered by whom or why he was killed.

At Stockholm, where the Party Congress assembled in April 1906, Koba appeared as the virtual spokesman for Bolsheviks of the Caucasus. The Fourth or, as it is somewhat humorously described in Party history, the Unity Congress was in fact the first Party gathering deserving such an exalted name. The two factions, plus their national affiliates, the Polish, Jewish (the *Bund*), and Lett Socialists, could boast more than 100,000 members and of course many more sympathizers. All the luminaries of Russian socialism were there, except Martov and Trotsky, the latter currently in jail awaiting trial for his part in the St. Petersburg Soviet. There was Plekhanov, who after a temporary rapprochement with Lenin now again gravitated toward the Mensheviks. Because of this and because of his acerbic wit, Plekhanov was not very popular among the more brawling type of Bolsheviks. One of them, Gregory Alexinsky, announced that he would beat him up, and two burly fellow delegates had to sit with Alexinsky during the sessions to make sure the Congress would not witness such a scandal.

Verbal assaults upon Plekhanov, however, were permissible, and Koba was not backward in this respect. Plekhanov, he declared, talked about Lenin's "anarchistic" mannerisms. Was this the way to bring about Party unity? He for his part could say something about Plekhanov's "Kadet" mannerisms. This reference was to a dilemma that perplexed the assembled socialists: the intertwined problem of the Duma and the nature of the Revolution. Elections to the Duma were still going on (they were indirect, and staggered through several phases), but it was already clear that it would have a radical complexion, with the Kadets as the biggest party. In Georgia the Mensheviks showed every sign of scoring a major success—which they did, capturing five out of seven seats for the whole country. The original idea of abstaining from the "parliamentary farce" now looked like a very bad one, and it was decided that socialists should participate in the last phase of elections and in all future ones. But both factions were almost unanimous in their proclaimed intention to use parliamentarism as the means for exposing the sham constitution, for pushing the Kadets toward more provocative acts against the government (at the time the Kadets did not need much pushing in that reaction), in brief, for calling a spade a spade, making the whole experiment of limited constitutional government unworkable and eventual progress toward a responsible one impossible.

But the Bolsheviks *knew* that those Mensheviks really longed for seats in the Duma, craved ministerial portfolios and other forbidden bourgeois-democratic fruit. Why, they were nothing but Kadets in Marxist disguise. The Mensheviks protested against these slurs, but they were handicapped by the circumstance that two people close to them did in fact profess scandalous democratic ideas. One was Akimov, who was one of those people with a fatal gift for saying what others feel like saying but do not dare to, in this case lest the noble ghosts of Marx and Engels rise and smite them for opportunism. At the Second Party Congress, in 1903, he had created a scandal by saying that the Party program and statute seemed like a blueprint for dictatorship. He now compounded his crime by wondering aloud whether the Duma should not be given a chance to work and, if it advanced the citizens' liberties, fine and well; if not, there would be time for armed uprising. The same ideas were expressed in a more cautious form by one Martynov which was even more embarrassing to the Mensheviks, since Akimov was but their fellow traveler admitted to the Congress at *Bolshevik* insistence, but Martynov was undeniably one of their own.

Koba laid it on thick. In one of two brief speeches to the Congress, and in his subsequent written report to the Georgian Bolsheviks, he described how the Mensheviks through "their leader Martynov" revealed their real intentions of helping the bourgeoisie to achieve hegemony and betray the working class. But for all his violent partisanship, he was not a blind follower of Lenin's. This was displayed in a remarkable speech on the Party's land program.

The Russian Marxist approached the problem of the peasant with almost as much distaste as that of the parliament. Everybody knew (i.e., Marx had said) that the individual peasant was by instinct a petty bourgeois with an unquenchable thirst for private property. In a socialist society, individual property in land would be abolished, agriculture would consist of huge grain factories modeled on industrial ones. But to tell this openly to the peasant meant to say goodbye to revolution for a long, long time. The countryside was currently in great revolutionary ferment but that was because the peasant wanted more land, not because he longed to become a rural or industrial worker. How, then, could one persuade the peasants that the socialists would give them more land, while at the same time keeping faith with Marx? The Bolsheviks proposed nationalization: all land to be vested in the state. The peasants would understand, said Lenin, that their rights in the land would be undisturbed and only the large landowners' property would be confiscated. But, expostulated the Mensheviks, that would mean that the bourgeois democratic state would hold the land, and would not the bourgeoisie work to strengthen private property? They opted for *municipalization*: the right to all land to be vested in the hands of local authorities. Ah, retorted the Bolsheviks, but would not local authorities be controlled by the peasants, i.e., petty bourgeoisie, would not *they* tend to preserve and strengthen the institution of private property? Here the future Stalin displayed revolutionary common sense: if you want the peasant to help you with the Revolution you must *give* him land. "We must support full confiscation and redistribution of the [proprietors' land] to the peasants. Thus both nationalization and municipalization are equally unacceptable."[34] Without the peasants, the Revolution will falter and fail.

And so the little-known delegate from the Caucasus outlined tactics which, endorsed by Lenin in 1917 with his "All land to the peasants," were one of the most important reasons for the Bolsheviks prevailing in Russia and, practiced by Mao Tse-tung in the 1930s and 1940s, carried the Chinese Communists as well to victory. The future Stalin is already discernible: with his brusqueness, his ability to cut the Gordian knot of Marxian dialectics and propose a simple and effective slogan: "The liberation of peasants must be the work of the peasants themselves." So it was in 1917–18, when the peasants did on a vast scale what they had done sporadically during the First Russian Revolution and themselves seized the state's and large proprietors' land.

Though he earned his spurs in an all-Party arena, Koba—or, to give him his Stockholm Party alias, Ivanovich—does not seem to have attracted any special attention. He was a Bolshevik from a predominantly Menshevik area. For all Baku's pioneering role in the revolutionary movement, to many Russian delegates the Caucasus seemed a distant and backward province, the activities there but peripheral to the great events taking place in central Russia. And there were linguistic difficulties. It was characteristic that one of the Congress chairmen, Fyodor Dan, remarked at one point that his fellow Menshevik, Noah Jordania, being a Georgian probably did not correctly understand a Russian phrase. One year

[34] Stalin, I, 237.

later Lenin told Jordania, "You Georgians stay out of Russian affairs, you do not understand our people." Yet very shortly those outsiders would reach the highest position in both branches of Russian Marxism.

At Stockholm the split between the two was only papered over, not healed. The new joint Central Committee included seven Mensheviks and three Bolsheviks. Lenin's decision to stay out of it reflected his determination, despite all professions to the contrary, to keep working toward a separate party of his own. A secret Bolshevik center was probably already operating in Stockholm, working out separate Bolshevik tactics and policies in defiance of Congress' decisions. And in Russia there would soon be organized separate Bolshevik Literary Bureaus. Koba, then, upon his return to Georgia, worked again in a double capacity, as a member of the Social Democratic organization and as a member of the Bolshevik "underground" within it. His partisanship, strong as it was, at times vicious, did not keep him from appreciating practical advantages of joint work with the Mensheviks, and we shall see how the time came when he found Lenin's obsession on the subject incomprehensible.

The Georgian Mensheviks were in plain ascendance, with the majority of their country's representation in the Duma. Some deputies elected from other regions declared themselves Social Democrats, and the Socialist faction in the Duma elected Jordania as its chairman. Koba's advancement in the Party, it was clear, would have to take place outside of Georgia. But only in mid-1907 did he definitely shift his base of operations to Baku.

In the meantime there took place an event about which we have but the barest information: Joseph Djugashvili married Catherine Semyonovna Svanidze.

The revolutionary code prescribed that a marriage or liaison was an entirely private affair, and the revolutionaries frowned upon any "human-interest" stories about them, except for propaganda purposes—as in the case of Nadezhda Krupskaya's highly elevating and exceedingly boring description of her life with Lenin. Some Bolsheviks, notably Krasin and Trotsky, do let us in on their private life in their memoirs, but Stalin adhered to the norm. Hence the numerous official biographies and chronologies preserve an almost uniform silence on the date of his marriage and the background and personality of his wife. A very unreliable account by a Georgian contemporary had led most of Stalin's Western biographers to place the marriage in 1903 (when he was in jail) and Catherine's death in 1907. But we know from Svetlana Alliluyeva's book that her half-brother Jacob was born in 1908. Revolutionaries sometimes scorned the bourgeois institution of formal marriage, but a church union had to be resorted to (since there was no civil wedding) when children were expected. The marriage then took place probably in 1906 or 1907, and Catherine Semyonovna Djugashvili died, we are told by Alliluyeva, in 1910.

As to her family, she was almost certainly the daughter of that Semyon Svanidze, a railway employee, who was named in a police indictment as the main organizer of the political strike in the depot of Alexandropol, and who, after the station was seized by the rebels, was named by them its director.[35] This Svanidze was a Social Democrat, and so was his son, Stalin's brother-in-law, Alexander Semyonovich Svanidze, who studied philosophy in Germany and was the author of a book on Ernest Mach. Alexander, as Alliluyeva details, was to occupy a number of economic posts in Soviet Russia, but eventually, like so many in Stalin's circle, was destroyed by him.

This is as far as we can go on the basis of current knowledge. How the marriage affected this unusual man, why he should first neglect his son and then treat him so atrociously are questions about which we can only speculate. Some men in his position would have recalled with fondness the early years of struggle, poverty, and insignificance. But there are people whom power and honor in middle and old age make even more resentful of the deprivations of their youth. "You are a Goddamned privileged class," he exploded when his daughter described to him how she and the other notables' children evacuated to Kuibyshev during World War II had a special school and privileged accommodations. In the all-powerful dictator, the conscious maker of that class, there still remained a rebel furious over his lost youth and early manhood with their privations and humiliations. For others he could remake his past, present it as a selfless and glorious ascent in the sacred cause. But not for himself.

[35] Academy of Sciences of the U.S.S.R., *The High Points of the Revolution of 1905–7*, Part 3, Book 2 (Moscow, 1956), pp. 881, 883.

THE
ASCENT AND
THE
ORDEAL

The second year of the Russian Revolution brought a marked change in its character. Previously the government had responded through a mixture of brutal repression on the one hand and panic and concessions on the other. Now its actions became more purposeful and its intention to save the framework if not the entire edifice of the autocracy more obvious.

In addition to the government's stiffened resistance, another force arose on the side of reaction. This was the coalescence of various reactionary and sometimes outright criminal elements to oppose constitutionalism as "anti-Russian" and to combat revolutionary movements with their own weapons: riots and demonstrations. The Union of the Russian People was its main expression. The Black Hundreds, as its detachments of hooligans became known, would demonstrate carrying ikons and the Emperors' portraits, and their demonstrations easily turned to looting and violence directed against Jews and the intelligentsia. The pogroms against the Jews were an old story in the Ukraine, where the bulk of the Jewish population of the Empire resided. But the new slogan of the Black Hundreds was "Beat the Jews *and* the intelligentsia and save Russia." Though most Tsarist officials combated such activities, there were some who looked the other way, and a few who actively encouraged them. Nicholas II, son of that Alexander III who once admitted that "in the depths of his soul" he could understand those who attacked the Jews, replied graciously to a declaration of loyalty by those protofascists with one of his inimitable messages of thanks: "May the Union of the Russian People be my trusty support, serving for all and in everything as an example of lawfulness and [a force for] civic order."

In the Caucasus, where there were few Jews and where the absence of universities deprived them of the other obvious targets, the forces of "lawfulness and civic order" had to be content with breaking into the high schools and roughing up those students who refused to join in singing "God Save the Tsar." The revolutionaries maintained that the "dark forces" and officials sympathetic to them were also involved in stirring up riots between the Armenians and Tatars. This charge is rather hard to substantiate: relations between the two nationalities were always strained, and any small incident might lead to an explosion. But it suited the socialists to accuse of instigating the Armenian-Moslem massacres those officials whom they wanted to get rid of. In early 1906 the Georgian socialists decided to remove General Gryaznov, chief of staff of the Caucasian district and very active on the side in organizing the right-wing elements in Tiflis. Sylvester Djibladze summoned the head of the Party's terrorist squad, who in turn selected one of his men, who carried out the deed. Arrested on the spot, the assassin refused to name his superiors and accomplices and went calmly to his execution. Such were the practices of an allegedly moderate wing of a party which allegedly condemned individual terror. Whatever one may think of the People's Will, which used terror as the means of political struggle in the 1870s and 1880s, one must note that its leaders not merely ordered assassinations but for the most part carried them out themselves. It would be preposterous to accuse the Krasins and Djibladzes of lacking courage: the story of their lives speaks for itself. But that moral insensitivity inherent in their behavior helps us understand how easily the Bolsheviks during the Civil War could turn to *mass* terror and how the soil was prepared for that "war upon the nation" which Stalin was to wage in the 1930s.

Terrorism and constitutional experiments—such were the incongruous elements of the situation in Russia in 1906. The revolutionary fever still ran high, so that it appeared incredible to recall the political apathy of only a few years before. Can one believe it, exclaims a writer in a revolutionary journal published legally in St. Petersburg in 1906, that in the 1890s the disinterest in politics among the university youth was such that at a students' meeting a speaker could say, "If you are studying to be a doctor then your main duty is to try to become a good doctor, if engineer to be a good engineer," that female students' circles sponsored courses in cooking![1] Another modern touch was provided by the current revolutionary fashion: radical Georgian youths grew their hair very long, and at least one police official who ordered the heads of some youths shaved paid with his life for his "derision of the revolution."[2] In view of such an atmosphere, the revolutionaries' and most particularly Lenin's fears of an accommodation through reform between the government and society were groundless. The Duma, dominated in the socialists' parlance by the "cowardly bourgeois liberals," i.e., the Kadets, pressed for a full democratic regime and a radical land reform. The government felt compelled to dissolve it after it had sat for less than two months. Thereupon two hundred of its deputies traveled to Vybory, in Finland, and issued a manifesto branding the act as illegal and calling upon the citizens to refuse to pay taxes and provide recruits for the army. The signatories of the Vybory Manifesto were not revolutionaries but members of the "Establishment," many of them lawyers, professors, and landowners.

On his part, the Tsar had already dismissed Witte. This enlightened bureaucrat was now hated in Court circles, where it was whispered that his ambition was to become the first President of the Russian Republic. In the summer the Emperor entrusted the government to Peter Stolypin, who had a reputation of being a "strong man" and who unlike many with such a reputation did in fact turn out to be one. Stolypin instituted courts-martial to deal with the revolutionaries peremptorily and without the inhibiting influence of the professional judiciary. But unlike most of the traditional bureaucrats, he understood the need for social reform and knew where the need was most urgent. A comprehensive land reform was initiated to erect a strong rural middle class of peasant proprietors as a barrier against revolution.

The incongruity of the situation deepened. Elections to the new Duma were going on through their laborious stages, and it was clear that it would be even more radical than the first. Revolutionary propaganda was being purveyed fairly openly: it would have been inconceivable even in contemporary England and France to publish legally what was being read in Russia with but little interference by the censor: virtual calls to armed rebellion, hardly veiled libels of the Emperor and members of the government. Yet at the same time gallows and firing squads were doing their work. In the first six months of their existence the courts-martial passed 1042 death sentences. Revolution, reform, repression coexisted.

---

[1] M. S. Alexandrov, *The Past* (St. Petersburg), No. 11 (November 1906), p. 4. The editor of the journal was Vladimir Burtsev, who became famous through his unmasking of notorious agents provocateurs.

[2] Gregory Uratadze, *Reminiscences of a Georgian Social Democrat* (in Russian; Stanford, Calif., 1968), pp. 135–36.

Amidst the many paradoxes in this strange Russia of 1906 none was greater than that concerning the role and activity of the Bolsheviks. They lived in "double illegality," as they put it: first, as revolutionaries working for the overthrow of the government; second, within the officially reunited Social Democratic Party working at cross purposes with its central organs elected in Stockholm and in defiance of the resolutions of the Party Congress which forbade factional activities. Neither aspect of this double life was much of a secret. As far as the government was concerned, information about the Bolsheviks' doings was provided through local agents and also by a man then in Lenin's confidence and not until much later unmasked as a police agent, Dr. Jacob Zhitomirsky, the Bolshevik center's representative in Berlin. Through him the Okhrana received fairly accurate intelligence about the Bolshevik leaders, their whereabouts, and their plans. Though Lenin often shifted his quarters in St. Petersburg and moved to Finland at the beginning of 1907, it is unlikely that the Okhrana was ever for long ignorant as to where he was. Why, then, was he not arrested? We have already considered this problem in connection with Krasin; with Lenin and other prominent Social Democrats not directly connected with armed activities, the authorities' dilemma was even more serious. The arrest of a political leader, even a self-proclaimed revolutionary, was bound to antagonize the liberals even further, something the government strove to avoid during the elections. There may have already been then, as there was certainly to be after 1910, an element of deliberation in the police indulgence toward the Bolshevik leaders, for the latter (and Lenin especially) provided the main obstacle to the Social Democrats' and, beyond them, the revolutionary movement's reaching real unity. There were probably elements in the political police and the ministry (it was almost as badly divided as the revolutionary movement itself) that were pleased by the Bolshevik's scorn for constitutional methods of penchant for violence. For many the greatest danger appeared that of a constitutional, truly responsible government; at times even Stolypin showed himself inclined to seek the collaboration of the Kadets, which would have been the first step toward a representative government. And no one was fighting more strenuously to make any constitutional experiment impossible than Lenin and the Bolsheviks.

The other aspect of Bolshevik illegality was represented by the "literary bureaus" which sprang up in most Party centers and were but a transparent device through which the Bolsheviks kept their faction together while working within the Social Democratic Party. We must be careful, however, not to view this arrangement anachronistically as a harbinger of future United Fronts, of Communist infiltration of left and radical parties. Until at least 1912, nobody except perhaps Lenin himself thought of permanently splitting the Party or of having one faction take it over completely. Factional strife, tempestuous and even violent as it occasionally became, was after all natural in a party that was still composed predominantly of young men and women, with all of youth's need for intense friendship and hostility, the alacrity with which it offers loyalty and feels betrayal.

The Tiflis "literary bureau" was composed of Makharadze, Tshakaya, Shaumyan, and Koba. The first two, as behooved elderly persons on the threshold of forty, were really more interested in literary work, so the burden of actual leadership of conspiratorial Bolshevik enterprises fell upon the two younger men, with occasional help from "Alyosha" Djaparidze, who was otherwise preoccupied by labor union work in Baku (i.e., with subverting the Shendrikovs' influence).

The bureau, like other organizations of this kind, reported to the Bolshevik center, the geographic location of which became Kuokkala, Finland, sometime in 1906. There Alexander Malinovsky, known in the Party as Bogdanov, prepared a hideout for the Bolshevik high command. Soon Lenin himself moved in, accompanied by his wife, mother-in-law, and sister. From Villa Vaza, his residence in Kuokkala, Lenin and his two lieutenants, Krasin and Bogdanov, consulted on strategy and issued orders on how to fight the Mensheviks and make sure that at the forthcoming Party Congress the Bolsheviks would regain the majority. It was to Kuokkala that proceedings of expropriations would be brought (but not always *all* of them), and there the women would sew the high-denomination notes into the coats and vests of couriers who would try to exchange them abroad. The villa was regularly visited by a stream of revolutionaries and terrorists, and it is not clear how seriously Lenin himself believed that the Okhrana was in the dark concerning his activities.

As one of the two principal agents of Bolshevism in the Caucasus, Koba faced an uphill fight. As a Bolshevik speaker was to bewail at the Fifth Party Congress, "The Caucasian Mensheviks, profiting by their crushing numerical preponderance and their official [*sic!*] lordship over the Caucasus, have taken all possible measures not to let any Bolsheviks be elected [to the Party Congress]."[3] One might think that such a complaint was disingenuous: if the other side has a crushing majority, how can you complain that you don't get elected? But the Bolsheviks were already imbued with the psychology that led Khrushchev in 1957, when outvoted in the Presidium of the Communist Party, to declare that the vote was not legitimate since it was merely an "arithmetical majority" which had voted to fire him! And so Koba's and Shaumyan's efforts were directed at discrediting and disrupting the Mensheviks. The

[3] *The Fifth* [London] *Congress of the Russian Social Democratic Workers Party, Protocols* (Moscow, 1963), p. 227.

methods used to undermine the Shendrikovs in Baku have already been related, but in Georgia one could not allege that the Mensheviks were being subsidized by industrialists. In fact Shaumyan, through his connection with some rich Armenian entrepreneurs, was able to secure their financial help. Still, the Mensheviks were guilty: their very majority indicated that they were really in a minority. How? Well, both the vote for the Georgian Mensheviks in the Duma election and their membership was much *greater* than the number of class-conscious proletarians in Georgia. So they were not a workers' party at all, and the Georgian proletariat looked with distaste at this petty-bourgeois group masquerading as Marxists! For their own part the Caucasian Bolsheviks were seeking localities where there were few or no members of the Party and were proclaiming them to be bastions of Bolshevism. Such arguments, it must be added, were being advanced in all seriousness and were far from being rejected out of hand by most Mensheviks. After all, when the Russian socialist movement was but a handful of intellectuals, hadn't they shared the belief that sheer numbers are unimportant, that this handful represented the true interests of hundreds of thousands of workers?

The depressing state of intraparty affairs may have affected Koba's literary work. Toward the end of 1906, as befitted his enhanced position in the movement, he tried his hand at a major theoretical treatise. This was a series of articles, *Anarchism or Socialism*, published in Georgian, but it was never finished. The quality of this tirade against anarchism may be best judged from the fact that even at the height of the cult of personality, when Stalin's most insignificant utterances were being paraded as evidence of his theoretical genius, no one had the heart to cite for this purpose his lengthy, repetitious diatribe where the author repeatedly tripped over his own argument and forgot what he was attempting to prove. Even faithful Beria praised this production rather guardedly, explaining that it had been necessitated by an influx of anarchists into the Caucasus. The only noteworthy aspect of the inept production is Koba's oblique reference to his father.[4]

The other aspect of Koba's activity in 1906 is surrounded by certain obscurity. That is the *extent* of his participation in the partisan activities, i.e., expropriations and terroristic acts against government officials and the like. That he was connected with them there can be no question. As we have seen, in the Caucasus both factions of the Social Democrats indulged in such activities. Andrei Vishinsky, then a Menshevik, was linked with a partisan group in Baku; an authorized

---

[4] "Imagine a shoemaker who had a tiny shop, but who not being able to withstand the competition shut it down and let us say hired himself as a worker in the Adelkhanov factory in Tiflis. . . ." Stalin, *Collected Works* (Moscow, 1946–52), I, 315.

biographical sketch states that he was "chief of the staff and led a number of partisan activities: participant and organizer of a number of terrorist acts against provocateurs."[5] The activities in Guria have already been related. The Stockholm Congress resolution on the subject was ambiguous: partisan activities and seizures of state funds were authorized in certain conditions, attacks on private persons and property declared impermissible. It was, of course, ridiculous to expect that such a fine distinction would be observed. The Mensheviks cannot escape a degree of responsibility for expropriations, and one must take with a grain of salt their subsequent expressions of horror on the subject.

Following the Revolution the Menshevik press, first inside Soviet Russia and after 1921 in migration, directed its main fire concerning expropriations against Stalin. And Soviet historians, obviously under official instructions, have treated the subject somewhat coyly: while not connecting the leader directly with such exploits, they let drop hints that, yes, it was Koba's brain and ingenuity that were behind the most spectacular feats of armed banditry for the cause. In fact his role in them was rather modest: he was principally a recruiter of personnel and expediter of funds. The overall direction of partisan activities belonged, as we have already seen, to Krasin. And in the most notorious Caucasian expropriation of all, that of June 13, 1907, in Tiflis, Koba played a secondary role. Its remote planner was Krasin and the local supervisor Shaumyan.

The incongruous subjects of terrorist activity and socialist tactics in the Duma preoccupied the attention of the Fifth Party Congress which assembled in London in April 1907. Some weeks earlier the second Duma had convened, more radical than the first: the socialists had scored a brilliant success with a total of sixty-five deputies.[6] But to Lenin this very success portended a danger. The socialists might yield to the temptation of playing the parliamentary game and forget about the Revolution. If he was worried, his principal lieutenants Krasin and Bogdanov were alarmed. Both of them were by temperament revolutionary adventurers, and the prospect of plodding parliamentary debates, ministerial coalitions, and the like replacing such exhilarating episodes as stealing guns to bombard the Winter Palace and blowing up the Prime Minister's residence was enough to drive them out of the Party if it authorized such a betrayal. However, there seemed to be no practical possibility of such a depressing development: the Bolsheviks had conducted the electoral campaign with gusto (in some districts obtaining the votes of dead people) but they used the Duma only

---

[5] V. I. Nevsky, ed., *Activists of the Revolutionary Movement in Russia—A Bio-bibliographical Dictionary* (Moscow, 1931), p. 1074.
[6] Thirty-six were avowed Mensheviks, eighteen Bolsheviks, and eleven stood apart from the factions.

for revolutionary propaganda. There were also the Mensheviks, of course; but they loudly protested that they were not in the Duma to pass legislation, only to push the Kadets into a new confrontation with Stolypin and at the same time to unmask them before the people, to destroy any constitutional illusions. The Menshevik revolutionary virtue was so great that when other parties raised the proposal of amnesty for political prisoners the Menshevik Irakli Tseretelli declared that it was ridiculous to talk of freeing selected persons: all of Russia was one huge jail and the only real amnesty was to overthrow the government! But such professions did not fool the Bolsheviks. They knew, declared Lenin, that the Mensheviks were dealing "secretly and in an underground fashion" with the Kadets. Proof? Already in November 1906 some Mensheviks had gone to a tea with Professor Paul Miliukov, leader of the Kadets.

The Congress that was taking place under such favorable conditions for intraparty unity was an amazing achievement in itself. This conspiratorial, illegal party managed to transport upward of three hundred delegates to London, where their arrival created a sensation. The delegates were barely recovered from seasickness[7] when they received a vivid reminder of the philistinism of the bourgeois world: the English Friends of the Russian People gave a reception in their honor but they were expected to attend in evening dress. We are not warranted the information whether the delegate from the Caucasus, Ivanovich-Koba, did indeed don a borrowed dinner jacket for the occasion. But there were gracious speeches hailing the Russian fighters for freedom—the British like Ramsay MacDonald little suspecting that in a few years they would be denounced as "yellow socialists" by the men they were entertaining. The spirit of tolerance must have very briefly infected the Russians, for when Lenin gave the reply, Plekhanov graciously agreed to translate it into English.

Ivanovich-Koba and other Caucasus Bolsheviks had their mandates challenged by the Mensheviks. Since the Bolsheviks, with the help of the affiliated Polish and Latvian socialists, disposed of a majority at the Congress, the mandate commission did not bar them. Shaumyan was allowed a full vote, Koba an advisory one. In these circumstances it was advisable for him not to be conspicuous, and so he did not speak during the entire deliberations, which occupied three weeks. It would be futile to speculate on the impression that London made on the young man from the Caucasus. The revolutionaries, even when they lived abroad, never really left Russia or the problems and quarrels of their own

---

[7] They had come by boat from Copenhagen, where it had first been proposed to hold the Congress. The travails of a sea route were so depressing that a Bolshevik delegate, A. Mandelstam (with the most inappropriate alias of *Ulysses*), demanded that a way be found for him to go back *entirely by land.*

movement, and (with a few exceptions, such as Plekhanov) could not look at Western culture and institutions as anything but monuments of a hostile bourgeois civilization. Generalissimo Stalin never mentioned his visit to London to the man who at the time was Under-Secretary for Colonies in His Majesty's Government, Winston Churchill.

Koba's impressions of the Party Congress itself, however, were subsequently printed in the *Baku Proletarian*, the Bolshevik journal he edited with Shaumyan and other Bolsheviks. Predictably the tone was one of rather impudent hostility toward the Mensheviks. "Menshevism represents the tactic of the semi-bourgeois segments of the working class";[8] the Bolsheviks represented the real workers, the Mensheviks only the Party bureaucracy. Gregory Alexinsky, who at Stockholm wanted to beat up Plekhanov (in a few years he would break with Lenin and try to beat *him* up), joked at the Congress that the Mensheviks were heavily Jewish in their leadership while the Bolsheviks more Russian, so the latter might organize a pogrom! Koba repeated this bon mot with some relish. Seriously, he went on, the Mensheviks *were* heavily non-Russian, not only Jewish but also Georgian in composition (a strange reproach coming from a Georgian). For Trotsky, whom he saw for the first time in London (Trotsky professes not to have noticed *him*), Koba already expressed dislike: this man represents nothing but "elegant uselessness." Already there is an inkling of that temperamental incompatibility which as much as political rivalry characterized the relations of the two men.[9] All in all, concluded Koba, presaging one of Stalin's famous non sequiturs ("It is well known that . . ."), the Congress brought greater unity in the Party as a whole!

The partisan tone of the article must have been judged excessive even by Koba's fellow Bolshevik editors, for the promised next installments of the reminiscences of London never appeared. But there was another reason for the Bolsheviks not to envenom the intraparty disputes during the summer of 1907: a major scandal broke out in connection with expropriations, and Shaumyan and Koba were directly involved.

The London Congress had passed a definitive prohibition on partisan activities and expropriations. Such activities, it was noted, encouraged criminal and anarchist elements in the population, led to similar feats attempted by the Black Hundreds, brought repression against peaceful and innocent people, and thus did incalculable damage to the revolutionary cause. Hence all the fighting detachments of the Party organiza-

---

[8] Stalin, II, 30.

[9] It is true that Trotsky's interventions at the Congress conveyed the impression of that intellectual arrogance which was to harm him so much in his political career. He tried to "rise above" the quarrel between the Mensheviks and Bolsheviks with the predictable result of alienating people in both factions.

tion were to be dissolved forthwith.[10] A hundred and seventy Bolsheviks voted for this resolution, though Lenin was among the thirty-five who voted against, while fifty-two withheld their votes.[11] Though Koba in his report of the Congress presented the resolution as one of no importance, passed only to give the Mensheviks something to be happy about, it is obvious that many in Lenin's faction believed the expropriations were a disgrace, and harmful to boot.

Barely three weeks after the London Congress concluded its deliberations, a new and sensational expropriation took place. At eleven A.M. a Cossack convoy escorting a cashier of the State Bank with a large sum of money was attacked at the Erivan Square in Tiflis. Several of the escorts were killed, the money scooped up by the assailants. It became immediately known to Social Democratic circles in Tiflis, if not to the police, that the attack was the work of the Bolsheviks, and the leader of the assailants none other than a certain Kamo, already well known for exploits of similar character.

Kamo's life has been a favorite subject for Soviet biographers. Semyon Ter-Petrosyan, or Kamo, was born in 1882 in Gori, the son of a meat dealer. Having broken with his father, the young Armenian proposed to enlist in the army, and for that purpose took lessons in Russian from his fellow townsman Djugashvili, who persuaded him to enter upon a more exciting career. His frequent arrests, escapes, and disguises, his feigning insanity for a long time in German, then Russian, jails—these add a touch of romance and heroism to the Party annals, otherwise filled with petty squabbles and intrigues. But it is odd that the Soviet writers do not seem to realize what light his story throws upon those who like Lenin, Krasin, or Stalin himself commanded this man to attempt apparently suicidal actions, or who did not try to keep him from returning to Russia from abroad when he faced a death sentence. Kamo himself hardly fits the stereotype of the class-conscious revolutionary. He was politically illiterate and quite clearly mentally unhinged. After his famous escape in 1911 he still dreamed of terrorist exploits, even though by now the Bolsheviks had given them up. And so, after a consultation with Krasin, he launched an attempt at expropriation on his own, during which he was wounded and captured. It would be interesting to know for what purpose he and Krasin proposed to use the money if the attempt had been successful.

The Revolution of 1917 freed Kamo from prison, and he now organized his famous partisan detachments for the Civil War. A feature of

[10] *The Fifth* [London] *Congress of the Russian Social Democratic Workers Party* (Moscow, 1959), pp. 581–82.
[11] The resolution was, however, weakened when the Congress accepted an amendment eliminating *mandatory* exclusion from the Party of those violating the prohibition.

their training was that their members would be "captured" by alleged counterrevolutionaries (in fact partisans from another detachment), who would give them the alternative of betraying the Soviet cause or being tortured to death. Would-be traitors were shot out of hand, but many who passed the trial succumbed to nervous shock. According to Svetlana Alliluyeva, her mother's brother, Fyodor, never recovered from this appalling test he underwent as a teen-ager and suffered from intermittent mental illness for the rest of his days.[12] The barbarous practice was finally stopped at Lenin's express order.

In Soviet Russia Kamo was like a fish out of water, and he was unable to learn some civilian skill. Stalin procured for him a job in the Tiflis customs office, where he might have worked peaceably and perhaps even survived the purges. But his friends, who treated him like a big child, bought him a bicycle, and one day in 1922, riding on the wrong side of the street, he ran into a car[13] and was killed.

Most accounts of the Tiflis robbery attribute its planning to Koba. It was indeed he who some years before had recruited Kamo for the Bolsheviks. But a recent Soviet biography of Stephen Shaumyan makes it clear that he was the main "strategist and planner" of the attack.[14] The threads of the conspiracy reached to St. Petersburg, where it was originally planned by Krasin, and to Kuokkala in Finland, where most of the money was delivered by Kamo himself. But not all of it: hurriedly leaving Tiflis, where the Party set up a secret court of inquiry, members of the Literary Bureau, Shaumyan and Koba took along with them to Baku at least 15,000 rubles from the spoils.[15] The money would come in handy to pay for the Bolshevik organization in Baku and for its publications. This, and the proceeds from similar exploits, explains the source of income for underground organizers like Koba, now a man with a family, who in 1908 was well enough off to offer to lend money to Alliluyev.

The repercussions of the Tiflis expropriation reached far beyond the frontiers of Georgia, and indeed of the Empire. Much of the money was in easily identifiable five-hundred-ruble notes, and Bolshevik couriers were dispatched to try to exchange them abroad. Unfortunately, the government had the banknotes' serial numbers, and to the shock of Europe's socialist and progressive circles, Bolshevik agents were being

[12] Svetlana Alliluyeva, *Twenty Letters to a Friend* (in Russian; New York, 1967), p. 60.
[13] Undoubtedly occupied by a member of the Soviet bureaucracy, adds Trotsky, never one to leave a story without a moral, even though he should have reflected that at the time he was very much a Soviet bureaucrat himself. Leon Trotsky, *Stalin, An Appraisal of the Man and His Influence* (London, 1968), p. 106.
[14] Vladimir Dubinsky Mukhadze, *Shaumyan* (Moscow, 1965), p. 123.
[15] *Ibid.*, p. 137.

arrested all over the Continent. Kamo was seized in Berlin, on the denunciation of Dr. Zhitomirsky (who added the piquant though improbable detail that the Caucasian terrorist was about to try his luck with the local bank of Mendelssohn and Sons); Maxim Litvinov and his traveling companion, Fanny Yampolsky, were arrested in Paris; the Latvian Bolshevik Yan Masters and "Olga" (the Party name of Sarah Ravich, the future wife of Gregory Zinoviev) were seized elsewhere in France. Though protests from progressive French circles led to the release of Litvinov and Yampolsky and to the return of "their" money, the attendant publicity provided ammunition for fresh Menshevik attacks upon Lenin. This time the attacks proved not merely embarrassing but dangerous. The Bolsheviks could not risk an expulsion or condemnation by the Second International, could not risk being branded by the organ of international socialism as anarchists rather than Marxists. This explains why expropriations were discontinued in 1908 and why in January 1910 Lenin was to agree to have most of the money the Bolsheviks had acquired by these means, and by those "Bolshevik marriages" arranged by Krasin, turned over to three German trustees to be held for further disposition. The de-emphasis of violence in Party activities was bound, in turn, to lead to Lenin's break with Bolsheviks like Bogdanov and Krasin. For them those exciting partisan activities were the essence of the underground struggle. They would not go back to peaceful Marxist propaganda, to advancing the Bolshevik cause in the Duma and in labor union elections.

It is remarkable that while the fuss over the Caucasian expropriations spread all over Europe, Shaumyan and Koba lived on peaceably in Baku. Koba was not arrested until March 25, 1908, and then on an entirely different charge. Out of the proceedings of the robbery he and Shaumyan were able to finance the *Baku Proletarian*, which appeared entirely legally—though with occasional interference by the authorities, who did not shut it down permanently until August 27, 1909.[16] That their share in the expropriations was a secret to the Mensheviks is most unlikely. But to name names and demand their exclusion from the Party would have meant, of course, denouncing fellow socialists to the police. (A bit later, as we shall see, Koba was arraigned before a Party court for a less-well-known expropriation.) So on June 25 the local Social Democratic organization passed a general resolution about the Tiflis attack,

---

[16] In Stalin's *Collected Works* the journal is described incorrectly as clandestine. The fact that it *was* openly published makes it at first incredible that Koba should have published in it his frank reportage of the London Congress, giving names of delegates, etc. But nobody was under the illusion that you could have a meeting of three hundred revolutionaries without some police agents among them. It is a testimony to what you could write *openly* in Russia (and especially in Baku) that he wrote there also about the socialists' armed activities.

urging the expulsion of the unnamed culprits. In subsequent attacks the Mensheviks named only those Bolsheviks who were abroad and whose complicity was public knowledge, like Litvinov. For all their post-Revolution condemnation of armed banditry for Party purposes, the Mensheviks' agitation on this issue between 1907 and 1910 was circumspect. Martov, who wrote a pamphlet on the subject, was even blamed by his fellow faction members for washing dirty linen in public.

Apart from the dramatic issue of expropriations Koba's attention was drawn to two more prosaic issues. One was the new Duma elections. The Second Duma had been dissolved in June, and the government followed it by decreeing a new electoral law that made sure the new parliament would be more docile: representation of national minorities was severely cut, and the radicals' membership was also to be reduced. Paradoxically this clearly illegal step by Stolypin's government only strengthened Lenin's determination that the Bolsheviks should participate in the new election: the new parliament was not likely to breed any constitutional illusions. The Mensheviks would have no more opportunities for their clandestine and sinful collaboration with the Kadets.[17] And the few Bolsheviks who would get in could spread propaganda from the privileged parliamentary rostrum. Most of the Bolsheviks were stunned by Lenin's position, but Koba followed it loyally. The Bolsheviks in the new Duma, he wrote, would be able to say, in the hearing of the whole nation, "that there is no possibility in Russia to free the nation peacefully"; they will unmask before the people not only the landowner–Black Hundred forces, but also the "treacherous liberal-monarchist party of the Kadets."

The Third Duma, which assembled in November 1907, satisfied these expectations as well as those of Stolypin. It had a pleasingly reactionary complexion, the largest bloc of seats going to the Right. There were now only eighteen Social Democrats, among them five Bolsheviks. Quite enough! ☆☆☆

T HE fires of the first Russian Revolution were dying down. In December 1907 Lenin, now seriously worried about the police, left Finland and followed the many other revolutionary leaders who had left for Western Europe. But in Baku the "practitioner" Koba stayed at his post. The ebb of revolutionary feelings was as yet not so pronounced

---

[17] Several of the socialist members of the Second Duma, including its Menshevik star, the twenty-five-year-old Irakli Tsereteli, were arrested for consorting with the illegal socialist organization among the soldiers and were sentenced to exile.

there as elsewhere. Strikes kept erupting in the oil industry, hurt by the damage done to the installations during the turbulence of the preceding years. The industrialists and the government finally agreed to let the workers elect representatives for collective-bargaining procedures, and in the election, with the Shendrikovs now gone, the Bolsheviks scored a success: more than half of the deputies of the workers' commune belonged to their faction. In the subsequent dispute as to whether the oil workers' union should enter into bargaining with the oil producers, Koba occupied a relatively moderate position, as against that held by the Socialist Revolutionaries, who rejected any negotiations with the capitalists. In his regular writing for *The Signal*, the organ of the oil workers' union, he characterized this position as anarchosyndicalist and condemned methods of economic terror, such as setting fire to oil installations, as harmful to the workers. He was for negotiation, provided the industrialists gave some prior guarantees about meeting the workers' demands. The Bolshevik position was supported by a majority of the workers.

The Baku period of Koba-Djugashvili's life lasted, with interruptions for jailings and exiles, until 1911. It marked his rise to a position of prominence within the Social Democratic movement, first in the Caucasus and then in the Bolshevik faction on the all-Russian level. This prominence in turn was bound to lead to bitter personal enmities, no longer caused merely by his brusque and offensive manner, but also by political rivalry.

One such rivalry was to lead to accusations which, repeated by some Menshevik sources, have found their way into practically all Western biographies of Stalin. Koba shared the leadership of the Baku Bolshevik Committee with Stephen Shaumyan. We have already alluded to the hostility that developed between the two men. In his family Shaumyan referred not infrequently to his fellow Bolshevik's "viperlike behavior." This undeniable fact, remembered by his children and recorded by his (post-Stalin) Soviet biographer, was used belatedly by some Menshevik writers as the basis of a story that in Party circles in Baku it was rumored that Koba wrote anonymous denunciations of Shaumyan to the police, that he revealed Shaumyan's conspiratorial quarters to them, which led to his arrest, etc. In the more extreme Western versions this story became a "proof" of how Stalin had all along been an agent of the Okhrana. Even a biographer as careful as Boris Souvarine assigns great weight to the Menshevik gossip: "It is a fact that an arrest of Shaumyan had been explained in the Party circles by an anonymous denunciation, and that denunciation attributed to Stalin."[18]

It would be fortunate for Stalin's reputation if some of the major

---

[18] Boris Souvarine, *Stalin* (in French; Paris, 1935), p. 107.

charges against him rested on evidence so flimsy, and so easily disproved, as that concerning his alleged denunciation of Shaumyan. For one, Shaumyan had no secret hideout to be betrayed—for the simple reason that he lived in Baku under his own name and papers, holding a regular job, first as the director of a workers' club, then as manager of an oil firm. In the second place, Shaumyan was arrested twice, both times while Koba-Stalin was in exile. The first jail term, in May 1909, did not last long: a friendly industrialist bribed the police officer and Shaumyan was released. The second case was more serious: he, along with some other Bolsheviks holding a secret meeting, was denounced by a provocateur, "Miron" Chernomazov, and arrested on September 30, 1911. This time he was held in jail until June 1912. But his sentence then was not overwhelming: he was exiled by administrative order to the Caspian port of Astrakhan—by comparison with northern Russia and Siberia practically a vacation spot.

In fact the circumstances of Koba's life and work between 1908 and 1910 planted the seeds of that bitter resentment of his fellow Bolsheviks and that persecution mania which Stalin was to exhibit so ferociously in the 1930s. The leading lights of the Party were now abroad, engaging in what from the perspective of an underground activist were senseless quarrels over abstruse philosophical theories, while in Russia the revolutionary movement was virtually shattered. Even by comparison with his fellow Caucasian "practitioners," Koba's lot seemed unduly harsh and unfair. Shaumyan, Djaparidze, and Spandaryan lived under their own names and were less molested, whether by the police or by the Mensheviks. Shaumyan was arrested but then released under the circumstances already described. Djaparidze was detained in 1908 but freed on the intercession of the oil workers' union. Koba lived under a false name and with forged identity papers—an exciting adventure for a youth but something quite different for a man now almost in his thirties, with a wife and child. In the division of functions among the Baku Bolsheviks, Koba was charged with the more delicate—i.e., more illegal and hazardous—work, and that, combined with his personal characteristics, made him the main target of attack by the local Mensheviks.

Early in 1908 Koba was brought before a Party court in connection with a local Bolshevik expropriation. Even before the Revolution this appearance was to become something of a cause célèbre, and after the Revolution the story grew apace with Stalin's stature in the Soviet regime: Koba had been excluded from the Party; he had been tried not for the Baku but for the 1907 Tiflis expropriation; the matter concerned not an expropriation at all but the denunciation of Shaumyan to the police. And so on.

Reviewing the available evidence, it is clear that Koba was not excluded by an all-Party court, still less by the Bolshevik faction. He continued writing in the Party press throughout 1908 and 1909, which would have been inconceivable had he been expelled. What little solid evidence remains comes from 1918. In an article in the Menshevik *Forward* (the Menshevik press had not yet been banned in Soviet Russia) Martov repeated the charge of the Party trial and Stalin's exclusion. The Commissar of Nationalities exploded: "I want to declare J. Stalin was never judged by a Party organization and still less excluded. . . . It is a despicable lie."[19] Martov's "slander" went before a Revolutionary Tribunal. Martov demanded that Jordania, then in Tiflis, and Shaumyan, then in Baku, be called in as witnesses since they were members of the Party Caucasian Committee in 1907 when the steamer *Nicholas I* was looted in Baku harbor. Another witness from the Caucasus, then virtually inaccessible because of the Civil War, was Isidor Ramishvili, the Menshevik chairman of the court that allegedly sat in judgment on Koba. The Revolutionary Tribunal declared itself unable to judge the case on its merits but reprimanded Martov for slandering a Soviet official. There was to be no sequel: both Bolsheviks and Mensheviks soon had more pressing worries.

In a dispute between Martov, a man of integrity, and Stalin it is difficult not to sympathize with the former. Yet it is undeniable that Martov was engaged in a fishing expedition. If we piece together the 1918 proceedings and some other accounts of the 1907 expropriation in Baku, the picture emerges as follows. The steamer *Nicholas I* was looted, and the worker who accused the local Bolsheviks of having perpetuated the robbery, one Charinov, was himself the victim of an attempted assassination. A Party court was convoked, but before it could sit in judgment Koba was arrested. In the literal sense his disclaimer was correct: he was never judged by, still less excluded from, the Party, though it was true that he had helped to organize the robbery. Still, it was somewhat disingenuous for Martov in 1918 to concentrate his fire on Stalin. He may not have known that other Caucasian Bolsheviks, notably Shaumyan, were as deeply implicated in the expropriations, but he must have realized that there were people right there in Moscow who bore a much heavier overall responsibility in the matter—notably the head of the Soviet regime and his onetime closest friend, Vladimir Ulyanov-Lenin.

Koba's imprisonment on March 25, 1908, was not in connection with the expropriation, whose real culprits remained undetected by the authorities, but because of his leadership of a clandestine and subversive organization. He was detained in the Bailov prison until November 9, then sentenced again by an administrative decree to two years' exile in

[19] Gregory Aronson, "Stalin's Trial Against Martov," *The Socialist Herald* (in Russian; Paris), No. 6 (434) (March 31, 1939), p. 55.

northern Russia. As was often the case, the jailing did not mean an interruption of the revolutionary's political activities: an article of his was smuggled out and appeared in the *Baku Proletarian* and *The Siren*. On February 8, 1909, while traveling to his place of exile, he fell ill with typhus and on February 27 was delivered to Solvichegodsk, in the province of Vologda. He was to spend only four months in this town of two thousand, escaping on June 24. After a few days in St. Petersburg he set out for Baku, where he arrived in July to find the affairs of Caucasian Bolshevism and of the Russian socialist movement as a whole at a low ebb.

"There was a time when our organization numbered thousands of members and could mobilize hundreds of thousands. Then the Party had its roots among the masses. How different it is now. Instead of thousands we count in our organization but tens, or at best hundreds of members. . . . Look at St. Petersburg. There in 1907 we had about eight thousand members and now barely three or four hundred."[20] Thus did the returning Koba appraise the state of the Social Democratic Party in August 1909. He was now on the threshold of thirty, and his article in the *Baku Proletarian* offers striking proof of that gift that was to astound his enemies after the Revolution and during the struggle for power. This apparently choleric and obsessed man was at the same time perceptive and eminently practical; the often petty and partisan polemicist evidences real statesmanship. A battle had been lost but not the war, he argued; though the Social Democratic Party was decimated, it still retained the respect of the masses of workers. There will come a moment of revolutionary upsurge, and the Party must be prepared for it and reunited.

There is but little partisan animus in Koba's assessment of "our tasks in the current Party crisis." The leaders of *both* factions have been delinquent. The Party cannot be reunited and made viable by those quarreling potentates abroad. There must be a Party journal and coordinating committee right here in Russia. The Social Democrats must devote more attention to the day-to-day needs of the workers. More rank-and-file workers must be brought into Party posts, he writes —the same Soso Djugashvili who a few years before had ridiculed the possibility of "simple" workmen serving on the committees. Now his prolonged experience with quarrelsome intellectuals makes him more indulgent. And although a conspirator of long standing, he is far from scorning the weapons of legal struggle against Tsarism: the Duma and labor unions offer excellent opportunities for spreading socialist propaganda and it would be folly to cast them away, he argues.

Koba's article implied a criticism of Lenin as well as of other émigré

[20] Stalin, II, 146.

leaders. And indeed, if tempestuous was the proper term for intraparty life in normal conditions, then the condition of the Russian socialists between 1908 and 1912 can only be described as a madhouse. It was no longer the case of a by now routine quarrel between the Bolsheviks and Mensheviks, the former charging the latter with opportunism, with selling out to the liberals—why, to Stolypin himself; the latter almost as insistently describing Lenin and his partisans as anarchists procuring Party funds through robbery. These charges now receded into the background, and a new series of epithets made their appearance to beguile and exasperate future Soviet and Western historians: "Idealists" (not good at all), "God-builders," "Recallers," "Liquidators." People bearing such epithets or shouting them in derision would in a few years overthrow one of the most powerful governments of the world and build a movement aspiring to inherit the whole world. But for the moment they appeared to many of their followers in Russia, and not only always figuratively, as mad. ☆☆☆

ALEXANDER MALINOVSKY, or Bogdanov, was between 1905 and 1907 one of Lenin's closest collaborators and lieutenants. Beneath a veneer of orthodox Marxism, Bogdanov was in fact a revolutionary of the modern New Left temperament, thrown anachronistically into the first quarter of the twentieth century, with its struggle between Marxism and liberalism, rather than into the third with its new cults and ideological passions. In turn biologist, psychiatrist, politician, as well as a novelist and organizer of expropriations on the side, Bogdanov fitted incongruously into a movement that had as its philosophy the materialism and rationalism of Marx, and as its organizational principle strict discipline and centralistic direction. He would be more at home, one feels, in the world of Jean-Paul Sartre and Frantz Fanon, of revolution preached for its own sake, as man's only significant form of self-assertion. Or, one might equally easily imagine him as one of the underground philosophers of contemporary Soviet Russia, preaching that Marx is not enough, that his doctrine's dry materialism and determinism are responsible for the horrors of Stalinism and its lingering echoes, and that what remains valid in Marx must be combined with a more voluntaristic and all-encompassing philosophy. As it was, what kept him in the ranks of Lenin's followers was the excitement of partisan activities and the promise of still more spectacular and romantic revolutionary struggle.

And then this whole exciting world of barricades, mutinies, and expropriations had to be given up. Bogdanov bitterly resented Lenin's recognition of the fact that guerrilla warfare was now harmful and unavailing and must cease. Lenin, who until 1908 was willing to overlook his lieutenant's suspicious philosophical proclivities, when confronted with his political insubordination decided to open fire on philosophical heresy among the Bolsheviks. Bogdanov had sought ideological nourishment not only in the only safe source—namely, Marx and Engels—but in the nineteenth-century bourgeois philosophers Mach and Avenarius. Strangers to the class struggle, indeed to politics altogether, they worked on the theory of knowledge as if materialism had not solved that question once and for all, and propagated phenomenalism and empiric criticism. Bogdanov followed in their footsteps. His "Empiriomonism" undertook to show in his own words "the world from the organization point of view, i.e., as the process of formulation, struggle and interaction of complexes and systems of various types and grades of organization." Some might smile at the presumption of such system-building, but not Lenin. His attitude toward philosophy was a variant of that ascribed to Caliph Omar concerning all books: they were useful to the extent that they repeated Holy Writ, scandalous and not to be tolerated otherwise.

If it were only Bogdanov and only the matter of his obscurantist hankerings! But now a veritable plague of philosophizing struck the Bolsheviks. Another prominent Party member, Lunacharsky, erupted, if you please, with a socialist *religion*. The real aim of socialism was to go beyond dialectical materialism into a religion of humanity. "You seek God? God is mankind. Build up God and mankind by joining with the leading elements in society." There were others. In distant Georgia a young Bolshevik, Alexander S. Svanidze, wrote a book on empiriocriticism asserting that Machism should provide the new philosophy for socialism.

To an orthodox Marxist like Lenin or Plekhanov, philosophical views could never be something apart from politics, or a matter of private preference. Just as you could not be a Christian and a Marxist, so you could not combine philosophical idealism with socialism. And you had the immediate proof in the political insubordination of these philosophical innovators. They opposed Lenin's insistence that the Social Democrats continue their work in the Duma. They objected to Bolsheviks' giving up the armed struggle. Here the Bogdanovs and Lunacharskys and their ilk were joined by people like Krasin and Alexinsky who had no interest in philosophy but who could not bear to give up that, to them, glamorous side of Party life. There now arose against Lenin the serried ranks of Recallers (those who wanted the Bolshevik Duma deputies to resign) and Ultimatists (those who would have the Duma deputies pledge to work illegally, in effect making their parliamentary position impossible), buttressed by Idealists and God-seekers.

As with many other developments in the history of Bolshevism, seemingly unconnected with his person, so this philosophical crisis of the revolutionary movement had a profound influence on Stalin's career. At a later stage he was pushed forward by his fellow Communist oligarchs, not because they particularly liked him but because they hated Trotsky. And so in this instance Lenin became between 1908 and 1912 heartily sick of the God-seekers, Ultimatists, etc.—for the most part people of the intelligentsia and with literary and theoretical pretensions: Bogdanov a dabbler in philosophy, Lunacharsky a second-rate dramatist, Bazarov a writer on economics, and even Krasin who, though contemptuous of theoretical scribbling, was still from an intelligentsia family. At such moments Lenin easily persuaded himself that the original sin at the source of all heresies was a middle-class origin, that one had to turn to "staunch proletarians." And here was this Caucasian Bolshevik who had won his spurs fighting the Mensheviks, an *intelligent* by training but of undoubted proletarian origin. Before as after the Revolution, Stalin was to be a beneficiary of Lenin's hatred of his own class, a class that first undermined and then brought about the fall of the Old Russia but that was to prove incapable of building a new one. And it was this class—writers, lawyers, thinkers, questioners of all established authority, enthusiasts of new trends and theories, alert to any threat to liberty except the one which its own feeling of guilt was breeding—that Lenin's successor was to destroy, as thoroughly as any class in history has been destroyed.

Lenin's esteem was not purchased by Koba through any servility toward him. Like most "practitioners," he was disgusted with the émigré theorists' squabbles, and in conversations and letters to Party comrades he characterized the Lenin-Bogdanov disagreement as a tempest in a teapot. (The practice of denunciation that was to reach such impressive proportions in Stalin's Russia was already taking root among the Bolsheviks.) Shaumyan took care that these seemingly innocuous remarks should reach the ears of Vladimir Ilyich, by conveying them to Michael Tshakaya, then in exile and sure to repeat it to Lenin. The great man had his first but not last moment of doubt concerning the man whom he was soon to call a "wonderful Georgian." How could Koba make such a philistine remark? he inquired of Orjonikidze, who succeeded in mollifying his anger.

If Shaumyan gained some points through his denunciation, through his tactlessness he soon managed to lose them. Along with some other Caucasian Bolsheviks (but not Koba), he appealed to Lenin to come to Russia and lead the revolutionary struggle in person! Such a request, and the prospect of arrests and exiles which it suggested, was not likely to be greeted by Lenin with enthusiasm. In 1900, when he was about to leave Russia, he explained to a follower who wondered how a revolution could be led from abroad that for a revolutionary leader to be imprisoned and exiled *once* (as he had been) was par for the course, but that it would be unpardonable folly to let it happen again. Perhaps this was to be among the reasons why in 1912 Shaumyan was elected only alternate member of the Bolshevik Central Committee, and why after the Revolution of 1917 he was left to carry on the struggle in Baku while his erstwhile rival began his fantastic ascent to power.

Koba's disagreements with Lenin were, of course, either glossed over or concealed in Stalin's Russia. It was only in 1961, when Khrushchev unleashed the more intensive phase of the campaign against his predecessor's ghost, that Party historians and litterateurs were given license to dig out those alleged criticisms Koba had made about his leader. Yet it is testimony to the enduring influence of Stalinism that these relatively mild, in fact quite sensible, observations of young Stalin's are supposed to damn him in the eyes of the modern Soviet reader.[21] Apparently it is deemed less scandalous that Stalin ordered or tolerated the deaths and sufferings of millions of his countrymen than that in 1909 or 1910 he wrote that Lenin might be mistaken. The Party writers unmasking Stalin miss the point that in those early years, even in the already intolerant intellectual atmosphere of Bolshevism, a disagreement with the leader was still not considered a state crime. Far from denigrating the young Stalin, they in fact offer rather favorable testimony as to the extent of his readings in philosophy and the independence of his judgment.

Koba's main crime was in connection with Lenin's most lamentable literary production, *Materialism and Empiriocriticism*. For much of 1908 Vladimir Ilyich neglected even pressing Party business and worked in the British Museum and elsewhere, collecting materials for this lengthy diatribe against philosophical idealism, Mach, Bogdanov, etc. His followers begged him to desist and to attend to political tasks. Even his sister Anne, who arranged for the work's publication in Moscow in 1909, pleaded that he soften the virulence of some of his attacks on people and theories having no earthly connection with Ultimatism, Godbuilding, and other ostensible subjects of his polemic. The work is one long denunciation before the Marxist gods of history of luminaries of philosophy, dead or alive, who indulged in or flirted with the nonmaterialist positions. It could be expected that Mach would be described as a plagiarizer, but it is more difficult to account for Lenin's attacks on figures as distant as Hume and Bishop Berkeley, of his

21 With Khrushchev's fall the revelations abruptly ended and Party historians set about to rewrite their histories once more. So that for some of them we have three versions: one before 1953, praising Stalin to the skies; one between 1960 and 1965, damning him for irreverence to the leader, and the later third one, striking the currently "correct" balance.

chastising the great French mathematician Henri Poincaré as if he were a Menshevik leader, of his forays into theoretical physics, his declaring that those who assert that there can be more than three dimensions are but theologians masquerading as scientists. In more rational moments Lenin subsequently and often admitted that he had no competence to judge scientific matters. But the harm was done. Many years later Soviet physicists were imprisoned and stripped of their jobs for propagating the philosophy of Einstein, "idealist and alien from the class point of view." And the whole mishmash is still an obligatory text for every Soviet student of philosophy.

The man who was to license and enforce such obscurantism showed himself at the time quite open-minded. Yes, Koba wrote to a Georgian party friend, Lenin's work was "a summary unique of its kind, of the theses of the philosophy of materialism." But this rather generous estimate was coupled with an acknowledgment that Mach's thought had its good side. It was not a suitable philosophical underpinning of socialism, but one could not gainsay that Mach and Avenarius were, like Holbach and Hegel, eminent philosophers. We needed, Koba thought, further study and development of dialectical materialism, such as Dietzgen had done, and in the process we must absorb the positive side of Mach's philosophy.

This is for us a virtually unknown Stalin, and we should be grateful to the Soviet author—or, really, to Khrushchev—for letting us steal a glimpse of him. A scholar might find it dilettantish that thinkers as diverse as Holbach and Hegel were grouped together, but here is a man who obviously reads widely and thinks occasionally about subjects other than power, Mensheviks, and expropriations. Could Khrushchev or Brezhnev identify Holbach or Dietzgen? Most unlikely. And Koba continued, "How did you like Bogdanov's recent book? I think that he correctly and precisely points out some *special* blunders of Ilyich's [Lenin's]. He is also correct in pointing out that Ilyich's materialism is quite different from Plekhanov's, although somewhat illogically (but for reasons of diplomacy?) Ilyich tries to gloss over that."[22] Not a single "as is well known." In fact, the tone of the letter is urbane and non-doctrinaire. The Soviet reader is supposed to rise up in wrath at this impostor who claimed to be Lenin's "most faithful disciple and comrade in arms" and in reality wrote so dispassionately of errors and illogicalities in Ilyich's immortal work. But we shall have to face a more difficult problem: what happened to this judicious and tolerant Stalin in his later life?

The truth is, then, that between 1909 and 1910 Koba was a "Conciliationist," i.e., one who believed that the warring Bolshevik factions

[22] Quoted in Mukhadze, p. 156.

should reconcile their differences and work for the common cause. This was not a real split, he wrote of the Lenin vs. Bogdanov war, but just differences of opinion on various practical tasks. "Such differences always existed and will always exist in a group as varied and lively as the Bolsheviks."[23] Strange words, again, for a man who was eventually to brook not even the merest shadow or suspicion of disagreement with himself. But we are beginning to see in Koba not only a conspirator and poisonous polemicist, but a statesman and diplomat; we can discern the qualities that would enable him to preserve the Communist Party on Lenin's illness and death, that he would brilliantly display in his bargaining with Roosevelt and Churchill. A resolution of the Baku Party Committee formulated by Koba in 1909 chided all the tendencies in Bolshevism which Lenin combated, but at the same time criticized him gently for turning a philosophical dispute into a political one, expressing hope for Bogdanov's and other dissenters' repentance. The same note of moderation characterized the Committee's resolution of January 1910: another plea for unity in the Party as a whole (not only among the Bolsheviks) and the expression of a hope that the means would be found to create a directorate *in Russia* for guiding the Party's practical work, thus diplomatically suggesting that the theoretical guidance could still be done from abroad.

Koba's common-sense position enhanced his standing among the Russian Bolsheviks. To them, he was now known as "one of the best and most active Baku Party workers,"[24] and if they heard rumors about his unattractive personal traits, they probably ascribed them to local rivalries. Vladimir Nogin, a member of the Central Committee, went to Baku in February 1910 to persuade Koba to agree to be coopted onto it, but Koba refused. It is not difficult to see why. Nogin was currently at odds with Lenin, and to become a member of the Committee meant that Koba would have to take a definite stand on several issues that divided not only the Party as a whole but the Bolsheviks themselves. It appeared to be, and was, wiser to await a definite turn in the affairs of Russian Marxism before accepting this hazardous distinction.

The situation at the socialist Olympus was in fact quite uninviting. The anti-Leninist forces among the Bolsheviks at first grouped around the journal V*peryod* (*Forward*), and thus, to the reader's undoubted relief, can now be referred to jointly as Forwardists. But there was little common ground among them except for their determination to annoy and attack their erstwhile leader. They now imitated his own tactics vis-à-vis the Mensheviks when they were in ascendance. No, they were not a faction, just a "literary group." He withheld Party funds, they com-

---

[23] Stalin, II, 164.
[24] L. Germanov (Frumkin), "From the Life of the Party in 1910," in *The Proletarian Revolution*, No. 5 (May 1922), p. 232.

plained; Lenin in turn accused Bogdanov of misappropriating them for the use of the Forwardists. They demanded a Party Congress, but Lenin's usual passion for such gatherings was now restrained: he might be attacked by the Mensheviks about the expropriations or by the *Forward* group for ignobly giving up the armed struggle. Besieged on all sides, he sought aid in what was for him strange quarters. The editorial board of his *Proletarian* wrote to Trotsky, inviting him to join. Somebody identifying himself as his secretary replied that Comrade Trotsky refused. Lenin gained Plekhanov's collaboration, but how long could that last? Plekhanov sympathized with his struggle against those who dared to defy dialectical materialism, but privately he expressed the opinion that not only they but other Bolsheviks as well should be chucked out of the Party for sponsoring armed robberies.

In the absence of Party Congresses, the *Forward* group sponsored Party schools where cadres could be trained and then sent back to do missionary work in Russia. The first such school, organized by Bogdanov, convened at Gorky's invitation at his current residence on the island of Capri. The second one in 1910 was in the city of Bologna. Workers' committees in Russian industrial centers were invited to send representatives, all expenses paid by the organizers (from the proceeds of past expropriations that Krasin and Bogdanov had withheld from Lenin). The Baku Committee refused this scholarship, explaining diplomatically that it did not have enough information about the school. As police agents infiltrating both schools reported to their superiors, some facets of the organization would have done credit to a well-run jail. Formally, the institutes were open to all factions, but the students were encouraged to spy on each other and Bogdanov, the director, regularly opened their mail. To be sure, some students at Bologna were caught having a clandestine correspondence with Lenin and were engaging, at his instructions, in what would be described in Soviet Russia as "wrecking and sabotage" activities.

In 1910 Krasin and Bogdanov were finally separated from the Bolshevik faction and forced to resign the seats they held on its behalf in the Party's Central Committee. Krasin's defection was deeply felt by Lenin. The mercurial organizer and terrorist for his part became distraught over his separation from the movement he had done so much to build. His depression took the form of strange dietary fads: as prescribed by Professor Mechnikov he abstained from meat and subsisted largely on mare's milk. He was not to return to the Party until after the Revolution, but in the meantime he would help some old comrade financially or, as we have seen, advise Kamo on an expropriation. Bogdanov also soon abandoned politics. After the Revolution he was to become a leading exponent of Proletkult (Proletarian Culture), an attitude toward cultural affairs which may be best summarized in the words of a young poet of the day: "And in the name of our better tomorrow we shall burn Raphaels." Proletkult was almost as distasteful to Lenin, whose views on literature and the arts were traditionalist, as empirio-criticism had been. Once again Bogdanov was reprimanded, and this time he turned back to his original profession. He ran an institute for the study of blood transfusion. In 1928 he died as had the Russian intelligentsia, victim of an experiment he performed on himself.

Splits and divisions were also rife among the Mensheviks. While continuing their uneasy coexistence with Lenin and his group, they divided on the issue of what importance to assign to legal activities in Russia vis-à-vis illegal ones. This rather involved problem appears in histories of the Party as a simple one: many Mensheviks (sometimes all of them) were "Liquidators," i.e., they wanted to abandon entirely all illegal work inside Russia. The term, needless to say, was Lenin's, and as in so many other things imprinted on the pages of history through sheer repetition and insistence, the term sticks in Russia and in the West. Yet it is palpably an unfair one. From the perspective of the Krasins and Bogdanovs, Lenin himself was a "Liquidator," for like most realistic revolutionaries, he had recognized that the time for guerrilla activities had passed. "Ilyich tends to exaggerate the importance of legal work," wrote Koba in 1909, but by and large he accepted his views. It was foolish for the socialists to throw away or slight the opportunities for educational and propaganda work among the workers. As for the possibility of *entirely* legal work in Russia, not even the most right-wing Menshevik could be under any illusions. To be a member of the Socialist Party was in itself a crime, for its program unambiguously called for the overthrow of the government. For reasons of their own the police often chose not to arrest well-known socialists who lived under their own name, such as the Menshevik Alexander Potresov, in Lenin's eyes the arch-Liquidator. But there were Bolsheviks in precisely the same position. A Bolshevik writer who in 1914 collected statistics on political exiles in one of the worst parts of Siberia, the Yenisei-Turukhan region (where Stalin was at the time), found that Mensheviks of all hues constituted 42 per cent of the Social Democrats currently there, and among them the Liquidators 9 per cent.[25] Thus a sizable number of those who allegedly lacked the spirit for revolutionary work and meekly believed in legality found their way to a most severe place of exile.

This is really the best commentary on the appropriateness of the term Liquidator. All that can be said fairly is that the Liquidators believed that in view of the limited opportunities that did exist for legal political work, *excessive* stress on conspiracy was both pointless and harmful,

25 Ilya Vardin, "Political Exiles on the Eve of the Revolution," in *ibid.*, p. 99. There were 350 exiles in the region at the time.

playing into the hands of the police by enabling them to arrest Socialist union organizers and Duma candidates, increasing the danger of infiltration by criminal elements and agents provocateurs. You could *say* and *write* almost anything in Russia of 1910, while equally clearly you could not overthrow Tsarism by any act of violence that a handful of revolutionaries could perpetrate. These were sensible observations, and the story of the Bolsheviks between 1910 and 1914 confirms their acuteness. But to Lenin the epithet Liquidator offered a convenient rallying cry against the Mensheviks, and obscured similar charges made against himself by his former partisans. This passion for conspiracy brought the Bolsheviks by 1914 to the brink of political destruction, with most of their leading activists in jail or exile.[26] ☆☆☆

KOBA-STALIN'S story during the four years before World War I offers a good illustration of the self-destructive effects of this excessive stress on conspiracy. He was arrested, escaped, and came back to Party work. But after 1913 he stayed in exile. There was very little to come back to. The Bolshevik conspiratorial organization in Russia was shattered, and played but a negligible role during the first days of the 1917 Revolution.

On March 23, 1910, the Baku police arrested a man they had long had under observation as a leading Bolshevik. He was found in possession of identity papers in the name of Zakhar Krikorian Melikyants, but under interrogation he admitted his true identity. And so on March 26 he was lodged in Bailov Prison.

We have a report concerning Koba's two stays (1908 and 1910) in that institution from Semyon Vereshchak, a well-known Caucasian Socialist Revolutionary who in an émigré Russian journal published his recollections of his fellow prisoner. The Soviet poet Demyan Byedny culled from them that small part which reflected well on Stalin and printed it along with some doggerel of his own in *Pravda* on the occasion of Stalin's fiftieth birthday in December 1929. Unfortunately, the account, which was given credence by several biographers, contains some palpable inaccuracies and is worthless.[27] But we do have another,

[26] For all the relative ease of escape, the repeated imprisonments were taking their cumulative toll. A prominent Bolshevik, Joseph (Innocent) Dubrovinsky, committed suicide in 1913, and Spandaryan died of tuberculosis in 1916—both in exile.
[27] Koba is characterized as taller than the average. He is alleged to have shared a cell with a forger, but we know that political prisoners were separated from common

reliable report on the place where the future leader spent altogether a year of his life. Here again we see that mixture of laxity and brutality which was Tsarist Russia. Inmates were locked in only at night and in the daytime could wander through the courtyard and corridors, left to their own devices. The "politicals" organized discussions, games, and concerts; Party courts dispensed rough and ready justice with the guards looking the other way. A Bolshevik who defrauded some anarchists was sentenced by his own comrades to be beaten, and died as a result. Criminals would attack or try to blackmail political prisoners, but the authorities tolerated measures of self-defense, and since among the politicals there were plenty of sturdy veterans of expropriations, they more than held their own. In fact, an author claims, he and his comrades put an end to the widespread sexual abuse of young boys by the criminals.[28] This is quite a different world from that of Party discussions about God-building, Mach, and Avenarius.

On September 23 Koba was again dispatched to Solvichegodsk to finish his previous sentence of exile. The Viceroy of the Caucasus rejected the Baku authorities' recommendation for a more severe term—five years in a distant region of Siberia. This time he patiently endured his sentence, which expired on June 27, 1911. But the end of one's exile term did not necessarily mean that one became a free man. Certain places—in Koba's case the Caucasus and the two capitals—might still be prohibited, and all freedom meant was that Koba now had the privilege of *choosing* his next place of exile, where he would no longer be under *open* police surveillance. He chose Vologda. But rather than spend five years there under *secret* police surveillance, as a law-abiding political criminal was supposed to do, he left in early September for St. Petersburg, where he contacted his Bolshevik friends Sylvester Todria and Sergei Alliluyev. During this "willful" escape, as the police record indignantly describes it, he was chaperoned by police agents who, having established his Petersburg contacts, arrested him after only three days at large. Now it was the St. Petersburg transit jail. The local authorities reported to the Vologda ones, they in turn to the Tiflis and Baku ones, and from that correspondence we get a glimpse of Koba's reading matter: his notes included some on "Problems of Political Economy," Volume I of *Capital, Notes on Sociology*, also a few phrases in German

---

criminals. The most unlikely detail concerns the story of how Stalin along with other political prisoners was made to run a gauntlet between two rows of soldiers and how he calmly endured their blows. At the time such practices were unheard of in the Tsarist jails, and the news and protests about the torture would have immediately swept Russia.

28 The boys, many of them only ten to fifteen years old, were detained along with their parents whose only crime was the absence of residence permits. A. Rogov, "Life of the Baku Prison," in *Hard Labor and Exile* (Moscow), XXXVII (1927), 126–32.

that a traveler might use—which confirms, adds the well-informed official, the secret reports that Djugashvili was planning to go abroad.[29] After three months of leisurely correspondence, the police simply sent Koba back to Vologda for three years of *open* police surveillance.

By the standards of the FBI, not to mention their own Soviet successors, the dreaded Tsarist Okhrana was indeed inefficient (and a thoughtful revolutionary must have reflected that *we* shall not make the same mistakes!). It was old-fashioned.[30] There was often no rhyme or reason in the pattern of its arrests or punishments. Of the Bolshevik notables from the Caucasus, Sergo Orjonikidze was treated more severely than Koba, let alone Shaumyan (this might have been influenced by his having been caught transporting arms). Twice he was sentenced to terms of strict prison regime and *lifelong* settlement in Siberia. Koba was never brought before the court and the maximum administrative penalty was five years of exile.

But the main defect of the Okhrana was its excessive subtlety. Its main concern was not so much to catch and hold the leading revolutionaries as that the revolutionary movement should remain divided. Secret Police agents in the movement were instructed to work and speak insistently on the theme "of the impermissibility of union of those organizations and especially of a reunion of the Bolsheviks and the Mensheviks."[31] A Baku police chief might wish Koba to be far away in Siberia, but the higher and subtler officials would prefer to have him in Solvichegodsk, in proximity to other political exiles, where he would keep the pot of intraparty dispute boiling.

When the police intercepted a letter of Koba's from Solvichegodsk to foreign Bolsheviks, they might well have congratulated themselves on the perspicacity of their calculations. The letter sent on December 31, 1910, to a comrade then in Paris, undoubtedly was intended for Lenin's eyes.[32] Here we have Koba the flatterer trying to dissipate the effects of his "tempest in the teapot" remark, which he may have heard had reached Lenin's ears. The Lenin-Plekhanov Party "line" is now the only correct one. Lenin is full of "peasant wisdom" (a shrewd thrust: if the

[29] *The Red Archive* (Moscow, 1941), II (105), 22.

[30] The very language of the police reports breathed archaism. Unmarried revolutionary ladies were invariably identified, often technically incorrectly, as "Maiden X." The male patronymic was given in its antiquated form: thus Joseph Vissarionov (instead of Vissarionovich) Djugashvili. The police seem not to have recognized that serfdom had been abolished in 1861. Koba is at times referred to as "peasant from the village of Didi-Lilo." That was where his *father* was born, but he himself never resided there.

[31] M. A. Tsiolovsky, ed., *Bolsheviks, 1903–1916, from the Files of the Former Moscow Security Department* (Moscow, 1918), p. 148.

[32] The letter was copied by the Okhrana but allowed to reach its destination. See Edward E. Smith, *The Young Stalin* (New York, 1967), p. 232.

hereditary nobleman and *intelligent* Vladimir Ulyanov had a vanity, it was about being considered a man of the people). Koba associates himself with Lenin's passions and obsessions of the moment. Trotsky's proposals—he was presuming at the time to try to unite the Party and was occasionally referred to by Lenin as "Little Judas" Trotsky—show nothing but a "rotten lack of principles." The *Forward* people? Not worth talking about. If they want to follow Lenin's line, all well and good; otherwise let them stew in their own juice.[33] But the Liquidators! Oh, they are clever: they threaten to take over all legal socialist activity in Russia and for that purpose have organized their own illegal center. So there is a crying need for Bolsheviks to organize their own center in Russia—needless to say, not to replace foreign guidance but under Lenin's direction. Koba himself has six months to go in exile. After that he is ready to serve in any capacity. If really needed, he is ready to escape before.

This was perhaps not very subtle, but to the besieged and harassed Lenin in Paris (he had just barely escaped being beaten up in a café by a group of *Forward* partisans led by Alexinsky) it was a heartwarming reassurance that real Bolsheviks in Russia understood and supported him. And the Stalin who would one day flatter the Zinovievs and Bukharins before destroying them was already in evidence, who drank to Hitler's health: "I know how much the German people love their Führer," who remarked to the Japanese Foreign Minister, "We are both Asians."

It is unlikely that Koba's views had changed drastically from a few months before, when he was quite critical of his leader. But he has reached the end of the line as a provincial Party activist. He now aspires to what he had rejected then: a seat on the Party Central Committee, possibly also a respite from jail and exile by working abroad.

In 1911 in Longjumeau, near Paris, Lenin opened his own Party school, an answer to Capri and Bologna. Like them, it seemed on the face of it a pointless venture. At some risk and expense, seventeen Social Democrats traveled from Russia to France, there to listen to what they easily could have read at home: the socialist view of political economy, the agrarian problem, and Party history as expounded by Lenin and his two current lieutenants, Kamenev and Zinoviev. But Lenin was in fact looking for organizers to go back to Russia and prepare the ground for his next step, a definite breach with the Mensheviks and the foundation of the *Bolshevik Party*.

And so in January 1912, in Prague—Paris and Geneva were full of the *Forward* people, Vienna was currently inhabited by the impossible Trotsky—a meeting hosted by the Czech socialists took place, known as

[33] Stalin, II, 209–10.

the Sixth Party Conference. It was a gathering of twenty people—fourteen of them voting delegates, two of the latter Okhrana members. The group usurped the rights of a Party Congress and elected an entirely Leninist committee (not entirely, for one member, Roman Malinovsky, divided his allegiance between Lenin and the police). Two committeemen were Caucasians: Orjonikidze, who with a life sentence hanging over his head had traveled the length of Russia preparing the Congress; and Suren Spandaryan. Though some alternate members were also elected (among them Shaumyan), the Committee went outside their list in coopting two new full members. One was Byelostotsky, who was to vanish into obscurity after the Revolution, and the other was Joseph Koba-Djugashvili.[34]

[34] Jacob Sverdlov, the main Party organizer in 1917–18, was coopted a bit later.

~4~

ON THE
CREST
OF THE
WAVE

Stalin[1] now became one of the ten top men of the Party. When his friend Orjonikidze personally brought him this news in Vologda in the middle of February, he also informed him that he had been appointed to the Party Bureau for supervising work within Russia. Other members of the Russian Bureau were Orjonikidze himself, Spandaryan, Yelena Stasova, and Roman Malinovsky. In his new job Stalin would have a salary of fifty rubles per month, hardly a princely sum (the police were paying Malinovsky five hundred), but an improvement on his government allowance as an exile of seven rubles and forty kopecks. He would have to flee again, for the job demanded that he travel throughout Russia and organize the workers, not so much against the Tsarist regime as against the Liquidators. Unbeknownst to him, his new eminence meant the certainty of new arrests and more severe treatment, for in 1912 police indulgence toward the Bolsheviks came to an end.

The reasons for this must be found in the general political situation in the country. The skillful hand of Peter Stolypin no longer guided Russia. In 1911 he had been killed—the assassin was an anarchist by conviction and police agent by profession—a fate he had long anticipated.[2] Before his death, he had fallen into disfavor with the right-wing elements, whose self-destructive propensity was even stronger than that

---

[1] As Koba began to use this pseudonym at this time, we shall refer to him as such.
[2] Once a would-be assassin broke into his office. "Hold my coat," commanded the Prime Minister, and profiting by the man's momentary confusion, disarmed him.

of the intelligentsia, because his reform allowing peasants to leave the commune and become individual proprietors (thus, it was hoped, building a rural middle class) displeased the conservatives. And he would not allow the Empress Alexandra's favorite, Rasputin, to interfere in politics. The more perspicacious of the revolutionaries, Lenin included, recognized that the history of Russia might well have been different had Stolypin rather than some bureaucratic nonentities been at the helm between 1911 and 1917.

As it was, there was an upturn in political and strike activity. Leo Tolstoy's death in 1910 had already given rise to widespread demonstrations—the great writer in his latter phase having been an opponent of Tsarism, indeed of all political authority. Stolypin may have believed in repression, but he had also believed in social reform and parliamentarism. The new Prime Minister, on the other hand, was able to say from the podium of the Duma, "Thank God we don't have a parliament in Russia." In April 1912, in the Lena gold field in Siberia, the police opened fire on striking workers, and when questioned in the Duma about the veritable massacre, which involved five hundred casualties, Minister of the Interior Makarov offered an "explanation" that could serve as part of the epitaph for the monarchy of the Romanovs: "Thus it has been done before, so it will be in the future." A wave of protest strikes and demonstrations swept the country. In view of this general resurgence of the workers' and students' movement, the police now took a more serious view of the leading revolutionaries being at large. In 1912 orders went out to stop the cat-and-mouse game and to arrest the main Bolshevik organizers.

As a local policeman notified the chief of Vologda's police in writing (where is the telephone?), Stalin "left unauthorized, destination unknown, at 2 o'clock the night of February 29, having taken with him part of his valuable [?] belongings." Excessive hurry was not in the style of the Tsarist bureaucracy. Local police searched Vologda for six days before their chief notified the head of the Petersburg Okhrana about the unfortunate event.

Stalin went to the capital and then, like other members of the Russian Bureau, toured Party organizations, explaining the Prague Conference. A definite break with the Mensheviks was still unacceptable to a majority of Bolsheviks in Russia. Thus the Baku conference held under his leadership called for an eventual reunion of the Party. Stalin wrote from Baku on March 30 that the Bolshevik meeting there "proposed to the [local] Mensheviks that a joint directorate be formed."[3]

---

[3] M. Moskalev, *The Bureau of the Central Committee of the Russian Social Democratic Workers Party in Russia* (Moscow, 1964), p. 197.

He was shadowed by the police as he was leaving Baku. On April 7 he was in Moscow, conferring with Orjonikidze and Malinovsky. But the two Georgians obviously could not be arrested in Moscow, for this would have thrown suspicion on Malinovsky, so they were allowed to leave for St. Petersburg on April 9 in the discreet company of three police agents. In the next few weeks the Bolsheviks' entire Russian Bureau was "busted." Orjonikidze was arrested on April 14, Stalin on April 22, then Spandaryan and Yelena Stasova, the Central Committee's new agent for the Caucasus.[4]

This time Stalin was sent to the town of Narim, in the Siberian province of Tomsk. "Town" is perhaps an exaggerated term for a bleak provincial hole of about a hundred and fifty houses. But the region had the heaviest concentration of political exiles anywhere in Siberia, in 1913 about three hundred of them. This made flight rather easy: having arrived on July 18, Stalin fled on September 1. The local officials were true to form: On *November* 3 the Governor of Tomsk ordered a general search for "the peasant of the village of Didi-Lilo, Joseph Vissarionov Djugashvili." How did the Empire of the Tsars manage to survive until 1917?

But in Russia proper they knew his whereabouts long before November. Stalin went to Moscow to take counsel with his fellow Party official Malinovsky. We are pleased to hear that the Moscow police moved with the times: they treated Malinovsky to a telephone! And so the Moscow Okhrana advised its branch in St. Petersburg that Stalin had departed for the other capital on October 29 and that he would try to leave through Finland for Cracow, in Austrian Galicia, where he had been summoned by Lenin.[5]

In St. Petersburg and then in Finland, Stalin was able to throw off his police "tail" and board a steamer in Abo to go abroad. How? Again, the police were oversubtle. They did not want to reveal that they knew that the Alliluyevs (with whom Stalin intermittently stayed in St. Petersburg) sheltered revolutionaries, or that Alexander Shotman, the Bolshevik agent in Finland, was expediting Party members abroad. So each time instructions were given to arrest Stalin only just before he departed —as he boarded the train for Finland, as he embarked on the ship in Abo—and in both cases he was able to give the agents the slip.

---

[4] This is another long-lived lady revolutionary. She died in 1966 at the age of ninety-three. Stasova came from the elite of the Russian intelligentsia; her father, of whom she writes warmly, was a leading lawyer and a connoisseur of music and the arts (he was a co-founder with Anton Rubinstein of the St. Petersburg Conservatory). The Stasova apartment in the capital was a frequent hiding place for Bolsheviks, the butler being privy to the conspiracy. In 1913 she was sentenced to exile for life. In the first months after the Revolution she was a secretary of the Central Committee. She then, no doubt fortunately, sank into obscurity.

[5] *The Red Archive* (Moscow, 1941), II (105), 28.

There is an undoubted element of mystery in Stalin's first trip abroad in November 1912. Why did he go so circuitously, rather than simply crossing the Russian-Austrian border, as he was to do in his second trip, in December? The implication is that he was charged by Lenin with a mission in Sweden or Germany prior to his arrival in Cracow, where Lenin now resided and where the Central Committee held a meeting around the middle of November.[6] Then, at the end of November Stalin was back in St. Petersburg.

To summarize Stalin's activity for 1912–13 is to realize the frantic pace of a revolutionary's activity. Fled February 29; arrested April 22; escaped again September; went abroad and returned in November; went abroad again in December, for his longest stay out of the country, returning the middle of February; and then, February 23, his last arrest, closing the chapter of his political activity before the Revolution. During that hectic year he managed to write several articles and his book on nationalism, help to organize *Pravda*, and participate in numerous Party meetings. While he did not singlehandedly do all the Party work, as his apologists represent, even hostile writers of the Khrushchev period bent on demonstrating his "errors" (i.e., even the slightest disagreement with Lenin) render unwitting testimony to his energy and enterprise.

His work during the few weeks he actually spent in St. Petersburg bore on two major Bolshevik endeavors of the time. In April 1912 there began to appear legally the Bolshevik paper whose name is now a household word, *Pravda* (*The Truth*).[7] The secretary of the editorial board was young Vyacheslav Scriabin, who was to become better known as Molotov and whose appointment to the position was probably influenced by the fact that a rich friend of his, V. A. Tikhomirnov, gave the Bolsheviks money for the enterprise. Though occasionally confiscated by the authorities, *Pravda* remained until the war the legal voice of Bolshevism, and with its circulation oscillating between 20,000 and 80,000, it was really the mainstay of their activity in Russia. Stalin, when he was not in prison, was its supervisor on behalf of the Central Committee. As such he faced the ungrateful task not only of assuring its continuation in spite of police harassment, but of defending it against . . . Lenin! For the great man continually contributed articles and editorials whose intemperance toward the Mensheviks and toward even some of his own supporters brought other contributors to the verge

---

[6] It may have been in connection with Party funds, which were still held by German trustees and which Lenin now desperately needed, threatening even to sue the German comrades for them. It would have been an interesting suit: for the recovery of monies obtained by fraud and armed robberies.

[7] The name was actually stolen from and probably chosen to annoy Trotsky, who had for some time been publishing a journal in Vienna under the same name. When he protested, the editors on Lenin's instructions wrote that they would not reply to his "vulgar" letters.

of quitting. The editorial board discreetly censored such writings, and this would lead to new outbursts and threats from Cracow. Stalin, for all his determination to cast his lot with Vladimir Ilyich, realized that in Russia the Bolsheviks had at least to pretend that they were working for a reconciliation, for otherwise whatever influence they had among the workers would dwindle catastrophically. And thus the scribes of the Khrushchev period classify him as a "conciliationist."[8] After Molotov's arrest *Pravda* got a new secretary, one Miron Chernomazov. Krupskaya did not like him and during a visit he made to Lenin she would not let him stay in their apartment, and the poor man had to spend the night on a Cracow park bench. Her intuition was justified: he was later unmasked as an agent of the Okhrana.

The other aspect of Stalin's activity was equally vexing: he was to keep an eye on the Bolshevik members of the Duma—that is, he had to make sure that they would make life impossible for their Menshevik fellow deputies. In the elections to the Fourth Duma, which assembled in December 1912, the Bolsheviks had won six and the Mensheviks seven seats. Since the workers voted for Bolsheviks on the understanding that they would strive for a reunion, the two factions established a joint Social Democratic club in the Duma. This led to a new explosion in Cracow: how could the Bolsheviks agree that a Menshevik should be chairman? Long before Khrushchev, Lenin made the discovery that if the majority is on the other side it is only "arithmetical," i.e., it shouldn't count. The Mensheviks had one more vote, but since they had really been elected not by the workers but by the middle class, *they* should submit to the Bolsheviks in everything, and anyway Bolsheviks should have nothing to do with "Liquidator riffraff."

Stalin's exasperation with this impossible leader may be judged by the fact that at one point he proposed that Shaumyan, then in exile in Astrakhan, should escape and take over the editorship of *Pravda*, a suggestion unlikely to have been inspired by any overly friendly feelings toward his Baku rival.

Practically the minute Stalin returned to St. Petersburg fresh orders issued from Lenin: back to Cracow for a new session of the Central Committee and the Duma Bolsheviks. How they viewed this entirely needless trip, with its attendant dangers of illegal frontier crossing, may be inferred from Lenin's own letter to his contact in Russia: "Write him [Stalin] that he must unfailingly come back here again . . . and, if need be, *drag along* the others. He will spend his time very profit-

[8] Molotov, who edited and helped to finance the paper, and who bore the brunt of Lenin's terrible wrath, is not even mentioned in a book on *Pravda* written when this faithful servant of Stalin enjoyed the salubrious air of Mongolia, where he had been exiled for anti-Khrushchev activity. V. T. Loginov, *Lenin and Pravda* (Moscow, 1962).

ably."[9] It says a great deal about the Bolsheviks' discipline that they all obediently trooped back to Cracow, though some two weeks later than their impatient leader wished.

Of his third clandestine crossing in seven weeks Stalin in later years was to tell two stories. One was about how he was smuggled across the border by a Pole who refused to be paid for his services on learning that Stalin was a Georgian: both Georgia and Poland were oppressed by Tsarism. The other was about a waiter at a railway station in Galicia refusing to serve him when he ordered in Russian, and how Lenin had to explain to him that the local Poles loathed everything Russian. But it is unlikely that a Russian revolutionary, Georgian or not, had to be instructed in the strength of Polish national feeling.

The Cracow meeting was what might be expected: the issue was how to straighten out *Pravda*, how to combat the Liquidators and "conciliationism." But undoubtedly to Stalin's surprise, he did spent his time "most profitably." Lenin had a boon for him. Lenin could at times be a charmer, and he knew how to flatter and attach to himself a man he needed. And so he proposed that Stalin should take a few weeks' vacation abroad and write a treatise on the nationalities problem. He could go to Vienna to study the Austrian Marxists' views on the subject. Why Vienna? Cracow had fine libraries and Stalin anyway did not know German and could read only what was translated. Lenin was being tactful. His wife had very definite ideas about the manners of people she entertained, and there was a danger that this invaluble man Stalin would soon be ordered out of the Ulyanovs' home. That mutual antipathy had already formed which was to last throughout Stalin's and Krupskaya's lives and to cost the latter dearly.

Stalin somehow never reminisced about his one-month stay in the wonderful city on the Danube, his longest sojourn abroad. It was there that he met his two future collaborators and victims, Trotsky and Bukharin. The then very young Bukharin (he was born in 1888) was already quite erudite and probably helped Stalin with some German texts relevant to his work. Unlike the relationship with Trotsky, Stalin's friendship with Bukharin remained cordial for a long time. "We shall not give you the blood of Bukharin," Stalin would say in 1925 to the Trotskyites . . . and then he took it himself.

Stalin's *Marxism and the National Question* was printed in Russia in 1913 in the journal *Enlightenment*, though its author was already in jail. It is cogent and well written. Trotsky suggests that it was virtually redone by Lenin and Bukharin, but though the work shows traces of help by others,[10] it is undeniably his work in content and style, with some editorial help by Lenin. He was, as we have already seen, a vora-

[9] Lenin, *Collected Works* (5th ed., Moscow, 1970), XLVIII, 130. Lenin's italics.
[10] In one place Stalin corrects a Russian translation of a German text.

cious reader, with a considerable stock of historical and philosophical knowledge. At times he faltered, e.g., in writing that at the beginning of the nineteenth century North America was called New England. But he was well informed about the nationality problem in Switzerland, in Poland during her autonomy under the Russian crown 1815–30, and elsewhere. And naturally he drew many of his examples from the Caucasus.

Stalin's analysis is far from a servile reproduction of Lenin's own views on the nationality question. Lenin saw the enormous importance of the problem for the revolutionary movement: it was national oppression in the Empire which was bringing disproportionate number of Poles, Jews, Latvians, and Georgians, etc., into the radical camp. Hence social democracy, in his opinion, had to commit itself uncompromisingly on the side of the right of every nationality for self-determination, even though Marx in his nineteenth-century way had minimized the problem: "Workers have no country." Stalin was far from endorsing the right of every nationality to secede from the future democratic and republican Russia. It all, he thought, depended on concrete historical circumstances. "The national question in the Caucasus can be resolved only in the spirit of bringing the backward nationalities into the general stream of a higher culture."[11] Just as the socialists were opposed to forcible denial of self-determination, so they were also against forcing it upon a nation that did not desire it. Were Russia a "cultured country" like Switzerland, he implied, Poles and Latvians would be seeking not independence but autonomy. The important thing was to grant complete national equality when it came to the use of one's native language, schools, etc. There is a veiled though unmistakable note of Russian nationalism in Stalin's essay, and it is somewhat surprising that Lenin (who was unaware how much of a Russian nationalist he himself was) did not take exception to this. But he was undoubtedly pleased by the work's general tone and its condemnation of the Austrian socialists and the Bund's position that Socialist Parties should be organized according to national lines. In a letter to Gorky he referred to the "wonderful Georgian" and his satisfaction with his work.

In the middle of February, after a stopover in Cracow, Stalin was back in St. Petersburg. (The hostess of his clandestine apartment of those days gives a rather untypical testimony to his thoughtfulness and consideration for others. He did not want his hosts to go to any trouble on his account, would subsist on beer and bread rather than share the regular meal with her children, was serious and taciturn.[12]) His days of

---

[11] Stalin, *Collected Works* (Moscow, 1946–52), II, 151.
[12] Quoted in Yuri Trifonov, *In the Light of the Fire* (Moscow, 1966), p. 53. These reminiscences were written *after* Khrushchev's denunciation of Stalin by a woman whose son and daughter had been exiled, and son-in-law shot, during Stalin's reign.

freedom were numbered. The Okhrana was picking up Bolshevik leaders one by one, its intention being to leave the field free to Malinovsky. There were already rumors about that gentleman's double role, and Stalin probably heard them in Vienna from the local agent of the Bolsheviks, Alexander Troyanovsky (his future ambassador in Washington). But Lenin still had unbounded confidence in Malinovsky and attributed insinuations about him to envy and to the fact that he was of proletarian origin and not one of the "intelligentsia riffraff."

Malinovsky's background was not only that of a worker but, unbeknownst to the Bolsheviks, also that of a common criminal. Already in his teens he had been arrested four times, three for armed robbery. In 1906 he became a union organizer. In 1910, at the suggestion of the police, he joined the Bolsheviks. About then he was suggested by some Russian comrades for the Central Committee, a testimony to his organizing gifts and to the Bolsheviks' then desperate need for personnel. In 1912, after his selection to the Central Committee, he became a favorite of Lenin's, whose letters for the next two years abound in complimentary references to him. The Okhrana facilitated his election in 1912 to the Fourth Duma in which he assumed the leadership of the Bolshevik faction. Unlike other Bolsheviks, who felt lost without a written or a memorized text (often composed for them by Lenin), Malinovsky had an oratorical gift, and his fiery revolutionary rhetoric from the Duma podium would embarrass his police superiors and lead to doubts concerning his role as a parliamentarian.

Jacob Sverdlov, who had been coopted as a member of the Central Committee, was picked up by the police on February 9, 1913. In view of that, Stalin's subsequent behavior was, for a seasoned conspirator, most imprudent. On February 23 a musical soirée was organized for the benefit of *Pravda*. In some Bolsheviks' memoirs it is stated that it was Malinovsky who persuaded Stalin to attend, telling him that the police would never choose such a public function to try to arrest people, but it is unlikely that the provocateur would have chosen such a time and place for the arrest for it was bound to lead to new suspicions about him. Whatever the circumstances, Stalin went to the entertainment where, in the words of the Okhrana report, "agents of our division spotted Djugashvili among the public and according to their instructions arrested him." The search yielded nothing compromising, only a traveler's manual entitled *A Russian in Germany* with specially useful German phrases underlined.

It would not be back to Narim this time. The authorities decided to sentence him to four years of exile in the Yenisei-Turukhan region. This was probably the most dreaded location for penal settlement. The incredibly vast, barren region in northern Siberia, twice the size of

Texas, had in 1913 a population of 12,000: apart from exiles and a few officials and traders, mostly local tribesmen and hunters. Escape, while not impossible, was much harder than from any other area. Many who tried perished of cold, temperatures in winter going to less than —40° C., or of exhaustion, hundreds of miles often separating a settlement of four or five huts from another one. Former exiles could not decide what had been harder on their nerves—the long Arctic night of winter or the brief, damp, bug-infested summer with its "white nights." On his arrival in the region in 1914 Suren Spandaryan fell into despondency, which he could not conceal in a letter to his wife: he was ill and local conditions would tax even the hardiest. How was he going to live? Everything—the most primitive furniture, food, wood, kerosene—was very expensive, and as one sentenced by a court he was left to his own devices when it came to money. Spandaryan was to die of tuberculosis. But even people who were physically well often broke down: suicides and cases of insanity were not infrequent. Sverdlov, who was exiled there, begged his wife to join him, and she came, bringing with her a small child and an infant. There was *one* doctor for the entire vast region; if you lived in a major settlement, i.e., one having ten or twenty houses, you might be visited by a *feldsher* (medical assistant) *once* a year.

In August 1913, when Stalin arrived in the region, there were about three hundred fifty political exiles sprinkled throughout it. Those in a given vicinity would greet a new arrival with a festive reception, pooling their resources for food and vodka; in return they expected a report on how things were at home (mail to more distant points was delivered only four or five times a year). Stalin, if one account is to be believed, violated the exiles' etiquette on such an occasion: freshly arrived, he went straight to his room and refused to come out for refreshments and conversation.[13] And another incident soon confirmed the bad reputation which preceded him to the Turukhan region: Stalin simply took over all the books and papers of a prominent Bolshevik, Joseph Dubrovinsky, who had committed suicide shortly before. This was a breach of the custom which ordained that in such a case books, as vital to the exiles' sustenance as food, be distributed among the comrades in the neighborhood. But when some of them dared to expostulate with him, he replied to them haughtily in his capacity as Party official.

The story of this episode is a bit suspect and possibly colored by Stalin's later role. Such a gross violation of comradely comity would have brought a hearing before a Party court, regardless of Stalin's rank in the Party. But it is undeniable that the people were taken aback by his behavior. It is impossible to say whether this was a case of his customary rudeness, or whether his brusqueness had been intensified by

13 *Ibid.*, p. 48.

a natural despair over his situation. Stalin was now in his middle thirties. There seemed to be no end to exiles and arrests. His inherent suspiciousness and misanthropy, the feeling that everybody was turning against him, now fed on four years of loneliness and the harshest exile he had yet endured.

There was, to be sure, some thought of escape, though the obstacles seemed insuperable. The Party was eager to recover its two principal Russian organizers. The man charged with expediting their flight and sending money for it was none other than Malinovsky. And so it is not surprising that in February 1914 Stalin and Sverdlov were transferred to a safer location, the settlement Kureika, fifty miles beyond the Arctic Circle. The two men did not get along. In March Sverdlov wrote to his wife, "With me is the Georgian Djugashvili, an old friend from another exile. A good fellow but too much of an individualist in everyday life." In May there is a different note: "We have come to know each other too well. The saddest thing is how under the exile and prison conditions a man reveals himself in all his petty characteristics. We are now in separate quarters and seldom see each other." And, still later, "You know, my love, under what vile conditions I lived in Kureika. The comrade with whom I stayed turned out to be impossible in personal relations. We had to stop seeing and speaking to each other."[14] Kureika had about fifty inhabitants! Sverdlov soon moved elsewhere, and Stalin would live apart from Party comrades. Money to enable them to escape reached Stalin and Sverdlov in September 1914, but by then a flight was impossible. Thanks to Malinovsky, they were being guarded especially carefully. And soon afterward the Bolshevik organization in Russia virtually collapsed.

It is to be kept in mind that though Stalin was unpopular he was not shunned by his Party comrades, and he saw them on Party business, including Sverdlov. With Spandaryan he remained on a friendly footing until the latter's death. But for the most part his company was that of Siberian peasants and natives. He appears also to have hobnobbed with the local policeman, for years later this worthy, unmasked as a former servant of Tsarism and threatened with ejection from a collective farm (which under the conditions of 1930 meant virtual certainty of starvation), wrote to his illustrious former charge. From the Kremlin came a letter which, if not a model of graciousness (of course Stalin could not have had "friendly relations" with the cops), still bore him good testimony and probably saved his life.[15] It was becoming safer to have been Stalin's jailer than his friend or relative.

[14] Jacob Sverdlov, Works, I (Moscow, 1957), 276, 298.
[15] M. Moskalev, The Russian Bureau of the Central Committee of the R.S.D.W.P. (Moscow, 1947), p. 166. This touching episode is omitted from the 1964 edition of this work.

The Turukhan exile must be taken as one of the major formative periods of Stalin's life. Isolated from his Party comrades, Stalin appears to have made an adjustment to the misery and monotony of Siberian life. The necessarily lonely and austere arrangements became in a sense habitual, and in fact he reverted to them after the thirteen years of his second marriage—the only period of his post-1913 life when he displayed sociability in the true sense of the word, not out of diplomacy or calculation. Somewhere in Georgia there was his little son, and he must have written to or about the child, but he later scorned to have any such letters reproduced for they interfered with the steel-like superhuman image in which he had come to believe himself. He hunted and fished not only as a diversion but of necessity, for administrative exiles were allowed only fifteen rubles per month, insufficient even for subsistence.[16] Some money was being sent him by the Party fund for exiles, managed by Alliluyev, but Stalin evidently refused any personal help from his future father-in-law.[17]

Following the outbreak of World War I, Lenin moved to Switzerland, and Stalin's contact with his leader ceased after August 1915, when Lenin recorded that "Koba sends greetings and news that he is well." Twice during 1915 Lenin inquired about Stalin's real name, which he had forgotten, undoubtedly to reestablish communications, but Stalin can be forgiven if he felt that the Party had forgotten about him, that other figures were moving to the fore and would lead the Party if the revolutionary movement ever were resuscitated. His state of mind can be partially inferred by the fact that there is a gap in his writings between 1913 and 1917. Many other exiles put pen to paper, writing political, historical, or ethnographic sketches for Siberian newspapers. If Stalin did write, he must have felt subsequently that the articles were too revealing of his state of mind in Siberia to be included in his published works.

Revolution had been Stalin's entire life since the age of nineteen. It is unlikely that even when deeply depressed he would have contemplated any other future than that of a revolutionary. But the long period of largely self-imposed separation from his Party comrades undoubtedly influenced his egotistical and eventually inhuman view of revolution.

---

[16] A bottle of vodka was five rubles. Martov, who at the turn of the century had been exiled in Turukhansk (population four hundred), was sure that it had the highest per-capita consumption of alcohol in the Empire. The annual shipment of the vital article would be met by a procession headed by the priest, carrying a cross.

[17] Sergei Alliluyev was then working as a master electrician in St. Petersburg. Unlike most highly skilled workers, he could afford to send both of his daughters to private schools. Just before the Revolution the Alliluyevs moved to a modern building with an elevator; their apartment had three rooms, a bathroom, and a kitchen—rather unusual for their station in life.

Among the Bolsheviks he was far from being alone in striving for personal power. But much more than in the case of any other, Stalin's actions expressed a conviction that politics was inherently corrupt, that not only did capitalism have to be destroyed but that afterward that product of its corruption, the revolutionary movement itself, did too.

Following the arrests of Stalin and Sverdlov, the disintegration of the Bolshevik high command continued apace. To replace them as his personal watchdog over the Duma Bolsheviks and *Pravda*, Lenin sent to Russia Lev Kamenev, a man of mild and scholarly temper. Kamenev was little suited for the role of leader of the underground, and it was a strange quirk of fate which thrust him forth as a militant revolutionary rather than as scholar and archivist of Marxism. The Bolshevik Duma faction finally succumbed to Lenin's badgering and broke with the Mensheviks, but almost immediately it was shaken by a scandal. The new Deputy Minister of the Interior, Djunkovsky, was a man of principles.[18] He fired Malinovsky's sponsors in the Okhrana and ordered the agent provocateur himself to lay down his mandate as deputy, which he did in May 1914. Malinovsky then fled to Lenin's protection in Cracow, and though his action was a gross violation of Party discipline, Lenin was ready to defend him and to attribute his breakdown to Menshevik and other slanders.[19]

The final act of self-immolation by the Bolshevik organization in Russia came following the outbreak of the war. Both socialist factions in the Duma voted against the military budget and joined in a declaration condemning the war. But in Lenin's eyes this courageous act—for it went against the popular sentiment of the moment—was not enough: to distinguish them from the Liquidators, the Bolshevik high command must endorse his theses on war. This was done at a secret Bolshevik gathering which included Kamenev and the remaining five Duma deputies. All the participants were promptly arrested and, because Lenin's theses called openly for the defeat of Russia, charged with high treason. It was only by a hairsbreadth that the conspirators avoided a court-martial and execution. The civil court before which the Bolsheviks were ably defended—among others by Alexander Kerensky—sentenced them to exile in Siberia. It is difficult to account for Lenin's surprise and shock at the news. For more than three years his passion for illegality had been claiming one needless sacrifice after another. Now the Bolshe-

---

[18] He authorized the arrest of Rasputin after the latter had created a brawl in a nightclub, the step which led to Djunkovsky's eventual dismissal.

[19] Malinovsky then disappeared, surfaced during the war in a Russian war prisoners' camp in Germany, where he conducted Bolshevik propaganda, Lenin still corresponding with him. His true role was definitely established with the seizure of the Okhrana's archives after the Revolution. Malinovsky came back in 1918, hoping for forgiveness, but was judged and ordered shot by the Revolutionary Tribunal.

vik organization lay shattered. A rational conjecture for the future had to assume that in any resurgence of political radicalism in Russia the Mensheviks would have a headstart, perhaps even that the Bolshevik faction might not recover from the damage inflicted upon it by internal divisions and scandals and by its leader's obsessions.

But here one recalls again Tolstoy's story of the man whose movements viewed from a distance suggested madness but who as he approached was seen to be sharpening a knife. As against the madness which seized Europe and convulsed it for four years, and as against the fatuousness which liberal and other radical forces displayed in 1917, Lenin's seeming irrationality stamped him as a genius. In 1915 he inquired of Alexander Shlyapnikov, his new liaison with Russia, then in Stockholm, whether he knew a single Party address in Moscow. After the February Revolution his followers were invited to the Presidium of the newly formed Soviet more as a courtesy than as representatives of a sizable revolutionary movement. And within six months the Bolsheviks would push aside the decrepit Provisional Government and open a new chapter in the history of Russia and the world. ☆☆☆

COMMUNISM was born in Lenin's mind the day World War I erupted, even though his Party would be renamed only in 1918. The war snapped the links between him and the Western Social Democratic traditions, especially those epitomized in the second part of the name. Gone was the notion of orderly stages of historical development, of Russia's requiring a full blossoming of capitalism and a period of a democratic republic before she would be ready for socialism. Socialism would not be born of capitalism, as Marx had decreed: it would come out of revolution. Parliamentarism and democracy—these were exposed, as the Russian revolutionaries had always suspected them of being, as false gods. Did not the West European socialists follow the lead of the capitalists and militarists in pitting the workers against the ruling classes in a fratricidal struggle? How relevant were humanity and legality now, and the oft-repeated statement of Russian revolutionaries that when their hour came, they would eschew Tsarist brutality and denial of liberty? Such squeamishness was nonsensical when the interests of a handful of imperialists required a holocaust which would dwarf the most severe revolutionary terror.

Lenin's relative equanimity concerning the disintegration of the Bolshevik apparatus in Russia reflected his now much stronger internationalist perspective. He believed—and this belief stayed with him long after October 1917—that a major *European* revolution was in the offing. At present the workers, misled by their leaders, were trooping under the colors of their respective countries, but eventually they would see that real war must be against their own masters. It was of secondary importance whether the revolution would begin in Russia, Germany, or elsewhere; eventually its flame would spread all over Europe. "Our slogan must be a civil war."

Many other Russian socialists viewed the war in a different light. For some it was a struggle against German militarism; allied with Britain and France, Russia was fighting for European civilization; a victory for the Entente had to result in real democratic and parliamentary reforms. Such venerable revolutionary figures as the anarchist Prince Peter Kropotkin and George Plekhanov became "defensists." The Mensheviks split. Martov, then in migration, took an "internationalist" position (i.e., against the war), which temporarily revived Lenin's affection for the closest friend of his revolutionary youth; Potresov, in Russia, became a "defensist" (and what else could one expect from an arch-Liquidator!).

Whatever the feelings of their leaders at home, rank-and-file members of the movement, Bolsheviks and Mensheviks alike, were *at first* swept by the surge of the patriotic and anti-German feeling. Many of them volunteered or, if called to the colors, certainly did not seek to desert.[20] The strikes which beset the capital on the eve of the war ceased completely on its outbreak. Under a repressive system a foreign war will often seem a release and a liberation, until the full extent of casualties and miseries is revealed—this was the phenomenon that was so striking in Soviet Russia during World War II. Moreover, to many radicals the very system of bureaucratic autocracy with which Russia had been saddled since Peter the Great was German in its inspiration and methods; the Imperial Family itself as well as many leading military and civil bureaucrats were of German descent.[21] It was then easy to rationalize the war as a populistic crusade: by fighting Germany abroad, one would bring the eventual downfall of the "Germany" inside Russia.

"They are ringing the bells, but soon they will be wringing their hands," said a British Prime Minister about one of those little (and by our standards civilized) wars of the eighteenth century. And reflective people, whether on the right or the left, could perceive how hollow such

[20] Lenin's brother Dmitri served as an army doctor.

[21] The Empress Alexandra, unpopular anyway because of her sponsorship of Rasputin, was born a German princess, which was to be an important factor in the growing unpopularity and eventual downfall of the Imperial House. People with German names, though Russian for generations, found themselves molested or barred from employment; mobs invaded and looted shops with such names. The capital was renamed Petrograd.

enthusiasm was, how short-lived it was bound to be. In 1905-6 a brief war with what was then a small Asian power had shaken the Russian Empire to its foundations. Now the country—still divided, still badly governed, with Stolypin's social reforms still not established—was being asked to enter a major conflict that was certain to be long, to bare Russia's social and economic weaknesses, and to pit her against what was then the most efficient army and war industry in the world. People as different in background and attitude as Witte and Rasputin believed that a prolonged conflict was a folly bound to end in the downfall of the regime.

While their leader was in Switzerland trying to recreate a new militant socialist movement from the ashes of the Second International, the Socialist Party high command assembled in Russia in July 1915. They met in the place where most high-ranking Bolsheviks, Central Committee members, and Duma members currently were installed, in Turukhan exile in the village of Monastyrsk. Sverdlov presided, Stalin and the gravely ill Spandaryan came from their distant locations. The conference reviewed the trial of the Duma deputies, and approved their conduct— i.e., Lenin's "line" on the war. One other matter was touched on which would be of importance to Stalin in the first years after the Revolution. At the trial Kamenev had taken a somewhat different position from that of his fellow defendants: in the natural hope of softening their sentences (they had been threatened with the gallows) he denied that the Bolsheviks' position amounted to all-out defeatism. The conferees debated whether this had breached Party discipline, could be called unworthy. Stalin, an acquaintance of Kamenev's since the days in the Caucasus in 1904, was among those who were against censoring him too severely, a position that prevailed against Sverdlov's and Spandaryan's. Kamenev, though often criticized by Lenin and other zealots for not being "hard" enough, went on to enjoy wide respect and popularity among the Bolsheviks; he sided with Stalin in the most important political disputes of the crucial years between the Revolution and Lenin's death.

As the war progressed—with its toll of casualties, its increasing food shortages, and, after some initial successes against the Austrians, its continued military reverses—the initial mood of political reconciliation and almost of euphoria gave way to impatience and discontent. It was folly that the Tsar did not take advantage of the first surge of patriotism by creating a government of national union. Perhaps the government handled its war effort no more incompetently than did the other European powers, though this is doubtful, but the social and political structure behind it was much more fragile. When the British ambassador hinted tactfully that the government ought to seek to gain the confidence of the people, the last of the Romanovs observed that it was the other way around: the people should try to earn *his* trust. The Empress and her circle were believed quite widely—and quite falsely—to be working for a separate peace, if indeed not engaging in outright treason. Elsewhere, the War Ministry and the rest of the government presented a bleak picture of incompetence. The Emperor was foolish enough to assume the role of commander-in-chief, and though he was one only in name, this burdened him with the responsibility for defeats. It also took him out of the capital, which enhanced the influence of the Empress and through her of Rasputin (although popular rumor exaggerated his role out of all proportion, as most books on the subject still do). The Russian soldier, as throughout his history, fought well, but he lacked vital supplies. Too many men were mobilized, the government not realizing that in modern warfare sheer manpower could not compensate for shortage of equipment, and the excess of course worsened the shortages of matériel and food. It also contributed to growing discontent and, eventually, to the Revolution: many overage men who could not be sent to the front because there was no equipment for them idled in the rear, deeply resentful of their needless separation from their families and jobs.

And thus it was that in 1916 a thirty-seven-year-old political criminal was summoned to be examined for induction. As the father of an eight-year-old motherless child Stalin could have claimed exemption, but he chose not to. Probably even army life seemed preferable to a continuance in Siberia.[22] Other exiles, we are told, envied those summoned up by the army—a striking commentary on their life in Siberia and on how little they suspected that a momentous turn of events was in the offing.

Stalin's deformed left arm kept him out of the army, but the summons turned out to be a great stroke of luck. He was examined in Krasnoyarsk, some six weeks' traveling time from Kureika. He was then not sent back, but allowed to spend the balance of his term in Achinsk, on the Trans-Siberian Railway line. And so, when old Russia crumbled, the future maker of the new one was but four days by express train from Petrograd and the Revolution. ☆☆☆

T HE events of February 1917 can be summarized under two headings: one, the collapse of the Imperial regime; the other, revolution in the proper sense of the word. It is important, especially for understand-

---

[22] Though his sentence had only a few months to go, he was sure to be forbidden to settle in European Russia or the Caucasus upon its expiration.

ing Stalin's future career and as a *partial* explanation of his purges in the 1930s, to distinguish between the two. The Imperial regime collapsed because there was *nobody*, whether the army, the conservatives, or the bourgeoisie, ready and willing to defend it. Thus a series of strikes and food riots in Petrograd, in themselves less momentous than the events of January 9, 1905, brought forth the collapse of governmental authority. In 1905 the soldiers, when called upon to suppress the manifestation, obeyed. Now the garrison in Petrograd—swollen by recent draftees, staffed largely by reserve officers, many of them with liberal and radical sympathies—refused to quell the disturbances, and soldiers occasionally fired upon police rather than demonstrators. When some days later the Emperor sought support from the field army, none of the principal commanders was ready to lift a finger on his behalf or, as it turned out a bit later, on behalf of the Imperial House. A long history of Romanov incompetence and a series of scandals, the latest of which was the assassination of Rasputin with the participation of a member of the Imperial Family, convinced them as well as most other thinking Russians that a change was imperative if the war was not to be lost. The Russian "Establishment" of the moment agreed with practically no dissent that the only other legal authority, the Duma, should assume the power which had slipped from the hands of Nicholas II and his advisors, that it should form the government and carry the war to a victorious conclusion, and that beyond this immediate goal it should bestow real freedom on Russia, whether as a republic or a constitutional monarchy. And the Duma did form a government. But that was only half of the story—the less important half, as history was to demonstrate.

The other was the history of the real revolution, the birth of a new authority, the Petrograd Soviet. Here again the Tsarist regime had, ironically, contributed to forging the weapon of its own destruction. In 1915 some industrialists and politicians,[23] appalled by the government's ineptitude in mobilizing the country's resources, prevailed upon it to let them organize a sort of war production board and to have on it not only industrialists' but also workers' representatives. The workers who joined were, needless to say, denounced not only by Bolsheviks but by many Mensheviks as renegade servants of capitalism. But it was precisely this group of worker members of the Central War Industry Committee who in January 1917 issued a condemnation of the government which, "incapable of dealing with problems raised by the war . . . uses it as a pretext to strengthen its oppression of the people of Russia.[24] Thereupon the workers' group was promptly clamped under arrest. Released in February, when the police no longer would even attempt to detain

[23] Among whom was Krasin, a staunch supporter of the war effort.
[24] Alexander Shlyapnikov, *Year 1917* (Moscow, 1923), I, 224.

political prisoners, it was those "socialist patriots" (among whom there was not a single Bolshevik) who on February 27 proposed and initiated the Petrograd Soviet of Workers' and Soldiers' Deputies.

By March 8, when Stalin set forth for the capital, Russia had in fact two governments. One was the Duma-spawned Provisional Government, headed by Prince Lvov, a liberal nobleman, and composed for the most part of Kadets and moderate conservatives, with only one member from a radical party (or from revolutionary democracy, as it was called), the Socialist Revolutionary Alexander Kerensky, already rumored to be the man of destiny of the Russian Revolution. The other was the Soviet of Workers' and Soldiers' Deputies, dominated by the Mensheviks and the Socialist Revolutionaries, and headed by none other than Nicholas "Karl Marx" Chkheidze. The duality fitted in with orthodox socialist doctrine. "Everybody knew" (that is, Marx would have said) that Russia was not ready for socialism, but only for a "bourgeois democratic" regime. Hence those lawyers, professors, and industrialists *had* to take power to administer, conduct the war, etc. But, of course, they could not be fully trusted by the people, and so the Soviet, as the representative of the people, had to watch over the bourgeois government, veto its actions if unacceptable to revolutionary democracy, and legislate on its own if necessary.[25]

As Stalin's train sped toward Petrograd it must have required considerable detachment for him to think of the distant future. The country was seized by an intoxicating feeling of freedom far more intense than that of October 1905. Russia was the freest country in the world, Lenin was to say, still in Switzerland and vexed at his inability to get home. This was a spring of freedom such as the Russian people had never known—and such, alas, as they have never known again. All forms of authority crumbled. In practically every town, every military unit, a soviet was being formed. For a year it would be a land of soviets, most of them deferring to the one in Petrograd, but far from feeling that they were subject to *any* central authority, whether that of the socialist leaders in the capital, or that of the group of industrialists and lawyers who called themselves the Provisional Government. Jails yielded up their political inmates. From distant points of Siberia exiles began their

---

[25] Thus on March 1 the Soviet issued its famous Order Number 1, commanding all Russian military units to form their own soviets. Military officials were now proclaimed to be under the authority of the Petrograd Soviet in all political matters and commanded not to obey orders of the Duma if they clashed with its own. All weapons were to be under the control of the soldiers' committees and "under no circumstances to be handed over to the officers even at their demand." Outside their actual war duties officers had no right to control soldiers' activities or to issue commands. Traditional forms of saluting and address of soldiers to their superiors were banned. It must remain a source of wonder why it took the Russian army six more months to disintegrate.

trek home. They were delayed not only by the slowness of transportation, but by the need to stop at practically every station to address the crowds that had gathered to see and hear the martyrs for freedom whose sacrifices had brought about this glorious day.

Freedom already bred dissent. People whom shared sufferings had made friends now began to recall that they were political rivals and even enemies. For an anarchist March was but the beginning of the destruction of all forms of political authority. The socialists engaged in heated dispute: How ready is Russia for socialism? Ought there to be freedom for everybody—even for landowners, bankers, former Tsarists officials, and grand dukes? How merciful should the Revolution be? A Bolshevik would later remember an argument which developed with his travel companion on the Trans-Siberian Railway, a friend of long standing. As an anarchist, he proclaimed that the Revolution should not stain its hands with blood. Yes, even the Emperor should be spared. The Bolshevik maintained that the first order of business must be exemplary justice to be meted out to the enemies of the people. By the time they reached their destination they were not on speaking terms.

Stalin, as his sister-in-law remembered (one of the few authentic-sounding touches in her rather silly book, *Reminiscences*,) ridiculed this wave of revolutionary bathos which engulfed Russia. She and her sister, both in their teens, were convulsed at his mimicking of homegrown orators who extolled him and other revolutionaries on their way from exile. The misanthropic "loner" of the exile was transformed again by events into businesslike politician, and there were some very practical concerns on his mind when on March 18 he reached Petrograd.

Already on the way he, along with his companions Kamenev and Muranov, a Bolshevik Duma deputy, sent a telegram of greetings to Lenin and Zinoviev, then his chief lieutenant. But Lenin was still abroad and the big question was what role the Petrograd Soviet would allow Stalin and Kamenev to play. Kamenev had been partly discredited by his behavior at the trial in 1915 and the subsequent censure upon him. Unflattering rumors about Stalin's behavior in exile must have reached some Petrograd comrades. It was perhaps fortunate that Sverdlov was still in Siberia. (He reached the capital only at the end of March, and then the local Bolshevik organization, i.e., Stalin and Kamenev, sent him almost immediately to work in the Urals.) Would they be allowed to resume their positions as senior officials of the Bolshevik movement? Or would Stalin drop back into the ranks, perhaps be forced to go back to Georgia (now bound to be ruled by the Mensheviks) or Baku, away from main events and because of its proximity to the front in some danger of capture by the Turks?

The Bolshevik organization in the capital, moribund after 1914, had revived somewhat in 1916. Its leader at the time of the February

Revolution was Alexander Shlyapnikov, his main assistants Vyacheslav Molotov and one Peter Zalutski. They had been of little consequence in the movement before 1914; Molotov, who always irritated Lenin, had been tolerated probably because of his rich friend who contributed to the Party. But since they were there when the Revolution began, they had been thrust among the leaders of "revolutionary democracy."

Shlyapnikov had been since 1914 Lenin's main liaison with what remained of the Bolshevik organization in Russia. This required him not only to work clandestinely in Petrograd, but to travel extensively abroad in quest of funds for Party work. More than once he had been approached with offers by German agents, but he declined, unaware that in 1917 his leader would be less squeamish. Some money would trickle in through the help of Scandinavian socialists, but it was hardly enough. In 1916 he set out for the distant United States—that fabled land, he wrote, the country of the Redskins, and of the tales of Jack London and Mayne Reid. But his business was with the Jewish socialists in New York to whom he hoped to sell materials on the mistreatment of the Russian Jews by the Imperial Army. Poor Shlyapnikov was a better revolutionary than businessman: all he got for his labors was five hundred dollars, half of which went for expenses.[26]

With the onset of the February events, Shlyapnikov's attitude became that of the French Revolutionary figure who, on seeing a demonstration from his window, exclaimed, "There is the crowd and I am their leader," and set forth to catch up with the head of the column. He and Molotov did a creditable job in putting the Bolshevik organization on its feet. For its use they confiscated the famous prima ballerina Kshesinskaya's house,[27] and started publishing *Pravda*, banned since the war.

Shlyapnikov was a forthright and rather engaging figure. One day he would lead the only truly ideological opposition to the growth of totalitarian and bureaucratic tendencies in the Soviet state. But at the time both he and Molotov felt they were leaders and should remain so until the arrival of Lenin, and they did not relish the prospect of being superseded by others.

The two tried to guide the Bolshevik group along lines suggested by Lenin's telegraphed instructions. This was not easy, since the great man,

[26] Alexander Shlyapnikov, *On the Eve of 1917* (Moscow, 1920), p. 198. He had some rather odd things to say of America: New York subways and buses ran only downtown in the morning and uptown at night; the police put down strikes by shooting into the crowds of demonstrating workers. "Few major strikes pass without provocateurs, without the arrest of union leaders, without some bloodshed." The revolutionaries took their Russia along wherever they went.

[27] It was among the prerogatives of the young ladies of the ballet to initiate grand dukes in the art of love and Kshesinskaya performed this service for the future Nicholas II. After the Revolution she married a grand duke and died in 1971 at ninety-nine.

like anyone else who was not on the spot, could not quite visualize what was going on. (As late as March 16 he wondered whether the government would legalize the Bolsheviks—when as of March 1 every party, even the outright Anarchists, had legalized itself.) But it was clear that he was against the Provisional Government (though not sure what could replace it) and against the war (though as yet without an idea how it could be ended). And so the Petrograd Bolsheviks attacked the capitalist government and assailed the imperialist war. On both counts the Shlyapnikov-Molotov position was unpopular, even among the workers. For a resolution assailing the Provisional Government the Bolsheviks were capable of mustering only nineteen votes in the Soviet, against four hundred. On the war, while the other left groups demanded a people's peace with no annexations or indemnities, most non-Bolsheviks agreed that the war could not be stopped unilaterally and that Russia must defend herself against German militarism. The Bolsheviks' position was doing them harm politically; by continuing defeatist propaganda, it was held, they were in fact helping Germany (the rumors that they were outright agents of the Central Powers came later).

"The arrival of our exiled comrades overjoyed us," Shlyapnikov writes most unconvincingly.[28] The newcomers demanded that in view of their Party seniority they be given immediately seats on the leading organs: the Russian Bureau of the Central Committee and the editorial board of *Pravda*. Their great joy notwithstanding, members of the Russian Bureau[29] passed a resolution containing a very unsentimental verdict on the returning Party potentates. "Concerning Stalin it was reported that he had been an agent of the Central Committee in 1912 and therefore it would be desirable to include him, but in view of certain personal characteristics of his the Bureau decided to invite him only in an advisory capacity."[30] Kamenev because of his conduct at the 1915 trial was allowed to write for *Pravda* only on condition that his pieces would be unsigned. Quite a greeting, after four years of Siberia! The insult to Stalin was all the greater in view of the fact that the third returnee, Muranov, was unanimously invited to join the Bureau as a full member.

Shlyapnikov does not mention this warm comradely welcome to the returning exiles (it was revealed only in 1962), but he attributes the attempt to keep Stalin and Kamenev out to their conciliatory attitude toward the Provisional Government and their failure to take a stoutly antiwar position. Yet this is palpably untrue: of the three it was Muranov who was most "conciliationist," yet he was voted in. Muranov,

---

28 Shlyapnikov, *Year 1917*, II, 179.

29 They now included several others in addition to Shlyapnikov and Molotov, among them two sisters of Lenin.

30 Cited in *Problems of the History of the Communist Party of the Soviet Union* (Moscow, 1962), No. 3, p. 143.

it was rightly felt, was not of leadership caliber, hence not a potential rival.

It is a piquant detail that of the local Bolshevik politicians in Petrograd the one who was most anti-Stalin was Molotov. He was undoubtedly the main source of information on Stalin's "certain characteristics," with which he had become acquainted in 1912–13 during his previous stint on *Pravda*. The paper, he felt with some justification, was his child; now Stalin and Kamenev wanted to snatch it out of his hands. Shlyapnikov mobilized some workers against the newcomers. They demanded that the three returning heroes be read out of the Party.[31] But it was no contest. Stalin and Kamenev within two days took over *Pravda*, pushing out Molotov and the other editors. Stalin not only became a full member of the Bureau, but also replaced Molotov on its presidium and became the Bolshevik representative in the executive committee of the Petrograd Soviet. And Molotov found his master. He would henceforth serve him—the worn-out simile is precisely right here—with doglike devotion, enduring kicks, taunts, injuries to those closest to him for over thirty years.

And Stalin had won his first open political contest. He could not have had too much assistance from the mild and indecisive Kamenev. But he had his self-assurance and his domineering manner, distasteful to his comrades and yet impressive at such a bewildering time. He was far from being the polished intriguer that he would become in a few years, but he towered over his opponents. Shlyapnikov was all right addressing a workers' meeting but he had no head for administration: affairs of the Bolshevik Bureau were in a mess. Molotov after long apprenticeship in knavery would one day become a skillful diplomat, but he was still young (twenty-six) and, with his prim bourgeois ways, overawed by the older and brutal revolutionary. Stalin was indisputably the senior Bolshevik on the spot. They were a revolutionary party and not a club whose members are judged according to their manners. And Kamenev was a talented writer; for all his past sins, his pen was needed for *Pravda*. With the politician's sure instinct Stalin allied himself with the man whose personality complemented his own, just as one day he would be helped by the humane and (by Bolshevik standards) moderate Bukharin. Kamenev's mild and intellectual manner made him unpopular among the hotheads, but by the same token he was well liked by more civilized Bolsheviks and respected by their political rivals. He would be repeatedly assailed and reviled for his half-heartedness, but it was he and people like him who saved the Bolsheviks from an all-out joint attack by other radical parties which might well have crushed them at various times between February and October and possibly even afterward. The

[31] Shlyapnikov, *Year 1917*, II, 185.

policies he now advocated and propagated in *Pravda* were much more moderate in substance and especially in spirit than those urged by its previous editors and Lenin. They amounted to a qualified support of the Provisional Government and to an acknowledgment that Russia could not end the war unilaterally. "When an army faces the enemy, it would be the most stupid policy to urge it to lay down arms and go home. That would be a policy not of peace but of serfdom, a policy contemptuously rejected by the free nation."[32]

Stalin supported Kamenev's position, though in a more guarded language. During the Khrushchev anti-Stalin campaign this was again called one of the most grievous sins of the late despot. He disagreed with Lenin! Stalin in his capacity as editor of *Pravda* censored or disregarded outright Lenin's articles sent from Switzerland which contained wild rantings against the Provisional Government and other revolutionary parties. But as Lenin himself acknowledged on his return to Russia, the Stalin-Kamenev position was at the time good politics. What would be permissible in the summer, advisable in the fall of 1917—an all-out antiwar and anti-Provisional Government position— was political folly in March. Lenin's vitriolic passages, which Stalin and Kamenev tactfully omitted, spoke of Chkheidze and other Mensheviks as "traitors to the cause of the proletariat, peace, and freedom." At the same time the Bolsheviks were badgering Chkheidze to facilitate Lenin's return home. Another passage referred to the Provisional Government as "robbers" (changed to "annexationists"). It would have been dangerous in the extreme to indulge in such provocative language when rumors were already circulating among the soldiers that the Bolsheviks were doing the Germans' work for them.

Another item of news from Russia that was bound to raise Lenin's temperature was that the Stalin-Kamenev leadership was not averse to a reunion with the radical wing of the Mensheviks. Again as in 1905, most of the workers could not understand why at a time like this socialists should be fighting each other rather than working for the common cause, and in some provincial areas the two factions had merged in a single organization. Stalin was far from advocating a reunion with *all* the Mensheviks. He was against those like Plekhanov who, he believed, had gone overboard in support of the war. But he advocated that those Mensheviks who took the "internationalist position"—which to oversimplify somewhat amounted to the demand for a speedy and negotiated peace with no annexations or indemnities—belonged in the same party with the Bolsheviks. For Lenin pacifism was repellent. From the beginning of the war he had held that the goal should be a transformation of the imperialist conflict into civil wars in the belligerent coun-

[32] Cited in *ibid.*, p. 183.

tries. Stalin did not ignore the possibility of a future struggle for power. On March 18 he wrote, "We need a force of armed workers connected with the main revolutionary centers. . . . Revolution cannot win without an armed force at its disposal."[33] But the same revolutionary common sense urged that the Bolsheviks could never seize power by themselves and needed allies. And he was right.

Minutes of the Bolshevik committee meetings of the time show again his amazing tendency to shed one personality and assume another. His interventions in the debates were crisp and businesslike. The misanthropic recluse of a few weeks before, shunned by and shunning others, was now listened to respectfully. His language was reasonable and moderate. His fellow committeemen foundered in doubts and fears: Should they meet with the Mensheviks and discuss a reunion? What would Vladimir Ilyich say? What if the Mensheviks tricked them? Stalin would go straight to the point: "We ought not to look too far ahead and foresee disagreements. There can be no party life without disagreements. Within a [united] party we would overcome mild disagreements. . . . The Mensheviks can be told that this position represents views of those present and is not obligatory for all the Bolsheviks. We ought to seek a meeting [with them] without presenting any preconditions."[34]

The same reasonable and tolerant tone emerges in his articles of the period. The Revolution, he wrote very perceptively, was made by Petrograd, and its source of strength was still in the capital; the bourgeois Provisional Government had its main support in the provinces. Hence the revolutionary parties must develop more fully in the provinces—otherwise the cause of revolutionary socialism would be lost when the Constituent Assembly met to prepare a new constitution for Russia. He still could not visualize how the Bolsheviks would solve the problem within a year by simply chasing out the Constituent Assembly.

Occasionally Stalin looked beyond the political passions of the moment. Should the Russia of the future be a unitary state or a federation? Practical sense in conjunction with his (as yet) latent Russian nationalism made him skeptical of the federal solution. Modern life condemned federalism, he held. Look at the United States. *In fact* though not in form it has been a unitary state since the Civil War, with the states having but limited political autonomy. He attributed the same trend toward centralization and weakening of the federal units to Canada and Switzerland. The thesis was debatable and certainly premature in its conclusions, but it was evidence nevertheless of considerable acquaintance with the history and political systems of other countries.

[33] Stalin, III, 13.
[34] *Problems of the History of the Communist Party of the Soviet Union*, No. 6, p. 140.

On April 3 Lenin returned to the city that would bear his name, and Stalin's role as the temporary leader of the Bolsheviks came to an end. From now until well after the October Revolution he was overshadowed not only by the leader but by several others in the Party: Trotsky, who returned in May and soon joined the Bolsheviks; Zinoviev, Lenin's inseparable assistant in exile, whom he brought back with him; even the figures of subsequently secondary importance in Soviet politics such as Lunacharsky and that Bolshevik patron saint of women's liberation, Alexandra Kollontay.[35] To Sukhanov, the chronicler of the Revolution, Stalin in those days appeared "a gray blur" as against these dashing and brilliant figures. Garrulous intellectual that he was, Sukhanov was naturally attracted to people like himself. Thus by reading only his account, one might conclude that the most important Bolshevik after Lenin and Trotsky was Lunacharsky, the old "God-builder" once again enrolled under Lenin's banner. And it was true that as a speaker at mass meetings Stalin could not compete with Trotsky and Zinoviev, and he did not try. But the qualities he displayed during those two weeks in March continued to make him indispensable to Lenin and the Party.

On his return to Petrograd Lenin loosed his thunderbolts: there would be no toleration of the Provisional Government, no support for the war. "The [alleged] defense of the Fatherland means the defense of one band of capitalists against another." On April 4 that joint consultation of the Bolsheviks and the Mensheviks took place at which Stalin was supposed to make the principal address and at which, it had been hoped, a platform could be laid down for a reunion. Instead of Stalin, Lenin appeared on behalf of the Bolsheviks, and what he announced was his famous April Theses. *All* power to the soviets. Immediate confiscation of landed estates and their transfer to committees of poor peasantry. No reunion with the Mensheviks. The Party ought to change its name to Communist, and a new militant Marxist International should exclude not only the "socialist patriots" like Plekhanov, but also "centrists," i.e., most Mensheviks.

The initial reaction to Lenin's position was one of shock and bewilderment. To some it was clear that the man was mad: his program promised anarchy. The proposal that the peasants should take over land, that the workers (*not* the state) should control industry and distribution was subject to the standard Marxist objection, the one he himself would make *after* the October Revolution: this was not Marxism but

[35] Of Polish descent and daughter of a general, Kollontay became a revolutionary and an advocate of women's rights early in her youth. Unlike the intense and prudish type of female revolutionary, epitomized by Krupskaya, Kollontay was charming and vivacious, the life of the party at international socialist gatherings. A Menshevik, she came during the war under Lenin's influence and in 1917 officially joined his Party.

anarchism, and it was bound to make shortages of food and the paralysis of industry much more severe than they already were. His followers, Stalin among them, were mainly puzzled: "*All* power to the soviets"? Since the soviets were led by Mensheviks and Socialist Revolutionaries, did this not mean that power should be given over to the "Menshevik scoundrels Chkheidze and Skobelev" and to the "windbag Kerensky"— to use Lenin's characterization of the president and vice-presidents of the Petrograd Soviet? To be that violently against the war meant risking a pogrom against the Bolsheviks by the soldiers. Already the very fact that Lenin had traveled through Germany to return to Russia aroused wide suspicion ánd indignation. Members of the guard of honor that had greeted him on his arrival at the Finland Station issued a public statement expressing the feelings of the rank-and file soldier. "Having learned that Mr.[36] Lenin came to us by permission of His Majesty the German Emperor and the King of Prussia, we express our deep regret that we participated in his solemn welcome to Petrograd. . . . [Had we known we would have shouted] . . . down with you, go back to the country through which you came to us." Crowds of veterans and wounded men marched through the streets with signs denouncing the defeatists and demanding Lenin's arrest.[37]

At the April 8 meeting of the Petrograd Bolshevik Committee two votes were cast for Lenin's position, thirteen against. But the strength of Lenin's convictions and prestige was bound to prevail. Stalin bowed to the will of the stronger man. He in turn was far from considering his follower's previous policies as apostasy, or seeing his behavior in March as revealing the- characteristics of a "plebeian democrat and oafish provincial forced by the trend of times to assume the Marxist tinge," as Trotsky was to write from the depths of his bitterness against his terrible rival.[38] Kamenev and Stalin continued as editors of *Pravda*, and as such they soon became loyal followers of Lenin's policies.

This was no mere kowtowing to the leader. In those days the Bolsheviks were still far from a "cult of personality." The main objection to Lenin's views had been that they were impractical. Now every day brought fresh evidence that perhaps they made good revolutionary sense. In view of the Bolsheviks' opponents' folly and irresolution Lenin's madness began to take on the appearance of geniuslike audacity.

[36] Already a term of opprobrium: if not "Comrade," it should have been at least "Citizen."

[37] N. N. Sukhanov, *Notes About the Revolution* (in Russian; Berlin, 1923), III, 109. And yet Deutscher, who cites the same source, writes that on Lenin's arrival "nobody reproached him for the journey through Germany." Isaac Deutscher, *Stalin: A Political Biography* (New York, 1967), p. 137.

[38] Trotsky, *Stalin, An Appraisal of the Man and His Influence* (London, 1968), p. 194.

Those crowds ready to surge upon the Bolshevik headquarters were restrained not only by the "Menshevik scoundrels," but by that arch-reactionary former chamberlain of His Majesty, the Duma's president, Rodzianko. The Revolution cannot countenance mob violence! The soldiers' section of the soviet continued to denounce Lenin's and the Bolsheviks' propagation of defeatism among the troops, but, they added, as long as the Bolsheviks limited themselves to propaganda, no repression should be used against them.[39]

"*All* power to the soviets" was also beginning to be seen in a different light. It was an effective slogan for weakening the government's authority throughout the land, thus enabling a determined and disciplined party (such as the Bolsheviks were, at least in comparison with others) to come closer to seizing power, the idea of which somehow no longer seemed so fantastic. The soviets were not stable in their composition, delegates to them being constantly recalled and new ones freshly elected by factions and military units, people with suspicious credentials or none at all in many cases remained unchallenged. So the Mensheviks and the Socialist Revolutionaries need not control them forever.

"All land to the peasants"? Marx, or even Lenin before 1914, would not have approved. But peasants who probably had never heard of either were already putting this principle into practice, in places seizing the landlords' farms and distributing land among themselves. Were the Bolsheviks to set themselves against this spontaneous movement because of some pedantic theoretical or legal objections, and forfeit the peasant's goodwill or at least neutrality? In an editorial of April 14 Stalin spoke approvingly of the peasants' helping themselves to others' lands: "We urge the peasants, the country poor of all Russia, to take this business [changing ownership of land] into their own hands and to move it ahead."[40] And he spelled it out for the Marxian purists: if you want the Revolution to advance, you must realize once and for all that the two elements in the population that have to be won over are the workers and the poor peasants whom the war has put in uniform. Before Lenin's arrival Stalin had wanted a speedy convocation of the Constituent Assembly to decide among other things the land question; now he condemned such scruples and delays as silly and antirevolutionary.

What a few weeks before had been seen as madness now appeared as revelation. The *next* revolution would come not according to some blueprint laid down by Marx, Kautsky, or Plekhanov, but from the ever expanding lawlessness and anarchy. And that anarchy had to be crushed if one wanted to preserve the Russia of February—"the freest country in

[39] They did not want the troops to desert or to stop fighting, protested the Bolsheviks. They merely urged them to fraternize with the enemy soldiers!
[40] Stalin, III, 35.

the world"—or nourished and exploited if one wanted a different Russia. There was no third choice.

The Bolshevik movement grew. No one knows how many members the party had before the February events, and estimates range from 10,000 to a generous 30,000. When the Seventh Party Conference assembled toward the end of April, the membership was approaching 80,000. This accession of strength was mainly in the two capitals and some other industrial centers. Even more important than this growth was the radicalization of the army and the fleet. While the war continued and a peace was not being negotiated, leaders of the Provisional Government and of the Soviet wallowed in bombastic oratory. It is clear why many without the slightest sympathy toward Bolshevism or even socialism began to be attracted to the one man and the one party that appeared to know what they wanted, while many others (especially soldiers in the rear) sympathized with a movement that defended them against the generals who would reimpose discipline and dispatch them to the front to fight in the interests of Russian and domestic capitalists.

At the conference Stalin was elected to the Central Committee and his current stature in the Party was attested to by the fact that in the secret balloting he received ninety-seven of the hundred and nine delegate votes. Only Lenin with a hundred and four and Zinoviev with a hundred and one were ahead. The barely known Caucasian of 1912, the man whom five weeks earlier it had been proposed should be kept out of the Party councils because of his bad temper and manners, was now freely acknowledged by his fellow Bolsheviks to be the leading "practitioner" in the Party. In the turbulent months ahead Stalin remained at the center, one of the principal leaders of the Party, though only a secondary figure of the Revolution.

At the April Conference Stalin also delivered the report on the question of nationalities. This was no longer a theoretical problem, as it had been in the prewar days, but an urgent and immediate political question. National separatism was yet another factor in the progressive disintegration of government and authority. Finland clamored for independence, the Ukraine for far-reaching autonomy; similar trends were asserting themselves in other non-Russian areas. Some Bolsheviks, notably the Ukrainian-born Gregory Pyatakov, and a Pole, Felix Dzerzhinsky, still would not acquiesce to Lenin's principle that every nationality had the right to secede. Perhaps they were impeded not only by Marxian scruples and their own cultural or, more properly speaking, revolutionary assimilation but also by the tantalizing prospect of power: Should the Russia they were aiming to inherit be stripped of vast and rich regions, be reduced to her sixteenth-century borders? Stalin, psychologically at one with them, could nevertheless sense the political appropriateness of giving in on this as on other political questions convulsing the country, even to the most extreme demands. The Bolsheviks, he explained, must not endorse the chauvinist policies of the Provisional Government and the "socialist patriots."[41] Would they deny the right of the Irish to fight for independence? Were the Bolsheviks to become accomplices of British imperialism? It was a rhetorical device to which he would often resort: the use of an example which has nothing to do with the case under discussion, but which in the heat of the debate somehow sounds very convincing and revolutionary. Pyatakov and Dzerzhinsky retreated in confusion, but he had some words of consolation for them: he was sure that in the future free Russia, more than nine-tenths of the other nationalities would not want to secede. And indeed in the "Stalin Constitution" of 1936 the right of every federal republic to secede was to be solemnly guaranteed. More realistic was the Soviet national anthem, which proclaims: "An *unbreakable* union of free republics was forged *forever* by Great Russia."

Stalin was now enjoying his first real freedom since he was arrested that April day in Baku in 1902, and we must not disdain the more obvious explanations for his relatively benign temper: the dramatic change in his personal life may have temporarily quieted his inner suspiciousness and irritability, just as later the enormous political success of the mid-1920s would make him appear, and to some extent be, a normal politician, comrade, family man. Anna Alliluyeva remembers the Stalin of those days often smiling. He adopted the Alliluyevs, and when they moved to a flat in a modern appartment building, he asked them to keep a room at his disposal. He did not use it often, though. Like everyone in politics, he was always on the run—to hurried consultations with colleagues, committee meetings, visits to Party cells in suburbs, his work on *Pravda*, which at times kept him in its editorial offices overnight. He was already developing that habit of nocturnal work and late-morning arising which later became so well known.

As during any revolution, life in Petrograd had an unreal, theatrical atmosphere. Politicians persisted in their incantations—"defense of the Fatherland," "interests of the international proletariat," "the sacred cause of freedom." In the Soviet (the Duma had by now faded away) they assumed roles they read about in history books—Roman senators, Whig noblemen of England of 1688, tribunes of the French Revolution. Historical imagination shaped hopes and fears. The bayonets of the freest army in the world would sweep Teutonic militarism off the face of the earth. Or a Bonaparte or Cromwell would emerge and with a few detachments of Cossacks sweep away the soviets, make short shrift of this orgy of oratory and resolutions. It was the Bolsheviks, bewailed the

41 Who as a matter of fact were in their hopeless way trying to deal with the problem partly by appeasing the nationalist movements and partly by persuasion: now is not the time, let us wait for the Constituent Assembly.

other socialists, who through their irresponsible behavior and demagogy were bringing that unhappy possibility ever closer to realization. But they could not agree on any steps of repression against their errant brethren: "history taught" that the threat to Revolution could come only from the Right.

History was very much on the mind of the Bolsheviks as well, but they looked to it to answer a very practical question: When is the moment to strike? You make your bid for power prematurely and you are crushed. This is adventurism. But you cannot afford to wait too long; the mood of the masses grows more and more feverish. Do you dare wait till you have a majority in the soviets? What if the *active* minority of soldiers and workers grows impatient with you, concludes that just like the Mensheviks you talk tough but cannot deliver?

The first time this dilemma appeared was in the beginning of June, when there was an All-Russian Congress of Workers' and Soldiers' Soviets. The Bolsheviks were still in a minority. They and their allies had about a hundred and thirty delegates out of seven hundred and seventy-seven, but it was a sizable minority, especially in view of the bumbling behavior of the leaders of the majority of Mensheviks and Socialist Revolutionaries. Now? At the Congress Lenin made his as yet most demagogic speech. One month before, leaders of the other socialist parties had joined the Provisional Government, with Kerensky becoming War Minister, but this step, Lenin declared, did not bring peace one step closer. The country wanted peace. The government, for all the participation of Menshevik and Socialist Revolutionary gentlemen, did not know how or want to bring it about. How could you achieve this goal? Very simple, declared Lenin: the capitalists want to continue the war. Arrest fifty or a hundred leading capitalists, bare their intrigues. Arrest them, force them to confess; blinkers will fall from the eyes of the masses in the belligerent countries. They will compel their governments to make immediate peace. Here in Russia food shortages will disappear, the soldier will be able to go back to his family, share in the redistribution of land. This was a call for class terror, playing upon the worst instincts of the masses, insinuating that their sufferings were due to a conspiracy by a handful of people

The majority of delegates sat in shocked silence. But when Lenin compounded his brazenness and declared that if they were unable or unwilling to perform this deed his Party was—"At any moment it is ready to take over power in its entirety"—there was general laughter. The idea was absurd that any single party could seize power, and yet more fantastic that it could govern Russia.

Even the Bolsheviks were stunned. Trotsky, already at Lenin's side though not yet formally a Bolshevik, felt constrained to soften the impact of the speech: nobody meant to *seize* power against the will of the soviets. This combination of Lenin's audacity and Trotsky's more prudent resolution was to be one of the keys to the Bolsheviks' victory.

But now the Bolsheviks had to prove that Lenin's words were not just empty oratory à la Kerensky. There was a discussion in the Central Committee about how far it was advisable to go. One version has Stalin advocating a very bold attack at the Provisional Government, and Zinoviev and Kamenev opposing any test of strength. The former is doubtful, although in view of Zinoviev's and Kamenev's behavior in October the latter is most likely. In any case it was decided to test the revolutionary temperature: an inflammatory proclamation of June 9 called upon the soldiers and the general population to take to the streets next day to demand an immediate peace and the resignation of the "ten capitalist ministers." The masses were advised to "state your demands calmly and convincingly, as behooves the strong." It was hoped that the demonstrators would march on the government building, that when the ministers, in the fashion of the times, tried their oratorical powers on the mob and preached on the famous themes "Now is not the time" and "The Revolution must not soil its hands with blood," the people's indignation would lead to their arrest; and then, if the mood was favorable, the Bolsheviks might try. . . .

But this time revolutionary democracy showed that it still had some strength left. The Congress of Soviets banned all demonstrations. Non-Bolshevik members were dispatched to barracks and factories to explain the Bolshevik game. Pro-Menshevik and Socialist Revolutionary military units were put on the alert. And on the morning of June 10 the Bolsheviks called off the "demonstration."

So the first rehearsal was unsuccessful—but perhaps not entirely so. The man mainly responsible for the resolute behavior of the Socialist Parties was the Menshevik Irakli Tseretelli, the same Georgian who at age twenty-five had been leader of the socialist faction in the Second Duma. Now a minister and a member of the Executive Commitee of the Soviet, he demanded that steps be taken to prevent a recurrence of the threat; the Bolsheviks' private army (the Red Guards) should be disarmed, their subversive propaganda banned. But to the majority of the revolutionary democracy such demands went too far. The Bolsheviks *did* submit peacefully. To disarm a proletarian, even if misguided, party? History has shown . . .

In three weeks the Bolsheviks were ready to try again. To be fair, this time their hand was forced. In June the Russian army launched an offensive ordered by the Provisional Government on the very dubious principle that inactivity was the main reason for the growing indiscipline and disintegration. After some initial successes the offensive had its predictable results: under a German counterattack the Russian army fell back and desertion became endemic. In the first days of July some Petrograd units found themselves in imminent danger of being sent to the front. After listening to Bolshevik orators, their soldiers concluded that this was indeed a counterrevolutionary plot. They proposed to march not to the trenches but on the Tauride Palace, the seat of that government which with tragic prescience had called itself provisional. The Bolshevik high command was in a quandary. Perhaps now? It was decided to urge moderation but to call the pro-Bolshevik sailors in Kronstadt to the capital, just in case.

Stalin, a famous story has it, was the member of the Central Committee of whom the sailors inquired by telephone whether they should bring their rifles along. He was not the one to advise them, Stalin is supposed to have replied. He was just a writer and as such always carried his weapon, a pencil, with him. And so they marched, stopping in front of Bolshevik headquarters to listen to the leaders (including Lenin), who extolled their revolutionary firmness and vigilance but refused to commit themselves.

On July 4 the capital was seized by anarchy. An armed rabble, shooting at random and looting as they marched on, surrounded the Tauride Palace, and when the ministers tried to deliver their lectures, its mood became nasty. A sailor who evidently understood literally the injunction "All power to the Soviets!" shouted to Victor Chernov, "Take power, you son of a bitch, when we offer it to you," and when the leader of the Socialist Revolutionaries droned on, the impatient sailors proposed to drag him off; it took Trotsky's oratorical skill and the intervention of the sailors' leader to save the veteran revolutionary from the threat of lynching.

Rumors that some pro-government troops were being summoned to the capital were enough to panic the demonstrators. The siege of the palace was lifted. After some hesitation by the Bolsheviks, the Kronstadt sailors were sent back to their base. They trooped meekly back, some 20,000 of them, to be disarmed.

Now the outcry against the Bolsheviks was universal. The editorial offices of *Pravda* were raided, its printing plant smashed. The Executive Committee of the Soviet decided to close down the Bolshevik headquarters. Stalin tried to bluff Tseretelli, the man mainly responsible for those energetic measures, by threatening him with bloodshed if anyone tried to occupy Kshesinskaya's villa. He should not talk nonsense, his fellow Georgian told him: the Bolsheviks will not dare to resist. Stalin left without a word. Tseretelli was right.

Stalin's other errand of those anxious hours during the night of July 4–5 took him to another Georgian: Would Chkheidze, as head of the Soviet, prevail upon the government and the press not to publish the allegations that Lenin was receiving money from the Germans? Information to that effect had been in the government's hands for some time, but now it was proposed to make it public. Though he was successful in his plea, and Chkheidze promised to stop this unproven libel of a fellow revolutionary, the story appeared on July 5 nevertheless. It was none other than Lenin's onetime close associate and then mortal enemy Alexinsky who had made sure that an extreme-right-wing journal should print it. And then of course it spread like wildfire.

Today there can be no doubt—we have seen the relevant German documents—that the substance of the charges was correct, though not the interpretation put upon them. Lenin did take money from the Germans, as he would have taken it for revolutionary purposes from any source, the Russian Imperial House included, but he was hardly a "German agent."[42] At the time, however, the story ironically enough redounded to his benefit. None of the anti-Bolshevik socialist leaders, not even Tseretelli, was ready to believe that their onetime comrade was capable of such behavior. And so, though on July 7 a warrant was issued for his and Zinoviev's arrest, it is clear that the government took special care *not* to catch them.

Already on July 5 Lenin had decided to go underground. Whatever the government's intentions, it was entirely possible that some patriotically minded soldiers or officers might take the matter into their own hands. But the comrades with whom he tried to take shelter greeted him without enthusiasm and urged the two "hot" leaders to move on. On July 6 Stalin found them more courageous hosts, the Alliluyevs. Zinoviev was panic-stricken, but Lenin was outwardly calm. He even found time during this frantic house-hunting to compose articles denouncing "the vile lies of the reactionary press and of Alexinsky." And yet, "This time they may bump us off," he said at one point, and bade goodbye to his wife, "We may be seeing each other for the last time." The Party high command discussed the next step: Perhaps it was safer for Lenin to surrender? Stalin and Orjonikidze negotiated with the Mensheviks: Would the comrades (it was the first time in weeks that they were addressed as such) guarantee that if the Bolshevik leaders surrendered, they would be put in a safe jail, i.e., one controlled by pro-Bolshevik soldiers? Finally it was decided to spirit Vladimir Ilyich and his shield-bearer out of Petrograd. The men had to alter their appearances, which meant for Lenin the sacrifice of his beard and mustache and for Zinoviev the trimming of his curly hair into a crew cut. Stalin, the barber, may silently have reflected on what Lenin had once recorded a working-class Bolshevik as saying: "The Russian *intelligent* needs a

---

[42] I dealt with the subject in *Lenin and the Bolsheviks* (New York, 1965), pp. 326–27, 349–50.

servant as he is himself incapable of tidying up."[43] He and Alliluyev
then accompanied their leaders to a suburban station where they
boarded the train for a hideout in the country not far from the capital.[44]

On the face of it the Bolsheviks had suffered an irreversible disaster.
"The masses," of which they spoke so often, had turned tail and fled
when confronted by the danger of real fighting. Those whom the government considered to be the leading Party members were under arrest:
Kamenev, Lunacharsky, Kollontay. Trotsky, eager to earn passage back,
declared that he was equally responsible and should also be imprisoned;
and his wish was granted. However, nothing had been done to destroy
the Bolshevik organization or to put into effect the order for disarming
the Red Guards. The other socialist parties became frightened of their
own success: Were they acting in the manner of the oppressors of the
Paris Commune of 1871? "This is how a counterrevolution always
begins," shouted Martov when it was announced that pro-government
troops were arriving in Petrograd. Martov was universally liked and
respected, and his influence began to offset that of the more sensible
Tseretelli, and thus confirmed the Mensheviks on their suicidal course.
Martov knew Lenin well, realized his total lack of scruples when it came
to politics. But, went his reasoning, one could not move againt a fellow
socialist party: the Bolsheviks, though exploiting them, were still expressing the real aspirations of the masses. One had to satisfy the masses
and "isolate the Bolsheviks morally." Already this reaction was beginning: mobs were attacking the Bolsheviks.

The Bolsheviks were then given an opportunity to rebuild. Stalin and
Sverdlov were left at large—a tribute to the current and fallacious belief
that in a revolution it is oratory rather than other less dramatic qualities
which is important and hence dangerous in the enemy. It was up to
them to pick up the pieces and prepare the Party for the next test.
During the four intervening months they were to be mainly responsible
for the developments which insured that when the Revolution took
place, the patched-up Bolshevik Party was there to gather its fruits.

With Lenin and Zinoviev in hiding the Sixth Bolshevik Party Congress took place at the end of July, uniting 276 delegates representing
more than two hundred thousand members, a dazzling accession of
strength since the April Conference. It fell to Stalin, who delivered the

[43] This was recorded for posterity in Anna Alliluyeva, *Reminiscences* (Moscow,
1946), p. 184. She does not mention, of course, that Zinoviev was hiding in her
parents' apartment along with Lenin.
[44] They lived near Razliv Station, with the family of the Bolshevik worker N. Emelyanov. Lenin was almost daily visited by Bolshevik dignitaries from Petrograd,
yet there were no arrests—vivid testimony on how vigorously he was being pursued
by the authorities. In Stalin's Russia, Emelyanov, who had sheltered Lenin and
whose sons had distracted Vladimir Ilyich, a great lover of children, was arrested
and, despite pleas by Lenin's widow, suffered long imprisonment.

main political report, to present Lenin's new and more radical slogans, but he did this with considerable skill, softening the tone if not the substance of Lenin's recommendations, making them appear ambivalent enough not to alarm the more fainthearted among the Bolsheviks who had not quite recovered from the recent turbulence. Before the Congress he had declared that "the peaceful period of the evolution of the Revolution has ended." And he had maintained that the Party would have to stake all on another, this time premeditated, armed uprising. But Stalin refused to state this as unequivocally as Lenin would have wished. The Bolsheviks do not propose to do anything illegal (!), he remarked, and they had not abandoned the idea of uniting with other forces of the Left. To be sure, there could be no union with "socialist jailers" like Tseretelli and Kerensky, but there were sound internationalist elements among the Mensheviks—take Martov—with whom it was just possible that one could cooperate in the future.

And so, with the same tactical skill in dissipating his followers' apprehensions and his enemies' worst suspicions, Stalin urged the rather confused delegates to drop Lenin's "All power to the soviets" as the Bolsheviks' postulate. Nothing so obvious was said as that the soviets had displayed too much power for the Bolsheviks' comfort. No, it was simply that the current moment demanded that somebody else should take power. The Bolsheviks? Certainly nothing so un-Marxist and undemocratic! The city proletariat and the poor peasants—*they* were to become heirs of the Romanovs and the doddering pseudosocialists of the Provisional Government.[45] The skill of this doubletalk was so great that the resolution embodying it passed with no opposition, which certainly would not have been the case had a more straightforward language been proposed, in keeping with Lenin's wish.

When it came to the ability to take liberties with facts, Stalin, it is fair to say, was not alone among the Bolsheviks. But already he was better at it and could do it with more apparent (and perhaps real) conviction. What of the July days? Had the Party erred, had it engaged in adventurism? Far from it: "What kind of a mass party is it which disregards the masses? Our Party always moves with the masses."[46] Who saved the day and prevented greater bloodshed? Why, the Bolsheviks. Stalin personally had had to beg the irate sailors to return peacefully to Kronstadt. As a group the Bolsheviks were as yet far from being cynical pursuers of power, and these arguments were reassuring and consoling to men who still clung to the belief that they were good Marxists and social *democrats*.

[45] In July, Prince Lvov finally faded out of the picture, with Kerensky becoming Premier in name as well as in fact.
[46] *The Sixth Congress of the R.S.D.W.P.(b), August 1917, Protocols* (Moscow, 1958), p. 20.

Stalin also had some words for those who were beginning to wonder what was going to happen *after* power had been snatched from the feeble hands of the people who currently held it. He now raised the hope that was to sustain the Bolsheviks in their venture in October: they would not be alone; revolutionary currents were apparent and growing in the West. Hence it was necessary to have ties with the militant socialists there, for without them "the Russian Revolution would be easily choked to death by the combined forces of Russian and Western imperialists."

He had something reassuring for everybody. To those who worried about what Marx would say about socialists trying to conquer a country as backward as Russia, Stalin declared: "There is dogmatic Marxism and creative Marxism. . . . It is quite possible that Russia will be the country that will show the path to socialism. No country until now has enjoyed such freedom as Russia does. . . .[47] The base for our revolution is broader than in Western Europe. . . . In Germany the state . . . apparatus functions incomparably more efficiently than do those untried rulers from among our bourgeoisie. . . . One should reject the obsolete concept that only Europe can show us the right path."[48]

Taken together his speeches are full of inconsistencies and ambivalence. But Stalin was not speaking to a congress of logicians, and considering the audience and the time, his was a masterful performance. A recent defeat was painted as a triumph of Bolshevik moderation and political sagacity. The delegates, many of them not realizing clearly what they were doing, were nudged into approving preparations for an armed coup d'état. Sharp disagreements and discriminations that might easily have arisen were avoided, and the Congress presented an impressive show of unity. Most of the resolutions proposed by the Central Committee were accepted unanimously. As against their rival parties, the Bolsheviks were becoming a cohesive group with disciplined forces at their disposal.[49]

Stalin had risen in his comrades' esteem. He was not among the four men who secured most votes for the Central Committee, but the choice of Zinoviev, Kamenev, and Trotsky in addition to Lenin is easily explained: the Congress wanted to honor those who were sought by the

[47] Who would remind him that elsewhere he had bewailed the oppressive rule of the Russian bourgeoisie and landowners?

[48] *The Sixth Congress of the R.S.D.W.P.*, p. 250.

[49] One may express some doubts, though, as to this description of affairs at the Bolshevik-dominated naval base of Kronstadt. "The Kronstadt Soviet rules firmly. By its decree drunkenness is not tolerated and the penalty for it is confiscation of all goods and immediate dispatch to the front[!] . . . All the prostitutes have been sent out. Gambling has been forbidden. There have been cases when militiamen have turned their guns on gamblers who would run away and never go back to playing cards." *Ibid.*, p. 77.

authorities or in prison.[50] Among the Party officials Stalin was preferred to his future rival, and this is well attested by the first acts of the new Central Committee. In the voting for the editorial board of the Bolshevik newspaper Stalin received the most votes, and the motion that Trotsky, if released from jail, should be asked to join it was rejected eleven to ten.[51] In view of the now larger size of the Central Committee (twenty-seven full members, ten alternates), it was decided to elect a "narrow" subcommittee of ten to guide its work, and Stalin again had the highest number of votes for membership in this ancestor of the Politburo. Until October meetings of the small and the larger body were, however, usually chaired by Sverdlov, who assumed the functions of the Party's secretary.

The next important turn in the Bolsheviks' and the Revolution's affairs came toward the end of August. The "man on horseback" so long awaited, whether fearfully or with fervent hope, finally seemed to materialize, only to vanish in a few days: not a Cromwell or a Napoleon but one of those befuddled Russian generals who became infected by the politicians' indecision and florid oratory. What appears to have happened—the details are somewhat lost in the crossfire of charges and countercharges—was that Kerensky wanted the commander-in-chief, General Lavrenti Kornilov, to concentrate the army corps in readiness to march on Petrograd in the case of a Bolshevik uprising. The very brave but not very intelligent general was then persuaded by some conservative politicians that the Prime Minister wanted Kornilov to become dictator and make short shrift of the soviets. Kerensky realized with a shock that his general meant to supplant him, and he dismissed Kornilov. Kornilov in turn assumed the posture of savior of his country and ordered some army units to march on the capital. The march bogged down, and the agitators sent by the soviets had an easy job of persuading the soldiers that they should not become the instrument of counterrevolution. The *Putsch* fizzled out.

The Bolsheviks were the main beneficiaries of this tragicomedy. Their imprisoned leaders were freed, their military force (the Red Guards) were allowed to come out in the open, since even the most right-wing Mensheviks and Socialist Revolutionaries concurred that every conceivable force had to be mustered to defend the Revolution. In the aftermath of the Kornilov affair Kerensky lost whatever credit he had with the officer corps and the more disciplined units of the army. The temper

[50] Trotsky and his "interfaction" group were now formally admitted by the Bolsheviks. There was some discussion as to whether the two hiding heroes should not turn themselves in and disprove in court the enemies' slanders. Many Bolsheviks were unaware that the substance of the charges was correct. But Bukharin with that imprudence in speech which will stay with him made a slip which shows that he knew only too well.

[51] *Central Committee of the R.S.D.W.P.(b), Protocols* (Moscow, 1958), p. 4.

of the urban masses, oppressed by inflation and food shortages, became much more radical. And so in September the focal point of the Revolution, the Petrograd Soviet, reached a pro-Bolshevik majority and elected Trotsky as its chairman. Moscow followed the other capital's lead, and in some other industrial centers the Bolsheviks, together with their allies of the moment, the Left Socialist Revolutionaries, and occasional Anarchists or even maverick Mensheviks, also achieved majorities. The slogan "All power to the soviets" became relevant again. It was only a question of time before the Second Congress of the Soviets, scheduled to meet late in October, deposed the Menshevik and Socialist Revolutionary–dominated Central Executive Committee elected by the First Congress in June and installed a new one led by Bolsheviks.

"It would be naïve to wait until the Bolsheviks achieve 'formal' majority, no revolution has ever waited for that."[52] The Bolsheviks must *seize* power. This was the gist of the letters from Lenin discussed at the Central Committee meeting on September 15. Party officials were shaken out of their complacency by this bombshell from their leader, who—still in hiding, now in Finland—was seething with impatience and fury at the news that his followers apparently proposed to wait with folded arms for that moment when majority would be theirs. It would be criminal, he thought, to wait. There might be a successful repetition of the Kornilov plot; Kerensky might surrender Petrograd to the Germans and thus decapitate the Revolution. But over and above such contingencies the Bolsheviks had to demonstrate that they *were* different from the Mensheviks and the Socialist Revolutionaries, that they were real revolutionaries, not worrying about majorities, legalities, the inviolability of this or that. Lenin sensed that an act of force, an insurrection, was a psychological as well as a political necessity if Communism was to be born.

Stalin along with most other Party hierarchs was not enchanted by Lenin's outburst. To stake everything on an uprising now, when things were going so well, to risk a repetition of the July days! He proposed to temporize, acquaint local organizations with Lenin's views, discuss them at the next Central Committee meeting. The unfortunate Kamenev, who at this time was constantly getting into one trouble or another,[53] moved to reject Lenin's proposals outright. Lenin should be told that he might publish a pamphlet embodying his views! This far the Central Committee was not ready to go, but it was decided to burn all copies but one of the dangerous letters and to take steps to prevent any outbreaks by the Party's soldier and worker sympathizers.

[52] *Ibid.*, p. 57.
[53] In August there were rumors that some documents established his prewar links with the Okhrana. An intraparty commission presided over by the Menshevik Fyodor Dan exonerated him of all charges.

For some time afterward the Central Committee appeared almost as fearful of Lenin's returning to Petrograd as of another Kornilov's entering it at the head of a Cossack force. It was solicitude for his safety, they pleaded unconvincingly, that made them ban his premature return, and he as a disciplined revolutionary should obey. Frustrated, he lashed out at his followers by mail. Hearing that the Bolsheviks were ready to participate in a so-called Democratic Conference, another talk-fest among the parties by which the Provisional Government sought to prolong its agony, he exploded to his lieutenants: "You are nothing but a bunch of traitors and nincompoops unless you surround the Conference and arrest those scoundrels." Zinoviev, well known for his unheroic disposition, was believed to be a good influence on his reckless leader. Hearing that the two had become separated, the Central Committee grew alarmed. It voted that "it was wholly impermissible for Comrade Zinoviev to separate himself from Comrade Lenin." The former was invited for a consultation, obviously on how to bridle that demonic force.[54]

After a great historical event it is difficult for people to reconstruct precisely their anticipatory feelings, hopes, and fears. It is thus important for us to realize—and this does not come out clearly in any account of the October Revolution—that the Bolshevik Central Committee, while committed in principle to the armed uprising and driven eventually into approving it because of Lenin's frantic insistence, tacitly decided to hedge its bets. And this explains a great deal about the events of October 24–25, including Stalin's absence among the leading actors of the drama.

On October 10 the Central Committee held a fateful secret meeting, with only twelve of twenty-one members present. Lenin, in hiding in Petrograd since October 7, attended in disguise, wearing a wig. As in April, one man's will prevailed over his followers' fears and doubts. By ten votes to two (Zinoviev's and Kamenev's), it was voted that "armed uprising is the order of the day." But the Committee still did not answer categorically the question: When? *Presumably before October 20*, when the Congress of Soviets was scheduled to open. But the still hesitant and temporizing attitude of the majority is seen clearly when we consider the implications of another act by the committee on that historic night. It elected "for political guidance for the immediate future" a Political Bureau of seven (the first time this institution appears). It included, of course, Lenin, Trotsky, and Stalin, but also those two who had declared their opposition to the uprising, Zinoviev and Kamenev! The Politburo, all accounts agree, and quite correctly, did nothing toward the preparation of the great day, and in fact never met as such. Some guidance during the "immediate future"! It is clear,

[54] *Central Committee of the R.S.D.W.P.(b), Protocols*, p. 65.

though after October 25 everybody forgot it or pretended to, that the Party was taking out insurance against the future. If the coup failed it could always be claimed that the Party as a whole was not really involved, and some leaders would, it was hoped, escape repression and remain at large since they could prove they had been against the venture.

But such calculations were at first rendered inoperative by the veritable panic into which the two intended "reserve" leaders were thrown —Kamenev because violence and precipitate action were not in his nature, and Zinoviev because he was a bully when on top and a coward in an emergency (one must record a rare agreement between Trotsky and Stalinist writers on this count), and they did not keep their objections to themselves. They circularized Party organizations with fearful visions of the forthcoming disaster: we don't have the right, they argued, to risk everything on this one throw of dice. Don't think that this time we will get off as easily as we did in July. Their fear had huge eyes: the disorganized and tottering Provisional Government was seen as commanding powerful forces in the capital: five thousand excellently armed military students. And they knew how to fight because of their class origins, added the unfortunate protestors in a rather indelicate hint that this knowledge was not widespread among Bolshevik partisans. And remember the Cossacks! And the artillery regiments surrounding the capital! One should not commit this folly when we are going to have a majority in the Soviets and probably as many as one-third of the seats in the future Constituent Assembly.

At a meeting of leading Bolsheviks on October 16 Lenin had to listen not only to another variant of this dire prediction and lament from the two dissenters, but to more practical objections from the others: there was no central organ to lead the uprising; in some regions of the city workers were apathetic or even hostile to an insurrection. Stalin endorsed Lenin's position but in a rather reserved way, without much apparent faith in success. "One must make sure to choose just the right day for the uprising," he said—a somewhat fatuous remark in the circumstances, as was also Sverdlov's contribution: the previous decision to have a rising should not, he thought, be reversed but only amended.

The two dissenters now compounded their treason in Lenin's eyes by conveying the news of Bolshevik intentions and of their opposition to *New Life*, published by Maxim Gorky and then strongly anti-Bolshevik. The smoldering volcano that was Lenin now erupted: Kamenev and Zinoviev were strikebreakers, he wrote from his hideout to the Central Committee. No one can betray you as shamelessly as one of your own. Throw them out of the Central Committee, out of the Party!

As far as Zinoviev was concerned, a Committee member contemptuously observed at the meeting of October 17, the demand was irrelevant: Zinoviev was hiding from his comrades and not doing any Party work. Trotsky, on the other hand, was all for an exemplary punishment of his brother-in-law Kamenev. Amid the frayed tempers Stalin once again emerged as conciliator and voice of moderation. Let Lenin's recriminations be considered at a future and better attended meeting of the Central Committee, he suggested. Kamenev and Zinoviev had now seen the error of their ways. It did not solve anything to exclude people from the Party in the heat of the moment. Let them promise to mend their ways. One must preserve the unity of the Party. When it was voted to exclude Kamenev from the editorial board of the Party organ, Stalin offered his own resignation, which was not accepted.

He was accumulating political capital for the future. One day Kamenev and Zinoviev, frightened by Trotsky, would help him achieve leadership of the Party. But it would be ridiculous to credit him at the time with such foresight and calculation. He *was* trying to preserve the unity of the Party, and to make sure that if the insurrection failed there would be something and somebody to start buidling again.

The same consideration must have been responsible for his detachment from the events of October 24 and 25, when the Provisional Government was overthrown and the Winter Palace stormed in the Bolshevik coup d'état. It was a source of embarrassment to the future makers of the Stalin legend that none of the dramatic political and military actions of the day can be associated with his name, that while every contemporary account is filled primarily with Trotsky, but also with various Podvoiskys and Chudnovskys, Stalin, who evidently spent most of the historic two days in the editorial offices of the paper *The Worker's Path*, is barely mentioned. But at the time, his absence, as well as that of some other Bolshevik notables, was taken as quite natural, certainly not as a matter for reproach. Though there was no actual disposition to that effect (the insurrection was far from being a carefully planned and conducted conspiracy) there was undoubtedly a tacit agreement that some Bolshevik leaders should not be directly connected with the armed uprising.

It was disingenuous of Trotsky to write of Stalin in those days, "The cautious schemer preferred to stay on the fence at the crucial moment."[55] Each Bolshevik leader had a specific task assigned to him. Stalin's was to stay away from the fighting, to be held in reserve.[56] And up to the very last moment the Central Committee was anxious to avoid

---

[55] Trotsky, p. 234.

[56] How deeply ingrained in the Bolshevik consciousness was the notion of "reserve centers" for the plot was shown in the Great Purge trials of the 1930s. Several of the accused were charged with belonging to such centers, i.e., of lying low but ready to spring to action if Kamenev, Zinoviev, Bukharin, etc., were unmasked as plotting against Stalin. The charges were false and absurd, but they reflected the psychology and experience of 1917.

a too direct identification with the uprising. In its meeting on October 24 it discussed a very practical problem: Where should the Bolsheviks establish alternate headquarters for the uprising if the government troops seized the Smolny Institute, the current seat of the Petrograd Soviet and of the staff of the uprising?[57] They settled on the SS. Peter and Paul fortress, whose garrison was solidly pro-Bolshevik. But Sverdlov insisted and obtained that the man in charge of the second headquarters would *not* be a member of the Central Committee but a Bolshevik of lesser standing.

With the Central Committee first dragging its feet and then trying to mask its complicity in the uprising, the center of the revolutionary stage belonged to the Military Revolutionary Committee of the Petrograd Soviet, and the proscenium was occupied by Trotsky. This committee was a convenient instrument for the uprising, for though it was dominated by the Party it was not exclusively Bolshevik in composition and was presided over by a Left Socialist Revolutionary, the eighteen-year-old Lazimir. Trotsky was of course its real head and director. Lenin inspired the insurrection, but since he did not emerge from his hideout until the night of October 24–25, its real planner and head was Trotsky. Lenin's actual schemes for the uprising verged on incoherence: at one time he favored its beginning in Moscow, at another somewhere else. He opposed any delay. Trotsky believed and maintained that it should take place in Petrograd and that its chances of success and acceptance would be infinitely greater if it coincided with the opening of the Congress of the Soviets, now scheduled for October 25. The Congress, with its pro-Bolshevik majority, would be able to throw a cloak of legitimacy over the act of force and maximize the Mensheviks' and Socialist Revolutionaries' indecision and paralysis of will.[58] There can be no question that this insight of Trotsky's saved the Bolsheviks' enterprise from disaster; it was true that those politicians and soldiers who were outraged by the armed seizure of the capital were thrown into uncertainty by the Congress' legitimizing the act, and when they recovered it was too late. Lenin wrote repeatedly in those days about the "art of insurrection," but Trotsky practiced it. Apart from being the brains of the undertaking, he was one of its main actors: one speech of his, and the soldiers of the SS. Peter and Paul garrison who had opposed the insurrection declared themselves on the Bolshevik side. He spoke elsewhere—here trying to infuse badly needed martial fervor in military units supporting the cause, there reassuring the Mensheviks and Social-

[57] Kamenev, who had skulked back, showed his continued diffidence by suggesting they should be on a Bolshevik man-o'-war!
[58] One of the more outrageous falsifications by Soviet historiography has been to assimilate Trotsky's position with that of Zinoviev and Kamenev.

ist Revolutionaries in the Soviet who were beginning to worry that the Bolsheviks might again start something.

Stalin's only ostensible contribution in those momentous days was made with his pen. In an article published on October 20 he poured scorn on the neurotics from *New Life* and their ilk who were asking anxiously what the Bolsheviks were up to: he was almost playful in his implication that they would know soon enough; the considerate, temperate Stalin of the intraparty councils becomes in this instance vituperative and vulgar. Gorky, at odds with the Bolsheviks, is compared to those extinct volcanoes of the revolutionary movement—like Plekhanov, Zasulich, Kropotkin—who wring their hands over the Bolsheviks' irresponsible behavior. But on the very eve of October 24, in an editorial in *The Worker's Path*, he was again ambiguous and noncommittal. Power must pass to the Soviets: unite and organize. He addressed the famous "masses" already being sent out to occupy strategic points of the city: "The stronger, more united, and more impressive in your might you are, the more *peacefully* the old regime will yield power to the new."[59] This was an attempt to deceive the enemy to the very end, but expressed also a certain hedging by the Bolshevik *politicians:* if there were unexpected and effective resistance, perhaps the takeover would have to be accomplished by the Congress of Soviets.

And so came the great day, October 25. The "armed masses" were certainly not "impressive in their might," and yet the takeover of strategic points in the city took place *almost* peacefully. Kerensky escaped in the morning to the front, hoping to bring back troops with him to subdue the capital. The headless government assembled in the Winter Palace, defended by some military students and by women's battalions. In front of it milled Bolshevik soldiers and sailors, the bolder among them squeezing into the building, where they were disarmed by the defenders, but in the process haranguing them about the futility of resistance. The same conclusion was reached late at night by the besieged ministers, who gathered around the cabinet table as if awaiting a photographer to record the historic moment when the only democratic government in Russia's history yielded not so much to force as to its own weakness and indecision. Instead it was the Bolshevik leader Antonov-Ovseenko who finally broke in, at the head of some Red Guards. There was the exit line of that rhetoric which between February and October had been thought mistakenly to be a substitute for policies: "Members of the Provisional Government submit to force and surrender in order to avoid bloodshed," they said. The Provisional Government collapsed with barely a whimper.

"The Provisional Government, headed by Kerensky, was dead and awaited only the broom of history to sweep it away," announced an

[59] Stalin, III, 390. My italics.

exultant Trotsky to the Petrograd Soviet the same afternoon. He added the incredible but true detail that "until now" there has not been a single fatality on the revolutionary side. At night Lenin announced the beginning of the new era to the Second Congress of Soviets. The Menshevik and Socialist Revolutionary minority in that body were prepared. They had ready a resolution condemning the whole disgraceful business. And after reading it, they trooped out of Smolny, being assured on their departure by Trotsky that they were marching straight "onto the rubbish heap of history." Next day the now overwhelmingly pro-Bolshevik and enthusiastic Congress approved Lenin's "decrees" on peace and on land. They declared the Bolsheviks' determination to conclude peace, expropriated all landlords' and church lands, and invited peasant committees to arrange for their distribution. The peasant masses, still following the right wing of the Socialist Revolutionaries, would thus be hard put to oppose the new regime, which proposed to do immediately what their leaders had talked about: bring their sons and husbands home and give them more land. To assure their survival, the Bolsheviks had to make the anarchy which gripped the land even deeper and more universal.

The man who would extirpate the last traces of that anarchy, and who upon the foundation of this most anarchic of all revolutions would build the most autocratic state, was included in the list of the new rulers—a rather grandiloquent term for the group that on October 26 controlled Petrograd and its environs. In the list of fifteen People's Commissars headed by Lenin, Joseph Djugashvili-Stalin appears as Commissar of Nationalities. The hastily improvised all-Bolshevik list already showed an element of political calculation: it was recognized that anti-Semitism was still a potent force in rural Russia; hence with the exception of Trotsky, Commissar for Foreign Affairs, there were no Jews and such luminaries as Sverdlov, Zinoviev, and Kamenev were not included. When it came to the designation of Chairman of the Executive Committee of the Soviets, the closest thing to titular head of state, Kamenev's origin as well as his past sins were felt to be of less importance than his gift for mollifying non-Bolshevik socialists and nourishing their illusions that Lenin and his followers would mend their ways. So Kamenev was elevated to the position which in the last mad twelve months had been occupied by people as diverse as Nicholas Romanov and "Karl Marx" Chkheidze.

The wheel of fortune turned even more fantastically in Stalin's case. Only eleven months before he had been a political exile, a recluse in a Siberian hamlet brooding over life's injustices and wondering whether his comrades would ever take him back. Now he was a key figure of the movement that no longer merely aspired, but actually had begun, to remake Russia and the world.

~⁄(5)~⁄

THE
TASTE
OF
POWER

Stalin was a man of uncommonly good sense and unusually vile as well as brooding temper. These characteristics came out vividly in his immediate as well as his later reactions to the October Revolution. On the morrow of victory some Bolsheviks were naturally exultant. Others, especially many of the new minister-commissars, were panic-stricken by their new and unfamiliar duties. Some complained to Lenin that their talents were in the political rather than the administrative sphere. One, Teodorovich, charged with perhaps the most unenviable post of all, the Ministry of Food Supplies, actually tried to flee, and when brought back, resigned, pleading that his bad health required him to go for a cure in Siberia!

Stalin's gloomy and apprehensive mood in the hour of triumph is described by Stanislaw Pestkovsky, one of those invaluable raconteurs for whom the drama of a great historic occasion does not obscure its details and nuances. Having participated in the armed takeover of the telecommunications centers under a fellow Pole, Felix Dzerzhinsky, Pestkovsky then sought a job with another fellow countryman, Vyacheslav Menzhinsky, then Commissar of Finance and the future head of the political police. There were not many job-seekers in those days, and the overjoyed Menzhinsky proposed to make Pestkovsky Governor of the State Bank. But its employees refused to have him, even though he boasted a diploma from the London School of Economics. He then went to Trotsky. Trotsky did not fancy Poles; there was no job in his ministry, he tactfully explained, that was worthy of a man of Pestkovsky's qualifications. Trotsky himself took on Foreign Affairs only to have more time for Party work. Next the persistent Pestkovsky tried Stalin: he would, he said, set up his ministry for him. He found a free room in Smolny, attached a card on the door reading COMMISSARIAT FOR NATIONALITIES, procured a typist, and borrowed three thousand rubles for current expenses (from Trotsky, who "liberated" the Foreign Ministry safe). "Comrade Stalin, here is your commissariat," he said proudly to the future dictator. He "emitted some nondescript grunt, either of approval or of dissatisfaction," writes our poor storyteller, who even in 1922 should have known better.[1] He then became Stalin's assistant. But working for Stalin was no fun. While other Party potentates were chatty and full of stories of the exciting doings in the Central Committee, Stalin was gloomy and taciturn.[2]

His gloom reflected not only the worries and confusion of a time when the Bolsheviks' power still hung by a thread and when nobody had the slightest notion of how to start administering the country. In the mood of many Bolsheviks of those days one also discerns a certain resentment of Lenin and Trotsky: Why did they get them into this predicament, where they had to tackle this unimaginable mess on their own rather than behind the comfortable screen of a coalition government? In Stalin's complex psychology there was also an element of envy. Things had gone far more easily than anyone could have predicted, and this spectacular success was due not only to the "theorists" Lenin and Trotsky, but also to the unspectacular yet vital hard labor of "practitioners" like himself. People were already forgetting this. Two and a half years later Stalin was to reveal this residue of bitterness at a birthday celebration for Lenin held in Moscow. Other speakers there emulated each other in flattering their leader; Stalin discoursed on Lenin's modesty, as evidenced in his readiness to admit his mistakes, one of which was the insistence on a premature uprising in 1917 "while we practitioners thought that such tactics were inexpedient,"[3] and insisted that the uprising coincide with the convocation of the Congress of Soviets. And Vladimir Ilyich "with a cunning smile" had to admit that the "practitioners" had been right. It was a clever thrust—Lenin hated excessive flattery[4]—but it was also more than that. We shall see that at

[1] Stanislaw Pestkovsky, "About the October Days," *The Proletarian Revolution*, No. 10 (October 1922), pp. 98–103.

[2] In 1937 Pestkovsky was to share the fate of so many of Stalin's former friends and associates.

[3] Stalin, *Collected Works* (Moscow, 1946–52), IV, 317.

[4] He walked out of the meeting when comrades started to eulogize him.

the very end of his life the deified dictator continued to show rancor at being a successor to and not the maker of the Communist world.

The immediate concern in the days following the October coup was, of course, the survival of the nucleus of Bolshevik power in Petrograd. Kerensky had fled to the front, whence he hoped to bring troops to subdue the new capital, but meanwhile the Bolsheviks encountered serious armed opposition in the old, and heavy fighting ensued in Moscow. In the circumstances the Bolsheviks felt constrained to negotiate with other socialist parties: would they not help them against *counterrevolution*? The Bolsheviks did not mean to seize power for themselves alone, they now said, and perhaps a place could be found in the government for representatives of other truly revolutionary parties.

For Lenin the whole purpose of these negotiations was to gain time, make sure that the wretched Mensheviks and Socialist Revolutionaries would not join the anti-Bolshevik forces while the issue was in doubt. "The negotiations should be considered as a diplomatic coverup for military operations." But there were other Bolsheviks—epitomized by (who else?) Kamenev—who genuinely believed that the Soviet government should be a broad coalition of all genuine Socialist parties. The Bolsheviks had made their point, Kerensky had been overthrown, and why not invite such worthy if occasionally misguided revolutionaries as Martov and Chernov to share the appalling burden of power? The negotiations on the Bolshevik side were conducted by Kamenev, assisted by David Ryazanov.

Inclusion of the latter was good proof of how desperately the Bolsheviks needed to nourish their opponents' illusions and, if worse came to worst, to get their support. For Ryazanov was a white elephant, a Bolshevik with genuine democratic instincts. For years he would not so much shock as amuse Bolshevik gatherings by denouncing terror, by chastising Trotsky and even Lenin for their authoritarian ways. Even in the beginning of the Stalin era this fearless man tried to protect and support former Mensheviks and Socialist Revolutionaries by employing them in the Marx-Engels Institute, which he headed. "No one here takes Ryazanov seriously" became a standard saying at Party Conferences and Congresses, for how indeed could one take seriously a man who preached toleration and strict observance of legal and humanitarian criteria?

The negotiators now brought the other side's representations before the Bolshevik Central Committee. They included the widening of the government's base, but also a request that Lenin and Trotsky be excluded from any future socialist coalition. Ryazanov was ready to agree even to the last condition. "We have already made a mistake by leading the [new] government." Kamenev, while unwilling to go that far, still favored a coalition with the Mensheviks and Socialist Revolutionaries.

By the beginning of November, with Moscow in Bolshevik hands and with Kerensky's attempt to recapture Petrograd a debacle, Lenin's position hardened. He and the majority of the Central Committee, including Trotsky and Stalin, demanded that Kamenev and those who sided with him submit. Thereupon five of the Central Committee members and five of the commissars resigned: "We leave the Central Committee in the moment of victory. . . . We cannot watch without protest as the policy of the ruling group of the Central Committee leads to the loss by the workers' party of the fruits of their victory, and to the crushing of the proletariat."[5] The majority denounced them as deserters, and recalled previous and similar behavior on the part of Kamenev and Zinoviev. Once more these two were threatened with dismissal from the Party unless they submitted. And submit they did, with only Ryazanov making a spirited rejoinder that it was against the principle of revolutionary social democracy to curtail criticism, and to maintain that any individual, even Lenin or Trotsky, was indispensable. Again Lenin was lenient after the dissenters surrendered, and they were readmitted to the Central Committee. But Kamenev was removed as titular head of the state and replaced by Sverdlov. Lenin's Party had made its first decisive step toward the one-party state. Some Left Socialist Revolutionaries were coopted into the government, but they did not stay long.

Thus the crisis passed. But crisis was to become the normal condition of Party life, and so it has been into our day. Never would a Soviet leader be able to relax, confident that changes or challenges to his power would develop through the normal political channels. Threats to him and his policies would always be lurking on the left or the right. When Lenin fell sick, or Khrushchev went on a trip or vacation, a new combination of forces and personalities would immediately crystallize in their absence and attempt to prevent the absent leader from resuming his position. Communism has never shed its birthmark of conspiracy, not even though the Party became a mighty bureaucratic institution ruling a powerful state. The dictator, or the oligarchs, can dispose of powers undreamed of by rulers of any other state, but they have never been able to achieve security.

The first post-victory crisis found Stalin on Lenin's side, and he was now considered an indispensable organizer and committeeman. Thus, at the session of the Central Committee of November 29 which appointed several subcommittees for dealing with current work, Stalin was put on practically all the important ones: the editorial board of *Pravda*, the committee to supervise the Bolshevik press, the group to deal with the Ukrainian question. He had inestimable gifts as a committeeman and organizer: brevity and the ability to get to the point.

---

[5] *Minutes of the Central Committee of R.S.D.W.P.(b)*, p. 135.

The Soviet government, as we now might call it, had already begun to display the characteristics with which we are now so familiar. It was not a government of or by the Soviets, despite its name: the huge unwieldy Congress of Soviets, though important on a few occasions in the early years of the regime, functioned mainly as a platform for the government's declarations, and not as a parliamentary or deliberative body. Its Executive Committee, soon to grow quite large, was to be the collective titular head of state, its chairmen men of little importance (Sverdlov's and, later, Kalinin's importance derived from their roles in the Party). The Council of Commissars was at least until 1922 an administrative body at most, the importance of its members again measured not by their ministries, but by their standing in the Party. Thus the center of gravity, the place where the weightiest decisions were made, was the Central Committee. And the most important administrative rules were in turn worked out by its various subgroups.

Among the adventurers who, guided by Lenin's vision, had seized power there were two avenues of advance: one through oratory, the other through committee work. Oratory—propaganda if you will—made the Revolution. Oratory was in ascendance as long as the Revolution needed to be defended: crowds of famished workers, of semimutinous soldiers would be galvanized into enthusiastic support of Soviet power, not only by Trotsky or Zinoviev, but all over Russia by a multitude of Bolshevik agitators on whom the oratorical gift seems suddenly and miraculously to have descended. The Revolution was saved as much by the tongue as by the sword, by the fact that those who spoke on its behalf did so with more conviction and fire than those who spoke against it. But the new Russia, the new structure of power, was built by the committeemen, by the men who saw the enduring problems of power in a cold unemotional light, who impressed their colleagues by prosaic practicality and dissipated their suspicions by a readiness to undertake unrewarding and unglamorous tasks. Such a man was Stalin.

☆☆☆

THE conflict between the romantic and the practical, between the vision of Bolshevism as the promise of a new world and its existence as a new system of power built upon old foundations, was epitomized by the sequence of events by which Russia was led to sign the Treaty of Brest-Litovsk. Nothing in the history of Communism, it can be asserted, was to be of equal importance. October 25, 1917, was the day of the Bolshevik Revolution; March 3, 1918, when the agreement (if such it can be called), was signed in that dingy provincial town, was the real day of founding the Bolshevik-Communist state. The political repercussions of the conclusion of the peace were enormous. The last trappings of revolutionary democracy disappeared. Soviet Russia became a one-party state. Lenin now not only led but towered over his followers. Trotsky's star, for all his glorious role in the Civil War, would never again shine as brightly.

Even those effects of the treaty and the events that led to it are dwarfed by the change in the nature of the Bolsheviks. With all the qualifications already stated, they went into the Revolution as ideological zealots. They emerged from the experience of Brest-Litovsk as politicians. Many of them still felt in the vanguard of world revolution, but all of them now realized that they were primarily masters of Russia. Rapidly there now developed those state institutions which even the most cynical among them had believed they were casting aside forever when they seized power: a standing army with an officer corps, a bureaucracy, a *permanent* political police. "Defensist" was the worst term of reproach one could use against a Bolshevik before October. After April, it would be "Soviet," and very soon unabashedly "Russian patriotism," which they would seek to evoke and which in fact saved Russia for them.

The Bolsheviks had to make peace. But how? As insistent as they had been before October that the war must be stopped, they decried violently any idea of a separate peace with the "German militarists." The most sanguine among them hoped that their own revolution would spark a European one; the more prudent believed that the governments of the belligerent powers, when confronted by an appeal from the new revolutionary regime, would be forced by their own people to go to the conference table. Yet this latter hope, which from our perspective appears as one of the more realistic premises on which the Bolsheviks sought power, was soon disproved by the facts. The Entente governments saw in the Russian Revolution the work of German agents and nihilists with whom they would have no truck; buoyed by the recent accession of the United States to their alliance, they proposed to persevere. To the German high command, now the decisive factor on the other side, the Russian situation offered the possibility of shifting the bulk of its forces from the front there to the West to deal a crushing blow to the French and British. Because of the obvious and now irretrievable incapacity of the Russian army to continue the war, the German generals did not propose to let Russia off easily, certainly nothing so ridiculous as a "peoples' peace" with no annexations or indemnities.

Having already thus compromised their original position by sitting down to negotiations, not with the representatives of the German and

Austrian workers but with those of the Emperors of Germany and Austria, the Soviet delegates made an even more painful discovery: their protagonists intended to carve out what today would be called satellite states from the body of the dead Russian Empire. It was the Bolsheviks' own principle of national self-determination that they proposed to put into practice, the German General Hoffman jovially explained, and demanded that the Soviet government yield Russian Poland, the Baltic provinces, and, toward the end of the negotiations the most devastating of all, the Ukraine.

Until this point, the Bolsheviks had been living in two unreal worlds: one of their own phraseology and messianic expectations, the other of the Russia of 1917, with nothing but political phantoms opposing them and interfering with their designs. "Until now our enemies have been miserable and pathetic . . . idiot Romanov . . . windbag Kerensky . . . a handful of military students and bourgeoisie. Now we have a giant against us." Thus mercilessly Lenin painted the picture for those of his colleagues who refused to come down to earth.

Whatever had remained of the Russian army's organization and discipline (admittedly not very much) was destroyed by the Bolsheviks in the first days of their power when, fearful of a generals' countercoup, Lenin called for the front-line regiments to elect representatives to fraternize with corresponding German units. He now knew that it was madness to expect any resistance from the Russian soldier if the Germans launched an offensive, and foolishness to try to stop the demobilization of the anarchic rabble which once had been the Russian army.

But the opposition Lenin encountered now over the matter of the peace was ferocious. Some cried about their betrayed hopes. "We are turning the Party into a dungheap," shouted Bukharin and burst into tears at one point. Others saw catastrophic consequences in such a capitulation. Russia would be stripped of all her territorial accessions since the sixteenth century. She herself might become a puppet state of Germany. Aroused national fury would sweep the Bolsheviks away. Better to fight the Germans with bare hands in a revolutionary war and perish than to make a peace in disgrace as puppets of the Kaiser and his generals. Lenin, said Dzerzhinsky, one of the most fearless and fanatical Bolsheviks, is showing himself as fainthearted as Kamenev and Zinoviev were in October.

On January 11 the Central Committee, after a tempestuous session, accepted a compromise position between Lenin's insistence on signing *any* peace, and that of the advocates of revolutionary resistance. This was Trotsky's formula of "neither war nor peace." The Russian plenipotentiaries would refuse to accede to the Germans' demands, but would declare that Russia was concluding the war and demobilizing her army. It was hope against hope: maybe the German soldiers would in such circumstances refuse to advance against their nonresisting Russian brothers, maybe their generals would fear to order them to. "The policy of Comrade Trotsky is no policy at all," Stalin said brutally. In October they had been told that one word, peace, would start a revolution in the West. Well, where was it? He supported Lenin's position, but his speech contained a barely discernible reproach of his leader. *Who* had told them in October that the word peace would start a revolution in the West?

In one of those astounding ironies of history, the Bolsheviks' desperate position now enabled them to do speedily and expeditiously what otherwise would have been fraught with great danger: chase out the Constituent Assembly. This body, to which generations of Russian revolutionaries and liberals had looked so longingly and hopefully, was elected after the Bolshevik coup but, as expected, contained an anti-Bolshevik majority composed largely of right-wing Socialist Revolutionaries. It met on January 5 and after one day of oratory reminiscent of the pre-October days was chased out by the sailors. That on the one hand this step led to no democratic soul-searching among the Bolsheviks and on the other encountered no serious resistance must be attributed mainly to the gravity of the overall situation. With the Germans likely to occupy Petrograd in a few weeks, the Zinovievs and Kamenevs had other things to fear than the wrath of the Russian people over this dispersal of the only democratically elected national body in their history.

On January 28 at Brest-Litovsk, Trotsky launched what he thought was a bombshell: Russia was leaving the war without signing a peace. Since the people across the table from him were old-fashioned diplomats and generals of a different mien than their Hitlerite successors, this declaration was greeted with some confusion and embarrassment rather than with hilarity. But neither was General Hoffman a Gandhi. On February 16 the Germans announced they would resume armed operations.[6] On February 18, by seven votes to six with one abstention, the Bolshevik Central Committee decided to seek peace. Five minutes of German artillery barrage, said Stalin, and not a single Russian soldier would stay at his post. He impatiently described Trotsky's proposals for a further delay as belonging in the realm of fiction rather than of politics.

Informed of the Soviets' readiness, the Germans still could not deny themselves the pleasure of teaching them a lesson, and they began to march. Stalin's prophecy proved in fact overoptimistic. The Russian soldiers had not even the will to flee, and whole battalions surrendered

---

[6] On February 1, 1918, the Russian calendar jumped thirteen days and from this point conforms with Western usage.

to single Germans. A new German ultimatum specified that the Soviets had to agree within forty-eight hours to negotiations that must not last more than three days. Lenin added his own ultimatum to the Central Committee: either they accept this or he would go.

On March 3 the peace treaty was signed. Russia lost the Ukraine, Finland, and her Polish and Baltic territories. At the meeting of the Petrograd Soviet, the Bolsheviks were assailed by their hitherto allies, the Left Socialist Revolutionaries, with shouts of "Traitors!" "German spies!" "They have sold out our country!" Several Bolsheviks, including Trotsky, resigned their positions and had to be begged to keep their resignations secret so as not to advertise the Bolshevik division and perhaps provoke another German move.

The intra-Bolshevik discussions of those desperate days offer an interesting sidelight on Stalin's already considerable ability to maneuver, to restrain his own ferocious temper, and to appease the opponent. His first reaction to the announcement that Trotsky and others were resigning was that they should be thrown out of the Party. But Lenin, usually so impatient and obsessed, was now the master diplomat that he would remain until the end of the Civil War. This was not, he realized, a question of overawing a few timid souls, as it had been with Zinoviev and Kamenev in October. It was imperative to heal the rift, otherwise the Party would divide and die. So he soothed Trotsky's feelings. There could be no question of losing the services of such valuable men, he implored. And Stalin beat a hasty retreat. He did not intend to blame anyone, he could not help expressing his pain at the behavior of those comrades; hadn't they realized they were irreplaceable?

For everyone concerned Brest-Litovsk was a veritable trauma. It left a permanent scar on the psychology of the Soviet rulers. The memory of those days was with Stalin in the summer of 1939, when he sought an understanding with Hitler, and in the spring of 1941, when he clung to the forlorn hope that Germany could be propitiated and would not strike.

The trauma of Brest was intensified by the events of the two weeks following the signing of the peace treaty on March 3. We have but a very imperfect knowledge of them—all the main actors chose subsequently to pretend to have forgotten them, and only a very distorted version of those dramatic days came out in the Great Purge trial of 1938.

The peace treaty had been signed but not yet ratified. Lenin faced danger on two fronts: the Germans might still march on and seize Petrograd; but there was a threat nearer home: the Left Socialist Revolutionaries were contemplating a coup against him, for they now were convinced he was a German agent. There was evidently some sentiment along the same line among *Bolshevik* opponents of the peace treaty, headed by Bukharin. Already in January one member of the Central

Committee had blurted that they must take over power *without* Lenin. The Seventh Congress of the Bolshevik Party assembled on March 6 in secrecy and amid rumors that such a coup might be forthcoming. Only sixty-nine persons attended it, and of those, thirty-two were denied the right to vote. This can be partly explained by the chaos in the country which prevented many delegates from reaching the capital and by the consequent difficulty of verifying others' mandates. But it is also clear that some delegates (such as Ryazanov) were disqualified because it was feared they would be against Lenin—Bukharin's antitreaty position was probably shared by the majority of the Party members. ☆☆☆

STALIN'S whereabouts during those anxious days is something of a mystery. His official chronology states that he participated in the work of the Seventh Congress. But this is palpably untrue for the Congress report published in 1923 lists him among neither the speakers nor the delegates. That Lenin would have dispensed with the services of such an important supporter except for some very special reason is most unlikely. Everything might have depended on one speech or one vote. So the implication is very strong that with real fear of a coup during the Congress, Stalin and some others were told to stay away (Kamenev's name is also missing from the proceedings), in order to be able to reconstruct the regime if Lenin and Sverdlov were seized.

Bukharin's speech at the Congress was a flaming appeal for a revolutionary war against the Germans. He accused Lenin of fostering the illusion that the treaty would provide a breathing spell for the Soviets, and there was an innuendo that Lenin himself did not believe it, and that the treaty would turn Russia proper into a satellite of the German warlords. Had Bukharin come to feel momentarily that his leader was obligated to the Germans? He was, as we have seen, one of the few Bolsheviks who knew the truth about the German money. But Lenin responded in a major speech—the best of his career—which while it did not alter his opponents' position, must have made them ashamed of questioning their leader's revolutionary probity. "Yes, we shall live to see the world revolution, but until now it has been a beautiful fairy-tale. . . . Does a serious revolutionary believe in fairytales?"[7] The Bolsheviks must learn discipline, for otherwise they would be ground under the German heel and would continue to be so until the nation

[7] *The Seventh Congress of the Russian Communist Party, Stenographic Report* (Moscow, 1923), p. 26.

learned to fight, until it had an army that did not run away. Lenin carried the day and, until his fatal illness, no Bolshevik from now on dared to think of overthrowing him.

Amid all the anxiety and strain the Congress found time to rename the Party. As Lenin had desired since 1914, "Social Democrat" was cast aside like "a child's soiled shirt" and in its place was now the Russian Communist Party (b).[8] The absent Stalin was reelected to the Central Committee and made a member of the commission to rewrite the Party's program. He received fewer votes than before. The memory of his venomous words against them still rankled some "Left Communists" (i.e., the supporters of Bukharin's anti-Brest position). ☆☆☆

T HE shift of the Soviet government to Moscow, which took place on March 10, was an equally symbolic act. We can now appreciate the symbolism as twofold. St. Petersburg had represented Russia joining the mainstream of European, Western culture. Now in Moscow, the new rulers, like the Tsars before Peter the Great, resided in the Kremlin, sought their inspiration in Russian history, made Russian nationalism the mainstay of their power. As Petrograd, the city on the Neva embodied the Russian *revolutionary* tradition. Much of that tradition would be destroyed by Stalin, and Moscow once more would become synonymous with autocracy, while Leningrad, the former capital's third incarnation, was treated with suspicion and conscious neglect, as if Stalin somehow felt it might rise against him.

But such perspectives were mercifully hidden when Lenin and his lieutenants hastily left Petrograd. For this was not an orderly transfer but a veritable flight, and it was arranged in deep secrecy. There was still the danger of the Germans' bagging the whole Soviet government, and the latter was far from being the master of the birthplace of the Revolution. The city was virtually in the hands of armed sailors whose loyalty was at least dubious, since some of them were partisans of the Left Socialist Revolutionaries while others were outright bandits, and practically all of them would have fought the removal of the government had they known in advance. In October there had been a rumor that Kerensky's government contemplated such a flight and a "decapitation of the Revolution," and it had been one of the most effective arguments

[8] The (b) stands for "of the Bolsheviks." This letter—so redolent of history, so indissolubly associated with Lenin—was dropped from the name in 1952, a small but symbolic expression of the resentment which the by then aged Stalin bore toward his great predecessor.

in mobilizing the sailors on the Bolshevik side. So the first act of the Communist regime was to flee from the very people who had enabled it to carry the day on October 25 and who had dispersed the Constituent Assembly. In a sense, it fled from the Revolution. ☆☆☆

I N Moscow Stalin began his administrative career, properly speaking. The first steps were rather harrowing. In those infant days of the Communist state each ministry was headed by a "collegium," i.e., a committee with the commissar considered only first among equals. While there was supposed to be a discipline of some sort within the Party, the notion of what today would be called "participatory democracy" was still prevalent, as it was in the Red Army, where officers were at first elected by the rank and file. "In the very office of the commissar mass meetings took place one after another. The collective of the employed [i.e., all employees including janitors] having still an unfortunate idea of the constitution of the republic attempted to arrogate to itself the right to conduct the foreign policy of Russia."[9] The collegium of the Commissariat of Nationalities was a miniature Tower of Babel, since it comprised representatives of the many nationalities of the former Empire: Jews, Tatars, Poles, Letts, etc. For most of them the official policy of the moment—i.e., granting each nationality the right to self-determination—was uncongenial, and though in most cases the whole problem had been rendered academic by the German occupation, they still quarreled and disputed, with quotations from Marx, Lenin, and Rosa Luxemburg. The regime had already begun to use drastic measures to restore some semblance of social discipline,[10] but nobody had yet invented a way to stop the Communists from talking. To a man with Stalin's temperament, this continuous talk was unendurable. One can believe Pestkovsky's story that when Stalin was unable to stand it any longer, he would leave the deliberations at his ministry and seek refuge at some neighboring apartment, where he would smoke and brood.

For actual policymaking his ministry had very limited scope. The most important nationality problem of all—that of the Ukraine—was solved for the time being by a fait accompli. The Germans had chased out the Ukrainian Bolsheviks, and the new regime in Kiev was at first not recognized by the Soviets. As late as March 14, in a published

[9] Ivan Maisky, *Foreign Policy of the Russian Soviet Federated Republic* (Moscow, 1923), p. 20.
[10] Ryazanov accused Trotsky of ordering the execution of six innocent people. *The Seventh Congress of the Russian Communist Party, Stenographic Report*, p. 113.

article, Stalin expressed the hope that the German-supported regime might be overthrown by a popular pro-Bolshevik uprising and "that a patriotic war begun in the Ukraine had every right to count on a whole-hearted support of all Soviet Russia."[11] And he allowed himself the vision of "the gluttonous imperialist beast [breaking] his neck in the encounter with the Soviet Ukraine"—testimony to how the logic of Brest-Litovsk still had not sunk in. But this was doubly unrealistic: the Bol-sheviks were unpopular in the Ukraine; their list got only 10 per cent of the vote in the elections to the Constituent Assembly. And the German "imperialist beast," having swallowed the Ukraine, began to chomp at the neighboring Russian territory. In violation of the peace treaty Ger-man troops entered the Crimea. Already mortally wounded in the West, Imperial Germany proposed to establish a protectorate over the Don Cossacks and Georgia. There was no patriotic uprising against the invader. It was the *Soviet* state which now had to face a civil war, begun in the south but soon flaring up around the periphery of central Russia. And so it fell to Stalin to conclude at the end of April a truce with the Ukrainian authorities.

On June 4 Stalin was sent to the south, close to the front of the Civil War. The first and ostensible purpose of his mission was to organize the supply of foodstuffs to central Russia. From now until the end of the Civil War he, like most Bolshevik potentates, would be constantly sent on special missions and serve as Political Commissar with the army.

"Delegate to somebody (or me) special plenipotentiary powers (of a military character) for the region of south Russia, so that he may take appropriate measures before it is too late." By the time Stalin sent this request to Lenin[12] on July 7, he had, on his own, assumed such powers. And so in Tsaritsyn, the city which would become famous as Stalingrad, he began his career as a dictator, albeit on a merely local scale.

There is no question that this was a role he preferred to sitting in Moscow and quarreling with his assistants on the Commissariat. To give him justice, however, it was not a role which a man who was interested *only* in power would have sought. Such a man would have preferred to sit in the relative safety of Moscow rather than shoulder hazardous responsibilities in the war zone. A mere politician would have opted for pulling the strings from the center, for building a power base at the head of one of the main Party organizations, as Zinoviev was already doing in Petrograd and Kamenev in Moscow. Stalin, like Trotsky, undertook jobs that could make and as easily break reputations. In the committeeman there was also a warlord.

His performance as such generated a legend and a passionate dispute.

[11] Stalin, IV, 47.
[12] *Ibid.*, p. 118.

In the heyday of Stalinism countless novels, plays, and histories extolled Stalin as the savior of Tsaritsyn in 1918 and Petrograd in 1919, the man who frustrated Trotsky's treacherous designs and saved Soviet power from the Whites. Those hostile to him, headed by Trotsky, paint a different picture—of a mutinous schemer against his superiors and rivals, a man who out of envy disobeyed orders and contributed to the Soviet military disaster before Warsaw in 1920, a military ignoramus who compensated for lack of knowledge by intrigue and wanton cruelty.

In fact, Stalin and Trotsky had characteristics in common when it came to their activity in the Civil War. Both men possessed ferocious energy and enterprise which enabled them to cut through the red tape and get things done, to conquer panic and dissipate apathy. Both men were ruthless. But there was an important difference on this count: Trotsky's ruthlessness was for the most part a product of a well-thought-out policy to break the anarchistic habits engendered by the Revolution, and to instill discipline and efficiency in the Red Army, which had been born in defeat and humiliation. Stalin's was an instinctive reaction to some dark forces he felt were crowding upon himself and the cause he represented. Thus a military setback or a strategy of which he did not approve became in his mind products not of error or accident, but of treason. The subtle and self-possessed committeeman was, in an emergency, driven by obsessions. His mentality mirrored that of Communism as a whole, though in hugely exaggerated form.

This ambivalence is pronounced in his messages to Lenin from Tsaritsyn in 1918, some of which verge on insolence. The tone is that of a "practitioner" writing to people in Moscow who have not the slightest idea of what is going on at the front. Why does Trotsky appoint commanders who are unsuitable and whom the local Bolsheviks do not trust? Lenin must expedite airplanes, armored cars, and guns to Tsaritsyn or the front will collapse. Stalin must have full plenipotentiary powers: he has already written about this but received no answer. "Very well. In that case I shall remove on my own, with no formalities, those commissars and commanders who are leading us to disaster. Such is my plain duty, and the absence of a piece of paper from Trotsky is not going to stop me."[13] Then, some time later, when the worst emergency has passed: "I clasp the hand of my dear and beloved Ilyich."

Whatever Lenin's private sentiments, and he disliked flattery as much as rudeness, Stalin's initial achievements made his removal inopportune. The emissary's energy infused a fighting spirit into the army guarding the front, his ruthlessness terrorized the inhabitants of the region into submission, and trains with desperately needed foodstuffs were beginning to roll north.

---

[13] *Ibid.*, p. 121.

It was in Tsaritsyn that Stalin's partnership with his future longtime war minister, Klimenti Voroshilov, began. Voroshilov had been an industrial worker, and began his military career only during the Revolution, when he was in his late thirties—all the more remarkable that he became an expert horseman and developed that martial bearing which he preserved into his extreme old age. It has been said of Napoleon's cavalry leader, Joachim Murat, that while a hero on the battlefield he was a coward at the council table, and this was true of Voroshilov too. Utterly fearless under fire, in World War II as an old man he continued to risk his life in the front lines before besieged Leningrad, but he squirmed before the dictator. In the 1930s Voroshilov, who had been built up ridiculously as a military genius, was probably the least vulnerable of Stalin's subordinates and as such the only one who might have mitigated the purges and saved some of his old comrades at arms from a terrible and infamous end. But he lacked moral courage to stand up to Stalin, and toward the end, the dictator treated Voroshilov with contempt.

Already in 1918 Voroshilov, although as the local commander he might have been expected to resent Stalin's high-handed ways, submitted to the stronger man. There was the bond of a previous acquaintance from Baku, but also and mainly of common opposition to some of Trotsky's policies.

As War Commissar Trotsky's main contribution to the building of the Red Army was undoubtedly his insistence that it be staffed largely with those former Tsarist officers who expressed willingness to work with the Bolsheviks, and his strenuous protection of those specialists from unjustified attacks upon them and from humiliations. Thousands upon thousands of these military officers served their new masters loyally, either because of a genuine ideological conversion, or in the majority of cases because they felt they were still serving Russia, or out of concern for their families (which were considered hostages for their good behavior); and it was this factor above all others that enabled the Bolsheviks to win the Civil War against the armies led by their former colleagues and friends. The more intelligent Bolsheviks came to appreciate the necessity and benefit of this infusion of professionalism: with all their native endowments, a Voroshilov or a Budenny probably could not read an ordnance map when first entrusted with a command. But it ran against the grain for many former noncommissioned officers and workers who rose in street or partisan fighting to accept the hated "gentlemen" as their commanders or colleagues.[14] Naturally enough, it was the

Their White counterparts when captured were often treated with exquisite cruelty: their epaulets were driven into their shoulders with nails. They were drowned in batches. Such was the legacy of hatred that officer ranks were restored imperious Trotsky—who was sponsoring and protecting these people, who often took their side against the political commissars (Communists attached at every level of command to watch over the officers' and the units' political reliability)—who became the main target of this proletarian resentment. And that resentment was in some cases strengthened by a covert anti-Semitic bias.[15]

One day Stalin would restore to the Red Army formal ranks, elaborate uniforms, and a kind of discipline unimaginable even in the old Imperial Army.[16] But in 1918–19 his feelings on the military question were ambivalent. The practical, authoritarian Stalin appreciated the need for discipline. He could see that though there were cases of betrayal of the Communist cause by former Tsarist officers, there were at least as many cases of indiscipline, anarchic behavior, and passing over to the other side by commanders who had risen from the ranks. On the other hand his class instincts and most of all his innate suspiciousness made him sympathize with Trotsky's opponents. In Tsaritsyn he dealt cruelly with some of the military specialists: many were dismissed, some imprisoned and then shot. About the same time Trotsky was using similar measures against *Bolsheviks* at another segment of the front. A local commissar was executed, as were twenty-six men who had deserted, and he accompanied the executions with an order that in case of mass desertion or unauthorized withdrawals it would be the commissar who would be shot *first*. What could impress itself on the mind of some of the more primitive Communists was that Stalin was shooting "gentlemen" for treason, while Trotsky was killing honest Communists for such a relative trifle as disobeying orders.

Terror by now had become endemic and was practiced on both sides of the Civil War. In the Communist camp the example came from the highest authority. In a telegram to Stalin, Lenin once gave the following advice: "Threaten to shoot the idiot who is in charge of telecommunications and who does not know how to give you a better amplifier and

---

only in the 1930s (until then ranks were expressed as "commander of . . ."), and the most evocative of all, "general," not until 1940.

[15] There was some recognition at the Eighth Party Congress, in 1919, of the importance of mollifying the peasants, who were by now outraged by the Communists' exactions and among whom anti-Semitism was a force. The peasants in his district, one delegate declared, were saying, "We used to have a Romanov, now we have an Abramov." Michael Kalinin was elected the President of the Republic, succeeding Jacob Sverdlov. Though he had been an industrial worker in his youth, rather than "a middle peasant from the Tver Province," as Lenin outrageously described him, Kalinin, with his appearance and folksy ways, could in fact persuade the peasants that he was one of them, and he played the role of a kindly peasant uncle with some success until his death in 1946.

[16] In the presence of a superior a Soviet officer would have to ask permission to speak, to light a cigarette.

how to have a working telephone connection."[17] Stalin did one better: the engineer Alexeyev, a man who had volunteered for the front and whose loyalty had been vouched for by leading Communists, and his two sons were shot as alleged White agents. Even in those brutal times this ferocious act led to protests and expressions of horror.

On August 30, 1918, a woman called Fanny Kaplan shot at Lenin and wounded him. Though the would-be assassin was clearly demented, and whatever political ties she had were with the Left Socialist Revolutionaries, the terror now struck mainly at the former bourgeoisie. A veritable "socialist competition" ensued among various Soviet agencies as to which could behave most savagely. The Commissariat of the Interior urged local soviets, "A considerable number of hostages must be taken among the bourgeoisie and the officers." The Cheka, the Soviet political police, ancestor of the OGPU, MGB, NKVD, and today's KGB, cleared the jails of Tsarist officials and capitalists, some of whom had been there since the February Revolution and who by the longest stretch of imagination could not have had anything to do with the attempt on Lenin's life. "Not more than six hundred people were shot by the Moscow Cheka alone," wrote its chief. And from Tsaritsyn, Stalin and Voroshilov wired to Moscow that the War Council of the north Caucasus region had answered the assassination attempt with "open, mass, and systematic terror against the bourgeoisie and its agents."[18]

Even in the civilized days before 1914 the Russian Marxists, while objecting to *individual* terror as practiced by the Socialist Revolutionaries, agreed that the victorious proletariat might have to resort to mass repression to prevent the former possessing classes from staging a comeback. But none of them—including, it is safe to say, Stalin—could have envisaged that repression as consisting of dragging innocent men from their homes and executing them for an act of terrorism committed by a member of a *revolutionary* group. Certainly no one thought of hostages. Even during the most brutal period of Tsarist repression, relatives of revolutionaries were not molested by the government. Every war, especially civil war, generates atrocities, erodes humanitarian and legal scruples, turns the ordinarily decent man into an oppressor. But while the more humane among the Bolsheviks deluded themselves into believing that all these phenomena were temporary and would stop once peace came to the land, it is undeniable that the Communists grew to think of terror as a *technique of government*. Some of them developed a weird theology of terror, reminiscent of those religious heresies which have maintained that until absolute human perfection is established, all forms of vice are permissible. Latsis, a high Cheka official, reiterated that

[17] Lenin, *Collected Works* (4th ed., Moscow, 1946), XXXI, 338.
[18] Stalin, IV, 128.

the ultimate goal of Communism was the abolition of the state and all forms of coercion, but until then coercion, indeed terror, were necessary and laudable.[19] He may have recalled this philosophy when his own turn came during the purges.

It must be an indelible stain on Lenin's record that for all his humane instincts he allowed this cult, a veritable mystique of terror, to develop. While he was quick to intervene when an individual case of injustice was brought to his attention, he allowed mass terror not only to be practiced, but to become legitimate and respectable.[20] It would have been better for the future of Communism and their country had the Bolsheviks regarded the whole subject of terror in an *entirely* cynical way: as a necessary but distasteful business to be handled by sadists and thugs who in any case infiltrated the security apparatus from the very beginning. Instead terror was extolled, the Cheka was presented as the sword of the Revolution, its first head, Felix Dzerzhinsky, is still and even in the most anti-Stalin literature described as a veritable Communist saint, a "knight without fear or blemish." He was, to be sure, a selfless fanatic who had suffered for the cause—but how often is the psychology of the martyr also that of the oppressor!

The facility with which Stalin fell in with the terrorist ways of the times contributed to his political success in the 1920s. The rougher type of Communists who sprang into prominence during a period which called for courage and enterprise of quite different nature than in the pre-Revolution days came to feel—and only time would show how mistaken they were—that Stalin was one of them. He was not one of those Jewish intellectuals who staffed the Party apparatus and looked on them with condescension and perceptible distaste, who begrudged them harmless fun with the "class enemy." He was not a Trotsky, who came to the front on his lightning visits and like a general of yore admonished them to behave or else. . . . Even about Lenin there was a feeling of distance from the revolutionary warrior; he was also, after all, a "gentleman." Stalin was agreeably coarse, "one of our own kind," and he seemed closer to that generation epitomized by the peasant and plumber's apprentice who joined the Party in 1918, Nikita Khrushchev.

Men are influenced by their own legend. In Tsaritsyn, Stalin was for the first time the object of flattery and adulation, and he found the experience pleasing. Local Communist and partisan worthies clung to him as the one man who stood between them and the wrath of the War Commissar, and who knew how to deal with those "bourgeois" military

[19] M. Latsis, *Two Years of War on the Domestic Front: A Popular* [sic] *Review of Two Years of the Cheka* (Moscow, 1920), p. 1.
[20] Blindness to this fact mars an otherwise powerful and moving indictment of Stalinism by Roy Medvedev, *Let History Judge* (New York, 1971).

experts with their arrogant ways.[21] And so, all the more strenuously, they cultivated their boss and protector. One of the legends which now sprang up, and which was later celebrated by Soviet writers in the 1930s, concerned Stalin's special gift, "second sight," you might say, for spotting "enemies of the people," traitors and saboteurs masquerading as loyal Soviet officials and military specialists. These people might plead, say, practical difficulties in constructing a row of trenches by a given deadline, or might submit an apparently sensible plan of military operations. But Stalin's revolutionary instinct would quickly instruct him that here was a traitor, and so with a nod of the head he would indicate to the guards to take the man away and have him "stood against the wall," as the popular euphemism for execution had it. There would be protests and the fuss of formal investigations, but at the end Stalin's insight would prove to have been right.

There is no question that Stalin contributed to the successful defense of Tsaritsyn from the Ataman Krasnov's Cossack bands in 1918, and thus an extremely important strategic bastion was preserved from the Whites. But, equally undeniably, his continuing defiance of the directives of the War Commissariat and the Supreme Revolutionary War Council[22] was interfering with the Red military effort as a whole. For all of Trotsky's expostulations with Lenin that Stalin must be transferred, it was difficult to detach Stalin from the place where he first tasted the voluptuousness of life-and-death power over men, and where he had convinced himself that he was indispensable. In September and October he traveled back and forth between Moscow and Tsaritsyn, but finally Trotsky prevailed. On October 19 Stalin was moved back to Moscow. This blow was softened by his being appointed to the Revolutionary War Council. Trotsky then proposed to have Voroshilov and Minin court-martialed, but he was dissuaded and Voroshilov went to another command in the Ukraine. There was some fence-mending on

---

[21] In addition to Voroshilov there were other interesting characters in the group. There was an ex-tailor, Shchadenko, who in 1941, as Assistant War Commissar, was one of those most responsible for the deplorable condition of the Red Army at the start of the German offensive. The local Communist boss, Sergei Minin, was considered by Trotsky as a troublemaker; he was later thrown out of the Party as a Trotskyite! There were two colorful partisan leaders, Dumenko and Budenny, whose detachments were half-bandit and half-Communist. Dumenko, after some legendary exploits, was accused in 1920 of having murdered his commissar and of planning to go over to the Whites. Shot by the order of the Revolutionary Tribunal, he was "rehabilitated" in 1964 and a street in a provincial town was named after him. The luckier Budenny emerged from the Civil War as the most renowned of Soviet military heroes, his cavalry having played a key role in defeating the Whites and the Poles. But in 1941 the dashing cavalryman, famous also for his ferocious mustache, was found incapable of waging modern warfare and was relieved of his command. He was employed in his old age as President of the Soviet-Mongolian Friendship Association.

[22] The highest military agency, also headed by Trotsky.

Stalin's part. On the anniversary of the October Revolution (it seemed not a year but decades ago) an article by Stalin contained an acknowledgment (subsequently excised from his works) of Trotsky's great services on that historic occasion!

Too much is usually made of this first major clash between the two willful men. Certainly neither Stalin nor Trotsky thought in terms of "succession" to Lenin, then still in his forties, and in view of the overall situation such thoughts would have been ludicrous. It was a clash between two points of view, aggravated by a strong temperamental incompatibility. Stalin's messages from Tsaritsyn bear witness more to his visceral reactions to the war situation than to a schemer's designs. Even a year later he was still writing to Lenin in a peremptory and violent tone rather than as a skilled intriguer: if his plan for military operations were not approved, he wrote in one message, then "my work on the Southern Front will become empty, needless, criminal, which gives me the right, or rather obligates me to go anywhere, to the devil, rather than remain here."[23] In addition to the taste for power the Tsaritsyn interlude brought out in him that passionate self-assurance which one day grew into a conviction of his political and military infallibility. ☆☆☆

THE collapse of Germany lifted from Soviet Russia the nightmarish threat that it might be reduced to becoming a vassal of the Kaiser's Reich. But the winter of 1918–19 brought no alleviation in the Civil War. The number of enemies of Soviet power multiplied, their strength grew. There was now the further perspective created by the victorious Allies rendering massive help to the forces striving to overthrow a regime that, by concluding a separate peace with Germany, had "stabbed them in the back." In the south, north, and east White armies were threatening the central Russian bastion of the Communist power. Poland, now independent, looked longingly at the Ukrainian and Byelorussian lands which between the fourteenth and eighteenth centuries had constituted part of the Polish-Lithuanian commonwealth. The French had landed in Odessa, in the Ukraine; the Japanese, soon followed by the Americans, in Siberia; the Caucasus was a welter of native regimes, fighting both the Whites and the Communists and intermittently among them the Menshevik-dominated regime of Georgia. Near and behind the front lines of the Civil War there ranged anar-

[23] Stalin, IV, 277.

chists, the so-called Green bands, some fighting in turn, and at the leader's whim, on both sides.

On paper the Bolsheviks' situation looked hopeless. In fact they enjoyed great advantages: there was unified direction at the center, wielded by Lenin, and what rivalries and dissensions did exist in the Communist camp paled in comparison with the situation on the White side. The White generals did not trust each other; their politicians were a motley crowd of the Socialist Revolutionaries, liberals, and monarchists incapable of agreeing on a common program or political philosophy; there were constant coups and changes within the White regimes. The White leaders not only were Russian nationalists, but they spelled out their chauvinism in painful detail, thus provoking intermittent warfare not only with the non-Russians, like the Ukrainians and Caucasians, but also with those groups which sought regional autonomy, like the Don Cossacks. And the foreign powers' Russian policies were a maze of contradictions and rivalries. Japan and some newborn states like Poland and Finland viewed a Communist Russia as a lesser evil—less threatening than a reconstituted Imperial Russia would be—a belief that history was to expose as one of the most fatuous ever. America suspiciously watched Japan's designs in Siberia. France wanted a revival of (White) Russian power to offset any future German threat. Britain, with her troubles in India and Ireland and with opposition to any intervention in Russia from the influential Labour Party, was unable to pursue a consistent policy. And so in the Civil War of 1918–21, just as in the Revolution in 1917, the Bolsheviks prevailed though their opponents' forces were much greater, and for the same reason: the foe was disunited, disorganized, and uncertain of its goals.

But such a verdict could not have been reached prior to 1920. Underlying forces of history are most convincing as ex-post-facto explanations of events. Throughout 1919, however, the survival of Soviet power often appeared to hang on the ability of some Red Army unit not to panic when surrounded, or on the success of a White cavalry charge. Lenin's political genius, and the already considerable skill of Soviet diplomacy that occasionally held out alluring prospects for the benefit of Western capitalists (a possible recognition of Tsarist international debts or permitting of foreign investments)—all that might be frustrated by a single act of incompetence in the field or by an accident. An unusually severe outbreak of typhus, which plagued all the armies, a drunken brawl between a Red commander and his commissar—and all might be lost. At another level everything depended on patient organizational and supply efforts, which seldom are acknowledged in the histories of the Civil War. Party potentates quarreled about politics and strategy, military commanders performed feats of daring and tactical improvisation, but the fate of a campaign often depended on whether there were enough shoes for the soldiers and fodder for horses. Krasin, now reconciled with Lenin, brought his expertise to the problem of supply; and while Trotsky and others indulged in heroics at the front, the day-to-day administrative work at the Commissariat and the Revolutionary War Council was carried out by his deputy, a twenty-seven-year-old former military doctor, Ephraim Sklyansky.[24]

Some Communists had a considerable psychological difficulty in appreciating the complex and extremely difficult administrative side of the war. They had been taught that (their) faith moved mountains, that the Communists had history on their side, that the correct "class" policies guaranteed success. So if a battle was lost, there had to be treason involved, and if not treason, then conscious or unconscious sabotage. In December 1918 Admiral Kolchak's White forces, advancing from Siberia, dealt a Soviet army a severe defeat in the vicinity of Perm. The Central Committee and the Revolutionary War Council delegated Stalin and Dzerzhinsky to investigate the causes of the debacle.

This time Stalin's companion was not Molotov or Voroshilov, but a man of strong character, utterly fearless in saying what he thought and devoid of outright political ambitions. It is thus all the more remarkable that Stalin managed to establish ascendancy over him, this time an intellectual ascendancy. But Felix Dzerzhinsky was content to second Stalin's opinions and directives, and, like so many with whom Stlain worked closely in those years and who presumably could observe the negative sides of his personality, Dzerzhinsky remained on the future dictator's side in the ensuing Party struggles.

In his reports from the front, one can discern a small token of Stalin's future megalomania, one form of which was the habit of referring to himself in the third person. In describing measures taken to succor the defeated Third Army, the delegates cite one of them as being "the sending to the front, *through the efforts of Stalin and Dzerzhinsky,* of nine hundred entirely dependable infantrymen needed to lift the fallen morale of the Third Army."[25] The source of trouble, Stalin believed, lay in the incorrect recruiting policy of the War Commissariat. *Everybody,* including hostile class elements, was being drafted, and it was no wonder soldiers deserted and went over to the enemy. New units should be trained in places far away from their native regions, he observed with melancholy realism, otherwise recruits fled back to their villages. His mania about traitors was similarly curbed by realism. Local officials in

---

[24] Since he was almost as unpopular with Stalin as Trotsky was, Sklyansky's contribution to the Soviet war effort has never been acknowledged. Dismissed in 1924, he was sent to the United States the following year on a trade mission and drowned there while taking a swim.

[25] Stalin, IV, 144.

one province complained that the attitude of the population in the rear of the front was hostile toward them because the province in question was inhabited mainly by "the exploiting classes." Stalin inquired how one could have only exploiters and no exploited. As usual he acted and wrote with brutal energy, not sparing Trotsky and the central military authorities ("which do not treat their own directives seriously") and the professional officers ("individual division and brigade commanders behave in the manner of feudal princes"). He did not hesitate to tread on the toes of other important Party officials. "[I] disregarded," he wrote, a nonsensical directive from the Party Secretariat "signed by one Novgorodtseva." He could not have forgotten that the lady in question was Sverdlov's wife.[26]

The terrible and miraculous year of 1919 began with the Soviet government ready to agree to a truce and a peace conference with the Whites. This could conceivably have led, on the analogy of the post-1945 fate of Germany and China, to the establishment of "two Russias."[27] But at the end of the year the Red Army had smashed the main White forces, and the Civil War in essence had been won.

Stalin's career progressed at a corresponding pace. At the Eighth Party Congress, held in March 1918, his was one of the six names found on every list of candidates for the Central Committee. The Party was growing those agencies which in an incredibly short time transformed it from a body with certain inherent democratic ways into an organization tightly controlled by an oligarchy, which in turn then yielded to the dictator. At the Congress two subcommittees of the Central Committee were organized: a Politburo of five members, for political guidance, and an Organizational Bureau (Orgburo), for problems of administration and personnel. Stalin was an original member of both bodies. There was now formally created the office he one day made world-famous: Secretary of the Central Committee. Stalin was not appointed to it (its first holder was Nikolai Krestinsky), but he added another Commissariat to his already imposing list of offices and committees—that of State Control, in which he had his hand over the now rapidly growing Soviet state bureaucracy.

Even at a time when many important Party officials toiled at several jobs, this was an unusual accumulation of offices, and it reflected Stalin's reputation for great capacity for work and for cutting through red tape.

---

[26] The fashion was for female Communists to use their maiden names. Jacob Sverdlov, President of the Republic and de-facto secretary of the Party, died in March 1919 of Spanish influenza.

[27] The Soviet acquiescence was submitted to President Woodrow Wilson's emissary, William Bullitt, on March 12. But the arrangement was blocked by the Whites, who were confident that all of Russia would be theirs within a few months, and the Supreme Council of the Allied Powers in Versailles decided not to proceed with the plan.

Some of the jobs were thought extremely unglamorous and politically unrewarding. Take State Control. Who would want this hopeless task of producing some order from the chaos that was the current civil administration; of quarreling with the local soviets, which still believed they exercised sovereign powers over their city or region; of finding people with some rudimentary knowledge of accounting and finance; of the almost inevitable prospect of confrontations with fellow commissars? Stalin's willingness to take on the job was in the eyes of a Zinoviev or Bukharin proof of his lack of political sophistication. History, it was felt, was made by oratory or the pen. Power in the Party was likewise thought to depend on the ability to entrance a Party Congress or other gatherings with a brilliant speech, with erudite references and citations from Marx and other classics. Among the pre-1914 Bolsheviks the notion of Stalin's one day inheriting Lenin's mantle would have met with incredulity. He lacked the theoretical and oratorical stature. And how could one even conceive a Marxist Party and a world socialist movement led by a man who did not know German? He would be, it was probably recognized by 1919, a useful *ally* for one who aspired to leadership: an able organizer and a man who could communicate with those primitive and rather boorish Communists who had flocked to the Party since the Revolution.

At the Eighth Congress Stalin spoke but little: mainly he supported Lenin and Trotsky (who was not present, having left for the front) in defending the military specialists against the "military opposition," which wanted to curtail the functions and prerogatives of the former Tsarist officers. Discussion of this issue was so tempestuous that the minutes of the session devoted to it were omitted from records of the Congress. V. M. Smirnov, the spokesman for what might be called the partisan point of view, decried the airs of the former officers—they insisted on being saluted, and some of them, if you please, had orderlies!—and Trotsky was strongly criticized for his alleged favoritism of these exploiters and Tsarist servants over honest Communists. Smirnov demanded that their privileges be abolished and that political commissars be given the power to command, with the specialist being just a consultant.

But Stalin saw the logic of Trotsky's position, though he might have sympathized with the opposition emotionally. "Facts show that the concept of a volunteer army does not withstand criticism, that we shall not be able to defend our Republic if we do not construct another regular army imbued with discipline. . . . Smirnov's proposals are unacceptable."[28]

On yet another issue his political instincts prevailed over his emo-

[28] Stalin, IV, 249.

tions. There was some sparring at the Congress between Lenin and Bukharin on the nationality issue. Bukharin, with his fatal passion for frankness and for elucidating what should remain vague, objected again to the principle of national self-determination. It was a fine principle to be used against the enemy, but do Communists mean that this principle is applicable even when it is invoked against themselves? Is it not ridiculous to proclaim this principle as valid in regard to every group, regardless of its stage of development? Should it apply even in regard to "Hottentots and Bushmen"? Yes, said Lenin, and about Bukharin, "Scratch a Russian Communist and you will find a Russian chauvinist." The Georgian who without any scratching would become the greatest Russian chauvinist in history still saw the marvelous political sense of Lenin's position. It gave the Communists a vast propaganda advantage over the White generals, who with their "Russia great and indivisible" slogan were practically forcing the Poles, Finns, and others to sit on their hands rather than join them. After the Communists won, they could decide what this self-determination meant in practice.[29]

Stalin moved from the dissensions and intrigues of the Party gatherings back to the front. The White threat to Petrograd in May 1919 brought him there on a special mission, and, predictably, he discovered there a major plot of treason, found the directives of the commander-in-chief (Trotsky's protégé) harmful, and saved the day by his initiative— all of which developments he communicated without inhibition to Lenin.

His communication regarding the treason plot already has the flavor of the Great Purges of some fifteen years later. The threads of the plot, he wrote, ran to some employees of the Italian, Swiss, and Danish legations. (They had to have been former consular employees of Russian nationality, since these countries had no diplomatic relations with Russia at the time.) He proposed to keep them under a severe prison regime "until the conclusion of the investigation, which *will unravel* a new rich vein [of treason]."[30] A search of the Swiss Consulate revealed that there were traitors on the Soviet General Staff working for the Whites! Would the Central Committee have enough courage to take the appropriate steps? ☆☆☆

---

[29] Why do Americans *talk* about unconditional surrender? wondered Stalin to Harry Hopkins in 1945. *After* Japan surrendered, one could *make* it unconditional!
[30] Stalin, IV, 263. My italics.

AND what had saved the day in the field? Stalin's "indelicate interference" had led to the Reds' recapture of the crucial forts of Red Hill and Gray Horse. The naval specialists resisted his orders, protesting that they violated the rules of naval science. But, said Stalin, "I feel bound to declare that for all my respect for science, I will act the same way in the future."[31]

One may well question Lenin's judgment in retaining Stalin in an important position, not to mention heaping additional powers and honors on him during the next three years. But there *had* been some cases of betrayal, and Petrograd *was* saved that spring from the White armies. Apart from the already considerable megalomania and the obsession with treason, Stalin displayed real talents in command. He did not panic. He immediately assessed the enemy's weak points: on the Northern Front the Whites had "neither sufficient rear space, nor adequate manpower, nor food." The hinterland lay in Finland and Estonia, countries interested in keeping their independence rather than being dragged into Russia's internal conflicts. Though Petrograd was to experience another serious threat in the fall, when Trotsky this time was dispatched to bolster Zinoviev's faltering local leadership, the factors Stalin discerned did lead to the eventual disintegration of the northern Whites. In June he argued that Petrograd should not be reinforced at the expense of other, more crucial fronts. This composure and reasonableness were valued higher than the lives of some innocent people shot as "White agents" and "enemies of the people."

Most of all, Lenin was inhibited by a complex of his own in dealing with Stalin. Stalin's brutality and occasional insolence were undoubtedly distasteful to him, but did his qualms spring from his own background as a bourgeois and *intelligent?* Stalin's behavior was perhaps the kind of proletarian forthrightness that was now so badly needed and that must not be curbed, lest the Communists share the fate of the Mensheviks and Socialist Revolutionaries. He never had occasion to admonish Stalin, as he did another front commander, "I am afraid you are mistaken in not applying utmost severity, but if you are absolutely certain that your forces are inadequate for a savage and ruthless repression, then wire all the details without any delay."[32] For all the ample provocations there is no record of Lenin so much as reprimanding Stalin for the tone,

---

[31] *Ibid.*, p. 261.
[32] Quoted in *Trotsky Papers* (The Hague, 1964), I, 380.

if not the substance, of his messages.[33] Occasionally Lenin marked an unusually boastful or insolent message of Stalin's with question marks, but it was only for his private archive. Finally in 1922 and on his deathbed Lenin's eyes were opened to the character of the Georgian, and he spoke out. But it was too late, and he must have realized it was partly his own fault: he had brought Stalin up badly.

This is no mere figure of speech. Stalin must have sensed how his very brutality and peremptoriness intrigued the older man, and while it certainly did not lead to the kind of domination he came to exert over Molotov or Voroshilov, it still gave him a strange kind of power over Lenin. As the Civil War progressed, messages to his leader no longer bore the "I clasp the hand of my dear and beloved Ilyich" character so evident in the summer of 1918. More characteristic now was the dry "Request: have it explained to the commander-in-chief that he does not have the right to declare wars. Request: to curb the commander-in-chief."[34] The closest Stalin came to being reprimanded was after one of his particularly violent outbursts, when the Politburo informed him that it was impermissible to issue ultimatums and threaten to resign if his plan were not adopted. Trotsky, and for that matter other Communist potentates, threw scenes occasionally and had to have their egos soothed by Vladimir Ilyich—who from the intemperate polemicist of yore had become, in the interest of the Revolution, a patient and long-suffering diplomat and conciliator. But none of them, it is fair to say, matched Stalin's occasional rudeness or insubordination.

It is thus a basic error to see Stalin's role in the Civil War as consisting mainly in rivalry with or intrigue against Trotsky. He was a skillful politician, intriguer if you will, while in a committee or at a Party gathering. Faced with a concrete task or with a threat, he would become driven by obsessions—he then was invariably in the right and any opposition to his ideas found its source in treason and envy. Surrounded by people impressed by his brutal energy, uncurbed by the one man who was in the position to do so, he was allowed to develop the habits of a tyrant while still far from being a dictator.

In November 1919 Stalin and Trotsky were among those given the then highest decoration of the Soviet Republic, the Order of the Red Banner. Stalin continued to spend the major part of his time in exacting military duties: after Petrograd, as a member of the War Council of the Western Front until September; of that of the Northern Front from October 1919 to January 1920; finally of the Southwestern Front from January to September 1920.[35]

[33] If there were, we may be sure it would have been brought up by Soviet historians between 1961 and 1964.
[34] *Trotsky Papers*, I, 600.
[35] Those councils—subordinate, at least in theory, to the Supreme Revolutionary

It is Stalin's role in the last post that is connected with the most controversial issue of Soviet military history before World War II: that of military strategy and tactics in the war against Poland. The controversy affected Soviet military thinking for the next fifteen years and was to compound the grisly fate of some leading Russian military commanders in the 1930s. ☆☆☆

T HE independent Polish state was in 1919 headed by Joseph Pilsudski, a former socialist and conspirator in Russian Poland.[36] It is remarkable that a man with knowledge of the Bolshevik mentality believed that a Communist Russia would be a lesser threat to the independence of his country than a resurrected nationalist Russia. Intermittent warfare between his state and the Soviet army was brought to a standstill at the most dangerous period of the Civil War for the Reds —in the early fall of 1919, when the White armies were marching on Moscow. Consequently the Communists were able to bring in reinforcements against the Whites from the Polish front.

By April 1920 the main White armies had been crushed. There remained only General Wrangel's, based in the Crimea, and though it still presented a considerable potential threat to south Russia, there was no question that barring some very unusual eventuality, like a massive Entente (i.e., mainly British-French) intervention, the Communists had won the war. With the danger (as they saw it) of a White victory over, the Poles struck.

Pilsudski's scheme, viewed skeptically by right-wing politicians in his country, envisaged Poland in a loose association with an independent Ukraine and Byelorussia. Though what might be called Soviet historio-propaganda has always claimed that the inspiration for Pilsudski's move came from London and Paris, the opposite in fact is true. The Western powers, or at least their governments, were opposed to what they considered Poland's adventurist and imperialist plans, and resentful that Poland had not intervened when such intervention could have swayed the military balance in favor of the Whites.

Having attacked Soviet Russia on April 25, the Poles scored dazzling

War Council of the Republic—consisted usually of three members: the commander, the political commissar, and the chief of staff or of supply.

[36] Pilsudski's older brother was involved indirectly in the plot against Alexander III which led to the execution of Lenin's brother Alexander. He himself was one of the most famous organizers of armed expropriations between 1905 and 1908.

successes, and within two weeks their armies were in Kiev. But like the Whites before them, they stretched their lines of communication and supply to the danger point. And the population of the Ukraine failed to respond to the appeals of Pilsudski's Ukrainian ally, Petliura. The Ukrainian peasantry, while not enchanted with the Bolsheviks, was exhausted from the years of warfare which had rolled over their unhappy land and fearful that the Poles would bring back the landlords. (A considerable proportion of Ukrainian landlords in Tsarist times was Polish by nationality.) In June the Soviets opened their counteroffensive. Budenny's First Cavalry Army cut the thin and vulnerable communication lines of the Polish army, and the Poles' retreat now became as rapid as its advance had been.[37]

At the end of July the advancing Soviet armies reached the line roughly corresponding to the frontier of ethnic Poland. At this point a debate ensued among the Soviet leaders over whether and how far the offensive should be pursued, and whether the Soviets should not agree to armistice proposals advanced by the British Foreign Secretary, Lord Curzon, which would establish a truce at this line. (This was the famous Curzon Line proposed initially by the British in 1919 and used so masterfully by Stalin in World War II as an argument for the retention by the U.S.S.R. of that share of Poland which accrued to it under the Nazi-Soviet agreement of 1939.) But the hitherto restrained and realistic Lenin now reverted to the pre-Revolutionary Lenin: the vision of a Communist Poland and, beyond it, of the Communist flame spreading westward to Germany and beyond now took hold of his mind. Other Soviet political and military leaders were more realistic, but with the Polish armies in apparent rout few of them could resist the vision of the Red Army in Warsaw, of a Communist Poland.[38]

One who could was Stalin. As early as May he said publicly that the Polish offensive in the Ukraine was doomed, but he warned that "if the Polish armies were operating in Poland, it would be undoubtedly very hard to fight them."[39] He rejected by implication Lenin's fond belief that the Polish proletariat would rise for Communism: "The rear of the Polish armies is monolithic and nationally united. . . . The dominant sentiment is the feeling for the Fatherland. . . . Hence the firm unity of the Polish army." In late July, when the heads of most leaders were

[37] The Polish offensive, like the Civil War, was a war of movements—with the armies poorly equipped, soldiers on both sides hastily trained and liable to panic at any and every insignificant threat from the rear. Hence the cavalry had an importance it had not had elsewhere since the Napoleonic wars. In World War II Stalin had to be dissuaded by his staff from creating a special cavalry army, so strong was his memory of Budenny's exploits.

[38] Trotsky's assertions that he was *definitely* opposed to a further march must be taken with a grain of salt.

[39] Stalin, IV, 324.

turned by military success, he again denounced the "braggadocios . . . who shout 'On to Warsaw!' and who will be satisfied only with a 'Red Warsaw.' "

Stalin's opposition was enhanced by the feeling of personal responsibility in the matter. "His" southwestern group of armies was responsible not only for the southern part of the front against the Poles, but for watching over Wrangel, who had just broken out of his Crimean lair and was only with difficulty pushed back. But the Soviet government, i.e., Lenin, was bent on securing a "Red Warsaw." Its counterproposals to Curzon were to concede armistice to Poland on the condition of the country's becoming a Communist satellite; the Polish army was to be reduced to 50,000; a "workers' militia" was to take over "the protection of order and the safety of the population in Poland. Conditions and the manner of organization of this militia will be spelled out while settling the details of the peace treaty."[40] A provisional revolutionary government of Poland was organized out of the Polish Bolsheviks in Russia; Dzerzhinsky was one of its members.

In order to remove Stalin from any connection with the Polish campaign, the Politburo decided to form a special front against Wrangel under his direction, and to attach the remaining units of the southwestern groups to the main body driving on Warsaw from the Western Front under Tukhachevsky. Stalin's reaction was the most insolent yet: "I have your note about the splitting of the fronts," he wired Lenin. "The Politburo should not occupy itself with such nonsensical trifles." Once more he asked to be relieved. Again, and amazingly, Lenin chose to ask, Would Stalin please explain why he was dissatisfied? Finally, three days later, a compromise was arranged: the Southwestern Front would remain with its previous tasks and Stalin with it, but some armies would be detached to help the drive on Warsaw.

The Soviet armies pursuing the Poles toward the Vistula were commanded by Michael Tukhachevsky. A former Tsarist lieutenant, now all of twenty-seven years old, he had distinguished himself in previous Civil War campaigns. Unlike most of the former Imperial officers in Soviet service, Tukhachevsky's accession was followed by a wholehearted conversion to Communism. Because of that and because of his age, he was viewed with some skepticism by many military specialists, some of whom suspected him of harboring Napoleonic ambitions.

The drama that now unfolded must be explained in terms of the Soviet command situation. Trotsky at one point in his autobiography states that he had absolute power of command, a statement sufficiently disproved elsewhere in his own book. There was, in fact, no such thing

---

[40] S. Budenny, *Life's Path* (Moscow, 1965), II, 304.

as a unified and monolithic supreme command. The so-called commander-in-chief, the post occupied in succession by two former Tsarist colonels, formulated operational plans and issued directives, but obviously could not secure their fulfillment. The same went for Trotsky and the Supreme War Council. In the last instance, a dispute over strategy had to be adjudged by the Politburo, i.e., mostly by Lenin; and even there, as we have seen, there was no guarantee that a strong-minded commander or his commissar would readily comply with orders.

On July 23 Sergei Kamenev,[41] the commander-in-chief, ordered Tukhachevsky's armies to secure the Vistula line and seize Warsaw, "not later than August 12."[42] At the same time the southwestern group, commanded by Alexander Yegorov, with Stalin as his commissar, was to continue to diverge south, with the aim of capturing the important Polish city of Lvov, and to guard against a possible Rumanian military intervention on behalf of Poland. Thus between Tukhachevsky's and Yegorov's forces there opened a dangerous gap, with but a very weak Soviet corps at the left flank of the advancing Western Front. About August 5 Tukhachevsky, worried by the Poles' stiffened resistance, demanded that the armies promised him be detached from Yegorov's command and march rapidly northwest to secure his flank. On August 11 the Supreme Commander ordered Yegorov to send Budenny's First Cavalry Army, along with the Twelfth Army, to help Tukhachevsky. Yegorov and Stalin temporized, alleging difficulties and the possible Rumanian threat. When Yegorov finally decided to send Budenny's mounted legions northwest, Stalin refused to sign the order; without the commissar's signature, it could not be put into effect.

On August 16 the Poles counterattacked along the entire Western Front. The most damaging blow came on Tukhachevsky's unprotected left flank, the one which might have been secured had Kamenev been able to overcome the dilatoriness, then the insubordination of Yegorov and Stalin (mainly the latter, since he obviously dominated Yegorov, as he had his previous commanders). The battle turned into a complete Soviet rout, with the Red Armies fleeing in disorder. In October an armistice was signed, in 1921 confirmed as the Peace of Riga. Far from becoming a Soviet republic, Poland now secured frontiers far to the east of the Curzon Line and including substantial Ukrainian and Byelorussian populations—a fact that would be of enormous importance in European politics between 1921 and the end of World War II.

Who was responsible for this disastrous debacle for the Soviet Army? The primary *political* responsibility was undoubtedly Lenin's, since he had persuaded himself that Polish workers and peasants were dying with

[41] Not to be confused with our old friend the pusillanimous Lev Kamenev.
[42] *The Party in the Period of Foreign Military Intervention and Civil War, 1918–1920, Documents* (Moscow, 1962), p. 506.

impatience to greet Dzerzhinsky and his fellow Polish Bolsheviks (many of them also employees of the Cheka), while, as Stalin had correctly predicted, the Communist offensive in fact generated a patriotic upsurge among all classes of the population. On the military side the primary responsibility must remain Tukhachevsky's, all of Yegorov's and Stalin's derelictions notwithstanding, for he advanced too fast without protecting his flanks, and in fact became vulnerable not only on his southern flank but also on the northern, where he lost contact with his Fourth Army (which was crushed, its remnants seeking refuge in German East Prussia).

Stalin's objections to the order detaching some armies from his group were eminently reasonable: the Southwestern Front did indeed have to watch not only the Polish forces around Lvov, but Wrangel's hundreds of miles to the east, and it was true that they had to be on guard against a possible Rumanian intervention which would have come from behind Lvov. It is most unlikely that France and Britain would have acquiesced in the fall of Poland. One year earlier the Western Allies had prevailed on the Rumanians to help crush the Communist regime in Hungary. With massive Western help forthcoming, even Wrangel's bridgehead might have become a deadly threat to Soviet Russia, close to the end of her endurance and resources. It is also improbable that Budenny's army, if it had moved on August 12 as ordered by the commander-in-chief, could have affected decisively the outcome of the battle, especially in view of its soldiers being fatigued and in need of a rest. Still, Stalin's behavior undeniably constituted the kind of insubordination for which people are shot, and he would later have *his* generals shot for much less than that. Most accounts explain Stalin's actions as being motivated by his envy of Tukhachevsky: if the young commander was to have Warsaw, *he* wanted Lvov. This is most unlikely. Stalin's megalomania ran along different lines: he was convinced all along he had been right and "they," including Lenin, wrong; he would act according to his beliefs, and to hell with the consequences.

In the immediate sequel to the Polish campaign none of the main actors of the drama was to be punished or disgraced for the defeat. On September 1 Stalin was relieved as Commissar for the Southwestern Front, and he did not participate in the epilogue to the Civil War: the crushing of Wrangel's forces and the Soviet occupation of the Crimea. But his position otherwise remained unimpaired. In 1921 Tukhachevsky was employed to command the Soviet suppression of two uprisings: the famous mutiny of the Kronstadt sailors and the much less known but actually more dangerous partisan-peasant rising in the province of Tambov. Both were suppressed with appalling cruelty: the captive sailors were shot in droves; in Tambov the families of insurgents were taken hostage and executed unless their menfolk turned themselves in.

Tukhachevsky then held a number of leading military posts until 1937, when his and other military figures' executions initiated Stalin's vast purge of the Red Army. Similar honors and the same terrible fate awaited Alexander Yegorov, whom Tukhachevsky rather openly blamed for his failure before Warsaw, and who in turn wrote a book (published in 1929) castigating Tukhachevsky and Kamenev for their operational errors in the Polish campaign.

Even in the 1920s Stalin's share of blame could only be whispered about rather than openly discussed in military and Party circles. But there is no question that again he felt "picked on" and blamed Tukhachevsky as the source of the rumors.[43] Yet in his strange way he highly valued Tukhachevsky's military gifts. Absolute dictator as he was after 1930, he could easily have consigned Tukhachevsky to obscurity or exile, but he kept him in high posts and in 1935 promoted him to Marshal of the Soviet Union. But when to the old grudge was added the (unjustified) conviction of Tukhachevsky's treason, the tyrant's ferocity was unleashed. After studying the chronicles of the terror of the 1930s, one loses somewhat the capacity to be shocked, and yet the tale of what happened to Tukhachevsky's family chills one's blood. Savage repression struck at *three* generations: he, a devoted Communist and patriot, perished on an infamous charge, and so did his two brothers (one a talented musician[44]), while his aged mother, his teen-age daughter, and three sisters were exiled to labor camps. He was fully exonerated of treason after Stalin's death. ☆☆☆

THUS ended the period of the Civil War, in many ways more formative of the character of Communism and of the character of Stalin than 1917 or the long underground years before the Revolution. Its heroics and savagery have been described in innumerable Soviet novels, the Stalinist version best depicted by the dictator's literary flatterer-in-chief, Alexis Tolstoy, in his *Calvary*, in which one finds a grotesquely distorted picture of Trotsky at the front. A more balanced version, even though Stalin himself lent his "editorial" help to it, is found in Mikhail Sholokhov's *And Quiet Flows the Don*, but even this does not do justice to the horror of the struggle. Memoirs or dry historical accounts are sometimes better than even the most realistic fictional description at making one visualize the dimensions of its horror.

[43] That Stalin disobeyed a direct order both of the Politburo and of the commander-in-chief became public only in 1962.
[44] The Marshal was himself a lover of music, his hobby violin-making.

Thus Budenny mentions an actual case of a Red cavalry commander's encountering his own father in hand-to-hand combat and, when the enraged old man refuses to surrender, killing him. This was not an isolated case among the Cossacks, whose political divisions often ran more along generational than class lines.

Reflecting on this lesson of inhumanity, Maxim Gorky, now reconciled with Lenin, had some bitter things to say about his own people. To the question who was more cruel, the Whites or the Reds, he answered, "Both, equally, because there were Russians on both sides."[45] Though one may not accept such national stereotypes, Gorky's anguish is a valuable testimony to the legacy of the fratricidal struggle. "I think that just as the English have a special gift for humor so do the Russians have one for cruelty. It is a peculiar, cold-blooded cruelty which tests the limits of human endurance for suffering, cruelty which [perversely] imparts a [sense of] tenacity and solidity to life." Gorky could not know in 1922 that he was describing Russian life in the 1930s and '40s, nor that another of his remarks, while debatable as a general principle, still offers a dazzling insight into the character of the man who would fashion those decades and make him, Gorky, an instrument of his tyranny. "History," wrote Gorky, "offers a clear answer as to gradations of cruelty: he who is most active is most cruel."

[45] Maxim Gorky, *About the Russian Peasant* (in Russian; Berlin, 1922), p. 19; the booklet was never published in the Soviet Union.

~~6~~

IN LENIN'S SHADOW

On November 6 a former inmate of the Baku jails addressed a solemn meeting of the Baku Soviet on the commemoration of the anniversary of the Revolution. Stalin came to the gathering as a victor. Azerbaijan, with its precious oil resources, had just been conquered for the Soviet cause; in the Caucasus only the Menshevik-ruled Georgia remained outside the Communist sphere, and the days of its independence were numbered.[1] Stalin did not indulge in any sentimental reminiscences. He chose rather to tell the story of the fabulous growth of the Soviet power. Three years before, he recalled, "a tiny group of Bolsheviks . . . the Red Guard, insignificant in numbers . . . the relatively small and not fully united Communist Party" overturned the bourgeois Russian government. Now they had "a multimillion-man Red Army, a seven-hundred-thousand-member Party as cohesive as steel . . . the Party which at any given moment can reform its ranks . . . and, responding to a single directive of the Central Committee . . . can throw itself at any enemy."[2] They now had a worldwide band of sympathizers, headed by the Third International.[3] There were revolutionary stirrings in the Orient. All in all, "in terms of revolution we were poor three years ago, but are rich now." With a flash of eloquence, Stalin paraphrased Luther's words at the Diet of Worms in 1521 at which he laid down a

[1] In Armenia the Soviets took over within a month.

[2] Stalin, *Collected Works* (Moscow, 1946–52), IV, 391–92.

[3] The Communist International was organized hastily, mostly from foreign Bolsheviks resident in Russia in 1919. Its first real Congress was the Second, in July 1920.

challenge to the Emperor and the Church: Russia might say, "Here I stand at the frontier between the old capitalist and the new socialist worlds. . . . Here I . . . draw together the strength of the proletariat of the West and the peasantry of the East to smash the old world. May the god of history help me."[4]

It was a typical performance. Some of Stalin's listeners, if they had studied the history of the Reformation, might have reflected that Martin Luther's voice was that of an individual conscience, and that in 1521 he did not have behind him a "multimillion-man . . . army" nor a "seven-hundred-thousand-member Party," nor that institution which Stalin delicately forebore to mention, "our excellent Cheka," as Lenin called it, the local branch of which was already functioning full blast in Baku. Conversely, the Communist Party was far from having that steellike cohesion of which Stalin spoke. In fact, in 1921–22 it was to be shaken by a serious ideological dispute, not to mention the web of intrigues in which its leadership was already entangled. But to a not terribly sophisticated listener, Stalin must have sounded very convincing, as he continued to do during the ascent to supreme power, even his occasional awkwardness of style contrasting favorably with Zinoviev's and Trotsky's polished, at times florid oratory. Here was an educated man (Luther!), but he did not drive one to distraction with citations from Marx and Engels as did so many other Communist dignitaries, including, to be honest about it, Vladimir Ilyich himself. Again Stalin appeared as "one of our own," the voice of the common people in the highest Party councils, councils otherwise rather unfortunately dominated by intellectuals of the "gentleman" background and Jews.

Stalin's visit to the Caucasus partook of a viceregal progress. The Azerbaijan Communist Party hailed him extravagantly as "the leader of the proletarian revolution in the Caucasus and the East," and announced that it forsook a special festive reception only out of consideration for the honored guest's well-known modesty.[5] The leader of the Caucasian Bureau of the Communist Party and, as such, the impresario of Stalin's visit was Sergo Orjonikidze, and again we have a testimony to Stalin's amazing ability to win over and dominate people who had every reason to know better. There was very little in Stalin's background, including those "certain personal characteristics," that Orjonikidze did not know about. He might have resented the national prominence and domineering ways of the man whose Party standing before 1914 was lower than his own. Yet Orjonikidze became Stalin's satellite.

---

[4] Stalin, IV, 393.
[5] Richard Pipes, *The Formation of the Soviet Union* (Cambridge, Mass., 1964), p. 230.

With his role as a warlord now temporarily in abeyance, Stalin was entering a new one, that of the "gatherer of the Russian lands."[6] It was largely his influence which led the Soviet government to complete its conquest of Armenia in December, thus disregarding its agreement of a few weeks before with the Armenian Dashnak (nationalist) government which stipulated a mixed Communist-Dashnak regime. And then it was the turn of Stalin's native land.

With the Polish armies thundering toward Kiev, the Soviet government in May 1920 had negotiated a treaty with Georgia which acknowledged the little country's independence. But the Georgian Mensheviks had not learned the lesson of rather recent history: they had agreed to legalize the Georgian branch of the Communist Party; its leaders were released from jail and of course immediately started planning an uprising against the new independent regime. (Noah Jordania's government included such former all-Russian Menshevik stars as Nicholas Chkheidze and Irakli Tseretelli, who certainly should have known better.)

For a few months the Menshevik-dominated Georgian government was the toast of Social Democratic circles in Western Europe. It amused rather than irritated Stalin when a delegation of Socialist notables led by Karl Kautsky, the idol of his (and Lenin's) youth, visited the little republic and enthused over its virtuous brand of socialism, so different from the naughty Communist ways. Kautsky, he joked, fearful of a Communist revolution in Germany, was seeking refuge in "backward Tiflis" with those "bourgeois socialists." In November he rather undiplomatically stated in a press interview that he was quite sure Georgia was in the throes of a "catastrophic economic crisis" and was "living out its last days."

This was a classical case of what is known as self-fulfilling prophecy. Orjonikidze and his assistant, Sergei Kirov, another man who would play an important role in Stalin's ascent to full despotism, and who was currently Soviet representative in Tiflis, were planning all along a Red Army invasion combined with an uprising by the Georgian Communists. The country was now surrounded on three sides by Soviet territory. But the main obstacle lay in Lenin's hesitation. He had just burned his fingers in an attempt to export revolution to Poland. Would Britain stand idly by? The British Labour Party, which in the main viewed Soviet Russia as a somewhat misguided yet in essence genuine workers' state, and which had energetically opposed helping Poland,[7] might have a different view of an attack on the undeniably socialist

---

[6] The name given to the Russian Tsars of the fifteenth and sixteenth centuries, especially Ivan III, who from the nucleus of Muscovy built up the Russian state.

[7] The chief figure in the "hands off Soviet Russia" movement was a dynamic trade union leader named Ernest Bevin, who one day had an occasion to reflect on this role.

Georgia. Lenin may have remembered his words to Jordania in 1907, "You Georgians stay out of our Russian affairs and we will stay out of yours."

But sentimentality was not one of Lenin's traits. Soviet power elsewhere in the Caucasus was not going to be firmly rooted unless this enclave of democratic socialism were liquidated. Krasin, his diplomacy and charm now enlisted in the Soviet cause, reported from London that Mr. David Lloyd George would not be unduly perturbed at a Soviet move. He had never been strong for intervention in Russia's internal affairs, undertaken largely because of the importunities of his friend and Cabinet colleague Winston Churchill. The Prime Minister was sorely troubled by Ireland and India, and since geography was not his strong point, it is questionable whether he knew exactly where and what Georgia was. (The current witticism had Lloyd George confuse Galicia with Cilicia, in Asia Minor!)

When the Communist uprising was finally organized by Orjonikidze, Lenin still had his doubts. He finally authorized military intervention in February 1921 but on the condition that the members of the Revolutionary War Council of the Eleventh Army, which was to be its instrument, signify in writing their agreement with the decision and pledge its success. Within a few weeks Georgian military resistance crumbled. The Menshevik government headed by Jordania fled to France, there to appeal to the "conscience of the West" and to meet with the same response that many who followed in their footsteps during the next fifty years were to receive. Lenin still wanted a transitional arrangement of a coalition government with the Mensheviks. But it was vain to expect that Stalin and Orjonikidze could acquiesce in such a compromise, could show moderation toward and regard for those who for so long had lorded over them. In fact, Orjonikidze's brutal ways in Georgia before long provoked a conflict with the Georgian Communists, one which almost ended his Party career and brought a fatal setback to that of his patron.

With the absorption of Georgia, the Communist state assumed the geographic extent it was to preserve until 1939.[8] Except for its Polish, Finnish, and Baltic parts and some small districts in the Caucasus, Nicholas' Empire had become a Communist one. ☆☆☆

---

[8] I am here disregarding the Far East, where it was thought desirable to preserve until 1922 the fiction of an independent Far Eastern republic, and northern Sakhalin, evacuated by Japanese troops as late as 1925.

THE Communists in turn now faced a struggle which, though more prosaic, dwarfed in difficulty their heroic struggle for power and its preservation: the restoration of their country's cruelly devastated economy, and the building of a modern industrial society. No Marxist, Lenin included, could make the error of assuming that Russia in 1921 *was* a socialist society. Socialism could be built only upon the foundation of a thoroughly industrialized modern economy. Tsarist Russia, according to Marxian categories, was barely entering its industrialized capitalist phase when Lenin decided to give history a push and to seize power, and so now he and his victorious Party had first to accomplish the work the capitalists and Tsarist bureaucrats had failed (or more properly, had not been allowed) to complete before they could even glimpse the promised land of socialism. There was to be no help, as Lenin had hoped as late as 1920 there would be, from the more advanced industrial countries of the West. Russia remained the only state ruled by Communists. There was some expectation that foreign capitalists out of greed would sell their technical expertise and invest in the nation which now was pledged to their eventual destruction. Krasin and other Soviet diplomats and trade negotiators scurried through the West in search of credits and favorable trade terms; defeated Germany gave some help in developing Soviet military technology, in return for being able to train her troops secretly in Russia, in circumvention of the Versailles Treaty. There would be some experts coming, foreign philanthropy would help to alleviate the great famine of 1921–22. All in all, however, it was but a trickle of foreign aid in the face of vast needs. "Backward, semi-Asiatic Russia," Lenin had called her long before, and as the result of the wars, she seemed more truly that than before. She would have to build the future on her own.

Apart from schemes, statistics, and ideological preferences, there was the reality of destitution, of the total breakdown in social relations—all the more apparent when the strain but also the exhilaration of the Civil War was gone; and no Communist directives or "steel-like cohesion" could conjure up food for the cities, rebuild entirely destroyed industries overnight, cut short widespread banditry. Once more the Communist Party was like a besieged garrison, struggling this time not against armies and political enemies, but against hunger, lack of manufactured goods, and that elemental anarchy which in Russian history has so often alternated with periods of tight repression. Hordes of homeless children roamed the streets and the countryside. Many people starved, even before the onset of the great famine—especially former "exploiters," who in some cases were refused food coupons. Epidemics raged throughout the land.

Again a small detail portrays Russian life in those years more vividly than volumes of statistics. Ilya Ehrenburg records in his memoirs how one winter toward the end of the Civil War he found that all his outer clothing was wearing out and soon he would be without even rags. It took an audience with the chairman of the Moscow Soviet, Lev Kamenev himself, for the writer to receive an authorization for the issue from government stocks of *one* article of clothing, and that only because of his job in a governmental artistic enterprise. Naturally he chose a long overcoat, and since he did not dispose of a single pair of trousers, he astounded his friends by never removing his coat, even when (as was rare) his office or apartment was heated.

To conquer power, the Bolsheviks had to license anarchy, allowing peasants to seize land, workers to take over factories, etc. To retain power they had to institute repression and terror, but always with the stipulation that this was a temporary measure, just for the duration, and that the anarchic Soviet democracy which existed in the first days after the October Revolution would return once the domestic and foreign enemy were defeated. They had learned well two techniques of ruling men: the appeal to the anarchic instincts of the masses and repression. The drama of Lenin's last years consisted in the struggle between those two tendencies within his Party, as well as in his grasping for another, different formula for rule, and discovering, on his deathbed, that it had eluded him.

In 1917, when he was striving to overthrow old Russia, Lenin wrote that within "twenty-four hours after the overthrow of capitalism" simple workers would be able to control production, there would be no need for material incentives, all officials, managers, and similar personnel would be paid a worker's wage. In 1921 he was trying to build a new Russia and he had different things to say: "Can any worker administer the state? Practical people know that that is fantasy. . . . After they [the workers] spend years in learning they will know how, but this takes time." Lenin the Marxist had to struggle with his anarchist ghost, the Lenin of October. But around the latter there now assembled a crowd of flesh-and-blood people who called for the redemption of the promises of the Revolution. This was the Workers' Opposition, a group which arose within the Party and which between 1920 and 1922 challenged Lenin's and official Soviet policies.

The Workers' Opposition has often but mistakenly been represented as the voice of democracy within the Party. To be sure, it objected to Lenin's and his lieutenants' high-handed ways. And it protested against the already considerable growth of Soviet bureaucracy, and the officials' higher pay and privileges;[9] but the Opposition's solicitude extended only to the Communists and workers, and took little account of the vast majority of the population, the peasants. Like practically every opposition within Communism, it pleaded not for tolerance but for a *different type* of intolerance than that practiced by the current Party oligarchy. The Opposition assailed the employment of "bourgeois specialists" in the economy and administration, where their professional abilities were in fact badly needed if the country was to recover from misery and chaos. That the former "exploiter who through neglect had not been finished off"[10] was again a boss, with special food rations and living quarters; that some Communist administrators like Krasin favored this species over Bolshevik veterans of the underground and the Civil War, it was held to be a scandal and a betrayal of all that the Revolution had been fought for.

Alongside such proletarian obscurantism and class hatred the Workers' Opposition represented genuine ideological postulates and aspirations. Most of all the Opposition wanted the workers and not the government or even the Party to run industry. The economy should be controlled by the trade unions. They in turn should have their leaders genuinely elected by rank-and-file union members, rather than, as increasingly was the case, having them imposed by the Party's Central Committee.

Leading the Workers' Opposition was the incongruous pair of Alexandra Kollontay and Alexander Shlyapnikov. The general's daughter and the former metalworker were now united in romance as well as in politics. Mme. Kollontay wrote a pamphlet bewailing the workers' hard lot in the workers' state and denouncing the growing bureaucratic rot allegedly caused by bourgeois and other alien class elements in administration and economic management. Shlyapnikov, never reconciled to his eclipse in Party affairs in those days of March–April 1917, took to the political struggle with gusto. He retained the mannerisms and freedom of speech of an earlier period of Bolshevism, but what had been considered proletarian forthrightness was now judged as want of discipline and lack of reverence for the leaders, and he sorely tried Lenin's patience.

Whatever its virtues and sins, the Workers' Opposition expressed a sentiment shared by many not within its ranks, a sentiment that something was wrong in the Soviet state, and that this something, far from diminishing, was in fact growing. Was it Lenin? One of the Opposition

[9] Considerable though these were by the standards and notions of 1918, Soviet Russia was in 1921 an egalitarian paradise, or more properly speaking, purgatory, in comparison with the situation from about 1930 to the present.

[10] An attempt at translation of a really untranslatable, much more succinct and colorful term then much in use.

members called him the bureaucrat-in-chief to his face, but as yet most Communists revered the man who had led them through such incredible trials and hardships.

Another group of oppositionists concentrated their fire on the erosion of democracy within the Party. Already at the Ninth Congress, in 1920, it was charged that the Party and the country were ruled by a despotic oligarchy. Why, said one delegate, there had been cases in which the entire executive committee of a city or provincial soviet had been imprisoned by order of an individual commissar, without his even bothering to ask the Central Committee for permission! But these protests ran into the quite logical rebuttal that the Communist Party as a whole was in fact an oligarchy, although for politeness' sake this was styled the "vanguard of the working class." "We don't believe in 'absolutes,' we laugh at 'pure democracy,' " said Lenin, and he could have reminded his opponents that they did so along with him when they overturned Kerensky and chased out the Constituent Assembly. "Comrade Lenin," said one exasperated delegate, "allow us ignoramuses to ask you a question. . . . Do you think that the only salvation of the Revolution lies in mechanical obedience?" But what answer did he expect? Some of the Opposition's ideas for bridging the gap between the masses and the rulers smacked of what today would be classed as Maoism: the Party was to be purged of all "careerists" (defined as people of nonworker and nonpeasant background who joined it after the middle of 1918); *every* member of the Party, including, presumably, Lenin, should be obliged to spend three months a year in *physical* labor as either an industrial or a rural worker.[11]

For all the mutually contradictory or actually absurd nature of the Opposition's demands, they brought to Lenin the realization that Communism was face to face with a danger as great as that posed by the Civil War and even more complex: the Party was slipping out of control, reverting to the turbulent ways of pre–World War I Russian Social Democracy. His campaign against what he conceived to be the anarchistic tendencies within the Communist Party was to be his last *successful* major political struggle. But he won it only at the price of sacrificing what still remained of the democratic spirit in Communism, and turning over the Party organization to the one man whose brutal and unscrupulous energy he knew was equal to the task.

The first and fundamental battle touched on the role of the trade unions. Here his success in repulsing the demands that the unions run the economy, and that Russia should have in effect workers' control of industry, was greatly helped by Trotsky's impolitic intervention in the debate. The War Commissar spelled out what Lenin was thinking but

[11] *The Ninth Congress of the Russian Communist Party (b)* (Moscow, 1963), p. 654.

was too diplomatic to say, and did so with brutal explicitness: it was sheer nonsense to babble about proletarian democracy when Russia's economy was in ruins and required military methods to get going again, he argued. The unions had to be strictly controlled by the Party. All democratic and egalitarian compunction had to yield to the drive for higher production. Marxism, he reminded the Party, never promised equality until the final stage of abundance of Communism was reached. Men work because they have to, and work well because of material incentives. Just as the Civil War could not have been won without military specialists, so the war for production for socialism could not be carried on without skilled managers and engineers.

Trotsky's frankness enabled Lenin to play the role of a moderate, of an arbiter between the "anarchosyndicalist" Shlyapnikov and the "militarist" Trotsky. God forbid that the workers' state should abolish the workers' unions or turn them into purely administrative agencies! No, trade unions should function freely, they should be "schools of Communism." But the state (i.e., the Party) should control the economy. With Trotsky once again serving as the lightning rod for antiauthoritarian and egalitarian forces, Lenin's position was endorsed by the Ninth and Tenth Party Congresses in 1920 and 1921.

Stalin eschewed a prominent part in this trade union dispute—wisely for his future career. Though there was some superficial similarity between the Workers' Opposition postulates and those of the "military opposition" during the Civil War, the background of the dispute was quite different. The opponents of military specialists had often been motivated by their own ambitions to command; here, whatever the personal motives of Shlyapnikov or Kollontay, there was a genuine grassroots feeling of resentment among the workers at the return of the "capitalist boss," rechristened "economic specialist." Stalin may even have shared this feeling. Class hatred was not the least prominent among his many hatreds. As dictator he licensed the trials of managers and engineers who were made to confess to belonging to a fictitious "industrial party," etc. But of course he was also the man who would subjugate trade unions and submit the workers to a discipline undreamed of by Trotsky at his most authoritarian, and who would create that Soviet managerial elite whose emoluments and privileges made the special benefits of the "bourgeois specialists" of the 1920s seem puny by comparison. Now he stood firmly behind Lenin and his allegedly compromise position. It gave him a welcome opportunity to assail Trotsky—a man, he said, who "does not understand the difference between the army and the working class." Persuasion rather than compulsion, as Trotsky would have it, should be used to harness the labor unions in the task of reviving the economy.

Another of Stalin's infrequent interventions in the issue that rocked

Russian Communism for about three years was on the opposite front, that against what Lenin called the "anarchosyndicalist deviation" of Shlyapnikov. Despite the several condemnations of Workers' Opposition postulates by Party Congresses and Conferences,[12] this "deviation" kept popping up like some medieval heresy condemned by Church councils but embedded in the simple faith of laymen. The regime therefore resorted to chicanery against the more prominent Opposition leaders. They were sent on missions abroad—thus began Mme. Kollontay's long diplomatic career. Michael Tomsky, who was enormously popular with workers, showed himself not free from error: it was discovered that he was badly needed for Party work in Turkestan. A few months among the sands of Central Asia, and he came back chastened and ready to support Lenin. In a secret vote the Tenth Party Congress authorized the Central Committee to throw out people from the Party for factionalism.[13] Still the damnable heresy persisted. It raised its head at the Fourth All-Russian Congress of Trade Unions in May 1921. And somebody in the Party Secretariat (it shows what a mess its affairs were in before Stalin took over) had the fantastic idea of delegating Ryazanov to defend the official Party line before the Communist caucus of the Congress.

To be sure, the old eccentric had supported Lenin on the issue. Always ready with a quip, Ryazanov convulsed the gathering by declaring that Mme. Kollontay's proletarian zeal reminded him of those wellborn maidens who in the 1870s went "to the people" to instruct the benighted peasants in the latest political fashions. But he was a hopeless individualist, and it occurred to him while he was speaking that, by God, it was true that the unions were being run in an undemocratic way! So he proposed an amendment, which carried, stipulating that union officials should be elected according to scrupulous democratic norms. Lenin, Stalin, and Bukharin had to rush in to try to undo the damage. This sudden emergency had the usual effect on Stalin of transforming him from a skillful and judicious political manipulator into a violent and threatening accuser. He lashed out at Ryazanov and those who supported him. "Shut up, you fool!" he shouted, when Ryazanov interrupted his speech.[14] It fell to Lenin to soothe tempers and to persuade the delegates to reverse their vote. Ryazanov, who had an-

---

[12] The Party Conference, which did not possess the powers of the Congress, was a gathering of officials rather than of elected delegates of the membership.

[13] The first of many to be so excluded was Gabriel Myasnikov, a renowned partisan leader of the Civil War, who was naïve enough to advocate freedom of the press "from the monarchist journals to anarchist ones."

[14] Roy Medvedev, *Let History Judge* (New York, 1971), p. 34. The author somewhat distorts Ryazanov's position. Stalin may well have been discomfited by the occasion, for his speech was booed. It is not included in the *Collected Works*.

swered Stalin tit for tat, was henceforth banned from any activity connected with trade unions.

To Lenin, Stalin's performance was evidently far from disgraceful. Lenin was already in bad health, and though maintaining outward composure, increasingly despairing of his ability to control his turbulent Party, fearful of the future of the experiment he had launched with such blind confidence four years earlier. Hence he increasingly relied on his vigorous lieutenant, whose very brutality exerted such a strange attraction. Stalin was charged with investigating the mess in the union movement, and it was following his recommendations that its leaders were reprimanded and transferred to other posts.[15] But Stalin avoided further overt interventions in the debate. He was a fast learner.

Stalin's main activities in 1921–22 removed him, in fact, from the attention of most politically minded members of the Party, and there-fore it is credible (though this has been much exaggerated) that many rank-and-file members were caught by surprise by his enormous and seemingly sudden prominence when Lenin fell hopelessly ill. Politics revolved around dramatic events at home and abroad, and in them Stalin seemed to play a very subordinate part. He avoided the impas-sioned oratory of the Party Congresses and Conferences, with the excep-tion already noted. And from the perspective of the average Party member, politics after the Civil War had reverted to its normal pattern of orators competing to persuade the audience that each knew the only correct application of Marxism to current problems, that this or that policy was the only one which would have secured the blessing of Marx or Engels. The center of the stage was occupied by Lenin—thundering against the un-Marxist distortions of Shlyapnikov and Kollontay; ex-plaining how Marxism in Russia's current condition demanded state capitalism, rather than workers' control of industry, sanctioning by the same argument the New Economic Policy, which relieved the peasant's lot and allowed the return of private enterprise to retail trade and small industry.[16]

Clustered around Lenin were figures like Trotsky, who spoke often with his customary brilliance and arrogance; Zinoviev, who in addition to resuming his role as Lenin's chief political assistant and frequent spokesman, was the executive head of the Communist International and as such wove tales of still intriguing revolutionary possibilities in Ger-many or the colonial world; Bukharin, the main political writer for

[15] Robert V. Daniels, *The Conscience of the Revolution* (Cambridge, Mass., 1960), p. 157.

[16] The NEP was introduced in 1921, its main feature the substitution of the tax in kind for the previous policy of requisitioning of what was arbitrarily declared the peasant's grain surplus. With the peasant now reassured that only a *scheduled* part of his crop would be taken by the state, Russian agriculture began to revive.

Pravda; Kamenev, who in view of his temper was considered the Party's elder statesman though he was not yet forty. For the dissenter who felt that members of this group, for all their past services, were a clique that inhibited intraparty democracy, the main stage of Party life was also occupied by other people whose names are now remembered only by scholars: people like Yurenyev and Sapronov, who not so much argued as pleaded with Lenin to change his ways. These, many felt, were men of the future. After all, whatever the machinations of the oligarchs of the Central Committee, the Party Congress was the sovereign body. One day Lenin would either not be there or would see his error in sheltering those men who had grown too used to power and were forgetting the comradely customs of the old days.

Stalin? He was mostly in the wings, appearing but infrequently on the main stage. He was thought of mainly as a specialist and as a Party workhorse (like, say, Dzerzhinsky, who in addition to this very necessary but rather unpleasant job of identifying and destroying "enemies of the people" had also been commandeered into tough administrative tasks as Commissar of Transport and head of the National Economic Council). Somebody had to attend to the necessary but not terribly important tasks of planning the formal constitutional framework of the Soviet state, working out the structure of those innumerable national republics and districts, and thus leaving the Party *statesmen* to discuss the real issues. Stalin appeared immersed in addressing Bashkirs, reassuring Byelorussians and Ukrainians that the Party was solicitous about the development of their national cultures, settling obscure tribal disputes in the Caucasus. It was difficult to think of him as a political figure.

Stalin's activity of those years is also downgraded by his biographers, eager to move on to his alleged intrigues to succeed Lenin. Yet it presents some interesting sidelights on the man and the times. He worked indefatigably to build the complex multinational structure which in 1924 was proclaimed the Union of Soviet Socialist Republics.[17] *Politically* there could be no question in his mind that all the "independent" as well as autonomous national subdivisions had to be strictly controlled from Moscow. But culturally the period of his intense Russian chauvinism was still in the future. And so the 1920s were a period of vigorous sponsorship of non-Russian languages and literatures. Stalin defended the regime from the charge of creating artificial national entities. Thus it was argued by others that Byelorussian was but a

[17] Until then the Ukraine, Byelorussia, and Transcaucasia were on paper independent. The Treaty of Riga with Poland had thus to be signed by the Ukraine and Byelorussia as well as by the Russian Soviet Republic. This led to a rather comic embarrassment when it turned out that none of the Soviet Ukrainian or Byelorussian negotiators knew "their" language, and it fell to a Polish negotiator to translate the text of the treaty into Ukrainian and Byelorussian.

peasant dialect because the region's city-dwellers (like those of the Ukraine) spoke Russian. But, retorted Stalin, this had been the pattern in the case of every oppressed nationality. Hungary's cities used to be German in character; with the growth of Hungarian culture and national consciousness they became "Magyarized." It was the duty of the Communists to help develop Ukrainian and Byelorussian cultures. This gives us another glimpse at a well-read man whose sensible views on the matter clash with those of the Stalin of twenty and thirty years hence, who sponsored cultural Russification and undoubtedly regretted his activities in creating the Ukrainian and Byelorussian intelligentsia.

The same impression is conveyed by Stalin's utterances on economic problems. Many Communists accepted the NEP reluctantly, viewing it as a capitulation to the peasant and an encouragement to the growth of capitalism in the countryside: the villager would now be able to dispose freely of his grain and meat surplus. But for Stalin this was a colossal step forward, "since it stimulated the productive energy of the producer." His analogy was vastly extravagant: still, it demonstrated acquaintance with economic history. "Russia is now undergoing an outburst of the forces of production of the kind experienced by the United States after the Civil War.[18] But there is also a new note: we perceive Stalin the social engineer, who will strive after gigantic "leaps forward" and will brook no interference by economic realities or human cost. When his prognosis turned out to be wildly overoptimistic, he subjected the Russian to the cruelest ordeal in his long experience with oppression.

To Lenin, it was Stalin's ability to work which was the main argument in his favor. Any dispute with one of the intelligentsia kind of Communists would bring to Lenin's mind how fortunate he was to have among his lieutenants one who worked so uncomplainingly at so many jobs. Adolf Yoffe, a leading Soviet diplomat (he had been the chairman of the first Soviet delegation to Brest-Litovsk), wrote to Lenin complaining about being shifted from one job to another, and was ill advised enough to blame this situation on Lenin himself: "You are the Central Committee," he wrote. Lenin was very sensitive about being identified as a dictator. He advised his old friend to take care of his nerves, and held up Stalin as an example of a proletarian who went from one job to another whenever the Party required him to do so.[19] In another letter Lenin spelled out the difference between the two types: "a decadent petty intellectual when he sees an untoward incident or injustice" whimpers, cries, and complains, while "the proletarian . . .

18 Stalin, v, 124.
19 Yoffe followed Lenin's advice and went to Vienna, where he became the first, possibly the only, prominent Communist to undergo psychoanalysis. He shot himself some years later.

seeing something wrong, goes about correcting it in a businesslike way."

Considering his considerable experience with "proletarians" (including Stalin) who threw fits, Lenin's stereotypes were not merely childish but self-revealing. In 1921–22 he was already ill, and increasingly harassed and irritable. In such a frame of mind he forgot the Stalin of the Civil War who threatened to resign and "go to the devil if need be," and saw only a patient administrator. When somebody at a Party gathering protested the accumulation of jobs in Stalin's hands Lenin launched into a veritable eulogy: in the Commissariat of Nationalities you need a man "to whom representatives of all nationalities can go and unbosom themselves." Who was such a man? *Everybody* would bring up one name: Stalin. As for the Commissariat of Control, "There you have a gigantic task. But in order to know how to deal with inspection, you need to have at its head a man of real authority, otherwise we shall sink, shall drown in a sea of petty intrigues."[20]

It is therefore at least fanciful for some Soviet historians, official and unofficial,[21] to suggest that Stalin was *not* Lenin's personal choice for the post of the General Secretary of the Central Committee to which he was elevated in April 1922 and in which he continued until December 1952. This appointment was the logical outcome of the Eleventh Party Congress, at which Lenin realized that he was losing his hold over the situation and that, unless decisive measures were taken, Communist politics would revert to a struggle between factions and cliques.

Though Lenin delivered the main political report and spoke in rebuttal to its criticisms, he did not attend most of the sessions. The regime, and he personally, were being assailed on several fronts. Some time before the Congress, in February, twenty-two Communists, headed by the incorrigible Shlyapnikov and Kollontay, petitioned the Third International with complaints against their own government. Their grievances make interesting reading for those who believe that it was Stalin who *began* chicanery and repression in the Soviet state. There was no freedom of criticism within the Russian Communist Party, the twenty-two asserted. They were being watched by the political police, their mail was intercepted, their apartments searched; a Cheka agent tried to involve Shlyapnikov in a political provocation, thus to provide grounds for his exclusion from the Party; in the alleged workers' state strikes were being broken with the help of the army.

The Executive of the Comintern—being of course the creature of the very same government against whom the twenty-two complained— exonerated the Soviet regime, though in somewhat embarrassed language. But at the Congress the same charges were repeated to Lenin's

[20] *The Eleventh Congress of the Russian Communist Party* (*b*) (Moscow, 1961), p. 143.
[21] Such as Medvedev, p. 18.

face. Ryazanov described how the right to strike was being suppressed in Soviet Russia,[22] how some bureaucrats had tried to prevent him from speaking at Party gatherings. Others cited similar instances of high-handedness and of falsification of election results in the labor union and Party local organizations.

Lenin's answer to these attacks showed little of his usual diplomatic persuasiveness. One senses instead a man close to the limits of his physical and nervous endurance. He was angry and threatening. As one delegate said: "Comrade Lenin struck a false note . . . he said one should beat, shoot, squeeze."[23] And some of the awe that had surrounded him ever since Brest-Litovsk was now dissipating. People joked about the leaders threatening them—always a danger signal for a dictatorship. They proposed to gun down all the opposition! exclaimed Shlyapnikov, pointing to the Presidium of the Congress, Lenin among its members. This, alas, proved not to be a joke but a fairly accurate prophecy of what would happen in about fifteen years, among others to himself.[24] The Central Committee is a very peculiar institution, said Ryazanov, more powerful than the British Parliament. The latter, it is asserted, can do anything but change a man into a woman. But the Central Committee "has already turned more than one revolutionary into an old woman and the number of such cases is multiplying in a most astounding manner.[25]

Lenin's ability to manage the Party he had created was clearly drawing to an end. His prestige was still great enough to get the Congress to approve most of the regime's policies. But on certain issues he had to compromise. He had tried to exclude Kollontay and Shlyapnikov from the Party, but the Congress would not have it, only some secondary troublemakers were kicked out and the two main culprits were merely reprimanded. On another important matter the Central Committee got its way only by falsifying the results of the vote.

This concerned the Party Control Commissions. These had been created in 1920 to do for the Party what Stalin's Commissariat of Control was supposed to do for the *state* administration: to act as a check on corruption and official privilege, to curtail red tape, to be the guardian of Communist morals. It was Lenin's fond and naïve hope that the control organs would keep the Party free of the vices which in

[22] The Congress passed a resolution of sympathy and support for the "striking workers of America."

[23] *The Eleventh Congress of the Russian Communist Party (b)*, p. 89.

[24] In 1933 Shlyapnikov was excluded from the Party, allegedly not for political reasons but as a "degenerate." This might well have been Stalin's personal revenge for Shlyapnikov's having tried to keep him out of the Central Committee "because of certain personal characteristics of his."

[25] *The Eleventh Congress of the Russian Communist Party (b)*, p. 79.

the past had afflicted every ruling group, that they would somehow, even in the absence of political opposition, keep it close to and accountable to the masses.

The control organs launched with gusto into the job of prying, not only into official activities but also into the private lives of individual Communists. Soon *subordinate* Communist officials had to watch their step if fond of vodka or wenching, if scandalously inefficient or indolent; the local Control Commission would get after them. But from the beginning it was clear that the same vigilance was not observed when it came to the high and mighty. To be sure, there were cases in those days when complaints were lodged against members of the Party oligarchy. A railway guard in Moscow cited Stalin in 1920 for abusive language and behavior. In 1921 Stalin's wife, Nadezhda Alliluyeva, had her Party membership suspended—possibly for nothing more heinous than her failure to attend the prescribed quota of her Party cell meetings—and it was restored only on Lenin's personal intervention. But from the beginning the special attention of the control organs was directed to the sins and transgressions of those Party notables who found themselves in *opposition* to Lenin and the Central Committee. Mme. Kollontay, it was discovered, lied about the length of her Party membership, dating it back to 1898 while everybody knew that the woman had been a Menshevik until 1917! Though the control organs were separate in personnel from other organs of the Party, and no member of the Central Committee could sit on the Central Control Commission, the latter in fact became an added instrument of the regime's repression of criticism. And under Stalin the control organs became one of his main tools for fastening his dictatorship on the Party.

At the Eleventh Congress the motion to abolish the Control Commissions, and to turn their functions concerning alleged breaches of law over to the state, and those concerning Communist ethics over to Party courts, was, according to the official count, rejected by a vote of 223–89. On the face of it, these figures are suspicious, since the Congress was attended by 520 delegates with the right to vote. And at a subsequent Congress an official of the Control Commission was to confess rather good-naturedly that the figures had been "fixed."

"Comrade Lenin may be laughing now, but we will see what he will have to say at the next Party Congress," said an opposition speaker at one point in the proceedings. Lenin would never see another Congress. But at the time he felt that something had to be done if the threat implicit in that statement was not to become reality. One day after the Congress closed on April 3, it was announced that the Central Committee had designated Stalin as its General Secretary. The office of Secretary (though not of General Secretary) had existed since 1919, but most Party members would have laughed had they been told that its incumbents were pretenders to the leadership. (Since 1921 there had been three Secretaries, principal among them Molotov.) And at the Eleventh Congress the bureaucratic ways and red tape of the Party Secretariat were the subject of much ironical comment. The Congress was convulsed when one delegate quoted what he called a typical interoffice memorandum of the Secretariat: "The telephone operator of the general section, Comrade Mutalova, is as of this date to be referred to as Mrs. Nezamedinova. Please furnish the information about the birthdate and the application of Comrade Mutalova-Nezamedinova." (The atmosphere of the Secretariat was not free of male chauvinism. The head of its women's section was invited to a conference only when affairs of her section were discussed; if the conferees then passed on to other topics she was invited to leave.) Nobody thought of the Secretariat, as distinct from, say, the Control Commission, as having any sinister powers or potentialities. Stalin's becoming General Secretary was thus unlikely to create much stir—just one more dull administrative post for this strange man who evidently preferred bureaucratic drudgery to politics (he did not speak once during the Eleventh Congress). Molotov and another Old Bolshevik of bourgeois antecedents, Valerian Kuibyshev, were named his assistants, and indeed they were to become more than that, his most loyal servants during his ascent to absolute power.

Lenin viewed the appointment in a different light. He may or may not have said, as Trotsky reports, "That cook will concoct nothing but peppery dishes," but certainly he hoped so. Stalin would free him from those humiliating and exhausting combats with the opposition. He would take the local Party organization in hand, make sure that they did not send to the Congresses so many people ready to applaud Shlyapnikov or Ryazanov, and to remain unscandalized when those impudent speakers called him "oligarch" or "bureaucrat-in-chief." The give and take of Party life, which he once enjoyed, now irritated and fatigued him. He wanted to have more time for state affairs, and not expand his dwindling energy in defending himself against charges that what he was doing in 1922 was exactly the opposite of what he had promised to do in 1917 or 1918. To an extent, his sentiments were shared by other members of the oligarchy. Much as they disliked and competed with each other, they all resented being criticized by some ignorant boor who, because he had joined the Party in 1910 or displayed animal-like courage in the Civil War, thought that he was the equal of Trotsky or Zinoviev. The mere idea that *they* should be required to spend three months of every year at physical labor! The insolence of denouncing them to foreign Communists on the Comintern! Stalin would know how to take care of all that. Some may have calculated with secret pleasure that in the process Stalin was bound to become unpopular among the rank and file, to be resented for the further curtailment of criticism and freedom within the Party.

Stalin was much too clever not to see through this. Superficially, his new post promised to add little in the way of tangible power or added prestige. Already, as the only man who was on both the Politburo and the Organizational Bureau, he was in a position to exert influence on the Party apparatus, and it would have seemed preferable to do it through a personal satellite like Molotov than to assume direct responsibility. Indeed, looked at in one light, it could well be chalked up as yet another grievance, another instance of "being picked on." But Stalin undertook the job because of his already enormous self-assurance. As he saw it, his colleagues were for the most part loafers, splendid at speech-making and posturing, but unwilling to tackle an arduous day-to-day job. As a result the affairs of the Party were in a mess. Now they wanted him to deal with a rebellious Party committee in Tambov or to chastise choleric trade unionists, so that they could have more time for their speeches and intrigues, hoping in the bargain that he would break his political neck and became another Molotov. Well, he would show them!

O N May 26, 1922, Lenin suffered a stroke which caused a partial paralysis of the right side and a loss of speech. Though his condition soon improved and in July he was able to speak and write again, it was suddenly clear (he was but fifty-two) that his days as an active politician were numbered.

Sentiment apart, Lenin's removal from the political scene had to be viewed with the utmost concern by the Party and especially its ruling group. He was more popular in the country than his Party was; and within the Party, for all the criticism he had recently incurred, more popular than the rest of the Politburo together. Without him, what would happen to the Soviet ship of state, which he had guided with such incredible skill—or luck, depending on one's view—through one cataclysmic storm after another? And would the ruling group be able to preserve its powers and privileges with him gone or incapacitated?

It is thus no surprise that the Party oligarchy strove desperately to keep alive the hope, which by the late fall of 1922 had become a fiction and deception, that Lenin's debility was but temporary and that he would be back, with his powers fully restored, guiding the Party and the state as before. Stalin's contribution to this campaign of reassurance could undoubtedly be rated very high as an exercise in public relations. He was asked by *Pravda*, he wrote in one newspaper account, to record some of his personal impressions of Vladimir Ilyich during the latter's convalescence in the country. Well, it was not quite appropriate to write about it now that Comrade Lenin had almost completed his vacations (*sic!*) and was ready to return to work. Besides, the interviews filled one with so many priceless impressions and memories, how could one summarize them in a brief article? But the newspaper editors insist. . . .

At his first meeting in July, Stalin wrote, Comrade Lenin reminded him of those old warriors who, having struggled without respite, collapse, but, after a brief rest, are fully refreshed and ready to plunge into the most strenuous activity again. And in truth, in July Lenin was exactly like that, fully refreshed with only traces of his former fatigue and strain. (He was just beginning to speak and write again.) The doctors tried to keep him from politics, "but we laugh at the doctors who cannot understand that two professional politicians when they meet cannot be kept from talking about politics." And so they talked about all the current issues: about the trial of Socialist Revolutionary "saboteurs,"[26] about the Genoa conference, where Soviet diplomats were then making their international debut, about prospects for the harvest (good!), about finances.

A month passed and Stalin saw Lenin again, "surrounded by a pile of books." Not a trace of the former residue of strain and fatigue: it is "our old Lenin who looks at you slyly, squinting his eyes." He is full of confidence: Russia's main difficulties are behind us, he asserts. The foreign capitalist powers? "Because of greed they hate each other." If the Soviets hold their course steadily, they have nothing to be afraid of. How about the Mensheviks and Socialist Revolutionaries who agitate madly against Soviet Russia from abroad? "For our working class they have long been dead." And all those lies about how mortally ill Comrade Lenin is? He "just smiles and notes, 'Let them lie if it makes them happy. One should not deprive the dying of their last consolation.'"[27] In its way this is a small masterpiece of propaganda. With a few lines Stalin conveys the impression of a Lenin fully recovered, ready to lead yet another triumphant advance of Communism, confident that everything is going splendidly in politics and the economy. Above all he conveys his own great political and personal intimacy with Lenin. According to Stalin, they discussed everything under the sun, Lenin

[26] This was perhaps the first of the Soviet "show" trials. Several Socialist Revolutionaries, though recently inactive politically, some of them jailed for several years, were put on trial for allegedly collaborating with White generals to subvert the Communist regime.

[27] Stalin, v, 184–86.

relied on him for information, and he did not intrude his own opinions but simply asked questions, listened, and modestly tried to memorize verbatim the weightiest of the great man's statements.

What reader of this heartwarming sketch who was not in the know could guess at the truth? Lenin was still exhausted, incurably ill, beset by desperate anxieties. To the old worries about the Party and the state of the economy were joined new ones. What were his lieutenants doing in his absence? Why weren't those Socialist Revolutionary leaders put to death?[28] Was the NEP really, as his opponents in the Party charged and the émigré Mensheviks gloated, leading to a revival of capitalism? Were the Soviet negotiators in Genoa being taken in by wily British diplomats? A frantic Lenin chafed under the restraints that kept him from politics at the same time as he despaired of ever being well enough to catch up with the work.

Lenin's absence brought out in full the oligarchic character of the Soviet government, somewhat obscured when he was at the helm. The top and intermediate oligarchy—members of the Politburo and of the Central Committee[29]—were already sliding into the habits and attitudes of a ruling class. There was as yet little material corruption in the strict sense of the word. Stalin, like many other Soviet dignitaries, lived with his wife in a very modest apartment in the Kremlin.[30] We know from Svetlana Alliluyeva's recollections that as early as the end of the Civil War her parents (as well as other notable families) acquired a country residence, or *dacha*; in many cases these had belonged to pre-Revolutionary capitalists. This could hardly qualify as a serious abuse— only a misanthrope would begrudge the government figures who had spent their youth and early manhood in prison and exile some comforts inaccessible to the ordinary citizen, and one ought not censor Trotsky for his unproletarian passion for hunting either. But by the still very

[28] The trial attracted a lot of unfavorable publicity abroad. Bukharin and Karl Radek, in negotiations with Western left-wing socialist leaders, promised that there would be no death sentences. Yet twelve leading Socialist Revolutionaries, convicted on false evidence, were sentenced to death. On Kamenev's motion (not, as Trotsky claims, on his) the Politburo authorized suspension of death sentences, i.e., the twelve received life imprisonment and would be executed if at any time some *other* Socialist Revolutionary attempted a terroristic act against the regime.

[29] There were at the time eleven full and alternate members of the Politburo, forty-six of the Central Committee.

[30] In 1918 he had married Nadezhda Alliluyeva, a secretary in his Commissariat of Nationalities. She was then seventeen, but it was not unusual for girls of this age from Old Bolshevik families to be working at such jobs. The girl's mother, we are told by their daughter Svetlana, was opposed to the union. There was, of course, a great disparity in age, twenty-two years, and the Alliluyevs knew their future son-in-law's personal characteristics better than most. To Nadezhda, who remembered Stalin from childhood as a revolutionary conspirator and martyr, he must have still appeared as a romantic hero. Their son, Vassily, was born in 1920. Stalin's son of his first marriage, Jacob, continued to live with relatives in Georgia.

egalitarian norms of revolutionary Russia this was a breach of etiquette. Leaders were not supposed to enjoy any material privileges! With the NEP licensing private trade there would soon be rich entrepreneurs, but a Communist was strictly forbidden to become one, no matter what his official position; even Lenin was not supposed to receive a salary exceeding the wages of the skilled workers. But as in almost every similar case in history, these established puritan norms could not prevent those in the ruling group from enjoying privileges unavailable to the ordinary mortal.

The main problem and the main abuses did not lie in the sphere of material privileges. It is arguable that it would have been better for Communism, certainly for Russia, if it had. But the main luxury the new rulers craved was power. And what made it worse was that this craving was based on the feeling—undoubtedly sincere in most cases—that the policies and tactics which either Stalin or Trotsky advocated were the only ones that could save the Revolution and move it forward, that history and Marxism were on his side, and ignorance if not indeed ill will or treason on that of his opponents.

Even before the period of the so-called struggle for succession and even among the oligarchs with no ambition for the top spot, there was a luxuriant growth of authoritarian habits and mentality. A Party office (this was much less true of state offices) was already not just a job to which one was elected by one's equals, but a piece of that magic dimension of life called power. The secretary of some petty Party committee viewed himself not as a mere administrator—that was the job of his corresponding number in the state hierarchy, the chairman of the local soviet, who worried about roads and street lighting, say—but as something much more elevated, as head of a congregation of the faithful whose spiritual life, or to translate into the Communist vernacular, whose "level of class-consciousness" and "ideological vigilance" were his responsibility. He could be removed by his comrades, but this was more and more unlikely if his superior, or especially some potentate at the center, were his sponsor. As one rose in the hierarchy one's conviction of one's own heroic stature and historical role became more pronounced. It is almost incredible that as early as 1922 Tsaritsyn became Stalingrad. It is unlikely that for all his megalomania Stalin *initiated* this christening; he was too wary a politician. But the local Communist notables sought to flatter him, in the way that medieval burghers sought the protection of some feudal lord or dedicated their town to a saint. There was also to be (not for long) a Trotsk and a Zinovievsk. (Prophetically, they were much smaller towns!) Stalin's "cult of personality" grew in a Soviet soil in which many such minor cults had already sprouted.

On October 2 Lenin returned to work, and insofar as outsiders, i.e., the vast majority of the Party members, were concerned, things returned to normal. But as those close to him noticed, he was not the same Lenin. And, as he gave every indication of sensing, it was not the same Party he had had to leave four months before.

There now ensued the extraordinary drama of Lenin's last months as a political leader, and then the tragedy of the helpless invalid watching as the man he had finally come to understand and loathe took over his life's work while he was unable himself to speak out.

Lenin's mood was brittle and irritable. Obviously he should have gone south for further recuperation instead of plunging into work more demanding than ever and facing the rigors of a Moscow winter. But he would not hear of any reduction in his work load. He suspected and was not far wrong about the existence of a veritable plot in the Politburo—conceived either from solicitude for his health or other less laudable motives—to reduce him to a figurehead while exploiting his prestige to rule themselves. And the main suspect was Stalin.

Even before his return to work in late September, Lenin wrote a letter to the Politburo members in which he criticized some details of Stalin's plans for the constitution on which he had been working. "Stalin has a tendency to be overhasty," he remarked, and asked that the Politburo wait for him, Lenin, before considering the whole matter. And the first people he wanted to confer with upon his return were the deputy chairman of the Council of Commissars, Rykov, on whom Lenin had leaned in state administration, and Trotsky: two Politburo members he felt he could count on. Rykov was straightforward and personally devoted; Trotsky certainly would not fall in with any scheme of Stalin's.

In a reply circulated to members of the Politburo the very same day, September 27, Stalin shows a different side of his relations with Lenin than the one he had so charmingly described for the readers of *Pravda*. He was obviously enraged, and anyone who thinks that he toadied to Lenin should read this document, in which he treats the man who still could destroy him politically with an insolence inconceivable on the part of any other member of the ruling group.[31] He took up Lenin's objections to his plan for federating the Soviet republics one by one. Yes on No. 1, Lenin's amendment was acceptable. No. 2, absolutely not! It would lead only to confusion and conflict. No. 3, "Comrade Lenin's correction is of only editorial significance." Concerning No. 4, Stalin grew sarcastic: Lenin has trapped himself! He proposes that several commissariats in the projected union exist only at the federal level, but "would not this overhastiness [an obvious retort to Lenin's characterization of Stalin] provide ammunition for our 'independentists' [i.e., Georgians, Ukrainians, etc., who had been resisting close federal ties]

[31] *The Trotsky Archive* (in the Harvard Library), T755.

and thus damage Comrade Lenin's reputation for liberalism on the nationality question"? Lenin's amendment No. 5 was "superfluous." And there was not a word to soften this harsh response to Lenin's rather polite and conciliatory memorandum, not a single expression of warmth toward his leader. Who, in a few years, would even dream of referring to Stalin in this vein?

Stalin's fury was enhanced by the knowledge that during his convalescence Lenin had seen Budu Mdivani, head of the Georgian malcontents, who undoubtedly complained about Orjonikidze's (i.e., Stalin's) arbitrary rule in the Caucasus. Here he was, doing all this work, holding the Party together, while Lenin was listening to gossip about the Georgian Communists! The old man was growing soft. If Lenin thought he could dispense with Stalin's services and enter on some combinations with Rykov and Trotsky, he would soon find out that he was irreplaceable.

And indeed this was the conclusion Lenin must have reached on his return to work in October. For the Party apparatus was for once running smoothly. Oppositionists were being put in their place—*out* of the Party offices and committees—so that the next Party Congress would not witness a rumpus like the Eleventh. "The masses decide everything" was a bracing Communist slogan, but Stalin knew that they would decide things *correctly* only with a proper guidance. You needed a well-oiled Party machinery whose officials had a personal stake in doing things right, that is to say, the way you wanted them to. Even before his formal installation as General Secretary, Stalin instructed Molotov to improve the material conditions of the "active Party workers." They were, he wrote, in a significant military simile to which he would return, the "noncommissioned officers of the Party" and had to be taken care of.

Wherever Lenin looked, there was Stalin or some confederate of his handling the main business. In the Central Control Commission, a body supposedly apart from factional politics and barred to leading Party potentates, the moving spirits were Aron Soltz and Matvei Shkiryatov. Soltz was an old pal of Stalin's from prewar days in St. Petersburg when they had once shared a conspiratorial hideout. A dull-minded bureaucrat who delighted in prying into and censoring the activities of his betters—Ryazanov called him a "governess in trousers" —he remained an obedient tool of Stalin's until the 1930s.[32] The Caucasus was a satrapy of Orjonikidze's. Even in the Politburo itself it

---

[32] When he objected to some features of the purges, he was carted off to an insane asylum, where he actually became mentally ill, and *then* he was released. A witness recalls the shattering picture of an old man constantly and in vain seeking an audience with the friend of his youth, and filling page after page with rows of figures, some private code of his demented mind. Yuri Trifonov, *In the Light of the Fire* (Moscow, 1966), p. 27. More fortunate, Shkiryatov remained the dictator's accomplice to the very end.

was obvious that Lenin's oldest lieutenants, Kamenev and Zinoviev, gravitated toward the General Secretary. Everywhere Stalin! "Ask Svidersky what Tsyurupa wrote; if he does not know, then ask Stalin," wrote Lenin in one of his frantic attempts to find out what was going on.

A dictator left in darkness as to what is going on in his Party! This was the ironic paradox of Lenin's situation in the last months of his active political life, between October 1922 and March 1923. And this was the picture that impressed itself on Stalin's mind and affected his actions in his own last years.

Trying to recover some grip on the situation, Lenin tried to have meetings of the Politburo tailored to his convenience and endurance: it was to meet once a week for not longer than three hours, its agenda was to be distributed at least one day in advance, additional material could not be presented except in the case of an extreme emergency. He bridled at suggestions to husband his strength, indignantly rejecting Rykov's suggestion that he see visitors only after they had been "cleared" by a Party secretary or deputy chairman of the Council of Commissars. The log of the secretaries attending Lenin in his last month shows how the sick man strove in vain to be informed about everything, with the predictable result that he got bogged down in minor details.[33] His overexertion hastened the inevitable: two minor strokes on December 13, a major one on December 16. This time he never recovered sufficiently to return to work.

Apart from his hopeless attempt to keep abreast of affairs Lenin during those two months of partial recovery tried to find a fulcrum to regain effective leadership. But it turned out impossible to find a Politburo member who in effect would do this work for him. Rykov was simply not cast for such a role. He was well liked in the Party, anxious to please everybody, but incapable of countering Stalin and his two current allies, Kamenev and Zinoviev. Trotsky was by now somewhat isolated in the Politburo, and much as he feared Zinoviev and loathed Stalin, he was unwilling to increase his isolation by fighting *all* of Lenin's battles.

Trotsky's literary skill has subsequently persuaded Western readers that the main reason for the Stalin-Zinoviev-Kamenev alliance was their fear of him as Lenin's logical successor. But that was only one and the less important reason why the Old Bolsheviks in the oligarchy clung to Stalin. They looked to him for salvation from the Party "masses," barely repulsed at the Eleventh Congress and now with Lenin incapacitated looming all the more dangerous. These "masses" had chafed under Lenin's rule; they would certainly not select Trotsky as his successor. All

---

[33] This was first printed in *Problems of History of the Communist Party* (Moscow, 1963), No. 2, pp. 70–91. This phase of Lenin's life is covered in my *Bolsheviks* (New York, 1965), pp. 555–75.

the members of the ruling oligarchy, not excluding Trotsky, thought with sinking hearts of the possibility of being supplanted on the Politburo and Central Committee by Shlyapnikovs, Osinskys, Sapronovs, et al.—the current advocates of these unruly democratic feelings which had been spreading in the Party since the end of the Civil War. It was Stalin who stood between them and this anarchic mob, as they viewed it. What Stalin was already accomplishing was well described in a lament of forty-six prominent Party figures written a year later, in October 1923: "free discussion in the Party has all but disappeared," they said, and it was not the body of the Party membership which elected the local committees and the Central Committee, but, "on the contrary, it is the *secretarial hierarchy* which more and more determines membership of Party Conferences and Congresses."[34] With his wretched sense of timing Trotsky was to appeal to this sentiment, but too late. Throughout most of 1923 he stood apart from those protesters, many of whom had viewed him as an exponent of the most authoritarian tendencies in the Party. And his vanity, unlike Stalin's, stimulated lassitude: everybody knew he was the second towering figure of the Revolution, the memories of his feats in October 1917 and in the Civil War would of themselves bring him the glittering prize.

Lenin's debility increased the oligarchs' dependence on Stalin. After December 16 it had to be recognized, though public communiqués about Lenin's health maintained the deception to the contrary till the very end, that he would never be able to shoulder political duties. But he might live semiparalyzed for years, able to communicate, to *intervene* in politics. Who could handle him, make sure that the sick man's resentment of fate would not also turn him against his old collaborators, lead him to pursue some whim that might upset the whole structure of political authority they had worked out so painstakingly?

On December 24 a committee of the Politburo composed of Stalin, Kamenev, and Bukharin held a conference with the doctors. It was decided that "Vladimir Ilyich has the right to dictate every day for five or ten minutes, but this cannot have the character of correspondence and Vladimir Ilyich may not expect to receive any answers. He is forbidden [political] visitors. Friends or those around him may not inform him about political affairs." Stalin was delegated the Politburo's liaison man with the doctors, in effect Lenin's guardian.

When these details were finally published in Russia in 1963, it was, of course, the intention of Khrushchev's regime, which authorized the release, to cast unfavorable light on Stalin. Yet as in the case of many such revelations, the story reflects more discredit on his colleagues than on him. He had not sought this assignment and, as a matter of fact,

---

[34] *The Trotsky Archive*, T802. My italics.

tried on at least one occasion to lay it down. It was bound to increase
Lenin's already increasing dislike and suspicion of Stalin, would almost
inevitably embroil Stalin with Lenin's family. And if Lenin had a spell
of recovery, Stalin would feel his wrath. The job called for a man of
tact, preferably for an old personal friend of the Lenin family like
Kamenev or the Commissar of Health, Dr. Semashko, an Old Bolshevik. The reasons the oligarchs turned this invidious job over to Stalin
were transparent, and he would not forget them.

Lenin took the "doctors' orders" as might have been expected: he felt
that he had been made a ward of the Politburo, and he did his
damnedest to frustrate the scheme, keep abreast of politics, and influence if not indeed direct policies from his sickbed. His political interventions between December and March thus sprang from a mixture of
motivations and moods: from a rethinking of some basic problems of
the Revolution, from rancor at his lieutenants' humiliating solicitude,
and from awareness of the approach of death and of the need to preserve and vindicate a life's work. The story of Lenin's last struggles is
full of pathos: it shows the old revolutionary's last conspiracy, in which
he involved his wife and attendants in trying to glean fobidden information and smuggle out articles and political directives. And too it reveals
how all along he had doubts about whether he was right in October,
whether some Marxist gods were not already taking their vengeance for
his having given history a push. The impatient authoritarian mood of
the man of destiny dropped off, revealing what Lenin was by heredity
and upbringing: a Russian *intelligent* of the old school, sensitive to
oppression and incivility.

The Lenin of this last phase amply justified the Politburo's forebodings. He became, if you please, a member of the intraparty opposition.
By threatening to go on strike and refuse medication, he won the right
to work on his papers for longer than "five or ten minutes." Some of
this "diary," as the old conspirator called it, he sought to have published
in *Pravda*; other, more sensitive items, more shattering to the oligarchy,
were for his own use if he ever again appeared at a Party Congress or, if
not, were to be communicated to the Party following his death. It is this
last document that became celebrated as Lenin's *Testament*.

Written in several installments between December 23 and 29, the
document is headed *Letter to the Congress*.[35] It began, "I would
strongly advise that this Congress adopt several changes in our political
system." The main change recommended was an increase in the number
of Central Committee members to fifty or a hundred. The additional
members ought to be rank-and-file workers and not those with governmental experience because the latter "have already formed well-known

[35] The Twelfth was scheduled to meet in March 1923.

habits and biases against which we must resolutely struggle." These workers, "being present at all meetings . . . of the Politburo, reading all the documents of the Central Committee . . . can add stability to the Committee . . . [can] renew and improve the [Party] apparatus."[36] Lenin then gives his reasons for this proposed "proletarization" of the Central Committee. There were currently dissensions on it, mainly between Stalin and Trotsky, he remarked: "Comrade Stalin, having become General Secretary, has accumulated enormous power in his hands, and I am not quite sure whether he will always be able to use this power carefully enough." Trotsky? To be sure, he was the most capable man on the Central Committee, but too self-confident, too much given to looking at politics from the administrative point of view. Kamenev and Zinoviev: Lenin recalled their less than heroic behavior in October 1917, but it should not be held against them, any more than Trotsky's separation from Bolshevism until 1917 should be considered a blemish on his record. Lenin then mentioned two younger men: Bukharin, a good theoretician, universally liked but, alas, weak on dialectics;[37] Pyatakov, again very able but like Trotsky an administrator rather than a politician.[38]

When the abovementioned gentlemen became acquainted with Lenin's document,[39] their feelings toward the deceased leader must have been less than kindly: what a plotter, even on his deathbed! This was a genuine plot against the "Leninist Old Guard," one which could not have been bettered by members of the Workers' Opposition. Sins of omission and commission were so indelicately sketched, and there was this intolerable insinuation that individually and collectively they were unworthy to fill his shoes, that they must be watched or supervised by some fifty boors fresh from the workbench or the plow!

Like the others, Stalin probably remained ignorant of the existence of Lenin's *Testament* until 1924.[40] But it must have been clear that the old man was up to something, getting his wife and secretaries to

---

[36] Lenin, *Collected Works* (4th ed., Moscow, 1950), XXXVI, 547.

[37] Read: not a politician.

[38] Pyatakov was not a member of the Politburo, and it is thus somewhat surprising to find him on Lenin's list, but he was probably there because of his economic expertise.

[39] It was kept in several copies marked "Secret, not to be opened except by V. I. Lenin and after his death by Nadezhda Krupskaya." Transmitted by her in 1924 to the Central Committee, it was read by a select group of delegates to the Thirteenth Congress. It was not acknowledged or communicated to the Soviet public until 1956.

[40] His wife Nadezhda, who had been a member of Lenin's secretariat, was evidently detached from it after December 18, 1922. At least, her name is not found in the secretariat log after that date.

smuggle him "forbidden" Party materials and news, dictating to them not only lofty historical reflections, as would behoove a dying leader, but scandalous subversive pieces designed to throw the Party into disarray. Stalin kept calling the poor women, asking who it was that was telling Vladimir Ilyich these things, reminding them that they were subject to Party discipline and had better watch their step. After one such call, on December 23, Krupskaya appealed to her friends Kamenev and Zinoviev to protect her from "invectives and threats." But when they mildly remonstrated with Stalin he declared that he would resign his charge— let somebody else deal with the impossible invalid, his busybody wife, his hysterical old-maid sister, and those gossipy secretaries—but he was prevailed upon to stay on as Lenin's guardian.

Krupskaya would not have sought to increase her husband's agitation, but he may have heard about this incident from his chief secretary, Lydia Fotyeva. For on January 4, he dictated to her a postscript to the *Testament*: "Stalin is too rude, and this defect, which is tolerable in the intercourse between us Communists, is intolerable in the man filling the function of the General Secretary." Hence, he recommended, the comrades must find a way to remove Stalin from the post. His replacement should have *just one* point of superiority over Stalin—be "more tolerant, more loyal, kinder, less capricious." There is a hint of embarrassment in Lenin's tone, in his stress on a point of manners that "may appear an insignificant trifle." But, in view of what he had said before— that he wished to prevent a Party split along the Stalin-Trotsky lines— "this trifle may assume a decisive importance."

Lenin's embarrassment is understandable: the history of Bolshevism can be written around the theme of manners as "an insignificant trifle" versus manners, in the widest meaning of the term, as a concern for human dignity and sensitivity transcending such categories as "objective forces of history," "class justice," "the interests of the proletariat." It was precisely because Stalin epitomized the former attitude that he was elevated to the General Secretaryship. After that, it was rather late in the day to worry about "manners."

This conclusion must have been reached by Lenin himself, for while the postscript was locked up with the rest of the *Testament*, he took another, different, and more circuitous route in his scheming against Stalin. First he sought openly to attack Stalin's record as an administrator. Mentioning no names, he launched a vigorous assault against the Commissariat of Inspection (its Russian initials form the acronym Rabkrin). Stalin vacated that office on becoming General Secretary, but anyone in the Party would know whom Lenin meant to criticize when he wrote, "The Rabkrin has not a shadow of authority. Everybody knows that no institutions function more poorly than those of the

Rabkrin." And more poignantly: "Let us say, by the way, bureaucratism is found not only in the state institutions but in the Party ones as well."

The Politburo had to consider whether these articles should be printed. Predictably Stalin said no and Trotsky yes, while the others in a somewhat embarrassed way held with Stalin. But the old fox managed to have them distributed to some other Party leaders (under pretense of seeking their opinion of the proposed reorganization of the Rabkrin), and so, after a delay, they appeared in *Pravda*. But they created no sensation. The references to Stalin were oblique enough, and everybody knew that the Rabkrin was hardly unique in Soviet administration as far as red tape and other bureaucratic evils were concerned.

The other avenue of attack against Stalin concerned the Georgian question.

We have seen how on September 27, after seeing Budu Mdivani, Lenin launched a criticism of Stalin's nationality policy, and how Stalin was infuriated by Lenin's seeing "his" Georgians behind his back. Throughout the fall Lenin kept receiving complaints from Georgian Communists about how Orjonikidze was treating them like a Russian viceroy of yore. Even before its absorption into the U.S.S.R., Georgia had been forced, against the overwhelming feeling of the local Communists, into a federation with the Armenian and Azerbaijan Soviet Republics, and they had seen this as a Russian means of still further repressing their legitimate aspirations. Coming from the people who had assisted the Red Army in conquering their country, such complaints were a bit disingenuous, and at one point in October, Lenin told them to stop fussing and obey the Stalin-Orjonikidze directives.

But as his health deteriorated Lenin was becoming more sensitive to tales of oppression and rudeness, quite apart from his growing dislike of Stalin. The Georgian dissidents kept complaining, and their leader, Mdivani, was a man of charm and eloquence. According to people who knew them both, his personality was the antithesis of Stalin's: handsome and sociable, a boon companion and a conqueror of hearts, he epitomized the Georgians' self-image. Mdivani knew how to win followers (among whom was Stalin's own brother-in-law, Alexander Svanidze, Commissar of Finance of the little republic), and his charm worked on Lenin too: as he wrote to his followers in Georgia, "In Lenin's absence they treated us like dirt, laughed at us; after I saw him and gave him detailed information, things took a more reasonable Communist course."[41] He hoped that Georgia would have only a loose federal relation with Russia, retaining, for example, its own currency, and most of all that the Georgians would be masters in their own house

[41] S. V. Harmandanyan, *Lenin and the Foundation of the Transcaucasian Republic* (Erivan, 1969), pp. 347–48.

rather than letting their country become a fief of Stalin's. The latter, however, instructed Orjonikidze that "we are determined to finish with the Georgian squabble and to punish exemplarily the Georgian Central Committee."[42] Orjonikidze purged this Central Committee of Mdivani and three of his followers. They again appealed to Moscow. Finally in November 1922 it was decided to dispatch a commission of the Russian Central Committee to Georgia to investigate the charges against Orjonikidze.

Since the commission was headed by Stalin's satellite, Felix Dzerzhinsky, Lenin did not believe that it could return an impartial verdict. So he asked Rykov, who happened to be vacationing in Georgia, to report to him personally. Dzerzhinsky's expected exoneration of Orjonikidze and Rykov's own report were brought to Lenin's attention in December, just before his health took a turn for the worse—the news quite conceivably contributed to his seizure on December 16. Lenin was particularly enraged by a report of a scene witnessed by Rykov: in his own apartment Orjonikidze engaged in a quarrel with a follower of Mdivani and, after an alleged insult, struck his visitor. The scene preyed on Lenin's mind for the next months: Is this what had come to pass after five years of Soviet power? Not even in pre-Revolution Russia would a high official lay his hands on a subordinate. This behavior was a throwback to the darkest days of the autocracy. In becoming assimilated, Stalin, Dzerzhinsky, and Orjonikidze absorbed the worst trait of old Russian officialdom—*khamstvo*, a barely translatable term imparting a combination of brutality and boorishness.

Feverishly on New Year's Eve 1922 Lenin dictated a memorandum on the nationality question, a most tragic and perceptive assessment of the Soviet experiment.[43] He felt, he wrote, that he had "sinned greatly before the workers of Russia" by not having paid more attention to the nationality problem, but he could not help it, he had been sick. He now saw the whole constitutional structure prepared by Stalin as a sham. This freedom to leave the Union "guaranteed" by the Constitution was bound to become but a scrap of paper! It would not protect the non-Russians "from invasion of their rights by this typical Russian man, the chauvinist, whose basic nature is that of a scoundrel and repressor, the classical type of Russian bureaucrat." Stalin's hastiness and authoritarian temperament had played a fateful role in the whole picture.

But when it came to concrete remedies, Lenin's suggestions were almost trivial when compared to the enormity of the danger he outlined: Orjonikidze was to be punished exemplarily, the Stalin-Dzerzhinsky "Russian chauvinist" line was to be reversed.

Throughout the next two months Lenin brooded about the Georgian affair and Stalin. On March 5 something, and we still don't know whether it was another piece of information or a premonition of complete incapacity, determined the sick man no longer to stay his hand. He dictated two letters, one to Stalin, the other to Trotsky. The communication to Trotsky went out the same day but the one to Stalin he wanted to reconsider. He did so on the morrow and asked that his secretary, Maria Volodicheva, hand it in person to Stalin and wait for a reply. But unbeknownst to him Krupskaya begged Volodicheva not to deliver it. On March 7 the latter felt she could no longer disregard Lenin's instruction: she waited on Stalin with the letter and received a reply.

Trotsky was asked by Lenin to take up the defense of the Georgian dissidents. "The matter is now being pursued by Stalin and Dzerzhinsky, on whose objectivity I cannot rely, quite the contrary." Lenin enclosed his memorandum on nationalities of December 31. If Trotsky took up the matter he was to keep it and use it in the Central Committee. If he returned it to Lenin, it would mean that he was refusing the assignment. Trotsky returned the memorandum, *but only after copying it*, something Lenin did not authorize him to do. Asked specifically over the phone by Volodicheva whether he proposed to take up the Georgian case, he refused on the grounds of ill health.

On March 6 Lenin, in addition to ordering the letter to Stalin delivered, sent a telegram to Mdivani and his group in Georgia (copies to Trotsky and Kamenev): "I am following your case with all my heart. I am appalled by Orjonikidze's coarseness and the connivance of Stalin and Dzerzhinsky. I am preparing a memorandum and speech for you." This referred presumably to speeches for the forthcoming Party Congress but was undoubtedly meant to shame Trotsky into action and to rouse some sentiment in Kamenev. Here Lenin was virtually killing himself over the matter. Wouldn't Trotsky take this chance to strike at the man he hated? Wouldn't Kamenev remember their old friendship and forget his fear of Stalin?

And the General Secretary, who probably heard from Kamenev about the telegram to Mdivani, found himself the next day in the receipt of the letter from Lenin:

Dear Comrade Stalin:
    You permitted yourself a rude summons of my wife to the telephone, and a rude reprimand of her. Despite the fact that she told you that she agreed to forget what was said, nevertheless Zinoviev and Kamenev heard about it from her. I have no intention to forget so easily that which is being done against me, and I need not stress here that I consider as directed against me that which is done against my wife. I ask therefore that you weigh carefully whether you are agreeable to retracting your words

and apologizing or whether you prefer the severance of relations between us.[44]

It is not known what Stalin's reply was. Curiously, in the most recent Soviet references to the matter, it is Lenin's sister Maria Ulyanova, rather than his widow, who is made the authority for information that Stalin did in fact apologize. Maria was described by Trotsky in exile as an "old maid, reserved and persistent," and jealous of Krupskaya's influence on her brother. Thus her testimony is perhaps a bit suspect. In any case Lenin's condition worsened on March 7. On March 10 there ensued paralysis of the right side and loss of speech. We do not know when or how he received Stalin's alleged apology.

But it is most unlikely that Stalin was panic-stricken by this turn of events or very apologetic. He was doing his duty as charged by the Politburo. Other Politburo men knew that following his tiff with the impossible Krupskaya, he had tried to lay down his charge, and that they had begged him to continue. Was the Party, whose policies Vladimir Ilyich had approved when well, to be thrown into a crisis because some women were feeding irresponsible gossip to a crippled man? Trotsky's imagination (though it is possible by then he came to believe it actually had happened) made him depict a cowering Stalin sending Kamenev to him to negotiate and he, in a fit of generosity, agreeing to let Stalin continue as General Secretary if he would mend his ways.[45] Trotsky's inventing and juggling of facts led his biographer to paint this fanciful picture of Stalin: "To find himself threatened with political ruin, to feel Lenin's anger bursting over his head, and at this moment to see Trotsky stretching out to him a forgiving hand was a quirk of fortune for which he could not but be grateful."[46]

In fact Trotsky's behavior was devious and unheroic. He was obviously planning to make use of Lenin's memorandum in his own good time and not before, and did not intend to let anybody know that he had in his possession this blast against Stalin. Thus on March 28 at a Politburo meeting he criticized Orjonikidze and moved for his recall from the Caucasus, without saying a word about Lenin's views on this question.

And so the "hot" memorandum would have stayed secret except for Lydia Fotyeva. The Party Congress was about to take place, and not a

[44] Khrushchev read this letter in his famous de-Stalinization speech to the Twentieth Party Congress in 1956.

[45] Trotsky, *My Life* (New York, n.d.), pp. 483–86, describes how on March 6 he learned from Kamenev about Lenin's letter to Stalin. But the letter and its copies to Kamenev and Zinoviev went out only on March 7 and by then Kamenev was on the way to Tiflis. Nor does Trotsky mention that Lenin had asked him by phone to take up the Georgian case and that he had refused.

[46] Isaac Deutscher, *The Prophet Unarmed: Trotsky 1921–1929* (New York, 1959), p. 92.

word had been spoken about a matter which she knew her paralyzed boss wanted to bring up. On April 16 she wrote to Kamenev, chairman of the Politburo, acquainting him with the whole story. Trotsky now had to release his "illegal" copy of the hot document. Far from cowering, Stalin took the offensive. He wrote to the members of the Central Committee, "I am greatly surprised that those articles of Comrade Lenin which without doubt are of a distinct basic significance, and which Comrade Trotsky received as early as March 5 of this year, he has considered admissible to keep his own secret for over a month without making their content known to the Political Bureau or to the Central Committee, until one day before the opening of the Twelfth Congress of the Party." The issue thus became not what Lenin had said about Stalin but Trotsky's being caught red-handed, violating the wishes of the crippled leader and deceiving the Party. Trotsky's inept excuses compounded his predicament. He had copied the memorandum only to make some corrections to Stalin's theses on the national problem, he said, and to help him with an article for *Pravda*. He did not want to carry the thing any further since the memorandum reflected unfavorably on three members of the Central Committee. Would not the Central Committee certify that he acted absolutely correctly?

In his agitation Trotsky passed to threats. On April 18 he wrote Stalin that Stalin had assured him *the day before* that he would circularize members of the Central Committee to the effect that Trotsky's action re the memorandum was correct. Here it was, *two o'clock in the morning*, and no such letter yet. Unless Stalin sent it this very day, Trotsky will ask for a special commission to go into the matter. "You better than anyone else can appreciate that if I have not done so until now it was not out of fear that it would be my interests which might suffer."[47]

Stalin must have smiled at this hysterical outburst. The Central Committee declared that Lenin's memorandum was revealed so late "not because of a dereliction on the part of any member of the Central Committee but because of Lenin's directives and the course of his illness."[48] The material itself was made known to chairmen of local delegations to the Congress who were then instructed to acquaint their groups with it. In the process it was explained that Vladimir Ilyich was the victim of incorrect information. If someone stirred up a sick man with tales of people being beaten and humiliated, it was no wonder that he got overexcited and lashed out against the people in whom he had put his full trust when he was well. It was Stalin who received credit for generosity: Didn't he show amazing restraint in dealing with Trotsky, in fact covering up for the latter's unseemly behavior?

[47] *The Trotsky Archive*, T796.
[48] *The Twelfth Congress of the Russian Communist Party (b), Stenographic Report* (Moscow, 1968), p. 821.

The Twelfth Congress took place at a turning point in Stalin's ascent to the top. He must have suffered some irritation on the still considerable gap between his actual power and his reputation. In those traditional greetings to the Congress from various factories, youth organizations, etc., which end with the ritual tribute to the leaders, Stalin's name was conspicuous by its absence. In some Zinoviev's name followed Lenin's, in others Trotsky's. The more prudent listed "Lenin, Zinoviev, Kamenev, and Trotsky." There was an occasional oddity such as hailing "the chief Red Army man, Comrade Budenny," or, from a women's organization, the old German Communist Klara Zetkin. But no Stalin, except once in the last place.

For all his megalomania, Stalin was still feeling his way cautiously. He refused the honor of giving the main speech—the political report of the Central Committee, which was in fact delivered by Zinoviev—for he was still somewhat diffident of his ability as a public speaker. Once before, in 1917, he had spoken at length before the Party Congress, but then the leading lights of the Party were either in jail or in hiding. Now, before delivering his "organizational" report, he begged the delegates' indulgence for speaking slowly. He alleged the bad acoustics as a reason, but more likely he was troubled by his Caucasian accent.

Stalin was rather anxious to appear before the mass of the Party membership in a moderate and statesmanlike light. Zinoviev, his head turned by this apparent recognition of him as *the* leader, was in contrast flinging threats right and left. He spoke ominously of oppositionists who managed to get elected to the Congress: let them mend their ways or the Party would deal with them the way it did with the Mensheviks and Socialist Revolutionaries! Indeed he was first to raise (albeit in a muted form) the prospect of the use of terror against the intraparty opposition; some of those people were incorrigible, he said, and quoted an old Russian saying, "I am afraid that those are the people of whom it will have to be said, 'Only the grave straightens out a hunchback.' "[49] He was vulgarly offensive about one of the founders of Bolshevism, Krasin, who had been stressing that the reconstruction of Russia's economy required that experts and not "newspapermen, litterateurs, and agitators" be put in charge. Zinoviev took this as a personal attack and again voiced a threat in return: Krasin, he said, was on the verge of making a "very, very serious mistake."

Stalin rather successfully tried to establish a contrast to this bullying tone, but he could not always keep his violent temper in check. At one point an Oppositionist, Kosior, made the charge that the ruling trio of Stalin, Zinoviev, and Kamenev were keeping such people as Trotsky and

[49] *Ibid.*, p. 52.

Shlyapnikov out of important jobs.[50] Stalin exploded: Trotsky was already War Minister, and Lenin and the Central Committee had tried several times to make him also a deputy chairman of the Council of Commissars. Trotsky always refused out of pride since there were already several deputy chairmen.[51] He could tell them some more things about Trotsky! And Shlyapnikov was working in the Institute of Party History (!). Kosior should shut up![52] By future standards this was a very mild outburst indeed, but Stalin requested that it be omitted from the records of the Congress, and so it was until 1968.

A follower of the proceedings of the Congress would very likely conclude that Comrade Stalin was firm but reasonable, different from the bullying Zinoviev. His ideas seemed sensible and nonpartisan. For example, he had said that the Party needs new blood, the old guard is becoming worn out. The current leaders were weary of their responsibilities, yet obviously could not lay them down just yet. New cadres must be trained. It would be splendid to have a department of instruction in the Secretariat where one could train two or three hundred people, say, who then would be sent out to be local Party secretaries, to help the regional organizations. One must think of the future and start to educate the leaders of tomorrow. "It is much easier to conquer a country with Budenny's cavalry," joked Stalin, than to bring up from the masses two or three people capable of leading the Party.

Somebody mentioned the need for more democracy in the Party. Did he mean, wondered Stalin, that important and urgent decisions should be made not by the Politburo, but through discussions in 20,000 primary Party organizations? If that were the system, the class and foreign enemy would rejoice at knowing in advance all Soviet plans, strengths, and weaknesses. The position of the Soviet Union unfortunately required secrecy to surround decisionmaking: "You must remember that you are surrounded by enemies, salvation may be in your ability to strike a sudden blow, to execute an unexpected maneuver, in speed."[53]

In addition, Comrade Stalin had eloquently and frankly described the need for new blood on the Central Committee: "We need men with an independent viewpoint on the Central Committee, independent to be sure not from Leninism, not from the Party line, no, God save us from that, but free from personal cliques, from those [bad] habits and

[50] This was Vladimir Kosior and not his brother Stanislaw, subsequently an important henchman of Stalin's who was liquidated in the 1930s sometime after his two brothers had met the same fate.
[51] Actually Trotsky felt, and with justification, that the job would be superfluous.
[52] *The Twelfth Congress of the Russian Communist Party (b), Stenographic Report,* p. 199.
[53] *Ibid.,* p. 200.

traditions of strife within the Central Committee which have caught on, alas, and alarm us so much at times."

Stalin's talent for sophistry, for warding off criticism with what might be described as an unanswerable irrelevancy, was already highly developed. For example, somebody complained about the lack of freedom of speech at the Congress. How could one say that? protested Stalin. No Party Congress since the Revolution had been so well prepared as this one. It would have required a very quick-thinking man to interject: yes, that was precisely the point.

The Congress *was* well prepared. The Oppositionists were given their opportunity to speak, and Stalin himself asked the Congress to grant Mdivani more time than the regulations allowed, but their voices lacked resonance. The Georgians' complaints were answered by other Georgians, henchmen of Stalin's, and to the average delegate it must have seemed like some intrafamily squabble of no great significance. Trotsky absented himself from the nationality discussion allegedly because he was preparing his report on industrialization. References to Lenin's explosive memorandum were adroitly parried by the General Secretary: *he* would not quote his "teacher Lenin" for fear of not quoting him correctly. He was sorry Lenin was not with them: were Lenin present he would say, "I have nursed this Party for twenty-five years, and I have raised it great and powerful." This was not so much hypocrisy—practically everybody present had some intimation of what Lenin had actually written about Stalin—but colossal and impressive brazenness. One day, when nearly every family had yielded a victim to his terror, Stalin would address the nation: "Brothers, sisters . . . I speak to you, my friends."

And so the Congress where Vladimir Ilyich had hoped Stalin would be chastised and demoted led to further increase in his power and prestige. It is possible that it was at the Twelfth Congress that Stalin was first seized with the idea of his personal dictatorship being both feasible and the only salvation for Communism and the Party. His current allies must have appeared to him almost as contemptible as his enemies. They expected him to do their dirty work, to keep the opposition from storming the seats of power, to prevent some irresponsible action on Lenin's part, and to contain Trotsky. At the same time Zinoviev was already showing signs of intriguing against him, Kamenev at one point almost betrayed him on the Georgian issue, and Bukharin, if not an intriguer, was a babbler: at the Twelfth Congress he teasingly attacked Stalin's nationality policy and said that if Lenin were present, "he would give the Russian chauvinists hell." He did the work, they played at leadership, basking in tributes from ignorant workers, silly students, and fawning foreign Communists. And there was no question that they would be happy to get rid of him if they only dared and thought they could manage without him.

But Stalin *was* indispensable. No Congress or resolution appeared capable of suppressing the ferment within the Party or the political danger from outside. Russia had not yet grown used to the dictatorship of one party. The beginning of economic recovery gave people leisure to ponder what had happened to the promises of the Revolution. Echoes of Kronstadt and of the Workers' Opposition's postulates reverberated in the lower ranks of the Party and among the workers outside it. And among the more restless of Communists, the NEP, though bearing fruit in the upward trend of industrial and agricultural production, was still considered a betrayal of Communism, a "sellout" to the peasant. The Politburo authorized Dzerzhinsky's GPU[54] to crack down and arrest members of the so-called Workers' Group, which advocated strikes as a political weapon and was led by Gabriel Myasnikov, previously expelled from the Party for his scandalous ideas such as advocating freedom of the press. Party members who knew but failed to inform of such subversive activities were now also subject to Dzerzhinsky's ministrations: it was the first official sanction of terror to be applied within the Party.

But terror could not as yet be applied to "straighten out" factionalism—to use Zinoviev's words—that is, to eliminate open defiance of Party policies by a group of its members. On October 15 forty-six prominent Communists issued the statement already referred to which criticized "the intolerable regime within the Party," the serried ranks of local secretaries who tried to suppress criticism and pack the Party gatherings, and various aspects of the current economic policy. It was an interesting group: many Party leaders of the second rank, some persistent Oppositionists of the last few years, others new to that role. Quite a few belonged to the burgeoning new group of Communist economic managers. Young Gregory "Yuri" Pyatakov had been spotted by Lenin as a man of great promise, and he would be a key figure in Stalin's great industrialization drive before being cut down in the Great Purge. Eugene Preobrazhensky, largely self-taught, was one of the best economic minds in the Party and he was probably the initiator of the petition. A passionate opponent of Stalin's, he caught on to the man's true character earlier than most. And Valerian Osinsky, a trained economist who was currently Commissar of Agriculture, had been one of Lenin's most persistent critics during the last years of his active leadership.[55] There were others of similar background—in brief, they were men of real achievement and talent. Stalin would exploit those

[54] The Russian initials of the new name of Cheka—the political police.
[55] His real name was Obolensky, and he evidently came, though he denied it in an autobiographical sketch, from a branch of the famous princely family.

talents to the full in his economic revolution, and then the entire group down to the last man would be struck down by the terror.

But the proclamation itself (it was sent as a letter to the Politburo but of course became widely known immediately) spotlighted the fatal weakness of the Opposition: it was divided, unsure of itself. Some of the forty-six signed the whole list of complaints, others only select points, some had an individual grievance to add. And it proposed no remedies except a Party gathering and consultation at which the Opposition could argue their case.

Trotsky, though not directly connected with the forty-six, took it as an evidence of the mountains coming to Mohammed or, prosaically, of the Party malcontents' recognizing the justice of what he had felt if not quite said about the evils and errors of the ruling trio's policy. He had addressed a letter of his own to the Central Committee on October 8, criticizing the leaders' policies.[56] And it suited the ruling group to link the forty-six with Trotsky, even though many of its members had in fact been his opponents. Here is Trotsky, Stalin was to say later, "the granddaddy of all bureaucratism," complaining about the bureaucratic degeneration within the Party! And who is he complaining against? The leaders—i.e., the Politburo—but isn't Trotsky a leader himself? It was felt advisable to let the steam off. The Central Committee authorized free discussion of grievances. On December 5 the Politburo announced a "new course," allegedly meeting the Opposition's demand. Trotsky in his fatal way first endorsed this resolution; then in a letter to *Pravda* he harped again on bureaucratic usurpations.

It was at this point that Trotskyism was born, or more precisely, was invented by Stalin. From now on he branded every opposition to the regime's (increasingly his own) policies, even if it came from people diametrically opposed to the War Commissar's views, as Trotskyism. The term eventually lost any concrete political meaning; it stood for some elemental malevolent force that believers in good, Leninism, must constantly combat and be on guard against. Even Stalin's subsequent invention, Bukharinism, would never be invested with the same intensity of evil, the same ominous power to pounce upon and devour all those who might have strayed from the straight and narrow path of Leninism-Stalinism.

The beginning of this transmogrification of a live politician into Satan

[56] In August Trotsky had offered to resign as War Commissar if he could be sent to Germany to help the German Communists, who were contemplating a revolutionary coup. Zinoviev then announced that as head of the Comintern *he* should go, which in view of his well-known characteristics was pure theater. Though the Comintern did engage in some half-hearted and irresponsible playing with revolution, the coup was finally called off, but not before the Communists rose in Hamburg and were suppressed in street fighting.

must be dated to the Thirteenth Party Conference, which met on January 16, 1924, as the conclusion of the period of "free discussion" ordained the preceding November. It was a different Stalin who stood before the delegates than the one who only a few months earlier had worried about his accent and tried to curb his venomous temper. The new Stalin launched on a heavy, rather liturgical indictment of "Comrade Trotsky's six principal errors."[57] He spoke with undisguised anger: Who was to guide the Party, its Central Committee or some individual who deemed himself a superman, agreeing with the Central Committee one day and criticizing it the next? People were saying that Trotsky was ill. How, then, did he manage to write all those articles and pamphlets against the Party?[58] Stalin was already perfecting that technique of guilt by association of which, for all the crowd of imitators, he remains unsurpassed master: X has said something against you, but at another point X said something which sounds like what Y, a Menshevik in Berlin, has said, and "as is well known" Y serves the White generals and capitalists. And so, "objectively," X, "under cover" of criticism, seeks to restore capitalism. In 1924 Stalin was just beginning. Of course, "not for a minute . . . would I count Trotsky among the Mensheviks, . . . but [I am] afraid" that Trotsky's writings will lead "some inexperienced people" in the Party into the "anarcho-Menshevik" path.[59]

Another technique of assault and intimidation which in a few years assumed enormous proportions was the evocation of the "guilty past." Preobrazhensky, irked by Stalin's use of Lenin's name to justify repression within the Party, was indelicate enough to recall, without naming the sources, Lenin's characterization of the General Secretary in his memorandum on nationality. This use of Lenin against him brought out a streak in Stalin that would become all too familiar in ten years or so. They *now* praised Lenin, called him a genius, but "Permit me to ask you, Comrade Preobrazhensky, why did you disagree with this genius about the Brest-Litovsk Treaty, why did you abandon this genius at such a desperate moment and disobey him? Where and in whose camp were you then?[60] Comrade Sapronov now falsely, pharisaically praised Lenin to the skies, but he was the same Sapronov who had had the impudence

---

[57] In Stalin's *Collected Works* "Comrade" is of course omitted, and there are other interesting editorial changes.
[58] *The Thirteenth Conference of the Russian Communist Party (b)* (Moscow, 1924), pp. 96–97. Trotsky had caught a cold and developed an infection while hunting and was now recuperating in the Caucasus; the psychoanalytically minded will note the frequency of Trotsky's indispositions at crucial points during his downfall.
[59] In the *Works* "not for a minute" is omitted.
[60] Preobrazhensky was allegedly among those Bolsheviks who, like the Left Socialists, toyed with the idea of deposing Lenin.

at a Party Congress to call Comrade Lenin an 'ignoramus' and 'oligarch.' Why did he not support Lenin at the Tenth Party Congress?"[61]

There was no mistaking the ferocity of the man. Even the hints of his deep resentment of the dying leader, the sarcasm that radiated from his repeated references to "that genius," were merely intimidating, rather than potential ammunition for the Opposition. Stalin would probably not hesitate to denounce Lenin himself for betraying Leninism! "You are terrorizing the Party!" shouted Preobrazhensky. No, said Stalin, he was just issuing a warning to those who brought discord and disunity into its ranks.

And yet one could not dismiss the man as a maniac with narrow-minded and fanatical obsessions who was bound sooner or later to alienate his partisans and break his political neck on some madcap venture of repression. Interspersed amid the heavy tautological oratory were rapierlike thrusts to his opponents' vulnerable points, evidence of an informed, quick-thinking mind which could appraise a situation lucidly and objectively.

There was his treatment, for example, of Karl Radek. Radek was one of the handful of Communist notables who were personally and genuinely attached to Trotsky. From a Polish-Jewish background, Radek, though not an Old Bolshevik, enjoyed considerable popularity because of his revolutionary heroics in Germany and his scintillating wit, which enlivened many a Party gathering. And now Stalin turned this man's gift against him and transformed Radek into a sort of political clown—and such he would appear even to his friends—useful as a journalist but hardly to be taken note of as a politician. For most men, said Stalin, speech serves as an instrument of thought. But Radek was an unusual man, his tongue runs his head. Here he says one thing, there another, as long as he can make a quip. And thus began the taming of Radek. The likable scoundrel became one of Stalin's most slavish flatterers and one of the most vulgar detractors of his old friend Trotsky—until even his servility and wit proved unable to save him.

Stalin was not superhuman. His position in the Party was not yet invulnerable, nor would it be for some years to come. A *healthy* Lenin would undoubtedly have carried the Party with him and against the General Secretary. Trotsky—and of course he should have attended the Conference even if on a stretcher—was not without serious political assets. To the Party youth, he was still a dashing and romantic figure. Students in military schools were his enthusiastic supporters, and at the time Soviet Russia was experiencing something in the nature of a youth

[61] Stalin, v, 152. Stalin distorted the incident. Lenin had talked about "ignoramuses" who opposed official policies, and Sapronov in a rebuttal had asked, "Who, then, is an ignoramus?"

rebellion against the regime.[62] (This was more grist for Stalin's mill: would the "battle-hardened old Leninist guard" yield meekly to immature youth?) Most incredibly and inexcusably, Trotsky still did not see Stalin as his real rival: a man of "third-rate, provincial mind," Trotsky believed, simply could not lead the Party and world Communism. It was Zinoviev and his hated brother-in-law Kamenev who were *using* Stalin to keep him, Trotsky, out of his rightful place as successor to Lenin. To attack Stalin too strenuously meant to play into their hands.

And so the Thirteenth Conference, with only three votes cast against the resolution, censured Trotsky and the forty-six Communist dissidents for engaging in "factional" activity and expressing the "petty-bourgeois deviation" within the Party.[63]

In the meantime the maker of this phantasmagoric world was approaching his end. In May 1923 Lenin had been moved to his country home in Gorki, a move which previously he had strenuously resisted, and the Politburo's supervision of his treatment was lifted. There was no chance that he could recover sufficiently to cause trouble. And though there were periods of improvement, his speech never came back. At times he managed to walk with a cane; he tried to learn to write with his left hand. And this was most cruel: he was perfectly conscious and rational most of the time, and yet helpless. He tried to preserve outward calm except when annoyed by the doctors' and nurses' ministrations, but a sudden visitor to his room might see tears running down his face.[64] His wife tried to interest him in seeing political figures, but except for permitting a brief visit from Bukharin and Preobrazhensky, he refused to see any of his main lieutenants, and it is not difficult to guess why. On January 19 and 20, 1924, Krupskaya read to him, rather ill-advisedly one should think, the *Pravda* report of the Thirteenth Party Conference, and noted his excitement. He suffered another stroke on the morning of January 21, and the end came in the evening.

Trotsky did not enhance his reputation by suggesting shortly before his own death that Stalin furnished poison to the desperate Lenin. Humanly, this accusation—absurd on its face—is understandable, coming as it does from a man whose children perished at the hands of the

---

[62] Trotsky, however, did not "have" the army as is sometimes assumed in the accounts of the period. Even in the administrative sense his control was curbed by the Revolutionary War Council, on which there sat Stalin and Zinoviev partisans. And most of the military commanders, whether former Tsarist officers or partisan leaders, were indifferent to his fate. Antonov-Ovseenko, of Winter Palace fame, who as the head of the Army Political Administration tried to build up support for Trotsky, was unceremoniously dismissed, and the Red Army officer schools were purged.

[63] This count seems to have been genuine, which would mean that some of the Oppositionists voted for their own condemnation.

[64] The best account of those last days is by Dr. V. P. Osipov in *Red Chronicle* (Moscow) No. 2 (1927), pp. 236–47.

tyrant's agents. Even so it is half-hearted: Stalin's deed was alleged to be more of a mercy killing than an assassination. Were the roles reversed, it is easy to imagine Stalin's convincing himself of and charging Trotsky with murder pure and simple.

It is doubly incorrect to write of Stalin as trying to usurp the succession to Lenin. For Lenin the historical figure, the "theoretician," Stalin preserved the highest respect and was content to represent himself as his best *pupil*. Only toward the very end of his own life did the frustrations of old age and the intimations of approaching death bring out in Stalin a feeling of retrospective envy, the desire to emulate and surpass his predecessor as the maker of Communism, of the new world. The cult of Lenin was to become an important foundation of his own cult, but was not its absolute prerequisite. A man with a more intellectual type of vanity than Stalin's—Trotsky, say—would have been content to leave Lenin as *one* of the great figures of the Revolution, a Plekhanov on a larger scale, rather than make him into a protective divinity, the source of and authority for everything done in the Soviet Union.

For Lenin as leader of the Party and state, Stalin's feelings were quite different, nor would he limit himself to aspiring to the degree of power Lenin exerted in that capacity. From Stalin's point of view, Lenin was in fact a naïve politician who in his last years had to expend most of his energy in wrangling with brawlers and intriguers who had infected the Party and who, no matter how often reprimanded and chastised, returned to threaten the survival of Communism. He surrounded himself with Zinovievs and Trotskys, poseurs and megalomaniacs who had already demonstrated that at the first opportunity they would throw themselves at each other's throats, split the Party into countless warring factions, and destroy the work of the Revolution. Lenin did not realize how the Party was held together by him, Stalin, how without him the whole structure would crash down and Communism become like Russian Social Democracy before 1914. Lenin's very modesty, even if partially a pose, was a grave political mistake. It encouraged any ignorant rank-and-file Communist to believe that he could talk back to the head of world Communism, and made his lieutenants indulge in scandalous intrigues with impunity. Without the patient and unrewarding work that he, Stalin, and his assistants were carrying on, the Party Congresses would long ago have turned into bedlam, and demagogic and soft-minded humanitarian objections would have prevented the adoption of urgent and beneficial policies. How could one run in this fashion a society barely beginning to recover from the ravages of war? How could one allow the luxury of internal dissension, the pretense of intraparty democracy, to a weak and backward country surrounded on all sides by hostile capitalists? If Leninism was to be saved, an entirely different style of leadership was required.

AT THE TOP —ALONE

Funerals have played an important part in the history of the Russian revolutionary movement. In Tsarist times the death of a prominent radical or intellectual, or even of somebody who while not a revolutionary epitomized opposition to the status quo (such as Leo Tolstoy), was an occasion for processions, speeches, and ceremonies which, from a commemoration of the deceased would often turn into a political demonstration against the regime. In the Soviet period this tradition, like so many others, was neatly reversed: funerals of Communist notables who died in good graces were turned into massive propaganda spectacles, occasions for the regime to congratulate itself on the strength and victories of Communism. Oliver Cromwell, in a letter to the mother of a fallen soldier, sought to console her with the assurance that the dying hero's only regret had been that he could not go on slaughtering God's enemies. Somewhat in the same manner, the last wishes of dying Soviet dignitaries always touched on the need to preserve and strengthen "the unshakable unity" of the Party, to raise production and the material well-being of Soviet citizens, to promote the cause of Communism throughout the world. The bier of the deceased would be presented to the newspaper reader as guarded by his "close comrades in arms," always somehow in even numbers, standing symmetrical and stony-faced, and including, if the man had been of an appropriate rank, the Leader himself.

In Lenin's case the ritual was all the more distasteful since it almost certainly contravened what would have been his last wishes, a simple funeral and burial near his mother, whom he had adored. The pomp of the proceedings, the preservation and permanent exhibition of his remains, must have been unpleasant to his family and was certainly so to his wife, who had rigid views of revolutionary ethics and demeanor. Legend has credited Stalin with the proposal for some of the grosser features of the proceedings and the cult, but he was not the only one capable of political exploitation of Lenin's death. The chairman of the commission charged with funeral arrangements was Felix Dzerzhinsky, head of the GPU, not a happy symbolism.

Stalin's contribution to the events was nevertheless rather unfortunate. After some years his famous "oath" eulogy became a subject for movies, books, and articles, but at the time its effect was embarrassing, almost to the point of making it a serious political gaffe. This was a speech before the Second All-Union Congress of Soviets, the Soviet parliament, where after a passage of purple prose Stalin intoned: "We swear to you Comrade Lenin . . . [to keep high and pure the vocation of the Party member, the unity of the Party, etc., etc.]." This florid oratory would have made some sense had it been delivered at the funeral proper as the only farewell to Lenin on that occasion (millions of Soviet moviegoers were led to believe that those were indeed the circumstances). But in its actual setting, following three other speeches to the Congress, its pathos seemed ludicrous. The first report of the world-shaking "oath" summarized it in two small paragraphs and gave far more extensive accounts of the speeches by Kalinin, Krupskaya, and Zinoviev which preceded it. Though later on it was printed *in extenso*, Stalin must have sensed the unfortunate impression it created. A quick learner, he henceforth tried to avoid purple prose.

Stalin's *faux pas* was only one among the many exhibitions of tastelessness by the ruling group. Zinoviev, now preening himself and strutting about as *the* successor, tried to answer the unspoken question of so many Communists as to why the government had not informed them about Vladimir Ilyich's hopeless condition, and had said instead that he would be back at the helm. The doctors had assured them, wrote Zinoviev mendaciously, that by the summer Lenin would fully recover his speech.[1] As for Trotsky, he did not return from Tiflis to the funeral. He may have felt that his colleagues would be thrown into panic and the "masses" into anxiety by the absence of the second giant of the Revolution from the funeral of the first. Or he may have felt simply that his health could not stand the trip and the rigors of an unusually severe Moscow January. In any case, his subsequent explanation that he was misled by Stalin as to the date of the funeral and that

---

[1] *Pravda*, January 30, 1924.

he could not possibly make it back to Moscow on time does not hold water.[2]

The official line held, of course, that no single leader could even aspire to the position held by Lenin. He would be succeeded by the collective brain of the Party, the "Leninist Central Committee." The "collective brain" assembled as a rule only once every two months. So those in the know undoubtedly assumed that the leadership would be exercised by the Politburo, and more precisely by the three who had led the Party since the onset of Lenin's illness: Zinoviev, head of the Comintern, and for long Lenin's closest lieutenant; Kamenev, who by now was a sort of political Siamese twin of Zinoviev's and whose dignified demeanor made him the logical choice for the unofficial head of the Politburo; and Stalin. Lenin's actual successor as Chairman of the Council of Commissars, Rykov, was assumed to be a step below the three. Rykov was universally liked in the Party, but by the same token was felt to lack that extra something—one is tempted to say frightfulness—which in the long history of the Russian land has been felt to be an important ingredient in the supreme ruler. A betting man among well-informed Communists would still lay odds on Zinoviev-Kamenev as the winning combination. Stalin was a bit *too* frightful. There were those harsh things that Ilyich had said about him. And in Zinoviev-Kamenev the frightfulness of the first was nicely balanced by the equable and mild temper of the second. Trotsky might still create trouble, but apart from everything else he was a newcomer to the Bolshevik ranks and as such unacceptable even to many of those already branded as Trotskyites.

Many accounts of Stalin's rise to power concentrate on his undoubted ability as an administrative "operator." There he was in the Secretariat, spinning a web in which one by one he enmeshed Trotsky, Zinoviev, Kamenev, and then Bukharin and Rykov. Outvoted in the Politburo, he would bring the Central Committee into play. When he still lacked sufficient weight, he found added support somewhere else: the Party's *control* organs—which in their inception were thought to be strictly separate from the political agencies and to which other ambitious leaders consequently paid scant attention—were used by him to increase his leverage. The Central Control Commission sat with the Central Committee to pass on important decisions, its Presidium held joint sessions with the Politburo to decide the still more important ones. His Secretariat and the Orgburo would appoint, transfer, and dismiss local Party leaders, extending his power over the provinces. Only after the

[2] He alleges being told on January 22 that it would be on January 26 (and not, as Deutscher states, on the next day), while it actually took place on January 27. Even so, only three days by *regular* train separated Tiflis from Moscow.

administrative web had swallowed Stalin's main rivals and opponents would it be discarded as no longer necessary. Behind it stood revealed naked personal tyranny, its main instrument sheer terror.

To a large extent this picture is true. Stalin's successors and would-be successors were to study his administrative campaign betwen 1922 and 1930 the way students in military academies study the tactics of Marlborough and Napoleon. In 1957 Khrushchev borrowed a leaf from his predecessor's book and prevailed over his enemies in the Politburo with the help of the Central Committee, but between 1961 and 1964 somewhat different but also borrowed tactics brought him to grief. In China, Liu Shao-chi would in the 1960s try to wall in Mao Tse-tung through administrative-parliamentary maneuvers, and it took the Cultural Revolution for the Great Helmsman to destroy the Party machinery which while promoting his worship threatened to strangle him as an active leader.

But sheer administrative skill and intrigue are far from providing a complete answer to the question of how by 1930 Stalin had achieved a degree of power which dwarfed that commanded by Lenin in his most active period of leadership.

In 1917 Stalin's transformation within a few weeks from a misanthropic recluse to a man acknowledged by a sizable group as their leader marked him as a skillful politician. By the mid-1920s and in the context of Soviet politics he became a superb one. He had all the essential ingredients: an excellent sense of timing; simple but effective oratory, which even in its certain crudity was reassuring to the average Party member; the appearance, which while not wholly correct was certainly more true then than at any time before or later, of a man free of internal complexes and problems, zestfully playing the political game. All these combined to gain him a widespread acceptance that sheer administrative intrigue alone could not have secured. Even some of his irritability seemed to have dissipated. The tyrant lay dormant in the politician.

In addition to his political acumen Stalin mastered a specifically Communist technique which might be called the expropriation of history. Here his indebtedness to Lenin is unmistakable. We have seen how Lenin would insist at every twist and turn that where *he* stood was Marxism, and that however orthodox-sounding the arguments of his opponents they represented only opportunism at best, a sellout and betrayal of the working class at worst. Young Stalin, like practically every one of Lenin's disciples at one time or another, had rebelled against these claims of infallibility. Why refuse to admit the possibility that a great man can make mistakes, why make such a fuss over some silly philosophical dispute, why *not* admit that Lenin in Switzerland was unable to see clearly what was happening in Russia in March 1917? As late as 1920 Stalin was expatiating with some satisfaction on the occasions when Lenin *did* admit he had made mistakes. But with the installation of the Lenin cult such an attitude became impermissible. "Our banner shall be Lenin, our program will be Leninism," declaimed Kamenev at the Thirteenth Party Congress. One could not lead the Party without seizing the banner.

Stalin's bid to do so was expressed in "reminiscences" of Lenin which he shared with students of the Kremlin military school on the evening of January 28. This was a clever performance, so clever that it has fooled many of Stalin's biographers, even those not basically hostile to him, who see in it nothing more than a revelation of the man's essential vulgarity. In this address Stalin wisely avoided the pathos of his speech of two days before, and the style is chatty and simple. His listeners are treated to a scene of the young exile in Siberia "discovering" Lenin by reading *Iskra* and then expressing his enthusiasm for the man in a letter to a friend abroad. Imagine his pride and exaltation when he receives a letter from Lenin to whom his friend has shown Stalin's tribute![3] Then some years later he meets the objects of his worship at a Party conference. Imagine the disappointment of the simple boy from Georgia when at first the admired leader turns out to be physically most unimpressive, lacking pomp and self-importance, ready to talk "with the most ordinary delegates about the most ordinary subjects" (how unlike a Zinoviev or Trotsky!). But then it dawns on him: this *is* greatness.

And how unaffected was Lenin by temporary reverses! Yet he would not be carried away by successes. Other leaders, Stalin has observed, become arrogant and proud when victorious. Not Lenin. "The important thing is not to defeat the enemy, but to finish him off," he used to say.

More on the theme of simplicity. Many leaders, erudite people to be sure, still suffer from an "unbecoming ailment": they are frightened of the masses. They become a sort of aristocracy looking down on the simple folk, try to rule them according to books. But Lenin believed in the masses, learned from them. He believed in bold improvisations, occasionally would "leap into the unknown"—but of course it was not really unknown, for Lenin's "prophetic sight" would assure him that victory would be his. Stalin was with the leader on one such occasion, and he could speak about the unusual radiance which illuminated Lenin's face as he made that seemingly foolhardy decision.

Stalin's speech had not a word about Marx, nor about Lenin's writings and theories; he knew that his listeners had been filled with that. There was just this intimate account of personal impressions, hints of a close master-pupil relationship, and how becomingly modest that he

---

[3] As pointed out earlier (see above, pp. 48–49) the story is almost certainly fabrication.

omitted all those occasions on which he must have rendered Vladimir Ilyich advice and help.

There was still the rather embarrassing possibility that the obverse—i.e., what Lenin thought of Stalin—would become widely known. But just as in the case of Lenin's "jumps into the unknown," so Stalin's "prophetic sight" must have reassured him that the dead leader's less than rapturous impressions of him would not become public property. On the eve of the Thirteenth Party Congress Krupskaya turned over her husband's *Testament,* and his explicit wish that it be read at the Congress, to the Central Committee. It was decided to follow the same procedure as with the nationality memorandum: it would be shown to select delegates, who would then explain it to their regional groups. The "explanation" was the same as with the other document: Lenin had obviously been sick and resentful of those close to him who wanted to spare him undue exertion. Publicity concerning the unfortunate document would compromise the whole Party, give ammunition to foreign enemies. Following the Congress, Stalin offered his resignation to the Central Committee. But it was almost a foregone conclusion that it would be rejected. For Zinoviev and Kamenev, Stalin was still an indispensable ally: Who would keep Trotsky and the Oppositionists in check? Trotsky did not want Stalin out since the job might go to a follower of Zinoviev-Kamenev. Other members kept their peace. And so Stalin was confirmed. ☆☆☆

T HE Thirteenth Congress marked for Stalin another accession of strength and prestige. Superficially Zinoviev was still the principal figure, and he delivered (for the last time) the principal report of the Central Committee. But in the eyes of the delegates Stalin was at least Zinoviev's equal. He was greeted by "applause turning into an ovation," Zinoviev merely "prolonged applause." At the end of the voting for the Central Committee Stalin rose to suggest that one comrade who "accidentally" did not pass be still voted in as an alternate member. And the Congress complied unanimously. It was a small and significant indication of his growing power.

This Congress, to use Stalin's terms, was even better "prepared" than the preceding one. The factory workers and youth organizations had gotten the point: no more of those unseemly greetings to Zinoviev or Trotsky; only the memory of Vladimir Ilyich was "hailed," respectfully. In his organizational report Stalin was composed and businesslike. However, in the course of the ensuing discussion it became obvious that not only Stalin's henchmen but Zinoviev and Kamenev wanted to have some fun at Trotsky's expense. And so in his concluding remarks the General Secretary obliged them.

As Stalin rose higher so the archoppositionist sank quite a bit lower. In his speech at the Congress, Trotsky did not repudiate his views, but with dignity if somewhat fatuously he announced his submission to the majority. "If the Party decides something that one or other amongst us considers unjust, he will still say whether the decision is just or unjust, it is my Party and I shall loyally carry out its decision."[4] There was some applause at this formula, and a naïve person might have assumed the issue of Trotsky's "deviation" was closed.

Professional politicians seldom follow the noble stricture that you do not kick a man when he is down. If not then, when? He might at other times kick back. And so instead of letting bygones be bygones, Trotsky's declaration encountered a storm of indignation. For once belying his reputation for moderation and judiciousness, Kamenev venomously assailed his brother-in-law.[5] Zinoviev performed as might be expected. There was the usual vulgar satisfaction at the discomfiture of a proud and brilliant man. Trotsky, said some insignificant delegate, had declared that he would follow the Party's directives. But which party? The one of which he had been a member for only *seven years*[6] or of some other party? But most of the assault had obviously been prearranged and was in concert with the aim, all too well realized, of driving Trotsky to make further and damaging outbursts. Trotsky had said that he disagreed and yet would obey. Could that be sincere? Did he not continue to excite the young, stir them up against the Party?

And so Stalin in his concluding remarks declared that much as he hated to rehash old material, he had to. Trotsky and other opposi-tionists, in their attempts to "outfox the Party," were compelling him to revert to the old material. They agreed and yet disagreed. They whined about the Party's not being democratic, but where, if you please, could they show a better party in the whole world? Why did they refuse to admit to representing a "petty-bourgeois deviation"? After all, a devia-tion is not such a serious thing *if* you admit it. (If you don't admit it, it might become very serious indeed.) Here an alumnus of the Tiflis Theological Seminary is speaking: "If you insist, comrades from the

---

[4] *The Thirteenth Congress of the Russian Communist Party (b), Stenographic Report* (Moscow, 1963), p. 159.

[5] Kamenev was married to Trotsky's sister.

[6] This was a supposedly devastating reminder that Trotsky had joined the Bolsheviks only in 1917.

opposition, the petty-bourgeois deviation might turn into petty-bourgeois policies."[7]

It is unfair to attribute to Stalin alone the perfection of the technique of recantation and its use as a political weapon. Zinoviev, who did not have a theological training, made similar demands. And at some future party congresses he himself would be compelled to perform the ritual, with the hall howling with derision: "Tell us more!" "What are you concealing?" It became a technique of political self-strangulation—stripping the man, first of his supporters, then of his self-respect, and thus readying him for the final act of self-denunciation in court. And then it would be a firing squad rather than the stake which awaited the lapsed heretic.

In 1924 it was impossible to foresee such atrocities. The Congress ended on a note of unity. Trotsky was retained on the Politburo, and Bukharin occupied the seat left vacant by Lenin. The Party had earlier decided to increase its membership by the so-called Lenin levy—more than 200,000 new members, largely industrial workers. All the rivals counted on this accession to improve their political situation. The new members, Trotsky felt, would not be so critical of the idea that he had been a member for only seven years; they would be respectful toward the *acknowledged* head of the Party, thought Zinoviev and Kamenev. But in fact the future was to show that the new members benefited Stalin more than anyone else. It would also become of some importance that the other three contenders were Jewish. The Lenin levy increased the proportion of Russians in the Party; new members were often politically ill educated and more prone to the anti-Semitic bias than a Communist of long standing.

It is difficult to say whether, with different personalities involved, collective leadership could have endured. One is inclined to say no: it would take forty more years, a more viable society, a more advanced economy, and status as a great world power for the establishment of a fairly stable oligarchy in Russia. Given the Communists' premises and goals, the country's conditions in the 1920s, the feeling that 700,000 Party members (this was the number after the inclusion of the Lenin levy in 1924) were still a tiny garrison in a hostile country—this situation seemed to call for a single authority at the top. Contestants for the supreme prize were vigorous men in their forties and not, as now, sexagenarian bureaucrats.[8] It is conceivable that had Stalin dropped out

[7] *The Thirteenth Congress of the Russian Communist Party* (*b*), p. 236. It is, of course, unclear what it is that Trotsky and Co. should *not* insist on: that they do represent the deviation or that they don't.

[8] Though the situation in China reminds us that there can be some brisk in-fighting even among oldsters.

of the running, even Zinoviev and Kamenev would have divided, hurling anathemas and Party resolutions at each other.

In retrospect it seems that Stalin could safely have just bided his time, waiting for his partners to stumble politically, and as for Trotsky it was virtually inevitable that he would sink even deeper in the quicksand of Party disgrace. Still, the General Secretary showed some signs of chafing under the conditions of shared power. There was always the danger that his partners would suddenly be stricken by remorse at not honoring Vladimir Ilyich's last request, freeing Stalin from the burdens of the Secretariat—a danger made more probable by his very success in stifling the opposition and trouncing Trotsky. If this process was pushed much further, there could be no question that Zinoviev's and Kamenev's consciences would start bothering them. And they had a considerable weapon in Krupskaya, who for all her disenchantment with their behavior was bound to assist them if they turned against the man she loathed.

Prudently Stalin began to take steps to ward off such danger. The Secretarial hierarchy had to be his to such a degree that, even without him at the head, it would follow his directives.

In June 1924, speaking before some three hundred local Party secretaries who had been attending, so to speak, a refresher course at the central secretariat, Stalin dropped hints about the unreliability of his partners. He "read in the paper," he said, the speech of a comrade at the Thirteenth Congress (it *seemed* to have been Kamenev) which contained a serious theoretical error.[9] The speaker had said we must transform NEPman Russia into a socialist Russia. (The NEPmen were private traders and small industrial entrepreneurs licensed under the New Economic Policy.) That was very, very wrong. Lenin had spoken of a NEP Russia—i.e., Russia in the period of the New Economic Policy; but that was completely different from a NEPman Russia—i.e., Russia ruled by NEPmen. Did Kamenev understand the difference? He did, but he was careless with these extremely important theoretical matters. Certainly he should correct his errors, otherwise all sorts of misunderstandings might arise in the Party.

A sophisticated audience would have greeted this whole passage with amusement. But here were at best semieducated people whose ideological training had consisted for the most part of a few weeks' hurried classes in which they memorized some historical data about Russian socialism and some citations from Lenin. Above all they had had it drilled into their skulls that is was impermissible to disagree with Lenin about anything. How *could* Kamenev have said that Russia was ruled by those speculators and traders who, though tolerated, were viewed by

---

[9] Stalin, *Collected Works* (Moscow, 1946–52), VI, 257. My italics. Stalin had been present, of course, at Kamenev's speech.

every Communist with indignation as a legitimate object of eventual repression? Was he careless, or was it something else?

Stalin's capacity for what might be called creative hair-splitting was to be of great use to him in the future. One day he would discourse at length on how criminally un-Marxist it was for Bukharin to say that the peasant should become *rich*, while his (Stalin's) slogan, "the peasant should become prosperous," was in strict accordance with Leninism. It is an untutored mind which is impressed by this apparent theoretical erudition; it is a sophisticated one which will demand simplicity and concreteness. What made Stalin devastating as a polemicist was his ability to vary his approach according to the audience and the needs of the hour. He wove abstruse scholastic distinctions for the benefit of provincial hicks, and at other times and places was a pragmatist scornful of dogmas and bookish learning: Would Trotsky tell them in plain words what is wrong with building socialism in Russia?—and please, no quotations from the Marxist classics!

In his speech to the provincial officials Stalin also made veiled criticisms of Zinoviev. As his partners were to confess later, they were taken aback when they read the General Secretary's "educational" discourse in *Pravda*. They were being invited, to be sure in a much milder form, to do what they had themselves demanded of Trotsky one month before: recant.

If Stalin's aim was to smoke out Zinoviev and Kamenev, he succeeded. They convoked a group of their partisans to take counsel; rather than taking the initiative, the political twins were thrown on the defensive. Why, they finally inquired of Stalin, did he give this speech and have it printed? The General Secretary now played his usual gambit: he was ready, he said, to resign. The nucleus of just three top leaders, he felt, was insufficient, and a wider collective leadership was needed. It is possible that Stalin was contemplating a somewhat risky maneuver: since he was unwilling to put up with Zinoviev and Kamenev he offered to resign in the hope that the Central Committee, in which he now had a majority, would either beg him to remain or name one of his satellites in his place. Either way, Zinoviev and Kamenev would be discredited and dropped a notch for allowing their intrigues to threaten the Party with the loss of Stalin's services.

But this gamble did not have to be put into effect, for before the year was over, fate—or, more precisely, Trotsky—delivered Stalin's partners into his hands.

Had Trotsky's timing been as good as Stalin's, he would have simply waited quietly for the almost inevitable split between Stalin and Zinoviev-Kamenev, which would have furnished him with an opportunity for a comeback. But he was a vain and impatient man. And so in the fall of 1924 he loosed what he thought was a thunderbolt against the ruling and discordant trio; in fact it was against himself. This was a lengthy preface to a volume of his writings from 1917, *The Lessons of October*.

Trotsky's story was very simple. Those Old Bolsheviks who had tortured him during the last two years—principally Zinoviev and Kamenev but also others, like Stalin and Rykov—were in 1917 either opposed to or lukewarm in supporting Lenin's plans of insurrection. Even after October 25 they had opposed an all-Bolshevik government. In fact, they were tainted with the Menshevik syndrome and harbored constitutionalist illusions. Of all the current leaders only he, Trotsky, had stood unfailingly on Lenin's side in preparing the Revolution. (As a matter of fact, Trotsky could not help himself from noting, and this point was enlarged by his worshipful editor, that he had improved on many aspects of Lenin's plan and, as head of the Military Revolutionary Committee, played the leading part in the preparation of the uprising of the Petrograd Soviet.)

The intended lesson was of course that the people who had shown themselves so fainthearted then were unworthy and unqualified to lead Communism now. The Comintern in 1923 had failed to exploit boldly the revolutionary situation in Germany and Bulgaria. No wonder! At its head was the very same Zinoviev who in 1917 had feared the Revolution and not believed in the masses. Kamenev? Even before Zinoviev joined him he had espoused an essentially Menshevik position. Trotsky also dropped transparent hints about Stalin's essentially "defensist" position in March, about Rykov and the others defying Lenin on the issue of an all-Bolshevik regime, etc.

As history Trotsky's reconstruction was essentially correct. But one does not have to sympathize with Zinoviev et al. to see it as a most ill-inspired work. (And not only in the political sense. It is illuminated by neither eloquence nor vivacity, as was Trotsky's *History of the Revolution*, but is, rather, a dry doctrinal treatise instructed by spite and wounded vanity.) In fact, Trotsky could not have written a more unfortunate piece had it been dictated by Stalin. Unlike Stalin, Trotsky did not understand how to exploit the "historical guilt" technique. Stalin used it, one might say, the way cavalry had been used in the Civil War—to raid the enemy's rear in order to cut off his lines and his path of retreat. But you must have solid forces facing the enemy, capable of exploiting his momentary confusion. It was only when the majority was his, or at least contestable, that Stalin raided the enemy's past. But here was Trotsky, practically alone, charging the enemy's entrenched positions. It was even worse: by dealing such a blow to Zinoviev and Kamenev, he rendered Stalin's position stronger. Of course, the Old Bolsheviks already knew about the two leaders' less than heroic behavior in October 1917. But to recall it now was humiliating and, in the eyes of new Party members who had heard something about it but not in detail, discrediting. There was no longer any question of competing with Stalin on anything like even terms.

Trotsky's raid was answered by a massive barrage from the Party leaders. Several of them contributed to *For Leninism*,[10] a systematic exposition of Trotsky's alleged sins: his falsification of history, his derogation of Lenin, his dictatorial ambitions and "cult of personality," his gross mistakes during the Civil War. Its general position may be gauged by this passage from Rykov's introduction: "The historical source of the disagreement of a huge majority of the Party members with Comrade Trotsky lies in the fact that Comrade Trotsky grew up and formed his political viewpoint as an active leader of the Party hostile to us, the opportunist Menshevik Party."[11] Even Krupskaya, basically friendly to Trotsky, was prevailed upon to contribute to the broadside; she accused Trotsky of trying to "revise" Leninism. To be sure, her piece is the most moderate, and it can be easily imagined what Zinoviev and Kamenev had to say about "Trotskyism," a term which now gained regular currency.

Stalin's contribution must have given him considerable satisfaction, for it is reprinted in his *Collected Works* even though its laudatory references to Zinoviev and Kamenev ten years after he had sent them before a firing squad make the inclusion somewhat embarrassing. It is, however, a clever piece of historical polemic. He presents Trotsky as *one of many* during the historic days of 1917. Trotsky fought well, but who among the Bolsheviks and even their allies did not fight well in October? Trotsky was important, but not so important as he claims. The main credit belongs to Lenin and the Party. Stalin does not drastically distort the facts. One might make the parallel of somebody writing of Britain in 1940 and pointing out that Churchill then spoke on behalf of the Cabinet as a whole, that the basic strategy in the Battle of Britain had been worked out by the military leaders, that the main credit belongs to the RAF, etc. This would undoubtedly be correct, and yet it would not be history, for it would omit the electrifying influence and presence of a man who did make the difference. And so with Trotsky in October.

With Zinoviev and Kamenev the General Secretary could afford to be generous. Surely they made mistakes, he argued, but who does not? Stalin himself, he confessed, took some time to realize the full greatness of Lenin's revolutionary concept. But eventually they all corrected their errors and worked together. As for Trotsky, remember Brest-Litovsk, remember his quarrels with Lenin before 1917, remember his occasional

[10] Moscow, 1925.
[11] *Ibid.*, p. 4.

slander of the great leader. "The task of the Party," said Stalin, "is to bury Trotskyism as an ideology."[12] Stalin was not as yet ready to "bury" Trotsky himself. An utterly discredited Trotsky sitting on the highest Party agencies suited him fine vis-à-vis Zinoviev and Kamenev. The latter (and it is instructive how power and vindictiveness had transformed this once equable man) had inserted into his polemical article a whopping lie: "Not a single member of the Central Committee has raised the question about a Party punishment for Trotsky."[13] One year later, when he was settling his accounts with Zinoviev and Kamenev (or rather giving them the first installment), Stalin had something to say about this. At the end of 1924, when Zinoviev and his Leningrad partisans were demanding Trotsky's expulsion from the Party, Stalin argued:

> We, the majority of the Central Committee, did not agree. . . . Afterward, the Leningrad people and Comrade Kamenev demanded an immediate exclusion of Comrade Trotsky from the Politburo, but we did not agree. . . . We did not agree with Comrades Zinoviev and Kamenev because we realized that the policy of cutting off heads is fraught with major dangers for the Party. . . . It is a method of bloodletting—and they *did* want blood—dangerous and contagious; today you cut off one, tomorrow a second, and then a third. Who would remain in the Party?[14]

While retaining Trotsky in his Party posts, the January 1925 meetings of the Central Committee once again condemned Trotskyism and ordered an "educational" campaign as to its malevolent influence beginning in 1903. Trotsky was also removed as Commissar of War and Chairman of the Revolutionary War Council. Politically this move was of little significance, his influence there having been previously reduced through the dismissal of his loyal subordinates such as Sklyansky and their replacement by Stalin's and Zinoviev's henchmen, some of them Trotsky's personal enemies. But symbolically the move was enormously important: he had been chief of the Red Army for seven years, and to many who did not understand the finer points of all those debates and deviations, this was visible proof that a giant of the Revolution had toppled.

There followed a rather silly maneuver by Kamenev to persuade Stalin to become War Minister. It is quite possible that he could have become Commissar and still retained the General Secretaryship, despite Kamenev's obvious hope. But he sensed that it would have been a

12 Stalin, VI, 357.
13 *For Leninism*, p. 85.
14 *The Fourteenth Congress of the All-Union Communist Party (b), Stenographic Report* (Moscow, 1926), p. 502.

psychological error to succeed Trotsky, and the post went to a secondary figure, a wartime commander and Old Bolshevik, Michael Frunze.

Largely due to Trotsky, the problem of supreme power in the Party and the state was thus transformed. Now, in 1925, there was no longer any question of Zinoviev or Kamenev demoting or getting rid of Stalin. The most that the political twins could hope for was to retain *some* share of supreme power, to keep Stalin from replacing them in the ruling "nucleus" with some other partners. As yet the idea of a single person ruling by himself was extravagant. ✩✩✩

B EFORE we pass on to the next phase of the struggle for power, let us consider the intricate problem of the relationship of this struggle to ideology and policies. It is probably true, though his detractors would deny it, that Trotsky sincerely believed that the ruling trio had caused "bureaucratic degeneration" of the Party. It is equally true, though his admirers would protest, that the main source of this feeling lay in the fact that *he* did not control the Party apparatus. In other cases the relationship is different: it is most unlikely that in objecting to Lenin's policies Kollontay and Shlyapnikov thought of themselves as candidates for the leadership. It is impossible, as Lenin had said on one occasion, to develop a "sincerometer," yet it is still possible to apportion the relative shares of self-interest and of ideological conviction which motivate politicians, always bearing in mind that, more than most, Communist members of the fraternity are prone to self-delusion on this score: their ambitions' whisper is identical with Marxism's demands.

And so we shall not quibble: Zinoviev and Kamenev grew progressively more unhappy with the powers of the Secretariat and the policy of the regime toward the peasant, because of both their being squeezed out by Stalin and from solicitude for the correct organizational form for the Marxist Party and fear that the country's economy was taking a non-Marxian direction.

For the Marxist the peasant problem is a veritable Procrustean bed. To put it simply, you squeeze the peasant, deal with him by compulsion—he does not produce; you appease him, respect his property, allow him to produce in peace—then you get food but at the same time capitalism in the countryside grows stronger, i.e., peasants get more attached to the principle of private property, insist on getting a suitable price for their produce. Since Communism "happened" in an overwhelmingly peasant country, the Russian Marxists' problem was even more complicated. Millions of peasant households were involved, rather than relatively few landowners, and Russian agriculture was backward and inefficient. What to do with the peasant thus was the number-one socioeconomic problem of Russian Communism.

In 1921, with the NEP, Lenin inaugurated the policy of appeasing the peasant. He would no longer be dragged into communes; his surplus (a most flexible term) would no longer be confiscated or paid for in worthless paper money; instead a regular tax would give him the incentive to produce. For most Communists the NEP was a temporary expedient, though, as Lenin promised, it was meant seriously and for a long time. If socialism was to come to Russia, one had at some point to grapple with the notion of private property in land, substitute for the millions of individual land*holders*[15] large-scale, scientifically organized farming.

In Communist phraseology, the peasant class, like Caesar's Gaul, was divided into three parts. There was the poor peasant, who had either no land or too little for the needs of his family, and who thus had to hire himself out to his more fortunate fellows. There was the middle peasant, who produced by his and his family's work enough for his and their needs. And there was the "class enemy"—the kulak—the rich peasant (and only in the wretchedly poor Soviet village could he have been called rich). It is obvious that these classifications were hopelessly imprecise, especially the last. The kulak might be just that, "the tight-fisted one," in the traditional peasant lingo, the village bloodsucker who for lending money, seed, or beasts of burden exacted exorbitant interest or work on his land. Or he might be simply a more efficient producer, a harder worker than most. Or he might be both. In any case, the "class enemy" was usually also an economic benefactor: the kulak produced most of the surplus which went to feed the cities and for export.

Even from this hugely oversimplified picture we can see why the formidable peasant problem seemed, in terms of the Communists' premises and Russia's situation in the mid-1920s, virtually insoluble. Strike at the kulak, as virtually every dissenting group within the Communist Party urged between 1921 and 1925, and the breakdown of the food supply is risked, a setback to the whole economic recovery, if not indeed vast famine (as at the end of the Civil War). Indulge the kulak, and he will dominate the countryside and withhold the grain unless high prices are paid. And then—a vision ever present to a Communist, like Doomsday to the medieval Christian—the moment might come when the peasants, led by these budding country capitalists, would advance *political* demands and seek their own political party.

Thus, quite apart from any economic considerations, the history of Russia in the 1920s and the very concept of (and ghastly sacrifices

---

15 Not proprietors, an important difference as we shall see.

involved in) Stalin's "great leap forward" can be understood only against the background of the almost superstitious fear with which practically all Russian Marxists viewed peasant Russia. It was a kingdom of darkness which had to be destroyed before the modern industrialized economy without which one could not have socialism could be built. For many Communists the kulak was a demonic force, dormant but stirring in the countryside, which if left alone for long might become more dangerous than all the White generals and their foreign allies combined. The city NEPman, those petty traders and entrepreneurs, could be swept away overnight, but to try to get rid of the kulaks (whose numbers were estimated at roughly 10 per cent of the peasant population) might mean civil war. Being "soft on the kulak" was, then, for whoever was on the outs with the ruling group, a slogan as convenient as the "being soft on Communists" charge on the American Right in the 1950s. It aimed to arouse the deepest apprehensions of the faithful, to hint at some dark betrayal at the top.

As events were to show, Stalin was abundantly endowed with the Communist obsession about the kulak, and he realized the strength of antikulak sentiment. Were they to raise the slogan "Strike at the Kulak," he said in 1925, ninety-nine out of one hundred Communists would applaud. But, he added, all the more important not to let our emotions run away with our judgment. Such a slogan and policy would mean civil war, for the vast mass of the middle peasants would think that the blow at the kulak was also directed at them.

There had already been a warning in that direction. In the summer of 1924 a violent revolt shook the Georgian countryside. It was largely a national uprising against Soviet rule and as such was suppressed ruthlessly. But it also expressed the peasants', and not only the rich ones', grievances, and an apprehension on their part that the regime was biding its time before proceeding to destroy private holdings in agriculture.

The Party leaders decided to conciliate the peasant still further. In April 1925 the tax on peasants (now collected partly in kind and partly in cash) was reduced. The Party legalized the right of individual peasants to hire labor and to lease land beyond their own allotment—this was of course mainly for the benefit of the kulak. Both practices had already been widespread, but the new ruling was intended to provide an assurance (which in a few years proved to have been a deception) that the regime would respect the rights of the individual cultivator.

That astute politician Stalin did not speak at the Party Conference, letting Rykov and Bukharin take the credit (in a few years it would be blame) for sponsoring these sensible measures, by which according to Marxian standards the regime committed the cardinal sins of expanding rural capitalism (leasing additional land) and encouraging exploitation (hired labor for private profit). He was not, of course, afraid of being identified with the policy, which was popular in the country at large and economically beneficial. Nor was he unduly worried about being accused of inconsistency sometime in the future. But until full and absolute power was his he preferred to let others stretch the doctrine, enunciate the details of a risky policy, and be the lightning rod for any ideological shock or partisan bitterness. The task of the leader is sometimes to stay behind and observe how his advance guard is doing before committing the gross of his troops.

His calculations were brilliantly vindicated. As incautious as Trotsky was with his pen, so Bukharin was with his mouth. Carried away with enthusiasm at being the official spokesman on agricultural policies, he announced even before the Conference that the Party slogan to all the peasants should be "Enrich Yourselves." The reaction to this innocent, if not indeed laudable sentiment was one of shock. This was encouraging the kulak, asking for perpetuation and expansion of capitalism in the countryside! It was as if after pronouncing "I want every Frenchman to have a chicken in his pot," Henri IV was accused by the Church of trying to abolish meatless Fridays and by cattle raisers of trying to sabotage the consumption of beef. Stalin admitted Bukharin had gone too far. The indiscreet theoretician withdrew his horrendous statement not once, but on three separate occasions.

But now Zinoviev and Kamenev had an issue. They agreed fully with the conclusion of the April Conference, but on thinking about their strategy for the forthcoming Party Congress they felt that their best bet would be to strike at Bukharin rather than tangle directly with the General Secretary. Stalin was trying to squeeze them out and to substitute Bukharin and Rykov. But Bukharin's slogan was obviously a revelation of his deep-seated right-wing deviation, and he was not alone. A whole school around him was trying to substitute state capitalism for socialism, to perpetuate the NEP and worse. An obscure Party member named Boguszewski unmasked this plan: he asked, if you please, that the Party should legalize the buying and selling of land![16] Boguszewski was now presented as an "agent" of Bukharin; and the more enthusiastic Zinoviev-Kamenev partisans asserted that he did not exist but was a pseudonym for Bukharin himself. If the plan worked, the aroused Marxian indignation of the Party representatives would force Stalin to repudiate Bukharin and Rykov and embrace again Zinoviev and Kamenev as his partners in the ruling team.

It was far from Stalin's intentions to let this happen. The Congress, traditionally held in the spring, kept being postponed. In the meantime

---

[16] One of the first acts of the October Revolution nationalized all land, providing at the same time for the peasants' free use of it. Thus only after 1928 would the peasants realize that the land was not *legally* theirs.

he consolidated his grip on the machine to make sure that the majority of the delegates would be firmly on his side, resistant to both Zinoviev's fiery oratory and Kamenev's Marxian erudition.

Ever since the Revolution the political twins had dominated the Party organizations in the two capitals, Zinoviev in Leningrad, Kamenev in Moscow. The Secretariat now moved to snatch those fiefs from their hands. In Moscow the task proved to be easy: Kamenev was not a forceful man. The local secretary, Uglanov, had personal scores to settle with Zinoviev—in 1921, after a quarrel with Zinoviev and his wife, he had been fired from the Leningrad organization—and he now came over to the Stalin-Bukharin side and managed to isolate Kamenev in his own bailiwick. But it proved impossible to pry Leningrad loose from Zinoviev, who ruled it with methods similar to Stalin's in the country at large. Infiltrators from the Secretariat who tried to undermine Zinoviev were chased out by the local Communists, who remained loyal to their boss.

The Congress was finally fixed for December 18. Significantly, its location was shifted to Moscow, though previously it had been decided that it would be held in Leningrad. There were some last-minute attempts at compromise. An open clash, coming in the wake of all the troubles with Trotsky, the forty-six Oppositionists, etc., could only be damaging to the Party, scandalous to foreign Communists. But Stalin would not agree to anything short of a qualified capitulation by Zinoviev and Kamenev. He agreed to making one of their followers a Party secretary, but in return he insisted that they refrain from attacking Bukharin and, most painful of all, that the Leningrad Party organizations and its newspaper, the Leningrad *Pravda*, which had recently engaged in open warfare with its Moscow namesake, be staffed by the Secretariat. Zinoviev was thus asked to surrender his political base in return for being retained as a junior partner. He decided to fight back.

And thus in December 1925 the Fourteenth Party Congress opened, the last one in the true sense of the term, for subsequent ones partook more of the character of festivals at which the Party rendered its collective homage to the Leader.

Though the Stalin delegates assembled at the Congress with a crushing majority—the ratio was ten to one—he could not be absolutely sure that there would not be some unpleasant surprises. Zinoviev's prestige, though declining, still stood high. His attack on the NEP and his plea for taking energetic steps against the kulak might create some trouble. The Leningrad opposition, as it was now being called, was bringing with them what they thought was a big gun: Krupskaya had been persuaded to abandon the role of grieving widow, uninvolved in politics, and to throw her great personal prestige into the struggle against the man she so disliked. Lenin's *Testament* might pop up again, and some simple-minded delegates might be influenced by the voice of Vladimir Ilyich posthumously condemning Stalin. The whole thing had to be meticulously planned.

It was. This time Stalin delivered the main political report; Zinoviev was reduced to the status of co-reporter on behalf of the dissenting minority on the Central Committee. In his opening speech, the General Secretary was all business, and merely referred to the unseemly squabbles. There was the danger of the kulak, he admitted, but for the time being it was even more dangerous to overestimate the kulak, to use forcible methods in the countryside, to alienate the peasantry as a whole, and to impede this economic recovery which was so visible and gratifying.

Zinoviev pursued his original strategy—strike at Stalin by attacking Bukharin—in the course of a speech which fills thirty-three large pages of small print. Apart from the copious citations from Lenin and his own writings, its gist is best seen in one sentence: "Who could have even imagined one year ago that it would be he, Comrade Bukharin, who would say 'get rich' in the hope and expectation that the kulak's grandchildren will be grateful to us?"[17] Cornered, the once brilliant orator had become a bore.

And it was easy to demolish this line of argument. One by one Stalin's henchmen got up to denounce Zinoviev for his unfeeling attacks on the man Vladimir Ilyich had called the favorite of the Party. "Bukharin is one of our best theorists, our dear little Bukharin, we all love him and will stand by him," exclaimed Orjonikidze. Bukharin had admitted that he had erred, so what else did Zinoviev want? It would be well for the Party if *other* leaders were man enough to admit their mistakes and apologize for them!

Zinoviev's biggest gun also misfired. As long as she castigated Bukharin and defended her old friends Zinoviev and Kamenev, Krupskaya was listened to respectfully. But her charge that the Congress was packed and her warning that Lenin had taught that a Party Congress may not always be right were greeted with indignant interruptions and catcalls. On top of this, the Congress was treated to the unseemly spectacle of Lenin's sister Maria Ulyanova, a friend of Bukharin's and always envious of her sister-in-law, being dragged in to denounce Krupskaya. "Lenin's relatives do not and cannot have any monopoly for the correct interpretation of Leninism,"[18] she remarked, and suggested that it was shameful and subversive to insinuate that Vladimir Ilyich approved of Communists disobeying the directives of a Party Congress.

Even this was felt insufficient to destroy the sentimental appeal the

17 *The Fourteenth Congress of the All-Union Communist Party* (*b*), p. 116.
18 *Ibid.*, p. 299.

Founder's widow might exert. One by one Stalin's spokesmen castigated the unfortunate woman for her presumption. "We love and respect Nadezhda Konstantinovna, not on account of her beautiful eyes, but for her [past] political work," said the gallant Voroshilov.[19] It was probably about the same time that Stalin made his famous "joke" that the Party might have to appoint someone else as Lenin's widow.

There was natural apprehension on the part of Stalin's henchmen that Lenin's views about the General Secretary might now be made public. Anastas Mikoyan sought to prevent, and failing that to offset, such an unpleasant possibility: "Do you think we don't know what kind of people Stalin, Trotsky, Bukharin, Zinoviev, and Kamenev are? Oh yes, we know. Ilyich has left a correct appraisal of each of our leaders. But why should we discredit our leaders before the masses?"[20] Stalin himself tried to blunt the edge of any possible revelation with a jocular admission: "Yes, comrades, I am a man who goes to the point and is coarse, that is true. I don't deny it." The gambit worked. No direct references were made to the compromising document. Only at the Twentieth Congress, in 1956, did the Party learn officially what Lenin had wanted it to know after his death. It is strange that Trotsky, who sat through the proceedings without a word, his hatred of Zinoviev and Kamenev balancing his envy of Stalin's power, did not seek to have the *Testament* read. When it was published abroad by an American follower of his, he denied the authenticity of the document. But he also may have felt that with the ruling trio breaking up, Stalin might soon seek his help.[21]

For amazing as it may seem now, there was still general disbelief that Stalin was capable of becoming a *sole* dictator. He was a man who was dangerous because of his organizational skill, it was thought, but he needed a more subtle theoretical mind to guide him in policy matters. Having emancipated himself from Zinoviev, he was now under the spell of Bukharin. Poor Rykov, the nominal successor to Lenin, who thought he was finally coming into his own as a member of a new ruling trio, spelled out this general belief. "The Party never has gotten and never will get on its knees before Stalin, Kamenev, or anyone else."[22] It was bad prophecy.

But there were more perceptive voices. Kamenev had known Stalin longer than most, and he deeply resented his "stealing" the Moscow Party organization from under him. He spoke with all the rage of a mild

[19] *Ibid.*, p. 368. Krupskaya had the protruding eyes of a goiter-sufferer.
[20] *Ibid.*, p. 188.
[21] Some of the leading Stalinists, e.g., Mikoyan, were referring to Trotsky in very conciliatory terms.
[22] *The Fourteenth Congress of the All-Union Communist Party (b)*, p. 418.

man who has been deceived and insulted beyond the limit of his endurance. Moreover, he felt a sense of personal betrayal on the part of a man who had once been his friend and who, in Siberian exile and in those March 1917 days in Petrograd, had rendered him help and support, a man whom Kamenev in turn had protected by turning a deaf ear to Krupskaya's expostulations and Lenin's injunctions. But even he did not see clearly enough: he thought Stalin had been captured by others. "Comrade Stalin has become the prisoner of that false policy whose creator and main representative is Comrade Bukharin."[23] Even though Kamenev thought that Stalin was ideologically a prisoner, he argued that politically the man had been seeking something unprecedented in the history of the Party: absolute power for himself and his factions. I and my followers, said Kamenev, oppose the theory of the Supreme Leader and oppose the attempt to impose such a leader on the Party.

He then went on to spell out his views in a most unfortunate fashion. "We are for an organization of our high command in which you would have an all-powerful Politburo, uniting the leading politicians of the Party, to which the Secretariat would be subordinate as a mere technical organ."[24] And, dotting the i, "I am deeply convinced that Comrade Stalin is incapable of uniting the Bolshevik guard." At these words there was bedlam. There were shouts of "So that is what they want!" "They have shown their true colors!" Then the majority started chanting, "Stalin, Stalin!" while the Leningraders, whose numerical weakness was partly compensated by their having in their midst some of the loudest rabble-rousers of the October days, took up a counterchant: "Long live the Communist Party! Hurrah!" Similar demonstrations and disorder interrupted a speech by Sokolnikov in which he advocated removal of Stalin as General Secretary or abolition of the post.

Even the most subtle political argument could not affect the decision of a Congress packed with Stalin's supporters. Still, as an appeal to Party ranks beyond the Congress, Kamenev's argument was inept and self-contradictory. He did not call for an intraparty democracy, but pleaded for the preservation of rule by a narrow oligarchy, the "all-powerful Politburo." It was easy to punch holes in this: Zinoviev was head of the Comintern, Kamenev was deputy chairman of the Council of Commissars and chairman of several important government committees, and both were members of the Politburo. Sokolnikov was Commissar of Finance. What more did they want? Obviously, to have absolute power in their own hands, or at least to have a feudal arrangement within the Party in which the bigwigs could have virtually independent principalities of their own, such as Zinoviev had had in Leningrad and Kamenev used to have in Moscow. He would let the Congress in on a secret, said

23 *Ibid.*, p. 253.
24 *Ibid.*, p. 274.

Voroshilov: Who did they suppose had presided at Politburo meetings since Lenin died? None other than Kamenev! Why was he complaining about Stalin? Well, the fact was that "nature or fate" had endowed Stalin with such an ability to formulate problems and practical solutions that the majority of the Politburo followed his suggestions rather than anyone else's.

In addition to such maneuvers, the General Secretary's principal lieutenants unraveled before the Congress the labyrinthine intrigues in which Zinoviev and Kamenev indulged, even when they outwardly collaborated with Stalin and depended on him to preserve their preeminence in the Party. There was a dramatic tale about Kislovodsk, a watering place where at the end of 1923 Zinoviev and some of his henchmen had taken counsel on how to limit the powers of the Secretariat. They had addressed a demand to Stalin, which he answered "in a coarse but friendly" fashion, saying that other members of the Politburo should be introduced into the Secretariat. But the resolution of the conflict, as confirmed by Zinoviev himself, could not but reinforce the impression of a conciliatory and hardworking Stalin vs. a scheming but lazy rival. The General Secretary agreed that three oligarchs be introduced into the Organizational Bureau, over which he presided. But what happened? Zinoviev, Trotsky, and Bukharin, who were thus given a chance to influence the composition of the Party apparatus,[25] found all those discussions about who should be secretary in Stavropol, or what should be the qualifications for Party officials at the county level, etc., to be boring and unworthy of their attention. And so they seldom bothered to attend sessions of the Orgburo.

It is not too fanciful to liken the Fourteenth Congress to a bullfight. The "Leningrad opposition" repeatedly charged the red cloak (Bukharin) rather than its real tormentor. Worn out by its own vain charges, bled by the matador's assistants, the bull was then ready for the kill.[26] Stalin performed the task elegantly and with a minimum of unnecessary motions. "The Party wants unity; it will achieve this unity with Kamenev and Zinoviev if they so desire, without them if they don't." He rose above personal attacks. It was absurd, he said, to talk of one man's leading the Party by himself. After Lenin's death the only possible leadership was collective. This conclusion was greeted "by applause turning into an ovation." The delegates, standing, broke into the "Internationale."

[25] Though Stalin undoubtedly removed much of the important business from the Orgburo to the Secretariat proper.
[26] There was even the equivalent of the picador's eviscerated horse. This was the heretical and unfortunate Boguszewski, whose views *everybody* agreed were too heinous for words. He had been exemplarily punished, announced Stalin, and the poor man dropped back forever into that obscurity from which he had so briefly and unhappily emerged.

Stalin was now the Leader, if not yet the absolute dictator. Though he already must have believed in the maxim he ascribed to Lenin, "It is not enough to defeat the enemy, one must finish him off," he still could not allow himself such a luxury. (It is probable that had the Congress been free rather than carefully "prepared" by the Secretariat, Stalin still would have obtained the support of the majority but certainly not by such a crushing margin.[27]) His chief opponents' downfall and disgrace, like Trotsky's, was gradual. This was purge by installments, which Stalin employed until the moment came to "finish them off." Zinoviev was thus retained on the Politburo, Kamenev was demoted to being alternate member; but then, step by step, they and the other Oppositionists would be stripped of their important jobs. A man treated in this fashion had two choices, both fatal to his self-respect and his political influence. He might try to atone for the past by servile support of the General Secretary, which would not in most cases restore him to a position of real power, since Stalin's suspiciousness though not as yet homicidal would make him further demote the victim. Or he might, while outwardly conforming, search for new formulas and arguments that would make the Party see the light and realize how Stalin was betraying Leninism; to do this, he would have to collaborate with his predecessors in disgrace and with any new malcontents, entangling himself ever more in the web of his own intrigues and hastening his doom.☆☆☆

I N the wake of the Congress, Stalin obtained a solid majority on the Politburo, to which were now elevated Molotov, Voroshilov, and Kalinin. Molotov was his principal assistant in the Secretariat. True to his assumed name,[28] he was used to hammer down the organizational details of his boss's political schemes. Following the Fourteenth Congress he led a special mission to Leningrad, and within a month the majority of Party members in the "birthplace of the Revolution" decided that their support of Zinoviev had been a great mistake.[29] For over twenty years he was to be Stalin's principal assistant, and some of his boss's meanness

---

[27] The vote for his resolution was 559 to 65.

[28] *Molot*—"hammer" in Russian.

[29] The methods used can be illustrated by an incident at the Congress. A Party official from Moscow related how Comrade Stalin had dressed him down for supporting Kamenev. For two months, he confessed, he was madder than hell—here a Leningrader interjected, "and unemployed"—but then decided Stalin was right and Kamenev wrong.

and sardonic humor was taken out on the faithful servant.[30] Voroshilov was, of course, an old pal from Tsaritsyn days. Though not credited with brains, he was a clever political operator, and his speech at the Fourteenth Congress was one of the most devastating thrusts at the opposition. The same was true of Kalinin, for all his pose of a simple-minded peasant. He was not to be among Stalin's more important assistants, and during the terror he tried to save some of the victims. All the more impressive, he succeeded in that most difficult art for an Old Bolshevik: surviving.

All these men were already in 1925–26 considered Stalin's lieutenants, if not yet his servants. But in addition, the General Secretary had partners who, though recognized as juniors in influence, were not merely subordinates but members of a new "nucleus" of the Central Committee, the ruling collective. These were Bukharin, Rykov, and, a shade below the other two, Michael Tomsky, head of the Soviet labor union. This new team was quite different from the old combination. None of the three, in contrast to Zinoviev and Kamenev, had any ambition to challenge Stalin's primacy or any chance to do so. Bukharin claimed, and was assumed, to be the theoretical guide of the new regime. It was only a question of time before he would take over from Zinoviev the leadership of the Executive of the Comintern, i.e., of international Communism, a field which the General Secretary, with his embarrassing ignorance of foreign languages and conditions, would surely trust to somebody more sophisticated in such matters. But when it came to tough political infighting, everybody including himself agreed that Bukharin was not the man. The same was true of Rykov, a dignified figure as Prime Minister, and a good administrator. Tomsky's past and present activity was mainly that of a trade union leader. A true proletarian in background (he was the illegitimate son of a locksmith), his formal education had ended with elementary school. But he was evidently a man of great personal charm: it was largely his personal influence which persuaded the British trade union leaders, whom he visited in 1924, to agree to a joint committee with the Soviet labor unions, which some Communists saw as the entering wedge of a social revolution in Britain. But Tomsky was not a forceful man. He had shown in the past some leanings toward the Workers' Opposition, but after a short period of exile in a Party post in Turkestan he had mended his ways. (It is at him that Ryazanov had aimed his barb that the Central Committee had managed to turn many an old revolutionary

---

[30] During one of the Allied wartime conferences the conversation took a light turn: What, Churchill asked, did Molotov do during his 1942 visit to the United States? He went to Chicago to meet with some fellow gangsters, volunteered Stalin.

into an old woman.) Still, he was a person of enormous popularity among the industrial workers, and he was an important ally when the opposition claimed that the worker had been sold out in favor of the kulak and the NEPman.

What brought these men to Stalin's side was, first of all, a shared dislike of the Revolution's prima donnas, Trotsky and Zinoviev, but also a genuine agreement on policies. They saw in Stalin—and fatuous though this belief may seem today, it was not without ostensible validity in 1925—a practical and reasonable man. While he was inordinately ambitious in the political field, he was not likely to rock the boat with wildly repressive policies in the countryside, or endanger Russia by embarking on some madcap revolutionary venture abroad. In some ways they were not too dissimilar from those reasonable and humane conservatives in Germany of the early 1930s who welcomed Hitler as a man strong enough to save the country from anarchy, and whose wild attitudes would undoubtedly be moderated and restrained by the experience and responsibilities of power. But one must hasten to add that Bukharin, Rykov, and Tomsky were in no sense conservative. They were good Marxists with a fervent hope of achieving an industrialized and socialist Russia and of seeing Communism prevail in the world.[31] But they hoped to achieve these ends gradually and without undue cost in human suffering. One is often tempted to exaggerate the virtues of the three men, and one must remember that certainly none of them was squeamish about the use of terror against non-Communist political opponents or repression against their intraparty enemies. But they were more humane than Trotsky and Zinoviev, not to mention their partner and eventual destroyer, and the history of Russia and Communism would surely have been happier had they been allowed to guide them.

Granted not only Stalin's personality but the nature of Soviet politics by the mid-1920s, there was no chance of collective leadership's becoming a permanent feature of the Russian revolutionary regime. As nature abhors a vacuum, so Communism abhorred divided leadership. Stalin's

---

[31] *As far as possible,* and except when quoting, I shall try not to classify Communists as *right* or *left* wing. This practice is part of that terror-by-semantics developed by Lenin and perfected by Stalin. It implies that objections to the regime's policy are never based on practical or humanitarian grounds but must spring from some deep-seated complex or heresy on the part of the protestor. Thus Bukharin is pictured as a "Left Communist" in 1918 and a "Right deviationist" in 1929. In fact, he objected in one case to Brest-Litovsk and in the other to violent measures against the peasants, objections which have nothing to do with being "left" or "right." Today, the Chinese Communists attack the Russian leadership as "right-wing deviationists" while they praise the Rumanian Communists, whose internal policies are essentially the same as Moscow's. It *does* make sense to talk of *policies* as being more or less egalitarian, traditionalist vs. Marxist, but almost never should one use the wretched "left" and "right," just as one should avoid that other semantic trap, "revisionist" vs. "dogmatist and sectarian."

power over the Party in 1926 was already much greater than Lenin's had ever been. There was no foreseeable chance of his being upset or removed through normal procedures, i.e, by vote of the Central Committee or the Party Congress. What Lenin had tried to achieve (without always succeeding) through prestige and oratory at Party gatherings was now Stalin's through mastery of the machinery. The tentacles of the Secretariat reached into the smallest territorial units throughout Russia— enforcing his edicts, making sure that his men constituted a majority at every Party gathering. Malcontents could be dealt with by his friends and servants on the Control Commissions, which also in pyramidal fashion were riveted upon the Party, scrutinizing every member's background activity and private life. A dissenter or even an incautious loud-mouth could be sure that this scrutiny would be particularly assiduous in his case, that some real or fictitious sins would be unearthed that would lead to his being cast out. The Control Commissions were already seeded with officials of the sinister GPU, the political police, and it was no longer unimaginable that factional activity would cost a Communist of humble standing not only his Party card but his freedom.

But this enormous power, equivalent already to that which Hitler exerted over his country at the height of his dictatorship, was not enough. There were contingencies which could not be warded off by the mere arithmetic of Party Congresses and committees. As he surveyed his position Stalin must have felt occasionally—and in a few years this feeling became an obsessive mania—that along with power grew vulnerability, that along with servility came hidden envy. The men for whom he was a usurper of Lenin's mantle were not the kind of people who respected formal votes and resolutions if they saw a promising opening for a new intrigue. His new collaborators would follow his lead, but only so long as he would agree with their policies. Even his lieutenants served him on the assumption that his luck was holding and that he would continue as the source of their power and preferments. Any untoward development, a prolonged indisposition (witness Lenin), an international crisis, a grave setback to the nation's economy—any of these might loosen his grip, set him on the path traveled before by Trotsky or Zinoviev. Dictatorship required of the dictator not only ceaseless vigilance and hard work, of which Stalin was more than capable until overcome by old age, but also political restraint, and this in the long run was against his nature.

An incident of 1926 illustrates how unfinished as yet was the structure of Stalin's dictatorship and how the very nature of Soviet politics drove this suspicious and vindictive man to respond with despotism.

Michael Frunze, Trotsky's successor as Commissar of War, had long suffered from an internal ailment which was finally diagnosed as a bleeding ulcer. A prominent official's medical treatment was considered of concern not only to the person involved and to his family but to the Party organs as well.[32] In 1925 the Politburo seconded the doctors in recommending immediate surgery, and Frunze, though like most people fearful of going under the knife, submitted to this joint political-medical pressure. The operation evidently disclosed only a healed ulcer, but sometime later the patient's heart stopped.

The story was not too unusual. If one reads Party journals of the period one often finds complaints about the incompetence of the Kremlin medical service, harrowing stories of how it pronounced some old revolutionary to be well when in fact he collapsed and died after release from the hospital, etc. One suspects that like everything else, Russian medicine had been hurt by the Revolution and not yet recovered. Many sick dignitaries wisely sought medical help abroad when stricken by more serious ailments or requiring even simple surgery (thus Trotsky repaired to Berlin for a tonsillectomy). The charges of medical malpractice aired in the wake of Frunze's death and the demands for an investigation thus followed a pattern which was not too unfamiliar.

Frunze died in October 1925 at the height of the Stalin vs. Zinoviev-Kamenev contest. He himself had taken no position in the struggle. His successor as War Commissar was Voroshilov. And so rumors began to circulate that his death had been more than simply another case of medical malpractice. The story exploded in the May 1926 issue of *Novyi Mir* (*New World*), then as now the leading Soviet literary journal, in an all too transparent fiction about an "army commander" whom "Number One, the unbending man," forces to submit to an unnecessary operation, during which he is medically murdered. The story, "The Tale of the Unextinguished Moon," was by the noted Soviet writer Boris Pilnyak. The issue was, of course, immediately confiscated, and the substitute number of *Novyi Mir* carried the editorial board's frightened apology for printing anti-Party slander.

This *was* slander, and it is probable that Pilnyak was put up to it by somebody who wanted to strike at Stalin. The remarkable thing is that nothing happened at the time to Pilnyak or to the editor. In 1937 they were both arrested, but on other charges, and since so many literary figures were liquidated at the same time, it is unclear what role their

---

[32] The reason for this practice lay in Lenin's rather peculiar form of hypochondria. Considering that prominent Communists often overworked and failed to take care of themselves, he insisted that Party authorities have the right to prescribe periods of forced rest for them, medical treatment, etc. This praiseworthy solicitude had, as his own case vividly demonstrates, the most unfortunate result of making a sick person's regimen and treatment subject to the Politburo's approval. A special Kremlin medical service was set up which treated ailing notables, and they were thus preserved from falling into the hands of a doctor who might be an "enemy of Soviet power."

fantastic imprudence of 1926 played in their fate. It could not have helped.

Whether out of contempt for the slander or a calculated restraint, or both, Stalin chose not to react to a libel which even in a democratic society would have provided ample grounds for criminal proceedings against its author and publisher. In eight years Osip Mandelstam was arrested, then released, hounded, and finally destroyed for reading an anti-Stalin poem in private to six people. Those eight years marked a terrible progress in Stalin's vindictiveness, as well as in his ability to indulge it without restraint. But it is at least possible that in 1926 the successful politician, so close to having absolute power, was reminded that this was not enough. Slander and spite still tormented him, as it had in the days when he was an underground agitator. But it would have been too easy to punish a foolish writer who had let himself be used by others. As for those others, Stalin could not yet deal with them in the way he thought they deserved. One day he would; they would be made to *confess* to crimes and intrigues of the kind they tried to pin on him.

For a mind like Stalin's it could not be mere coincidence that the Pilnyak story was scheduled for publication at the very time another kind of opposition raised its head. Throughout the 1920s, a decade which carried Russia from a one-party dictatorship to a personal one, from rule by political repression to rule by terror, oppositions were reborn and continually dashed themselves against the ruling machine in ever more desperate and suicidal attempts. Here, Communism seemed tainted by an original sin of its own: a lust for power which made those who actually wielded it feel they could never have enough. And for those who tasted power and then lost it the addiction seemed to remain as strong as ever. They could not be appeased with positions of honor and influence, ministerial and ambassadorial posts that were still freely distributed to Party leaders in disgrace. These were but temporary stops in their descent, they felt; if *they* had sent Stalin as ambassador to Germany or had made him the head of an industrial commission, would he forsake his ambitions? Would they forsake their fears and forget his past sins? But above all it was a craving for "real" power, and a strange metamorphosis which occurred once power was no longer theirs: a metamorphosis of shrewd and realistic politicians into visionaries, impractical schemers, or childish intriguers.

For the first generation of Russian Communist leaders, the main reason for this transformation undoubtedly lay in their own historical experience. They had seen Lenin perform what might be called ideological magic. Often beaten, outvoted, and deserted, he always came back. With a propitious timing and a felicitous theoretical formula the

Party became his, its founders and former leaders cast aside. Another "correct" formula and new slogans, and the Provisional Government, backed by all the other political forces in Russia, crumbled before a handful of the Bolsheviks. And so, they reasoned, there *had* to be a formula, a combination, that would bring down the Bukharin-Stalin usurpation and open people's eyes. What were all of Stalin's secretaries and Control Commissions compared to the massive Tsarist police and bureaucracy before 1914? What were the odds now compared to those the Bolsheviks faced in March–April 1917? Lenin had prevailed because he had been right, and so would they!

This kind of reasoning helps explain the foolhardy ventures of the fallen greats, but it explains much else besides. Against this background one can begin to understand how in the 1930s Stalin saw these men not as human or political ruins, most of them genuinely longing to be allowed to live out their lives in obscurity, but as vengeful spirits, ever watchful and plotting. The very depths to which they had fallen in this view would make them all the more vicious. They would not disdain any means to try to recover what had once been theirs. Stalin certainly wouldn't in their place.

In the spring of 1926 the outcasts—as they viewed themselves, for all the high Party and state positions they still held—Trotsky, Zinoviev, and Kamenev joined hands against the ruling group. Two years earlier this combination would have been almost unbeatable, but now the dissidents simply added to each other's weaknesses. Everybody remembered what Trotsky had once said about his new partners, what Zinoviev and Kamenev had said about him—and in case someone did not remember he would be reminded. "What used to be the strength of the Zinoviev block?" Stalin asked. "It was in its resolute struggle against Trotskyism. But now that it abandoned that struggle, Zinoviev and Company emasculated themselves." And Trotsky's strength lay, of course, "in the resolute struggle against the Zinoviev-Kamenev errors in October 1917 and their repetition of them today." So now you had a bloc of political eunuchs![33]

What did the three men count on in entering on this repulsive union? asked Stalin (who one day would form some rather startling alliances of his own). "I think they count on the situation worsening in the country and the Party."

This was quite close to the truth. The three men were politically foolhardy, but not entirely mistaken in believing that there was growing restlessness within the Party and mounting dissatisfaction in the country at large. The main reason for this dissatisfaction lay, paradoxically, in

[33] *The Fifteenth Congress of the All-Union Communist Party* (b), *Stenographic Report* (Moscow, 1927), p. 427.

the very success of the Soviet experiment. We might use the analogy of a besieged fortress: so long as the situation is desperate the garrison does not mind the danger, the inhabitants acquiesce in short rations. Then the danger grows less imminent, food stocks more plentiful: the garrison chafes under its inactive confinement, and the population demands normal living conditions. And so with Soviet Russia in 1926: the NEP returned the economy *almost* to the prewar level. The Soviet state had *almost* become an accepted member of the community of nations, all the major powers except the United States having recognized it. But as throughout the history of Communism, and as is true of the Soviet Union today in some ways, it is "normalcy," relative economic prosperity, which breeds political danger and restlessness. The regime was congratulating itself, said Trotsky, making a telling point for a change, that at the present pace the Russian economy would reach the 1913 level by 1930. Hadn't they all denounced *that* Russia as an impoverished, backward, and barbarous society?

And so the average Communist was bound to wonder: Where was socialism in this tenth year of Soviet power? Where was its modern, industrialized economy? In fact, wasn't the NEP making the individual peasant landholder's situation, especially the kulak's, even stronger? It was undeniable, on the other side of the ledger, that the peasant was no longer grateful for the NEP but was becoming, as almost any Communist would phrase it, more insolent. He was taking it for granted that his grain surplus would no longer be confiscated as it had been before 1921, and he was demanding high prices for his products as well as cheap manufactured goods. So the recent good harvest failed to bring with it a corresponding increase in grain procurements for the cities and for exports. With low prices and with very little his money could buy, the peasant preferred to eat better than to sell.

Another variety of ideological disenchantment touched on the role of Communism on the world stage. The year 1926 was, as the ritualistic Marxian phrase goes, a year of stabilization of international capitalism, i.e., of relative decline in Communist prospects, certainly in the West. Weimar Germany seemed no longer on the brink of collapse as it had in 1923, though in three years this would be shown to be an illusion. The Locarno agreements of 1925 had ushered in an era of reconciliation (again illusory) between Germany and France and Britain, hence of European peace. Ever since 1917 the Communists had lived in daily expectation of a cataclysmic crisis of capitalism, an economic depression, a conflict or perhaps a war between the main capitalist powers, which would open new and glittering opportunities for revolutionary Marxism and end Russia's isolation as the only Communist state. Now these hopes had to be deferred.

Whoever was in opposition in Russia tended to blame global as well as internal reverses of Communism on the leadership of the Russian Communist Party. To us this seems vastly more unfair than the practice of those in opposition in the United States who blame Washington for the shrinkage of the "free world." How could the Soviet Union be held responsible for Communism's not advancing in 1926? How could Stalin be the cause of Germany's economic recovery, of the electoral reverses of the French Communists, or of the failure of the British General Strike? But it was felt, and not only by Trotsky and Zinoviev, that the Marxian gods of history were punishing Stalin, who of course dominated the Comintern, for his essentially lukewarm attitude to world revolution. Did he not weaken the Communist Parties in the West by insisting that they purge their ranks of Trotsky's and Zinoviev's partisans? Hadn't Stalin and Tomsky, by their collaboration with the British labor leaders, helped to deceive the British workers into believing that the latter had their interests at heart, when in fact they called off the General Strike after nine days and betrayed the cause of the class struggle?

Stalin was no longer merely director of a Party apparatus and concerned with *some* aspects of internal policies of the Soviet Union. He was now the Leader of Communism at home and abroad, and he acknowledged his role and responsibility as such. He would be a *working* dictator. Unlike Hitler, who left vast areas of governance to others— economic planning and administration to Hjalmar Schacht and Hermann Göring, state administration to Meissner—Stalin displayed jealous proprietary feelings for power in all its aspects and details. Already in 1926 he astounded and possibly chagrined his associates, like Rykov and Bukharin, by initiative and interest in fields they had assumed would remain their preserve: the economy and international Communism. "The peasant from the province of Tiflis" laid down the law to the German and Polish Communists, expounded ambitious and (as they must have felt) unrealistic views as to how Russia would be industrialized. Stalin the Marxist was revealed, a man for whom power was a mandate to build and transform. But there seemed to be in his approach to power something like an atavistic feeling inherited from the suppressed longings of his serf ancestors: an ambition to own *completely* what one had, and greed for more. Not merely would Russia and world Communism be his to command; he would make them his property. Not only would he be the Leader; in Party circles he soon came to be referred to as *Khozyain*, the master of the household, the Boss.

As yet the property was not fully his, and most of all it was poor and primitive. The Marxist and the grasping proprietor were combined in Stalin when in 1925 he advanced the slogan "Socialism in One Country." While Marxist in its feeling, it appeared to clash with what the economic realities and the classics of Marxism taught. How could agrarian, backward Russia acquire that advanced industrial economy on which alone, as Marx had taught, socialism could be built? Lenin had urged a socialist *revolution* in Russia, but with the proviso that actual socialism could be built only with external help; an advanced industrial country, Germany, say, would soon become Communist and then would help with capital and experts. But now? The capitalists were not going to give credits to Russia as they had before 1914. Lenin had counted on their greed to overcome ideological hostility, but greed and antipathy to Communism combined to render the flow of foreign capital and technical expertise into Russia a mere trickle, for the Western bankers and industrialists neither forgot nor forgave the Revolution for confiscating foreign investments and repudiating foreign loans. Both Marxist purists and trained economists shook their heads at Stalin's formula. How could peasant Russia pull herself up by her own bootstraps? How could the regime extract from her population, a large part of it living at subsistence level, the wherewithal for industrialization?

And yet it was an effective political slogan, especially before Stalin gave his terrible answer as to how precisely the rapid industrialization would be accomplished. Socialism in One Country meant that the Russian Communists would not remain content to mark time, waiting for the distant moment when red flags would wave over Berlin and Paris, spending their time in intraparty squabbles. It meant doing something now, giving history a push, just as politically the Bolsheviks had given it a push in October 1917. Why—after performing a political miracle, giving the lie to the laws of history—shouldn't the Communists be able to perform an *economic* miracle?

In choosing Socialism in One Country as the main target of attack, the Trotsky-Zinoviev opposition again committed a major psychological and political error. Not that it mattered seriously in the actual resolution of the intraparty conflict. The preponderance of forces on Stalin's side made his victory a foregone conclusion even if the slogans had been reversed and the Trotsky-Zinoviev group had urged the rapid industrialization of Russia regardless of Communist developments abroad. Still, the opposition cast itself in a ludicrous light. It was they who had urged a more rapid tempo of industrialization, who had accused Stalin of being a prisoner of Bukharin's and acquiescing in an indefinite continuation of the NEP. Now that Stalin stood by this bracing slogan, they cast themselves as constant faultfinders, men of little faith who with copious quotations from Marx and Engels sought to bar the road to an exciting and essential venture, who sowed defeatism and distrust for ulterior, selfish reasons.

But just as this generation of Communist leaders could never overcome its lust for power, so it could never think of politics in *entirely* cynical terms. Cynicism would have urged the oppositionists to lie low and bide their time. If Stalin meant Socialism in One Country seriously, then sooner rather than later he would clash with Rykov and Bukharin, for they would surely not go along with the pressures on the peasant that any plan for rapid industrialization would require. Zinoviev, a better politician than Trotsky, saw the possibility of a new division, with Rykov and Bukharin ranged against Stalin. But even he, not to mention the much more impetuous Trotsky, would not consider delaying their attack until a more propitious time. As for Trotsky, he saw Socialism in One Country not as a program or a promise but as a deception; its real meaning was not to speed up the economic revolution at home, but to abandon the struggle for political revolution abroad.

And so the opposition marshaled its meager forces. Along with the assault on Stalin's slogan, there was a rehashing of old charges about bureaucratic degeneration in the Party, about the worsening lot of the industrial worker and the growing power of the kulak. In Party cells in factories and Soviet institutions, reckless partisans of Trotsky and Zinoviev brought up those accusations only to be shouted down by the followers of the apparatus (the names of the oppositionists and the more compromising points they made being transmitted to the Control Commissions and the GPU). Stalin's agents jotted down punctiliously the more scandalous doings of the enemy: Lashevich, a burly Civil War commander who was Zinoviev's man in the War Commissariat, held a conspiratorial meeting in the woods near Moscow! Karl Radek had dared to exercise his wit at the expense of the General Secretary: Stalin's Socialism in One Country, he said in a public speech, washing the Party's dirty linen before a non-Party audience (and thus undermining Soviet power!) reminded him of a story by Saltykov-Shchedrin. The great humorist fantasized how some landowners deep in the provinces of nineteenth-century Russia, having read about England and her liberal institutions, decided to proclaim "Liberalism in One County."

In its counterattack the apparatus did not disdain the most demagogic argument. Though two of Stalin's leading hatchetmen, Lazar Kaganovich and Yemelyan Yaroslavsky, were themselves Jewish, anti-Semitism was undoubtedly an element in the whisper campaign against Trotsky, Zinoviev, and Kamenev. Uglanov, head of the Moscow Party organization, was prominent on this score. In March 1926 Trotsky complained indignantly in a letter to Bukharin of a Party cell meeting in Moscow at which someone had charged that he, Trotsky, was being paid for his speeches. Another worthy had interjected, "You know, those Yids in the Politburo!" The Party authorities were constrained to issue pious declarations that such methods of fighting the oppositionists were impermissible. Stalin himself was far from the anti-Semitism of his later years, but as always in battling the enemy, he did not disdain any weapons.

In July a joint meeting of the Central Committee and the Central Control Commission dealt the new opposition some preliminary blows.

Zinoviev was expelled from the Politburo, Lashevich was dismissed as Assistant War Commissar. Stalin chose to dwell on Trotsky's most vulnerable charge, his quite silly complaint about the committee of collaboration between the Soviet and British trade unions. The British labor leadership was from their viewpoint quite conservative, allowed Stalin. So what? Did Communists refuse to enter into political combinations and arrangements, even with reactionaries, when it promised ultimately to suit the interests of the Revolution? Had not Lenin negotiated with representatives of William II? "The policy of grandiloquent and empty pose has been the characteristic of Trotsky ever since he joined our Party."[34] Who would profit by the Soviets' breaking up this, at worst, harmless "dialogue" with the British unionists? None other than Winston Churchill.[35] This made excellent sense.

Stalin had a gesture of his own: he moved that Lenin's *Testament* be made public. By now the revelation could hurt him very little, and possibly it might redound to his credit. Let the whole Party know how "the old woman" (Krupskaya) had managed to poison her sick husband's mind against this selfless man.[36]

Little was left for the opposition—ever more futile and suicidal appeals to the masses, speeches in factories where the once proud and distant greats pleaded for the support of Party rank and file and were met with heckling, hoots, and laughter. As the vernacular has it, Trotsky did not know what had hit him. Rather than acknowledging the solid organizational assets in Stalin's hand, he kept imagining sinuous and obscure ideological betrayals by members of the majority. In a letter to Radek, Trotsky interpreted Tomsky's position as the result of his contacts with Western labor union leaders.[37] And he saw Voroshilov and Kalinin as the kulak element of the Politburo. Both gentlemen had peasant antecedents, but now they were simply Stalin's henchmen, and tied to him for reasons other than their class origin.

The aim of the ruling group was now to eliminate the leaders of the opposition as persons of consequence in the Party. On this the mild and humane Rykov and Bukharin were at one with Stalin; they failed to see how retaining Trotsky and Zinoviev could provide at least partial insurance for themselves. But then no one could really believe that the three dissident leaders would cease criticizing and plotting, no matter how many times they pledged good behavior. There *was* one solution, so

---

[34] Stalin, VIII, 190.

[35] Chancellor of the Exchequer in the Conservative government, advocate of strong measures against the trade unions during the General Strike in May.

[36] She was only fifty-seven, but was referred to as "the old woman" in Party circles. Somehow the document was never widely circulated until 1956. It was published in 1927 in a bulletin of the Fifteenth Congress, which had a limited distribution.

[37] *The Trotsky Archive*, T890.

brilliant in its simplicity that no one thought of it until an obscure Party member named Ossovsky broached it in a magazine article in September 1926. Factions *within* the Communist Party were forbidden,[38] but why not form another party? Neither Marxism nor the Soviet Constitution prescribed that there could be only one party.[39] For contributing this original suggestion Ossovsky was kicked out of the Party. Would you believe, asked a henchman of Stalin's, that Kamenev and Trotsky voted against throwing out this "hidden Menshevik," this "wicked enemy of Communism"?

Despite the opposition leaders' attempt to retract some of their statements, the regime tightened the screws a bit more. In October a Central Committee–Control Commission meeting ejected Trotsky and Kamenev from the Politburo. And then the Fifteenth Party Conference met to ratify and publicize the errant leaders' ever deeper disgrace and to elevate the General Secretary still higher.

Less than a year before, at the Fourteenth Congress, the opposition had fought for power, though against hopeless odds. Now they were to struggle merely to stay alive politically. Bukharin used an appropriate figure of speech: they were drowning and calling on each other for help. But instead of helping, they were in fact dragging each other down. At the Conference Stalin denied any intention to expel the oppositionists from the Party. Let them acknowledge, he asked mildly, the even graver charges against them, and all would be well. This was unlikely to have been conscious hypocrisy. Stalin the cautious politician preferred to have his enemies disarm themselves, preferred to offer the lesson that salvation lay in submission. A sadist relishes the vision of people once superior and condescending to him retained in insignificant positions and helplessly thrashing about, torn between hope and fear. We must not credit the General Secretary with a degree of introspection greater than that of ordinary people, to make him aware of that other Stalin, incapable of forgiving or forgetting. Shortly before the Conference, at a Politburo meeting, Trotsky had called Stalin "the gravedigger of the Revolution" to his face. Few of those present could believe that Stalin would ever forget this insult. Within a few months he had been accused of ordering a medical murder and of trying to destroy the cause he believed he had worked for ever since his adolescence. But the full revelation of the tyrant who ordered assassinations lay in the future. Now he was still a politician.

There is no doubt that he enjoyed himself in this role. The hideous

---

[38] This was according to the decision of the Tenth Party Congress which barred factional activity. This meant that once the competent Party organ made a decision after a free discussion, Party members had no right to form groups to agitate or plot to undo the decision.

[39] But Soviet law does ban counterrevolutionary activity.

strains and fears which would lead to holocausts still lay in the future. The Fifteenth Party Conference marked the point at which he could feel he had been genuinely accepted by the majority of the Party. His preeminence was a deserved reward for his hard work, for his correct application of Marxist and Leninist teachings. His self-image was helped by the belief that he was genuinely popular with the rank and file, and by the fact that people like Bukharin and Tomsky were happy to follow his leadership (so different from Zinoviev and Kamenev, who had intended merely to *use* him). Slander and intrigue proved unavailing, for he had been right. Before the Conference Krupskaya capitulated and abandoned the opposition. Harassed by Stalin's adherents, troubled by the thought that her husband would not have approved of tearing the Party apart, she felt she could not endure the strife any more. For the remaining thirteen years of her life she remained a docile witness to tyranny and tried to intercede only on behalf of some of the humbler victims of the terror.

And so at the Conference Stalin appeared confident and radiant. "Yes, we can and we ought to conquer the capitalist elements in our economy, we can and must build socialist society in our country."[40] To be sure, this victory could not be secure so long as Communist Russia was surrounded by the capitalist world. "To win fully, to win definitely, we must see to it that the current capitalist encirclement be changed to a socialist one; we must strive for the proletariat's winning in at least a few other countries. Only then will our victory be full and final." In twenty years Stalin had occasion to recall these words, and then a little later they took on yet another and ironically threatening meaning. Yes, Russia exchanged a "capitalist encirclement" for a "socialist" one: Stalin looked unusually wistful in the photographs with Mao Tse-tung in 1950.

But for the time being this formula was as convincing to himself as it undoubtedly was to the majority of the delegates. They were not betraying the cause of the Revolution by trying to build socialism in Russia. Quite the opposite. The opposition was and seemed confounded and bankrupt. Its leaders' speeches sounded hollow, and would have been so even without the hostile audience. It is a measure of Trotsky's biographer's emotional attachment to his subject that he can describe his speech as "one of his greatest . . . moderate in tone yet devastating in content, masterly in logical and artistic composition, gleaming with humor," and the audience's reaction as one of "breathless suspense and respectful hostility."[41] It is impossible to endorse this judgment on the basis of the actual text: the speech runs to more than thirty pages of close print, most of which is strings of quotations from Engels and

[40] *The Fifteenth Conference* (Moscow, 1927), p. 440.
[41] Isaac Deutscher, *The Prophet Unarmed: Trotsky 1921–29* (New York, 1959), pp. 301–302.

Lenin, labored attempts to prove that what Trotsky was now saying was in no way different from what Stalin had said in 1922 or 1924, that Bukharin himself had sometimes agreed, that the opposition was not really guilty of all the deviations it was charged with, that though denying the accusations they would still work loyally within the Party after it had condemned them, and so on. Repeatedly the speaker begged to be allowed more time, as if persisting in the vain delusion that one more citation, one more felicitous phrase, and the audience would understand him. The noise which punctuated his speech was, alas, not in tribute to his powers. The audience was laughing at the proud and once powerful man now being humiliated.

> A TYPICAL INTERRUPTION: Do you think you are speaking to children? . . .
> TROTSKY: I think I have the right to appeal from my words of 1917 to what Lenin said in 1921.
> VOICE FROM THE FLOOR: And what did Lenin say afterward?
> TROTSKY: Afterward he said some other things.
> *General laughter.*[42]

By the time Zinoviev took the floor the delegates had tasted blood and were reveling at the discomfiture of the man, for while he had sometimes been hated as strongly as Trotsky, he had never been equally respected. If Trotsky pleaded, then Zinoviev begged. He piteously quoted a line of Blok's: "Are we then guilty if our body is being crushed in the embrace of your heavy paws?" to be answered by laughter and shouts, "Well written! Very well said!"[43] He begged for forgiveness. Did they remember that Bukharin and others had said terrible things about Lenin and yet had been forgiven? Would they show a similar generosity in regard to the present opposition? He ran out of his allotted time. Would they give him ten or fifteen more minutes to talk about this important problem of Socialism in One Country? Would they, please? Stalin had talked about it for three hours. If not about that, how about the Comintern? He was about to be dismissed from it, so couldn't he have just five more minutes? Amid general derision he was cut off. In the Roman circus the audiences occasionally refused to spare the fallen gladiator, but it is not recorded that they ever laughed at him in his agony.

Stalin enjoyed the spectacle from his Presidium seat (one is tempted to say the imperial box). He did not have to render the mortal blow to the prostrate enemy. That task was performed by Bukharin, with a gusto on which in the years to come he may often have reflected. Why,

[42] *The Fifteenth Conference*, pp. 519–20.
[43] *Ibid.*, p. 558.

he asked, did the leaders of the opposition prattle all those formulas and quotations? Why did they not repeat what they had said before: the country and the Party were being ruined and the working class betrayed? How about the Thermidor? (With his gift for politically disastrous historical allusions Trotsky had picked up this theme from a follower of Zinoviev's, Zalutski. Already in 1925 Zalutski had been roundly rebuked for comparing the situation in the Communist Party to that in the French Revolution after the overthrow of Robespierre and the right-wing Thermidorian reaction of 1794.) Who called whom the gravedigger of the Revolution? And hadn't Trotsky maintained that a *good* harvest was a dangerous thing? (Here again, Trotsky had been imprudent. He had said that as long as agriculture was not socialized a good harvest *might* be dangerous, for it would embolden the kulak. This was rumored to mean—and it became a persistent theme in the 1930s— that the opposition was praying for economic disaster and might resort—in the 1930s this became: has resorted—to sabotage.)

Bukharin's brilliant, if in some ways contemptible polemical feat was also interrupted from the floor, but this time with applause and expressions of delight. Stalin joined with shouts of approval at the orator's wittier and more venomous thrusts. At one point, unable to contain his admiration, he yelled "Bravo, Bukharin, bravo! He does not speak but cuts with a knife!"[44] Seldom was he to express pleasure in a collaborator's performance so vividly and characteristically.

He now advanced to the position of superleader. For all the opposition's "points," they were being punished mainly for their attacks on him. They had dared to say, recalled Yaroslavsky, that Stalin could not unite the Party. "I ask you, do you dare to repeat such accusations before the whole Party? Can't you realize, can't you see that Comrade Stalin, because at such a difficult time he protected Leninist policy, has gained the still greater respect of every member?"[45]

In his concluding address Stalin was at some pains to show himself able to juggle quotations from Marx, Engels, and Lenin as well as the others. It was a creditable performance, and though by this time he must have had secretarial and research help in preparing it, the style and content are unmistakably his. He departed occasionally from the written text to deal with points raised from the floor. His theoretical sophistication went beyond anything which the later Khrushchevs and Brezhnevs were able to muster in their reports, but he was clearly impatient of the scholastic mumbo-jumbo; he invoked it to show—and this was still important—that he could meet Trotsky and Zinoviev on their own terms, as well as massacre them politically. If Engels were alive, he

[44] *Ibid.*, p. 601.
[45] *Ibid.*, p. 497.

assured his listeners, he would not drone on with old formulas; he would most likely say, "To hell with those old formulas. Long live the victorious revolution in the U.S.S.R.!"[46] He was more in his element when issuing ominous threats and conditions against the defeated, in his recital of what the Party "cannot and will not tolerate."

The Fifteenth Party Conference heaped new and heinous charges on the heads of the oppositionists. If in 1925 they had been adjudged guilty of the Menshevik deviation, this time they were convicted of the Social Democratic one. The vote on it was unanimous, and so would be every vote on every issue at every Party Conference or Congress of the Communist Party of the U.S.S.R. to this very day.

What could Stalin's enemies do now? They had been branded with a new and shameful stamp. It was ironic that the honorable name of Social Democrat, once proudly born by both Marx and Lenin, became a brand of infamy, an epithet implying not only heresy but also weakness. They would soon descend still farther—the General Secretary was operating the elevator carrying them—to a lower level of employment. It was ironic how many oppositionists landed abroad in various diplomatic and trade mission jobs. The embassy in France headed by Trotsky's friend Christian Rakovsky was seeded with them. Kamenev was for a short time envoy to Mussolini's Italy. (This was, of course, a technique that antedated Lenin's use of diplomatic exile for dissidents: the chief of police under Alexander II was foolish enough to remonstrate with the Emperor about his young mistress,[47] and as a reward for his solicitude found himself ambassador to Great Britain.) Abroad, Stalin knew, these people could not but be faithful servants of the Soviet state. They would not defect. But by the same token they would not acquiesce in what seemed not only honorable but luxurious exile. The taste of power was still too fresh in their mouths: what were all the splendors and amenities of Rome or Paris compared with that? Better some wretched flat in Moscow if along with it they could recoup real power, engage in ideological discussions, talk over schemes of economic and social reform determining the fate of millions of Russians. For others the descent was more precipitous: an obscure job at home, expulsion from the Party in some cases, and even in 1927 imprisonment.

One did not have to be Stalin to believe that this could not be the end. The craving for power was an essential part of the Old Bolsheviks' makeup. Some of them might or would "forgive and forget" if chastised repeatedly, but never Trotsky and Zinoviev. (Kamenev, if separated from Zinoviev, was a somewhat different case, and perhaps would have been content to spend the rest of his life editing Lenin's writings and engag-

---

[46] *Ibid.*, p. 721.
[47] The Tsar's friends were worried that his amorous exploits were sapping his strength and prematurely aging him.

ing in similar scholarly endeavors.) For them power was their whole life. They had owned what Stalin has stolen: the glory of October had been Trotsky's; the Comintern Zinoviev's. It was inconceivable that these two would be content to serve as mere members of the Central Committee, as subordinate bureaucrats while Stalin and Bukharin marshaled the forces of world revolution, ordered around not only men but history itself, transformed Russia, summoned the revolutionary masses of Germany and China. This was not just power, this was immortality. How could one be denied the right to fight for it by some vote of a Congress or Conference? Trotsky's terrible obsession was much more than envy: he believed he knew where history was going, how the Russian Revolution could be saved from the fate of the French, the one correct formula which would electrify the German masses, bring out the revolutionary potential of China. It is strange that with his passion for historical analogies he did not think of Socrates: his "demon" would not let him remain silent. He had to cry out against this boor, this provincial ignoramus who was ruining the Revolution, betraying world Communism. The demon would rob Trotsky of all his children, would make him a homeless exile, would bring him death at the hand of a faceless assassin. And only in this death was he fortunate, dying without first groveling before the tyrant and befouling his own past. And, the greatest mercy of all, he died before he could see his terrible rival acclaimed in victory, fawned upon by world statesmen, accomplishing what Trotsky believed only he himself could accomplish, bringing Communism into the heart of Europe and seeing the red flag unfurl over the largest nation in the world.

And so for Zinoviev and Trotsky and many, many others, the defeats of 1925–26 marked the end of their careers as political leaders and the beginning of that calvary that would fill out the rest of their lives.

For Stalin too 1927 was an end and a beginning. The politician completed his role, consolidated his grip. By the end of the year he had disposed of the opposition which had dogged his steps ever since he seized Lenin's mantle; this Party "nobility," as he called them, was cast into outer darkness. His future struggles and purges were not in defense of leadership and dictatorship—*that* was conceded by the end of 1927—but in pursuance of his new role: tyrant-demiurge now forcing all Russia to bend to his will. He owned to his nature. Yes, he would say again, but this time not jocularly, as he had at the Fourteenth Congress, Lenin was completely right: "I am coarse, comrades." Before an awed assembly of Party officials he picked up this description with pride and defiance: "I am coarse and heavy-handed toward those who perfidiously try to divide and destroy the Party. I have not concealed it. Perhaps you need a certain softness in dealing with rebels. But that is not in my nature." He would show them, show the whole world, that softness was not in his nature.

It is fair to say that had the opposition behaved in the most exemplary and docile way following its defeats, it still would have been subjected to further repressions. The ruling group's cohesion was forged as much by hatred of Trotsky and Zinoviev as it was by loyalty to Stalin. Stalin was not just being sly when he said at one point in 1927 that his own followers were "accusing" him of being too lenient with the fallen greats. Early in the year Trotsky addressed a letter to Yaroslavsky, one of the most persistent of his tormentors and among the most repulsive of Stalin's henchmen, protesting some new attacks and the way that anything untoward happening in the Party was blamed on him and his followers. Yaroslavsky replied that, yes, there was trouble in some Party organizations. He did not blame Trotsky for having inspired it, but the opposition could not escape *all* responsibility if somebody somewhere attacked the ruling group. Yaroslavsky's venom brought protests even from some of Stalin's staunchest supporters. At a meeting of the Central Control Commission, Orjonikidze cut him short when he started on the old theme of how, during the Civil War, Trotsky had ordered Communists shot. Those were deserters, said Orjonikidze, who may have been not a more tolerant man but simply a shrewder one: excessive taunting of Trotsky could gain him sympathy, and it was better to wait for his next move. Soon enough it was forthcoming.

In April 1927 the opposition exulted. Trotsky and Zinoviev believed that now they had *proof* of how Stalin's policies had led world Communism to disaster. They pointed to what was happening to the Chinese Communists, whom they saw as the victim of Stalin's policy of collaboration, with the Kuomintang imposed upon them. Through Stalin's blindness, if not outright betrayal, they were now being massacred by Chiang Kai-shek. ☆☆☆

COMMUNISM in China! Who among the early Communist leaders could ever have believed that one day the greatest victory of world Communism since October 1917, its conquest of China, would turn out to be Soviet Russia's greatest defeat and greatest danger? In the 1920s there seemed to be new and dazzling opportunities in China to strike at imperialism and capitalism from, so to speak, the rear. China lay in complete political and social chaos. But the country's economic primitiveness, much greater than that of prerevolutionary Russia, precluded an outright Communist coup. The Chinese Communist Party, born in 1919, was at first but a handful of intellectuals and students, epitomized by two whose names would become household words in Stalin's lifetime: Chou En-lai, scion of a Mandarin family who had imbibed his Marxism as a student abroad; and Mao Tse-tung, son of a well-to-do peasant, librarian by profession and largely self-taught.

In *Imperialism* Lenin laid down the future tactics for Communism in underdeveloped areas. And following the Revolution he drew the logical conclusion from the stabilization of capitalism in Europe and from the continuing ferment in the colonial areas. The Communists must support what today we would call national liberation movements. Such movements, even though bourgeois-nationalist in orientation and leadership, still work indirectly for Communism, he argued. They strike at the imperialists' spheres of influence, and activating the masses can only bring the day closer when Communist power is established.

It was in pursuance of this policy that in 1923 a Soviet emissary, Adolf Yoffe, of Brest-Litovsk fame, signed the celebrated agreement with Dr. Sun Yat-sen of the Kuomintang. Soviet Russia would help the Kuomintang, until then holding power only in an area in the south, around Canton, in its attempt to unite China and free it from warlords and foreign imperialists alike. The Chinese Communists would enter the Kuomintang without giving up their own party.

During the next three years both sides profited by this agreement. Communist influence, Soviet experts, and Soviet advice transformed the Kuomintang from what it had been prior to the Sun-Yoffe agreement—a group of intellectuals seeking leverage within this or that warlord group—into a modern well-organized party. Like its Bolshevik prototype, the Kuomintang developed techniques for exploiting the numerous social ills and grievances of the unhappy country: the peasants' exploitation by the landlords, the workers' struggle to exact a living wage from their (mostly foreign) employers, the almost universal resentment against Western imperialism. The Communists, in turn, gained in numbers and influence. Many foreign observers concluded overhastily that the Kuomintang was but a front for the Communists. Certainly Chiang Kai-shek, its leader after Dr. Sun's death in 1925, leaned heavily on Soviet advisers. The most prominent of these were Michael Borodin, a Russian Communist with an American background, whom many in 1925–26 considered the real ruler of South China, and the chief military expert, "General Galen," whose real name was Vassily Blücher, a famous Red officer in the Russian Civil War and a future Soviet marshal.

The Sun-Yoffe agreement included a specific pledge by the Russians that they would not try to export Communism to China. But of course the Soviet aim all along was to employ the Kuomintang to the limit of its usefulness; as Stalin was to say in the spring of 1927 of the Chinese

Nationalists: "They have to be utilized to the end, squeezed out like a lemon, and then thrown away." These tactics foresaw the Kuomintang expanding its power over more and more of China, when Chiang would be pushed aside or replaced by more left-wing elements within the Kuomintang who eventually would give way to a Chinese October Revolution. The trouble with this scheme was that Chiang had read about the Russian Revolution and was determined to be a *successful* Kornilov.

But in 1926 the Moscow scenario for China appeared to be working out. To be sure, in March Chiang staged a coup which expanded his powers and limited that of the Communists in the Kuomintang. But in October Borodin persuaded a number of Chiang's rivals to set up their own regime in Wuhan (the joint name of three industrial cities on the Yangtse), and this included some Communists. The Soviets now had three balls to juggle in the struggle for power in China: Chiang, still professing friendship for the Soviet Union, still tolerating Communists and Soviet advisers; the Left Kuomintang government in Wuhan; and of course the Chinese Communist Party.

Trotsky's supporters were to claim that from virtually the beginning he had seen the sinfulness and the disaster lurking in the Communists' arrangement with the Kuomintang. But the fact is that only in early 1927 did he begin to voice doubts. Though faithfully obeying the Comintern's (i.e., Stalin's) directives, some Chinese Communists had been fearful that the Kuomintang, instead of serving as the Trojan Horse, might turn out to be a live beast that would devour them before they could split its belly. On March 17 Trotsky in a confidential memo to Radek wrote that indeed the Chinese Communists should now leave the Kuomintang. But he still favored continued collaboration with Chiang.[48] In another letter to a supporter he formulated the Communist philosophy of alliances: "One can be an ally of Kuomintang, but an ally is to be watched like an enemy; one should not be sentimental about one's allies."[49]

The intra-Soviet discussion of the Chinese situation was couched in those ideologicohistorical formulas which are the staple of the Communist political rhetoric. Was China now at the phase corresponding to Russia in April or in July 1917? Was the Left Kuomintang analogous to the Martovs and Chernovs of the Russian Revolution? But in plain speech the problem could be put less elegantly: Who would manage to doublecross whom first, Chiang the Communists, or the Communists

---

[48] He also complained about the Chinese Communists. Many of them still want to stay within the Kuomintang. The Communist Party of China must itself be purged of its "Menshevik elements."

[49] *The Trotsky Archive*, T938.

Chiang? Stalin, despite what is implied in the Trotskyite literature on the subject, did not love or trust Chiang; he simply underestimated him.

In the spring Chiang's armies, helped by a Communist-led uprising within the city, conquered Shanghai. Now the future Generalissimo, an honorary member of the Executive of the Comintern, threw off his mask. On April 12 he ordered a massacre of the Shanghai Communists.

Stalin was to claim, and there is a hard core of common sense in his argument, that though the Chinese policy failed, the premises under which it had been conducted could not be faulted. The Communists *had* to take the risk inherent in collaboration with the Kuomintang. Certainly the latter's successes curtailed the influence of imperialist powers on China and set the stage for Communist successes some time in the future. The Chinese Communists could never have grown so impressively in membership and influence without collaborating with the Kuomintang, and it would have been sheer fantasy to imagine that in 1923 or 1927 they could have conquered a sizable part of China by themselves. There were occasions, he implied, when ideological incantations and citations from Marx and Lenin are powerless to change the disposition of class forces. Was it wrong to have the Revolution of 1905? he asked. It had ended in disaster, but it had also set the stage for 1917. ☆☆☆

THE day was still distant when such *Realpolitik* was convincing to all Communists. (One day nobody would think it strange that the Soviet Union should help and protect Egypt though at the time Gamal Abdel Nasser was jailing Egyptian Communists en masse.) The opposition now exulted in what it believed was a golden opportunity. For all the General Secretary's machinations and chicanery, everybody would see how Stalin and his satrap in the Comintern, Bukharin, were in fact the gravediggers of the Revolution. As soon as the news of the Shanghai massacre reached Moscow, Trotsky and Zinoviev sprang into action. In a letter to the Central Committee they and eighty-one of their followers demanded an immediate and secret Plenum of the Central Committee to discuss the disaster. What had happened in China, what was happening elsewhere, in Poland,[50] in Germany, was the obvious fruit of the "petty-bourgeois theory of Socialism in One Country." Now the danger of war threatened the U.S.S.R., because world capitalism, emboldened by its success in China, would strike at Russia. The Central Committee had

[50] Where in 1926 Piłsudski carried out a coup and established a semidictatorial regime.

to authorize a free discussion and allow Trotsky and Zinoviev to expound their views in print.[51]

Though revivified, the opposition was just as blind as before. Trotsky and Zinoviev again fell prey to a fatal delusion that Stalin himself would see that he was out of his depth as leader of world Communism. In a letter to Krupskaya, Trotsky attempted unsuccessfully to draw the poor woman back into the struggle against the General Secretary: Stalin, he wrote, had become weaker and the bankruptcy of his policy had been exposed; the out-and-out right-wingers (i.e., Bukharin) will soon turn against him. But even in this wildly overoptimistic assessment there was a touch of hopeless prescience. "The more our prognosis is confirmed by the facts, the more cruelly they oppress us."[52] And thus with hope and despair the opposition rushed to a new struggle and doom.

There was no danger to his power, yet these renewed attacks were for Stalin more than a mere embarrassment. It was not his power but his authority that was being threatened. In substance the Trotsky-Zinoviev charges about China were absurd. To visualize how much so, we may compare them to the outcry of the American right wing a little more than twenty years later about how Truman and Acheson "lost China." Those charges were unfair enough: how can one nation in peacetime determine the course of events in another vast and distant country? But at that time the United States was unquestionably the most powerful nation in the world, its industry producing more than half the entire global output. The American protégé, Chiang, was until well into 1947 in control of most of mainland China, and it was his own policies as much as the Communists' clever ones that brought about his doom. But here was a weak and impoverished Soviet Union, with its clients, the Chinese Communists, mustering a strength of only about 60,000. Could the most brilliant understanding of dialectic, the most "correct" directives sent to the Chinese comrades, have affected the issue of the struggle? Suppose that by some miracle the Chinese Communists had seized southern China: would the imperialist powers have tolerated their attempt to conquer the whole country? In his memoranda throughout 1926 Trotsky himself stressed the absolute necessity of not provoking Japan, of respecting her sphere of influence in Manchuria and north China. Any likely Communist conquest would have brought the capitalist powers together, would have presented the *Soviet* Far East with the danger of Japanese invasion, an invasion which, everybody recognized, the Soviet Union was in no position to defeat.[53]

[51] *The Trotsky Archive*, T941.
[52] *Ibid.*, T950.
[53] The international side of the Chinese question then is dealt with in my *Expansion and Coexistence: The History of Soviet Foreign Policy, 1917–1967* (New York, 1967), pp. 167–81.

Fair or unfair, the charges inflicted a wound that went deep. There was still among Communists a belief in the magic power of incantation, as opposed to common sense. Why hadn't the slogan of worker and peasant soviets been raised in China in 1926? asked Trotsky. Everyone remembered how in April 1917 Lenin had advanced the then barely comprehensible formula of "*All* power to the Soviets," and like the walls of Jericho, the Provincial Government had begun to tumble down. And there was an added element of superstition, common to all ideological systems. Stalin's dictatorship was still not established firmly enough, and he was vulnerable to the feeling that he was unlucky. Before, he had brought the Party out of the dangers it faced during Lenin's illness, and after Lenin's death he had curbed the opposition, chastised the quarreling oligarchs. But had he now failed as the leader of world Communism?

The greatest danger he had to overcome, however, was to his self-esteem. Stalin said that he did not claim to be infallible, and he still and probably genuinely repulsed the grosser type of flattery. But he was also already establishing a legend, building an image which in due time he would fully believe in: as an imperturbable and omniscient man to whom history granted knowledge of its laws. He now often referred to himself in the third person. But on the Chinese issue he had been brought down to earth: a Chinese warlord had tricked him. His apparent self-assurance had been his main asset in his ascent to power. Through it he had mastered people like Orjonikidze, Molotov, and Dzerzhinsky. Show a sign of faltering, admit that you have made a mistake, and these people would be at your throat. This was what Zinoviev and Trotsky were counting on: they could not really hope to get a majority or even a sizable minority of the Party behind them, but they could hope that Stalin would begin to apologize, perhaps ask for their assistance in helping to run the Comintern. It would be the first step.

Stalin did not make it. In a fashion that became standard, Stalin proclaimed that the Comintern's Chinese policy had been right all along, at the same time as it was being rapidly changed. With Chiang now an enemy, the Chinese Communists were instructed to lean on the Left Kuomintang regime in Wuhan. When the latter turned against them and most of its members sought a reconciliation with Chiang, the Chinese Communists were unleashed by Moscow. They were commanded to undertake a series of armed revolts in the countryside and seizures of the urban centers against the Kuomintang forces. By the middle of 1928 most of these were suppressed, some only after bloody fighting, as in Canton. A few scattered bands of guerrillas remained in isolated countryside far from the main centers. It would have required considerable imagination to prophesy that two of their leaders, Mao and

Chu Teh, the latter a reformed opium-smoker and warlord, would forge their half-anarchist and half-Communist motley bands into an army and a movement which would conquer China. For the time being their names were virtually unknown in Moscow. The debacle of the Chinese Communist Party was blamed on its leadership, which had so docilely followed the lead of the Comintern. Its head and one of the founders, Chen Tu-hsiu, was purged. ☆☆☆

O N the domestic front the Stalin regime readied fresh measures of repression against Trotsky and Zinoviev. In return the opposition thought itself very clever by raising the specter of war. It so happened that about the same time, in May, the Conservative government of Stanley Baldwin broke off diplomatic relations with the U.S.S.R. In the suspicious mind of the Soviets there always lurked an apprehension that Great Britain, leader of world capitalism, would one day mount an offensive against Communism. The Comintern considered Britain Enemy Number One: it conducted agitation in Britain's colonial empire; its alliance with the Kuomintang had been inspired largely by the desire to deal a blow to the British interests in south China. In Communist eyes Imperial Britain was the bastion of that world order which had to be overturned if Communism was to inherit the world. The British lion was not only rapacious, but full of guile. As J. Edgar Hoover and many Americans in the 1950s saw the hand of the Kremlin behind every untoward development in the United States and the world, so in the 1920s for the more imaginative Soviet leaders the sinister influence of the fabled British Intelligence Service was blamed for every blow to Communist interests, whether Chiang's coup or the recent assassination of a Soviet diplomat in Warsaw. And now this government, of the arrogantly monocled Sir Austen Chamberlain (Foreign Secretary) and the inveterate Bolshevik-hater Winston Churchill (Chancellor of the Exchequer), was mounting a war against the U.S.S.R.[54]

How anyone conversant with what was going on in Great Britain could think the British willing and able to attack the Soviet Union is another matter. But the war scare was thought to be grist for the opposition's mill. Could the Soviet state face it without summoning Trotsky to a leading position, without availing itself of the talents of those fabled Civil War commanders like Lashevich, Yevdokimov, and Muralov who were currently in opposition and disgrace?

[54] The pipe-smoking Mr. Baldwin was evidently thought to be a poor hate symbol and was seldom mentioned.

The Stalin camp turned the argument neatly around and employed the war scare for its own propaganda. The war was threatening, and Trotsky and Zinoviev, instead of abandoning their opposition and presenting a joint front with all the loyal Soviet citizens, were through unpatriotic and un-Communist behavior encouraging the would-be aggressor. The phrase "fifth column" had not yet been coined, but that was what the regime was insinuating that Trotsky and his partisans were. A *united front from Chamberlain to Trotsky* was threatening the Fatherland of Socialism—this was the slanderous charge of Stalin's henchmen. But even some of the General Secretary's partisans were shocked by this insinuation. Had Trotsky not compounded his previous mistakes by a yet more fantastic one, it is likely that his downfall would have been postponed. But he did make one, probably the most foolish and inexcusable in his long struggle against the hated enemy.

In a letter to Orjonikidze[55] the former War Commissar protested the accusation that he was a defeatist. His real position Trotsky likened to that of Georges Clemenceau during World War I. The French statesman continued to attack the government even though the war was going on because he felt it to be his patriotic duty. And finally, with the Germans but fifty miles from Paris, power was turned over to him and Clemenceau led France to victory! The proud and doomed man could not resist the temptation to dazzle his readers with historical erudition. But whatever sympathy he had gained by being the target of slander was now dissipated and replaced by indignation. He had delivered into Stalin's hands the knife with which his own jugular would be cut. "Clemenceau—it is Trotsky and his group," exclaimed Stalin before the joint Plenum of the Central Committee and the Central Control Commission summoned to sit in judgment on the opposition. "If the enemy finds himself fifty miles from the Kremlin, then this new Clemenceau, this musical-comedy Clemenceau, will try first to overthrow the regime, and then deign to undertake the defense [of the Soviet Union]."[56]

The joint Plenum met at the end of July to consider the expulsion of Trotsky and Zinoviev from the Central Committee. Stalin's parliament was in a bloodthirsty mood. Gone were the last remnants of comradely comity. Trotsky and Zinoviev tried to talk about China, Germany, England, but were incessantly interrupted: "Trotsky! Tell us about the charges against you. . . . Tell us about the Communists you had ordered shot in the Civil War . . . about the demonstration you organized at the Yaroslav station."[57] Attempts to deal with ideological

[55] Currently chairman of the Party Control Commission.
[56] Stalin, x, 53.
[57] Trotsky and his partisans had bidden a tumultuous farewell to an oppositionist "transferred" to the Far East.

issues were met with shouts. "Look! He is reading his collected works! . . . Read us something from Chekhov."[58]

But then Stalin stayed his hand: the two men were not expelled from the Party. The reason usually adduced for this is that Stalin's scheme encountered opposition among his own followers. But this is unlikely. He was a master of the art of timing. It is more likely that he wanted Trotsky and Zinoviev to recant once more before their final doom. He realized that in the Party and the country there was by now real apprehension about the possibility of war. This was not the moment to increase this apprehension. The war scare must pass. The two rebels made a declaration of submission to the regime and of unconditional support in the case of war. They gained a few weeks' stay of their political execution. . . .

The tyrant was reawakening within the politician. However phony the war scare was in its inception, there is no doubt that in the course of the passionate debate Stalin and his opponents came *almost* to believe in its imminence. What begins in the Communist mind as a coldly calculated gambit not infrequently turns into hysteria. And Stalin epitomized this tendency. Were the capitalists really so foolish to pass up this opportunity to strike at the U.S.S.R., torn by internal strife? In June 1927 the GPU rounded up and shot twenty people whose only sin was that they had belonged to the prerevolutionary nobility and upper bourgeoisie. No proof was ever offered that these peaceable people had been "spies and diversionists." In fact this act of wanton terror was aimed at strengthening the "vigilance" of Soviet citizens as well as being an "answer" to the assassination of a Soviet diplomat in Warsaw by a demented White émigré. In one speech Stalin raged at Communists who like Kamenev deplored this barbarity, not so much out of humanitarian scruples but on the grounds that it would alienate progressive circles abroad. "The shooting of twenty 'noblemen' met with approval and understanding on the part of the millions of workers in the U.S.S.R. and in the West . . . with the sentiment, well done to those scoundrels. . . . To hell with those liberal-pacifist philosophers and their 'sympathy' for the U.S.S.R."[59]

Stalin was impatient to proceed with his great design to remake Russia, to make his country powerful and invulnerable in war as well as peace. But first he had to get rid of those people who at every step, at every setback, made trouble, who just had declared in so many words that in the case of a real emergency they would not hesitate to try to overthrow him.

For all their recantation Trotsky and Zinoviev were at it again almost

---

[58] *The Trotsky Archive*, T3085.

[59] *Ibid.*, pp. 45–46.

immediately. The Fifteenth Party Congress was approaching, and they were marshaling support. Meetings of their supporters were disrupted. GPU agents provocateurs infiltrated their ranks so that the regime might have "proof" of how the opposition had not only *talked* of treason but had even allowed former White officers in their midst. Since as a rule Trotsky and Zinoviev were now refused the right to write in the Party journals, the opposition undertook the desperate step of establishing a clandestine press, and this printed its platform for the forthcoming Congress. But Stalin's police were already more efficient than the Tsar's had ever been. Within a few days the printing shop was raided by the GPU, and its alleged founder, S. Mrachkovsky, a noted partisan leader of the Civil War, was expelled from the Party and arrested.[60] In October the curtain rose on Trotsky's last appearance before an organization of the CPSU, another joint Plenum. This time there was no doubt that Trotsky and Zinoviev would be cast from the Central Committee, and few could doubt that their expulsion from the Party and worse would follow in short order.

Stalin was undergoing yet another transformation. To an outsider, he might seem a passionless intriguer, coolly maneuvering his pieces on the vast chessboard of politics and repression, and so in a way he was. But he was changing, and the period of his life as a happy warrior zestfully enjoying the game of politics was drawing to an end. The persecutor felt persecuted. He was donning the hairshirt of a man of destiny, he was ready to destroy not only the enemy but what remained of the humane and tolerant in his own makeup. Sometime before, he had discussed Trotsky with foreign Communists in the Comintern in a most unusual manner. What, Stalin had asked, does this man want? Why does he persecute me and the Party? Obviously he wants power. But why does power not come to him? Does Trotsky lack ability? No, he is a man of great abilities. As a speaker he stands way above the current leaders of the Party. Why, then, has the Party rejected Trotsky? Because he holds them in contempt, believes them to be sheep blindly following the present leadership.[61]

This was not a pose: Stalin saw himself as a coarse Georgian peasant called upon by history to assume the burden of leadership. History and the Party rejected the Trotskys and Zinovievs, even though they were more brilliant and clever, because they were false. But they did not let

---

[60] The GPU was headed by Vyacheslav Menzhinsky, Dzerzhinsky having died in 1926. The latter remained faithful to Stalin to the very end: he collapsed of a heart attack after finishing a violent attack on Zinoviev and Kamenev before the Central Committee. The death of this fanatical and fearless man facilitated the General Secretary's use of the GPU for intraparty struggles.

[61] Stalin, x, 159. It is revealing that Stalin allowed this passage to remain in the *Collected Works.*

him carry on with his superhuman task, they schemed and intrigued. This made him reveal the full depths of hatred and cruelty which lay in his nature.

At the joint Plenum Stalin reverted to the same perverse and frightening humility that fed his most awesome megalomania. Once more he was taunted with Lenin's *Testament*, which the opposition now screamed at him from the rooftops. So he talked about himself. "But what about Stalin? Stalin is a small man. . . . You have heard how elaborately and forcefully the oppositionists curse Stalin. This, comrades, does not surprise me. This is explained by the fact that Stalin better than most knows all the swindles of the opposition; it is not so easy to fool him."[62] But Stalin, an insignificant man, was comforted by the reflection that Trotsky used to attack and abuse Lenin, a man to whom Trotsky in comparison was just a pygmy. He felt honored that those people hated him. "It would be strange and shameful if the opposition which tries to destroy the Party should praise Stalin, who stands as the defender of Lenin's principles."

The virulence of Stalin's venom makes one recall the observation of a fellow revolutionary of many years before about Koba-Stalin's "viperlike" moods and thrusts. Had the assembled Party notables perceived the full import of the man's words, they would have shivered. This man was going not only to sweep away Trotsky and Zinoviev, but to try to destroy anything and anybody who stood in his way.

But the assembled Party officials enjoyed themselves too much for such ominous reflections. Like schoolboys given license to torment the teacher's erstwhile pets, some of them amused themselves while Trotsky spoke by tossing heavy books and water glasses at him. He had never endured such sadism and indignities before a Tsarist court or in the pre-October soviets dominated by his political enemies. He and Zinoviev were expelled from the Central Committee. We might sympathize with Trotsky more if, in recounting the disgraceful scene, he had regretted that he himself had once consigned the Mensheviks, leaving an assembly to the accompaniment of Bolshevik taunts, to the "rubbish heap of history." He did not.

In their flight to doom the oppositionists took to the streets. On the tenth anniversary of the Revolution, on November 7, 1927, little groups marched in Moscow and Leningrad. They carried banners with inscriptions demanding the publication of Lenin's *Testament*, an end to indulging the kulak and the NEPman, and, rather humorlessly, the restoration of unity in the Party. Zinoviev personally led the desperate and fatuous demonstrations in Leningrad; Trotsky toured Moscow and tried to address the workers. But the demonstrators were set upon by the

[62] *Ibid.*, p. 172.

284

police and by specially instructed gangs, and failed to elicit any response from the masses. It was Stalin's Russia, not Kerensky's.

Repression kept gathering momentum. On November 15 Trotsky and Zinoviev were expelled from the Party. Their last followers on the Central Committee and the Central Control Commission were removed. And in December 1927 the Fifteenth Party Congress met to ratify those and other measures of punishment. ☆☆☆

THE Congress marks the end of the Lenin era of Communism. In approving the directives for the New Economic Plan, the delegates voted, unbeknownst to most of them, for a new Russia, Stalin's, which was ushered in with the great national tragedy of forced collectivization and then became the stage for almost ceaseless purge and terror. The Russian country and people were pushed to the limits of their endurance in building a mighty industrial and military base and background for the despot, whose stature itself grew to superhuman height, dwarfing the modest man who began it all.

It was also at the Congress that what remained of the opposition, many of them members of Lenin's Old Guard, was ground into political nothingness. Who, two or three years before, could have imagined a Party Congress without Trotsky and Zinoviev! Kamenev was allowed to appear, a ghost of the once powerful and popular Party great he had been, to plead for one more chance for himself and his friends. Yet while the assembly was still meeting, he and some previously unpurged oppositionists were expelled. They crawled back again, denouncing their own "un-Leninist views" and begging to be taken back, only to be told contemptuously that they had to wait and that their cases would be considered individually. Trotsky and some of his friends spurned this final act of self-abasement. They would be dealt with by the GPU.

"Only the grave straightens out the hunchback," Zinoviev had said when he was administering and exulting in repression. But now even the grave was incapable of erasing a man's sins, of protecting him from savage attacks and slander. Adolf Yoffe committed suicide shortly before the Congress. The famous Soviet diplomat left a letter to his friend Trotsky, explaining his desperate act. He had been suffering from recurrent nervous crises, he was also ill with consumption. The medical committee of the Central Committee would not authorize his going abroad for a cure. They alleged the need for economy, but Yoffe had been offered twenty thousand dollars by a foreign publisher for his memoirs, which the Central Committee would not allow to be printed.

Now he was refused free medicine from the Kremlin pharmacy. He begged Trotsky to continue his struggle, recalled Lenin's praise for him. One day, if he persevered, Trotsky would again occupy a position worthy of him. Would he then take care of Yoffe's family? He was leaving behind a wife, a small son, and a chronically ill daughter.

This heartrending document was circulated by the opposition as part of its propaganda. However reprehensible this exploitation, it pales in comparison with the indecency of the treatment by Stalin's henchmen. To the applause of the Congress, the unspeakable Yaroslavsky castigated this cry of despair as "a testimony of the worst kind of decadence, moral rottenness . . . Karamazovlike degradation." It was the deed of a drug addict, and its exploitation by the opposition showed its depths of moral degradation, the likes of which one meets in Dostoevsky's most decadent characters. Some worthy shouted from the floor: "Even after death they carry on their factional activity!"[63] In fact it is Yaroslavsky and his listeners who evoke the lurid scenes in *The Possessed*.

It might have been centuries earlier, rather than barely two years, that Stalin had protested that the Party could not afford to "cut off the heads" of the dissident leaders. Now he sounded more like Ivan the Terrible, venting his wrath on treasonous noblemen who abused his trust and fled to his enemies, than a twentieth-century politician celebrating a victory. Kamenev's speech, in which this erstwhile friend and partner offered complete submission and begged that he not be unduly humiliated, was for Stalin "the most lying, pharisaic cheating of all opposition speeches we have heard here." This was not as yet the cold-blooded and contemptuous wrath with which Stalin would in a few years consign his victims to destruction. This was still a man gathering his resources for hatred, paying back the former Party potentates for the humiliations he had suffered at their and Lenin's hands. Did they think that complete recantation, complete self-abasement, was unworthy of a Bolshevik? Then they were not Bolsheviks. They were—and this is the word he actually used—"filth." They should all have been arrested when they took to the streets on November 7, Stalin said. Never, since becoming General Secretary in 1922, had he come so close to losing his self-control.

And so the politician receded into the background. Power brought with it an enhanced sense of insecurity, increased an already considerable vindictiveness. Politically Stalin's victory had been as complete as any reasonable man could have wished. In the elections to the Congress the opposition garnered only one half of one per cent of the votes. No doubt without chicaneries and without the fear in which Party members

[63] *The Fifteenth Congress of the All-Union Communist Party* (b) (1961 edition), I, 395.

286

already lived, the vote for the Trotsky-Zinoviev position would have been considerably larger, but equally certainly Stalin and his group still would have commanded an overwhelming majority. But that very majority portended danger. How many of those who now gloated over their downfall had previously applauded and fawned upon Trotsky and Zinoviev? How many of them would turn against him if he faltered or if he showed a sign of being able to forget and forgive?

In the period now drawing to a close power had not yet crowded everything else from Stalin's life. He was husband of a young wife, father of two small children. And incongruous as it seems to think of him as a family man, this was evidently a time when he relished this role. His daughter's recollections—i.e., what she must have heard from her aunt and nurse, having been at the time too small to remember herself—portray a man still capable of sociability, of having friends. He takes time out for picnics and other amusements with the Voroshilovs and Orjonikidzes, the latter evidently being particularly close to Stalin and his wife. A man of such completely different background and temperament as Bukharin was a welcome visitor to Stalin's *dacha*, and it is no wonder (and not only because of the animals he brought for the children) that he became the family's favorite. Svetlana Alliluyeva dates the abrupt end to this happy period with her mother's death in 1932. But a change must have taken place before. It is unlikely, for instance, that Bukharin could have continued his visits after 1928. And the terrible ordeal of collectivization reverberated in Stalin's household, even if it was not, as was rumored, connected with Nadezhda Alliluyeva's suicide.

Having been born only in 1926, Svetlana's account of her father's married life is also second-hand.[64] But it is clear and not surprising that the terrible tensions and passions of his political life also invaded his household. His wife was sensitive, refined, at least in contrast to him, and twenty-two years younger than he. On at least one occasion Nadezhda Alliluyeva tried to leave her husband. Having been brought up in an old revolutionary's family and a Party member from her adolescence, she had an independent outlook on politics, which came out in such gestures as her attendance at Yoffe's funeral. Yet given the personality of the man, the period of the middle 1920s was for the Stalins, as it was in a way for Russia, one of calm before a terrible storm.

To us, it must appear paradoxical if not perverse that those closest to the dictator—the long-neglected son of his first marriage, his young wife—could retain a measure of devotion for him. Both were to become

---

[64] And because of the passage of time, hazy. It is unlikely that Anna Alliluyeva or anyone else dared to discuss it at any length in Stalin's lifetime.

victims of his terrible temper, but both were to seek release in suicide (unsuccessful in his son's case) rather than in rebellion and flight. But to them, his personal tragedy—which to us appears utterly insignificant compared with the sufferings he imposed upon his people—took on a different dimension. Unlike his other victims, they could see the evolution of a bad-tempered and suspicious man into a tyrannical and obsessed one; could appreciate how the more power he achieved, the more he destroyed—including, eventually, his own family.

That evolution was caused, as we have seen, not only by his inner development, but also by the system in which he lived and strove for power. As for an underground revolutionary, so for a successful Soviet politician suspiciousness and ruthlessness were necessary means of self-preservation. They became implanted in the character of most active Communists.

There was another Stalin, the one who once wrote that there could be no Party life without differences of opinion within it. This Stalin appeared, perhaps for the last time, in a speech delivered in the city where he began his fabulous political career. On June 8, 1926, he talked in Tiflis to the workers in the local railroad shops. Their representatives had previously eulogized him, and Stalin, currently vacationing nearby between two acts of the intraparty struggle, was at some pains to appear modest and unassuming. "In all honesty I should tell you, comrades, that I do not deserve as much as half of those praises which here have been bestowed upon me. It would appear that I was *the* hero of October, *the* leader of the Communist Party and Comintern, a veritable miraclemaker. All that is fantasy, comrades, a completely needless exaggeration. One talks in such terms over the grave of a revolutionary. . . . But I am not ready for the grave."[65]

A pose? Perhaps—but even if it were, it is nonetheless significant that Stalin was capable of striking it. This was still Soso Djugashvili, recalling his fantastic rise from obscure agitator to master of one-sixth of the earth's surface, allowing himself that most pleasant prerogative of success and vanity: a disavowal of flattery. It would have been fortunate for him and his country had he remained capable of such very human enjoyment of power, of such very human vanity. But now he became Stalin the agent and maker of history, who would demand and need not flattery, but worship.

[65] Stalin, VIII, 173.

THE
WAR AGAINST
THE
NATION

It has been called the great leap forward. At tremendous human cost Soviet society was propelled within a few years, 1928–34, into the industrial age. To some, this is the greatest crime of modern history. To others it is a grandiose feat of social engineering, ruthless in conception, cruel in its effect on millions of human beings; but still it laid the foundations of a richer and more rational economy, enabled Russia to withstand a foreign invasion and become a superpower. But in trying to describe it, one runs out of metaphors and superlatives. Was it a new and particularly fearsome type of civil war? One gropes in vain for historical analogies. The main architect of the transformation has been compared by his detractors to Genghis Khan or Tamerlane. And yet even this comparison is imprecise. When the Mongols conquered Russia in the thirteenth century, they slaughtered those who resisted them, laid waste the great cities of the land. But from those who submitted they exacted a tribute and allowed them to live their own way, left them their own institutions and their faith. In the twentieth century the conquered were most of the nation, the bulk of its peasantry. Within a few years they were forced to change their entire manner of life, forsake their immemorial customs and rights. It was not a civil war. It was, as a Soviet poet justly called it, a war against the nation waged by Stalin at the head of the Communist Party of the U.S.S.R., and from this war he emerged victorious.

It would be untruthful to deny this victory or to qualify it with some hollow moralism. The dimension of the holocaust which accompanied the forcible collectivization awed even its maker. In a conversation during World War II with Churchill, Stalin acknowledged that the ordeal surpassed in its severity even those disaster-filled first years of the Nazi invasion. It was a demonstration, unique in recent history, of how much can be accomplished by force and violence. And this violence was not exerted against a foreign nation, an isolated class, a racial minority; it was directed against one's own people, with victims' sons and brothers serving as the instrument of their kin's oppression.

What made Stalin and the Party enter upon this path of open warfare against the Russian people? At its beginning it may have been seen as suicidal, this attempt to force millions of Russians to enter the collective farms. Like everything else about Stalin, the drive to collectivize through compulsion has been explained by inordinate lust for power. But no one who thirsted *only* for power would have pursued this policy, which every cold calculation warned was bound to end in a catastrophe—for himself, for the Communist regime he headed, for the country he increasingly thought of as his own. Was it, then, ideology, the faith of Marxism-Leninism which urged it? No: properly understood, Marxism would have required a safer, more reasonable method of transforming Russia into a modern industrial society.

Like all manmade disasters, the war against the nation was a product of ignorance and obsession. These were not uniquely Stalin's. To a greater or lesser extent they were shared by other Communists, his enemies in the Party and the enemies of collectivization included. What was uniquely his was the indomitable resolve to carry the campaign through to the victorious end, no matter what the cost. He did not falter when the peasantry appeared to rise as a body against it, nor when millions of starving human beings were strewn along the road toward his goal. And so this experiment in inhumanity succeeded, from his point of view anyway, and probably even beyond his expectations. The victory was secured not only over those who starved or were exiled or jailed, but also over the minds of the majority who were forced to submit to the collective farm. They accepted their new status as their ancestors had been forced to acquiesce in their serfdom, and met the cataclysmic change in their lives in the manner the Russian peasant has always met the plague or a crop failure. And their sons and grandsons would go into battle against an invader "for the country, for Stalin." A recent Soviet dissenter entitled his indictment of Stalin *Let History Judge*, but history does not judge; it records facts.

What enabled one man to "get away with" this? What enabled him to find a multitude of enthusiastic accomplices? Faith, and the most pernicious faith is the one which justifies inflicting suffering on human beings in the name of benefits to future generations.

Faith alone would not have wrought such havoc. The Marxist goal for Russia was eminently sensible and practical. A modern industrialized economy presupposed a drastic transformation of Russia's agriculture. It was primitive, inefficient, and wasteful. There was no hope of applying more rational, mechanized methods so long as the cultivation of land was spread among 25 million individual peasant households. There was no way of gauging and controlling the grain supply for the cities and for export under such a fantastically diffuse and primitive system of production. There would be no labor force for the industrial enterprises of the future until the villages, with production organized more rationally in a more concentrated way, could release their millions of superfluous farmhands to become workers in the cities.

Where was the solution? Stalin paraphrased what had been the Communists' bible on the subject when he said at the Fifteenth Party Congress: "The solution lies in the transformation of small and scattered peasants' plots into large consolidated farms based on the joint cultivation of land using new superior techniques."[1]

How was this transition to be accomplished? Here again Stalin followed Lenin's wise dictum: it must be done through persuasion and education, by demonstrating to the peasant the incontrovertible benefits of the new ways. "The small and tiny plots must be consolidated gradually but steadily, *eschewing forcible methods*, but through demonstration and persuasion. . . . [One could then use] agricultural machinery and tractors and apply scientific measures for increasing agricultural production."[2]

Had Stalin adhered to this formula, his role as the benefactor of the Russian peasant would remain undisputed rather than being, in view of what was to transpire within the next few years, a cruel mockery. But, of course, Stalin's formulation of the problem (like Lenin's before him) begged the crucial question. The peasant was going to be won over to collectivization through its obvious material benefits. He would *see* how much more convenient and rewarding was the use of machinery in lieu of draft animals and primitive plows (in places, peasants used wooden plows identical to those used by their ancestors a thousand years before). His reluctance to give up his own plot would be dissipated by a higher standard of life; he would be able to procure a variety of goods, rather than being barely able to afford such necessities as kerosene, matches, cloth. But here was the catch: where was that machinery, where were those goods? Russia did not have the industry to provide

[1] Stalin, *Collected Works* (Moscow, 1946–52), x, 305.
[2] *Ibid*. My italics.

them. And so this seemed a vicious circle: the country did not have a well-developed industry because of a deficient agricultural base; agriculture remained backward because of the absence of a strong industry.

There were two ways of breaking this vicious circle: one was through foreign credits and investments, the other through internal saving. The first possibility was by the mid-1920s exposed as a mirage: foreign capitalists were not going to lend money to the country which had expropriated foreign investments. There remained the more painful and seemingly slower way for Russia to lift herself by her own bootstraps: exacting forced savings from the population (the majority of whom lived not much above the subsistence level), and turning them into the seed stock of industrial development. This was what was happening under the NEP: both in agriculture and in industry the country was recovering from the losses incurred through the terrible ordeals of the 1914–21 period. By 1927 Russia made good those losses and by and large reached the prewar level of economy. But it was slow. What was the point of the October Revolution, of the prodigious human sacrifices, if after ten years of Soviet power the country had barely climbed back to the level of the poor backward Russia of 1913? How much longer would it take for this potentially fabulously rich land to reach the level of economic development of even the more backward capitalist countries (not to mention the United States and Germany)?

We have seen how the opposition upbraided the Stalin regime for "selling out" socialism, purchasing power and tranquillity in the countryside at the price of postponing industrialization indefinitely. Both Trotsky's and Zinoviev's partisans had an essentially simple recipe for a faster pace of industrialization: *more* should be extracted from the countryside. A variety of fiscal and economic measures could exact more, especially from the kulak.[3] And we have seen what Stalin and Bukharin kept retorting to those taunts: Trotsky and Zinoviev wanted the Party to treat the peasants the way the capitalists exploited their colonies, to exact tribute from them, to incur the terrible risk of a civil war to have the countryside rise up against Soviet power. There is no reason to

[3] Trotsky and his followers (and after them some Western economic commentators) were subsequently to claim that (1) Stalin's economic policies in 1928–34 represented a steal of Trotsky's program of the years before; (2) *their* policies would have avoided the terrible losses and sufferings of those years since they would have been more carefully and humanely put into effect. As to (1), it was axiomatic for Stalin as for every other Communist that *sometime* the NEP would have to be abandoned and a drastic advance attempted in industry and agriculture. It might be argued that had such an advance been attempted before Soviet industry and agriculture recovered to the almost prewar level, the attempt would have resulted in even greater disaster. As to (2), Stalin's capacity for ruthlessness undoubtedly surpassed that of Zinoviev and Trotsky. But how could any policy premised upon the oppression of a whole class fail to bear fearful fruit?

believe that Stalin, any more than Bukharin, was dishonest in these protestations, that he was (as was subsequently alleged) waiting to get rid of his political opponents in order to put their policy of squeezing the peasant into effect and much more brutally than they had ever intended.

The Fifteenth Party Congress charged the government with working out a Five-Year Plan for the development of the country's economy. Thus began the series of comprehensive plans which to this very day regulate the economic life of every Soviet citizen. Every Soviet producer, whether in agriculture or industry, would become a soldier in the war to attain the goals prescribed from above. Fulfillment or nonfulfillment of quotas would become equivalent to soldierly behavior and desertion under fire. Stalinism came to mean many things, but chief among them was this relentless struggle to produce, to sacrifice everything but the dictator's personal power at the altar of industrialization. Totalitarian government took on a new and awesome dimension: its subjects were judged not only according to their degree of submission, but also according to their ability to produce what and as much as the despot commanded. One's daily work would become a test of one's loyalty. Karl Marx described the process of alienation under early capitalism as consisting in the capitalist's power to transform the worker into an adjunct of the machine. In the heyday of Stalinism this phenomenon became much more intense and widespread; the peasant would be tied down to his collective farm, the worker to his workbench, not only through the operation of economic forces, but through the sanctions of the omnipotent state. The margin allowed for error, accident, nonfulfillment of unrealistic targets would almost disappear, for the state seldom recognized error or human frailty in such cases but called it treason and sabotage. There would be stupendous achievements under this tyranny but also stupendous failures, both compounded in a fantastic system of deception and self-deception practiced by the entire regime from Stalin down to the lowest bureaucrat. And so Stalinism strained the human capacity to suffer and also to believe.

To be sure, no such perspectives could have been anticipated from the economic program of the Fifteenth Congress. It was, on the surface, a reasonable call for a mobilization of economic resources in the struggle for industrialization. On the agricultural side the directives for the Plan foresaw a considerable increase in collectivization, yet it was assured and believed by everybody, and stated by Stalin himself, that the end of the plan would see individual household farming as the prevailing form of production in the countryside.

What, then, conspired to make the First Five-Year Plan a chart of unparalleled human suffering, the end of individual peasant holdings, the death sentence for millions of peasants? Partly an accident, but mostly, again, ignorance and obsession.

Like a devout Christian who seeks in the Bible an answer to all problems of man and society, so have the Russian Communists sought an answer to the question of how to industrialize their country in the writings of Marx and Lenin. But no precise answer can be forthcoming from these scriptures. Marx wrote about the economy of Western capitalism during the first sixty years of the nineteenth century, and there is not a line in his economic writings suggesting how to transform an agrarian society like the Russia of 1927 into an industrialized one. Lenin, as we have seen, admitted that the *logic* of Marxian economics would require postponing the socialist revolution until such a time as individual peasant lots had given way to a relatively few scientifically run farms. But beyond emphasizing that this sin against the Marxian gods of history could be atoned for by voluntary growth of cooperation in the countryside, he left no economic guidance to his successors. In trying to find an answer to Russia's economic problems in Marx and Lenin, the Communists, and this was as true of Bukharin and Trotsky as of Stalin, were engaged in a hopeless pursuit. One cannot find out from Marx how to build socialism in a prevailingly agrarian society any more than one can learn how to build a nuclear reactor by reading the works of Newton.

But if not in Marx, one could find a partial answer in common sense: one tolerates *some* capitalist development in the countryside, as well as gradually introducing socialism there. The kulak and the more efficient peasant might well squeeze out less efficient cultivators, who join the cooperative farm or go to the city and become industrial workers. Agricultural production thus becomes more consolidated and efficient. With the state controlling trade and enjoying the monopoly of foreign trade, such a *temporary* growth of capitalism in the countryside could not be considered dangerous to Soviet power. Once the kulak had grown into a reasonable facsimile of a Western farmer, then legal measures could be taken to limit or eliminate the private-property element in the countryside. These were the premises which seemed to underly the NEP policy toward the peasant. And under the NEP Russian agriculture made a spectacular recovery from the days of War Communism, when violent measures, euphemistically dubbed class policy in the countryside, had helped to produce the famine of 1921–22.

But the continuation of these sensible policies ran into terrible obsessions of the Russian Communists, obsessions which again were shared by all of them, and not just Stalin and his group. Even the father of the NEP wrote hysterically about where toleration of the "private principle" in the countryside would lead: "Petty production gives birth to capitalism and the bourgeoisie—continuously, every day, every hour, spontaneously, and on a mass scale."[4] The Communists were frantically impatient. How long would it take for agriculture to become ripe for socialization, through the kulak's growing into a farmer and a simultaneous *voluntary* growth of rural cooperation? Decades? Would they have in the meantime to endure a slow growth of industry, delay their dream? Would they allow the peasant to be the arbiter of the tempo industrialization would take by paying him high prices and thus having less capital for industrial investment?

In addition to this impatience, there was yet another, verging on irrationality. The kulak was not only a stratum of the rural population, he was *the class enemy*. He was the personification of evil on the social scene. Other class enemies such as the NEP private trader or small industrialists were few in number, and once the regime decided to wind up the NEP they could be liquidated overnight (as they were in 1928–29) without too much fuss and danger. But the kulaks ran into millions.[5] Moreover if left undisturbed, allowed to grow richer and more insolent, they would demand political power: they would want their own party or even would rise in open warfare against Communism. They were assumed to be mortal enemies of Soviet power.

And so statistical and economic data cannot by themselves explain the tragedy of collectivization. One must take into account this superstitious and deep-seated fear of the peasantry as a whole, this feeling on the part of the Communists that a vast, inert, and yet somehow threatening mass of people barred Russia's path to industrialism, modernity, socialism; that a kingdom of darkness must be conquered before the Soviet Union could become the promised land.

Ignorance of the economic facts of life together with obsessions about the kulak led the masters of the Soviet Union to launch in 1926–27 a complex of social and economic policies which were bound to bring on disaster. The only question could be whether this economic disaster would lead to a political one, a collapse of the regime, or whether the government, by an unprecedented display of resolution and force, could confine it *just* to the people of Russia and save itself. The latter was to be the case, and the credit for this feat of resolution and inhumanity belongs to Stalin.

Even before the Fifteenth Party Congress, in 1926 the regime had embarked on the policy of squeezing the kulak. (This policy was subsequently alleged to have been designed by Stalin, to blunt the accusation by oppositionists that the regime was selling out to the kulak. This may

[4] Lenin, *Collected Works* (4th ed., Moscow, 1970), xxxi, 8.
[5] There was, of course, no agreement upon the actual number of kulak households, just as there could be no precise definition of who qualified as a kulak. Those who tried estimated the number of "rich peasants' households" on the eve of collectivization at 3 to 5 per cent of the total. Let us repeat that most kulaks were—by, say, a German farmer's standard—quite poor.

have been a partial reason, though it is pertinent to observe that (1) *every* opposition within the Party ever since 1920 claimed that whoever was in power was "soft on kulaks," and (2) by 1926–27 the Trotsky-Zinoviev forces were already effectively beaten, and there was no need for Stalin to try to steal their thunder.) There were new legal chicaneries against the more prosperous peasants, who were now banned from voting in the elections for the Soviet legislative bodies. More important (since the legislatures by now were purely decorative), the kulak was kept out of his village assembly, which still retained some important functions in peasant life. Most important of all, the Party developed a policy of economic pressure: the better-off peasant was to be heavily taxed. In addition the peasantry as a whole was affected by the government's decision to cut the prices for grain by as much as 20 per cent, a simple administrative fiat completely unrelated to the existing state of supply and demand. Increased pressure and growing persecution of the most efficient producers, lowering incentives to the peasantry as a whole to produce and sell grain—had the government planned to cause food shortages it could not have devised a more effective way! Why should the middle peasant strive to produce more and improve his economic status if by doing so he might pass into the kulak category, which, as the Fifteenth Party Congress announced, was scheduled for liquidation? Why should any peasant, including that alleged ally of the industrial proletariat the *poor* peasant, sell his surplus grain if by withholding it he could hope to persuade the government to raise prices to a more reasonable level?

By January 1928 the regime had reaped the fruit of its policies: government purchases of grain stood at 300 million poods as against 428 million for the corresponding period the year before.[6] There was no grain for export, thus no foreign-currency earnings for the purchase of machinery, etc. Much worse, Russian cities faced the prospect of famine.

A schoolboy would have known the remedy: let the government raise the price for grain it was buying, and the peasants would then empty out their barns. But to Stalin this meant a personal as well as a political humiliation. Did the peasants think they could bargain with Soviet power? Could Stalin be defied by the peasant, just as he had been defied by Trotsky and Zinoviev? He would never forgive the peasant, just as he never forgave his political enemies.

In January 1928 Trotsky and the hard core of his followers were deported from Moscow to various distant locations. Trotsky himself was sent to Alma-Ata in Turkestan. He spent one year in Central Asia

---

[6] Alec Nove, *An Economic History of the U.S.S.R.* (New York, 1969), p. 150. One pood equals thirty-six pounds.

before beginning that life of a wanderer through foreign lands which ended in Mexico with a blow from a pickaxe by an agent of the GPU. . . . At about the same time, Stalin set out from Moscow to confront and chastise the fresh enemy: the Russian peasant. ☆☆☆

"I HAVE been commandeered here to Siberia for a short time. I have been charged to help you to fulfill the quota of grain procurements." We have seen how a self-deprecatory tone was often with Stalin a prelude to wrathful outbursts. He had ordered his most trusted lieutenants to visit the areas which were lagging in grain procurement, to whip up Party and state officials in a campaign to extract more grain. And to show how this was done, Stalin himself was making a lightning trip of inspection through west Siberia. At every stop the assembled officials were treated to the same speech.[7] Didn't they know that there was a deficit of some 100 million poods in grain deliveries? Didn't they realize what it meant? Hunger, widespread starvation threatened cities, industrial centers, the Red Army! "You say the plan for procurements is too ambitious, that it cannot be fulfilled." Nonsense, there is plenty of grain. The kulaks' barns and sheds are overflowing. *Every* kulak's household has 50,000 or 60,000 poods he has not surrendered to the state. The kulaks want the state to double or triple prices before they condescend to sell the stuff of life. There is a law to deal with those gentlemen, Article 107 of the Penal Code.[8]

The frightened local officials could only stand openmouthed at these outbursts from the ruler suddenly materialized in their midst. Braver ones feebly objected that the use of Article 107 was an "extraordinary measure" which the courts had not dreamed of applying against the peasant who was doing merely what the law allowed him to, holding on to his *own* grain until he decided to sell it. This brought another outburst: obviously the judges and prosecutors were tools of the kulaks. Throw *them* out! The kulaks' grain was to be confiscated, they were to

---

[7] Stalin, xi, 1.

[8] This statute, put on the books in 1926, provided for up to three years' imprisonment and confiscation of the property for "speculation," defined as buying and hoarding in order to cause an increase in prices. No one until now had thought of invoking this law, since obviously under it every commercial transaction by a private person could be considered a crime, and the NEP had authorized private trading. But what had been assumed until now to be the product of careless drafting turned out now to be one of those helpfully elastic laws which allowed the regime to declare any activity hitherto widespread and officially encouraged to be criminal.

be tried and sentenced by new judges and prosecutors free from the influence of the class enemy.

And so there returned to many regions of Russia the days of violent requisition and confiscation of grain, days that Lenin had pledged were gone forever when in 1921 he announced the NEP, which was designed to secure the peasants' trust and cooperation. It is almost superfluous to add that violence was used against not only the kulaks but the mass of the rural population. Stalin had a recipe for securing the cooperation of the lowest group of peasants (i.e., for inducing them to denounce their richer neighbors): in each village 25 per cent of the confiscated grain was to be distributed among the poor. But the local authorities were unlikely to stick to this once the visiting divinity from Moscow was gone. Nor were they likely to deliberate for long on how much grain each peasant needed for his family's consumption or for sowing.

Stalin's speeches were not reported in the press.[9] Undoubtedly he knew that the tenor of his Siberian speeches would shock some of his staunchest supporters. But he had also said many things he had not meant to say—not yet, anyway. Whatever happens, he had clearly implied, the Red Army and the cities must be fed. Here was his sense of history: the Russian Revolution was set in motion because of *food riots* in Petrograd, because of the mutiny of the capital's garrison. In contrast, half of *rural* Russia might have been in upheaval and yet the Empire would not have been overthrown. And so there was not only Communist hatred of the peasant emanating from his speeches, but also an incongruous contempt. It was as if he were thinking, you can push those people around all you want, they are used to it. They are a danger to the regime only if you betray softness in dealing with them. However, a demonstration by a few thousand workers in Moscow or an uprising by an army unit, and the whole Soviet regime, not to say his own power, would be in mortal danger.

The same impulsiveness led him to say, "There will be sabotage of bread procurements as long as the kulak exists."[10] The government had just announced that liquidation of the kulak was a matter for the fairly distant future. Yet here on his own Stalin was proclaiming a drastic change in policy, and in the context of what he was saying it was clear that he meant not a long-drawn-out process of social change through education, taxation policy, etc., but something much more direct and ominous. No, the Soviet government was not going to regulate the tempo of industrialization according to the whim of "these kulak gentlemen." No, Russia needed collective and state farms in a hurry. Here again he was way ahead of what the Central Committee and the

[9] They were not printed until twenty-five years later, and then in condensed form (omitting, one assumes, his more violent threats and gross expressions).
[10] Stalin, XI, 5.

recent Party Congress had been saying on the subject of collectivization.

Stalin returned from Siberia on February 6, his long trip (mainly by rail) having taken but three weeks—an indication in itself of how sketchily he must have investigated the local conditions and learned that "every" kulak had "vast" hoards of grain. Then the General Secretary held conferences with his henchmen sent on similar missions into other regions. He had confirmed what he had expected: violence and coercion worked. As a Soviet author of the Khrushchev era puts it unblushingly, "These energetic measures brought their results. Already in January a breakthrough took place in many areas. Deliveries of grain by the middle peasant increased everywhere. Squeezed from every side, even the kulak had to deliver grain."[11] By April the deficit in grain procurements was *almost* made up. This was a pleasing proof of how, if one destroyed sabotage and knew how to deal with the peasants, one was bound to succeed. Those alleged economic laws existed only in the imagination of the doddering fools on the Planning Commission. Or *were* they only fools? Perhaps something much worse? It would be strange if widespread sabotage existed only in agriculture.

The great procurements victory threw Stalin's more reasonable supporters into despair. Rykov, Bukharin, and Tomsky now realized that this man was not only a shrewd and realistic politician who had kept the Party out of the hands of Trotsky and Zinoviev, and saved the country from their madcap schemes, but was on occasion a maniac. In a few weeks' time he had destroyed the policy that had enabled the country to get on its feet after the catastrophes of foreign and civil wars; he had undermined the whole basis for a gradual and prudent advance toward industrialization and socialism. And now what? One could use force to extract the existing stock of grain from the peasant, but how could one force him to produce above his own needs when he had seen what happened to the fruit of his labor?

Stalin was to stamp such doubters as "right-wing deviationists." Such is the hypnotic power of Communist name-calling that this term has stuck, and Western as well as Soviet sources often refer to Bukharin, Rykov, et al. as right-wingers. But it is obvious that they were nothing of the kind and deserve neither blame nor credit for opposing Stalin's policies. They objected to his methods, not out of any humanitarian scruples but on the ground that they were bound to bring disaster to the regime. In that they were mistaken: they were to bring about a national catastrophe, not a political one.

But their objections for the moment brought out the other Stalin: the realist and the wary politician. Within a week of his return from the

[11] Y. Moshkov, *The Grain Problem in the Years of Mass Collectivization of the Rural Economy of the U.S.S.R., 1929–1932* (Moscow, 1960), p. 32.

Siberian tour he addressed a circular to all Party organizations. The raving tyrant of a few days before became again a practical and understanding administrator.

How regrettable, he wrote, that "they" had to threaten the Party officials in such peremptory tones. He of course realized that those conscientious men worked for the good of the Revolution and not for any career reasons! But it was a most unusual situation, and it would not recur. "The countryside is growing stronger and becoming richer[!]."[12] To be sure, there were still problems, like the kulak. But one should not believe the rumors about the regime's plans to destroy them, restore forcible requisitions of grain, abolish the NEP; all that was "counterrevolutionary rumormongering which must be resolutely combated."[13] True, "the local authorities," in coping with the emergency, committed some excesses such as "illegal confiscation of grain," the use of police to bar peasants from selling their products to private traders, etc. And perhaps the Central Committee was not entirely blameless in such abuses, Stalin allowed generously. But that was all in the past! What were the practical lessons? One must, "whatever happens, strengthen the procurement campaign, fulfill the annual quota of grain delivery . . . strengthen the struggle against any direct or indirect attempts to raise the price of grain." The regime must continue the pressure on the kulak while "observing strictly the principle of Soviet legality." Only the "evil-intentioned" among the kulaks were to be dealt with under Article 107. Please, avoid the recent abuses. —One can well imagine the sentiments of a local Party official upon reading this circular.

Stalin displayed the same ability to talk out of both sides of his mouth at the April meeting of the Central Committee. "Only enemies of the Soviet power can talk about the NEP having been discarded," but, he warned, "if unusual circumstances return and the capitalist elements attack . . . Article 107 will reappear on the scene."[14]

Was this, as is universally considered, another example of his famous hypocrisy? No, hypocrisy is a product of cynicism, and Stalin was seldom cynical. Usually he was worse than that: he was sincere and obsessed. The source of his obsession and the reason so many intelligent and humane people nevertheless followed and obeyed him is well illustrated by a phrase he used in his speech to the Central Committee. He said, "Our policy is a class policy. He who thinks that one can conduct in the countryside a policy that will please everybody, the rich as well as the poor, is not a Marxist but an idiot, because, comrades, such a policy does not exist in the nature of things."[15] The Central Committee members,

12 Ibid., p. 12.
13 Ibid., p. 15.
14 Stalin, XI, 46.
15 Ibid., p. 48.

most of whom sat through the speech in gloom and apprehension about where this man was taking them, broke into applause and approving laughter at these words.

Here, then, was the clue. Russia is a fabulously rich land, Stalin was arguing. Those who rule her are guided by the true science of society—Marxism-Leninism. So why do things not go better than they do? Why is the economy wretchedly poor? The answer is clear: it has to be the work of the class enemy. Now that Russia is to embark on a grandiose task of socialist construction, the enemy who hitherto lay concealed and but intermittently indulged in sabotage and terror would embark on offensives of his own. He would obviously change and adjust his methods to the new type of war; he would exchange—already had exchanged—the gun and bomb for wholesale economic sabotage. His agents in the planning and economic agencies would claim that the production targets set by the Party were unrealistically high and would try to slow the march toward socialism. Bourgeois engineers and special-ists would cause "accidents" in the plants and mines, would produce defective machinery and inferior products so that the Soviet worker-consumer would become disgruntled. And need one say anything about agriculture?

Years have passed since then. Part of the truth about Stalin and the hallucinatory madness that seized Russian society under him has been told by Khrushchev and others. But in 1960 a Soviet author could still write, "In the course of 1928–31, wrecking organizations were uncovered in the following industries: coal mining, defense, textiles, machine, chemical, rubber, oil, in transport, retail trade. Wreckers penetrated into the most important key institutions of the national economy. They infiltrated the leading bodies of the whole economy: the Supreme Eco-nomic Council and the Planning Commission."[16] No. Stalin was not a hypocrite.

He was, however, the man for whom the expression "there is method in this madness" might well have been coined. For most people who believe in it, the notion of demons and witches being on the loose in the world is depressing and frightening. But Stalin greeted every fresh manifestation of the class enemy with the élan and zest of an early Christian saint whom the Evil One has incautiously challenged to a new test of strength. Treason, wrecking, sabotage were soon seen everywhere. And "the honest Soviet people," with the help of the GPU, would invariably (though often regrettably late) unmask those enemies and deal them "decisive blows." As Stalin saw it, every Soviet toiler would work harder, produce more, stand ever more firmly behind the Party as

---

[16] I. Trifonov, *The Outlines of the History of the Class War in the U.S.S.R.* (Moscow, 1960), p. 153.

STALIN / THE MAN AND HIS ERA

his answer to these plots and activities; thus wrecking had its positive side: it enhanced people's vigilance and mobilized the masses behind the Party in the struggle for socialism.

Early in 1928 production difficulties affected the coal mines in the Shakhti region of the Donets Basin. These were industrial accidents such as flooding of pits, difficulties due to shortage in trained personnel, red tape, etc. In addition, the unfortunate managers ordered coal-cutting machinery from abroad only to discover—and how often was this tale repeated in the history of Soviet industrialization?—that improper use increased the wear and tear on the machinery and no spare parts were to be had in the U.S.S.R. It was a typical case of mismanagement. A few years earlier, the culpable "specialists" would have been dismissed, perhaps a few punished by administrative jail sentences or exile. Now, in view of what might be called the growing need for hysteria, such quiet disposal of the case was not enough. "The organs of the GPU," it was announced, "with the collaboration of rank-and-file workers, have discovered a major wrecking organization . . . having as its aims the disorganization and destruction of the coal industry. . . . Twenty per cent of engineers and technicians are engaged in diversionary activities."[17] A public trial of fifty-three "wreckers" on the charge of "economic counterrevolution" was scheduled for May 1928.

Speaking at the April Plenum, Stalin had shown remarkable fore-knowledge of what the trial would establish: "Facts show that the Shakhti affair is an economic counterrevolution, plotted by a number of bourgeois specialists . . . who received money for wrecking from the former [mine] owners, currently abroad, and from counterrevolutionary capitalists in the West."[18] To be sure the trial did establish precisely that. The first of many such spectacles with which Soviet citizens were to be regaled in the years to come, it was presided over by Andrei Vishinsky, whom Stalin had known as a Menshevik in the old Baku days; he was beginning a career as judge and prosecutor which, it is fair to say, has no parallel in the annals of the law.[19]

Now an interesting thing about the Shakhti affair is that Stalin could not have initiated the enterprise, and indeed the whole affair could not have been staged, without the approval of Rykov, still Prime Minister and in overall control of Soviet industry. (Of course, the General Secretary must have sanctioned the gruesome business.) Was Stalin con-

---

[17] *Ibid.*, p. 161.
[18] Stalin, xi, 58.
[19] By later standards the trial was not a complete success. Some of the accused refused to confess. Three of them were German engineers who could not be unduly "investigated" or sentenced in view of the premium the regime put on good relations with Germany. A few Russians were also acquitted. Of those convicted, eleven were sentenced to death, and only five were actually executed. One should perhaps add that the charges were fraudulent.

vinced of the men's guilt? From the class point of view—and never mind some unimportant details—he undoubtedly was.

The beauty of "the class point of view" was that it bridged the gap between the actual and the potential, between fact and theory, and accounted for otherwise inexplicable failures of Soviet industry and agriculture. *All* bourgeois specialists and kulaks were potential enemies of the Soviet power; any breakdown of grain deliveries, every flooded mine *must* be the work of the wrecker, the class enemy, Q.E.D.

This demonology—the class point of view—made it extremely difficult to oppose the General Secretary's policies on the agricultural front effectively. The most reasonable and enlightened Communist still had to admit that every kulak was a potential enemy. Could a medieval Christian have openly avowed disbelief in the existence of witchcraft? That would have made him a candidate for the stake. The Russian regime could and did claim that the very failures of its policies testified to their correctness: if the offensive on the agrarian front were *not* inspired by true Marxism and did *not* promise to bring about socialism, would the kulaks sabotage it so viciously? What was left to the Bukharins and Rykovs was a rearguard action: they could only argue that many of those accused of and being dealt with as witches (kulaks) were in fact innocent (middle peasants). The regime (though Rykov was still Prime Minister and Bukharin head of the Comintern, they were no longer real rulers by the middle of 1928) would thereupon acknowledge some excesses and beat a temporary retreat. But then the "kulak danger" would become "acute" again. The analogy with witchcraft may seem far-fetched, and so it is: the most extensive medieval witch hunt was a puny affair in comparison with what was soon to take place in the Soviet Union. ☆☆☆

I N trying to fight Stalin, whom they saw clearly as leading the country to unimaginable catastrophe, Rykov, Bukharin, and Tomsky thus labored under two grave handicaps. First, they were fighting the man who was a master politician and manipulator. That need not have been fatal, for they were themselves people of wide popularity and influence in the Party. But they could not counter his obsessions with common sense, because—and this was the second handicap—to a very considerable degree they were victims of the same obsessions.

No sooner had Stalin finished congratulating himself on the famous procurement victory of the first three months of 1928 than the situation again took a desperate turn. As he said later in the summer, while 300 million poods were collected from January through March, the April deliveries fell to 100 million. And so the extraordinary measures banished "forever" in April returned in May: "administrative exactions, breaches of revolutionary legality, search of the peasants' quarters, illegal seizures."[20] This imperiled the alliance of peasants and workers on which, as is well known, Soviet power rested. Fortunately, good prospects for the harvest brought an alleviation of the crisis and the "extraordinary measures" could be *partly* discontinued.

This remarkable admission was contained in a speech to the Central Committee in July. Some time earlier, in June, a secondary Party figure named Michael Frumkin, Assistant Commissar of Finance, tried to suggest that unless reversed, the current policies would lead to disaster. In a letter to the Politburo, Frumkin sounded the alarm: growing economic chaos and consequent political troubles might lead to a capitalist offensive against the U.S.S.R., and the regime ought to stop pressing the kulak: "because the kulak has been declared outside the law, lawlessness has become the rule in regard to all the peasantry." It was imperative, Frumkin said, to raise grain prices. Stalin exploded. Of course the capitalists had become more hostile, but that was because the U.S.S.R. was growing stronger and its economy was more flourishing. It was a lie to say that the kulak had been put outside the law. He had merely been deprived of his civil rights! Did Frumkin propose to restore them to him, to stop the offensive against the kulak ordered by resolution of the Fifteenth Party Congress? Was Frumkin wiser than the Politburo and the Central Committee?

This intimidation accomplished its purpose. The July Plenum of the Central Committee,[21] theoretically the highest organ of the Party (it could, even more theoretically, dismiss Stalin), eschewed any discussion of the bases of agricultural policies. Those who felt along with Bukharin and Rykov that they were leading to disaster pleaded simply for the elimination of excesses—which could hardly be very effective, since the very author of those excesses also condemned them.

Still, the picture was dismal, and it is fair to say that except for the factors already mentioned, no dictator would have survived the revelation of the terrible plight into which he had plunged the country and the very idea of Communism. Bukharin's speech painted a picture of how the policy was bearing fruit. Last year they had exported 277 million poods of grain and had still had enough bread to feed everybody. Now, even without any exports, they faced the prospect of famine. They had destroyed the peasant's incentive to produce. In one of the richest areas of the nation, the north Caucasus, the average yield from one

[20] Stalin, XI, 206.
[21] Held, as has been the custom, jointly with the Central Control Commission.

desyatina[22] in 1925–26 was seventy poods; this year it would be fewer than thirty. In conjunction with the lowered prices for grain, this meant that in 1925–26 the peasant earned seventy-two rubles from the unit's crop, this year only twenty-four. Where were the "extraordinary measures" decreed by the government taking them? Already more than a hundred fifty major peasant demonstrations and riots had broken out against requisitions.

There was a commotion in the room as these grim figures delineated the march of the Soviet regime toward the fate which had overcome the Romanovs!

But Bukharin revealed the fatal weakness of those who opposed the ruin of Russia's agriculture. *He was not against squeezing the kulak,* he said. There was, precisely, the danger that the kulaks might "organize peasant uprisings. The wave of peasant unrest would overturn the dictatorship of the proletariat." Here Stalin contemptuously interjected a Russian proverb: "The nightmare is frightening, but God is merciful." Prospects were terrible, but he would be ruthless in dealing with any threat to Soviet power, to *his* power.

Many others echoed Bukharin's forebodings. Russians had been living above their means; the country could not afford a vastly overambitious program of industrialization when it could not feed its own people. Why, said Uglanov (hitherto one of the staunchest of Stalin's henchmen), workers in Moscow had to send food to their families in the country, from whom grain had been taken by force. There must be no more talk about collectivization, which only scares the peasant; industry would be ruined as well as agriculture.

No direct challenge was made to the General Secretary's power but his situation appeared unenviable. Stalin could readily deal with a crisis within the Party, and would face unblinkingly an economic disaster that claimed millions of lives. But he could not risk coping simultaneously with both. And yet, while conceding or temporizing on either front, he dared not show himself other than steel-like in his resolution. Otherwise his strongest supporters would be at his throat, and his would be the fate of Trotsky and Zinoviev. And so on the most urgent problem he conceded: state prices for grain would be raised. And Russia, which before the World War had exported up to 12 million tons of grain and during the late NEP years on the average of 2 million, in 1928 *imported* 250,000 tons. But, Stalin hastened to make clear to his listeners, he was far from changing the basic policy. He chose to speak with brutal frankness of how the peasant was and would continue to be squeezed. How did they think the industrialization was going to be financed? Everyone was enthusiastic about such projects as the Dneprostroi dam

22 2.7 acres.

and hydroelectric station, the railway lines in Central Asia. Where was the government getting the means for such huge investments? They were getting them out of the peasant: by taxing him heavily, by making him *over*pay for commercial products he needs, by *under*paying him for grain and other agricultural products. "Of course this is an unpleasant business. But we would not be Bolsheviks if we tried to cover up this fact, if we shut our eyes to the truth that our country, our industry, cannot for a while do without this extra exaction from the peasant."[23] And having just said how the main burden of financing industrialization was being put on the broad shoulders of the Russian peasant, Stalin then proclaimed (as if this followed, rather than glaringly contradicted the preceding): "[by definition] the socialist state cannot exploit the peasantry. . . . The payment of this extra contribution takes place in the circumstances where the peasant's standard of living continually improves."[24]

It was only if one closed one's mind resolutely to "the class point of view" that one could believe that this was not merely a matter of statistics, crops, and industrialization, that it was in truth more like a bad dream or a surrealist play in which the main character has just announced that the peasant while being skinned alive was not being "exploited." For Stalin's supporters his performance was welcome assurance that the Boss was not losing his grip and was just biding his time. And his opponents by now had enough evidence that this was not another case for the medical department of the Central Committee: Stalin knew how to impose his own brand of madness on others.

And so Nikolai Bukharin felt an anachronistic and, as it was to turn out, fatal impulse to do what a Russian *intelligent* would have done in the good old days when confronted by a personal or political crisis: to have a heart-to-heart talk with someone with whom he could discuss the terrible things in the offing. There was no point talking with Rykov and Tomsky: they already knew, and anyway they tended to seek solace in strong spirits rather than in conversation. But there was another *intelligent*, the judicious Kamenev. True, not so long ago Bukharin had helped to destroy him politically and Kamenev was currently out of things. But he was a wise man whom one could trust, and Bukharin perhaps had a morbid craving to find out how it felt to be in his shoes.

And so a meeting was arranged through Sokolnikov, another former oppositionist currently restored to grace. On the evening of July 11, without even ringing the bell, Bukharin and Sokolnikov crept into

---

[23] Stalin, XI, 160.

[24] *Ibid.* The speech, need one add, was not published at the time. It was inserted in his *Works* twenty years later and unlike what was done in similar instances, it is not pointed out that this was being printed for the first time.

Kamenev's apartment. He was sworn to secrecy. He must not even call Bukharin since, the latter was sure, his phone was tapped.[25]

Bukharin's agitation was unmistakable. Though still officially one of the Party's top leaders, he had been teased at the Central Committee's meeting, which was just ending. He, the leading theoretician of the Party, had been interrupted by the crude Voroshilov with the shout, "Give us your panaceas, Bukharin!" The sensitive and rather engagingly childish man smarted under these boorish ways of his recent allies. Take Molotov, who presumed to give him lessons in Marxism. "We call him 'the iron ass,' " chuckled Bukharin, in one of the few lighter moments of his visit.[26]

But there was nothing humorous about his attitude to Stalin. "He will slaughter us," he kept repeating. The General Secretary was a new Genghis Khan, and Bukharin, Rykov, and Tomsky would *now* prefer to have Zinoviev and Kamenev on the Politburo instead of Stalin. Another item of the conversation must have attracted the General Secretary's special attention when it was placed on his desk. Among the potential allies in disaffection whom Bukharin named were two high GPU officials, Henryk Yagoda and Michael Trilisser.[27] One did not have to be Stalin to see in this an avowal that the Bukharin-Rykov bloc would, if it dared, stage a coup against him.

A realistic reading of this garrulous and frightened recital must confirm, however, the impression of the Bukharin-Rykov bloc's ineptitude. Even more than Zinoviev and Trotsky they were incapable of wresting power from Stalin's hands. Bukharin was grasping at straws: at one point he declared Voroshilov and Kalinin had been on their side on the peasant issue, although now they had gone over to Stalin. But there was never a good reason to think that those two were not completely under Stalin's thumb. Kalinin looked like a peasant elder, and Voroshilov as head of the army should have been worried about policies which harmed the families of the rank and file; those were the only grounds for such fatuous hopes.

Bukharin was full of illuminating gossip: Tomsky, he related, in a drunken moment had told the General Secretary that some worker would

[25] *The Trotsky Archive*, T1897. Kamenev wrote down the conversation for the benefit of a few friends. They in turn circulated it to their friends, including Trotsky. In a few months the report of the secret meeting was published abroad. The exiled oppositionists—i.e., Trotsky's group—were accorded the right to correspond on political subjects, the right to which they availed themselves voluminously, to the great enlightenment of the GPU.

[26] The credit for this characterization belongs evidently to V. I. Lenin.

[27] Henryk R. Yagoda, then deputy head of the GPU, eventually succeeded to its leadership but not surprisingly was never fully trusted by the Boss. He was removed for "insufficient vigilance" in 1934. In 1938 he was to share the bench of the accused with Bukharin and Rykov and receive the same sentence.

try to shoot him. (One is not surprised that Stalin referred to Tomsky, in a private letter he wrote in August, as "a malicious and devious man.") Stalin, he went on, was constantly wheeling and dealing: he had bought the support of the Ukrainian members of the Central Committee by removing, as boss of the Ukraine, Kaganovich, who as a Jew was not very popular in that post. (In fact, Stalin needed this ruthless and capable man at the center. And even more than Molotov, Kaganovich was his right hand in running the Party in the difficult days ahead.)

It is interesting to note another bit of information. Stalin, declared Bukharin, was left-wing on the peasant policy but right-wing on some other issues. Thus he wanted to throw the Comintern offices out of the Kremlin and opposed even a single death penalty for those found guilty in the Shakhti trial; on the last he was outvoted in the Politburo "by us." This item does not help Bukharin's reputation as a humanitarian, but it suggests how unrealistic it is to use "left" and "right" to describe sides to disputes within the Communist Party of the U.S.S.R.

For all his naïveté, Bukharin had a sober premonition of the future. Were he and those like-minded to oppose Stalin's policies openly,[28] Stalin would destroy them politically by claiming that they had split the Party in its moment of danger. Were they to go along with and simply try to moderate his policies, he would get rid of them through "chesslike" organizational moves. In either case, "he will slaughter us," concluded the unhappy Bukharin, who according to Lenin did not quite understand dialectic but whose greatest political vice was that he did not know how to keep his mouth shut.

There was, however, a basic error in Bukharin's analysis of Stalin. "He is not interested in anything except power," Bukharin had said. That hardly did justice to Stalin's nature. A man whose horizons were limited by considerations of personal power would hardly have embarked on this terrible crusade against the peasant. The notion of Stalin as being concerned *only* with power led Bukharin to fear that the General Secretary would now start to woo the Trotsky-Zinoviev camp. They had, after all, urged vigorous measures against the kulak. This would be a chesslike move: having defeated Trotsky and Zinoviev with the assistance of Bukharin and Rykov, he would turn the tables. "Don't praise Stalin's policies," Bukharin kept pleading with Kamenev.

To be sure, there was rising excitement among the disgraced oligarchs and their followers: Stalin was adopting their "left" policies and might need their help to counter the intrigues of the "right" Bukharin-Rykov bloc, they thought. Letters were being exchanged between the exiles in

[28] All previous disputes had taken place within the bosom of the Politburo and the Central Committee, and the average Soviet citizen did not hear about "right-wing deviation" until the end of the year.

which they discussed in what conditions they would agree to help Stalin. The more Machiavellian among them suggested that perhaps they should support Stalin's policies but join with Bukharin and Rykov on the issue of "Party democracy," i.e., demand their old jobs and the curbing of the General Secretary's powers in exchange for joining Stalin's campaign against the kulak and for industrialization. It was said of the French Bourbons that they returned in 1815, having forgotten nothing and learned nothing during their period of exile. This could not be said of the defeated opposition within the Communist Party. They learned nothing from their predicament, to be sure, but they kept forgetting the character of the man who visited it upon them. And so throughout 1928 Trotsky half-expected Stalin to turn to him for help: an emissary of the General Secretary's might appear in Alma-Ata to ask, Would Trotsky resume his proper place in the Party, on the Politburo? What conditions should he attach to a generous agreement to let bygones be bygones, and to show Stalin and everyone else how one should pursue the offensive against the kulak and for industrialization? How much should he dwell on Stalin's past mistakes? In what way should he deign to negotiate with Bukharin? Even Trotsky's biographer and admirer winces when he recalls the doomed exile's words that he was ready "to negotiate with Bukharin in the same way that duelists parley through their seconds over the rules and regulations by which they will abide."[29]

It suited Stalin's purpose perfectly that such foolish rumors should circulate. Though Bukharin, Rykov, and Tomsky feared the General Secretary, they still hated Trotsky more: better Stalin's chicaneries than Trotsky's insufferable arrogance. It is clear that some of Stalin's supporters already lusted for an all-out attack against Bukharin, especially since with his precious intellectual's ways he aroused the sadism of the brawling type of Party member and, though less offensively than Trotsky, conveyed to them the impression that they were ignorant boors. But Stalin was wiser than Molotov or Voroshilov. His strategy, as before, was to let the new opposition discredit itself; then it would be destroyed. Still, to his intimates he let drop hints about the villainy of these men. Here he was, being knifed in the back by people, by the same "dear Bukharin," whom he had defended so strenuously against Trotsky and Zinoviev when they were howling for his head. In a letter to his lieutenant Kuibyshev, currently in charge of industrialization, he pledged his support in Kuibyshev's quarrel with Tomsky, who was opposing pressure for the nationalization of industrial labor. Stalin overlooked the possibility that Tomsky's objections were those of a trade

[29] Isaac Deutscher, *The Prophet Unarmed: Trotsky 1921–29* (New York, 1959), p. 448.

unionist. No, he was "a malicious and often devious man." And all this in a business letter about a visit from an American engineer and a proposed tractor plant in Stalingrad.[80] ☆☆☆

RUSSIA was hovering on the brink of economic disaster, but Stalin still contained his impatience for an all-out offensive on the peasant front. First he must destroy the opposition within the Party. His opponents must not be allowed to appear as defenders of the peasantry as a whole or as proponents of reasonable and painless economic policies. They would be painted as friends of the kulaks, carriers of the "right deviation," as loathsome to every good Communist as the Trotsky-Zinoviev "left" one.

And so in the fall 1928 Stalin announced to the faithful a startling discovery: it is true, he said in a speech to the Moscow Party organization, there is a right-wing deviation and danger in the Party. Where? Who? Well, said Stalin, it is not so simple. Some comrades had asked him to name the carriers of this loathsome deviation so they could deal with them forthwith, but personalities were not really that important. The main thing is to spot the disease and define its characteristics. They had neglected the right deviation because, and understandably, they had concentrated on the left one. The essence of the right-wing deviation consisted in this: it was an underestimation of the danger of restoration of capitalism in the U.S.S.R. Its carriers denied the fact that as long as there was petty production (individual peasant plots) this danger existed and was growing.

Imagining you are a Communist in this year of grace 1928, try to find any fault with Comrade Stalin's logic. *Everybody* knew—and Marx, Engels, and Lenin had said so—one had to be on guard against people who underestimated the capitalist-kulak danger. Hadn't Bukharin just published an article which, for all the learned economic mumbo-jumbo, seemed to defend the individual peasant proprietor? And hadn't he said at one time that the peasants should become rich? One had to watch this man!

But if a great logician, Stalin did not appear to the Moscow audience to be his usual ever-vigilant self. He had masterfully sketched the danger of the right-wing deviation but seemed not to know who the right-wing schemers were. Were there any in high Party positions? Well, hardly.

---

[80] Which he called Tsaritsyn—a double Freudian slip you might say. How fond he must have remained of his memories of Tsaritsyn in 1918.

"In the membership of the Central Committee there are, to be sure, most insignificant elements of a conciliatory attitude toward the right danger, one must admit." In the Politburo? "In the Politburo there is neither right nor left nor any attitude of conciliation toward them. One should say this categorically. One should deny the nonsensical gossip spread by the ill wishers and enemies of all kinds about the presence of the right deviation and the conciliatory attitude toward it in the Politburo."[31] The cunning of this was remarkable. Bukharin, Rykov, Tomsky, and all the members of the Politburo were now trapped: they would be unable to oppose Stalin's policies before the Party. In his own good time they would all be "unmasked" as right-wing deviators, and the befuddled rank-and-file member would then be made to wonder at the General Secretary's patience and generosity.

Before that moment when Stalin would publicly recognize how ill-founded was his trust in Bukharin and Co., he was diligently destroying any potential organizational support for them. The Moscow Party organization was headed by Nikolai Uglanov, who to Trotsky and his friends appeared as the most vicious of Stalin's supporters. He had "stolen" Moscow from Kamenev, he had been the main instigator of the anti-Semitic slander campaign against Trotsky and Zinoviev. But now, more than others, he saw and opposed the folly of Stalin's peasant policies. So the General Secretary, by insinuation rather than direct attack, undermined his rebellious satrap's position. There was obviously, he intimated, some right-wing danger in the Moscow organization. One of the borough leaders offered a manly avowal of his past errors, but criticism and self-criticism should not be limited to the lower ranks of the Party hierarchy. And so this democratic procedure was applied to the First Secretary of the Moscow organization, alternate member of the Politburo Uglanov. Within a month Uglanov was replaced by Molotov.[32]

Stalin's tactical skill ought not to blind us to the fact that it cost him dearly in terms of self-control. He was burning with impatience to go ahead with the task of reconstructing the country, of building industry, of pushing the peasantry into collective and state farms. He made himself believe that the task could not wait. In November he said to the Central Committee, "To gain a final victory of socialism in our country, we must catch up with and pass capitalist countries in technology and economy." To catch up and to overcome—this was his slogan and constant theme from then on. His followers were seized by the same lust

---

[31] Stalin, XI, 235.

[32] Uglanov became, not for long, Commissar of Labor, eloquent testimony to how unimportant a state position was considered, as compared with one of the main Party satrapies. But then Rykov, the chairman of the Council of Commissars (Lenin's old position), was by now politically emasculated.

for industrialization, for huge projects which took no account of human cost. He would have to appease this lust or be destroyed by it. What he proposed for Russia could not be done, he felt, slowly and cautiously. Enthusiasm had to catch up with and overcome the suffering which lay in the future. The expected economic debacle would be made to appear insignificant as against the vision of a grandiose future. He now began to grasp for parallels in Russia's past, to see the Tsars as his predecessors: "When Peter the Great, competing with the more developed Western countries, *feverishly constructed* industrial works and factories to provide supplies for the army and *to strengthen the country's defense, this was an attempt to liquidate backwardness.*"[33] Stalin now wanted to emulate and surpass what the great Tsar had done. But Peter did not have to negotiate with his Bukharins and Rykovs. Peter cut off their heads.

Stalin could not yet do this. At the November meeting of the Central Committee he still had to temporize with Bukharin and Tomsky, who threatened to resign. Once more, abuses in extorting grain were condemned, once more a unanimous vote of the Central Committee promised moderation on the agricultural front and in overall economic planning. Bukharin and his friends were taken in by this apparent victory. They now joined in the condemnation of the "danger of the right-wing deviation," thus completing the preliminaries for their own doom. But for the time being one real live right deviationist would do, and Stalin found him for the benefit of his audience. Frumkin, of course! The same man who had written that sensible letter to the Politburo in June, and who even now was making fun of the "deterioration" of the rural economy. Frumkin, said Stalin, tried to hide behind Bukharin's skirts, and they all knew that Bukharin was free from any deviation. What Frumkin was saying was both grotesque and outrageous, he suggested. "Can you imagine the Soviet regime, in the eleventh year of its existence, bringing about the deterioration of the rural economy? Why, were it so, it should be chased out rather than supported!"

But such games could not be pursued with the zest and exhilaration of the campaigns against Trotsky and Zinoviev. Time was growing short for a breakthrough on the economic front and, therefore, for making short shrift of Bukharin and his friends. The news from the countryside was again grim. At the end of 1928 the regime began to introduce bread rationing. It became universal in 1929 and then was applied to other foodstuffs and consumer goods. When even greater hardships and strains came, Stalin could not have people around in positions of influence (even if no longer of power) who could say "We told you so."

[33] Stalin, XI, 248. My italics.

They must be disgraced before that. And so the tempo of intraparty repression was speeded up. There were renewed arrests and exiles of real and alleged Trotskyites and Zinovievites, mostly of the rank and file. And in January 1929 a messenger from Moscow arrived at Trotsky's domicile in Alma-Ata. But it was not, as he had intermittently hoped during the past year, to conduct him back to Moscow and install him in the Kremlin again. The Politburo had voted to expel him from the U.S.S.R. Trotsky, said Stalin—answering the anguished protests of Bukharin and Rykov, who well understood what such a step portended for them—has passed from attacking the leadership of the Party to an open anti-Soviet position. "He has urged strikes and sabotage of collective agreements, and he is preparing his cadres for the possibility of a new civil war."[34] No longer "factionalism" or "deviation," but treason! He laid before his colleagues the record of the voluminous correspondence of the Trotskyites in exile, and to the Communist mind there was enough in it to justify dark suspicions and insinuations. Did they not expect, i.e., *hope for*, a complete breakdown of the economy? Did they not view with delight the growing conflict between Stalin and Bukharin? Was that not preparation for civil war?

The "revelations" about the Trotskyites which Stalin placed before the Politburo contained, of course, much that was compromising for Bukharin and his friends. As if to help the GPU, which was doing an excellent job in this respect anyway, some of the Trotskyites abroad leaked the story of the Bukharin-Kamenev conversations and other details about the ripening "right-wing deviation" to a Menshevik journal published in Berlin. Devout Stalinists once more had occasion to admire their idol's political foresight and perception. For indeed he had taught that right-wing deviation led to the left-wing one, that in turn to Menshevism, and where that led everyone knew. . . .

And so in February 1929 Bukharin was invited before the Presidium of the Central Control Commission to explain, as Orjonikidze, its chairman, put it, his "notorious secret negotiations" with Kamenev. It was part of Stalin's cunning that he assigned his main lieutenants to different roles which served to confuse and bamboozle his actual and potential opponents. Kaganovich and Molotov were hard and unyielding, so much so that the more naïve could believe that they were leading Stalin into repressive policies he himself would not have devised. Voroshilov and especially Kalinin were in private contacts soft and understanding: yes, they could not quite see this attack upon the peasant, but perhaps Joseph Vissarionovich could be shown how dangerous it was. Kalinin played with considerable skill the role of advocate of the peasant, even made some "right-wing" speeches, but when it came to

---

[34] *Ibid.*, p. 315.

voting on actual policies in the Politburo, he somehow always went along with Stalin. Orjonikidze was equally adept at the role of the Party's father confessor. He would sigh over his fellow Georgian's unreasonable moods and harsh manners, but ask his interlocutor to go along for the sake of the Party unity. Sooner or later Stalin would see the light, he argued, although not if people like Bukharin publicized their disagreements and thus gladdened the hearts of Trotsky and the class enemies. "We took all measures to preserve Comrades Rykov, Bukharin, Tomsky, and Uglanov in the leading posts in the Party," he sorrowfully told the Party Congress after all those worthies had bit the dust.[35] And he pleaded with "our dear little Bukharin," as he had called him two years earlier, to confess his errors publicly. At the time Bukharin almost did; his conversations with Kamenev, he admitted, were a political error. But he would not indulge in self-criticism and refused to retract his warnings on the need for patience and caution in dealing with the peasantry.

Impractical as he was, Bukharin could not but realize that self-criticism and avowal of error was merely the first major step into the quicksands of "deviation." In addition to Uglanov, there was another mournful example of such "democratic" methods being used to undermine his supporters. Stalin's machine had already moved against Tomsky. For all of his popularity among the workers, Tomsky's firm hand in running the trade unions—there was a bit of Stalin in all of the Communist oligarchs—was resented by some of their officials. So it was easy to produce speakers at the All-Russian Trade Unions Congress in December 1928 who assailed Tomsky's bureaucratic ways, and the chairman in turn admitted that in some respects he had sinned. Such extorted self-criticism served Stalin well as one of the most useful tools of his craft of despotism. An official's admission of his errors was an indication to his career-minded supporters that his days in power were numbered. It was also important as a camouflage and explanation for failures in policy and management. Food and housing shortages were already beginning to affect the cities, hence the industrial workers. It was not difficult to argue that this was in large measure the fault of those like Tomsky who were supposed to look after the workers' interests.

One of Tomsky's supporters defined with dazzling insight this standard Soviet use (Stalin was merely the most skillful practitioner) of self-criticism. "It is clear that the slogan of self-criticism serves Stalin as a lightning rod [for popular discontent], just as the Tsars used pogroms against the Jews for the same purpose. Officials, especially in the

[35] *The Sixteenth Congress of the All-Union Communist Party (b), Stenographic Report* (Moscow, 1931), p. 325.

economic apparatus, are now being used in the same way as were those wretched Jews of yore."[36]

The democratic principle was then satisfied by placing on the Trade Unions Council five henchmen of Stalin's, chief of them Lazar Kaganovich, who now took over the management of the unions' apparatus, even though Tomsky was not fired officially until June 1929. The General Secretary had conquered another bastion of relative autonomy within the Soviet system. The task of the Soviet labor unions from now on became quite different from that in capitalist countries. They would collaborate with the employer (the government) to achieve more and cheaper industrial production, and the workers' interests and freedom were sacrificed (though not nearly so drastically as those of the peasant) on the altar of industrialization.

In February, Stalin dropped the other shoe: in the privacy of a Politburo meeting he confronted his former allies. "Comrades. Sad though it may be, we must face facts: a factional group has been established within our Party composed of Bukharin, Tomsky, and Rykov." This group wanted to slow down industrialization, prevent the expansion of collective and state farms, preserve and expound private free trade—in brief, a pro-kulak right-deviation group. Stalin seemed to be in one of his nastier moods during this diatribe. The three culprits wanted to resign from their Party and government posts to protest the regime's economic policies, but this offended his sense of propriety as well as his tactical sense. Deviationists should not resign, they should be chased out in disgrace when *he* had decided the moment had come for it. The Bukharinites (this term, ominously reminiscent of Trotskyites, was now used for the first time) must not be allowed to resign! He was already listing some of the particulars of the act of accusation for the moment when they would be dismissed. Lenin, he continued, had as early as 1916 complained about Bukharin. Tomsky, of whom he now spoke with ill-concealed hatred, was in 1921 ordered by Lenin to Turkestan so that in the salubrious desert air he might ponder how wrong it was to oppose the Party's policies.[37] All in all, Stalin concluded, the Bukharinites' transgressions were worse than those of many people who had previously been thrown out of the Party, and yet the Party was displaying incredible liberality by ordering them to stay in their high positions.

[36] This perceptive, and for its author fatal, observation was made by Boris Kozelev, one-time chairman of the Metalworkers Union. It was cited by Orjonikidze to a chorus of shouts: "Infamy!" "Throw him out of the Party!" One does not have to speculate what happened to this perspicacious man.

[37] Here Tomsky interrupted to shout that it was Zinoviev and Stalin who had persuaded Lenin to send him away. It is interesting that in this exchange Stalin and Tomsky both used "thou" rather than "you," usually a mark of intimacy in Russian, but also at times of disrespect.

It was a madhouse. The prime minister, the head of the union movement, and the principal government publicist were being declared to be enemies of the state, one of the proofs being that they wanted to resign their high charges. But as usual there was method in this madness. Stalin would allow them to resign only after they had been made to approve of the policies they felt were ruinous. And this strategy worked: the culprits were for the moment persuaded to withdraw their resignations.

The ritual of the purge had two main variants. A man in full panoply of power might be struck suddenly, transferred from the Kremlin straight to the cellars of the GPU. This happened frequently in the 1930s. Or it could be slow, an ordeal by hope. The victim might make a verbal concession, admit a deviation, and be allowed to stay on the job. A little later it would be a less important post where by hard work he might "regain the Party's confidence." The "Bukharinites" stayed on, according to this second formula. They continued to hope. . . . Perhaps Voroshilov and Kalinin . . . Orjonikidze was so understanding. . . . Krupskaya, to whom they confided their hopes in Orjonikidze, displayed her common sense: Orjonikidze sympathized with everybody he talked to, she told Bukharin.

How vain were the hopes of both old and new opponents of Stalin comes out well from another piece of inside information conveyed by *The Socialist Courier*, published in Berlin. Its Menshevik editors, gleefully kibitzing on the intra-Bolshevik intrigues, revealed that as late as December and January Bukharin had continued to seek solace from Kamenev. But the former "left oppositionists" were not very encouraging: many of them had made their peace with Stalin (or so they thought). Even Zinoviev and Kamenev were given, respectively, minor administrative and educational jobs. Pyatakov, once so cruelly tongue-lashed by Stalin as a hypocrite and liar, was now completely sold on supporting him. Don't come out against Stalin, he told Bukharin, the majority of the Party is behind him. And if somehow Stalin could be gotten rid of, who would take his place? Somebody like Kaganovich. And for Kaganovich one could not work. And so many of Stalin's victims were content to be minor cogs in his machine. It was something, after all, to be allowed to play a part, however small, in the exciting venture of moving Russia toward socialism. Things could be worse.[38]

It would be tedious to recount all the details of the downfall of Bukharin and his friends. To be sure, they were never a faction as Stalin charged, an *organized* group systematically trying to oppose Party policy. Unlike Trotsky and Zinoviev, Bukharin had never tried to organize such

[38] *The Socialist Courier*, May 4, 1929.

a group. Being a typical Russian *intelligent*, who as the saying went "knew about everything but could do nothing," he just wrote and spoke. But nevertheless he and his friends, repeatedly assaulted and condemned, recanting their views,[39] finally stripped of their posts, had by the end of 1930 sunk into political nullity. They were tolerated in minor posts—Rykov in an unimportant ministry, Bukharin as an editorial writer and publicist, Tomsky as an economic functionary—but the odor of the "right-wing deviation" clung to them, until later on they were charged with much more than a deviation and, with their predecessors in opposition, merged into "the Bloc of Rightists and Trotskyites —the enemies of the people."

Bukharin's quarrel (it could never be called a contest) with Stalin was not over power. Though at times he sought to warn his antagonist ("Don't think that the Politburo is just an advisory body to the Secretariat"), he and his friends acquiesced in Stalin's primacy and sought only to moderate his policies. And now their fate served as a warning to anyone who would so much as even question Stalin's policies.

Stalin was now ready to take the Party into his war against the nation. It is well to recognize the perverse grandeur of this enterprise before considering its absurdity. Stalin tried to do what the most absolute ruler before him would have shrunk from attempting: to change in a few brief years an entire nation's way of life, to mobilize the nation's energy and resources *against itself*. During the period 1928–33 the Russians' already pitifully low standard of living fell by as much as a third. The peasants, some 80 per cent of the population, were forcibly torn from age-old ways of living and working. Many starved. Millions were deported and resettled. The city-dweller was also made to suffer: he had to endure food and housing shortages, was made to work harder and longer, was deprived of any freedom to move from one place of employment to another.

One cannot explain this by alluding to what had happened in Russia before: Lenin and his tiny group of Bolsheviks secured power because they promised and delivered "peace" and "land." Comparisons with other totalitarian systems are misleading too: Hitler at the height of his power enjoyed the support of most of the Germans and the blind devotion of most members of the Nazi Party. But in 1930 Stalin's removal from power would have been greeted by most Russians with indifference, in 1932 with relief. And the very instrument of this intended national change, the Communist Party of the U.S.S.R., was treated cruelly and repressed. Within a few weeks in 1930 as many as

---

[39] On November 25, 1929, Bukharin, Rykov, and Tomsky publicly repudiated their views and supported Stalin's economic policies.

130,000 people, more than 10 per cent of its membership, were struck from the rolls. Many, many more were purged and some arrested for their inability to extract more grain from the starving peasants in 1932. No ruling group in any other society, it is fair to say, would have endured such an ordeal without turning against the man who was the cause of their and their nation's suffering.

Faith, as we have said, provides a large part of the answer. An early father of the Church said, "I believe in it because it is absurd." It was absurd to set about improving Russia's agriculture by destroying the most efficient group of cultivators. It was absurd to strive for unrealistic and unrealizable goals in industrialization and in the end achieve less than a more rational plan would have accomplished. It was absurd to seek to make Soviet Russia invincible through methods which turned the majority of the nation against the government and which led to the death and debility of millions of potential soldiers and producers.

And yet a believing and determined handful of men embarked upon those absurdities with the enthusiasm of members in a religious crusade. And they were spurred in this effort by the will and resolution of Stalin. One cannot avoid the unpalatable conclusion: it is unlikely that an enterprise which would not have demanded so much suffering could have evoked so much enthusiasm.

Perception of this frightening propensity in human nature constitutes Stalin's best claim to fame as a political thinker. Marx's "class war" was an intellectual concept expressing a clash of economic interests in society. For Stalin this was a real war of violence and bloodshed. He ridiculed Bukharin's very Marxian notion of peaceful liquidation of class differences under socialism. "Bukharin's formula calls for the liquidation of class differences through the dying out of the class war and through capitalism evolving into socialism." He then gave his own formula, ascribing it, falsely, to Lenin. "[Exploiting] classes can be liquidated only through *the ruthless class war by the proletariat.*"[40] And so, whatever the production goals and statistics, the essence of what happened in Russia between 1928 and 1933 was *ruthless war* in which casualties did not count.

In embarking on its decisive phase, Stalin could not have been motivated by *personal* vanity. On his fiftieth birthday, in December 1929, he was eulogized as the leader of his country in a manner surpassing any praise lavished on Lenin in his lifetime. Doubters and political enemies were crushed. No dictator could or would have wished for more. Now a fifty-year-old man might in such circumstances turn to hedonistic rewards of power. Not a few despots would seek the laurels of foreign

---

[40] Stalin, xii, 33. Stalin's italics.

conquest. But neither mistresses nor military glory attracted Stalin. For the moment his megalomania took the form of vast schemes of social engineering. While never an ascetic, his habits remained simple, his foreign policy (in startling contrast to the domestic scene) pragmatic and prudent.

Stalin's ignorance of economics contributed to his underestimation of the extent of the catastrophe he was about to visit on Russia. But he could be under few illusions as to the risks he and the Soviet regime were assuming. The opposition which materialized along the way dwarfed all the previous endeavors of Trotsky, Zinoviev, or Bukharin. Once, in talking about the man he so admired and resented, Stalin referred admiringly to Lenin's capacity to gamble, to take a "leap into the unknown." He was now taking such a leap. So many things could go wrong: a real foreign threat (as distinguished from those half-believed, half-invented dangers of capitalist aggression he often invoked as a rationale for going faster, faster on the road to industrialization); a series of bad harvests, which might not only lead to famine in the countryside, but would require spending foreign currency to import food rather than machinery and experts; even a temporary indisposition or illness that removed him from the helm for a few weeks might be fatal. For in the last analysis it was only Stalin's continuous presence at the command post that could assure victory. Others would slacken, fall for the stratagems of the enemy: the kulak seducing the whole peasantry into resisting collectivization, Party officials tainted with Bukharinism failing to deal ruthlessly with the recalcitrant peasant, bourgeois experts on the Planning Commission who because of their Menshevik convictions and ties with foreign capitalists would do their damnedest to slow down industrialization. Only Stalin, he believed, had the insight to unmask these plots, to spot treason and the class enemy. "It is not so easy to fool Stalin," he wrote in 1929.[41]

The war he undertook required him more than ever to be the "most active Communist." Not for him Hitler's essentially indolent manner of absolute rule. As against the Austrian possessed alternately by Wagnerian reveries and hysteria, Stalin was a hard-working dictator. The capacity for detail and suspicion blended in his nature and made him strive to control and keep informed about all aspects of politics and administration, the social and cultural life of his country. Thousands of economists and officials for years and years produced volumes of plans and figures, but essentially the Five-Year Plans emanated from Stalin's brain and took little count of economic reality or expertise. Why not conclude the Five-Year Plan in four? And if one tried hard, *complete* collectivization

41 *Ibid.*, p. 113.

of Russian agriculture could be concluded within a few months rather than decades, as the defeatists (or perhaps wreckers?) from the Planning Commission suggested.

And not only plans. One had to keep watch on details of performance and in touch with the masses. A simple worker might spot what the GPU (itself not free from suspicion—so many of its officials had been friends of the fallen Party leaders) failed to unmask: his director might be a hidden Bukharinite who under cover of "industrial accidents" was sabotaging production targets. Such people had to be encouraged to write to Stalin directly. Sabotage, wrecking, or simply an unwholesome residue of the capitalist past might hide in a work of literature, in an innocent-sounding article in a provincial journal. Stalin was a great reader.

You could not trust anybody. Even the roles which he himself assigned to his subordinates became grounds for suspicion. Was Orjonikidze becoming too convincing as the father confessor to and negotiator with the deviationists? Kuibyshev was frantically whipping the economic planners and officials into faster and faster production schedules, but in time he would succumb to "professional" advice. Kaganovich was his right-hand man in Party affairs, but it was not wise to allow one man so much power in the Secretariat. Kirov did a splendid job in erasing the last traces of Zinovievism in Leningrad, but perhaps he was becoming too firmly entrenched there himself.

In general Stalin could not be sure about the Old Bolsheviks. They all remembered a different Party, a different Stalin, and the very extent of adulation of him that they displayed was to Stalin a proof of their insincerity and corruption. Wasn't there something more than that in some cases? One had to remember Roman Malinovsky, and the fact that except that some Tsarist police files had not been burned he might now be in a leading state or Party position. High-ranking Party and government officials leaked secrets to foreign Mensheviks, and to Stalin this was *objectively* the same as working for foreign governments.

Such a bizarre assortment of works, concerns, and fears might well have made another man a mental invalid. But Stalin was one of the few who thrive on suspicion and hatred, for whom they provide a stimulus for mental effort and physical vigor. His historic sense and now growing identification with the *Russian* national past suggested parallels and remedies from the history of that "prison house of nations," as Lenin had called Tsarist Russia. Tsars like Ivan the Terrible and Peter the Great, when they met with opposition to their absolutist cravings and reforms among princes and noblemen, sought "new men": they raised plebeians to the highest positions in the government. Ivan even built a separate state within the state, his famous *oprichnina*, so he could be surrounded entirely by men of his own choosing and indebted solely to him, with none of the traditional constraints which had attended even the most absolute Grand Duke of Muscovy. The examples of Ivan and Peter stayed in Stalin's mind to the end.[42]

Stalin's administrative innovations were in some fashion, in fact, indebted to Ivan's *oprichnina*. Though already in control of the Party's central organs, he built a machinery to double- and triple-check on them. His Secretariat became a state within a state, a party within the Party. Its operations extended into every government and Party institution. It is instructive to look at the organizational scheme of this institution as set up in 1930. It listed six major subdivisions: the organization and instruction department, which took care of the Party organization proper; agitation, charged with the elaboration of the slogans and propaganda themes that impinged on every Soviet citizen's consciousness, shouting at him from the headlines and loudspeakers; the cultural and propaganda department, controlling intellectual and artistic activity; the Administrative branch; the Cadres or Assignment Section, which made and approved appointments in all branches of the government administration, political and economic; the secret department, keeping tabs on political police and intelligence activities at home and abroad.[43] This was a prodigious web for collecting information, exerting control, and cross-spying, and all the threads reposed ultimately in Stalin's hands. A powerful state or Party figure could be sure that somewhere in the Secretariat there was a man checking and reporting on his policies and performance. Even the most favored lieutenant—Orjonikidze or Kaganovich—was aware that everything he said and did was recorded, most likely by at least two groups: the GPU and the Secret Department of the Secretariat (which after 1934 had the innocent-sounding name Special Department). Spying ceased to be a mere feature of the system: it became a way of life. ☆☆☆

[42] Stalin was not the only Russian Marxist to consider the paranoid Tsar as a *progressive* historical figure. There is extant a letter by Suren Spandaryan from his Siberian exile in 1915 to his children in which he advises them not to accept the textbook interpretation of Ivan. The common people, he wrote, kept a grateful memory of the Tsar, who while terrible to the nobles was solicitous of Russia's national interest. We shall have occasion to return to Stalin's view of Ivan and Peter.

[43] See Merle Fainsod, *How Russia Is Ruled* (Cambridge, Mass., 1963), pp. 192–93. Though this reorganization of the Secretariat was announced in 1930, it is likely that its main features were introduced some time before in preparation for the industrialization and collectivization campaign.

WITH the party as his army and the Secretariat as his general staff, Stalin launched his war in 1929. The blueprint of the campaign was the First Five-Year Plan. Officially, the Plan was to cover the years 1928–33. But like so many things about Soviet society at the time, almost everything about the Plan had an air of unreality. Officially begun in 1928, it was not voted on by the Sixteenth Party Conference until April 1929. It was pronounced to have been concluded by the end of 1932, but many of its main industrial targets were not fulfilled until years later. Conversely, the planned expansion of collectivization was fulfilled many times over within a few months of 1930. The First Five-Year Plan in fact belongs to the same fictional category as the "left" and "right" deviations: it is largely a semantic mirage, one of those terms so continuously and insistently used by the Soviets that even the most critical Western writers have been obliged to employ them and in fact believe that there *was* a plan rather than just bracing slogans. This naturally encourages the assumption in this case that the Soviet economy during the years in question was being rationally planned. Yet the most authoritative statement on the subject was this: "People who babble about the necessity to slow down the tempo of our industrialization are enemies of socialism, agents of our class enemies."[44]

What saved the First Five-Year Plan from complete unreality was that it was possible to pinpoint and carry through to completion a number of specific industrial projects. It goes without saying that if the economic and political resources of a country like Russia are thrown behind tangible and spectacular projects such as the great Dneprostroi dam and power plant or the tractor factory in Stalingrad, they have a high probability of fulfillment, but this is often accomplished at the price of a number of smaller—although in sum equally or more desirable—projects being denied resources and attention. And while Stalin could not compel production figures to bend to his will, he could and would compel human beings to do what he wanted. Quotas for kulak families to be exiled or resettled, people to be drafted into the industrial army, peasants to be forced into the collectives—these targets were met and overfulfilled.

The First Five-Year Plan can be called a propaganda broadside in figures. The April 1929 Conference set targets for steel production to increase from 4 million tons in 1927–28 to 10.4 million by the end of the

[44] Stalin in June 1930, XII, 274.

Plan. Actual production in 1932 was below 6 million. The respective figures for coal were 35 million tons to go to 75 million, and 64 million was achieved; for electricity, 500 million kilowatt hours to go to 22 billion, and 13 billion achieved; chemical fertilizer, 175,000 tons to go to 8 million tons (!), and 1 million achieved. And still the final figures remain suspect.[45] Even after the experience of the First Five-Year Plan, the planning continued to exude fantasy. At the Seventeenth Party Conference the target for 1937 production of automobiles and trucks was listed as 300,000–400,000. This was much too low, declared Osinsky, one of the leading Soviet economists (soon to be purged); the figure should be 1 million. Stalin voiced his approval. But only in 1936 did Soviet automobile production pass 100,000 and only in 1971 did the U.S.S.R. produce more than a million cars.

Still, it might be retorted that the industrial growth was in most cases enormous and perhaps production of even 6 million tons of steel in 1932 would not have been achieved unless the target was 10.5 million. Before we answer this argument, we must turn to Stalin's war against the peasant. If considerations of national defense were, as he claimed, the primary reason for attempting to do within five (or four) years what might reasonably have been expected to be done in ten, then why did he embark simultaneously on a program bound to bring about virtual civil war, pursue policies that filled most of the nation with hatred of the regime? What good was even 50 million tons of steel a year if the average peasant looked upon his own government rather than a foreign invader as his enemy?

The First Five-Year Plan envisaged an ambitious but sensible and practical program for increasing the socialist sector of agriculture. Sovkhozes and kolkhozes (state and collective farms), which in 1927–28 provided just under 2 per cent of total agricultural production, were by 1932–33 to produce 15 per cent. It was also assumed that most of this growth would take place within the loosest form (hence the most acceptable to the peasant) of the collective farm, the so-called toz.[46]

[45] See *The Communist Party of the U.S.S.R. in Resolutions,* IV (Moscow, 1970), 201–2; Roy Medvedev, *Let History Judge* (New York, 1971), pp. 105–6; Nove, p. 191.

[46] Classically, the collective farms were divided into three main types: the *toz,* where the peasants, retaining their individual holdings, banded together for the purpose of acquiring or renting the implements of cultivation or of jointly working some land; the *artel,* where the ownership and cultivation of *all* land (except for the individual peasant's small garden plot) were in common; and the *commune,* where the principle of private property was entirely erased and the members worked and lived communally. Needless to say, these categories have never been more precise than those of the kulak, the middle, and the poor peasant. The artel was eventually imposed as the dominant form, but its history to this day has been zigzag: the regime sometimes allows, sometimes cracks down on, individual peasant ownership of cattle, at one time curtails and then allows the expansion of the individual household plot.

Stalin himself did not address the April Conference on this or other matters. It fell to Kalinin, with his folksy joviality and somewhat phony reputation as the peasants' friend, to enunciate rather vaguely and, as soon became apparent, completely deceptively the Party's forthcoming drive into the countryside. Stalin did not want to tip his hand. It is quite possible that had he announced what he had in his mind, dictator or no, he would have been shouted down by indignant delegates. For in fact he was fully determined to finish off individual peasant farming in something like a year.

This determination had been with him ever since his Siberian tour of February 1928. Now the enthusiasm and drive generated by the announcement of the Five-Year Plan's industrial goal provided the cover and the psychological stimulus for this offensive against the peasant. The moment had come and one had to act fast. Any dallying, any talk of percentages and of educating the peasant to the advantages of collective farming, risked political disaster. The peasant had to be hit hard and pushed into the collective before his befuddlement and inertia could turn into organized resistance. The offensive force—the Party— had to find itself in the struggle before the individual soldiers could reflect and recoil from the enterprise.

"On August 12, 1929, the Central Committee's department for agriculture held a special conference about collectivization which approved the idea of mass and rapid collectivization of whole regions." Thus, the signal for a clear departure from the directives of the Party Conference was given by a division of the Secretariat, not by the Central Committee proper. "After that meeting, the central and regional organizations intensified their work to draw[47] the peasants into kolkhozes."[48]

The methods used were those partly of persuasion but mostly of compulsion combined with what was officially described as "intensification of the class struggle in the countryside." The latter meant a campaign against the kulaks, more relentless and systematic than the one in early 1928. The "rich" peasants were assessed high quotas for grain deliveries; if they were unwilling or unable to meet them, they would be subject not only to seizure of their crop, but to confiscation of their property and to imprisonment or exile. This violence was planned to accomplish several aims and not just to "disarm" the class enemy and to seize his grain. The kulaks' confiscated land and cattle would become the nucleus of the collective farm, thus, it was hoped, providing material incentive for other peasants to join the kolkhoz. His cottage might be turned into the village club, his personal belongings distributed among

[47] The Russian word for "to draw" has a secondary meaning: "to drag in."
[48] M. Bogdenko, "About the History of the Initial Phase of Massive Collectivization of the Rural Economy of the U.S.S.R.," *Problems of History of the Communist Party of the Soviet Union* (Moscow), No. 5 (1963), p. 21.

the impoverished of the locality, thus giving tangible proof of the Soviet regime's solicitude for the element it hoped to enlist on its side—the poor peasant. Most of all, "dekulakization" was meant to have an important educational influence on the "middle peasant." Seeing what was happening to a neighbor who might have only a couple of cows more than himself, realizing how flexible the definition of the kulak was, he would have a mighty incentive to recognize the advantages of large-scale agriculture and to apply for membership in the kolkhoz.

There were, to be sure, other consequences of this campaign:

As reports of killings and arson multiplied, Party members were warned to stay away from the windows when working in Soviet institutions and not to walk the village streets after dark. . . . The procurator of the Western Oblast, meanwhile, reported a substantial increase in the number of "terrorist" acts as the grain delivery campaign gained momentum. . . . In September their number reached twenty-five and during October mounted to forty-seven. . . . Of the 122 persons who were apprehended in October for committing "terrorist" acts approximately half were *kulaks* . . . and another 45 per cent were middle and poor peasants. The latter group, observed the procurator, was closely allied with *kulak* elements by "family and economic ties" and still manifested a "petty bourgeois" ideology.[49]

From the point of view of Stalin and that handful of his lieutenants who were privy to his design, this spread of terrorism and peasant resistance was not entirely unwelcome. The class enemy has dropped his mask and, instead of merely sabotaging the economy, was openly attacking Soviet power. Now those Communists who were frightened of or lukewarm to collectivization would see that this was not just a matter of economic policy but a question of life and death for the Party, for Communism.

And so, when the Central Committee met in November 1929, Stalin and his henchmen could congratulate themselves on what they viewed as the splendid success of their policy. The state grain collection exceeded the preceding year's by some 50 per cent. The level of collectivization set for 1933 had already been surpassed in several regions where the "experiment" with mass collectivization has been tried. "Now we have, as you see, the material base to replace kulak production by that of the kolkhozes and sovkhozes. . . . And that is why we have turned recently from the policy of *limiting* the exploiting tendencies of the kulak to the *policy of the liquidation of the kulak as a class*."[50] Those terrible words of Stalin's speech in December reverberated through the

---

[49] Based on a report from the Party files of the Smolensk region, which at the time was *not* among those undergoing mass collectivization. Merle Fainsod, *Smolensk Under Soviet Rule* (Cambridge, Mass., 1958), p. 241.

[50] Stalin, XII, 169.

whole land. Upward of 5 million human beings would find themselves subject to complete destitution, imprisonment, exile to "distant locations," as the phrase went, death by starvation or before the firing squad for "wrecking." Some would spare the regime the trouble: they killed their families and took their own lives. With one very significant exception, about which more later, there seemed no way out for these accursed people, who became like lepers. Give up their property voluntarily and join the kolkhoz? In his jocular preview of the benefits of collectivization Kalinin had conceded that "good" kulaks would be allowed to join. But five months later Stalin would not hear about it. "If you cut off someone's head, you don't worry about his hair. And no less ridiculous is the other question: Can the kulak be allowed to join the collective farm? Of course not. He is the accursed enemy of collectivization."[51]

The November meeting of the Central Committee, having acknowledged the success of mass collectivization in select regions, sanctioned an offensive all along the front. There was no reason, implied Molotov, why they could not collectivize Russian agriculture 100 per cent within a year. A special Center for Collectivization Affairs and an All-Union Ministry of Agriculture[52] were organized to speed up the drive. They would report to Stalin and the Politburo every week; the figures they gave him were testimony of ever widening peasant accessions to the collective farms.

The Soviet writer of the Khrushchev era must have winced when he wrote of this process in the following words: "Not infrequently the artificial hastening of the tempo of collectivization led to the violation of the Lenin principle that the accession to the collective farms must be voluntary."[53] Party officials down to the lowest level found themselves under severe pressure to drag the unwilling peasants into the collective farms. The slogans were "Who will collectivize fastest?" for the Party and state functionaries, and "Who does not join the kolkhoz is an enemy of Soviet power" for the peasants. The campaign was merged with that for grain deliveries. At the regional level this war against the peasant was commanded by a trio (*troika*) composed of the secretary of the Party committee, the chairman of the regional soviet, and the local GPU head. Stalin's lieutenants traveled to the main segments of the front, always bearing the same message to the local officials: "Get your quota of grain deliveries and of peasants in kolkhozes, or else." But the war also required special personnel. At the village level the local official

[51] *Ibid.*, p. 170.
[52] Previously, Ministries of Agriculture existed only at the federal-republics level.
[53] N. A. Ivnitsky, "About the Initial Phase of Mass Collectivization," *Problems of History of the Communist Party of the Soviet Union* (Moscow), No. 4 (1962), p. 65.

and/or Party member (if there was one) would often be inhibited in his attempts to coerce his fellow peasants by friendship, family ties, or simple fear. So the Party mobilized some 25,000 of its urban members to go into the countryside and to act as shock detachments. They were, in the main, industrial workers and Civil War veterans, and they were not only used as propagandists, but they were put in positions of authority, often as chairmen of the kolkhoz-to-be. Fired with zeal, usually entirely ignorant of rural life, they often exceeded their instructions and evoked resistance from even the most submissive peasants. The Party activists loosed upon the countryside had been taught to think of rural Russia as a kingdom of darkness and of their job as dragging the peasant (and never mind the fine distinction between kulak and middle peasant) into socialism, even if he was kicking and screaming. In many cases they would shut down the local church, strip it of its bells and other religious articles, denounce as a kulak any peasant who proved recalcitrant, and bring in the GPU and the militia to deal with him. Theoretically, very theoretically, the decisions as to who was a kulak, and whether and how to collectivize, were subject to the decision of the village meeting. But we shall see how even contemporary Soviet literature described the practical application of this village democracy. ☆☆☆

THUS the collectivization drive proved to be a great success. At the beginning of 1930 Stalin decided to go even faster. A commission of the Central Committee prepared a project of the new schedule for the campaign, but he judged it still too timid. And so in *one day*, on January 4, Stalin (with some technical assistance from his agriculture minister) wrote an "improved" version. The Central Committee in turn displayed remarkable speed in determining how some 120 million Soviet citizens should live and work, for it approved Stalin's project *the next day*.

The decree of the Central Committee of January 5, 1930, not only doubled and tripled the tempo of collectivization in some regions, but proposed to alter its character considerably. It ordained that the main form of the collective farm should be forthwith not the toz but the artel, "in which the main means of production are owned in common (live and mechanical inventory, farm buildings, draft animals)."[54] The state tractor stations were ordered to service "mainly if not exclusively" collective farms rather than individual peasants (one can well imagine

[54] *The Communist Party of the U.S.S.R. in Resolutions,* IV, 385.

how many individual peasants were after that able to avail themselves of the agricultural machinery owned by the state).

But even this latest directive was overtaken by events and quite deceptive. It spoke of *completing* the collectivization in all grain-producing regions by the fall of 1931, but in fact the regime was hell-bent upon finishing the business by the fall of 1930. The resolution talked about the artel being the standard form, but even before, in December 1929, the Center for Kolkhoz Affairs, i.e., Stalin, was urging a "higher" form of socialist organization of agriculture. In many places the peasants' cows and even poultry were being expropriated for the collective as well as his land and draft animals. In some regions peasants were chased into outright communes, even their tiny cottage plots and their dwellings being collectivized.

In addition to ordering mass coercion which in scope and tempo had no precedent, the edicts created indescribable chaos and confusion. It bordered on lunacy for the regime to think it could in three brief pages provide a blueprint for reshaping the whole way of life and work of more than 100 million people. These pages did not contain a word about how members of the collective farm were to be remunerated, hardly anything about the structure of the kolkhoz beyond the bare statement already quoted and presumably meant to apply everywhere, whether to a collective farm in the Ukraine or to an association of hunters in Siberia. All these petty details were, presumably, to be settled later. "The Central Committee directs the Commissariat of Agriculture . . . to work out in the shortest possible time a Model Charter of the artel form of the collective farm, *as a transitional stage toward a full commune*, taking into consideration the impermissibility of admitting kulaks into it"[55]—which suggests that had the plan worked as intended, even then the fully collectivized peasantry would not be left in peace: there would be (sooner rather than later) a *new* campaign to turn all the remaining artels into communes. It is not difficult to see where Mao Tse-tung got the idea for the Great Leap Forward and for turning Chinese collectivized farms into communes—with the result that famine and other catastrophes struck the Chinese economy in the late 1950s and early 1960s.

The Great Helmsman's predecessor—and the obvious model on which he based his statesmanship and self-image—must of course bear the brunt of responsibility for those disastrous policies—if that be the word. Soviet historians who in the 1960s wrote of that hideous period of their country's history blamed Stalin, and after him Molotov and Kaganovich, for what is delicately referred to as the "excessive" tempo of collectivization. But of course Stalin had other willing collaborators—

[55] *Ibid.*, p. 385. My italics.

such as Kirov, Orjonikidze, and Mikoyan, who because they remained in good odor during the Khrushchev era were not mentioned in this connection. Few among Stalin's closest associates tried to slow or even moderate the madness. Anyone who might ask "Joseph Vissarionovich, can't we go more slowly?" risked being branded as a Bukharinite and a kulaks' friend. There was only one, very characteristic note of "moderation": instructions from the center were explicit that the kulaks with *sons in the Red Army* were not to be touched. Such lucky fellows might be called "honorary" middle peasants (as some Jews were called "honorary Aryans" in Nazi Germany). On the other hand, their sons were less lucky; lists of people in this category were forwarded to the political administration of the army. They were carefully watched. To be a kulak's son, nephew, or relative by marriage usually meant you could not become so much as a corporal (this was true until the war with Germany), and unless you concealed your family connections you could not dream of an officers school. (And if you concealed them and then were "unmasked," it was much worse.)

There is no single word to describe what happened in the Russian countryside during the eight weeks following the January decree of the Central Committee. The pace of collectivization during the preceding five months had already been frantic—a pallid and insufficient adjective in this connection—but now in less than two months the number of collectivized households was more than doubled. On March 1 the number stood at 55 per cent of all peasant farms and enterprises. On March 2 Stalin gave a signal for retreat, with a famous article in *Pravda*. Well, Moscow was far away, and during the next ten days the number of collectivized households grew apace everywhere except in the Moscow region (there it fell from 73 per cent to 58) and on March 10 stood at 57.6 per cent for the whole country. But then the number shrank, peasants having been told that now they could flee the kolkhozes as rapidly as they had once "spontaneously acknowledged the superiority of socialized agriculture." On June 1, 1930, the number stood at 23.6 per cent.[56] Imagine today some 120 million Americans being forced within seven months to change drastically their manner of living and working and to surrender most of their property, in effect to the state; then, within ten weeks, some 75 million of them returning to their previous condition and recovering some, though by no means all, of their property. But worse was to come. . . . ☆☆☆

---

[56] M. L. Bogdenko, "The Collective Movement in Spring and Summer of 1930," *Historical Notes* (Moscow), VII (1965), No. 76, p. 31.

A PHOTOGRAPH, evidently and incomprehensibly used for propaganda, epitomized the mood of the period of "mass and rapid collectivization." A crowd of peasants advances behind a banner carrying the legend: "On the Basis of Mass Collectivization We Are Liquidating the Kulak as a Class."[57] The group may be, as the caption states, returning from work in the fields. But it is at least possible that this was an incident of "spontaneous class justice" being meted out: the village poor advancing on the households of their well-to-do neighbors. The only men clearly visible in the forefront are the leader (perhaps one of the 25,000 sent from the city) and the two sign-bearers, undoubtedly members of the village soviet. Behind them, armed with pitchforks, staves, and shovels, are mostly women, their grim faces not boding well for the "tight-fisted ones" who are about to be looted and roughed up.

To be sure, the drive did have some support among the most destitute of the peasant class: the landless and the very poor who had little to lose in joining the collective. But even among them the drastic form of collectivization such as the "communalization" of milk cows and poultry met with resistance. And many among the village riffraff recoiled at the class sins of the fathers being visited on small children. "I will not go. I have not learned how. I don't know how to fight children. . . . For God's sake!" screamed a poor peasant and former Civil War partisan at the Party instructor who was preparing a "dekulakization" expedition against a rich peasant with eleven children.

The novel by Sholokhov in which the incident takes place (entitled in Russian *Upturned Virgin Soil*[58]) is on the surface a eulogy of collectivization. But the author, as Stalin's favorite, could afford to inject a note of grim realism. The village Communist is a psychopathic fanatic who drives the middle peasants at gunpoint into signing for the kolkhoz and who goes into convulsions when anyone objects to violence against the kulak. True, the hero of the novel, one of the 25,000, tries valiantly to educate the peasants and to restrain his mad assistant, a literary embodiment of all those "leftist" mistakes which brought the collectivization to grief. But the hero himself messes things up: orders the collectivization of all cattle and poultry, thus alienating the middle peasant; entrusts the management of the communal farm (he is

---

[57] There is a glaring grammatical error in the sign—"class" is in the wrong case, a sad testimony that even in the Moscow region, where the picture was taken, there was widespread peasant ignorance of Marxian terminology.
[58] Translated into English as *The Seeds of Tomorrow*.

"elected" its chairman though entirely ignorant of agriculture) to a "hidden" kulak whose wrecking leads to destruction of the livestock; etc. It is when he faithfully follows the official propaganda themes that Sholokhov sometimes insinuates a grotesque sense of unreality. Wrecking and sabotage in the area are directed by two former Tsarist officers, cogs in a vast anti-Soviet plot stretching to émigré circles in Berlin and Warsaw, and sheltered by the treacherous manager. Few, even among the most credulous Soviet readers, could fail to notice the patent absurdity of two people of a completely different background and manner of speech being able to remain undetected in a small, tightly knit Cossack village.[59]

This mad speed on collectivization reflected Stalin's belief that there was no social or economic problem which could not be solved by force. He knew that the effort to collectivize through compulsion would mean civil war; he had said so in 1924 and 1925 when urged to adopt a more modest policy of collectivization and of "squeezing the kulak." But it would be a civil war he could win. The enemy's forces would be divided and dispersed, his united and resolute. There would be instead (and there were) tens of thousands of little civil wars: in every soviet village. The poor peasants would help the Party and the GPU and, if need be, though this was to be avoided, the Red Army could also be used in the struggle. Once the kulak was done with and the peasants were on the collective farms, what could they do? They might be unhappy, might rebel here and there or sabotage deliveries, but one could take care of this by increasing the GPU forces in the countryside (as was done). And then tractors would come to make the work easier, and more and more village lads would find industrial employment in the cities. The peasant would acquire socialist consciousness and would be grateful to the Party and Comrade Stalin for saving him from what Marx had called "the idiocy of rural life" and enabling him, after a painful but short interval, to enjoy the benefits of a cultured existence in a modern industrial society.

But as Stalin read the local reports and letters piling up on his desk, it became clear that while the famous percentages were growing, so was the situation: from being desperately bad it was growing cataclysmically disastrous. There *were* things the peasants could do in protest, and they were doing them. They were slaughtering their livestock, consuming it,

[59] The action in Sholokhov's novel (published in 1931) ends in 1930. Sholokhov, even though a convinced Communist, was unable to go on with the second part, planned to show the triumph of collectivization in his native Cossack country. In 1933 he wrote to Stalin protesting the excesses perpetrated there, a rare act of courage for which he may be forgiven much of his more recent and repulsive behavior. The second part of his novel appeared only in 1960, and it is mechanical and lifeless compared with the first.

and giving it away rather than surrender it to the kolkhoz. In January and February alone 14 million head of cattle were destroyed. In 1928 the U.S.S.R. had 32 million horses; in 1934, after the regime had made some concessions on this issue and the situation improved, the figure stood at 15.5 million. For cattle, the figures are 60 and 33.5 million; for pigs 22 and 11.5 million; for sheep 97.3 and 32.9 million.[60] The peasants' resistance assumed ominous proportions also in a more direct sense—riots and terrorist acts against officials were reaching epidemic proportions. The Party's ban on not touching the kulaks with sons in the Red Army or with children in the teaching profession was not being observed in most places: it seemed impossible to make the village riffraff make these fine distinctions or to dampen the fervor of the people in charge of gaining the highest possible number of "dekulakized" or collectivized peasants. In some places 15 to 20 per cent of the peasants were being peremptorily classified as kulaks. Army commanders in a number of regions were reporting growing unrest among their troops when they were used to put down peasant insurrections.

It now occurred to Stalin—and he shared this unpleasant discovery with the readers of *Pravda* on March 2—that for all the enormous success of collectivization, some abuses had been allowed to creep in. How did he explain it? Many "local" workers, he said, had become "dizzy with success." They had lost their sense of balance, their feeling for reality. It seemed to them that they could do anything. But most of all they had lost sight of the Leninist principle on which the Party based its whole collectivization drive: accession to the kolkhozes must be voluntary. He had just heard some stories of peasants being compelled to join. "Who would wish for such abuses, for that bureaucratic ordering of the collectivization movements, for those unworthy threats against the peasant? None other than our enemies."[61] The U.S.S.R. was a vast country, Stalin reasoned, and one could not do things everywhere the same way. Would his readers believe that dizzy people went about organizing collective farms the same way regardless of whether they were in the black earth country of the Ukraine, the cotton fields of Turkestan, or the tundra of the north? And how many overzealous collectivizers had alienated the peasant by taking every square foot of his ground, not leaving to him even the strip around his cottage, his last cow, why, even poultry! Did they not realize that this was strictly forbidden by the Model Charter of the Collective Farm, *which was being published today?*[62]

If the word hypocrisy was found to be inaccurate in describing Stalin's actions and arguments before this time, at this point it must be judged

[60] From Alec Nove, *Was Stalin Really Necessary?* (London, 1964), p. 28.
[61] Stalin, XII, 195.
[62] My italics. It appeared in the same issue of *Pravda*.

inadequate. This was gall so colossal, so self-confident, so unself-conscious, certain that the nation and those thousands of Party activists who had been carrying out his commands would "take" it, that it partook of the maniacal quality of the original directive for mass collectivization. But, as in most of his *political* calculations, Stalin was right.

At the higher level, certainly in the Central Committee, nobody could be fooled by the "Dizzy with Success" article. But the very extent of the actual catastrophe acted as a bond between Stalin and the Party elite (a situation which, we shall see, recurred in June and July 1941). He got them into this indescribable mess; he was the only man to get them out of it. What would happen to the morale of thousands of rank-and-file Communists who were convinced they were building socialism if dissent was expressed in the Central Committee? Could they now be told that they had in fact been the victims of one man's economic folly? The extent of the national disaster was so great that no administrative intrigues, no GPU, could have saved Stalin if some forty members of the Central Committee had found the strength to express what they felt and risked their power in order to succor their people's sufferings. But they did not. Instead, they decided to wait until things settled down and the crisis passed. Then perhaps one could take up the whole business of the General Secretary's powers and make sure that he would not get them into such a mess again.

And thus the Central Committee in a resolution of March 14 echoed Stalin's articles. Regrettable errors had been allowed to creep into the collectivization drive and mar what otherwise had been a wisely conceived and beneficial policy, it said. It was necessary to reemphasize the *voluntary* character of collective farms; to rehabilitate and make restoration to middle peasants falsely classified as kulaks, especially those with relatives in the armed forces and the teaching profession; to allow collective farmers to retain their garden plots, nondraft animals, poultry; to stop shutting down the churches. . . .

The Russian peasant won not a victory but a brief reprieve and a slight amelioration of his bondage. The regime, Stalin certainly, was as determined as before to carry out complete collectivization. It would now simply have to take longer; the methods of "persuasion" would have to be more varied and subtle. The only lasting concession of the March retreat concerned the main form of the collective farm. The regime abandoned its previous intent to dragoon most of the peasants into the communes and state farms, where they would be stripped of all their productive property, and allowed them to retain garden plots, milk cows, and poultry. Even so, the regime continued to look with distaste upon those relics of capitalist production and periodically tried to abolish or limit them. The vision of peasants assimilated completely into the way of life of industrial workers, purged of their "petty-bourgeois class consciousness," stayed with Stalin to the end and cost the Russian peasant dearly.

In April and May the peasants were leaving collective farms in droves. Those who had brought them there in the first place were now suffering real dizziness; some were being fired and punished for "leftist deviation" and violation of the "voluntary principle." But new chicaneries were already beginning. Yes, he could leave, many a peasant was told—Comrade Stalin had said that no one should be kept against his wish. Could he have back his horses and seed? Well, that was more complicated: maybe after the spring sowing and maybe after the harvest. At the end of May the oracle spoke again in terms that could leave no doubt as to what was coming. The Party was not in retreat on the collectivization front, Stalin insisted, it was just correcting some mistakes. The offensive would continue. "In leaving the kolkhozes [the peasants] go against their own interests, because only the kolkhozes can save the peasant from poverty and backwardness. . . . They worsen their situation because they deprive themselves of those tax privileges and general conveniences which the Soviet power is extending to the collective farms."[63] And to be sure, tax concessions were granted to collective farms while the screws were tightened on the individual farmer. "Is it not clear that only by returning to the kolkhoz they can secure all those concessions and conveniences?" The most ominous was Stalin's promise of further campaigns against the kulaks—"those bloodsuckers, spiders, vampires"—which would be conducted "with all the insistence and resoluteness of which the Bolsheviks are capable."

Stalin's self-confidence was displayed and buoyed up at the Sixteenth Party Congress of June–July 1930. Not one of some twenty-one hundred delegates so much as alluded to the fact that Russia was enduring a most severe social and economic crisis, that the directives of the previous Congress had been completely disregarded, that thousands of peasants had been killed and hundreds (if not more) of their oppressors assassinated. Stalin exuded pride at the success of the agricultural policy. Think how few peasants had been collectivized one year ago, how many are now (the peasants were in fact still fleeing from the kolkhozes, though at a slower rate: the nadir was reached on August 1, with 21 per cent, as against 53 on March 1). Did they remember, asked Stalin, those horrifying prophecies of the "right oppositionists" that collectivization and squeezing the kulak would bring disaster? Yet experience had fully vindicated the wise policy of the Party. *They* squealed hysterically about the "extraordinary measures" of 1929. "And now we are carrying out the policy of liquidating the kulak as a class, the policy compared with

[63] Stalin, XII, 220.

which the previous repression of the kulak was nothing. And look, we are alive and well."[64]

Like Kamenev and Zinoviev before them, so Rykov, Tomsky, and Uglanov were but the ghosts of their political selves when they appeared before the Congress.[65] Had they retained but an infinitesimal part of that courage which had brought them into the revolutionary movement, of that solicitude for their suffering countrymen, they would have flung the challenge back in Stalin's face. Perhaps they would have found support among the delegates. Rykov was still Premier, still a member of the Politburo—recognition of the lingering latent support his views enjoyed among many Party members. But instead they recanted, pleaded to be forgiven, promised to mend their ways. At this moment, said Tomsky, the duty of every Communist was to do nothing "which might even for a minute bring hesitation or confusion among the ranks of the builders of socialism, which even for a single moment might undermine the authority and the trust in our Party among the millions of toilers, or bring satisfaction in the ranks of our enemies."[66] Such self-abasement availed them but little. It was not enough, said Stalin; it just showed "that if you don't press those people, you don't get anywhere with them." The lowliest delegate was encouraged to treat (and did treat) with insolence and contempt these fallen greats, among whom was the nominal head of the government of the U.S.S.R.

The "victory of the Party line" at the Sixteenth Congress, the tumultuous applause which met Stalin's most brazen statements about the successes of the agricultural policy undoubtedly had an important effect on him. It is easy to see, and part of him undoubtedly realized, how much of this unanimity and enthusiasm was spurious, the product of fear, of the careful preparation of the Congress by his subordinates. And yet not one out of more than two thousand people found a word of criticism of his policies or his leadership.[67] So he must be right. The Party was behind him, and his war could be renewed. "There are no fortresses which we Bolsheviks cannot storm and seize."[68]

[64] *The Sixteenth Congress of the Communist Party of the U.S.S.R. (b), Stenographic Report* (Moscow, 1931), p. 293.

[65] Bukharin was absent, pleading illness.

[66] *The Sixteenth Congress of the Communist Party of the U.S.S.R.*, p. 148.

[67] The closest anyone came to mentioning the disastrous side effects of collectivization was the famed Civil War commander Budenny. He was supposed to lead cavalry in any future war, he declared, but how was he going to do it without any horses? Would the Party take steps to prevent the current wholesale slaughter of horses? The delegates found his peroration, delivered in the racy and blunt manner of a cavalry sergeant, very amusing, and the minutes noted "homeric laughter" at several points.

[68] From a speech to industrial managers in 1931. Stalin, XIII, 41.

Nature at this point conspired to reinforce his determination. The year 1930 produced a bumper crop. This made it much easier to argue that all the difficulties on the rural front had been exaggerated; that with all the "mistakes" now eliminated, one could renew the offensive, push the peasants even harder, and expect even more grain in the years to come. Industrialization went on at a feverish pace. Severe sacrifices would be required from that mainstay of Soviet power, the industrial worker. One could not dilly-dally with the peasant.

The renewed drive to collectivize that began in the fall of 1930 bore a more deliberate and cruel character than the one between January and March. The former was to a large extent the product of ignorance and overoptimism. Now the regime advanced more slowly and cautiously, knowing the cost but resolved not to be deterred by it.

It now also became clear, at least to Stalin, that Russia's economic troubles were due not so much to good if misguided Party members dizzy with success, but to outright wreckers. His melancholy thought at the time of the Shakhti trial that the Soviet economic administration had been penetrated by saboteurs, agents of White exiles, and foreign governments was now amplified. In September the GPU unmasked a . ring of wreckers in the state food industry who had contrived to create those food shortages which increasingly plagued the Soviet consumer. The ring was financed by "foreign firms which had provided it with a million rubles for subversive work."[69] Forty-six of the "traitors" were shot. More unpleasant events—you could not really call them surprises—were in the offing. A whole wrecking party, no less—the Industrial Party—was uncovered, whose members in high industrial and planning posts were sabotaging the Five-Year Plan. The fertile imagination of the GPU investigators made the accused confess to a variety of crimes committed at the express orders of high foreign potentates, including a former President of France, Raymond Poincaré. This time, though the court bowed to the demands of the workers' mass meetings that the accused be sentenced to be shot, the sentences were later commuted to prison terms. The men were highly skilled engineers and might prove useful in the future. (And some of them did: engineer S. Ramzin, one of the chief wreckers, one day became head of an institute and a Stalin Prize laureate. What were his feelings when he was handed it?)

The Industrial Party, the confessions established, maintained close links with the Working Peasant Party, a counterrevolutionary group supporting the kulak, hoping for the victory of the right-wing deviation in the Communist Party, and, through its agents in the planning agency, sabotaging collectivization. "The smashing of the wrecking

[69] Trifonov, p. 163.

counterrevolutionary kulak-S.R. group laid the basis for a speedier construction of socialism in the countryside, removed serious difficulties in the way of reconstruction of rural economy."[70] The "rich threads of treason," to quote Stalin on the discovery of a similar group in beleaguered Petrograd in 1919, were then found to lead to some former Mensheviks who had been working in Soviet institutions. In arranging *their* trial the regime showed delicacy of feeling: Andrei Vishinsky, who had presided over previous wreckers' trials and very ably too, was excused; he had been a Menshevik himself. The court was instead presided over by Nikolai Shvernik, not a lawyer by profession but thought to be well qualified as head of the trade unions to spot an economic wrecker; fourteen people were sentenced to long terms of imprisonment. Among them—and they would never again live free— were V. Groman, one of the main figures in preparing the data for the Five-Year Plan, and N. Sukhanov, the celebrated chronicler of the October Revolution. Like many Mensheviks, they could easily have emigrated after 1921 but instead had chosen to stay to serve their country.

The Central Committee drew the conclusions and lessons to be learned from the unmasking of traitors. "The more successfully the proletariat of the Soviet Union conducts its offensive, the more the counterrevolutionary elements inside the country (from Ramzin and Kondratiev to the Mensheviks Groman and Sukhanov) placed their wagers on the attack of foreign imperialists against the U.S.S.R. The answer of workers and peasants . . . must be even a more resolute socialist offensive all along the front. . . ."[71]

Thus the Soviet regime now *had* to demonstrate that the kulak and Professor Ramzin worked for Poincaré and the foreign capitalists. To be sure, this was most embarrassing for Comrade Litvinov, the Foreign Commissar, who had to make all sorts of excuses to foreign governments. And the regime was currently paying a lot in hard currency to entice foreign capitalists, managers, and engineers to come to Russia and work on industrial projects—some of them undoubtedly to replace Russian managers and engineers who had gone to jail or been shot on charges of serving foreign capitalists. Dialectic, as Lenin said, is a science of creative contradictions. ☆☆☆

---

[70] *Ibid.*, p. 167. Let us repeat, this was published in 1960.
[71] *The Communist Party of the U.S.S.R. in Resolutions*, IV, 506.

AND indeed, problems of dialectic were not far from Stalin's mind. One might think that at this moment all his thoughts and energies would be absorbed by the problems of peasantry, of industrialization, not to mention the darkening international horizon. But he was still "the most active" Communist. Beyond that he was a genius at devising systems of control and oppression. A society cannot be controlled fully by merely political and economic chains, he recognized; a nation's energies cannot be mobilized for mighty endeavors, for enduring frightful sacrifices, if its spiritual and intellectual nourishment is neglected. The edifice of Tsarist absolutism was undermined long before 1917, even before 1905, not by the revolutionary movement, not even by military defeats, but by the work of a handful of writers, philosophers, and satirists. Their testimony to the regime's brutality, inefficiency, and preposterousness took hold in the intelligentsia and then seeped down to the masses. Leo Tolstoy in his last antistate phase influenced more people than all the Social Democratic groups put together. It was only when the belief in the Tsar and Orthodoxy had crumbled that a new faith in the Revolution could take root.

Stalin saw that his system of ruling could not acquiesce in philosophers who allowed relativism in their teaching, in instructors who taught that Marxism was just one system of thought among many, rather than the only correct one as expounded by Lenin and applied to current problems by Stalin. A worker coming home from work to his flat or hovel should not reach for a novel extolling *individual* pursuit of happiness or other noxious themes. "How sad is our Russia," said Pushkin on reading Gogol's *Dead Souls*, passed by the Tsarist censorship. Well, no one should feel that way after reading a *Soviet* novel. And those Party histories which still mentioned the Trotskys and Zinovievs without painting them in true colors!

One must grant that Stalin was a great teacher. He had a feeling for the psychology of his people such as is seldom given to an outsider.[72] He knew how to evoke that blend of idealism, romantic craving, and brutality which is often typical of the young. Indoctrination cannot entirely explain the worship of him among them, often by the very children of his victims. He appealed to their need for action and enthusiasm, and he did it without Hitler's theatricality and without

---

[72] "Did you know," Vassily Stalin told his six-year-old sister, "Papa *used* to be a Georgian!" And for all his awkward accent and occasional ungrammatical phrases, Stalin had by now become Russian.

Mao's grotesque exaggerations. Unlike Mao, Stalin knew how to prevent young people's censoriousness of their elders from turning into undisciplined hysteria. He encouraged his own cult but was careful to make himself appear as an executor of the Party's will and as Lenin's pupil. Like every great teacher, he had a gift for simplicity and a passion for detail. He not only remade his country, he reeducated his people, and it has been Russia's tragedy that in the twenty years since his death the impact of his teaching has not worn off.

In the middle of the new push for collectivization, Stalin found time, on December 9, 1930, to have a lengthy session with philosophers "about the situation on the philosophical front and the plans for the war on both of its segments"—i.e., against both bourgeois "idealist" philosophies and the Trotskyite and Bukharinite perversions of Marxism. A bit later, the editors of *Proletarian Revolution* received a letter from an attentive reader in the Kremlin: "I categorically protest your printing an anti-Party and semi-Trotskyite article by Slutsky. . . ."[73] After this promising beginning, Stalin lashed out against the whole body of the historiography of the Russian revolutionary movement. Not even Yaroslavsky, his most craven follower, the author of what had been assumed to be the model Stalinist history of the Party, was spared.

And so the Soviet Union's journals lapsed into exemplary dullness. *Proletarian Revolution,* until the late 1920s a mine of objective information about Party history, took the hint and struggled valiantly on the ideological front. Yaroslavsky and others started to rewrite their histories, but since they would never quite catch up with the latest revelations of Trotsky's villainies, etc., it fell to Stalin himself to write a definitive account. Soon many writers on subjects ranging from ancient history to Romance philology found it judicious to seed their writings with quotations from Comrade Stalin. The Stalin cult became preposterous.[74]

Not that flattery would always help. Stalin's suspiciousness made him wary of writers who tried to smuggle in undesirable themes while quoting him copiously, and his irritability made him occasionally turn on the most slavish and insistent of his sycophants. Poor Demyan Byedny, an indefatigable writer of propaganda doggerel, was perhaps the first to glorify Stalin in verse and prose. He had wittily and forcefully devoted his pen to the theme of the First Five-Year Plan—to the idea that the time had come to end Russia's immemorial slovenliness and indolence, to break with all the barbarism and backwardness of the nation's past—

---

[73] Stalin, xiii, 84.

[74] A story has a candidate in Romance literature being asked about Stalin's contributions to his field. He confessed ignorance, and was chastised by his indignant examiner with forgetting that in a Party discussion in the 1920s Stalin had qualified his opponents' views as "sheer Don Quixotism."

in his two pieces *Get Down from the Stove* (on which the Russian peasant has slumbered for centuries) and *Without Mercy* (a self-explanatory title in the period of "dekulakization"). Readers liked them; Comrade Molotov had some nice things to say to the author about the timeliness of the subject. And then out of the blue, a devastating blow: a Central Committee edict condemned writings which slandered Russia's past and cited Byedny's recent writings as a case in point. The agitated writer addressed himself to the man he had thought of as his protector and friend. Why, he asked Stalin, were they persecuting him, why had the Central Committee "fixed the noose" around his neck? Stalin's answer is all the more interesting since it was meant at the time as a private letter and was not published until 1951. Yet it is not as a former friend and boon companion but as the official Stalin that he chastises Byedny.[75] So Byedny expected to be praised all the time! The Central Committee "protected you (not without stretching it a bit) from attacks of various groups and comrades from our Party." Having delivered this kick to the poetaster who had licked his boots and vilified his enemies (like Trotsky), Stalin went on to more serious things. How did Byedny dare to slander Russia's past, concentrate on just the dark incidents in the history of this glorious nation? "Aside from reactionary Russia revolutionary Russia always existed. . . . All this fills (and must fill!) the hearts of Russian workers with the feeling of revolutionary *national pride*, capable of moving mountains, of forging miracles."[76] Here, then, is a foretaste of how before long Stalin would appeal to national, not only Soviet, pride and not only to the workers but to all Russians who "will move mountains and perform miracles," like saving his bloodstained regime.

The theme of Russian, not even Soviet, pride was increasingly evoked by Stalin, with an intuitive knowledge that much would be forgiven him if he appeared as the architect of his country's greatness. None of his biographers has failed to be impressed by a famous passage in his speech to industrial managers:

> To slow down the tempo [of industrialization] means to lag behind. And those who lag behind are beaten. The history of Old Russia shows . . . that because of her backwardness she was constantly being defeated. By the Mongol Khans, by the Polish-Lithuanian gentry, by the Anglo-French capitalists. . . . Beaten because of backwardness—military, cultural, political, industrial, and agricultural backwardness. . . . We are behind the leading countries by fifty-one hundred years. We must make up this distance in ten years. Either we do it or we go under.[77]

[75] Stalin, XIII, 23.
[76] *Ibid.*, p. 25. My italics.
[77] *Ibid.*, pp. 38–39.

The hypnotic eloquence of this evocation has blinded the commentators (many of whom do not credit Stalin with being much of a public speaker) to its patent historical absurdity. How had Old Russia, "constantly being defeated," managed to stretch over one-sixth of the globe, to swallow up her alleged victors "the Tatar khans" and "Polish-Lithuanian gentry"? The true sense of Russia's history was different: "the state became swollen while the people shrank," as a great Russian historian wrote. Her own rulers had "beaten" her people and always on the same pretense: the greatness of the state required it.

And so with Stalin. He was now inebriated—and he conveyed this intoxication to others—with a vision of a mighty and industrialized Russia "overtaking and leaving behind" Britain, Germany, even America. Inebriation is accompanied by self-deception, and so in February 1931 he convinced himself that the main breakthrough had been accomplished:

> We have built heavy industry under socialism. We have converted the middle peasant to socialism. The main things from the point of view of [socialist] construction have already been done. Relatively little is left for us to do: to learn technology, to master science. And when we accomplish that, we shall have rates of industrialization of which right now we do not even dare dream. And we can do it if we really try.[78]

"The main things have already been done." This was now the most dangerous of his delusions, for it fed the others. What were those stories about peasants still resisting collectivization, workers grumbling because of worsening living conditions, industrial targets being unrealistic? Only panicmongers could circulate such stories, only traitors and class enemies could be responsible for what little truth was in them, hoping through their wrecking to dampen and divert the mighty surge of popular enthusiasm for the Plan. Thus skepticism about the economic fantasies woven by the regime, doubts expressed even in private conversation about the official statistics, would soon be treated as treason.

It is clear that it is for such indiscretion rather than for any political activity that two of Stalin's hitherto most faithful henchmen incurred disgrace and chastisement in the late fall of 1930. It is unlikely that T. I. Syrtsov and Ivan Lominadze had been guilty as charged of any factional, still less conspiratorial, activity. Syrtsov, a coming man and Stalin's protégé, was Prime Minister of the Russian Soviet Republic, possibly being groomed to become Rykov's replacement as Premier of the U.S.S.R., and as recently as July 1930 he had been made an alternate member of the Politburo. Lominadze had been employed on a number of confidential missions. Their real sins evidently consisted in having divulged to others, in whom they had mistakenly placed their

[78] *Ibid.*, p. 42.

confidence, their concern about the real economic situation and their indignation about the falsity of official statistics and the regime's brutal disregard of the workers' and peasants' needs. They were stripped of their official posts and thrown off the Central Committee. And in December Rykov was finally discharged as chairman of the Council of the People's Commissars and member of the Politburo, relegated to Commissar of Posts and Telegraphs. The Party will never get down on its knees before anybody, he once had said. ☆☆☆

STALIN'S wrath against the peasant in 1929 was largely motivated by fear of what would happen in the cities if the worker did not have enough food. But now even that concern was cast aside. In 1929 the city-dweller consumed 47.5 kilograms of meat, poultry, and fat; in 1930, 33; in 1931, 27.3; and in the terrible year of 1932 less than 17. He was saved from near and actual starvation by a somewhat increased consumption of bread and potatoes.[79] In January 1933, reporting on the results of the First Five-Year Plan, Stalin would say (probably the high point of his brazenness and his self-deception) to the Central Committee, "We have undoubtedly reached the situation where the material conditions of workers and peasants has been growing better year after year."[80] Only sworn enemies of the regime could deny it, only some of the foreign correspondents in Russia could fail to see it. But of course they could not understand how socialist planning must lead to a higher standard of living.

The city-dweller was hit hard and not only on the food front. Finding housing became a nightmare when the industrial working force almost doubled between 1928 and 1932. (Even so, to the recent conscripts into the industrial army their chaotic and strained existence must have appeared almost luxurious compared to what was happening in their villages.) Unemployment disappeared as industrial managers, confronted with impossible targets and a shortage of skilled workers, tried to sign up all the labor force they could get their hands on. But the competition, and the lack of living quarters, led in turn to a fantastic labor turnover. The regime tried to discourage this wandering from one job to another. Partly for this reason, but also for police purposes, detailed identity papers listing one's national and social origins, employment record, and domicile were reinstated and made compulsory for

[79] Moshkov, p. 136.
[80] Stalin, XIII, 200.

every Soviet citizen in 1932. The Revolution had abolished the internal passport as it had existed under the Tsars and been branded by Lenin, among others, a "document of barbarism." But now, within twenty-four hours of his arrival in any location, each Soviet citizen had to submit his identity papers to the police. During the Great Purge and, much more, during the war loss of the papers was considered prima-facie evidence of criminality or treason.

But it was the countryside which remained the primary battleground of the war against the nation. By June 1931 the proportion of peasant households in kolkhozes almost reached the figure for March 1930—52.7 per cent, by September 60 per cent. One cannot endorse the judgment of the Soviet author that "unlike during the winter of 1929/30 this time the vigorous growth of collectivization was laid on a more healthy foundation."[81]

The flames of class war were once more kindled in the countryside. Most of the kulaks had apparently been gotten rid of during the terrible winter of 1929–30. But once more the quotas for kulaks in the three official categories were being sent to local authorities, and those quotas were being translated into millions of human beings harassed, stripped of most or all of their property, exiled. (Kulaks, since the beginning of mass collectivization, were divided into three categories: (1) "active counterrevolutionaries," their families exiled to the "distant regions," heads of families often subject to "the highest measure of punishment"; (2) "counterrevolutionary elements," resettled outside their native region, most of their property confiscated. Those in the third category, for which the classifiers could not find a clear-cut term, but presumably the best possible type of the horrid species, were generously allowed to stay where they were but were stripped of their own and given the worst land, forced to clear swamps, improve eroded areas, etc. In the language of an official source, "In this category were about 5 million people, who had to be drawn into socially useful labor and who were given the opportunity for reeducation through socially useful production."[82]) The highest Western estimates of the number of peasants treated as kulaks and subject to repression and confiscation have ranged around 5 million. But, as we see, this is the number given by an authoritative Soviet source merely for the "good" kulaks and their families, and only for the initial period of mass collectivization. This source, after amply demonstrating how the quotas for each category of the kulak were fixed by the central authorities, goes on to say coolly: "The measures of the Soviet authorities in the struggle against the kulak had as their aim to

[81] Moshkov, p. 99.
[82] N. A. Ivnitsky, "A Critical Analysis of the Data of the History of the Beginning Stage of Mass Collectivization," *The Historical Archive* (Moscow), No. 2 (1962), p. 199.

turn the spontaneous mass movement into an orderly path so as not to allow incidents of mob justice."[83]

The time had come, however, when the plight of the real or alleged kulak was not substantially different from that of the poor peasant dragooned into demanding the expulsion of the class enemy and the confiscation of his land and goods. After the very good crop of 1930, nature had withdrawn her bounty. The harvests of 1931 and 1932 were poor: bad weather combined with a continuing decline in draft animals, with breakdowns in transportation and in collectivized agriculture as a whole. But this time there was no retreat. The regime had grown greedy for the grain. In 1930 it exacted in state procurements 22 million and exported 5.5 out of 83.5 million tons of grain. The value of grain exports was one-fifth of Russia's total. Now it went on exacting the grain and exporting, though millions of Russians were starving. In 1931, though the country produced 14 million tons less,[84] it squeezed out 22.8 million tons and exported 4.5. In 1932 unmistakable portents of famine in large areas of the land were visible as early as the spring, and yet the procurement plan was fixed at 29.5 million tons (eventually reduced to 18 million). Peasants were already starving—the state had exported 1.5 million tons for the year.[85]

R. Terekhoy, who strangely enough lived to tell the tale, recounted how in 1932, as Party secretary of the Kharkov region in the Ukraine, he begged Stalin to rush food shipments to his area, which was on the verge of famine. He was a good storyteller, Stalin told him in the presence of other notables. "You made up a story about hunger, you mean to frighten us, but nothing doing. You had better leave the posts as regional secretary and on the Central Committee of the Ukraine and go to work for the Writers' Union: you will write fables and morons might read them."[86]

If in 1928 Stalin was sure that every kulak in western Siberia was hiding huge quantities of grain, so now he was certain that all peasants were cheating, even those who had entered the "socialist path in agriculture." Those local Party workers who in 1930 were "dizzy with success" were obviously trembling with fear as they listened to fairy tales about the drought, the approaching famine, and the like. To him it was obvious that the real cause for the alleged shortages and nonfulfillment of procurement quotas was that the peasants were stealing from the collec-

[83] Ibid., p. 200.
[84] Official figures for 1931 and 1932 are 69.5 and 69.9 million tons, almost certainly overestimates.
[85] Statistics in L. Volin, A Century of Russian Agriculture (Cambridge, Mass., 1970), p. 232, and Moshkov, p. 135.
[86] Pravda, May 20, 1964. The story is repeated in Medvedev, p. 94.

tive farms' stocks. *They* wanted to starve the country, he wrote in a private letter to Sholokhov. He would show them.

"He hammers in decree after decree like horseshoes to be flung out; this one is to be struck on the head, this one in the groin, this one in the eye," wrote Osip Mandelstam in his famous poem. And so in the summer of 1932 a decree was flung out at the peasant: stealing of socialist and kolkhoz property was to be punishable by death or, if there were mitigating circumstances, by no less than ten years of forced labor or jail. The law, a Soviet author acknowledges, was used not only against thieves but also against those "who maliciously refused to turn over grain for state procurements,"[87] i.e., in practice against many who simply kept bread for their families' needs. Under this law the father of Paul Morozov was shot for concealing grain, having been denounced to the authorities by his fourteen-year-old son. (The young monster, having been garroted by a group of peasants led by his uncle, was then extolled by propaganda as a patriotic saint of the Young Pioneers—the Party's youth auxiliary.)

But of course much of the trouble was in Stalin's eyes again due to these local Party workers, the collective and state farm chairmen. In January 1933 Stalin ruminated about the sins of these incorrigible people, who became so engrossed in the affairs of their farms that they forgot that their primary duty was to deliver grain to the state: "Instead of pressing the grain procurements they began organizing all sorts of kolkhoz reserves. . . . They did not understand that the *negative side* of kolkhoz trading can do incalculable harm to the state if they, i.e., the Communists, do not from the *first day of harvesting* whip in the procurement campaign."[88] Stalin worked himself into a fury about the collective farmers: they had cheated him out of 11 million tons of additional grain he had planned to collect during the year. Those collective farms, he exclaimed in a speech to the Politburo (so unbalanced that it is not included in his *Collected Works*), must be dealt a "crushing blow."[89] And those officials who set aside reserves so their peasants might have enough to eat during the winter must be taught a lesson. "Communists who proposed to give grain to the state only after satisfying the needs of the collective farm were ordered to be thrown out of the Party."[90] Rural Communists were in fact being thrown out right and left. In the northern Caucasus, where Kaganovich was sent in November 1932 to demonstrate how things were to be done, half of the Party officials were discharged, many arrested for "sabotage," and many

[87] Moshkov, p. 215.
[88] Stalin, XIII, 218.
[89] Moshkov, p. 217.
[90] *Ibid.*, p. 171.

followed the kulaks into exile in "distant locations." In fact, the collective farms in 1932 were being treated precisely as the kulaks had been. If by some miracle they fulfilled their delivery plan, this was merely proof that they could and must deliver more. "All the grain without exception was requisitioned for the fulfillment of the Plan, including that set aside for sowing, fodder, and even that previously issued to the kolkhozniks as payment for their work."

Stalin won his battle against the collectivized peasant just as he had defeated the kulak. It was no mean achievement to extract 18 million tons of cereal grains from a country on the brink of a famine. Another regime might have retained that million and half tons which the Soviets sold abroad during 1932, since it was enough to save some four million (this is a very conservative estimate) Russian peasants from starving in 1933.

"Many kolkhozes experienced great difficulties with provisionment. There were mass cases of people swelling up from hunger, and dying."[91] The Soviet author of this statement may or may not have realized how startling its effect is—these two sentences appearing in the midst of a lengthy technical article, which of course takes a highly approving view of collectivization and of the regime's policy, even if, as was the fashion under Khrushchev, it reprimands Stalin and Kaganovich for their mistakes. A number of rather shattering descriptions of various incidents of the great famine of 1933 appeared during the 1960s.[92] In an underground Soviet novel an eyewitness is made to recall a Ukrainian village: "Then I came to understand the main thing for the Soviet power is the Plan. Fulfill the Plan. . . . Fathers and mothers tried to save their children, to save a little bread, and they were told: You hate our socialist country, you want to ruin the Plan, you are parasites, kulaks, fiends, reptiles. . . . But these are words, and that was life, suffering, hunger. . . . When they took the grain, they told kolkhoz members they would be fed out of the reserve fund. They lied. They would not give grain to the hungry."[93] But the most dramatic evocation of the great famine cannot match in stark horror that learned article of twenty pages in which, having discharged his debt to historical truth in one line, the author concludes: "And thus strengthened, the collective system be-

[91] I. Zelenin, "The Political Department of the Machine Tractor Stations, 1933–34," *Historical Notes* (Moscow), No. 76 (1965), p. 47.

[92] They are listed in Medvedev, pp. 94–95.

[93] From a novel by Vassily Grossman, completed in 1963 and translated into English in 1972 under the title *Forever Flowing*. The quotation is from the Russian text published in West Germany in 1970, p. 123. Grossman, much praised during World War II for the patriotic themes of his novels and reportage, fell into disgrace after 1946. He died in 1964.

came even more firm and dependable as the foundation of the Soviet power in the countryside."[94]

At the time, of course, no public reference to the famine could be made, and we have seen what happened to a high-ranking official when he alluded to it in a closed meeting with Stalin. Naturally Stalin knew. According to him it was all the fault of the peasants. Why were they fighting collectivization, stealing grain, and slaughtering livestock? To succor the starving would be to reward them for their previous crimes. And where would the regime get the food? They could not afford to underfeed the army, the GPU troops, the industrial worker. They could even less afford to import grain: foreign currency was needed for industrialization. Besides, it would have been a shocking admission of failure. Here was Stalin, upbraiding the capitalist economies whose farmers were burning crops and leaving land waste, and pouring out rivers of milk in a frantic effort to keep the prices of their produce from falling even more disastrously. Progressive circles in the West commented with awe on the fact that in the midst of the Great Depression one country had avoided mass unemployment, in fact had abolished it altogether, one industrial economy kept growing by leaps and bounds, that of the U.S.S.R. To acknowledge even a small part of the truth would be to hand a ready-made weapon to the foreign enemy, to risk a real capitalist attack.

With a fairly efficient system of control, the regime could keep the news of mass starvation from spreading too much even within the U.S.S.R. People were not allowed, as they had been during the famine of 1921–22, to wander far afield looking for bread. In the most severely stricken regions, the Ukraine and the north Caucasus, militia and GPU detachments barred people from leaving their villages. Lots of urban workers of course had close ties with their native villages, but since most Russians were already inhibited against sharing observations of a socioeconomic nature even with close friends, many undoubtedly remained under the impression that things were particularly bad only in their own region. A foreign physicist worked at the time in Kharkov, the capital of one of the most cruelly stricken regions. But it was only when he found himself in jail during the Great Purge and met peasants from that area that he realized, or so he tells us, what had been going on. How many in Moscow or Leningrad could know that in the steppes of Central Asia half of the Kazakh nation was dying of starvation?[95] Of

---

[94] Zelenin, p. 61.

[95] Kazakhstan lost 73 per cent of its cattle and 88 per cent of its horses during the collectivization. Since this was the main basis of the Kazakhs' largely nomadic economy, it is not surprising that in their case collectivization had the effect of a veritable genocide. Four million Kazakhs were listed in the census of 1926, 3 million in that of 1939, a figure 1.5 million short of what should have been the population,

course everybody suspected, everybody had knowledge of some particular horror. But in many cases of massive persecution of a class, caste, race, and not only in a totalitarian country, people often develop a kind of filtering device: their eyes see, their ears hear, but their minds do not register.

Stalin did not have to fear that as in Tsarist times a Leo Tolstoy would rise to denounce the regime's inhumanity. Sholokhov protested, but in a private letter to *him*. "Ten paces away and our voices cannot be heard. The only one heard is the Kremlin mountaineer, the destroyer of life and the slayer of peasants," wrote Mandelstam in his terrible poem. But how many heard it—some eleven persons to whom the unfortunate poet read it, at least one of whom denounced him to the GPU. When it was brought to his attention, Stalin was probably as amused as indignant. He was to call writers "engineers of the human soul," a statement repeated with rapture by his literary sycophants. Well, he had shown them how to deal with real engineers when they "wrecked" and sabotaged.

Within the Party there was hardly a peep of protest. The Bukharins and Rykovs had learned their lesson and were content to be allowed to function as minor subordinates of the man who was once their partner. Many of the former "Left Oppositionists" were even happier to participate in the task of socialist construction, nurturing quiet pride that they had urged it even before Stalin. Pyatakov, "the insolent pharisaic Pyatakov," as Stalin had called him to his face, was now one of his most valuable industrial managers and troubleshooters. Radek once joked about the uncouth Georgian who presumed to usurp Trotsky's and other true leaders' position. Now he wrote of Stalin reviewing the May 1 parade: "Waves of love flowed toward the massive figure, calm as a rock; waves of love inspired with the trust that here, on the Lenin Mausoleum, stood the leaders of the future victorious world revolution."[96] Of course the object of this adulation was not fooled. These people kept hoping, perhaps did more than hope, that his great experiment would fail, that he would bite the dust and their beloved Trotsky and Zinoviev would come back. It was not quite fair that the peasants—not really criminal, many of them, only stubborn and ignorant—were dying while these hypocrites in the Party were let off with prison or exile. Should one put an end to such privileges?

Stalin tried to set an example in that direction in 1932 when it came to light that a group of rather obscure Party figures headed by M.

---

given normal growth, at that time. Frank Lorimier, *The Population of the Soviet Union* (Geneva, 1946), p. 140.

[96] Karl Radek, *The Architect of Socialist Society* (Moscow, 1934), p. 32.

Ryutin[97] had circulated a lengthy memorandum urging the removal of the General Secretary. The Central Control Commission and the GPU dealt with Ryutin and his fellow miscreants in a dilatory and overlenient fashion, Stalin was to feel subsequently. They were expelled from the Party and given prison terms. But the Politburo did not take to hints, and it balked at the "highest measure of punishment" against former Party officials.[98] Were his closest associates hedging their bets? A plot had been hatched against the commander-in-chief of an army engaged in a war, and yet the plotters were let off with prison sentences. Did the GPU really work hard to unravel "the rich threads of treason"? It seemed unlikely that somebody as insignificant as Ryutin would have instigated a plot like that on his own. Stalin, still a master of the art of timing, did not insist on this viewpoint, but neither would he forget. For the moment he was content with pruning the Party rolls: in one year they were reduced from about 3.5 million members and candidates in January 1933 to 2.7 million in December. Such a purge of the rank and file always had a bracing effect. Those retained would be grateful and less inclined to listen to troublemakers; those excluded would be eager to earn their way back by hard work and exemplary loyalty—say, by unmasking some real enemies. A real job of cleansing the Party and especially its hierarchy had to wait until he concluded his campaign against the peasant.

Stalin and his closest collaborators had not willed the famine, and even though it had a positive side from the regime's point of view in teaching the peasant how useless it was to struggle against history, it was painful to lose so many potential workers and soldiers. And agriculture as a whole continued to suffer through the loss of livestock. Stalin's reaction to the disaster took a twofold form. In the first place, he predictably argued that it was the work of the class enemy, and secondly, conversely, a result of lack of vigilance on the part of the local authorities, who failed to understand that the "appearance of the class enemy in the countryside has changed." They still kept looking for kulaks such as those portrayed in the posters, "men with beastlike expressions, jutting-out teeth, fat necks." But such kulaks were long gone! The new type of class enemy sat right in the kolkhoz, often as manager, bookkeeper, secretary, etc. They professed full devotion to collectivized agriculture, but how they wrecked and sabotaged! And they insinuated

---

[97] Ryutin had been a henchman of Uglanov's in the Moscow organization and shared his disgrace in 1929. The case is discussed in Robert Conquest, *The Great Purge* (New York, 1968), pp. 28–31.

[98] Stalin's manner in such matters was seldom a direct command or motion. Had he demanded it, there is little doubt that Ryutin et al. would have been shot then rather than later.

that more grain than in fact was needed should be saved for the kolkhoz rather than turned over to the state. "To unmask such a clever enemy, one must have mastered revolutionary vigilance. . . . But do we have many rural Communists with this ability?"[99] Unfortunately not, Stalin answered his own question. And so he devised an additional form of political control in the countryside. The Machine Tractor Stations now being set up to service a number of kolkhozes would have a political department, officers of which would be selected with special care so that most of them had no local ties. Among the deputies of the political director, one had to be a representative of the political police. The latter in many cases went about unmasking the new kind of class enemy in the village without any reference to their nominal bosses, the director of the MTS and the chief of its political department.[100] And so in addition to the local Party and state organs, and the local militia, another structure of control and oppression was erected upon the prostrate form of the Russian peasant.

But it was by now clear even to Stalin that new and better ways of squeezing the peasant were not enough. In January 1933 the agricultural procurement system was put on a more regular basis: the collective farm's delivery quota would be set in advance of the harvest; the kolkhoz would be allowed to retain the rest of the crop for use of its members or for sale in the free market where prices were higher than those the government paid for compulsory deliveries.[101] Thus in principle, at any rate, the unregulated and repeated exactions which had brought on the horrors of 1932–33 would not recur in years to come.

Simultaneously, the regime rediscovered, as it had in the past and would intermittently in the future, that the socialist path in agriculture must be supplemented by material incentives to the individual peasant if Soviet agriculture were to hobble along. A benign, jocular Stalin materialized on February 19, 1933, before the first All-Russian Congress of Leading Kolkhoz Workers. Even though the delegates present were presumably those who distinguished themselves by zeal in the cause, it still required gall as well as physical courage for Stalin to appear before any peasant gathering at this time. Collectivization, he assured them, and correctly, "has already been an achievement of the kind the world had not seen and no other government could have put into effect." But, he said, it was just the first step. Here his listeners' hearts must have sunk, in expectation that he would proclaim another socialist offensive, turning artels into communes or state farms. But no, he had a great

[99] Stalin, XIII, 230.
[100] One such GPU stalwart informed his chief: "I am not your subordinate. I work according to the special instructions of the GPU. These instructions have nothing to do with you. I simply go about my own operations." Cited in Zelenin, p. 54.
[101] Volin, p. 242.

boon to announce: the regime aimed, he said, *to make all collective farmers prosperous.* Such was the shock of relief that he had to repeat the phrase before the gathering exploded in applause. He had some details to spell out as to how the regime would bring all the collective farmers up to the level where "they would have an abundance of goods and enjoy a cultured existence."[102] Take the cow: the regime had a bit of misunderstanding with peasant women about cows (i.e., it took cows away from them). But that was in the past! Another year or two and every collective farmer would have *one* cow. Peasant women should be especially grateful for collectivization: it brought them equality with their menfolk. (Again this was true, but in a much grimmer sense than Stalin intended: "The men died first, then the children, then the women," wrote a contemporary author about a Ukrainian village at that very time.[103])

Stalin indulged in some earthy humor. A widow from the Volga region had written to him to complain that "they" would not admit her to the kolkhoz. He inquired of the officials why. It appeared that on the occasion when the villagers first discussed joining the collective farm, the lady in question had lifted up her skirt, displayed her backside, and announced that *that* expressed what she thought of collectivization. Stalin persuaded the officials to let the woman, who now sincerely repented of her incivility, into the kolkhoz and she was now its leading worker. There was general merriment at this tale and at Stalin's jocular approach. Some of those who laughed must have seen their fellow villagers trying to eat tree bark.

In the spring the regime moved to moderate its repression of the peasant—to a large extent the famine was rendering repression superfluous; besides, the overcrowding of the jails had led to outbreaks of typhus. Under the signature of Molotov as Prime Minister and Stalin as Secretary of the Central Committee[104] a secret circular was sent to the state and Party organs. Under the heading "To Bring on Order in the Matter of Jailings" it prescribed that *only* judicial organs, the GPU, and the militia had the right to arrest. The jail population was to be reduced forthwith to 400,000 for the whole of the U.S.S.R. But of course the excess was not to be freed. Those with sentences of under three years were "pardoned" to one year of compulsory labor. Those with sentences of between three and five years would be sent to "the labor settlement of the GPU"; of upward of five years, to forced labor camps—peasants in

[102] Stalin, XIII, 249.
[103] This is again a single sentence smuggled into a lengthy novel that otherwise eulogizes the socialist experiment in the countryside. Ivan Stadnyuk, *People Are Not Angels* (Moscow, 1966).
[104] For some reason Stalin was not using the word "General" in his title in official documents, which throws light on a question we shall consider in the next chapter.

both categories to be accompanied by their dependents. Special commissions were empowered to substitute forced labor for jail sentences in the following categories: "Those not capable of physical labor [sic!], cripples, mothers with infants, pregnant women." And the main reason for this humane measure was that authorities had to eliminate outbreaks of typhus in jails within one month.[105]

The crucial year of the war against the nation was 1933. By 1937 practically all of the peasants were absorbed in collective and state farms. Through its system of procurements at low prices the state exacted even higher tribute from the peasant than in the tragic years of 1928–32.[106] But the peasant population was now much lower (some 20 million fewer in 1937 than in 1928), and the individual garden plots, cows, and poultry provided a cushion against starvation in a bad harvest year. And so the great famine of 1932–33 did not recur. The peasant did not have an "abundance of goods and enjoy a cultured existence"—on the eve of the German war his standard of living was still below the not very splendid level of 1928. But he would live.

Forgiveness was not an outstanding characteristic of Stalin's. To the very end his attitude toward the Russian peasants was a bit as if he were dealing with a multimillion-headed Trotsky or Zinoviev. The concessions the peasants has wrested through their ordeal—that half-acre plot, that cow, the right of the kolkhoz to market its produce after the state's quota has been satisfied—were tolerated but grudgingly and with periodic attempts at their curtailment. To Stalin, these were regrettable concessions to that "individualistic psychology" in the peasant which he had pledged to eradicate.

The regime's continued vendetta against the peasantry stands in even starker relief when viewed against some other economic issues in which Stalin and his collaborators were able to discard their ideologically begotten obsessions. In his speech to industrial managers of June 1931 he had spoken a lot of sense about the industrial sector of the economy. Factories and industrial trusts required unified direction rather than, as the old Soviet practice had it, management by boards. This was the beginning of the rehabilitation of the industrial manager and engineer. *He* will no longer be considered an ex-officio hidden class enemy. Many, of course, were victimized during the Great Purge, but probably fewer proportionately than in such other segments of the Soviet hierarchy as the Party elite and the officer corps. Those who remained in good standing

---

[105] This document comes from the Party archive of Smolensk which, captured by the Germans, reached the West. It is quoted in Fainsod, *Smolensk Under Soviet Rule*, p. 186.

[106] Volin, p. 250, gives the average state procurement figure for 1933–37 at 27.5 million tons of grain, or 37.7 per cent of the total crop, as against 18.2 million and 24.7 per cent for 1928–32.

were free of interference by labor unions and lower Party organs, and many a visiting Western entrepreneur rather shortsightedly envied the Soviet manager's position and power. And those who delivered would be especially pampered with high salaries, bonuses, and other emoluments. For in the same speech Stalin pronounced a death-sentence on any lingering economic egalitarianism. It was a lot of nonsense, he said, to argue that Marxism advocates equality of wages and material rewards. People, whether managers or workers, should be paid according to their qualifications and performance. Wide disparities in salaries and wages, rigid labor discipline, extensive authority for the manager and specialist —these would be the features of Soviet industrial organization. They bore their fruit in better economic performance but also in the creation of an elite of managers and "shock" workers who disposed of an "abundance of goods" (often purchased in special stores with the prices way beyond the horizons of the average Soviet wage-earner) even when conditions of political life did not let them enjoy a "fully cultured existence." For such people—Alexei Kosygin is the classical example— the Stalin era was a time not only of purges and fear but of exhilarating competition in which those who succeeded were rewarded by quick advancement, villas, chauffeured limousines, and the like. And since *retrospectively* people enjoy danger, it is no wonder that the current rulers of the Soviet Union retain a bit of nostalgia for the time when opportunity raced danger and when ambition more than fear was their usual companion. ☆☆☆

COMMON sense was now allowed to intrude into other aspects of Soviet economic life. The Second Five-Year Plan, 1933–37, was not so bad as the first fantasy-set-to-figures. Its targets for the most part were more realistic. Though the emphasis on heavy industry continued, there was a real effort to increase and improve the production of consumer goods. For the industrial worker, once he was doing what he was told—i.e., working hard with no nonsense about strikes or absenteeism— Stalin's attitude was quite different than toward his rural counterpart, a faint echo of his Marxian upbringing. It comes out in his very manner of speaking. He would announce what the regime proposed to *grant* to the collective farmer. As to the worker, "he demands the satisfaction of his material and cultural needs, and we are under an obligation to meet his demands."[107] The peasant of Stalin's speeches "sees," "feels," "needs,"

107 Stalin, XIII, 59.

but dares never demand anything, for if he does, it will be due to the influence of the class enemy.

And so at the end of the war against the nation there emerged Stalin's Russia such as it substantially remained until March 1953. Or rather, Stalin's two Russias. One, comprising the urban and industrial part, was to his mind like a strict-regimen school: those who failed or showed the slightest sign of indiscipline were severely chastised, but those who adopted, obeyed, and passed examinations would be warmly praised, rewarded, and even elevated to be senior prefects. But there was the other, rural Russia, still comprising more than two-thirds of the population. This one was more like a reform school or a vast correctional camp. It included people with almost incurable antisocial tendencies, longing for sinful private property and their old uncultured life, people who unless constantly watched and prodded would loaf rather than work for the state, steal and destroy socialist property. All in all Russia was a vastly superior, better organized, purposeful society than the one he had inherited from Lenin, that Russia of continuous Party wrangles, of a countryside dominated by the kulak. And the main work had been done in four brief years, and only because he had not faltered or been deterred by his enemies' intrigues.

Among the casualties of the war was Stalin's wife, who took her own life on the night of November 8–9, 1932.[108] There is no reason to doubt the accuracy of the account as it was passed on to her daughter many years later.[109] Her husband addressed Nadezhda rudely in front of others at the banquet on the fifteenth anniversary of the October Revolution, and with the words "Don't you 'Hey, you' me," Nadezhda left the room. She walked around the Kremlin court with her friend Pauline Molotov and then, seemingly calmed, retired to her apartment. The same night[110] she shot herself with a revolver given to her by her brother Paul.

The funeral was public, Stalin walking in the cortege. For several days running, messages of condolence kept appearing in the press. It does not require much speculation why a young woman would have found life unendurable with such a man and at such a time. Nadezhda Alliluyeva was a student in the textile branch of the Industrial Academy, and she may have heard tales of what was happening in the countryside from

---

108 There was really no attempt to conceal the fact. The press announcement spoke of her "sudden death" on the night of November 9, which in the case of a young woman has to be construed as a suicide. It is therefore not correct to say, as does Roy Medvedev (p. 368), that the death was reported as due to appendicitis. That was the story her small children were told.

109 Svetlana Alliluyeva, *Twenty Letters to a Friend* (in Russian; New York, 1967), pp. 103–5.

110 This is one doubtful detail, since the banquet ordinarily should have been held on the night of November 7.

her fellow students. There is no reason either to doubt the daughter's story that her father felt the loss deeply. Years later the aged tyrant would fall to brooding as to who turned his wife against him and visited his wrath on those he suspected, including Molotov's wife. But at the time, and for him rather inexplicably, he did not even punish the brother-in-law who had presented Nadezhda with the fatal gun. He was *Stalin*, rather than a bereaved husband, and as such he had to concentrate on the savage task at hand. It is a legend that he broke down and offered to resign his Party post, and it is incorrect to assert, as Deutscher does, that "months of sullen silence" followed the suicide.[111] On November 27 he delivered a speech before the Central Committee which was so intemperate in its tone and threats against the peasantry that it was never published.[112] Private sorrow only enhanced his public ferocity.

We cannot get the sense of what happened in Russia between 1928 and 1933, or of Stalinism in general, by trying to apply purely rational criteria, by talking about models of economic development or even about Stalin's love of power. The decision to collectivize rapidly was made by him on an impulse, even if it was cunningly pursued later on. There has been in recent years much discussion in economic literature in the West, and some in the Soviet Union, to the effect that the statistics Stalin used to justify the policy in 1928 were largely incorrect, or that he had intentionally misinterpreted them. The performance of Soviet agriculture in 1927 was not nearly so bad as depicted: in view of the low government prices for grain the peasants simply preferred to favor other crops and feed grain to their cattle since meat prices were relatively high.[113] With higher prices and some capital investments noncollectivized Soviet agriculture could have given Stalin all he subsequently extracted by collectivization and more. But we have already seen that this was not a mere question of price indices and statistics. In the placid Soviet countryside of 1927 Stalin had seen not peasants trying to earn a few more rubles, but millions of class enemies trying to ruin his benevolent designs and overthrow Soviet power. So it was war, and the enemy had to be dealt a crushing blow.

Then collectivization is seen sometimes as an excessively cruel but necessary breakthrough enabling the Soviet regime to dispense with negotiating with the peasant via the price mechanism—a mechanism that indirectly allowed the peasant to determine the pace of industrialization. It was the only way, the argument goes on, to scoop up additional labor for the cities in a hurry. But this argument only shows the

[111] Isaac Deutscher, *Stalin: A Political Biography* (New York, 1967), p. 334.
[112] We know of it from a hair-raising excerpt subsequently quoted by Kaganovich.
[113] This literature is summarized in Jerzy Karez, "Thoughts on the Grain Problem," *Soviet Studies*, April 1967.

hypnotic power of Soviet propaganda: the most objective foreign, not to mention Soviet, commentator is forced to seek a rational explanation for something conceived in ignorance and obsession. Quite apart from its immediate catastrophic effects, collectivization has been an economic disaster in the long run. After forty years Soviet agriculture still remains the Achilles' heel of the entire national economy. For all the zigzag course of repression and incentives, it still performs poorly in comparison with agriculture of other countries, still ties down an unnecessarily large proportion of the country's labor force.

In a somewhat schizophrenic way the regime recognized as early as 1933 that economically collectivization had been a failure. It was then that systematic falsification of crop statistics began. Instead of, as before, reporting crop figures in terms of the grain actually collected, the regime began to give out the so-called biological yields, i.e., visual estimates of the crops standing in the field. This was practiced until after Stalin's death, thus overestimating harvests by 15 to 20 per cent. Khrushchev, who as one of the main architects of Soviet agricultural policy under Stalin was excellently informed of what was going on, *after* Stalin's death gave vent to pious indignation. How dishonest it was, he exclaimed, "to use the so-called biological harvest, though everybody knows that the biological harvest is greatly in excess of the grain eventually collected in the bins. . . . How can you, if you please, bake bread out of grain which has not been collected? It is baked out of grain gathered in the barns."[114] He went on to say that if fraudulent statistics were discarded and only the grain collected and usable were considered, the performance of Russian agriculture in 1953 was in no sense superior to that in 1913.

Can it thus be said of collectivization that it enabled the regime to control the peasant better politically? To be sure, the peasant "was taught a lesson," and this lesson he would not forget for decades to come. But as to the logic of collectivization in terms of control, we might turn to that great authority in matters of control and repression, J. V. Stalin. More than once he urged his Party audiences to bear in mind that the peasant was now potentially more dangerous than before. Before, the regime had dealt with a diffused mass of 25 million households, now it faced peasants organized in some 200,000 groups. What if the class enemy should seize the control of the collective farms?

The only logic, then, was that in terms of the art of repression Stalin's regime had showed that it could do what no other could: repress a vast majority of the population and yet survive the effects of both folly and crime. ☆☆☆

---

[114] *The Plenum of the Central Committee of the Communist Party* (Moscow, 1958), p. 13.

THERE is a story in Boccaccio's *Decameron* of Abraham the Jew who was pressed by a friend to become a Christian. Abraham, still hesitant, goes to Rome to study Christianity at its center. His Christian friend is ready to concede the game: no one can observe the real state of affairs in the capital of the Church and yet arrive at the conviction of its divine mission. Abraham returns, appalled by the corruption and degeneracy he has found, but his conclusion is the very opposite of his friend's fears: an institution whose highest representatives are so corrupt and which yet "continually grows and becomes more bright and clear" must be divinely ordained. And he becomes a Christian.[115] I have seen the future and it works, wrote an American after visiting Russia in the 1930s.

---

[115] Giovanni Boccaccio, *The Decameron*, trans. by Frances Winwar (New York: The Modern Library, 1955), p. 15.

9

"LIFE HAS BECOME BETTER, COMRADES, LIFE HAS BECOME GAYER"

Stalin seldom failed to impress foreigners with whom he spoke. The Georgian cobbler's son was in this respect greatly superior to his predecessor. Lenin with a capitalist visitor was always conscious of his own sinful class origins and by way of compensation was obsessively doctrinaire and condescending. The Father of Communism did not suffer fools gladly, and he placed in this category people like well-meaning Western progressives and Labour politicians. They could always be counted on to ask a silly question—Why was terror being practiced? or the like. As for Stalin, "We Russian Bolsheviks have for long learned not to be surprised at anything," he told Emil Ludwig. And so, when Lady Astor, combining American forthrightness with a British aristocrat's unceremoniousness toward lesser breeds, inquired how long he proposed to go on killing people, Stalin was unfazed: As long as it is necessary, he answered. Reading his interview with Emil Ludwig, one is struck again by Stalin's intuitive ability to gauge his visitor's personality. Ludwig, a German writer of rather facile biographies then very much en vogue, probed into Stalin's family and personal background in a way which would have made Lenin show him the door. But Stalin was calm, courteous, and "one-up" on him. He managed to convey the impression of reasonableness but also just the right touch of mystery and steely resolution which his visitor would convey to Western readers. He did not lecture, still less orate, in the manner of Hitler. Ludwig kept fishing for some revealing and characteristic clue from which to draw the personality of this mysterious potentate. Did Stalin consider himself a continuator of Peter the Great? No, he was just a disciple of Lenin's, and of course between the maker of Communism and the Tsar there could be no comparison: Lenin was like an ocean; Peter, for all his work in modernizing Russia, was but a drop in the sea. Frustrated in his "Red Tsar" image, Ludwig tried other tacks. He had heard of Stalin's youthful "expropriations"—what did he think of Stenka Razin and Pugachev ("Stalin, inspired by the Cossack bandit chieftains of yore"). But, Stalin explained patiently, those semibandit, semirebel figures of the Tsarist past expressed only a primitive popular reaction to oppression. They had nothing to do with Bolshevism, which pursued humane goals and is based on scientific truth. Doctor Freud did not help either: Stalin's childhood was quite normal, his parents, though uneducated, treated him well. Ludwig turned to his theological training—what did Stalin think of the Jesuits? Stalin would not swallow this bait. The Jesuits based their system on indoctrination and spying; how different from what Communism tried to impart to Russia's young! No, this capitalist scribbler would not be able to interpret him according to such philistine categories. And for his oversubtle visitor he had a sardonic remark: "You in Germany will soon see things you would never have believed possible."[1] It was 1931.

A perfectly reasonable man, a devout believer but not a fanatic. This was the impression that many a foreigner would carry away from an interview. "I have never met a man more candid, fair and honest," wrote H. G. Wells in 1934, when the tyrant's whims and passions had already led to several million Russians' losing their lives.

He could be so convincing and impressive—after all, he impressed such connoisseurs of human nature in politics as Winston Churchill and Charles de Gaulle—because unless something touched off the inner springs of suspicion and rage, he *was* a most reasonable and perceptive man. A politician's sense of timing and an intuitive grasp of the protagonist's mentality had served Stalin well in intraparty struggles, and they contributed to making him a superb diplomat.

Whatever their respect for his guile and internal maneuverings, his enemies were always sure of one thing: Stalin could never become the leader of *international* Communism. He had hardly been abroad, he had not mastered a single foreign language, his pretensions as a theorist were ridiculous. How could a man like that step into Lenin's shoes or even replace people with such cosmopolitan background and outlook as Zinoviev or Bukharin? Yet here again he fooled them. By the early 1930s his mastery over foreign Communism was unprecedented, all the more amazing since it extended over people who were not within his physical

[1] Stalin, *Collected Works* (Moscow, 1946–52), xiii, 119.

359

power. Foreign Communist notables who had argued with Lenin and quarreled with Bukharin and Zinoviev bowed to Stalin. Whatever their private feelings, people as different as Palmiro Togliatti, Mao Tse-tung, and Maurice Thorez echoed the eulogies of him pronounced by Kaganovich or Molotov. The rank-and-file Communist in Paris or New York believed in him as uncritically as the most devout member of the Komsomol (Communist Youth) in Russia. Fastidious Communist intellectuals who later looked down their noses at Khrushchev extolled his name. The emotion experienced on Stalin's death by Louis Aragon, the French Communist bard, would make him recall the last moments of his own mother: "She turned towards me those green eyes which had watched over my childhood and whispered against my cheek, 'Stalin. . . . What is Stalin saying?' "[2] If one persists in denying Stalin's gift of mastery over men, and the tragedy of twentieth-century politics which it epitomizes, one must explain the behavior of foreign Communists between 1930 and 1953.

To do this, one can resort to a variety of psychological explanations which cannot concern us for the moment. But the key reason for Stalin's ascendance was the same in foreign as well as in domestic politics: he was "the most active" Communist. Beginning in 1927–28, when the leadership of the Comintern was still in Bukharin's hands, and when the recent Chinese fiasco would have led another person in his position to eschew a direct identification with international affairs, Stalin stepped to the forefront of the world Communist movement.

Conspiracy was his craft and power his passion. And so, with its Sixth Congress, July–September 1928, the world Communist movement took on a new appearance. The last vestiges of autonomy and freedom of decision for the individual parties were dropped. "International Communist discipline must be expressed in the subordination of local and particular interests of the movement and in the execution without reservation of all decisions made by the leading bodies of the Communist International."[3] This was but a reiteration of the principle formulated in Lenin's time, but Stalin meant it much more literally. The Comintern Executive in Moscow, i.e., eventually Stalin himself, must make all the decisions on tactics and policy of the French, say, or Guatemalan Communist Parties. There was little point in spending good Soviet money on foreign Communists unless they became disciplined fighting detachments, just as the Russian Communists had. They had to be purged of the last lingering remnants of Trotskyites and soon of the Bukharinites as well. The Comintern Executive, hitherto the preserve of the more intellectual and independent-minded Communists,

---

[2] Quoted in J.-J. Marie, *Stalin* (Paris, 1967), p. 8.
[3] Jane Degras, *The Communist International, 1919–43, Documents*, II: 1923–28 (London, 1960), p. 525.

now became staffed by Stalin's servants. After Bukharin's fall it was presided over by Molotov, and when his undivided attention was soon needed on the domestic front, it was turned over to a third-rank Soviet figure, Dmitri Manuilsky. The foreigners, Stalin seemed to say, should get it out of their heads that they need a Politburo member to hold their hand. There were no more Congresses of the Comintern until the seventh and last in 1935. Comintern affairs no longer required discussion, but only orders conveyed by Moscow's special representatives, or by Party leaders on their return from a pilgrimage to the Kremlin.

It has often been alleged that Stalin did not care for foreign Communists and did not believe in the world revolution. This is certainly overstating the case: foreign Communists were for him a valuable asset that should not be squandered. It goes without saying that the interests of the Soviet state—his state—took absolute priority over those of any foreign Communist Party, or of all of them. But he was not much different in this respect from Trotsky, or from Lenin after his phase of internationalist enthusiasm in 1918–19, when for a Communist Germany he would *almost* have sacrificed Communist Russia. Where Stalin was different from many of his fellow Bolsheviks was in his thoroughly unromantic view of foreign Communism. For them it was an exciting adventure, the stuff of dreams and passions. Stalin was in love with production figures: for an additional million tons of Soviet steel he would gladly have sacrificed a sizable foreign party. Foreign Communists were advance detachments of the main army, which was the Soviet Union, and as such they might on certain occasions be expendable. He was a true believer: to his mind capitalism was doomed. But of course the eventual triumph of Communism abroad would not come through some ridiculous revolutionary adventure and improvisation in Germany or China. It would come through the growing military strength and industrial might of the Soviet Union, combined with the growing debility and chaos of the capitalist world.

Capitalism was the enemy, and in its appraisal of this enemy, whether domestic or foreign, the Communist mind (and not only Stalin's) has always been schizophrenic: the enemy was weak, divided, condemned by the forces of history; and yet it was infinitely dangerous and resourceful. The capitalist ruling class was foolish and irrational: Why hadn't the capitalist powers combined to choke the infant Communist state in Russia rather than continue to fight over a few square miles in the West? Why did they let the Soviet experiment grow in strength and stability, why did they recognize and trade with the U.S.S.R., allow their scientists and engineers to help with industrialization? Yet there was the constant threat of capitalist intervention; "objectively" every internal trouble in the Soviet Union was the result of capitalist plots; every foreigner in the U.S.S.R., including every Communist, was a potential spy. Hope and fear were intertwined in this surrealist view of the capitalist world. Vast new conflicts were about to seize the West: Germany against France, Japan against the United States; or—a bizarre notion seriously entertained by otherwise quite sober Soviet international experts—the United States, representing a new and dynamic type of capitalism, grappling for empire with Britain. But then these pleasurable visions would fade, and their place would be taken by a nightmare: the capitalists were planning a concerted action against the U.S.S.R.; the Japanese attacking in the East, Ukrainian and Byelorussian uprisings in the West, helped by a Polish invasion sponsored by the French, while the British from India provoke an uprising of the Muslims of Soviet Central Asia! Sober and efficient Soviet diplomacy operated in the real world of the 1920s, but those phantasmagoric hopes and fears were never absent from the mind of the rulers. ☆☆☆

STALIN epitomized the Communist mind at its most realistic and its most suspicious, in foreign policy as in other matters. This innate suspiciousness as well as certain lack of subtlety marked Stalin's initial period of guidance of the world Communist movement. The recent fiasco in China was to his mind a strong argument against the Communist Parties' collaborating with any other radical or, in Asia, nationalist forces. The Sixth Comintern Congress laid down that the socialist parties were "a particularly dangerous enemy of the proletariat, more dangerous than the avowed adherents of predatory imperialism." European Communists made socialism the number-one target of their attack. The propaganda school for Asian Communists in Moscow had once been called Sun Yat-sen University, symbol of that tactic of alliance with nationalism in colonial areas which, for all the setbacks in China, had brought Communism such handsome dividends in the past and would bring more after World War II. But after 1928 the Chinese Communists were ordered to "eliminate what remained of the ideology of Sun Yat-sen." In India the momentous struggle for independence associated with Gandhi and the Congress Party was in the eyes of Moscow a reactionary movement. "More and more, Gandhism is becoming an ideology directed against the revolution of the popular masses. Communism must fight against it relentlessly." Whomever one could not control directly was the enemy: such was Stalin's unsubtle directive for world Communist Parties. It was only when there was a real and tangible danger to the Soviet state, in 1934–35, that this directive was reversed.

With the onset of the Great Depression in 1929 this line was intensified. Obviously some Western capitalist states were going to experience a revolutionary crisis. So much the better. As it had for many Russian radicals in the nineteenth century, so for Western Communists the slogan became, at the signal from Moscow, "The worse it is, the better." Communists had no reason to shed tears at the economic and political breakdown in Germany or France, or to try to prop up those countries' failing bourgeois systems. Fascism? One need not be unduly alarmed at the prospect of its seizing power in parts of Europe. Soviet Russia's relations with Fascist Italy and semi-authoritarian Poland were correct. National Socialism in Germany was a beast of a different color, and the Depression turned it from a sort of lunatic fringe on the right into a claimant for power—after the elections of 1930 more than one hundred instead of twelve Nazi deputies sat in the Reichstag. But the approaching demise of Weimar Germany was viewed by Stalin with more than equanimity, for all the friendly relations which had prevailed between Germany and the U.S.S.R. since 1922. Hitler was preferable to the Catholic and Social Democratic politicians who had been seeking a rapprochement with Britain and France. Hitler and his followers might destroy what remained of German democracy, but they certainly could set up a viable and long-lasting regime of their own. A Hitlerian interlude would only serve to radicalize the German working masses, turn them toward the only party that could solve the social and economic problems—the Communist Party. The prospect of a Communist Germany must have been contemplated by Stalin with special pleasure. How much Lenin had hoped and prayed for such a development! Trotskyites and Bukharinites had prattled that he, Stalin, misunderstood and neglected the interests of world Communism. Now, through his understanding of historical forces, he was going to add the country of Marx and Engels, more importantly of the most advanced industry and technology in Europe, to his domain. The German Communists (to be sure they did not need much encouragement) were ordered to avoid any common front with the socialists—the "social fascists" in the Comintern's parlance—and were forbidden to try to save the tottering republic.

The realist in Stalin was not entirely absent during those grim years 1929–33, when after an illusory brightening of the international political and economic horizon, mass unemployment afflicted the West and the fragile remnants of the pre–World War I liberalism and rationality in politics were under increasing attack from extremists. In 1931 the Japanese seizure of Manchuria initiated a period of neither-peace-nor-war which lasted until September 1939. With Japanese "militarist adventurers" now increasingly influential in the government of their country, the Soviet Union faced a real threat, and not merely one of those half-

363

believed, half-imagined dangers invoked in the past which could be countered by denouncing Trotsky and shooting some White Guardists. A real threat for the Soviets had the effect of an electric shock on a patient: it brought them out of the realm of imaginary fears and hopes into a sober appreciation of reality. The Soviet Far East and Mongolia, a virtual Soviet satellite, were vulnerable to Japanese attack. Even a local defeat in an undeclared war might start a sequence of catastrophic events in a country bleeding from collectivization, for a regime hated by the mass of its population, for the man who had trampled on the Party.

The year 1932 saw the beginning of a new look in Stalin's foreign policy. The U.S.S.R. signed nonaggression treaties with the Baltic states, Poland, and France. This was in the way of protecting her Western flanks, and while the treaty with France could be only symbolic, it was the first step toward eventual alliance. In the same year diplomatic relations were restored with Chiang's China. The man who had massacred Communists in 1927 and was conducting an intermittent civil war against the still obscure Communist chieftain Mao Tse-tung and his "Soviet republic" in Kwangsi Province, now became a valuable potential ally. How desirable it would be if Chiang were to take a forthright anti-Japanese stand and thus make Tokyo forget the vulnerability of the Soviet Far East and become mired in an endless war in China!

In 1933, the decisive year of the war against the nation, the Soviet Union became the most vocal exponent of peace, of the inviolability of frontiers, of wide-ranging regional treaties of nonaggression. Even the old Soviet hope-expectation of a new intraimperialist war had abated. In view of the overall international situation, no major war (as distinguished from a local conflict between Japan and China) could be guaranteed not to entangle the U.S.S.R. For the next three years, at least, there is no reason to question the Soviet Union's self-estimate as a peaceloving country. The war against the nation had made any war of nations too hazardous to contemplate.

Foreign policy, like everything else in Russia, was Stalin's, but his spokesman and main technician was Maxim Litvinov. Who would recognize in the rotund, amiable, and articulate Soviet diplomat the erstwhile "Papasha," the Bolshevik courier of 1905–10, the man detained by the French authorities for exchanging the ruble notes expropriated in the 1907 Tiflis affair in which the present dictator had taken a hand? Now this man epitomized the new Soviet policy of (let us call it prematurely) peaceful coexistence, of collective security, and soon on antifascism and antimilitarism. The able Foreign Minister became one of the most valuable of Stalin's subordinates. It showed amazing good sense on Stalin's part that he retained Litvinov, whom he inherited from Lenin's era (when he was already Assistant Minister), rather than replacing him with one of his more sinister henchmen, who would never have been able to impress liberal public opinion in the West so favorably or to display such consummate knowledge of European politics. And such was Litvinov's value (at least until as a Jew he would be considered unsuitable for confidential dealings with Hitler) that the man's usefulness would restrain the tyrant's inordinate suspiciousness. An Old Bolshevik married to an Englishwoman, Litvinov would have been a logical target in the Great Purge. He himself was well aware of this: for years he went to sleep when in Russia with a loaded pistol on the night table, determined to take his own life rather than confess to a fantastic tale of treason and "wrecking" in a show trial—a fate which befell his two deputies. But for Litvinov the dreaded knock on the door during the night never came, as it did to most Soviet diplomats during that period.

It fell to Litvinov in a speech of December 1933 to spell out the new look in Soviet foreign policy: Soviet Russia needed friends abroad. She would seek them among the countries hitherto depicted as sworn enemies of the Soviet Union, as having incited every type of internal trouble, from a kulak uprising to the wrecking of a coal mine. "Any state, even the most imperialist, may at one time or another become profoundly pacifist." And why such compliments about Britain and France? Since he had to educate the Soviet public about the real dangers now facing the country, Litvinov was forthright: "[A] revolution . . . brought a new party to power in Germany preaching the most extreme anti-Soviet ideas. . . . Japanese policy is now the darkest cloud on the horizon."[4] The Soviet Union did not deserve such a cruel turn of affairs, continued the Foreign Minister: "Enormous advantages, both for Germany and for us, followed from the political and economic relations between us. Excellent good neighbor relations existed between us and Japan. . . . We had such confidence in Japan . . . that we left our Far Eastern frontier practically undefended." After a year in power Hitler no longer appeared as a transitional figure who by destroying the Weimar Republic would clear the path for German Communism. Perhaps he really meant his anti-Communist and anti-Soviet rhetoric. As for the Soviets, they were not really angry with the Nazis: "We understand very well the difference between doctrine and policy." The fact that Hitler was putting German Communists in concentration camps was no bar to good relations, argued Litvinov: "We as Marxists are the last who can be reproached with allowing sentiment to prevail over policy." So the appeal went out to Hitler to promise not to attack Russia, not only now but also at such time "when Germany will have

---

[4] Jane Degras, ed., *Soviet Documents on Foreign Policy*, III: 1933–41 (New York, 1953), p. 49.

greater forces with which to put those aggressive ideas into effect." Only something approaching panic could make Soviet statesmen sound so candid and so fatuous, make them forsake their usual "Come what may, the Red Army is ready," or "The working class of the imperialist countries will frustrate the anti-Soviet designs of their masters."

Litvinov pleaded even more about Japan, currently the main focus of Soviet worries—Germany, after all, was just beginning to rearm. The U.S.S.R., he recalled, refrained from joining any anti-Japan move at the time of the Manchurian invasion. "We declined to take part in the international action taken and prepared at that time, firstly because we did not believe in the sincerity and firmness of purpose of the states which did take part, but chiefly because we did not then and we do not now seek an armed conflict with Japan."[5] So, would those "intelligent and influential people in Japan" who had resisted the militant clique now realize how "dubious at best" the results would be of a Russo-Japanese conflict? When confronted by extreme danger, most people, it is said, "get religion." The Soviets lose theirs.

But of course Stalin's foreign policy did not content itself with such Chamberlainlike pleas with would-be aggressors. It pursued any conceivable avenue to avoid or postpone an armed conflict into which the Soviet Union might be drawn. The League of Nations was traditionally, in Soviet semantics, "the League of Imperialist Robbers" which threatened to stabilize the capitalist world and thus unite it against Communism. Now even this tottering institution was recognized as a potential brake, as Stalin phrased it, or delaying device on war. In 1934 the U.S.S.R. entered the League. Most of all the Russians were aware that by joining it after Japan and Germany had left it, the country's image would be enhanced in the eyes of the democratic West.

Even in this grim and foreboding atmosphere of 1933–34 the Soviet Union scored one diplomatic success which, though it did not have the immediate and favorable effects the Soviet leaders expected, was to have incalculable long-range consequences: the U.S.S.R. was recognized by and entered into diplomatic relations with the United States.

It was Franklin Roosevelt's Democratic administration which greeted Maxim Litvinov on his arrival in Washington in November 1933. The Foreign Minister's charm and amicability smoothed the way to an agreement, even though there had been some knotty problems in its way: the Americans were still unhappy about the Tsarist and Kerensky debts owed them, not to mention the Comintern and the threat it presented to what in those days was proudly called the American Way of Life. On the debts, the Russians first proposed to brazen it out by presenting the Americans with a bill for their intervention in Siberia.

[5] *Ibid.*, p. 58.

But the clever Litvinov soon dropped this approach and in a very handsome way avowed that, after acquainting himself with the relevant documents, he had discovered that the American intervention had been directed not against the infant Soviet republic but against an unnamed third party (Japan). This was close to the truth and flattering to his hosts in their current rather anti-Japanese mood. And the debts would be discussed once the relations were restored. The second obstacle was more insurmountable: the Americans would not buy Litvinov's argument that the Comintern was a private organization with which the Soviet government had no connection and which just happened to be situated in Moscow. American labor leaders, some of them renegade Communists, kept reminding the public that in 1928 the Comintern, over their impotent protests, had ordered the American Communists to work for an independent Negro republic in the South, and that Comrade Stalin himself had been in the commission which prepared this resolution of the Comintern, then repeated more emphatically in 1930. It must have been with an inward sigh of relief that Litvinov finally signed a declaration which pledged his government not "to injure the tranquillity, prosperity, order, or security of any part of the United States, its territories or possessions. . . . Not to permit the formation or residence on its territory of any organization or group . . . which has as its aim the overthrow or the preparation for the overthrow . . . of the political or social order of the whole or any part of the United States."

The beginning of Soviet-American relations was attended by a rosy glow such as would not return until the wartime alliance. The American ambassador, William Bullitt, appeared well suited to inaugurate what the Russians hoped would be a period of close relations with the capitalist colossus. As a young man he had been President Wilson's unofficial envoy to Lenin. He subsequently married the widow of John Reed, patron saint of American Communism. He was the first of that rather remarkable group of American patricians and businessmen who felt that they understood the Russians as no striped-pants diplomat could, and that hence it was incumbent on them to forge a friendship of two dynamic nations slated to inherit the world.

Stalin's hopes, for his part, were of an unsentimental nature. To be sure, he genuinely admired America for her economic might. He was told, he observed characteristically to Ludwig, that in America, unlike Germany or Britain, you could not tell a manager from a worker by his dress or demeanor. Phrases like the "American style of work" were frequently on his lips. But for the moment he was understandably interested in only two things: what assistance the United States could render the Soviet economy, and what kind of diplomatic help, at least, he could expect from the Americans in the situation vis-à-vis Japan.

The Russians gave the new American ambassador a reception unprecedented for any foreign diplomat, in fact any foreigner in the Soviet Union. Stalin, hitherto a "private person" who would not see foreign envoys, appeared at a dinner in Bullitt's honor tendered by Voroshilov, and attended by a galaxy of Politburo members and by some lesser lights who had been in opposition: Pyatakov, Sokolnikov, and others. It was heartwarming old Russian hospitality at its best, with the dictator raising his glass to Roosevelt and amazing his visitor with references to American domestic politics, such as the trouble Roosevelt was having with Hamilton Fish of isolationist fame. No one could be more open and informal when he wanted to be than Stalin—who in a few years was to send some of the evening's dinner companions to the gallows. Roosevelt, he told Bullitt, was one of the most popular men in the Soviet Union. It was quite likely that Japan would attack in the spring, he went on, and he introduced Bullitt to Chief of Staff Yegorov, the man who according to him would lead the Red Army in victorious defense. (He would be shot before he could get the chance.) Mixing business with conviviality, Stalin inquired whether the Soviets could purchase 250,000 tons of steel rails needed for the second line of the Siberian railroad which, for obvious reasons, they were eager to complete in a hurry. And the ambassador must have been swept off his feet when the allegedly sinister despot assured him that he would be at his command to see at any time of the day or night.

Unfortunately, this cordial spirit did not last. It did not take the Russians long to ascertain that in her present mood America would not risk any entangling alliance, nor an appearance of one, would not even pretend that she might come to Russia's aid in the case of a Japanese attack. Americans turned out to be of a literal turn of mind: when asked about credits, about military and industrial supplies, they kept talking about the old debts. Bullitt grew first impatient then angry with these people who had been so friendly. The height of his indignation was reached in 1935 when, with the Seventh Congress of the Comintern approaching, he asked Litvinov how it could be squared with the solemn Soviet promise not to interfere in American domestic affairs. What Congress? said Litvinov with a grin. He had just seen Stalin and mentioned to him the rumors circulating in Moscow that there was to be a Congress of the Third International. Stalin, he said, had been quite surprised.[6] This was a definite end to what had promised to be a beautiful friendship, and as far as Bullitt was concerned it was the beginning of a furiously anti-Soviet phase that did not abate during the war and led to a personal break with his patron and friend President Roosevelt. The Russians discerned that for the moment the United States could not do anything for them, and in her isolationist mood would not do

6 *Ibid.*, p. 222.

anything *to* them either. So there was no reason to humor them any more than, say, the Rumanians. In fact, at that point the Rumanians were probably more important from the Kremlin's point of view. ☆☆☆

WE have seen how the very depth of the national emergency in 1931–33 served to inhibit any move against Stalin by the ruling oligarchy. By the end of 1933 the worst was over, and there was a certain economic upturn. It is not surprising that it would have occurred to some Party leaders that now if ever was the time to get rid of or restrain this terrible man before he could propel the Party and the nation into another catastrophe. But precisely at this point another danger—this time foreign—loomed on the horizon. Could the Party risk another split and crisis in its leadership when a war in the Far East was imminent, and when Hitler, instead of looking westward for his territorial vindications, was talking openly of Germany's need for living space in the East? The Party had survived the earlier ordeal very largely because of the myth that had been established of Stalin's firmness, wisdom, indeed infallibility. To destroy this myth now risked not only cataclysmic internal consequences, but also the dispelling of the would-be aggressor's hesitations and scruples. To his closest colleagues, Stalin by now appeared as an obsessed and whimsical tyrant. But he was also, especially in the eyes of the average Soviet citizen and of foreign statesmen, a national leader who in an emergency exuded resolution and confidence. We have seen Litvinov's almost panicky assessment of the international situation of the Soviet Union. But Stalin knew that he had to strike a different tone: "We stand for peace and work for it. But we are not afraid of threats and are ready to return blow for blow any aggressor's provocation. He who wants peace and seeks businesslike relations with us will always be welcome. And those who would dare attack our country will receive a crushing blow, so that in the future they will not be tempted to stick their piglike snouts into our Soviet garden."[7] And thus in 1934, as was again to be true in June 1941, the very degree of the nation's danger proved to be Stalin's great luck.

Had the international situation not been what it was, it is at least possible that Stalin's career as dictator would have come to an end in 1933–34. He did not as yet rule the Party through terror. The organs of physical repression used on the country at large, the GPU and the army, were

[7] *The Seventeenth Congress of the All-Union Communist Party* (Moscow, 1934), p. 14.

his to command because he spoke for the Party. But for all his organizational grip on the ruling body he was not invulnerable. A majority of the Central Committee, some forty people or so, could always vote to demote or dismiss him, and he was not as yet in a position to order their arrest and liquidation. The credit he had accumulated with the rank-and-file members as the preserver of the Party's unity after Lenin's death and the conqueror of the Trotskys and Zinovievs had by now been largely dissipated through the horrors of collectivization. There was the "cult of personality," which the Party had built assiduously ever since 1929. But unlike Nazism, under which the Leader came first and the Party second, if it was not indeed incidental to him, the cult was still of recent origin, and to many it was a superimposition or an excrescence on a Party, which stood above any individual. And so while at the beginning of 1934 Stalin's power was considerably greater than Hitler's, it was far from being equally secure. In the last analysis it still depended on his skill as a politician and on his colleagues' conviction that for the moment they could not do without him. For a man of his temper such a situation was intolerable.

This, then, was the background of the fateful year 1934, which for the Communist Party opens and closes with a mystery. We must tackle those mysteries, for in them lies the clue to a fresh tragedy which was to overcome the nation and open a new and terrible chapter in Stalin's career.

The first and basic mystery concerns the Seventeenth Congress of the Communist Party which assembled on January 26, 1934. As the Party history of the Khrushchev period states, "The Congress was the scene of the most excessive praise of his [Stalin's] services."[8] And in the same paragraph there is this tantalizing statement: "The abnormal situation which the personality cult was creating in the Party caused deep concern to some of the Communists, above all to the old Leninist cadres. Many Congress delegates, particularly those who were familiar with Lenin's testament, held that it was time to transfer Stalin from the office of General Secretary to some other post." Here the reader is understandably panting with excitement: What happened next? But, cruelly, history does not satisfy his curiosity and does not inform him what those "many delegates" proposed to do or did. The book goes on to mention the other mystery with which 1934 closed: the murder of Sergei Kirov on December 1, 1934. Incorrigible, the authors again insinuate that there was more to the murder than meets the eye, but do not say what; it was still being investigated (in 1962). As of 1973, the investigation evidently has not yet been concluded. If Stalin was peremptory in decid-

8 *History of the Communist Party of the Soviet Union* (2d rev. ed., in English; Moscow, 1962), p. 486.

370

ing who committed various real and alleged crimes, his successors have certainly set some sort of record in the thoroughness with which they investigate them. All that they say in 1962 about the murder serves merely to tease: "Stalin seized upon it to begin dealing summarily with people who did not suit him." The most consummate writer of mystery stories could do no better than that in concluding his next-to-last chapter. But the last chapter is missing and we are not likely to get it for a long time—if ever; for Khrushchev, the man who was really weaving the plot, was shortly afterward dismissed and since then has departed this world.

In his absence others have tried to finish the story (though not his successors, who decided—logically, from their point of view—that Khrushchev had already said too much about the man who had given them their start in life). Roy Medvedev collected some evidence from unpublished memoirs and recollections of the survivors of the period. His verdict is that there was some plot to get rid of Stalin. "At the very beginning of the Congress, or before it, a group of Party officials including . . . Orjonikidze and Mikoyan had a talk with Kirov touching on the need to replace Stalin. But Kirov would not agree either to get rid of Stalin or to become General Secretary himself. The reports also say that Stalin somehow found out about this discussion."[9] Medvedev then goes on—and this theory was espoused even before by many Western and Russian émigré writers—to attribute the responsibility for Kirov's murder to Stalin.

What happened at the Congress? Here the one indisputable item in the official description (Khrushchev's) is that Stalin was subject during it to "excessive praise." But even the word "praise" is insufficient: Stalin was extolled, worshiped. Open at random to any of some seven hundred pages of the proceedings and you will find at least one worshipful reference to him. If previously Stalin had been hailed as the leader of the Party and the nation, he now became the "leader of the working classes everywhere," ". . . of progressive mankind," "the outstanding genius of the era." It is not too much to say that this is the first occasion on which he was acclaimed as standing above the Party, not merely as an executor of its will and the continuer of Lenin's work, but as an embodiment of the Revolution, of Communism. To quote from Kirov's speech, "It seems to me, comrades, that as the result of this detailed consideration of the report of the Central Committee which has taken place in this Congress, it would be useless to think what kind of resolution to adopt on the report of Comrade Stalin. It will be more correct, and more useful for the work at hand, to accept as Party law all the proposals and

[9] Roy Medvedev, *Let History Judge* (New York, 1971), p. 155.

considerations of Comrade Stalin's speech."[10] And so the Congress adopted this brilliant suggestion, voting, in place of the usual resolution on the report of the Central Committee, "that all the Party organizations be guided in their work by the proposals and tasks presented by Comrade Stalin in his speech."[11] This was unprecedented. It conferred upon Stalin virtually all the powers and attributes possessed by the Congress, the sovereign body of the Communist Party. If before it was barely conceivable that he might be dismissed by the Central Committee, it now became unthinkable: even in theory he was no longer its servant but its master.

What, then, of the alleged plot to remove Stalin as General Secretary? It is clear that there *was* such a plot, and it is also clear why its nature was misrepresented by Khrushchev in those tantalizing insinuations which appear in the Party histories written during his rule. As the First Secretary between 1956 and 1964 unfolded each new installment of the Awful and Unbelievable Crimes of Joseph Stalin he was confronted by the same question: What was the Party, what was the Central Committee (of which Khrushchev became a member in the very same year of 1934) doing all that time? And so there was established for the benefit of the new Party generation the legend, or rather half-truth, that the Central Committee finally stood up to Stalin in 1934 and was ready to remove him when he seized the pretext of Kirov's murder ("whose circumstances are still being investigated") to initiate a reign of terror and decimate this brave Central Committee.

But all the pieces fall into place if we see in the Seventeenth Party Congress what might be called a plot-by-adulation. The Party leaders who by now were fed up with Stalin reached a consensus, for the reasons already mentioned, that it would have been too dangerous for themselves, for the Party, for the country to try to get rid of this great and unbalanced man. The clue is provided in the Khrushchev history: ". . . it was time to transfer Stalin from the office of General Secretary to some other post." No one in possession of his senses could have believed in 1934 that one could "transfer" Stalin the way he had Trotsky or Rykov: appoint him head of the Concessions Bureau or Commissar of Posts and Telegraphs. But conceivably you could play on the man's megalomania and on the undeniable national danger. The "struggle for socialism in Russia" had already been "won" under his "brilliant leadership." Now foreign, military, and state affairs in general cried for his undivided attention. Why should the leading genius of the era, the father of his country, continue to hold the job which in its inception was but that of a chief clerk of the Party? Why should he, now entering his fifty-fifth

---

[10] *The Seventeenth Congress of the All-Union Communist Party*, p. 251.
[11] *Ibid.*, p. 659.

year, expend his energy on day-to-day petty details of running the Party? It was more fitting that a new position, of Party leader or chairman, be created, someone else freeing him from the vexing and exhausting work of the Secretariat. Possibly he might also assume the job of chairman of the Council of Commissars: the national emergency required the hand of the supreme ruler on the tiller of the state.

If this is how it happened, all those hints and suggestions were intended to mislead us. Instead of the Central Committee and the Party being ready in 1934 to smite down the "cult of personality" and remove Stalin, they prostrated themselves before him even more completely than in the past, hoping that the dictator, his megalomania appeased, would be content to become sort of tutelary divinity–elder statesman and leave the management of Party affairs to his faithful comrades at arms. This kind of strategy would bear a startling resemblance to what part of the Chinese Communist hierarchy tried to do with Mao in the early 1960s. In China the enraged dictator replied by unleashing the Cultural Revolution and politically liquidating his solicitous admirers. Stalin, when he became convinced in 1936–37 that the adulation of the Seventeenth Congress had been a cover-up for treacherous designs (which, of course, was not quite true), reacted with savage terror: of the 1966 delegates to the Congress, 1108 were arrested; of the 139 Central Committee members and alternates elected at it, 98 were shot. They contributed to their own doom: had Stalin's stature not been built up at the Congress to the point where he stood above the Party, it is unlikely that he could have undertaken or succeeded with such a decimation of the ruling group.

But at the time, and possibly genuinely, he showed signs of going along with the plans for his "transfer." He had been General Secretary for twelve years, he was nearly fifty-five. His inordinate suspicion must have been allayed by the extraordinary tribute to him at the Congress. One by one, former oppositionists, "right" and "left," mounted the tribune to denigrate themselves and to grovel at his feet. Kamenev's performance was typical: "I want to say from this tribune that I con- sider the Kamenev who fought the Party between 1925 and 1933 to be dead, and I don't want to go on dragging behind me that old corpse. . . . This era in which we live . . . will be known in history as the era of Stalin, just as the preceding era entered history as the time of Lenin."[12] Bukharin hailed him "as the field marshal of the proletarian forces, the best of the best."[13] And it would be tedious to describe the efforts

[12] *The Seventeenth Congress of the All-Union Communist Party*, p. 521.

[13] Poor Bukharin in denouncing Hitlerism quoted a Nazi philosopher who wrote, "The nation needs priest kings who spill blood, blood . . . who strike and slaughter," and he contrasted this barbarism with the humane philosophy which prevailed in the Soviet Union.

made in the same direction by his henchmen, and just plain delegates, as well as foreign Communist guests. For the moment he must have been almost convinced the Party loved him: this was the first Congress at which there was complete unity, this was the "congress of victors," as Kirov said in a felicitous phrase. Nobody was indiscreet enough to ask who were the defeated.[14]

The dictator was, for him, in a generous mood. Some of the erstwhile oppositionists were elected to the leading organs: Pyatakov, full member; Bukharin, Rykov, and Tomsky, alternates in the Central Committee. The Congress laughed with as much as at Radek, currently an authoritative journalistic spokesman on foreign affairs, when he recounted how he had been cured of Trotskyism. Some may have wondered at his handsome tribute to the Party. "All that we have gone through in the last years has shown how, having destroyed the freedom of the press and all other bourgeois freedoms, the working class under the Party's leadership has erected such freedoms for the creative activity of the masses of workers and peasants that the world had not seen before." But he got away with it. By Stalinist standards the Congress was a veritable love fest. The delegates must really have felt that the worst was over—with the peasant subdued, the economy on the upturn, the former oppositionists put on probation—that, as Stalin was to say later, "Life has become better, comrades, life has become gayer." Now, if only this terrible man would confine himself to frustrating the designs of the Japanese and German militarists, and to making occasional lofty theoretical pronouncements befitting the Leader.

That Stalin may have contemplated laying down his *administrative*

14 We cannot admit the story, or rather stories, which have circulated ever since the Congress that in the election to the Central Committee Stalin got fewer votes than anyone else. *The Socialist Courier*, published in Paris by the Mensheviks, reported on February 25 that Stalin got fewer votes than two others, the most votes going to Kalinin. Medvedev reports (p. 156) the recollections of a delegate that two hundred seventy delegates voted against Stalin, as against only three who crossed out Kirov's name, and that Stalin was elected only because there were as many candidates as members to be elected. But the story is suspect, since the alleged recollections show unfamiliarity with the voting procedures for the Central Committee. The voting was secret, and ever since 1923 the announced results had not included the number of votes received by successful candidates. Only one list was proposed. Delegates could then show their disapproval by crossing out names on the ballot, and the candidate crossed out on at least half of them would fail of election. There were about twelve hundred people voting, and for anyone to be disqualified his name would have had to be crossed out on some six hundred ballots rather than two hundred seventy. There is every reason to believe that the election of the Central Committee was unanimous. Medvedev's story is weakened further, as he acknowledges, by the fact that the Central Committee members who were elected comprised Stalin's most recent favorites, such as Nikolai Yezhov. Why should a hitherto obscure choice of the dictator get more votes in the election than he himself? But there are also good reasons why someone would have been interested in spreading rumors of Kirov's popularity with the delegates and dealing a setback to Stalin.

duties is also suggested by another fact. He had been confirmed as General Secretary of the Central Committee following the Sixteenth Congress, in 1930. Since 1932, there had developed the custom of decrees issued jointly by the Council of Commissars and the Central Committee. They would be countersigned first—a nice sense of protocol—by Molotov, Chairman of the Council, and then by Stalin, identified only as "Secretary of the Central Committee." This was undoubtedly with an eye to the possibility of someone else's assuming the primary responsibility for the Secretariat without inheriting the momentous title so clearly identified with his person.

Following the Congress, an official announcement of the meeting of the freshly elected Central Committee omitted the hitherto sacramental phrase: "The Central Committee confirmed Comrade Stalin as General Secretary." But we certainly cannot interpret it as Stalin's having been defeated in the Central Committee. *He* chose not to emphasize the existence of the office, so that in the case of his resignation from the Secretariat, no one would draw wrong conclusions or expect someone else to succeed him as the *General* Secretary. That his dominance over the Party was now enhanced is clearly indicated by the fact that the list of Politburo and Secretariat members was published, not in alphabetical order as after the previous Party Congresses, but in order of importance with his name of course coming first and others ranked in terms of their standing in the Party. The list of the secretaries went: Stalin, Kaganovich, Kirov (with the stipulation that he was being retained as secretary of the Leningrad organization), Andrei Zhdanov (who unlike Kirov resigned his territorial secretaryship of the Gorki region on his elevation to the Central Secretariat).

And thus we turn to the Kirov mystery. It is natural that in casting about for his successor in the Secretariat, Stalin would have thought of Kirov. His main deputy in Party affairs had been Kaganovich. But Kaganovich had been in the Central Secretariat since 1928. Stalin did not believe in leaving officials for very long in a position from which they might build an independent power base, and Kaganovich as one of the most brutal enforcers of collectivization was not too popular in Party circles. He was also a Jew, and by now Stalin was already in his intensely Russian phase. Kirov, on the other hand, was Russian, very much so in physiognomy and manner. He had been a faithful servant of the dictator; after rendering yeoman service in the Caucasus, where he struck up a great friendship with Orjonikidze, he was in 1926 transferred to the then crucial segment of the front in the struggle against the opposition—Leningrad. Here he purged the Party of its hitherto dominant Zinovievite elements and otherwise displayed an exemplary Stalinist zeal. It would have been quite in Stalin's style to authorize Mikoyan and Orjonikidze at the time of the Seventeenth Congress to

375

canvass other Party notables about the possibility of Kirov's eventually taking over his duties in the Secretariat. He might have genuinely contemplated elevating his Leningrad satrap to the principal administrative post in the Party. And it would be interesting to find out who his dear colleagues thought could take over his job. It was natural and sensible for Kirov to resist the idea of such a dangerous promotion. He knew his boss. Therefore, though selected to the Secretariat, he begged to be allowed to retain his provincial post. For the time being, Stalin agreed to let Kirov stay in Leningrad but indicated that before long he would insist on his transferring to Moscow. Kirov knew the predicament he was in: Moscow meant a dangerous advancement, the probability of arousing this terrible man's suspicion, not to mention the unavoidable hostility of those he would then outrank, like Kaganovich and Molotov.[15] But to keep refusing Stalin's offers of advancement meant also the danger of losing his favor. He returned from the Seventeenth Congress to his beloved Leningrad quite ill, and perhaps this was more than a simple case of influenza.

The spring and summer of 1934 must have reinforced a casual observer's impression that as far as internal policies were concerned the U.S.S.R. had turned the corner and the worst of the repression was over. It certainly could be taken as a reassuring sign that the dreaded GPU was now renamed the Commissariat of Internal Affairs.[16] A skeptic might have pointed out that the previous change of name, from Cheka to GPU, had not affected the sinister character and operations of the political police, and that the Commissariat was headed by former GPU officials, notably its former head and now Commissar, Henryk Yagoda. But the average citizen in his search for crumbs of comfort saw a good sign even in this change in nomenclature. Russia was now trying to move closer to the Western democracies—the danger of fascism was growing. It was reasonable to expect more liberal policies at home now that the public opinion in Britain and France was being courted, and now that Litvinov was so eloquently presenting the U.S.S.R. as a peace-loving law-abiding state—so different from Germany, with its open threats and its *publicized* concentration camps.

The war with Japan had not come, though the Japanese and their Manchurian puppets were subjecting the Soviet-owned Manchurian Railroad to increasing chicaneries.[17] But the German danger *was* grow-

15 In the list of the Politburo members after the Seventeenth Congress, Stalin's name was followed by Molotov's, Kaganovich's, and Voroshilov's. Kirov was ranked eighth in the list of ten.
16 The Russian initials for this were NKVD.
17 The Soviet Union inherited from Tsarist Russia the Manchurian and East Chinese Railway, which also included land and industrial holdings. It was to be sold at much below its real value to the puppet government of Manchukuo in 1935, reclaimed in 1945, and finally yielded, this time to Mao's China, in 1952.

ing. And when it came to politics and propaganda, the Nazis showed that they had learned a lesson or two from the Communists. Thus by now all the competing political parties and organizations in Germany had been liquidated or absorbed by the National Socialist Party. To be sure, in some respects they were slow learners. There must have been some chuckling in GPU-NKVD circles when Hitler staged his show trial in Leipzig to prove that the Communists were responsible for burning the Reichstag in 1933. Its star victim was to be the then Comintern representative in Germany, the Bulgarian George Dimitrov. But far from confessing, Dimitrov fought with and baited the Nazi dignitaries who appeared as witnesses, goading none other than Hermann Göring into a most unseemly and embarrassing outburst of rage and threats. And so, though the actual incendiary, the halfwitted Marinus van der Lubbe, was sentenced to death, Dimitrov had to be released. Now covered with world fame as a man who had unmasked Nazi "justice," Dimitrov was back in the U.S.S.R. and slated for big things in the Comintern.

But any illusions as to the Nazis' incompetence in the totalitarian craft were dispelled by the famous "Night of Long Knives"—June 30, 1934—when Hitler slaughtered the high command of his private army, the SA, throwing in for good measure a few inconvenient politicians and generals. He thus got rid of some of his more unruly and potentially dangerous supporters and cemented his alliance with the Reichswehr. (The Führer's delicate moral sensitivity had also been outraged by the discovery, evidently sudden though he had known them for years, that his chief victims were homosexuals.)

No, this man had style and resolution, and no one was going to snatch power from his hands. The pleasing vision of a Communist Germany now faded away and was replaced by the grim one of Hitler in a few years disposing of the most powerful and efficient military-industrial machine in Europe. Could Britain and France, yesterday's "imperialist bandits," today's "peaceloving countries," be counted upon to stand firmly against Hitler? The German dictator had fooled the Communists in yet another respect. Before 1934 it was fondly imagined that his anti-Communist tirades were mostly for propaganda purposes and his real territorial ambitions lay in the West and against Poland. But now Hitler was putting himself forth as defender of Western civilization against Communism. He signed a nonaggression agreement with Poland and his message was finding a sympathetic echo in some circles in Britain and France. Any attempts on the Soviet Union's part to keep relations with Germany tolerable had for the time being been frustrated. In late 1933 Russia's clandestine military collaboration with Germany, which had gone on ever since 1922, was terminated, and the

377

secret German military installations on Soviet soil, which enabled Weimar Germany to circumvent provisions of the Versailles Treaty, were shut down. The Germans now were rearming openly and no longer needed them, and in view of Hitler's threats it would have been folly for the Russians to tolerate German military advisers and observers in their midst.

It is the measure of the ordeal through which Russia passed between 1929 and 1933 that the threat of a foreign war was almost welcome since it was credited with making the regime more humane and rational. Large-scale deportations of peasants had ceased; a largely peasant Red Army would have to defend Russia and Communism. The hunt for wreckers and saboteurs slackened. It could be taken as a good sign that the newspapers in addition to their constant report of new triumphs of industrialization gave an inordinate amount of space to the First Congress of Soviet Writers. The erstwhile sinners Bukharin and Radek were featured prominently at the Congress, at which they gave authoritative talks on the Party "line" in literature and the arts. It was another demonstration of Russia's link with Western culture, as foreign guests to the Congress repeatedly emphasized. In Germany the Nazis were publicly burning books. Here in Russia high officials of the Party and the state reaffirmed the importance of the arts. You would not find a Communist saying, as did the Nazi hero of a drama popular at the time in the Third Reich, "When I hear the word culture, I undo the safety on my gun." Stalin pointed out the difference between the two systems in his talk with H. G. Wells. The English writer mentioned how the International PEN Club, of which he was president, propagated the right to freedom of all opinions including those which clashed with existing political systems. He was not sure whether this salutary principle was being acknowledged in the Soviet Union. Oh yes, said Stalin, among Communists this was called "self-criticism," and it was very widely practiced in the U.S.S.R.

The dictator's behavior since the Seventeenth Congress lent some substance to the rumors that he was going to lay down his administrative duties in favor of loftier tasks. His speeches and public appearances had been infrequent. He was displaying an increasing interest in historical and pedagogical problems, which was perhaps a good sign. His colleagues in the Politburo must have shaken their heads, though, when in July they received a rather unusual communication from him. He had learned, Stalin wrote, that the Party theoretical journal *Bolshevik* was about to print an old pamphlet of Frederick Engels' on the foreign policy of Tsarism. He thought it would be most unsuitable. What did they think? Engels' piece was an attack on Russia as a fortress of reaction and barbarism. To be sure, this was Tsarist Russia he was talking about, but still hardly suitable reading for a wide audience in this day and age. Stalin more than implied that the socialist patriarch was something of a wrecker. Engels had on another occasion written that in the case of a Russo-German war, all progressive people should be for Germany, and if "Russia begins a war—forward against the Russians and their allies, whoever they may be." His colleagues must have appreciated Stalin's point and implication, but they may have wondered why the man who started on his own a revolution in Russian agriculture needed their agreement to ban an article.

This must have been also the conclusion of the would-be reluctant successor Kirov when in late summer he received the summons from Stalin to join him in vacation on the Black Sea. Kirov could not have been enchanted: troubled by insomnia and fatigue, he had looked forward to a hunting expedition with his beloved dogs, certainly a more relaxing prospect. But one did not refuse Stalin's invitations. On his arrival in Sochi there was another surprise: Stalin and his other house-guest, Zhdanov, were going through various history textbooks, noting their deficiencies and needed corrections. Kirov, though he helplessly pleaded that he was no historian, was drafted into this editorial work. Hitler's guests were made to suffer endless tirades and had to fight off drowsiness, but it was worse with Stalin: visitors must have felt that they were being subjected to a constant examination and scrutiny; an incautious phrase, lack of enthusiasm for an idea of their host's, or, conversely, excessive rapture, and the man's terrible suspicion would be aroused, with perhaps fatal consequences for the hapless guest. Stalin must have also relished having in such close proximity and under his vigilant gaze two people who, whether they aspired to it or not, were currently considered competitors for the principal role in the Secretariat. For all the beauty of the surroundings, not one's idea of a restful vacation.

After partaking of his gracious hospitality, Stalin desired Kirov to go to Kazakhstan to help the local Party organization with the completion of collectivization and the harvest. Then, he indicated, Kirov should assume full-time duties in the Secretariat. Kirov balked once more: Would Stalin allow him to remain in Leningrad until the end of the Second Five-Year Plan, i.e., until 1937?[18]

Kirov spent September in what could not have been very congenial work in Kazakhstan. Hundreds of thousands of Kazakhs had starved in the last two years, and the heat, as he wrote his friends in Leningrad, was insufferable. He tried to avoid any undue prominence and warned the local organization not to expose him to any festive receptions or

---

[18] Most Western authors who hold to the theory of Stalin's role in Kirov's assassination believe he resisted Kirov's move to Moscow, while Soviet writers who espouse or imply the same theory see him insisting on the move.

special tributes. In October, to his undoubted relief, he could finally get back to his little kingdom and resume rule over Leningrad.

He was in Moscow a few days before his tragic end. The Central Committee held a meeting, November 25-28. The decisions reached seemed to emphasize the return of "normalcy" to the country. The rationing of bread and flour was to end in 1935. The special political departments in the Machine Tractor Stations were abolished. From now on the director of each station was to have a political deputy subject to the regular local Party organs. Again this could be taken as a sign of a certain normalization of the situation in the countryside—for the time being, no new "offensives." The peasant would be left in peace.

After the meeting Kirov spent another day in Moscow with his friend Orjonikidze and, despite his plea to stay longer, on November 29 boarded the train to Leningrad and his doom.

On December 1, having worked late into the night on November 30 (this being the pattern now in high Soviet circles), Kirov got up late. There was going to be a conference of Party officials in the evening. Lachrymose Soviet accounts of his last moments agree on one fact: before setting out for his office at 4 P.M., he extracted a promise from his wife that she would serve his favorite dish for supper: cabbage dumplings.[19] But beyond that there is considerable disagreement. One version has Kirov leaving for his office in his limousine.[20] Another would have Kirov walk for several blocks and then be picked up by his car.[21] At any rate, he arrived at the Smolny Institute of October Revolution fame, now Party headquarters, at about 4:30. "Having entered the building, Kirov stopped, hearing behind him the steps of his bodyguard. He smiled—'He finally let me be'—and without waiting started for the third floor."[22] This melodramatic detail is supposed to be very sinister, in line with the whole Khrushchev version of the murder. It is in fact ridiculous. How could the author know what Kirov thought a moment before he was shot to death? More important, why should a bodyguard accompany him within the Party headquarters, access to which was by pass? But it is indisputable that just as he was entering the office of Michael Chudov, second secretary of the Leningrad Party district, Kirov was shot. He died instantly.

His assassin, caught on the spot, was identified as Leonid Nikolayev, born in 1904, a Party member and former official of the Leningrad

[19] Alas, even this homely detail, testimony to the Communist martyr's simple tastes, is suspect. He must have expected to work late and to grab a bite with his subordinates.
[20] S. Krasnikov, *Sergei Kirov* (Moscow, 1964), p. 200.
[21] S. Sinelnikov, *Kirov* (Moscow, 1964), p. 363.
[22] Krasnikov, p. 200.

branch of the Commissariat of Inspection.[23] He had been excluded from the Party earlier the same year but then readmitted. It is thus idle to ask, as does a Soviet defector and former political police official, "How did he manage to sneak into the heavily guarded Smolny?"[24] In the pre-terror days a Party member would easily be admitted into its regional office.

Political assassination is a highly contagious business. In any society, it is fair to say, there are a number of people who for political or psychotic reasons, or usually a combination of both, contemplate such a step, and their resolve may be triggered by news of a successful venture of this kind. Stalin's first concern had to be to impose a ferocious terror which would nip such an infection at the start. Even before leaving for Leningrad on the evening of December 1 to investigate the murder, accompanied by Molotov, Voroshilov, and Kaganovich, Stalin had Yenukidze, secretary of the Presidium of the Executive Committee of the Congress of Soviets (the Soviet parliament), sign a savage directive: all investigation of terroristic acts was to be speeded up; judicial organs were not to hold up the execution of death sentences for such acts or attempts since no appeals would be considered. Death sentences would have to be put into effect immediately. Needless to say, the decree was thoroughly unconstitutional in terms of state and Party law. The Presidium had not even assembled to consider the law, and since its chairman, Kalinin, was evidently not around to sign it, it was illegal even on the face of it. And there was no time even to consult the Politburo, which approved it formally only two days later. Yet even this decree was deemed insufficient. A more precise instruction, issued on December 5, specified that all investigation of terroristic acts and attempts was to be completed within ten days, indictments were to be handed to the accused only on the day before the trial, the court proceedings were to take place without contesting parties,[25] and absolutely no appeals were to be considered. And to show that the law was not an idle threat, newspapers on December 6 carried the news of the execution of several dozen people in Leningrad and Moscow. It was not even pretended that these people had anything to do with the Kirov murder: they had already been held for some time on various charges of wrecking or espionage on behalf of Poland and Latvia.[26]

Was Kirov's murder an isolated act of a single demented individual?

---

[23] *Pravda*, December 2, 1934. The Commissariat was abolished in January of the same year.

[24] Alexander Orlov, *The Secret History of Stalin's Crimes* (New York, 1953), p. 3.

[25] Why, then, bother with handing the accused the indictment?

[26] It was never explained why tiny Latvia should have maintained a spy network within the territory of its powerful neighbor.

It would have been worth the life of any Soviet magistrate to sign a report presenting such a version of Nikolayev's deed. And not only Stalin or the NKVD but the average Soviet citizen would have found such an explanation, no matter what the weight of evidence behind it, preposterous. By now they were accustomed to living in a society in which there was no such thing as an industrial accident, no such thing as the failure of a collective farm to deliver its quota—but, rather, sabotage and wrecking, conscious plots by the class enemy. To believe that it was Nikolayev alone who had the idea to shoot one of the highest officials of the Party—that was ridiculous.

Beyond discovering the real plot, which *had* to be there, Stalin was also interested in what might be called the educational aspect of the murder. What was the best way to capitalize politically on the assassination? What if it were called the work of foreign agents? At the time this would have been awkward: the U.S.S.R. was trying to draw closer to France and Britain, had not quite given up trying to reach an agreement with Germany and Japan. White émigrés and the Paris Mensheviks? Hardly worth bothering with. On the other hand, there were cogent reasons to try to connect the murder with the erstwhile intraparty opposition. To be sure, that opposition, "left" and "right," had disarmed itself entirely (to use Stalin's words) by the time of the Seventeenth Party Congress. But the murder might give them ideas. Also it had taken place in Leningrad (conveniently), a former bailiwick of Zinoviev's. The "rich threads of treason," to use Stalin's phrase of 1919, would no doubt lead to Zinoviev. But it would be unreasonable to stop there. How about Zinoviev's political twin, Kamenev? And hadn't the two of them at one time formed an anti-Party (i.e., anti-Stalin) group with Trotsky?

On December 27 a long statement signed by Andrei Vishinsky, Deputy Procurator of the Soviet Union, revealed the existence and unmasking of a terrorist "Leningrad Center" composed, in addition to Nikolayev, of several former Komsomol officials of the Zinoviev era. The conspirators had planned to kill Stalin as well as Kirov, it was said. There were additional touches: through the Latvian consul the wretches had been furnished with funds that came from none other than Trotsky. The trouble was that most of the accused did not want to confess to this crime, and since the law provided for a speedy investigation and trial, there was really no time to work on them so that they would change their minds and recite a convincing confession in court. Also, Nikolayev was obviously unbalanced, and who knows what he might say? So they were tried behind closed doors. On December 30 the papers announced the execution of all the accused.

Though we shall return to the matter, we must sketch briefly here the future development of the question, Who was behind the murder of

Sergei Kirov? In January 1935 Zinoviev, Kamenev, and some of their former political allies were tried for *moral* complicity in the murder. They were all sentenced: Zinoviev to ten years, Kamenev to five. Someone must have felt that this differentiation was unfair to Zinoviev, and so Kamenev was retried and also given ten years. In 1936 the more or less same cast, with a few other ex-oppositionists thrown in, appeared in the first of the three great open purge trials of the Bolshevik Old Guard. The proceedings, in August 1936, were public this time, and the sixteen accused confessed to the planning and instigation of Kirov's murder. For good measure, it was also established (to quote the verdict) that "not confining themselves to the assassination of Comrade Kirov, the Trotskyite Zinovievite center prepared a number of terroristic acts against Comrades Stalin, Voroshilov, Zhdanov, L. M. Kaganovich, Orjonikidze, Kosior, and Postyshev."[27] At the second trial, in January 1937, in which Pyatakov and Radek were the star accused, Kirov's murder was barely alluded to. This was more than made up in the third, final, and most famous spectacle, in March 1938, which featured Bukharin and Rykov as well as the man who had presumably prepared materials for the 1936 show trial, Henryk Yagoda. And now the final Stalinist version of the murder of his faithful comrade-in-arms was revealed: not only the former "left opposition" but the "right" one as well, Bukharin and Rykov, were in on the murder. To quote from the verdict of the court:

> As the preliminary investigation and the Court proceedings . . . have established, the dastardly assassination of S. M. Kirov on December 1, 1934, was organized in accordance with a decision of the "Bloc of Rights and Trotskyites." A direct part in the organization of this terrorist act was taken by the accused Yagoda, who gave special instructions to his accomplices working in the Leningrad Administration of the People's Commissariat of Internal Affairs not to hinder the perpetration of this crime.[28]

Yagoda's personal assistant, Paul Bulanov, also accused and subsequently shot, filled in alleged details: Yagoda acted through the deputy head of the Leningrad branch of the NKVD, Ivan Zaporozhets. The local agents arrested on *one* occasion a man acting suspiciously in the vicinity of the Smolny. In his briefcase there were found a gun and a diary. This was Nikolayev, and on Zaporozhets' instructions he was released to proceed with his dark designs. Zaporozhets was also instru-

[27] *The Case of the Trotskyite-Zinovievite Terrorist Center*, published by the People's Commissariat of Justice (Moscow, 1936), p. 176. Molotov's absence from that exclusive list led to rumors that he was in disgrace.
[28] *The Case of the Anti-Soviet "Bloc of Rights and Trotskyites" Heard Before the Military Collegium of the Supreme Court of the U.S.S.R.* (Moscow, 1938), p. 796.

mental in arranging an "accident" in which Kirov's head bodyguard, Borisov, was killed just as he was being brought to be questioned by Stalin on the murder.[29]

Now we turn to Khrushchev's version. In his "secret" speech of 1956, when for the first time Stalin was attacked, he said the following:

A month and a half before the killing Nikolayev was arrested on the grounds of suspicious behavior, but he was released and not even searched. It is an unusually suspicious circumstance that when the NKVD official assigned to protect Kirov was being brought for an interrogation, on December 2, 1934, he was killed in a car accident in which no other occupants of the car were harmed.[30]

By the time he came to refer again to the murder, in 1961, Khrushchev must have realized that he had not done his homework properly in the first version. He had stated that Nikolayev had not even been searched, but Bulanov's testimony had spoken of a gun and a diary (presumably expressing his intention to do Kirov in) found on his person. And so now, "It is worthy of notice that the future killer of Kirov had been detained by the agents twice before in the vicinity of the Smolny, and they found a weapon on him."[31]

For all the resources and archives at his disposal Khrushchev was unable to improve in 1961 on the version of the murder given out by Stalinist justice in 1938 except for that one detail—Nilolayev had been detained twice rather than once before he killed Kirov—and it must be connected to his slip in the 1956 speech.

Who lies? Everybody. It is admittedly impossible for someone writing in 1973 in Cambridge, Massachusetts, to establish the circumstances of a murder committed in Leningrad on December 1, 1934. But there are certain probabilities as well as facts.

Robert Conquest, in his masterful survey of Stalin's terror,[32] and Roy Medvedev in his book endorsed the explanation at which Khrushchev seemed to be hinting: it was Stalin who was behind the murder, acting through Yagoda, who issued the appropriate instructions to Zaporozhets.[33] The reason was twofold: Stalin's envy of Kirov's popularity in

[29] Borisov was presumably the man who abandoned Kirov as he entered the Smolny on the fateful occasion.

[30] Quoted in Bertram D. Wolfe, *Khrushchev and Stalin's Ghost* (New York, 1957), p. 130.

[31] *The Twenty-second Congress of the Communist Party of the Soviet Union* (Moscow, 1962), II, 583.

[32] Robert Conquest, *The Great Terror* (New York, 1968).

[33] This individual, along with other officials of the Leningrad NKVD, was tried *in camera* in 1935 on charges of neglect of duty in failing to prevent the murder. They were sentenced to several years of penal labor, but in the Great Purge of 1937–38 they were all shot.

the Party and his need for a pretext to unleash a bloody repression of Communist notables.

Assuming that Stalin wanted to get rid of Kirov, would he have chosen this way to do it? He had good reasons not to trust Yagoda. In 1928 Bukharin, in his conversation with Kamenev, had stated that Yagoda was sympathetic to his own and Rykov's position on the peasantry. We know also from other sources that the head of the NKVD was friendly with Bukharin. In September 1936 Stalin dismissed Yagoda, suspecting him of protecting people who were against him. In 1938 he sent him to his death. Could he in 1934 have entrusted him with such a terrible mission? Short of assassination, there was in 1934 only one eventuality through which Stalin himself could be overturned, and this was precisely Yagoda's communicating a secret of this nature to other Politburo members. It is a very clumsy and dangerous way to get rid of somebody: to instruct the chief of police, whom one does not trust, to instruct his subordinate not to interfere with the would-be assassin who had already wandered (twice?) into the arms of the police. Only after Yagoda was replaced as head of the NKVD by a man Stalin himself had trained, Yezhov, did Stalin abandon any restraint in using assassination as an instrument of his whim and vengeance.

It is unlikely that Stalin would have wanted to establish the precedent of a successful assassination attempt against a high Soviet official.[34] Anyone familiar with the history of the Russian revolutionary movement must know how intoxicating the news of a successful political assassination can be to victims of political oppression. "A sixteen-year-old student was said to have declared, 'They have killed Kirov; now let them kill Stalin,'" states one of the many similar reports found in the archives of the Smolensk Party organization.[35] One finds there also reports of Komsomol members from rural regions singing a ditty, "When Kirov was killed, they allowed free trade in bread; when Stalin is killed, all the kolkhozes will be divided up." There was every conceivable reason for Stalin to try to keep assassination as a state monopoly, rather than to encourage the notion that it could be the product of private enterprise.

As to his real feelings concerning Kirov, we cannot go beyond conjecture. It was entirely in Stalin's character to grow suspicious of the man whom shortly before he had considered for the principal post in the Party and of whom he had personally been very fond. That Kirov had

---

[34] Many people were subsequently made to confess to unsuccessful designs of this kind against Stalin, Molotov, etc. The only allegedly successful murder attempts which the regime chose to publicize were those by doctors attending high Soviet officials, and these, of course, could not offer much encouragement to the average person entertaining murderous designs.

[35] Merle Fainsod, *Smolensk Under Soviet Rule* (Cambridge, Mass., 1958), p. 422.

been a leader of the "liberal wing of the Politburo," that he was popular with the Party to the extent that he aroused Stalin's jealousy—all these are later reconstructions with no basis in established fact. It is said that the ovation accorded to Kirov at the Seventeenth Congress rivaled Stalin's, but this is certainly not supported by reading the report of the Congress. The average delegate's enthusiasm was rationed in accordance with the given notable's proximity to and assumed standing with the Leader, and so Kirov, just like Voroshilov or Molotov, received the quota of cheers prescribed for "a close comrade-in-arms of Great Stalin"—"loud, long-lasting applause, a warm ovation by the whole gathering, everybody stands up." And it is extravagant to claim that assassination was the only means by which Stalin could get rid of Kirov without encountering Party opposition. The average Party member, unless situated in Kirov's principality, Leningrad, had no particular reason to form any special impression of him. It is quite probable that he was popular in a negative sense, i.e., not hated and feared as much as Molotov and especially Kaganovich, who had been associated with the worst incidents of repression during the collectivization drive. And Stalin, even when his power was considerably less, had still managed to demote and humiliate without too much trouble people as genuinely popular with the Communists as Bukharin and Tomsky. Why, especially after he had been enthroned as a Marxian divinity at the Seventeenth Congress, should he have had trouble with Kirov?

Only in 1936 did Stalin's suspicions about the whole train of events surrounding the Seventeenth Congress ripen into a murderous rage, and it is then that he may have retrospectively come to question Kirov's role in 1934. Within the next two years Zhdanov, who had succeeded Kirov in Leningrad, purged the local organization of all of his predecessor's lieutenants. But this was not very different from what was happening elsewhere in the U.S.S.R.

In his artful hints Khrushchev was of course aiming to titillate the Party about Stalin's possible role in the murder. But he had also a more practical aim in mind. Among his colleagues and enemies on the Politburo in 1956 were still Molotov, Kaganovich, and Malenkov. In 1934 all three of them had reason to fear Kirov's coming to Moscow and becoming Stalin's principal aide. Molotov had been Stalin's right-hand man in state affairs, Kaganovich in the Party's; Malenkov was a rising figure in the Cadres Division of the Secretariat. In 1961, after he managed to overcome their plot against him and to remove them from high positions, Khrushchev hinted openly at their complicity. "There are many, many unclarified circumstances of this [Kirov's] and other affairs of a similar kind. . . . You can imagine how difficult it was to investigate such problems when you had in the Presidium of the Central Committee people who themselves had been guilty of abuse of power and of mass repressions."[36] Conceivably in 1961 Khrushchev was laying the groundwork for yet another trial of Kirov's "real" assassins, this time with Kaganovich and Malenkov in star roles. But his colleagues must have objected. They presumably never heard of the American baseball immortal Satchel Paige, but his words appear to have guided their attitude toward further revelations of the crimes of the Stalin era: "Don't look behind yourself, something might be catching up with you."

Without their help, then, what can we say about the background of the Kirov murder? The hypothesis of what might be called the Renaissance type of crime cannot be supported by facts and reasonable conjectures at our disposal.[37] We begin with one undeniable fact: Nikolayev's shot. And here is another: in no subsequent trial was Nikolayev's own deposition cited or so much as alluded to. One might well have expected Vishinsky at one point or another to say, "Here is what Nikolayev said and here is what establishes his link with Zinoviev, Yagoda, Bukharin, et al." But he did not. The "evidence" consisted solely of the confessions of the various accused, and to what should have been the key point of the prosecution, the testimony of the undoubted murderer and of those tried and executed with him on December 29, there was no reference at all.[38] The assumption then must be that the assassination of Kirov was an act conceived and executed by a single

[36] *The Twenty-second Congress of the Communist Party of the Soviet Union,* iii, 584.

[37] In his *Civilization of the Renaissance* Jacob Burckhardt cites the case of the leading citizens of an Italian city-state who were discussing how to reward a mercenary leader who led their forces to a victory. It was finally decided to arrange for his assassination and then have him proclaimed the patron saint of the city.

[38] Why, it may be asked, was Nikolayev's testimony not tampered with, following his death, or simply falsely quoted? Here we come to a very curious and at first glance inexplicable characteristic of Stalinist justice. There was not the slightest compunction in securing false confessions and depositions through torture or blackmail. Yet there was great reluctance to tamper with actual documents. One would think it would have been a relatively simple matter to forge a letter of Trotsky to connect him with any of the innumerable crimes to which he was linked in the 1936–38 trials. Yet this was never done. Letters from and to Trotsky were mentioned in the trials, never produced. In fact, very few written documents apart from confessions were used. But what appears at first a strange delicacy on the part of Soviet justice conforms well to the "method in madness" so characteristic of Stalin. One must keep control over the facts, be able to distinguish what might be called real reality from the "objective" one. It is the latter which required in 1936 that Zinoviev and Kamenev, and in 1938 also Bukharin and Yagoda, be connected with the murder. And so one can well imagine Stalin telling Vishinsky and the NKVD to get their confessions but leave the Nikolayev file alone. It was the same with foreign policy: one "knows" that the capitalists are planning an attack on the U.S.S.R., that Hitler wants to detach the Ukraine, Poland Byelorussia, etc. But this must not get in the way of finding out the actual dispositions and plans of the German and Japanese general staffs, the chances of coming to an accommodation with the rulers of Germany and Poland. This was, to be sure, institutionalized paranoia, and even Stalin found it difficult to keep the two realities from getting mixed up. But he tried.

individual. Nikolayev and the people connected with him had been connected with Zinoviev, but only in the sense that any Communist who had been resident in Leningrad prior to 1926 was connected with the man who had dominated the city and the region from the October Revolution to his political downfall in December 1925. Official post-Stalin literature has dropped any reference to Zinoviev-Kamenev-Trotsky complicity in the affair, and though this might seem premature in view of the fact that "the circumstances are still being investigated" it is still convincing proof of the absurdity of the 1935 charges—not to mention later ones—especially since the three men remain in exceedingly bad odor. ☆☆☆

THE reverberation of the Kirov murder set the stage for what might be described as the preliminary phase of the Great Terror, 1934–36. The reports which filtered to Stalin from all regions of Russia must have contained material similar to that already quoted from the Smolensk Party archive: young people's expressions of glee at Nikolayev's deed, regrets that it was not Stalin who met the bullet, and incredulity that people with the revolutionary past of Zinoviev and Trotsky could have become enemies of the people. This last element was undoubtedly instrumental in setting the stage for the Great Purge trials.

Stalin might well have deluded himself that, while hated by the class enemy and his rivals in the Party, the great adventure of industrialization and the building of a new Russia won him the hearts of the young. And now this! Well, the younger generation would soon hear from the mouths of those alleged heroes of the Revolution how they plotted, assassinated, and wrecked, how the suffering of the last few years was the result not of collectivization but of sabotage and dark machinations of Trotskyites and Zinoviev. In his preoccupation with the national economy and foreign affairs, Stalin had perhaps neglected his role as the educator of the new generation. Now he would have to make up for this neglect. The youthful propensity toward rebelliousness against established authority would be combated by capitalizing on youth's need to believe, to see the world in terms of heroes and villains. Such a world would now be painted in garish colors. There would be the realm of darkness, with the famous revolutionaries revealed as politically bankrupt, dissimulators, people who had plotted against Lenin or worked for foreign powers. Even the most skeptical and sophisticated among the young would come to despise them: even if not guilty, why did they confess, how could a real revolutionary behave in such a craven and cowardly fashion? The minds of the growing generation, Stalin must have reflected ruefully, had been affected by tales of revolutionary heroics, of young people throwing bombs and shooting Tsarist ministers. (Zhdanov complained openly about the undue prominence and praise given to such figures as Zhelyabov and Perovskaya, who plotted the assassination of Alexander II, and other famous terrorists. This lends credence to the reports that Nikolayev rationalized and explained his deed in such terms.) Those terrorists had not confessed in open court but hurled defiance at the prosecutor and the Tsar. The Zinovievs, Kamenevs, and others would have to behave differently; they would have to acknowledge their crime, grovel, and beg for mercy. No Komsomol member would then feel like saying, as did some young idiot in Smolensk, "They have slandered Zinoviev enough; he did a great deal for the Revolution."[39]

Stalin now surrounded himself with an aura of martyrdom. How steadily and inflexibly he had pursued his chosen path, even though surrounded by villainy and treason, being the target of countless plots! How stern his devotion to duty, which kept him from interfering with justice even for those who had been close to him and whom he personally liked, but who had betrayed the trust of the Party! Crumbs of his glory fell to others: the handful of his faithful comrades-at-arms who stuck it through with him. The work of the political police, which until then had seemed rather sordid, became respected and even glamorous. NKVD people were not to be thought of as mere policemen who dragged off a peasant for concealing a few pounds of grain, or unmasked some innocent oldster as a member of the prerevolutionary ruling class. They were fighters, engaged in an intricate and dangerous struggle to catch the incredibly cunning people's enemy. Their work was all the harder because so often they had to combat the indifference or even hostility of the older generation. How gloomily, rather than with relief, they greeted the fresh news of spies and saboteurs unmasked. It is not hard to see why the young could be impressed with Vishinsky's performance as the prosecutor at the trials. Day after day he patiently and even courteously countered the lies and evasions of the accused. To understand one of the main purposes of the Moscow trials one must try to see them through the eyes of a sixteen-year-old Soviet citizen. Stalin was a great educator.

As such, he did not make the mistake of assuming that most young people are interested in politics. For all its official solicitude about education, post-Revolution Russia had, from his perspective, been neglectful of the real needs of the young. Until the early 1930s progressive education—reflecting partly John Dewey's ideas and partly Marx's—was

[39] Fainsod, p. 422.

the rule in Soviet schools. This bred disrespect for authority, and a premature and possibly dangerous interest in social and economic questions. Authority, traditional methods of instruction, and discipline had to be restored. Old dodderers like Krupskaya (who until her death in 1939 was retained as Assistant Commissar of Education, but without the slightest influence on educational policies) might protest that this was restoring the Tsarist school and destroying the Marxist-Leninist principle of combining education with productive labor. But the young people, the future workers and soldiers, had to be educated in the new spirit rather than unduly exposed to the influence of an older and unregenerated generation. How silly to submit schoolchildren to the atmosphere of a factory or a collective farm brigade, and thus to initiate them into the daily grievances and problems of workers and peasants. Much better that they should be exposed to socialist labor on just a few festive and well-chaperoned occasions.

Even worse was the uncritical cult of the revolutionary past. Unformed minds were made to enthuse about incidents of rebellion and defiance of authority. The people offered as objects of veneration and emulation were all old: gray-bearded veterans of Siberia, quite likely former partisans of Trotsky or Rykov. Much better that Stalin should embody revolutionary heroism and suffering—with Lenin, of course, in the background, blessing and applauding his endeavors. All other heroes and models for the young should themselves be young products of *his* Russia. People were tired of those endless tales of ideological disputes, clandestine printing shops, raids on the Tsarist treasuries. Stories of today's heroism were more appropriate, exhilarating, and unlikely to lead to dangerous associations. And so in the Soviet newspapers of the middle and late 1930s the news of the purges competed for space with feats of a coal miner who sensationally surpassed his work quota, of daring Soviet fliers who established new altitude records, of Arctic explorers whose sagas were followed by the whole world. These were "real people" who should and would be looked up to.

Stalin's conviction of the harmfulness and danger of commemorating many incidents from the revolutionary past extended even to those associated with his own name. Thus he ordered the destruction of the Tiflis monument to Kamo, his Caucasian pupil and companion who had led armed expropriations and was a master at escaping from jails. Those were not achievements to be celebrated in Stalin's Russia. "From the midst of the people there has arisen a mass of organizers, leaders, inventors, courageous explorers of hitherto unseen regions of the Arctic, hero-conquerors of the stratosphere . . . depths of the ocean, mountain peaks, and the interior of the earth."[40] Let the young emulate *these*,

[40] *Pravda*, August 29, 1935.

and not the Kamos of the past. At about the same time the Society of Old Bolsheviks and the Association of the Veterans of Exile were ordered dissolved.

In Stalin's scheme of things, education supplemented but could never supplant repression. Diseases had to be stamped out and their carriers exterminated before the new hygienic measures could produce beneficial results. The Party and the Young Communists would have to be purged more thoroughly. The purge of Party ranks ordered in 1933, which was to have ended around the time Kirov was murdered, was continued until the end of 1935. No new members were admitted until mid-1936. And the locus of the infection was burned out: all through the early months of 1935 thousands of Leningraders, many of them former Komsomol members, others of "hostile" class origins, were deported to forced labor camps or to "free" exile in Siberia.[41]

With Nikolayev's shot the plot to contain Stalin by adulation, as conceived at the Seventeenth Party Congress, lay in ruins. If he had ever seriously considered laying down his Party duties, Stalin now reversed his mind. The enemy was shooting at the Party and he would not leave his post under fire. The murder must have refreshed and revivified his previous suspicions and grievances. Tomsky had told him in a drunken moment in 1928, "Some worker will take a potshot at you." Bukharin had told Kamenev at about the same time that high GPU officials including Yagoda were sympathetic to his position. In 1932, after Ryutin and others wrote about getting rid of him, his Politburo colleagues seemed strangely unconcerned. But if Ryutin had been shot then and there, people would not now be going around saying, "They got Kirov, let them now shoot Stalin." Was all that praise lavished on him at the Seventeenth Congress designed to lull his vigilance, to fool him? During the coming year these suspicions arranged themselves into a coherent pattern.

For the time being, there were no premonitory signs of the bloodbath which was to envelop the Party in 1936–38: Kirov's assassination as well as the death of another Politburo member, Valerian Kuibyshev,[42] led to a reshuffling of high Party posts announced on February 2, 1935. Advanced to full membership in the Politburo were Anastas Mikoyan and Vlas Chubar. Kirov's position on the Secretariat was taken over by

---

[41] As in Tsarist times exile was a generic term. It could mean settlement in a specified locality for a period of time, or prohibition of residence in cities, usually one of the capitals, but sometimes more. In 1934 Osip Mandelstam was given a "minus twelve" exile—i.e., he could reside in any but the twelve major urban centers.

[42] He was in 1938 declared to have been a victim of a medical murder ordered by Yagoda. In fact, he died of a heart ailment complicated by the heavy intake of alcohol.

Nikolai Yezhov. And the other rising star, Andrei Zhdanov, was promoted to alternate member of the Politburo.

What a story we would have if Anastas Mikoyan gave us his true recollections! The old phrase about "wily Armenians" takes on real meaning when we view the career of this man, now a venerable elder statesman. In thinking of the art of political survival, we turn to the example of Talleyrand, bishop under Louis XVI, one of the leading figures of the early phase of the French Revolution, then successively the servant of Napoleon, Louis XVIII, and Louis Philippe. But he was a rank amateur compared with Mikoyan. In 1918 he was a Communist leader in Baku, but he miraculously (and a bit suspiciously) avoided the fate of Shaumyan and the other "twenty-six Commissars" who were executed by the local regime. An early henchman of Stalin's, he might have been a prime candidate for the fate of so many of that breed between 1936 and 1939. "Don't we know what kind of people those Stalins and Zinovievs are!" he exclaimed at the Fourteenth Party Congress in 1925, a jocular remark which was designed to blunt any revelation of Lenin's *Testament*, but which Stalin, whose memory in such matters was phenomenal, could not have relished in the years to come. As Commissar of Trade, he was in charge of grain procurements in 1928. Then in 1934 he was one of those charged with ascertaining whom the Party would have as First Secretary should Comrade Stalin retire to some lofty height. After World War II, when Stalin turned against the handful of his old servants who survived simply because they had been around too long, nothing happened to Mikoyan, apart from his son's arrest. After Stalin's death, a new political life: Mikoyan cast his lot with Khrushchev, and nobody appeared to remember that this leader in the struggle against the "cult of personality" had been Stalin's close lieutenant for almost as long as Molotov had been. Mikoyan helped to save Khrushchev from a plot hatched by the latter's old pals in 1957. He went to Castro in 1962 to persuade that young man (not even born when Mikoyan was a key figure in subduing the Russian peasantry) to agree to have Russian missiles and bombers withdrawn from Cuba—and thus helped Khrushchev to extricate himself from the consequences of what Mikoyan, along with other Soviet leaders, was later to declare was one of his "harebrained schemes." In October 1964 it was Mikoyan who was delegated to detain and amuse Khrushchev in the Crimea while in Moscow Brezhnev and Kosygin were putting the finishing touches on the plot which unseated him. But, alas, Mikoyan's official recollections are, as we would expect of a wise man in the circumstances, dull. And when Anastas Ivanovich is gathered unto his ancestors, we may be sure that his grief-stricken colleagues will thoroughly and nervously scrutinize each scrap of paper he leaves behind.

Yezhov's career, by contrast, was short-lived. But how momentous! As long as there is history, *"Yezhovschina,"* "the Yezhov time," from the end of 1936 to late 1938, will figure in it. More people undoubtedly perished in the years of forced collectivization, 1929–33, than during the "Yezhov time." But in the later period it was everybody, and not just the peasant, who suffered and feared. It was a hideous democracy of fear: a Politburo member as well as the humblest citizen went to bed not knowing whether this was the night "they" would come after him. In fact, the influential, the hitherto successful, the oppressors themselves, were struck hardest—as if Providence, acting through the instrumentality of the tyrant, sought to punish them for their indifference and complicity in the ordeal of millions of their peasant countrymen. But like all great disasters, this one defied all rationalization, classification, and moralizing. Never since the outbreak of the Black Death in the fourteenth century could so many ordinary people have felt so alone and afraid, so deprived of any mooring in reality, so much a plaything of blind fate. But this was a manmade disaster. People did not pray but cursed and denounced themselves as well as others. Dishonor walked hand in hand with death.

Yezhov, it is almost superfluous to say, does not deserve to be considered the architect of this evil grandeur. He was its chief technician, an instrument of Stalin's will and design. Yezhov joined the Party in April 1917—a date of some importance, as is his age at the time, twenty-three. It is unlikely that people who joined the Party then possessed the sophistication or the concept of revolutionary morality characteristic of an Old Bolshevik. Nor were they likely to be mere careerists, as were so many who gained entrance after 1918. A Bolshevik of Yezhov's vintage was likely to be a narrow-minded worshiper of Lenin and his successor, a man who joined the Bolsheviks because it was the most radical party on the horizon, promising to deal most uncompromisingly with the class enemy and avenge most ruthlessly the past abuses of power and privilege. In the 1920s Yezhov was an obscure Party official in Kazakhstan. For a Russian Communist to be relegated to such a backwater meant, unless he was a former oppositionist, that he was thought of as a man of zeal rather than intelligence. But he must have caught Stalin's eye, for in 1929 he was appointed to the then very important post of Assistant Commissar of Agriculture, Stalin's eyes and ears in a ministry headed by an Old Bolshevik.

Short, almost a dwarf, with a lame leg, Yezhov is the epitome of that "rabble of fawning half-men" who surround Stalin in Mandelstam's poem and who "whinny, purr, or whine as he prates and points a finger." We have this incongruous picture of him as a vacationer in a government villa in the Caucasus in 1930: "The Sukhumi Yezhov was a modest and rather agreeable person. He was not yet used to being driven about in an automobile and did not therefore regard it as an exclusive privilege to which no ordinary mortal could lay claim. We sometimes asked him to give us a lift into town and he never refused."[43] Mme. Mandelstam recalls him offering roses and flirting with a young literature student, and being, despite his leg, a vigorous and enthusiastic dancer. It is easy to imagine such a man being filled with gratitude and devotion to the Leader who had brought him up from the ranks and whom one must protect from traitors and ingrates. He was never a comrade of Stalin's, as Orjonikidze, Molotov, or Kaganovich had been, but was in every sense of the word his creature. In 1930 Yezhov became head of the Appointments Section of the Party Secretariat, in 1934 a member of the Central Committee and deputy head of the Party Control Commission under Kaganovich. Stalin thus installed a new favorite to check or, more indelicately, to spy on the work of an old one.

The three men Stalin employed as his chief architects of terror were all monstrous, each in a different way. Yagoda was a hardened scoundrel and intriguer who grew up with the GPU and whom Stalin never trusted. Yezhov started out as a sort of Communist Boy Scout, and was then consumed with zeal to prove himself to his master, uncovering and uprooting every conceivable and inconceivable spy or people's enemy. And then there was Beria—the courtier policeman, attuned to the mentality of his fellow Georgian but, had Stalin lived longer, a man who would have been dispatched to join his predecessors in that very special corner of Hell. No one, it is fairly safe to assume, will ever say a word of defense on behalf of the monstrous threesome. But let us be fair: it is unlikely that a prudent, as distinguished from an ambitious (or, in the case of Yezhov, stupid), scoundrel would have aspired to the job they held.

At about the same time in 1935 that he became Party secretary and assumed overall supervision of the security organs, Yezhov took over from Kaganovich the chairmanship of the Control Commission. (The number-two man on this body now became Matvei Shkiryatov, a man hitherto slighted by history; but he belongs with the trio as one of the chief architects of Stalin's terror—his services to Stalin, as a matter of fact, antedating those of the others. But perhaps because he was never given much public prominence, Shkiryatov cheated the executioner. He died a year after Stalin, still a high Party official at a ripe old age.) And Zhdanov was now Stalin's principal coadjutor in the Secretariat, thus further weakening the influence of Kaganovich.[44] Zhdanov's and Yezhov's elevation

[43] Nadezhda Mandelstam, *Hope Against Hope* (New York, 1970), p. 322.
[44] In 1932–35 messages of tribute, etc., to the Central Committee were often addressed to "Comrades Stalin and Kaganovich." After 1935 the latter remained a person of great prominence, one of the most energetic and brutal purgers of the local Party organizations in 1937–38, but in 1935 he was also given the time-consuming job of Commissar of Transport and relieved as Secretary of the Moscow committee.

marked the rise of a new team of Stalinists, people who were his creatures rather than former-allies-become-servants like Molotov, Kaganovich, and Orjonikidze. Two other people were appointed to important
positions at about the same time: young Georgi Malenkov (he was
thirty-three) became assistant director of the Appointment Section of
the Party Secretariat, where he became an éminence grise of the purge
period and came into public prominence in 1939. Stepping more directly into the limelight was Malenkov's future nemesis, Nikita Khrushchev. The world would come to know him as a cheerful and oversubtle
contriver, as the destroyer of the Stalin legend. But in 1935, when he
became the head of the Moscow Party, he was very much Stalin's idea
of a desirable satrap, a new Soviet man entirely free of an Old Bolshevik's ideological baggage,[45] bursting with energy and devotion to the
Leader.

It was clear what was on Stalin's mind: he had to think of the
possibility of being incapacitated and then of becoming, like Lenin in his
last two years, a virtual prisoner of the Politburo. He was at an age when
as a veteran of jails and exiles, a man with a terrible temperament, he
might be expected to have a stroke—as his colleagues probably reflected,
recalling piously the cases of Lenin and Dzerzhinsky, to mention just
two. What then? People like Kaganovich and Molotov might well overlook their rivalry in order to insure that he would not return to lord it
over them. And in their quest for popularity they might decide to
become "liberals" (as Malenkov and Beria were to do in 1953), to turn
to people like Bukharin and Tomsky and others who still enjoyed the
secret attachment of many in the Party. But there were new men with
their hands on various levels of power who had to look to Stalin for
further advancement: Yezhov (who would never become a full member
of the Politburo), Zhdanov (not until 1939), Malenkov (only in 1946).
If a crisis occurred, every motive of self-interest would impel them to
stick by an ailing Stalin and counter any intrigues by their senior
colleagues.

This mock struggle for succession eventually, of course, compounded
the horrors of the Great Purge. The newcomers to high positions strove
to demonstrate their zeal and loyalty by uncovering new plots and
dangers and by mercilessly hounding those of their rivals' subordinates
whom they felt they could safely pursue. And then older Politburo
members felt that they could not remain backward in this competition.
The object was no longer to have influence over the Party elite, as it had
been in in the 1920s, but over the tyrant's unpredictable mind. On his
appointment as Commissar of Transport in 1935 Kaganovich, possibly

---

[45] Even when he became head of the government and the Party, Khrushchev showed
an embarrassing ignorance of Marxist theory and Party history.

fearful that this might be taken as a sign that he was growing soft, conducted a veritable pogrom of the managerial personnel and personally requested the arrest of eighty-three completely innocent leading managers and specialists of the Soviet railways (a matter not revealed until 1961). How eager the older oligarchs were to appear no softer than Yezhov or Malenkov is well illustrated by another incident related at the Twenty-second Party Congress. A disgruntled functionary wrote a letter to Stalin in 1937, denouncing his superior, Lomov, for having been friendly with Bukharin and Rykov (something which, of course, used to be true of Stalin himself). Stalin, in his hideously indirect manner, sent the letter to Molotov with a note: "To Comrade Molotov. What is to be done with this?" He received the answer: "Immediately arrest that scum Lomov." And so Lomov, a Bolshevik since 1903, a member of the Central Committee at the time of the October Revolution, a former minister, was shot.

Stalin's tactics thus made sure that the various threads of power and information were drawn together in his hands and that the Politburo could no longer stand between him and his designs, but could be bypassed and serve as a mere advisory body. Even if ailing, he could not be insulated as Lenin had been from news of what was happening in the Party and the country. There could be no new "Stalin" waiting in the wings, since the prospective candidates for that role—Kaganovich, Zhdanov, and Malenkov—were watching each other like hawks, conscious that an undue elevation of one might mean more than just political death for the others. As if this were not enough, there was now also Stalin's personal secretariat, headed by Alexander Poskrebyshev.

The interlocking apparatus of despotism was bound by its very momentum to produce a bloody harvest. It would have been implausible for, say, Yezhov, when charged with supervision of the security apparatus, to report to Stalin that the NKVD was functioning well, displaying just the right kind of vigilance. He had to find plots, treachery, inefficiency.

The first such "plot" spelled the eventual doom of Stalin's oldest friend and political associate, Abel Yenukidze. Ever since 1918, Yenukidze had been Secretary of the Presidium of the Executive Committee of the Supreme Soviet, a sort of secretary general of the Soviet presidency, in charge of the administration and personnel of the Kremlin. It was in this enclave of government offices and official residences that early in 1935 there was "discovered" an alleged conspiracy against Stalin, a conspiracy involving a number of the Kremlin guards. The trial was held in secrecy and of the forty condemned only two were shot—which lends substance to the theory that no actual attempt on Stalin's life had been made and the whole affair had been the fruit of provocation. In any case, in March 1935 Yenukidze was relieved of his post but blamed, evidently, only for negligence rather than complicity, for he was slated to receive an honorific post in the Transcaucasian Republic. He was never allowed to settle down in his homeland, however. On June 7 a cryptic announcement in *Pravda* revealed that the Central Committee had heard Comrade Yezhov's report on the situation in the Secretariat of the Presidium and on Yenukidze. It was decided to approve the measures taken by the Party *control* organs to improve the security in and supervision of the Secretariat's personnel. "For political and moral degeneracy" Abel Yenukidze was ejected not only from the Central Committee but from the Party.

Yenukidze had been a man of no power but of considerable influence. He had acted by virtue both of his office and of his personal reputation as a one-man complaint bureau and receiver of petitions from those struck down by Soviet justice. It was to him that Osip Mandelstam's friends went to beg him to intercede after the poet had been dragged off by the GPU. Seemingly no one, except for Orjonikidze, could have been personally closer to Stalin, whom he had known since 1900, whose wife was his goddaughter, and whose children called him uncle. But Stalin's new favorites must have sensed that the ties and recollections had become cumbersome to him, that Yenukidze's memoirs were distasteful, with their mention of the young and taciturn Soso Djugashvili, whom he had met that afternoon in 1900 in Tiflis when the latter was lieutenant to Sylvester Djibladze. And they *had* uncovered White Guardists and former Trotskyites in the Kremlin personnel. The commandant of the Kremlin was none other than an officer who during the Civil War had commanded Trotsky's armored train! Why hadn't the security organs spotted those wreckers and potential assassins on the Kremlin staff? Could Yenukidze have been scheming with Yagoda? Beria was encouraged or commissioned to come out with "historical" lectures, and his historical survey of Bolshevik organizations in the Caucasus, delivered and printed in the summer of 1935, contained violent attacks on Stalin's fallen friend: Yenukidze, said Beria, had falsified and magnified his own role while detracting from that of the dictator in the revolutionary underground.

We shall have to consider later to what degree Stalin believed the charges or—to put it more precisely—the absurdities which accompanied the destruction of so many Party and government leaders. But it is clear that when it came to suspicion it was "easy to fool Stalin," or rather that Stalin chose to fool himself. If a man had grown obnoxious or inconvenient to him, he was ready to listen to and accept any accusation, no matter how absurd. It is not recorded whether Henry VIII believed the charges on which his two wives were sent to the scaffold, but undoubtedly his decision to get rid of them preceded the preparation of the indictment. Stalin's passion for power and the conviction of his historical mission were those of a jealous lover. Even in his pre-Revolution days, his language about his opponents had sexual overtones; the Mensheviks, he wrote in 1907, were "unclean." He used the same epithet in a private letter in 1928 in reference to Tomsky. Now he felt that Yenukidze had abused their earlier intimacy and had betrayed him. The official communiqué branded him as "dissolute" in his political and his private life. (All that meant was that Yenukidze, like most kind-hearted people, was a hedonist. His interest in the ballet, it was rumored, extended beyond a concern for the art of the dance.) Did Stalin believe every letter of the charges under which his old friend went to his death? Did Henry VIII believe that Anne Boleyn had actually committed adultery with her brother? Yenukidze was executed in December 1937, but since the trial was secret, it was only in the next year, during the great case of Bukharin, Rykov, et al., that it was revealed how he had plannned a palace coup against Stalin and how, with Yagoda and others, he had contrived the death of Kirov.

The Yenukidze case is as essential to an understanding of the atmosphere and mechanics of Stalin's reign of terror, as is Kirov's. By sacrificing a man who had been so close to him, Stalin set a precedent: past services or personal loyalty did not count if one got in his way. It also set an encouraging example for denunciation of those in high position. Stalin might well have intended at first to let Yenukidze spend the rest of his days as President of the Transcaucasian Federation, but Yezhov and Beria were quick to transform the original charge of negligence with additional evidence, first into crime and then into treason. One need not have compunctions, evidently, about fabricating evidence even against a Politburo member. For the NKVD and ambitious newcomers like Yezhov and Beria, the former oppositionists now held in jail and camps, like Zinoviev and Kamenev, became a stock-in-trade, a foundation on which further plots could be built, reaching into Stalin's closest entourage. "We Russian Bolsheviks learned long ago not to be surprised by anything," Stalin once said. He certainly had. If Yenukidze, why not Kaganovich or Molotov? One had to stay informed about what they were doing and saying.

Other portents of horror were to be found in the various new extensions and additions to the criminal code. One law prescribed imprisonment for members of a serviceman's family who, knowing of his intention to defect abroad, did not report him to the authorities, and those in the family unaware of the traitor's plans to be exiled to Siberia. Another extended penal sanctions, including "the supreme penalty," to children over twelve. (The legalization of this system for obtaining hostages, which had been practiced before, would explain many of the features of the purges, such as the readiness of the accused to confess to even the most absurd charges.) And directly reflecting the murder of

December 1, 1934, unauthorized carriers of weapons, including knives, were now subject to severe punishment. ☆☆☆

THE machinery for terror was set, the mood for it was becoming propitious, and yet Stalin did not loose Yezhov on the Party and the country for another year. The reason must be sought in the developments in the international situation. In 1933–34, when war was thought to be imminent, Stalin's response had been to authorize a certain liberalization of internal policies. Now, in the wake of the Kirov and Yenukidze affairs, he became convinced of widespread disloyalty and potential treachery. When the international situation heated up again in 1936, he saw danger, almost certainly war, no longer only in the Far East but on several fronts: against Hitler's Germany, with the probable connivance of Poland, in the West; against Japan in Asia. And so he conceived a frightful plan: to destroy anything and anybody who in case of war *might* turn against him; to stamp each past, present, and potential enemy with the brand of traitor to his country; to let denunciation run rampant, suspicion be prima-facie evidence of guilt; to let his lieutenants compete in savagery, since those who survived would be linked with him in crime, incapable of plotting against him, as he was sure they had been in 1934, or of wresting power from his hands. But this plan ripened in his mind only after Hitler had sent the Reichswehr into the Rhineland and after it was clear that Hitler meant war and in a few years would have the capacity to wage one.

In 1935 the Russians still believed that war could be postponed indefinitely. In that year they sold their interest in the Manchurian Railroad to Manchukuo, thus giving de-facto recognition to this puppet of Japan's. This clear act of appeasement of Tokyo—the railway was sold for a fraction of the sum the Russians had originally demanded—led to vigorous protests by the Peking government, but it was passed over in silence by the Chinese Communists, who no doubt with Soviet blessing had declared war on Japan as early as 1932. And in Europe too, Soviet diplomacy sought (in a much more realistic way than that of Britain and France) to avoid war. To do Stalin justice, he never made a secret of that objective or pretended that his destestation of fascism was greater than his desire to avoid war, or more precisely to avoid Russia's military involvement in one. And it would be erroneous to assume that in 1935 Stalin already thought he could avoid such involvement by signing an alliance with Hitler.

The Führer had betrayed Stalin's expectations, as we have seen, first by staying in power and then, more ominously, by continuing to talk of

Germany's need for expansion in the *East* and of her historic mission to free European civilization from the threat of Bolshevism. Moscow's first priority thus became to convince Paris and London that Hitler did not mean these words, that they were really a smokescreen for his aggressive designs in the *West*. When Anthony Eden, then minister without portfolio, went to Moscow in March 1935, Litvinov was quite emphatic on this point: "The Reichswehr . . . is always ready to bargain with the Soviet Union. I have evidence of this from a secret source. The plan of the Reichswehr is always to dispose of France first rather than to waste valuable time and energy on Russia. . . . Hitler's assurances are not to be believed even when he says he has renounced Alsace-Lorraine."[46] Stalin, much preoccupied at the moment, took time out to receive Eden, an unusual courtesy. He too insinuated that Russia did not really need the West but the West needed Russia to meet the danger of Hitler. Behind this somewhat disingenuous pleading was a growing concern that the West might really fall for Hitler's anti-Communist rhetoric. Even if France and Britain did not join Hitler, a general capitalist crusade against the Fatherland of Socialism—something the Russians always talked about but never really believed—they still might do what Stalin would undoubtedly have tried were he in their shoes: stand on the sidelines and cheer as the two dictatorships belabored each other.

It was therefore a triumph of Stalin's diplomacy when the Franco-Soviet treaty of mutual assistance was signed on May 2, 1935. The treaty pledged each country to come to the other's aid "in case of an unprovoked attack on the part of a European state." The alliance turned out to be very much a paper one. No discussions betweeen the two general staffs took place following its signing. There was for the moment not even any attempt to spell out how, in case of a German attack on France, the U.S.S.R. would come to her aid: the Soviet Union and Germany were separated by Poland and the Baltic states, and the former, despite her alliance with France, was believed—at least in Russia—to be a potential accomplice of Germany's. There were thus ample excuses for Russia to plead inability to come to her ally's help in case of a German aggression in the West, conversely, in case of a German aggression (with Polish help) against Russia, France had no such excuse. But neither of the partners had an *actual* war in mind when signing the alliance. The French hoped to discourage Hitler by invoking the vision of millions of Russian soldiers somehow coming to their aid. Stalin hoped to shatter Hitler's dream of securing Western acquiescence in a move in the East. The French proved to have been wrong and

[46] The Earl of Avon, *The Eden Memoirs: Facing the Dictators* (New York, 1960), p. 155.

Stalin right. Hitler, disabused of his hopes of securing a free hand against Russia, had to reexamine his anti-Communist phobia. Would he, or his generals with memories of what had happened in the World War, again risk a war on two fronts?

The Soviet plan of building barriers against German aggression in Central Europe was supplemented by an alliance signed on May 16 with Czechoslovakia. It included the provision that Russia was obligated to help the cosignatory *only* if France, which had a long-standing treaty with Czechoslovakia, came to her help too. Again, while enhancing Russia's reputation as a staunch defender of collective security, the treaty did not significantly increase her commitments: she did not have a common frontier with her new ally.

Stalin's game on the chessboard of European politics can best be understood if we keep in mind that *at the time* the Kremlin's objective was not to destroy Hitler. The danger of war with him was thought to be real but not imminent: Germany's rearmament was far from complete. The Russians considered the French army (as they continued to do in 1939) to be the best in Europe. The war might come, but certainly not this year or next, and if it came, one hoped that the Soviet Union would not be involved or, if worse came to worse, would not be without powerful allies.

Stalin's reputation as an international statesman grew. In the West liberals and socialists disgusted by their governments' pusillanimous policy toward fascism were taking another look at Stalin—evidently the only world leader with enough guts to stand up to Hitler. Even non-leftists of an anti-German persuasion were encouraged by the Soviet Union's international posture. Stalin, it was explained by experts in such things, was really a national Communist. Had he not, after all, chased Trotsky out for trying to promote world revolution?[47] One could do business with such a man, and perhaps those stories about terror in Russia were exaggerated.

This new image of the man who was then on the point of launching one of the bloodiest periods of terror in the history of the world, was fortified by incidents like the visit of Pierre Laval to Moscow. What the French Foreign Minister wanted was the help of his host: his (right-wing) government was having trouble with pacifist elements about launching even a moderate rearmament program to meet the growing German danger. Stalin obliged: a joint Soviet-French communiqué set a new precedent in international relations. "It is precisely for the sake of maintaining peace that these states are obliged above all not to weaken in any way their means of national defense. On this point, in particular,

[47] This sophisticated argument neatly paralleled a similar one made in different circles about Hitler: that as an Austrian by birth he was alien to the militaristic tradition of Prussia!

Comrade Stalin expressed complete understanding and approval of the national defense policy pursued by France with the object of maintaining its armed forces consistent with its security requirements."[48] And Stalin was sympathetic to Laval's stories and to his complaints that the French Communists, for all their changing "line," were still obstructing France's defense effort.[49]

Stalin's words had the expected effect on the French Communists, then already embarked on the policy of the Popular Front. But again we must remember that Soviet solicitude about the strength of this future Western ally had definite limits. The Soviets had no intention of encouraging the Anglo-French part of the imperialist camp to be unduly powerful vis-à-vis the German one.

The same qualification applies to the famous policy of the Popular Front. Beginning in 1934 and culminating in the Seventh Congress of the Comintern, in July–August 1935, Moscow reversed its former directives to the world Communist Parties. Socialist and liberal movements denounced in 1928 as "social fascist" were now proclaimed to be desirable allies, to be wooed and joined in a common struggle against the fascist danger, against the threatening alliance of Germany, Japan, and Italy. But contrary to what is still often and erroneously believed in he West, the Popular Front policy was not intended to be a clarion call for joint action of Communists and democracies in a sacred war against fascism. It was thought of primarily as a *prophylactic* policy: one designed to prevent a configuration of forces in the democratic world that would incline the Western powers to preserve neutrality, if not indeed to join the fascists in a venture against the Soviet Union. France should be strong enough to make her alliance with Russia deter Hitler from attacking the latter, but it was far from Stalin's mind to make France once again the dominant military power in Europe. Thus the French Communists were to vote for the French defense budget but in 1935 they opposed extension of compulsory military service to two years—the only step which would have enabled France, in view of her smaller population, to match the buildup of the Reichswehr. The French Communists joined in an electoral bloc with the Socialists and Radicals, but *not* to lead the Third Republic in an effort to terminate Hitler's career before Germany became too powerful, only to prevent a victory of the Right that *might* seek accommodation with the Führer by giving him a free hand in the East.

Stalin's international game was far from simple. He courted the democracies. But he did not abandon the possibility that Hitler might come to his senses, see that he needed Soviet neutrality, and forsake his

[48] Degras, *Soviet Documents on Foreign Policy*, III: 1933–41, 36.
[49] It is doubtful that, as legend has it, he suggested to Laval, "Why don't you shoot them?"

dreams about the Ukraine in favor of trying to recover what Germany *should* want: Alsace-Lorraine and the Polish Corridor. And so, incongruously, for all the anti-Hitler rhetoric and for all the copious tears shed over German Communists in Nazi concentration camps—the German Communist Party in its official program echoed nationalist aspirations. "For the complete annulment of the Versailles Treaty. For the unification of all Germans not through war but on a voluntary basis. . . . For the abolition of the Polish Corridor."[50]

For the moment Hitler was not inclined to contemplate any Soviet-German agreement. Discreet probes from the Soviet side took place as early as the summer of 1935. The Soviet commercial envoy in Berlin, David Kandelaki, intimated to Dr. Schacht that he had talked not only to his immediate superiors but to Stalin and Molotov, and he implied that he had their authorization to express the hope that commercial and political relations between the two countries could be improved. For all these and subsequent hints, and Germans as yet were not biting. The Führer still hoped that he could make the French and especially the British see that by establishing hegemony over Europe, he was doing them a favor. As he did not think that they would counter any of his designs by force, there was no reason for him to approach the Russians, whom he genuinely loathed. It would be some time before he felt that, in view of British and French ingratitude and incomprehension of his plans, he would have to approach Stalin, and even then he did it on the premise that he would be able to doublecross him and that, confronted by the Nazi-Soviet Pact, the Western powers would not go to war.

Russia's new, more cordial relations with the West were probably one of the main reasons behind the new "Stalin Constitution" which was elaborated in 1935 and came into effect in the Soviet Union in 1936. As a propaganda move the constitution was a masterpiece—so much so that even the Mensheviks in migration experienced a momentary surge of hope. Was the Soviet regime, as they had been prophesying ever since October 25, 1917, finally compelled to bow to the will of the masses? Their illusions did not last long, but others continued to be impressed. No doubt about it, the document was as advertised, "the most democratic constitution in the world." Elections were to be free, equal, and secret.[51] To the list of individual rights found elsewhere the Soviet document proudly added the right of every individual to demand that his government provide him with employment. Neither J. S. Mill nor Thomas Jefferson could have objected to a single provision. In brief, as Stalin shrewdly if ungracefully concluded, "Now, when the muddy wave of fascism denigrates the socialist movement of the working class and

[50] *The Communist International*, XIII, No. 13 (March 1936), 42.
[51] Disenfranchised members of the former exploiting classes were now allowed to vote.

tries to cover with filth the attempts of the best people of the civilized world, the new constitution of the U.S.S.R. is an act of accusation against fascism, a proof that socialism and democracy are invincible."[52] Even people with a fairly realistic notion of Soviet realities, and even during the purges, were buoyed up by the constitution and its impressive array of individual rights and immunities: psychologically it was an important stimulus in the right direction, and how different from Hitler, who even verbally spat on democracy!

Again, Stalin was not entirely cynical nor was he thinking merely of propaganda. For him the constitution was welcome proof and reassurance that the U.S.S.R. was becoming a "respectable" state and that the revolutionary mumbo-jumbo of its previous documents was being discarded. Similar considerations made him restore the ranks of marshal and general in the armed forces, substitute "minister" for "commissar," and, after World War II, put his diplomatic corps in fancy uniforms just as the British were putting theirs in plain civilian clothes. *His* Russia was now a Great Power, entitled to the appurtenances possessed by the British and the French; the revolutionary language invented by Trotsky and Zinoviev was obsolescent and out of place. One day he would authorize a new national anthem in place of the "Internationale," which had hitherto served this purpose, and it would be a paean of praise to Russia and Stalin. The "Internationale," with its references to "prisoners of starvation" and "wretched of the earth," was fine for Party occasions but the national anthem had to celebrate *his* Russia, a powerful union of nations cemented by their love for Stalin. ☆☆☆

THE year 1936 saw the collapse of the apparent equilibrium in Europe that had been reached through the Franco-Soviet alliance and the entrance in 1934 of the U.S.S.R. into the League of Nations. And in the same year the intensive phase of the Great Purge began. The two developments are closely connected.

The international situation was transformed by the entrance of German troops into the Rhineland on March 7, a violation of the Versailles Treaty and of the voluntary German pledge under the Locarno agreements to keep this area demilitarized. About the same time Italy, in defiance of the League of Nations, conquered Abyssinia, and the whole system of collective security, believed only a year before

[52] Stalin, *Works* (in Russian; Stanford, Calif.), 1, 115. This edition is supplementary to the Soviet one, whose contents end with 1934, and it will be referred to henceforth as the Stanford edition.

to be at least a "brake on aggression," as Stalin had put it, was exposed as an illusion. Italy now drew close to Germany, and Hitler became for Mussolini no longer a parvenu imitator but a desirable partner in profitable blackmail and a model of emulation.

With German troops in the Rhineland, the Franco-Soviet alliance lost much of its original value, from Stalin's point of view, and Moscow had to revise its whole assessment of the nature and timetable of the German danger. As long as the Rhineland was demilitarized, it lay at the mercy of France in case of war. But now it was quite easy to foresee a situation such as actually arose in 1939–40: Germany making an aggressive move in the East, while France, even if choosing to honor her treaty obligations, being unable to come speedily to the aid of her Eastern ally, whether Czechoslovakia or the U.S.S.R. What would be the situation in Russia, if she suffered even an initial defeat and if a part of her territory were occupied by the enemy? Stalin did not have to go very far to look for an answer. This had been the situation in World War I. It availed Nicholas II very little that his allies eventually won the war and defeated the Germans: his regime had crumbled before then. Stalin, with his political realism, must have feared that his position was bound to be worse. Why should *Soviet* Russia's *capitalist* allies refuse an attractive peace offer from Hitler and continue to fight after Russia had been defeated? No Communist, certainly not Stalin, could really believe that. But supposed the unexpected happened, and the French (or British?) went on fighting Germany? Russia might eventually emerge as part of a victorious coalition. But would it be *Stalin's* Russia? The decrepit Tsarist regime had endured two and a half years of an unsuccessful conflict, but it had not uprooted every peasant family in the land, had not starved 4 or 5 million people on the eve of the war. A few thousand revolutionaries took advantage of military defeats and food shortages to start a sequence of events that led to the overthrow of the Romanovs. How many thousands of Stalin's enemies were even now in the Communist Party itself, waiting for an opportunity to strike? There were would-be pretenders. Trotsky now had virtually no followers in Russia, but how many of Lenin's followers had there been in February 1917? Perhaps 10,000. Zinoviev and Kamenev were in jail, but so had Stalin been at the time of the Revolution. All around him, in the Central Committee, in the army, there were men whom he had humiliated. They might eagerly seize an opportunity offered to them by Soviet military reverses. Were they not hoping—i.e., working—for such an eventuality? The Bolsheviks' proud boast during World War I was that they were defeatists because only through a defeat of their country could the tyranny be overthrown. It was foolish to imagine that all those Zinovievs, Bukharins, and Radeks might not secretly feel the same way now. Stalin's megalomania was no greater than his suspiciousness; his conviction in his historic mission and in the gratitude that all "real" Soviet people bore toward him did not preclude a belief in the essential baseness of human nature. He, Russia, Communism—Stalin no longer distinguished clearly among them—were in mortal danger.

Diplomacy might still avert the war danger. Or, if war came, Soviet arms might parry the enemy's blow and begin the war victoriously. But one could not take chances. The imperialists, even if not wicked, were certainly weak and undecided. After Hitler's move, the French did not do so much as to order a general mobilization, even though this, with Germany far from fully rearmed, would probably have made Hitler back down on the Rhineland. As to Russia's chances in a military confrontation two or three years hence one had to be realistic, and keep in mind the German genius for war and technology. Russia's great military asset, her space, could be of little comfort to a regime that believed it could not afford initial military reverses. And the German blow would most likely come through the area most cruelly hit by collectivization, the Ukraine.

Stalin was not overlooking any possibilities. Soviet diplomacy officially stood by its obligations to France, but not in an entirely unambiguous way: "Help would be given in accordance with the treaty and with the political situation as a whole." In a newspaper interview Molotov professed to see the remilitarization of the Rhineland as a threat mainly to Germany's *western* neighbors. He then dropped an ingenious hint which, if overlooked at the time, was possibly remembered in Berlin in the summer of 1939: "There is a tendency among certain sections of the Soviet public toward an attitude of thoroughgoing irreconcilability to the present rulers of Germany, particularly because of the ever-repeated hostile speeches of German leaders against the Soviet Union. But the chief tendency, and the one determining the Soviet Government's policy, thinks an improvement in Soviet-German relations possible."[53] This was a shrewd thrust, designed to make the French solicitous of their alliance with Russia rather than taking it for granted, while at the same time it titillated Berlin. In their manner, at once sinister and childish, the Nazis saw deception and intrigue everywhere, so somebody in Berlin might prick up his ears: perhaps the pro-Western and anti-German orientation of Moscow was the work of "Jews" like Litvinov and "fanatical Communists of the Comintern," while "Russian nationalists" like Stalin and Molotov looked for ways to reach an understanding with Germany. All too transparent a device, one might think, but this was quite close to what poor Ribbentrop, if not quite his Führer, came to believe in 1939.

Hitler "got away with" the Rhineland, as he was to get away with so

53 Degras, *Soviet Documents on Foreign Policy*, III: 1933–41, 184.

many things during the next three years. And the facility with which he worked his bluff militated against any need to seek an understanding with the "chief tendency in the Soviet Union."

There is strong circumstantial evidence that the idea of physical liquidation of all his intra-Party opponents germinated in Stalin's mind following the Rhineland crisis. The enhanced foreign danger triggered his resolve not only to kill all potential rivals and opponents, but to dishonor them in death by "revealing" their part in the Kirov assassination, their even more ambitious terrorist designs, their links with Trotsky and, of course, with hostile foreign governments. The first and key step in the progression toward the holocaust was the show trial of Zinoviev, Kamenev, and their alleged accomplices in August 1936. But a key element here was that some of the accused should also implicate the former "Right Opposition" in their treasonous doings, and so they did, mentioning Bukharin, Rykov, Tomsky, and others. As late as February 1936 Bukharin, still editor-in-chief of the government organ *Izvestia*, still an alternate member of the Central Committee and of the commission preparing the "Stalin Constitution," was allowed to go abroad. He was not even required to leave a hostage for his return, for his young wife, then pregnant, accompanied him on the trip. It is thus unlikely that the outlines of the dreadful scenario were elaborated by Stalin prior to March. But one can well imagine Stalin one spring day summoning Yezhov and the chiefs of the NKVD and ordering them to seek out and uproot treason in a more systematic and wide-ranging way than hitherto. To them the international situation would justify extreme measures and ruthless methods of investigation. The guilty should be tried so as to prove to the Soviet people an organic link between any opposition to the Soviet regime and treason on behalf of hostile foreign powers.

The first of the Moscow trials, that of Zinoviev, Kamenev, and fourteen others, took place in public between August 19 and 24, 1936. Among the defendants, some, like Ivan Bakayev and Gregory Yevdokimov, had been associates of the two former triumvirs and had gone down to defeat with them in 1925; some had followed Trotsky; there were also a few quite obscure figures, as well as one or two agents provocateurs. The primary objective of the trial was not to destroy Zinoviev and Kamenev and the others—they had been in jail for some time and it would have been easy to make their treatment there such that none of them would leave prison alive—but to let the Russian people hear from the mouths of the accused themselves how they had plotted murders and with Trotsky's connivance sold themselves to a foreign power. A precedent would thus be set: former greatness in the Party, closeness to Lenin, could not protect anybody either from the bacillus of ambition-turned-to-treason, or from being punished by the "supreme penalty." Links would be discovered leading from the

"Trotskyite-Zinovievite Terrorist Center"[54] to the "Right Oppositionists," then to the army and to loyal Stalinists who still at one point or another might appear lukewarm in their loyalty or might become cumbersome and distasteful to him. There would be hysteria and spy mania. Even Stalin must have realized that many completely innocent and personally loyal people would perish. But anybody even remotely suspect, likely even by the furthest stretch of the imagination to turn against him if the foreign enemy struck, must perish. Would this turn the nation against him? What about prophecies that if you struck down the kulaks the peasantry as a whole would rise? Millions of peasants now worked in the collective farms, relieved that they had been spared—why, even grateful for the "more cultured" existence he had forged for them. The country as a whole would grow stronger, the nation healthier through this blood-letting. If war came, millions of the best sons of the nation might have to die. Should one hesitate to destroy those who might or would betray?

One must not credit Stalin with conceiving this plan all at once. His war against the nation had begun with the impulse and policy to repress *just* the kulaks, to collectivize in good time *just* 20 to 25 per cent of the peasant households. And similarly in 1936 he may have desired to strike out just the leaders of potential treason: those few thousand Party officials who in the past had been connected with his rivals. But the mechanics of terror, like the mechanics of collectivization, soon acquired its own momentum. The more he killed, the more he was bound to suspect. Since his mind evidently made no distinction between actual and potential treason, slander became a prima-facie proof, a reproach or hesitation on the part of an associate as much of a challenge to him as some old vitriolic diatribe by Trotsky or Zinoviev. The purge could not be limited to the elite; there had to be, though *proportionately* a much smaller number, many "two-faced traitors" among the population at large.

Considerations of personal vengeance played an increasing role. Stalin had always been a vile-tempered and dangerous man to cross. But before 1929 there was still an element of zest and enjoyment in his attacks and polemics against his opponents. Now, as he grew older, the strains he had endured between 1930 and 1933 turned his attitude into one of meanness and sadism. A more cynical man might have enjoyed the spectacle of Trotsky as a homeless exile with no support in Russia and barely a handful of partisans abroad loosening his impotent diatribes

[54] This was the name by which the plotters' group was identified as if they had proudly adopted it themselves. Absurd, even in the context of the obscene absurdity of the purge trials as a whole. But behind this absurdity there is a shrewd insight. The Soviet people, even if skeptical about the trials, were bound to refer to the "case of the Trotskyite-Zinovievite Terrorist Center." How unsound psychologically it would have been to let the accused be identified by the name they actually adopted in their struggle against Stalin in 1926–27, "The Leninist Bolsheviks."

against one of the world's most important leaders. A more civilized man might have tolerated Zinoviev and Kamenev as petty officials of his empire. But quite apart from the fear of war, Stalin now hated them more than he had when they had been his rivals. They defied and sullied his self-image as a man of destiny. His passion for revenge was not merely atrocious, it was vulgar. Wives and children of his victims were to suffer, for *no one* was to curse him, even in silence, with impunity.

Stalin's inhumanity fed on the idea of his own historic mission. He was the embodiment of the Revolution, the foundation on which Soviet power rested. It is possible that in his paradoxical fashion Stalin liked Bukharin. (In 1934 Bukharin's personal intercession with Stalin temporarily saved the life of Osip Mandelstam, denounced for having written his famous poem about "the slayer of peasants.") Roy Medvedev has described how on November 7, 1936, Bukharin, already sensing his forthcoming doom, was attending the anniversary parade. Stalin spotted him in the stands and sent an officer to ask Bukharin to join him and the other leaders on the top of the Lenin Mausoleum. Bukharin thought at first the officer was coming to arrest him. Refined sadism? Perhaps. It is at least possible, however, that Stalin meant it as a friendly gesture, one he would never have extended toward Zinoviev or Tomsky, who were personally loathsome to him. But as a dictator contemplating the possibility of war and defeat he would not allow himself the luxury of personal feelings. One had to destroy Bukharin, associate his name with murder and treason. Of all rationalizations for inhumanity, the reason of state is the easiest.

The Zinoviev-Kamenev trial and the other two great Moscow trials—the one of January 1937 of Pyatakov, Radek, and Sokolnikov, and the March 1938 spectacle featuring Bukharin, Rykov, and Yagoda—were the focal points of the Great Purge. Indeed, for an outsider they *were* the Great Purge—a view which largely obscures the fact that millions of others were being arrested and hundreds of thousands killed after trials behind closed doors or with no trials at all. A foreigner, even a well-informed non-Communist foreigner, was bound to miss the fact that the period of the Great Purge was also one of great fear which affected everybody from the Politburo member down to the street cleaner.[55] But even for the Russians the trials served as a major explanation of the horrors going on in society at large. Beginning in 1937 the educational purpose of the trials was enlarged, and they were to serve also as a lesson in recent history: food and goods shortages, economic failures, industrial accidents going back to the First Five-Year Plan were all interconnected

[55] A lifelong student of Russia, a Fabian Socialist in his beliefs, Sir John Maynard could thus write of Stalin: "It is the men in responsible places who have cause to fear. The rank and file are happy with their hero, and confident he is their friend." *The Russian Peasant and Other Studies* (London, 1942), p. 420.

pieces of a vast design of treason and crime, its ultimate source Trotsky and the intelligence services of several imperialist states, its main agencies the former "Left" and "Right" oppositions, its accomplices marshals, high officials of the NKVD, of all other state agencies and Party organizations. ☆☆☆

WHILE we cannot here consider the trials in detail,[56] we must review those elements which remain important to the story of Stalin and to the tragedy of twentieth-century politics.

The central point of the trials, and the precondition for holding them, was the willingness of the accused to confess, and the ability of those who were staging the trials to persuade Stalin that the defendants would repeat their confession in open court in a convincing manner. Why should people, some of whom had displayed great courage as revolutionaries, confess to heinous crimes they had not committed? At the time those who did not believe the confessions felt impelled to seek answers in the alleged "Russian soul" and its alleged need for self-humiliation, in the defendants' being drugged, etc. Even Medvedev, writing recently, grasped for explanations, like these: "It is said that Bukharin, Kamenev, and Rakovsky and others did not really appear in court; skillfully made up and specially trained NKVD agents supposedly took their place. . . . Today some comrades say the investigators may have used hypnosis and suggestion. . . ."[57] Did they, as Arthur Koestler argues in *Darkness at Noon*, plead guilty to false charges out of a perverse feeling of loyalty to the Party and Communism?

But the question should really be turned around: What enabled some individuals who were logical candidates for the hideous ritual, such as Yenukidze and Preobrazhensky, to resist all the manifold pressures for confession and thus compel Stalin to authorize their executions without a public trial? There was certainly nothing specifically Russian about the trials, and the ritual of confession would be repeated in trials in Central Europe after World War II, such as those of Slansky and Rajk. From the point of view of the prosecution, physical tortures or hypnotism would not have produced satisfactory performances in court. And the notion of the accused discharging their duty to the ideal of Communism is hopelessly romantic.

The problem of the false confessions is puzzling only if one takes an

---

[56] This has been done in masterful fashion by Conquest in *The Great Terror*.
[57] Medvedev, pp. 186–87.

unrealistic view of man's[58] capacity to endure constant battering and pressure by teams of inquisitors working for hours at a stretch; verbal abuse; confrontations with those who had already been broken and confessed, alternating with periods of solitary confinement; sleeplessness and terrible fatigue; fear threaded by hope that in submitting, one might still escape with life. Physical torture was used for the most part to extract confessions from those not slated for a public performance. With those who were, any experienced NKVD operative knew he needed mainly one thing: time. Having been worked over for two months to a year, most victims would greet a public trial with relief, even gratitude: for some it was an exciting *facsimile* of freedom—after a cell a large room with sounds and sights of many people—while for others it meant one step closer to getting it over with, to the final release.

It is at this stage that the regime ran some risk: the accused might again start having normal human feelings. And indeed some of them tried in court to repudiate part of their confessions, others "cheated" by employing double meanings or by verbal fencing with the prosecutor. But undoubtedly there were solid guarantees against the possibility of a really damaging outburst, such as a denunciation of Stalin: it is unlikely that anyone produced in court did not have someone close and dear to him—a wife or children—whose life depended on his performance. The proceedings could always be suspended. And a few might have hoped, or perhaps have even been promised, that their lives would be spared. All in all, one admires the fortitude of that handful who refused to be false witnesses for Stalin; one has no right, and it would be inhuman, to condemn those who were.

As for the reasons for the insistence on public self-incrimination by the accused, they are fairly obvious, and the practice antedates Stalin. From the beginning of the Soviet regime, the notion of a political trial was bound up with the accused confessing to the crime as charged. The technique was already being developed in Lenin's lifetime, as in the trial of the Socialist Revolutionaries in 1922. Most politically conscious Russians still remembered how political trials under Tsarism turned into indictments *of the regime* when the accused hurled defiance at the authorities and declined to collaborate with the prosecution. And so the pattern in a Soviet trial had to be different: the accused had to acknowledge his villainy, demonstrate that there could be no political dissent under the Soviets. The logical objection that such avowals would be greeted with widespread skepticism and at least suspicions that the confessions had been extorted seems very strong. "Who will believe a

---

[58] Especially middle-aged man's: none of those put on trial were really young or, except for the two doctors in the Bukharin trial, really old.

single word of ours?" said Yevdokimov at the August 1936 trial, a question that could not have pleased Vishinsky. But in the climate of Soviet Russia of the 1930s most people did.

The eight-year-old girl who wrote to the columnist of the *Baltimore Sun* inquiring whether Santa Claus really existed posed the kind of question that every totalitarian regime must strive to answer convincingly. Is there really such a thing as the class enemy? Of course there is! Sometimes one cannot see him, but one can observe the results of his nefarious strivings every day: goods shortages, train wrecks, attempted assassination of leaders who work so selflessly for the good. The child's simple query was echoed in the Russia of the purges by that simple soldier who asked of the Party instructor: "Why do enemies of the people always occupy the leading posts?"[59] But most people are neither sophisticated nor simple enough to ask such questions. Tales of wrong-doings in high places exert a great fascination on people's minds, especially at times of confusion and crisis. Even in the skeptical, pluralistic atmosphere of the United States in the 1950s, how many people professed to see all its internal and external troubles explained by the existence of a "Communist conspiracy," and how many in the late 1960s found the villain in the "military-industrial complex"? Here is the dialogue between the prosecutor and one of the accused who had been head of the consumers' distributive network:

VISHINSKY: That is, the public was offered felt boots in the summer and summer shoes in the winter?
ZELENSKY: Yes.
VISHINSKY: Was this your plan?
ZELENSKY: Yes.
VISHINSKY: Was this accidental, or was it a plan and a system?
ZELENSKY: Seeing that it was wrecking work, there can be no question of its having been accidental.[60]

And so the purge trials were a great morality play, illustrating that objective reality which Communism has imposed on 170 million inhabitants of the Soviet Union.

There can be no doubt that the man who inspired the trials came to believe in the *essential* veracity of the fantastic tales of treason and sabotage woven by his servants and confessed to by his former rivals and opponents. This to us may seem the most fantastic component of the whole story. How could this realistic politician, this subtle and skillful negotiator, *really* believe that Trotsky was working for the German

[59] Unlike the American newspaperman, the unfortunate instructor could not answer the question and as a result was expelled from the Party as a Trotskyite. Fainsod, p. 427.
[60] *Report of Court Proceedings in the Case of the Anti-Soviet "Bloc of Rights and Trotskyites"* (Moscow, 1938), p. 333.

General Staff, that Bukharin was plotting to detach Soviet Central Asia from the U.S.S.R. at the behest of the British Intelligence Service? But he was the same man who, once his passion and fury had been aroused, could readily believe, as in 1928, that *every* kulak was hiding 50,000 or 60,000 poods of grain, or, as in 1932, that the *peasants* were trying to starve the country. Was it really more fantastic to credit his enemies, and soon his former friends, with those plots and villainies to which they had confessed? The Bolshevik mind—and not only Stalin's, though his was the extreme case in point—was unable to distinguish between theoretical and factual reality, between the world of ideologically inspired dreams or suspicions and the world of hard facts. Who among the future victims of the purges raised his voice in 1928 against the trial of "bourgeois specialists" in the Shakhti case, or in 1930–31 against the similarly fraudulent trials of the "Working Peasant Party" and the formed Mensheviks? People as humane and rational as Bukharin and Rykov, both of them in 1928 still in positions of power, found themselves incapable of pleading for the falsely accused.[61] They must have realized, as Stalin did during the purge trials, that the indictment was manufactured and the confessions exacted through pressure. But these were "details"; the essential fact was that the accused were of hostile class origin and hence *capable* of the crimes of which they were charged. The principle "innocent until proven guilty" is not so much alien as incomprehensible to somebody nurtured on Communist dogmas and categories. Does one have to *prove* that the *kulak* is an enemy of the Soviet power? Even Bukharin in his most pro-peasant "liberal" period would have found such a question ridiculous. Freedom, wrote an English jurist, was secreted in the interstices of procedure. Stalinist terror bred upon Communist semantics: terms like class war, class justice, enemy of the people, encouraged a frame of mind in which individual guilt or innocence was the consequence not of facts but of political and social imperatives of the moment.

To be sure, the Zinoviev-Kamenev trial marked a new phase of this ideology-generated progression toward terror. Hitherto it was only the class enemy who was assumed to be capable, hence guilty, of treason and sabotage. Here were Lenin's closest companions confessing to actual—no longer, as they had in 1935, merely to moral—complicity in murder and treason. As Zinoviev was made to say, "My defective Bolshevism became transformed into anti-Bolshevism and through Trotskyism I arrived at fascism. . . . We filled the place of the Mensheviks, Socialist Revolutionaries, and White Guards who could not come out

[61] Conquest, pp. 549–50, reports some evidence that Rykov did in fact object in 1928. But the source from which the evidence is drawn is dubious: in the undoubtedly authentic report of the Bukharin-Kamenev conversations in 1928 there is no hint of any opposition within the Politburo to the trial.

openly in our country." And Kamenev, his inseparable partner in power, then in disgrace, and soon in death, asked, equally instructively: "Is it an accident that alongside of myself [and] Zinoviev . . . are sitting emissaries of foreign secret police departments, people with false passports, with dubious biographies and undoubted connections with the Gestapo? No! It is not an accident!"[62] It fell to I. N. Smirnov, the one among the accused who refused to accept any responsibility for actual terrorism, to spell out what might be called the positive message of the trial: "There is no other path for our country but the one it is now treading, and there is not, nor can there be, any other leadership than that which history has given us. . . . Trotsky . . . is an enemy."[63] While the trial was going on, mass meetings all over the country passed resolutions urging death for the traitors. Pyatakov and Rakovsky, old friends and associates of the accused, soon to share their fate, chimed in with letters to the press praising the vigilance of the security organs and urging that there should be no mercy.

It is possible that some of the accused had been promised their lives if they confessed. But they must have realized that it was unlikely Stalin would honor such a bargain: the whole educational effect of the trial would be spoiled and it would indeed appear as a contrived affair. Vishinsky demanded that "dogs gone mad should be shot—every one of them." Stalin was vacationing in the Caucasus when the Presidium of the Supreme Soviet rejected all the appeals for a commutation of death sentences, and all of the sixteen condemned were shot.

The story of the preparation and management of the Moscow trials must be a high point of both human depravity and human irrationality. We must not neglect the latter aspect by focusing entirely on the former. The trials were the product of Stalin's conscious designs, but they also fueled even further his pathological suspiciousness. Though the NKVD was told what they *must* produce, they were not limited to the basic scenario and were encouraged to discover, i.e., fabricate, additional plots. Yagoda and his subordinates then had a hunting license to discover ever wider-ranging treason and crime.[64] Stalin's manner, as

[62] *The Case of the Trotskyite-Zinovievite Terrorist Center*, p. 170.
[63] *Ibid.*, p. 171.
[64] It is unlikely that Stalin was concerned with the preparation or details of the accusations or with the mechanism of the trials. It is so alleged in a former NKVD official's revelations. A. Orlov, *The Secret History of Stalin's Crimes* (New York, 1953). But certainly this account is rather suspect. For one thing, it shows the NKVD operatives as unusually garrulous about matters on which any Soviet citizen, not to mention people in their position, would have realized how dangerous loose talk was. One assumes that the procedure was as follows: depositions would be taken or extorted from the accused and then circulated to Stalin and among the Politburo members. They would then be returned to the investigators with appropriate instructions.

behooved a true tyrant, was to keep even those closest to him in a state of uncertainty concerning his real thoughts and intentions. The chief of the police was then left in the unhappy predicament of trying to guess whom the Boss suspected or wanted to get rid of next. For two of them this proved to be a fatal dilemma. Should he cast his net wide enough to involve one of the Leader's "trusted comrades in arms," of whom he seemed to be growing tired? Or should he remain on the conservative side and unmask just those with undoubted Trotskyite and Zinovievite credentials? But then one might be accused of failing to display proper vigilance and Bolshevik initiative or, worse, of covering up for two-faced traitors and criminals.

The preparation of the Zinoviev-Kamenev trial was Yagoda's swan song as head of the NKVD. There are several aspects of the trial that must have increased Stalin's determination to get rid of a man whom he distrusted even more than most of his lieutenants. Yagoda had obviously been charged with the task of "uncovering" the story of a terrorist plot against a number of Soviet leaders. In the trial it came out as follows:

> The materials of the investigation have established that the united Trotskyite-Zinovievite Terrorist Center, after it had killed Comrade Kirov, did not confine itself to organizing the assassination of Comrade Stalin alone. The terrorist Trotskyite-Zinovievite Center simultaneously carried on work to organize assassinations of other leaders of the Party, Comrades Voroshilov, Zhdanov, Kaganovich, Kosior, Orjonikidze, and Postyshev.[65]

This is a very curious list. It includes Zhdanov and Postyshev, then alternate members of the Politburo, but does not include Molotov, then the second person in the state, nor four other full Politburo members (as of 1936): Kalinin, Mikoyan, Andreyev, and Chubar. No wonder that rumors immediately circulated that Molotov was in disgrace and that his days in power were numbered.

This select list must then be considered in conjunction with another element of the drama. The network of treason was to be broadened by implicating many others, including principally the former "Right Oppositionists." Thus Kamenev testified:

> They sympathized with me. When I asked Tomsky about Rykov's frame of mind, he replied "Rykov thinks the same as I do." In reply to my question as to what Bukharin thought, he said "Bukharin thinks the same as I do, but is pursuing tactics of persistently enrooting himself [*sic:* the English of the official translation of the first trial transcript is atrocious] in the Party and winning the personal confidence of the leadership."[66]

[65] *Ibid.*, p. 35.
[66] *Ibid.*, p. 68.

No wonder that on August 21 Vishinsky interrupted the session to inform the court and the Soviet public that, "Yesterday I gave orders to institute an investigation of these statements of the accused in regard to Tomsky, Rykov, Bukharin. . . ."[67] Tomsky did not wait for the investigation but shot himself upon the announcement, undoubtedly to Stalin's fury, since he disliked him more than any other alleged "Right Oppositionist." But then, surprise of surprises, on September 10 it was announced that the proceedings against Bukharin and Rykov were being dropped because of lack of evidence.

From Stalin's point of view this was an extremely bad show. Worse than that, clear evidence of bad faith on the part of those staging the trial, primarily Yagoda. By not including Molotov and four others of the Politburo on the select list of those to be assassinated along with the Leader, his chief of police meant more than just to hurt their feelings. They were bound to wonder whether it was Stalin himself who had deprived them of this signal honor, thereby signifying his doubts about their loyalty, perhaps an intention to correct this startling oversight on the part of the "Trotskyite-Zinovievite Terrorist Center." At best it was throwing an apple of discord into the Politburo: some of its members were now unlikely to take a positive view of the need for further purges and show trials. It was undoubtedly an attempt by Yagoda to sabotage the trial and punishment of his old friends from the "Right Opposition." Tomsky had now definitely escaped having to confess his nefarious schemes in open court, and the Politburo insisted on quashing the proceedings againt Bukharin and Rykov. If they escaped this fate, the whole effect of the Zinoviev-Kamenev trial would be spoiled and the momentum of the purges interrupted. Stalin's predicament in regard to the purges in September 1936 was analogous to that he faced in regard to collectivization in the spring and summer of 1928: he had drawn the first blood but then faced political complications which forced him to delay putting his full plan into effect.

At first glance it seems unrealistic to credit Yagoda with either the ability or the courage to stave off Stalin's plans. But he had the best of all reasons, that of self-preservation, to try to limit the purges. Perhaps if there were enough opposition in the Politburo, Stalin would be content to liquidate the remaining former partisans of Trotsky and Zinoviev and spare the rest of Lenin's old guard. Yagoda was an Old Bolshevik, having joined the Party as a teen-ager in 1907. It was not sentimental concern for Bukharin and Rykov that prompted him—what could personal friendship mean to such a man at such a time?—but the realization that

---

[67] A pedant might have observed that since these incriminatory statements had been made already in the pretrial deposition by the accused, such an investigation should have been ordered long before.

if they went, most prerevolutionary Communists would follow. Stalin did not trust him, and had Yezhov supervise the security organs. But Yagoda may well have deluded himself by believing that his professional expertise rendered him indispensable to Stalin. He had been with the dreadful organization practically from its inception and had all along functioned as its actual head, in view of his predecessor's illness long before 1934, when he formally took over. How could any newcomer familiarize himself overnight with all the intricacies of repression and provocation, of espionage and counterespionage, all those secrets of the trade? Unlike other Soviet institutions where constant flux of personnel was the rule, most of the high officials of the NKVD had grown with it from the days of the Cheka. How could the regime, how could Stalin, dispense with him? He was the guardian of so many secrets, the supreme expert on the distinction between "objective" reality and real reality. This professional pride did not abandon Yagoda even in his fall. He was to beg the court to remember the vast construction projects and canals built by convict labor—all of them the fruit of his enterprise. And while he was to plead guilty to various crimes, he would not admit to having been a spy: "I am not jesting when I say that if I had been a spy dozens of countries could have closed down their intelligence services—there would have been no need for them to maintain such a mass of spies as have now been caught in the Soviet Union."[68]

Yagoda should have realized that in Stalin's scheme of things there was no room for an organization with even a shadow of independence. The anomalous position of the security organs in this respect had long displeased Stalin, and he had tried to control it through his Special Department of the Secretariat. But, of course, under Soviet conditions, and being Stalin, he could never overcome the suspicion that the political police were not telling him everything.[69] In the Zinoviev-Kamenev trial alleged attempts on Stalin's life were described in realistic detail. It was, of course, right and desirable for the accused to confess to plotting against him, but what was the need for such vivid, one might say suggestive, details? It is likely that of all those who were tried and condemned on fictitious charges, Yagoda was the one whom Stalin came to believe was *literally* guilty of scheming against him.[70]

---

[68] *Report of Court Proceedings in the Case of the Anti-Soviet "Bloc of Rights and Trotskyites,"* p. 786.

[69] In World War II Stalin tried to draw Churchill out on the subject of Rudolf Hess: Hadn't he been charged by Hitler with a secret mission to the British Government? Churchill replied with some heat that he could never have countenanced such negotiations, and it was all nonsense, whereupon Stalin replied soothingly that perhaps the Prime Minister did not know the full story. *His* secret police, Stalin observed, sometimes kept things from him too!

[70] The alleged would-be assassin delegated by Trotsky was supposed to shoot Stalin at a session of the Seventh Comintern Congress, but could not get close enough. In

With Stalin on vacation, ruminating on the untrustworthiness of human nature, preparations were going on in Moscow for another show trial. The Politburo members who had stopped the proceedings against Bukharin and Rykov may well have believed that their absent leader would be appeased if some of the surviving notables of the Left Opposition were subjected to the ordeal. In his announcement concerning further investigations Vishinsky had mentioned Pyatakov, Radek, Serebryakov, and Sokolnikov. These men were now arrested. It is improbable that Stalin's colleagues could have been pleased with what was being prepared. Unlike the defendants in the first trial, the new batch had been working in fairly high Soviet positions: Sokolnikov as Assistant Commissar of Foreign Affairs, Pyatakov as Orjonikidze's deputy at the Commissariat of Heavy Industry. But perhaps Stalin was just settling old scores. They had all actively opposed his rise and their condemnation might quench his thirst for blood.

Molotov for one was making sure that at the next trial his name would be included in the roll of honor, i.e., among those who had been slated for assassination along with the "greatest genius of the era." After his return to Moscow from vacation on September 1, Molotov soon had another reason for irritation and, if he was superstitious, for apprehension: *Pravda* had discovered a horrid case of journalistic "wrecking." A story on September 3 reported that a provincial newspaper, while referring to the second man in the Soviet Union, had *skipped three letters,* with results so ghastly that *Pravda* could not reveal them to its readers but assured them that both the editor and copy editor in question must be "two-faced Trotskyites."[71] This story may well have made Stalin's day when he read it, and it is possible that the editor in question was not even shot. But Molotov now conveniently remembered that during a tour of Siberia in 1934 he had been involved in an automobile accident. The security organs were cooperative. On September 21 Molotov's driver on that unfortunate occasion was already confessing to the NKVD that "the Trotskyite terrorists . . . attempted to kill Comrade V. M. Molotov by causing an automobile crash."

Yagoda's star still shone brightly. Pictures of festive occasions—opening of a new canal built by convict labor or welcoming the Soviet

future trials such realism concerning alleged attempts on the life of the Leader was omitted.

71 Most Russians had no difficulty in deciphering what had happened: if you skip three letters in Molotov's title, you come out with—oh, horror!—"traitor Molotov" instead of "Chairman Molotov." (The press, according to *Pravda*, was full of such wrecking. Another provincial paper had mixed up its headlines and under "Death to the Trotskyist Traitors" had carried the story of a triumphant reception of Soviet aviators who had just beaten some records, while "Hail to the Heroes of the Skies" graced a discussion of the purge trial. As *Pravda* observed, "Even to the most inexperienced eye, this is obvious sabotage and provocation.")

aviators returning from a new triumph—featured the General Commissioner of State Security next to bigwigs like Molotov or Kaganovich. But both he and the Politburo members lived in a fools' paradise if they believed that they had "fooled Stalin." To be sure, they must have been worried by the fact that though the vacation period was over Stalin was not returning to Moscow. Was he sulking in his tent, about to threaten them with resignation, or what? On September 25 he let them know. On that day a telegram was sent to Kaganovich, Molotov, and other members of the Politburo over the signatures of Stalin and his houseguest in Sochi, Zhdanov: "We consider it absolutely necessary and urgent to appoint Comrade Yezhov as Commissar of Internal Affairs. Yagoda has definitely proved himself unequal to the task of exposing the Trotskyite-Zinovievite bloc. The NKVD is four years behind in this matter. This is noted by all Party workers and most of the NKVD regional agents."[72] The next day Yezhov was so appointed. Yagoda was transferred to the Commissariat of Post and Telegraphs from which Rykov had been dismissed. The full import of Yagoda's fall was not immediately realized, since the announcement had been accompanied by his picture—which would not have been done had the people below the Politburo level known that his new post was to be but a brief interlude before a prison cell.

The telegram marked a new stage in Stalin's dictatorship. For now the Politburo's function even as an *advisory* organ was challenged. Stalin (his current favorite not a full member of the body) was ordering it to do something which would have required at least the formality of discussion before. Stalin eschewed even the seemingly simpler way of calling Molotov or Kaganovich on the phone. It is clear that he meant it as a test of will: he wouldn't even argue; let them refuse or temporize if they dared. They did not.

The NKVD was, as the phrase went, the "unsheathed sword of the Revolution." As such its functions went beyond those pertaining to political police even in other totalitarian systems, since even prior to 1936 its activities were not limited to uncovering and uprooting *actual* treason and dissent, but were meant to uncover and destroy every *potential* threat to the regime, to serve as the instrument of class justice (that is, to repress "hostile class elements"), and to collect information about the *real* political feelings of the population. We get a more adequate, but still not complete, description of it by imagining an institution which combines the functions of the ordinary police, the FBI, the Internal Revenue Service, and the Holy Inquisition. Ever since Dzerzhinsky's death, it was tacitly assumed that its head and high officials

[72] This telegram was revealed by Khrushchev in his 1956 speech and its somewhat differing texts are given in Medvedev, p. 171, and in Wolfe, p. 130.

should *not* be Party leaders of the first rank, nor people taking active part in intraparty decision making.

With the appointment of Yezhov, the security apparatus was taken out of the hands of a professional and a cynic and entrusted to a newcomer, a man (as Stalin realized) deranged in a way that made him particularly suitable for this position at this time. The job called for a man with no compunctions about liquidating the Old Bolsheviks and hence with no ties to the pre-Revolution Party. Yezhov had no connection with any past or present greats; he would not keep Stalin in the dark concerning the schemes or plots behind his back. Already in 1936 Stalin must have given some thought to appointing Beria to the post. But Beria was too much of a politician. For the job at hand Stalin needed an unreasoning and fanatical scoundrel, not a clever one, a warped idealist rather than a contriver.

Stalin's desperate realism now led to an incredible plan of repression and terror. The Spanish Civil War erupted on July 28. Italo-German support for the Spanish rebels made it clear that fascism was going on the offensive. Another signal that a war was now almost inevitable was the Anti-Comintern Pact between Germany and Japan. For all the pious language of the public part of the treaty, which pledged both countries to cooperate in opposing the *spread* of Communism, it had to be taken as a clear preliminary to an attack on the U.S.S.R. from both East and West. If so, who could believe that the advancing aggressors would not find ready support within the U.S.S.R.? "Fifth Column" was just coming into fashion in connection with the events in Spain. How many such columns would form in the Soviet Union on the day of a foreign attack? Could Stalin rely on the army, many of whose leaders were injured by him during or since the Civil War and some of whom owed the beginnings of their careers to Trotsky? Would the Ukrainian peasant, first in the path of aggression, fight for a regime that had exiled or starved members of his family? The first defeat—and how could one avoid initial defeats if attacked from both sides?—would mark the end of the legend of "the greatest genius of the era." Would the Bukharins, Pyatakovs, and all the rest continue to serve him in an hour of defeat and danger? It now became clear why they had submitted so meekly and stomached all their demotions and humiliations. War was what they had been waiting for. *Objectively*, they were nothing but spies and wreckers praying for a national emergency, for an opportunity to destroy Stalin. But not only they: colleagues and servants who had chafed under his leadership had tried to sabotage his plans and, as recently as 1934, flatter him into semiretirement. It would be strange and contrary to human nature if many of them were not waiting for the opportunity to get rid of him, to offer him as a sacrifice to national unity.

The purge had to strike beyond the elite. At every level of society there were potential traitors. Prudence dictated that those with even the most remote inclinations in such directions be exterminated. A whole generation was to be struck down. Many innocent and valuable people would be lost. But there were others, brought up in unquestioning obedience to the Soviet state, who would be able to step into their places. Stalin could have no illusions as to the risks this dreadful course would incur. But the experience of collectivization suggested that repression, if swift and concentrated, can be amazingly effective. Fear and the gratitude of having been spared combine to smother inclinations toward actual disloyalty. During the next three years most thinking Russians were too preoccupied by the possibility of a false accusation to do anything that would incur a true one. When war came, treason might—in fact, probably would—be reborn, but it would be headless and diffused treason, for he would have destroyed its main potential reservoirs, killed off everyone who might proclaim that you could fight for Russia, for Communism, without fighting for Stalin.

This entire scheme was one of political and psychological realism pushed to the border of madness. The chorus of worship and adulation which grew all the more insistent the deeper Stalin waded in blood was for Stalin more than something required by his megalomania, it was the one barrier keeping him from stepping over this border into actual and debilitating insanity. For himself as well as for simple-minded believers it was a constant and needed reassurance that it was not one man's irrational whim and suspiciousness but the interests of Russia and of the new social order that were exacting these appalling sacrifices.

In his famous telegram Stalin had asserted that the NKVD and Yagoda in particular were "four years late" in exposing the Trotskyite-Zinovievite bloc. The thrust of this remark was obvious. The security organs began to catch up with the traitors only in 1934, after Kirov's murder. But of course the treasonous plotting by Trotsky et al. against the Soviet government and people must have gone on long before then. Stalin's charge, which the NKVD would try subsequently to implement, was to characterize the period since at least 1930 as one of constant "wrecking" by the Trotskyites and Bukharinites. All the suffering during the collectivizations, all the failures and privations during the First Five-Year Plan, were to be laid at the door of his former opponents, explained to the Soviet people as part of a design conceived in the first place in Berlin and Tokyo. Here again Yagoda managed to give the Zinoviev-Kamenev trial an unduly narrow political character. Much as the good Soviet people were expected to be horrified at the story of the assassination of Kirov and similar attempts on the life of Stalin and other leaders, it was also necessary to demonstrate to them how the same scoundrels plotted to injure little people. And to be sure, intriguing stories of plots against the high and mighty alternated in the trials to come with vivid details of how the traitors arranged to cause shortages and confusion, to have nails mixed with butter, how "the German intelligence service, through the Trotskyites," made a special point of organizing wrecking in horse-breeding "in order . . . to deprive the Red Army of horses," how "the task set for me by Rykov was to arouse the anger of the peasants against the policy of the Party . . . by extending to the middle peasants the repressive measures established for the kulaks, and to rouse discontent among the workers by disorganizing the supply of bread."

There is no reason to think that this seemingly crude technique was not to a large extent effective. It enabled Stalin to dissociate himself in the popular mind from many of the oustanding economic failures of the past and present. The point often made about the irrationality of the purges touches on the general impression they must have produced on the people: one after another high official of the Party and the state are unmasked as criminals and traitors; how could Soviet citizens retain trust in or respect for the Party and their rulers? But this was *precisely* the lesson Stalin was striving to teach: apart from himself, not even a Politburo member was to be above suspicion. He was the rock, the foundation upon which the whole system was built. It may seem insane, but it is probably true that a successful coup against Stalin in 1937 or 1938 would have been taken by most Soviet citizens as added confirmation that treason was widespread. People close to Stalin whom he was eventually to kill or drive to suicide may have given some thought at least to the possibility of taking the tyrant's life rather than or in addition to their own. But someone in that position, like Orjonikidze, must have been restrained by the reflection that by this act he would bring down the Soviet system and stamp as a lie his whole life as a Communist. To strike down Stalin would have required the kind of courage which only complete criminality or inflexible morality can muster. Stalin knew his closest collaborators, and only they stood a chance of assassinating him: they were capable of neither. They were, as Mandelstam called them, "half-men," who even in their criminality were pale imitations of their leader. ☆☆☆

THE second Great Purge trial opened in Moscow on January 23, 1937. Its proceedings reflected improved preparations and management (from Stalin's point of view) of the spectacle. The Kirov assassination was now relegated to second place while the main element was a vast panorama of "wrecking" and sabotage in the economic field, in which the accused indulged at the command of the German and Japanese intelligence services,[73] transmitted to them by Trotsky. This time there was no clear-cut hierarchy of those who had been slated for assassination in addition to Stalin, but only the "leadership," or "leaders." To be sure, the attempt on Molotov's life was given great prominence, probably to compensate the Prime Minister for being neglected previously. Some upcoming Party figures were mentioned—Beria, the Party boss in the Caucasus, and an alternate Politburo member, R. Eikhe—but in the increasing flux of Soviet politics such indications were no longer reliable as portents of future greatness. Beria, to be sure, was to go on to bigger things, but among the people he was to liquidate at Stalin's order was none other but Eikhe. The regime was now more self-confident about the educational and propaganda value of the trials. More spectators were allowed. And there was a touching faith that the trials were having a positive effect abroad. Of the Zinoviev-Kamenev trial, only a summary was published in (very bad) English; this time the Ministry of Justice went to the trouble and expense of a handsome *verbatim* version competently translated. Let the whole world know the truth: the Soviet government had nothing to hide.[74]

The accused—to give them their official and self-adopted name, the Anti-Soviet Trotskyite Center—included such recent high officials as Pyatakov, Sokolnikov, and Radek. In other words, it was the second team or, in the words of the indictment, the "reserve center" of the old Left Opposition. The moral of the trial was clearly spelled out by Radek when he revealed the following passage from a letter he received from Trotsky (which, needless to say, was never produced):

> It must be admitted that the question of power will become a practical issue for the bloc only as a result of the defeat of the U.S.S.R. in war. For this the bloc must make energetic preparations. . . . Since the principal condition for the Trotskyites [*sic*] coming into power, if they fail to achieve this by means of terrorism, would be the defeat of the U.S.S.R. it is necessary as much as possible to hasten the clash between the U.S.S.R. and Germany.[75]

Trotsky was evidently full of such succinct and vivid instructions. As Pyatakov testified: "I advised my people (and did so myself) not to scatter their wrecking activities, but to concentrate their attention on the principal big industrial enterprises of defence and national importance. On this point I acted on Trotsky's directives: to strike blows at

[73] In view of the Anti-Comintern Pact, Japan was added to Germany as an employer of traitors and Trotskyites.
[74] We shall take up the subject of foreign reactions at the time of the Bukharin trial.
[75] *The Case of the Anti-Soviet Trotskyite Center* (Moscow, 1937), p. 9.

the most sensitive places."[76] For all the conspirators' laudable resolve to eschew such normal appurtenances of their trade as coded messages, indirect language, for all their eagerness to present their motivation in the most straightforward unambiguous form, some of the plots revealed in the trial were amazingly complex. It must have taken the accused quite a while after they consented to confess to memorize all the details of "their" wrecking.

That the security organs and Vishinsky should have gone to all this seemingly unnecessary trouble reflected two things. First, their shrewdness. People are often willing to believe the most thinly established slander when it concerns human motivations, but when it comes to actual plots, credulity and interest grow in proportion to the richness of detail. It would have been suspect for Pyatakov to say: "I just 'wrecked' whenever and wherever possible." So the usual story ran something like this: "I contacted my deputy, X, who checked and issued appropriate instructions to Manager Y. He in turn decided that Mine Number Three was the best place for sabotage. Engineer Z was then told to stop the pumps and have the mine flooded while at the same time fire was started in the offices. . . ." Who would invent, nay, remember, such details unless they were true?

There was also an element of professional pride, of career considerations. Yezhov was now purging the NKVD of Yagoda men. Most of the investigators must have hoped that if they wove a pretty and complicated tale of sabotage and if the accused recited it well, their chief might be persuaded to retain them, or the Boss himself might be impressed in reading it. Alas, such hopes were unfounded: most of the NKVD officials who composed confessions prior to 1937 were making them within a year before a new batch of inquisitors, and, since they were not slated to be produced in court, they were beaten and tortured in the process.

One man who escaped this fate was, of course, Vishinsky. The ex-Menshevik, promoted from judge to prosecutor, was the star of all the big Moscow trials, and as such he acquired fame throughout the nation rivaling that of the record-breaking pilots and "shock workers."[77]

---

[76] *Ibid.*, p. 11.

[77] In an enormously popular novel describing the heroics of Soviet youth under the German occupation (much of it based on a real-life story) two of the teen-age heroes discuss the pros and cons of a legal career: " 'All in all it is awkward to be a defender in our system,' said Jerry. 'Remember the trial of those saboteur scoundrels. I always think how silly the defenders' situation was.' And Jerry laughed, showing his dazzling white teeth. 'Well, to be a defender is of course not interesting, since we have people's court, but it would be very interesting to be an investigating judge. You get to know all sorts of people.' 'Best of all to be the prosecutor,' said Jerry. 'Remember Vishinsky. How splendid.' " A. Fadeyev, *The Young Guard* (Moscow, 1966); p. 98. This passage was allowed to remain, even though by the time the

Vishinsky's mastery of all the fictional evidence with which he had to deal, his brutal and sarcastic manner with the defendants, the Ciceronian prose of his accusatory speeches must have impressed Stalin. How amusing it might have been to have Vishinsky himself confess, and what interesting tales could his prosecutor be made to avow! In 1908, when they were both in Baku, it might have been Vishinsky who turned him in to the Tsarist police! And being Polish and an ex-Menshevik, he was a natural for a spy. But Vishinsky was too valuable to sacrifice. Fortunately for him, his connection with successive NKVD chiefs was not too close; he was evidently not on the planning end of the purges. And so the hideous man not only was spared but went on to new honors in diplomacy.

The prosecutor's main task was to avoid any major slipups in open court; this, despite the fact that the accused had been carefully tested for their dependability on this score, was not always easy. Radek readily recited the prepared material, as ordered, implicating people like Bukharin, throwing out first hints of the treason of Marshal Tukhachevsky. But the irrepressible jester could not miss his last opportunity to display his famous wit and must have given the prosecutor some difficult moments. "I was arrested," he said at one point, "but I denied everything from beginning to end. Maybe you will ask my why." And when Vishinsky was pressing him a bit too much: "You are a profound reader of human hearts, but I must nevertheless comment on my thoughts in my own words. . . . You are the State Prosecutor and may demand that I repeat it ten times." Radek managed to reveal that for two and a half months he had resisted the pressure to make him confess. He said it in his own inimitable way. "The question has been raised here whether we were tormented while under investigation.[78] I must say that it was not I who was tormented but I who tormented the examining officials and compelled them to perform a lot of useless work."[79] In his last words, the nimblewitted man managed to convey what looks suspiciously like a message for foreign Communists to keep out of Russia: "We say to the Trotskyite elements in France, Spain, and other countries—and there are such—that the experience of the Russian Revolution has shown that Trotskyism is a wrecker of the labor movement. We must warn them that if they do not learn from our experience, they will pay for it with their heads."[80]

Radek was among the four defendants who were not sentenced to

---

edition appeared, Vishinsky had been denounced and the Moscow trials, though not officially repudiated, acknowledged to have been based on fraudulent evidence.

[78] To be sure, no one had raised it before him!

[79] *The Case of the Anti-Soviet Trotskyite Center,* p. 549.

[80] *Ibid.,* p. 550.

death, but "only" to ten years in a camp. It was quite possible that Stalin thought of the use his brilliant pen and his knowledge of world politics might play if the U.S.S.R. should find itself in war on the side of the democracies. But he did not survive until June 1941. Simultaneously with the appointment of Yezhov, Stalin ordered an end put to any favored treatment of the "politicals" in prisons and labor camps, to those indulgences and special treatments which had lingered on since Tsarist times and which had enabled Koba-Djugashvili to try to escape several times without additional penalties. The regime for political prisoners was to be much harder than that for common criminals, with whom they were to be indiscriminately mixed. At the hands of one of the latter, Radek, a man whose wit lightens the grim story of Stalinism and provides one of its few elements of relief, met his end in 1939.

Radek knew why he was being destroyed. "We are living in times of great strain, we are on the verge of war." In Western liberal and progressive circles the Spanish Civil War tended to blunt much of the criticism of the Moscow trials. The Soviets were being unreasonable and uncivilized in dealing with their political opposition, but Stalin's Russia was the only country to provide real help to Republican Spain. This contrasted with Britain's and France's pusillanimity (even though in France one was speaking of a Popular Front government which the Communists supported though they had refused to participate in it). It took Stalin some time to decide on a public gesture in favor of the embattled Republicans. The insurrection started on July 28, 1936, but it was only on October 4 that Stalin in a telegram to the head of the Spanish Communist Party asserted his support of the Republic. He was eager that his policy in Spain should not alienate his prospective French and British allies, though judging by their performance on Spain, any vigorous anti-fascist stand on their part grew more and more unlikely. In December he, along with Molotov and Voroshilov, warned the new Spanish Prime Minister, the left-wing Socialist Francisco Largo Caballero, to avoid any radical social policies and thus win the middle class to his side. He should spare no effort, the letter went on, "to prevent the enemies of Spain from presenting it as a Communist republic." The Soviets were careful to avoid a close identification with the Republican military effort. Soviet military experts and equipment were dispatched, but unlike Germany or Italy, the Soviet Union dispatched no regular army or air units of its own. The Comintern recruited Communists all over the world to fight in the International Brigades, but even here the note of prudence was unmistakable: their subdivisions bore names like that of Ernst Thälmann, currently in a Nazi concentration camp, or Abraham Lincoln; it was an oddity, though nobody seemed to have noticed it at the time, that none was named after Lenin or Stalin.

The fact remained that Russia was doing something to try to stop the march of fascism, that Communism appeared to extend a helping hand to an embattled democracy, while the French and British statesmen prattled on about nonintervention in Spain, where German planes and pilots and fascist legions were openly assisting Franco. And so the anguish over the behavior of their own governments stifled what would otherwise have been a reaction of mixed horror and incredulity at what was going on in Moscow.[81]

The Pyatakov-Radek trial was a fitting opening for 1937, a year of horror stamped indelibly on the memory of those then alive and beyond infancy. Even for many who were then small children the memory of that terrible year would linger to their grave, for many of their parents, brothers, and other relatives disappeared, some forever, others to reappear years later from the camps. The sufferings and losses of the years of World War II did not erase the peculiar horror of 1937: one's own government, one's own countrymen, were perpetuating those crimes. To prepare for war, Stalin and his servants imposed havoc and fear such as few wars in modern history have been able to equal.

Symbolically the first major victim following the trial was a man from Stalin's closest circle. Gregory "Sergo" Orjonikidze was his oldest friend, a member of the Politburo, Commissar of Heavy Industry. In Party circles Orjonikidze enjoyed genuine popularity. Unlike Molotov or Kaganovich, he was reputed on occasion to stand up to Stalin and to try to soften his cruel disposition. It is quite possible that the very fact of their early intimacy, the memory of the pre-Revolution days when Orjonikidze ranked him in the Party, now grated on Stalin. Later on it was alleged that the tyrant's new favorite, then head of the Trans-caucasian Party, Lavrenti Beria, had for a long time intrigued against Orjonikidze and worked systematically to arouse Stalin's suspicions against him. But it is oversimple to see Beria as Stalin's evil spirit and a *major* cause of the Great Purge. Still, with his ever deepening suspicions and a growing apprehension of what might happen when war came, Stalin was not unwilling to listen to tales about people closest to him and came to resent those who had known him as Koba. Beria's rise was enhanced by the very fact that those who knew him, like Orjonikidze, considered him a scoundrel and advised Stalin accordingly: a man like that had to be personally loyal; perhaps the very hostility against him

---

[81] Something parallel was to occur some thirty years later. The excesses of the Chinese Cultural Revolution were greeted in the West at first with a mixture of indignation and amusement. But as time went on, America's role and performance in Vietnam tended to obscure the Chinese drama. Mao, who in 1966 was the butt of so many jokes in the Western press on account of his famous swimming feats, and whose sanity was questioned because of the vast repression he had loosed on the Party and the country, reemerged at the end of the decade as a wise and masterful statesman.

was prompted by fear that he would unmask their intrigues, tell Stalin what they were saying behind his back. In his new phase Stalin subjected some of his leading collaborators (Kaganovich, Kalinin, Molotov, Mikoyan) to an inhuman test: close relatives would be arrested and held on fictitious charges while they were supposed to go on serving him without interceding for their dear ones. Now Orjonikidze, to the public one of the first men in the state and a "close comrade-at-arms of great Stalin," was expected to be working at his desk, appear smiling in photographs at the side of the Leader, while somewhere in an NKVD jail his older brother Papulia was being tortured.[82] Orjonikidze was not a healthy man: he had undergone operations and suffered from high blood pressure and a heart ailment. And now on February 19 the Central Committee was to assemble to consider the "lessons" of the Pyatakov-Radek trial and to order new measures of repression against wreckers and saboteurs. Orjonikidze's part was a key one: his deputy Pyatakov had been shot, several of his most important subordinates and industrial directors had been arrested. He was to make a report on "wrecking" in industry and on further measures of repression to deal with spies and saboteurs.

But the meeting had to be adjourned. On the very day it was slated to open, newspapers carried the news of Orjonikidze's sudden death on the preceding day from a heart attack.

That Orjonikidze in fact committed suicide was well known in top Party circles, and it is incredible—as Khrushchev, in 1937 head of the Moscow Party organization, was to allege in 1956—that Khrushchev learned the true facts of the death only many years later. We know[83] that on the morning of February 17 Orjonikidze had a tempestuous interview with Stalin. He wanted to know why his office had been searched by the NKVD. Nothing unusual about it, replied Stalin; why, the NKVD might very well be ordered to search his own office! Orjonikidze worked for the balance of the day in his Commissariat, attending to various items of business, issuing dispositions for the future. He returned to his Kremlin apartment at two A.M. The next morning he refused to get out of bed, and at five-thirty in the afternoon the shot rang out. Zinaida Gavrilovna Orjonikidze phoned Stalin, but he refused to see the widow of his lifelong friend alone, and arrived only after a while, accompanied by other members of the Politburo and Yezhov. According to Roy Medvedev, who collected evidence from eyewitnesses, Zinaida Gavrilovna shouted at the dictator, "You did not protect Sergo

[82] It is not clear whether Papulia was executed prior to or following his brother's suicide.
[83] The facts are presented in the 1963 edition of Ilya Dubinsky-Mukhadze, *Orjoni-kidze*. They were omitted in the 1966 edition of the same book.

for me or for the Party"[84]—certainly in the circumstances a masterpiece of understatement. Stalin's unsentimental reply was, "Shut up, you fool." His reaction on the death of the man whose recommendation had been instrumental in Lenin's appointing him to the Central Committee in 1912, and whose help had been essential at several other crucial points of his career, was one of wonder: "What an odd disease. Man lies down to rest, has a heart attack, and there." This, it is hardly necessary to add, was the official verdict of the medical certificate signed by four distinguished doctors, three of whom were subsequently liquidated.

"Why did Orjonikidze shoot himself and not Stalin?" asks a Soviet author. We have already tried to answer this question. Knowing him well, it is unlikely that Orjonikidze could have thought that his act of desperation would bring any remorse in Stalin or make him abandon or temper his bloody designs. The tyrant must have viewed his friend's suicide as an attack upon *himself*, a stab in the back: Orjonikidze deserted his post, tried to bring confusion and doubt into the highest Party ranks, discredit that essential work being done by the NKVD. It was undoubtedly great generosity on his part, Stalin believed, to cover his dead comrade with honors, to give him a hero's funeral, and to leave that chatterbox, Orjonikidze's wife, free. But Stalin's suspicions pursued a person even after his death. As after his wife's death, Stalin now brooded over the meaning of Sergo's suicide: What had he really meant by this act? Would his relatives talk, spread the true story, breed defeatism through gossip? One by one Orjonikidze's closest relatives and co-workers who knew the facts were arrested. In 1942, the year of supreme danger, when the Germans approached the Caucasus, Stalin remembered his fellow Caucasian, and orders went out to change the names of several cities and towns called after Orjonikidze. There was no point in commemorating the man who had betrayed him.

The Central Committee session began on February 23 and lasted for ten days. For most of its members it must have been a most unusual experience: they were discussing a rationalization of their own liquidation. Few of them could have been under any illusions on this count when on March 3 Stalin listed three "basic and indisputable facts" which he said had emerged from the meeting. "First, the wrecking and spying activity of foreign agents, in which the Trotskyites played a sizable role, hurt to a lesser or greater degree all or almost all our institutions—economic, Party, administrative. Second: foreign agents, among them Trotskyites, have infiltrated not only the lower ranks but also some leading posts." After this promising beginning, Stalin turned on those present, telling them in so many words and to their faces that

[84] Medvedev, p. 195.

they had been unable, because of their "carelessness, indifference, and naïveté," to unmask the "wreckers, spies, and murderers."[85] What had been the source of this political blindness? In the first place it was another case of being "dizzy with success." People were so impressed with the successes of the U.S.S.R. that they forgot that as long as there are capitalist states there will be spies and wreckers. This was an almost exact copy of his famous pronouncement of nine years earlier and that as long as there were kulaks there would be sabotage and wrecking. Will there *always*, a skeptic might ask, be spies, etc., etc.? Will there never come a time when a Communist will be able to say with the poet, "Moment stay, thou art fair," when no more vigilance would be required? Precisely, said Comrade Stalin, again the logician: it is a "rotten and dangerous theory" to claim that as things get better the enemy becomes less dangerous or, in Marxist-Leninist terms, "the more we succeed, the less dangerous and tamer becomes the class enemy." What blindness! It was obvious that the more the U.S.S.R. and Communism succeeded, the more dangerous the class enemy became. Here, then, Stalin formulated his famous contribution to Marxian theory and logic: the closer you get to socialism, the sharper becomes the character of the class war. The ignorance of this salutary principle, Stalin continued, had led to strange and dangerous practices. Many people believed that the wrecker was simply a man engaged in sabotage. But a clever wrecker would obviously not wreck all the time: "A real wrecker will from time to time do good work, because it is the only way for him to gain confidence and to continue wrecking." Finally, the ultraclever wreckers did not wreck at all! They fulfilled and overfulfilled the production quotas and waited for war, when they could display their real talents and wreck to their heart's content.

It was at this point that someone of the audience with little to lose anyway might have covered his name with glory by calling upon Comrade Kaminsky, the People's Commissar for Health, to take this man in charge. But no one did, and Stalin continued with the practical deductions from his law: *every* Party official from the secretary of the primary Party organization up to the Union Republic level should immediately choose two assistants and train them in his duties. Of course you could find such "new" people, said Stalin, lapsing into biblical language: "Seek and ye shall find." There was no misunderstanding the clear meaning of this injunction: Stalin planned to liquidate two-thirds of the Party apparatus, an assessment which events were to show to have been on the conservative side. The expression "like sheep led to slaughter" hardly applies to the members of the Central Committee who listened and applauded: sheep *don't know* they are going to their slaughter. But Stalin made certain that even the most stupid among his listeners would not miss his implication. The Central Committee should forthwith organize a special course to train regional Party workers in "problems of internal and foreign policy." These students should be numerous enough to provide "not for one but for *several teams* capable of replacing the leaders of the Central Committee of our Party."[86] One could hardly come closer to saying: I am one and you are many, but I am going to kill off most of you.

The famous German Communist poet Bertolt Brecht once said, "The victim is always guilty." His American interlocutor took it as an expression of cynicism. But in the case of the Soviet leaders of February–March 1937 this statement would be factually true. Stalin told them what was in store for them. For once he did not maneuver or dissimulate. Who among his listeners, and after the lesson of Orjonikidze's fate, could reasonably feel safe? Which members (except for a handful like Yezhov) did not wish that this possessed man be struck down? For all the instruments of force at his disposal it was on Stalin's part a fantastic challenge: he was daring some one hundred and thirty men to fight not for power or a principle but for their very lives. Among them were veterans of Tsarist jails and exiles, military officers who had displayed intrepid courage under fire, many who had shown no scruples when it came to killing or authorizing killings to advance their careers. But here they sat, hypnotized by Stalin's will and malevolence, hoping against hope that they would be allowed to remain his accomplices rather than join his victims.

Stalin's rage on this occasion has been attributed to the opposition he encountered at the meeting of the Central Committee in respect to his plans against Bukharin and Rykov. Yet if we examine the scraps of recollections which are available from the meeting (the minutes of which have never been published), this reading has to be amended. His attitude was one of contempt for people who, while they dared to cross his designs while he was away, could, in his presence, only beg him to soften his resolve. Thus the best example of opposition that Khrushchev could dig up in 1956 was that of Paul Postyshev, alternate member of the Politburo, second secretary of the Ukrainian Party (in fact its leader, in view of the ineffectiveness of the first secretary, Stanislaw Kosior). Postyshev had been close to Stalin. He had distinguished himself as one of the main engineers of mass collectivization and as late as 1936 was honored by being included on the list of those slated for assassination. Now in February 1937 he incautiously pleaded for one of his subordinates, Karpov, who had been arrested as a Trotskyite. He did not believe, said Postyshev, that a man who had been with the Party through

[86] *Ibid.*, p. 222. My italics.

its most difficult days would in 1934 allow himself to be recruited by Trotsky. But here was the rub: Postyshev could not bring himself to ask, "Where is the evidence?" For the evidence that existed against Karpov was no less substantial than that on which he, Postyshev, had authorized many arrests in the past. So his was not a plea for justice or an attack on the system of denunciation and forced confession. It was a demand for a special privilege for the Party bigwigs: those whom they liked and trusted should not be touched by the NKVD.

The Plenum howled down Bukharin and Rykov when they tried to defend themselves. The Central Committee set up a commission to "examine" their case. Its members, polled in alphabetical order, repeated until Stalin's turn came up, "Arrest, try, shoot." But such unseemly prejudging of the case was not for the Leader, and he spoke the verdict, "Let the NKVD handle the case."[87]

In his concluding remarks, Stalin expressed measured satisfaction with the outcome of the meeting. "The speeches have shown that now we view things with full clarity, we understand our tasks, and are ready to liquidate the defects in our work."[88] Everybody could see that the wreckers "under whatever flag, whether that of Trotsky or *that of Bukharin*"[89] have long ago ceased to be a political movement and are just spies and saboteurs. They have to be smashed and rooted out as traitors. "This is clear and needs no further explanations."

Now to further tasks. Many, to all appearances and in all probability loyal Party officials, still conducted themselves incorrectly, Stalin observed. They resented criticism; they refused to admit their errors. Most regrettable of all, they behaved undemocratically, refused to learn from the masses. Take the Kiev Party organization (where Postyshev had been the boss). There an intrepid rank-and-file member, Comrade Nikolayenko, had written letter after letter to the authorities unmasking people's enemies in high and low positions and denouncing the local leaders' lack of vigilance. Did the Party Committee pay heed to the warning signals transmitted by this patriotic woman? Not only did they not, but they kicked her out of the Party as a slanderer. It took the Central Committee to right this wrong and establish that Nikolayenko was right and the Kiev authorities wrong. So much for Postyshev, though Stalin did not name him. Soon he was transferred to Kuibyshev, where, possibly trying to make up for his lapse into liberalism, he distinguished himself by persecution savage even by the standards of those terrible years. But all in vain. Within a year he was arrested and in 1940 he was shot.

87 Medvedev, p. 174.
88 Stalin (Stanford ed.), I, 225.
89 My italics.

The laurels of Nikolayenko may have aroused a desire to emulate her in the breast of every literate maniac or gossipmonger in the country. It was a brilliant stroke of Stalin's thus to acquire a whole army of unpaid assistants in his campaign against the Party. Previously those people satisfied their morbid needs by denouncing kulaks, White Guardists, or acknowledged Trotskyites. Now a "little woman," as Stalin touchingly called Nikolayenko, had humiliated and prevailed over a mighty Politburo member. As they slunk back to their satrapies and ministries the Party oligarchs must have reflected that for all their power and privileges they no longer stood above mere mortals. Russia, though not in the sense proclaimed by the Stalin Constitution, was a democracy, a democracy of fear.[90] ☆☆☆

W E must now pose the question whether the Stalin of the period was insane, whether his pathological fear of betrayal and the extraordinary courage he displayed on occasion (to be fair, his performance at the February Plenum must be classified as such) were the workings of a sick mind. If our definition of insanity includes utter lack of moral sensitivity, then Stalin *in his fifties* must be so adjudged. If it does not, then we cannot hold Stalin in this period to have been insane. (The problem must be considered separately in the context of his old age.) The pathological elements of his nature reinforced and exaggerated those of the system in which he lived, whether as conspirator, high official, or dictator. It is characteristic that Soviet authors who discuss this problem, even those who are as emancipated from Stalinism and as forthright in its condemnation as Roy Medvedev, do it invariably in connection with the Great Purge of the middle and late 1930s and never in connection with mass collectivization, which claimed more human lives. Yet Bukharin or Postyshev were certainly no more innocent of the charges preferred against them than the anonymous peasant shot or exiled in 1931 as a class enemy. Stalin's mentality made him peculiarly suitable for operating and succeeding within the context of Soviet reality (it is, of course, erroneous to see him as *the* inevitable product and result of that reality). We might go even further: it is unlikely that a man *without* unusual suspiciousness and proneness to intrigue would have

[90] "If I may be pardoned for attempting to raise a corner of the veil which covers Stalin's inner thoughts, I suggest that his constitution of 1936, with the accompanying hints of a desire to construct a true democracy, show that he has no successor in whom he is able to repose full confidence, and that he seeks to protect his people against the consequence of a less able rule than his own." Maynard, p. 420.

prospered in Soviet politics of the 1920s, let alone reached Stalin's heights. Those "personal characteristics" of Stalin's which made the Petrograd Bolsheviks reject him as a committeeman in March 1917 were precisely the ones that enhanced his value in Lenin's eyes and led to his appointment as General Secretary in 1922, that induced the Voroshilovs and Molotovs to look to him in the later 1920s. What made him appear close to insane in the eyes of the Soviet elite in the 1930s was that, having fastened Soviet rule on Russia and having imposed Communism's obsessions on the land, he refused to fade from the scene or to relax. He knew how they felt or how they would feel if he would accord them leisure from fear, so now he proceeded to decimate them.

"The closer we get to socialism, the sharper becomes the character of the class war." As a theoretical formula this was, of course, absurd. But politically and for Stalin it made a lot of sense. Here it was, 1937. The class enemy had been decisively smashed. The international situation called for a relaxation of internal terror, for political reconciliation and national union going all the way to Trotsky and beyond. What, then, of the rationale of his own despotic rule? Stalin's successors condemned and rejected his terrible formula for perpetual terror, yet were he alive today he would smile over their predicament. They try to be both "liberal" and to run a tight totalitarian society, they condemn his excesses and attempt to practice what he taught them. For Stalin, this would be a clear formula for failure. Here are the Solzhenitsyns and Medvedevs "slandering socialism," Jews who demonstrate against the regime with impunity, and in some cases are rewarded for it by being allowed to emigrate, troubles in the Ukraine and Lithuania. . . . To think that he is being criticized for anticipating and preventing such horrors!

◅ 10 ▻

THE
TERRIBLE
INTERLUDE

Great and evil men always retain certain characteristics of malicious and stubborn children. In the "most active Communist" at fifty-seven one could discern the Gori youngster who answered his schoolmates' innocuous jokes with blows, the young revolutionary who broke out in vituperation at a comrade's unintended slight, and the Civil War commander who, stung by a reproach of Lenin's, was ready "to go to the devil" rather than put up with his leader's fatherly admonition. Now that this childish impatience and despotism were clothed with absolute power, the adolescent's fears and secret shame were mitigated but never completely dissipated by a nation's and world Communism's worship. To the end Stalin retained even some physical boyish characteristics. His daughter recalls introducing him with some trepidation to her son (the father was Jewish). The seventy-year-old dictator was enchanted by the child and ran rather than walked around the grounds with him, but he never asked to see his grandson again; he was easily bored with every game but that of politics. He could seldom sit still. People summoned for conferences recall how he would walk around the room while questioning them, how the stated business of the meeting would often be changed or terminated by a sudden question or gesture. At his less and less frequent public appearances, the audience's dutiful applause would be cut short with an impatient wave of his hands. Between 1934 and his death only two Party Congresses and one Conference took place, undoubtedly—among other reasons—because he found it tedious to sit still in the Presidium while fools and hypocrites tried to surpass each other in praising and flattering him.

Even his favorite forms of relaxation seemed somewhat childish. He was an insatiable viewer of movies, his taste running from musicals to historical dramas about Alexander Nevsky or Peter the Great. (But a director had to watch his step: Eisenstein's intimations of the psychotic and homosexual elements in Ivan the Terrible's makeup led to his film's being banned.) Stalin's sociability increasingly took the form of ghastly all-male nocturnal banquets, of which we have a fine description from Milovan Djilas.[1] Judging by his and Svetlana Alliluyeva's accounts, they had the atmosphere of a college freshman outing—with middle-aged men inappropriately indulging in drinking bouts and bad practical jokes—and a festive Mafia gathering. Stalin would watch, smoking his pipe, while one of his companions placed a tomato on the chair someone else was to sit in. When the weather was fine, the merrymakers played outside. Poskrebyshev, chief butt of Stalin's practical jokes as well as his chief secretary, would be pushed into a shallow pond.[2] It is characteristic that as the years passed Stalin's sadism grew and so did his inclination to indulge it at the expense of those who were close to him.

But this inherent vulgarity of Joseph Djugashvili was concealed from the world by the awesome dignity of Stalin. Early in his life as a politician he would occasionally get drunk and sing indecent songs in mixed company,[3] but we do not hear of such incidents after 1930. A characteristic story, which was widely circulated in Moscow, concerned Alexis Tolstoy: once, emboldened by alcohol, Stalin's chief literary flatterer approached the dictator with a proposal of *Brüderschaft*, a traditional embrace and toast after which friends begin to call each other "thou." Recoiling, Stalin said, "You must be joking, Count." Awareness of his historic role grew along with his dislike of approaching old age. After Mandelstam's arrest in 1934 he called Boris Pasternak and reproached him for not trying to help his fellow poet: "He is a genius, he is a genius, isn't he?" he asked. It was obvious what was on his mind, and why Mandelstam got off relatively easily after his first arrest. Stalin wanted to be immortalized in verse by a real genius (as well as by countless hacks).[4] He understood the necessity of keeping a distance between himself and those who he hoped would glorify him in poetry and prose. Much as they longed to, Pasternak and Ehrenburg were never brought into his presence, never saw at close quarters the small man with bad teeth and a pockmarked face. This tactic worked: Ehrenburg confesses he thought of Stalin as a kind of Old Testament god and

---

[1] To be sure, the one he attended was in Stalin's old age.

[2] Svetlana Alliluyeva, *Only One Year* (New York, 1969), p. 386. Mme. Alliluyeva points out that this kind of entertainment became common only after World War II.

[3] Roy Medvedev, *Let History Judge* (New York, 1971), p. 329.

[4] Mandelstam tried but could not, and went to his doom during the Great Purge.

recounts how at the height of the terror Pasternak exclaimed, "If *he* only knew." Stalin was careful to stage his appearances according to the occasion: at an audience with a military officer he would be an impassive man of steel, at a youth or workers' meeting a jovial father of his people, to a foreign journalist an unpretentious and businesslike politician. A small but significant detail: he was almost never photographed smoking a cigarette though he smoked quite a lot—there is something more reassuring and folksy about a pipe-smoker (witness how much the pipe contributed to the success in British politics of Baldwin and Attlee). The same was true of his worker's blouse and cap, which he habitually wore until the war gave him an opportunity to exchange them for a marshal's uniform. And since he wanted to be associated in his countrymen's minds with the pathos and glory of the victory, he never returned to the earlier costume. ☆☆☆

A N inflexible, wise, and all-seeing statesman; a benevolent dictator whom evil counselors kept in ignorance about the sufferings of his people; a mysterious Oriental potentate—the ability of this nervous, sardonic, and vengeful man to produce so many incongruous versions of his personality paralleled his ability to impose several layers of unreality on the society he ruled. The Soviet people, inspired with patriotism and love of socialism, marching from one victory to another, its army invincible, the Party undivided in its dedication to the goals of Communism: this was one version. At the same time the Soviet people were asked to believe—and many did—that treason and crime were rampant, that the highest officers of the Red Army were agents of foreign powers, that the enemies of the people penetrated the top positions in the Party state, that Trotskyite and Bukharinite wreckers roamed in every sphere of national life. In 1937 the most democratic constitution in the world came into effect, the freest elections in history were held. At the same time each citizen knew that his neighbor, subordinate, or washwoman might be a spy reporting or misrepresenting his words and activities to the police. The people were warned to prepare for an enemy attack at the same time as they were told that the invincible Red Army would never let a foreign aggressor seize one foot of Soviet territory. The fascist enemy was said to be filled with cruel designs to enslave and destroy, and yet logically it was difficult to imagine what even the most ferocious foreign enemy might do in excess of what the Soviet government had already done to the peasant and what between 1937 and 1939 it would do to the population at large.

How could people function in this atmosphere—work, make love, talk to friends, play with their children? A martyred poet's wife gives a partial answer:

> Our way of life kept us firmly rooted to the ground and was not conducive to the search for transcendental truths. Whenever I talked of suicide, M. used to say "Why hurry? The end is the same everywhere and here they even hasten it for you." Death was so much more real, and so much simpler than life, that we all involuntarily tried to prolong our earthly existence, even if only for a brief moment—just in case the next day brought some relief. . . . In a strange way, despite the horror of it, this also gave a certain richness to our lives.[5]

But there must be also other answers. For Stalin and for many others, it was faith that enabled them to function amid the nightmarish reality. For him it was a belief in his historic mission, for others quite often a belief in him as the epitome of Russia or Communism. One should not be too cynical or censorious about those who profess to have held to such beliefs even in prison or in a camp, since for people who really felt that way it may have been the only anchor in sanity, an irrational way of making sense out of something which yielded to no rational explanation. ☆☆☆

AFTER the February–March meeting of the Central Committee in 1937, the purge was in full swing. Bukharin and Rykov had been arrested while the meeting was going on. But the search for and elimination of real or alleged former Trotskyites and Bukharinites now became almost secondary. In accordance with Stalin's directives the purge took on a quantitative character, the goal being the destruction of most of the existing higher and intermediate Party cadres as well as that of a sizable proportion of the rank-and-file membership. And a similar process was inaugurated in other spheres of national life, from the army to the arts and sciences. The problem now becomes not so much to explain why X, a person of prominence in his field, was arrested or destroyed, but why Y was spared. It is clear why those with a history of even the slightest opposition to Stalin, or those who had given an unsatisfactory performance from his point of view, were destroyed: thus Postyshev or another Politburo member, Yan Rudzutak, who as the head of the Control Commission from 1930 to 1934 failed to display proper "vigilance." But why did the axe not descend on, say, Andrei Andreyev,

[5] Nadezhda Mandelstam, Hope Against Hope (New York, 1970), p. 261.

the most obscure member of Stalin's Politburo? He had had links in the old days with the Workers' Opposition, balked at some features of terror during collectivization, and then performed miserably as Commissar of Transport. Yet he remained alive and on the Politburo until 1952. To be sure, he was one of the most enthusiastic executors of the terror,[6] but that was far from being a guarantee of safety. Short of some personal link with Stalin (and we have seen how much that was worth) the only explanation can be found in Stalin's whim. Military men were arrested and shot wholesale, but Yeremenko, the future defender of Stalingrad, committed a crime as serious as helping the wife of an imprisoned colleague; yet he stayed free and advanced in his profession. Isaac Babel, the brilliant writer and storyteller of the Civil War, was destroyed along with numerous other literary figures, yet Pasternak remained untouched, though he was forbidden to publish. Ilya Ehrenburg's journalistic though not literary talents were highly estimated by Stalin (he was right on both counts); scores of talented Soviet publicists were destroyed, but not Ehrenburg, for all of his connection with the Spanish Civil War (a lethal factor for most of the Soviet diplomatic, military, and journalistic personnel in Madrid). The famous physicist Lev Landau was imprisoned, but not Peter Kapitza, though he had stayed abroad for a long time and was foolhardy enough to intervene on Landau's behalf. It became almost miraculous if a major Soviet diplomat of 1937 was still alive by 1940, but Alexandra Kollontay, a very early heretic and a close collaborator of Lenin's at one time, continued as envoy in Scandinavia and was one of the very few Old Bolsheviks to survive Stalin.

When we look for criteria by which certain people were saved, we are on very uncertain grounds. Some men were well-nigh irreplaceable: Litvinov and Ambassador Ivan Maisky in London were in this category because of their contacts and knowledge of the West, even though they fitted the requirements for *the* enemy of the people perfectly. Andrei Tupolev, the greatest talent in Soviet aircraft engineering, was grotesquely accused of selling airplane blueprints to the Germans, something which would have meant automatic death in the case of a less valuable man, but Tupolev was generously allowed to go on working for the socialist Fatherland in one of those prison institutes set up for scientists and technicians too valuable to be shot or killed in the camps. Considerations of sentiment played a scant role for the man who imprisoned or destroyed most of his in-laws by both marriages and who joked about his eldest son's unsuccessful attempt at suicide. Robert Conquest suggests rather diffidently that it may have been sentiment which made Stalin spare the five Bolshevik deputies to the Fourth

[6] Mme. Mandelstam records the inside information that it was Andreyev who ordered the second and fatal imprisonment of her husband.

Duma whom he knew from his St. Petersburg days in 1912–13. But the only one among them who reached prominence in Soviet Russia, Gregory Petrovsky, President of the Ukraine, was dealt with more cruelly that most of those who were "just" liquidated. Stripped of all his dignities in 1938, he was left at large while both his sons and his son-in-law were arrested. During the war one was released and died a hero's death. The old man then wrote a pathetic letter to Stalin, urging that the other two be freed and allowed to fight the Germans. The plea was not heeded; both men were shot. In regard to the Duma veterans it was Stalin's good-natured contempt, rather than sentiment, that allowed them to survive. They were now old dodderers, so why bother? (One of them, Samoilov, head of the Museum of the Revolution, wrote the Leader asking for the manuscript of his immortal *History of the Communist Party of the Soviet Union—Short Course*. Since in fact Stalin himself had not written most of it, he was not pleased by this ingratiating but imprudent request. Why in his old age did he concern himself with such nonsense? he asked poor Samoilov. Stalin had burned the manuscript![7])

Though conceived for an emergency, mass terror now became a regular technique of Stalin's rule. From 1937 and until his death it was to be of quite different character, and varying in intensity, from anything which had gone on before. "Normal" Soviet terror prior to 1934 was directed against the class enemy; between 1934 and 1937 it was at least purportedly aimed against former oppositionists. But now it became an everyday feature of life, a reflection of its maker's belief that this was the most efficacious and economical way of ruling the country, and that nobody (himself excluded), should be beyond its reach. During its intensive phase, 1937–39, its clear goal was not only to catch actual and potential "spies and wreckers," but to remake entirely the instruments of power: the Party, the army, and the security forces, as well as the nation's intellectual and artistic elite. This emerges clearly in Stalin's speech at the notorious February–March Plenum of 1937. They did not want a Party which was composed of people who *mastered* Marxism-Leninism, he remarked. "Were we to take this road, we would leave in the Party only intellectuals and learned people. Who needs such a Party?"[8] He certainly did not. He wanted a Party of simple people, doers rather than thinkers who would unhesitatingly denounce any "wrecker" no matter how high his position. And so by 1939 some 850,000 Party members had been purged, more than one-third of the 1937 membership, some half million of them replaced by those "simple people" whom Stalin liked.[9] And it is a safe assumption that the great

7 Medvedev, p. 512.
8 Stalin, *Works* (Stanford ed.), I, 245.
9 Leonard Schapiro, *The Communist Party of the Soviet Union* (New York, 1960), p. 436.

majority of those purged suffered more than the mere loss of their Party cards.

At the higher level it was more of a pogrom than a purge. A typical occurrence of 1937–39 was the descent on some important Party center of one of the chief hatchetmen: Kaganovich or Malenkov. Ostensibly it was a visit of inspection, such as had been usual before. But the visitor would not confine himself to an edifying speech or two and conviviality with the local satraps mixed with some criticism. He *had* to find Trotskyites and two-faced people in high places. After an appropriate telegram to Stalin and with his approval, the local Party commmmittee would be summoned to vote (unanimously) for the removal of its top officials as enemies of the people or, a bit more hopefully, as guilty of blindness and lack of vigilance. Then the NKVD would take over. In the case of small fry the pomp and circumstance were dispensed with: the NKVD would arrest the head of the city or regional Party organization, then his subordinates, often his family, even the chauffeur.

By mid-1937 Stalin brooked no interference with the momentum of terror. Commissar of Health Kaminsky spoke in defense of some accused at the July meeting of the Central Committee. There was no dilly-dallying, no transfer to a less important position, as would have been the case one year earlier: Kaminsky was arrested the very same day. In his hurry to create the maximum numbing effect on the Party and the country Stalin no longer showed any concern over protocol, nor did he often indulge in that protracted destruction of an official which had once suited his fancy. Commissar of Education Andrei Bubnov, an Old Bolshevik and historian of the Party, repaired in October to the Kremlin to a session of the Central Committee, of which he was a member. He was not allowed to enter, and the NKVD official on duty explained that in addition to membership one had to have a special permit! Bubnov was dismissed the same night and arrested within a few days. Once in jail the procedure was more leisurely: Bubnov was not shot until 1940.

These later delays reflected the hideous legalism of the NKVD, the maniacal insistence that the accused be "proven" guilty, i.e., made to write and sign his confession. There were, of course, pragmatic reasons for this ritual: the prisoner was expected to implicate others, and some NKVD officials undoubtedly worked under the impression, if not under an actual directive, that they had to produce a certain quota of "enemies of the people." But the main reason was the pathological craving for "proof," for a written and signed confession; the Boss wanted it this way, and it was a black mark on an interrogator's record if he failed to produce one. With vast numbers of people being handled by the security organs, there was no time for subtle, psychological methods of extracting confessions. Beatings and other forms of physical torture were now standard. After Yezhov's removal at the end of 1938 Stalin became

STALIN / THE MAN AND HIS ERA

concerned that his dismissal might be interpreted as a sign that such practices were now being discontinued. On January 20, 1939, the local NKVD organs were notified that "the Central Committee considers that physical pressure should be used obligatorily, as an exception applicable to known and obstinate enemies of the people, as a method both justifiable and appropriate."[10] If an accused resisted torture and still refused to sign a confession, as some did, it *might* help him. General Gorbatov was rather surprised when, having endured beatings for weeks and still not signing, he was sentenced to fifteen years at hard labor, after a "trial" before three members of the NKVD tribunal that lasted all of five minutes. Ironically, his heroism probably contributed to his future rehabilitation and restoration to the army on the eve of the war. But in the case of more prominent people against whom he had a personal grudge, such "stubbornness" under investigation only served to enhance Stalin's fury. To petitions for mercy or professions of innocence that were in some such cases circulated to members of the Politburo, he would attach comments: "A scoundrel and a male whore," he wrote on the letter from the army commander Yona Yakir. He liked cases against his victims neatly wrapped up. It was a personal challenge to him if any of those "unclean" people refused to acknowledge their crimes and thus slurred Soviet justice—*his* justice.

From Kaganovich and Yezhov down to the lowliest interrogator, every operative of the purge worked in the awareness that if he failed to produce, his turn might be next, that somewhere in the files was at least one written deposition naming him as a participant in some "Trotskyite-Bukharinite center," or one of the German and Japanese espionage networks which had been sprouting all over Russia like mushrooms. It is difficult to assess the exact degree of "responsibility" for the purge among people other than Stalin. It is clear that Kaganovich and Molotov threw themselves into the bloody task with some zeal, unclear whether other Politburo members, including those who were eventually liquidated themselves, ever tried to temper the horror. Only of Michael Kalinin is it actually recorded that he tried (timidly) to rescue some less prominent victims, and he paid for it. Kalinin was President of the U.S.S.R., recipient of the state's highest decorations. Important cities were named after him. Early in 1939 his wife was summoned to Moscow from the vacation she was spending at the side of her sick husband. As befitted her station, she was arrested by Beria himself. Only seven years later, with her husband suffering the advanced stages of cancer, was she released and allowed to go to his side; she was banished from Moscow following his death.

[10] Revealed in Khrushchev's 1956 speech, quoted in Bertram D. Wolfe, *Khrushchev and Stalin's Ghost* (New York, 1957), p. 160.

442

At the lower levels the huge army of officials who supervised the details—officers of the forced labor camps, interrogators, judges, etc.—worked under feverish constraints, knowing that they had an even chance of ending up as prisoners themselves. The Yezhov period saw the virtual extermination of two previous types of NKVD personnel. The first to go was the handful of veterans of the Dzerzhinsky era, who, we are assured in the anti-Stalinist Soviet literature, though ruthless toward the class enemy and devoid of "rotten liberalism" were still characterized by a certain revolutionary integrity and incorruptibility.[11] Then came the turn of the typical official from the Yagoda period, the cynic who would compose the accused's confession and beg him to sign and not to complicate everybody's life. Their successors mirrored the mentality of the current boss, Yezhov: they were narrow-minded fanatics, exuding hatred of the "people's enemies," whom they grilled and tortured. The selection process ensured that many of them should be sadists who displayed special enjoyment when working on and torturing former bigwigs or their erstwhile colleagues.

Once the "unsheathed sword of the Revolution," the NKVD now became a vast politico-military-economic organization. It ran enormous complexes of forced labor camps where millions of convicts worked on important construction projects; it had its own troops and an extensive network of agents in foreign countries to supplement the work of the regular intelligence agencies. It became guardian of the Soviet past, having been entrusted with the care of the history of the Party and state archives. The NKVD also assumed many functions of a scientific institution, its jail institutes, such as Alexander Solzhenitsyn describes in his novel *The First Circle*, working on numerous problems of pure and applied science and engineering. According to an alumnus of one such institute, the NKVD sponsored the following contributions by imprisoned scientists and engineers: ". . . the 1-5 fighter, by Gregorovich and Polikarpov, the FD and IS steam engines, and . . . the communications systems devised by Kuksen and Berg; artillery pieces of Blagonravov and Pobyedonostsev; tank designs of Kotin and Kosotsior; the PE-2 and TU-5 airplanes . . . interplanetary rockets by Korolyev[12] and even the nuclear research of Landau, Frank."[13]

After 1937 the NKVD thus became both the epitome and the moving force in Soviet society, virtually replacing the Communist Party

[11] The "honest Chekist" is a standard figure of Soviet novels about the period. He is severe but humane, contemptuous of his younger colleagues—who are portrayed either as simple-minded and brutal, or as soulless bureaucrats capable only of acting according to the book and incapable of insight into human nature.
[12] The man mainly responsible for the Soviet satellite and cosmonaut program.
[13] A. Sharagin (pseud.), *The Tupolev Jail Institute* (in Russian; Frankfurt, 1971), p. 10.

in these respects. But one thing it was never allowed to become: a rival of Stalin's, a threat to his power.

It suited Stalin prefectly that he should have been widely considered a dupe of misinformation provided by the NKVD. A man as perspicacious as Bukharin still saw Stalin as a victim, manipulated by the security organs: "At present most of the so-called organs of the NKVD are a degenerate organization of bureaucrats . . . who use the Cheka's bygone authority to cater to Stalin's morbid suspiciousness (I fear to say more) in a scramble for rank and fame."[14] Yet we know that Yezhov took no important step without obtaining Stalin's sanction. The lists of important people to be shot or otherwise repressed were sent to Stalin by the Commissar for his approval. During the period 1937–39, 383 such lists were submitted to Stalin, which means that hardly a working day went by without the tyrant imbruing his hands in blood. There were excesses and mistakes, of course, even from his point of view—people whom he would have preserved had he known the full circumstances; in some cases his subordinates were settling personal scores rather than working selflessly for him. But he knew that to interfere unduly with the terror before the lesson had sunk in would strip it of its educational effect. Mme. Alliluyeva records an instructive story: a schoolmate whose father had been arrested prevailed on her to give Stalin a letter. At dinner his case was discussed; it turned out that Molotov knew the man and had a good opinion of him (something which from our point of view does not argue in his favor); a human life was saved. But Svetlana was strictly forbidden to repeat such errands of mercy. In a Soviet novel a rehabilitated general tells Stalin that he is not up on modern military technology because he "sat," as the euphemism for imprisonment went, under Yezhov. "Chose quite a time to 'sit,' eh," observed the dictator jocularly.

To be sure, a few did manage to "fool Stalin" and get away with it. One to whom this honor undeniably belongs is Trofim Lysenko. By training an agronomist, and evidently quite a capable one, he decided to branch out and become a scientific charlatan on a national scale. He cleverly exploited Stalin's predilection for scientists who refused to be intimidated by alleged scientific laws and who, if higher production was at stake, overcame those laws in the spirit of "There is no fortress that we Bolsheviks cannot take." Helped by faked experiments and Stalin's growing patronage, Lysenko opened his campaign against respectable scientists and for the domination of Soviet biology. It is partly to Lysenko that Stalin referred in his famous toast at a reception of scientific workers in 1938: "To the flourishing of science, of that science

14 Medvedev, p. 183. Bukharin, prior to his arrest, made his wife memorize a "letter," which she put down in writing after her release from imprisonment. This passage comes from it.

whose exponents, though they understand and exploit the strength and meaning of scientific tradition, refuse to be slaves of those traditions. To the science which has the courage to break with old traditions, norms, directions if they have outlived their usefulness, if they have become a brake on progress."[15]

While it would be ridiculous to imagine Stalin as deceived and as not, in the main, in firm control of the purge, it is also true that his suspiciousness fed upon itself and grew along with the number of victims. He would appoint a man to a new post, perhaps promote him, and then an item in the man's dossier would strike him: perhaps the fellow was alleged to have said something derogatory about the dictator, or he had studied abroad, or his wife was a relative of someone repressed. Orders would go out to have him investigated—and the usual results of such investigations followed. "Better safe than sorry," must have been Stalin's justification as he signed yet another authorization for execution. The widow of the Komsomol leader Alexander Kosarev recalls this extraordinary incident: her husband, long Stalin's favorite, attended a big reception at the Kremlin. In the Slavic manner, men whom Stalin toasted went up to him to clink glasses. When it was Kosarev's turn Stalin embraced him and whispered in his ear; the youth leader paled and hurriedly left the reception. Stalin had said, "If you are a traitor, I shall kill you." He did, shortly afterward.[16] Along with Kosarev the whole "Kosarev gang," i.e., the leadership of the Komsomol, was liquidated, and those who denounced them were installed in their place.

The aspect of the terror which is most often held up as an illustration of Stalin's paranoid fears is his purge of the Red Army. By today *every* prominent military and naval victim of the Great Purge has been fully rehabilitated, which is far from being the case with the Party and state figures. The post-Stalin regime has found it impossible to acknowledge publicly the innocence of Bukharin and Rykov (though by now, in a very quiet way, they have been absolved of having been foreign agents and wreckers), not to mention Trotsky and Zinoviev. But the memory of Tukhachevsky, Yakir, Blücher, et al., has been fully vindicated, and numerous biographies have appeared to render justice to the victims' great services to their country and Communism. In contradistinction to other kinds of official anti-Stalin literature, the flow of these biographies did not cease with Khrushchev's fall. And so today the loyal Soviet

---

[15] Stalin (Stanford ed.), I, 276. The bitterness of those Soviet scientists who suffered under Stalin may be judged from the following passage. "Let us admit 'they' don't want to have trials of our own brand of SS men who ran the forced labor camps and the NKVD: too much may come out. But it would be right to shoot Lysenko and Prezent. Having lost ten million lives of its citizens in torture chambers, the country can afford to add to their number two scoundrels who lacked the courage to do away with themselves." Sharagin, p. 10.

[16] Medvedev, p. 333.

citizen, who is expected to believe that Trotsky was a traitor, that there was something not quite right about Bukharin, is allowed and expected to be indignant at Stalin for having destroyed the flower of the Red Army. One winces when one reads this tribute from the pen of a daughter of one martyred officer: "But then, justice has prevailed. The Party of Lenin has restored the good name to those innocent people who were destroyed. The Party has given me back the honor of my father. For this first of all I bow to the earth, to Nikita Khrushchev."[17]

To contemporaries, things appeared in a quite different light. We might bring up as an example the émigré Mensheviks. These humane democratic socialists had a better reason than most to realize the preposterousness of the charges on which people were being repressed in the Soviet Union—they themselves, after all, were regularly listed as Hitler's agents and Trotsky's accomplices. But here is the *Socialist Courier*, published in Paris on March 25, 1937: "There is no question that the Germans have managed to have their agents in the U.S.S.R. penetrate the most responsible positions." And there is grim irony in a Menshevik writer's stating on May 28, 1937, just a few days before the announcement was made of the execution of Red Army leaders: "I will not say that Stalin is already a prisoner of the army but . . . within a short time political leadership will pass into the hands of the army."[18] How prone is the Marxist mind, even the enlightened democratic variety, to suspicion! But, to be fair, people as far from Marxism as Winston Churchill also swallowed the story that there had been treason afoot in the highest ranks of the Red Army. ☆☆☆

THE purge of the Red Army in 1937–38 illustrates vividly the incredible omnipotence of Stalin and, conversely, the utter absence of any effective opposition to him. Here he was dealing not with politicians and bureaucrats who had grown soft and ineffectual through years of good living, political compromise, and complicity in his tyranny, but with people of legendary military exploits and courage. The political purge had after all been protracted; its victims in a grim way became accustomed to their fate. But the army was struck as if by a thunderbolt.

---

[17] *Army Commander Uborevich: Recollections* (Moscow, 1964), p. 239.
[18] It is appropriate here to bring this story of Captain Dreyfus of the famous case. In his old age the victim of a historic injustice liked to play bridge. At one such session his partner mentioned the case of Officer X who was under the suspicion of espionage and then catching himself tried to undo his tactlessness in bringing up such painful associations by observing that this must be a mistake. "Ah, ah, there is no smoke without a fire," said Dreyfus.

There is something pathetic in Marshal Blücher's story. As a soldier in World War I, wounded in eighteen places, he was taken to the morgue, and it was noticed only at the last moment that he was still breathing. After a convalescence he volunteered for further soldiering, further fantastic exploits. Yet this same man, as required by Stalin, sat in judgment and passed the sentence of death on comrades at arms whom he knew to be perfectly innocent. Then came his own turn: without the slightest resistance he was lifted from his command (where he was worshiped by the troops) to await his own doom: the marshal who had trounced the Japanese was arrested and tortured to death on charges of having been a Japanese spy.

It took Hitler a great deal of trouble just to *dismiss* his two top military leaders in 1938, and then his original choice for the commander-in-chief was vetoed by the Reichswehr on the grounds that the man was too much of a Nazi. It must have been with some professional envy that he watched his fellow dictator's unceremonious ways with generals. Stalin had them shot, with or without a trial, and en masse: three of the first five marshals of the Soviet Union; three of four full generals; all twelve lieutenant generals; sixty of sixty-seven corps commanders, a hundred and thirty-six of one hundred ninety-nine divisional ones.[19] The holocaust in the Soviet navy was even worse, and in the armed forces' political branch the loss among the lower grades of officers was considerable, though not on the same scale. No army officer corps in wartime, observed a Soviet author, ever suffered on the scale of what the Soviet military establishment underwent in peace. And, to repeat, these were people who knew how to use arms, individually and collectively. Apart from the vast sum of personal suffering and injustice, this was a hideous insult to the Red Army as a whole: every survivor had to acknowledge that his superiors and comrades at arms had been traitors to the country, and many of them must have felt inwardly dishonored when they reflected that they had not dared to lift a finger to help or to protest against the fate of their colleagues and friends, their wives, children, and parents.[20] Why did none of them turn his weapon against the tyrant? Stalin occasionally appeared before the graduating classes of the military academies, and sat in conferences with the higher officers, men who had no illusion that their death and dishonor were only a question of time. Or if not against him then against some of the main perpetuators of the purge: Yezhov, Mekhlis, Beria? How could the ordinary soldier go on obeying his commanders, when more than half of them, from the company level up, had been "unmasked" as traitors?

[19] Figures are from Medvedev, p. 23. "General" is used here, though officially the rank was restored only in 1940.
[20] It appears that relatives of the military men liquidated were treated with more systematic cruelty than those of other categories of victims.

Even in comparison with collectivization and with the purge of the Party apparatus, this looks at first glance like a miracle of repression: one man, with a nod of his head, ordering the decimation of brave and armed men. Then, on top of it, another miracle: thus dishonored, stripped of its most experienced leaders and officers, the army would (after initial defeats) become an effective defender of the country, and Russian soldiers, led in some cases by the very men who had been beaten and tortured as traitors, went into battle "for the Fatherland, for Stalin."

Confronted by such apparent miracles, one gropes for answers. Perhaps after all there *was* a military conspiracy against Stalin? If not, why not? A cynic might inquire whether by shooting generals one does not in fact increase the fighting efficiency of an army. How different would the fate of France and Europe have been if, prior to 1940, a similar purge had been performed on the French high command? (It took the war to make Charles de Gaulle, age fifty, the youngest *acting* brigadier general in the French Army.) Yet from all available evidence it is certain that there was no military plot against Stalin. And as to the salutary effect of removing elderly generals, most of the Red Army commanders who were liquidated were vigorous men in the prime of life, whose absence undoubtedly contributed to the military catastrophe of the first months of the war and of the summer of 1942.

That the army command played such a small part in Soviet politics, and that it displayed no instinct or ability at self-preservation in 1937–38 may indeed appear, at first glance, incredible. Certainly Communist leaders since 1917 displayed a healthy fear of a "man on horseback." And there were many occasions for him to make an entrance: the crisis and divisions in the Party following Lenin's debility and death, the national catastrophe of collectivization, the beginning of the purges. How responsive, one should think, the people might have been to a military hero who promised to save them from doctrinal excesses and the stifling rule of the bureaucracy while preserving the gains of the Revolution. But in fact such a view is naïve.

We must recognize first of all that the military mind, whether collective or of an individual, tends to be politically inert[21] if not indolent. Within the Soviet system the ubiquity of Party control was from the beginning a further guarantee against political interference by the army. A military man in Soviet Russia was not precluded from seeking a political role, but the world of Soviet politics—of ideological formulas and contentions, of constant speechmaking, of paperwork and journalism—held no temptations for professional military men. Their own

---

21 Of the two most famous exceptions, Caesar was a politician long before becoming a general. Napoleon's decisive coup was largely the work of politicians, who only afterward discovered they had a master and not a servant.

life was pleasant and fulfilling; even before the Party bigwigs learned to enjoy the appurtenances of power the army officers became a privileged class. With their villas, servants, and cars, they felt little inclined to plunge into intraparty debates and risk their professional advancement.[22] That was best left to politicians in uniform, like Frunze or Voroshilov. Stalin's elevation was at first viewed with favor by the officer corps. He pampered the army, stressed the themes of Russian patriotism, of discipline, and of industrialization, and he honored and rewarded the top military leaders. Prior to 1936 few officers, except for those clearly identified with the opposition, suffered at the hand of the dictator. He favored his old pals from the Civil War, especially those of the Tsaritsyn period, but he showered honors and advancements even on Tukhachevsky, despite what must have been unpleasant and embarrassing recollections of their clash in 1920.

The army and the officer corps, then, displayed exemplary loyalty to the regime and to Stalin. This was of crucial importance during the collectivization, when troops were used against rioting peasants and the officers had to display special care to prevent the spread of disorders to the soldiers, most of them peasants' sons.[23] In foreign policy the army also unquestioningly followed directives of the Party. After close collaboration with the Reichswehr ceased, when Hitler came to power, the Soviet military leadership shifted to planning for a war against Germany, with France as a probable ally. Except on technical matters it is unlikely that their views were ever sought by Stalin, or that they were privy to his inner thoughts and fears. Official propaganda portrayed the Red Army as invincible: any blow by the fascists would be answered a hundredfold by the Soviets.

Some military men were evidently apprehensive over the officially sponsored overoptimism about the threatening conflict. Even as late as 1938 a brave soul in the army political branch appealed to Stalin to prepare the nation for possible setbacks, to permit a more realistic propaganda line about what might be expected in a war: "Many propagandists and some newspapers take the oversimplified view that we are

---

[22] A capsule representation of one aspect of Soviet life is contained in a fragment of recollections by the servant of the purged General Uborevich: she had been a cook in a Tsarist general's house. When the Revolution came, her brothers told her, " 'An end has come to your poverty, Mary. You will live like a human being.' General Fomin's big house was taken over by Comrade Belenkovich's detachment. Soon Belenkovich became garrison commander and I the cook for the commanders' men. I was also Belenkovich's maid." M. Vlasova, in *Army Commander Uborevich: Recollections*, p. 224. To be fair, we must add that her son grew up to be a general.

[23] Only one of the commanders, Blücher in the Far East, expostulated about this, and he obtained the regime's agreement that, in view of the Japanese danger, collectivization in his region should be carried out with moderation.

so strong that the capitalists would be afraid to attack us. This propaganda does not offer a sober estimate of the potential of the Red Army. . . . This leads to 'Hurrah-patriotism' . . . to excessive and unbalanced epithets 'great and invincible,' 'the crushing force' [of the Red Army]."[24] For many years the Soviet commanders could observe the Reichswehr at close quarters, and they knew its terrifying efficiency, supplemented now by Nazi fanaticism and the lust for conquest. Initial reverses in the case of a German attack had to be anticipated, although Russia's traditional advantages—superior manpower reserves and vast distances—should eventually right the balance.

It is likely that such views when urged on Stalin only fed his secret distrust of military men. As we have seen, he believed that Russia's first military defeat might spell the end of his power, and he was under no illusions as to what his fate would be then. Were his military commanders perhaps too much impressed with Germany's military power? Or was there more to it than that? They had long hobnobbed with the German officers, many of them had attended German military schools in the pre-Hitler days. Until now the Red Army was the only institution that has escaped the impact of Stalin's personal rule: its higher commanders were virtually the same people who had emerged as leaders during the Civil War—some of them promoted by Trotsky, all of them with vivid recollections of Stalin as just one among several Party leaders. To be sure, they *appeared* loyal. But he himself had developed the brilliant insight that the most dangerous traitor is the one who seems in fact most of the time to be perfectly loyal, awaiting the opportunity to reveal his "two-faced" character. How would Tukhachevsky act if appointed commander-in-chief in the case of war—as he probably would have to be, since most military commanders didn't think much of the military talents of Voroshilov or Budenny? Perhaps there was even a more immediate danger: the Party and state leadership was being purged; would the army people start getting ideas? Did one have to attend to them before it was too late?

If he were to strike at the army, Stalin had to do it faster and more resolutely than in the case of other institutions. If one dawdled, one risked the buildup of a sense of outraged professional solidarity. There was on the other hand the danger that, while people might become used to the idea of widespread treason and wrecking by politicians and bureaucrats, the idea of similar behavior among those who shed their blood for Soviet power would appear incredible. To be sure, the people at large could be made to believe anything. But what of the officers who

24 See Y. Petrov, *The Party Organization in the Soviet Army and Fleet* (Moscow, 1964), p. 335.

were *not* going to be liquidated? The purge of the army required caution and speed—a difficult combination.

Stalin seldom required prodding for his bloody designs. But everything points to the conclusion that when it came to the army the NKVD was especially assiduous in manufacturing evidence. It must have offended their sense of propriety that with the Party and state apparatus being massacred wholesale the army had remained until now virtually untouched. What had restrained Stalin was obviously what, using Marxian jargon, might be called the inherent contradiction within his lust for power: it urged on the one hand that he should get rid of people who could be dangerous on the first day of the war, and on the other hand those were precisely the people he would need if war came. Some of the survivors of the purge were subsequently baffled when Stalin, in talking with them, praised highly the military gifts of such executed "traitors" as Tukhachevsky and Uborevich. But it was typical of the man: he valued some of his military victims, just as he had personally "liked" Bukharin, but personal preferences could not justify *not* shooting a man if he might be a traitor to Stalin and Russia. The NKVD people decided to free their boss from these torments of uncertainty by preparing an especially handsome case of provocation and forged evidence against the high command of the Red Army.

The details remain obscure, but it is clear that the web of provocation began to be spun in 1936. The figure with whom the trap for the army was baited was Vitovt Putna. Of Polish-Lithuanian origins he had been a division commander in the Civil War. In the mid-1920s he reached the important position of Director of Military Training. But then his career suffered a setback: he imprudently signed the "letter of 180," the platform of the Trotsky-Zinoviev opposition in 1927, as well as a letter to the Central Committee criticizing Voroshilov's administration of the army. He was then sidetracked to being a military attaché—the work, one might say, of an official and respectable spy—in Berlin and more recently London, where he had attended Tukhachevsky during his visit as Soviet representative at the funeral of King George V. Putna was thus a logical man to be involved in the "Trotskyite-Zinovievite Terrorist Center," and he was mentioned as such in the Zinoviev-Kamenev trial in 1936. In the January 1937 trial, Putna's name was brought up again, this time by Radek, who said that Putna had come to him with an errand from Tukhachevsky. But in the interrogation by Vishinsky, Radek exonerated Tukhachevsky from any wrongdoing. The latter continued as Deputy Commissar of War, and in May 1937 was again slated to represent his country in London at the coronation of George VI.

The arrest of Putna as well as of two second-rank army commanders took place in mid-1936. It was a classical case of provocation: the arrested could be made to talk and to implicate others, and they, in turn, could be drawn into an incautious move—or at least into talk—that would make up Stalin's mind about their doom. The army's privileged position would then end. The generals, with their all too obvious distaste for the security people, would soon be made to realize that they no more than the Party bigwigs were immune to the ministrations of the NKVD.[25]

A yet more intricate provocation followed: through double agents the NKVD planted within the German intelligence service the idea of manufacturing fake evidence that implicated top Red Army commanders, principally Tukhachevsky, in treason.[26] This "evidence" then reached Stalin from several sources early in 1937.

It is unlikely that Stalin was fully taken in. He was an experienced conspirator and appreciated the story's several aspects of improbability. Germany had an obvious interest in decapitating the Red Army. People who contemplate treason on such a scale do not put it down in writing, appending their signatures! Who could *really* believe that Tukhachevsky and the other officers (three of whom were Jews) became German agents? But once aroused, his suspicions had to be appeased with blood: perhaps they were not traitors in the literal sense but they were capable of scheming against him. To present them as traitors had obvious advantages: what other officers would dare to defend them? Stalin liked to have documents "proving" what he was ready to believe, and here they were: by their own avowal Marshal of the Soviet Union Michael Tukhachevsky, Yan Gamarnik, head of the Political Administration of the Army, Yona Yakir and Jerome Uborevich, commanders of two of the three most important military districts (the Ukrainian and the Byelorussian), were unmasked as traitors scheming, at the bidding of Germany, to seize the government of their country. It is likely that the German list included more than the names of nine commanders Stalin *publicly* struck against in May–June 1937, but for his own good reasons he confined himself for the moment just to those.[27]

25 The theme of the hostility between the army and the security organs comes out strongly from Soviet novels about World War II. After Stalin's death the army had a belated revenge for its sufferings at the hands of the NKVD. It was Marshal Konev who presided at the trial which sentenced Beria and other high NKVD officials to death.

26 Because of his official dealings with the Reichswehr until 1933, it was easy to obtain a facsimile of Tukhachevsky's signature as well as a sample of his style. The fake information was then planted with, among others, the Czechoslovak government, and conveyed in good faith by President Eduard Beneš to Stalin. Various versions of the story are reviewed by Robert Conquest, *The Great Terror* (New York, 1968), pp. 204–21.

27 This is why the military court which on June 11 condemned Tukhachevsky and seven others to death was not furnished the forged German document, but only told about it. The document most likely listed some of the judges among the traitors.

Once Stalin's mind was made up, he moved with lightning speed against the leaders of the alleged military plot. Tukhachevsky's mission to London was revoked only a few days before he was due to depart. On May 20 he was demoted from being Deputy Commissar of War to commander of the Volga military district. He arrived there on May 26 and was arrested the next day. Toward the end of the month Yakir and Uborevich were urgently summoned to Moscow. They were arrested on the train. Hearing the news, Gamarnik, more realistic than the others, shot himself. Yakir, a member of the Central Committee, rather anachronistically asked for the Committee's authorization of his arrest. He was being taken to Moscow, he was told, and there he would be shown all the necessary papers.

The circumstances of the arrests show that Stalin at least half seriously believed there was a plot, and conversely that there could not have been any. If there had been, why did Yakir and Uborevich, hearing of the arrest of their alleged chief Tukhachevsky, not try to raise a mutiny within their districts (where they had commanded for over six years and were surrounded by friends and protégés); and if their treacherous plans had not yet ripened to that extent, why did they not try to flee? They went dutifully to Moscow, though they could have but few illusions as to why they were being summoned.

A success in the initial phase of his schemes of violence always acted on Stalin as a drug does on an addict: having tasted blood, he wanted more. There was now a clear indication that his previous fears of the army had turned into contempt. They schemed, they made fun of his performance during the Civil War, but when the moment came, they put their head on the block without the slightest resistance—all of which *proved* they were waiting for the war and for a chance to strike at him. They were cowards as well as traitors.

The Military Council, the body which included most of the army's leading commanders and administrators, met on June 1 and deliberated for five days. Its only item of business was to discuss the consequences of the uncovering of "the counterrevolutionary fascist organization within the armed forces." Stalin's tirade, of which we have only scraps, appears to have been a fair copy of his performance at the February–March meeting of the Central Committee. Once more he was a man possessed. How could they all have been so blind for so long? He offered his own example for them to emulate: he had come, then very foreign to things military, to Tsaritsyn in 1918 to help save it from the White armies. He immediately discovered that the former Tsarist officers pretending to serve the cause of the Revolution were in fact two-faced traitors. He had them arrested and executed. Tsaritsyn was saved. (We see once more how crucial the Tsaritsyn episode was in his development: a misanthropic and insecure conspirator, turned politician and journalist, is suddenly invested with the power of life and death, and finds his life's mission.) Now he was caustic about the commanders' inability to uncover traitors among those whom they had known for years. Here were documents and depositions amply proving the existence of the fascist plot! But not all the traitors have been unmasked, far from it! They all now had to make up for their former negligence and lack of vigilance! There were no protests, only shameful inquiries for guidance: How far should one go in denouncing one's comrades-at-arms? Someone wondered whether "one should speak publicly about the enemies of the people [within the army]." Stalin had a quick answer: absolutely, before the whole world.[28] Again, there was method in his madness: what army commander would now even dream of calling upon his men to help overthrow this man who was massacring the officer corps? The slightest gesture of opposition or criticism would be proof of treason. Any officer who might be tempted to strike a blow for his suffering country not only realized the fatuousness of such an endeavor, but also knew that if by some miracle he were successful he would die not as a martyr for freedom, but cursed as a traitor by his countrymen. As of June 1937 individual courage as well as professional honor became irrelevant to the situation of the Russian officer corps.

It is said that when the Mongols invaded Russia in the thirteenth century such was the hypnotic influence of the terror they exerted that when inhabitants of a locality were assembled and told not to stir but to await the return of a Mongol detachment from a raid so they could be massacred at leisure, few dared to seek safety in flight. Perhaps that is a fable, but now in the twentieth century the behavior of the Red Army leaders was even more craven: they had to lend a hand in the destruction of their friends and colleagues, while knowing that they had more than an even chance of following in their footsteps.

The only possible way out of the trap lay through collective resistance to the tyrant, but of that the military men were no more capable than the Party leaders. The years during which they praised Stalin to the skies, helped him to subdue the peasants, and stood apart while he decimated the Party leadership had paralyzed their will. Few of them would have hesitated to charge an enemy position to certain death; now at a word from this ranting man they denounced and cursed their closest friends, closed their ears to pleas for help from their wives and children.

The reader of the Soviet press that spring had little inkling of what horrors were soon to be unveiled. The journalistic fare consisted of endless accounts and praise of the feats of the Soviet aviators who had just flown over the North Pole in a nonstop flight to the United States.

<hr/>

[28] Petrov, p. 300.

Equal prominence was given to the achievement of the Russian Arctic explorers who from distant Francis Joseph Land were sending a continuous stream of reports and greetings to Comrade Stalin. Readers bored by these monotonous tales of heroism were undoubtedly titillated by one rare story of a nonpolitical crime[29]: a distinguished Soviet heart specialist, Professor Pletnev, had been unmasked as a "violator and sadist." The victim of this foul violation of Soviet medicine's humane tradition recounted her pitiful tale in a public letter. Some three years earlier Pletnev had received her at midnight and proceeded with "suspicious methods of medical inspection." Suspicions hardened into certainty when the doctor, belying his sixty-four years, proceeded to bite her breasts and to indulge in other behavior of which she could not bring herself to give the details. The result was lasting emotional as well as physical damage.

A more perceptive reader must have concluded that there was more to the story than met the eye. Why had it taken the NKVD three years to catch up with the lustful doctor, while all the while he was attending such notables as the late Orjonikidze and the American ambassador, Joseph Davies? This could not be taken as a welcome sign that medical rather than political wrecking was now occupying the attention of the security organs. All over Russia medical associations passed resolutions condemning the unprofessional behavior of Dr. Pletnev. The Procurator General, Vishinsky, promised an investigation. . . .

If anyone was apprehensive that the NKVD and the Procuracy were neglecting their more important tasks, he must have been reassured by *Pravda's* editorial of June 5: "The punishing sword of the proletarian dictatorship has become neither dull nor rusty. It will descend on the heads of those who want to tear our beautiful country to pieces and to subject it to the yoke of German-Japanese fascism." There was a long, dull, and seemingly pointless series of articles on espionage and counter-espionage drawing heavily on the more lurid Western literature on the subject. On June 11 the point of all such allusions became clear. The announcement was made of a trial before a military court of Tukhachevsky, Yakir, Uborevich, Putna, and four others of general rank. Their judges included two Marshals of the Soviet Union, Budenny and Blücher, the head of the Soviet air force, and five other top military commanders.[30] The verdict after one day's secret session: guilty. On June 12 came the announcement of the executions, as well as a patently

[29] Crime, as is well known, is the product of the conditions in capitalist society, and as the Soviet Union draws closer to socialism, it becomes less and less frequent there, the proof being the virtual absence of crime news in the Soviet press.
[30] The presiding judge was not, as the regulations required, the top-ranking officer but V. Ulrich, the purge specialist who presided in all the major Moscow trials.

455

untrue statement that all the accused had confessed.[31] A wave of national indignation against the "traitors" swept the country. The tenor of the countless resolutions passed by factories, schools, professional associations, etc., is well epitomized by one from the workers in the Stalin Automobile Factory which expressed thanks to "the illustrious sons of our Socialist Fatherland, workers of the NKVD led by their fighting Commissar N. I. Yezhov, so indefatigable and ruthless in unmasking the people's enemies" and in striking off the "viperlike head of the manyheaded enemy monster"; pledged that "we shall all be faithful helpers of the NKVD"; and concluded, "Long live the famed and vigilant Soviet counterespionage, with its iron commissar Yezhov."

Now the carnage began. The victims' families, aides, and servants were all rounded up. Virtually every Soviet officer of any standing had served at one time or another under one of the eight; and everybody in the Political Administration had been compromised by Gamarnik, now joined in treason to the others and violently condemned for cowardice in taking his own life. And so every officer's dossier was scanned and those with favorable testimony or recommendations from one of the victims were liquidated in their turn.

It is characteristic that with the nine "traitors" in their graves the investigation into their treason continued. Their aides continued to be questioned about suspicious incidents in their careers. Uborevich's servant was asked to recall anything and everything her master might have said about Stalin. It is clear that the tyrant still wondered whether his victims were only *objectively* guilty or whether they had in fact actively plotted against him. It is likely that he now convinced himself of the latter. Certainly even by his standards the vengeance he exacted against the nine murdered generals' families was ferocious. We have already mentioned the fate that befell three generations of Tukhachevsky's family. But we might add another detail. Uborevich had been born in a small Lithuanian village, where his family had continued their peasant existence while in Russia their brother became a famous commander and then perished. In 1940, with the war approaching, the Soviet Union annexed Lithuania. The NKVD could not leave Uborevich's family alone. Though in fact most of them had had no contact with Uborevich since 1917, his surviving brother and four sisters and their children were all sent to camps and exile in distant regions of Siberia.[32] Those who survived returned to Soviet Lithuania only in the late 1950s.

Stalin did not see fit to preserve even a shred of professional self-respect in the officer corps. It might have been given out, for example,

[31] A post-Stalin report has Tukhachevsky saying, when confronted with the charge of treason, "I must be dreaming."

[32] Vlasova in *Army Commander Uborevich: Recollections*, p. 6.

that it was the army's own intelligence services that were uncovering these heinous plots and treason. But, as his favorite proverb went, "If you cut off the head, you do not worry about the hair." On June 26 the newspapers prominently featured the award of high decorations to ten leading officials of the NKVD, led by Assistant Commissar of the NKVD Leonid Zakovsky and Yezhov's special aide Nathan Schapiro, who for "exemplary and selfless performance of duties entrusted to them by the Government" were given the Order of Lenin.[33] In the context of the recent news it is not difficult to divine for what services they were being rewarded. After June 11 there was not even any pretense at trying accused officers according to military law and custom. If accorded a trial at all, it was a few minutes' affair before a three-man NKVD collegium.

There was an element of shrewdness in spotlighting the NKVD, allowing the monstrous Yezhov to bask in his role as wielder of the sword of the proletarian revolution. The "If Stalin only knew" interpretation of the purges was gaining ground, even within the army. Those who were inclined secretly to disbelieve the fantastic charges were often ready to blame the "excesses"—as they are delicately called in the post-Stalin literature—on evil and criminal people in his entourage and the NKVD. One day, they believed, the Leader would see the light, punish the guilty, and restore honor to the army.

But it would be erroneous on the other hand to exaggerate the element of design and guile in Stalin's plan. His feelings must have been those of what might be called controlled panic. The army may have been incapable of rebellion, but the ever widening repression would come close to destroying it as a fighting force. Stalin's thrashing about amidst his terrible and contradictory fears is well illustrated in the history of what happened to the political commissars. A relic of the Civil War period, the institution of the political commissars had been abolished some years before as prejudicial to the authority of the commander and to the fighting efficiency of the army. In 1937 political commissars were reintroduced and put on the basis of equality with the commander. In 1940, after the disastrous experience of the Finnish War, unitary command was once again restored. The commissars returned at the supreme moment of Stalin's panic in 1941, after the outbreak of the German war, to be relegated again to the position of political assistants in 1942.

In 1937 there were only a few military figures on whom Stalin felt he

[33] "Selfless" was the right word. In a year and a half Zakovsky himself was liquidated, and though we do not have any information about the other nine gentlemen it would be most surprising if they escaped the same fate. Zakovsky, with his genial cynicism, was a survivor of the Yagoda era. Khrushchev was to quote him as telling one victim that he did not have to rack his brain about what to confess: the NKVD would prepare the scenario, and he just had to sign it and thus secure lifelong room and board at the government's expense.

could rely (the word "trust" is incompatible with the man)—mostly his old pals from Tsaritsyn and the Civil War. The army's political administration was entrusted to a Party hack and journalist by profession, Lev Mekhlis, until 1937 the editor of *Pravda*, a narrow-minded fanatic whose subsequent career suggests that he believed his own bloodcurdling editorials. The Tsaritsyn clique was epitomized by Ephim Shchadenko, successor of Yakir in the Kiev district, who became Assistant Commissar of War and as such contributed mightily to the catastrophe of the Soviet Army in the first months of the conflict with Germany. There is hardly a memoir by a Soviet wartime commander which does not speak with loathing and contempt of Mekhlis and Shchadenko.

"I would like to get my hands on your man Ryabnikov," said a local NKVD man to a regimental commissar in 1939. The latter was shaken by such formalities being observed toward what must be an "enemy of the people." Ryabnikov was promptly excluded form the Party; the NKVD was told he was all theirs. "Soon the mistake was cleared up. Ryabnikov was a good Bolshevik, and the counterintelligence people wanted him to work with them. The error was righted, but Comrade Ryabnikov was seriously disturbed." The man who recounted this story at the Eighteenth Party Congress then exclaimed indignantly: "The time has come for all of us, army Bolsheviks, to deal with people in the Stalin way, not to allow men to be excluded because of some back-street gossip, but only on the basis of documents and facts."[34] But in 1937 and for most of 1938 the procedure observed toward most suspects, especially military ones, was arrest, conviction, and sentence first, investigate later.

General Gorbatov's case was typical except that he was to be among the more lucky ones. He had served under Yakir. He compounded this crime by hobnobbing with a foreign Communist, something that was highly recommended in the 1920s but in the 1930s required fantastic naïveté and imprudence. And so came the arrest. Then beatings, which he endured without signing. Then the sentence: fifteen years at hard labor. Gorbatov comes out as an unusually brave man. Writing his memoirs at the age of seventy-four,[35] he recounts many acts of suicidal daring he witnessed during the war. But none of them, he says, matched the courage of his commanding officer when after Gorbatov's arrest he succored Mme. Gorbatov, gave the desperate woman (wife and sister of convicted enemies of the people) money for a ticket to rejoin her mother.

General Gorbatov endured the horrors of the Kolyma camp in the

34 *The Eighteenth Congress of the Communist Party* (Moscow, 1939), p. 276.
35 Alexander Gorbatov, *Years and Wars* (Moscow, 1965).

Far East for several months. Then came a lucky break: depositions of many convicted "traitors" (still alive) were being reconsidered by the Military Council. In this fresh atmosphere of liberalism Marshal Budenny mustered courage to say he never considered Gorbatov guilty. And so he was returned to Moscow for a new investigation. His luck continued: half of those whose cases were reviewed were being sent back to the camps, but after four months of questioning Gorbatov was exonerated. At this point the NKVD investigator became solicitude itself: he ran errands for the general, made sure that he had a spic-and-span uniform for the moment he stepped outside the prison gate (which like his arrest occurred at two A.M.). On bidding goodbye to the officer whom at first he had greeted by bursting into laughter,[36] this representative of humane tradition in the Soviet security organs said warmly, "Here is my telephone number. If you need to, call me at any time. You can count on me."[37] Released and restored to his command, Gorbatov soon had another close call. He went to visit his old friend, the German Communist Wilhelm Pieck. His faith in international proletarian solidarity appeared unshaken. And so next night there was another knock on his door: the NKVD conveyed the general into the presence of Mekhlis and Shchadenko. "They evidently did not teach you enough at Kolyma," said Shchadenko. But the war had already begun. Marshal Timoshenko wanted Gorbatov at the front, and at the time Stalin had to pay heed to Timoshenko. And so the erstwhile "traitor" went on to martial exploits in the war, concluding it as the Russian Commandant of Berlin. An unusually lucky fellow, General Gorbatov, and for a Russian officer highly eccentric—a lifetime tee-totaler.☆☆☆

W ITH the end of the army's immunity to mass repression, terror in mid-1937 assumed a comprehensive character: in Soviet life there was now no sphere free from it, no leading group or profession that would not be decimated within the next year and a half. We have, of course, no reliable figures as to its extent. A Soviet author who studied

---

[36] Undoubtedly because it was so amusing to see somebody who had *not* confessed.
[37] Gorbatov, p. 168. Gorbatov relates this without comment. How much he remains infected by the atmosphere of the times, despite his experiences, comes out in another story. He was very taken aback by the fact that one of his fellow prisoners at the time of the arrest was also released and restored to rank. The man had belonged to the former "exploiting class," while he, Gorbatov, came from a poor peasant family. The other one signed a confession, he hadn't. And yet the other general got off even without going to a camp!

the subject estimates the total number of the repressed during 1936–39 at 4 to 5 million. These were people arrested and/or exiled to the vast networks of forced labor camps, or sentenced to "free" exile in a given locality.[38] How many were killed outright? The same authority gives the figure at 400,000 or 500,000. Of one thing we can be reasonably sure: a great majority of the 170 million inhabitants of the Soviet Union spent that time in fear, bewilderment, or anguish. The memory of those years sank deep in the national consciousness and will linger there for long. In the post-Stalin era many foreigners were surprised by the Russians' seeming indifference to tales of wartime suffering among nationalities like the Jews, Poles, and Yugoslavs. But these reactions are not necessarily due to insensitivity or anti-Semitism. Often they spring from the conviction—a guilty secret shared by all the survivors of the period—that no other people could have suffered so much (and that at the hands of their own countrymen) as did the Russians and other peoples of the Soviet Union.

The national shame is compounded by realization that the fear was no more widespread than the belief that those being liquidated and repressed were in the main guilty. People could whisper about "excesses," about Stalin's being misled; people knew of course about their own innocence and that of their families and close friends; they could, as in the case of most military men, be incredulous about the *extent* of treason in their profession. But about the others one believed. There were different gradations of this belief, ranging from the Komsomol members' certainty that Vishinsky was a hero, to the more sophisticated and conscience-soothing belief that while most of the victims were not *precisely* guilty as charged, they were guilty of something and the international situation required that their guilt be painted in violent hues, that one could not be too vigilant, etc. Human nature recoils at the notion of apparently senseless criminality on a vast scale. It would have been easier to believe that Stalin was a German agent bleeding the country at Hitler's behest than to conceive of the purge not having *some* justification.

For many the period was one of weird exhilaration. Young Paul Morozov had undoubtedly thought he was serving the Cause when he denounced his father for concealing grain. A young officer might well believe he was striking at the fascists by reporting to the NKVD that his commander once had spoken well of Tukhachevsky, or that the lecturer in the military school cast doubts on the superiority of the Soviet air force over the German one. The tone was in many ways already one of war, and the official nomenclature recognized this by dropping all references to "deviations" and "inefficiency," speaking instead of "enemies" and "sabotage," regardless of whether the transgression in

[38] Medvedev, p. 239.

question was some typographical error in reproducing Comrade Stalin's speeches or a supply of bayonets that allegedly bent too easily.

Beyond the real or alleged need for terror due to the danger of war with Germany, it must have struck Stalin that he had discovered a new technique and philosophy of government applicable also in normal times. "Violence is often very useful; without violence we would not have had the Revolution; violence is the midwife of politics," he said to a young protégé. If one looks at the Soviet press of the period one senses the currents of fear and exhilaration that ran through the whole society. "We were set on our fellow men like dogs, and the whole pack of us licked the hunter's hand, squealing incomprehensibly."[39]

There it is set in vivid colors: the kingdoms of light and darkness. From the yellowed pages of *Pravda* and *Izvestia* the smiling heroes peer at us: those very Russian faces of the record-breaking pilots, the Arctic explorers under Professor Schmidt who sent a message of homage to the Leader, as well as a resolution approving the execution of the army traitors. (Khrushchev's propaganda exploitation of Sputnik was but a pale imitation of Stalin's achievement in this respect.) How could one believe that the Leader hailed so continuously by these brave and handsome young men—shown clasping them to his bosom, inquiring solicitously about the details of their feats—was a bloody tyrant, who after a triumphant reception sat down and signed another list of victims to be murdered and deported? And here are articles on other people who in a different manner are still heroes: in an "exemplary and selfless way" they have fulfilled the government's orders and unmasked the people's enemies. Wisely, one should think, the announcements of these awards are seldom accompanied by photographs. But the reader's curiosity is occasionally gratified. There is the chief of them all, the iron commissar Yezhov—smiling shyly at the camera, being embraced by President Kalinin on receiving the Order of Lenin, in immediate proximity to Stalin and Molotov at one state occasion after another. To think that such a small, delicate-looking man had accomplished so much! And he was not without a certain eloquence. "For us in the NKVD our work is its own reward," he declared modestly on receiving the highest order of the Soviet Union. Regrettably there are no pictures of his "close comrades in arms," who also received high orders at a festive reception in the Kremlin on July 27, 1937. Among those honored was Leonid Ushakov, whose special talents as torturer enabled him to survive the liquidation of his boss, and who as late as 1939 and 1940 was reported working on such important "enemies" as former Politburo member Eikhe. Not many were to be so lucky. Of that proud group which gathered at the Kremlin on that summer evening, most shared the fate

[39] Mandelstam, p. 107.

of Yezhov and perished under Beria. Among them was Stalin's own brother-in-law, Stanislaw Redens.

Against the world of heroes exuding strength, resolve, and gaiety was the murky realm of traitors and enemies. Stories about them appear as often as those about the heroes. Here was a rich opportunity for the humble citizen to do his bit: to report to *Pravda* that, say, a secretary of a Party cell, though unmasked as an enemy, had merely been transferred to another post, how the new chairman of the city council had previously worked under six convicted traitors, how his warnings on this count were being brushed off by local authorities. Not for nothing did Stalin attack "the silent ones," those officials and citizens who because of "ideological spinelessness" were often as harmful as the traitors themselves, and who out of misplaced modesty or pride refused to join in the task of denunciation. In a sense Russia in 1937 and 1938 presented the ultimate of egalitarianism: every citizen was endowed with the potential power of life and death over his neighbor; no man save one was above suspicion or immune to the nocturnal knock on the door.

Stalin appeared to stand like a rock amid the flow of violence and hysteria shaking the Soviet world. Even to his victims he was an element of stability and a source of hope. "Why don't you write to Stalin?" asked an aide of Tukhachevsky before the Marshal's fatal trip to his last assignment. And Tukhachevsky, who could have no illusions about Stalin, confessed he just had. Before the firing squad, Yakir exclaimed, "Long live the Party! Long live Stalin!" Much as one is amazed by the extent of Stalin's megalomania before, one is now impressed by his ability to go on being a working dictator, politician, and statesman in the midst of this carnage. ☆☆☆

IT was as a candidate to the Supreme Soviet from the Stalin district of the city of Moscow that the god Stalin appeared before his electors on December 11, 1937. Here he immediately became a politician and showed that he had lost none of that folksy quality which stood him in such good stead when he really had to plead for votes. He did not intend to speak, said Stalin, but the chairman on the occasion (none other than Nikita Khrushchev) "brought me here, you might say, by force, and ordered, 'give a good speech.'"[40] Yet everything that needed saying, he remarked, had already been said by Comrades Molotov, Kalinin, Yezhov, and others. And so he would just like to assure them,

[40] Stalin (Stanford ed.), I, 237.

The Terrible Interlude

"You can fully depend on Comrade Stalin, you can depend on him to fulfill his duty toward the people." It was not a long or significant speech, but it showed that Stalin had not yet lost either the patience or the ability to speak to his subjects. On occasion he could still play the role of a genial father of his people.

He had other surprises in store for those who might believe that he was a figurehead and that the NKVD exercised the real power. Nothing suggests that during this time he slackened his hold on the reins of government or that ceremony and list-checking occupied most of his time. He was still "the most active Communist." The enjoyment of absolute power had not weakened his ambition—indeed it grew stronger as he grew older—to become a great historian and philosopher of Marxism. This ambition led him, as it has led many busy people with literary pretensions, to employ ghostwriters. Thus in 1938 there appeared *The History of the Communist Party of the Soviet Union—Short Course*, before which Russia's philosophical and historical professions, calling it a work of genius, immediately prostrated themselves. Only with Khrushchev was this work revealed as having been written by a committee of the Central Committee with Stalin's participation, rather than by the dictator himself as the title page asserted. Khrushchev's unsentimental revelation is hardly likely to detract from Stalin's literary reputation. The merit of the work can be sufficiently judged by the fact that its real authors have not bothered to come forward and put in their claims. In any case, one chapter clearly bears the imprint of Stalin's didactic style—a lengthy, lucid, but thoroughly unoriginal disquisition on dialectical and historical materialism. Let us be fair: neither Khrushchev nor Brezhnev ever learned enough Marxism to be able to write it.

And if he could speak in his own defense, Stalin might find much of this later criticism equally unfair. Hadn't he made his successors what they were? Not only Khrushchev but Brezhnev, Podgorny, Kosygin, et al. would be retired minor bureaucrats if he had not cleared their path by liquidating all the dead wood left by the Revolution—dullards, talkers, journalists who, if not actually traitors and wreckers, were useless.

In advancing people, Stalin was mainly drawn to two types. For the more delicate tasks, he liked people who aped his own manner with his conviction, who could instantly spot the enemy, who were quick and brutal with no humanitarian compunctions. Such were Yezhov and Mekhlis. Such was the fantastically incompetent Kulik, another Assistant Commissar of War, who in issuing orders would add, "If you do it well, a decoration; if not, jail." (Came the war and Kulik, after contributing to the destruction of a Soviet army, was demoted from Marshal to brigadier general. Even that rank was above his abilities, adds one of his former subordinates.)

Vice is attracted by innocence, and the other category of people to receive preferment during the purges were young people who impressed Stalin as doers and believers. The Soviet Union's leading aircraft designer, Alexander Yakovlev, may well think of the late 1930s with a certain nostalgia. One day back then, the thirty-two-year-old engineer found himself summoned to Stalin's office in the Kremlin to report on his latest design. Yakovlev was nervous, but Stalin's kind manner and calm voice quieted him. After hearing the report, Stalin nodded to Voroshilov, who scribbled on a piece of paper and then read that it was proposed to award Yakovlev the Order of Lenin, an automobile, and one hundred thousand rubles.[41] Another summons, this time to the offices of the Central Committee, came later. Since there was no explanation, Yakovlev was understandably exercised: he does not say so, but after all, at the time many people were being called out from their work to return only after years away, if ever. But who should meet him in the reception room but Stalin! In a fatherly manner, taking him by the arm, the dictator introduced him to a group of assembled generals and engineers as the young man who was going to design a new fighter in a hurry, show "what a young Soviet engineer can do." This time his reward was going to be even more substantial: Stalin would invite him for a cup of tea. Some months later a telephone call came. "How goes it? Will the fighter be ready in December?" "It will be, Comrade Stalin, just as promised." "Well, then, the drink is on me."[42] Yakovlev adds modestly, "I have no doubt that similar telephone calls went out to other engineers, participating in the construction of new planes." Well, not always. Several of Russia's most distinguished aircraft designers, including of course the famous Tupolev, were doing their sketches while in jail, and for progress reports they were summoned not to the Father of the People, but to the head of the NKVD; for incentive they were offered not decorations and money, but a promise that if they didn't come through, it would be hard labor camp for them.

Yakovlev, an intelligent and perspicacious man, was still taken in not only by Stalin's favors but also by his theatrical ability. After the outbreak of the war, Stalin once bemoaned in his presence the lack of competent men. Yakovlev, now an assistant minister, seized the opening: "Comrade Stalin, it has been more than a month since they arrested our Assistant Commissar for Engines, Balandin. . . . We cannot believe that he could be an enemy." Stalin fell into his role of humane leader misled by his entourage: "Yes, he has been sitting for forty days without making any confessions. Maybe there is nothing to him. Quite possible. Such cases do happen. . . ." And then the end result, undoubtedly intended all along by Stalin: "Next day Vassily

[41] Alexander Yakovlev, *The Life's Aim* (Moscow, 1970), p. 185.
[42] The tea was all along a euphemism.

464

Balandin . . . was working at his desk in the ministry as if nothing had happened." Yakovlev reports naïvely on a yet more impresssive bit of playacting by his benefactor. Summoned to the Kremlin at one of the most critical moments in the fall of 1941, the airplane designer was reassured by Stalin's calm. But what soothed his nerves most was the sight on Stalin's table of an open book. With the Germans advancing on Moscow, Stalin was still able to relax by reading Gorky! (We know from other sources that before the arrival of visitors appropriate literature would be placed on Stalin's working table, and the visitor would thus be struck by the breadth of his host's interests.) "We left Stalin with a firm belief that no matter how heavy the coming setbacks, in the end the indisputable superiority on our side will assure us victory."[43]

Though Yakovlev, writing in the late 1960s, mumbles dutifully about the evil of the "cult of personality," those were not such bad years from his point of view. And for many others the time of terror was also a time of opportunity. Those like Yakovlev who could win distinction and advancement through their work were fortunate (and even they cannot escape the charge of complicity through silence in the fate of their comrades and the whole nation). For others the road to preferment was not so straightforward, nor bereft of dark and shameful episodes.

The "new men" brought up in this period have continued to dominate Soviet life up to our own day. And through them Stalin has come close to changing the traditional Russian character. Gone is the volubility, that "broad Russian nature" which even the Revolution had not managed to suppress. By some miracle Nikita Khrushchev kept some characteristics of the old stereotype, but he was born in 1894. Others of the Stalin generation, and often even their children, gaze at us with watchful eyes, as if still scanning for enemies or denouncers. The countrymen of Gogol and Shchedrin appear incapable of wholehearted gaiety, but retain that sardonic humor which was so amply used when unmasking the lies of the bourgeois press or observing an apprehended enemy of the people wriggle hopelessly in the net. Nor is the new Soviet man prone to that philosophical volubility which permeates the pages of *Dr. Zhivago*. Watchfulness seems to be the key characteristic of Stalin's generation, a feeling that the individual is indeed very much an island, or must be, in order to survive. These characteristics do not disappear even in the face of the freer ways of the young, and despite the fact that Stalin has been dead for twenty years and a return of full-fledged Stalinism appears inconceivable. To those who lived through 1937, nothing is inconceivable.

The approaching war was the purported reason and justification for terror. It is remarkable that in all the accounts of the purges—whether

[43] Yakovlev, p. 297.

Western or Soviet post-Stalin ones—there is not so much as *one* authenticated case of a real traitor or spy among the thousands of victims listed by name. (A defector from the Soviet political police mentions one spy, but the case is at best dubious.) Following Yezhov's downfall, the NKVD chief in the Far East did flee to the Japanese, but neither in his case nor in that of a handful of Soviet diplomats and foreign agents who refused to return when summoned from abroad is there any documented evidence of previous disloyalty. ☆☆☆

I F internal policy smacked of insanity to those who did not know Stalin's mind, in foreign affairs an unbiased observer must assess Stalin in the years 1936–39 as prudent and realistic. The contrast is instructive: it demonstrates not only the inherent difference between two spheres of his activity, but also how different a man he was when absolute power was his and when it wasn't. In foreign affairs he could not gratify his whims, indulge his every suspicion, slacken his thirst for blood. Here there was only one reality, not an "objective" one and a real one. One could not "liquidate" Hitler the way one did Bukharin or Pyatakov. Nor did Stalin overreact to Japanese provocations. His policy in the Far East was a prudent blend of appeasement and firmness vis-à-vis Tokyo. Stalin's personal feelings, so ferociously stamped on internal policies, were not allowed to interfere with rational calculation in foreign affairs.

How different, again, from Hitler. After 1938 the Führer needlessly liquidated the stump of Czechoslovakia, already a virtual German satellite (or, rather, group of satellites). Inordinate vanity also made him forsake Japanese assistance in the attack on the Soviet Union which he could have had if he pressed for it. And just as visions of a triumphant entry into Prague, and of Russia conquered solely by the German sword, pushed away practical considerations and cautions, so Hitler's ignorance and sentiment made him declare war on the United States (he believed it was well known that American soldiers could not fight) and dissipate German armies in Italy and Africa (to succor Mussolini, his faltering partner in crime, he sent troops which in the summer of 1942 might well have spelled the difference at Stalingrad and in 1943 at the great battle of Kursk). In contrast, in foreign affairs until well after World War II, Stalin continued being what he had been in domestic politics until the late 1920s—a ruthless realist, unaffected by ideology or sentiment, unmoved by vanity.

Even in 1936–39 one great success of Soviet foreign policy was already

466

indisputable. Hitler's dream of isolating the Soviet Union, still more of leading a great European crusade against Communism, had already failed. Instead, the piecemeal aggression on which Germany embarked helped Soviet rapprochement with the West. No one, least of all Stalin, could yet be sure that at the crucial moment, and despite the Franco-Soviet alliance, the Western powers would not let the Russians fight their wars alone. But in 1937 the probabilities already looked the other way. The Western governments—slowly, to be sure, and ineffectively, as it later turned out—were rearming, thus strengthening Hitler's conviction that he would have to begin the battle to preserve European civilization by fighting the decadent democracies rather than half-Jewish and half-Mongol Bolshevism. The policy of the Popular Front and Russia's recent democratic transformation under the Stalin Constitution was bearing fruit: a growing body of public opinion in the West (no longer confined just to left-wing and liberal circles, witness Mr. Churchill) was clamoring for a tougher stand against Hitler and firmer collaboration with the U.S.S.R. The depredations of the Fascists and Nazis in Spain blurred the impact of the Russian purges. The Second (Socialist) International denounced the Moscow trials, but at the same time it was negotiating with the Comintern for a joint front against Hitler.

Such developments could not in themselves reassure Stalin. His thinking was dominated by the fear of *any* war in which the enemy might reach Soviet territory, and against such an eventuality even the firmest alliance with France and Britain offered no guarantee, certainly not after the reoccupation of the Rhineland and Hitler's construction of the Siegfried Line of fortifications in the West. That a general European war could be avoided Stalin, like any realist in those years, could have but little hope. But perhaps Russia could stay out of the war, or at least out of its first phase? Hitler's irritation was growing as his sublime plans for saving Europe and the Aryan race failed to be appreciated in Paris or London. He lacked that patience which, when it came to plans of foreign conquest, his fellow dictator manifested so strongly. If he could not have the Ukraine right away, he would have to take Austria and the Sudetenland. Eventually even Stalin miscalculated the extent of Hitler's irrational impatience, but in the 1930s he had a more realistic appreciation of it than most: he knew that Hitler was not only a master bluffer playing on the weak nerves of the democratic politicians, but a warlord who would one day cast aside both the bluff and the ideological crusade.

This is not to say, as some have done, that the 1939 scenario was already in Stalin's head by 1937. Soviet diplomacy kept probing discreetly (under the cover of trade negotiations) for the possibility of an accommodation with Germany, but Hitler seemed obdurate. Until the spring of 1939 Stalin had to assume that the Nazis meant what they were saying, and had to act accordingly: to present the Soviet Union as a probable ally of the democracies. The widespread belief in the West that quite apart from her national interest the U.S.S.R. "had" to be on the side of the democracies against fascism was, of course, assiduously cultivated and assisted by Soviet propaganda, was inherent in the concept of the Popular Front, was loudly proclaimed in speeches by Litvinov and other Soviet diplomats in the West. Yet Stalin himself never phrased the problem in such terms, not even when extolling the unequaled democratic virtues of his constitution. He preferred to list Russia among the "peaceloving states"—a statement of his which for once was sincerely meant and true: no other statesman, not even Neville Chamberlain, feared war as much as he.

While Russian military, air, and naval personnel helped the Republican side and the U.S.S.R. furnished it with supplies, Soviet participation in the Spanish Civil War was veiled in much more mystification than that of the fascist powers. After mid-1937 it became clear that the legitimate government was losing. From an overall perspective, the setback to the Soviet position was slightly more than balanced by enhanced Soviet prestige and a larger following in the West.

It was only to a handful of Western radicals—on whom, however, as to George Orwell, it was to have a decisive influence—that the Soviet intervention in Spain revealed some of the true meaning of Stalinism. Among the fantastic profusion of radical parties on the Spanish Republican side one bearing the initials POUM had a fairly clear Trotskyite coloring. It was not out of the range of possibilities that the POUM and the anarchists, both especially strong in Catalonia, might coalesce to create a semi-Trotskyite regime; the heresy might then acquire a territorial focus. Orders went out from Moscow and, with them, agents of the NKVD. The latter, assisted by Spanish Communists, then conducted a campaign of assassination and purge against real and alleged Trotskyites in the Republican ranks, a campaign which at one point assumed in itself an aspect of a civil war. The Comintern put its seal of approval on this extension of Stalinism to foreign soil: "Since the Trotskyites in the interest of fascism are carrying on subversive work in the rear of republican troops, the presidium approves the policy of the party aimed at the complete and final destruction of Trotskyism in Spain as essential to the victory over fascism."[44] And then inevitably the purge extended to Soviet advisers and diplomatic personnel serving in Spain. On their return to Russia, if not before, those who had been exposed to the germ of Trotskyism in foreign parts were, in a majority of cases, liquidated. Among them was the consul general in Barcelona, the commander of the detachment which in 1917 had seized the Winter Palace, Antonov-Ovseenko. It was only the unusually lucky ones among

44 Jane Degras, ed., *The Communist International* 1919–1943, *Documents*, III: 1929–43 (New York, 1965), 398.

the "Spaniards," such as the future Minister of Defense, Rodion Malinovsky, and the chief of Soviet artillery in World War II, Voronov, who escaped execution or imprisonment. ☆☆☆

EVEN the most perspicacious and powerful tyrant cannot control the course of history beyond his death. Stalin never indulged in nonsense on the order of Hitler's flamboyant oratory about a "Thousand-Year Reich." But if there was one legacy he hoped to leave, it was that of a monolithic Communist camp and of Russia, world superpower in her own right, absolutely controlling it. And yet in 1937 he contributed to a sequence of events which frustrated this dream and helped to erect a giant state which ended Russia's undisputed domination of world Communism. In 1937, however, the turn of events in China looked like an undoubted success for Soviet diplomacy and for the cause of Communism.

After their famous Long March in 1934, the position of the Chinese Communists still remained precarious. A truce with Japan enabled Chiang Kai-shek to concentrate on destroying his Chinese rivals. With the help of German military advisers he was preparing in 1936 yet another campaign against the Communists. The Chinese Nationalists at the time (and since then) were widely blamed for their policy between 1931 and 1936 of concentrating on the internal enemy while acquiescing in Japan's seizure of Manchuria. But in the Kremlin Chiang's policy could be more dispassionately appraised if not approved: Chiang's tactics and reasoning were not too dissimilar from Lenin's when he signed the seemingly disgraceful and ruinous Treaty of Brest-Litovsk. Like Lenin, Chiang wanted a breathing spell in the struggle against the external foe, and time to solidify his power. The Japanese, said the Generalissimo, were a disease of the skin while the Communists were one of the heart. The defeat of Japan in the 1930s was beyond China's means, just as the defeat of Germany in 1918 was beyond Russia's. But Chiang could hope that in due time the United States would rid China of her foreign enemy, as the victory of the Entente in 1918 undid Brest-Litovsk.

The success of this policy of Chiang's would mean a catastrophe for the Chinese Communists and a grave danger for the Soviet Union. With the situation in China stabilized the Japanese would be free to move against the Soviet Far East. Not for nothing was German diplomacy striving to turn the informal truce between Chiang and the Japanese into a definite agreement.

How different the course of world history would have been if, say, the Left Socialist Revolutionaries had managed to capture Lenin in the spring of 1918 and force him to renew the war with Germany! In China such a conspiracy did dramatically change the course of events; world history is affected by personalities, accidents, and plots, no less than by the proverbial underlying social and economic forces. While preparing a campaign against Mao's forces, Chiang was imprisoned by one of his subordinates. There followed negotiations between the Generalissimo, his captor, and the Communist emissary and probable instigator of the coup, Chou En-lai. A drastic change of policy was exacted from Chiang in return for his release: he was to cease the fratricidal war, and collaborate with the Communists against the foreign invader. The Communists, in turn, acknowledged his leadership in the struggle against Japan while retaining their own political organization and armies.

The Japanese did not wait for these negotiations to be completed. They struck in China on July 7, 1937. The formal agreement between the Chinese Nationalists and the Communists was announced on September 22. Even before, in August, the U.S.S.R. signed a treaty of nonaggression and friendship with the Chiang government. Soviet munitions, credits, and military instructors began to flow once more to China. The threat to the Soviet Far East was not ended—there would be sharp border fighting between the Russians and the Japanese in 1938 and 1939—but with the Japanese occupied in the seemingly endless process of wresting one province at a time from Chiang's control Stalin, as well as Mao, could breathe more easily.

Stalin's policy in China demonstrates yet again how in a situation where he did not have absolute power Stalin could be subtle and diplomatic rather than tyrannical and whimsical. The leaders of Chinese Communism, Mao, Chu Teh, Chou, were not his men. They had advanced to the top in an intraparty struggle pushing aside in some cases people previously favored by Moscow. Of course, nothing suggests that they were not, at least until 1947, fully respectful of his wishes and ready to fulfill his commands. Trotskyites were liquidated within the Chinese as well as in other Communist Parties. But even absolute obedience did not save many foreign Communists, whom Stalin destroyed on the same principle that he liquidated many Russian supporters: when they had political associations and memories antedating his absolute power, when they were not "his" men. But in the case of China he resisted the temptation to show that heads could roll in Yenan as easily as in Moscow or Kiev. And the Chinese Communist leaders wisely contributed to his self-restraint: none of them is on record as visiting Moscow in those terrible years 1937 and 1938. (Only as master of China did Mao step onto Soviet soil, in December 1949. And his Oriental prudence did not abandon him even then. He had once entrusted his life to American pilots, and he went to Russia by air in the more relaxed atmosphere of 1957, but in 1949 he made the trip to and from Moscow by train.)

The years of the Great Purge were also years of horror for foreign Communists. To be sure, Communism the world over throughout these years displayed exemplary loyalty to Stalin. This loyalty was the product of faith rather than of fear. To be sure, nowhere was a prominent Communist completely safe from the long arm of the NKVD—as Spain, isolated assassinations of Soviet officials who defected to other countries, and finally Trotsky's fate amply demonstrate. Still in Paris, London, or Greenwich Village one was not under the same constraints as in Moscow. One knew people and read literature that denounced Stalinism and the grotesque Moscow trials. And yet the faithful abroad prostrated themselves before Stalin's name, cursed Trotsky and Bukharin, applauded every execution in the Soviet Union as just and necessary, as if they themselves lived in the nightly danger of a visit by the NKVD. This behavior demonstrates most strongly the irrational appeal of tyranny, and one may also note the marked decline in this faith that characterized foreign attitudes toward Soviet Communist leaders once the latter had renounced Stalinism and unveiled some of its horrors.

Yet even these blindly loyal people, if they were unlucky enough to live in the Soviet Union or even to visit there, were purged as mercilessly as if they had been Soviet officials or military officers. The NKVD took Stalin's warning to heart about the most noxious spies and wreckers often being those who appeared entirely loyal. Who could answer this description better than all those foreigners, each of whom at one time or another had had some connection with Zinoviev and Bukharin, former heads of the Comintern, and who in any case were automatically suspect on account of being foreigners? The Constitution of the Soviet Union had proudly proclaimed that any revolutionaries of any nationality on claiming asylum in the U.S.S.R. enjoyed all the rights and responsibilities of the Soviet citizen. In 1936–39 this principle was fully observed. General Gorbatov's friend Wilhelm Pieck was one of a small handful of German Communists in Russia who were *not* liquidated. The Polish Communists in the Soviet Union were decimated even more thoroughly than the German ones. So convinced was the NKVD that the Polish Party was shot through with provocateurs that it was ordered dissolved in 1938, and its members (many of them in jail in their own country) were branded as Trotskyites and agents of the Warsaw regime's police. The Central Committee of the Yugoslav Party was invited to Moscow in 1936; with one exception they were liquidated there. The exception and the new secretary general, "Walter," later better known as Tito, left hurriedly with his assistants for Yugoslavia.

The Party was illegal there, but the worst that could happen was arrest. The whole colorful elite of international Communism of the early days was destroyed. Gone were such heroes as Béla Kun and the resourceful German propagandist Willi Münzerberg (he refused to leave Paris for Moscow, was expelled from the Party, and murdered on French soil, presumably by an NKVD agent, in 1940). The Swiss Communist Fritz Platten, who arranged Lenin's historic trip to his homeland in 1917, was not spared. He was accused of having been in German employ ever since that year! (It would have been hard for Lenin, one feels, in 1937: Trotsky, Zinoviev, and the man who arranged his passage through Germany in 1917 were all now unmasked as German agents.) NKVD officials were not endowed with a sense of historical irony, but their supreme boss was, and he well might have reflected that after all "objectively" all those people worked in 1917–18 in Germany's interest.[45]

Though all Communist parties suffered in the purge, there were significant variations in the way they were treated. To some extent this reflected the availability of their personnel: obviously if you lived in Moscow your chances of ending up in the clutches of the NKVD were higher than if you were just an occasional visitor or prudently stayed home. (But as we have seen entire central committees, not to mention individual leaders and activists, could be and were summoned to Moscow.) But an important variable was also the place the country and Party occupied in Soviet foreign-policy calculations. The French Communists fared relatively well. They, like most of their countrymen, were loath to leave their beautiful land for foreign parts, and French representation in the Comintern apparatus was negligible. The Franco-Soviet alliance and the elections also argued against any tendency to treat the French Communists harshly. The English and American parties, on the other hand, were always thought of by Stalin with contempt. Thus, though in the mythology of the terror the British Intelligence Service was not far behind the German and Japanese espionage agencies in plotting against Soviet power, it evidently failed to recruit a single British Communist, though in Russia it scored handsomely in enlisting all sorts of important Soviet leaders from Central Asia among its agents. The American intelligence services were held in as great contempt as the American Communists, and unique among the major capitalist powers (except for the ally, France), the United States was not credited with a single act of espionage or wrecking in the Soviet Union: a sad record for the mainstay of world capitalism. Only after World War II did the

---

[45] The NKVD apparently inherited the files of the Tsarist Secret Police and so at the 1938 trial there was one piquant and little-noticed detail. Rakovsky was accused of receiving money from the German government in World War I, which he owned to. Uniquely among all the accusations in the trial, this story was probably true.

activities of the CIA occupy a place of honor in the black book of Soviet propaganda.

Meanwhile, the Soviet Union's own espionage efforts were, like everything else, gravely handicapped because of the purges. If humdrum Soviet officials so often turned out to be two-faced, what of the men whose very profession required them to be two-faced? It goes without saying that several successive layers of command in both the military and NKVD foreign intelligence services were liquidated. One of the most successful Soviet spies of the period, Richard Sorge, escaped this fate by a hair's breadth. He just failed to be recalled to Moscow at the height of the purge, at a time when both his immediate superior and his Russian common-law wife were arrested. Sorge was able to continue at his Tokyo post whence, utilizing his German and Japanese connections, he provided Moscow with warnings about the probable date of Hitler's attack on Russia and about the Japanese decision to move against Pearl Harbor rather than Siberia. His spy ring was then broken, he was arrested, and the Soviet Embassy in Tokyo denied any knowledge of him. Sorge was executed by the Japanese in November 1944, when, fearful of the Russians joining the war against them, Tokyo would have gone to almost any lengths to appease Moscow. Only in 1964 did the U.S.S.R. recognize the services of Richard Sorge: he was named, posthumously, Hero of the Soviet Union.

With most Soviet diplomats and intelligence operatives unmasked as traitors, it is difficult to see how Soviet foreign policy could operate at all. But the same question may be posed in relation to every other sphere of Russia's political, social, and cultural activity. The problem of how any information could be conveyed and then acted upon in the Soviet Union of those days is among the most perplexing ones about the whole purge. By 1938, if one believed the official line, one had to grant that beginning with the Revolution, Soviet society had been in the main organized and run by traitors and foreign agents. Not even the most inveterate enemy of Communism could have imagined or invented the picture of Soviet reality that was trumpeted daily in official propaganda.[46] But the problem that confronted Soviet policymakers who had somehow escaped the net was how to secure the data on which any policy must be based. How did one appraise a diplomatic dispatch filed by a man whose superior had just been shot as a foreign agent? How did one approve a construction project when one of the architects had confessed to being a wrecker whose blueprints caused the collapse of several edifices? *Every one* of the higher Red Army commanders had at

---

[46] Among certain Russian émigré reactionary circles the purge was viewed not so much with satisfaction as with sympathetic interest in Stalin's work and—this was not so much off the mark—as a contribution to the rebirth of the Russian national spirit and the demise of Bolshevism.

one time or another served or studied under a traitor. One recalls the harm done to the efficient functioning of the American government in the 1950s through the extravaganza of McCarthyism, yet to compare McCarthyism to Stalinism (and some writers have attempted this in all seriousness) is to compare a fly to an elephant. Much of even the most extreme criticism of Stalin in the post-1956 Soviet literature is tempered by a certain wonder if not admiration: how did he manage to keep the Russian state in any kind of running order?

Part of the answer must be found, unsophisticated though it may appear to believers in "deeper causes," in Stalin's fantastic luck, which accompanied him throughout his fantastic career. What if Lenin's health had improved decisively for a few months in 1923? What if there had been one resolute man among the Right Oppositionists between 1928 and 1932? The luck persisted in the 1930s, for the world of Hitler, Mussolini, and the Japanese generals appeared to lend a certain plausibility and justification to the surreal landscape of Soviet life which Stalin and the NKVD were painting.

Part of the answer must also be provided by Stalin's undoubted mastery of the craft of oppression. He was a master of the art of brinkmanship, to borrow John Foster Dulles' term, and practiced it not against foreign countries but against his own nation. The "dekulakization" campaign of 1929–30 had been intended to destroy the spirit of, and any possibility of collective resistance by, the peasants. The purpose of the terror in 1937 was similar: in fear for their careers and lives, officials as well as the intelligentsia would lose their capacity for group solidarity, for critical thinking: one has no time to think in terms of right and wrong if one's mind is preoccupied by the question of how to avoid a nocturnal knock on the door or how, if it does come, one can somehow preserve one's wife and children. Yet if pressed beyond a certain point, terror may destroy fear. In 1930 the peasants became quite ready to kill their last head of cattle, give up their spring sowing. It was then that the divinity spoke: it has all been a mistake, Stalin argued at this critical point, the result of misdirected enthusiasm on the part of those "dizzy with success." The trick worked. So the indifference of despair yielded to hope, coupled with what might be called functional fear.

Similarly, in January 1938 the Central Committee met to "consider the question of the errors of the Party organizations in expelling Communists from the Party, the formalistically bureaucratic attitude towards those appealing their expulsions, and measures to remedy this situation."[47] The Leader, it was obvious, had heard the anguished cry of the nation, and was moving speedily and decisively to right injustices.

---

[47] *The Communist Party of the U.S.S.R. in Resolutions,* v (Moscow, 1971), 303.

Who was guilty? This time the abuses were the work of "careerists trying to gain merit by throwing people out of the Party, trying to gain security for themselves through mass repressions against the rank-and-file members," careerists who lacked that essential for a Communist, concern and solicitude for the individual. "They think it a trifle to exclude from the Party thousands and tens of thousands, reasoning that our Party is large and what harm can be done to the Party by excluding tens of thousands."[48]

The Central Committee resolution went on to give some examples of the soulless bureaucratic attitude toward individuals. Take the former secretary of the Kiev organization, Kudryavtsev, now unmasked as a careerist and enemy of the people. His conversational gambit in meeting a Party member was: "Whom have you unmasked recently?" Not surprisingly, half of the Party members in Kiev had been victimized by written denunciations. If he could speak in his defense, Kudryavtsev could have pointed out that his predecessor Postyshev had been removed for his efforts to curb denunciations. (Speaking of Postyshev, the Central Committee removed him from the Politburo, a rather belated step since he had already been arrested. It turned out that the incorrigible man had gone from one extreme to another: "liberal" in Kiev, he turned out to be a savage purger in Kuibyshev; not content with expelling honest Communists from the Party, he transmitted their names to the NKVD as enemies of the people. Of one such list of fifty people, the NKVD established that forty-three were entirely "innocent.")

The most piquant story of an unjust exclusion and arrest throws some interesting light on the functioning of the Great Stalin Constitution. At an electoral meeting for the Supreme Soviet, a non-Party worker was to give the nominating speech, in which, after recounting his happy life under Communism, he was to propose Comrade X as a candidate best embodying the qualities essential to a representative of the Soviet people and a faithful follower of Comrade Stalin. The female Party instructor duly wrote the speech and rehearsed it with the representative of the non-Party masses. But the latter, when delivering the address, became flustered and could not remember the name of the man whom the workers of his factory had unanimously nominated. The Party instructor was therefore branded an enemy of the people. Another case of abuse concerned a woman who testified *against* a Trotskyite. Her boss then proposed her exclusion from the Party on the grounds that she was

---

[48] In a year Stalin would say good-naturedly: "At the current Congress one represented about 1,600,000 members, i.e., 270,000 fewer than at the Seventeenth. But there is nothing bad about it. On the contrary it is good because the Party grows stronger as it cleanses itself of foulness." *The Eighteenth Congress of the Communist Party*, p. 28.

connected with an enemy, while her brother-in-law was fired from his job for being the relative of a Trotskyite.

The purpose of the Central Committee meeting was clearly to reassure the "little people" in the Communist ranks that while severe measures would continue to be applied against bigwigs, indiscriminate terror as far as the masses were concerned was a thing of the past. It is interesting to note here that Stalin chose to discredit and throw blame for the "excesses" on the Party hierarchy. The NKVD, in contrast, was presented as a humane institution scrupulously protecting honest Communists from persecution by the higher-ups. It was still in the Party leadership, decimated and terrorized though it had been, that Stalin saw the main danger for himself should war come.

Stalin was not the first despot to project the image of a benevolent ruler striving against evil and incompetence among his subordinates. But he was more successful in this masquerade than most, just as undoubtedly he was more directly and deliberately responsible for the sufferings of his people than any tyrant of the past.

Both terror and unlimited power were, then, byproducts of Stalin's ability to create an artificial reality, to transform the country into a vast theater where everyone had to play a role assigned to him. This was not merely outward theatricality of the kind every totalitarian system strives for—a matter of parades, feasts in honor of the Leader, other obligations after which every citizen can return to his own work, cares, and thoughts. By the late 1930s theatricality possessed every aspect of Soviet life. One was not working at one's job, one was building socialism; there was no amusement or relaxation, one was exhibiting cheerfulness and a joy of living characteristic of society where exploitation had been abolished. It took intervention by the Central Committee, i.e., Stalin, to establish that one might honestly forget a name. It is easy to see how even silent rebellion or dissent became well-nigh unendurable: how could anyone be sure of one's thoughts if everybody else evidently was a believer? Some of the most severe critics of Stalinism were to confess after 1956 that in those years they themselves had believed in him. One must not be cynical about such avowals or pity people for being taken in by official propaganda. Propaganda is a pallid and insufficient term. The war, for all its horrors, was in a way a liberation, as Pasternak observes in *Dr. Zhivago*: one experienced human reality rather than the contrived Stalinist one.

The stage manager was at the same time the leading actor. And it was at this time that Stalin exhibited most strikingly his consummate acting talent. Only those very close to him got a glimpse of the Stalin whom it had been proposed in 1917 to keep out of a Party committee "on account of certain personal characteristics," an ill-tempered, whimsical man who scribbled obscene insults on petitions of mercy, who visited his bad humor even on those whom he needed by torturing their wives, children, or brothers. For others he was a godlike figure of iron resolution—filled with benevolence on the one hand, but, for the enemy, with merciless retribution. To the masses he was the genial father of his people: embracing an Arctic explorer, kissing a little girl who handed him flowers. Visitors of these days still recall his calm demeanor: he never raised his voice. They were impressed by his knack of looking the visitor straight in the eye: thus the master of men in one glance plumbed the depth of human souls, discerned the slightest residue of Trotskyism or any other impurity. (The object of scrutiny was well advised to reciprocate this searching glance rather than to lower his gaze.) One had to be careful not only in facing Stalin but in the manner of departing his presence. It was rumored that many a fate was determined by Stalin's impression of the man as he was leaving—presumably a bowed back or hurried and unsteady step could undo all the efforts to display trust and devotion. Soviet writers who reported such details still do so not only seriously but with awe.

Perhaps even Stalin's closest collaborators failed to perceive behind the godlike calm the panic that had unleashed terror and swelled its ferocity. The probability of war fulfilled for Stalin one of the functions which conscience does for most men: it made him assess with brutal realism his fears and weaknesses. Throughout his life he had the knack of attributing in public his own fears and failings to others—thus the "dizzy with success" episode. And so after victory had finally dissipated the nightmare which had brought about the Great Purge, he chose to exorcise it by mocking it: "In the foreign press one can find statements that the Soviet system is a 'risky experiment,' that it is a 'house of cards' without roots in the life of the nation *but imposed upon it by the Cheka; one push from the outside,* and this 'house of cards' would crumble into the dust."[49] But that was said in 1946. Between 1936 and 1941 it was Stalin himself who believed that the Soviet system was held together by the Cheka, that one push from the outside and Soviet reality and his power with it would fall like a house of cards.

The Marxist believer in Stalin tempered his cynicism and his realism. Future generations would be grateful for the sacrifice he offered at the altar of his and Russia's power. But the tyrant had no illusion as to the outcome of a *premature* testing of the system he had erected on so much blood and suffering. War, unless fought on the enemy's territory and under conditions of overwhelming superiority, would bare the true reality, and the spell of terror and worship would be broken. In the spring of 1941—with his calculations deceived, his stratagems exhausted—Stalin awaited news of the German attack in a mood not dissimilar to

[49] Stalin (Stanford ed.), III, 6. My italics.

that in which his countless victims expected a nocturnal knock on the door: half-convinced it must come, half-incredulous it could happen to him. "For what?" asked one victim before he was shot. "What had we done to deserve this?" Molotov inquired of the German ambassador on June 22, 1941. ☆☆☆

THE scenario of Stalin's fears comes out vividly from the third and in a way most important (because of its victims and the themes developed) of the Moscow trials. This was the case of the Anti-Soviet Bloc of Rights and Trotskyites, heard before the military section of the Supreme Court in March 1938. The stage managers were the same as before, Vishinsky and Ulrich. But both the main defendants and the supporting cast, so to speak, represented a wider spectrum of Soviet history than in the two preceding show trials. Here, listed with a scrupulous regard for their previous importance in Soviet life and hence their current importance as traitors, were former Politburo members, ministers, diplomats, stars of the medical profession. The list opened with Bukharin and Rykov, Stalin's partners in power during 1925–27. Then, with a nice concern for *his* former partner, Vishinsky placed the name of Yagoda before those of Krestinsky and Rakovsky, who though distinguished figures in the early days of the Party were eclipsed by the mid-1920s. Then a sprinkling of ministers and regional Party secretaries. Three doctors followed, and the list closed with the evidently least important figure of all the defendants, the secretary of the "great proletarian writer" Maxim Gorky, whose death in 1936 was now declared to have been caused by a medical murder.

In the number and variety of crimes "unmasked," in the richness of horrifying detail, the Bukharin trial might appear as the finest flowering of the Yezhov school of investigation and confession. Public tributes to the "iron commissar" now drew dangerously close to the level reserved for the Leader himself. The national poet of Kazakhstan, Djambul, sang of him: "[He] who has been brought up by Lenin and Stalin, who is firm and severe as if poured from steel, braver than the badger, more sharp-eyed than the eagle—the beloved of the country, Yczhov."[50] But in fact Stalin, though he authorized the general format of the trial, must have considered it less than a success: no more major show trials took place in Russia during his reign (though it is probable that preparations were being made for one at the time of his death).

The main lesson the trial was intended to convey was the identifica-

[50] *Pravda*, March 2, 1938. The badger as a symbol of courage must be a local peculiarity of Kazakhstan.

tion with treason of any past, present, or potential opposition to Stalin. This theme was stressed even more than it had been in the 1936 and 1937 trials, and was made more explicit and detailed. There were no more coy references to contacts between the accused and "representatives of a foreign power" in Berlin or Tokyo. This time the victims were supposed to acknowledge openly their services for Germany, Japan . . . and Poland and Great Britain. The last two states must have been introduced after considerable hesitation. At the time the Kremlin believed that Poland's rulers were flirting with the idea of joining Hitler against the Soviet Union, but it was also well known that influential circles in Warsaw considered Germany rather than Russia the main threat to Poland's independence. But if the idea of Poland's having designs on Soviet territory was farfetched, then the similar charge about Britain was fantastic. The British at the time were having no end of trouble in India, but for the Russians the British lion was undaunted, its appetite as voracious as in the days of Benjamin Disraeli. It proposed to help itself to Soviet Central Asia! That this theme should have been written into the Bukharin trial demonstrates a certain touching anachronism in the thinking of the NKVD. Earlier generations of Soviet statesmen, beginning with Lenin and Trotsky, had a superstitious awe of Great Britain. It was difficult to give up the traditional motif about the British Intelligence Service, especially since, because of the Franco-Soviet alliance, no use could be made of French intelligence. But immediately after the trial Stalin evidently realized that this bow to tradition was a potentially ruinous error. Hitler had just taken over Austria, and a general European war might break out in a matter of months. Since French foreign policy was now in a state of complete dependence on Britain, any French support or aid to Russia would hinge on Britain's readiness to stand by France. Yet this was the time that Yezhov chose to bring in this nonsense about Britain designing to annex Uzbekistan!

But though Stalin was to change his estimate about which danger was most acute, the trial still reveals a fairly accurate chart of his nightmares. It is clear that he was concerned that Soviet border regions would gravitate toward the neighboring states. The whole Byelorussian Party leadership in 1937 was represented as having been in the pay of the Poles. What more natural than that traitors among the Uzbeks should look toward the British in India? The Ukraine, though not as yet a neighbor of Germany, was well known to be an object of Hitler's territorial ambitions, and so the "representative" of Ukrainian nationalism in the trial, Gregory Grinko, confessed to having been an agent of both the German and the Polish intelligence services.[51] This is a picture

---

[51] Grinko was a former Commissar of Finance of the U.S.S.R., a run-of-the-mill bureaucrat with no record of any opposition to Stalin. The only sin in his dossier

painted in garish colors, but it emanates from a sober and realistic assessment in Stalin's mind: what must happen when the foreign invader sets foot in a region so cruelly oppressed as the Ukraine? He could not foresee what still appears almost incredible: after a few months the behavior of the Germans dimmed the Ukrainians' memories of the sufferings they had endured at the hands of their own government.

The theme of nationalist uprisings against Soviet power is blended with that of enemies of the people inciting general discontent and rebelliousness through wrecking. Here the weapons employed were not just a few acts of sabotage, as unmasked in the 1937 trial. One had instead the former Minister of Agriculture, Michael Chernov, whom his superiors in treason instructed "to incense the middle peasants by extending to them the repressive measures which the government laid down for the kulaks. I was to accentuate the distortion of policy . . . to take special account of the national feelings of the Ukrainian populations, and to explain . . . that these were a result of the policy of Moscow . . . to rouse the peasants against the Soviet government."[52] Or another example: How did Grinko "wreck" on his own as Commissar of Finance? Listen to Vishinsky: "We all know how abominably the savings bank business was organized under Grinko when depositors had to waste an enormous amount of time and encountered . . . insolence, rudeness . . . and when every attempt was made to incense the public and to scare them away from the savings banks."[53] And then there was the confession of the head of the Soviet cooperative-stores system, who took care that the stores were issued winter footwear in summer and sandals in winter and who, impatient of subtler methods, ordered nails mixed with butter. Crop failures in the early 1930s and the widespread mortality in the cattle herds were now exhibited as the result of wrecking. How could it be otherwise if a high official of the Ministry of Agriculture avowed that "my criminal activities consisted first of all in wrongly planning the sowing of vegetables . . . secondly . . . retarding the development of fruit-tree nurseries." It would be tedious to repeat the details of how the crop areas were planned incorrectly so that the peasants were unable to practice "proper crop rotation and would be obliged to plough up meadows and pastures for growing corn," or how the German intelligence service even in the pre-Hitler days issued

---

may have been an altercation with Kaganovich during the latter's reign in the Ukraine. But in any case the previous Party and state leadership in the Ukraine was now being liquidated.

[52] *The Case of the Anti-Soviet Bloc of Rights and Trotskyites* (Moscow, 1938), p. 91. The man who was issuing these instructions was none other than the then head of the government, Rykov!

[53] *Ibid.*, p. 672.

instructions for "wrecking activities as to seed selection, crop rotation, machine and tractor stations and stock-breeding." Chernov's inclusion among the accused was indeed directly related to the fact that, unlike most Communist officials concerned with agriculture, he had a high degree of technical proficiency. He was thus able to answer when Vishinsky asked: "Tell us in greater detail about the cattle mortality, where you got the bacteria from, what kind of bacteria *and so on.*"[54]

It would be imprecise to say that most of the facts presented in the "agricultural" part of the trial were untrue. During the collectivization cattle did die, crop rotation and seed selection were messed up, and collective farming was "conducted in such a way that the collective farmer received next to nothing for his work." If one was a Russian peasant in 1938 and listened to the broadcast of the trials in the collective farm club, or had the newspaper transcript of it read to him by the local Party worker, this sounded quite realistic, as did another undeniable fact: all this had been due to orders from above. Thus many propaganda elements of the Moscow trials were in the context of Russia in the 1930s quite effective. The ability to capitalize on past crimes and follies was in fact a considerable contribution of Stalin's art of government.

In the case of war, the twin themes of treason and wrecking as developed in the trial were to provide the first line of psychological fortifications against popular rebellion and betrayal. But while the picture of economic wrecking and sabotage it presented was effective and convincing, the one of treason was much less so. Bukharin and Rykov were to be destroyed so that not only they but anyone invoking their name would be unable to rouse patriotic opposition to Stalin. Stalin wanted a pattern of consistent and long-standing criminality and treason to be established in the case of the two fallen greats, especially for Bukharin. He was to confess that as early as 1918 he had plotted to kill Lenin, that he had been an agent of every conceivable and inconceivable intelligence service (thus Vishinsky asked him whether he was connected not only with the police of Austria and the United States, where Bukharin lived for some time *before the Revolution,* but even with that of Japan, where he had once spent a week!), that he was *directly* connected with the assassination of Kirov and the alleged murders of Kuibyshev and Gorky, et al. Not even Trotsky has been charged with such a mass of opprobrious crimes. But Bukharin foiled all these attempts. Yes, he answered, he had had a political disagreement with Lenin at the time of Brest-Litovsk and contemplated a coup that might for a time remove Lenin from the government so that the war could continue. He stoutly defended himself against the charge of being

[54] *Ibid.*, p. 103. My italics.

in the employ of foreign states or of sharing in the alleged assassinations. He admitted his *general* responsibility for the opposition and its crimes—that was undoubtedly the minimal concession he had to make to the NKVD for the promise to spare his wife and young son.

In fact, Bukharin's behavior at the trial comes close to what in the Russia of 1938 and in his own situation must be defined as courageous. At times he baited the monstrous prosecution, acting as if he were about to open up about things Vishinsky wanted to keep quiet. Which crimes was Vishinsky interested in? "These crimes are so numerous, Citizen Prosecutor, that it is necessary to select the most important." He went far to expose the phoniness and absurdity of the evidence against his fellow defendants: he was alleged to have been a co-plotter with those people, some of whom he was seeing for the first time in court; and how could the "Bloc of Rights and Trotskyites" have been wrecking in the 1930s when officially it had been smashed by the NKVD in 1928? At times the chairman of the court would become nervous, and humiliatingly the prosecutor would have to change the subject of interrogation or announce that he would soon call a recess. Vishinsky was to pay back Bukharin—"that damnable cross of a fox and a pig"—for tarnishing his laurels as a master inquisitor. And Bukharin's final statement left no doubt in the mind of anyone with an ounce of critical spirit that if he had confessed at all, it was because of blackmail and because of the international dangers now threatening the U.S.S.R.

To Bukharin's performance we must add that of Rykov, who, though a ruin of a man—enfeebled by his treatment and by alcoholism—managed to parry some of the most infamous charges; and also the scandal that another of the defendants refused to plead guilty.[55] In all, the trial did not produce the effect Stalin might have expected. But Stalin's fears proved excessive, for the ghosts of Bukharin and Rykov did not rise to threaten him during the weeks of panic and disaster in 1941 or in the summer of 1942, politically an even more dangerous time. Terror had worked better than expected. Not even in the 1970s has the Communist Party found the fortitude to nullify the mendacious verdicts of the Moscow trials. In a left-handed way, at an obscure historians' meeting in 1962, Bukharin and Rykov were graciously acknowledged not to have been spies and traitors, but attempts to rehabilitate them fully have so far been fruitless. Even sadder, neither the Party nor the Russian people has retained a clear memory of these men who believed that Communism could be built in a more humane and rational way, and who eventually were to pay for that belief with their lives. ☆☆☆

[55] Krestinsky during his first questioning repudiated his statement during the investigation, and despite Vishinsky's shocked "Why this lack of respect for investigation?" denied all the charges. Only the next day did Krestinsky repudiate his repudiation and recite as he was supposed to.

$\mathbb{S}$CANNING the trial transcript, Stalin must have recognized, as does anyone who reads it today, that the NKVD had laid it on too thick: the story of crimes attributed to Yagoda was indeed so horrible as to be unbelievable even in the Russia of 1938, and most important of all it detracted from, indeed overshadowed, the much more important themes of treason and wrecking by the Bukharin-Rykov group. Stalin had believed that Yagoda was one of those who had tried to "fool" him, and hence he authorized his being charged with a list of crimes in comparison with which those of Cesar Borgia appear amateurish. Yagoda was now made the central figure in the plot to assassinate Kirov; with Yenukidze (shot without a trial late in 1937) he planned to seize the Kremlin; he had ordered the poisoning of his predecessor, and schemed to do the same for his successor, Yezhov; he had arranged the medical murders of Gorky and Kuibyshev; and, taking time out from public crimes to indulge his bestial lust, had done in the husband of his mistress. Such were the activities of the man who for years had been called the wielder of the "unsheathed sword of the Revolution" that for once Vishinsky's eloquence failed him in trying to characterize the monster: Yagoda must have been inspired by Joseph Fouché, Napoleon's minister of the police, master of duplicity. But then catching himself—what an anticlimactic comparison!—the worthy prosecutor owned that Yagoda could not have been inspired by Fouché, for, as expected of a monster, he read no serious literature at all. All that the careful investigation could establish about Yagoda's literary tastes was that he had read Dumas' *Three Musketeers*.

It was generally recognized that Yagoda was a scoundrel beyond the call of duty, but those few who were still capable of laughing must have done so reading the allegation that he had tried to assassinate his successor: here one had Yagoda instructing his assistant to go around the office to be occupied by Yezhov with a flit gun, spraying rugs and curtains with mercury and an "unidentified substance of foreign make." (And indeed the "iron commissar," Yezhov, incurred serious damage to his health by inhaling the odorless substance.) Even within the generally absurd context of the trial the absurdity of this story was so patent that Vishinsky felt constrained to recall various seemingly incredible murders of the past. Did his listeners recall how Pope Clement II was killed by inhaling the fumes of a poisoned candle? "The path Yagoda selected was suggested by a detailed study of the history of crime," he remarked.

If the story of the attempt on Yezhov's life was too silly, then the theme of the medical murders of Menzhinsky, Kuibyshev, and Gorky was too horrifying to suit the main purpose of the trial. The masses would hardly recall, or properly abhor, the politically important stories of economic wrecking and treason as they contemplated the absorbing business of poisons, of doctors prescribing lethal treatments, of how the tubercular Gorky was dragged out for long walks in cold weather after being previously overheated, etc. This Gothic tale was so striking that some Western analysts have been constrained to speculate that in essence it was true: that during his tenure Yagoda, on Stalin's orders, did contrive the medical assassinations of Kuibyshev and Gorky, both of whom were embarrassing and potentially dangerous to him. This thesis may appear to have certain plausibility: why should people balk at committing these crimes if they broadcast that others have? If Stalin sanctioned the assassination of Trotsky, would he have winced at a poisoning or two?

But as with Stalin's having been an agent of the Okhrana, so with the story of his share in the medical murders: it is not only psychological improbability but solid evidence to the contrary that requires that we reject the charge. It is now accepted that the three alleged victims died of natural causes. Menzhinsky had for long been a sick man. Kuibyshev had a bad heart, aggravated by alcoholism. Gorky had suffered since his youth from tuberculosis, which led to his death in 1936 at the age of sixty-eight. Isaac Babel, who frequently visited Gorky in his last years, confided to Ehrenburg that the story of his having been poisoned was insane.[56] And two of the doctors alleged to have been Yagoda's accomplices in the poisoning cases have been referred to in some recent Soviet books as honest and skillful practitioners.

The introduction of the theme of medical murders was connected with the one undoubtedly morbid trait of Stalin's that grew stronger as he grew older. From his earliest days as a revolutionary he felt himself being "picked on," a victim of slander. His henchmen well knew his masochistic interest in what was being secretly said about him.[57] Stalin believed that "they" whispered about his complicity in the deaths of Lenin, Frunze, and Kirov, and it is just possible that he believed Yagoda had been the original source of the libel about Frunze's death.[58] Some strategist of terror may well have thought that it would please the Boss to use Yagoda as the lightning rod for these sinister medical rumors.

56 Ilya Ehrenburg, in *New Life* (Moscow), No. 5 (1962), p. 153.
57 After his execution Uborevich's maid was closely questioned as to what Uborevich had been saying about Stalin.
58 Even if he did not read much, Yagoda had connections and relations in the literary world. And Boris Pilnyak, the author of the fantastically imprudent "Tale of the Unextinguished Moon," subsequently sought patronage and protection from none other than Yezhov.

It was easy to terrorize Yagoda's physician, Lev Levin, who as a member of the Kremlin medical service had attended many other bigwigs, including Gorky and Orjonikidze. As the old doctor said at the trial, "My family is a good, working Soviet family." The other supposed accomplice of Yagoda's, Dr. Pletnev, had been broken before in the famous "breast-biting" provocation. The publicity given to Pletnev's case was a good lesson to other doctors, some of whom were to give "expert" testimony at the trial, not to have any ideas that their profession entitled them to greater consideration from the NKVD than that accorded generals and Party secretaries.

Even at the trial Yagoda failed to measure up to Stalin's expectations. When called upon to recite his piece the ex-inquisitor-in-chief confessed as he had agreed to, but something in him rebelled when he heard his medical "accomplices" list his crimes. To the court's undoubted horror, he confessed only to some of the assassinations he had previously agreed to acknowledge: "I gave Levin instructions to bring about the death of Gorky and Kuibyshev, and *that is all*."[59] Vishinsky's scandalized rejoinder concerned Gorky's son and Menzhinsky: "Why did you make a false deposition?" This brought from Yagoda a reply he repeated several times: "Permit me not to answer this question." When it came Yagoda's turn to testify, there was a certain note of respect in the court president's command, and instead of the brusque "Tell the Court about your crimes," Ulrich was almost pleading: "What do you wish to tell the Court about your crimes?" Yagoda did not refrain from hinting that the evidence was rigged in a most unprofessional way: if the head of the NKVD had been a foreign spy, why did foreign powers go to the expense and bother of maintaining vast espionage networks in the U.S.S.R.? Even begging for his life Yagoda brought up the same point.

Eighteen of the condemned were shot; Rakovsky and Dr. Pletnev and another secondary figure were given long sentences and were never heard of again.

The great trials were over. Similar spectacles would be held after the war in Russia's satellite states. But the three Moscow trials remained unique in Soviet history. They are not only the most lurid incidents of the great terror, not only another stage in the development of a propaganda technique evolved as far back as 1922, at the trial of the Socialist Revolutionaries, but in fact the most ambitious and concentrated attempt to destroy and distort the historical truth that history has known. They stand as a monument to the immense vindictiveness of Stalin. Many despots of the past killed their victims and desecrated their memories; Stalin in addition killed his victims' self-respect. They used corrupt judges and henchmen; he made the whole nation his accom-

[59] *The Bukharin Trial*, p. 525. My italics.

plice—hundreds of thousands of Russians cheered the resolutions demanding that enemies of the people be shot like mad dogs. Not only the present but future generations were tricked into a kind of complicity. Thirty or forty years later people realized the absurdity and falsity of the crimes, but they still could not respect the people who had confessed to them, finding it difficult to separate a Yagoda from a Bukharin, a despicable victim from an honest one. Even the best-intentioned of Stalin's successors were baffled as how to undo this perversion of truth. It is relatively easy to rehabilitate victims who went to their deaths without public confession. Their tragedy can be blamed on human malevolence: on Stalin, Yezhov, or Beria. People can withstand the shock of tragic truth about the past and still believe there is nobility and logic to the Soviet system, which if it made them suffer, now it has opened their eyes; it can purge itself of abuses. But the trials played a monstrous joke on the whole nation, as well as on the idea of Communism. Dare one tell them that what they had been made to believe was not only false but ridiculous? Though some of the men convicted in the Moscow trials have been more or less quietly rehabilitated, there has been no formal, public nullification of the verdicts.

Yezhov's days at the head of the NKVD were now numbered. Stalin was displeased by the artistic shortcomings of the 1938 trial. Most of all he was sensitive to others developing their own "cult of personality." His "iron commissar" appeared no longer to be inspired by the laudable sentiment that work is its own reward. His lack of humility and a sense of proportion was shockingly demonstrated by this silly story of his own attempted assassination. Incorrigible in its constant misreading of the tyrant's character, the Russian émigré press now referred to the "Stalin-Yezhov regime." Yezhov's actual standing with the dictator was probably something of a puzzle even to Politburo members. Yet they could be under no illusions that the nature and extent of the terror were being determined by no one else but the Leader, even if they did not know as we now do (which is quite possible) that the arrest and liquidation of notables and their families had to be personally sanctioned by Stalin. It would also be wrong to suppose that Stalin with his passion for detail did not regularly demand and obtain estimates of the number of those who "sat" in forced labor camps and prisons. (We also have on record a letter from Molotov to Yezhov which sounds like a peremptory order, rather than a communication between equals.)

But with the war imminent, Stalin needed a subtler man as his policeman, a counselor rather than a fanatical disciple. In July 1938 Beria, hitherto the Party boss of Transcaucasia, a fellow Georgian, was brought to Moscow to be Yezhov's deputy. In August the "iron commissar" got an additional job as Minister of Water Transport. In itself this was nothing unusual. Water transport—witness the canals built with convict labor—went together with police work. But in conjunction with Beria's arrival the appointment was quite significant. On December 8 Yezhov was finally replaced by Beria. For a few weeks he lingered at his other job, then he vanished from the news. No further public reference to him, no attribution to him of any crimes. Just gone.

The only epitaph that Stalin left to his faithful servant was recorded in a private conversation. Over a luncheon with a young protégé Stalin confided, "Yezhov was a scoundrel. He killed our best people. The man went to the dogs. You call him at the Ministry, they say he is gone to the Central Committee. Call him there, they say he is at work. You send after him to his house, he is lying in bed dead drunk. How many innocent people he destroyed! For that we had him shot."[60] That his terrible duties induced Yezhov to take to drink is the most favorable testimony we are ever likely to obtain about the man with whose name is connected one of the most horrifying periods in the life of any nation.

Being head of Soviet police forces in 1938 was not the kind of job that promised a secure and tranquil tenure. Yet Beria prospered in it for fourteen years. Not only was Beria allowed to staff the top positions in the NKVD with his personal henchmen, and to branch out into other areas of the state machinery, like diplomacy and the Party organization in Transcaucasia (whose boss he remained, even though in Moscow); he also achieved personal influence over Stalin. Marshal Voronov tells a story illustrating the extent of this influence. During the war he and some other generals were checking orders for military equipment with Stalin. In view of the general shortage of arms, Stalin found excessive the order for an additional fifty thousand rifles for NKVD troops. Beria, who was summoned, argued vigorously for the original figure, contradicting Stalin several times and shifting the conversation into Georgian. Stalin finally told him to speak in Russan and cut down the order, but who else would have behaved this way before Stalin and in the presence of witnesses?[61] Beria's influence may have been connected with some personal services he rendered the aging dictator. But, most of all, Stalin must have been reassured by the almost universal distrust that surrounded Beria.

By the end of 1938 mass repression obviously had to be slackened. The prisons and forced labor camps were overcrowded to the bursting point. Turnover of personnel in every state and Party institution was fantastic. Ehrenburg, returning to Moscow after a stint as war correspondent in Spain, was surprised to discover that there were no name-

[60] Yakovlev, p. 509.
[61] After they all had left Stalin's presence, the police chief turned on the generals: "You just wait. I'll have your guts cut out." Marshal Voronov tells us, not very convincingly, that he took this to be some sort of *Oriental* joke.

plates on the doors of editorial offices at *Izvestia*. When asked about this, an officeworker shrugged his shoulders: people were often gone by the time their new nameplates were ready. And so the Beria era was to be the period of "correction of abuses." Prisoners' cases were reinvestigated, and quite a few among the lesser victims were released.

But among the elite the purge continued unabated. Its major target now became the NKVD itself. Beria did not feel comfortable with the relics of the Yezhov and Yagoda periods, and a veritable pogrom of regional heads of the security forces occurred. Among them was Stalin's brother-in-law, Stanislaw Redens. It is difficult to establish the exact extent of Beria's rascality—after all, between 1953 and 1956 he was presented as the evil spirit of the entire Stalinist era—but it seems true that his personal contribution to terror was to defame and destroy those who on one count or another were close to the dictator, such as Yenukidze, and Stalin's brothers-in-law from both marriages. This was a dangerous game, but Beria evidently liked to live dangerously. One story credits him with arranging a fake assassination attempt against Stalin and himself as they were boating on the Black Sea.[62] And after the war, piqued that the aircraft engineer Yakovlev continued to enjoy Stalin's special favors, Beria accused him of making false claims for his planes.

But the main thrust of the purge remained the same: to destroy any conceivable danger, any remotely conceivable internal foe in the case of war. The books were closed on the whole pre-1938 leadership of the Ukrainian Party and state—the Ukraine would be the main route of aggression. Since Ukrainian nationalism was the most advanced among those of non-Russian nationalities in the U.S.S.R., it was logical to brand leading Ukrainians as foreign spies. On this charge, Stanislaw Kosior, a Ukrainian of Polish descent who was a longtime staunch follower of Stalin's and a member of the Politburo, was shot. It was "natural" that he should have been accused of and confessed after beatings to having been an agent of the Warsaw government.[63] Another Ukrainian potentate of long standing, a full member of the Politburo and former U.S.S.R. Commissar of Finance, Vlas Chubar, was liquidated at the same time. Nikita Khrushchev, a Russian, was now the head of the Ukrainian Party, charged with the purging of what was

---

[62] Medvedev, p. 299. This came out in the trial of some of Beria's henchmen in 1955. American Ambassador Joseph Davies reported that rumors to this effect were circulating in Sochi when he visited there in 1938. *Mission to Moscow* (New York, 1943), p. 307. It was supposed to have happened in 1936.

[63] There were five brothers Kosior, all of them Bolsheviks. One, Wladislaw, encountered Stalin's hostility as early as 1923 and was shot in 1937 as a Trotskyite while his brother was still one of the leading men in the country and First Secretary of the Party in Kiev. Joseph had the luck of dying of natural causes and in good standing in the same year. Stanislaw's death in the purge was followed by the deaths of Casimir and Michael.

left of the entourage of Kosior, Postyshev, and Chubar. This sturdy, loyal, and uncomplicated man of the people was currently among Stalin's top favorites.

Top army and navy commanders continued to be purged up to the very day of the German attack, though as we saw some lucky officers were released and returned to their duties. The purge of men who during the war might become invulnerable to the long arm of the NKVD had an internal momentum which was difficult to stop. Consider the navy: Stalin had great ambitions for the Soviet navy; he wanted Russia, for the first time in history, to take its place among the world's great naval powers. He had little patience with the argument that the day of great surface vessels was over—he liked big things. Poor though Russia was, he said, they would save pennies and build battleships like Britain's and Japan's. Zhdanov, whom he considered the ablest of his lieutenants, was put in overall charge of naval affairs. Yet for all this solicitude, the navy's personnel was being cut down more pitilessly than the army's. (Ships ply the high seas, put in at foreign ports, and people who repeatedly meet foreigners *must* be foreign agents.) At one point in 1938 there was literally no officer left of sufficient stature to take over the Commissariat of the Navy, and an NKVD official of sinister reputation, Michael Frinovsky, was made Commissar. Almost immediately his NKVD past caught up with him, and in March 1939 he shared the fate of his professional colleagues. Nicholas Kuznetsov, who only one year before was a simple captain, was made head of the navy.

With military men beyond a certain rank the presumption of guilt was automatic. And so to survive for a leading military figure in those days required a special combination of circumstances. The Tsaritsyn veterans were saved not only through Stalin's sentimental recollections, but also because of his quite justifiably low estimate of their intelligence. Who could credit Voroshilov or Budenny with initiative or enterprise sufficient to turn the troops against him? Another marshal of the first creation, Alexander Yegorov, failed this test. In 1920 Stalin had been his Political Commissar and had refused to countersign his orders to shift the army in the direction of Warsaw. Perhaps there was a clash then and perhaps its memory offset Yegorov's otherwise punctilious obedience. He was dismissed and then arrested in 1938. The date and manner of his death are uncertain.

The extensive list of qualifications needed for survival is best seen in the case of Yegorov's successor, Marshal Shaposhnikov. A former Tsarist colonel, he (like Yegorov) had passed over to the Red side in the Civil War. By 1939 he was old, ailing, a staff officer rather than field commander, not the stuff of which Bonapartes are made, yet at the same time most capable. Reassured by such a combination of virtues, Stalin developed a great liking for the veteran. Shaposhnikov had the manner and appearance of a military patriarch from the great period of Old Russia, and his fatherly, courteous ways toward his subordinates—he would address them as "my dear"—were a striking and welcome anachronism in the era of Shchadenkos and Mekhlises. Stalin in turn behaved toward him as if he were a Tsar dealing with Kutuzov or Suvorov. To others in his entourage, the dictator now referred dryly by their title and last name, and he required that they follow his example. He himself was always Comrade Stalin. But Shaposhnikov he addressed as Boris Mikhailovich—the use of the first name and patronymic conveying both courteous formality and the affection due a distinguished servant of the state.

If one was on guard, as Stalin constantly was, against a possible Bonaparte, one could not overlook Marshal Blücher. In fact to Tukhachevsky's alleged qualifications for this role he added a particularly important one: he came of peasant stock, had been a proletarian, had started in the army as a private. Renowned for his heroic exploits in the World War and the Civil War, there was a certain mystery attending his mission in China in the mid-1920s when he taught the Chinese Nationalists to beat the warlords' armies. But nothing suggests that Blücher even remotely aspired to political influence or that he ever clashed with Stalin. Blücher's Far Eastern command had been purged earlier. His turn came in the late summer of 1938, after his troops had beaten off Japanese incursions over the Soviet frontier (and had thus destroyed Tokyo's hopes that the purges had undermined the Red Army).

"Search for compromising evidence and ye shall find" was the device of the NKVD when dealing with any of Stalin's intended victims. Blücher was recalled to Moscow in obvious disgrace in August, but he was not arrested until October. Beria in person conducted the first interrogations. And then the Marshal, like countless of less distinguished victims of the terror, was put through the "conveyor"—subjected to continuous questioning by a team of investigators. He died, evidently under torture, in November. The interrogators' absurd purpose—to make him admit that he had been a Japanese agent *ever since* 1921—appears preposterous even by the standard of the times, and no public announcement of the charges or of Blücher's fate was ever made before 1956. But Beria and his crew were still working with a purpose and for a public: Stalin had to know that those whom he destroyed were guilty.

At the beginning of 1939 Stalin's Russia had already been ravaged by death and fear. Few, himself included, could be confident that Soviet society would be able to endure a war or that his own power would not crumble. But, fantastic and unpredictable as it may be, the moment came when he would be able to say to the Russian people, "Brothers, sisters, I speak to you, my friends." And they would listen.

~⁌ 11 ⁍~

DANGEROUS GAMES

The fear of war had spawned mass terror. But terror in its turn increased Stalin's fear of war. The generals and politicians who had "schemed with foreign powers" or were ready to scheme—the difference was unimportant—had been liquidated. Millions of "unreliable" people had been safely put away in concentration camps. The nation had been taught the lesson: political dissent or even passivity equals treason. But Stalin could not afford the equanimity of that dying Spanish dictator of yore who, when asked by his confessor whether he forgave his enemies, replied that he had none; he had had them all shot. He was too suspicious to believe that all the enemies had been fished out, too intelligent not to realize that fear bred inward hostility as well as outward obedience. It was inconceivable that treason would not be reborn if the enemy occupied Soviet territory. The scenario of his fears was vividly illustrated in Bukharin's trial: the Germans, with the probable assistance of Poland, enter the Ukraine and Byelorussia, where they appeal to nationalist feelings in this border region; they gain acquiescence if not indeed support by abolishing the collective farm system. National troubles erupt in other parts of the Soviet state—say in Central Asia. Then there might well be some Party leaders and generals who would blame Stalin for the disaster and would try to save Russia by overthrowing him and his system.

Fear was not Stalin's only consideration about the approaching war. Young Soviet citizens had been brought up in a spirit of fanatical loyalty (it was not only sadism that dictated that children of his victims, on reaching young adulthood, were themselves sent to the camps: no tellers of tales thus), and patriotic Russian history must also have buoyed up his spirit. How often had the Russians fought bravely against their enemies, even for the rulers who had used them harshly. The Red Army and air force, purged of traitors, were powerful weapons. It was not so much that he feared the war itself, as that he feared what might happen if the war punctured that Soviet reality which he had erected. If the enemy entered Soviet territory, then like air from a pierced balloon the people's trust in his own infallibility might evaporate, their trust in those slogans on which the whole system in many ways rested: "the unbreakable friendship of the nations of the U.S.S.R."; "the invincible Red Army"; "the indestructible socialist system." The only war Stalin could afford was a war on enemy territory.

"If tomorrow a war, if tomorrow we shall have to march, then already today we are ready to advance," were the words of an enormously popular Soviet song of the late 1930s. How official propaganda prepared the Russian people for the possiblity of war may be judged from a book that appeared in the summer of 1939 and was hastily withdrawn from circulation after the Nazi-Soviet pact. Written by one N. Shpanov and entitled *The First Blow: The Story of the Coming War*, it was published by the Ministry of Defense and recommended especially for the armed forces. If there is such a thing as an idyllic description of war, then Shpanov's book was certainly that. The reader was invited to participate in an air show on Soviet Air Forces Day, August 18 of an unspecified year. Barely do the viewers witness a Soviet pilot breaking a world altitude record when a loudspeaker announces that as of 5 P.M. German planes treacherously breached the Soviet air frontier. There follows a *Blitzkrieg*, but of quite a different kind than Hitler had in mind. Within *one* minute, enemy planes are met by Soviet fighters. Twenty-nine more minutes, and the last undestroyed fascist plane turns tail and flees the airspace of the socialist Fatherland. And now the fun begins: within two hours, seven hundred and twenty Soviet bombers set forth for Germany. Having destroyed most of the German defending planes on the way, they reach the Nüremberg–Fürth industrial complex at 12:01 A.M. Here German workers begin to feel the stirrings of proletarian solidarity. "In the Dornier aircraft plant all lights are extinguished. The German workers await with impatience the descent of bombs on the factory *in which they are sitting, singing the 'Internationale.'* " Their expectations are not 'disappointed. "Our planes methodically and with striking accuracy drop bombs on the planned objects." And at 3 in the morning of August 19, with German industry, air force, etc., utterly destroyed, the Red Army begins its victorious march across the frontier.[1] Some Russian pilots taking to the air in the early-morning hours of June 22, 1941, may have recalled this book.

For Soviet military and industrial leaders, this attitude toward the approaching war was far from a laughing matter. Russia's strongest asset would be, as it had been in the past, her vast spaces in addition to her

[1] Quoted in Alexander Yakovlev, *The Life's Aim* (Moscow, 1970), pp. 265–67. My italics.

vast manpower. But as of the middle 1930s any planning for a defensive war, for utilizing space and retreat as weapons, was first frowned upon and then declared equivalent to treason. Military men, in their way often simple-minded, could not understand why the Boss would not hear of any strategy that authorized temporary withdrawal from as much as a foot of Soviet territory. It seemed folly to preclude the possibility or utility of retreat in case of an attack by a technologically superior enemy. But about the same time it became extremely unfashionable, and then worse, to allege or warn that the German army might be technologically more advanced and superior in modern weapons than the Red Army. In the early 1930s the Soviet general staff had prepared for the possibility of retreat. Fortified points were built at some distance from the country's Western border as well as concealed communication and supply depots to service partisans who would harass the advancing enemy. Predictably, in 1937 all such plans were unmasked as a scheme of traitors (notably the executed commanders of the western regions, Yakir and Uborevich) to strike the Red Army in the back. The prospective leaders of the guerrilla detachments were arrested and executed. The same fate befell Soviet intelligence officials who reported German technological advances accurately.

The anathema laid on the concept of defensive war was reflected in the orientation of the Soviet air force and aircraft industry. Stalin wanted heavy bombers that would be able to "strike at the beast in his lair," a favorite expression. Aircraft designers were under constant pressure, often presented with (then) unrealistic demands to construct ever heavier bombers with ever greater radii of operations. The development, not to say production, of fighters was, by contrast, neglected. And so in the first months of the war German planes dominated the Russian skies.

Stalin could ban as defeatism any discussion of war fought on Soviet territory, shoot as traitors those who as much as mentioned the possibility. But how could one ward it off? This was a task for statemanship and diplomacy. Stalin may have recalled his maneuvers in the 1920s—how he had used Zinoviev and Kamenev to cut Trotsky down to size, how he had embroiled the "left" and "right" factions in fights with each other while building his own power. Could he repeat the same maneuver with the capitalists? His policies and Litvinov's diplomacy had already enmeshed Russia's interests with those of the Western powers, or so at least the French and British statesmen now believed. Hitler's hopes of invading Russia had been frustrated. His attempt to inveigle others into the schemes of conquering *Lebensraum* in the East—the Ukraine to be settled by the Germans—was also meeting with setbacks. The Japanese had gotten bogged down in China. Poland's leaders, while hostile toward Moscow, realized that the passage of the German army through her territory would render them Hitler's vassals. And so the Führer had to seek conquests closer to home. Threats and rhetoric were now accompanied by action. In March 1938, even though the Soviet reader may hardly have been aware of this—the bulk of the news was occupied by the Bukharin-Yagoda trial and its reverberations—the German armies began the march that would end only four years later on the Volga. Austria had fallen.

Czechoslovakia followed. The little country had a treaty of alliance with France and, conditional on France's honoring her obligations, also with Russia. If Czechoslovakia fell undefended, Russia's turn might be next. Unlike many European statesmen, Stalin did not see Hitler as a bluffer, bent on getting whatever he could through blackmail and threats but too reasonable to resort to war. But like everyone else in Europe, including the German generals, he had considerable respect for the French army. If France, Britain, and the Soviet Union jointly confronted Hitler, he might recoil from the prospect of repeating Germany's fatal experience of war against such a coalition. He might nurse his resentment, rearm further, and then strike again. Russia still did not have a common frontier with Germany.

On March 17 the Soviet government announced its readiness to consult with other interested states for the purpose "of checking the further development of aggression and of eliminating the increased danger of a world massacre." Litvinov specified Czechoslovakia as the area threatened.

But the British politely declined the Soviet initiative. Chamberlain's government was bent upon exploring the possibilities of appeasement— a word which had not yet acquired an unpleasant connotation. And so the Führer, who when he was swallowing Austria reassured the Czechoslovak ambassador that his country had nothing to fear, now began his campaign to rescue his fellow (Sudeten) Germans groaning under Czech oppression. The term war of liberation had not been invented, but Hitler's skill in exploiting the theme of Germans in foreign lands who longed to be united with their brethren had the same effect on the average citizen in the democracies that the anti-imperialist motif was to have in the years after World War II.

Up to our own day the Soviet position and the lessons Stalin drew from the Czechoslovak crisis of 1938 are presented by official Russian sources as follows: the U.S.S.R. was ready to stand loyally by her obligations to Czechoslovakia and her commitment to collective security. Britain and France, however, by yielding to Hitler and sacrificing Czechoslovakia, showed that they were not interested in collective security. More than that, Munich demonstrated that the Western powers not only appeased Hitler, but excluded the U.S.S.R. from the conference and thus implied to the Führer (in the more extreme Soviet versions they more than implied) that he had a free hand in the East.

To some extent this version still finds adherents in the West, where it competes, however, with an opposite interpretation, which argues that the Soviets acted a charade, pretending their readiness to help Czechoslovakia and the West if it stood by Prague, when in fact Stalin was all along preparing to sell out to Hitler.

Both versions are absurd. The first one credits Stalin with the kind of virtues and idealism in foreign affairs which, when it comes to domestic affairs, his countrymen are no longer willing to accord him. And the second interpretation, while realistic about his lack of scruples, vastly exaggerates his ability to foresee and control the future.

As stated before, the Soviets had sound reasons to try to save Czechoslovakia. Though he had probed the idea before, the thought that he might be able to strike a bargain with Hitler did not occur to Stalin as a real possibility until March 1939. If we keep these two facts in mind, the actual game of Soviet diplomacy in the Czech crisis can be seen much more clearly.

Russia's promise to stand by her obligations if a European war broke out over Czechoslovakia did not provide much reassurance to the British and French, nor any particular worry to Hitler. How could one count on, or seriously fear, an army whose highest officers had just been shot, or a government whose highest officials vanished into thin air? On May 30, with the crisis entering its most crucial phase, the German Deputy Minister for Foreign Affairs, Ernst von Weizsäcker, a level-headed man and not an admirer of Hitler's, confided to a fellow German diplomat: "Russia hardly exists in our calculations today. As long as Stalin makes himself as ueful as now, we need not particularly worry about him as regards military policy."[2]

Was Stalin ready to throw his daily and mercilessly purged army into a war? To answer this question, we must consider the geographic realities of the moment.

In order to get at the Germans, Soviet armies could intervene in one of three ways. They could cross Latvia and Lithuania to attack German East Prussia. They could cross Rumania to join the Czech army. Or they could march the width of Poland to strike at the heart of Germany. The first possibility was so absurd from the military point of view that it was not even mentioned during the feverish summer months of 1938. The second one was hardly less so. Soviet troops would be required to move across wretched Rumanian roads and railways to the mountainous region of eastern Slovakia, far from the decisive theater of war in

[2] *Documents on German Foreign Policy, 1918–45*, Series D, 1 (Washington, 1949), 864.

Bohemia and Moravia. In the circumstances a division might be sent, but no military man in his senses would dream of sending an army. The only way that Soviet troops could be deployed en masse, and create a second front, was through Poland. The Polish government would not acquiesce in Soviet passage, even if it had been ready to help Czechoslovakia—which was far from being the case. In fact, confident that France and Britain were ready to throw the Czechs to the wolves, Warsaw was ready to join the pack and to help itself to a slice of the unfortunate country.

The eruption of a European war in 1938 thus left Russia a considerable latitude of military action. The U.S.S.R. might plead technical inability to come to Czechoslovakia's help. She might attack Poland if that country joined Germany (which was unlikely). She might try to force the passage of her troops even through a neutral Poland. But in any case Poland's refusal to allow Soviet troops on her territory even if she herself fought on France's side[3] gave Russia a quite legitimate excuse to weigh her options carefully during and according to the course of the opening phases of any hypothetical conflict. In any case, there was no imminent threat to Soviet territory. If the French army carried the war into German territory—a contingency which to us in retrospect seems fantastic but which in 1938 was seriously entertained—then the Red Army would march in for the kill and perhaps it might eventually encounter German workers singing the "Internationale"!

It is unlikely that even Foreign Commissar Litvinov knew what Russia might do—i.e., precisely what was in Stalin's mind. His conversations with the French ambassador show that he was told what to do, say, and ask but hardly more than that. At one point he stated that Russia could not force her passage through an unwilling Poland: "We would appear as aggressors and that is something we cannot do." At another time, he inquired what France would do in the case of Poland, having invaded Czechoslovakia, being in turn attacked by the U.S.S.R.[4] Litvinov's expertise concerning the West, the favorable reputation he enjoyed among Western statesmen and in public opinion there helped to save him from the fate of his two former assistants, Sokolnikov and Krestinsky, but he was not privy to Stalin's inmost thoughts.

They, in turn, as events were to show, combined the traditional Soviet half-suspicious, half-contemptuous assessment of the Western statesmen's political capacity with peculiar quirks of his own. The British seemed so naïve and unrealistic, yet would the British Empire have spread over a fourth of the globe if this apparent naïveté were not offset by craftiness and capitalist villainy? As for Hitler, ever since the Night

---

[3] Poland, after all, had a treaty of mutual defense with France.
[4] Robert Coulondre, *From Stalin to Hitler: Memoirs of Two Embassies,* 1936–1939 (Paris, 1950), p. 156.

of the Long Knives in 1934, he had his fellow dictator's professional respect. Above all, the Wehrmacht and German technological and organizational ability added up to fearsome force.

In early September Stalin, like everyone else, must have realized that Britain and France would back down on Czechoslovakia. Chamberlain's first two pilgrimages to Hitler must have led not only to that conclusion but to the rebirth of an old fear: might not the British try to steer Hitler eastward, after and beyond Czechoslovakia? With the Czech government now under pressure from London and Paris to cave in to Hitler's demands, the Soviets sought to fortify the Czechs' weakening resolution. Litvinov wired the Soviet minister in Prague to tell President Beneš that "the U.S.S.R. will in accordance with the treaty render immediate and effective aid to Czechoslovakia *if France remains loyal to it* and also renders aid."[5] This wasn't quite explicit: Moscow did not say, "We shall declare war if . . ." But it indicates that Stalin was ready to risk a war if France entered it. Litvinov's statement on September 21 also expressed Moscow's *conditional* commitment. "We intend to fulfill our obligations under the pact, and together with France to afford assistance to Czechoslovakia *by the ways open to us.*"[6] The meaning of these statements is fairly clear: fearful that Britain might be launching some anti-Soviet intrigue, the Soviets preferred that the Czechs and the French should fight, in which case they would render assistance "by the means open to us."

We now know—and the Soviets realized it within the next few days, though they would never admit it—that while Chamberlain was capable of appeasement, he was morally and intellectually incapable of Machiavellian machinations. The elderly statesman was beguiled by Hitler's sincerity. Stalin would have relished if not approved of the way the Führer opened his heart to his visitor and was able to dissipate his fears: these were tactics much like his own. Understandingly, rather than indignantly, Hitler acknowledged to Chamberlain that "people in Britain had often reproached him because they thought that the appetite grew with eating," and that probably after the attainment of one objective he would again and again make fresh demands. "But all that because of a complete misunderstanding of the National Socialist doctrine." It was in certain respects the antithesis of imperialism . . . "the racial basis of the National Socialist Party and with it of the German people . . . [it] excluded any form of imperialism." Once he acknowledged the sanctity of another country's frontiers, that was that. Look at

[5] From *Documents and Materials Relating to the Eve of the Second World War*, I (Moscow, 1949), 204. My italics.
[6] From Jane Degras, ed., *Soviet Documents on Foreign Policy*, III: 1933–41 (New York, 1953), 303. My italics.

the case of Poland![7] If he read this account after the war, Stalin may have recalled his own interview with Roy Howard, when the American journalist asked him whether the Soviets proposed to impose Communism on other countries: a *ridiculous* misunderstanding of the Communist doctrine! Why, as Lenin said . . .

From Munich the Soviet leaders drew, as the world did, the lesson of British and French faintheartedness. But there was another lesson learned in Moscow but overlooked in Berlin. Between September 22, when Hitler brutally rejected Chamberlain's offer to agree in principle to cession of the Sudetenland and demanded *immediate* German military occupation of the districts in question, until September 28, Europe was on the brink of war. Having conceded the substance of the German demands, the British and the French countenanced war over the means and timing of putting them into effect. This could hardly be a part of some sinister anti-Soviet plot by everyone concerned. And it was a reassuring sign that while the political intelligence of the Western leaders was limited, so were their patience and their willingness to endure humiliation.

The September conference of Hitler, Chamberlain, and Daladier, with Mussolini playing the role of the dishonest broker, evoked the kind of official Soviet reaction one might have expected. But nothing suggests that it led to a profound trauma in Moscow, that the Russians lost their illusions about the Western powers' devotion to collective security, etc. Stalin had precious few illusions about human nature in politics, domestic or foreign.

Whatever his calculations and subsequent reflections, Stalin that summer must have felt war to be quite close. The Japanese probing actions on the Soviet frontier continued between the beginning of July and August 11. Apart from testing whether the Red Army was still capable of organized resistance, this was a clear warning that if the U.S.S.R. became involved in a European war its Asiatic extremities were far from safe. The threat may have speeded up the fate of a number of army and state officials, arrested before at different times, who were shot within the last days of July. From now until the summer of 1942 an international and later military emergency would spell the doom of those repressed notables of whom Stalin stood in fear, should they remain alive on the morrow of Russia's major defeat. He would demand lists of people in such categories, and with a flick of the pen appease, but not for long, his fear of the future. And then he would turn his attention from the world where he was the absolute master, the world of Yezhov and Beria, to the world of Hitler and Chamberlain, where he must negotiate, plead, and dissimulate.

[7] *Documents on German Foreign Policy, 1918–1945*, Series D, II (Washington, 1953), 789.

For all the mitigating circumstances of the Munich settlement, the Soviet diplomatic position following it was unenviable. Had Hitler been capable of even feigned and temporary moderation, Russia would have become isolated as she had been before 1934. After a suitable interlude, Hitler in conjunction with the Japanese might have reverted to his professed aim of freeing Europe from "Bolshevism." But the Führer was as capable of moderation as Stalin was of trusting his colleagues. The relative ease of his triumph left him with a certain anticlimactic feeling. He longed for the role of the warlord; in fact a psychologist studying his moves after Munich might well conclude that he craved war more than conquest. It was thus impossible for him to remain quiet for long or, even when not issuing threats and demands, not to rub salt in the wounds of his Munich partners—"worms," as he called them in private conversation—by declaring that peace was jeopardized so long as there was the possiblity of warmongering politicians like Churchill coming to power. And so the "Peace in our time" mood that reigned for a few short weeks in London and Paris gave way to "Where is he going to strike next?"

In contrast to Western nervousness, Soviet diplomacy exuded confidence, almost indifference, about the threat of war. "Anyone who wants to be convinced of the strength and power of our forces is welcome to try," said Molotov in a speech on November 6, 1938. Litvinov and his collaborators were casually sympathetic in their conversations with Western diplomats: yes, the Western powers were in for a hard time from Hitler. The Soviet Union was not particularly concerned. Were the Russians nervous over the German designs on the Ukraine? Of course not: Hitler would attack only those countries unwilling or unable to defend themselves, so why should they worry? There were playful suggestions that the Germans might be seeking an accommodation with Moscow. Speaking with the French ambassador about Munich, Assistant Commissar for Foreign Affairs Potemkin dropped the proverbial studied indiscretion: "My poor friend, what have you done? As for us, I don't see any other conclusion than a fourth partition of Poland."[8] Soviet taunts, hints, and insouciance had the expected effect on the Western official circles and undid much of the negative impression of the purges: strong and confident Russia was once more included in the calculations in London and Paris. Stalin's moves between Munich and the Nazi-Soviet Pact provide a classical example of how skillful (and to be sure unscrupulous) diplomacy can change the course of world history. Some of the premises on which this policy was based were to prove fallacious. But as a technique of juggling opposing sides, in its alertness for openings and opportunities, it must be judged masterful.

[8] Coulondre, p. 165.

In contrast, Hitler's diplomacy was increasingly clumsy. The successful blackmailer's skill consists in two main ingredients: concentrating on one issue at a time, and making it appear convincing that this is absolutely his last demand. This technique served the Führer well through Munich, but afterward he was no longer capable of it. He wanted to swallow what was left of Czechoslovakia, but in addition, apparently forgetful of what he had said on the subject to Chamberlain, he began to look greedily on Poland. To be sure, to Hitler there was no inconsistency between the lofty renunciation of German territorial claims on Poland and his current demands. On the contrary, he proposed generously to settle all outstanding differences and problems so that from then on nothing could mar the course of Polish-German friendship. As a beginning he proposed to incorporate the Free City of Danzig into Germany and to have an extraterritorial road linking East Prussia with the rest of Germany, running through the Polish Corridor. And not a word about the Corridor and Polish Silesia, areas that had been German for centuries until Versailles wrested them from her! But the Polish foreign minister, Beck, to whom those demands were communicated, refused incredibly to see them in their "true light"—i.e., as a German *concession*. For him it represented a disastrous bankruptcy of his policy based on the fatuous assumption that Hitler's word could be trusted. Fearful of the reactions at home and elsewhere, the Warsaw government kept the mounting German pressure secret and the Polish crisis did not become known to the world until April 1939.

It is unlikely, however, that the Russians were kept in the dark. In November 1938 the Polish ambassador in Moscow approached the Kremlin with a query whether something could be done to improve Polish-Soviet relations. This was quite a change from Warsaw's rather haughty attitude of a few weeks before when the U.S.S.R. warned Poland not to press her territorial claims on Czechoslovakia. On November 26 both governments issued a joint declaration reaffirming the Polish-Soviet Non-Aggression Pact of 1932 valid until 1945, and pledging friendly relations. Russia had a good, indeed desperate reason for wanting the Poles to stand up to Hitler. If Poland made the first fatal concessions, she was bound to become a German satellite, and Stalin's nightmare—a foreign aggressor in immediate proximity to the Soviet Ukraine and Byelorussia—would be a terrible reality.

What was happening to the rump of Czechoslovakia was a good object lesson to the Kremlin and to Warsaw. What remained of the unfortunate country after the Munich surgery was in an obvious state of dissolution; all its parts were in varying degrees satellites of Hitler's. The Prague government was constrained to grant substantial autonomy to Slovakia, and some Slovaks, egged on by Berlin, were pressing for "independence"—i.e., direct rather than indirect status as

Germany's satellite. There was also within this living corpse an autonomous Carpatho-Ukraine also clamoring to be independent. In November a slice of Slovakia was presented as Hitler's gift to Hungary.

The Poles and to some extent the Soviets had to be especially worried by the Carpatho-Ukraine. This minuscule creation of some 700,000 inhabitants became with discreet German encouragement the center of nationalist Ukrainian propaganda directed at the brethren in eastern Poland and in the Soviet Ukraine. Warsaw would have liked this troublesome phantom state to be absorbed by Hungary. But Poland's pleas for a joint Polish-Hungarian frontier were answered playfully in Berlin with questions as to why such a frontier was needed. The Hungarians who had held the area before 1918 were warned against such unseemly greed and reminded that the Führer was a staunch believer in national self-determination. The Soviets, not very convincingly, tried to minimize the importance of what they could not at the moment prevent. How ridiculous, Stalin was to say, to think that a "gnat"—i.e., a few hundred thousand Carpatho-Ukrainians—could absorb the "elephant," i.e., 30 million Soviet Ukrainians who in any case were joyful and proud to be citizens of the U.S.S.R.! Yet how many of his listeners could really believe he was that unconcerned? The entire leadership of the Ukrainian Party, practically every person of consequence before 1939 in the province's capitals of Kiev and Kharkov, had been liquidated on charges of being Polish and/or German spies and plotting to detach their beautiful land from the U.S.S.R.

Stalin's avowal was made at the Party Congress that met on March 10. Five years had elapsed since the Seventeenth Congress, at which he had been made a divinity and then, as behooves one, had visited incomprehensible sufferings on his worshipers. According to Party statutes such an interval was illegal, and all the rights and competence of the Party officers should have lapsed. But does one demand an accounting from a god and restrict him by statutes? Stalin summoned the survivors among his priesthood to announce that he had taken pity on his people. "There is no doubt that we will not use again the method of the mass purge."[9] In purging the country of "unclean people," his priests had not always understood his merciful intentions. "One cannot say that the purge was conducted without serious mistakes. Unfortunately, more mistakes were committed than one could have foreseen." The delegates were undoubtedly impressed. Few of them could have known that on the lists submitted by Yezhov to Stalin there was often a postscript: "and the following people are being investigated," and that Stalin sometimes returned these secondary lists with a note: "Never mind investigating. Arrest."

[9] *The Eighteenth Congress of the Communist Party* (Moscow, 1939), p. 28.

Yezhov's name was not mentioned, tempting as it must have been to Stalin to link the past abuses to his executioner who at the time of the Congress was still alive, being "investigated"—i.e., getting a taste of his own medicine. But, psychologically it was sounder to make Yezhov just disappear. Stalin now ruled through mystification almost as much as through terror. Had Yezhov been punished for crimes so horrible that they could not be mentioned? Was he kept in reserve to be brought back if the people failed to appreciate the Leader's new and merciful mood? A divinity is not expected to behave in a neat, logically predictable way. There was also an excellent practical reason. It would not do, Beria must have argued, to present *two* successive heads of the NKVD as people's enemies. Soviet citizens might draw unfortunate conclusions concerning *his* prospects. They might even laugh, the greatest danger to a totalitarian system. In addition, Stalin had now decided that undue publicity given the purge of notables could be a mistake. Hitler, as well as London and Paris, took it as a sign of weakness and as a reason to downgrade Russia as an enemy or ally. So Kosior, Blücher, et al., had to be disposed of quietly. The foreign danger required sacrifices, and it was only within Politburo circles and to a few protégés like Yakovlev that Stalin could indulge his love of slandering those he destroyed.

In fact, Stalin felt constrained to deny, in a rather disingenuous way, that the bloodbath over which he had presided could be taken as either a sign or cause of Russia's weakness. What are all these lies in the foreign press, he exclaimed, about the "weakness of the Soviet army," the "decomposition of the Soviet air force," "unrest in the Soviet Union"? Their purpose must be to suggest to the Germans, "You just start a war with the Bolsheviks and everything will go easy."[10] Yet he had irrefutable proof that each purge made the Soviet Union stronger. Think of this: after Tukhachevsky, Yakir, and the rest had been shot in 1937, elections to the Supreme Soviet had taken place and 98.6 per cent of those voting approved of the policies of the regime. In 1938, Rykov, Bukharin, et al., were shot, and then there were elections to the federal republics' legislatures. The latest shootings must have reassured some diehard opponents of Soviet power, for this time "the Bolshevik and non-Party" list received 99.4 per cent of votes. The English parliamentarian who coined the immortal remark, "Give me but leave to use statistics and I shall manage to prove anything," would have been pleased.

Stalin's speech, the last report he delivered to a Party Congress as General Secretary, was dominated by foreign affairs. And here he was as shrewd and subtle as he was disingenuous and brutal when talking of domestic affairs. After August 23 everybody would say that already in

---

[10] Stalin's salient points, the transcript notes, were often interrupted by "applause" or "laughter." Nobody laughed at this one.

March he was making an oblique advance to Hitler, and they would recall that he had said that the U.S.S.R. would not enter a war "to pull somebody else's chestnuts out of the fire." Yet in fact his March speech was in line with every aspect of Soviet policy after Munich: through taunts, expressions of self-confidence, and hints of an as yet nonexistent (in fact despaired of), rapprochement with Germany, it was meant to draw out the Western powers. "We don't need you, but you may need us; if so, better hurry up" was the gist of his message for Paris and London.

He *was* hinting to Hitler, as in his statement that "the Anglo-French and American press" was raising a fuss over the Ukraine with the intention of "incensing the Soviet Union against Germany, to poison the atmosphere, and to provoke a conflict when no sensible reasons for such a conflict exist.[11] But he was clever enough to realize that there would be no reason for Hitler to swallow the bait and approach the Russians until and unless the latter were on the point of signing a binding military agreement with France and Britain. And so the subtle hints to Hitler were matched by broad ones for the benefit of London and Paris. They should not be afraid of standing up to Germany. Lapsing into language unusual for a Communist, Stalin proclaimed that "peaceful, democratic states taken together are without doubt stronger than the fascist countries, both economically and militarily." He allowed that there might be some "madmen" in Germany who dreamed of wresting the Ukraine from the U.S.S.R., and in defining the general outlines of Soviet policy, he stressed that "we support the nations which have fallen prey to aggression, and which fight for the independence of their country." Litvinov, very unusually for a Foreign Commissar, did not speak at the Congress. Stalin knew this would titillate the foreign chanceries. Someone in Berlin might perk up his ears: "Is the Jew out of favor?" And the Western experts would conclude that the leading Soviet advocate of collective security was losing out in the struggle with those in the Kremlin who were disgusted over Munich—all the more reason to propitiate Moscow before it was too late.

Stalin played it cleverly. In the great game being played over the destiny of the world, it is unlikely that anyone else would have been accorded high marks by a Talleyrand or Bismarck. Still, he probably would not have succeeded in his desperate goal of steering the war away from the Soviet Union except for the unwitting assistance of Hitler and Chamberlain. ☆☆☆

[11] *Ibid.*, p. 13.

Hitler moved while the Eighteenth Party Congress was still in session. On March 15 Germany swallowed what had remained of Czechoslovakia. Bohemia and Moravia became a Reich protectorate. Slovakia became "independent" and was immediately occupied by German troops. After some hesitation Berlin allowed the Hungarians to seize the Carpatho-Ukraine. Subsequently the Germans were to claim that this was done to remove the focal point of Ukrainian irredentism and thus an obstacle to an understanding with Moscow. But at the time the main reason was Hitler's conviction that after such a generous *concession* on *his* part, the Poles would be less likely to quibble over Danzig.

Hitler's move was a prodigious mistake. In the first place, it was unnecessary. There was very little that the post-Munich Czech government would not do in order to placate its terrible neighbor. In the second place, Hitler's argument, hitherto found so unanswerable (especially in Britain), that he merely sought to reunite the Germans and did not want Slavs to spoil the racial purity of his Reich, now stood completely exposed. It is possible that he could have managed another Munich over Danzig (though the Poles would probably have fought, even if alone) if he had not previously succumbed to the temptation of bullying yet another foreign statesman into surrender, staging yet another triumphant entry into a foreign capital.

On March 17 Neville Chamberlain exploded with the anger of a patient and credulous man who has been deceived and made ridiculous. His indignant speech on that day marked the death of appeasement and the beginning of a determined British effort to bar further aggression by Hitler.

The Kremlin had to be alarmed by this latest turn of events. The "gnat" Carpatho-Ukraine was disposed of, but the German army was moving eastward closer to the border of the Soviet Union. It was becoming difficult to preserve the mask of cheerful unconcern. A Ukrainian official was permitted to say on March 19, "Let those base hypocrites, the German fascists, this scum of mankind, realize that Soviet Ukraine is strong and powerful. . . . Every attempt by the enemy to cross the frontier of the U.S.S.R. will be met by his devastating and lightning destruction *on his own territory*.[12] This is a good commentary on the theory that Stalin already *knew* he would be able to make a bargain with Hitler.

[12] *Ibid.*, p. 597. My italics.

The sound of marching German boots seemed to provide the distant background music to the last half of the deliberations of the Eighteenth Party Congress. It was reflected in assurances, this time extended by Zhdanov, that no further mass purges would be undertaken and that past errors were being rectified. The Leningrad boss, who was now finally elevated to full Politburo membership and who had obviously nudged out Kaganovich as Stalin's chief lieutenant in Party affairs, gave incredible examples (although not so incredible to those present) of the atmosphere of terror and denunciation which had permeated the Party, speaking in the vein of "Wasn't it all too ridiculous? It will certainly never happen again." Here, he said, was one vile character who having written a hundred and sixty-four denunciations, none of which was confirmed,[13] applied for a subsidized stay in a resort because "I am at the end of my powers on account of fighting enemies of the people." Some Party members sought to escape the terror by means of a medical certificate, Zhdanov said, and quoted one of them: "Comrade X because of the state of his health and understanding could not conceivably become a tool of the class enemy." The Congress laughed—but one wonders how lightheartedly.

There were other attempts to reassure the delegates—who, when they dispersed to their farms, factories, and military units, would carry words of comfort to their constituents. Voroshilov gave figures designed to show that "our army is unbeatable." There was further comfort in data which "demonstrated" that the French air force was not much inferior to Germany's, and the French army formidable and well equipped. Soviet military intelligence, much of its personnel recently purged, was obviously in a deplorable state. It is difficult to account otherwise for the fact that Poland was credited with having a thousand combat planes.[14] The military data on which Stalin based his diplomatic stratagems were to be exposed in September 1939, and then much more ominously in May 1940.

But the main antidote to the fear of a terrible German war machine, a fear which no phrases or statistics could quite dispel, had to lie in the faith in one man. In the emergency, and against all logic, even Stalin's past frightfulness had something reassuring about it. He had brought the country through the horrors of collectivization and the purges. So now, though nobody could quite understand how, he would find a way to keep Russia out of war, or if it came, he would see to it that it was brief and victorious. It had to be this way. All the unspeakable sufferings of the last year had been endured so that Russia might be invincible— he had told them so. As Stalin listened to the paeans of praise, now at once so extravagant and repetitive, it must have occurred to him that

[13] They may not have been confirmed, but it is a sure bet that many were acted on.
[14] When the war began, Poland had barely two hundred obsolete planes.

there was a burdensome side to being a divinity: people expect you to produce miracles.

And it would have to be a near miracle to avoid war for the U.S.S.R. Hitler was bent on war, and one could not avoid it but only deflect it from Russia's frontiers. But how? The Western powers would have to be ready to rush to the help of the next victim of German aggression. Hitler would have to forget his hatred of "Jewish Bolshevism" and his predilection for joint world mastery with "Teutonic Britain," and would have to make a bargain with the former, war on the latter. As of March 21, when the Congress finished its recitations, both contingencies seemed unlikely.

On March 23 Hitler helped himself, with Lithuania's helpless acquiescence, to that country's Memel region. Ever closer to Russia's frontiers! On March 28 Litvinov warned the governments of Latvia and Estonia that any similar concessions to Germany on their part would not be tolerated by the U.S.S.R. It would not allow any "abatement or restriction of [their] independence and self-determination," no matter what agreements were signed, whether voluntarily or not. In plain words, the Soviet Union declared its readiness to go to war if Germany sent troops or established bases in those states.

Litvinov asked the two governments not to broadcast Moscow's warning. And no wonder. The satellitization of the two Baltic states would present Russia with only a fraction of the political and military danger if a similar situation arose with respect to Poland. Someone in the West might ask why they should worry about Hitler's threat to Poland—it was primarily the Russians who could not afford to have Poland go under, to have German troops and autonomous Ukrainian and Byelorussian states on Soviet frontiers.

If Chamberlain had been endowed with an ounce of that Machiavellianism he was subsequently to be credited with by Soviet sources, he would have said to the Kremlin, "We will guarantee Poland's independence provided you do it first or simultaneously." But the Prime Minister—justly condemned for ineptitude, most unfairly condemned for having some alleged scheme to push Hitler eastward—was now under great public pressure to do something to stop Hitler. He was now informed that Poland was next on Hitler's menu. So he issued a declaration on behalf of the British and French governments pledging to lend support to that country if it were attacked. Before this historic declaration was delivered in the House of Commons on March 31, the Foreign Secretary met with Ivan Maisky, the Soviet ambassador, to acquaint him with its gist and to ask for permission for the Prime Minister to say that the U.S.S.R. supported his pledge for Poland.

Maisky could not tell Lord Halifax that Stalin not only would appreciate such a declaration, but would be wildly overjoyed to have the British and French rush in to pull his chestnuts out of the fire. But he had obviously been briefed on what to say in case of such a delightful surprise. It struck him that the guarantee to Poland was not categorical enough, he remarked. While he could not speak officially for his government, it was well known that Stalin had said that the Soviet Union was ready to help all "those who fought for their independence." So the Prime Minister might say on his own authority that the Soviet Union did appreciate the principles on which the British government acted. And so did Chamberlain say, in a speech which marked a historical and fateful reversal of the tradition of British foreign policy. Neither he nor his equally obtuse Foreign Secretary noticed how terribly eager the Russians were to have the declaration made, and to have this challenge to Hitler made as strong as possible.

Now that the trap was baited, the Soviet government pretended great surprise. Maisky had been misunderstood, they remonstrated; he could not commit Moscow to any "sympathy and understanding," i.e., possible support, in a war for Poland. So Litvinov told the British ambassador in Moscow. But Britain was now committed: on April 6 the British pledge, now accompanied by a reciprocal pledge from Poland, was reiterated in London. The first part of Stalin's scheme was, though as yet on paper, complete. Not only Poland but also Britain and France stood between Hitler and the Soviet Union.

Here Stalin's script called for the Germans to make an approach. But they did not. Until the lust for war completely overcame him, Hitler could appreciate Stalin's game; as the German councilor in Moscow wrote: "The Soviets . . . desire also a development which would preferably bring about war between Germany, France and Britain, while they, to begin with, preserve their freedom of action and further their own interests."[15]

The trap had to be baited more heavily. The British went on to give similar guarantees to Greece and Rumania. Here came a two-pronged Soviet initiative. The Soviets told the British on April 18 that they were interested in discussing joint military guarantees for all the "Eastern European states situated between the Baltic and the Black Seas and bordering on the U.S.S.R." Obviously the discussions were bound to be long. The British were unlikely to comply readily with the condition that they should come to Russia's aid should she fight Germany in Latvia, while the Russians would have no corresponding obligation in case of an attack on Belgium or Holland.

And on April 17 Alexis Merekalov, the Soviet ambassador in Berlin,

[15] *Documents on German Foreign Policy, 1918–45*, Series D, VIII (Washington, 1956), 139.

paid his first call in a year on an important German official—Deputy
Foreign Minister Weizsäcker. "The Russian asked me frankly what I
thought of German-Russian relations. . . . There exists for Russia no
reason why she should not live with us on a normal footing. And from
normal the relations might become better and better."[16] With this
tantalizing hint Merekalov vanishes from the scene. Future contacts in
Berlin would be made more "conveniently," i.e., surreptitiously, by
officials of a lower rank, some working under the cover of membership
of the Soviet trade mission.

Still no German response. The situation was heating up—on April 28
Hitler renounced the Polish-German nonaggression treaty (why should
the stubborn Poles be protected by Germany's well-known respect for
her international obligations?) and, for good measure, the Anglo-
German naval treaty (this would punish the British for their encouragement of the Poles). On May 3 Litvinov was replaced as Foreign
Commissar by Molotov. In his desperate anxiety, Stalin was showing
more of his hand than he might have wished. A Jew was obviously not
particularly suitable for diplomatic contacts with the Germans. To be
sure Molotov could hardly qualify under the Reich's racial laws: he was
impeccably Aryan himself, but he had a Jewish wife! German diplomats
in Moscow, most of them proponents of a Russo-German understanding, withheld this embarrassing fact from the temperamental Führer.
While London and Paris should have drawn ominous conclusions from
the shift, it could be and was presented to them that with Soviet-
Western negotiations and the international situation entering the decisive phase, Stalin wanted his closest collaborator in charge of foreign
affairs. So they should hurry and negotiate with Russia in earnest.

How did Berlin view the replacement of Litvinov? asked a Soviet
embassy councilor, Astakhov, of a German contact of his. Hitler's
favorable reaction to this racial improvement in the Soviet government
was slow in coming. On May 30 the bait was swallowed. Weizsäcker
wired the German embassy in Moscow: "Contrary to the policy previously planned, we have now decided to undertake definite negotiations
with the Soviet Union."

What had happened? On May 23 Hitler instructed his generals that
he intended to smash Poland even if it meant war with Britain and
France. They were horrified by his intimation that he would not be
restrained even if Russia should join against him. Into this breach
stepped Ribbentrop with a brilliant insinuation: if Hitler got an agreement with Russia and secured her neutrality, Britain and France would
not fight, and wouldn't that be a joke on Stalin! The prospect of having

[16] R. J. Sontag and J. S. Beddie, eds., Nazi-Soviet Relations 1939–1941, Documents
from the Archives of the German Foreign Office (Washington, 1948), p. 2.

a splendid little war on Poland and doublecrossing Stalin overcame the Führer's aversion to dealing with the Bolsheviks.[17]

Stalin never read *Dangerous Relations*, that elegant eighteenth-century French novel recounting how the prerevolutionary aristocracy amused itself with stratagems of love and betrayal. Yet his game in the summer of 1939 was an intrigue of the classical type that evokes the sensuous feeling of diplomacy of the old school, cast anachronistically into the era of mass politics. Everything hinged on timing, on a correct appraisal of men and situations. Would Britain and France go to war, or would they draw back at the last moment? Then Hitler would swallow Poland and deal with Russia at leisure, treaty or no treaty. Would Hitler sign a pact with him? In May the Japanese attacked Soviet forces in Outer Mongolia, and a sizable frontier war ensued through the summer. Was it another probing operation, as of the last year, or a prelude to all-out war in the Far East? If the latter, would Hitler still need a treaty with Russia?

In order for Hitler to sign with Russia he would have to be convinced that Russia was *almost* on the point of entering into a binding agreement with the West. And so the negotiations with London and Paris progressed, if that be the word, through the spring and summer months, to the accompaniment of publicity, while contacts (wary on both sides) were maintained with Berlin. On June 29 another Soviet move: Zhdanov in an article in *Pravda* expressed his "personal opinion," which his "friends do not share," that Britain and France might not really want a binding military agreement with the U.S.S.R. This was to become a regular ploy in Soviet diplomacy: the intimation that there were "hard-liners in the Politburo" who did not want this or that agreement, so hurry up before they converted Stalin (or Khrushchev, or Brezhnev) to their point of view. After 1953 this ploy occasionally contained an element of truth. But at the time one man only weighed the chances and made the decisions.

On July 27 a breakthrough occurred—Julius Schnurre, in charge of commercial negotiations with Russia, invited Astakhov and Babarin, supposedly a Soviet trade delegate in Berlin, to some very noncommercial discussion over dinner, coffee, and brandy in a private room of a luxurious Berlin restaurant. Herr Schnurre, speaking on behalf of Ribbentrop, gently reproved the Russians for carrying on with the West. Was there not more similarity between the *Weltanschauungen* of their two dynamic, virile nations than between Russia and the decadent

---

[17] For obvious reasons the Germans kept hinting to the Western powers that if they did not behave, Germany might reach an agreement with Russia. One such leak was through General Bodenschatz, an aide of Göring's. He maintained what Ambassador Coulondre indiscreetly describes as a "tender friendship" with a young French attaché, and combined business with pleasure by feeding him hints of a German-Soviet rapprochement.

plutocracies? Astakhov politely agreed, but wanted to know what would happen to the Ukrainian and Byelorussian parts of Poland if Poland disappeared for some reason or other. Schnurre was quite encouraging. Astakhov continued: did Germany understand how deeply the Soviet Union was interested in the Baltic states and in Rumania? Yes, the Germans understood and sympathized with the Soviet solicitude for those countries. Astakhov promised he would report to Moscow, and he "hoped it would have visible results in subsequent developments there."[18]

The "visible results" was Stalin's conviction that the Germans were not only willing but eager to reach an agreement. As a consequence, the Russians *now* appeared in no hurry to spring it on the world. The legacy of past distrusts was so great, the Russians kept explaining in Moscow to Ambassador Schulenburg, that it was best to move slowly, first to sign a trade treaty, then gradually to arrive at a political one. But it was already August, and the Germans were bursting with impatience. Autumn rains would soon transform the Polish roads into quagmires; the Wehrmacht could not wait much longer.

What was Stalin waiting for? In brief, he saw through the German game, and he had to be sure that a war *would* break out following his making a pact with Hitler. Otherwise, for all the territories which would accrue to him, it would be a terrible trap: Russia would merely be fattened up to provide Hitler's next feast. If he could have had his way one hundred per cent, Stalin would have preferred a war to break out *before* the Soviet signatures were affixed to the treaty.

In the prelude to this terrible drama there was now a comic relief. An Anglo-French military mission was finally making its way to Russia—by slow boat. Indeed, Messrs. Daladier and Chamberlain seemed almost determined to provide future Soviet historians and propagandists with abundant material to justify the charge that the Western powers acted in bad faith and that Russia hence had no option but to sign with Germany. To add a Gilbert and Sullivan touch to the whole affair, the mission was headed by Admiral Sir Reginald Plunkett-Ernle-Earle Drax. But Stalin could not afford to take a humorous view of the matter, nor was the invitation to the mission only the latest move in a game of deception. He truly needed to know the Western powers' *military* intentions. And if the deal with Hitler fell through, he might need their help. And so the conversation which opened on August 12 between the Anglo-French mission and Soviet military leaders, headed by Voroshilov, ought not to be considered merely a feint on the Russians' part— they helped Stalin make up his mind.

He must have concluded that while Britain and France would go to

[18] Sontag and Beddie, p. 35.

war if Germany struck Poland (and he, unlike the British and French, now knew there was no if about it), their aid to that unfortunate country would be ineffective. The French, amazingly enough (it is not clear whether they were deceiving themselves or the Russians), stated that the Maginot Line extended all the way to the sea.[19] This could only mean that, as he had thought all along, the French in case of war would simply sit snugly behind their fortifications and let Poland and perhaps Russia take the brunt of the Wehrmacht attack. By the same token, there was every pleasing probability that a war between the two Western powers and Germany would be long, nor would it end with Poland's destruction.

While the military men were having their leisurely meetings,[20] Hitler was panting with impatience: he needed the August weather for his tanks and planes. On August 18 Ribbentrop wired Schulenburg that the Führer could not wait much longer; he, Ribbentrop, must come to Moscow and sign a treaty. Otherwise, if conflict broke out without it, *Russia's interests* might suffer. In other words, Russia must sign right away, otherwise no Polish Ukraine, etc. But Molotov would not be hurried: such a trip needed preparations, and so on, he said. But after giving this discouraging message to Schulenburg, within half an hour he recalled him. It had taken Stalin only those few minutes to decide that one could not push the game with Hitler too far. The Soviet government, Molotov now said, would be happy to welcome Ribbentrop on August 26 or 27.

For Hitler this would not do: he planned to start the war August 26. He sent a personal message to "Herr Stalin." Ribbentrop must be received *at the latest by August 23.* Two hours after receiving this virtual ultimatum, Stalin, undoubtedly with a sigh, agreed.

In the face of the approaching cataclysm two of the subordinate actors in the drama displayed some incongruous concerns. Molotov could not help teasing the Germans. Schulenberg was worried that one couldn't prepare a Soviet-German nonagression treaty so hurriedly. Nothing to it, said Molotov: the Soviet Union had such treaties with Poland, Latvia, and Estonia, any of which could serve as a model of the Russo-German one. And Schulenburg had a personal reason for wanting Ribbentrop to come: Schulenburg was scheduled to attend the Nazi rally in Nuremberg, and there he would have to wear a Nazi uniform, something the veteran diplomat and aristocrat found very distasteful.

To the amazement and horror of the world, the two tyrants struck a

[19] *Documents on British Foreign Policy* 1919–1939, 3d Series (London, 1950) VII, 567.
[20] *As proposed by the Russians,* there was one working session per day of four hours—i.e., two hours of discussion and two of translation—and this with the world teetering on the brink of catastrophe!

bargain. Ribbentrop arrived in Moscow on August 23. The same night the two powers signed and announced a nonaggression pact. A secret additional protocol provided for the distribution of the prospective loot. Should a "territorial and political rearrangement" take place with respect to Poland, as it was delicately phrased, the two signatories' "spheres of influence" would run through the middle of the country. Thus Russia was scheduled to receive not only the Ukrainian and Byelorussian territories, but also a sizable portion of ethnic Poland. Russia was to have a free hand in Estonia, Latvia, and Finland, Germany in Lithuania. The U.S.S.R. declared its "interest" in Rumania's Bessarabia; Germany took note of it.

With Ribbentrop burning to produce his great coup, the Germans conceded to Soviet demands on almost every point. And the social hour that followed the signing was most amiable. Stalin drank to Hitler's health: he knew, he said, how much the German nation loved its Führer. Again he displayed his remarkable ability instantly to size up the people he was dealing with. Ribbentrop, who had been ambassador in London, had a parvenu's feeling of social inferiority and bitterness toward the British. Stalin craftily played up to the former champagne salesman's resentment of the English. The Anti-Comintern Pact, said Stalin, scared mainly the City of London and the British merchants. Ribbentrop chimed in eagerly—the British would never fight, he said— and offered a sample of Nazi humor: the joke was making the rounds in Berlin that Herr Stalin would join the Anti-Comintern Pact! Stalin had his own little joke: he "knew the Germans desired peace." To be sure, said Ribbentrop, but they had to crush Poland. Stalin, possibly to reassure himself, opined that the British "would wage war craftily and stubbornly," and, his sense of humor now somewhat faltering, gave his personal "word of honor" that the Soviet Union would never betray Germany. Millions would die as a consequence of this amiable evening.

On his return to Berlin, Ribbentrop was proclaimed by Hitler a "Bismarck" (an indication of how modestly he viewed his own stature). But the Foreign Minister basked in this glory for only two days. To Hitler's surprise, the British, far from caving in, reaffirmed on August 25 their pledge to Poland. "What now!" exclaimed the Führer furiously to his "Bismarck." Marching orders for August 26 were postponed.

The next seven days were for Stalin, as for everyone else, a period of great anxiety. But his reasons were the opposite of everyone else's: he was afraid war might *not* come. And there were some rather strange doings that could not inspire Berlin's confidence in Stalin's word of honor. Why, wired the Germans on August 26 to Moscow, were Russian troops rumored to be withdrawing from Poland's frontiers, thus encouraging the Poles to concentrate all their forces in anticipation of the German blow? Russia was a constitutional state, Molotov explained to Schulenburg, and in order to become binding, the Nazi-Soviet Pact had to be ratified by the Supreme Soviet, but the Supreme Soviet kept tending to other business and the Foreign Commissariat was powerless to interfere with it. The Germans were not amused, and somehow on August 31 the Supreme Soviet did find time to ratify the pact. On September 1 Germany struck and on September 3 Britain and France declared war. "May God have mercy on us if we lose," said Göring—probably the most extravagant request ever made of the Deity. But Stalin could breathe more easily. Ribbentrop had been wrong, and he was half right: the British would wage war "stubbornly" but, alas, not "craftily."

Unlike most of Stalin's other actions, the Nazi-Soviet Pact has never been criticized in the post-1956 Russian literature. Even such an uncompromising enemy of Stalin's as Roy Medvedev offers a partial extenuation of Stalin's reasons in signing with the Germans. And it is unreasonable to assume, as some Western commentators do, that other Communist leaders would have acted differently in Stalin's shoes, or that the purges were largely motivated by the desire to get rid of those who would oppose a deal with Hitler. To a devout Communist, be he Trotsky, Bukharin, or Stalin, the difference between Hitler and Chamberlain was only one of degree, and Russia's imperative need in 1939 was to stay out of war. It is probable that no other leader would have conducted the game of deception so cynically or cleverly as Stalin did in the summer months of 1939. But the ambition to reunite all the Ukrainians and Byelorussians within Great Russia was shared not only by the Communists but by the most liberal of the Russian émigrés.

With the first part of his gamble an unqualified success, however, Stalin was soon in for an unpleasant surprise. The Poles and the French let him down. His scenario envisaged several months of fighting in Poland, with the German army, while undoubtedly victorious, getting bled in the process. And while he correctly suspected that the French would not mount a major offensive, he must have expected (as did the unfortunate Poles) that the fabled French army would at least make a demonstration in force to relieve pressure on her ally, while the Franco-British air force would give the Germans a lesson or two. To the amazement of even the German General Staff, no fighting of consequence took place in the West. British bombers did appear over Germany to drop . . . leaflets containing Chamberlain's indictment of Hitler's naughty behavior. Within five days, outnumbered and with no modern equipment whatever, the Polish army was destroyed. Isolated units and besieged Warsaw fought on valiantly, but after the first few days the issue could no longer be in doubt.

On September 2 the Soviet ambassador in Warsaw asked the Polish government why it was not applying to the U.S.S.R. to purchase war matériel (another commentary on Stalin's "word of honor" to Ribbentrop). The Polish request for aid reached Moscow on September 6 and by now Molotov informed the Poles frostily that there could be no question of helping them. A new and fearful anxiety seized the Soviet leaders. Hitler's legions were racing through Poland. Would they stop at the German-Soviet line of demarcation? Or, for that matter, at the Polish-Soviet frontier? Schulenburg pressed the Soviets to march into Poland and claim their share. But the Russians saw it as another possible trap. What if they marched into Poland prematurely, the Germans concluded an armistice with the Poles, and the Russians found themselves at war with the latter and possibly Britain and France? German hints to the Russians to march into Poland began in the first week of the campaign, but apart from wariness the Russians were militarily unprepared to do this, even though they were sure not to encounter any organized resistance.

On September 10 the Soviet government publicly ordered a partial mobilization. It is poignant and piquant to note that this step had not been taken in connection with the fighting with the Japanese that had been going on since May, nor would it be taken in the face of the genuine German threat in the spring of 1941 *until June 22*. But now they made war preparations on a scale that obviously could not be justified by the mere need to mop up the remnants of the Polish army milling around in eastern Poland. Molotov was eager to have the Germans know the vast extent of the Russian mobilization. "More than three million have already been mobilized," he told Schulenburg, who on his own noticed the "sudden disappearance of important foods, the preparation of school rooms for hospitals, curtailment in issuance of gasoline." Did this sound like preparations for an operation in which the Soviet army was to suffer a total in casualties of only twenty-five hundred? In any alliance it is not unusual for partners to suspect treachery, but this alliance was only two weeks old.

Stalin, ever careful to maintain his mysterious detachment from day-to-day negotiations, and to ration carefully his audiences with foreign envoys, took a hand in dealing with the Germans; not even Molotov could be trusted to penetrate the true intentions of these people. He received Schulenburg on September 17, as the Russian troops finally entered Poland to "liberate" the territories allotted to the U.S.S.R. under the agreement of August 23. Stalin, usually so composed, the master of every situation, could not help blurting out his fear. He said, "somewhat suddenly, that on the Soviet side there were certain doubts as to whether the German High Command would stand by the Moscow agreements and would withdraw to the line that had been agreed upon."[21] Schulenburg jotted down another observation that he chose not to convey to Berlin: "Indicative of Stalin's mistrust is his comment that there may be people in Germany who think that the Soviet Union might make common cause with the defeated Poles against Germany."

Ambassador Schulenburg, although a veteran expert on Russia—nay, on the Caucasus[22]—failed to appreciate the true import of this revelation of Stalin's state of mind. The August 23 agreement allotted Russia a sizable slice of ethnic Poland: the province of Lublin and part of that of Warsaw. Why would Stalin want that slice? It was, in fact, his insurance against an improbable but not impossible chain of events. Suppose the French armies poured into Germany following Poland's defeat. He could then argue that Russia had never aimed to assist Hitler in destroying Poland, proof being that he had preserved part of the Polish state from the invader and now, with a Franco-British victory approaching, was happy to become champion of the Poles and to help this gallant nation restore its independence! But as of September 17, this Polish enclave Stalin had secured posed a terrible threat. Hitler might see through his game. If there was one thing the Führer hated, it was ingratitude—witness how he had dealt with the Poles who had refused his generous offer on Danzig, and how angry he had become with the French to whom he had "guaranteed" Alsace-Lorraine. There would be grave danger if he thought that Stalin was ready to stab him in the back if Germany began to lose in the West. And so this Polish present of Hitler's had to be gotten rid of in a hurry. It is strange that the Germans did not catch on. But Schulenburg missed the clues, and in Hitler's glee over the victorious carnage and in his growing fury against the ungrateful West, he overlooked Stalin's stratagems. Ironically enough, he would turn against him later when Stalin loyally and fearfully abided by his agreement with Germany.

The *Blitzkrieg* in Poland and the Western powers' inactivity convinced Stalin that he could not, for the moment, afford even the appearance of a double game. The alliance with Germany had to be renegotiated; he now would be on his good behavior so that there could not be a shadow of a doubt in Hitler's mind that he was true to his word of honor. Ribbentrop came to Moscow again on September 27. (The negotiations could not be conducted in Berlin, Molotov pleaded, since on the Russian side they required the participation of "the highest personage" and he would not go abroad.) The Germans were in a position to drive a hard bargain, but the Soviets were helped by Ribbentrop's vanity. He liked coming to Moscow and conversing on terms of equality with Stalin. In Berlin there were other Nazi potentates and

[21] *Documents on German Foreign Policy, 1918–45*, Series D, VIII, 92.
[22] Before World War I he had been German consul in Tiflis.

generals looking over his shoulder, not to mention the Führer, who might not like meeting an actual Bolshevik. Ribbentrop spared no effort to smooth the course of the beautiful friendship. Russia, he insisted to Hitler, was now a nationalist state and international Bolshevism a thing of the past. Jews in high places? Even on this extremely touchy point the enthusiastic Foreign Minister was most reassuring if not outright deceptive. He had met Kaganovich at a reception, but he looked more like a Georgian than a Jew, he told Hitler.

Ribbentrop's second visit of September 27–28 produced a new agreement. Stalin skillfully persuaded him that "to partition the Polish population would . . . create sources of unrest from which discord between Germany and the Soviet Union might arise," so Germany should have all the Poles! Stalin, if pressed, would have given up his share of ethnic Poland for nothing, but profiting from Ribbentrop's mood, he exacted Lithuania in exchange. The new Bismarck, having accepted the idea of Germany's getting more of the troublesome Poles instead of the less anti-German Lithuanians, did not, however, let friendship moderate his greed. Would Russia surrender also the oil-rich districts of Drohobycz? She already had so much oil and Germany had no deposits. Stalin demurred: "The Ukrainian people had strongly pressed their claim to the area." But he would sell Germany oil for coal and steel tubing.[23]

The territorial rearrangement was agreed upon without too much difficulty. For Stalin, then almost sixty, it was a hard day's and night's work. The negotiating session began at 3 P.M. and lasted until 5 A.M. And even when the Germans broke off this trading in millions of human beings to enjoy a cultural interlude (the inevitable *Swan Lake*), the dictator kept working. He was receiving the Latvians who were negotiating their treaty of friendship with the U.S.S.R. (i.e., were being told to provide for Soviet bases on their territory). One had to cash in on the agreements: soon the Estonians and Lithuanians would also be invited to "negotiate" the first stage of their absorption into the Soviet Union.

The altered power relationship between Germany and Russia was underscored by Stalin's being constrained to drop the pretense of Soviet neutrality which still characterized the *public* part of the August 23 agreement. The joint declaration of September 27 stated that now that the collapse of Poland was a fact there was no reason for the war to continue. "Should, however, the efforts of the two governments remain fruitless, this would demonstrate the fact that England and France are responsible for the continuation of the war." Both powers pledged in such a case "to engage in mutual consultations in regard to necessary

23 *Documents on German Foreign Policy, 1918–45*, Series D, VIII, 160.

measures."[24] This was meant to sound like a threat that Russia might enter the war on Germany's side. (Ribbentrop wanted to make the insinuation stronger, but Stalin balked.) That Britain and France should continue in the war was, of course, Stalin's most devout wish, yet he had to declare public support for a peace that would spell out a catastrophic bankruptcy of his policies. There were other provisions in the new agreement, hardly momentous, but perhaps of interest to chroniclers of international morality. Both countries promised to synchronize their police measures to combat Polish agitation in their territories. The principle of mutual *voluntary* exchange of nationals was interpreted by the NKVD to include the surrender to the Gestapo of German Communists in Russian jails, many of Jewish descent. One is not surprised that a member of Ribbentrop's entourage, describing the visit to Moscow, enthused over the cordial nature of the reception: "One might think oneself in a circle of old [Nazi] party comrades."

For all such cordiality and Ribbentrop's amenability, the new agreement was from the Soviet viewpoint both humiliating and ominous. Russia was linked to Germany's triumphant chariot. Stalin, an arbiter of Europe's fate only one month earlier, was now a virtual satellite of Hitler's, his policy for the moment more attuned to Germany's wishes and needs than even Mussolini's were.

It was comforting that the Germans did keep their part of the bargain. In the Far East the Japanese, disheartened by the German rapprochement with Moscow, relaxed their pressure. The fighting between Soviet and Japanese troops stopped, and on September 15 the two countries pledged to settle frontier questions through negotiations. For Stalin, perhaps, the gamble was working; he was gaining time. But he had to pay much more than he had bargained for the German alliance. The U.S.S.R. now had to provide Germany with vast quantities of raw materials. It was to act as Germany's agent in neutral countries, thus evading the British blockade, and the terms of trade were not equal. "Soviet deliveries [of grain, iron ore, and oil] of the first six months are to be compensated by us within twelve months"[25] with industrial products. Much of the latter, especially war matériel, proved to be obsolete. The Soviets agreed to have German submarines use one of their naval bases.

Hitler could not be trifled with. He would not believe that Stalin meant to be loyal if foreign Communists continued to fight and to denigrate the Nazis. At the beginning of the war the Comintern did not plan to accommodate the Germans. The French Communists, considerably bewildered by the Nazi-Soviet Pact, pledged support of their gov-

[24] Sontag and Beddie, p. 108.
[25] *Ibid.*, p. 132.

ernment in the war over Poland, their deputies voted for war credits, their leaders answered the call to colors. But at the end of September they along with other Communist Parties changed course drastically and demanded peace with Germany. French Communist leaders deserted from the army, and the Party, soon banned, entered on a defeatist campaign that was to contribute to France's collapse in the summer of 1940. Their efforts in this respect were highly appreciated by the Germans, though they felt the French Communists could do even more.

On one occasion, in January 1940, Ribbentrop asked Schulenburg to tell the Russians that it was planned to send a special courier to Moscow, and would the Soviets be kind enough to let him inspect "Soviet information files on French Communists"? To be sure, the tactful Ribbentrop suggested that this request be phrased in very delicate language: "the German Government assumed that the Soviet Union was greatly interested in freeing French domestic politics from the repressive measures of the present War Government and in restoring democratic liberties." It would be a fine token of joint German-Soviet devotion to these ends if the files were to be shown to the courier, "Herr Nikolaus Rost, a man born in Russia and familiar with conditions there."[26] The Soviet official to whom this model diplomatic approach was made transmitted the request to Molotov, but he subsequently became ill, so that he could not receive Herr Rost and discuss with him ways of restoring democratic liberties in France. It would be interesting to know what became of the mission, indeed of Herr Rost—for whom after 1945 the NKVD, with its elephantlike memory, must have searched up and down Germany.

The Soviets on their part were also capable of delicacy. In the fall of 1940 Beria issued secret instructions to his administrators of camps and jails, forbidding their personnel to refer to political prisoners as "fascists." This term was now too flattering to be bestowed on the "enemies of the people," many of whom were sent to camps on charges of premature friendship toward Russia's current ally. It was only after June 1941 that things became less confusing and one could call a prisoner a "fascist" to one's heart's content.

The nonaggression pact with Germany was accepted by the Soviet people with that acquiescence which years of totalitarian rule might be expected to produce. It was undoubtedly popular in the sense that there was general relief that Russia was to be spared the horrors of the war, at least for the moment. There was a vague uneasiness among the people, and one more than vague among military personnel about the speed of the German campaign in Poland and Hitler's ultimate designs on Russia. Except for Molotov, and possibly other members of the Politburo,

26 Documents on German Foreign Policy, 1918–45, Series D, VIII, 597–98.

no one was privy to Stalin's plans. The Commissar of the Navy, Admiral Nicholas Kuznetsov, was apprised of the Soviet move into Poland only a day before it took place. But it was believed that Stalin knew what he was doing and foresaw every eventuality; as one might expect of him, he had wrought a miracle, recovering for Russia, and at practically no cost, the lands for which the Tsars had striven and fought bloody wars for more than four hundred years. Western Ukraine and western Byelorussia, as the territories seized from Poland were dubbed, were promptly absorbed into the corresponding Soviet republics. No one could doubt that a similar fate awaited the Baltic states, which for all their formal independence had to admit Russian garrisons. Lithuania was given the proverbial condemned man's breakfast: out of the Polish loot the U.S.S.R. ceded her the province and city of Vilna. Though the city had long been sought by the Lithuanians, they accepted this present tremblingly, knowing what it portended.

To Stalin's territorial greed was now joined haste: how long would the Germans tolerate his cashing in on their victories? Finland and Turkey were invited in the fall of 1939 to discuss treaties of friendship on the order of those signed with the luckless Balts. Rumania was warned that she would soon have a similar honor—Stalin had not forgotten how, in 1918, the Rumanians helped themselves to Bessarabia. And indeed, these activities were not creating a good impression in Berlin—weren't the Finns a Nordic race?—and Mussolini was trying to stir up Hitler against the Russians. The Duce's feelings were at the time nicely balanced between the cupidity that would make him join Hitler, and fear that after all Britain and France might win. All the greater his bitterness about those "Russian crooks," as he called them, who were carving out a new empire without any apparent risk.

Mussolini might not have been so envious had he realized to what extent suspicion accompanied Stalin's greed. Stalin was now feeling constrained to participate in routine commercial negotiations with the Germans: he felt that his subordinates would be cheated without him—the Nazis would send junk instead of up-to-date industrial and defense equipment—or, conversely, that they might become provocative and rouse the Nazis' anger. And so, painstakingly and patiently, Stalin went over all the Soviet requests himself. Would the Germans please sell them the blueprints of their newer aircraft and their latest battleships? (He still had an unrealistic and costly passion to acquire a fleet of capital ships for the high seas.) He tried to deflect the Germans' often quite rudely expressed demands that the Russians hurry up with their deliveries. Yes, they would deliver 100,000 tons of chromium, but first they would have to complete a railway line—and that might take ten months. He haggled and pleaded, but in an almost deferential manner. In reading the record of these negotiations, it is hard to decide what is more remarkable: the dictator's grasp of technical and business details or his willingness to submit to apparent humiliation at the hands of subordinate Nazi officials. "Ambassador Ritter rejected the view of Herr Stalin as unworkable in practice and contrary to the Agreement of September 28."[27] How long had it been since anyone had addressed him so peremptorily? He would return to this point later, the absolute master of the Soviet Union replied meekly.

So long as Britain and France held out against any peace with Germany that would not resurrect independent Poland, Stalin could breathe more easily. Even Hitler would not risk conflict with Russia with the French army poised on the Reich's frontier. But the period of the "phony war" was as hard on the Russians' nerves as on the others'. It would have suited Stalin to have real and, needless to say, indecisive fighting going on in the West rather than this disturbing peace barely marred by a minor skirmish here and there. So long as Germany was not actually fighting for her life, one had to grit one's teeth and bear the Germans' nonfulfillment of promised deliveries with composure, their increasingly rude and insolent demands.

Stalin had strong nerves, but he was also sixty years old and of a violent temper. There was a terrible day in October 1939 when he was informed of the latest request from Nazi Foreign Minister Ribbentrop. Though not a collector of stolen goods on Marshal Göring's scale, Ribbentrop had a passion for real estate. His chief of protocol transmitted to Schulenburg a most unusual request: the Foreign Minister would like to "lease" an estate in Soviet Western Ukraine. Renowned hunter that he was, Ribbentrop had been grieved to learn that "royal red deer" were practically extinct in Poland; but he had heard that on the Russian side of the frontier there was a huntsman's paradise, "with shooting boxes, hunting paths, and gamekeepers almost exclusively of German descent." Schulenburg was asked to tell either Herr Molotov or Herr Stalin himself that there were no stags in Augustow (in German Poland) and "suggest that he be leased one of the two hunting grounds in the Carpathians." Such a gift—"lease" was, of course, a euphemism—would, Ribbentrop felt, be of great benefit to the Russians. He would then visit the Soviet Union to hunt; the Russians would have the pleasure of his company often, and not, presumably, only on those occasions when a country or two had to be carved up. Schulenburg, an honorable diplomat of the old school, must have been deeply humiliated by this brazen request of his thieving superior,[28] but orders were

---

[27] *Ibid.*, VIII, 594.

[28] Ribbentrop was not above petty thievery as well. In the same letter he asked that Schulenburg keep sending him caviar. Oh, not for himself! The humanitarian Foreign Minister was distributing it to "badly wounded soldiers who can take no other nourishment."

orders and he kept importuning Molotov. Molotov kept promising to look into the matter while putting him off. Such were the Nazis at their friendliest. Stalin, "the greatest genius of our times," was expected to attend to Ribbentrop's private needs. If only one could make the great huntsman engage in some other invigorating exercise—say, cutting timber in Siberia.

To personal humiliation there now was added a national one of almost disastrous consequences. The Finnish government refused to follow in the footsteps of the other Baltic states, and rejected Soviet proposals for a territorial readjustment that would push the frontier further from Leningrad and for Soviet bases on Finnish soil. ☆☆☆

I N ordering an attack on Finland, Stalin probably felt like the French minister of war who, on entering the conflict with Prussia in 1870, said, "We enter this war with a light heart." This was going to be a brief and glorious exercise against a country of fewer than 4 million people. By December 1, 1940, it was decided to deal with the Finnish problem in a wholesale fashion. On that day the Soviet Union recognized and signed a treaty with the "Government of the Democratic Republic of Finland," i.e., with a few Finnish Communists resident in the Soviet Union headed by a veteran Comintern official, Otto Kuusinen. Obviously the armies of one military district (Leningrad's) would be sufficient for the task. The whole business, Assistant War Commissar Kulik told the future Marshal Voronov, should be over in ten or twelve days.[29]

The Soviets were in for a big surprise. The Finns fought stubbornly and well. The disastrous effects of the purges in the Soviet armed forces now became evident. The command was incompetent, field officers lacked experience and initiative, coordination between the various branches of the armed forces was chaotic. The Red Army kept attacking frontally en masse and suffering fearful casualties—by the Soviets' own admission these amounted to more than 200,000, a number greater than that of the whole Finnish army, including 50,000 killed, in a war which lasted a little more than three months.

The repercussions of the conflict threatened to be even more calamitous. There w s a wave of indignation in the democracies, of barely concealed amusement and satisfaction at this revelation of Russia's weakness in the fascist countries. Sympathy for Finland plus bitterness

[29] N. N. Voronov, *On War Service* (Moscow, 1963), p. 136.

at the Soviet "betrayal" led the British and French governments to formulate a plan which, if put into operation, could have drastically changed the course of the war and world history. The French prepared to send 50,000 "volunteers" and a hundred bombers to help the Finns; the British, though more cautious, promised a bomber force. The French command in the Near East also toyed with the idea of bombing the oil centers in the Caucasus. The ever ingenious Mussolini now had some startling advice for his Axis pal: Why fight Britain and France, which are strong, when there is Russia, which "is not a power but a weakness"? And against a "weakness" the Duce was ready to throw in the full might of his new Roman Empire: "The day when we shall have demolished Bolshevism we shall have kept faith with our two Revolutions."[30] Then, he enticingly continued, the turn of the big democracies would come. Italy, he wrote with laudable candor in this New Year 1940 message to Hitler, was ready to join in any scrap but only "at the most profitable moment."

Unlike Hitler, Stalin knew how to be moderate when the situation required it. By March, with more than a million men thrown into the war against the Finns, Soviet troops finally breached the Mannerheim Line and could be expected to overrun the country and to foist the Communist government on it. But the international situation was menacing. So the Kuusinen government was told to disband, and on March 12 the U.S.S.R. concluded a lenient peace (considering every-thing) with Finland. The frontier was pushed away from Leningrad, the U.S.S.R. obtained military and naval bases; but Finland kept her independence. Later, the memory of the international reaction to his Finnish move made Stalin spare Finland's independence again in 1945, when Finland might have been expected to be enrolled among Russia's satellites.[31]

Some lessons were drawn from the Finnish affair. A few generals were shot. But Stalin was lenient on those bearing the primary responsibility for the chaos in the army. Voroshilov, he recognized, was incompetent to supervise a modern defense establishment, so he replaced him with a much younger veteran of the Civil War, Marshal Semyon Timoshenko. Still his old Tsaritsyn pal kept a high position on the War Council. Mekhlis, Shchadenko, and Kulik—the three main culprits—were repri-manded but retained. Stalin had few illusions about the harm they had done. Mekhlis, he observed, interfered with field commanders. Kulik was dressed down for military illiteracy. (This worthy was elevated in

---

[30] *Documents on German Foreign Policy, 1918–45*, Series D, VIII, 608.

[31] Deutscher touchingly suggests that Stalin's forbearance on both occasions may have been due to sentimentality: in 1918 it had fallen to him as Commissar of Nationalities to acknowledge Finland's independence. Isaac Deutscher, *Stalin: A Political Biography* (New York, 1967), p. 447.

May 1940 to the rank of marshal. His contribution to the Red Army's strategic doctrine was a strong disparagement of mechanized warfare and an insistence that military transport should continue to rely on the horse.) But Stalin needed them: Mekhlis and Shchadenko were assiduous sniffers-out of treason and political unreliability, and Kulik was stupidly loyal.

The Red Army, Stalin realized, however, had to become more of a *Russian* army—hence an even greater emphasis on the continuity with the Imperial past. In the course of 1940 the rank of general was restored—the title was thought at one time to be so redolent of Tsarism that it had not been used even when the rank of marshal had been introduced. Political commissars were stripped of their equal status with the military commanders. Reforms were instituted to restore the authority and self-confidence of the officer corps. Discipline and the privileges of officers were strengthened. Count Ignatiev, an officer in the Tsarist army who since the Revolution had rendered some discreet services to the NKVD in Paris, had been brought to Russia in the late 1930s to teach Red Army commanders manners appropriate to officers and gentlemen. The gap between officers and enlisted men had already widened; now the salute was reintroduced. But all these privileges and amenities could not undo the fatal effect on the rank and file of seeing so many officers denounced and arrested as enemies of the people. When the Germans eventually struck, units dissolved into fleeing rabbles, the soldiers paying no attention to their commanders' orders (even pleas). On July 3, 1941, Stalin would be constrained to repeat the question posed by millions of his subjects: "How could it happen that our famous Red Army has surrendered so many of our cities and regions to the fascists?" He would not be able to give the true answer.

The fearful coexistence with Hitler continued. In public Stalin continued to plead for the negotiated peace that privately he feared more than anything else. A French report in the fall of 1939 that Russia might be changing her foreign policy elicited the kind of contemptuous, derisory reference to the West which the Russians hoped would reassure Hitler. He did not know, wrote Stalin in a message to *Pravda*, in which *café chantant* the report was manufactured, but here were the facts. "It was not Germany which attacked France and Britain, but France and Britain, having attacked Germany, assumed responsibility for the war." Germany was trying to achieve peace and the Soviet Union was seconding those efforts, but "the ruling circles of Britain and France have rudely rejected" the efforts of the peaceloving countries.[32] He awaited with mounting impatience the news that a long and inconclusive war in the West had begun.

[32] Stalin, *Works* (Stanford ed.), I, 404.

In April Hitler obliged him, but not very satisfactorily: the Germans seized Denmark and Norway. It was good that the chances of the Germans reaching an accommodation with the Western capitalists were growing increasingly remote, but bad that the Germans had such an easy time of it. Surely the French Army . . .

And this must have been Stalin's hope when in the early morning of May 10 Molotov awakened him with the long-awaited message. This was it: the Germans (with little consideration of the Soviets' nocturnal habits) were going to telegraph their latest intention via Schulenburg, demanding to see Molotov as instructed "at 7 A.M. German summer time." Informed of the German invasion of Holland and Belgium, Molotov said that he understood that "Germany had to protect herself against British-French attack. He had no doubt of our [German] success."[33] This was the big test of Stalin's gamble.

Stalin had miscalculated. Within two weeks the Anglo-French armies in the north were either destroyed or forced to evacuate. Unlike World War I, no "miracle" followed on either the Marne or the Somme, on which the French tried to establish a new line of defense. What had seemed inconceivable to practically everybody in Europe became, on June 23, a fact: France capitulated. Again oblivious to his word of honor to Hitler, Stalin concentrated substantial forces on the Soviet-German frontier following the German attack in the West. This was intended to become known in Germany, making her retain some divisions against a possible move by her Soviet "ally" and thus slow down the German drive in France.[34] But such was the speed of the German advance that by the time this movement was confirmed by the High Command of the Wehrmacht it was too late. It was June 20. The French had already collapsed. (In June 1941 Stalin would be so eager to undo the effects of this belated and awkward perfidy that the Soviet frontier *then* remained relatively unprotected.) But Stalin had managed to confirm Hitler's worst suspicions. And so, like the Poles, the French, and the British before him, he was ungrateful; he would have to pay for it. On July 31 at a meeting with his military chiefs, the Führer announced his verdict: "In the course of this contest Russia must be disposed of. Spring 1941. The quicker we smash Russia the better."[35]

The Führer's decision was also prompted by Russia's unseemly greed for yet more territory. With the campaign in the West reaching its climax, in June the U.S.S.R. proceeded to annex the three Baltic states. This had been provided for under the Nazi-Soviet Pact, but the timing was unfortunate. It was yet more proof that ungrateful Stalin did not

---

[33] *Documents on German Foreign Policy*, 1918–45, Series D, IX (Washington, 1958), 316.
[34] *Ibid.*, IX, 636.
[35] *Ibid.*, X (Washington, 1958), 373.

trust the Germans and wanted to close down the bargain while they were busy and before they could have second thoughts. What followed was even worse. Under the Ribbentrop-Molotov deal Bessarabia was also scheduled to go Russian. But now the Russians gave an ultimatum to the Rumanians to surrender not only Bessarabia, which once had been theirs, but also northern Bukhovina, which though it had a large Ukrainian population had never been part of the Russian state. The Rumanians pleaded with Hitler to protect them but were told to acquiesce to the Soviet demands, which they did on June 28. The unfortunate country had then, under Germany's prodding, to cede further territory to Hitler's greedy satellites, Hungary and Bulgaria. But Moscow's fond expectation that Rumania's rump would now become *her* satellite was cruelly disappointed. Hitler was gracious enough to take the Rumanians under his protection (though they had first to get rid of their king, who unmindful of his German descent and of being a Hohenzollern lived in notorious concubinage with a Jewess): Germany guaranteed "the integrity and inviolability" of what remained of Rumania, and the Wehrmacht soon moved in.

Hitler was master of the Continent. The French Army, which in a manner of speaking had stood between him and Stalin, had disappeared. Britain was still fighting against Germany, but could Britain resist the air and submarine warfare, and the invasion (which seemed inevitable in those summer months of 1940) by the invincible Wehrmacht? Few outsiders thought so, but devout prayers for the security of the British Empire emanated from the Kremlin. In receiving the British ambassador, Sir Stafford Cripps, Stalin was "formal and frigid,"[36] and an account of the interview stressing its "frigidity" was conveyed by Molotov to Schulenburg. But in a speech on August 1 Molotov gave unwitting expression of Soviet hopes: "The end of the war is not yet in sight. . . . The war between Germany and Italy on one side and Britain assisted by the United States on the other, will become more intense."[37] And to be sure that archimperialist Winston Churchill, for years the *bête noire* of Soviet propaganda, did not let Stalin down.

As the season for sea invasion passed and Hitler still had not made a triumphant entry into London, Stalin grew bolder. Perhaps it was a mistake to appear so submissive to Hitler. German troops were moving into Rumania and Finland. On September 27 Germany signed a Tripartite Pact with Italy and Japan—one of those pompous declarations in which fascist diplomacy excelled. The treaty specified that the three powers' relations with Russia were not to be affected, but the Russians grew irritable. The treaty was really intended against Britain and to

[36] Winston L. S. Churchill, *Their Finest Hour* (Boston, 1949), p. 136.
[37] Degras, III, 462–63.

keep the United States from joining the war, the Germans kept explaining, but Molotov was not appeased. He would have to see the secret Protocol to the treaty. There wasn't any, Schulenburg insisted. A treaty without a secret protocol! Who would believe it? asked Molotov. He grew petulant and sarcastic, and Stalin, previously so readily accessible to the Germans, now became unreachable.

The Germans were angry but also puzzled. Was there some power play going on in the Kremlin? Was Molotov sabotaging Stalin's pro-German policies? Ribbentrop hoped to keep the alliance with Russia: the 1939 agreement was the high point of his career. He kept arguing his point with the Führer, but Hitler was interested only in concealing his unpleasant surprise for Stalin until the very last moment. He agreed to let Ribbentrop try once more to make Stalin fall in with the Führer's sublime schemes for the future of the world. Overjoyed, the Foreign Minister addressed a lengthy letter to the man he fondly imagined was his great friend, Stalin, ending with the kind of flattering offer which Ribbentrop believed Stalin simply could not refuse: "In the opinion of the Führer, it also appears to be the historic mission of the four powers, the Soviet Union, Italy, Japan, and Germany, to adopt a long-range policy and to direct the future development of their peoples into the right channels by delimitation of their interests for the ages."[38] Would Stalin send Molotov to Berlin to discuss these exciting prospects with the Führer?

Stalin replied to the garrulous and bombastic communication in a few paragraphs. He thanked Ribbentrop for his "instructive analysis of recent events," and assured him that Molotov would come in November. Stalin knew that this brusqueness might offend the vain man, who probably expected him to open his heart, so to compensate for this he sent Ribbentrop an inscribed portrait.

While the faithful Molotov set out for Berlin, the German General Staff was completing its war games for the forthcoming operation against Russia. The Foreign Commissar was accompanied by a numerous suite: being valuable to Stalin, he was guarded by a detachment of the Secret Police headed by the NKVD's Assistant Commissar, Merkulov. And for all his loyalty he could not be fully trusted—who could?—so another Secret Police man, currently designated as ambassador to Germany, Paul Dekanozov, also watched over Stalin's "faithful comrade-in-arms." Both Dekanozov, a Georgian, and Merkulov were Beria's men, and they were shot along with their boss in 1953. But there were also less sinister companions: aircraft and other armaments experts charged personally by Stalin to find out as much as they could about

---

[38] *Documents on German Foreign Policy, 1918–45*, Series D, xi (Washington, 1961), 296–97.

German military technology. The circumstances of the trip could not be conducive to free and uninhibited conversation, especially because the whole entourage had to switch at the frontier into a German train and there was a frantic search for hidden listening devices.

In the land of the Nazis, the representatives of the socialist state were given the kind of reception the Germans believed would impress their guests and prospective victims. The Russians were introduced to marshals and generals whose names had sown terror throughout Europe. In their hotel rooms they could skim through illustrated magazines with artistic depictions of European cities being obliterated by the Luftwaffe and of German artillery decimating enemy columns. There was the grandiose expanse of the Reichschancellery, its walls lined with blond giants in SS uniforms who snapped to ominous attention as the small Foreign Commissar and his suite of aides and spies trooped to an audience with the Führer. Hitler himself, observed a Soviet witness poisonously, looked very un-Aryan in comparison, and so did "little, lame, and monkey-like" Joseph Goebbels.[39] The intended effect was also somewhat spoiled by the British, who chose Molotov's visit as an occasion for some bombing raids on Berlin. This led to a meeting's being adjourned in the midst of one of Hitler's lengthy harangues, and on another occasion to Molotov's indulging his penchant for sarcasm: in an air-raid shelter with Ribbentrop, who assured him that Britain had already lost the war, he asked, Why are we, then, in an air-raid shelter and who is dropping the bombs?

This last story is a bit suspect.[40] Certainly in his conversation with Hitler, Molotov was deferential and his slight stutter was more pronounced, but as instructed he was a tenacious bargainer, occasionally interrupting Hitler's geopolitico-philosophical disquisitions—something Hitler was unaccustomed to. The Germans tried to entice the Soviets by the prospect of sharing in the loot of the "bankrupt British Empire" and evoked the prospect of India, which could be theirs if they joined the Tripartite Pact. Molotov, unmoved by these riches of the Orient, kept asking about Finland and Rumania: what were the German troops doing there? It was only a temporary measure, the Germans explained, to protect those countries against the British. Well, Molotov was ready to thwart British plans by having *Soviet* troops in Finland. Here Hitler, his patience and caution strained, opined as a "military expert" that this might lead to war. How? wondered the Foreign Commissar. Sweden might come to Finland's help, Hitler replied, and when Molotov did

[39] Yakovlev, p. 243.
[40] Molotov related it during the war to his British colleagues, and it is found in Valentin Berezhkov's account in the magazine *New World* (Moscow), July 1965, p. 154.

not blanch, the Führer added that the United States might come too. How would the Russians like that?[41]

And so the conversation concluded with the Russians feeling that the Germans wanted to entangle them in a war with Britain, and with Hitler more than ever convinced that there was only one way of dealing with the Russians. Hitler's disposition was not improved by reports from "the confidential agent working in the Soviet Russian Embassy" that its councilor, Kobulov (another Georgian and NKVD man, also shot in 1953 along with Beria), had been personally charged by Stalin to secure texts of the Führer's secret speeches to his officers and to find out "which military men were opposed to Ribbentrop's policy and which German personages were opposed to collaboration with Russia."[42] Ribbentrop suspected that Molotov was sabotaging Stalin's pro-German policy. Stalin, on his part, suspected—this was an error of enormous importance in the spring of 1941—that it was the military men who were trying to provoke Hitler against Russia.

Molotov's report must have strengthened this suspicion, inclining him to seek to appease Hitler still further. On November 26 Stalin had Molotov transmit to the Germans an agreement to join the Tripartite Pact and share in the disposal of the British Empire "in the general direction of the Persian Gulf" (read: Iran), provided German troops withdrew from Finland and Russia could have military and naval bases in Bulgaria and Turkey. Hitler might well have accepted this offer: it would have been an ideal cover-up for his preparations to attack the U.S.S.R., but he was too disgusted with the Russians' greed even to pretend. The Soviet proposals never received a formal answer. And on December 18, 1940, the Führer signed the directive for Operation Barbarossa: "The German Wehrmacht must be prepared to crush Soviet Russia in a quick campaign," preparations to be completed by May 15, 1941.[43] (The name chosen for the operation was not auspicious: Frederick Barbarossa, the great German emperor of the Middle Ages, drowned while leading a crusade in the East.)

Hope and despair now fought for mastery over Stalin's mind. It would be insane for Hitler to attack Russia with Britain still unconquered, with the United States edging ever closer to active participation in the war. But then he may have reflected on the Russian proverb: "Excessive fat drives one mad." Hitler was fat with the spoils of the whole Continent. And in the winter of 1940–41 reports multiplied of a forthcoming German attack on Russia. Several Soviet espionage rings, the British, and the Americans all conveyed intelligence that the Ger-

---

[41] *Documents on German Foreign Policy*, Series D, XI, 557.

[42] *Ibid.*, XI, 1086. Kobulov evidently mixed pleasure with business, since his spies were also to report on "people who call on the actress Eyck."

[43] *Ibid.*, XI, 899.

mans were switching the bulk of their troops to Poland. Violations of Russian air frontiers by German aircraft became endemic. But Stalin remained wary: obviously the British and their American friends were trying to push him into a war with Germany, as were some Prussian generals. For class reasons those aristocrats might try to provoke a border incident and then trigger a war against the Bolsheviks against Hitler's wishes.

In Solzhenitsyn's *First Circle* Stalin is made to say that Hitler was the one man he trusted. With all due regard for the great writer, this interpretation is absurd. Stalin trusted his own judgment of men: Hitler was not as intelligent as himself, but being a man of the people, he had got where he was by hard work and being clever. To attack Russia now would be foolish. Hitler was under the strong influence of Ribbentrop (this was an exaggeration), and *he*, Stalin knew, was an inveterate hater of the British, and in love with his own success in bringing about the Soviet-German rapprochement.

The important thing was not to let oneself be provoked. Russia scrupulously kept up her schedule of deliveries of foodstuffs and raw materials, even though Germany fell behind in hers. Soviet batteries were strictly forbidden to fire on German planes violating Soviet airspace. When Admiral Kuznetsov issued an order in March 1941 to force down those planes—they were now almost openly photographing Soviet naval bases—he was summoned to Stalin and, in the eloquent presence of Beria, told to countermand the order.[44] German pilots forced to land on Soviet territory would explain that they had gotten lost on a metereological mission, and the local Soviet commanders would grit their teeth, entertain them hospitably, and then allow them to take off for home, even though intelligence officers had ascertained that it was not weather maps but photographs of strategic objects that their guests were taking back with them. To think that in 1938 a Kiev veterinarian was sent to jail for treating the German consul's dog!

Others might be agitated; Stalin was the picture of calm and confidence. What should the navy do to prepare for a possible conflict with Germany? What "line" should political officers take with sailors about the possibility of a conflict? asked Kuznetsov. "At the appropriate moment you will receive all the necessary instructions," said Stalin. But how in fact could one prepare for an offensive war against Germany if the news of such preparations was bound to trigger off Hitler's resolution to attack? This terrible dilemma meant that no clearcut instructions could be given, that the armed forces in turn labored under the frightful disadvantage of having no plan, not even an organizational setup for a war that everyone felt, even if they did not believe, was

[44] Nicholas Kuznetsov, *On the Eve* (Moscow, 1969), p. 344.

coming. The last war games held by the Soviet General Staff in December 1940–January 1941 epitomized the strain under which the Russian generals worked in those last months of peace. What Russian commander would dare to summarize their result as indicating that in the initial phase of war Germany might defeat Russia? But when the chief of staff, Kiril Meretskov, fell back on the hackneyed theme of a Russian division's always being superior to a fascist one, Stalin angrily reminded him that he was not at a propaganda meeting. General Meretskov "froze" and became incoherent. The very same night he was replaced by George Zhukov, but the future victor of Moscow was unable to improve on the work of his predecessor. The purges, as well as Stalin's inability to adjust to the possibility of a conflict with Germany, entirely sapped the power of initiative of the Soviet generals, and it took the shock of the war itself to restore it—and then at a hideous cost.

As with the army, so with the defense industry: ultimate decisions even on minor matters could be made only by one man. On military strategy Stalin did not know his own mind, but when it came to military technology, for all his talent for mastering facts and details he very often simply did not know. Yet from the design of the infantryman's rifle to that of a heavy bomber, the decisive word was Stalin's. People with creative ideas were often shunted aside (or worse) while sycophants and dull-witted bureaucrats got the dictator's ear. Boris Vannikov, an extremely able supply expert, recorded his travails as Commissar of Armament.[45] He was set to order mass production of 76-mm. tank guns which, mounted on the famous T-34 tanks, were to serve the Red Army so well during the war. Stalin suddenly got the idea that 76 mm. was not big enough. During the Civil War he had seen the 107-mm. gun in operation. It was bigger, so it had to be better. (It was, of course, a field gun, utterly unsuitable for tanks.) The production of the 76-mm. gun was discontinued, and Vannikov, who quite uncharacteristically for someone in this situation continued to expostulate with Stalin, went to jail as a "wrecker."[46]

The horrors of the late 1930s left their print on industry as a whole. In many crucial fields production fell or leveled off in 1939 and 1940. Many able managers were gone, others worked as if in shock. Stalin lashed out at inefficiency in his customary manner: threats, dismissals, imprisonments. At the Eighteenth Party Conference, in February 1941, several commissars in charge of financial ministries were dismissed. Stalin paid off some old scores: Litvinov was among those dropped from the Central Committee. But a special, though by this time, one should

[45] *The Military History Journal* (Moscow), No. 2 (1962), pp. 78–86.
[46] He was lucky. The war broke out in three weeks and Stalin asked Vannikov, then in solitary confinement, to write a memorandum on armaments production. He was then restored to his ministry, which he headed until 1962.

Dangerous Games

think, unnecessary warning was given that even those closest to the highest men in the state would suffer for administrative derelictions. Pauline Molotov was dismissed as candidate member of the Central Committee. Michael Kaganovich, previously removed as Commissar of Aviation Industry, was given an especially severe reprimand.[47]

It would be unfair to accuse Stalin of neglecting the country's defense. In 1940 new regulations lengthened the working day and week. By 1941 the army was more than double the size it had been in 1939. In a number of cases capable people were put in charge of vital departments. But his complex feeling about the approach of war prevented Stalin from *preparing* the Soviet Union for it.

By the early spring of 1941 Hitler did not bother to conceal his contempt for Soviet diplomatic maneuvers. It was enough for Molotov to indicate his interest in a foreign country and fumblingly inquire whether the Germans would mind if the Soviet government "guaranteed its independence," for serried masses in field-gray uniforms to move in, saying in effect, Halt! this is protected by the Führer! After Rumania and Finland came Bulgaria's turn. Bulgaria acceded to the Tripartite Pact on February 28, 1941, and was rewarded by German troops moving in. Stalin now tried briefly what might be described as a get-tough policy with Hitler. The pro-Axis Yugoslav government was overthrown by a group of Serbian officers, and the Soviets hastened to fortify Yugoslav resolve to stand up to Germany. There was some hope that the Germans might get bogged down in the Balkans if they tried to punish the Yugoslavs. Mussolini's armies were currently being trounced by the Greeks. On April 5 the U.S.S.R. signed a treaty of friendship with the Royal Yugoslav Government. A smiling Stalin was photographed in the company of the Yugoslav ambassador. Neither the smile nor the friendship was to last very long. Within a week the German war machine had rolled over the Greeks and Yugoslavs. The Russians might well have believed that the Balkan terrain would strain the resources of the German Panzer, but then it was another hope that crumbled. Stalin made an unseemly and belated attempt to undo the effect of this

---

[47] He had held a number of important industrial offices, more because of his powerful brother than because of his ability. During the war he was threatened with arrest on the absurd charge that he (a Jew) was a Nazi agent, and he shot himself. The third brother, Yuri, at one time Party satrap in Gorki, had vanished even before then.

There was another important Kaganovich, but this one was a production of fiction. Troubled by Stalin's solitary status after Nadezhda's death, and mindful how many of his Politburo colleagues had Jewish wives, some Russian émigré bestowed on him a nonexistent Rosa, "Stalin's third wife." This fiction found widespread acceptance. According to a recent biography of Stalin, Rosa was a "dark-haired beauty" (rather surprising, in view of the appearance of her brothers) and encouraged her husband's cultural interests by holding little soirées for writers like Pasternak (who in fact never met Stalin).

531

defiance of Hitler: on May 9, in flagrant violation of "friendship," recognition was withdrawn from the Yugoslav government, now in exile in London, and for good measure the same step was taken in relation to the exiled Belgian and Norwegian governments.

There was one last diplomatic success before all hell broke loose. On April 13 Russia signed a nonaggression treaty with Japan. The Japanese Foreign Minister, Yosuke Matsuoka, had been in Berlin, where he hinted about Japan's designs against America, and was rewarded by Hitler's opening up his "impenetrable bosom"—to quote Ribbentrop—with hints of Germany's intentions vis-à-vis Russia. But Hitler was at the very height of his hubris; he did not seek to dissuade Matsuoka from signing with Russia, and nonchalantly promised to join in the war against the United States. "In a period when he was still young and vigorous he should make use of favorable circumstances and take upon himself the risk of war which was eventually unavoidable."[48] Even after the American landing in North Africa in 1942, Hitler's opinion was that the only Americans who were not afraid to fight were gangsters.

In Moscow Stalin shamelessly courted the vain and garrulous Matsuoka. They were both Asians, he proclaimed, and when his visitor became tiddly from too much vodka, Stalin pretended to be drunk too and divulged confidentially that he was an adherent of the Axis and angry with Britain and the United States. At Matsuoka's departure Stalin and Molotov came to the station to wish him a pleasant journey. Then the dictator embraced Schulenburg, who was present, and asked for the German military attaché, Colonel Hans Krebs. "We will remain friends with you in any event," said Stalin to the latter. (In 1945 it was Krebs who was charged with surrendering the ruins of Berlin to the Russians.)

April 13, 1941, must have appeared a good if not a great day for Stalin. If Germany let Japan sign a treaty with the U.S.S.R., there was still hope that Hitler did not really want war.

On May 6 Stalin became chairman of the Council of Commissars, the first *government* office he had chosen to occupy since 1922. Why did he bother? There were two reasons. The Russians were playing the old game of pretending to "discord in the Kremlin." Several highly situated Germans, Ambassador Schulenburg among them, believed that Stalin headed a "peace party" while Molotov had become anti-German. Stalin's assumption of the chairmanship might reassure Hitler and avert or postpone the blow. The second reason was that if war came, the informal kind of dictatorship which Stalin exercised might become vulnerable. Otherwise trifling matters—such as who has the *legal* right

[48] *Documents on German Foreign Policy, 1918-45*, Series D, XII (Washington, 1962), 456.

to negotiate, issue decrees, sign a peace—can become of life-and-death importance. Stalin left nothing to chance. He now became the highest executive official of his country.

In 1939 Hitler confessed to the British ambassador in Berlin that he preferred to have war when he was fifty, since he was not sure he could shoulder such a burden at fifty-five or sixty. At sixty-two Stalin, the veteran of Tsarist jails and Siberian exiles, had the agonizing task of leading a nation he had martyrized in the "war of nations." We have already spoken of his fears of what such a war might portend for the Soviet regime, and for himself. But there was another element in Stalin's makeup that kept him from utter despair: self-confidence. Over the years, as he passed from one fantastic gamble to another and emerged victorious, the phrase "It is not easy to fool Stalin" had become more "There is no one Stalin cannot fool." (Where were those who had contested him, or who had sought to lie low, awaiting such a moment as now in the spring of 1941 to denounce and overthrow him? He had had them shot. And on August 20, 1940, near Mexico City, an NKVD agent's pickaxe had been buried in Trotsky's brain.) He might still fool Hitler.

Was he also fooling his own people? No, he was ruling them the only way they could be ruled, and they would recognize that it was for their own sake he had to be ruthless. In the spring of 1941 the author Ilya Ehrenburg was almost as unhappy if not as frightened as he had been during the purges. His beloved Paris was in the hands of the Nazis. Moscow was full of subdued fear. Ehrenburg was finding it difficult to have his *Fall of Paris* published. The first part came out all right, but the publisher objected that in the second part Ehrenburg had the French crowd shout "Down with the fascists!" Would it not be more tactful, in view of Russia's current alliance, to change in this and similar passages "fascists" to "reactionaries"? How was he going to reach the culmination of his epic? He could not very well say that Paris fell to otherwise unidentified "reactionaries." He was afraid to appeal again to Stalin, now in his mind the God of the Old Testament. On April 24 the telephone rang in the Ehrenburgs' apartment: Jehovah's secretary was speaking: the writer was to call such and such a number and "Comrade Stalin will talk with you." From behind this telephonic burning bush came the god's voice asking when Ehrenburg would describe the villainies of the "German fascists." How could he? Ehrenburg asked. The publishers did not let him use the word fascist, and he was almost ready to give up. Stalin soothed him. "You just go on writing, and *we shall together* try to push the third part through."[49] The story, as Stalin

[49] Ilya Ehrenburg, "People, Years, Life," *New World* (Moscow), No. 6 (1962), p. 150.

intended, made the rounds of Moscow. The publisher called that very same day—of course Ehrenburg's second part would be published, fascists and all. People who had been shunning the author now besieged him with invitations. Stalin had said that they could use the word fascist again; that must mean that he is expecting war.

He was, and he wasn't. There were now very precise warnings from several sources—the Americans, the British ambassador, Soviet spies in Tokyo—that the German invasion originally scheduled for May 15 and postponed due to the campaign in the Balkans would take place around June 20. But perhaps this was part of some German general's provocation; therefore Stalin should indicate to Hitler that he stood by his word of honor. On June 14 all Soviet newspapers and radio stations carried a Tass announcement bearing the imprint of Stalin's own style. "Despite the obvious absurdity of rumors about a forthcoming war, German and Soviet troop concentration," "responsible circles" in Moscow had authorized the statement that "according to evidence in the possession of the Soviet Union, both Germany and the Soviet Union are fulfilling to the letter the terms of the Soviet Non-Aggression Pact." German troop movements to the "eastern and northern parts of Germany" (i.e., German-occupied Poland) were mysteriously "explained by other motives that have no connection with Soviet-German relations." It was false to state that "the Soviet Union is preparing for a war with Germany."[50]

Stalin must have realized that the communiqué represented yet another gamble. It was bound to lull the vigilance of the Russian people, and especially of the army. But the risk had to be taken. Perhaps Hitler would be impressed, perhaps the troop concentrations were simply a way of pressuring the Russians. (There was an oblique hint in the communiqué that the Soviet Union would welcome new negotiations, perhaps stood ready to make concessions.)

Even at 9:30 P.M., June 21, with German units in a jumpoff position, Molotov kept on trying. Was the German government, he asked Schulenburg, dissatisfied with the Russians? If so, why? Was it over Yugoslavia? The Soviets had straightened this out. Schulenburg was noncommittal: he would report Molotov's words to Berlin, said the ambassador.

Mistake upon mistake, miscalculation upon miscalculation! Yet Stalin would not pay for them. The war, like collectivization, would be a monumental national catastrophe, and yet it would be a tremendous political success, and it would end with Stalin towering like a giant over prostrate Europe, unwilling to moderate in the slightest his tyranny over a heroic people. In the years to come he must often have reflected on

[50] *Documents on German Foreign Policy, 1918–45*, Series D, XII, 1028–29.

this outrageous favoritism of Providence. In the end he had managed to fool them all: Hitler; the Allies; people who thought things would be different in Russia after the war; his generals, who thought *they* had won the war and could give themselves airs. In his youth the Georgian Mensheviks had branded Stalin a *kinto*—a tough, sardonic street urchin. And he retained to the end some characteristics of an impossible adolescent. It is hard to resist the impression that there he is, Joseph Vissarionovich Djugashvili, thumbing his nose at his successors, at moralists, and at historians.

⤙ 12 ⤚

FOR
OUR COUNTRY,
FOR
STALIN

Saturday was now a regular eight-hour working day, and most Muscovites on June 21 were preoccupied by one thought: how to rest or amuse themselves tomorrow. With the Tass communiqué of June 14 the fear of war had been allayed. Issues of *Pravda* and *Izvestia* that went to the press the same night contained the usual reassuringly dull stuff: production achievements in Kazakhstan, a report on the Moscow Party conference. The war was far away—news of military operations in North Africa and Syria appeared on page 5—and most readers were expected to be more interested in the announcement of an exhibition of aquatic sports that was to open on Sunday. No other European capital awaited the summer of 1941 so calmly and unconcernedly. There was still uneasiness among the intelligentsia: people remembered Stalin's words to Ehrenburg, and if they had short-wave radios they heard rumors of Hitler's next move: Would it be through Spain against Gibraltar, or finally, against England? The prospect of yet another German conquest was depressing. But after the communiqué and especially in view of the fact that Stalin had chosen to become head of the government, one could be confident. He knew how to keep Russia out of the war.

By contrast, the highest agitation ruled among officers in the War Commissariat and General Staff. On June 21 they received confirmation of the intelligence reports pinpointing the night of June 22 as the beginning of the German attack (reports that had met with derision when brought to the attention of Stalin or those closest to him, like Malenkov and Zhdanov). A German deserter informed a Soviet frontier commander that his unit was ordered to go into action at dawn. At 5 P.M. War Commissar Marshal Semyon Timoshenko and Chief of Staff General George Zhukov waited on Stalin with the news, as well as with an order that would put all Russian border units on a war alert.[1]

Stalin's first reaction was to dub the business with the alleged German deserter as an obvious provocation. The term provocation, which had been on his mind all those months, appeared to have lost all concrete meaning and was simply an exclamation of despair. The generals insisted, and Stalin authorized the alert. But the directive had to make clear that what was expected was not war, but . . . provocations. With every minute of delay costing tens of thousands of lives, the military men spent hours trying to execute this impossible charge: to warn their field commanders that the German attack was expected, but not that it would mean war. At 12:30 at night the order was ready to be sent out. It speaks for itself: "There has arisen the possibility of a sudden German attack on June 21–22. . . . The German attack may begin with provocations. The main task of our armies—not to be taken in by any *provocations*. . . . It is ordered: in the course of the night of June 21 [it was already June 22] to occupy *secretly* the strong points on the frontier: . . . to disperse and camouflage planes at special airfields . . . to have all units battle ready. . . . No other measures are to be employed without special orders."[2] How could the Russians, on the shortest night of the year, move hundreds of thousands of troops and thousands of planes before dawn? Timoshenko would not dream of having his commanders called simultaneously by phone: this was Stalin's Russia, where everything had to be in writing, so that the dictator could be shown that his orders were obeyed explicitly. Out went the telegrams to the district commanders. By the time the latter in turn sent theirs to the field units, it was 2:25 A.M. Then the local commanders had to decipher what was meant by "no other measures are to be employed without special orders." Were they to order their units to shoot at the Germans when they crossed the frontier, or not? The commander of the Baltic district did not think so: "in the case of provocations by the Germans . . . withhold fire."[3] (Rather idiotically, he added, "In the case the enemy attacks with major forces he is to be smashed.") But most of the frontier units had not received Timo-

---

[1] This story of the first night and day of the war on the Eastern Front is drawn from several Soviet accounts, and as far as Stalin's movements are concerned mainly from what purports to be a factual account in a story by Alexander Chakovsky, "The Blockade," *The Banner* (Moscow), No. 11 (1968), pp. 42–56.

[2] Victor Anfilov, *The Beginning of the Great Fatherland War* (Moscow, 1962), p. 48. My italics.

[3] *Ibid.*, p. 49.

shenko's "directive" by the time the Germans struck at 3:15. For all the months during which information had accumulated as to precisely when the Germans would strike, many a Soviet frontier soldier had not as much as a minute's warning when his post was overrun by the enemy. The man bearing the main responsibility for this appalling negligence was at the time asleep in his suburban villa. Not even in the face of the news would Stalin vary his routine and spend the night in the Kremlin. Close to midnight a fleet of limousines had driven out of the Kremlin and speeded to his villa in Kuntsevo. Perhaps especially tonight and in view of the possible German "provocations," he wanted to be away from the people of the big city and in his country retreat (about the existence of which few Muscovites knew). Yet Stalin was apprehensive. Moscow Party officials were warned not to leave town on Sunday—a bit paradoxical, since he himself did not plan to return to the capital until the afternoon. Alone in his hideaway, Stalin must have experienced further agonizing uncertainty, for at two o'clock he called army General Ivan Tyulenev, commandant of the Moscow district, and ordered him to have its antiaircraft defenses "at seventy-five per cent of war readiness." By three o'clock he was asleep, and all over Russia Party leaders, ministers, and managers slept too; they could now be reasonably certain until noon that the phone would not ring with the frightening message "Comrade Stalin will speak to you."

But this was not a night like most nights. General Vlasik had just retired himself, after making sure that all the approaches to the villa were properly guarded, when at four o'clock the phone rang. Yes, insisted General Zhukov to the scandalized policeman, Comrade Stalin had to be awakened immediately: war.

Even an hour later in the Kremlin, in the presence of his generals and Politburo members, Stalin clung to the fatuous "provocation" theory. How could this be a mere provocation, pleaded the generals (still no one dared to shout, though obviously the situation called for it), if Soviet cities from Odessa to Murmansk were being bombed and German soldiers were miles inside Russia and advancing. There was one thin thread of reason in Stalin's otherwise irrational compound of despair and hope. In 1938 and 1939 the Japanese had attacked suddenly and with large forces, but it had turned out to be a "provocation"—i.e., a probe of Russian strength in the Far East rather than full-scale war. Perhaps Hitler was playing the same game, and perhaps it was not Hitler but his generals. This hope crumbled when Molotov arrived from an interview with Schulenburg: Germany had formally declared war. But even if it was war, perhaps the Germans would stop, and start negotiating, once they had convinced themselves that the Russians were fighting. So Stalin instructed his commanders to repulse the enemy attacks but make sure that no Soviet units crossed the frontier until the situation was clarified. A ridiculously superfluous order but what a testimony to his state of mind!

News of the war was moving through Russia with the speed of lightning, but the machine of the totalitarian government was for the moment like an overturned car, its wheels spinning in the air, the driver in a daze, no one able to order it to be righted. Until noon the Soviet radio broadcasted music, instructions for calisthenics, and similar trivia. And when the time came to tell the people the frightful news, Stalin—the man who had been deciding everything, who was his country's chief executive as well as its absolute ruler—could not bring himself to do it. At noon, in a halting voice, Molotov spoke of Germany's "faith-breaking" deed. "Our course is just . . . we shall prevail." Only now did orders go out for mobilization. Late in the evening Stalin, accompanied by some members of the Politburo, arrived in the operations room of the Commissariat of Defense. The war had been going on for only twenty hours, but the magnitude of the disaster was already clear. German armored columns had cut deep into Soviet territory, communication with many frontier units had been lost, others were known to have disintegrated. By *midday* on June 22 twelve hundred Soviet planes had been destroyed, eight hundred of them on the ground.[4] What was to happen on December 7 at Pearl Harbor was a trifle compared with this.

Stalin exploded. He seemed clearly unhinged. Why were the Russian troops retreating? Did they not know they had to carry the war into the enemy's territory? But such was the terror he exuded that at 9:15 P.M. Marshal Timoshenko issued an order although, in view of the situation, it was sheer lunacy: the advancing German units were to be "surrounded and annihilated"; by June 24 Soviet armies in the north and center were to advance sixty to ninety miles and to seize strategic points within German Poland. As a result the Soviet armored divisions of the second line of defense, which should have been carefully husbanded, were prematurely thrown into battle. Their personnel incomplete, many of the tanks and armored vehicles unavailable because of repairs, this precious force was cut to ribbons. By June 24 the Germans were in many cases one hundred miles and more inside Soviet territory.[5] The fatal directive had facilitated German encirclement of sizable Russian forces.

On June 23 the Soviet press carried Molotov's speech and a huge picture of Stalin. The war communiqué was reassuring: the Germans were being repulsed. The Luftwaffe had incurred heavy losses while the Russian air force had lost only seventy-six planes. On June 24, over the

[4] *The History of the Great Fatherland War of the Soviet Union*, II (Moscow, 1963), 16.
[5] *Ibid.*, pp. 30–31.

newspapers' mastheads: "Under Stalin's name we scored victories. With Stalin's name we shall win. For our country, for Stalin. Forward." Not a word from or about the dictator.

Stalin had left the country rudderless—or, to use the by now proper term, he had deserted his post. After the scene at the Commissariat of Defense on the evening of June 22 which led to Timoshenko's fatal order, he returned to his villa in Kuntsevo. As far as it can be gleaned from the shamefaced Soviet accounts, for the next several days he suffered from nervous prostration, which completely disabled him. The "man of steel" was incapable of issuing commands, even of participating in consultations. Everything seemed to be lost; the whole edifice built on the fiction of his infallibility was crumbling. The Germans were an enemy who could not be conjured away by bracing slogans, tricked by ruse, or taken in charge by the NKVD.

In his absence Russia in effect ceased to be ruled. The Stavka—an old Russian word for Supreme Field Headquarters, now synonymous with the High Command—was officially set up on June 23. It included military and political officials, Stalin simply being designated as a member, its chief and Supreme Commander being Marshal Timoshenko. For seven days supreme power was in Timoshenko's hands and, had he been made of a different stuff, Stalin might well have met the fate which in wartime, not to mention according to his own standards, is usually reserved for those who through dereliction of duty have been responsible for a military disaster. But there was little of Bonaparte in Timoshenko's makeup. Admiral Kuznetsov, who attended the Stavka sessions, testifies that during the seven days when Stalin was absent Timoshenko and Zhukov conceived their roles as that of *rapporteurs* before fellow committee members rather than supreme leaders of an embattled country requiring unquestioning obedience from soldiers and civilians alike.

Stalin was outrageously the beneficiary of the magnitude of the disaster. If the defeat had been less precipitous and catastrophic, if the front line had become stabilized within a few days, the story might well have been different. But as it was, those who during the week tried to fill in for him felt, probably realistically, that the deposing of Stalin would remove the last barrier to an uncontrollable and irremediable panic. The very extent of his crimes and mistakes had rendered him irreplaceable. And so the people whom he tyrannized now begged him to pull himself together and come back.

There must have been some doubt whether he would be able to do so. Between June 25 and 29 Stalin's name was absent from the newspapers. The patriotic poems now printed so profusely carried not a single reference to the man who had been for more than twelve years the central figure in all evocations of patriotism, all appeals to the people. Ambassador Cripps and members of the British military mission who hastened to Moscow to sign an alliance were received on June 28 by Molotov—a clear indication that Stalin was still incapable of functioning. The next day the Council of Commissars and the Central Committee addressed a circular to Party and state organizations in the frontier regions, acquainting them with what was still being concealed from the public—namely, territorial losses had already been severe, the Germans had seized most of Lithuania and a large part of Byelorussia, and now was "being decided the question of life and death of the Soviet state, whether the nations of the Soviet Union live free or become slaves."[6] The task of the Bolsheviks, the circular concluded, was to "unite the whole nation around the Communist Party, around the Soviet government." Not a word about Stalin, the man who had been synonymous with the Party and the government.

The Soviet citizen's bewilderment must have been enhanced by the fatuous and inept war communiqués. In trying to conceal the magnitude of the defeat and the territorial losses of the first days of the war, they failed to convey the desperate urgency of the struggle. If one lived away from the front, one might well have conluded that what was going on was a frontier war on the order of the conflicts with Japan in 1938 and 1939. Fighting, proclaimed a communiqué of June 29, was severe in "the direction of Minsk." ("Direction of" soon acquired notoriety, and most Soviet people within a few days read the term as indicating that the given locality was about to fall.) Elsewhere, the public was urged to believe that Soviet armies had beaten off the German attacks and were holding the frontier—here a Soviet corporal disabled a German tank, there a flier downed a couple of Messerschmitts. The men responsible for this idiotic prevarication did not seem to realize that one could not falsify data about a military disaster the way one did figures on a harvest or on industrial production.

But as of July 1 Russia again received a government. On June 30 there was instituted the State Defense Committee, "uniting in its hands the plenitude of state powers." Joseph Stalin was designated as its chairman, Molotov vice-chairman, the remaining members being Voroshilov, Beria, and Malenkov. Millions of Soviet citizens could again feel some relief. The Boss was back.

On July 3, for the first time in two weeks, the voice of authority was heard throughout the land. Stalin addressed his people on the radio. "He spoke in a dull, slow voice with a strong Georgian accent." At one point he lifted a glass with a trembling hand, making a sound against the table, and the radio listeners could hear him drinking water. "His

---

[6] *The Communist Party in the Period of Great Fatherland War* (Moscow, 1961), p. 87.

voice was low, soft and he might have appeared calm, but for his heavy, tired breathing and for his drinking water during the speech."[7] Ambassador Maisky gives a more forthright version; "It came out badly. Stalin spoke in a dull, colorless voice, often stopping and breathing heavily. . . . He seemed ailing and at the end of his strength."[8]

Yet for all the unwitting testimony that Stalin was hardly well, the speech was the first essential step in his ascent to a new position. For his countrymen he now became the national leader, not because of his vast powers and the machinery of terror at his disposal, but because they saw him as the only man capable of lifting Russia out of the depths of defeat and leading her to victory. Even his apparent anguish and agitation for the first time brought him close to his subjects. And there was a note of stark frankness in his speech, welcome after the would-be soothing but in fact disturbing lies of the official propaganda. The enemy was advancing, Stalin admitted; he had already seized Lithuania, Latvia, Western Byelorussia, large parts of Western Ukraine. "Our country is in serious danger."[9]

Yet there was also a hint of the old Stalin, the master of men who let no obstacle keep him from reaching his objective. For one thing, he began with a colossal, but in the circumstances reassuring, effrontery. Who else, addressing a country where virtually every family bewailed a victim of his terror, could have dared to begin "Brothers, sisters, I turn to you, my friends"? Who else, barely recovered from a debilitating shock, could have called upon the people "to unite around the Party of Lenin and Stalin"? *Excessive* contrition, he must have sensed, might produce a bad impression, and so he still defended his treaty with Germany. No "peaceloving country" could decline a treaty of nonaggression, he remarked, even if offered by such "perfidious and monstrous people as Hitler and Ribbentrop." And by signing the pact, Russia had gained a year and a half of peace. He welcomed the "historic declaration" of Churchill that Great Britain would help and the statement of the government of the United States, which stood ready with material aid. These "arouse the feeling of gratitude in the hearts of the nations of the Soviet Union."

But most of all Stalin's speech was a call for a relentless struggle against the enemy, for a scorched-earth policy in the areas to be surrendered, for partisan warfare at the enemy's rear. It dispelled any illusion about a "frontier war" and about the "Soviet troops firmly holding on to the positions." As the hero of a Soviet novel says of the

[7] Constantine Simonov, *The Living and the Dead* (Moscow, 1966), p. 67.
[8] Ivan Maisky in *New World* (Moscow), December 1964, p. 165.
[9] Stalin, *Works* (Stanford ed.), II, 1.

speech, "The truth was bitter, but finally it has been said, and now one felt firm ground under one's feet."[10]

This hope of firm ground underfoot was vastly overoptimistic, for the worst defeats, the most trying moments, were still ahead. But for Stalin, July 3 was the turning point. He had conquered his own panic and despair, and for *him* this was by far the most important victory of the war. The extent to which the Party bigwigs were relieved to feel again the familiar yoke may be judged by the heading of an article in *Pravda* of July 9, in the circumstances so disingenuous and grotesque as to come suspiciously close to "wrecking": "Long live Great Stalin, the inspirer and organizer of our victories!" And Stalin's name reappeared in patriotic appeals and poetry.

Stalin returned chastened but unrepentant. The tyrant has not dissolved in the war leader. Execution squads were soon at work, and their victims were not limited to "saboteurs, panicmongers, and deserters" for whom Stalin had promised this fate in his speech. The main German blow had been directed at the central section of the front—i.e., at the Byelorussian Military District commanded by General Dmitri Pavlov. (This was a surprise within a surprise, since it has long been axiomatic in Soviet military thinking that for political reasons the Germans would strike hardest in the south, through the Ukraine.) Pavlov, most accounts agree, was not qualified for his command, though even the most capable general would have been hard pressed to do well in view of the complete tactical surprise of the assault and the enemy's superiority along this crucial sector of the front. He was relieved of his post on July 1, and a few days later Stalin's resumption of supreme authority was signaled by the fact that General Pavlov, as well as his chiefs of staff and communication, were summarily executed as traitors. And NKVD firing squads were also not idle. Many former "oppositionists," disgraced Party and military leaders who had somehow survived in jails and camps, were ordered shot.

Now that he had overcome his debility, Stalin was eager to grasp all the levers of power. In mid-July he became Commissar of Defense. On August 7 he assumed the title (since the beginning of July he had exercised the power) of commander-in-chief. He must have hesitated to take on this last: the title identified him directly with the military conduct of the war, and it was foolish not to anticipate further defeats. But there was no choice, and after July 3, as before June 22, only one man was conceivable in the post. So Stalin, in his mid-sixties, carried the burden of supreme authority in the state and in the army. He did not make the mistake of Nicholas II, who, after taking over the High Command, compounded this error by leaving the capital for field head-

10 Simonov, p. 68.

quarters, nor that of Hitler, who also left the government to squabbling bureaucrats while secluding himself in his appropriately named "Wolf's Lair." Stalin stayed at the nerve center of Russia and conducted the war from the Kremlin, even when Moscow became the front line and when most government agencies had been evacuated. And though some criticized him for eschewing the theatricalities of front-line visits, his staying in the embattled capital, like his speech of July 3, was not forgotten by his people, and as long as the war lasted dimmed the memory of his crimes and errors.

All that, however, was in the future. In the summer of 1941 the only urgent task was to survive, to stop the German advance somewhere, to gain breathing space for training and for bringing fresh troops into battle to replace the millions of soldiers who had already been lost.

Though he was the only possible commander-in-chief, Stalin was not a good one. He was, of course, a military dilettante. Stalin's only military experience had been in the antediluvian campaigns (by World War II standards) of the Civil War. He had quick intelligence and an enormous capacity for work and for mastering details. But these qualities were offset in large measure by his inordinate suspiciousness and stubbornness, which did not allow him to judge men on their professional ability alone, or to accept strategies merely because of their military soundness. Considerations of power and politics reigned supreme except in the moment of the most desperate danger. As the war progressed, Stalin improved, learned to reward generalship over political reliability, to delegate some authority in the military field. But how costly in human lives his education was!

It is not surprising that his first steps in directing the war were almost as disastrous as his failure to prepare the country and army for it. He was obsessed by the necessity of defending every square foot of Soviet territory, blind to the advisability of tactical retreats so that the battered Soviet armies could be re-formed and re-equipped. And his choices for commanders-in-chiefs of the main fronts (this was to be the Soviet designation for an army group) were to prove most unfortunate. On July 10 Voroshilov was made commander-in-chief of the north, Budenny of the south, and Timoshenko of the central front. Apart from their personal loyalty to Stalin, the first two had little to recommend them. Voroshilov was incapable of commanding a major army unit, let alone a front. Budenny lived in the military past, in the era of cavalry raids before such inconvenient innovations as tanks and aviation.[11]

---

[11] In late summer Budenny got lost and Zhukov was sent to find him. He finally tracked him down in an abandoned town and the following conversation ensued. "You are coming from where—asked Budenny.—From Konev's headquarters.— Well, how are things with him? It has been two days since I lost contact with him. Yesterday I was at the Forty-third Army headquarters. In my absence the staff of my

Within a few weeks both had to be relieved, but not before they had aggravated an already critical situation. Much younger than the other two, Timoshenko would have been a capable division or corps commander, but in 1941 and again even more disastrously in 1942, he showed himself unqualified to be commander-in-chief of a front.

Zhukov, Stalin's chief of staff in those few weeks, grew increasingly exasperated at his leader's unwillingness to sanction timely withdrawals. At the end of July Zhukov finally gathered up enough courage to argue that it was imperative for Soviet armies in the south to retreat beyond the Dnieper if they were to avoid encirclement. Stalin exploded: How did he dare to propose that Kiev be surrendered to the enemy? Zhukov offered his resignaton; he offered to go to the front, even as a division commander. Stalin: "Well, if you put the question this way, we can do without you." Zhukov was replaced by Shaposhnikov, but he, for all his experience and his military gifts, was in failing health and functioned more as a consultant than as a chief of staff.

The military disaster grew. To the shock of the initial surprise and defeat, there now was added dull horror at the continuing German advance. Here and there a Soviet unit broke out of an encirclement; on occasion a resourceful commander would carry out a successful counterattack; but the situation as a whole remained bleak. When and where and how would the Germans be stopped? Stalin's re-emergence buoyed up the spirit of the people, but in a little while it became obvious that this had not been followed by a military miracle. And people brooded over the question which he himself posed but could not quite answer in his July 3 speech: "How could it happen that our famous Red Army had to surrender to the fascist so many cities and regions?" When the war started, the Soviets were far from being inferior to the Germans in numbers, whether of soldiers, tanks, or planes. The official figure for the army was 4.2 million and this was not counting the sizable frontier and other NKVD troops or the vast reserves in the paramilitary organizations. Even with a considerable army guarding against the Japanese in the Far East, this should have provided a solid defense against the some 3 million German and satellite troops that struck on June 22. But unpreparedness, poor deployment of the troops, and the calamitous first days of the war—when among other things practically all Soviet fighter planes were destroyed—removed the Soviet advantage and gave momentum to the Germans.

Yet by the end of July the Wehrmacht was feeling the effect of overextended supply lines—a grave obstacle to mechanized warfare in a country of limitless space. Soviet manpower losses were not as yet of

---

front has moved and now I don't know where it is." George Zhukov, *Recollections and Reflections* (Moscow, 1969), p. 310. It says a great deal about Stalin's attachment to the old warrior that he was not shot or at least demoted.

catastrophic proportions, and new tanks and planes, some of the tanks qualitatively superior to anything the Germans disposed of, were being delivered to the Red Army. The German threat appeared to be blunted. Sensible strategy and organization promised to stabilize the front line. Indeed, Stalin was quite hopeful. He told Harry Hopkins, President Franklin Roosevelt's emissary, that "the line during the winter months would be in front of Moscow, Kiev, and Leningrad, probably not more than 100 kilometers away from where it is now."[12] And after the winter the fact that the population of the Soviet Union was three times that of Germany was bound to assume its due significance.

But the gravest, most costly Soviet defeats were to come during the next two months. The Red Army reeled from those catastrophes for a year and a half. For all the incalculable psychological effect of the Wehrmacht's defeat in front of Moscow in December 1941, the Germans did not lose their mastery in the field, nor would the Red Army recover technically and, much more important, morally until the battle of Stalingrad, in the winter of 1942–43. And not until then did Stalin learn the job of commander-in-chief; not until then did Soviet leadership in military affairs cease to have unfortunate if not disastrous results.

The first six weeks of the war eroded most of the varnish of propaganda and uniformity which Stalin's rule had superimposed upon the life of the nation. In the first shock, soldiers either fled or died bravely; civilians either silently cursed the regime or volunteered to fight "for the country, for Stalin." But when the German pressure slackened temporarily, the initial panic and then resolution were succeeded by realization of the appalling truth: the system under which they lived was grotesquely inefficient, to the point that the war made it appear unreal, yet as before the man who had built and epitomized this system was exempt from criticism. Only a few in his immediate circle knew that Stalin's stubbornness in the face of expert advice was costing hundreds of thousands of lives, that decisions to extricate and save whole armies or to evacuate invaluable supplies were not being made because Stalin said no or was too busy to come to the telephone. But for the Soviet citizen, whether soldier or civilian, there was simply the shattering realization of yet another and fatal aspect of his country's life: he was governed by Stalin, the Party, and the NKVD, but he was now more than ever a slave of rules and documents. In a situation which called for enterprise and initiative, he was alone, bound hand and foot by regulations that made little or no sense.

Life was governed by "papers." Marshal Rokossovsky in his memoirs recounts how in the first days of the war (he was then a corps commander) he received from his immediate superior orders to unseal secret

12 Robert E. Sherwood, *Roosevelt and Hopkins* (New York, 1950), p. 339.

emergency instructions. On drawing these from the safe, he was stunned to read on the envelope, "Not to be opened except by express orders of the Chairman of the Council of Commissars." Being one of the few Soviet generals who then would have dared to display such bold initiative, he broke open the seal and read the instructions to march forward—which would have meant straight into the jaws of the enemy pincers. Simonov's novel *The Living and the Dead* purports to tell the story of the first months of the war as seen through the eyes of Ivan Sintsov, a Red Army political officer who gets separated from his unit, but the second hero of the novel is Sintsov's identity papers. He loses them while fleeing German captivity. To the world he then ceases to be a soldier and Soviet citizen and becomes, at best, a deserter who threw away his papers so that the Germans would not know he was an officer and Party member if they captured him, or at worst an enemy spy. Once in the Russian lines, Sintsov tries to flee again, because the officer into whose unit he has wandered proposes to turn him over to the NKVD. He is picked up by an old acquaintance driving to Moscow in a military truck, but then ejected from it unceremoniously when his friend hears the fatal words, "I lost my documents." And so, on foot and like a real spy, Sintsov steals into the capital. It takes an unusually bold and humane official to allow Sintsov to join a militia unit being sent to fight in the defense of Moscow. The story has a happy ending: Sintsov gets new papers for heroism under fire, he is readmitted to the Party. Not so happy is the ending of a short story by Solzhenitsyn whose hero, a soldier without papers who escaped from an encirclement, is turned over to the NKVD with the inevitable consequence.

These stories stand not for isolated incidents but for hundreds of thousands of cases. Whole units that after stubborn fighting broke through a German encirclement were, once in the Soviet lines, disarmed and sent back for "investigation." Once the superficial layer of unanimity and enthusiasm was peeled off by the war, what was found underneath was "papers," a synonym for that total distrust of people which was the cornerstone of Stalinism, proclaiming every Soviet man from Politburo member to an army private guilty until proven loyal. In peacetime this distrust enabled Stalin to build his personal power to an extent unprecedented in history; in war it nearly led to an irretrievable disaster. It took him some time to gather enough fortitude to appoint people who were competent rather than safe to principal commands. And not until the winter of 1941–42 did he find the right language in which to speak to his people, when he finally urged them to fight not for "the Party of Lenin and Stalin" but for Russia.

On August 20, with the Germans approaching the old capital, Voroshilov and Zhdanov set up a Leningrad Military Council. Stalin exploded: he had not authorized this. Were they perhaps inching toward the establishment of an autonomous regional regime? He dispatched emissaries from the High Command and the State Defense Committee, including Molotov and Malenkov, to check up on the doings in Leningrad. By October 30 the Council was dissolved, Voroshilov and Zhdanov reprimanded, and their authority curtailed and severely delimited.

Similar fears also dictated Stalin's revulsion against strategic withdrawals. How could one abandon Kiev, the capital of the Ukraine, where the Germans might proclaim a nationalist Ukrainian regime? How could one give up Smolensk, the first sizable *Russian* city threatened by the enemy, where the Germans if they had any sense might proclaim an anti-Soviet Russian regime? Political commissars were again given equal authority with commanders of military units at every level, thus further complicating and hamstringing the decisionmaking. Stalin's recurring political nightmare helped make the summer of 1941 one of continuing military defeat. In just two battles, at Smolensk and Kiev, the Soviets incurred over a million casualties. By November 1 the Germans had, incredibly, taken more than 2 million prisoners.[13] The figure reflected not only the extent of the military defeat but also the discouragement of the Soviet soldier thrown into one suicidal counterattack after another; shot at the "rear barrier" by NKVD units even when retreating in good order; treated as a deserter when breaking out of an encirclement. Many a Red Army man sought to purchase safety through surrender.

By now the tragedy—in his savage mind it was disgrace—was also Stalin's: a son of his was a war prisoner. His younger son, Vassily, was to perform creditably in the war, first as a fighter pilot, then in a training command.[14] But Jacob Djugashvili, though brave, met in war with the same bad luck which had dogged his steps since childhood. With his mother dead and his father first in exile, then in Russia, Jacob had been brought up by his Georgian relatives. As a grown man everything he did—from choosing a profession to choosing a Jewish wife—irritated his terrible father. But one cannot avoid inferring from Svetlana Alliluyeva's touching reference to her half-brother that hidden beneath Stalin's severity and neglect of his oldest born there was an element of

---

13 George Fisher, *Soviet Opposition to Stalin* (Cambridge, Mass., 1952), p. 3.

14 He had already evidenced the character defects which were to lead to his untimely death, and the proneness for riotous living which on one occasion led the Supreme Commander to punish him by ten days' arrest. Even before the war, in the air academy, Vassily Stalin, then barely twenty, showed himself overbearing and partial to alcohol. The commandant of the school, who must have been a very brave man, dealt him a public reprimand and then expelled him. Colonel General Andrei Stuchenko, *Our Enviable Fate* (Moscow, 1964), p. 78. Despite its title, the book contains some grim episodes of the time of the purges, which claimed members of the author's family.

affection that he could not or dared not reveal.[15] Jacob, an artillery captain, became a prisoner of the Germans during the very first days of the German attack. His father's characteristic reaction was to order the arrest of his wife "to find out what was behind it." From all accounts, Jacob bore himself bravely and honorably while in captivity. In 1943 there was a German offer to exchange Djugashvili for a German commander captured by the Russians.[16] But Stalin would neither negotiate a swap nor even acknowledge publicly the disgrace of having a son who had fallen alive into enemy hands. Worthless as propaganda or bargaining asset, Jacob was transferred to a regular prisoner of war camp, where (versions vary) he either was shot or committed suicide by throwing himself at the electric wire surrounding the prisoners' enclosure.

This tragic story may serve as more than a personal digression to a political history. It stands as the epitome of that destruction of human values which Stalinism had wrought. What Stalin was metaphorically for millions of other Soviet men under arms, he was literally for Jacob: a heartless and tyrannical father, one whom he and they sought to obey and please despite the blight he had brought on their lives. It was not a mystique that impelled this obedience to the Leader, it was a recognition, partly logical but partly a product of indoctrination, that the destiny of Russia was bound up with him. Yet judging by the number of prisoners in Germans' hands by the end of the summer, this loyalty was wearing off. Continued defeats and glaring examples of military incompetence could not indefinitely be blamed on "others." Many Russians now realized that the system was not only inhuman but also inefficient, and that it was fighting its inefficiency with enhanced inhumanity.

As he read the secret reports on Soviet casualties, before Stalin's eyes the vision must have again arisen that had haunted him before June 22 and paralyzed his will thereafter: while Russia's vast manpower and space might ultimately prevail, he and the whole Soviet edifice would crumble long before.

His struggle for the loyalty of the Soviet people merged, but was not completely identical, with the war against the Germans. It is not entirely inconceivable that Stalin's fear might have become a reality; but in the fight to survive, in the struggle for the Soviet people as well as for victory in the war, Stalin had one invaluable ally. This was Hitler. ☆☆☆

---

[15] Svetlana Alliluyeva, *Twenty Letters to a Friend* (in Russian; New York, 1967), pp. 148–54.

[16] Piquantly enough, this seems to have been Field Marshal Paulus, whom Hitler, whose ideas on surrender in war were not much different from Stalin's, wanted to get his hands on to have shot.

THE lust for war did for Hitler what morbid suspiciousness did for Stalin: it warped the workings of an intelligent mind, interfered with brilliant political and strategic concepts of which they were otherwise capable. Hitler himself had recognized, before intoxication with victories had turned his head, that a war with Russia could never be won by military means alone. But by 1940, when he ordered Barbarossa, he had not so much forgotten as felt impelled to reject Clausewitz's dictum about war's being a continuation of politics by other means. What he craved was not conquest but continuous war. Considerations of power, always supreme in Stalin's mind, were for Hitler now secondary to the vision of continuous slaughter. Unlike his Soviet protagonist, he sought, not to be the ruler gathering in his hands ever more numerous threads of control over every field of activity, from the economy to cultural life. The everyday business of government and administration bored and frustrated him. With the war he surrendered the government of the Reich to rival cliques of bureaucrats. He himself was, as he had always longed to be, the Warlord. One can even detect in his utterances during the planning phase of the Russian campaign certain apprehension at the prospect of a complete and speedy victory: this might bring about peace, an end to the exciting business of deploying armies, of millions of men risking their lives at his command.

By comparison with Hitler's puerile militarism, even Napoleon must appear a civilian in temperament: after all, he marched into Russia with a *political* aim in mind: to make the Tsar sign a peace recognizing France's domination in Europe. But even on paper Hitler's master plan contemplated no end to the war. In fact, by an insane paradox not one but two separate wars with Russia were to continue after the German "victory." Having destroyed the bulk of the Russian armies, the Wehrmacht would occupy the country up to a line running from Archangel along the Volga down to Astrakhan. Of course there would be no peace treaty with whatever Russian regime (Hitler implied it still would be Stalin's) ruled the not inconsequential area between the Volga and the Pacific Ocean. Some sixty or eighty German divisions would be sufficient to ward off thrusts from the east, while the Luftwaffe would keep busy by intermittently bombing the industrial complex in the Urals. This invigorating frontier war would presumably go on for generations.

The other war, needless to say, would have to be conducted west of the "Archangel-Astrakhan line" in the area occupied by the Germans but inhabited by some 140 million people. Nazi plans on what to do

550

with this uncomfortably large number of "subhumans" never really went beyond a combination of genocide and slavery. The solution for the Ukraine Göring observed in a light moment—he was reputed to be one of the more humane of Hitler's satraps—was to kill off all the men and then "send in the SS stallions." The Führer himself would never listen to any suggestion that the German war effort might be helped by a political appeal to the population of an occupied territory, any promise of autonomy (not to mention independence) for the Ukrainians, Byelorussians, etc., any propaganda effort to convince the local population that their lives would be freer than under Stalinism. In 1938 Hitler told Chamberlain that the Nazis' social ideas precluded any attempt by Germany to establish an empire. Though this was meant to deceive, Hitler unwittingly expressed a profound and fatal truth. Every durable empire has been based, in principle at least, on toleration of racial and national differences. None has endured if in addition to oppressing the subject peoples, it treated them with *unconcealed* contempt.

It would be a considerable oversimplification to assert that a more humane and rational treatment of the population in the conquered territories would have assured a German victory over the U.S.S.R. No nation in this century is likely to prefer a foreign invader to its own government, no matter how oppressive. People in Ukrainian and Byelorrussian villages and towns who sometimes welcomed the first wave of German soldiers as liberators still would not have acquiesced in having them as masters—even if they behaved with restraint and even if the military had not been followed by the notorious SS Special Detachments which murdered, burned, and looted. But Nazi barbarism made it inevitable that the Russian victory would also be Stalin's. As the mounting crescendo of the German occupation's atrocities continued, the prewar horrors of the collectivization and purges, while not forgotten, were dimmed. And tales of mass murder and starvation in German war prisoners' camps soon made the Soviet soldiers genuinely prefer death to captivity.

Yet this was precisely the period when Hitler believed he was winning, and the chance of him and the gangsters around him authorizing any half-humane treatment to their subjugated peoples was on a par with Stalin's proclaiming a multiparty democracy. After all, in September when it was already evident that the campaign was not a parade march, he would not hear of pressuring the Japanese to join him against the Russians: "This would be interpreted as a sign of weakness (as if we had need of Japan)."[17] And to share the laurels of victory with a Russian or Ukrainian anti-Soviet movement? In an inspired moment,

[17] *Documents on German Foreign Policy*, Series D, XIII (Washington, 1959), 466.

the Führer formulated the occupation policy as follows: "Naturally this giant area would have to be pacified. The best solution was to shoot anybody who looked askance."[18]

It was only after the battle of Stalingrad that half-hearted efforts were made to exploit anti-Soviet feelings among the war prisoners and the populations of the occupied territory. Even then they ran against Hitler's and most Nazis' grain. It was late: with the Nazi empire crumbling, the most notable Soviet defector, General Andrei Vlasov, was allowed in November 1944 to form a Committee for the Liberation of the Peoples of Russia and then to organize an army that would amount to perhaps fifty thousand people.[19] After the war most of them ended up in Soviet forced labor camps. And for twelve of their leaders, headed by General Vlasov, the end came in July 1946, when by a verdict of the military board of the Soviet Supreme Court they were sentenced to death, not by the firing squad customary for military men, but, as prescribed for traitors, by hanging.

That the Germans would prove as foolish politically as they were brilliant militarily was something that was only gradually realized on the Soviet side. In the early fall of 1941 Stalin could not allow himself the luxury of optimism on any count. Most of the armies with which Russia began the war had been destroyed. The enemy now occupied an enormous expanse of Soviet territory with a population of approximately 65 million. Would he be able to reimpose the Soviet system if the invader were to be chased out? What if the Germans restored private property in agriculture and abolished the hated kolkhozes?[20] Would the Soviet system have to conduct another war against the peasant after finishing a ruinous one against the foreign enemy? If victory were to come after all, it would redound to the glory of the generals, some of whom had only recently been freed from his jails; would they forgive and forget the dishonor and disaster he had visited on the army and revert to the terrified prewar docility?

At this point Stalin's luck again held true. First intervened a danger so frightful and pressing that it did not give Stalin or those around him the time or leisure to think of the future, and so possibly saved him from a collapse on the order of that of June. And on the heels of this came a victory, which to the world and to his people was *his* victory, and it enabled him to recoup his image as wise and intrepid leader.

If the Germans had stopped their offensive with the beginning of the

---

[18] *Ibid.*, p. 154.

[19] Fisher, p. 97.

[20] Which they most probably did not, despite vague promises in that direction. They preferred the short-run convenience collective farms offered for squeezing the grain out of the peasant, to the vast political capital which would have accrued to them by abolishing kolkhozes.

late fall rainy season and consolidated their lines, Stalin and the Russians would have faced a grim and dangerous winter. After consolidating their grip on the areas already conquered, the Germans were bound to resume their offensive in the spring. In fact they scored dazzling victories in 1942; how much worse would the situation have been if it had not been shown meanwhile that the Germans could be beaten?

By the end of September the Germans decided to resume their advance on Moscow. There ensued two weeks of intense fighting in which the Wehrmacht succeeded, in the battles of Vyasma and Briansk, in surrounding and destroying two major Red Army groups. By the middle of October Moscow stood exposed, the Russian forces in front of it battered and inferior to the Germans.

"Comrade Stalin, shall we be able to hold Moscow?" asked Alexander Yakovlev, who on October 11 had an audience with the dictator. "He did not answer right away, but walked silently around the room for a while, stopped at the table and filled his pipe with tobacco. 'I think that this is not the main problem at this time. The most important thing is to gather reserves. Then we shall grapple with the Germans and will chase them back.' "[21] But Stalin's calm, which impressed Yakovlev, was feigned or at any rate did not survive the events of the next few days. By October 15 he was *almost* convinced that the capital was lost. At about this time he called the future victor of Moscow, George Zhukov: "You are convinced we shall be able to hold to Moscow? I am asking this with pain in my heart. Answer truthfully, answer as a Communist."[22]

Belatedly, on October 15, the regime ordered Moscow evacuated of state and Party apparatus as well as of most of the defense plants, cultural institutions, etc. *Politically*, the next two days represented for Stalin and the Soviet regime a period as dangerous as that of the June days. There is no question, though this is not explicitly stated in any Soviet source, that on October 16 Stalin himself fled the capital and was away for two days. And October 16 panic broke out in Moscow. For the next three days civil and military authority virtually disappeared. A Soviet novelist describes this terrible time: "People would lose one another, and they would seek and not find, they would break into apartments, some waited in dumb despair at the crossroads . . . others cried and shouted, milling in the human whirlpools of the railway stations."[23] The NKVD and the militia vanished from the streets. Many Communists who could not get away were tearing up their Party cards. On October 17 the *local* Party secretary, Shcherbakov, appealed on the radio to the Muscovites not to panic. That the Leader himself was not immune to this panic and that for the second time in a year he

21 Alexander Yakovlev, *The Life's Aim* (Moscow, 1970), p. 296.
22 Zhukov, p. 366.
23 Simonov, p. 280.

had lost the ability to command is vividly confirmed by the fact that not until October 19 was a state of siege proclaimed in Moscow—the step which logically should have been taken the minute it was realized that the city was in danger. By that time, Stalin was back in the Kremlin in command of himself and the situation. He personally drafted the order putting the city under martial law, ordering shooting on the spot for panicmongers and agents provocateurs. And it was announced that the overall command of the approaches to Moscow was in the hands of the army General George Zhukov.[24] Moscow would be defended, if necessary in its streets.

A fascinating historical is, What would have happened if the Germans had realized the extent of panic and disorganization that gripped the Soviet regime between October 15 and 19? They were pursuing the textbook strategy of clearing pockets of Soviet resistance, preparing not a frontal assault but yet another pincers operation to encircle the capital. What if they had thrown caution to the wind and sent a Panzer division racing the fifty miles that separated their advance units from Moscow? The capital might still not have fallen or been promptly recovered, but Stalin would have had to leave it and join the rest of the government in faraway Kuibyshev. Russia might still have won the war. Would Stalin? Instead, the next two months raised him to new heights.

Though the military situation remained dangerous up to the first days of December, it never became again so desperate as in October. The German attack slowed down in the last days of the month, resumed in force in mid-November, but then the Germans ran out of steam and became vulnerable to the Soviet counteroffensive that began on December 6 and within six weeks threw the Germans back, in places sixty to two hundred miles. Moscow was saved and was never threatened again.

It would be superfluous to review and try to assess all the reasons given for the German defeat: the late-fall mud which paralyzed tanks; then winter; tactical errors of the German command; new Soviet armies brought from Central Asia and the Far East. The fact is that the Wehrmacht came close to accomplishing what was humanly (and inhumanly) possible for any army invading Russia. The losses inflicted on the Red Army in the first five months of the fighting surpassed the number of soldiers Germany had at any time on the Eastern Front. Winter and tactical errors played their part in the debacle, but the main reason for the eventual victory was that, confronted by stubborn defense, the German army was bound to bog down, and *militarily* it

---

[24] Constantine Telegin, in *Problems of the History of the Communist Party of the U.S.S.R.* (1966), No. 9, pp. 104–7. Telegin, then Commissar of the Moscow front, offers further corroboration of Stalin's absence from the capital. On Telegin's arrival at the Kremlin on the night of October 19, Stalin's first words were "What is the situation in Moscow?"

made little difference that it happened before rather than after the capture of Moscow.

After the beginning of November Stalin could feel some confidence about the outcome of the battle. Fresh divisions from Siberia arrived, and the main question was whether they should be thrown into the battle piecemeal or kept in reserve for the counterattack. Perhaps equally important, the overall command was in the hands of Zhukov, in whom he and the army had full confidence.

It was the measure of the gravity of the situation that Stalin should have overcome his suspiciousness to the point of entrusting the command of the several "fronts" surrounding Moscow to a single general. Before and after Moscow, his fears and restlessness were expressed in a continuous change in important commands. Generals were dismissed or shifted after a few weeks or even days in their posts, subjected to constant interference not only from Stalin himself but from civilian and military leaders whom he would send to field headquarters to look over the commanders' shoulders. But for once, if not for long, he let Zhukov have free hand. Marshal Rokossovsky recalls how he appealed an order of Zhukov's to the Supreme Commander and had it countermanded, only to be sternly reminded by Zhukov that it was he who was in charge and that his order stood. Writing years afterward, Rokossovsky still can hardly contain his amazement at the incident he witnessed in Stalin's office, when Zhukov told the dictator rather brusquely that an order of his was impractical. "I was impressed by George Konstantinovich's straightforwardness, but when we left, I told him that I would not be so brusque with the Supreme Commander. Zhukov answered, 'That's nothing. You should see us on other occasions.' "[25] To Rokossovsky, who had spent three years in jail as a "people's enemy," this was a new world. Yet writing in 1968, he feels constrained to volunteer, most unconvincingly, that Stalin usually addressed his subordinates with "fatherly warmth."

Other memoirs written at the time support the impression of Zhukov's commanding role and exceptional position vis-à-vis Stalin.[26] General Belov, who saw them both in November, recorded his impression that of the two it was Zhukov who was giving orders, Stalin at times becoming flustered. Yakovlev saw Zhukov at lunch in Stalin's villa. Having barely said hello to his host, Zhukov sat down and in peasant fashion gobbled down his food without a word and only then deigned to join the general discussion at the dictator's table.[27] To be sure, with

---

[25] K. K. Rokossovsky, *The Soldier's Debt* (Moscow, 1966), p. 92.

[26] Ironically not so much the Marshal's own. Despite Stalin's treatment of him after the war, Zhukov is quite generous in appraising the Supreme Commander's contribution to the victory.

[27] Yakovlev, p. 337.

the turn in the fortunes of war in December, his relationship changed again and Stalin resumed his habit of command. But he leaned on Zhukov—who in August 1942 was officially designated as Deputy Supreme Commander—until the end of the war. Soon after, the victor of Moscow was relegated to the obscurity of a provincial command.

On November 6, the eve of the anniversary of the Revolution, the Moscow City Council held its customary solemn meeting, but in unusual circumstances, with the Luftwaffe regularly bombing the city, the meeting was held in the Underground. But it was the old Stalin who addressed the celebration and the nation. There was no trace of weakness or irresolution. His didactic manner returned with his self-confidence. He read to his people a seemingly unnecessary lesson: the Hitlerites were neither nationalists nor socialists, they were a bunch of imperialist robbers. (Yet this was not entirely pointless. One still had to undo the residue of the official propaganda of the period of the German-Soviet alliance, which had painted the Nazis in a favorable light, as well as the popular belief which the news from the occupied zone had not yet dissipated that the Germans were "a cultured nation.") He told them what they needed for the war effort: more tanks, planes, and guns. He explained the reason for the continuing successes of the German army: the absence of the second front in Europe. "But there can be no doubt that the appearance of the second front on the continent of Europe—and there is no question it ought to appear very soon—will basically improve the situation of our army and will deal a blow to the Germans."[28] He told comforting lies: the Russian armies had suffered 1.7 million casualties (this figure must have shocked listeners, but it was a million and a half below the true one), while the Germans had lost 4.5 million (the actual number was 750,000, the total number of the German soldiers on the Eastern Front never being much in excess of 3 million). He compared the ironlike solidarity of the nations of the U.S.S.R. with the growing domestic opposition to the war in Germany, where "hunger, misery, epidemics" prevailed. More realistically, he likened the Nazi "New Order" in Europe to a volcano that would soon erupt and bury German imperialism. Of the man whom not so long ago he had toasted as "beloved by the German nation" he now said contemptuously that Hitler resembled Napoleon as much as a kitten does a lion.

But this dry lesson was soon succeeded by an inspired gesture. With incredulity the Soviet people, who daily expected the dreaded news of the fall of Moscow, heard from their radios on November 7 that there in Moscow Stalin and other leaders had taken their customary place on

---

[28] Stalin (Stanford ed.), II, 19. There was an intentional ambiguity in this phrasing. The word "ought," in Russian as in English, could be taken to mean "will."

the Lenin Mausoleum to review the anniversary parade. This idea had been Stalin's own, and its execution depended on the skies' being overcast till the last minute to minimize the chances of an air raid. His luck held, and on this day Stalin found the right words to address the troops who, straight from the review, would march to the front, and to fire the will to resist and the confidence of millions throughout Russia. "The war in which you are fighting is a war of liberation, a just war." And then came his famous evocation of the heroes of Russia's past: "May you be inspired . . . by the gallantry of our great ancestors." He began with Alexander Nevsky, who in the thirteenth century defeated the Teutonic Order, and concluded with two famous commanders of the eighteenth and nineteenth centuries, Suvorov and Kutuzov.[29] Stalin, the Georgian Communist, proclaimed this to be *Russia's* national war.

And within six weeks he would win *this* war. For if the aim of war, according to the famous definition, is to break your opponent's will to resist, then the chances of the Germans doing this to the Russians lay shattered before Moscow on December 6. The war that continued was then for the preservation of the Soviet system and his own power, and Stalin was sure of being victorious in this war only in 1943, after Stalingrad. And then *for him* there was a third war, for Russia's domination of Eastern Europe, for her status as a superpower; this one he won as much at the conference table at Teheran and Yalta as on the battlefield.

Stalin for a while continued to be a bad Supreme Commander. The Soviet victory in Moscow was not so decisive in the military sense as might have been hoped. On the German side the credit belongs to Hitler, who this time wisely overruled his generals. They wanted the Wehrmacht to withdraw all along the line, but in the winter conditions a retreat like this would have turned into a rout. By insisting that the armies stand their ground, Hitler was able to slow and then stop the Russian advance. On the Soviet side, much of the blame for not exploiting the victory more fully is Stalin's. With the turn of the tide he reverted to the norm, ordered his commanders around, and at times overruled Zhukov. On one occasion he detached an army from the front, and when Zhukov protested over the phone, Stalin simply hung up. As if to compensate for his previous moments of weakness, he tended once more to be peremptory and capricious in his orders. He insisted that attacks be pursued all along the front—something the Red Army, in view of its prodigious bloodletting, simply lacked the resources to do successfully. The German generals' memoirs notwithstanding, *all* Russians do not live in the realm of eternal snows or thrive on subzero temperature; hence the burden of attacking fortified positions in winter was almost as frustrating for the Red Army as it had been for the

[29] *Ibid.*, p. 35.

Germans. And so militarily the results of the victory were disappointing. Once again the Russians' casualties were much higher than the enemy's. And the imprudent strategy laid down by the High Command contributed to further disasters in the spring and summer of 1942.

Yet psychologically the battle of Moscow made all the difference. Hitler and the Wehrmacht stood humbled. The enraged Führer now dealt with his generals in Stalin's manner: dismissals, courts-martial, demotions were their rewards for military craftsmanship that foundered on his mad ambition. Stalin's military reputation grew, conversely, by leaps and bounds: it was he, the official view now argued, who devised the cunning strategy of luring the enemy deep inside the country, then dealing him the devastating blows at Moscow and later at Stalingrad. Only a few insiders knew the secret of Stalin's two breakdowns, but the entire country would be taught about "Stalin's ten offensives," which had ground the Wehrmacht into dust. So persistent was the legend of Stalin's military genius that to combat it Nikita Khrushchev had to resort to a fib: this reputed military genius, he told the Twentieth Party Congress in 1956, used to plan military operations on a globe!

The effects of the December victory on the morale of the Russian people were electrifying. Prior to Moscow the partisan movement in the enemy's rear was sporadic and confined mostly to bands of the Red Army soldiers who had become isolated and were abandoned during the retreat. Now, with faith in an eventual victory restored, the underground in the occupied territory became a formidable force, harassing the German communication lines and sabotaging their exploitive economy. The great patriotic surge, the War for the Fatherland, really began in December.

To the world at large, Russia's victory was a revelation and a beacon of hope in that grim winter of 1941–42. When the war began, "best-informed sources" in the West shared the estimate of the German General Staff: in three months or so the war in Russia would be all over. The junior senator from Missouri expressed the sentiment of many Americans: it would be a good thing if the two dictators could finish each other off. (During the Cold War the Soviet people were often reminded of Truman's impulsive remark.) Yet even here Moscow worked a transformation. Stalin was no longer a cynical despot, but a great national leader; the Russians were no longer a nation of slaves but the first heroes to deal a military setback to the fascists, to defeat them on the ground, where the Nazis had seemed invincible. People and politicians in the Allied countries badly needed reassurance that fascism was not the "wave of the future," and the battle of Moscow provided it. ☆☆☆

THE grand and strange alliance of Britain, the United States, and the Soviet Union was a child of Hitler's folly. He could have had Japanese help in the war against Russia if he had tried hard enough, and then the defeat at Moscow would not have happened, for it was the Soviet divisions brought from the Far East that had swung the balance. He then compounded his folly after Pearl Harbor by declaring war on the United States. Japan did not and would not help Germany militarily. Without Hitler's gesture, it is conceivable that though the United States would have entered the European conflict eventually, it would for a while have concentrated its fighting strength and resources on the Pacific war. The news of Hitler's almost nonchalant entrance into war with the greatest industrial power of the world must have been comforting to Stalin.

Paradoxically enough, Stalin's greatest gift and accomplishment has been given least recognition, even in his own country, even during the period of the "cult of personality." His greatness as a diplomat transcended his skill at personal diplomacy; for it was rooted in a shrewd appreciation of elements of strength and weakness (psychological as well as material) in Russia's partners and enemies, of national characteristics and idiosyncrasies, of human passions and fears. When he sat down with Roosevelt and Churchill, he—who had never been abroad except briefly, whose life had been spent in the confines of conspiracy and Communist politics—knew much more about the politics and economies of their countries than they or their expert advisers knew about his. More important, he grasped and deciphered the character of his two partners as they never did his.

Stalin's diplomatic performance during the war was dazzling. Russia's position during its first phase, until 1943, seemed after all not so much different from Chiang Kai-shek's China's: it was a country that had suffered defeats and a great loss of territory and was fending off the enemy only thanks to its vast space and manpower. Even with the Soviet victories in the last two years of the war, it ought to have been obvious that peace would find the U.S.S.R. weak and vulnerable, its economy in ruins, its political system facing new and perhaps intolerable strains. Yet from the beginning there was no question that Russia, unlike China, entered the alliance on the basis of complete equality with Britain and America. And it was as much the magic of Stalin's diplomacy as the Soviet victories at the war's end that created the illusion of a giant Russia threatening to engulf the continent, a power to be propitiated and appeased.

It was mainly after 1943 that Stalin's diplomacy reached its height of refinement. Until Stalingrad, he had to be a supplicant, and supplicants can seldom determine the course of a coalition. Yet even then he was a supplicant with a difference. He demanded rather than asked for military and material aid. Not even when the Soviet Union's military fortunes were at their nadir did he adopt the posture of a humble petitioner. Nor would he ever acknowledge or feel inhibited by the fact that it was Soviet Russia's pact with Hitler that had precipitated World War II, or that during the year when Britain stood alone against Germany the public Soviet attitude was one of bland unconcern. From the beginning his official stance was that Britain, and later the United States as well, were in Russia's debt. His first message to Churchill, on July 18, 1941, demanded an immediate opening of the second front in France: "This should be done not only for the sake of our common endeavor but also for that of England."[30] He referred but obliquely to his pact with Hitler: the Germans would be now in a better position, he remarked, if Russia had not acquired further territory to the West. There was not a single word of tribute to Britain's splendid year of solitary defiance of Hitler, or to Churchill's instant readiness on June 22 to forget his anti-Communism and declare unconditional support for the U.S.S.R. To be sure, Stalin was under fearful pressures, but his brusqueness was intentional: excessive politeness and gratitude, apologies for the past would be seen as a sign of weakness.

Roosevelt's confidential adviser, Harry Hopkins, visited Russia for the first time late in July 1941. Like practically every Westerner who was to come in contact with Stalin during the war, he was impressed and reassured. Stalin was "an austere, rugged, determined figure in boots that shone like mirrors, stout baggy trousers and snug-fitting blouse. He wore no ornament. . . . He's built close to the ground, like a football coach's dream of a tackle."[31] Hopkins saw Stalin when the military situation had momentarily eased, yet the dictator must still have been very nervous, judging by a detail which Hopkins reported without realizing its significance: he chainsmoked cigarettes throughout their interview. He was usually very careful, when with people he meant to impress, to smoke a pipe.

Hopkins *was* impressed: here was a busy politician and commander-in-chief who yet showed mastery of the technical details of the Soviet

[30] *The Correspondence of the Chairman of the Council of Ministers of the U.S.S.R. with the Presidents of the United States and Prime Ministers of Great Britain* (Moscow, 1957), I, 11; hereafter cited as *The Correspondence*. . . .
[31] Sherwood, p. 344. (See, in Mandelstam's famous poem: "his cockroach whiskers leer and his boot tops gleam.")

supply problem, knew precisely what kind of an antitank gun and how many tons of aluminum they would need from the United States, was thoroughly businesslike and untheatrical. How could such a sensible, attractive man aspire to be a dictator, how could one square his unassuming personality with all the stories about his purges and cruelty? In Hopkins' mind the idea germinated that perhaps those mysterious and repulsive aspects of Soviet reality were due not to Stalin but to others. "He never gained any clear idea as to how the Politburo really operated and neither did Roosevelt. As time went on . . . they became more and more aware of it as an unseen, incomprehensible and unpredictable but potent influence on Stalin and thus on all Allied long-term policy."[32]

Stalin's composure of late July had to give way to the extreme anxiety of September: the Germans had resumed their victorious advance. For the first and only time during the war he descended to begging for rather than demanding Allied aid. In a letter of September 3 to Churchill he acknowledged the possibility of the Soviet Union's defeat: the British must immediately establish a second front in France or the Balkans capable of drawing off thirty or forty German divisions. They must by October deliver 30,000 tons of aluminum and every month they must deliver at least 400 planes and 500 light or medium tanks. "Without those two species of help the Soviet Union will either suffer a defeat or will be weakened to the point where for long it will lose the ability to help its allies." He, Stalin, realized how unpleasant this message must sound, but experience had taught him to face the unpleasant truth.[33] On September 13 Stalin gave vent to still further anxiety and even more desperate and unrealistic demands. Could the British send twenty-five or thirty divisions to Archangel to fight along with the Soviet armies? That he should have asked that the "British imperialists" put their soldiers on Soviet soil was a measure of Stalin's anxiety, if not his despair. He was so suspicious of any contacts with Westerners that he did not allow Allied observers with his army and tolerated only briefly a single American airbase for shuttle-bombing of Germany, yet here he was contemplating having some 300,000 British soldiers alongside his own. In the same letter he found for once the right words to thank the British for their *material* help: "I hope that the English government[34] will find many occasions to see that the U.S.S.R. knows how to reciprocate in a worthy manner the help of its ally."[35]

The second front in Europe was then and remained throughout 1942 a military fantasy. Not only militarily but ideologically and emotionally,

[32] *Ibid.*, p. 345.
[33] *The Correspondence* . . . , I, 19. Soviet *heavy* tanks were superior to anything the Germans or the British had, but they were not yet being produced in quantity.
[34] Like most Europeans, Stalin seldom used "British."
[35] *The Correspondence* . . . , I, 22.

however, it was for Stalin as for the Soviet people the touchstone of their attitude toward their Western allies. One part of Stalin's mind urged that it was foolish to expect Churchill to establish the second front even if it were militarily feasible. Yet, like most Russians, Stalin resented his allies' "privileged" position in the war (and would until June 6, 1944, and even thereafter). His country was being bled; all the casualties the British and Americans sustained in North Africa and Italy did not amount to those the Russians suffered in *one* major battle; how could all the billions of Lend-Lease compensate for these millions of Soviet lives lost?

But even in the desperate summer and fall of 1941 Stalin was not giving anything away. On July 30 the Soviet Union signed a treaty of alliance with the Polish government-in-exile (the "London Poles"). Needless to say, the treaty nullified the Molotov-Ribbentrop pact, but the Poles' attempts to have Russians committed to restoring the Polish-Soviet frontier of September 1939—i.e., to returning the territories they had seized then—foundered on the Soviets' stubborn refusal. It was a small but ominous warning of the travails which the Grand Alliance would face: even in the hour of their extreme peril, the Soviets were not conceding anything of what they had gained through their collusion with Hitler. How would they act in the hour of their victory?

Western leaders now began to travel to Moscow. At the end of September W. Averell Harriman and Lord Beaverbrook arrived to assess and to expedite the flow of munitions to Russia. They were received with little of the proverbial Russian hospitality. Churchill was to write: "it might almost have been we who had come to ask for favors." But in view of the military situation, Stalin's behavior must be taken as a model of self-control and courtesy. At times he was harshly demanding: "Why is it that the United States can give me only 1,000 tons of armor plate for tanks—a country with a production of over 50,000,000 tons of steel?"[36] But the Western memorandum listing the proposed shipments to Russia met with Stalin's enthusiasm. And Litvinov, who had been brought out of retirement after June 22, exclaimed on hearing the figures, "Now we shall win the war!" The erstwhile "Papasha," whose retirement during the Nazi-Soviet honeymoon had threatened to become something worse, was soon dispatched to Washington.

Harriman explained to Stalin, whose mind at the moment must have been on the advancing German Panzer, that American public opinion was very keen on religious freedom. Would the Soviets take steps "to allow freedom of worship not only in letter but in fact"? Yes, said Stalin wearily. Molotov, less perceptive than his boss, sought clues to the

[36] Sherwood, p. 388.

Americans' obsession with such a subject at such a time: "He asked me [Harriman] whether the President, being such an intelligent man, really was as religious as he appeared or whether his professions were for political purposes."[37] Harriman's answer is not recorded. But the erstwhile theological student soon realized on his own how "the opium of the people," like other drugs, has its uses in wartime. Stalin would one day receive and chat amiably with the Patriarch of the Orthodox Church (it is unlikely that it occurred to him that *professionally* he was more qualified for this job than he was for that of Supreme Commander).

The feverish days at the beginning of December brought to the Kremlin the Polish Prime Minister, General Wladislaw Sikorski. Even at such a time, Stalin would not entrust the meeting with him to Molotov. One would have thought that he had not a minute to spare from military business, but on December 3' he held a two-and-a-half-hour conversation with Sikorski. (The same day a German patrol caught a glimpse of Moscow's spires.) Those thousands of Polish officers who, captured by the Russians in 1939, had subsequently disappeared in the Soviet Union, Sikorski asked. Where were they? They must have fled, said Stalin, without a trace of embarrassment. Where to? Possibly to Manchuria.[38] Though he paid tribute to the traditional gallantry of the Polish soldier, Stalin saw no reason to be excessively outgoing or courteous to representatives of a nation which already had endured much and a million of whose citizens had been deported to Russia after the Soviet seizure of its eastern part. There was little reason to make a fuss over a government which he was already determined to destroy once Russia recouped her full power. If at the time he was still patient with the "London Poles," it was because of public opinion in the West and especially because (as General Sikorski poignantly reminded him) 5 million American citizens were of Polish origin.

For centuries the Poles had intrigued against their Slavic brethren, and in the seventeenth century they had twice occupied Moscow, Stalin reminded the Polish ambassador. Now this nation of troublemakers threatened to throw a spoke in the wheels of the Grand Alliance. Already in London and Washington the Poles were slandering Russia and the Soviet system. Well, he would teach them in good time. Right now there was the issue of some 1.5 million Polish citizens in Russia who, after the German attack, had to be amnestied and released from confinement. It was dangerous to have so many people no longer under

---

[37] *Ibid.*, p. 392.

[38] Stanislaw Kot, *Letters from Russia* (in Polish; London, 1955), p. 125. As it was afterward ascertained, some 10,000 of them had been shot by the NKVD in 1940.

full Soviet control milling around. Best to have them out of the country as fast as possible (a conclusion which most non-Communist Poles reached independently of Stalin).[39]

The Polish problem, which in 1943–45 hovered over the Grand Alliance like a thunderhead, was in 1942 a mere cloud. But it was already intimately, and from the Polish point of view fatally, linked with the overall war strategy. The great issue was the second front, for which the Russians clamored insistently and at times insultingly. Whatever one thinks of the Allies' reasons for not establishing such a front in France after 1942, it was then out of the question. America's war effort was only gathering momentum. Britain's manpower resources were inadequate— throughout the first half of 1942 she suffered signal reverses in North Africa and Burma. The shipping and supplies needed to carry out and sustain operations in northern France were not available. But whatever experts and the logic of the situation argued, the fact remained that the momentous, most bloody battles were being fought on the Eastern Front. The British victory of El Alamein in October 1942 was secured against an Italo-German force of about 100,000. The Red Army suffered more than that in casualties in only a few weeks' spring fighting in the Crimea, one of many Eastern fronts. This contrast could not but be embarrassing and then galling to the Western leaders, as well as to public opinion in Britain and America. Unable to satisfy the Russians *militarily*, Churchill and then Roosevelt tried to appease Stalin *politically*. And the most logical object and victim of this appeasement was Poland. Already in the summer of 1941 the British government hinted that it would not insist on the restoration of Poland within its September 1939 borders.[40]

The psychologico-military-political complex of the second front thus had incalculable consequences for the war, the postwar settlement, and indeed the world in which we live. What should have been an element of weakness in Stalin's position within the Grand Alliance became instead a source of strength. Incomparable political strategist that he was, he used this advantage to chisel at the Allies' superior position. The

[39] Victor Alter and Henryk Erlich, two leading Jewish socialists from Poland, were released from a Soviet prison on December 4. They subsequently disappeared, and repeated inquiries from the West and from the Polish government-in-exile brought no response until December 1942, when the Soviet Embassy in Washington was constrained to declare that they had been shot as German agents. Erlich was a man with a considerable knowledge of the Russian revolutionary movement: he had been a member of the first Executive Committee of the Petrograd Soviet in 1917. The NKVD did not want such people in the West and believed, unfortunately correctly, that the fuss over the news of their execution would not last long, especially as the crime was revealed amidst the glorious tidings from Stalingrad.

[40] The Americans began by being harder with the Russians than the British but, as we shall see, as the war progressed the respective positions of both governments, or more plainly of Roosevelt and Churchill, were neatly reversed.

millions of Russian lives expended in fighting were exploited by him to erase the stigma of his past collusion with Hitler and his future rape of Eastern Europe. The moral capital accumulated by Britain in her year of lonely struggle against Hitler appeared as nothing against the bill presented by Stalin for the Russian lives lost (and who dared to throw in his face the fact that they had been lost largely because of his policies and errors?). Statistics of America's outproducing the rest of the world paled against the memories of Moscow, Stalingrad, and Kursk. Even the atomic bomb seemed a puny weapon when contrasted with the Red Army.

But in 1942 such perspectives of Stalin's future diplomatic and propaganda triumphs could be only perceived. Anxiety about the course of the war took precedence over all other concerns.

The Germans were on the march again. Stalin's main subordinates in the summer of 1942 have placed the main responsibility for the Soviet defeats in that season squarely on his shoulders.[41] Having frittered away the fruits of the Moscow victory by costly and ineffective attacks against entrenched German positions, Stalin in the spring compounded his mistakes by ordering Soviet attacks in places where the Germans were strongest. The most basic of his errors, the professional officers have claimed, was to order attacks in too many places, not leaving sufficient reserves for any single operation.

These criticisms are difficult to assess. It is clear, however, that after the Moscow victory the generals again did not dare to resist his dilettantish ideas. Stalin's favorites were even retained or restored to important command positions. The southern front remained under Timoshenko, even though his performance the previous summer was at best dubious. The important Briansk army group was given to General Philip Golikov. It was he who, as chief of army intelligence before June 22, had catered to Stalin's obsessions and pooh-poohed reports of Germany's preparation for aggression. Now given command of the one section of the front where the Russians enjoyed a clear superiority over the enemy, he proved himself incompetent as a field commander. The German breakthrough on his front in July contributed heavily to the Soviet military catastrophe farther south. Only then was Golikov dismissed and replaced by Rokossovsky, the erstwhile "enemy of the people" who was, along with Zhukov, the most successful Soviet field commander of the war.

If Timoshenko and Golikov were unfortunate, other commanders of large army aggregations were simply disastrous. The moronic Kulik had previously been demoted from marshal to brigadier general, but subsequently Stalin softened his attitude toward his old friend from the Civil

---

[41] See A. M. Samsonov, *The Battle of Stalingrad* (Moscow, 1968), p. 47.

War. Kulik was promoted to major general and given command of an army, which he promptly led into an encirclement. Whereupon Kulik vanishes from the pages of history, and there must be a strong presumption that he was shot. But Lev Mekhlis, who much more amply deserved this fate—he was not only incompetent but vicious as well—survived the war and held important political assignments after it. Assigned in the spring of 1942 to be the High Command's representative in the Crimea, Mekhlis terrorized the local commander, issued conflicting orders, and greatly contributed to a Soviet debacle which concluded with the Germans not only throwing back the Red Army's attacks but completing their conquest of the peninsula with the seizure of the great fortress of Sevastopol on July 4.[42]

The lesson of 1941 had still not sunk in as far as Stalin was concerned. On one hand he was eager, for national and personal reasons, to defeat the Germans decisively and to clear them from Soviet soil by the end of 1942—hence the overambitious Soviet operations in the spring. On the other hand, victorious generals challenging his monopoly of power was an ever-present fear. And so one had to have Kuliks and Mekhlises to offset the Rokossovskys and Zhukovs.

The result was a military catastrophe on the order of the one in June 1941, though this time confined mostly to the southern theater of operations. Once again the Soviets had been forewarned (by their espionage network in Western Europe) as to the direction of the main German blow: it would come in the south. And once again Stalin refused to believe the warning: obviously the Wehrmacht would try again for Moscow. To divert the German strength from the central front, Timoshenko's armies were thrown in May into an attack in the Kharkov region. This was precisely what the German General Staff would have ordered. We have Khrushchev's account, undoubtedly correct in general though somewhat suspicious in detail: a member of the southern front's army council, he tried to obtain authorization for a withdrawal, for after a few days it had become obvious that Timoshenko's forces were driving into a trap. He called Vasilevsky, the new chief of staff, who informed him that he would not even speak to Stalin since the latter's mind was made up. Khrushchev then telephoned Stalin in his villa. But the dictator did not deign to come to the phone and ordered Malenkov to instruct Khrushchev and Timoshenko that the offensive must continue.[43] Two whole Russian armies were destroyed in an encirclement,

---

[42] One must bear in mind that in the post-Stalin military literature Kulik and Mekhlis were, for a variety of reasons, selected as the official scapegoats—hence we have an abundance of details about their sins of omission and commission. The incompetence or dereliction of other Soviet commanders who remain in good odor politically (e.g., Budenny) are passed over in silence or with a slap on the wrist.

[43] Bertram D. Wolfe, *Khrushchev and Stalin's Ghost* (New York, 1957), p. 180.

the remaining severely mauled. After that Timoshenko was in no position to resist when the Germans opened their major offensive in late June.

Suddenly the summer of 1942 seemed to be a replay of the preceding one. German motorized columns were racing across southern Russia, encountering only sporadic Soviet resistance. Within the first three weeks of fighting the Soviet armies in the south were thrown back some two hundred and fifty miles. The Donets Basin, with its mineral deposits, was lost. By the end of July, with the German troops overrunning the northern Caucasus, it seemed certain that Transcaucasia would be cut off from the rest of the Soviet Union and then occupied by the invader. Germany would thus procure Russia's main source of oil and sever her supply route through Iran. The latter, in conjunction with the heavy losses suffered by the Allied convoys to northern Russian ports, would virtually seal off Russia from any Western help. The northern prong of the German offensive was reaching toward Stalingrad, threatening to paralyze the Volga waterway.

On July 28 the desperate situation evoked Stalin's Order of the Day: ". . . Not a single step backward. . . . You have to fight to your last drop of blood to defend every position, every foot of Soviet territory."[44]

Militarily, the crisis of 1942 might seem to have been less threatening than that of the preceding summer. Then the enemy was advancing all along the front from the Baltic to the Black Sea; now he was scoring gains mainly in the southern region. The most ambitious variant of the German plans envisaged, after the capture of Stalingrad, a thrust northward with the aim of creating a front *east* of Moscow, leading to encirclement and capture of the capital. Yet in view of the long distances involved and the attrition of German manpower, this would have remained in the realm of military fantasy even if the German summer campaign had gone as scheduled and Stalingrad fallen by the end of August. If it is dubious, to say the least, that Germany at this point could have won the war, there can be no doubt that a German victory at Stalingrad and subsequent occupation of Transcaucasia would have immeasurably prolonged it. Germany would have acquired the oil riches of Baku and a passageway to the Middle East,[45] where Erwin Rommel now appeared ready to sweep into the Nile Delta and the Arab world was seething against the British.

Politically, for Stalin the gravity of the situation surpassed that of the preceding year. Then the initial Soviet defeat could be attributed to the factor of surprise, and it was also clear to everybody that Russia's sur-

---

[44] *The History of the Great Fatherland War of the Soviet Union*, II (Moscow, 1963), 430.

[45] The Soviets firmly believed that Turkey was on the point of joining Hitler against the Soviet Union. And so a Russian army had to be kept on the Turkish border.

vival was bound up with his leadership. Now this was no longer so clear. The Red Army had won a signal victory; Stalin allowed its gains to be dissipated. A whole year had passed—and again defeats, encirclements, incompetent commanders, political commissars interfering with command decisions. The Soviet soldier was urged to fight "for the country, for Stalin" and in many cases did so, bravely. But some, even if only in their innermost thoughts, must have questioned the "for Stalin": Had one year of war really taught Stalin anything, had it made him forget any of his tyrant ways? It is obvious, though nowhere in the available records is it explicitly stated, that widespread discontent seized the Soviet officer corps. It is symptomatic that in the summer of 1942 and only then did the Germans manage to secure the collaboration of a captured Russian general. Andrei Vlasov, who in the winter of 1941–42 had been one of the more prominent army commanders before Moscow, was captured in May while deputy commander of an army group engaged in one of the disastrous Soviet spring offensives. While it is difficult to unravel the anatomy of Vlasov's treason, it is clear that among other reasons he was motivated by a genuine conviction that Stalin's military and political leadership was bringing disaster to his country. Few among Soviet officers, even if in captivity, were ready to follow Vlasov's path. But at no point of the war, either before or after, was the feeling that Russia's destiny could be separated from Stalin's as strong as during the summer of 1942.

The heroic defender of Stalingrad, General Vassily Chuykov, recounts in his memoirs that at a crucial period of the battle his political commissar arranged for Dmitri Manuilsky to visit the beleaguered city. Chuykov would have none of this; neither he nor the troops had the time or leisure for ceremonial vists and the usual propaganda drivel from a Party bigwig. It would have been inconceivable a few months before, and became so a few months hence, for a general to tell a Central Committee member to stay away.[46] But the renewed danger brought out in the military men the kind of courage in which they had hitherto been deficient: they no longer concealed their impatience with humiliating political control, with the whole paraphernalia of politics and propaganda "as usual."

With his superb instinct in such matters, Stalin sensed the latent political danger. At the same time as he worked feverishly on ways to stop the German advance, he took steps to quash what with a few more defeats might become a threat to his power. As usual, he employed a

[46] Vassily Chuykov, *The Beginning of the Road* (Moscow, 1962), p. 226. Chuykov not very convincingly says that one reason for his refusal was the fear for Manuilsky's safety. In World War I Rasputin proposed to visit the front "to bless the soldiers." Let him come, the commander-in-chief, Grand Duke Nicholas, informed the charlatan. He would be delighted to order him hanged in front of the troops!

mixture of blandishment, terror, and administrative reforms. To a degree, he would appease the generals. In June the hated Mekhlis was
removed as head of the political administration of the army. His place
was taken by Stalin's current jack-of-all-trades, Alexander Shcherbakov,
head of the Moscow Party, a former political supervisor of literature. It
was also to please his generals that in the same month he relieved
Shaposhnikov as chief of staff. The old marshal was well liked and
respected by his colleagues, but he was held, because of his health and
his excessive docility toward Stalin, to be unable to represent the professional point of view with enough firmness. His successor, Vasilevsky,
a much younger man, was a fortunate choice.

Two other measures were even more symptomatic of Stalin's desire to
propitiate his military leaders. In August, with the situation at the front
at its most critical, Zhukov was designated Deputy Supreme Commander. The importance of this appointment transcended its military
significance. A professional soldier now became in fact the second most
important man in the Soviet Union. His elevation seemed to suggest
that Stalin might turn over the actual control of military operations to
Russia's most prestigious general. But again, as after Moscow, victory
restored Stalin's self-confidence and determination to keep his hand on
every lever of control. Zhukov's appointment was never revoked, but
following Stalingrad his authority as such virtually lapsed and he no
longer enjoyed a special status or powers over other senior Soviet commanders such as Konev or Rokossovsky.[47]

In October the unified command was reintroduced, the political
commissar again became the military commander's subordinate and
deputy for political educational work.

Those measures would not have been taken by a suspicious and power-
greedy man except under the prodding of an extreme urgency. But there
was another and more sinister consequence of Stalin's fear that his
regime, even more than Russia, was in danger. As at the height of the
German advance the previous year, so in July–August 1942 a number of
political prisoners were ordered shot. Among them was Peter Petrovsky,
whose brother Leonid, a general, had died a hero's death at the front.

[47] It was Zhukov's unenviable fate to be exploited politically, first by Stalin and then
by Khrushchev. When occasion demanded it, he would be brought into the limelight so that his prestige and popularity would reflect on his political sponsor. Then,
with the emergency over, those very attributes were felt to make him dangerous; he
would be dropped down a notch (in 1943), relegated to obscurity (in 1946), and
dismissed (in 1957). In some ways, his career is oddly similar to Douglas Mac-
Arthur's. Like America's Presidents, Russia's dictators remained firm believers in
civilian control over the armed forces. And George Konstantinovich Zhukov, the
savior of Moscow, the man whose prestige was exploited to bolster the panicky
regime after Stalin's death, who saved Nikita Khruschchev from being overthrown in
1957, did finally, as old soldiers should, in the words of his American counterpart,
fade away.

The two brothers were guilty of the same crime: their father, once a prominent politician in the Ukraine, had been purged (though not arrested). Why one should have been entrusted with a military command while the other was kept in prison and executed must remain the tyrant's secret. The 1942 "list" contained also the name of Stalin's brother-in-law, Alexander Svanidze. ☆☆☆

W̄HILE propitiating his generals and executing people who *might* become dangerous, Stalin was taking his place as one of the leaders of the Free World.

London and Washington were eager to host a Soviet potentate. Stalin could not leave the country, and he would not even if he could. The prospect of extensive travel by air never attracted high-ranking Soviet leaders. (What an opportunity for sabotage!) And so Molotov again had to go, just as he had had the unenviable task of negotiating with Hitler in 1940. The prospect of what was then in fact a long and dangerous flight (Molotov had to fly over some German-occupied territory, since Russian planes did not then have the range to take a round-about route, and it was out of the question to go in a British or American plane) could not have enchanted Stalin's faithful servant. He also could not take some one hundred NKVD people with him as he had to Berlin. The few agents whom he did take were, however, most assiduous. In England and America Molotov's hosts were taken aback by the precautions their guests observed. The Russians always locked their rooms even when at Chequers, the Prime Minister's official country residence. Molotov slept with a gun at his bedside. These precautions did not reflect, as Churchill believed, the Russians' lack of confidence in the official hosts. But could one be sure that the domestic staff at Chequers or the White House did not contain a German agent or a Trotskyite?

Molotov's trip had two main purposes. First and foremost, the second front. The Americans were quite agreeable; but in 1942 the landing and fighting in France would have had to be carried out almost exclusively by British troops, and Churchill and his advisers were understandably less enthusiastic about the idea. To appease the insistent Molotov, the British rather unwisely stated officially that they were "making preparations for a landing on the Continent in August or September." They then qualified this pledge by adding "We can . . . give no promise in the matter." It would have been better to say plainly what was true, that the British had neither the intention nor the resources to invade the

Continent in 1942. As it was, the Russians had half a case for accusing their allies of bad faith.

The other Soviet concern was to procure London's and Washington's formal agreement that the U.S.S.R. should retain after the war the territorial gains she had secured between 1939 and 1941. The preceding December, when Foreign Secretary Anthony Eden had been in Moscow, Stalin had tried to beguile him into such an agreement by saying that in return Russia would support any British demands for bases in France, the Low Countries, and Scandinavia. And that the whole business did not have to be made public, but could be stipulated discreetly in a secret protocol! But neither then nor in May 1942 would the British agree to such an arrangement, somewhat reminiscent of the Ribbentrop-Molotov deal. *At the time*, Churchill, just to get the Russians off his back on the second front issue, would have been willing to promise Stalin almost anything he wanted in Eastern Europe, but the voice of Washington was as yet sternly moralistic: no sinful territorial bargains. And so the treaty of alliance between Britain and the U.S.S.R. signed on May 26 contained no secret protocol and no territorial provisions.

On less substantive matters Molotov could give Stalin more encouraging reports. Stalin's great fear had to be that within the Grand Alliance Britain and America would present a united front vis-à-vis Russia. And on this count Molotov could tell him that Roosevelt was very far from being under the sway of Churchill. Indeed the President had been eager for Molotov to visit Washington first, so that the Soviets would not enter into any deals with the British—which is precisely why the Soviet leader insisted on seeing Churchill before setting off across the ocean. Once in America, Molotov was treated to some of the President's ideas on the postwar world. What made Roosevelt so expansive with his Russian guest? First, he was acting in line with his stated belief: you make people trust you by showing trust in them. Then he was eager to prove to the Russians that he and Churchill were not going to gang up on them. And so he confided to Molotov, who had a long experience as an attentive listener, his anti-imperialist ideas. "There were all over the world many islands and colonial possessions which ought for our own safety to be taken away from weak nations."[48] Among the "weak nations" the President evidently included not only France, the Netherlands, etc., but Britain, for some of Britain's Asian possessions would also have to be "internationalized." What would Stalin think of the idea? Molotov believed that the "President's trusteeship principle would be well received in Moscow." He might have added that Stalin was a great believer in taking "possessions," and never mind whether "islands" or "colonies" or something else, from "weak nations."

[48] Sherwood, p. 572.

For the moment there were more pressing worries. Stalin was not at his diplomatic best when in August Churchill alighted in Moscow to "meet the great Revolutionary chief and profound Russian warrior and statesman with whom for the next three years I was to be in intimate, vigorous, but always exciting and at times even genial association."[49] The message the Prime Minister brought with him, though anticipated, still had to be infuriating: there would be no second front in 1942. In the fall the Allies proposed to land in French North Africa, from the Soviet point of view a piddling operation not likely to help them at all.

During their first conference, Stalin took the bad news calmly and even showed great interest in the proposed North African venture. But the next day, August 13, when he saw the Prime Minister at 11 P.M. his behavior was so different as to baffle Churchill. The dictator was cutting and insulting: Were British soldiers afraid to fight the Germans? He was insistent that the second front be established forthwith. Churchill attributed this change of mood to "his council of Commissars [who] did not take the news I brought as well as he did." But we now know the real answer: Stalin had spent the whole day presiding over a meeting of Stavka—the High Command—that sought ways to alleviate the catastrophic military situation in the south. The German offensive had by now in some places pushed the Red Army back three hundred miles. It was decided, without too much faith, that it would be possible to try to stop the Wehrmacht on the Volga at Stalingrad. One had to assume the probability of the enemy's reaching Baku and destroying, if not seizing, the vital oil wells. Several army commanders were dismissed on grounds of incompetence or nervous exhaustion. After a session like that it is no wonder Stalin was in no mood for polite conversation with a man who was in his eyes reneging on the pledge to help the Red Army in the moment of its extreme danger.[50]

It says much for his self-control that the next day Stalin recovered his composure and became a genial host. He was now eager to make amends for his behavior and to mollify Churchill. The Prime Minister responded to his mood: at the dinner he observed that Molotov on his American trip took a day off for a private visit to New York.[51] The Prime Minister noted that Molotov took this jocular remark and implication of private misbehavior rather seriously. Stalin was equal to the

---

[49] Winston L. S. Churchill, *The Hinge of Fate* (Boston, 1950), p. 477.

[50] The story of the High Command session is in Marshal A. Yeremenko, *Stalingrad: Notes of the Front Commander* (Moscow, 1961), p. 87.

[51] Much as he trusted his servant, the dictator, of course, had not let him go on his Western excursion completely unchaperoned. Molotov was accompanied by *Stalin's* personal interpreter, even though the Soviet ambassadors in London and Washington were perfectly fluent in English.

occasion: no, Molotov did not go to New York; he went to Chicago to see his fellow gangsters!

Once in command of himself, the dictator knew how to charm the people whose good will was important to him. What would impress the Englishman most? Why, to see how this mysterious potentate actually lived. When the Prime Minister bade him goodbye, the night before his departure, Stalin suddenly proposed that they go over to his place and have a few drinks. Thus Churchill saw Stalin's private quarters—"of moderate size, simple, dignified." Soon an impressive array of hors d'oeuvres was laid down while Stalin busied himself uncorking various bottles. And Svetlana made her appearance, completing the picture of a simple, hospitable family. This led to a discussion of Churchill's family and a demonstration of fatherly warmth on the part of Stalin toward his daughter. The Prime Minister believed that Stalin's invitation had come on the spur of the moment, and that the touching domestic scene he witnessed was a daily occurrence. He would have been disappointed to learn that Svetlana had been summoned in the morning from Stalin's villa where she lived and that the whole affair had been carefully planned in advance.[52] In his mellow mood, Churchill even "bought" Stalin's explanation of collectivization: ". . . very bad and difficult—but necessary." One could not argue with the kulaks and hence the majority of them "were very unpopular and were wiped out by their labourers."[53] The Prime Minister left Moscow feeling one could really get to like this man. If only the mysterious commissars did not have such a baleful influence on Stalin's moods. . . .

Within three months Stalin's mood improved markedly, though not in the direction of greater cordiality toward his allies. The fall of 1942 was—for once the trite phrase is here precisely accurate—the turning point of the war. From being on the offensive all over the world, the forces of the Axis were thrown into retreat. By the beginning of 1943 there was no more questioning whether the Grand Alliance would win decisively, but only when. One word epitomized the changed situation and mood: Stalingrad. The Soviet victory, in fact three separate victories connected with the famous city, overshadowed even the great successes of the Allies—the American victories in the Pacific, the landing in North Africa, even the defeat of Rommel's legions at El Alamein. And it was Stalin, the desperate pleader for help of the summer of 1942, who in the winter of 1943 stood as the colossus of the Grand Alliance, having scored the greatest triumph of all: his armies broke the spine of the Wehrmacht, and the once most fearsome military machine in history was now great only in retreat, in its ability to postpone the inevitable retribution for two years.

[52] Alliluyeva, p. 161.
[53] Churchill, p. 498.

At this point fortune's favoritism toward the bloodstained tyrant becomes positively reprehensible. Why was it that of all the galaxy of Soviet cities it was the one bearing Stalin's name that became the synonym of the Russian soldier's heroism, the scene of Germany's greatest defeat and utmost humiliation—for the first time in history a whole German army, commanded by a field marshal, was taken into captivity? Why was it that the Russian soldier fought for Stalingrad as he had not fought for Kiev, Kharkov, or Smolensk? And it was Stalingrad where the Germans committed their most glaring strategic and tactical blunders. And of course the local Soviet commander happened to be the most intrepid of all Russian generals, one of the few with enough resolution and fortitude to deny the ruins of the city to the enemy. It would be unreasonable to attribute these near miracles to the magic of Stalin's name, except perhaps that it hypnotized Hitler and his generals and made them persist in storming the city in the face of the growing probability of a military disaster.

The Germans' fascination with Stalingrad in late summer made them neglect the primary objective of their offensive, which until then had been the Caucasus. Politically as well as militarily, this was a major folly on the Germans' part and quite lucky for the Soviets. For geographic reasons, Soviet forces in the Caucasus could not have been easily or substantially reinforced had the Germans aimed their main blow there. Incredibly enough, the commander of the northern Caucasus front in the summer of 1942 was none other than old Marshal Budenny, and it is probably fortunate that his generalship was not put to yet another test. There was also another and major weakness in the Soviet military posture in the area: since this was a satrapy of Beria's, the defense of the Caucasus was largely in the hands of NKVD troops whose generals insisted on having their separate chain of command and cooperated but badly with the regular army.[54]

Equally troublesome in the Soviet perspective for the defense of the Caucasus was the attitude of the local population. In the non-Russian region of the northern Caucasus, collaboration with the Germans was probably more widespread than in any other occupied area.[55] It is quite possible that the Germans would have been welcome at least initially among the nations of Transcaucasia, even in the homeland of the

---

[54] Just as Himmler had his SS divisions, so did Beria have his own and sizable army.

[55] This was due in part to the German army's keeping the civil administration in its own hands and the population's thus being preserved from the horrors perpetrated elsewhere by the SS security detachments. After the Soviet reconquest the population of the northern Caucasus was to pay a fearful price for the incidents of collaboration with the invader. Whole nations were deported from the area and resettled in distant parts of Soviet Asia. The same mass repression and deportation were applied to Crimean Tatars and Volga Germans.

dictator.[56] But with the increased concentration of the Wehrmacht's manpower and equipment in the direction of Stalingrad, those tantalizing Caucasian opportunities were never exploited.

The city where Stalin had first made his name as a ruthless war leader and which from the early 1920s bore his name was by 1942 an important industrial center with a peacetime population of about 450,000. With the German approach, civilians were evacuated and the new Soviet commander in the area, General Yeremenko, decided, not without misgivings (his predecessor was dismissed after only twenty-one days in command) to try to defend the city. Success in that enterprise appeared dubious. Stalingrad stretched like a long thin ribbon along the western bank of the Volga, without any natural or artificial defenses, except from the east. By the end of August Stalingrad was already more of a ruin than a city; most of its wooden buildings had burned in the course of almost uninterrupted bombing by the Luftwaffe.

The main German force thrown against the city of Stalin was the ill-fated Sixth Army of General Frederick Paulus. Not having succeeded in seizing Stalingrad before its defense could be prepared, the indicated course for Paulus would have been to invest the city on three sides and to shell and bomb the river crossings, its only supply route, and link with the bulk of Soviet armies and supplies. But the German offensive was already behind schedule—Stalingrad was supposed to have fallen by the end of July—and a siege might be a prolonged business (Leningrad was to endure more than two years of an almost complete German blockade). There was no one to give Paulus precise instructions; the German High Command was in disarray: Hitler was again sacking generals right and left. And so the unfortunate commander decided to take the city by a frontal assault. By the middle of September the Germans controlled half of the city, but in the remaining two months of attacks and street fighting they did not manage to throw the Russian defenders into the Volga.

Paulus might have succeeded, though at an exorbitant price, except for the personality of the man who barred his way. On September 12 General Vassily Chuykov assumed command of the Sixty-second Army, charged with the defense of the city. His predecessor, General Anton Lopatin, who in other Soviet accounts is represented as a brave and resourceful soldier, was according to Chuykov at the end of his nervous endurance, convinced that Stalingrad must fall.[57] The artillery, tank, and communications commanders of the Sixty-second Army fled under various pretenses to the left, "safe" bank of the Volga. Chuykov and his chief of staff, Nicholas Krylov (both future marshals), pledged that they

[56] *Prolonged* experience with the German occupation invariably led to strong anti-German feelings.
[57] Chuykov, p. 112.

would stay and, if need be, die on the right bank. Their command post was never more than a few hundred yards from the enemy position, and was frequently under direct artillery fire.

Inspired by their commanders, the Soviet soldiers fought as they had never fought before. This was not field fighting, in which German tank columns would isolate groups of Soviet infantry who were then bombed by the Luftwaffe. In street and house-to-house fighting, superiority in tanks and planes was at a discount, the Soviet infantryman's tenacity at its premium. Repeated German attacks yielded only yards at the price of huge casualties. The city was turned into a sea of rubble, with islands of half-ruined stone and brick buildings inside which fighting continued for days on end, but all this reduced still further the advantage the Wehrmacht enjoyed in armor and planes. Constant replacements kept depleting German manpower and supplies at other fronts. Some 300,000 German soldiers and the strongest air fleet were immobilized before and in the ruins of Stalingrad, and by the beginning of November it was obvious that their exertions have been in vain; they would not be able to seize the mile and a half or so separating them from the great river.

On November 8 Hitler had to come down a notch from his previous assurance that the city bearing the name of his rival had been virtually conquered. "What we have we shall hold," he told his anguished people, for whom yet another series of glorious victories had turned to ashes. A much better prophecy was contained in Stalin's Order of the Day on November 7: "Some day, soon, there will be a parade on our street." To his listeners this Russian saying conveyed the promise that the period of the Red Army's being on the defensive was drawing to an end.

On November 19 the armies of three Russian "fronts" of Rokossovsky, Yeremenko, and Vatutin struck at the weak flanks of the German group between the Volga and the Don. Within a week the Sixth and parts of the Fourth Panzer armies had been encircled. The besieger had become besieged. There followed two and a half months of agony—in its way also heroic—of the surrounded German troops. Hitler would not sanction an attempted breakthrough by Paulus when it still seemed feasible. Such a maneuver, even if successful, could have led to the German army group's in the northern Caucasus being in its turn cut off. But the main reason was that Hitler's obsession with Stalingrad took a new form: if it was not to be the scene of a decisive victory, then it had to become the stage of a Wagnerian *Götterdämmerung*. The Sixth Army, if it could not hold out, was from its commander-in-chief to the last soldier to lay down its life for the Führer and Germany. And so in January, when the Russians threw overwhelming forces against the half-starving, unsupplied, and exhausted remnants of what had been Germany's most powerful army, Hitler would not hear of capitulation. And, in his own mind, he made quite sure that no such disgrace would take place by raising Paulus to the rank of field marshal. A German marshal letting himself be captured alive or surrendering his army—unheard of and inconceivable. The very next day, January 31, Field Marshal Paulus, bedraggled, his hands shaking, and suffering from a nervous tic, was interviewed by his captors. On February 1 the remaining German pockets of resistance were wiped out or they surrendered. Upward of 100,000 soldiers were herded into captivity. This was the third and final victory of Stalingrad, the war's greatest and most decisive victory for Stalin.

The outcome brought out vividly how strong the Russians' sense of military inferiority vis-à-vis the Germans had been until then. The Red Army men literally danced in the streets after hearing the news that a field marshal and twenty generals had been taken prisoner. Until then no German officer of that rank had fallen into Russian hands. February 1, 1943, was a day of rebirth for the Red Army: Russia in her own estimate had succeeded to the military laurels once held by France and then by Germany as the possessor of the most formidable fighting machine in the world.

Stalin was quick to appropriate to himself a considerable share of this new military glory and symbolism. He now made himself a Marshal of the Soviet Union, and to the end of his days he wore a marshal's uniform. To his title of Supreme Commander was added the redundant and, to the Russian ear, odd-sounding "Generalissimo." There was a profusion of new decorations: Orders of Suvorov, of Kutuzov, the highest one—of Victory—set in diamonds, *two* of which the modest dictator bestowed on himself. For the traditionalists in the Red Army the most startling innovation was the institution of shoulder tabs and epaulets for the general officers: they were evocative of the military atmosphere of Tsarist times. Returning to Moscow from the Stalingrad battlefield, Marshal Voronov thought for a minute that he was hallucinating: all around him at the airport were figures costumed like grand dukes and adjutant generals of yore—the new uniforms had just been introduced.[58]

Stalingrad wrought a subtle change in Stalin's attitude toward his generals. He became more relaxed and benign in dealing with them, obviously pleased to be associated with them. They in turn were loaded with honors: medals that covered the warriors' tunics down to their navels, laudatory mentions in the Orders of the Day, and, for those who had fallen on the field of honor, statues in their native cities and generous pensions for their families. There was, most important of all,

[58] At the height of the battle Voronov received the message that he had been elevated to Marshal of Artillery, and would *he* design an appropriate uniform?

more new respect for their professional and human dignity. In dealing with his senior commanders, Stalin no longer barked out orders or cut short objections or arguments. "Think it over," he would suggest when his operational suggestions were disputed by Zhukov or Rokossovsky. "Would it please you," he would ask, to have X as chief of staff or an army commander, and sometimes he honored their refusals.

But gratitude and honors were not accompanied by trust. The structure of command and decisionmaking in the Soviet army remained bizarre, and one cannot help feeling that it must have hampered the efficiency of the army even during its period of victories and advance. Imagine that General Eisenhower in command in Europe had a political figure, say Harry Hopkins, continually at his elbow; that not content with having a political watchdog over the general, Roosevelt from time to time sent the Chairman of the Democratic National Committee to his headquarters; that the American or British chief of staff and his deputy dropped in on him and kibitzed on his every major decision; and finally that in the midst of a military operation Eisenhower was summoned to Washington to report in person. These were conditions in which the major Soviet commanders had to operate, and there is no wonder that some of them broke under the strain. A front's commander would have a Party figure as a member of his military council. Thus at Stalingrad Yeremenko was chaperoned by Khrushchev. But what if the general and the commissar got too chummy? Malenkov would be dispatched to check on their doings and report back to the Boss. An important victory obviously should not become in the army's or the public's mind associated with the name of a single general. Moscow and Zhukov remained so linked, but whom can history call the victor of the November and January battles of Stalingrad? To be sure, Rokossovsky was in overall field command. But Zhukov, Vasilevsky, and Voronov were at various times overseeing his plans and operations. An *occasional* inspection trip by a representative of the High Command was of course the practice in every belligerent's army, but nowhere else were field commanders so closely and continuously, obviously wastefully, supervised as in the Red Army. Even some of the Stavka's emissaries were sent out for nonmilitary reasons: Budenny and Voroshilov continued to be employed in this capacity even after they had been judged unfit to hold field commands and when their opinions on military matters could not be taken seriously.[59]

[59] On one such trip to the Crimean front Voroshilov astounded his staff and threw it into a panic by insisting they all should carry out the inspection on horseback. No arguments as to waste of time, enhanced danger, or even inability to ride could persuade the old warrior to avail himself of the automobile. (Sergei Shtemenko, *The General Staff* [Moscow, 1968], p. 214.) Though himself not a horseman, Stalin had a weak spot for cavalry. He was persuaded only with difficulty that in the conditions

578

In addition to his suspicion and envy, Russia's commanders suffered from their leader's restlessness. All plans would be virtually almost perfected, the battle was about to start, and the general would be summoned to report in the Kremlin in person. This often meant taking off and landing in the midst of a snowstorm with Russian fliers navigating "by the seats of their pants," only to report what could perfectly well have been said on the phone. It was of course inconceivable that *Stalin* should expose himself to the danger of wartime travel and front-line inspections, as Zhukov or Vasilevsky were constantly called upon to do. But could one deprive the people, or future generations, of the legend and picture of Stalin at the front? A sensible compromise was agreed upon between those two imperatives: Stalin would go *toward* the front. One August day in 1943 Marshal Voronov was summoned from the front to an urgent conference well to the rear. During the long and dusty ride Voronov inwardly cursed whoever was responsible for the inopportune interruption of his work. Arriving at the destined location, he was amazed to encounter Stalin. The cabin where their interview took place was transformed: its usual furniture had been removed and replaced by rough-hewn chairs and table and a field telephone. All the necessary ingredients for the picture: "Comrade Stalin listening to a report in a front-line command post."[60] There were even more fraudulent posters and pictures, e.g., Stalin on the edge of the forest observing a Russian attack on the German lines.

The interlocking system of political controls—or, to put it bluntly, of spying on the officers—existed at all levels of the military hierarchy. The restoration of the principle of unitary command diminished but did not abolish the authority of the commissars. Quite apart from them, there was a special department of the political administration, known to the readers of Ian Fleming's James Bond stories as Smersh, which dealt not only with alleged spies and deserters but also with those suspected of harboring disloyal thoughts. There were also "unofficial" informers. A Soviet novel mentions a general who upon discovering that his aide kept a meticulous chronicle of events and conversations in his headquarters was about to chase him out as a spy until the young man convinced him that he kept a diary as the basis for a future war novel. During lulls in the fighting, Marshal Voronov and a fellow commander would while away their evenings in conversation (over, he assures us, a cup of tea!); "What are you and Sokolovsky doing drinking tea together all the time?" were the first words of his watchful and well-informed Supreme Commander when Voronov went to see him on returning to Moscow.

---

of modern warfare it would be foolish to have a separate horse army on the order of his beloved First Cavalry Army of the Civil War.

[60] N. Voronov, *On War Service* (Moscow, 1963), p. 385.

It is unlikely that following Stalingrad the dictator could still feel politically threatened. The generals, like everyone else, had to be watched, but for the moment one did not have to worry unduly. The winter of 1942–43 signified a decisive victory for Soviet power as well as for Russia. There were some military setbacks in 1943, but by then Germany had lost the power to sustain an offensive on the order of the one in 1942 not to mention that in 1941. There remained worrisome problems of internal politics, and a staggering economic problem: to rebuild Russian industry and agriculture from the ruins of war. But for the man for whom power was the key to economics and politics alike, the center of gravity now shifted to the problem of Russia's international position. From being a struggle for Russia's life, for Soviet power and his own power, the war in February 1943 shifted to being one for Russia's place in the world, for his own power to determine the shape of peace and of the postwar world.

How far would he be able to do that? America would emerge from the war as incomparably the world's greatest power. Fortunately, the Americans did not appear to realize their own strength. The British Empire, for years the object of awe and fear, no longer seemed such a colossus. Even before the war, this aggregation of nations and colonies was on the point of breaking up and now Britain was bound to emerge poor if not bankrupt, dependent on American help. But the British were wily. Churchill obviously dreamed of a combination of Britain's agelong experience in managing the world's affairs with America's resources, and thus keeping Russia from assuming her rightful place in Europe and the world. But Stalin had ample experience of being isolated within an alliance and yet in the end prevailing over his partners. To be sure, Churchill and Roosevelt could not quite be compared with Zinoviev and Kamenev. The British would try all sorts of tricks: perhaps a new *cordon sanitaire* of small East European states, perhaps even using the post-Hitler Germany as the counterweight to Russia.

There was Asia. Incomprehensibly, the Americans seemed to think that China could become or—they never distinguished between wishes and reality—already was a world power. Soviet advisers who had been with the Nationalist regime since 1937 told a different story: Chiang's government was as far from being an efficient totalitarian regime as it was from being a Jeffersonian democracy, the latter image being the one used by Chiang's more unrestrained American partisans. China's army was in fact a conglomeration of various warlords, with the Generalissimo just in nominal control. The Chinese Communists might come in handy to offset what otherwise promised to become the preponderant American influence in the world's most populous country.

And, though he was at the most intense phase of his thinking of himself as Russia's national leader, Stalin neither forgot nor scorned to use Marxism-Leninism. All over the world Communists could now combine their devotion to him and the Soviet Union with their own nationalism. More properly, they could combine their loyalty and fervor for *both* their countries, their native one and the land of Soviets. June 22, 1941, had freed them from the secret doubts and humiliations over the Soviet-German collaboration. All over occupied Europe Communists used to clandestine operations now often were the mainstay of the Resistance. All the old tortuous debates, the hunting for Trotskyites and Bukharinites, were forgotten. Here was another solid asset for the future. It was amazing how these foreign Communists, to whom in the last few years Stalin had paid so little attention, worshiped him. In Yugoslavia the Partisan movement was headed by one Josip Broz-Tito. Stalin had never met Tito and perhaps this was lucky, for Tito might have been liquidated as were all other members of the Yugoslav Central Committee unfortunate enough to find themselves in Moscow in 1937. And now this once obscure Communist official was leading the Partisans in an effective struggle against the Germans; his loyalty to Stalin and the Soviets was great, in fact embarrassingly so. It was perhaps awkward that they were so *obviously* Communist, protesting their faith in Stalin at every opportunity. The Chinese Communists were more sophisticated in this respect. They kept up a makeshift arrangement with the Nationalists, though not without occasional clashes. They did not itch to tell the world how much they loved Soviet Russia and Comrade Stalin. (As a matter of fact, their restraint on this count, though desirable at the moment, was suspicious.)

As against these opportunities beckoning all over the world, there was growing uncertainty about the United States. Long, long before, Stalin had written about the American federal system, issued instructions on how the American Communists should exploit the Negro question. And by 1943 Lend-Lease supplies were reaching the U.S.S.R. on a massive scale. Words like "Willys" (the almost invariable vehicle of conveyance for Soviet officers behind the front line), "pickup," "antifreeze" had become domiciled in Russian. But for Stalin the country was still, to paraphrase Churchill about Russia, a puzzle within an enigma. Would Americans after the war again pull back from world affairs? Would Roosevelt succumb to Churchill's blandishments and try to contain Russia? It was hard to reconcile America's economic power with her reluctance to play an imperial role. It was also puzzling to see how eager President Roosevelt appeared to be to build yet another international organization in the wake of the defunct League of Nations. All in all, the American approach toward problems of war and peace offered interesting possibilities for Soviet diplomacy. ✩✩✩

BEFORE following Stalin in his intricate diplomatic game, we get a brief glimpse of him as an irate old-fashioned father. To those of a sentimental turn of mind, it must be encouraging to know that the man who instantly knew what one general said to another over a glass of vodka could be kept in the dark for several months about what his own daughter was doing, that the grim walls and checkpoints of the Kremlin could not keep love from stealing in. Stalin's feelings toward Svetlana were of normal fatherly warmth. Reading letters that he exchanged with his daughter when she was a child and then a young girl, it is startling to reflect that on many a day when he scribbled some chaffingly affectionate note to Svetlana he also read and approved one of Yezhov's or Beria's lists with its invariable postscript: "Special measures to be taken in regard to the wives and children of the people's enemies named above."

Svetlana sought a release from the depressing atmosphere of war and her father's household in an innocent romance (could it be otherwise with a bodyguard always present?) with a much older man, a film director and script writer. She had encountered him, she tells us, at one of Vassily's parties, for which, somewhat in a manner of a young prince, he liked to commandeer figures from the artistic and sports worlds.[61] For about three months the middle-aged suitor managed to "fool Comrade Stalin," i.e., occasionally to squire his daughter on walks, to movies and to the theater. When she could not see him, Svetlana, in the manner of teen-agers all over the world, talked to him on the phone "for not less than an hour."

The dangerous idyll could have had only one conclusion. Even among Stalin's bodyguard there were some whose hearts melted at this romance and who warned the reckless swain to get as far out of Moscow as soon as possible. But the prospect of a penal battalion at the front or worse finally prevailed over their discretion. On March 3, 1943, the "greatest genius of our times" became a very ordinary father. Except that unlike most fathers in this melodramatic situation, he really did know all, for as he burst upon his daughter and demanded her beloved's literary compositions, which the man had imprudently entrusted to Svetlana, Stalin's pockets were bulging with transcripts of the telephone conversations and with detailed accounts of the sinful walks. Stalin, who never raised his voice in conversation, even when consigning men to their doom, now yelled and screamed and slapped his daughter. What infuriated him most was that Svetlana's suitor, Alexis Kapler, was a Jew. One

---

[61] Alliluyeva, pp. 163–64.

of Stalin's more innocent delusions was that he was a master of Russian prose, and now, as he scrutinized Kapler's writings before throwing them into the wastebasket, he pronounced him an illiterate. "You could not find yourself a Russian!" he kept repeating to his stunned daughter.

It was not, however, on the charge of doing injury to the Russian language that Kapler was sentenced to five years of "free" exile in the north. He was, Stalin triumphantly announced to Svetlana, unmasked as an English spy. This throws an interesting light on Stalin's definition of a spy—Kapler, like most members of the journalistic and artistic crowd, was encouraged to have occasional drinks with foreign correspondents. In view of what might have been expected, his punishment was rather lenient. But in 1948 when the poor man, having been released from "free" exile, violated the prohibition against visiting Moscow, he was dealt five years at hard labor. When this sentence drew to a close, he petitioned to be allowed to resume the life of an exile in the north, but instead he went back to an NKVD jail. Then Stalin died and in July 1953 freedom came to Kapler, as to countless other innocent victims; he was allowed to go and live anywhere, even in Moscow.[62] ☆☆☆

A T the same time as this domestic drama was taking place within the precincts of the Kremlin, the discovery of a vast tragedy enabled Stalin to complete his first move toward the future control of Eastern Europe. In the spring of 1943 the Germans uncovered in the Katyn Forest near Smolensk a mass grave of Polish officers. It was claimed by the Germans, and all the impartial evidence since then has supported their contention, that these were corpses of some of the 15,000 Polish officers who had been in Soviet camps until April 1940 and about whose subsequent fate the Soviets, when questioned by the Polish government, had professed ignorance. The Poles now requested that the International Red Cross investigate the charges. The Soviet government indignantly denied the implication that the Polish officers had been disposed of by the NKVD, and blamed the murders on the Germans.

The Russians now had a rare opportunity to do what they had planned for some time: to break off relations with the Polish government-in-exile. They denounced the "London Poles," as henceforth they would be called, as a bunch of reactionaries who in their hatred of Russia lent themselves to the purposes of German propaganda. Few in

[62] *Ibid.*, p. 171.

the West were ready to believe that their heroic Russian allies had been capable of such a crime, and those who did, like Churchill, felt they had to keep silent. To Ambassador Maisky, who brought him Stalin's indignant message about the Poles, the Prime Minister said, "We have got to beat Hitler and this is no time for quarrels and charges."[63]

The Soviets now had a bridgehead on the Polish issue: if the Polish government wanted to be recognized again, it would have not only to repudiate the infamous charges but to agree to the 1939 Soviet territorial gains at the expense of Poland. This bridgehead would be enlarged as the war went on; in the end it was Soviet diplomacy as much as the Red Army that conquered *all* of Poland.

The enemy was still deep in Soviet territory, but in 1943 Stalin was already accumulating counters with which he would gamble for Russia's postwar position. In March there emerged in Moscow the Union of Polish Patriots, this to offset the pro-West "London Poles."[64] If the latter would behave and grant his demands, then the Union would vanish overnight; if not, it would provide the nucleus of the future pro-Communist government of Poland.

In July there was another hedge against the future: the Free German Committee was set up. Now this did have *some* Communists among its founders, but its personnel included aristocratic German officers and even generals captured during the war. Its program for a free democratic postwar Germany eschewed any Communist rhetoric, and its official flag was that of Imperial Germany. It is unlikely that Stalin suspected the Allies of harboring dark designs to make a separate peace with Hitler, but there was always the possibility (which almost materialized in July 1944) of German generals and bureaucrats overthrowing the Nazis and pleading for peace before the Soviet armies reached the territory of the Reich. Would London and Paris really refuse such an offer, which might enable them to keep Soviet power and Communism away from the heart of Europe? Stalin had his own respectable and democratic Germans just in case.

One did not have to be too explicit about what one proposed to do with the enemy once one beat him. Privately Stalin must have shaken his head when he read that Roosevelt and Churchill proclaimed that they would accept only an unconditional surrender on the part of the Axis powers, though of course this suited his designs. Even at the height of Russia's danger, Stalin wisely avoided appeals to national hatred. In contrast to the many intemperate utterances in the West, he sought to draw a distinction between Nazism and Germany. "The experience of

---

[63] Churchill, p. 761.
[64] It is fair to add that many in the Union were not Communists, but believed that the new realities of international life forced Poland to seek an accommodation with Moscow.

history shows that Hitlers come and go but the German nation, the German state remains."[65] It was good propaganda and common sense as far as Germany's postwar fate was concerned, and both were currently in short supply in London and Washington.

Propaganda reasons and common sense dictated another Soviet move. In May 1943 the Comintern was told to dissolve itself; needless to say, this body of Soviet pensioners complied with the request. Communists might be expected to be postwar contenders for governments such as Yugoslavia and France, and it was essential to remove the handicap and stigma of the accusation that they were Moscow's agents.

War was increasingly seen through the spectrum of Stalin's postwar plans and needs. And thus with the second front. In his view the British reneged once more on a real second front. Instead of invading France, they landed in Italy. It was fairly clear that Churchill wanted to put the Anglo-American armies in the Balkans and Central Europe, which Stalin had already marked out for his own. Following the meeting in Casablanca with Roosevelt, Churchill traveled to Turkey. Stalin inquired directly what the Prime Minister was doing in that neutral country and equally directly let him know that he was up to his tricks: "I have no objection to your making a statement that I was kept informed on the Anglo-Turkish meeting, though I cannot say the information was very full."[66]

In fact, the Allied invasion of Italy *did* help Russia's war effort. Mussolini, "Hitler's tattered lackey" in Churchill's immortal jibe, fell. When Hitler felt constrained to send additional divisions to Italy, he weakened his forces in the east at the crucial moment in July 1943 at the great battle of Kursk, the last great offensive effort against the Russians. And so Germany lost the greatest tank battle in history.

The Soviet's advance and reconquest of their land was still agonizingly slow. In fact, to give them their due, the German armies' ability to retreat in good order surpasses as a military feat their previous victories. All the hope of victory had gone, the news from home was of continuous massive Allied air raids, defeat followed defeat. In such conditions most other armies would have turned into fleeing rabble; yet the German soldiers fought stubbornly and skillfully all the way back to Berlin.

That the Red Army did not exploit its opportunities better and faster must also be ascribed to defects in its command structure and organization. If Hitler harmed his armies by insisting that they stand their ground elsewhere, rather than shortening their defense lines and applying a flexible defense, then Stalin hobbled his generals by ordering them to attack all along the retreating German front rather than employing

---

[65] In his Order of the Day, February 23, 1942, in Stalin (Stanford ed.), II, 42.
[66] Churchill, p. 710.

the tactics of localized breakthrough and encirclement that had brought such a dazzling success in November 1942. The cumbersome structure of Military Councils and Stavka delegates, the constant shifts of army commanders, had a woeful effect on the latters' initiative and judgment. Most Soviet military memoirs exude an air of amiable unrealism. If one believes a typical account of a meeting between two generals, say, it would begin by their falling into each other's arms and reminiscing about the happy times they had as classmates at the General Staff Academy (this at a time when many of their instructors and fellow students were disappearing one by one, with no questions asked). "Vanya, can you push Fritz[67] out of city X?" the superior would ask. "Glad to try, old chap," the local commander would answer. In fact, as can be gleaned from the few realistic accounts, the dialogue was more often as follows: "Ivan Ivanovich, he himself has called. You are to take the fortified position by noon tomorrow, or it will go hard on you." "Yes, sir, Comrade Army General." The same harshness and brutality prevailed all down the line. Officers who through no fault of their own could not complete their assignments would be stripped of their rank, sometimes reassigned to penal battalions sent straight into enemy fire. At the slightest suspicion of cowardice or nonobedience soldiers were also sent there, if not shot outright.

Stalin kept a tight rein on military operations, and though he now deferred to opinions of Zhukov and Vasilevsky, they were kept so busy with flying trips to the fronts and field commands that it was probably difficult for them to have an overall view, especially as political considerations increasingly affected military decisions. The actual chief of staff after December 1942 was General Alexis Antonov, who was formally installed in the office when Vasilevsky was appointed to command a "front." (Antonov, a man of unusual ability, must have incurred Stalin's displeasure, since he was never promoted to marshal.) He and his closest collaborators had to endure an incredible regimen—a working day of seventeen to eighteen hours; nightly reports in person to the Supreme Commander. More considerate than before, Stalin still pulled up his subordinates, sometimes for very minor details: a city announced as having been taken some hours before it actually was, an army commander's name skipped in an Order of the Day. This partly reflected his nervous despotic temper, but it was also deliberate: they must never grow lax or unafraid; they must always know who was boss. Yet this frantic pace and the nervous tension in Supreme Headquarters could hardly contribute to their efficiency. ☆☆☆

[67] The common sobriquet for the Germans.

I N November 1943 Stalin set out for what was to be the scene of *his* greatest victory of the war: Teheran. What Stalingrad had been militarily, Teheran was diplomatically. And it was also Stalin's first meeting with the man in whose hands, if he chose to exercise it, lay the preponderant power to shape the postwar world: President Roosevelt.

Modern technology made it possible, and the realities of the Grand Alliance made it imperative, that the great issues of war and peace be decided in person by the three Allied heads of government. So, though Roosevelt was a cripple, Churchill nervous about flying, and Stalin nervous about leaving his country, the Big Three had to get together. Courtesy would have called for a meeting on American soil, in deference to the President's infirmity and his status as chief of state. But Stalin would go only where he could count on the reassuring presence of the NKVD. The farthest he would agree to go was Teheran, then under joint Soviet-British occupation.

This unprecedented trip "abroad" took place in such secrecy that his principal military adviser on it, General Sergei Shtemenko,[68] was not informed of the destination until the journey's last lap. From Moscow to Baku the party went by train, but from Baku there was no direct rail communication with the Iranian capital, and the commander-in-chief of the Soviet Air Force, Marshal Novikov, had to take time out from his pressing duties to arrange the momentous flight. There were two planes, he explained to the somewhat apprehensive Stalin, to take them to their destination. Stalin's would be piloted by a lieutenant general; the lesser mortals would go in one with a mere colonel at the controls. Stalin exhibited sensible preference for safety over pomp and circumstance: lieutenant generals did not get much practice flying, so he would go with the colonel. Escorted by three squadrons of fighters, both planes made a safe landing in Teheran.

The President was eager to work his famous charm on the mysterious dictator and to dissuade him from any notion he might have that he and Churchill were ganging up on the Russians. In a message on the eve of the conference, Roosevelt noted pointedly that the American legation, where he was supposed to stay, was some distance from the Soviet and British ones. How inconvenient for them to be so separated, how potentially dangerous to have to traverse the streets so often![69] The

---

[68] Chief, operations section, the General Staff. Voroshilov went along for show.
[69] *The Correspondence* . . . , II, 109.

Russians took the hint: Axis agents in Teheran, they announced, were up to no good; it would be safer for the President to stay in the Soviet compound. And thus it was in November 1943, for the first time in history, the President of the United States became a guest of the Union of Soviet Socialist Republics. (It is most unlikely that there were any hidden recording devices in Roosevelt's suite. Stalin would not jeopardize the great game he was playing for the sake of tidbits of trivial information.)

Stalin's eagerness to detach the President from any schemes Churchill and the British might devise to limit Russia's postwar role paralleled Roosevelt's keen desire to gain Stalin's trust. The President labored under no delusions that the Soviet Union was a democracy and Stalin a benign avuncular figure. But he believed that he could take the measure of, and conquer, Boss Stalin. More important, he believed that he *had to try*. The future of the world and avoidance of a third global conflict depended, Roosevelt believed, on building an effective United Nations. The American people would not enter or support such an organization unless the big powers showed that they could work together in it and forsake power politics. So he had to try to dissipate Soviet suspicions, their feeling that they would be isolated in the United Nations, that capitalists could never be trusted. The key was to win over Stalin. He was obviously more reasonable and willing to trust the Americans than the shadowy figures in the Politburo who, because of their lack of contact with the West and their diehard Communism, persisted in uncomprehending hatred of capitalism. It is unfair to accuse Roosevelt of naïveté on this score. He no more than Churchill or anyone else outside Russia realized the full extent of Stalin's omnipotence.

A French poet described his ideal woman as one "who is never quite the same, nor completely different." This is not a bad description for a master politician and diplomat. Which is what Stalin was in his encounters and dealings with his famous partners. As he had others, he impressed them by his simplicity, businesslike brevity of speech, toughness (which appeared to reflect self-confidence rather than inner fear), courtesy without obvious ingratiation. He could be shrewdly candid. He did not believe it was good psychology to *talk* so much about unconditional surrender by the Axis, he told the President; and he demurred from Roosevelt's enthusiasm for partitioning Germany into several states. At another point he was politely skeptical about the American vision of China as a great power.

And yet he was also different. Stalin, who seldom sat still during a meeting or while listening to a report, presented in the sessions with the two other arbiters of the world's fate a picture of statesmanlike calm and repose. It was Churchill who sprang from his seat to argue agitatedly. When, during the discussion of the future Soviet-Polish border,

Eden interjected that the Russian proposal conformed to the Molotov-Ribbentrop line, Stalin replied calmly, "Call it what you wish."

Who could divine in this dignified and self-possessed statesman the man who raved at and terrorized his subordinates, who scribbled on an appeal for mercy from a general "scoundrel and male whore"? In Teheran Churchill, on behalf of King George VI, presented the Russians with the Sword of Honor in commemoration of the heroic struggle of Stalingrad. As naturally as it might have come to a Tsar honored by an ally, "Stalin raised it in a most impressive gesture to his lips and kissed the blade." The Prime Minister, sensitive to the pathos of great historical occasions, had tears in his eyes.

No wonder that this masterful performance affected the course of history. In Roosevelt's mind the Teheran meeting implanted the conviction, a belief not eroded until the very last days of his life, that Stalin could and would be a loyal partner in building the free world of the future. Stalin also scored as negotiator. His insistence helped finally to nail down the date of the Allied invasion of France and defeated Churchill's last-minute attempts to schedule additional operations in the Mediterranean that might have diverted or postponed the second front, as well as put the Anglo-American armies in the Balkans ahead of the Russians. Stalin appealed to his partners' sense of fairness: the Russian people still bore the brunt of the war. He was intermittently forthright and sly in his prompting on the issue. How could his allies say that the invasion of France would definitely take place if they still had not designated the commander-in-chief for the enterprise? And he offered a hint that his generals would press for a separate peace with Germany[70] if the second front did not materialize in the spring: "It would be difficult for the Russians to carry on. . . . He feared a feeling of isolation might develop in the Red Army."[71]

On the key Polish issue, Soviet diplomacy scored an impressive breakthrough. Prior to Teheran there had been no real discussion among the Big Three of this thorny problem. But at Teheran the Soviets in effect got what they wanted; Yalta and Potsdam mostly sealed the deal. And the way the Polish problem was discussed in this distant Asian city determined much more than just the fate of Poland: it went far to shape postwar Eastern and Central Europe.

Churchill felt embarrassed and guilty. At the beginning of the conference he still hoped to convert Stalin to a deferment or modification of the second front—not because, as the Russians believed, he wanted the Red Army to bleed and hurt as long as possible, but because, like many Englishmen, he remembered the awful lesson of World War I, when

[70] The fear that the Russians might make such a peace was always and unreasonably in the back of the Western statesmen's mind.

[71] Winston L. S. Churchill, *Closing the Ring* (Boston, 1951), p. 380.

the flower of a generation had died on the battlefields of northern France. Perhaps if he propitiated Stalin about something else, he might tolerate a delay or change in the invasion of France. And so, "I suggested that we should discuss the Polish question. He agreed and invited me to begin."[72]

The dictator was a good listener; it fell to the Prime Minister to outline a solution to the Polish problem which the Russians could hardly have improved upon. Churchill proposed to "move Poland westward," i.e., granting the Soviet Union's territorial demands and compensating Poland with German territory up to the Oder River. Stalin must have been enormously pleased (possibly surprised) at thus being offered on a silver platter what the most powerful of Russia's rulers had not dared to dream of. He must also have been amused: "Stalin asked whether we thought he was going to swallow Poland up." He elicited from Churchill what was in fact the death sentence for the hapless Polish government-in-exile—the Big Three would solve the Polish question among themselves, and only later would they inform the Poles about it. The nature of the postwar Polish regime was not discussed, but Churchill's shamefaced account of the conversation makes it clear that he let Stalin understand that he could have his way in that respect too.

The resolution of the Polish question was bound to determine much of the German issue. It effectively barred any possibility of a "deal" by a post-Hitler regime with the Allies; no German group would voluntarily surrender large areas of ethnic Germany. And after the victory the millions of German refugees from the territories granted to Poland would throw the rest of Germany into economic chaos that would last for decades. It did not turn out that way, but in 1943 the chances of its happening looked overwhelming.

Stalin now had a bridgehead on the Polish issue, and he enlarged it throughout the conference, abandoning his previous restraint. The Soviet Union *had* to have its frontiers of 1941, "for they appeared to be ethnically the right ones," he insisted. And he became violently abusive about the "London Poles": "The Polish Government [in London] and their friends in Poland were in contact with the Germans. They killed the Partisans."[73] No objection was made by the Prime Minister or the President to this outrageous slander.

Roosevelt was pleased to let Churchill carry the ball (or rather to fumble it) on the Polish issue and obligingly explained to Stalin his reasons: there were quite a few American voters of Polish descent. Stalin was understanding: "Some propaganda work should be done among them."[74] (And during the coming year he showed Roosevelt how:

[72] *Ibid.*, p. 361.
[73] *Ibid.*, p. 395.
[74] Sherwood, p. 796.

Professor Oskar Lange, a distinguished economist from the University of Chicago, and Father Orlemanski, an obscure parish priest—both of Polish extraction—were invited to Russia amidst a blare of publicity. Stalin received them and assured them how fervently he desired a strong and independent Poland.) Roosevelt was at pains to assure Stalin that on many points America's views on the postwar world were closer to Russia's than to Britain's—or rather, Churchill's. The President said he believed that colonial peoples should be given independence, but this should not be discussed with Winston. He was so sensitive about India. "Stalin agreed that this was undoubtedly a sore subject."[75] Churchill, though not so outgoing, intimated in his private meetings with the dictator that the Americans, for all their great virtues, were childish when it came to subjects like territories, bases, etc. He and Stalin were of course realistic statesmen, but they should be careful not to offend the President's rather otherworldly idealism.

It was, however, in Roosevelt's presence that Churchill made a sly gambit to enlist Stalin as a fellow imperialist. Would Russia like a warm winter port? It was obviously unfair that "the Russian Empire, with its population of 200 million, should be denied during the winter months all effective access to the broad waters."[76] A fine idea, Stalin agreed, and asked immediately where this warm-water port might be—in the Dardanelles (at the expense of Turkey) or the Far East (at that of China)? Churchill was not prepared for such concreteness; did not Russia have Vladivostok in the Far East? Yes, said Stalin, but it is icebound in winter (a partial fib: Vladivostok is kept ice-free). Roosevelt tried to stop sinful conversation by observing that the Baltic Sea should be free to all nations' shipping. At this point the interpreter made a slip; Stalin thought the President had said that the Baltic *states* should be free. For once evidencing some heat, he declared "that the Baltic states had by an expression of will of the people voted to join the Soviet Union and that this question was not therefore one for discussion."[77] The mistranslation was rectified, and Stalin applauded the idea that the Baltic Sea should be open to ships of all nations and the Kiel Canal internationalized.

Churchill's uneasiness mounted. The climax of his unhappiness came one evening when Stalin proposed at the war's end to shoot 50,000 German officers, beginning with the General Staff. The Prime Minister exploded: this was barbarism that his government would never countenance. Roosevelt, not very happily, tried to be jocular, and suggested that only 49,000 should be executed. Churchill left the room, but in a

[75] *Ibid.*, p. 777.
[76] Churchill, *Closing the Ring*, p. 381.
[77] Sherwood, p. 782.

minute he was followed by Stalin and Molotov, who, grinning broadly, declared that this was all a big joke. The Prime Minister let himself be mollified. "Stalin has a very captivating manner when he chooses to use it," and he returned to the table. It did not occur to him to reflect that his genial host had no doubt shot or imprisoned more than 50,000 *Russian* officers.

Though he was accompanied to Teheran by Molotov, the burden not only of decisionmaking but of detailed negotiations was clearly Stalin's. He now appeared to have considerable confidence in his ability to handle the Western statesmen. In the course of 1943 Stalin replaced his ambassadors in London and Washington. Maisky and Litvinov were men with wide contacts and considerable expertise, but the voice of Soviet diplomacy had to grow a bit harsher; it would be better to have people in those posts who were formed in his school, who would not be tempted to let their British and American friends in on the changing mood of Soviet diplomacy. The replacements, Fyodor Gusev in London and Andrei Gromyko in Washington, were relatively junior officials with no foreign ties, and they had the cold manner of the "new Soviet man," much in contrast to the mercurial and cosmopolitan ways of their predecessors.[78]

There were other signs of Russia's growing confidence within the Grand Alliance and of her future role in Europe. At Teheran, the Western leaders believed, they had merely explored postwar plans and arrangements. But the East Europeans, though ignorant of what had been discussed and *almost* promised to Moscow there, saw the writing on the wall. In December 1943 President Beneš of the Czechoslovak government-in-exile traveled to Moscow. Previously his regime had been planning a Polish-Czech federation, but now, conscious of Soviet enmity toward the Polish exiles, he abjured such notions. In reward he got a treaty of alliance and friendship with the Soviet Union and the promise of Soviet support for the pre-Munich frontiers. Privately, he was told the U.S.S.R. might need some rectification of the northeastern frontiers of his country when the Red Army got there. And to be sure in 1945 the Soviet Union would claim and receive the Carpatho-Ukraine. And it would be helpful, it was also hinted, if his government contained the representatives of *all* the democratic forces in his country, i.e., some Communist and non-Communist friends of the U.S.S.R. The Czechs were ready to comply.

[78] George F. Kennan recounts a scene he witnessed at the Kremlin on the occasion of a diplomatic dinner in honor of Churchill during his 1944 visit to Moscow. Stalin was in high spirits as his eye spotted Gusev. "There are all sorts of people in this world," said the dictator. "Take Gusev: it is said he never smiles. But I believe he can. Come on, Gusev, let us see you smile." The Ambassador of the Union of Soviet Socialist Republics to the Court of St. James's got unsteadily to his feet and a sickly grin appeared on his face.

Russia's national leader now loomed as a giant on the international horizon. There was an ample paradox in the style of his leadership becoming more and more traditionalist and nationalistic, while at the same time his worship by foreign Communists grew ever more fervent. Dressed in a marshal's uniform, Stalin received leaders of the Russian Orthodox Church, commissioned a *Russian* National Anthem to replace the "Internationale," which until now had served this purpose.[79] At the same time his name was celebrated in songs of the Yugoslav Partisans, in poems of the French Resistance. It seemed absurd to suspect any threat to his absolute rule of the Soviet Union. Surely his inordinate thirst for adulation must have been satisfied by this apotheosis, his ferocious suspiciousness must have slackened, a feeling of gratitude and generosity must have tempered his harsh rule over his people—of whom so many, despite all he had done to them and to their families, went into battle to fight and die for their country and for Stalin.

But Stalin remained very much the same. With the war now going well, he did not relax his constant supervision of and interference with military affairs.

In the course of 1944 the Red Army dealt the enemy "ten Stalinist blows," as they came to be known in the Soviet military literature until 1956, liberated the still considerable Soviet territory the Germans held at the end of 1943, and chased the Germans home. The key Soviet offensive in the summer phase of the fighting was the attack by the First Byelorussian Army Group. In twelve days they had advanced a hundred miles and inflicted more than 100,000 casualties on the enemy.

During the planning of the operation in April–May, Marshal Rokossovsky, its commander, decided that the directive of the Supreme Headquarters which envisaged a single massive attack and breakthrough was unsound. The nature of the terrain and the dispositon of the enemy forces made it advisable to attack en masse in two separate locations: the Germans would not be able to shift their reserves easily; the cost in Soviet lives would be much lower. Rokossovsky's proposal aroused strong opposition within the General Staff. Reasons were adduced that would have done credit to those Austrian generals who claimed that Napoleon's successes were due to his ignorance of the art of war and his flouting of the wise principles on which that art had solidly reposed since the seventeenth century. The sages of the General Staff proclaimed that Rokossovsky's idea was at variance with everything they had been taught in the War Academy. Did not Lenin himself pronounce that one should attack at a single decisive point with the maximum of men and supplies? It is weird to find such rigidity in Soviet military thinking in the fourth year of war, yet this explains partly why

[79] The new anthem began: "An unbreakable union of free republics was forged forever by Great Russia," and continued: "Stalin has shown us the way. . . ."

it took the Red Army two and a half years to get from Stalingrad to Berlin.

Stalin endorsed the single-blow plan of his staff. He stuck to formulas, and also he perhaps thought it wise to put a proud soldier down a peg or two. But Rokossovsky persisted. "Go out and think it over," said the Supreme Commander. The Marshal did, but returned unconverted. Now in an ominous tone Stalin told Rokossovsky to go out again and give serious thought as to whether he would disobey his order. Molotov and Malenkov whispered advice: it was foolish to disagree with the Boss. But Rokossovsky stuck to his guns and did something unprecedented: he asked, if his plan was not adopted, to be relieved. Everyone present was aghast: would Rokossovsky, who had already "sat" some years as an "enemy of the people," be again arrested or worse? Instead Stalin was all smiles: of course they would attack in two places. Why weren't there more commanders who spoke out and stuck to their views? Why did he always have to deal with yes-men?[80]

Such generous sentiments notwithstanding, Stalin decided that the stubborn Marshal needed a special watchdog. Nikolai Bulganin was sent to serve as the political member of the military council of the first Byelorussian front. (Most of us remember Bulganin as a grandfatherly and bibulous character who was Nikita Khrushchev's constant traveling companion until, having tried to trip up the First Secretary, he was dismissed as Premier and consigned to obscurity.) His arrival at Rokossovsky's headquarters was greeted without enthusiasm. The man whom he superseded, Telegin, paints a very unflattering picture of Bulganin. He threw his weight around, gave everybody to understand he had special access to Stalin, insisted on having a private kitchen for which provisions were brought by plane from Moscow. Altogether, according to Telegin, and nothing worse could be said by a Russian general about a political commissar, he was another Mekhlis.[81]

The feats of Rokossovsky's armies constituted but one part of the great Soviet summer offensive and victory. The whole operation was given the code name Bagration, after the Russian commander in the 1812 war who happened to be of Georgian descent. At the central front four Soviet army groups disposed of 1.5 million men, 31,000 artillery and mortar pieces, 5000 tanks, over 6000 planes. This secured the Russians' superiority over the Germans of two to one in men, three to one in

---

[80] A description of the debate is in Constantine Telegin's article in *Problems of the History of the Communist Party of the U.S.S.R.* (Moscow, 1964), No. 6, pp. 86–90.

[81] Speaking of that gentleman, he had popped up again. For all the reprimands he had received and demotions he had suffered, Mekhlis in the great summer offensive of 1944 occupied the post of Political Commissar of the Second Byelorussian Army Group, then of the Fifth Ukrainian. He proved true to form, victimizing commanders as well as subordinate officers.

artillery, more than four to one in planes and tanks.[82] In fact, Soviet superiority was even more crushing than the official account indicates. Germany's defeat was decisive. When the Red Army stopped at the end of August, it had chased the invader out of most of the Soviet territory he had ever occupied, cut deep into Poland, entered Rumania. In July men of the Wehrmacht made their entrance into Moscow, but in a manner unanticipated by Hitler. Crowds of Muscovites watched silently as about 60,000 German war prisoners were paraded through the streets of the capital, a captive general marching at the head of the column.

Stalin, victorious, forgot none of the ways of the oppressors. Simultaneously with the army, the NKVD moved into the liberated areas. It is difficult to object to the severe retribution dealt to collaborators and traitors, but drastic penalties were dealt out to entire national groups, their republics or autonomous districts being officially dissolved, entire populations being shipped out of the areas where their ancestors had lived since time immemorial. This fate befell groups in north Caucasus as well as the Crimean Tatars. Khrushchev may not have exaggerated when he said that it would have pleased Stalin to deal in the same way with the Ukrainians, but that there were too many of them. As it was, some 4 or 5 million individuals are alleged to have been thus transferred, even with the war going on and transportation facilities being strained to the utmost.

Stalin sensed the mood of his people: surely the war's end, now not so distant, would bring them a reward for their unparalleled sufferings, for the exemplary loyalty and heroism of so many. The war has formed a bond of trust and affection between the Leader and the people, and the bond should render the NKVD and that frightful "vigilance" of the past superfluous. Some undoubtedly hoped that with the victory Stalin would be content to ascend to Olympian semiretirement. But Stalin was very conscious that in the struggle for peace Russia would find herself face to face with the enormous power of America, supplemented by the still not inconsiderable assets of the British Empire. Just as he believed that he had held the country together in the years of mortal danger, 1941–42, so now there arose an equally justified conviction that victory in peace depended on him.

He undoubtedly believed, and not without reason, that it was mainly his insistence and diplomacy which finally made the Allies throw their armies where he wanted them, into northern France. (So much for Churchill's schemes to get to Vienna and the Balkans ahead of the Soviet soldiers.) But there was also a note of unfeigned admiration in his tribute, printed in all Soviet papers, one week after Eisenhower's armies landed in Normandy. The Americans and the British had suc-

[82] *The Great Fatherland War, Short Version* (Moscow, 1965), p. 344.

ceeded in an enterprise which had defied Napoleon and Hitler. "One must admit that military history does not know a similar enterprise so broadly conceived, on so huge a scale, so masterfully executed." In July he sent Churchill and Roosevelt his photograph, with suitable dedications. When things were going his way, he was capable of generosity and just the right gesture. In two years he was to represent the Allied invasion as a niggardly and belated enterprise undertaken to forestall the nations of Western Europe liberating themselves with the help of the Red Army. And Churchill again became a villain. But in the summer of 1944 he felt genuine admiration for and gratitude to his great partners. The Soviet press was ordered to remind their readers how much the West had contributed to *Russia's* war effort.

This great outward cordiality which the victories of the summer of 1944 produced among the Big Three also had its practical uses. Churchill's suspicions would be allayed (he might be a wily imperialist, but as Stalin had an occasion to observe, he was also a sentimentalist); Roosevelt's vision of Soviet Russia as a trusting partner in the United Nations would be reinforced. And public opinion in the West was growing impatient with minor, entangled squabbles that threatened to disrupt this impressive harmony of the Big Three and endanger the foundations of a lasting peace.

One such issue was still Poland. Since Teheran, Stalin had raised his stakes. Now he insisted not only on the Polish territories he had annexed in 1939, but on a pro-Soviet, if not as yet outright, Communist government. To American Ambassador W. Averell Harriman he said, "Again the Poles, is that the most important question?" And to many in the West the problem now appeared in the same light. The unfortunate government-in-exile was still recognized by Britain and America. Roosevelt received its Premier, Mikolajczyk, in June and in a message to Stalin was at pains to excuse himself for this step.[83] The Polish official made a good impression on him: "He understands fully that the future of Poland depends on her thoroughly good relations with the U.S.S.R." Would Stalin see Mikolajczyk? Ambassador Harriman offered an additional explanation: 1944 was an election year, and the President had to think of the Polish votes.

It is not surprising that following this incident the dictator felt encouraged to tighten the screw. He would be glad to see Mikolajczyk, but any Polish government that he recognized would have to be wholly reconstructed to "include Polish politicians in the U.S. and the U.S.S.R. and especially Polish democratic leaders who are in Poland." To show whom he had in mind, he authorized the formation, on Polish soil now occupied by the Red Army, of the Committee of National Liberation,

[83] *The Correspondence* . . . , II, 145.

headed by a Communist, Boleslaw Bierut. To this body the Soviets turned over the civil adminstration of the part of Poland wrested from the Germans.

The Soviets had claimed all along that the underground which operated in German-occupied Poland and which in fact enjoyed the clandestine support of the vast majority of the population was a figment of the "London Poles' " imagination. To disprove this contention, but also most unwisely, the government-in-exile ordered a general uprising in Warsaw. It was foolish, even its more realistic members realized, to try to shame Stalin into action that lay against his plans. The uprising could succeed only if the Russians, who had now reached the eastern bank of the Vistula, would continue their offensive and cross the river. The uprising began on August 1. The ability of the Polish underground to mobilize forces that engaged several German divisions for sixty-two days obviously surprised the Russians. But the Red Army, ironically enough headed by the Polish-born Rokossovsky, did not cross the river. It is safe to say that had such an operation been among the Red Army's summer plans, which appears doubtful, it would have been postponed until the Germans' suppression of the uprising.

When directly defied, it was sometimes difficult for Stalin to remain a genial diplomat. Did those émigrés think they could force his hand, make him use Soviet soldiers to install them in triumph in Warsaw? To Western appeals to help the insurgents, he replied first with impatience, then with brutality. "Sooner or later the truth about the group of criminals who have unleashed the Warsaw adventure will become known to everybody."[84] No, the British and American planes that were attempting to drop supplies to the fighting Poles would not be allowed to land on Soviet soil. (Consequently, they had to fly from distant bases in Italy.)

By September, when the prospect of the uprising's success was gone, Stalin decided to change his tactics. Much of the good will the Soviet Union had amassed in the West was being undermined by the repercussions of the Warsaw affair. Therefore some Soviet supplies were dropped for the Poles; American and British planes bringing in munitions were finally permitted to land on Soviet territory; and a Polish unit attached to Rokossovsky's army made an unsuccessful attempt to cross the river. (It is not clear whether this was sanctioned by the Soviet command.)

When the insurgents surrendered to the Germans on October 2, Warsaw was by now utterly destroyed and it was clear that Warsaw was another of *Stalin's* victories. Once more he had displayed savage determination not to be swayed in the pursuit of his goals, no matter what

[84] *Ibid.*, I, 258.

moral pressure was brought on him. For many Poles, even anti-Soviet ones, Warsaw became proof that the only hope of saving some shred of Polish independence, if not indeed of saving the nation itself, lay in submission to Stalin's will. And the same tragic lesson would be studied in Czechoslovakia, Hungary, and elsewhere.

There was a lesson there also for Stalin. At one point Churchill proposed to Roosevelt that the Allies threaten to cut off supplies for Russia unless Stalin allowed their planes to land on Soviet territory. Roosevelt vetoed this, but it is possible that Stalin learned of this secret exchange between the Western leaders—hence the belated permission for the planes to land. (What if Roosevelt had said, "You must help the Poles or else"? Even in rage Stalin was a very practical man. He knew that one must capitalize on one's assets fast, that he should exploit his allies' current mood—a mixture of admiration and certain fear of Russia—before it passed.)

He was in a hurry to stake his claim in Eastern and Central Europe. After the great successes of the spring and summer offensives in 1944, the most logical and the shortest path for the Soviet armies to take to Berlin was through Poland. But he was anxious to step into the Balkans, Hungary, and Austria before the British could get there from Italy. So two entire army groups were diverted in that direction. In October he telephoned Marshal Malinovsky: Budapest must be taken forthwith; for political reasons he could tolerate no delay. Malinovsky pleaded that he needed more time and additional troops. Stalin hung up. As it turned out the premature attack cost the Red Army huge and needless casualties in what was militarily a secondary theater of operations. The Rumanian King Michael carried out a coup d'état, overthrowing his fascist premier-dictator, and brought his country and army over to the Soviet side. Stalin had the bad taste to award this young and not very important man the Order of Victory, reserved otherwise to prestigious Soviet marshals and foreign leaders of the caliber of Eisenhower and Montgomery. (Two years later King Michael was unceremoniously kicked out of his country.)

Finland quit the war in September, and there was some amazement in the West that judging by the usual standards the Soviet Union dealt with Finland quite generously: no Soviet occupation, Soviet territorial acquisitions restricted to what had been obtained in 1940. But Stalin knew that the Americans had a thing about this little country; at Terheran they had argued with some heat for a lenient treatment of the Finns. Why endanger the Americans' good will for the sake of a "peanut," as he characterized Finland to a Yugoslav Communist visitor? He was after bigger game.

Except in Finland, the obvious Soviet intention was to establish in every East European country they occupied, whether a former satellite of Germany or a victim, a solidly pro-Soviet regime with some Communist participation. There was yet no effort or perhaps even intent to impose out-and-out Communist governments.

Churchill viewed the whole process with a sinking heart. Britain after all went to war in 1939 to keep East Europe from being absolutely dominated by Germany. Now Soviet hegemony in the east and southeast was to be even greater than that which Hitler would have achieved had he been allowed to have his way with Poland—and much more entrenched, for the local Communists were bound to be enthusiastic helpers of Soviet imperialism. He almost despaired of securing American assistance in containing the Russians. Washington was preoccupied by the problem of the United Nations. Currently there were prolonged discussions going on between the Big Three at Dumbarton Oaks as to how this edifice was to be constructed. At practically every point the Russians were raising objections to American proposals, objections voiced mainly for debating purposes—permanent members of the Security Council had to have the right to veto not only on substantive but on procedural questions; each of the sixteen Soviet Union republics should have a seat in the Assembly; Argentina ought not to be invited to join. It was clear—but not to Roosevelt and his advisers—that these objections were raised only to be dropped at a point when the Americans would be grateful for Russian "concessions" and would therefore be embarrassed to quibble about Bulgaria or Poland.

But Churchill hoped that perhaps he might interest Stalin in a businesslike discussion of spheres of influence between the Russians and the British in the postwar world. And so in October 1944, while FDR was busy with the forthcoming election, Churchill went to Moscow. This was not *quite* going behind the Americans' back, but surely Stalin would appreciate some talk about the facts of international life rather than about those seating arrangements, votes, etc.

As usual, the Americans were more alert to trickery on the part of close allies than from potential antagonists. Roosevelt's message to Stalin showed that he saw through Churchill's naughty designs: "In the current world war there is literally not a single problem, military or political, in which the United States is not interested. . . . Only we three, and only together, can decide the hitherto unresolved problems."[85] Stalin must have been hugely amused. He really did not know why Churchill was coming to Moscow, he wired the President. He had assumed he was coming also on behalf of Roosevelt.[86]

In a rather imperious way Roosevelt had demanded that the Stalin-Churchill meetings be chaperoned by Ambassador Harriman. The

[85] *Ibid.*, II, 160.
[86] *Ibid.*, II, 162.

latter, Roosevelt informed the crestfallen Prime Minister, would not be empowered to commit the United States—only he, Roosevelt, could do that—but he would keep Roosevelt fully informed.

The visit was not one of Churchill's finest hours, for it was on this occasion that, having managed to shake off the friendly but inhibiting presence of Harriman, the Prime Minister eagerly propounded his famous percentage plan. Influence in various Balkan countries was to be apportioned between the two powers. In Rumania, Britain was to have 10-per-cent influence, Russia 90; in Greece, vice versa; in Yugoslavia, 50-50, etc. Stalin knew when to be silent; he took the paper with these sinful and preposterous figures and with his pencil "made a rather large tick upon it," which Churchill fatuously took as a token of agreement. "After this there was a long silence." Churchill wondered whether they should not burn the compromising document. "No, you keep it," said Stalin.[87]

On the same Moscow visit Churchill acted, again atypically, like a bully. The unfortunate Premier of the "London Poles," Mikolajczyk, was in Russia at the same time, and Churchill added his own threats to the Russians' to make him break with his government and join the Polish National Committee of Russian puppets. Representatives of these latter (the "Lublin Poles," as they were known) were produced for Churchill's inspection, and they echoed the Soviet demands. "I looked at Stalin and saw an understanding twinkle in his expressive eyes, as much as to say 'What about that for our Soviet teaching.' "[88] From Stalin's point of view Churchill's was a most successful visit.

Foreign statesmen were now eager to visit Moscow and seek audience with one of the two arbiters of the world's fate. In December 1944 De Gaulle journeyed to "dear and powerful Russia," as he called her when trying to make Roosevelt and Churchill take more notice of him, hoping to enlist Stalin against the Anglo-Saxons, as he quaintly referred to them, in restoring to France her rightful place in the world. But Stalin saw little reason to make a fuss over the sensitive Frenchman. He was not going to endanger his intimacy with Churchill and Roosevelt by exerting himself on behalf of France, which currently could do nothing for the Soviet Union, or on behalf of De Gaulle, who he knew was heartily disliked by them, especially by Roosevelt. He kept them informed of De Gaulle's maneuvers and plans and sanctioned a treaty of

[87] Winston L. S. Churchill, Triumph and Tragedy (Boston, 1953), 228. Some historians have shared the Prime Minister's delusion that there was an agreement between him and Stalin on spheres of influence. But all that Stalin did was to put a "tick" on a meaningless piece of paper. The fact that the Soviets did not object to British suppression of the Greek Communists' insurrection in November–December 1944 was due not to the British having been allotted "90 per cent" of Greece, but to the presence of British and absence of Soviet soldiers there.
[88] Ibid., II, 235.

alliance and friendship with France only when his partners informed him they did not object to it. The one thing France could do for him was to recognize his Poles as the official government of their country, and when De Gaulle balked at this, Stalin became quite rude. In his reception of De Gaulle, there was little of the tact and dignity Stalin displayed when entertaining Roosevelt and Churchill or other people whom for the moment he wanted to impress. De Gaulle may have expected an intimate discussion of how Europe could be rebuilt under joint Franco-Soviet auspices, or tributes to French culture. Instead, Stalin was alternately boorish and clowning. If he were De Gaulle, he remarked, he would not shoot the French Communist leaders, not right away, anyway. (His visitor probably did not realize that it was Stalin's orders that kept the French Communists in line after the liberation. Some of them grumbled that because of their leading role in the Resistance and their popularity in the country, this was the moment to bid for power. But again Stalin was not going to endanger relations with America and Britain by allowing irresponsible adventures by French and Italian Communists. First things first. Anyway, what could they do with the Allied armies on their soil?) Or again, to his interpreter Stalin said, "You know too much. I'd better send you to Siberia"—a piece of buffoonery which the Frenchman took seriously.[89] Stalin made De Gaulle sit through a terrible movie. Why abandon one's usual amusement on account of the representative of a second-rate power? Released from the torture at the end of the performance, De Gaulle asked to be excused. Wouldn't he stay? Stalin inquired; they were going to show another movie. De Gaulle's account of this episode virtually smolders as he relates how, after bidding his host adieu, he walked to the door alone while Stalin remained at the table, munching a late snack.

It was time, Stalin believed, for his allies to do something for him. With the election over and Roosevelt reelected, there was no reason for the United States to withhold official recognition from the "Lublin Poles." The President, for his part, wanted a decent interlude to elapse between his reelection and his turning his back on the "London Poles." They would soon meet, he wrote Stalin; perhaps the Soviets would "be able to withhold the recognition of the Lublin Committee as Government of Poland until our meeting?"[90] No, Stalin answered, encouraged by the pleading tone; if the Lublin group proclaimed itself the government of Poland, the Soviets would have no reason not to recognize it as such. They had new evidence about the heinous activities of the London regime, whose agents in Poland were killing Soviet soldiers. Roosevelt's further and feebler pleas were answered by Stalin more

---

[89] *The Complete War Memoirs of Charles de Gaulle* (New York, 1964), p. 757.
[90] *The Correspondence* . . . , II, 173.

categorically: the whole thing was out of his hands. As of December 27 the Presidium of the Supreme Soviet had recognized the Lublin group as the legal government of Poland. "This circumstance renders me powerless to fulfill your wish." He could not have expected the Americans to be unduly impressed by this constitutional punctilio. But what could they say in retort: that he should defy the highest legislative body of his land? Churchill and Roosevelt were spared the knowledge that the wife of the Chairman of the Presidium of the Supreme Soviet was currently under lock and key.

Things were going Stalin's way. In the fall the Red Army scored new successes, linked up with Tito's Partisans in Yugoslavia. There were some temporary setbacks in Hungary, where the Germans were fighting for Budapest as if it were Berlin. But his fantastic luck held. With the British and American armies now advancing from many directions upon the center of Europe, the Allies' bargaining position might have been expected to be noticeably improved. But a defeat and an embarrassment intervened. In December the Germans unexpectedly counterattacked in the Ardennes, breached the American lines, and raised the fear of a serious military debacle. Not until the middle of January did it become clear that this was but a futile last gasp rather than a major offensive, of which the Wehrmacht was no longer capable. In the same months the British had to use their troops to cope with a Communist insurrection in Athens. There was a chorus of disapproval from liberal circles in Britain and especially America, discreet silence from Moscow. It is therefore not surprising to hear the note of anxiety in Churchill's and Roosevelt's queries as to when the Russians planned to open their winter offensive. Not bad, not bad at all.

On New Year's Eve, General Shtemenko received an unusual message from Stalin's secretary: he was to report that night at Stalin's villa, as usual, but need not bring maps or documents. Soon his telephone rang again; other military leaders around Moscow had received the same message and wondered what it could mean. Things had been going well, but it was not difficult to be apprehensive about the unusual summons. Among those summoned were people like the Minister of Armaments, Boris Vannikov, who had already enjoyed Stalin's hospitality of a very special kind, and they must have reflected, as Bulganin told Khrushchev on another occasion, "When you are invited to Stalin's, you can never be sure you will get back home." Someone lightheartedly suggested they might be going to a party, a joke the others felt was in poor taste.

The nervous group assembled some minutes before midnight; Stalin entered shortly after with his suite of Politburo members. "Happy New Year, Comrades!" It *was* a party! A feeling of relief swept among the guests. They "hastened to enjoy their freedom, people broke into little clusters, laughter could be heard, voices became natural and loud." And then the proverbial "broad Russian nature" came into its own. Marshal Budenny, always the life of the party, pulled out his accordion. When he stopped playing, to the assembly's applause, the host put on records; there were folk tunes and dances. Since there was only one lady present, the wife of the Italian Communist leader Palmiro Togliatti, there could not be much dancing. But when it came to the gopak, Budenny could not resist. The sixty-two-year-old marshal performed his famous specialty, squatting and kicking his legs out, to the cheers and rhythmic clapping of the crowd. It was a scene that Hollywood could never match.

The guests dispersed in the morning with the feeling that this was indeed going to be a happy new year. Shtemenko and his superior, General Antonov, went home to sleep rather than simply snatching a catnap at their desks in the General Staff headquarters. It is unlikely that they would have taken such unprecedented license without an authorization from the Supreme Commander.[91]

Stalin's amiable mood reflected his conviction that not only the military but the diplomatic victory could not be long delayed. In the middle of January Soviet armies opened a new major offensive along the central front in Poland. The Soviet attack began somewhat earlier than originally planned—Stalin was able to tell his allies that he had heeded their pleas and advanced the date of his attack to relieve German pressure in the Ardennes. (Though by this time the German drive there had been repulsed.) All his military moves were now synchronized with his political aims. He was solicitous of the real estate he was acquiring. Marshal Konev's First Ukrainian Group was to bypass the rich industrial region of Silesia. "Sheer gold," said Stalin to Konev, placing his hand on the Silesian sector of the map. Though it complicated his task, Konev was moved: how deep was Stalin's solicitude for "fraternal Poland"? As of January 5 the official government of "fraternal Poland" was, as far as the U.S.S.R. was concerned, the Lublin Committee, and it was a Polish unit with the Soviet army which on January 17 liberated the ruins of Warsaw. While freeing, in a manner of speaking, the capital of its ally, the Red Army was also beginning the occupation of "the lair of the fascist beast," as the Soviet phrase went. Two army groups struck at East Prussia: 1.6 million Soviet soldiers, 22,000 artillery pieces, four thousand tanks, and three thousand planes attacked the German province, defended by some half million soldiers with eight thousand guns, seven hundred tanks, and five hundred planes.[92] ☆☆☆

---

[91] Shtemenko, pp. 301–3.
[92] *The Great Fatherland War, Short Version*, pp. 464–65.

STALIN / THE MAN AND HIS ERA

W ITH the Red Army's advance units some fifty miles from Berlin, its Supreme Commander welcomed the President of the United States and the Prime Minister of Great Britain at Yalta, in the Crimea, between February 4 and 11. The very day the conference opened Stalin called up the commander of the army group advancing on Berlin, Marshal Zhukov, and ordered him to stop the offensive.[93] Zhukov's army commanders, notably Chuykov of Stalingrad fame, subsequently felt that they had thereby missed a great opportunity to seize Berlin in February. With additional artillery and supplies, they were to argue, they could have easily advanced the remaining fifty miles, and the cost would not have been so great as it was to be in April.

Caution dictated Stalin's decision. Up to then the Russian offensive had rolled at fantastic speed but at prodigious cost in casualties; some Soviet divisions were by now at half their nominal strength. Zhukov's group had far outdistanced its right-wing neighbor, Rokossovsky's Second Byelorussian Group, and there was a chance (not a significant one in view of the Germans' losses and demoralization) of the Wehrmacht's striking at his right wing as he pushed on to Berlin. Before Stalin's eyes there arose the memory of Warsaw in 1920. Then the Red Army, pushing ahead to seize the capital, exposed its flanks and suffered a crushing defeat. There was no earthly possibility that the Red Army could be beaten now, but a major setback and a retreat while he was negotiating with the Allies were risks he was unwilling to take. The legend of the Red Army's inexhaustible manpower and awesome might was his main card in the game for the distribution of the spoils of war. What if it were realized that the Soviet armies had bled and were almost as exhausted as the Wehrmacht?

As it was, the Yalta conference taxed his diplomatic skill to the utmost. Take Poland. The Anglo-American position on this key issue had stiffened somewhat; Stalin had laid it on too thick with the Supreme Soviet story. Also, the President's attitude toward Stalin was imperceptibly changing. Still determined to do everything in his power to get his trust, Roosevelt could not help feeling a certain resentment that he, a sick and weary man, had had to travel halfway round the

---

[93] This version is from Marshal Chuykov's article in *Modern and Recent History* (Moscow, 1965), No. 2, pp. 6–7. It was vehemently denied by Marshal Zhukov in his memoirs published in 1969 (Zhukov, pp. 629–31). But while Chuykov, who was then one of Zhukov's army commanders, may err as to the exact date, his story in general rings true.

604

world for another conference, while his host, though deferential, had not even seen fit to meet his plane.

One side of the territorial aspect of the Polish question had been pretty much settled in Teheran. The President feebly tried to rescue the city of Lvov for Poland. But, as Stalin explained, the frontier between the two countries which he had in mind (i.e., the Molotov-Ribbentrop line) had originally been suggested by Lord Curzon in 1919. Could he be less pro-Russian than Curzon? Also, if he yielded, he would arouse great dissatisfaction and incur political trouble among the Ukrainians. So the official communiqué put the Big Three on record as sanctioning the Soviet demands.

Stalin found the going harder on getting his Polish regime recognized. But he showed himself indefatigable as a negotiator. He kept asking his partners to be fair and to realize that ominous results would ensue if they persisted in their stubbornness on the issue. True, the Lublin government was not a product of elections, but was De Gaulle's, which the Allies had fully recognized? Was the London Polish government? Say what you will, politicians who had been out of their country for four or five years inevitably lost touch with their people. To the query whether British and American observers should not report first as to what was going on in Poland, Stalin retorted that the Poles were a proud nation: they resented foreign interference. Then the President wanted to see the "Lublin Poles." Stalin regretted that his people could not locate the Polish officials to bring them to the Crimea! You could not treat the Poles like the Egyptians (sticking a pin into Churchill); you had here a highly cultured nation with a prewar literacy of 70 per cent. You had to treat them with respect. He sympathized with the troubles Roosevelt and Churchill had with *their* Poles; good people, excellent fighters, great scientists and musicians, but oh how quarrelsome and vain when it came to politics.[94] Wearily, the Western statesmen yielded to this combination of persuasiveness and prevarication. The Soviet protégé, the "Provisional Government of Poland," was to be the nucleus of the future Government of National Unity. Democratic leaders from Poland and abroad would be invited to join it—the process to be supervised in Moscow by a commission composed of Molotov and the British and American ambassadors.

The Polish issue crucially and intimately affected the most important postwar problem: the fate of Germany. Churchill's enthusiasm for moving Poland westward had now abated; a truncated Germany was bound to enhance Russia's domination of the Continent. Stalin was a

[94] As usual, he took a clue from a previous incautious statement by the President, who had said most Poles are like the Chinese and want to save face. *Foreign Relations of the United States—Conferences at Malta and Yalta* (Washington, 1955), p. 677; hereafter cited as *The Yalta Papers*.

fervent advocate of Poland's being compensated for her losses in the east by a sizable chunk of Germany up to the Oder–Western Neisse Line—a shift that would mean, and has meant, the displacement of 6 to 7 million Germans. The principle of Poland's thus being compensated was endorsed by the conference, with the precise details and boundaries to be settled later.

Contrary to what is often believed, Stalin had no clear idea what kind of postwar Germany he wanted. Roosevelt, reflecting America's currently fiercely anti-German mood, still talked of partitioning the country. Churchill, for obvious reasons, was against it. For Stalin, though he felt it diplomatic to agree with the President, the question was academic: Germany was going to be divided into zones of occupation by the Great Powers and (at Churchill's insistence) France, anyway. The Americans were unrealistic to think one could bind the future by agreements and clauses.

He had some pleasant surprises for them—concessions that made Roosevelt feel that his arduous journey had not been in vain. After putting up a show of resistance, the Soviet leaders announced that they agreed to the American proposal that procedural questions in the Security Council should be decided by a majority vote and that a permanent member would not be able to veto discussions of a dispute to which it was a party. For the President, "this was a great step forward which would be welcomed by all peoples in the world."[95] The Soviets' obstinacy concerning Poland seemed insignificant compared with this great concession they were making to the idea of true internationalism. The Americans had hardly recovered from this delicious surprise when Stalin threw in another. All during the Dumbarton Oaks discussion the stony-faced Andrei Gromyko had insisted that Russia had to have sixteen seats in the Assembly. Before Roosevelt's eyes there had arisen a vision of querulous senators proclaiming that they would never sanction American membership in that body unless the United States had forty-eight or forty-nine seats. But now Stalin announced he would be happy with just three additional seats—for the Ukraine, Byelorussia, and Lithuania. These republics had suffered most in the war. What would they think of him if he told them they were not going to have their own representation in the world parliament? Quick thinking might have produced the objection that the arrangement would be patently unfair to the "leading nation of the Soviet Union": the Russians, 100 million strong, who, unlike the 2 million Lithuanians, were to be denied this signal honor. But in their relief, the Americans demurred only, and with some embarrassment, about Lithuania; the United States had never acknowledged its absorption into the Soviet family of nations. Stalin did not quibble: he would settle for the Ukraine, Byelorussia, and the third seat for the U.S.S.R. as a whole, and, if the senators still raised difficulties for his American friend, he would be happy for the United States to have three seats too. Yes, one could do business with Stalin. If only those Politburo members did not get hold of him again when he got back to Moscow. . . .

Much of the Americans' attitude was epitomized in a note Harry Hopkins passed to the President during the discussion of the question of reparations: "The Russians have given in so much at the conference that I don't think we should let them down."[96] And Roosevelt still believed that the way to Stalin's heart was to criticize the British. The British, he remarked to Stalin, "were a peculiar people and wished to have their cake and eat it too." And he expressed the hope that Stalin "would propose a toast to the execution of fifty thousand officers of the German army."[97] The need to do away with imperialism was very much on the President's mind and he shared his reflections with his Russian friend. Hong Kong should go back to China and become a free port. How about internationalizing Indochina and Burma? Stalin gravely nodded. Then, when it came to Russia's territorial and other demands the President was understanding. The Soviet Union was pledged to enter the war against Japan after Germany was defeated. Yet, Stalin pleaded, it would be difficult for him to get popular support for a war with a "country with which they, the Soviet people, had no great trouble" unless they got something for it, such as southern Sakhalin and the Kurile Islands. The President saw no difficulty about that but felt a bit more constrained when told Russia would like some goods which, one might think, after Japan's defeat should revert to China—the Manchurian Railway complex, Port Arthur, and Dairen. If he were promised them, Stalin would find it easier "to explain the decision to the Supreme Soviet,"[98] he said. The President sighed, but thought he could make Chiang Kai-shek see that generosity would lay a firm foundation for Sino-Soviet friendship.

Churchill was not happy, though fortunately he was spared the knowledge of Roosevelt's ruminations with Stalin, details of which might well have brought on his stroke right then and there. At the general sessions Stalin gently teased him about Greece, countered his complaints about Tito's now openly Communist behavior (what happened to that 50-per-cent influence in Yugoslavia Britain was to have?) with a statement that he had occasion to remember three years later: "Tito is a proud man . . . and might resent advice."[99] But Stalin knew

[96] Sherwood, p. 860.
[97] *The Yalta Papers*, p. 571.
[98] *Ibid.*, p. 769.
[99] *Ibid.*, p. 129.

how to be charming and how to undo the effect of his chaffing; he drank a toast "for the leader of the British Empire, the most courageous of the Prime Ministers of the world," and he recalled that most glorious hour when Churchill said "that Britain would stand and fight alone against Germany, even without allies." After many years, in recalling this tribute, Churchill could not bring himself to comment on Stalin's subsequent statement: "In an alliance the allies should not deceive each other. . . . I as a naïve man think it best not to deceive my ally even if he is a fool."[100] How he could put it on: "We will not give you the head of Bukharin, the favorite of the Party"; "I drink to the Führer's health, I know how much the German nation loves him."

And thus they argued, feted each other, and decided the fate of hundreds of millions: three elderly men, on one of whom the shadows of death were already closing. Stalin's quick mind registered instantaneously the slightest hint of weakness or hesitation on either ally's part. Indeed, a whole volume might be written on the influence of one of Roosevelt's statements on the future course of Russian strategy for postwar diplomacy. On February 5 the President said that "he did not believe that American troops would stay in Europe much more than two years. . . . He could obtain support in Congress and throughout the country for any reasonable measures designed to safeguard the future peace, but he did not believe that this would extend to the maintenance of an appreciable American force in Europe."[101] To Stalin this meant one could go along with the Americans' schoolmasterish ideas and declarations about free elections in all countries liberated from Germany; in two years they would be packing up and going home anyway.

How strange some of the American ideas were! Among the American delegation there was the incongruous figure of Ed Flynn, Democratic boss of the Bronx. His presence was due to Roosevelt's hope that it would be a fine thing if Stalin and the Pope estalished a rapport, and on his way back from Yalta, Mr. Flynn was to make some discreet explorations in Rome. But the age of ecumenism was not to dawn for some twenty years. Still, it is slanderous to attribute to Stalin the rejoinder, "How many divisions has the Pope?" He was too urbane for that, and besides, how many divisions did Lenin have in 1917?

It would be wrong to see Stalin—at this in many ways most triumphant moment of his career—as entirely cynical. He had a sense of great historical occasions. The final victory, he knew, would in a sense be anticlimactic; it would bring out the inevitable dissonances and basic contradictions between the partners. For the moment, he enjoyed the

100 Churchill, *Triumph and Tragedy*, pp. 361–63.
101 *The Yalta Papers*, p. 617. American officials have often, to this very day, been reproachfully reminded by their Soviet opposites of this "commitment."

glow of camaraderie with two men whose greatness he clearly appreciated, for all his ruthless exploitation of their vulnerabilities, and whose attentions to him he valued. There was also a note of wistfulness, of something which looks suspiciously close to sentimentality in his avowal that he was an old man, in his assertion (for a brief moment he was sincere) that they must work together to spare the world the horrors of another war. Perhaps in his meetings with Roosevelt and Churchill, Stalin felt that he was taking a vacation from his job as a tyrant and his mellowness was not entirely spurious.

The mood could not endure. Within a month of the conference Soviet action contrasted so much with what the Americans took to have been the spirit of Yalta that they were thrown back on the standard explanation: "It was the opinion of the State Department group who were on the President's staff at the conference that Stalin had difficulties with the Politburo when he returned to Moscow for having been too friendly and for having made too many concessions to the two capitalist nations."[102] The Soviet government vetoed most candidates proposed by the Americans and British for the future Polish Government of National Unity as fascists or as otherwise unacceptable to its Polish protégés. In Rumania, King Michael was mercilessly bullied by Vishinsky, whose talents were now applied in the job of Deputy Foreign Minister, and was coerced into appointing a Communist-dominated government. Thereupon President Beneš hastened to designate as head of the Czech government Zdenek Fierlinger, who though nominally a Social Democrat had become during his tenure as ambassador in Moscow a thoroughgoing fellow traveler. The Americans' unhappiness was increased by the undue delays incurred during the repatriation of American prisoners of war whom the Red Army liberated from German camps as it swept westward. Some of the delays could be attributed to the inevitable red tape and chaotic wartime conditions. But the Soviets refused to let members of the American military misson in Moscow inspect the Soviet facilities where their countrymen were being detained on Polish soil. They were not eager, it was easy to divine, to let stories of what was being done in Poland reach America. The tone of the President's messages to Stalin grew sharp: "The American government has done everything to meet your every wish. . . . Speaking frankly, I cannot understand your unwillingness to allow the American liaison officers to help their countrymen."[103] The amiable Stalin of a few weeks ago had now disappeared: Soviet commanders in Poland were too busy to entertain visiting American officers, and as to the former prisoners of war, they were being better treated in the Soviet rest camps than the

---

[102] Edward R. Stettinius, Jr., *Roosevelt and the Russians* (New York, 1949), p. 309.
[103] *The Correspondence* . . . , II, 194.

Soviet prisoners of war who had been liberated by the Allies in the West.

Stalin's bad humor was mounting. His Polish government was finding it hard going. For all the ordeal of the German occupation and the exhaustion of the people in its wake, most Poles were resisting the Moscow-imposed regime. Stalin had believed that it had been accepted by the Allies and that all it needed was a few democratic trappings. But here the Americans and the British (it was mainly Churchill, he believed) were insisting on its thorough reorganization. Would he have to fight this battle all over again?

He took drastic measures. Sixteen leaders of the Polish underground connected with the London government were contacted and assured of immunity if they came out in the open. They were then invited to a conference with the Soviet military authorities in late March. On their arrival at Marshal Zhukov's headquarters they were seized and taken to Moscow. It was two months before any news of their fate reached the West.

For Roosevelt, Stalin had a bitter pill. The President's hopes were focused, he knew, on the founding meeting of the United Nations scheduled to open in San Francisco on April 25. On March 25 the Americans were informed that the Soviet delegation would not be headed by Molotov, who was needed at the April session of the Supreme Soviet. Implicit in the Soviets thus downgrading the conference was the threat that Russia might not enter the United Nations at all unless the Americans stopped bothering about Poland and other East European problems!

Stalin was treading a perilous path. The President's messages to him, though drafted by another's hand, now reflected unmistakable anger. On April 1 a long and imperious message reached the Kremlin. The Soviets' behavior in and concerning Poland, Roosevelt stated, threatened the Yalta agreement. If the Soviets continued along this line, the whole basis of Soviet-American relations might be undermined. "In America, I trust you realize, every policy, whether internal or foreign, depends on the support of the people."[104] The implication was clear that Roosevelt had done everything to build up support for the Soviet Union among the American people, and would be unable to continue assuring the public that the Russians were to be trusted unless Stalin changed his ways.

Through his impatience Stalin was risking what all his diplomacy since the inception of the Grand Alliance has been designed to avoid: a clash with the United States, a giant at the height of its industrial and military might, barely bloodied in the war. And to compound his errors,

[104] *Ibid.*, II, 202.

Stalin now made a huge and inexcusable mistake, one which but for a quirk of fate could have had momentous consequences for Russia and for the world.

He was seized by a panic: he had assumed all along that except for some unpleasantness over Poland and for all the transparent intriguing by Churchill, he was leading his allies where he wanted them. But now suddenly it occurred to him that they were fooling *him*. They were about to make a separate arrangement with Germany; the Wehrmacht was going to capitulate in the West and continue fighting the Russians in the East! He would be robbed of the fruits of victory by the capitalists. For the first time we see in Stalin's handling of foreign affairs an outburst of that paranoid anxiety and irrepressible suspiciousness which had marked his rule over his people.

The occasion was rather trivial. An SS general, Karl Wolff, arrived in Switzerland in March to ascertain possible Allied conditions for a surrender of German forces in northern Italy to Field Marshal Harold Alexander, the Anglo-American commander-in-chief. The British loyally informed Moscow of this secret Nazi proposal and expressed their readiness to have a Soviet representative present when and if the Germans capitulated.

Why should this routine information, the kind to be expected at this stage of the war, throw Stalin into a veritable panic? We now know the probable reason. Some "foreign friend" of the Soviet Union, presumably in the government of Britain or the United States, informed Soviet intelligence that what was discussed in Switzerland was not merely a *local* capitulation by the Germans, but a separate peace in the West.[105] In a sense the information was correct: there had been German soundings of the Allies through various channels about the possibility of a separate peace—though evidently not in this case. The anonymous "wellwisher" of the Soviet Union (who has never been identified) then informed the Soviets that the Allies had rejected the Germans' entreaties. But for Stalin it was the first part of the intelligence report that was important. "That Churchill!" he exclaimed in Zhukov's presence. "He is capable of anything." Orders went out to speed up the opening of the drive on Berlin. At the same time Molotov demanded that the Allied representatives in Switzerland break off their negotiations with the Germans.

On March 29 Stalin dispatched a wire to Roosevelt explaining Molotov's demand. It was restrained in tone though it carried an implication that the British and Americans were dealing with the Germans behind the Russians' backs. Roosevelt's patient expostulation—after all, there were no British or American representatives pres-

---

[105] This story comes out in Marshal Zhukov's memoirs (pp. 641–42).

ent when Field Marshal Paulus was capitulating, etc.—arrived in Moscow probably at the same time as some other disquieting intelligence from the Soviet source in the West. And now Stalin exploded; if the President were still capable of concentrated thinking on politics he must have seen that his correspondent was no longer the dignified, occasionally affable "Uncle Joe" of their meetings. It was now the authentic Stalin who spoke to him, in his obsession and panic addressing the President almost as if Roosevelt were one of his generals or satraps. "You maintain that there have been no real negotiations. One must assume you have not been fully informed." Stalin had reliable information that the German commander on the Western Front had agreed to open the front to the Anglo-American armies in return "for a lenient truce." Why had the British been silent on the whole business? And now the Anglo-American armies would march on while the Red Army fought and suffered. The Germans had stopped the war in the West while they went on fighting the Russians. Why had Roosevelt concealed all this "from your allies the Russians"? How could the British and Americans have resorted to such trickery? He and his colleagues would have never done this. They would never think of buying a temporary advantage at the price of trust among the Allies.[106]

Had the facts been as Stalin alleged, it would still have been fantastically imprudent to address the President in such terms, implying that he had been cheating the Russians, was a figurehead ignorant of what was being done in his name, or was being led by the nose by the British. To a degree unprecedented before or since World War II, all the threads of American foreign policy were in the President's hands. To offend Roosevelt personally, to destroy the impression he had so assiduously cultivated of Russia's constructive and loyal partnership in the Alliance, threatened Stalin with a fatal setback for his whole diplomacy. The President could now endorse the "get tough" attitude toward the Soviets which Churchill had always urged; his great ability to sway public opinion would be employed to dissipate American illusions about their Soviet allies and prepare his countrymen for some very unsentimental bargaining, no holds barred, over the shape of the postwar world.

The reply sent in the President's name to Stalin's outburst was chilling in its reproof: "I was astounded on receiving your message. . . . I cannot but feel extreme indignation about those who feed you such information, whoever they are, because of their disgraceful, false interpretation of my actions or those of my trusted subordinates."[107]

Stalin replied that he never doubted the President's or Churchill's "honesty and trustworthiness." But in the manner of a man whose

106 *The Correspondence* . . . , II, 204–5.
107 *Ibid.*, II, 206.

aroused fears do not allow him to follow his better judgment, he kept alluding to new complaints and suspicions. American intelligence had told the Red Army to expect a German counterattack in Pomerania; actually, it had come in Hungary! And the people who fed him the information which aroused the President's wrath were "honest and humble." A message sent in the President's name which reached Moscow on April 13 suggested drily that the subject be dropped and they get on with fighting the war.

On the same day there was inane rejoicing in Hitler's underground bunker: the news had just reached Berlin of President Roosevelt's death on the preceding day. Soon Hitler and Goebbels were brought back to reality: nothing could save them. But quite possibly the mournful event was lucky for Stalin. It is unlikely that Roosevelt would have persisted in his illusions about Stalin. In Soviet literature Roosevelt usually is eulogized and the Cold War blamed on Truman, but Stalin probably realized that Roosevelt's death removed a man who, once aroused, was a formidable opponent.

The new President had to be sized up, so the Supreme Soviet somehow relented and let Molotov go to the United Nations, and on the way to San Francisco he stopped in Washington to see Truman, who dressed him down in a way which was soon to become familiar to various American political figures. He had never been spoken to like that before, exclaimed the "iron bottom." One must assume Molotov meant "spoken to by a foreigner." But in general his report must have been reassuring, as were those of anonymous well-wishers who provided the Soviets with information about what the British and Americans were up to. President Truman was feeling his way in foreign policy; his advisers believed in the possibility of accommodation with Russia.

The Great Fatherland War, as it is styled in the Soviet literature, was nearing its end. Stalin's men got first to Berlin. On April 16 the greatest cannonade in history ushered in the final Soviet drive. Twenty-two thousand artillery pieces opened fire. On the First Byelorussian Army Group front 98,000 tons of explosives rained on the German positions. Zhukov's group would be the one to capture Berlin, helped by Konev's First Ukrainian Group. (In Western literature it has been suggested, not on very solid grounds, that Stalin encouraged rivalry between these two commanders.) It was a rare gesture of generosity on Stalin's part to permit the man who saved Moscow to take Berlin. But for the time being, he was very fond of the outspoken soldier. At one point he felt emboldened to ask Stalin a very personal question: What, he inquired, has happened to Jacob Djugashvili? Though now he knew what had happened, Stalin chose to place it in the future: the Germans could not make Jacob betray his country, he replied, and undoubtedly they *will* shoot him. To Zhukov, he appeared genuinely moved; he must have reflected how he could have saved and chose not to save his child's life.[108] But the incident shows he genuinely liked Zhukov—a feeling which after the war probably saved Zhukov from something much worse than the obscurity of a provincial command.

It was appropriately enough the choleric General Chuykov of Stalingrad who negotiated the surrender of Berlin. And the German general with whom the offer of capitulation came was Hans Krebs—the same Krebs who, as assistant German military attaché in Moscow in 1941, was embraced by Stalin and told, "We must always remain friends."[109] Coincidences abound. The first Soviet commander of Berlin was none other than our old friend General Gorbatov. He whose friendship with a German Communist had been instrumental in having him declared an "enemy of the people" and sentenced to hard labor now presided over the first steps in setting up Communist East Germany.

Berlin fell on May 2. On May 8 the war ended. The war with Japan, which they would soon enter, carried for the Russians none of the emotional meaning of the struggle against the hated German invader.

The feeling of great relief which Stalin must have experienced—Germany conquered, no last-minute tricks played by his allies—contributed to his generous mood. At a great Kremlin banquet in honor of his commanders he toasted the Russian people, the leading nationality of all in the Soviet Union. He acknowledged (uniquely) that the government, i.e, himself, had made many mistakes before and during the first phase of the war. Any other nation, he said, would have made short shrift of this government. Not the Russians! But he did not mention what rewards the grateful Leader was to bestow on his people.[110]

On May 18 Stalin summoned his first soldier. Did he still remember how to ride? he asked Zhukov. He would have to review the Great Victory Parade on June 24. Zhukov was embarrassed; it was he, Stalin, the Supreme Commander-in-Chief, who should be thus honored. No, he was too old for such things, insisted Stalin. He might also have added a very prosaic reason: *he* could not ride. Thus it was Zhukov on a white horse who was the central figure in a spectacle such as had not been seen even in Tsarist times: led by Marshal Rokossovsky, all the leading marshals and generals, accompanied by representative units of all armies, filed past Lenin's tomb to the strains of massed bands fourteen hundred strong.

And so, fantastically, the war which Stalin had feared so much, which

108 Zhukov, p. 638.
109 Krebs shot himself before the surrender.
110 After the First Fatherland War (against Napoleon), the Emperor Alexander I also expressed his public gratitude. His edict named various classes and their rewards. When it came to the peasants, the Emperor acknowledged that their services had been so great that their reward must come from God!

he had been sure would mean the end of his power, if not a defeat for his country, ended with the Soviet flag over Berlin, and with him vastly more powerful than ever before. There seemed to be no reason any more to fear for his power, even less so any conceivable foreign enemy. Now for him as for millions of his countrymen came the moment when, as a poet wrote during the war, "After the victory we shall call a halt, drink a cup, and rest to our heart's desire."[111]

But the mood soon passed. There could be no halt. The country was ruined, 20 million Soviet lives had been lost. One had to mask one's weaknesses and make up all those losses in a hurry. And he was sixty-five years old.

---

[111] Alexis Surkov, in *New World* (Moscow), No. 1–2 (1946), p. 49. The poem was written in 1944.

THE
AGING
GOD

Writing to a friend near the end of the war, a Russian artillery officer made a mildly deprecatory reference to the dictator, a remark which before his elevation to a divinity would have been laughed off by Stalin and hardly taken any notice of by anyone else. The letter was intercepted by the security organs; in the prevailing atmosphere of liberalism the culprit received what by 1937–39 standards was a lenient sentence: eight years at hard labor. Stalin undoubtedly never heard of the incident or of the incautious officer. For Alexander Solzhenitsyn this was the beginning of his calvary, but also of a glorious career as the voice of his great nation's conscience and pride.

Another, more worldly-wise writer deferred his reflections of the tyrant until he could seemingly be safely criticized.[1] Ilya Ehrenburg then concluded that Stalin had missed a great chance by not dying at the end of the war. People would have remembered him as a great war leader, and the horrors of the past would have been attributed to others: Beria, Yezhov, and Yagoda.

It is unlikely that Stalin, for all his concern for a posthumous reputation, would have agreed with Ehrenburg. Though he felt acutely the indignities of old age, he was far from wishing for or expecting an imminent departure from this vale of tears. He would often talk about getting old and about the approach of death, but this was mainly to register his companions' reactions to such statements and to gauge the intensity of their indignant protestations. In a 1948 play, which earned its author the Stalin Prize, and which was lovingly edited by its main

---

[1] Seemingly, because Ehrenburg's ruminations brought him a severe dressing-down by Khrushchev.

hero—himself—the theatrical Stalin says that he will live to be a hundred![2] What a joke *that* would be on all those scoundrels, his faithful comrades in arms (to give them their press appellation), whose unspoken thought, he was sure, was "When will the old bastard die?" and who were watching him (as well as each other) for any sign of debility. His anguish at getting old was to take a characteristic expression: he would turn on old servants whose aging appearance reminded him of his own. In a few years not only Voroshilov and Molotov, but his personal attendants of long standing—people like Poskrebyshev and Vlasik, people of no political importance—found themselves in disgrace, with all that that implied in Stalin's Russia.

If his subordinates did not actually wish him dead, they might well have expected Stalin to choose a dignified semiretirement. But he strove to rule as ubiquitously as before. People expected from the victory an easement of their burdens, but in fact they were going to have to work as hard as before, and who else could make them? This was no time to "drink a cup, and rest to our heart's desire." The western regions of the country, including its granary, the Ukraine, had been devastated. The achievements of the Second and Third Five-Year Plans had largely been undone: in 1941, had it not been for the German attack, Russia would have produced over 22 million tons of steel; in 1945 she produced barely over 10 million. People would have to work harder to make up for those millions who had died during the war. To catch up with the West, never mind overcoming it, was as crucial as in 1930 when Stalin had first advanced the slogan. How long before the Americans realized their power and were tempted to use it? What if at that moment Russia were still weak and backward?

Other dangers and fears crowded his suspicious mind. No one could think that the Soviet system or his own power was in danger. But certainly one had to be on guard. People would forget the German atrocities and would suffer their discontents more acutely now that they had been led to expect a better life. (In some German-occupied regions the Soviet underground had sponsored rumors that after the war collectivization would be either abolished or greatly modified.)

Thousands, if not millions, had proved to be disloyal. Unless one dealt with them with exemplary severity and promptly, one was asking for trouble. Soldiers who had let themselves be taken prisoner, the population of the Baltic states—why, there were regions in the Ukraine where nationalist partisans were fighting the reestablishment of Soviet authority! Millions had seen foreign countries; even though in ruins, they must have been impressive for their incomparably higher standard

[2] This is in Nicholas Virta's piece about Stalingrad, *The Great Days*, about which more later.

of life. Foreign wars, even victorious ones, have always been dangerous to Russian society. With his sense of history, Stalin must have thought of the First Fatherland War of 1812–13. At its end Alexander I was worshiped by the whole country. But within three or four years the Tsar-Conqueror had become hated among the educated classes, and plots and conspiracies were springing up all over the Empire. In 1825 poison brought from the West almost took effect, and the Decembrist plot shook the empire of the Romanovs.

The intellectuals! There was a class which had to be watched even more strenuously than before. Scientists, writers, artists were always prone to go into raptures over foreign ways and now they obviously hoped some of the so-called bourgeois freedoms of Russia's allies would rub off on them.

Yes, there was a foreign danger—different from and yet in a way more pressing than the one Stalin had faced before 1941. He now knew enough about the democracies not to fear an imminent war. They would envy and fear Russia's new power. Their governments, especially that of Churchill, would spare no tricks to deprive him of some of the fruits of the victory, but they always reacted so sluggishly—witness how belatedly and ineffectively they moved against Hitler. Their people lacked a sense of discipline, and once peace was restored, even Churchill would find it difficult to stir them up. But there was this intangible danger of demoralizing ideas and notions seeping in from the West, damaging the sense of cohesion and discipline on which Communist society must rest. Churchill phrased it straightforwardly: "They fear our friendship more than our enmity." Saltykov-Shchedrin (Stalin was a devoted reader of the great Russian humorist) once wrote about the nobility of a backwater Russian county which got stirred up by tales of strange institutions and customs in distant America, whereupon the local governor issued an order: "Shut down America." The Tsarist government never succeeded in "shutting down" foreign countries and it had paid for it. Stalin would know how. After the war Russia would be unable to keep up close contacts with her Western allies, Stalin told Ambassador Harriman, in one of those moments of frankness which made it so difficult for people to conceive of him as a master deceiver, she would have to attend to her own problems.

The feeling of his own indispensability for the guidance of Russia (and also, now that the war had been won, of world Communism) was especially strong when it came to foreign affairs. None of his lieutenants was fit to take over this burden. At the height of his generous mood, at the victory banquet on May 24, Stalin drank to the health of "our Vyacheslav." But even then his appraisal of Molotov was rather modest: a good foreign minister was worth two or three army corps, he said. But *his* diplomacy was at least as valuable as the entire Red Army. Who else could size up foreigners instantaneously, was up to all the capitalists' tricks, and knew their weak spots so well? Could Zhdanov or Molotov be surrounded by so much awe in the foreigners' eyes? Could they or anyone else inspire so much fear, exact the same deference?

The war with Germany was over, but the arrangement for this ramshackle peace had to be wound up. Just before the demise of the Thousand-Year Reich, there had been a flurry of diplomatic activity which enabled Stalin to undo much of the damage he had done to his cause during his altercation with Roosevelt. As late as April Heinrich Himmler tried to interest the Allies in a separate peace. Churchill rejected these overtures and loyally informed Stalin of them. Again, for a moment, the dictator found a way to the Englishman's heart. "That Churchill is capable of anything," he had exclaimed to Zhukov only a month before, but to the Prime Minister on April 25 went this handsome tribute: "Knowing you, I had full confidence that you would not act differently."[3] Yet Churchill's attempt to exploit this charmed moment to soften the Soviet position on Poland and to reserve some shadow of independence for the unfortunate country met with a harsh refusal: "You, it is clear, do not agree that the Soviet Union has the right to demand for Poland a regime that would be friendly toward the U.S.S.R." Did he, Stalin, interfere with any arrangements the *British* might make in regard to Belgium or Greece?

The Prime Minister, with the famous percentages in Eastern Europe melting into nothingness before his eyes,[4] thought of another stratagem. After the capitulation of Germany the Anglo-American armies should not retreat to their occupation zones, as agreed previously with the Russians, until and unless the latter became more amenable about Eastern Europe. The vision of Russian and Anglo-American soldiers standing eyeball to eyeball and glaring at each other until such time as the Soviets would behave did not meet with approval among the Americans. President Truman, an admirer of Churchill's, perhaps would have gone along with the policy of pressuring the Russians, especially because at San Francisco Molotov was again making trouble about voting procedures and membership in the United Nations.[5] But the American

[3] *The Correspondence of the Chairman of the Council of Ministers of the U.S.S.R. with the Presidents of the United States and Prime Ministers of Great Britain* (Moscow, 1957), I, 339.

[4] Stalin must have smiled on receiving this plaintive message from Churchill: "The trend of developments in Yugoslavia is such that I do not think that the ratio 50:50 as between our interests is being observed. Marshal Tito . . . himself admits he is warmly devoted to the Soviet Union." *Ibid*, p. 349.

[5] It was there that Molotov shocked Edward R. Stettinius and Anthony Eden by announcing that the sixteen Polish underground leaders who had disappeared were being held prisoners on charges of sabotage against the Red Army. Asked what was going to happen to them, he gave the famous answer, "The guilty ones will be tried."

chiefs of staff, whose advice was now decisive, were against any such confrontation with the Soviets. The Americans' attention was on the Pacific war, and contrary to what has sometimes been alleged, military opinion in this country was nearly unanimous on the need of Soviet assistance against Japan. Quite apart from professional advice, Churchill's scheme was impractical for psychological and political reasons. Public opinion in both Britain and America was eager for peace and continued friendship with Russia. Few would endanger that friendship for the sake of some Balkan country, or because one person rather than another with an unpronounceable name should become the Prime Minister of Poland. The Soviets were well aware of the facts of life of democratic politics. With the war coming to an end, the almost dictatorial powers which the British Cabinet and the American President exercised over their respective countries' foreign and military policies were bound to be terminated. Churchill begged Stalin not to ride roughshod over the "deepest convictions of the English-speaking democracies." But the dictator remembered what Roosevelt had said at Yalta: Congress and American public opinion would not allow American troops to stay in Europe beyond two years after Germany's capitulation. What good were "deepest convictions" without any troops to back them up?

Before Truman and his advisers there now arose the specter of a forthcoming Big Three meeting breaking up in a fight between Stalin and Churchill. The Russians then might not want to enter the war against Japan, American public opinion might pronounce a plague on both houses—i.e., the British imperialists' and Russian Communists'— revert to the view that the United States should have nothing to do with the quarrels and squabbles of the Old World; the Senate might balk at the United Nations. To prevent such dire contingencies, special emissaries hastened to Moscow and London.

To London went Joseph Davies who, by virtue of his brief tenure as Ambassador to Russia and a silly book he had written about it, enjoyed the reputation of a Russian expert. The aim of his mission was to persuade Churchill to countenance a private meeting between Stalin and the President before the Big Three assembled. It cost Churchill a great deal to write with relative composure about the envoy and his message, but his memorandum on Davies' plea speaks for itself! ". . . The representatives of His Majesty's Government would not be able to attend any meeting except as equal partners from its opening."[6] Once again someone in the State Department (the idea could not have been Truman's) thought that a good way to mollify the Russians was to

[6] Winston L. S. Churchill, *Triumph and Tragedy* (Boston, 1953), p. 578.

show the American detachment from Churchill and his "imperialist" schemes. The attempt fell through, but Stalin got wind of it and drew appropriate conclusions.

Harry Hopkins, who was very ill, traveled to Moscow. Washington believed he was one man who could restore a friendly dialogue between the two countries. Known as a confidant of Roosevelt's, Hopkins it was thought could pull Stalin away from the anti-Western views and suspicions which someone—was it Molotov, or those shadowy Politburo members?—was urging.

Stalin was ready. The differences between his two allies would enable him to have pretty much his own way on Poland and the rest of Eastern Europe. Needless to say, in his talk with Hopkins, he indulged in anti-British innuendos (the British desired a *cordon sanitaire* around Russia; they had encouraged the "London Poles" in their obstinacy) and flattered the Americans. The defeat of Germany would have been impossible without the United States; "The United States has more reasons to be a world power than any other state." Did the Americans really believe he wanted to swallow up Poland? True, he had ordered the arrest of the sixteen Poles, but in wartime one had to have recourse to arbitrary measures. In Britain they had the Defense of the Realm Regulations, which empowered the government to arrest suspects and hold them without a trial. He could not interfere with their case, since it was a judicial matter, but he had a feeling they would not be judged too harshly.

And so to the Americans' great relief the Polish issue was settled. A few outsiders from London, headed by Mikolajczyk, would be allowed to join the Provisional Government (where they would have no power). London and Washington would drop their recognition of the "London Poles" and acknowledge the Soviet creature as the legitimate regime of Poland. The day scheduled for this event was to be July 4, but at the last moment someone in Washington had the delicacy to move it to July 5.

With Poland in his pocket, Stalin became all amicability. Oh, there were still problems. At the end of the war against Germany, Lend-Lease had been abruptly stopped.[7] Did someone think Russia could be pressured in this way? "If the Russians were approached on a friendly basis much more could be done, but . . . reprisals in any form would bring about the exactly opposite effect."[8] But he now withdrew the Soviet reservations about the structure of the United Nations. (The Russians still felt obliged to go through their famous act, which never failed to

[7] This was also true in regard to Great Britain.
[8] Robert E. Sherwood, *Roosevelt and Hopkins* (New York, 1950), p. 897.

621

impress the Americans: Molotov would be obdurate and seemingly unyielding; Stalin had to plead with him to accept the American position.) And on the matter which was now uppermost in the Americans' minds, Stalin was very accommodating: on August 8 Russia would be able to enter the war against Japan. Of course, argued Stalin; the Russian people had to have some reward for this sacrifice, and that "depended on China's willingness to agree to proposals made at Yalta." But, again respecting the Americans' delicacy, he expressed his willingness to discuss the matter with Chiang. Though the American love affair with the Chinese Nationalists was already beginning to go sour, Stalin was at pains to praise the Chinese leader to Harry Hopkins. Chiang was the only man to guide his country, he said. "No Communist leader was strong enough to unify China."[9] And China *must* be unified, including Manchuria and Sinkiang, about which troublemakers were spreading the rumor that Russia might want them. Of course, he added, the United States would have to play a leading part in helping China get on her feet. The Russians would be plenty busy with their own problems.

His good mood led Stalin to impart some advice to his American guest. He understood the American insistence on Japan's unconditional surrender (here he sank another harpoon into the British—he heard they were secretly negotiating with Tokyo), but was it really necessary to be so literal? Suppose you let them capitulate on terms short of unconditional surrender? Then once the country is occupied, terms or no terms, you give them the works. And of course Russia would like to have an occupation zone in Japan too.

It would be a great oversimplification to see the Stalin-Hopkins episode as a typical encounter between American gullibility and Soviet Machiavellianism. Many of Stalin's statements represented what he *then* genuinely believed. In 1945 he could not have foreseen how *all* of China would come under Communist sway, and if he had he would very likely have recoiled from the idea. He could not know how far he could or wished to impose an openly Communist system on Poland. The main secret of his personal diplomacy was the same one which some twenty years before had enabled an awkward and not well-liked Communist to seize control of the Party apparatus: hard work. Hopkins knew precious little about the main business of his trip to Russia. Stalin's knowledge of the facts and complexities of the Polish problem, however, compared favorably with that of the holder of the Polish desk in the Foreign Office or the State Department. And he viewed China realistically, by comparing the information obtained from the local Communists with that brought by his own diplomats and advisers, many of whom had served as Soviet advisers to Chiang's forces between

---

[9] *Ibid.*, p. 902.

1937 and 1941.[10] The Nationalists' army was, he knew, a conglomeration of feudal levies controlled by various warlords who acknowledged only vague allegiance to Generalissimo Chiang. Perhaps the Communists' was not much better. Mao and his people seemed to believe that they could take care of Chiang, but that was undoubtedly an exaggeration. To Secretary of State Byrnes, Stalin said in December 1945, "All Chinese are boasters who exaggerate the forces of their opponents as well as their own." But it would be a fine thing if, with some discreet Soviet help, the Communists could establish their rule over Manchuria and perhaps northwest China. One had to watch one's step carefully. The Americans had this proprietary interest in China as well as inexplicable attachment to Chiang though, as he understood, that was changing. . . . ☆☆☆

THE Potsdam meeting, the last one between the Big Three, which opened in the middle of July was in many ways a replay of Teheran and Yalta. Some of the main actors were different. The new American President, who for all his self-assurance felt some anxiety at meeting his already semilegendary partners, brought with him the new Secretary of State, his *then* great friend James Byrnes. It is not recorded what impression Stalin formed of either, yet he must have felt relieved at not facing Roosevelt. And it was with mixed emotions that Stalin viewed Churchill's replacement before the end of the conference by Clement Attlee. Chivalry was not one of his strong points, yet as both his daughter Svetlana and Miloyan Djilas astutely recognized, Stalin had a sneaking admiration for Churchill. It was exhilarating to cross swords and best the last real leader of the British Empire, an object of emulation and certain awe by Russia's rulers for over a century. For the British Labour Party, on the other hand, as for socialists everywhere, the Soviets have always had little respect. If Attlee and his Foreign Secretary, Ernest Bevin, ever believed that their alleged ideological propinquity would assure them of warmer relations with the Russians than those enjoyed by the old "imperialist" Churchill, they soon found that the contrary was the case.

To tell the truth, there was a touch of snobbery about Stalin. He had just introduced uniforms for his diplomats in obvious imitation of the British (who were about to abolish them for theirs). Colonies (called,

[10] Soviet generals who had served with Chiang then included Chuykov and Vlasov. Service in China at the time was sought by Soviet officers: it kept them out of Russia at the worst period of the Great Purge.

of course, trusteeships), naval bases all over the world, even battleships were very much on his mind. And to think the English were now ready to exchange all that imperial splendor for planned economy and the welfare state!

But the business meetings of the conference were not unlike those of its predecessors'. Churchill argued, pleaded, occasionally fulminated: Germany should not be required to pay unduly onerous reparations; Poland should not be allowed to help herself to an unduly large part of Germany; the Russians should cease their scandalous goings-on in Bulgaria and Rumania, where the British and American members of the Allied Control Commissions were virtual prisoners of the Soviet authorities. Stalin imperturbably parried these arguments: Russia had to be compensated for her vast losses, Poland must get German Pomerania and Silesia; Rumania and Bulgaria had democratic governments that should not be interfered with. The Americans sometimes feebly took the British side; more often they appealed for harmony and compromise. Stalin usually had his way.

The main item of business had been largely settled before: Germany was to be divided into occupation zones. It is obvious that not even Stalin had expected this provisional arrangement to endure for generations, or he would not have insisted that so much German territory go to Poland—which, of course, meant a diminution of any future Communist East Germany. Berlin itself was to be divided, and it is also unlikely that it occurred to him *at the moment* how convenient this arrangement would be for himself and his successors as a means of pressuring the West and by the same token how bothersome it would be to his German Communist protégés.

Stalin's appetite for territory was growing. Churchill, he reminded the Prime Minister, once talked touchingly about Russia's need for warmwater ports. It would be then appropriate for the U.S.S.R. to get a military and naval base in the Dardanelles. This would also help Turkey, since she was too weak to protect the entrance to the Black Sea and Russia would generously assume the burden. And hadn't the Americans once stated that Russia *in principle* was entitled to trusteeship of one of Italy's former colonies? He was ready to accept Tripoli. Here the Americans joined their objections to those of the British. It was up to Stalin's successors to make Russia a Mediterranean power, and they then had to wonder whether it was such a good idea.

Throughout the generally unhappy time Churchill was having before and during the first sessions of the conference, one consoling thought stayed with him: the Americans were about to test the atomic bomb. The Prime Minister and the President agreed that they should tell Stalin about the weapon without, needless to say, going into any details. And so after the news of the momentous flash in the New Mexico desert reached Potsdam, Truman went to Stalin and informed him that the United States had a weapon of unusual force. It would have revived Churchill's spirits if Stalin had blanched or asked in a broken voice for details. But Stalin greeted the announcement with aplomb: he was pleased to hear the news and hoped the Americans would use the new weapon against Japan. Marshal Zhukov, who watched the scene, provides some dramatic details. Churchill was closely watching Stalin's expression as Truman gave him the news, and Stalin, according to the worthy Marshal, did not betray his feelings. Only later, in the Soviet quarters, did he turn to Molotov and say smilingly that they were trying to scare him: "Tell Kurchatov[11] to hurry up with the work."[12] Alas, this tale, designed to reveal Stalin's iron nerve, is largely untrue. General Shtemenko gives a more reliable version. Stalin told his chief of staff, General Antonov, about Truman's revelation: "But neither Antonov nor obviously Stalin realized that this was an entirely new type of weapon. In any case, the general staff received no special instructions."[13] Soviet nuclear research had begun on a modest scale in 1942, gathered momentum only in January 1945, when espionage reports indicated the Americans were making progress on the weapon. Stalin must have been kept informed but it is unlikely that he realized the full impact of the bomb until after Hiroshima. In any case, Churchill's day was spoiled, though there remained the consoling hope (false, as it was soon to turn out) that the Russians were ignorant of what had been going on in American laboratories and testing grounds.

At Potsdam, Stalin loyally informed his allies that the Japanese government sought Soviet help in arranging peace with the United States and Britain.[14] He reaffirmed his determination to enter the war with Japan on August 8. And it was assumed that the Big Three would reconvene after Japan's capitulation. But Churchill, who was going home for the announcement of the results of the elections, perhaps sensed that he would not return to the conference, perhaps never again see this man, of whom in a perverse way he had become quite fond. There was a last social hour, at a banquet given by the Prime Minister. After the dinner Stalin went around the table collecting everybody's autographs. He caught Churchill's surprised and amazed look and

[11] Academician Igor Kurchatov, the J. Robert Oppenheimer of the Soviet atomic project.
[12] George Zhukov, *Recollections and Reflections* (Moscow, 1969), p. 732.
[13] Sergei Shtemenko, *The General Staff* (Moscow, 1963), p. 359. Soviet generals should read each other's memoirs. Shtemenko's was published only one year before Zhukov's.
[14] If one is of a cynical turn of mind, one may explain Stalin's openness by the probable knowledge on the Soviet part that the Americans had broken the Japanese code.

laughed delightedly. This was the moment to elicit some historic statement that would make all the present and past disagreements fade away. Churchill filled their glasses with generous portions of brandy and gave his friend and antagonist a significant look. They drained their glasses, bottoms up, which in the case of an inveterate brandy drinker can be excused only by the weightiness of the moment and of his anticipations. But then, sadly, Stalin from being a collector of autographs became again a collector of territories. He said: "If you find it impossible to give us a fortified position in the Marmora, could we not have a base at Dede Agach?"[15] The spell was broken.

Not quite so anticlimactic was Stalin's leavetaking of Truman. The President hoped that they might meet again in Washington. "May God grant this," replied the dictator in one of those references to the deity which never ceased to puzzle the Americans: wasn't Communism supposed to be godless? Privately Truman was not so sure that God should. Writing to his mother in Missouri, he confessed that though he was impressed by Stalin, the Russians in general and Molotov in particular were awful. He wished he had seen the last of them, but he supposed that there would have to be more conferences.

Soviet preparations for attacking Japan had been veiled in deep secrecy. Stalin was eager that the blow should fall upon the Japanese units in Manchuria and northeast China suddenly and devastatingly. Any setback or stalemate threatened to jeopardize his political designs in the Far East. The following story, though in itself trivial, is of great human interest. On August 3 the General Staff's chief of operations, Shtemenko, received a letter from a private citizen informing him that in a "public place" (read: bar) he had heard a Red Army colonel boast loudly that he was attached to the Far Eastern headquarters and that very soon big things would be going on there. The culprit was soon identified and dismissed from the service, but not punished otherwise. Stalin was not told about the incident. The story is credible only within the context of the national euphoria following Germany's defeat. Certainly at any previous time the babbler would have been lucky to get away with several years at hard labor. And by concealing the incident from Stalin and the NKVD, Shtemenko and the others concerned risked much more than their generals' epaulets. Perhaps they thought of so many of their innocent comrades who had perished as victims of "vigilance." In any case, it is a rare case of humanity and compassion in Stalin's Russia.

August 6: Hiroshima. On August 8 the Japanese ambassador paid a visit to Molotov with yet another plea to have the Russians transmit Tokyo's peace proposals to the United States. This was the kind of

[15] Churchill, p. 667.

occasion the "iron bottom" enjoyed above all. What a happy inspiration for the diplomat to visit him just now, for he had something to tell him: as of August 9 the U.S.S.R. would be at war with the Japanese Empire.

Soviet historians have a legitimate grievance against Westerners who allege that the Soviet entrance was precipitated or hastened by the dropping of the bomb. August 8, as we have seen, had all along been the target date. Less legitimate is their argument that it was the Soviet intervention rather than the bomb which precipitated the Japanese surrender. The victory was easy: the Soviets enjoyed a crushing superiority in men and equipment.[16]

A glance at the map of the operations will show how closely they were attuned to Stalin's political aims. The Soviets were eager for the speediest possible occupation of Manchuria and northern Korea and a linkage with the forces of the Chinese Communists. To facilitate the latter, the main Red Army thrust was through Mongolia into northeast China. As usual, political aims were pursued with no thought of human cost. It made little sense for the Russians to attack southern Sakhalin, away from the main theaters of operation and assigned for return to the U.S.S.R. in any case. Yet Sakhalin was attacked on the first day of the war. The announcement of the general Japanese capitulation on August 14 did not stop the Soviet offensive. Rather than wait a few days, thousands of Soviet lives were expended. The twenty-three-day campaign of the Red Army in the Far East has been credited by recent Soviet sources not only with delivering the decisive blow to the Japanese, but also with being the key factor in the future successes of the Chinese Communists. And indeed, while to their great bitterness the Chinese Communists were not allowed to move into Manchuria alongside the Red Army units, the very considerable stocks of Japanese arms seized by the Russians were turned over to Mao's forces. But this fact did not become publicized until many, many years later when the Russians had occasion to reflect ruefully on Mao's ingratitude.

The closer Stalin got to success in any of the great historical tests he faced, the sharper his anxiety became, the more apparent his morbid suspiciousness. So it had been with collectivization and the war with Germany. And now there was fear again: would the Americans really keep their word and allow him to cash in on Japan's defeat—in which the Red Army's role, whatever he might say, he knew was secondary? On August 16 he addressed an anxious message to Truman. In his general order on Japan's capitulation General MacArthur, as Supreme

16 The official Soviet source, *The History of the Great Fatherland War of the Soviet Union*, v (Moscow, 1963), 551, places this superiority at two to one in men and planes, five to one in tanks. In fact, the Soviet superiority was even more crushing: few of the Japanese planes were battle ready, half of the troops were from the puppet Manchurian army and of little fighting value.

627

Allied Commander, specified that Japanese units in Manchuria, Sakhalin, and North Korea ought to surrender to the Soviet command. How about the Kurile Islands? Under Yalta they should go to Russia; hence they should be surrendered to the Soviets. And for good measure he tried now to slip in something which had not been agreed before—a Soviet share in the occupation of Japan proper. Half of the northernmost island of Hokkaido should be occupied by the Soviet Union, he argued. This would have a beneficial effect on Russian public opinion, which remembered so bitterly the Japanese occupation of the Soviet Far East between 1919 and 1921. "I should fervently hope that my modest requests do not meet with objections."[17]

Truman's answer was not likely to satisfy Russian public opinion. All of Japan proper was to be under MacArthur, and that was that. A *symbolic* Red Army detachment might be allowed to participate in the occupation, at the discretion and under the command of MacArthur. As to the Kurile Islands, they would go to the Soviet Union, but the United States wished to have airbases there "for commercial and military purposes."

Truman's answer was quite peremptory, and it brought out in Stalin some of that near panic which he had experienced in March–April when he convinced himself that his allies were ready to make a separate agreement with Germany. Were the Americans going to throw their weight around now that they had this bomb? He acquiesced in the Americans' refusal to give him a slice of Japan to occupy, but with almost tragicomic petulance: "I and my colleagues did not expect such an answer from you." But the demand for bases in the Kuriles made him frantic, and again it is amazing that he should betray his feelings so clearly. Why did the Americans want this base? It had never been discussed before. Demands like this were addressed only to defeated or weak states, went on the inveterate base-seeker. "Speaking from the heart, neither I nor my colleagues could understand what made the United States address this demand to the Soviet Union."

Though he protested how much he was hurt by the demand, Stalin was cautious enough *not* to reject it categorically. Now, had America at the time practiced atomic diplomacy, as has tediously been alleged in recent years, this would have been an excellent occasion for Truman to continue hurting Stalin's feelings. Yes, the United States gets the base or Russia doesn't get the islands. Or, let us talk now about Poland. But in fact, Truman explained, all he meant was for the Americans to have landing rights in the Kuriles for any emergency concerning the occupation of Japan. He would not insist, if the Russians objected.

Relieved, Stalin's answer was sweetness and light: of course the

17 *The Correspondence* . . . , II, 264.

Soviets would be happy to welcome American planes in the Kuriles! Eager to undo any previous impression of weakness and panic, he asked for reciprocal landing rights in the Aleutians. The U.S.S.R., he gravely explained, was eager to establish a commercial air route to Seattle. Strangely enough, no Soviet commercial plane is known to have landed in Seattle before or since then. And everybody was glad to forget about the Soviet occupation zone in Japan, and so this country was spared the ordeal endured by postwar Germany and Korea. Thus passed the only occasion on which it can be said with some assurance that America's monopoly of the atomic bomb filled Stalin with anxiety. But of course no one in Washington realized it!

In fact, the whole unpleasant but instructive episode was forgotten in the warm glow of exultation over Japan's formal act of surrender. On September 2 Stalin wired Truman his congratulations to "the U.S. armed forces for their brilliant victory," more than implying that they had carried the main burden of that victory. He dispatched his auto-graphed picture to the President which, the latter assured him, would always be treasured by him "in happy remembrance of our cordial collaboration at Potsdam."[18]

V-J Day could not have for the Russians the same meaning as it did for the Americans and, of course, could not approach in emotional impact the day of victory over Germany.[19] But in his victory proclamation he stressed Japanese perfidy, going back as early as 1904, when they suddenly attacked the Russian warships (just like Pearl Harbor, he added). People of *his* generation had waited for forty years for this day of retribution. This motif was a bit unhistorical: in 1905 Koba-Dju-gashvili, like most Russian revolutionaries, welcomed the defeat of Tsarist Russia. His proclamation was his most nationalistic yet—nothing about the "Party of Lenin and Stalin," no hint of an ideological theme, only the evocation of the great national endeavor at victories: "Long live and flourish our Fatherland." And he painted the prospect of a permanent peace. No conceivable enemies now threatened the Father-land. "For all nations of the world there has come the long-awaited peace."

And, so on September 2, 1945, Stalin shared the emotion of millions of his countrymen: "Glory to our victorious nations." He seemed to

---

[18] Truman's reciprocal gesture was to ask Stalin to receive an American artist, so that his portrait might join "the historic mementoes of the United States," presum-ably in the White House. But, like many American dreams at the end of the war, this one failed to come true.

[19] Stalin initiated the practice of hailing victories by army salvos: they could not use the old custom of having churchbells ring, he explained to his intimates. He regulated personally the magnitude of the salvos: on V-E Day the Muscovites were treated to thirty salvos of one thousand guns each; on V-J Day to twenty-four salvos by three hundred and twenty-four artillery pieces.

share the relief and the fervent wish of millions of human beings everywhere. But in four months the tyrant-teacher had returned. On February 9, 1946, he appeared before his "electors" (elections to the Supreme Soviet were going on) and his listeners (as well as the whole nation) must have realized that this was the pre-June 1941 Stalin who was speaking, that he had never stopped being a tyrant while leading the nation in defeat and victory. The wartime form of address was discarded: no more "Brothers, sisters, my friends, my countrymen." It was again the dry "Comrades." And the same dialectic tone, the same question-and-answer format. Who won the war? No longer the Russian or even the Soviet *nation:* "Our victory means above all that our *social* system has won. . . . Our *political* system has won."[20] And Stalin had built this system. He kept reminding them, as if they needed it, how he had had to fight to overcome the intrigues of the "Trotskyites and the Right," to force through collectivization and rapid industrialization. Did they expect a better deal for the consumer after their sacrifices during the war? Well, he reminded them, under Communism heavy industry must have a priority over light. Did they think that the collective farm system would be modified, and were some even foolish enough to believe it would be abolished? Collectivization was the cornerstone of the Soviet system. Stalin's general tone left little doubt that most of the burden for future rapid industrialization would continue to be borne on the Russian peasant's broad shoulders. Peace had come to the world? How could one expect lasting peace if capitalism and with it imperialism remained? They had to work harder than ever before. They had to achieve annual production of 60 million tons of steel, 500 million of coal, and 60 million of oil. "Only then will our country be guaranteed against all kinds of eventualities." How it all sounded like 1930 or even 1937!

As he had then, Stalin chose to accompany his bitter lessons with the promise of (largely illusory) boons. Soon, he said, rationing would be abolished and prices for consumer goods would be lowered. His listeners applauded. They did not know that when these blessings arrived in 1947, they would be accompanied by a revaluation of the ruble that would wipe out the life savings of a considerable number of them, especially among the peasants.

Stalin talked with that barely suppressed fury which one might have thought would never return after the war, after the victory. So "they" had said the Soviet system was a risky experiment, "a house of cards"? That it was held together by the Secret Police; that one push from the outside and the whole Soviet Union will come tumbling down? Few could perceive that he was reliving his own fears and humiliations of the

[20] Stalin, *Works* (Stanford ed.), III, 7.

first years of the war, that in his mind he was already searching for new traitors and victims, that he was angry at being old and alone.

There was no ostensible reason for the serene, confident, and grateful Stalin of September 1945 to revert to being a harsh taskmaster. Mme. Alliluyeva informs us that following the end of the war with Japan her father fell ill with a "long and difficult sickness."[21] But it could not have been too long, for in December of the same year, Stalin received Messrs. Byrnes and Bevin at the Big Three foreign ministers' meeting in Moscow, and neither of them noticed any traces of a major ailment.

Nothing on the international or the domestic scene seemed to warrant the dictator's displeasure. Soviet Russia's star shone brightly. Eastern Europe was firmly under Soviet sway. An interesting and promising situation was developing in China. All over the world Communist parties displayed new strength, reflecting the might and glory of the biggest of them. They were linked into a monolithic bloc—more than they had ever been by the formal machinery of the Comintern—by their worship of the greatest Communist. The Grand Alliance was coming to an end, but slowly, amid constant wrangling among the Big Three, disputes which unlike the wartime ones were taking place in the full glare of publicity. There was so much to wrangle about: division of reparations, payments from Germany, the Soviet-sponsored Bulgarian government, the Russians' separatist regimes in northern Iran, etc. But on almost all issues the diplomatic offensive was Russia's, and her allies were reduced to pleading that what the Soviets were doing was not in accordance with previous pledges or the Yalta Declaration on Liberated Europe, documents which had seemed so weighty only a few months before. With Churchill and Roosevelt gone, Stalin felt emboldened to push once more for Soviet bases on Turkish soil. And public opinion in Soviet Armenia and Georgia now raised its voice to demand the return of those parts of Russian Transcaucasia which Turkey had snatched in 1918.

In December, at the last Allied international conference in which he participated directly, Stalin demonstrated that he had lost none of his diplomatic flair. Yes, he would pull Soviet troops out of northern Iran *eventually.* For the moment they had to stay there because of the threat (from the Iranian army?!) to the oil fields of Baku. And he would be happy to withdraw the Red Army from Manchuria. But the Americans should also take their own troops from China. He was worried about Chiang, he explained. "If the Chinese people became convinced Chiang was depending on foreign troops . . . Chiang would lose his influence." Byrnes did not think of retorting that the Soviets had a wonder-

---

[21] Svetlana Alliluyeva, *Twenty Letters to a Friend* (in Russian; New York, 1967), p. 176.

ful opportunity of enhancing their East European Communist friends' popular support by pulling *their* troops out of these countries! There were flashes of the old, if somewhat spurious wartime intimacy. When at a dinner Molotov began to tease James Bryant Conant, the scientific expert brought along by Byrnes, and asked him whether he had an atomic bomb in his pocket, Stalin brought him down sharply: there was no reason to joke about the achievements of American science, he said. American "revisionist" historians have argued that all this while Stalin was deadly afraid of as well as humiliated by America's sole possession of the dreaded weapon. But as we have seen the Americans evidently did not know how to scare Stalin with atomic diplomacy. For Stalin the worst folly would be to display any anxiety on the subject, give the slightest impression that Russia's policies and claims were affected by it. What would the Americans do if they thought that their possession of the weapon could induce him to conduct more "reasonable" policies in Poland or Rumania? Why, soon they would be demanding that he introduce a two-party democracy *into Russia!*

For America's potential power Stalin had unfeigned respect, never mind the atomic bomb. How could one not respect and fear the country which at the war's end was outproducing the rest of the world, while having more men in its armed forces than the U.S.S.R! But he was confident he knew the Americans' political mind, could gauge their probable reaction to his moves, and could avoid what some years later was dubbed confrontation. American foreign policy lacked that essential ingredient of statesmanship: patience. Americans grew weary of, hence disinterested in, political disputes of long standing. It was by now obvious that beyond some tedious diplomatic notes and protests, they would do nothing about the Russian domination of Eastern Europe, hence one could go faster there than originally intended. Perhaps the same might be true of Germany when after a two-year period the Americans, as Roosevelt had promised at Yalta, pulled out their troops. One had, however, to be alert to the sensitive spots. You could not be sure about Finland, for example. Logically there was no reason to treat this little country differently from, say, Bulgaria. Yet Roosevelt had displayed incomprehensible solicitude for Finland at Teheran, greater than that for Poland—despite all those Polish voters in the United States.

When it came to the Far East, Stalin knew that American imperialism was purposeful and tenacious—witness the short shrift he got when he requested Soviet participation in the occupation of Japan. But there was a tantalizing inconsistency in American policy. They were really and seriously trying to bring about a lasting peace and harmony between Chiang and Mao rather than pulling out all stops in helping their man. The Chinese Communists were somewhat bitter that Stalin was not helping them more and openly, that the U.S.S.R. had signed a treaty with Chiang (where in exchange for the Generalissimo's agreeing to all the *Chinese* concessions Roosevelt had promised Stalin at Yalta, the Soviet solemnly pledged their noninterference in Chinese domestic politics). On the eve of signing the treaty Mao had thought to cheer up his partisans in Yenan in words also intended for Russian ears: "Relying on the forces we ourselves organize we can defeat all Chinese and foreign reactionaries. . . . U.S. imperialism, while outwardly strong, is inwardly weak."[22] Foreign Communists, it seemed to the Russians, were now very ready to have Russia fight their battles and were chagrined and uncomprehending if she did not. After Japan's capitulation Mao declared touchingly—but at the time it was foolish and tactless—that it was the Red Army rather than American power that brought about the end of the Pacific war. He was a bit like Tito, who could not understand why the Soviet Union should not risk a major confrontation with the Anglo-Americans so that some minor Adriatic port could go to Yugoslavia rather than Italy. True, on China the Americans' views and behavior were rather bizarre. Stalin could recall with amusement President Roosevelt's special envoy, General Hurley, assuring him and Molotov that the Chinese Communists were interested mainly in "creating a free, democratic, and united government in China."[23] With patience and luck one might be able to build a Communist state *within* China. But to think that Chinese Communists were capable of, and that the Americans would tolerate, conquest of the vast country? That seemed much less likely than an early American withdrawal from Germany.

Even a man as suspicious as Stalin could not discern any threat to his power in the Russia of 1945–46. What, then, accounted for the harsh tone of his February 9 speech? Lack of *overt* dangers of course never stilled his suspicions for long. As the war began to recede in time, so did the memory of those millions who died "for the Fatherland and for Stalin." Stalin's thoughts now evidently dwelt on those other millions who more or less willingly were returning from German captivity and from voluntary or forced labor outside wartime Russia. Here was another fertile breeding ground for enemies of the people. Many, to be sure, exchanged German captivity for imprisonment at home. Yet one could not imprison tens of millions of people who had been under German occupation and had thereby, even if absolutely loyal, suffered from some ideological pollution. In any event the whole society had to some extent been exposed to it; the mood of patriotism, so desirable during the war and in general, had been allowed to weaken that ideological vigilance on which in the last analysis the Soviet system must

---

[22] Quoted in Tang Tsou, *America's Failure in China* (Chicago, 1963), p. 304.
[23] From *U.S. Relations with China, with Special Reference to the Period 1944–49* (Washington, 1949), p. 95.

rest. One no longer had to worry about German and Japanese spies penetrating the highest ranks of the army, government, and Party. But a new danger loomed: admirers, whether overt or secret, of the West and of Western ways were infiltrating the world of the arts and sciences.

How could a man of Stalin's intelligence fear a returning Russian's impression of a higher living standard in Germany, a journalist's or engineer's envy of the freer ways among Englishmen or Americans he had encountered during the war? Crowds were not going to storm the Kremlin demanding civil liberties, plots were not going to be hatched within the Moscow Writers' Union or the physics faculty of a university to wrest power from the Communist Party of the U.S.S.R.! Yet a sense of their system's vulnerability never abandoned the Communists of Stalin's generation, nor the memory of how a handful of people inspired by *foreign* ideas had in 1917 in fact overturned the government of a powerful empire. During wartime collaboration with the West, too many subversive ideas had penetrated Soviet society as if by osmosis; now they had to be suppressed and strict ideological vigilance restored. For all his paeans to the Russian nation, Stalin had a very unsentimental view of certain national characteristics. Russians had to be ruled with an iron hand. Relax controls the slightest bit and people again became loafers, the educated classes started to imitate foreign ways. A large part of the awe in which the Soviet Union was held abroad was due to a belief in the monolithic unity of Soviet society, in the people's absolute loyalty and devotion to the leader and the Communist system. One must allow nothing which might shake that belief.

During the war a number of Britons and Americans stationed in Russia had married local girls. After the armistice no pleadings from the West, official or private, could persuade Stalin to permit the wives to depart with their husbands. Never mind public opinion in the West, never mind that it was but a handful of people involved. He would not let these "unpatriotic" women flee to easy life abroad, babble slanderous tales about Soviet reality. Only after his death was this policy, more amazing in its pettiness than its inhumanity, reversed.

Stalin's deification never quite quenched his lust for power. He was a jealous god. It was not enough to be worshiped and obeyed—he must know everything being done in his name. And at his age this was becoming impossible. He could no longer keep abreast of all the details—from problems of aircraft design to NKVD personnel procedures. How to make sure they were not fooling Comrade Stalin? More than ever before he shuffled his lieutenants around, made them compete against and inform on each other.

Even before the war Stalin was aware of how pervasive the influence of Beria had become, and he was taking steps to curtail Beria's powers. But then war came and Beria was for him in security affairs what

Zhukov was in military matters: a man he had to lean on.[24] Beria was named a Marshal of the Soviet Union, an insult which the officer corps of the Red Army never forgot and which in 1953 was an important factor in bringing about his downfall.[25] After the war the dreaded Georgian still held manifold reins of power: overall supervision of both police ministries, control of secret scientific projects (including atomic energy), his private empire in Transcaucasia. As before, the main factor in his indispensability was Stalin's realization of how deeply he was hated by the other oligarchs and hence the conviction, shaken only in Stalin's very last years, that he therefore had to be uncompromisingly loyal. Still, it was not healthy to have one man wield so much power. In 1946 Beria was raised to full membership in the Politburo, a belated promotion for a man whose influence now dwarfed that of such old-timers as Kaganovich and Andreyev. Yet at the same time, a Central Committee secretary, Alexis Kuznetsov, was made Party watchdog of the security apparatus. For Beria this must have been an ominous warning: Kuznetsov's role was unpleasantly reminiscent of that played by Yezhov in 1935–36 vis-à-vis Yagoda. Stalin was not quite ready to strike at Beria: he was too useful.

The vision of himself coming to Lenin's end—incapacitated, surrounded by sorrowful lieutenants who from solicitude would keep him out of things—was now very much on Stalin's mind. In Party affairs he had leaned in the last eight years on Malenkov. This intelligent pudgy man was also resented by his other "comrades-in-arms." Though in general fraternal love was not a strong characteristic of the group, Malenkov was felt to be an especial *parvenu* by people like Kaganovich and Molotov; others thought of him as a backstairs type who had never headed a big territorial Party organization like Zhdanov or Khrushchev. During the war Malenkov had shouldered the main responsibility for the state and Party administration. He took on some of the airs of an heir-apparent. A Soviet airman recalls Malenkov's visit of inspection to the Stalingrad front, when one by one he proceeded to dress down high-ranking military and air force leaders. This was par for the course from a representative of the State Defense Committee, but no one could suppress his amazement when Malenkov read a lesson to Vassily Stalin, then a major in the air corps.

---

[24] In 1941 the NKVD was to have been divided into a Commissariat of Internal Affairs, which would perform ordinary police functions, and a Commissariat of State Security, which inherited the secret police-terror role. Because of the outbreak of the war, this division was not effected. In 1946 "commissariats" became "ministries" in accordance with the general tendency to substitute respectable terminology for a revolutionary one. There was thus the *MVD* (Interior) and *MGB* (Security).

[25] He had personally supervised Marshal Blücher's investigation-torture in 1938. In December 1953 Marshal Konev presided over the special panel which sent Beria and his main accomplices to death.

Stalin liked the fat little man. But, again, he would not have Malenkov play Stalin to his Lenin. Toward the end of 1946 Malenkov's role as principal Party Secretary was temporarily terminated and his talents diverted to state administration. To offset this recent partiality, Stalin brought an old favorite back to the Central Party apparatus, Zhdanov. Until the last phase of the war he had stayed in Leningrad: we have seen how his activities there in 1941 earned him Stalin's displeasure and how his subsequent identification with the epic of the Leningrad siege could not have been too pleasing to an envious and suspicious man. But now Zhdanov—who for a high Party officer of the time was uncharacteristically articulate and had a certain polish—was again Stalin's right-hand man, until his death in 1948. Perhaps Stalin was reassured by the fact that Zhdanov was not well. What was an asset in a political lieutenant was a nuisance in a companion: suffering from a heart ailment and forbidden to drink, Zhdanov could not keep up his end in the frightful boisterousness that reigned around Stalin's table. Mme. Alliluyeva recounts how her father once turned on him for no reason except irritation at his guest's sickly and pained expression amidst the inebriated gaiety.[26] Stalin was not an easy man to work for.

Marshals and generals whose names had rung out all over Russia and the world were soon in decent professional obscurity. The most famous of them, Zhukov, remained until the spring of 1946, with Vishinsky at his elbow as political adviser, as Soviet commander-in-chief and member of the Allied Control Commission in Germany. General Dwight D. Eisenhower, during his visit to Russia in 1945, received the impression (evidently shared by the Marshal himself) that Zhukov was high in Stalin's favor and number two in the country. After the recall from Germany, Zhukov received a subordinate position in the Ministry of War; provincial garrisons followed. Nicholas Virta's play about Stalingrad, produced in 1948, has not one word about the man who at the time of the victory was recognized as its main planner.[27] No other leading commanders were treated so shabbily. But on Stalin's relinquishing the Ministry of War in 1947, the post went to Nikolai Bulganin rather than a professional soldier.[28]

The generals were put firmly in place. It was now discovered that the

[26] Svetlana Alliluyeva, *Only One Year* (New York, 1969), p. 384.

[27] One does not have to spell out who in the play is the main architect of victory. In fact it portrays Stalin, already in August 1942, outlining the precise tactics through which the Red Army's offensive in November would trap the Germans in Stalingrad.

[28] Bulganin's star was rising. He was named a Marshal of the Soviet Union, an appointment only a bit less outrageous than that of Beria. In March 1946 the same session of the Central Committee which elevated Beria and Malenkov to full membership made Bulganin and another up-and-coming man, Alexei Kosygin, alternate members of the Politburo.

contribution of Zhukov, Vasilevsky, et al. to the final victory was really secondary: all along they were executors of plans conceived by the greatest military leader of all time. Early defeats? What defeats? It was all part of the grand design of the genius strategist who lured the Germans deep into the country in order to deal them crushing blows. This discovery was announced by Stalin in a letter to a military historian who wrote to him for guidance on military doctrine. It turned out that Stalin was full of ideas on this subject, and was willing to share them not only with his correspondent but with the historical profession and the public at large. He gently chided the letter-writer for his praise: "One's ears hurt from your praising Stalin to the skies, it is too embarrassing to read."[29] But for all this usual modesty he adopted a rather haughty tone about the alleged authorities on the subject. The ideas of Clausewitz, for a century the bible of military thinkers, Stalin pronounced to be quite obsolete: "It would be ridiculous now to take lessons from Clausewitz." Engels' pretensions in the field were also dismissed. And for all of Lenin's greatness, he was not a military expert and so his ideas on war were a bit amateurish. Stalin the military historian then sought the clue to the greatness of Stalin the military leader, and he concluded that it lay in his innovative and creative development of the technique of *counteroffensive*. The ancient Parthians knew something about it when they annihilated the Romans deep in their territory. And Field Marshal Kutuzov in 1812 also lured Napoleon deep into Russia to destroy the Grand Army. But the reader must conclude that all these were rank amateurs when compared with Stalin: certainly no one else had ever lured the enemy so persistently and so deeply into his territory.

Stalin's revelations must have been greeted by his generals with some very private gnashing of teeth. But unmindful of his modesty, they all now joined in homage to the world's greatest theoretician and practitioner of the military art.

In addition to the intended effect of cutting the generals down to size, Stalin's excursion into military theory had another significance. He was increasingly eager to add the laurels of philosopher and theoretician to those of statesman and war leader. Though he intended to live to be a hundred, realistically speaking time was growing short, and he had to hurry to acquaint the world with the profundity of his views on history, economics, and linguistics. He now authorized publication of his *Collected Works*, perhaps they would look puny, in size and in content, when compared with those of Lenin. Stalin hinted in the introduction that Lenin could write so much because unlike himself he was not a *practitioner* of revolution. But on second thought, even Lenin's theoretical pre-eminence was rather irritating. Some ground might be gained

[29] Stalin (Stanford ed.), III, 33.

by a judicious rearrangement of past authors' credits. The *History of the Communist Party of the U.S.S.R.—Short Course* to which Stalin had contributed a chapter was after the war attributed to him in its entirety and proclaimed to possess theoretical significance approximating that of Marx's *Capital*. But it was difficult for Stalin to have frequent recourse to ghost writers. His vanity clashed with his ambition.

Alas, his famous oratory would also have to be curtailed. There were pressing reasons to call a new Party Congress, since none had been held since 1939. But a Congress would compel him to be on his feet for six or seven hours, delivering the general report. To delegate this task would mean to acknowledge his growing infirmity. People would draw outrageous conclusions. Yet public appearances and speeches, for which he never cared very much, now grew increasingly burdensome and were to be avoided. And why draw attention to his aging appearance? The only occasion on which Stalin made a speech to a wide audience after 1946 was at the Nineteenth Party Congress, in 1952. One might think that radio provided an ideal way out of Stalin's dilemma, but then he was sensitive about his accent. Everyone knew he was Georgian, yet the young believed that somehow he was also a Russian and might be unpleasantly surprised at his pronunciation. His favorite way of communicating with the outside world was through interviews: sometimes he received questioners in person, more often foreign or domestic persons submitted questions in writing and the oracle made a pronouncement.

"Lately a *Pravda* correspondent turned to Comrade Stalin with a request to clarify a number of questions connected with Mr. Churchill's speech."[30] Stalin obliged the readers of *Pravda*. The speech in question was the famous Fulton, Missouri, address by the former Prime Minister during which he gave world currency to a term he had used for some time: the "iron curtain." In the presence of President Truman, Churchill had argued that democracies must maintain unity and vigilance in the face of Soviet encroachments. His speech could not in any sense be construed as a call for a preventive war; it was a plea for negotiating with the Russians from a position of strength—to use a phrase as yet unborn—and Churchill was sure that if they remained united, the United States and Britain had such a position. Stalin chose to wait a week before commenting on his old partner's recipe. By this time it was clear that the reaction in the West to Churchill's speech was far from favorable. Truman himself was criticized for lending his presence to this anti-Soviet outburst. Many Americans (some of whom would in three years' time orate about the threat of "godless Communism") thought that Churchill was making yet another bid for America to pull British

[30] *Ibid.*, p. 35.

chestnuts out of the fire. In Britain the Labour Government was embarrassed: the belief that the Soviets were in a sense fellow socialists, and hence easier to live with, had not yet been entirely dispelled. *The Times*, always close to government thinking, offered an editorial rebuke to Churchill: Why talk about things which divide the Allies? The democracies could learn from Russia in the "development of economic and social planning." It had been only a few months since the end of the war, and most people in the West were eager to do some social and economic planning on their own and forget international conflicts, territories, etc., for a while.

When Stalin on March 13 loosed his thunderbolt against Churchill, he very astutely sought to cater to these fears and objections. Speeches like Churchill's, he seemed to say, made the Russians mad: if you listened to them, you might have to forget the pleasant private life you have embarked on, you might have war. Churchill, he said opprobriously of the man with whom he had frolicked a few months before, "reminds one startlingly of Hitler and his friends." Churchill wanted the English-speaking nations to dominate the world. The comparison was outrageously slanderous, but the latter statement was not far off the mark.

Churchill wanted war. He denigrated Russia's East European allies. What he said about the current regimes in Poland, Hungary, etc., was "not only slanderous but vulgarly tactless,"[31] since those countries had exemplary democratic regimes—more so, in fact, than Great Britain. In England the Labour Party was in power, with other parties "deprived of the right of participation in government," whereas in Poland, for example, Socialist, Peasant, and many other parties had joined in government coalitions with the Communists. "And that is called by Churchill totalitarianism, tyranny, the police state." As before, Stalin was a great master of logic. To be sure, the Communists played a leading role in the People's Democracies, but they deserved it. This was the case of the "common man," something an old Tory could not understand. And in England those "common men" decided they did not want Churchill in power.

It was also useful to have a message for home consumption. Churchill, Stalin proclaimed, was trying to organize a new crusade against the Soviet Union, just as he attempted to and failed after World War I. Of course he was not likely to succeed: millions of "common men" were guarding the world's peace. But the Soviet people must remain vigilant, so that if he tried anything, the foreign foe would be crushed as he had been twenty-six years ago!

All in all, it was an effective performance. It was some time before the

---

[31] *Ibid.*, p. 37.

diffident and sluggish American colossus adopted the kind of policies Churchill had in mind at Fulton: a Western military alliance, economic and military assistance to countries fighting Communism, etc. But Churchill would have been consoled for the initial failure of his plea had he realized that through the very fact of uttering it, he had helped to save another country.

Prior to March 1946 the Soviets gave every indication that they planned to retain troops in Iran, where, under their aegis, two puppet regimes had been established in the northern part of the country, and where the central government had been under Soviet pressure to grant the U.S.S.R. a variety of concessions. U.S.-British complaints about this, whether in Moscow or in the United Nations, did not meet with success. On March 26, however, Moscow pledged to withdraw its troops and within six weeks did so. Throughout the rest of the year the Soviets watched passively while the Iranian government liquidated the separatist regimes and executed their leaders. The Iranian parliament rejected any economic concessions to the U.S.S.R. and the pro-Communist Party was suppressed. Stalin was still prudent in foreign affairs. The chances were that on Iran as on Eastern Europe the British and Americans would talk a lot but do nothing, but the coincidence of Churchill's Fulton appeal and the Iranian crisis was awkward: better to pull back, allow time for passions to cool, and anti-Soviet impulses in the West to dissipate. ☆☆☆

WHAT were Stalin's ambitions and aspirations following the war? Once the Soviet Union demonstrated it would not play ball (at least not according to the American rules) in the United Nations, a considerable body of public opinion in America reverted to the theme that Stalin aspired to world domination. The legend grew of the Red Army's being able and ready to pounce on Western Europe, to march to the English Channel, and its being restrained only through the fear of the atomic bomb. An opposite but equally fatuous view held that Stalin's ominous and puzzling behavior was due to his fear and sense of humiliation from the treatment he was experiencing at the hands of the Western statesmen, who chose to withhold knowledge of nuclear technology from Russia. They *virtually* threatened him with the bomb, so he had to seize Eastern Europe and assure his security (so it was widely believed in the West and to some extent still is) by not demobi-

The Aging God

lizing the Red Army. America would not help Russia with a loan—small wonder the Soviets exploited their new empire and looted Manchuria.

Both appraisals expressed what their American exponents felt would be *their* reactions were they in Stalin's shoes. Churchill for his part offered another view of Stalin. He told Secretary of the Navy James Forrestal, the Washington official perhaps most agitated over the alleged Russian threat, the Russians "will try every door in the house, enter all the rooms which are not locked and when they come to one that is barred, if they are unsuccessful in breaking through it, they will withdraw and invite you to dine genially that same evening."[32] But Stalin's personality and hence Soviet policies defied such simple formulas. He was not a man bent on the world's conquest as Forrestal imagined. He would not, as Henry Wallace believed, collaborate wholeheartedly in the United Nations provided that the Americans rejected British blandishments and followed progressive anti-imperialist policies. And he was not quite Churchill's genial plunderer.

Churchill's view overlooked a considerable residue of Marxism-Leninism in the dictator's mind. To be sure, what was good for Stalin was good for world Communism: he could not conceive of any conflict between the two. *Eventually* Communism would inherit the world, but not in his time. And in a way this was comforting: he would not want to deal with a Communist United States and would not be altogether pleased at the sudden emergence of Communist China. World domination? He was not Hitler to think in such terms, to believe the main key to power lay in military escapades. Let Russia outproduce all other countries in steel and other aspects of industrial power—again something which will not happen in his lifetime—and then there might be some sense in such speculations. When his terrible suspiciousness was not aroused, he was the most realistic of statesmen. The Red Army, which the capitalists believed was ready at his nod to surge toward the Channel, was being demobilized almost as fast as the American: men were needed in factories and on farms.

Could anything have made him different, made him trust and collaborate with the West? He would have found this question hilarious: he had not gotten where he was by trusting people. Of course, much of the unpleasantness could have been avoided had the West been more forthright. He understood the Americans, but their ways were exasperating. They were Indian-givers and busybodies. They gave him Poland at Teheran and then started all that fuss about elections and democratic procedures. They would have spared themselves and him much agitation had they realized that he wanted for the Soviet Union what any self-respecting state would demand in her new position, a sphere of

[32] Walter Millis, ed., *The Forrestal Diaries* (New York, 1951), p. 145.

641

interest of her own, sòme rewards for her sacrifices and victories. He would not have disagreed with Mao's characterization of American imperialists as "the newly upstart and neurotic."[33]

If the Americans had been less neurotic, Soviet-American relations following the war could have been "correct," if distant. Of course, they could not have been friendly. For the Soviet Union, friendship with any democratic country was dangerous; with America it would have been suicidal. To have Americans as friends was like having a meddlesome wife: they always wanted to change you. If by some remote chance a Soviet "well-wisher" had furnished the Kremlin with a copy of the memorandum Henry Stimson addressed to President Truman on the subject of Russia and the atomic bomb, the dictator would have found startling confirmation of this. The veteran statesman suggested that Russia might be given atomic secrets in return for Stalin's "putting into effect" the Constitution of 1936 and granting his people democratic freedoms.[34]

Many in the West had believed that after the war the Soviet Union would moderate her foreign policy, if not from fear of the bomb, then in exchange for American economic aid. And there can be no doubt that many in Russia hoped for the latter. A large American loan was discussed in 1944 and 1945. Such a loan would have facilitated Russia's recovery and a quicker fulfillment of Stalin's dream of the U.S.S.R.'s acquiring a mighty industrial plant. But even if the Americans attached no political condition to a loan, the Soviets considered that it would be fatal to give them the impression that they needed it, that they were weak. Ambassador Harriman in 1945 reported that Molotov had proposed a loan of $6 billion in terms suggesting that by taking it, Russia would be doing a great favor to the United States: there was fear of a postwar depression in America, and that might be avoided or alleviated if the U.S.S.R. took American goods on credit. The subject was not raised again, and as we shall see, after momentary hesitations Stalin decided not to seek Soviet participation in the Marshall Plan.

Unlike the constant altercation with the West which in 1947–48 blossomed (if this be the proper word) into the Cold War, Russia's earlier isolation from the West was a deliberate decision of Stalin's, and it had its positive effect in foreign affairs. People are fearful of what they do not understand. In the West the image of a mysterious and incalculable despot began to replace that of "Uncle Joe."[35] "What does the

[33] *Selected Works of Mao Tse-tung* (in English; Peking, 1961), IV, 442.
[34] Henry L. Stimson and McGeorge Bundy, *On Active Service in Peace and War* (New York, 1947), p. 644.
[35] At Yalta Stalin exploded when told he was known in the West under this endearing name, and only with difficulty was persuaded that it meant no disrespect. Later on he accepted the sobriquet. In Virta's play, to the undoubted surprise of the

Soviet Union want and how far is Russia going to go?" asked the new American ambassador in his first audience with Stalin in April 1946. You don't ask such questions of a kindly uncle. "We are not going much further," replied the Boss not very reassuringly.[36]

But the main reason for this isolation was domestic: the whole society was again going to school to undo the effect of untoward influences and illusions of the last few years and one could not allow any foreign ideas to interfere with the lesson.

"Does it become us, representatives of advanced Russian culture, Soviet patriots, to play the role of worshippers of bourgeois culture, or the role of pupils? . . . Where do you find people and country like ours?"[37] The voice is Zhdanov's, but the sentiment and probably even some of the language are Stalin's. (When it came to formulas rationalizing repression, he did not insist that they be directly attributed to him.) It fell to Zhdanov (as of the summer of 1946 again his chief lieutenant[38]) to launch the drive against alien influences on Russian cultural and scientific life. This drive did not end with Zhdanov's death in 1948, but went on gathering momentum. The "Zhdanov times" turned into something reminiscent of the Yezhov era, if on a much smaller scale, in the repression of all potential opposition in society as a whole. (Had Stalin not died, it would perhaps have approximated the earlier horrors quantitatively as well.) In the place of Trotskyites and Bukharinites of yore, there were new villains: purveyors of foreign influence, proponents of decadence and pessimism, denigrators of great Russian culture and tradition. And it was discovered that those cultural saboteurs, like their predecessors of the 1930s in the army and the economy, carried on their wrecking in the interest if not at the actual bidding of foreign powers. Many of them were identified, in line with Stalin's growing prejudice, as Jews.

The opening salvo in the campaign was a now-famous Central Committee resolution of August 14, 1946. There can be no doubt that it was written by Stalin; in fact in the awkwardness of its prose it is startlingly reminiscent of his written debuts in Russian, with their occasional grammatical lapses, excessive use of the passive tense, and senseless piling up of venomous invective. "The Central Committee notes that the literary-artistic journals published in Leningrad, *The Star* and *Leningrad*, carry

---

Soviet theatergoing public, the Americans were allowed to refer to him by that name.

[36] Walter Bedell Smith, *My Three Years in Moscow* (New York, 1950), p. 50.

[37] Andrei Zhdanov, *Essays on Literature, Philosophy and Music* (New York, 1950), p. 42.

[38] In March he had still been listed after Malenkov among the Party's secretaries. In September he signed all government–Central Committee edicts as the principal Party representative, Stalin countersigning them as Chairman of the Council of Ministers.

themselves perfectly unsatisfactorily."[39] And then the Central Committee–Stalin proceeds to spell out this "perfectly unsatisfactory" record: the two journals have opened their columns to the writer Mikhail Zoshchenko, "whose mischievously hooliganlike representations of our reality are accompanied by anti-Soviet attacks," and have "popularized productions of the female writer [Anna] Akhmatova whose literary and sociopolitical physiognomy has long been known to Russian society [and who] appears a typical representative of empty idealless poetry which is foreign to our nation." (In Russian this sounds even worse.) Writing in white heat as if he were duelling against Trotsky or Bukharin (although there he was lucid and occasionally eloquent), Stalin commences to pile invective on the heads of his two helpless subjects: one a talented writer ("hack writer") and the other a woman who along with Mandelstam and Pasternak was recognized as one of the greatest Russian poets of her generation ("decadent, drawing-room poetess"). They and some other sinners printed in the unfortunate journals aimed to "disorient our youth and poison its consciousness."

As usual there were both genuine fury and cold calculation behind this outburst. Both culprits had been in disgrace before the war because of their "individualistic, non-Party" approach to literature, their unwillingness to sing of the collective farm, of the new joyful life, of Stalin. Akhmatova's personal calvary is immortalized in her "Requiem": her son and her husband were imprisoned during the Great Purge.[40] During the war they were allowed, indeed encouraged, to publish their works. Russian literature as well as every other national resource was mobilized, and perhaps it was perceived that personal non-Party literature was especially needed to give the people hope that the terrible but heroic present would not be followed by a return of the terrible and sordid past. But in Stalin's current mood these people, by continuing to write as they had during the war, were showing dark ingratitude and subversive interests. He had forgiven them for their past sins, even rewarded them: Zoshchenko had received a medal and Akhmatova's son had been released from prison so that he could serve in the army. And how were they repaying his generosity and trust? By continuing to write trashy art-for-art's-sake stuff, by sighing audibly for the old Russia—as if he had not built a better and more powerful Russia. He would show them!

But there was also an element of deliberation in Stalin's choice of the Leningrad journals as his initial targets. He could easily have selected other examples to make his point. Leningrad was Zhdanov's bailiwick; the journals' and writers' transgressions could not have taken place without a deplorable lack of vigilance on the part of local Party organs.

[39] *The Communist Party in Resolutions*, II (Moscow, 1953), 1028.
[40] Her first husband, the poet Nikolai Gumilev, from whom she was divorced, was shot for anti-Soviet activity in 1921.

How could the Leningrad Party Committee confirm as late as July a new editorial board of the *Star* including none other than Zoshchenko? This, then, in Stalin's hideously indirect way, was a hint to and a test of Zhdanov. Would he put on hurt airs and try to argue, or would he loyally go to work correcting *his* mistakes?

Possibly to the chagrin of people like Malenkov, Zhdanov passed the test with flying colors. He personally undertook to elucidate the meaning of the Central Committee edict to the Leningrad Party organization, and while it cannot be said that he improved on Stalin's language, he certainly elaborated it. He was amazed at the "lack of principle, looseness and slackness displayed by the people who paved the way for Zoshchenko," that "unprincipled and conscienceless literary hooligan." Anna Akhmatova was a denizen of "the reactionary literary swamp . . . with her little narrow personal life, her *insignificant experiences* and religio-mystical eroticism."[41] Stalin's faith in Zhdanov must have been fully restored; he liked a neat turn of phrase, and this was Zhdanov's capsule characterization of the great poet: "Not exactly a nun, not exactly a whore, but half nun and half whore, whose whorish ways are combined with praying." Yes, he has found the right man for the job.

As the Beria of intellectual life, Zhdanov now fell on other victims. Once one was a favorite of the Boss, one was encouraged to display socialist initiative and not just wait for instructions, and if one went cautiously about it, one could even settle a personal score or two. George Alexandrov, the head of the propaganda department of the Central Committee and a protégé of Malenkov's, had written a completely unexceptional and dismally orthodox history of Western philosophy. It was recommended for the Stalin Prize before its patron and distributor decided that this was not the felicitous moment to write about *Western* philosophy. But the fervor with which Zhdanov fell upon this work and upon Alexandrov went clearly beyond the call of duty. It was par for the course to accuse Alexandrov of such sins as that he found it possible to say something good about every philosopher of the past and hence was "a captive of bourgeois historians." But Zhdanov's critique was full of personal touches. Alexandrov, he remarked, had said that the barometer forecasts the weather, yet this was absurd: people had not yet learned to forecast the weather, "as is well known to you from the practices of our own Weather Bureau." The discovery of dialectic, according to Alexandrov, was made possible by the advances of natural science in the late eighteenth century. Heresy! Engels said that the dialectic method was prepared only by the discovery of the cellular structure of organisms and that, Zhdanov announced triumphantly, was discovered only in the nineteenth. All in all, the

---

[41] Zhdanov, p. 23. My italics.

ideological watchdog concluded, Alexandrov should have realized that such a book was beyond his own powers and should have enlisted a wide circle of competent authors, with himself acting as just the editor—a patently unfair remark, since like most such books, this had been written by a number of anonymous collaborators, with the Party bigwig just checking its general "line" and affixing his name.

Zhdanov also used the critique of the unfortunate textbook for discharging salvos against various targets of the cultural offensive: "followers of Einstein," with their absurd ideas that the universe was finite when it was well known it was infinite; "bourgeois atomic scientists" and their attempts to represent matter as only some "combination of waves and other such nonsense." In their current mood the Soviets were not sparing even some of their Western friends. Jean-Paul Sartre was severely taken to task for his Existentialism and his sponsorship of people like Jean Genet: "Pimps and depraved criminals" were portrayed by bourgeois writers as philosophers and were "showered with invitations to visit America."[42]

Zhdanov, it must be repeated, was an intelligent and well-read man, and much of this absurd obscurantism resulted from a frantic attempt to please his master. But who, beginning in August 1946, refused to join in the chorus of abuse against foreign influence in cultural life, against "cosmopolitanism," as it was dubbed? Writers and critics who later showed themselves enlightened and liberal-minded defenders of dissent who bravely defied Khrushchev and the Party line were in Stalin's lifetime at one with others. Konstantin Simonov, after 1956 an intrepid critic of Stalinism, in the 1940s denounced "deserters" in literature. It was courageous to denounce the noxious trends without naming their alleged propagators, it was heroism to remain silent, and it would have been madness to protest. No one, perhaps not even Zhdanov, could be sure how far Stalin wanted to go with cultural repression. The more intelligent among the purgers and denouncers went at their frightful task with an uneasy feeling that all of a sudden *he* would rap the knuckles (or worse) of those "dizzy with success." The reasonable, understanding Stalin would reappear: "But comrades," he might say, "it is shamefully un-Marxist to denounce everything foreign. How dare you slander a talented Soviet writer because he shows that all is not rosy in our Soviet life?" But for the moment—and a long moment it turned out to be—it was dangerous to fall behind in the competition to denounce most loudly, most critically.

As before, one could be a most loyal Stalinist, hew to the most orthodox line, and still get entangled in the net. No other Soviet writer had such irreproachable ideological credentials, worshiped the Leader so

---

[42] This was prophetic, but certainly not true at the time.

strenuously and wholeheartedly, as Alexander Fadeyev. There were two people he loved and feared, he told Ehrenburg, his mother and Stalin. His loyalty was rewarded by high offices in the Writers' Union. Yet Stalin became displeased with him—it is not clear why. He had intermittent moods of irritation with the more starry-eyed of his worshipers; perhaps that was it. Or was it his displeasure that Fadeyev, in his way an honest person, tried feebly to help his friends when they were in disgrace? Was it sheer sadism? Or was it irritation that his most strenuous admirer among writers was a man of mediocre talent? Fadeyev's *The Young Guard*, on its appearance in 1945 widely acclaimed by the Party press, became an instant best-seller. The success of the book—as a novel inept to the point of being grotesque in places—was due to its patriotic theme. It is based on the true story of heroic teen-agers who under German occupation carried on underground activity and paid for it with their lives. No one could fault the ideological purity of the book; the young people were Komsomol members—not only patriots, but exemplary Communists. For good measure it contained a touching reference to Vishinsky and his brilliant work in uncovering and prosecuting Trotskyite scoundrels, etc. Great, therefore, was the surprise in literary circles when all of a sudden *The Young Guard* was pronounced to be ideologically harmful, in fact a slander on the Communist Party. What was the matter? Well, it was explained, the author slighted the role of the Party in organizing and leading the underground struggle. He conveyed the impression that all that heroism was the work of the young, while Party elders either fled or let themselves fall into the Germans' hands. Fadeyev acknowledged his errors and set about rewriting his book—it took about four years until its general "line" was pronounced correct, and the book fit for public consumption. All the while, as Stalin's literary satrap, he continued denouncing other writers. He had become an alcoholic by 1956, and after the condemnation of his idol, Alexander Fadeyev shot himself. Such is the tale of a successful Soviet writer.

The cultural pogrom continued. The theater, movies, music, painting were in turn subjected to scrutiny by the Party and found wanting. Modern music, said Zhdanov, in one of his more fortunate metaphors, often reminded him of the whirring of the dentist's drill. To think that young composers muttered that Tchaikovsky and Glinka were old hat! It was well known that the leader did not like the kind of music one could not hum. And Shostakovich, long disliked by Stalin, was among those violently attacked. The composer now tried to atone for his sins with an "Ode to Stalin's Afforestation Plan."

In two fields the impact of the purge was rather less than might have been expected. No one acquainted with Soviet painting since the 1930s (i.e., with that which was publicly displayed) could have detected the slightest tendency to formalism or nonobjective art, and in fact it was rather difficult to produce a few sinners to offer as a warning to others. The cinema was very close to Stalin's heart, practically his only innocent form of relaxation. And so he was rather lenient with film producers, even when they strayed and their movies had to be banned. Certainly somebody like Eisenstein got off rather easily.

For Soviet sympathizers abroad the cultural purge created as much embarrassment if not more than the infinitely more frightful events of 1936–39. At the war's end Soviet Russia's standing in intellectual and artistic circles of the West was at its peak. It must have been presented to Stalin that the anticosmopolitan campaign and its growing anti-Semitic undertones were risking the alienation of an influential and important body of sympathizers abroad, an alienation whose importance could no longer be gauged in terms of *moral* support alone. There was a considerable fund of sympathy for the U.S.S.R. among Western scientists. The head of French atomic research, Frédéric Joliot-Curie, was an avowed Communist. Einstein, though apolitical, never concealed his friendly feeling toward Soviet Russia. Would such people's loyalty or friendship endure in view of the continued campaign "against the followers of Einstein and Planck" and the denunciation of their views as reactionary? Pablo Picasso's art and personal prestige were an invaluable asset to French Communism; soon they would be also to the Soviet peace campaign. But in Russia the master's paintings had to be kept in museum cellars, along with other treasures of decadent and nonobjective art, Russian and foreign.

But at the Soviet Olympus these arguments met with derision. Foreign sympathizers, no more than foreign governments, could not be given a veto power over Soviet policies. And the test to which the sympathizers were exposed now was surely no greater than what they had had to endure in the 1930s when so many associated with the glorious story of Communism were unmasked as traitors, or in 1939 when the interests of the Socialist Fatherland required a treaty with Hitler. And so to Stalin the ones who were worth their salt would bear up under this test, and the ones who would not were renegades, not worth bothering about. This appraisal was to prove realistic. Few foreign Communists were as well informed about the Russian intellectual scene and the havoc that Stalin-Zhdanov policies were wreaking as Louis Aragon, the French poet and writer. Yet it was he who left the heartrending recollection of his mother's last moments, her whispered: "Stalin, what is Stalin saying?" Among foreign Communists faith in Stalin was in many ways stronger and more genuine than among the countrymen of the "genius leader of mankind." As a Soviet poet says in his poem on the departed tyrant, "Explain it if you can, history."

Apart from Stalin's personal whim and the obscurantist zeal of his lieutenants, the cultural offensive had more serious motivations. It was a cardinal tenet of Stalin's that intellectual and literary trends were of enormous political importance. One could not afford any laxity in this respect. The whole propaganda apparatus and effort would be of little use if people, especially young people, were allowed to read and view things which clashed with what the Party was teaching them. One should be happy to live in a country where literature was thought important, Mandelstam observed to his wife with terrible irony: Where else do they kill people for writing poetry? What was the point of barring would-be dissenters from leaving the country if they could "migrate internally," find in a novel or in music a different private world separate from that of the Party, of Stalin? Nor could admiration of foreign ways be anything but harmful: one began innocently enough by being impressed with the scientific achievements of the West, and one ended up suspecting that there was something better and freer in life under capitalism. Quite apart from elements of political calculation, there was personal exasperation and fury in Stalin's attitude. Would the people, especially those damned intellectuals, never stop looking longingly at the greener pastures abroad? What other nation had a recent history so tragic and heroic as Russia's? Would the Americans be able to enjoy their automobiles and alleged freedoms if the war had cost them 20 million lives? It was indecent that the Russian people should have gone through all that suffering and privation so that some woman scribbler could write of love and old St. Petersburg, or some scoundrel should disseminate literary poison, avow that in the midst of Soviet reality, on the morrow of the greatest victory in history, *he* feels lonely and depressed.

Appeals to crude nationalism have on occasion been effective in every society. And it would be mistaken to see the Zhdanov offensive as something merely imposed from above which did not find a largely genuine response among the mass of the people. The theme—"What is so wonderful about foreigners? Could they have endured what we endured?"—was undoubtedly very effective. People's frustrations with daily life, the bitter taste of "normalcy" as it returned after the war, were channeled into a rage against "them." All those writers and scientists allegedly had stayed safely far behind the front, were paid and coddled by the state and yet sighed because Moscow was not Paris or New York. Even after his death and after Khrushchev's revelations, Stalin continued to enjoy the sneaking admiration of more unthinking Soviet "common men": *he* knew how to deal with bureaucratic Party bosses, with precious intellectuals and others of their ilk.

Soviet xenophobia during 1946–52 soon took on a more specific *Russian* coloration. Great though the achievements of the Ukrainian and Georgian and other nations may have been, they had been made possible only through the solicitude and protection of their "elder brother," the great Russian people. Excessive stress on and admiration of a purely Ukrainian or Kazakh past, ignoring how at every step in their development those nations drew nourishment and strength from Russian culture, became as deplorable and dangerous as uncritical praise of German philosophy or American technology. Even the traditional Communist critique of Tsarist Russia as an imperialist state had now to be modified and softened: oppressive though she had been, Imperial Russia had brought higher culture to the nations she had conquered. Stalin must have viewed his work as Commissar of Nationalities with retrospective disapproval: he had encouraged and insisted on the use of local languages, promoted the development of native cultures—thus creating Azerbaijan, Byelorussian, and other intelligentsias, as if the Russian one were not enough.

One aspect of the horrors perpetrated on Soviet culture and science under the ostensible auspices of Zhdanov is clearly connected with a long-standing prejudice of Stalin's. He had never liked "theoreticians," people who scorned the practical aspects of life, and even now when to his satisfaction he had established himself as the supreme authority in several fields of theoretical endeavor, the dislike was firm. What good was theory unless it could be applied to the solution of real-life problems, help him and the state? What good was a science if its exponents were interested only in discovering and expounding alleged laws of nature, which could not be transgressed or were lost in scholastic mutterings? *Real* science should adopt as its motto "There are no fortresses which we Bolsheviks cannot storm," should abandon superstitious awe, especially of foreign authorities.

This stress on what today would be called relevance was combined in Stalin with a certain populist bias against "pure" research. There was something aristocratic, "lordly" he called it, about scientific endeavor unconnected to the real needs of the people. Those gentlemen sat in their laboratories and studies, generously provided by the state, and scorned practical tasks. And indeed, for all of Zhdanov's threatening nonsense, the atomic bomb actually saved theoretical physicists and mathematicians from further unpleasantness: their "impractical" concerns were suddenly endowed with some very practical consequences. But the ordeal of Soviet science generally during the Zhdanov period approached that in the arts. The sufferings among applied scientists have already been alluded to. They sprang from the conviction of the authorities that "useful" scientists were a natural prey for spies and "wreckers." The havoc wrought among the Soviet technical intelligentsia by the spy mania of the prewar years was repeated, though on a much smaller scale, between 1946 and 1952.

Until a few years ago, a visitor to a Ukrainian town could admire a prominently situated monument of a rather unusual nature. With impeccable socialist realism, the sculptor portrayed an encounter between science and political wisdom, and unwittingly commemorated the most successful scientific fraud of modern history. The seated figures, in intimate discourse, are Stalin and Trofim Lysenko. We have already encountered the notorious charlatan before the war when his at first genuine and then faked experiments with developing new strains of wheat earned him the support of the regime and its protection against an enraged scientific community. But the pinnacle of his fame, fraud, and influence was to be reached in the 1940s, when he became the virtual Stalin of Soviet biology. His was truly a false idea whose time had come. Lysenkoism swamped Soviet biological sciences and threatened to invade other disciplines.

The main ingredients of his success were obvious. Like the Leader himself, Lysenko began as a humble practitioner but then, through attention to "real-life problems," was able to formulate sublime theories such as no ivory-tower academician had ever dreamed of. His was real *Soviet* science—no wonder bourgeois scientists and their Soviet imitators denounced and slandered him as a faker! He preached—and this synchronized with what Marxism taught about human society—that man was not a slave of his past nature, not bound by allegedly immutable laws, but that a man armed with the ideas of Lenin-Stalin and his own theories could go about improving and *transforming* species for the benefit and glory of the socialist economy. The biological equivalent of Trotskyites were geneticists. And no wonder: the science had been invented by a monk (Gregor Mendel) and it preached fatalism and resignation in the face of the laws of heredity.[43] Environment, not heredity, was Lysenko's key to unlocking nature's secrets, forcing her to abide by the rulings of the Central Committee and the dicta of Comrade Stalin. Lysenko (and it is probable that he eventually arrived at believing his own nonsense) exuded energy and confidence; he was what in Soviet parlance is described as a "real man," a person analogous to what American magazines mean when they call someone "dynamic and tough-minded." In fact he was of a type reminiscent of those American captains of finance and industry whose innovative ways enthuse the press and stockholders for a while, but who eventually find themselves in federal court or in a country with which the United States has no extradition treaty.

But Lysenko was more durable. In the summer of 1948 the Central Committee gave official blessing to his views and pronounced anathema

[43] "Not only was the gene proscribed and the chromosome under suspicion: Lysenko's more extreme followers denounced plant hormones and viruses as metaphysical vaporings of the bourgeois mind." David Zhoravsky, *The Lysenko Affair* (Cambridge, Mass., 1970), p. 142.

on his foes. With this in his pocket the indefatigable faker proceeded with a veritable pogrom of Soviet geneticists. Some of them had been victimized before, but now the handful that still resisted was compelled to recant, shift to other pursuits, or lose their professorships and laboratories. Soviet genetics, like Soviet modern art, went underground; its public practice for the balance of Stalin's life became as unimaginable as that of psychoanalysis.

Lysenko is a general Soviet, rather than specifically Stalinist, phenomenon. After Stalin's death he retained an important position in the Soviet scientific establishment, although he lost his dictatorial powers: Nikita Khrushchev, himself not free of a penchant for "harebrained innovations," had a weakness for the man who promised to work such miracles for Soviet agriculture.

But the official enthronement of Lysenko in 1948 must be connected with Stalin's mental decline, which becomes so apparent in the same year and of which we shall note some other symptoms. Prior to that time his sponsorship of Lysenko had been somewhat limited. It had run against the grain to turn absolute power in any field to a single person, not to have several people compete for his favor and denounce each other. But now fatigue and senile obstinacy apparently curtailed both his enjoyment of intrigue and his attention span. Reservations about Lysenko and his methods in suppressing scientific opposition were voiced by people for whom he had a high regard, such as Zhdanov's son, then head of the Central Committee's scientific section and soon to become his own son-in-law, and the head of the agricultural academy, Professor Nemchinov (who in 1928–29 had collected statistical data about Russian agriculture for Stalin). But the dictator could not be swayed, and Lysenko prospered. Among foreign scientists sympathetic to the Soviet Union the repercussions of the Lysenko reign were serious: people can tolerate or rationalize disgrace or the arrest of a colleague, but how can one acquiesce to the suppression of an entire discipline, especially if it is one's own? ☆☆☆

THE "Zhdanov times" set in perspective the whole problem of coexistence between Stalin's (and perhaps not only his) Russia and the West In the few interviews he granted to visiting Americans in 1946–47, he was undoubtedly sincere in emphasizing his wish and hope for peace and for amicable relations with the United States. As during the war, he was on occasion amazingly frank—e.g., in his statement of October 1946 that Soviet military contingents in Germany and some East

European countries amounted to barely sixty divisions and would be soon reduced to forty,[44] a statement which, had it been believed in the West (and he knew it would not), might have led to a tougher policy on the part of the United States, stripped of the illusions and fear that Stalin had millions under arms. But he was definitely untruthful when in answer to Elliott Roosevelt's question of whether he favored a wide cultural and scientific exchange between the two countries, inclusive of "students, artists, scientists, and professors," he replied, "yes, of course."[45] American fears of Russia fed upon and were compounded by Russia's isolation. Stalin's fears required that isolation. There were many things that a more skillful and forcible American policy could have extracted from Stalin without raising the specter of war: perhaps a united, if severely demilitarized, Germany; the survival of some elements of national independence and a freer political life in the countries of Eastern Europe. But paradoxical as it sounds, the one thing Stalin was not going to concede was precisely a "wide exchange of scientific and cultural information" and personnel. Both his tyrannical instinct and his Russian national pride made him abhor the prospect of a friendly intercourse between the two societies, the prospect of Americans, or for that matter Frenchmen or Britons, luring his people with wealth and licentious ways. And any other Communist ruler of Russia would have felt the same way. As a state of mind the Cold War had its origins in the Americans' fear of things and people they do not understand and in Soviet Russia's fear of being understood.

That a real war might come Stalin at the time had no fear. Milovan Djilas heard him say in an intimate Communist circle in the spring of 1945 that a war might come in fifteen or twenty years. In 1946 the growing tension with his allies (as late as 1949 he said to the British and American ambassadors, "We are still allies") made him denounce those he believed wanted to instigate war against the U.S.S.R., such as Churchill. But neither in his words nor (more significant) in his activities is there the slightest apprehension of imminent danger. This seeming unconcern puzzled those friendly and those opposed in the West to the Soviet Union. Certainly *they* would be nervous if they were in his shoes and confronted a disapproving transatlantic colossus armed with atomic weapons. And in view of everything that has been said here about Stalin's suspiciousness, we might wonder too. But, as we have seen, unless something triggered his suspicions, he had excellent common sense. Who, reading the news in 1946–47, would think that Washington and London were planning a war or capable of starting one against the Soviet

[44] Stalin (Stanford ed.), III, 61. A Soviet division would amount to 10,000 men in full complement.
[45] *Ibid.*, p. 69.

Union? Of course the capitalists wanted to see the Soviet system collapse, but how could they ever make their "millions of common men" don soldiers' uniforms and start the march from the Channel to the Volga? The bomb—and by now Stalin no longer thought of it as merely a more powerful type of explosive—did not interfere with his calculation. In his interview with a Western newspaperman he professed little concern: "Atom bombs are designed to scare those with weak nerves, but they cannot decide wars, because there are not enough of them. To be sure, atomic monopoly is a threat, but against it are two remedies: (a) monopoly of the bomb will not last, (b) the use of the bomb will be forbidden."[46]

Stalin's answers were a mixture of common sense and shrewd audacity. The atomic bomb did prove to be so formidable a weapon that it scared its possessors more than those who did not have it. The Russians found this out, to their discomfiture, a short ten years later, when they tried to alarm the Chinese with the prospect of an atomic war and at the same time persuade them, as the Americans had attempted to persuade *them* in the 1940s, not to construct their own nuclear weapons, but join in an international agreement banning their spread. Like Stalin before him, Mao refused to be alarmed. And neither Mao nor Stalin was so lighthearted about the bomb as he chose to pretend. But each realistically gauged the mentality of his opponent. To gamblers of their mettle, the prospect of a worldwide conflagration would always appear less fearful than attrition of their own power. Better to take the *small* risk that the bomb might fall on the Kremlin or the Forbidden City than to accept permanent inferiority vis-à-vis a rival. Fear of the unknown will always be more of a restraint on a democracy or, as in the case of present-day Russia, an oligarchy than on megalomaniac dictators for whom life is no more precious than power, whose nations' destinies are subordinate to their own.

Until 1948 Stalin was a prudent gambler, much more prudent in many ways than Khrushchev was to be. Whereas his successor tried to carry the day by threats and bombast, Stalin employed subtler means of intimidation. To be sure, he did not have to work at it so hard: by now he was mysterious and awesome. Khrushchev was to appear merely devious and, even at his most threatening, a bit ridiculous. The postwar Stalin just had to smile, hint that things were not so bad as they seemed, and stocks went up in the West, audible sighs of relief would be heard in the Western chanceries, and people would congratulate themselves that the war danger had passed and Uncle Joe was coming back. More often he succeeded in producing an impression of chilling distance, not of unfriendliness but of scant interest and no fear of Americans with

[46] Stalin (Stanford ed.) III, 52.

their bombs and money. Oh, if one could only find some way to his mysterious mind, assuage his heart, persuade him that Soviet apprehensions were groundless, that America did not threaten the U.S.S.R. but only wanted a peaceful world where everybody observed the United Nations Charter. In 1948 Harry Truman, depressed by U.S.-Soviet relations and by his bad prospects for re-election, sought an improvement in both by proposing to send the Chief Justice of the Supreme Court, Fred M. Vinson, on a special mission to Russia. "If we could only get Stalin to unburden himself to someone on our side he could trust, I thought we could get somewhere," Truman was to explain in his memoirs.[47]

Stalin played up to his image. Here, in written answers to an American journalist's anxious questions, he is pithy—half-ominous, half-reassuring.

> Q: Are you in agreement with the opinion of Secretary Byrnes . . . about the growing strain in relations between the U.S.S.R. and the United States?
> STALIN: No.
> Q: Who represents at present in your opinion the main threat to peace in the world?
> STALIN: The instigators of a new war, above all Churchill and those like-minded in England and the U.S.
> Q: Can the U.N. guarantee the inviolability of small countries?
> STALIN: From the evidence up to now it is difficult to judge.
> Q: How does the U.S.S.R. regard the presence of British troops in Greece?
> STALIN: As unnecessary.
> Q: Is Russia still interested in obtaining a loan from the United States?
> STALIN: Still interested.[48]

Abroad, those pronouncements of the oracle were eagerly scanned for clues. Optimists were encouraged by their content: he did say that the tension was *not* increasing. Pessimists would be depressed by the form: only extreme irritation with the West would explain Stalin's contemptuous brevity.

Soviet diplomacy mirrored the style of its master. The staccato of Soviet vetoes in the Security Council—*nyet* became a household word in America—saddened the hearts of believers in the United Nations. The Baruch Plan for the international control of atomic energy, with its elaborately worked out inducements for the Soviet Union and guarantees for the United States, was brusquely rejected by Stalin. One might have supposed that so long as the U.S.S.R. did not have its own atomic bomb, it would have been advisable for the Russians to go along in

---

[47] Harry S Truman, *Memoirs*, II, 215.
[48] Stalin (Stanford ed.), III, 57–63. The date was October 23, 1946.

principle with a plan for setting up an international agency, and to quibble about details to gain time. Though undoubtedly there were voices in the Kremlin arguing for such a course, Stalin scorned subterfuge. No, it would be a mistake even to pretend that the U.S.S.R. might agree to abandon its veto in the Security Council, allow inspection of its territory by an international agency. They might get the idea he was afraid of the bomb.

At other times, the amicable Stalin would make a brief reappearance. He was friendly and chatty in an interview with Elliott Roosevelt. How sad, he remarked, that since his visitor's father died, relations between their two governments had grown more strained! Was not the recent Republican congressional victory due to the American people's disappointment that Truman's administration has dissipated "the moral and political capital accumulated by the late President?" (It was April 1947, and the Truman Doctrine has just been announced.) But Stalin chose to be most engaging in a discourse with another American visitor, Harold Stassen. Of course, he said, the two countries can cooperate. They call each other names: for the Soviets the American system is monopoly capitalism, for the Americans the Soviet one totalitarianism— but so what? Every nation holds on to the system it likes, one that history has chosen for it. Stassen was solicitous about freedom of the press—why did the U.S.S.R. expel American correspondents? Stalin patiently, and to some extent convincingly, explained that the American press wrote a lot of nonsense about the U.S.S.R. One correspondent had "revealed" that he, Stalin, personally beat up Marshal Timoshenko! Another Kremlinologist reported that Molotov was scheming against Stalin and he in turn was going to chase Molotov out! The "Soviet people" were enraged by their country's being portrayed as so uncivilized and insisted that foreign correspondents' dispatches be censored.

Stalin then shifted to asking questions himself. Was America due for another depression? How did the American businessmen take to the federal government's attempts to regulate the economy? He did not think they would like it. Oh, happy America—with its two main rivals on the world market, Japan and Germany, prostrate and exports playing an increasing role in the American economy. And how lucky that Canada and Mexico were weak and presented no threat! Yes, he had learned a great deal from his discussion with Harold Stassen and hoped he would stay in the U.S.S.R. longer. He should not miss seeing Leningrad! Stalin had not lost his capacity to charm a foreign visitor, especially one whose dossier undoubtedly contained the remark, "thought by many to be the next Republican nominee for President."

Such amicable interludes could not seriously affect the course of Soviet-American relations. A democracy's unfounded hopes had given way to unfounded fears: a despot's wariness was bound to turn into groundless suspicion. And so in 1947 wrangling turned into hostility. The American people became convinced that Stalin aimed for world mastery; the dictator professed to see that America (now she became synonymous with the West) was preparing a crusade against the Soviet Union—not a war but, in their indirect sly way, conditions for such a war.

The Truman Doctrine announced in March of 1947 did not unduly disturb the Kremlin. The United States stepped in to assume what had been Britain's burden, to help Greece and Turkey economically, to re-equip and modernize their armies. The Greek government was fighting Communist-led insurgents; Turkey was under constant Soviet pressure to provide the naval base with which Churchill so unwisely titillated Stalin's cupidity at Teheran, and to return the territory Russia had exacted from Turkey in 1878 and to which the Turks helped themselves after the Bolshevik Revolution. It was irritating to have the Americans step in and deny what Stalin considered to be legitimate fruits of Soviet victory and Britain's imperial decline: a nice rounding-out of his Balkan preserve, Russia's flag in the Straits. Why should America's President deny him what Britain and France had promised Nicholas II during World War I? But despite very considerable nervousness in the United States as to how Stalin would take this departure from traditional American policy, not to mention the violently anti-Communist rhetoric in which it was couched, it was not seen by the Kremlin as a threat. Stalin did not even mention the Doctrine in his chat with Stassen. But then came another American initiative. Soviet apprehensions about it and American failure to understand them exerted a fateful influence on the course of world history. Everything during the next fifteen years— the Communist triumph in China, the successive confrontations over Berlin, the Stalin-Tito dispute, the Cuban Missile Crisis—were at least to some degree traceable to Stalin's reaction to the Marshall Plan.

That it should have been so is one of the supreme ironies of history. The Marshall Plan, even if not an example of unalloyed altruism—certainly it would not have been possible without American fear of Communism on the march—still deserves to be classed, in Churchill's apt words, among the "most unsordid acts" of history. It proposed to throw America's resources behind the economic recovery of Europe. It recognized the obligation of advanced countries to help the economy of less fortunate ones—something which has come to be an accepted maxim of international life but which in 1947 was still a fantastically revolutionary concept.

The less altruistic premise of the Plan was the conviction that, to quote Truman, the Communist way of life "spread in the evil soil of strife and poverty"—in other words, if their factories hummed and their standard of living rose, French and Italian workers would be unlikely to continue to vote Communist, so that their (and other) European countries would be saved for "free elections . . . guarantees of individual liberty . . . freedom of speech." This assumption, the first part of which history has not confirmed, was certainly necessary for "selling" the Plan to the American voter and taxpayer. The drafters of the Plan conceived of it as an attempt to restore the European economy as a whole. And at the insistence of some of them, the offer to participate in it or, to put it vulgarly, to share in the American largesse was extended to Russia and her satellites. There was a shrewd suspicion—and hope— among the proponents of this risky gambit that the Russians would refuse. As George Kennan, one of those mainly responsible for the Plan and this aspect of it, put it, "If they responded favorably, we would test their good faith by insisting they contribute constructively to the program. . . . If they were unwilling . . . we would simply let them exclude themselves."[49]

In the State Department there was certainly some surprise, not unmixed with apprehension (to put it mildly), when, following General Marshall's famous speech, the Soviet government accepted the British-French invitation for ministers of the three powers to meet and examine the American initiative. Many a heart must have sunk in Washington on June 27, as Molotov, accompanied by a goodly number of economic experts, alighted in Paris. The Plan was in for a tough going at the hands of the Republican-controlled Congress in any case. But how could one persuade Senator Robert Taft that Communism could be fought by handing over money to Stalin!

If there is one session of the Politburo for which the minutes could be procured, we should opt, in preference to the more blood-and-thunder ones, for the session which debated this extraordinary American offer. For here ordinary human logic must have clashed with the Stalinist one. With one part of his mind Stalin must have realized that Russia could not lose by joining in the Marshall Plan. Whatever happened, he stood to gain by such a decision: either Congress, stricken with horror at the prospect of subsidizing Soviet steel and nuclear plants, would veto the whole enterprise and Western Europe would continue in economic chaos; or if by some miracle the Americans went ahead, *his* economy would get a badly needed shot in the arm.

But the other Stalin saw the whole proposal as a trap. He had barely restored order and discipline in his society, taught the people not to expect an easy life or absurd freedoms. Could he now lean on the capitalists, acknowledging to them and his own people that he needed their help? How could he preserve Russia's healthy isolation? There would have to be foreign experts, congressional and parliamentary dele-

[49] George F. Kennan, *Memoirs, 1925–1950* (Boston, 1967), p. 342.

gations traveling over Russia. There would be no way to conceal the terrible weaknesses of the Soviet economy, the frightful state of agriculture, the plight of the consumer. Stalin himself must have realized that official statistics in agriculture, at least, had been systematically falsified since the mid-1930s.

The Stalin of two years earlier might well have taken the risk. But by 1947 he had become much more obsessive. In his personal life he had grown afraid not only of what the people were doing, but of what they were saying behind his back. Still he hesitated. Molotov's initial statement in Paris, while not a model of graciousness ("The United States in its turn is interested to use its credit facilities to enlarge its foreign markets, especially in view of the approaching crisis"), still appeared to foreshadow Soviet participation. Great, therefore, was the surprise (and relief on the banks of the Potomac) when four days later, on July 2, Molotov broke off the negotiations and announced that the machinery envisaged under the Plan would infringe on the national sovereignty of the participants. He warned the British and the French not to taste the poisoned grapes of American aid. The Plan, he said haughtily, had as its goal "not to unify the nations of Europe in postwar reconstruction, but other things which have nothing in common with their real interests."

Stalin had evidently seen through the designs of the American capitalists and their alleged solicitude for Europe. Since when do capitalists give away money to help restore the economy of their commercial competitors? Western Europe was being helped for one purpose, and that purpose must be to turn it into an armed camp against the Soviet Union and its satellites. As during the Russian Civil War the capitalists were going to fight Communism with other people's armies.

The danger was real but not imminent. It would take some time to set up the machinery of the Marshall Plan, a strong West German state, a network for anti-Communist subversion. But this threat had to be warded off by taking speedy measures in the most vulnerable area, the East European satellites. Hitherto the pace of subjugating those countries had not been hurried. Czechoslovakia was ruled by a coalition which, though headed by the Communist Party, left considerable scope for free political life. Elsewhere—except in Yugoslavia, where the local Communists on their own were eager to mold their country in the Soviet image—shreds of democratic freedoms persisted, and the more strenuous Soviet policies, such as forced collectivization, had been avoided. Now this all had to be changed, politically and socially. These countries had to be made immune to the expected onslaught of Western propaganda and subversion. Were the local Communist parties there entirely reliable? During the war all sorts of unreliable elements had been let in and the usual vigilance against ex-Trotskyites had slackened. Some of the local leaders, now advanced from petty Comintern officials to national leaders, had developed swelled heads. All in all those countries and parties had to learn some of the lessons Stalin had taught his own country and his own Communists in the 1930s.

How badly such lessons were needed became obvious within weeks of the Paris foreign ministers' meeting. Invitations now went out for a more comprehensive multinational discussion of the American proposals for the European recovery program. Despite the Molotov anathema, the Polish government was strongly tempted to accept, and the Czechs actually did. Warsaw was told that such greed would not be tolerated, and the Czechs were summoned to Moscow and pressured to withdraw their acceptance.

The major Communist Parties of Europe had to go back to school. This school, organized in September 1947, was called the Communist Information Bureau. If the title had reflected its true purpose, the Cominform would have been known as the anti-Marshall Plan Bureau. Representatives of the Eastern European as well as French and Italian Parties assembled in Poland, and there they were read the lesson.

The circumstances of this meeting throw interesting light on Stalin's political mind in its decline. The participants were representatives of ruling parties and, as in the case of the Italian and French, powerful and perfectly legal organizations in their countries. They were meeting in a Communist-dominated state under the reassuring presence of Soviet troops. Yet the date, existence, and subject matter of the meeting were kept secret until it was over. (The conference was stated mysteriously to have taken place "near Warsaw," yet in fact it met in Silesia.) This absurdly conspiratorial air now characterized Stalin's behavior: the less "they" knew about him, about Soviet moves, about Communism, the better. In his last years the all-powerful dictator reverted to the habits and mentality of a hunted revolutionary and conspirator.

The Soviet delegation was headed by two rivals, Zhdanov and Malenkov. What they had to say the assembled foreign leaders might well have read in *Pravda*. They did not need to travel to a Polish resort to learn that American imperialism had opened a new offensive, that the Marshall Plan was a subterfuge to enslave the European economy to Wall Street, that the Communist Party of the U.S.S.R. placed special importance on the fight against "cosmopolitanism" and against other types of infiltrating bourgeois ideology.

Still, there was a lesson which the foreign Communists could not have garnered from Soviet newspapers. It must have irritated Stalin that the very top leaders of Yugoslav, French, and Italian Parties—Tito, Thorez, Togliatti—had chosen not to attend the conference. Now they all received a lesson in humility.

Zhdanov instructed the Yugoslav participants, who soon had occasion to remember the event with shame, to deliver vituperative attacks on the Italian and French Communists. The two parties during the war had played a leading role in the anti-fascist underground and gained support among the masses. Now, it was alleged, when the liberating Anglo-American armies landed in their countries, the Italian and French Communists meekly surrendered their arms, forsook any idea of seizing power, and supinely collaborated within the bourgeois governments. These were absurd charges. It was Stalin who in 1944–45 reminded the more hotheaded among the French and Italians that this was no time for revolutionary adventurism, that Allied unity took absolute priority over narrow political interests of their own. And now for their exemplary obedience they were being crucified. Jacques Duclos left the room and, sitting on a park bench, cried in impotent rage. But in their public statements, the French and the Italians admitted their sins: yes, they had erred gravely. They would try to atone by leading their countries' working classes in a resolute struggle against the Marshall Plan and enslavement by American capitalism.

This submission meant, as the French and Italians soon realized, an end to any serious expectation that they could come to power through legal means, i.e., by winning a majority in elections. West European Communism's new look of respectability would become tarnished by the fresh proof of subservience to Moscow. Though the two parties for long retained the allegiance of the majority of the working class, they were unable to secure enough support from other left-wing groups to win a majority. It was a cruel predicament, to be thrown into a fight against policies that to everybody else promised vast economic benefits for their countries. And they were not allowed to try to *seize* power.

And so the Cominform was launched on its short and inglorious career. Its first seat was Belgrade, where its Soviet functionaries could combine their official tasks with a little spying and subversion on the side: Tito and his people were getting too big for their boots. The journal of the ill-fated organization bore the name *For a Lasting Peace, For a People's Democracy*. When at the founding conference some delegates objected that the title, while irreproachable in the sentiments it expressed, was journalistically speaking rather awkward, they were silenced by the revelation that Stalin himself had deigned to choose it. ☆☆☆

Ⅴ ICTORY over Germany, the new Soviet Empire in Eastern Europe, prospects of future Communist conquests in Asia and elsewhere —these presented exciting new perspectives but also problems for the man who loomed like a colossus over the whole edifice. Would he pass into history as the founder of another universal empire on the order of that of Rome and Britain? Would he be remembered as the creator of a new, Communist, civilization that eventually inherited the world? As both? Would Stalinism appear as a symptom of decline of one world (Western civilization)? Would Stalinism be remembered like the Mongol invasions of the thirteenth century: as an eruption that brought about or hastened the destruction of several civilizations but that in itself proved incapable of creating a new one, that dissolved into warring hordes which eventually were absorbed into the culture of the countries they had conquered?

For the moment there was a simple test of the enduring power of the new Stalinist order: would it be able to combine Soviet domination with some respect for the national peculiarities of the countries it had conquered; would it be able to supplement force with a bond of self-interest or ideology; or would it, by relying only on force, carry within it the seeds of self-destruction? One did not have to wait long for an answer.

Since the war's end, Czechoslovakia had been ruled by a Communist-led coalition of political parties. With the approach of elections in 1948, the Communist Minister of the Interior began to purge the police force of non-Communists to make sure that when the elections did come they would not reveal his Party's decline in popularity. Twelve non-Communist ministers resigned in February 1948, hoping to bring about an election before it could be "fixed" by the Communist police. There was no need for the U.S.S.R. to take alarm at this crisis. Whichever governmental combination ruled Czechoslovakia, she was bound to remain within the Soviet sphere, all parties agreeing that when it came to foreign and defense policies Czechoslovakia had to abide by the wishes of its powerful neighbor. But the combination of what he believed to be the West's long-term designs on Eastern Europe and its current helpless acquiescence in Soviet domination there determined Stalin to bear down on the Czechs. A special Soviet envoy bullied President Beneš; the Communist-led unions and workers' militia organized strikes and manifestations. Beneš yielded and entrusted formation of a new government to the Communist Clement Gottwald, who soon replaced the heartbroken Beneš as president. There were diplomatic protests from the West, debates in the United Nations Security Council. But when on May 24 the Soviet Union vetoed a U.N. resolution to investigate the Prague coup, it became clear that the Soviet order in Eastern Europe was to be a Communist one—democratic governments even when most deferential toward the U.S.S.R. were not going to be tolerated (Finland remaining, and at the time precariously, the only exception).

But even within the new formula there still remained a further question. Would Stalin allow his Communist satellites a modicum of independence? Or would he insist on being obeyed in Warsaw and Belgrade the way he was in Kiev or Tiflis? A younger, more flexible Stalin might have appreciated the need for leaving his Communist satraps some shreds of autonomy, for showing some respect for national traditions and pride. Their self-interest (where would they be without the Soviet Union?) and Communist faith provided obvious guarantees of loyalty. All they craved was a chance to appear to their people not only as faithful followers of Great Stalin but also as national leaders. Indeed, in some ways the personal devotion to Stalin of Tito, Gomulka, and others of the breed was greater and more genuine than that of his Soviet servants. But at his age and in his mood Stalin was less and less capable of diplomacy. Patience, the one element of his statesmanship that had moderated his predilection for force, was eroding. He was humiliated by old age, hence the increasing need to humiliate others.

It was natural that Stalin's resentment should center on Tito. Here was a man who had lived in Russia, who was a Communist of long standing, and who should know better than to give himself airs. As early as the spring of 1945 Stalin felt constrained to tease the Yugoslav leader, then his guest. It was both irritating and absurd that the Yugoslav Communists had persuaded themselves that, unlike other Soviet protégés, they had won their country through their own exertions rather than by the grace of the Red Army. Even then, in the flush of imminent victory, Stalin chose to remind his guest that the famous Yugoslav Partisans had never been able to stand up to the Germans in a pitched battle. Without Stalin's cleverness and generosity, Tito and his followers would most likely be in the current predicament of the Greek Communists, fighting and losing a civil war against a royalist government supported by the Americans and the British.

In the immediate postwar years Stalin felt constrained to indulge the collective vanity of the Yugoslav Communists and what he felt was the personal megalomania of their leader. There was no denying that they were devoted to him and the Soviet Union, in fact embarrassingly and almost dangerously. They could not understand why he did not tell the British and Italians to get out of Trieste and hand it over to them. They took to shooting down American planes which had wandered over Yugoslav territory and were surprised when the Soviets warned them in private to cease such playful activities. And so Tito was accorded by Moscow a place of honor among the East European satraps. To massage Yugoslav vanity Belgrade was made the seat of the Cominform. More important, until the end of 1947 Stalin went along with the Yugoslav idea of a federation of Balkan Communist states which would include, to begin with, Bulgaria, Albania, and Yugoslavia. Albania had in a way already become a subsatellite of Belgrade's. This silenced the objections of many Bulgarian and Albanian Communists, who did not relish the prospect of playing second fiddle to the Yugoslavs and becoming vassals of Tito's.

But Stalin was now often changing his mind. It has been a myth that he always stuck to his decisions, come hell or high water. But his changeability as well as his suspiciousness took on a new twist in his old age: he began to distrust his own judgment. He might approve, say, a book or a policy statement by a subordinate, and then the thought would strike him that this was slanderous, scandalous stuff! They were fooling Stalin! And so with the Balkan federation. In January 1948 Stalin decided he had been victimized! Tito wanted to build his own empire in the Balkans; all along it had been a mistake to trust this man. The news from Belgrade confirmed his suspicions. Honest Yugoslav Communists who, as was their bounden duty, brought the Soviet ambassador tales of Tito's misdoings, were being persecuted by their treacherous leaders. Members of the Soviet missions were hampered in collecting information corroborating Tito's treachery, in fact spied upon by the Yugoslav security organs. And so Tito joined the long list of those who paid dearly for their attempts to fool Comrade Stalin.

And here Stalin experienced the most bitter defeat of his political career. The man who had been an obscure Comintern functionary, of whose existence Stalin was probably barely aware prior to the war, now defied him for the remaining few years of his life. (And after his death it was Stalin's heirs who traveled to Belgrade, asking that bygones be bygones. Tito in 1956 triumphantly toured the Soviet Union. He went there repeatedly—a living reminder that the Stalinist era of Communism had passed, that the "unshakable unity" of the socialist camp had begun to break down even before the tyrant's death.) Stalin's awareness of his defeat, even though he believed it was a temporary one, at the hands of Tito forced him to swallow another humiliation: to accept China's Mao as *almost* his equal, to die in the knowledge that Communism's greatest victory would become Russia's greatest danger.

In destroying people, Stalin had hitherto acted with lightning speed or with painstaking deliberation. But in tackling Tito, he appears to have lacked both his old resolution and his old cunning. Milovan Djilas presents a vivid description of Stalin's machinations preceding the momentous split.[50] In January 1948 Djilas—then thirty-six years old—was summoned to Moscow. He was then very close to Tito, one of the four most influential men in Yugoslavia, but he was also known as a zealot and a worshiper of *the* leader. He was a man, in other words, who might be very useful to Stalin in an intra-Yugoslav Party intrigue.

[50] Milovan Djilas, *Conversations with Stalin* (New York, 1962).

Writing many years after the event, Djilas may well exaggerate the extent and immediacy of his disenchantment on that visit to Moscow. But what comes out vividly in the narrative is the crudity of the efforts to make him turn traitor. It is no reflection on Djilas to say that Stalin might have sown seeds of doubt in his mind concerning Tito had he, still the ruling deity of the young Yugoslav's world, opened his heart to him in one of those acting performances at which he once had been so skillful. But he was no longer the master psychologist, only an irascible and vain man with occasional flashes of cunning. He sought to impress rather than win people with that famous frankness which had fooled so many in the past. He grew impatient, and whereas before he had been awesome at such moments, now there was an element of an old man's petulance in the outbursts.

The central episode in Stalin's attempted seduction of Djilas was the signal honor of an invitation to a late dinner at Stalin's villa. Already in 1945, when along with Tito he had participated in a tasteful soirée of this kind, Djilas, a fastidious and puritanical man, had been somewhat repelled by the grossness of these occasions. And now this impression was strengthened, as was the picture of vulgarity on the part of Stalin and his "comrades-in-arms." Djilas could not help noticing how much older Stalin appeared, how his memory faltered occasionally, and how in the place of the quick wit and gaiety of three years earlier there was senile amusement at the inane and obscene jokes of his companions, who in their obsequiousness had grown even more repellent. To be sure, Djilas looked at the scene no longer as a worshiper and disciple but as a politician. His regime's fate hung in balance, his loyalty to Tito and to Yugoslavia was being tested. And indeed, he was supposed to be impressed by this sordid spectacle of gluttony and inebriation, flattered at being admitted (the only foreigner) to this feast of the Leader and his servants. It was not surprising that amid the spontaneous vulgarity of this gathering of more than six hours' duration the discussion grew increasingly critical of Tito. For all the ravages of age, Stalin was alert to his reactions, Djilas acknowedged, in turn insinuating and flattering. Aided by his abstemiousness and growing revulsion at the revelry, the Yugoslav was able to remain noncommittal.

Djilas stayed on in Russia a few more weeks, at times wondering whether he would ever see again his native hills and forests. An invitation went out to Tito to sample Soviet hospitality. Would he come and help clear up all the misunderstandings? But Tito remembered Moscow in 1937. Tito pleaded indisposition and instead sent some of his lieutenants to join Djilas. They also proved unshakably loyal. Frustrated, Stalin vented his fury on the Bulgarians, also summoned to Moscow, and on Molotov who, he felt, had botched the job. Finally, after weeks of cajolery, of being harangued and spied upon, the Yugoslavs were told they could go home and that the Soviet government was providing them with a plane for this purpose. Few people ever embarked on an air trip with more trepidation than those fearless veterans of Partisan warfare. Only after several hours in the air did Djilas relax and begin to feel happy as a child. Mao later chose to make the trip to and from Moscow by train. Yes, as Tvardovsky says in his poem on Stalin, "Such things were really happening in our time."

In fact, Stalin's vanity rendered the Yugoslavs' fears groundless. From Stalin's point of view there was no need for extraordinary measures against the Yugoslavs. While Stalin may not have *said*, as Khrushchev later alleged, that he would get rid of Tito by shaking his little finger, he certainly felt that way. He could announce his displeasure, and the Yugoslavs would fall on their knees, would themselves take care of their Titos and Djilases. Had he not told his own Central Committee in 1937 that he proposed to liquidate some two-thirds of them, and hadn't they all applauded?

In January 1948 all the talk about a Balkan or a Yugoslav-Bulgarian federation was condemned in the Soviet press. In March, when the Yugoslav police interefered with the more flagrant cases of spying by Soviet personnel in Belgrade, *all* Soviet military and civilian experts (who had been paid by the Yugoslavs) were withdrawn. Tito asked politely for an explanation, and Stalin let him have it: scandalous anti-Soviet rumors were circulating "among the leading comrades in Yugoslavia," he said. The Yugoslav Communist Party was run undemocratically: "the Party cadres are under the supervision of the Minister of State Security."[51] Having made all those irrefutable points, Stalin communicated this remarkable example of epistolary art to other Communist Parties in Eastern Europe and confidently waited for Tito to explain.

Later on Stalin may have had cause to appreciate that Party fights, like lovers' quarrels, are best not committed to writing. The Yugoslavs' answer was dignified: "No matter how much each of us loves the land of Socialism, the U.S.S.R., he can in no case love his country less." Where were the proofs of the truth of all those accusations? Tito spelled out the exploitation which went under the name of fraternal assistance: for Soviet services (i.e., spying), the Yugoslavs were expected to pay a Soviet colonel three times the salary of a Yugoslav minister. The people whom the Soviet letter branded as spies were being investigated: "We would not care to remove and destroy a man on the basis of suspicion."

---

[51] The Royal Institute of International Affairs, *The Soviet-Yugoslav Dispute* (London, 1948), p. 14. While the actual drafting of the correspondence on the Soviet side was probably done by somebody else, possibly Molotov, its general tone is unmistakably Stalin's.

Would the Russians send a representative to see for himself how groundless the charges are?[52]

No Communist since at least 1928 had dared to answer Stalin in such terms, and now his cunning was almost forgotten in an explosion of petulance. A few years before he might have masked his rage and waited for another opening, but he was now sixty-eight and appeared unable to put up with this insolence. The Soviet answer bristled with his personal resentment. And he forgot that if one wants to appear ominous, one should be brief: the Soviet diatribe of May 4 covers twenty pages of close print. Almost certainly Stalin himself wrote certain sentences in it, though officially it was signed by the Central Committee of the Communist Party of the U.S.S.R. Who else would characterize the Yugoslavs' letter, full of restraint and devotion to the Soviet Union, as "exaggeratedly ambitious," or say that "Comrades Tito and Kardelj . . . do not understand that this childish method of groundless denial of facts and documents can never be convincing, but merely laughable."[53] None but Stalin would have dared to make the generous admission that "in his time Trotsky also rendered revolutionary services . . ."—and thus delicately suggest to Tito that *his past* revolutionary services might not exempt him from Trotsky's fate!

It is revealing that all the substantive issues of the quarrel did not irritate Stalin nearly so much as Tito's actually talking back to him. This upstart, he now exploded, made ridiculous claims that the Yugoslavs *invented* guerrilla warfare (the Yugoslavs never made such claims). Why, he retorted pedantically, Marshal Kutuzov, and before him the Spaniards, used partisans against Napoleon. The Yugoslav Communists should be "less boastful about their merits and successes and . . . behave with greater propriety and modesty." The past and present seemed all mixed up in Stalin's mind. Three years before, Djilas had complained about the behavior of the Red Army in Yugoslavia. Since then he had repeatedly apologized to Stalin for his incautious though well-justified complaints. He had been forgiven and, as we have seen, was even thought to be good material for a Soviet agent. But now Stalin returned to this, just as he dwelt on what Tito was alleged to have said years before. And he added some really childish attempts to arouse the Yugoslavs' suspicions against each other: in 1945, he said, Tito's principal lieutenant, Edward Kardelj, had criticized his boss in a talk with the Soviet ambassador.

Thus the correspondence (which Belgrade very wisely, from its point of view, hastened to make public) is most revealing of Stalin's mind at this juncture: the old malevolence, the undying suspiciousness which

[52] *Ibid.*, p. 19.
[53] *Ibid.*, p. 31.

latches onto the most minuscule pretext, is still there. But the old skill at intrigue, the ability to overcome even those who are not within his physical power, is largely gone. Stalin is no longer the man who could turn Trotsky against Zinoviev, attract Bukharin, charm Roosevelt and Churchill. There were still flashes of his old self, of his cunning and insight. But in his remaining years, he was not only monstrous, as before, but at times ridiculous.

That Stalin had not lost all of his cunning and prudence can be seen by the sequel to the Tito episode. True, with an ounce of diplomacy tempering his hurt vanity, the Yugoslav issue could have been contained as late as the summer of 1948, for it was difficult for Tito's people to face the reality of breaking with the Soviet Union and the living god of Communism, and Tito, a clever man, was leading them into the wilderness cautiously. At the Yugoslav Party Congress in July 1948, at the end of Tito's speech recounting the indignities suffered at the hand of the Soviets, delegates took up the chant "Stalin–Tito–Party." But Stalin would not relent, and his megalomania reinforced his caution, rather than prompting him to act recklessly. Had he struck then, had the Red Army moved through Hungary and Bulgaria against the rebellious vassal, few in the West would have been seriously disturbed at this intra-Communist war. But Stalin knew that the Yugoslavs would fight. They could not hold out forever against the Red Army, but Yugoslavia's mountains might make it a war of some duration. Things might get sticky elsewhere. There was the warning example of the miscalculation over Finland in 1939. No, it was not worth the risk. In any case, in a year or two Tito would topple and the Yugoslavs would beg for forgiveness. ☆☆☆

I
N the meantime, others paid for Tito's defiance. All over Eastern Europe Communist leaders were purged, some for their hidden sympathy for Tito (which, however, they could not conceal from Soviet agents or their intraparty rivals), others for standing up, no matter how feebly, for their countries' economic interests against Soviet exploitation. But as in 1936–39 in Russia, so now in Hungary or Bulgaria the lightning might strike the staunchest Stalinist as well as a man with a Trotskyite past. It was Stalin's position that if the East European Communist parties were to be protected from the machinations of the Titoists and the intrigues of American imperialists, they had to absorb some of the lessons which he had taught his own Party and society, and which he now believed had been so helpful in enabling him to survive the war. He had employed public trials to unmask and illuminate the basic con-

nection between Trotskyism and Bukharinism and treason on behalf of Hitler's Germany and Japan. So now it was imperative that the new "rich threads of treason" be exposed: how they ran from Washington through Belgrade to conspirators in Prague or Budapest. Some local leaders pleaded that they be allowed to deal with their "people's enemies" in their own way. No, they were told, it was Comrade Stalin's express wish that the educational experience gathered in the Soviet Union now be shared by the People's Democracies. Soviet advisers would teach them how such things were arranged. And so the obscene drama of the Moscow trials was repeated between 1949 and 1952 in Sofia, Prague, and Budapest. The world now had vivid proof that it was not the "Russian soul" which had made Bukharin and so many others "confess" to opprobrious and absurd changes.

The East European countries were expected to initiate more than simply Soviet methods of terror. Conceit and personal treachery, it was believed, could not fully explain Tito's anti-Soviet moves: there had to be more basic, ideological roots of treason. As he advanced in years, Stalin reverted to the simple verities of his youth. The Soviet Union's victory in the war was no longer merely a national victory: it was a victory that would not have been possible without the vast social transformation he had wrought through his creative application of Marxism-Leninism. Perhaps it had been a mistake all along not to insist that the countries within the Soviet sphere carry out a thorough program of collectivization. Tito had betrayed not only him, Stalin, but Marxism-Leninism. He had allowed the peasants to remain the dominant social element in Yugoslavia and they had applauded his betrayal of socialism. As behooved a petty-bourgeois politician, Tito had told the peasants that they were the strongest pillar of his state, had tolerated the scandalous situation "where private ownership of the land exists and land is bought and sold . . . where hired labor is used."[54]

And so as of 1948 rapid collectivization became the order of the day all over Eastern Europe. The local Communists had hoped to delay this day as long as possible. Even the most fanatical among them had seen what an ordeal forced collectivization had been for Russia. They hoped, after consolidating political power, to proceed cautiously and gradually with developing farm cooperatives and to be spared the horrors that took place in the Soviet Union between 1929 and 1934. Their peasants were more individualistic than their Russian cousins, and many believed that to embark on rapid and forced collectivization in Poland and Czechoslovakia would mean to risk a civil war. But now they had to fall in with the Kremlin's orders.

[54] *Ibid.*, p. 42. In fact, the Yugoslav Communists started and by 1948 had pushed collectivization of agriculture farther than any of the People's Democracies.

Other aspects of the class war had also to be spruced up and intensified. In many East European countries, notably Poland, the Catholic Church represented a formidable force, and the Communist politicians there hoped to be allowed time to re-educate the masses before they frontally attacked this "bastion of reaction and superstition." Such caution had previously been not only approved but highly recommended by the Kremlin: there was no reason, it was said, to incense Catholic opinion, which was so influential in the United States and of some importance for the electoral prospects of the French and Italian Parties. (In Italy, as a matter of fact, at the end of the war, the Communists displayed more solicitude for the Vatican's susceptibilities and prerogatives than their Socialist allies, and it was largely due to their attitude that divorce remained banned.) But this prudent toleration, and with it the lingering ideological coexistence of Marxism-Leninism with Christianity, in the People's Democracies was declared impermissible. And struggling against the peasants and against the churches, trying to destroy other non-Communist forces and ideologies, the leaders of Eastern Europe had no stomach, indeed no time, for trying their own brand of Titoism. In their struggle with the majority of their countrymen they became more dependent than ever on the Soviet Union.

So, at least, thought Stalin. There can be no doubt that the whole plan of action against actual, budding, and imaginary Titoism came directly from him. No other aspect of his foreign policy was modified so rapidly and drastically after his death as the methods of rule over other Communist states. Stalin's successors—and it seems on this point they were virtually unanimous[55]—thought that it was neither possible nor desirable for Russia to control their vassals' policies down to every detail, that this was asking for unnecessary trouble, especially in view of China's having now joined the Communist family of nations. In turning on Tito, Stalin alienated Soviet Russia's most genuinely devoted followers, destroyed the legend of the unity of world Communism, showed how vulnerable Communism was to the virus of nationalism. Above all, he failed: with a thoroughness which proved that they had learned something from their expensive Soviet advisers, the Yugoslavs liquidated Moscow's agents in their midst. To his non-Communist subjects, Tito now appeared as a champion of national independence; to the leaders of other satellite states he was an object of secret envy; to Mao Tse-tung and his followers he was living proof that to incur Stalin's and Soviet Russia's wrath need not be fatal. Yes, Tito had fooled Comrade Stalin, or rather, for once Stalin had made a fool of himself.

---

[55] Khrushchev later charged Molotov with opposing the Soviet-Yugoslav rapprochement, but in 1953 he certainly supported a détente between Moscow and Belgrade.

But who would dare to throw this failure in his teeth, even point out respectfully that while still infallible, "the greatest genius of our times,"[56] he could not be expected at his age to cope with all foreign and domestic problems. In fact, the style of his despotism did change. Of the 1930s Mandelstam could write: "But everywhere is heard the voice of the Kremlin mountaineer, the destroyer of life, the peasant killer." The country was full of his voice, the nation reeled under his ferocious energy. Now, in the words of Tvardovsky's famous poem, "Like a dread spirit he stood over us; though alive, cut off from life by the Kremlin wall; of others we knew not the names."[57] He was like a disembodied spirit of tyranny hovering over society, seldom seen, almost never heard, yet his name was everywhere, in the first and last paragraphs of the most scholarly books on the most rarefied subjects, in every novel, every speech and report; his pictures and photographs (now usually retouched to conceal the ravages of age) gazed everywhere on his subjects. They "knew not"—i.e., did not care about—the others' names. Before, those subtyrants Kaganovich and Molotov et al. had appeared to have some personality and significance of their own; one could be heartened by Yezhov's disappearance, depressed by Orjonikidze's death. Now most people recognized that all such hopes and fears had been delusory: politically those "comrades-in-arms" of Stalin's did not really exist but were expressions of the tyrant's different moods and designs: it was one Stalin who replaced another, rather than Beria replacing Yezhov.

Who apart from a handful of people could assess the importance of Zhdanov's death in the summer of 1948, with Malenkov again the heir-apparent and chief priest of the ruling deity? In 1950 foreign observers and a hundred or so Soviet bureaucrats were perplexed by the apparent division within the Politburo on the future of the collective farm. Andreyev, in a speech, suggested loosening the structure of the kolkhoz. Khrushchev then criticized Andreyev and proposed on the contrary a merger of existing kolkhozes into larger units, looking eventually toward veritable giant farms: "agro-cities." Then a lesser priest, the secretary of the Armenian Party, criticized the idea of "agro-cities" and, by implication, Khrushchev. What was going on? The Soviet common man, even if a peasant whose entire way of life would depend on the resolution of the debate, could not get excited: soon Stalin might speak with yet another man's voice and order something entirely different for his peasant subjects.

---

[56] This formula was now felt inadequate and was being replaced by "the greatest genius of mankind."

[57] Alexander Tvardovsky, "Horizon Beyond Horizon," *New World* (Moscow), No. 5 (1960), p. 9.

With succeeding years, mystification became an ever greater part of Stalin's technique of despotic rule. Conspiracy, as we have seen, was natural to Communists of his generation. But with Stalin this characteristic was stronger than in most Bolsheviks, and in his old age it became a veritable obsession, extending to his personal as well as political life. He no longer could keep abreast of everything happening in the Party and the state, and from his point of view this meant that more than ever he must not only be feared and worshiped but appear mysterious and unfathomable. There was always the object lesson of his own rise to power. He had correctly read Lenin's character, and he had known how to become indispensable to him. And then the dreadful warning of Lenin's last illness. That must not be repeated. He must not let anyone get close to him, become indispensable, understand his fears.

His daughter's recollections lift the veil on the old man's mental struggle between his need for human companionship and his desperate need to protect his divine status.

In 1946 Anna Alliluyeva, Stalin's sister-in-law, was allowed to publish a book of recollections of prerevolutionary times. Quite understandably, and to a biographer infuriatingly, what her book has to say about Stalin is relatively trivial: heartwarming human-interest stories about a modest and intrepid young revolutionary. Anna Alliluyeva was helped in her labors by an appropriate person so that nothing untoward should appear in the book (thus the story of Lenin hiding at the Alliluyevs' house in July 1917 does not say a word about how they also concealed Zinoviev). Stalin undoubtedly read and sanctioned the manuscript for publication. He was never partial to women writing about subjects touching on the Party, but it is possible that he felt sorry for Anna.

A year and a half later *Pravda* published an extensive "review" of the book, which by then had probably been forgotten by most people who looked at it. Some idea of the tenor of the review is conveyed by the title: "Irresponsible Fabrications." The signature was of some hack journalist, but nobody could be in doubt who commissioned it and suggested some of its most venomous epithets. Had Trotsky written a book on the subject, it could hardly have been attacked more scurrilously than this harmless account of the Alliluyev family. Not only Anna, "who presumed to write about things she did not know and could not have known," but her literary helper and censor were viciously attacked.

This fury, this lack of any sense of proportion are explicable only in terms of the evolution of Stalin's fears. In 1946 the mood born of victory had not been entirely dissipated: so let the people read about the simple and strenuous beginnings of their father and savior. But a year and a half later! This silly chatterbox portrayed him as one of many revolutionaries, rather than someone who was always *the* leader. She dared mention such embarrassing details as how he fell asleep with his pipe lit and almost burned down the Alliluyevs' apartment. How he personally shaved Lenin before his escape from Petrograd: the "greatest genius of mankind" had been a barber!

Svetlana Alliluyeva attributes her father's growing misanthropy, if this be the word, and his anger toward his relatives to his feeling of loneliness and guilt over his wife's death. Such an explanation does credit to a daughter. But she herself recounts that in 1948, after the arrest and exile of her two aunts, Anna and the widow of Paul Alliluyev, her father said, "They babbled too much. They know too much. This might help the enemy."[58] Who was the enemy? The real enemy was his own old age and growing infirmity. He must get rid of those who knew too much about him: his oldest lieutenants, his old servants, his relatives. What might they not say or do if he became helpless?

On February 24, 1947, Stalin indulged in one of his favorite forms of relaxation: a chitchat with "leading cultural workers." The second part of *Ivan the Terrible* was to be put into production, and to give the correct direction to the work, the Boss invited its director, Sergei Eisenstein, and Nikolai Cherkasov, the portrayer of the psychopathic Tsar, to have tea at the Kremlin. Cherkasov—who gazes at us from the screen as the iron-willed Alexander Nevsky, as the mad (and reactionary) Tsarevich Alexis in Peter the Great, and as the tormented (but progressive) Ivan the Terrible—has left us a recollection of that social occasion.

As usual, Stalin was generous with his insights about art. What characterized a great actor, he opined, was his ability to assume the personality of the man portrayed.[59] But then he shifted to historical reflection. Ivan should be seen as a great and progressive ruler who strove for his country's good and unity. Even Malyuta Skuratov, whom bourgeois historians painted as a monster (he was Ivan's Yezhov), was in fact a patriotic citizen, a worthy comrade-in-arms of his leader. But, alas, continued Stalin, no one is perfect. Ivan did not liquidate enough people. He left behind several oligarchs whose struggles for power after his death brought decades of anarchy and foreign intervention to Russia.

[58] Alliluyeva, *Twenty Letters to a Friend*, p. 182.
[59] There was, to be sure, a certain risk in too faithful an identification with a fictional character. In the evening of his life Stalin was very much taken with a Ukrainian actor who portrayed negative characters—traitors and the like. And then the thought struck him that a man who puts on such convincing interpretations of "enemies of the people" must have been one himself. Instructions went out to deal appropriately with the man who had hit upon this novel way of concealing his "two-faced" personality. But then the believer in the theory that art expresses life's deeper truths died, and the artist was saved. This charming tale is recounted by Nadezhda Mandelstam, who had it from Ilya Ehrenburg, who in turn claims to have gotten it from Khrushchev. The last two, it is fair to add, were not above telling fibs.

Though this motif could not have been pleasant to Molotov and Zhdanov, who were present, Stalin expanded on the danger of allowing powerful subordinates to survive their boss. Ivan would liquidate a princely family, and then would waste a whole year in prayers and contrition, rather than cheerfully going on with the purge: "God would get in his way." "As usual, Comrades Stalin, Molotov and Zhdanov knew how to make us feel at ease, so that we not only listened but participated in the discussion," notes the enchanted narrator, who possibly because of his great height was never called upon to represent the man he so admired.[60]

During Stalin's last years, Russia partook even more of the theatrical and surrealistic than during the horrors of 1936–39. Stalin had destroyed anybody and anything which *might* prove troublesome in the case of war. Now the alleged rationale for repression became more intangible and preposterous. Before, one had been asked to believe (and many did) that the Party bigwigs, generals, and one's own neighbor were somehow connected with Trotsky, with Tokyo and Berlin. Few could now understand how the threads of treason ran from "personal" poetry or a geneticist's study to the "Mad Haberdasher"[61] in the White House. The quieter postwar years of repression had none of the populistic gloss given to the Great Purge: no mass meetings howled for death penalties. In a way, as time went on, this seemed more terrifying. Terror itself became subordinate to mystification: no one must know when, how, or why Stalin would proclaim a new war against the nation.

And perhaps Stalin himself did not know. It would be reasonable to suppose that there were moments when he must have felt that he had killed off his real enemies, and that the potential ones were safely locked up in Russia's vast network of camps and jails. One had to be on guard against intrigues in his immediate entourage, but one might show indulgence for the simple folk who worshiped him so much. Svetlana Alliluyeva recounts a few occasions which sound suspiciously like Stalin attempting to get close to the people and to vary his routine of being "cut off from life by the Kremlin walls." In 1946 he set out by automobile for his vacation in Georgia and visited Party organizations on the long route south. This must have been the only tour of this kind since the beginning of his absolute rule, when in 1928 he traveled through the Urals and western Siberia. In view of the state of Soviet roads and in view of his age, it was a rather startling sacrifice of the comfort to which

---

[60] Nikolai K. Cherkasov, *Notes of a Soviet Actor* (Moscow, 1953), p. 380.

[61] The title of a 1949 play about President Truman. This was a rare departure from the Soviet etiquette of vituperation: the abuse of hostile heads of state is not supposed to include references to their previous occupations or personal lives. This rule was breached again in the 1960s, when the Soviet press informed us that in her youth Chiang Ching (Mao's wife) had been a member of the oldest profession.

he had grown accustomed. For years he had barely deigned to visit a farm or a factory in or near Moscow. Perhaps he felt a sudden impulse to see how Soviet reality compared with the charts, reports, and statistics which his trembling subordinates submitted. A few other times while in his native land, we are told, he would venture out of his villa to visit some locality he remembered from his youth. But the tumultous reception organized for him by local Party and security organs made him furious and drove him back to his usual routine: solitude interrupted by that gross nocturnal conviviality. He had lost the ability to pretend to like crowds and contacts with simple people.

At times—and rather inconsistently, in view of Anna Alliluyeva's dreadful experience—Stalin allowed a less than Olympian image of himself to be presented to the public. In 1948 Soviet theatergoers must have been considerably surprised to see a quite human Stalin speak to them from behind the footlights in Nicholas Virta's play about Stalingrad. To be sure, he was a genius who knew in August precisely how he would crush the Germans in January, and who was up to every trick of Churchill's. And yet how endearingly human! An "old friend" from revolutionary days appears to reprimand "Joseph" for not taking care of himself: he smokes too much, never rests; how long can he carry on like that at their age? Instead of sending him where he has sent most of his old friends, the affable Stalin asks his pal to repair to his villa: there they can talk about the good old times to their hearts' content. But, alas, enters Poskrebyshev, a typical comically fussy secretary who runs his boss: no time for chitchat with old friends, important decisions and committees are waiting. Don't I get any free time, even at night? asks Stalin in mock despair. The schedule does not allow for any free time, retorts Poskrebyshev severely. But what a model of solicitude Stalin is himself! On every important question he sees and values Molotov's opinion; he is fatherly toward Malenkov and toward his chief of staff, General Vasilevsky. There is even an anachronistically friendly reference to the Americans, good people even if naïve, who call Stalin "Uncle Joe," a name which somehow never caught on in the Soviet Union.

This glimpse behind the Kremlin wall, at the exhilarating and comradely life of Soviet gods, was being served to the public at the same time as Pauline Molotov was arrested and then exiled from Moscow, not to return until her husband's great friend was safely under the glass in the mausoleum. Subsequent years brought a demotion to Molotov. And that model of all faithful secretaries, Poskrebyshev, spent the last months of Stalin's life disgraced and waiting to be arrested. They all knew too much.[62]

---

[62] Stalin was probably unique among despots in his ability to inspire worship among his victims. People forget what *he* had been through, Anna Alliluyeva told her niece

Yet is is doubtful whether even they really believed that they knew the man for whom they had worked for decades. In reading his daughter's account, one must conclude that Stalin acted a role even with her, and that after his outburst at her first romance he was careful not to reveal too much of himself, even to a person whom he had no reason to fear or suspect. Stalin the choleric father gave way to an understanding one. He would not stand in the way of her marrying a Jew. This was in 1944—when he came closest to being the normal human person he had been before 1928. In him it was a sign of fatherly tenderness, rather than the opposite, that he would never see his daughter's husband: this precluded his being struck by an irresistible dislike of him. He chaffed his daughter about her husband's not being in the army; but it is reasonable to see his hand in this: how the Germans would gloat at capturing Stalin's *Jewish* son-in-law! After the war Stalin enacted for his daughter's benefit the role of a lonely old man, abhorring the worship which surrounded his person but helpless to do anything about it. There was undoubtedly an element of truth about the first point. His talk would revert to his wife and her death. But recollection of his personal grief spelled tragedy for others: who were the enemies who had turned Nadezhda against him at a time when he needed all his strength and resolution to keep Russia and Communism from going under? By imprisoning his sisters-in-law and Nadezhda's friend Pauline Molotov, he gave a partial answer to his old question. The passage of time served only to ripen his suspicions into certainty and a resolve for vengeance.

Of the usual consolations of old age Stalin could have none. His surviving son, Vassily, was now an alcoholic.[63] He, like other children, had sought an escape from an impossible household (Stalin can hardly be said to have had a *home* following his wife's death) via an early marriage. He became a general while still in his twenties. It is unclear whether it was his father's direct favoritism or the others' dread of his name which led to his rapid promotions. But though he threw his weight around (at least one senior air commander is alleged to have been disgraced and imprisoned because of Vassily's enmity), the son, like Stalin's other favorites, suffered from his intermittent whims and rages. Vassily's alcholism finally compelled Stalin to relieve him of his command and order him grounded. After March 5, 1953, Vassily went

---

about the man who had killed her husband. And in Khrushchev's era both Molotovs used to express regrets for the good old times. There have been even more startling examples.

[63] His wife believed, and perhaps thus explained her husband's terrible temper, that there was a hereditary predisposition toward alcoholism in the Djugashvili family. This at least must be the explanation of the pledge she extracted from her daughter —then six years old!—never to drink. Alliluyeva, *Twenty Letters to a Friend*, p. 102.

to pieces, was discharged from the air force and later imprisoned. He died of alcoholism but also, like countless others, of Stalinism.

Following her divorce from her husband in 1947 (she insists that her father had nothing to do with it), Svetlana was occasionally sent for by Stalin to accompany him on his vacations. But as she describes persuasively, for all of his undoubted affection for her, he simply could not endure close human relations. He lived in a state of constant irritation with those close to him. Still, there were occasional flashes of the younger man—for example, at his daughter's second marriage. Svetlana sought to escape her father's too frequent and depressing presence by marrying someone he approved of: Zhdanov's son, Yuri. The dictator behaved like any peasant father, pleased that his girl was marrying a well-connected cultured man. And in the same vein he became anxious. Svetlana was planning to move in with the Zhdanovs. The household was full of meddlesome womenfolk; she would be devoured by mother-in-law![64] For a moment he forgot that even that formidable institution the Russian mother-in-law was not immune to his power. And, judging by Mme. Alliluyeva's account, Zinaida Zhdanova stood up fearlessly for the prerogatives of her position. Few women would have been so domineering with a daughter-in-law whose father could send one to Siberia, nor so free with her tongue—Zinaida and her dead husband's two sisters were uninhibited in their criticism of the new favorite, Malenkov.

But for all his stratagems to keep his grown-up daughter close to him, at which he was no more successful than ordinary fathers, he would occasionally reveal deep-seated emotions. The old revolutionary and former political prisoner would at times show resentment at the privileged Soviet caste which he himself had created. All those bigwigs' children, his daughter included, with their fine education, their contempt for physical labor. He resembled a self-made capitalist upbraiding his daughter for her precious radical ideas and sensitivities. "You are a goddamned privileged caste," he exploded during the war upon hearing that Svetlana, along with other evacuated officials' children, had been sent to a special school in Kuibyshev. He shared in the universal gift that parents have for embarrassing their better-educated children. "An idler," he called the young woman in the presence of his usual company.[65]

But in addition to the eternal father and the old socialist, there would also emerge the other and frightening Stalin. In 1948 he announced to his daughter that her first marriage had been a plot. Her first husband "had been thrown in her path" by Zionists. Svetlana was astounded,

[64] *Ibid.*, p. 179.
[65] *Ibid.*, p. 181.

even though in view of her experience—hadn't her first swain been unmasked as a spy for the English?—she should have been accustomed to such surprises. ☆☆☆

THE anti-Zionist and, as it soon became, anti-Jewish motif grew very prominent in Stalin's last years, crisscrossing his domestic life, internal policies, and foreign affairs. It illuminated the working of his mind: how from small personal and political irritations there grew a suspicion that was finally allowed to harden into certainty of the existence of some vast plot. The anatomy of his feelings on this issue was in no way different than that which in the past inspired the purge of kulaks, Trotskyites, or army officers. He was not a simple anti-Semite, any more than he had been anti-peasant, anti-Old Bolshevik, or anti-military. In each case the suspicion—up to a small, very small point rational—that a given group, class, or nationality harbored actual or potential enemies, was allowed to grow into a nightmarish plot. "They" all must be somehow mixed up in treacherous machinations. Treason for Stalin and, to be fair, for many Bolsheviks of his generation (though for none of them to the same degree), was like the Devil to the medieval Christian. His manifestations need not be blatant; he would not only lead one into mortal sin, he would tempt one into committing trivial sins. Stalin's famous speech of March 1937 was for all of its Marxian terminology a very medieval document: the class enemy may not manifest itself through major acts of wrecking and sabotage; the Evil One may ingratiate himself through his devotees' lying low, even doing good socialist work while waiting for an opportune moment to strike.

And so now: a Jewish critic writes scathingly about a classic of Russian literature; his own daughter marries a Jew; Soviet Jews cry with joy at the appearance of an Israeli minister in Moscow; America, where Jews are so influential, adopts an increasingly anti-Soviet attitude. Were these separate phenomena which simply happened to coincide? Stalin had never believed that treason or dissent—and the two became identical in his mind—could be an isolated phenomenon springing from an individual's decision, and not also be a state of mind. Marxism-Leninism taught that whole classes are guilty, become dangerous to the state and socialism. Even the most altruistic and patriotic kulak was still an enemy. So if classes, why not, at certain junctures in history, professions and nationalities? Once absolute power was his, Stalin acted upon this perverse and frightening logic.

He was never partial to the Jews; many of his rivals had been Jewish.

Quite apart from politics, the Georgian peasant who found a spiritual home in Russian culture resented the volubility and glittering cosmopolitanism of Trotsky and Radek. They were so prone to sneer and criticize. Stalin adopted some popular prejudices of his adopted country: the Jews, he believed, shirk physical labor. They make poor soldiers, he told the Polish ambassador during the war. But there was enough of the Marxist left in him to keep the prejudice from hardening into racial hatred. Some of his chief lieutenants had been Jewish. His children married Jews: he did not like it, but if he had been the classic type of anti-Semite he would have never stood for it.

At Yalta Roosevelt asked him whether he was pro-Zionist, and Stalin answered evasively that he was in principle. Both branches of Russian Marxism, and especially Jews within them, had traditionally opposed Zionism. Stalin himself before the war would not tolerate the creed, just as he would not tolerate any movement that claimed the loyalty or even sentimental attachment of some group of his subjects. If after the war Soviet diplomacy supported the Zionist claim for Palestine, the reasons were purely political. The creation of Israel would further weaken the crumbling British imperial position and would provide a festering sore in the relations of the Arab world with the United States. The Czechs furnished arms to the Jewish underground in Palestine, which they could not have done without express Soviet permission. When Israel was born, the U.S.S.R. was the first state to recognize it. (The changed Soviet attitude toward Zionism has nothing to do with anything Israel has or has not done subsequently. Soviet hostility to Israel and Zionism has a twofold explanation: Zionism has had a for them unexpected and scandalous impact on a number of Soviet Jews, and Soviet diplomacy had found it advisable in the struggle for influence in the Near East to adopt a pro-Arab stance. For this latter situation Nikita Khrushchev has been much more responsible than his late boss.)

When in 1948 Mrs. Golda Meir, the Foreign Minister of the new state, visited Moscow, she found herself the recipient of a tumultuous demonstration when she visited a synagogue. One can imagine what kind of impression this spontaneous outburst produced on the Soviet authorities and on Stalin. A relative handful of· mostly elderly folk created the demonstration, but it was more than enough to trigger Stalin's resolve to nip the danger in the bud. Since the war, his country had been virtually sealed off from the capitalist world. The very few women who had married Britons and Americans had been prevented from leaving the country. People had been put in camps for having received presents and decorations from the Allies during the war. Thousands of Armenians, whom nostalgia induced to return to their native land, were carefully screened in a search for imperialist spies and isolated from their fellow nationals. In 1947 Stalin sent Kaganovich to rule the Ukraine to make sure that Khrushchev was not being too soft on those who had been exposed to bourgeois and nationalist influences during the German occupation. He had almost persuaded himself that Russia was spyproof, and that except for a few writers and scientists there was no conduit through which noxious foreign ideas could leak. But he had been living in a fools' paradise: there was this vast reservoir for spies, dissenters, and troublemakers of all kinds: the Jews.

The anti-Jewish compaign would probably have taken place even without the Golda Meir incident. The younger generation of Soviet bureaucrats had been brought up on the tales of treachery of the older one, of whom quite a few had been Jewish. Many a Komsomol member has absorbed the impression, conveyed by his Party instructor through hints rather than explicitly, that most Trotskyites were Jews, that all the negative aspects of Communism had been due to Jews. It was even whispered that Beria was a Georgian Jew! It was probably the Jewish security people who, by distorting the Leader's wise and compassionate directives, had made the forcible collectivization such hell: what did they know or care about the peasants? *After* the war the regime discouraged excessive publicity about the Nazi massacres of Jews. Anti-Jewish jokes and gossip became fashionable among Soviet officials: Djilas's Soviet chaperon confided to him that General Antonov was unmasked as having non-Aryan antecedents. It is possible that this fact or rumor cost that architect of Soviet wartime strategy his marshal's baton. People whose nationality was entered in their identity papers as Jewish found it almost impossible to enter the officers corps or the diplomatic service after the war.

Perhaps the anti-Jewish drive would have continued in a low key except for the world situation. What had once been merely undesirable became treason with the onset of the Cold War. "The imperialists of Europe and America . . . are trying by all means to slander our nation, to discredit its successes in socialist construction, and to undermine its faith in Communism. Those who spread bourgeois theories in the arts serve the purposes of our enemies. Can our Soviet nation tolerate attacks by bourgeois esthetes on our national art? Our people brand with shame those rootless cosmopolites who lack the slightest feeling of patriotism."[66] The *rootless* cosmopolite was a particularly vicious subspecies of cosmopolite species: denigrators of Russian culture and of socialism, imitators and worshipers of Western ways and ideas. To make sure that the readers would catch on that most people in the category were Jewish, the unmasked rootless cosmopolites, if they had changed

[66] From "Hold Aloft the Banner of Russian Patriotism," *The Bolshevik* (Moscow), No. 3 (1949), p. 43.

their names to Russian-sounding ones, would be identified with their real names in parentheses. The rootless cosmopolites were cultural "wreckers"; not satisfied, like other cosmopolites, with just unduly admiring the West, they sneered at the treasures of Russian culture and tradition. They gravitated to literary, dramatic, and musical criticism ("those people never create, just criticize"), wrote condescendingly about Tschaikovsky, found fault with Gogol and Gorky. One "aesthete, Schneiderman," for example, professed that literature should deal with human feelings and emotions; political ideas, he wrote cynically, belonged in propaganda lectures.[67]

The hue and cry was now on. Jewish critics were discharged, forbidden to write for Soviet journals. Stalin could not deny himself the pleasure of the cat-and-mouse game. After the campaign identifying the racial origins of rootless cosmopolites had gone on for a while, editors of the journals which displayed special zeal in the effort were summoned to the Leader's presence and admonished that this was an impermissible and bigoted practice. Ilya Ehrenburg might well have believed that he purchased immunity for himself by writing for *Pravda* (on September 29, 1949) an article portraying Israel as a bourgeois state and a creature of Anglo-American capital, decrying the notion of any suprastate, single Jewish nation. But, "as for myself, from the bginning of February, 1949, I was not allowed to publish anything. My name was deleted from the critics' reviews. . . . Every night I expected the front door bell to ring," writes Ehrenburg.[68] Stalin was a discriminating torturer who varied the treatment of his victims. As Mandelstam had written, "This one is to be hit on the head . . . that one in the groin." Ehrenburg's share was the ordeal of uncertainty. He might still be useful. He was not an obscure critic or a Yiddish writer; as behooved a real rootless cosmopolite Ehrenburg had a lot of friends and connections in the West. But of course he had to prove himself, had to show that he was not proud; and beg. "I wrote a short letter to Stalin saying that for the last two months I had been denied all journalistic work and that the day before so-and-so had announced my arrest; in fact, however, I had not been arrested and I wished to have my position clarified." This time, unlike a similar occasion in 1941, Stalin did not choose to call Ehrenburg in person. It was Malenkov who called: "You wrote to Stalin. He asked me to ring you up. Tell me, how did all this start?" Why hadn't he let Stalin know sooner about the chicanery to which he had been subjected? But he had tried to, protested Ehrenburg. He had com-

[67] *Ibid.*, p. 42.
[68] Ilya Ehrenburg, *The Post-War Years, 1945–1954* (Cleveland and New York, 1967), p. 132.

plained to Comrade Pospelov (then head of the propaganda department of the Central Committee). Strange, said Malenkov, Pospelov, "a very reliable man," had not said a word about this to the Boss.[69]

Again, Ehrenburg's work became much sought after. Having passed the test, he was named a member of the Soviet delegation to the World Peace Congress in Paris. Who else could combat so eloquently all the slanders about the Soviet Union? But before he left he was made to write and submit for approval the speech he was going to deliver. It was a stirring reassertion of human brotherhood and condemnation of all forms of racial and national intolerance. When the text was returned to Ehrenburg, it had on the margin "the words 'well said!' in a handwriting that looked to me painfully familiar."[70] But even a visit to his beloved Paris was ruined by the thought of what he was coming from and to what he would have to return. Stalin must have known and relished this agony of his favorite "rootless cosmopolite." There was more than one way of dealing with the breed.

But playful sadism never dominated Stalin's mind for long: fear and wrath claimed their due. Zionist plotting and Jewish influence in cultural life were no laughing matters. The older generation of Soviet Jews was shot through with Zionism, he announced to his daughter, and they were trying to infect the younger generation. This was not the simple matter of a few book reviews or sympathy for Israel. These *had* to be real threads of treason leading from America through Zionism to Soviet Jewry. Stalin developed and proved his hypotheses of treason the way a mathematician solves a theorem. Once "proven" in theory, treason had to be found in nature. A security officer would risk his head if he sent back a dossier on Zionist espionage with a note that no actual spies had been uncovered. Some MGB[71] men set to work with the melancholy knowledge that if they found only a few spies, they would be guilty of "criminal blindness and negligence." (Conversely, an overzealous performance might well at some time in the future render them guilty of "slandering honest Soviet citizens" and of "the use of impermissible methods of investigation.") But by now few of the security officers were cynical or sophisticated. They had been conditioned through their work to believe that treason, like evil, rests in every man. The only question is how deeply one has to probe to uncover it.

How were such campaigns viewed by the top echelons of the bureaucracy of terror—by Beria, say, still the overlord of the apparatus, or by Abakumov, since 1946 Minister of State Security? Quite likely even they by now could not tell whether the Boss believed his theories of treason,

[69] Later on, Ehrenburg learned that Pospelov *had* talked to Stalin!
[70] Ehrenburg, p. 134.
[71] The current name of the former NKVD.

whether the "Zionists" were to be prosecuted for "educational" reasons, whether Stalin had turned against Jews in general, whether he thought there had been an actual plot, or what. Beria, cleverer than his predecessor as inquisitor-general, was far from being the wholly evil genius he has been portrayed since his fall. He pandered to Stalin's suspiciousness but in the main remained an instrument of his boss's designs rather than a mastermind of the terror. Was Stalin mad, then? No more so than in the 1930s. The madness lay in the system that gave absolute power to one man and allowed him to appease every suspicion and whim with blood.

Early in 1948 Solomon Mikhoels, a People's Artist of the U.S.S.R., met his death while visiting the city of Minsk. Mikhoels was a brilliant actor and producer, mostly of Yiddish drama, but also famous for his portrayal of King Lear. His death was officially blamed on a traffic accident; in fact he had been a victim of a criminal assault. He was given a state funeral and his memory was eulogized in the press. Yet rumors were rife that this was not an ordinary death. Years later Mikhoels' murder was ascribed—as what wasn't?—to Beria's machinations. Mme. Alliluyeva records that she heard Stalin discuss the assassination on the phone and issue instructions that it be treated as a traffic accident. "Automobile accident was the official version, the cover-up suggested by my father when the black deed was reported to him."[72]

Now it is possible that Mikhoels was assassinated at the orders of Beria and/or Stalin. But it is much more likely that, like Kirov's, it was an ordinary murder which then led to a series of political ones. That the official version should have claimed it to be a traffic accident is not surprising: ordinary crimes are not supposed to take place in a socialist society which has abolished exploitation and where consequently thieving and murder for gain are virtually unknown. And Stalin was not a man to allow funeral honors for those whom he had ordered killed.

Mikhoels had been chairman of the Jewish Anti-Fascist Committee, set up by the government during the war. On its behalf he had traveled in the United States, giving speeches and collecting funds for the devastated Jewish community in the U.S.S.R. But the Committee's main function was of course to funnel pro-Soviet propaganda among Jewish communities abroad. Hence its existence continued after the war, and like any Soviet organization with contacts abroad, it was, one must presume, the object of special vigilance and surveillance by the MGB. All of the Committee's activities, members, contacts, and pronouncements at home and in foreign parts must have been scrupulously checked and approved by the appropriate Soviet authorities. But in Stalin's Russia an individual's guilt depended not only on what he did or did

[72] Alliluyeva, *Only One Year*, p. 154.

not do: events beyond his control might render his previously permissible activities, even those urged upon him by the state, a retrospective treason. Hitler's coming to power rendered every Soviet officer, such as Uborevich and Yakir who had studied military art in Weimar Germany, a presumed traitor. And so the Marshall Plan and then the establishment of the State of Israel transformed all these innocent contacts and soliciting of funds among Americans Jews into the cause of espionage. In December 1948 the Anti-Fascist Committee was dissolved and its leading members were arrested. Sharing their fate was the original sponsor of the Committee, a former Assistant Foreign Minister, Solomon Lozovsky. Of Jewish origin, a member of that interfaction group which under Trotsky's leadership joined the Bolsheviks in August 1917, the veteran Communist was thus guilty on several counts. But the arrests spread to completely apolitical figures whose only crime seemed to be that they were prominent writers in Yiddish—a seeming paradox since their alleged treason, Zionism, decries the use of Yiddish instead of Hebrew. But precisely: Would not a clever "two-faced" Zionist use Yiddish, or for that matter Russian or Ukrainian, as a cover?

Those separate threads of dissent and subversion—"rootless cosmopolitanism" and the "Zionist agents of American imperialism"—were bound eventually to be combined into a single mosaic of treason. The moment came in January 1952 when Mikhoels, whose death four years earlier might well have spurred an "investigation" into the suspicious doings of the Jewish Anti-Fascist Committee, was named as a key figure in the by now notorious Kremlin Doctors' Plot. He was, it was "established," a liaison man between the murderous doctors (most of them Jewish) and "the international Jewish bourgeois nationalist organization 'Joint' established by the American intelligence [for] . . . extensive espionage, terrorist and other subversive work in many countries, including the U.S.S.R."[73] It may appear incongruous even within the Stalinist context for the murdered artist to be assigned this role as master spy: other leaders of the Anti-Fascist Committee had by now been shot on different fictitious charges; most of the crimes charged to the Kremlin doctors took place *after* Mikhoels' death. But Mikhoels was a stage name; his real name was Vovsi, and this happened to be also the name of the chief conspirator-doctor, possibly a relative. The coincidence was evidently too tempting for some ingenious investigator. But his labor was in vain. Stalin died, the doctors were rehabilitated and (except for one who died under torture) released, Mikhoels' good name was fully restored, though the mystery of his death remains.

The anti-Jewish campaign, to which we shall return, is thus one of the great paradoxes of Stalin's reign. His concern for agriculture led to

---

[73] *Pravda*, January 13, 1952.

policies that turned Soviet agriculture into a permanent cripple of the national economy; fear of war with Hitler induced him to condemn much of his officer corps as German agents and thus to facilitate Hitler's task in the case of a war; and now again, the logic of absolute power led to what in ordinary logic was nonsense. He began with the rational assumption that some of his Jewish subjects would be attracted by Zionism and thus develop conflicting loyalties. He acted on this premise by instituting a system of persecution and discrimination bound to accentuate the danger he feared, and he ended by viewing the Jews as he had the kulaks and the generals: a collective enemy. It is possible that had he lived a few more years, the Jews would have been subjected to wholesale deportation as the kulaks had been between 1930 and 1934, their elite massacred in the manner of the Red Army's from 1937 to 1939. ☆☆☆

T O most people such behavior is hard to explain except in terms of mental aberration. But most people have never exercised absolute power with its fears and temptations; have never been in the position to appease every suspicion, to satisfy their every whim and resentment.

The test of Stalin's rationality must then be sought, as before, in those areas where his power was not absolute, most notably in foreign relations. And here even during the last phase we find a sense of realism which keeps us from branding him as mad. If there was an element of passion in his thinking about the world outside of the Soviet Union, it was an ideology-induced paranoia no different in its essence from that which characterizes the thinking of every devotee of a rigid doctrinal system. The outside world was full of capitalists who plotted the destruction of the Soviet Union, of traitors within the Communist movement who schemed against him. Yet in counteracting their designs, he took careful stock of his own and their resources, calculated probabilities and contingencies. The conviction that the Marshall Plan was a plot against the Soviet empire did not make him command the Red Army to march into Western Europe. Tito's defiance, probably the most damaging wound to his vanity since he became master of world Communism, did not make him order an immediate liquidation of the impudent rebel and his gang. For all of his enormous megalomania, he realized when he sat down with Mao that he would have to bargain and concede on some points, rather than issue orders. This is not the behavior of a madman, nor even of a man like Hitler, in whom impatience and sense of historical mission stilled prudence and calculation.

Yet even in foreign policy, Stalin's last phase was one of decline in his powers, of vanity and megalomania increasingly encroaching upon intelligence. His attitude toward the West bore the imprint not only of ideological prejudice but of sullenness. He had reached the limit of his power on the world stage.

Probably for the same reason Stalin showed scant interest in the Third World, which his successors would court so assiduously. A younger and more flexible man would have been more alert to all the opportunities which the breakdown of the Western imperial systems presented to Soviet diplomacy. The Soviets stressed the anti-imperialist motif, and Stalin took it up in his last public speech. But he could not be bothered with Nehru, Sukarno, Nasser. He viewed them through the prism of his experience in the 1920s with Chiang Kai-shek: they were eager for Soviet material help and support against the West, but they would end up by doublecrossing him as Chiang had. He was interested in tangible absolute power, not in influence: he sought vassals, not allies.

The same considerations determined his attitude toward foreign Communists. The excessive servility expressed toward the Soviet Union and toward Stalin personally hampered the Italian and French Communist Parties; his private grievance with Tito dealt the death blow to the Greek Communists in their Civil War. Until the outbreak of the Yugoslav dispute, the Greek guerrillas had found shelter and supplies in Yugoslavia. Now they had to denounce Tito, purge their movement of the alleged Belgrade agents, and proclaim that in the case of their victory, part of Greek territory would go to an independent Greater Macedonia.[74] Not surprisingly, the Yugoslavs closed their border to the Greek rebels and the Civil War soon came to an end.

Before World War II, Stalin's major foreign-policy errors could be traced to ideological misperceptions or an excusable if faulty reliance on lessons of history. Thus the German Communists were enjoined *not* to fight for the continuance of the Weimar Republic because Marxism-Leninism indicated that Hitler would be unable to solve Germany's economic problems and would be quickly followed by a revolution. Similarly, the Nazi-Soviet Pact found its rationalization in the belief, virtually universal in 1939, that as in World War I Germany would be unable to prevail over the Franco-British forces and the conflict would be a long one. But in 1948 Stalin's conviction of his infallibility, though not so heady and ultimately fatal as Hitler's belief in his, led him into a most dangerous gamble: the Soviet blockade of Berlin.

It is necessary to appreciate both the limits of and the reasons for this imprudence. It was not an irretrievable act of aggression—no Pearl Harbor, no march into Poland. The blockade could be raised momen-

[74] Which Moscow started promoting to stir up trouble in Yugoslav Macedonia.

686

tarily if the danger of World War III became imminent. While it lasted Soviet diplomats kept the door open to an agreement. Indeed, Stalin himself was at pains to appear conciliatory: "We are still allies," he said to the Western ambassadors whom he received in August. Unlike Khrushchev, he would issue no ultimatums on which he would have to back down. His intelligence sources undoubtedly communicated to him that the desire to avoid war was at least as strong in Washington and London as his own. The United States was in the middle of a Presidential election.

And yet this was playing with fire, and it was a risk that a younger, less megalomaniac Stalin would not have undertaken. The Soviet Union still did not have the atomic bomb. Growing exasperation in the United States with Soviet policies *might* trigger a "let's get it over with" feeling. If Stalin contemplated, as he probably did, an abrupt lifting of the blockade in the case of a threatening American reaction, this might have serious consequences for the Soviet position in Eastern Europe; Stalin had just embarked on his conflict with Tito and begun to tighten screws in the satellites. Withdrawal in the face of a Western ultimatum might precipitate rebellion in Poland, Czechoslovakia. . . .

Why, then, did he do it? From Stalin's point of view there were compelling reasons for a blockade: the Western powers were in the process of unifying their occupation zones, the first step in setting up "their" West German state. Once this was accomplished, the Soviets guessed that German rearmament would follow. It would be a question of time before a new Wehrmacht stood on the border of the Soviet empire, ready to assist, perhaps to intervene, in uprisings against Soviet domination in East Germany, Czechoslovakia, and elsewhere. Democracies moved sluggishly, but it was a real danger. So one had to press the Americans now. Surely they had wearied of "foreign entanglements." Had troops not been in Europe for more than two years? And a Presidential election was coming. The evil intentions of the American capitalists until now had been balanced by the unwillingness of millions of "common men" to get involved in another war. But once the German militarists were installed in power, they would know how to implement the designs of Wall Street and present a confrontation with the U.S.S.R. in an alluring light. Now was the moment to make the Americans desist from erecting the West German state. They would tire and get frightened. Perhaps they would go home.

There must have been voices in the Kremlin who pleaded with Stalin that pressure on Berlin was likely to bring about what he was most afraid of. But of course no one argued, and Stalin's luck held. He was proved half right. The Americans neither issued an ultimatum nor backed down. There was in fact a very imperfect realization in the West of the Soviet Union's real fears and aims. The common assumption not only among the people but also among politicians was that the Soviets wanted to push the West out of Berlin. Truman was damned if he would let them do that, but was inhibited from a more vigorous reaction by a genuine fear of war and the fact that this was an election year. The challenge from Henry Wallace's Progressive Party, then estimated a much greater danger than it turned out to be on election night, made him circumspect and unwilling to appear bellicose vis-à-vis the Russians. He liked Uncle Joe, he said at one point in his campaign, but, alas, he was a prisoner of the Politburo. Stalin for his part was not without discreet hints to the democratic electorates. On the eve of the election he granted a reassuring interview to a *Pravda* correspondent. "All that Churchill, the main instigator of a new war, has achieved is that he has lost the confidence of his own people and of democratic forces in the whole world. . . . The peace-loving forces in the world are too strong for Churchill's pupils to overcome them and to drag them into a new war."[75]

The Western response to the blockade of West Berlin (which had began on June 24 with the cutting off of passenger and freight traffic) was a massive airlift. The blockade and tension continued even after the menstrual period of American politics had passed. But by the spring of 1949 it was obvious that Stalin's designs and hopes had been disappointed. The West German state was coming into being; in April the North Atlantic Treaty was signed in Washington; the United States was going ahead with its military support of Western Europe. In May the blockade was lifted. It had been a draw: the Americans had not grown weary of foreign entanglements; but the Western response to the blockade was not vigorous enough to discourage the Soviets from threats and chicaneries over Berlin in the future.

The full price Stalin paid for his Berlin move became evident to him only in December 1949, when he had to sit down and negotiate with another Communist leader. It had fallen to him to mark the end of Russia's centuries-old expansion in Asia, in fact to signal a retreat. For the first time in his career as dictator, he authorized cession of Soviet territory to a foreign power, and had to agree to an abrogation of Soviet rights and privileges on foreign territory.

It is inconceivable that as late as 1947 Stalin either wished for or expected to see *all* of China dominated by the Communists. In August 1945 the Soviet Union and the government of the Republic of China signed a Treaty of Friendship and Alliance, and Chiang Kai-shek paid most of the price Roosevelt had promised Stalin for Russia's entrance into the Pacific war: China surrendered her claim to sovereignty over Russia's satellite Mongolia; the area of Port Arthur was granted to the

[75] Stalin (Stanford ed.), III, 107.

Soviet Union, along with the port facilities of Dairen; the Manchurian Railway, which the Russians had sold to Japan's Manchukuo in 1935, was to return to Soviet co-ownership—and since this was by now a multifaceted business and industrial enterprise, the U.S.S.R. was bound to obtain thereby a powerful say in the economy and politics of China's most important industrial region.

These concessions, painful to Chinese national pride, were balanced by the Soviet pledge of noninterference in China's internal affairs—i.e., in the forthcoming contest between Chiang and Mao. How this pledge was observed following the entrance of Soviet armies into northeastern China may be judged from a letter of Mao Tse-tung to the Communist Party's representative in Manchuria. On November 19, 1945, Mao wrote, "Due to the support of our Elder Brother [the U.S.S.R.] and the growth of our party in Manchuria, the armies of Chiang could not move into the area and could not take over power in Manchuria."[76] Before the Soviet entrance into Manchuria, Communist forces combating the Japanese were below 10,000; by November they grew to 215,000, the Soviets equipping them with captured Japanese equipment.[77] By the time the Red Army evacuated Manchuria in May 1946, the Communists had a well-equipped force in northeast China: the United Army, under the command of Lin Piao, which was to play the key role in the Chinese Civil War.

Soviet help for their Chinese comrades was discreet and indirect and fell short of what Mao and his colleagues had expected. To the Chinese Communists' pleas for more help and to their anguish over the treaty with Chiang, the Soviets retorted that they could not risk a conflict with the United States. Furthermore, it was in Mao's interest that the Americans should not identify his cause with Moscow's and thus throw their weight decisively on Chiang's side. The Chinese Communists in 1945 could no more understand such caution on the part of the all-powerful Soviet Union, than Tito did when the Russians refused to force the Anglo-Americans to turn Trieste over to him. But it was out of the question at the time for *any* Communist to dare criticize Stalin. Up to the very moment of his final victory on the mainland, Mao had to worry more about what the Kremlin rather than the Americans might do. So the official Chinese Communist argument to their friends in Moscow was, You don't know your own strength and America's weakness and ineptitude, so don't be so afraid of provoking the Americans. Early in 1947 the chief of the Chinese Communist Party's propaganda department published an article, spelling out this view. "The American

[76] Quoted in A. M. Dubinsky, "The Liberating Mission of the U.S.S.R in the Far East," *Problems of History* (Moscow), No. 8 (October 1965), p. 61.
[77] *Ibid.*, p. 60.

imperialists cannot attack the Soviet Union before they have succeeded in suppressing and putting under their control the American people and all capitalist colonial and semi-colonial countries."[78] Mao's message to the "Elder Brother" was clear: Do not sell us out; we are helping you by fighting America's puppets.

Until the end of 1947 Stalin could feel complacent about China: How could *he* lose? The Americans were engaged in the hopeless task of trying to reconcile the Nationalists and the Communists and form a coalition. They were growing disgusted with the inefficiency and corruption of the Kuomintang. Chiang had wasted his best armies by trying to hold on to Manchuria. But then in the middle of 1947 the Communists got the upper hand and now controlled most of the countryside. The perspectives were still quite pleasing. The Chinese Communists might establish a state in the northeast of China—it would be dependent on Soviet support and would be a faithful ally-satellite. The Civil War might then go on, as it had already done, for decades. Or Chiang might ask the Soviet Union to help end it and then might stabilize his own power over *most* of the country—there would be two Chinas, both on the mainland. (The Soviets in fact did hint at several points in 1946–47 that they might help Chiang to secure a truce, in return for economic concessions and the Generalissimo's detachment from the Americans.) But that Mao might conquer all of China must have appeared to the Kremlin improbable: the Communists were not that strong. And even if they were, surely the Americans would not let it happen. The United States had started down the road to Pearl Harbor clearly because of its determination not to let China pass under Japan's influence. They would hardly now wash their hands of the whole business and consign the country to the Communists. Obviously, Mao was being overambitious in disregarding Soviet advice that he should consolidate his gains in Manchuria before embarking on further adventures. The most he could achieve was to bring America's massive support for the Nationalists. Such help would not be a bad thing from the Kremlin's viewpoint. With U.S. troops becoming involved in China, the Americans would have to become more restrained in Europe, would have to bargain with the Soviet Union.

The Chinese Communists were the main beneficiary of both America's and Stalin's fears about Europe. When the Berlin blockade began, they were still some way from conquering *all* of Manchuria; when it ended, there could be little doubt that they soon would be in control of the entire Chinese mainland. How could Washington assess the situation in China carefully, when it believed that there was a

[78] Quoted in *U.S. Relations with China, with Special Reference to the Period 1944–1949* (Washington, 1949), p. 713; hereafter cited as *China Paper*.

serious danger of the Red Army's moving in Western Europe? Why should Stalin try to brake Mao's advance, when he wanted the United States diverted from Europe and believed that unless so diverted, the Americans might in a few years' time threaten him with a revived Germany army?

Could Stalin have ordered Mao to stop and not to pursue the goal of conquering all of China? In 1973 such a conjecture may well appear fantastic. But at the time it would have seemed even more fantastic to think that any Communist Party or leader would or could defy his orders. The Yugoslavs did, but in a way they had stumbled into this defiance—until 1949 they believed that Stalin was being misinformed about their case and that once the true facts were brought to his attention, he would return the Yugoslavs to his fatherly affection.[79] In any case, Tito was firmly in control of his Party and state. Mao was fighting a civil war; he was by no means invulnerable to challenge within his Party ranks, were such a challenge backed by the Kremlin. He was to display a not inconsiderable megalomania of his own, and so it is remarkable how carefully he catered to the Elder Brother's. This is what he had to say on the occasion of Stalin's sixtieth birthday in 1939: "Stalin is the leader of world revolution. . . . It is a great event that mankind is blessed with Stalin. . . . Marx is dead and so are Engels and Lenin. Had there been no Stalin who would be there to give directions?"[80]

Mao continued this attitude or pose of a humble disciple until he was master of all mainland China. When Tito was excommunicated by Stalin, the Chinese Communists denounced him vigorously (thereby greatly disillusioning the Yugoslavs who could understand why the Eastern Europeans chimed in but did not see why the Chinese could not afford to show some independence). When the North Atlantic Treaty was signed, the Western European Communist parties were called upon to declare, and did so, that the workers of France, Italy, etc., would never fight against the Soviet Union. There seemed to be little ostensible reason for a Communist Party in *Asia* to take such a stand, and in the Chinese case—its victory still not complete, the possibility of a last-minute American intervention still not out of the question—there were persuasive reasons against it. But on April 3, 1949, the Chinese Communists publicly denounced NATO and affirmed their loyalty to their "ally the Soviet Union"—a declaration all the more curious since the Chinese Communist state had not as yet been officially proclaimed

---

[79] How far Tito himself believed this is a moot point, but he probably could not have at first carried many of his followers along with him had they not clung to the hope that Stalin would see the justice of their cause.

[80] Chen Po-ta, *Stalin and the Chinese Revolution* (Peking, 1953), p. 1.

and hence officially could not have allies. As if that were not enough in the way of identification with the Russian side, on July Mao himself spoke: "We must lean to one side. . . . Not only in China but throughout the world, one must lean either to imperialism or to socialism."[81]

The Chinese were well advised to play on Stalin's vanity. It has always been enormous, but old age has rendered it all-consuming. Prior to these last years, he could still laugh about tributes to him, would mimic flatterers in the presence of intimates. For the edification of a favorite like the aircraft designer Yakovlev, Stalin once read some florid homage and then exclaimed with mock despair: "And here we come to the usual 'Hurrah, hurrah, long live the Communist Party and its leader the great Stalin.' "[82] But now flattery became his sustenance, and vanity along with suspicion his strongest passion. And so it was pleasant to hear how the Chinese worshipers were conquering the world's largest nation, and creating confusion and alarm in America.

One must not treat them in a way that would give them excessive ideas about their own importance. The Chinese Communists might well have expected that the Elder Brother would recognize them, if not as the *de-jure* then as *de-facto* government of China during 1948, certainly by January 1949, when they occupied Peking. Nothing of the kind! A reader of the Soviet press as late as the summer of 1949 was fed news about the Greek Civil War—then in its last, and for the Communists disastrous, phase—and only after that about the feats of China's People's Liberation Army. The fact that Russia was not ready to recognize the People's Republic of China meant that Mao and his confederates could not proclaim it.[83] When in April the Communists occupied Nanking, the Kuomintang capital, most of the ambassadors including the American stayed on. The Soviet representative almost demonstratively followed the fleeing Nationalist regime to its temporary abode in Canton. In May there were negotiations between the Soviets and the Nationalist governor of Sinkiang. Even more ominous from Mao's viewpoint was that in July 1949 Kao Kang, the Communist head of Manchuria, was invited to Moscow, where he concluded a trade agreement between Manchuria (as if it were a separate country) and the U.S.S.R. After Stalin's death, and with his successors eager to propitiate Mao, Kao Kang was to be purged by the Chinese Communists as a tool of "re-

---

[81] Stuart R. Schram, *The Political Thought of Mao Tse-tung* (New York, 1963), p. 506.

[82] Alexander Yakovlev, *The Life's Aim* (Moscow, 1970), p. 499.

[83] In contrast the U.S.S.R. and China were officially to recognize Ho Chi Minh's government as early as 1950, four years before Dien Bien Phu and the establishment of North Vietnam!

actionary interests at home and abroad," and in 1954, according to the official story, he committed suicide.

There must be a strong presumption that Mao had been invited to Moscow several times before he actually went there in December 1949.[84] But the prudent man would go there only as official head of the People's Republic of China, recognized as such by the Soviets. That was the minimum insurance against the possibility of an unfortunate "incident" befalling him while visting the Fatherland of Socialism. He had done nothing to incur Stalin's displeasure, but he probably knew that the "genius leader of progressive mankind" preferred to have people he himself had selected at the head of Communist Parties. There were Chinese Communists in Moscow and in Mao's entourage who had been closer to the Russians. One of them was Lin Piao (who years later was to meet a mysterious death), who along with Peng Teh-huai (disgraced in 1959) had been an outstanding leader in the Civil War.[85] Mao had made it to the top through his own exertions. And he was the only living Communist of whom Stalin had a good reason to be envious: what a career it had been, from chieftain of a handful of peasant rebels to master of China! At no point did the senior dictator deign to address his most famous associate with a public message of greeting or congratulation. Leaders of the European Parties were usually hailed by Stalin on their birthdays. Thus to Maurice Thorez on his fiftieth: "The Soviet people . . . know and love you as their friend and intrepid fighter for the friendship and alliance between France and the Soviet Union."[86] His German puppets, Wilhelm Pieck and Otto Grotewohl, received a handsome message of congratulation at the establishment of the German Democratic Republic in October 1949. At about the same time the Chinese Communists finally proclaimed, and the Soviets recognized, the People's Republic of China. If Stalin chose to celebrate this with a message to its chief maker and chairman, he did not see fit to make it public. In view of the great stress the Chinese place on considerations of "face" and protocol, this was more than a snub: it was a warning.

In fact, the average Soviet citizen could be excused for overlooking

---

[84] In his talks with Yugoslavs in January–February 1948 Stalin referred to his conferring with some Chinese Communist leaders after Japan's defeat and to having advised them against an all-out attack on Chiang. The story is somewhat suspect. He was by then convinced that the Yugoslav state and Party apparatus was seeded with British intelligence agents, and so perhaps the story was designed to reach London and Washington. Such Machiavellianism was quite in his style.

[85] Lin Piao had spent some time in the Soviet Union. When in the late 1960s he was proclaimed Mao's closest comrade in arms and heir-apparent, the Soviet press volunteered the information that the lady who eventually became his wife had been put in his household by Mao to spy on him!

[86] Stalin (Stanford ed.), III, 110.

the momentous importance of this event. Throughout the summer newspaper stories about China were overshadowed by news of the dying embers of the Greek Civil War, but even more by *the* great event of the year: the approaching seventieth birthday of the Boss. A mass of birthday greetings, articles, stories, books tried to find new superlatives—the most extravagant form of praise and worship possible. To a devout Communist, there could not have been a more appropriate birthday present than this fulfillment of Lenin's dream: Asia going Red, the world's most populous nation becoming Communist. But to Stalin it was also an infuriating refutation of his expectations. Mao had been right about the United States being a "paper tiger," "outwardly strong, inwardly weak." He had been proven wrong. When in August 1949 Washington chose to publish the celebrated *China Paper*, baring the whole inner story of the misperceptions, illusions, and mistakes that had attended American policies in the Far East, the Kremlin finally understood that the United States would not intervene.

Inwardly, Stalin could echo Mao's jibes at the *China Paper* that the American imperialists were "the newly upstart and neurotic," and that Britain or even "some smaller imperialist countries" would never have revealed publicly such sinister and childish machinations.[87] But it was too late to do anything about it, with Chiang fleeing the mainland and his feudatories' surrender of vast provinces to the Communists. Beginning in August, the Soviet press finally began to present the Chinese situation in its true dimensions. And on October 3 the Chinese Communists for the first time made the front page in *Pravda* with a story of the proclamation of the People's Republic. The former Soviet ambassador to the Nationalist regime, who had been recalled only in May, was assigned to Peking. Again, this was a deliberate slight of the Chinese Communists' sensitivities: surely the occasion should have called for more ceremony, surely the post of ambassador to Peking should have gone to an important Soviet figure and not to an obscure diplomat.

On December 16 Mao Tse-tung debarked from a train at the Yaroslav Station in Moscow. With parts of China still to be wrested from the Kuomintang warlords, with thousands of problems requiring his personal attention at home, Mao would spend two months in the Soviet Union.

The erstwhile humble disciple became, as of the formation of the People's Republic of China, a man determined to win for his country and Party the status at least of junior partner of the Soviet Union. Stalin discovered he had to bargain with Mao and could not just command him. For the remainder of his life he addressed or referred publicly to Mao on only two occasions, and this was during the Korean War, when

---

[87] *Selected Works of Mao Tse-tung* (in English; Peking, 1961), IV, 442.

he answered the Chinese leader's felicitations on the anniversary of the end of the war with Japan. He graciously allowed that "the struggle of the Chinese nation and its People's Liberation Army lightened . . . the Red Army's task"(!) in defeating Japan. The style of his messages also was hardly a model of graciousness. Mao was addressed drily as "Comrade Chairman," and there was a studied omission of any reference to his personal role in the Chinese Communist epic. This was quite different from Stalin's messages to Thorez and Togliatti, "tested leaders" of the French and Italian "Communists and working people, known and beloved by the Soviet people."

Mao must have been deeply hurt by his reception in Russia. He was greeted upon his arrival by Molotov, just as if he were the head of, say, the Bulgarian Party. There was no special festive session of the Supreme Soviet in his honor. The main reception for the Chinese delegation was given not in the Great Hall of the Kremlin, but in the old Metropole Hotel, the usual place for entertaining visiting minor capitalist dignitaries. The official communiqué spoke of Stalin's "receiving" Mao—again a grating expression implying unequal status (during the war Stalin used to "meet with" or "receive visits from" Churchill and Roosevelt). It is no wonder that Mao conceived, if he secretly had not nurtured it before, an abiding hatred of the Soviet Union. He undoubtedly was awed by his host's barbaric grandeur, and he was to model his own "personality cult" on the best available example. To annoy Stalin's successors and to put them on the defensive, he played the role of defender of the tyrant's reputation. But the seeds of his bitterness against the Elder Brother, and his determination to seek revenge when he could afford to, took root when he was detained at the threshold of the Kremlin, almost as much captive as guest.

Yet both sides knew they had to reach an agreement. For Stalin the illusion that prevailed abroad—that China had become a satellite of Russia's—was an inestimable political asset. (In transmitting the *China Paper*, the Secretary of State had given expression to this belief: "*Ultimately* the profound civilization and the democratic individualism of China will reassert themselves and she will throw off the foreign yoke."[88] For Mao a break with Stalin would have meant utter isolation, the probability of a revived Civil War, possible troubles within his Party.

It is easy to see what they quarreled about. In a speech on his arrival Mao paid special tribute to the Soviet Union for being the first country to nullify unequal treaties with China. But of course the Russians had an unequal treaty with China at the time, and it was clear that far from abandoning their special rights now that their ideological brothers held China, the Soviets sought to expand them. There was the example of

[88] My italics.

those joint-stock companies which the fraternal socialist nations in Eastern Europe had established with the Soviet Union: the host country provided natural resources, the Soviet Union's managerial skills (for which they received 50 per cent of the profits!), and of course the Chinese would wish for similar Russian help in developing civil aviation, mining deposits in Sinkiang, factories in Manchuria. . . . Mao may have referred circumspectly to China's hope for another form of help: credits. During the period when the Red Army assisted the Chinese people against Japan and Chiang in Manchuria, it looted the area of industrial and mining equipment to the tune of some $2 billion. China was just emerging from three decades of Civil War and faced the possibility of Chiang's attempting a comeback, perhaps with American assistance. Would the U.S.S.R. provide industrial equipment, modern arms? Would she protect China by a mutual assistance pact?

The agenda was extensive; the bargaining must have been spirited. One may well imagine Stalin representing that the Soviet base at Port Arthur and Soviet ownership of the Manchurian Railway were the best protection for China: the Americans would never dare to attack knowing that Soviet troops were on Chinese soil, or bomb the industrial complexes of Manchuria knowing that the U.S.S.R. held a share in their ownership. (Khrushchev later revealed that Stalin put out demands "of a colonial nature" vis-à-vis the Chinese.) Stalin might have further hoped that Mao's absence from Peking would undermine his position as leader of his Party and make him amenable to pressure. Representatives of the Manchurian Communist government and that of Sinkiang joined the negotiations, thus underlining the Soviet tendency (insulting to Peking) to treat them as semi-independent regimes and to encourage separatist tendencies in China's border regions.

Then, on January 21 China's supreme diplomat arrived in Moscow. Chou En-lai, then as now the Prime Minister and in charge of foreign relations, brought what was to Stalin undoubtedly unwelcome news that the leadership of the Chinese Communist Party stood firmly behind Chairman Mao. Chou had negotiated previously with Chiang and the Americans; one day he would with Alexei Kosygin and Richard Nixon. Now his diplomatic skills and charm were put to their hardest test. In three weeks a Sino-Soviet agreement was patched up and a public clash between the two Communist giants was postponed for a decade.

Mao had won a point: the Soviets made concessions and China *was* accorded the status of a junior partner. But on many points Mao had to bow to Stalin. Soon, at Stalin's bidding and to save him from the consequences of a miscalculation, Mao had to risk committing China's troops against the Americans in Korea. It was only on Stalin's successors that Mao took out his feelings of hurt personal and national pride. Alone of the world's top Communist leaders, he did not attend Stalin's funeral. And after that Khrushchev had to go to him to deliver what Stalin had refused to or had reneged on.

The Sino-Soviet Treaty of Friendship and Alliance and related agreements were signed on February 14, 1950. The only part of the document that was wholly satisfactory to China was the preamble: "A new People's Government was formed which has . . . proved its ability to defend the state independence and territorial integrity of China, the national honour and dignity of the Chinese people." But it was like pulling teeth to make Stalin give anything back: the Manchurian Railway and its industry were to go to China, but the transfer was to take place after the conclusion of a peace treaty with Japan. Since at the time there was no earthly prospect that the Soviet Union and the United States would agree on such a treaty, the Chinese demanded and obtained that in any case the transfer should not take place later than the end of 1952. It is difficult to see why the transfer was to be postponed, unless the Russians expected something interesting—possibly not to the liking of their Chinese friends—to happen in the Far East in the next two years. The same provisions and time schedule were applied to the reversion of Port Arthur to China. And here, to be sure, when 1952 came around, both sides decided that in view of the Korean War, the Soviet troops and navy should stay at the base. Only in 1955 was Port Arthur, symbol of Russian imperialism on Chinese soil, returned to the People's Republic.

The handsome words in the preamble about China's "territorial integrity" were also made suspect by the fact that after Mao, Chou, and their entourage had departed on February 17, the Manchurian and Sinkiang delegations stayed on in Moscow. In March and April a series of agreements was announced setting up joint Sino-Soviet companies for the exploitation of Sinkiang's mineral resources, for air communications between China and the U.S.S.R., etc. Having thus received what amounted to a free gift of part of China's natural wealth, the Soviet Union generously accorded China all of $300 million worth of credits to be spread over five years at one per cent interest—a sum minuscule in proportion (fifty cents per inhabitant!) to the country's needs and to what the Russians had looted in Manchuria. One wonders why the loan was publicized. Mongolia's "independence" was acquiesced to by Peking. No sooner was Stalin dead than Mao demanded point-blank the return of this satellite of the Soviet Union to Chinese sovereignty.

The Sino-Soviet alliance provided for mutual assistance against aggression by Japan or "any other state which should unite with Japan directly or indirectly in acts of aggression."[89] But what security did this provide for the Chinese Communists? Japan was completely disarmed,

[89] *Documents on International Affairs, 1949–1950* (London, 1953), p. 543.

and it was laughable to think that the nonexistent Japanese army could invade the Chinese mainland. Mao's greatest fear had to be of American planes from Formosa bombing China, of the American navy transporting Chiang's troops back to the mainland and possibly landing American troops there too. What would the Soviet Union be obliged to do in such a contingency? Nothing. Conversely, in the case of a Russo-American conflict, U.S. planes and ships would operate against the Soviet Far East from Japanese bases; this would be proclaimed by the Soviet Union as aggression by Japan and would require Chinese entrance into the war. It is hard to recall another military alliance so one-sided: when most of the benefits accrued to the stronger party, most of the burdensome obligations reposed on the weaker. The Russians did not even undertake to equip the Chinese forces with modern arms. It was only when the Chinese "volunteers" entered the Korean conflict that the People's Liberation Army got Soviet arms, and Peking *had to pay for them*. "Long live the teacher of revolution to the whole world, the best friend of the Chinese people, Comrade Stalin," said Mao before boarding the train for Peking.

Though in a way he had put Mao in his place, Stalin could derive but little satisfaction from the encounter. What of the future? His visitor was fourteen years younger and he ruled a nation of 400 million.[90] Even now Mao had argued with him, made veiled complaints about Russia's stinginess and imperialistic ways. The last Communist who had dared to complain about Russia's economic exploitation of his country, the Bulgarian Traicho Kostov, had just been hanged after a public trial.[91] And the presumption of the Chinese! They had just dared to recognize the Viet Minh rebel government of Ho Chi Minh, thus forcing the Soviets to do so too—a step that was bound to make the outraged French government more inclined to fall in with the American scheme of rearming Germany.

The signing of the Sino-Soviet Pact was prominently featured in the Soviet press. The Soviet man in the street must have welcomed it, in view of the growing fear of war. Surely the Americans would not dare to attack, now that the world's largest nation stood at Russia's side. He may well have been puzzled that Mao and his fellow delegates were throughout the story referred to as "Messrs." rather than "Comrades." And in looking at the picture of the ceremony of signing, he might well have felt certain foreboding. In previous photographs on similar occa-

[90] This was the belief at the moment. An official Chinese census soon claimed the figure to be close to 600 million.

[91] In the course of it, Kostov repudiated his confession. Shortly before he was executed he corrected this faux pas in a letter to the tribunal in which he again acknowledged Titoist machinations. In *First Circle* Solzhenitsyn makes his Stalin erupt with fury at the recollection of Kostov's repudiation of his confession.

sions, the Boss certainly looked much happier. One recalled him grinning happily when Molotov was signing the agreement with Ribbentrop, in an affable pose with Roosevelt and Churchill, with an expression of fatherly solicitude entertaining a satellite leader. But here is the picture of February 15: Foreign Minister Vishinsky is signing the treaty; standing behind the table are members of the Politburo and their Chinese guests; Stalin's head is slightly bowed, his expression wistful; on his left Mao is looking rigidly into the distance. Others have unsmiling somber expressions, and the whole tableau conveys the feeling of strain and apprehension. The great illusionmaker did not choose to exercise his craft on this occasion. The great dissembler for once did not quite conceal his apprehensions: an era in the history of Communism, in the history of the world, *his* era, was passing.

~(14)~

THE
LAST PLOT

An impenetrable mystery appears to surround the events of the last four years of Stalin's life and reign. We start with an alleged conspiracy, the details of which are so murky that when the Khrushchev regime rehabilitated one of its chief figures, the official statement gave an incorrect date for his execution. Not long afterward Stalin decided to publish a treatise on linguistics, of all things, then one on economics. With just months remaining in his life, he convoked the first Party Congress in thirteen years, a Congress that authorized drastic changes in the personnel of the highest Party organs. At the subsequent meeting of the Central Committee, Joseph Stalin stepped down from the post he had held for thirty years (though he had not used the title since 1934), that of the General Secretary of the Party.

Then, with his death but few weeks away, there erupted the Kremlin Doctors' Plot. A number of distinguished Soviet physicians, most of them connected with the Kremlin Medical Service, were arraigned on charges of crimes against leading Party and army officials done at the bidding of foreign agents. Clearly another purge was coming. From a Politburo member to the humblest citizen, the people lived in daily expectation of new revelations, confessions, and arrests striking high and low.

Stalin died, and even his death compounded the atmosphere of mystery and terror. His successors feared universal panic, perhaps rebellion. The official communiqué lied about the place where Stalin had suffered the fatal stroke and died. The people were divided in their feelings between relief and fear of the unknown.

Years have passed since then, and we still have not had an official acknowledgment of what was really going on. Many of Stalin's victims of those years have been rehabilitated, *some* of his accomplices denounced and punished, but what all these events meant, what *he* intended them to mean, we have not been told. And so we are left with a chapter in the history of a great nation which reads like a tale by Kafka, with an occasional scene that seems to come from the chronicle of gangland warfare in Al Capone's era.

Yet though we may never know the full details of that incredible period, we have certain clues that enable us to pierce the mystery that hangs over Stalin's last years. Like all men at his advanced age, he must have feared death. But much more than most he had to fear physical debility which would render him a helpless prisoner of his creatures. The suspicious and vengeful man thus spent his last years in growing terror of being "found out." Secrecy and mystification had for long been an essential part of his technique of governing, but now he was not only afraid that the "enemy" might find out the true figures for grain production, say, or some military and state secrets. "They" might learn he was no longer the man he used to be. Young men of his entourage reminded him of how old he was; the older ones, the Voroshilovs and Molotovs, had been witnesses to his physical decline, knew his vulnerabilities. He envied the young, loathed the old, feared both. The key to Stalin's purges before 1941 must be sought in his fear of a military defeat, to the ones after 1946 of a biological one. In both instances wanton and arbitrary destruction of men were rationalized by solicitude for the Party and the people. He was not joking when, in talking of Ivan the Terrible, he accused one of history's cruelest tyrants of being insufficiently ruthless. "God got in Ivan's way" and prevented him from doing a thorough job. There was no god to restrain Stalin.

Fear of those closest to him is a despot's occupational disease. In the past Stalin could reshuffle, put to a test, or humiliate his lieutenants with relish resulting from self-assurance and innate cruelty. But with advancing years he must have viewed his colleagues not as potential rivals but as possible successors and, worst of all, probable custodians should he become incapacitated. His dislike of them grew, almost proportionally to their length of association with him and the strength of their former intimacy. To the Soviet people, to the world, Molotov remained to the end Stalin's second-in-command, a faithful alter ego of thirty years' standing: yet insiders after the war grew aware of Stalin's rising rancor with his oldest intimate, knew that the second man in the Soviet Union could not protect his own wife from exile. What could turn Stalin against Voroshilov, now utterly discredited as a military leader with no power base of his own? One must surmise that his old pal of Tsaritsyn days, barely two years younger than himself, irritated Stalin because of his robust health and bearing, as well as his friendship with and knowledge of Stalin before he had become a god. The old fool might survive him, and he was exactly the kind of man that other scoundrels might choose as a figurehead leader: a straightforward soldier unsullied by the terror and intrigues of the past.

Absolute power combined with old age made every aide appear either as an embarrassing witness or a future threat. Thus Malenkov, nurtured in Stalin's own Secretariat, did not possess that potentially dangerous influence which the past or present headship of a regional Party organization confers, and was judged the safest of his lieutenants, i.e., the one most conscious of his own limitations and of his inability to succeed Stalin. But he certainly knew too much. Malenkov's temporary eclipse between 1946 and 1948 might well have been due to an irritating recollection: Malenkov, then closest to him, knew best the full extent of Stalin's collapse in the first days of the war. A similar reason combined with envy dictated Zhukov's removal to a provincial command. And Admiral Kuznetsov, a great prewar favorite of Stalin's, was in 1947 demoted in rank and demoted too from commander-in-chief of the navy to its deputy commander: he too had witnessed a moment of near panic on Stalin's part, when in the late summer of 1941 Stalin had told him that Leningrad might have to be abandoned to the Germans.

The atmosphere of total distrust and self-felt isolation of Stalin's old age is well portrayed in one of the most characteristic, and undeniably true, stories Khrushchev ever told about his late employer. In his last years, he revealed, Stalin seldom presided over the Council of Ministers, leaving this task to one of his deputies. One particular session was to deal with an economic plan, and a vigorous discussion was anticipated, since it was well known that some of the ministers were complaining that targets for their branches of the economy were unrealistically high, funds assigned to them inadequate, etc. But to everybody's consternation, the session had hardly begun when Stalin appeared and took the chair. "Here is the plan," he said, indicating the huge sheaf of documents. "Any objections?" The ministers looked at each other and kept silent. In that case the meeting was adjourned, declared Stalin, and they all could go and see a movie he had ordered for that afternoon. As they trooped out, he said to no one in particular, "We fooled them but good!" Such were the amusements of his declining years.

When it came to anything not touching on power, domestic or foreign, the attrition of Stalin's sense of reality was virtually complete. Mme. Alliluyeva is very convincing when she describes how her father lost the comprehension of the value of money.[1] Official orators spoke of the continuing increase in the well-being of the Soviet consumer, and Stalin no longer had the endurance or any incentive to penetrate the

---

[1] Svetlana Alliluyeva, *Twenty Letters to a Friend* (in Russian; New York, 1967), p. 193.

rigged statistics. He hardly ever made any public appearances; few foreigners, whether Communist or not, were granted audiences in those years. It is not surprising that the American military attachés attending the Air Force Day parade in 1952 concluded that the Stalin on top of the Lenin Mausoleum must have been a dummy.[2]

Stalin's dislike of granting interviews and audiences, like the rest of his behavior, was due partly to the misanthropy of old age and partly to the fear of being found out. People would notice how old he had become, how unlike his portraits, how thin and white his hair was. Most important, they would notice how he no longer had his exceptional memory and the ability to attend to minute detail. "No, Benelux did not include the Netherlands!" he shouted in a conference. "It was a customs union comprising only Belgium and Luxembourg!" Djilas, who was present at this embarrassing episode, felt like protesting that the "Ne" in the name had to stand for the Netherlands, but since none of the Russians present dared point out the error, he also, and wisely, kept his peace. But how humiliated Stalin must have felt when, having realized his mistake, he reflected on what the others must have thought. He once had impressed his visitors with erudition and alertness, and now! In 1951 Yakovlev designed a plane that allegedly needed only a very short runway. Stalin decreed that this new model be used to bring his mail and papers from Moscow and land right in front of his villa in the Caucasus on a strip all of fifty yards long. When the pilot prudently refused to try this, the incensed dictator ordered Beria to conduct an investigation, and the latter ordered the new model grounded and its production suspended. A few years earlier Stalin, with his interest in technological novelties and in view of the fact that Yakovlev was a favorite of his, would have himself attended to the business. Now he must have felt he couldn't. People would hear and laugh at how Comrade Stalin thought transport planes could land and take off in a meadow fifty yards long.[3]

There were ways of masking Stalin's decline and combating this most ruthless of his enemies. He would write theoretical treatises to show everyone that his mind was functioning as brilliantly as ever. He had, in any case, to prove that in theory, not to mention in practice, he was at least equal to Lenin. How increasingly irksome it was to read of the Party of Lenin and Stalin, the All-Union Communist Party (b), the

---

[2] George F. Kennan, *Memoirs: II, 1950–1963* (New York, 1972), 132.

[3] Alexander Yakovlev, *The Life's Aim* (Moscow, 1970), pp. 488–89. The designer ascribes the decision, possibly correctly, to Beria's malicious intent toward anybody who enjoyed Stalin's favor. But the business was quite likely much more serious than he describes: Yakovlev's claims on behalf of his plane could have been represented as a case of "wrecking," if not indeed a covert attempt to have the plane crash into the villa.

wretched small letter standing for "Bolsheviks," always evocative of Lenin. How unfair that the man who, for all his undoubted services, had left the Party and the state in a mess should take precedence over the real founder of the Soviet Union and Communism.

Secrecy was another line of defense. Stalin's old collaborators, people who could best tell how he had slowed down, had in any case outlived their usefulness. The Mikoyans and Molotovs had been around too long. The same was true for his immediate entourage: his confidential secretary, Poskrebyshev, and his chief bodyguard, Vlasik, had been there for ages. It would be strange if they were not looking about in anticipation of his disappearance—making arrangements, perhaps leaking secrets. And then there was this uncomfortable fact that his doctors were precisely informed as to the state of his health. Could one trust them? Of course not. Vigilance was an attitude, he had preached for decades, obligatory for every Soviet citizen. It would be criminally negligent if he himself settled down to enjoy the flattery, forgot that the enemy was everywhere.

The government of the Soviet Union was a standing conspiracy. It is through understanding this fact and acting accordingly that Stalin had preserved and enhanced his power. But even his mastery of the art of conspiracy and purging had been affected by the passage of years. Theoretically, he could with a stroke of the pen order the doom of the highest official. In fact he had usually been too prudent to do just that. As long as there were trials, confessions, testimonies, and the like, even if palpably forged for the most part, the oligarchs would always cling to the illusion that their fate was dependent not just on his whim; the people at large would always try to see some logic behind the events. Condemned Politburo members and marshals had gone to their deaths with words of loyalty and affection for Stalin, and though in some cases this was explained by concern for their families, in many cases it went deeper than that. The power of one man to destroy so many with impunity depended on his ability to convince, to impose his "objective" reality in the place of a real one.

This ability to cast a spell, to mesmerize the whole nation as well as the potentates, depended on self-confidence and physical vigor. In February–March 1937 Stalin appeared before the Central Committee undaunted by the fact that many of those present knew he had just driven his closest friend to suicide, and like a man possessed, he mesmerized and bullied the group to authorize their own decimation. Could he do it now, or would people feel, though fear would keep them from speaking out, that this was an old man mumbling nonsense? Stalin was a well-read man; he may have also recalled Robespierre during the French Revolution. There was no possibility of Stalin's sharing the fate of Robespierre—he was a dictator with powers vastly greater than those of the French leader and he was the symbol and living god of Communism—but he might be rebuffed, and such a rebuff might lead to loss of the substance if not the appearance of power. There was the disturbingly suggestive problem of Tito: he had lashed out at Tito without making absolutely sure that he could expeditiously destroy him. And he had been rebuffed, at least temporarily. Could he afford a similar humiliation over, say, Molotov?

Circumstances required a much more circuitous way of disposing of his older lieutenants. They could not be attacked frontally. There is an old story of Stalin in his cups telling some companions how sweet it is to plan a man's destruction down to the last detail and then to go and have a good night's sleep.[4] Old age interfered with such pleasures. As in the first years of his absolute power he had to plot rather than hint to order a man's destruction. ☆☆☆

I N March 1949 the Soviet public was informed of a reshuffle in the highest state positions. Molotov surrendered the portfolio of Foreign Affairs to Vishinsky; Bulganin relinquished the Ministry of Defense to Marshal Vasilevsky; and Mikoyan gave up the Ministry of Foreign Trade to Mikhail Menshikov.[5] On the surface the changes were unsensational: the personages relieved were given or retained positions as deputy prime ministers of the U.S.S.R. There was not even a hint of demotion within the Party or as Stalin's "closest comrades in arms." Presumably they would also retain general supervision of their previous spheres of activity, their replacements being technicians and people of no political importance. Such shifts were not unusual—a parallel case being that of Beria, who, though no longer *directly* in charge of the security apparatus, was assumed to be the overall supervisor of the twin Ministries of State Security and Internal Affairs. Yet in the light of subsequent events, it is clear that the changes were intended to curtail the influence of gentlemen being replaced. Soviet satraps hated to part with a power base, whether a ministry or an important provincial Party post. Even so apparently unpromising an agency as the Ministry of Trade meant vast patronage, meant having one's fingers in and contacts with various branches of Soviet and other Communist countries' economy. A deputy premiership, of which there were several, could be, on the contrary, just

---

[4] The story is possibly apocryphal, but Bukharin referred to it in his famous "secret" conversation with Kamenev in 1928.
[5] Later the Soviet ambassador to the United States (in the late 1950s).

a title. There was an unpleasant recollection of how in the 1930s Kosior's and Chubar's appointments to lofty-sounding positions were mere way-stations on the path to liquidation. For Molotov, who had been Foreign Minister since 1939, dismissal was undoubtedly a hard blow. Soviet relations with non-Communist countries currently consisted of little more than the exchange of frigid notes and protests, but the change meant that the Boss did not trust him to manage foreign policy if he himself became incapacitated. And while in no sense could it be said that Bulganin, an oligarch of much more recent creation, controlled the army—during the war he had, as we have seen, rubbed many military men the wrong way—he still had important contacts with some generals: he had been close to Zhukov.

To those in the know, the changes bespoke Stalin's suspicions of his closest lieutenants, the first step toward eventual demotion, or perhaps worse. How the people concerned felt about their "promotions" to deputy prime ministerships can best be judged by the fact that no sooner was Stalin dead than Molotov, Bulganin, Mikoyan, and Beria repossessed their old ministries, the latter snatching back the complex of security agencies he had not headed since 1946.

Molotov's removal as Foreign Minister coincided with the arrest of his wife, who was subsequently exiled from Moscow. (This was, of course, known to only a few.) By itself the arrest did not portend Molotov's fall. In the past close relatives of a high official might be arrested or liquidated without ostensibly affecting his position: witness Kalinin's wife and Kaganovich's brothers. Pauline Molotov was Jewish; she had been a close friend of Nadezhda Alliluyeva, and Stalin had currently turned against both the Jews and those who reminded him of and who he decided had been involved in Nadezhda's tragedy. Yet for all this and whatever the Molotovs' conjugal relations, his wife's exile was a cruel affront to Molotov.

The Stalinist old guard had suffered a decline in influence. At the same time, and seemingly illogically, a much worse fate befell some of the younger satraps. The term Leningrad Affair is not the invention of a foreign Kremlinologist. It has been used in the Soviet Union since 1954 to describe a purge that took place in 1949–50 involving a number of Party and state officials most of whom were then or before connected with Leningrad and its longtime boss, Andrei Zhdanov.

The most prominent of these officials were contemporaries of the people who rule the Soviet Union in the 1970s. Like Brezhnev and Kosygin, the doomed "Leningraders"—Nicholas Voznesensky (b. 1903), Alexis Kuznetsov (b. 1905), and Michael Rodionov (b. 1907)—were beneficiaries of the era of the purges. In their early thirties, they were projected into important positions vacated by several successive echelons of victims of the Yezhov times. Their whole past and training bespoke absolute loyalty to Stalin, untainted by the slightest trace of old Party disputes, men for whom Stalin was not merely a benefactor, but the object of worship since their early adulthood. They were the obvious replacements or successors to the Molotovs and Mikoyans. Instead, in September 1950, all three, along with a number of associates, found themselves before the firing squad.

Voznesensky appeared to epitomize that professional intelligentsia which Stalin proposed and did create to take place of the "bourgeois specialists" whom he had destroyed. Trained as an economist, Voznesensky never held a purely Party or political position. Professor, then head of the economic planning office for Leningrad in 1935–37, he was in 1938 elevated to the top economic job in the country, head of the Gosplan. That is, at the age of thirty-four he was entrusted with direction of the Soviet Union's economic planning apparatus. In 1941, while retaining general supervision of the Gosplan, he became Deputy Prime Minister of the U.S.S.R. At the same time he was elevated to candidate member of the Politburo. While not an original member of the State Defense Committee during the war, he joined it in 1942 and became its deputy chairman.[6] In 1943 Voznesensky received the highest honor available to Russian scientists and scholars: he became a full member of the Academy of Sciences. (A cynic might attribute this less to his professional eminence than to the fact that most of the academicians in the economics section were his employees. But the distinction was unusual even for a very high political personage: Molotov was received into the Academy only in 1946.) He resumed direction of the Gosplan after the war and in 1947 became a full member of the Politburo. That Stalin continued to favor Voznesensky and did not think of him as merely a useful bureaucrat is testified by another signal honor: in 1948 Voznesensky's little book *The War Economy of the U.S.S.R.* was awarded the Stalin Prize, with its handsome emolument of 200,000 rubles (which he donated to the fund for children rendered fatherless by World War II).

In brief, Voznesensky's was a dazzling career reflecting, as everybody realized, not only Voznesensky's managerial ability, but the favor of the Boss. It was widely believed that if Stalin decided to abandon the presidency of the Council of Ministers, Voznesensky would be his choice for successor.

And then, suddenly, in March 1949, at the time of the ministerial reshuffle, Voznesensky lost his positions as chairman of the Gosplan and

---

[6] He was identified as such in an article in *Pravda*, December 1, 1963. The committee, as set up on June 30, 1941, had Stalin as chairman and Molotov as his deputy. Presumably, Voznesensky became Deputy for Economic Affairs—i.e., in view of Stalin's preoccupation with military foreign affairs, the virtual economic dictator of the U.S.S.R.

Deputy Prime Minister. Soon afterward his name was stricken from the rosters of the Politburo and the Central Committee. It had for long been assumed that he was arrested at the same time: his name vanished from the press around June 1949. But now we know that his ordeal was much more protracted.

The initial frameup of this outstanding representative of the Soviet managerial elite involved a secret trial in which he, along with a number of officials of the Planning Commissariat, was accused of allowing important documents containing state secrets to become lost or stolen.[7] Voznesensky was acquitted; his subordinates received a few years' jail sentence which, under Soviet conditions of the time, indicated that the "crime" was not thought to be serious, their guilt being "lack of vigilance" rather than treason. But the inspirers of the trial succeeded in their main objective: Stalin's trust in his favorite was undermined, his career blighted. Stalin may well have realized that the whole case was spurious—hence Voznesensky's acquittal—but his suspicions, once aroused, generated a frightful momentum. Was there more to Voznesensky's case than just the misplacement of some documents and statistics? He had read Voznesensky's book in manuscript, made corrections in it, and cleared it for the prize. But was the book really as innocent as it then seemed? Was there perhaps some hidden meaning to it, an oblique criticism of Stalin's policies, some data which in the hands of the enemy might become a dangerous weapon?

Reading this book, it is difficult to accept either the verdict of those who awarded it the prize on the grounds that it was a valuable contribution to Marxian economics, or Khrushchev's subsequent allegation that it was Stalin's envy of its theoretical and literary merits which led to Voznesensky's doom. Most of it consists of statistics (compiled, no doubt, by diligent research assistants), and its brief theoretical part is quite banal. Nor could Stalin feel hurt by the references to himself, a typical one reading, "The Stalin way of selecting leaders means choosing them according to their abilities, qualifications, and devotion to the cause of the working class. . . ."[8] It is also nonsensical to allege, as did the Central Committee resolution condemning the book, that it espouses the voluntaristic principle and denies that the socialist economy must develop according to certain laws. In fact, this issue is not even touched on in Voznesensky's humdrum description of the losses which the Soviet economy suffered during the war and the measures taken to keep it going and to assure victory.

But here, precisely, was the rub. As Stalin reread the fatal document, he must have seen that it spelled out in painful detail how the war had

---

[7] *Literary Gazette (Literaturnaya Gazeta)* (Moscow), November 30, 1963.
[8] *The War Economy of the U.S.S.R.* (Moscow, 1948), p. 152.

weakened the Soviet Union; it was a covert criticism of his own inability to prevent or anticipate the German attack; it informed the capitalists how much stronger they were economically than the U.S.S.R. and how weak and vulnerable Russia was because of her wartime losses. What other purpose could be behind the following passage: "No capitalist country in its entire history and during the past war had ever suffered such losses and barbaric destruction at the hands of aggressors as did ours."[9] And it was obvious, palpable treason for Voznesensky to advertise wartime achievements of the capitalists, to give figures for American production which, when read by Soviet citizens, would throw them into panic:

> War production in 1942 amounted to $32.5 billion, in 1943, $60 billion. Of planes of all kinds, the U.S. constructed 48,000 in 1942; in 1943, 86,000. Ships: in 1942, 5 million tons; in 1943, 12 million. Naval vessels: 860,000 tons in 1942; in 1943, 2.6 million tons.[10]

How could this boost national morale at the time of the Berlin blockade—when many believed that war with the United States was just around the corner?

The mania of secrecy was part and parcel of Communist psychology, but in Stalin's case it reached its extreme. When his aircraft industry proposed buying some jet engines advertised for sale abroad, he was amazed by what he thought was their naïveté: "What kind of fool will sell you his secrets?"[11] Following the war, Admiral Galler was disgraced and imprisoned for revealing naval "secrets," and Admiral Nicholas Kuznetsov, who sought to defend his subordinate by pointing out that the alleged secrets were common knowledge and for years had been described in *Jane's Fighting Ships*, barely escaped the same fate. And now here was a man he had trusted and rewarded who was broadcasting for the whole world to see data from which any statistician could extrapolate the vulnerabilities of the Soviet economy. Was it just naïveté and lack of vigilance on the part of a man who had not much experience in politics? If so, who could have put him up to it?

Was there perhaps a conspiracy? Some of those younger men whom he had promoted on the recommendation of Zhdanov might be chafing at the bit. Were they critical of his management of the Party and the economy, fearful of the risks he was undertaking in foreign affairs? With their own protector gone (Zhdanov died on August 31, 1948), were they trying to hurry things up, remove the old guard, isolate him? He had not clipped the wings of his old lieutenants only to become a prisoner of a bunch of upstarts.

[9] *Ibid.*, p. 163.
[10] *Ibid.*, p. 19,
[11] Yakovlev, p. 464.

The other central figure of the Leningrad case was Alexis Alexandrovich Kuznetsov. Between 1937 and 1945 he had been second secretary in Leningrad, and since Zhdanov had a multitude of other state and Party matters to attend to, Kuznetsov was the virtual ruler of the area until the war, when with Zhdanov back he shared the direction of the defense of the beleaguered city. In addition, he was a member of the war council of the army which in 1943 finally broke the blockade of Leningrad. In 1945, with Zhdanov recalled to Moscow, Kuznetsov succeeded him as first secretary; in 1946 came promotion to a secretaryship of the Central Committee. In line with his custom of pitting his lieutenants against each other, Stalin entrusted him with the Party end of the supervision of the security organs—i.e., made him a watchdog over Beria.

Unlike Voznesensky, who was often eulogized following his rehabilitation, Kuznetsov was referred to but infrequently in Soviet publications of the 1950s and 1960s. The *Soviet Encyclopedia*, 1959 edition, places his death in 1949. Yet we know that following his dismissal as a Central Committee secretary, which occurred about the same time as Voznesensky's disgrace, Kuznetsov was transferred to a minor position. On January 17 *Pravda* listed the dignitaries who were on hand to greet Mao Tse-tung, then visiting the city, and among them was A. A. Kuznetsov, chairman of the city soviet. He evidently had briefly returned to the city he once ruled, but now in an inferior position. It was a frequent trick of Stalin's: a doomed man was sent back in an inferior capacity to his former bailiwick, so that he might lead security people to those of his friends and accomplices they had hitherto overlooked.

But Voznesensky on his dismissal was not given another job to keep him busy. He sat at home, his wife wrote subsequently, torn between hope and despondency. Appeals to be allowed to see Stalin were rebuffed; his letters to the dictator pleading innocence and personal devotion to him remained unanswered. This refined cruelty reflected Stalin's conviction of Voznesensky's guilt; all that remained to be established was the extent of the conspiracy. Once Stalin took this attitude, it was obvious that the security organs would find incriminating evidence. There was a veritable raid conducted on the Leningrad Party and state organs. Kuznetsov's successor, Peter Popkov, and scores more of his and Zhdanov's former appointees were arrested; others were transferred or demoted. Another prominent victim, Michael Rodionov, Prime Minister of the Russian Federal Republic, had never served in Leningrad, but he had been a protégé of Zhdanov's since the days when the latter ruled the Gorki region.

Was the Leningrad Affair an intrigue of a new favorite, Malenkov, against the followers of the deceased one, Zhdanov? During the Khrushchev period responsibility for the purge was put squarely—as what crime of the Stalin era was not?—on Beria. Following Malenkov's downfall in 1957 the official version was amended to include him as a fellow instigator: "Malenkov, in addition to Beria, lent his hand to the so-called Leningrad Affair, which was from the beginning to the end fiction and provocation. Malenkov has on his conscience the deaths of completely innocent people and the repression of many others."[12] But these variations usually reflect the political needs of the hour rather than the truth about the past.

The one solid piece of information concerning the Leningrad Affair that has come out since Stalin's death is the identification of its stage manager and his assistants. Victor Abakumov was Minister of State Security between 1946 and 1951; during the war he had served as the Red Army's head of counterintelligence (the celebrated "Smersh"). In December 1954 a special session of the Military Collegium of the Supreme Court of the U.S.S.R., *sitting in Leningrad,* condemned to death Abakumov and several of his assistants (identified as officials in the Ministry of State Security's section "For Investigating Specially Important Cases") for falsifying "the so-called Leningrad Case."[13] The Abakumov trial was, unlike Beria's in the preceding year, an open one. Clearly it was a gesture of reparation, a ghoulish Christmas present for the Leningrad Party organization.[14] The original victims could not be resurrected, however, and Abakumov and his fellow monsters were, of course, mere tools in the intrigue, rather than its instigators.

People of Voznesensky's and Kuznetsov's stature could be destroyed only at Stalin's express orders. (A lesser official might be liquidated at the whim of Beria and/or Malenkov.) And without crediting Beria and Malenkov with excessive humanitarianism, it is clear that they must have wished that the purge of their potential or actual rivals should stop short of the firing squad. What possible inducement could they have to demonstrate—after ten years since high Party officials had been dealt with in this fashion—that a Politburo member or a secretary of the Central Committee could be arrested on spurious charges, tortured, and executed? The craving for power or the fear of its loss sometimes leads people to illogical and very destructive action. But Beria and Malenkov were not novices at intrigue; they had enough intelligence

[12] From a speech by Ivan Spiridinov (then secretary of the Leningrad organization), *The Twenty-second Congress of the Communist Party of the U.S.S.R.* (Moscow, 1962), I, 284.
[13] *Pravda,* December 24, 1954. Two of Abakumov's fellow defendants, V. I. Komarov and M. T. Likhachev, were Soviet experts who helped to arrange and supervise purge trials in the satellite countries between 1949 and 1952. See Artur London, *The Confession* (New York, 1970), p. 170. London was sentenced to life in the Slansky trial in Prague in 1952. The book gives a most complete description of the methods used to procure confessions and the atmosphere attending the purge trials.
[14] "The sentence was received by the whole audience with great satisfaction." *Pravda,* December 24, 1954.

and knowledge of Stalin to realize that if Voznesensky could thus be dealt with, so could they.

It is much more likely that if they were indeed the key figures in the original intrigue, their aim was to discredit Voznesensky and Kuznetsov rather than destroy them physically. The first was to be framed on charges of choosing assistants who were careless with state secrets. Other "Leningraders" would be charged with complicity—Stalin was always sensitive about high officials forming cliques and sticking up for each other rather than spying on each other and reporting to him. The aim of the intrigue was to topple these rival potentates, to assure their demotion and cast them into political oblivion.

But again Stalin "fools them but good." They had thought he had lost his grip, that they could play games with him. No, this could not be just a case of officials negligently misplacing state documents, of economists naïvely leaking out information, of all those Leningraders getting together just for sociability.

There is a suggestive parallel in some of the purges that took place in the Soviet Union's satellite countries. After the war there was keen rivalry in the Czechoslovak Communist Party between Clement Gottwald, Prime Minister and then President, and the Party's General Secretary, Rudolf Slansky. Slansky lost out, was stripped of his position of power, and transferred to the Deputy Prime Ministership. But then the Soviet "advisers" with the Czechoslovak security organs declared that even a further demotion for Slansky and his gang was not enough. It was high time for Czechoslovakia to have a trial tying Slansky, Great Britain, the Zionists, and the American imperialists into one neat package. Gottwald, we know, resisted this pressure but finally had to yield. Slansky and twelve others were tried, confessed, and were shot.

And so with the Leningrad Affair. What in another system might have been a political squabble or dispute among administrators ending in the dismissal of some, the demotion of others, assumed under Soviet conditions the sinister form of plot and counterplot, with the conflict's final resolution being death for those who lost. Stalin believed—and who can tell that he was wrong?—that if people could scheme and plot with the feeling that no matter what happened their lives were not at stake, sooner or later collective interest would prevail over mutual hatred, and they would combine to isolate him. But this way, no matter how much of his authority he had to delegate in view of his age, there was still one decision which no one could usurp and which he alone could make: who would die and who would live. The end of his power would come only when a doomed Politburo member could ask "Why?" and require an answer.

And so Nicholas Voznesensky had to wait while the most accomplished investigators of the Section for Specially Important Cases wove their "novels" (as they were known in Security Police circles)—those Kafkaesque tales of crime and plot compounded of some fact, but mostly gossip and fiction. In July 1949 he was ejected from the Party; his brother, Minister of Education, was dismissed and arrested. At the same time a secret Central Committee circular condemned his book and reprimanded those publicists who had praised and cited it. People must have been shocked out of bureaucratic complacency: here was a book that Comrade Stalin himself had helped edit and that he had praised only a year or so ago. What was going on? It had been premature to think that things had settled down. If today it was Voznesensky, then next year it might be Malenkov's turn. The only safe course was to praise and cite only Stalin.

While he might decide on a man's destruction in cold blood, Stalin sometimes would then develop a violent hatred of his victim. It is difficult, otherwise, to account for his treatment of Voznesensky. In late November security agents came to arrest him, as he must have half expected since March they would. During the interval he evidently had tried to keep busy and sane by working on a book on the political economy of Communism. This sizable treatise (822 typewritten pages) was just completed at the time of the arrest. One can visualize Stalin wrathfully and impatiently flipping through its pages, with their numerous references to himself, before ordering that all the existing copies be destroyed. On January 13 it was announced that in answer to considerable popular demand(!), the Presidium of the Supreme Soviet had decreed that the death penalty, abolished in 1947, was to be restored for crimes of treason. The 1947 law, though undoubtedly frequently honored in the breach, still could have been taken as a guarantee of sorts that terror of the variety of 1937–39 would not recur. While it was in effect it certainly must have complicated the life of the security people: it is difficult to extract false confessions if one cannot threaten victims with death, offer them the hope of life if they confess. And Stalin, though not planning any public trial, still wanted confessions: this minimized the chances of other Politburo members raising a fuss about one of their colleagues being shot. One must assume that when, in September 1950, the Military Collegium of the Supreme Court condemned Voznesensky, Kuznetsov, and their accomplices to death for treason and, as was the custom in such cases, the record of the case was circulated among the Politburo members, each and every one of them signed his name under "to be approved."[15] All that Khrushchev could bring himself o say in his indignant account of the Leningrad Affair given in his "secret speech" of 1956 was that the case was never *dis-*

[15] The date of the trial and execution was first revealed in *Pravda's* notice on the sixtieth anniversary of Kuznetsov's birth, February 20, 1965.

cussed in the Politburo. Once again Stalin had fooled his lieutenants. In signing the authorization for Voznesensky's death, they also in effect signed a warrant for other executions, the names of the future victims to be inserted at the tyrant's pleasure.[16] ☆☆☆

W HILE a number of his former lieutenants and favorites were awaiting the end of their calvaries, Joseph Stalin sought distraction in Marxian philosophy and in linguistics. What made the "supreme genius of mankind" turn his attention to linguistics, and that at a time when a serious Far Eastern crisis had alarmed the world and led many to believe that war was imminent? Preparations had been completed and approved in Moscow for an invasion of South Korea by the North Korean army when Stalin chose to publish a lengthy article on linguistics. Then the Korean War started (contrary to his original calculations, the United States intervened), and the world waited breathlessly—would Stalin say this means war? Would he ask for a summit meeting with Truman? Lower the international tension by a conciliatory gesture? No, the lord and master of world Communism was busy chastizing a Soviet scholar called Marr, dead these fifteen years. His comrades in arms, chastened by what was happening to Voznesensky and Kuznetsov, must have exchanged meaningful glances as they raised their eyes from an issue of *Pravda* which was mostly devoted to yet another pronouncement of Comrade Stalin's on the vexing question of whether language is part of the superstructure or, on the contrary, of *basic* social relations. A few paragraphs dismiss the news of the American troops landing to aid the South Koreans, the special session of the United Nations Security Council, the war fever in the United States. This is too much. . . . Is he really. . . ? But others at home and abroad anxiously seek some hidden meaning in these strange utterances. What is he trying to say? Does this mean a downgrading of Marxism vis-à-vis Russian nationalism? Or, on the contrary, is this a call for ideological purity? Does it portend a more ferocious effort at expansion of Communism, a tightening up the screws at home? Earl Browder, who at the Kremlin's request was at the end of the war dismissed as the head of the American Communist Party

---

[16] We have not been given the names of the judges in the case, but the chairman of the Military Collegium of the Supreme Court at the time was E. L. Zeidin. On December 14–19, 1954, the same gentleman presided over the trial of Abakumov and his associates, and pronounced their guilt in fabricating the Leningrad Affair and "many other cases of the falsification of trials and criminal violation of Socialist legality." *Pravda*, December 24, 1954.

and who since then had been bombarding Moscow with requests to be reinstated or at least be told what he had done wrong, saw Stalin's treatise as a document of momentous importance and as a beacon of hope for the world. In "Language and War," a little pamphlet he printed at his own expense in 1950, Browder perceived the hidden implication of this apparently esoteric exercise: Stalin was pleading for freedom and rejecting the dead dogma of authoritarianism. By denouncing the rule of Soviet linguistics by the followers of the late Professor Marr, Stalin wanted everyone to understand that their intolerant way of dealing with opposition—perhaps Browder had in mind the unfeeling treatment he had received from the American Communists since his downfall—was absolutely wrong.

Others who studied the document closely were not so certain that it is a ringing reaffirmation of freedom in all spheres of intellectual and political activity. To be sure, at one point Comrade Stalin came out strongly for what John Stuart Mill called the free market of ideas: "Everyone acknowledges that no science can develop and progress without a struggle of opinions and the freedom of criticism."[17] But there was a rather ominous reference to those who held (or rather, had held) ideas on linguistics different from his. "Were I not convinced of Comrade Meshchaninov's and of other linguists' honesty, I would say that their behavior constitutes 'wrecking.' "[18] And to be sure, despite Professor Meshchaninov's prompt repudiation of his erroneous views and his expressions of gratitude to Stalin for opening his eyes, he was subsequently dismissed from the directorship of the Institute of Linguistics.

Though Stalin's interest in linguistics destroyed the careers of several people, it must be taken—in comparison with so many other things then going on—as something which comes close to providing comic relief in the grim context of Stalin's Russia. But it was uncharacteristically comic only because those Stalin suddenly denounced did not pay for it with their lives or, so far as we know, with terms in camps or jail. And it illuminates a point which is obscured by the incredible human suffering that attended collectivization, the Great Purge, the Leningrad Affair: in the whole tragedy of Stalinism there was a hard core of sheer preposterousness.

There was no "deeper" reason impelling Stalin to burst out with his contribution on linguistics. It was sheer whim, to which was added a recent determination to leave behind him philosophical treatises and a great theory. Once having indulged this whim, Stalin went into his usual rage: How did those people dare to disagree with what he *was*

17 Stalin, *Works* (Stanford ed.), III, 144.
18 *Ibid.*, p. 145.

going to say—those scoundrels who, just because he had had no time to attend to the business, presumed to persecute honest scholars! The paradoxical nature of Soviet reality comes out well in this episode. Common wisdom teaches that it is better to be alive than dead. It is reasonable to assume that celebration of a dead scholar's anniversary would enhance his reputation, would bring tributes even from those who had disagreed with some of his theories. But in the topsy-turvy world of Stalin's Russia, these verities were neatly reversed. Certainly, everyone in 1950 must have felt that it was a fantastic piece of luck for Professor Marr to be dead: were he alive, it is unlikely that his eighty-five years would have saved him from something much worse than what befell his pupils, the loss of their professional positions and emoluments.

Comrade Stalin would probably not have turned his attention to the matter except that Marr's disciples chose to obey the biblical injunction "Let us now praise famous men and our fathers who begot us." The year 1949 marked the eighty-fifth anniversary of Marr's birth and the fifteenth of his demise. It was thus proper for the Academy of Sciences and the Party organization to order nationwide celebrations and discussion of the legacy of this "inspired Soviet scientist and founder of the new materialist teachings on language, who through his outstanding work brought fame to our fatherland's science,"[19] as the official journal put it. At a solemn session of the Academy, Professor Meshchaninov, the outstanding pupil and continuator of Marr's work, recalled his impassioned last charge to his successors: "Neither fainthearted retreat nor conciliatory appeasement. Forward, young comrades." Alas, in a few months, Meshchaninov would write, "These and many other errors of Marr himself and of his pupils, particularly myself, led to stagnation in Soviet linguistics. . . . In his article, Comrade Stalin laid a foundation for Soviet linguistics and opened a new era in its history."[20]

To give the Devil his due, most professional linguists would wholeheartedly agree with Stalin: Marr had written a lot of nonsense; his followers bullied and persecuted linguists who tried to point this out. Marr, who was half Georgian, had begun as respectable scholar and researcher on the structure and origin of various Caucasian languages. But then he grew into a crank and, as such, encountered hostility and ridicule within his profession. One of his more bizarre assertions, for which he refused to give any proof, was that all spoken languages were traceable to four sounds uttered by primitive man: *sal, ber, roch, yan.* The Bolshevik Revolution enabled Marr, who first among the linguists hastened to jump on the Communist bandwagon, to get even with his colleagues. To his previous nonideological inanities he now added

[19] *Problems of Philosophy*, No. 3 (1949–50), p. 326.
[20] *Pravda*, July 4, 1950.

Marxian-oriented ones: language, like everything else, was determined by the forces of production in the given society, part of the superstructure, just like politics or religion. The whole science of comparative linguistics was bogus and bourgeois in orientation: one had to study language by studying social relations; language was a tool of production. But this time nobody laughed or objected; until his death in 1934 Marr remained the Stalin of linguistics, and even after his departure his pupils, led by Meshchaninov, exercised what might be called dictatorial collective leadership. As Stalin indignantly and quite correctly described, "Talented scholars and language researchers would be dismissed or demoted for a critical attitude toward Marr's ideas, for the slightest token of disapproval of his teaching."[21] In other words, the situation in linguistics was similar to that in many branches of Soviet science and other fields: little Stalins ruled and bullied at will.

Well, not quite. A brave or ambitious man who felt he was being persecuted by one of the little Stalins could always appeal to the great and supreme one. Quite often such a step would have fearful consequences for the complainant: the divinity's wrath could turn against him, and the "unprincipled slanderer of honest Soviet workers" would be delivered into the hands of the official against whom he complained or, more directly, to the security apparatus. But occasionally one would draw a prize in the endless national lottery of denunciation: the whole country would resound with praises of the man who drew Comrade Stalin's and the Central Committee's attention to the intolerable state of affairs in . . . , the violations of socialist legality by officials of . . . , the abrogation of freedom of criticism and undemocratic ways practiced by. . . .

It is quite likely that for some time a few Soviet linguists had petitioned Stalin to take a look at the "intolerable situation in the field of linguistics." One whose name is mentioned in this connection was a fellow Georgian, Professor A. Chikobava. For years he and some other scholars had pursued what in official Stalinist parlance was called a "two-faced" position. While loudly praising the contribution of Marr, they discreetly pointed out that some of Marr's formulations seemed to run afoul of Comrade Stalin's lofty dicta. When in the spring of 1950 the linguistics debate became featured in the Soviet daily press, a connoisseur of these matters would have immediately perceived that the "Marrists" were making a fatal mistake: such was their attachment to their dead master and anger at those who surreptitiously denigrated him, that they cited only infrequently the man who was the supreme authority in all fields of knowledge. In a lengthy article Meshchaninov quoted Stalin only once. To be sure, it was hard as yet to find any words

[21] Stalin (Stanford ed.), III, 144.

of Stalin's that bore the slightest relevance to the matter under discussion. But his sly opponent, Chikobava, was unhampered by such superficial obstacles. His articles were full of passages like the following: "Comrade Stalin's words are a hymn to the development of the socialist nations, their cultures and languages."[22] Flattery did not always have the desired effect on Stalin, but lack of flattery by now invariably had ominous results for those guilty of the oversight. On June 20 Marr and his followers got their comeuppance.

He was not a linguistic scholar, Stalin wrote in his article in *Pravda*, but perhaps people would agree that he was something of an expert when it came to the relationship of Marxism to linguistics. In answer to queries from "young comrades," he would share with them his reflections on Marr and linguistics. Marr (as with people he has decided to liquidate, Stalin called him by his last name, omitting "Academician" or "Comrade") was not a Marxist but a vulgarizer and oversimplifier of Marxism. Language as part of the social superstructure? What nonsense! Language, wrote Stalin, is neither superstructure nor "basis": language is language. And what a conceited fellow! One would think, listening to this vulgarian (and here, as with everyone who became the object of his wrath, even though dead, Stalin shifted to the present tense), that until he and his so-called pupils appeared, the science of language did not exist! "You are dealing here with a clique, people who proclaimed themselves to be infallible and have ruled arbitrarily and without any consideration for others."[23]

Stalin's intervention was immediately acclaimed as a fundamental contribution to linguistics and epistemology, the philosophy of history, etc. It is clear that had not an international crisis intervened, he would have followed his first with several other lengthy articles on the subject: linguistics was such an inviting field. As it was, through the following months he had to content himself with a few brief articles—answers to those who wrote begging for further elucidation of his ideas. One such correspondent confessed puzzlement that what Stalin had just written seemed to be in clear contradiction of a dictum of his of 1939. There was no discrepancy at all, came the answer. Both of Stalin's formulas were correct: they were meant to apply to different epochs of history.

Was Stalin aware of the grotesque nature of this business? Did he really believe that the platitudes he enunciated constituted a fundamental contribution to knowledge? Or did he simply enjoy having all those professors and academicians jump through the hoop? Did he take in good faith the chorus of sycophantic praise that rang through the Communist world, celebrating his immortal work? By now, even in his

22 *Pravda*, May 9, 1950.
23 Stalin (Stanford ed.), III, 199.

own mind, Stalin would have been incapable of answering these questions. The linguistics affair, despite its apparent triviality, is one of the most telling episodes of Stalin's entire career. The urge to struggle, to seek out and destroy enemies, which had prompted young Soso Djugashvili to enter the revolutionary path, continued unabated in the aging tyrant. The middle-aged Stalin, like all successful politicians, advanced his career by seeking and gaining allies, by impressing people with reasonableness and tolerance. But in the end as in the beginning there was the terrible passion to destroy the "impure" ones, be it a loyal servant like Voznesensky or a professor he had never known; a cynic would have poured good-natured ridicule on Marr's absurdities; a more ordinary sadist would have relished having Voznesensky vegetate in an obscure provincial post. But now, even Stalin's passion for power and adulation was no greater than his passion and determination to punish the "impure" ones. Perhaps Voznesensky would have been spared had he humbly acknowledged his sins and begged for forgiveness, rather than pleading his innocence and having the presumption of working on his book. As if traitors could expect to teach Stalin and the honest Soviet folk about economics! And Marr had fooled him by dying before being unmasked.[24]

It is not quite correct to see Stalin simply as obsessed by power. Rather, the politician in him moderated the man bent upon extirpating treason and sin, be it in Trotsky, the kulaks, scheming aides, self-serving intellectuals, or artists masquerading as Marxists. This is how one can account for the seemingly baffling phenomenon that a man so obsessed was yet a skillful diplomat and a clever statesman. In foreign affairs one faced an open enemy, not one who pretended to be a loyal follower, friend, fellow Communist. One expected trickery from Churchills and Trumans. It was in domestic politics that one had constantly to be on guard against "two-faced" people. ☆☆☆

VANITY and not obsession flawed Stalin's direction of Soviet foreign policy in his last years. To be sure, its most signal failure, Yugoslavia, reflected also his "domestic" manias: too late he realized that a presumptuous Communist chieftain in Belgrade could not be dealt

---

[24] In at least one instance a distinguished Soviet figure who had been buried in the place of honor in the Kremlin wall was subsequently unmasked as a "wrecker"; he was at Stalin's order disinterred, his remains burned, and his ashes dispersed. A. Sharagin (pseud.), *The Tupolev Jail Institute* (in Russian; Frankfurt, 1971), p. 30.

with in the same way as one in Kiev. But his miscalculations in Berlin and Korea sprang from a conviction that he knew and could anticipate the reactions of capitalist leaders. Yet the Berlin blockade did not work out quite as anticipated. Still, Stalin's perception that the West would not try to *break* the blockade was vindicated, and the precedent of West Berlin being the West's hostage within Communist territory was established. Everything indicated that German rearmament, the real cause of Soviet fears, was, if it were to happen at all, years away. To his own mind, Stalin had frustrated the main objective of the Marshall Plan. And the Tito affair was not a complete loss: it had led to the elimination of Titoists and Zionist-imperialist agents throughout Eastern Europe, and it had brought new vigilance and vigor to the loyal Communist Parties. The Soviet Union had exploded its first atomic bomb, and the Americans were visibly shaken. European readiness to pull Washington's chestnuts out of the fire had virtually evaporated, now that the American atomic monopoly had ended and the bomb would no longer assure Western Europe's immunity from the Red Army. Any fool could tell that the Americans would use the bomb only if absolutely sure of not being paid back in kind, and after the autumn of 1949 how could they be sure? Prior to the Soviet development of the bomb, Soviet propaganda eschewed excessive discussion of nuclear weapons at home and abroad. But now a vast peace campaign was mounted, the main theme of which was the necessity of banning the bomb.

Some of Stalin's lieutenants must have felt that international tension resulting from Russia's isolation and from the manner rather than substance of her foreign policy was intolerable and dangerous. Certainly his successors hurried to lower the temperature of international relations immediately upon his death. But he stuck to his analysis: the Western leaders were not Hitler; they wanted to subvert Communism, but without making an all-out war. They wanted a new Wehrmacht to blackmail East Germany, new Titos to snatch Eastern Europe from him. And their willingness to play these games would be enhanced if they confronted a reasonable and accommodating Russia. Abroad as at home, people should worry about what Stalin might do next.

He did not want war. In many ways Stalin was more cautious and conservative in foreign affairs than Khrushchev. He feared war; but he needed tension. Where could he pressure his erstwhile allies with the least risk and the most profit to himself? In the Far East the Americans were rather amazingly acquiescing in Mao's conquest of mainland China, a not quite welcome surprise. But a pleasant one was that, unlike the case of West Germany, nobody even talked of rearming Japan. Perhaps there one could push harder. A Communist Japan would nicely balance Mao's China. Both would seek Soviet support; neither would dare to enter the Titoist path.

But it was more likely that the Americans would respond to a new Far Eastern crisis by clinging on desperately to Japan, sending in more troops to guard against an actual or potential uprising. Perhaps they might still try to deny Mao the fullness of victory by throwing a protective ring around Taiwan, and sponsoring an invasion of the mainland by Chiang. This would have a twofold desirable effect: the United States would have fewer resources, less stomach for adventures in Europe; and Mao would become dependent on Soviet arms and advisers.

When the Soviet Union on March 17, 1949, signed a treaty of friendship and cooperation with North Korea, this treaty, in startling contrast to those between Russia and her other satellites or with China, did not contain a mutual defense pact.[25] There must have already been some thought in the Kremlin of using North Korea to precipitate a crisis in the Far East in such a manner that would not involve direct risks to the Soviet Union.

Late in 1949 the Soviets redoubled their campaign against General MacArthur's occupation regime in Japan. There were war-crime show trials of Japanese generals still held as war prisoners in the U.S.S.R. The Soviet government demanded that Emperor Hirohito be tried as a war criminal. At the same time Moscow ordered the Japanese Communists to pursue more militant and disruptive tactics.

Then on June 25, 1950, the North Koreans struck across the 38th Parallel. South Korea would be occupied within a short time: the invading force was equipped with up-to-date Soviet weapons. Surely the Americans would not budge. Had they done anything when a year before Mao's forces crossed the Yangtze and moved on to conquer vast areas of south and west China, a prize compared with which South Korea was nothing? Secretary of State Dean Acheson, in a speech of January 1950, had clearly avowed that South Korea was not within the perimeter of America's defense commitment.

Yet the Americans proved unpredictable. Truman's reaction in ordering first naval and air and then ground forces to help the South Koreans fight off the Communist aggression must have thrown some Soviet officials into a panic. There were voices—to be sure, isolated ones—in America who argued for getting it over with, for striking at the source of the trouble and not dealing piecemeal with local manifestations whenever it pleased the enemy. That the specter of an armed conflict with the United States arose before the Soviet officials is vividly demonstrated by the growth of the Soviet armed forces. Following the Korean miscalculation they began increasing from the postwar low of 2.9 million to twice that number by the end of 1954, most of the growth coming

[25] See Allen S. Whiting, *China Crosses the Yalu* (New York, 1960), p. 42.

between 1950 and 1952.[26] And here Stalin was engrossed in Marr and in the question of whether mankind under Communism would speak one language or several! It is possible that, in addition to their other real and imaginary sins, Voznesensky and company had been arguing that the state of the Soviet economy required more conciliatory foreign policies: Why waste manpower that was so badly needed on the farms and in factories? The date of execution of the Leningrad Affair is suggestive: it was in September, when the tide of the Korean war turned and General MacArthur's forces appeared about to liquidate North Korea.

But if he was temporarily disturbed, Stalin's equanimity evidently soon returned. It is doubtful that Mao had been forewarned of the Korean gambit, most unlikely that he could have wished for the North Korean attack, although the Americans thought he was to blame. The Chinese Communists had plenty of unfinished business in their own country: how could they wish for anything that would rock the boat, which would bring the Americans back into the picture? And that is precisely what happened. The Chinese, not to mention the North Koreans, had to foot the bill for Stalin's miscalculation. The first installment came on June 27, when Truman ordered the Navy to "quarantine" Taiwan. Then, in September and October, as the tide of the war abruptly shifted, they were confronted with a much more serious danger and an excruciating choice. General MacArthur's forces were sweeping *north* of the 38th Parallel. The Americans had piously abjured any intention of reopening the Chinese civil war; the Navy was to keep Chiang out of the mainland as well as to prevent an invasion in the opposite direction. But one did not need to have the proverbially suspicious Communist mentality to disbelieve such assurances. The reason for their not having intervened before in Asia was fear of a world war, of Russia. But now the precedent was being set of *Asian* Communists being trounced without the Soviet Union lifting a finger.

When Chinese "volunteers" entered Korea and, between November 26 and January 15, inflicted defeats on the United Nation forces under MacArthur, they did so with obsolete civil war arms—some Japanese, some American (captured from the Kuomintang forces). In the course of their bloodletting over the next two years, the Chinese armies were re-equipped with modern Soviet arms, for which they had pay. When 1952 came, the Soviet garrison remained in Port Arthur, with Mao's undoubtedly exasperated acquiescence.

What would Stalin have done had nuclear bombs fallen on Peking and/or Chiang's forces escorted by the United States Navy made a landing *en masse* on the mainland? Most likely, nothing. This would not

[26] The statistics are given in Khrushchev's speech; *Pravda*, January 15, 1960.

have been an act of aggression by "Japan or states allied with Japan." At no point did the Russians choose to warn the Americans in so many words that such an action would mean war with them.

It is not surprising that the Chinese should have decided to intervene once the United Nations (mainly American) forces approached their frontiers. General MacArthur may have been a great expert on Oriental psychology, as he believed, but he failed to realize that a newly established Communist regime had to view the destruction of another one as a grave threat. The Chinese must have felt and demanded that Soviet "volunteers" should join theirs in Korea; that failing that, they should receive explicit Soviet commitment of aid if they found themselves in a full-fledged war. But they got neither.

When in June 1951 the Soviet representative in the United Nations proposed the opening of truce talks, the agenda submitted for the negotiations omitted those items which would have been of greatest interest to Peking: the problems of Taiwan and of the admission of Communist China to the United Nations. A prompt armistice was obviously in Peking's interest. An authoritarian regime often thrives on war—the Korean venture, even though undertaken by Mao with trepidation and costly in terms of his best troops (among those killed was his son), had enhanced the Chinese feeling of national pride and self-confidence—but in fighting the Americans, the Chinese Communists reached the limit of their successes, yet not of dangers. Domestic affairs desperately needed attention: China has not known real peace for forty years. But Stalin could see no reason for hurrying with an end to fighting.

Only after his death did the Kremlin heed the Chinese pleas, and then the Korean armistice was signed.

And so, once again, it was not Stalin who paid for his miscalculation. And how often his policies bore disastrous fruits and yet resounded to his glory and power: collectivization, the Great Purge, the pact with Hitler, and the calamitous war. His fame grew and fed upon disaster. "And so on this earth he lived and ruled, holding the reins in his relentless grip."[27]

Was the grip by now that relentless? Of all the legends about Stalin, this one has proved to be the most enduring—witness the poet (himself one of the most liberal influences in Soviet literature of his time) giving us this image seven years after Stalin's death, four after he has been cast down from his pedestal by Khrushchev. Was it really that, as Tvardovsky said, "This son of the East till the very end showed how relentlessly cruel he was, whether dealing out justice or injustice"?[28] There had

[27] Tvardovsky, "Horizon Beyond Horizon," *New World* (Moscow), No. 5 (1960), p. 10.
[28] *Ibid.*, p. 11.

always been another Stalin, different from the one of the legend. We have seen him, on arriving in Siberia for his last exile, giving vent to despair; crying out in self-pity when incidents from his past were brought against him after the Revolution; becoming prey to depression when reprimanded by Lenin during the Civil War. Power and adulation assuaged this sense of inferiority and life's unfairness, but they never quite removed it. At the happiest period of his career, when absolute power was *almost* his, but not quite, Stalin seemed more benign: "Yes, it is true, comrades, I am a coarse fellow," he said jocularly to a Party Congress in 1925. But after he had crossed the threshold of despotism, the old fears and despair began to return: "Oh, how they vilify Stalin, what names they call him," he exclaimed in similar surroundings in 1926. We do not know the state of his health during his very last years, but a man who when young and middle-aged had been unusually sensitive about what people were and might be saying about him, had by now fallen prey to the universal fears of old age, fears of senility and infirmity. ☆☆☆

THIS is, then, the setting of what looks like an impenetrable mystery of his last year. Its *full* story will never be told, for the key to it lies not in secret archives not yet unsealed, nor in details that a few survivors privy to Kremlin secrets have not been allowed to tell, but in the mind of one man who is dead. What did he plan to do? Was there a connection between his leaving the office he had held for so long and the blood-chilling announcement of the discovery of the Doctors' Plot? Did the enlargement of the Politburo augur a demotion or worse for his chief lieutenants—Molotov, Beria, Malenkov, and the others? Did Stalin, as is sometimes alleged, comtemplate a wholesale deportation of Jews into distant regions of the country?[29]

There has been no coherent explanation of the events and rumors current at the time. Stalin's successors—and of the present ruling group, Kosygin, Brezhnev, and Suslov were already in high positions in the period 1949–53—undoubtedly know much more than they have chosen to tell us. But it is clear that even they must have been perplexed as to what was really going on in Stalin's mind.

A Western Kremlinologist is greatly tempted to construct a neat, logical tale of Stalin's last plot. Perhaps he was scheming to get rid of his lieutenants, and feigned an intention to retire at the same time that he

[29] See Roy Medvedev, *Let History Judge* (New York, 1971), p. 495.

ordered the security organs to fabricate the Doctors' Plot. He was then planning to charge Beria, perhaps Molotov and Mikoyan, with complicity in the doctors' crimes. And having gotten rid of those inconvenient relics of the past and having unleashed a new wave of terror, he would rule with the aid of the newcomers to the Politburo. But death struck him in the midst of all this scheming, saved the oligarchs, and spared Russia from a return of the "Yezhov times."

Yet this is at best an oversimplification. Everything we know suggests that there was no clearcut design in Stalin's mind. The evidence seems to suggest that he was torn between two conflicting emotions. One was a genuine weariness and a desire to lay down his awesome duties before he would be "found out" to be incapable of discharging them. He would elevate new men—second-rank bureaucrats and younger Party bosses. They, unlike the Molotovs and Berias, would not dream of replacing him; they would rule in his name, with him still a deity. This comes out plainly in Khrushchev's 1956 speech: "His proposal after the Nineteenth Congress concerning the selection of twenty-five persons to the Central Committee Presidium was aimed at the removal of the old Political Bureau members and the bringing in of less experienced persons so that these would extol him in all sorts of ways."[30]

Yet with another part of his mind Stalin still clung to absolute power. He must have also half realized that a man in his position cannot really retire, that one cannot be a part-time despot. Would the Molotovs and Berias acquiesce in their demotion, abandon the ambitions they had cherished so long of succeeding him? Perhaps, with his passion for Russian history, he reverted to the old Muscovite practice of "placement." The Tsar was an absolute master of life and death, even of his highest born and placed subjects. But there was one ancient custom which even the most absolute monarch found it virtually impossible to break: he could not force a nobleman of high rank to take, whether at the grand ducal table or in the command of armies, a place lower than that held by someone of lesser ancestry. Princes often preferred imprisonment or even death rather than serve or yield the step to someone whose family ranked lower in the register of nobility.

Now, though his power was greater than that of the most absolute Tsar, "placement" became a feature of Stalin's court. Nothing short of imprisonment and execution would make the most tenacious of his lieutenants give up their places in the hierarchy. Despite what had happened to his wife and despite his own secret disgrace for two years, Molotov clung to the position of second man in the state. For some years, Stalin, with what for him was great delicacy, tried to suggest to Voroshilov that he should retire. "Stalin forbade him to attend the

[30] Bertram D. Wolfe, *Khrushchev and Stalin's Ghost* (New York, 1957), p. 244.

Political Bureau sessions and to receive documents. When the Political Bureau was in session and Comrade Voroshilov heard about it, he telephoned each time and asked whether he would be allowed to attend. Sometimes Stalin permitted it but always showed his dissatisfaction."[31] A younger Stalin might have dealt with the "placement" problem in a forthright manner, and as the Voznesensky case showed, even at seventy he had not entirely lost his ability in this respect. But could one pin the charge of treason on Molotov or Voroshilov? Once Stalin had been confident that he could order the whole Politburo shot and be obeyed. Now he could not be so sure. Could he at seventy-two, as he had at fifty-seven, bully the Central Committee and through his ferocious energy infuse its members with the belief that Lenin's companions were traitors, make them deliver their own lives into his hands? He must have noticed that even his most slavish henchmen were startled when he confided to them that Voroshilov *might* be an English spy.[32] Khrushchev told us that Voroshilov's home was bugged. And it is unlikely that he was the only one of the Politburo members to enjoy this distinction.

And so perhaps one could not get rid of the old guard by simply turning over their offices to his young worshipers. Fear, which had once driven Stalin to audacious gambles, was now a debilitating influence, rendering the old man indecisive. He would chip at the oligarchs' positions rather than strike at them directly. With Kuznetsov gone, there was no one to balance Malenkov in the Party Secretariat. And though Malenkov was now as close to being a favorite as anyone, he would still have a senior Party man looking over Malenkov's shoulder. At the end of 1949, Khrushchev was brought back to Moscow to be a Secretary of the Central Committee. It was a felicitous choice: the two men's personalities, as well as official positions, were bound to make them bitter rivals.

There was Beria. It is difficult now to get a clear picture of his personality and role. *Every* Soviet regime since 1953 has found Beria a convenient scapegoat for the horrors of the past. Clearly, he managed to become a person of much greater consequence and power than Yezhov or Yagoda had ever been. Unlike them, he not only built a following in the security forces; he also became the overlord of the Party organizations in all of Transcaucasia. Even if we discount much that has been written about him, there still emerges the strong impression of an in-

[31] Khrushchev in *ibid.*, p. 242.
[32] As we have seen in the case of Svetlana's suitor, "spy" in Stalin's vocabulary could mean anyone who had had social contact with a foreigner. Voroshilov might have earned this title by something as innocuous as having been drunk at a reception in the British Embassy or during the war having received, along with other Soviet military leaders, a major British decoration.

triguer who would constantly fuel Stalin's suspicions. By the same token, a man of that sort is seldom an outright sadist; he seeks to get people within his grip, to make them his tools and accomplices, rather than— unless they clearly stand in his way—destroy them. After the war Stalin, as we have seen, took steps to curtail Beria's powers. But to purge the security apparatus of Beria's men, to strike directly at him, would have meant chaos on the order of 1937–39, and unless it was absolutely neces- sary, Stalin did not want and could not afford a repetition of that ex- perience. Beria, he must have ruefully realized, was for him what he himself had been for Lenin in 1922: an almost indispensable man, the machinery of terror holding the Soviet system together just as the Party apparatus did then. The man had his hand on everything: he supervised much of the defense, including nuclear research; the tentacles of his apparatus gripped the East European parties and intelligence services; his slave empire was an important element in the Soviet economy. He certainly had proved himself efficient—witness the absence of political trouble at home during the war. Would another man be able to cope with the task? Would he feel safer with him?

Beria's position was only gradually eroded as Stalin pondered his dilemma. In 1951–52 alleged conspiracies were uncovered in Georgia; the local Party organization was purged, some of the victims having been protégés of Beria's. Another former henchman, Victor Abakumov, was dismissed early in 1952 from the Security Ministry and replaced by a man with no previous connection with political police, a former Party official, Semyon Ignatiev. Outwardly, Beria's position was unaffected by these changes. To the average Party worker as to the world, he was still Stalin's high executioner, next to the Boss himself the person to be feared most in the whole Communist empire. But to those in the know, Beria was no longer invulnerable.

Ignatiev's role, as subsequent events were to make clear, was not so much to direct as to watch over the machinery of terror. There is a clear and credible suggestion in Khrushchev's speech that Stalin himself took a hand in running security affairs, indicating to subordinate officials which people were to be investigated, etc. The year 1952 marked the height of the "anti-Zionist" drive. It was in that summer that Lozovsky and some other Jewish literary and public figures, imprisoned in 1949, were tried and shot. The international Jewish conspiracy was now very much on Stalin's mind. In Czechoslovakia the noose was tightening around the necks of high Party and state officials headed by Rudolf Slan- sky, once the country's number-two Communist. In November 1952 they were sentenced—eleven to death, three to life imprisonment—on the fantastic charges of having been Western agents recruited by the Zionists. Eleven of them were Jewish, and their public trial had strong anti-Semitic undertones.

As was obvious by their actions after Stalin's death, his Politburo colleagues must have been strongly opposed to, and so far as it was within their power resisted, preparations for a new wave of terror. And they also believed that the international situation was reaching an intolerably dangerous degree of tension. The United States, frustrated by the Korean stalemate, would probably soon have a new Republican administration; its putative spokesmen were talking in terms of "getting tough" with the Soviet Union. Eastern Europe was a powderkeg. There were growing strains with China. The Chinese were eager for a peace in Korea, increasingly angry that their pleas for economic and technological help were being met with impossible conditions on the Soviet side.[33] If Soviet policies were allowed to continue unchanged, the country, while going through a repetition of 1937–39, would face a real threat of war.

The summer of 1952 is the first time since the "plot by adulation" in 1934 that we see opposition to Stalin crystallizing in the highest ranks of the Communist Party. Under current conditions there was, of course, no possibility of a real plot's being hatched, or even of Stalin's opponents getting together just to talk about a strategy. But there was probably something in the nature of a silent meeting of minds: things could not go on this way.

On August 20 an official announcement apprized the Soviet public that the Central Committee, in a plenary session, decided to convoke the Nineteenth Party Congress on October 5, 1952. The communiqué was signed by Stalin in his capacity as Secretary of the Central Committee—the first time in many years that he chose to sign an official document as such. There can be little question that he agreed to the convocation of the Congress reluctantly and only under pressure from all the remaining members of the Politburo. Did he fear their revolt? This sounds ridiculous, but even in 1937–39 he could not have managed to liquidate *all* of his senior colleagues simultaneously. One can visualize them pleading respectfully but insistently that a Party Congress was necessary: none had been held since 1939, seven years had passed since the war, and the nation needed a new set of directives, a public reaffirmation that the Communist Party was still the leading force. There was still a fiction of collegiality as far as such decisions were concerned. There was obvious logic behind this argument; it was not Stalin's way directly to oppose the collective judgment of his colleagues.

Yet it was a decision he could not have relished. There is a great deal to indicate that a Congress had been planned for 1949, possibly in

---

[33] At Stalin's death Chinese trade and technological experts had been in Moscow for several months. On March 26, 1953, the Soviets granted the Chinese extensive credits and agreed to offer considerable technological and scientific aid by helping train the Chinese personnel.

conjunction with his seventieth birthday, and that the idea was abandoned. He was no longer able, did not trust himself to accomplish the physical effort involved in delivering the main political report. Of course, even if he did not deliver the political report, he still would be the central figure of the gathering; he would determine the Congress' order of business, would appoint the people they "elected" to the central organs. But the solid front which his lieutenants now established frustrated Stalin's intention of getting rid of Molotov, Voroshilov, and perhaps Beria at this time. For the sake of appearances, they would have to be reelected to the Politburo.[34]

We must assume, then, contrary to other Western interpretations of events in 1952–53, that Stalin's lieutenants, including Malenkov, presented a united front in urging the convocation of the Party Congress. Of course, Stalin could have said no, but he never clashed directly with his lieutenants when they stood together.

On the very eve of the Congress, Stalin confounded his lieutenants by publishing his treatise *Economic Problems of Socialism in the U.S.S.R.* There is no doubt that it was written with the Congress in mind. The main part of the work was dated by him as having been completed on February 1, but this was tomfoolery. Why should he have waited to give the world the latest product of his genius? (Or did he send the pamphlet to *Pravda* and other journals, only to receive a reply that because of lack of space and other commitments, his contribution could not be printed until October?) The truth is that following a discussion among Soviet economists in November 1951 about the contents of a projected textbook on political economy, Stalin prepared brief observations concerning its proceedings. These then were expanded in the summer of 1952 and supplemented by some letters he wrote to a few participants in the discussion between April and September. All this appeared on the eve of the Congress—and distracted public attention from the fact that he was unable to deliver the main report. Stalin was too busy with sublime theoretical verities to attend to the pedestrian business of writing and delivering the key address!

The work itself seldom rises above the level of the commonplace and then does so only to sink into confusion. It is startlingly reminiscent of Stalin's outpourings in the early years, with little of the clarity and crude vigor that characterizes some of his writings and utterances of the middle period.

[34] By 1952 Stalin managed to ban one of his old pals, Andreyev, from the Politburo. In the public eye Andreyev did not have a standing comparable to that of the others. How deeply the idea of "placement" was ingrained in the oligarch's mind can be judged from Khrushchev's reference to the affair. After detailing various crimes of Stalin's and hinting at worse, he described Andreyev's removal from the Politburo (he did not suffer worse) by Stalin's personal decision as "one of the most unbridled acts of wilfulness" on the part of the dictator.

He was writing, he said, to affirm that even under socialism, even in the Soviet Union, there are economic laws that cannot be disregarded or overcome through planning. This unsensational statement is then immediately and confusedly qualified by the assertion that the law of value cannot be applied to determine manpower distribution as between various branches of production, the prices. Of what use, then, is such a "law"? Stalin forecast a new era of instability and crisis for world capitalism, hence new conflicts and war between the imperialist powers. What was the basic law of socialist economy? It was "the maximum satisfaction of constantly growing material and cultural needs of the whole society through the uninterrupted growth and perfection of socialist production with the help of advanced technology."[35] But, of course, in the Soviet Union the needs of heavy industry must have priority over consumer goods. Then, all of a sudden, Stalin made some observations on the economy of feudalism, only to assert that the projected textbook on economics should point out that in the U.S.S.R. every kolkhoz member may own at least one cow and, depending on local circumstances, several hogs, goats, etc., plus an unlimited number of geese, turkeys, etc.! The textbook should have five hundred to six hundred pages. He allowed that the projected chapter "On the Creation of the Political Economy of Socialism by V. Lenin and J. Stalin" was not needed, since "It repeats in a pallid form what has been said in greater detail in previous chapters."[36] This is one statement in *Economic Problems of Socialism in the U.S.S.R.* to which no one can take exception.

One must sympathize with those, whether in the U.S.S.R. or abroad, who tried to decipher some meaning, hidden or otherwise, in these senile outpourings. There is a bit less mumbo-jumbo in those parts of the opus which consist of Stalin's replies to economists who asked for his opinion on various theoretical and practical matters. (It was not always safe to write Stalin, even if one did so in the most deferential form. Take one Yaroshenko. This ambitious man petitioned the deity to be commissioned to write the textbook on political economy, a task he was confident he could discharge in a year if provided with two research assistants. Something in Yaroshenko's letter struck Stalin as being a veiled criticism of himself, so he let Yaroshenko have it: thirty-one pages of close print on "Errors of Comrade Yaroshenko"—veritably a god swatting a fly. The presumption of this fellow! His views were un-Marxist and false. They smacked of Bogdanov's obscurantist ideas. Much worse, "Comrade Yaroshenko follows in the footsteps of Bukharin." Possibly work was found for Yaroshenko, but undoubtedly it was of the

[35] Stalin (Stanford ed.), III, 236.
[36] *Ibid.*, p. 242.

kind in which one doesn't have assistants and was of quite a different character than he had in mind. Under Communism, as Stalin repeated after Marx, the difference between mental and physical labor is constantly being attenuated.)

And in the jumble of would-be profundities, editorial comments, bilious criticism, and plain nonsense, there were some flashes of lucidity. Two economists had proposed that the Machine Tractor Stations be sold or turned over to the collective farms which they were servicing. (In a few years Khrushchev did, in fact, do that.) This proposal brought out the true believer in Stalin for whom even the collective-farm system was insufficiently socialist. No, to turn over the MTS to the kolkhozes would be a step back, toward capitalism. On the contrary, "Kolkhoz property should be raised to the level of national property." This signaled that Stalin had in mind yet another assault on the peasantry: the curtailment or destruction of the peasants' household lots, possibly the transformation of collective farms into state farms, with the inevitable expropriation of the peasants' animals and private ownership, which in another part of his work he asserted to be an immutable feature of the Soviet agricultural system.

Economic Problems of Socialism in the U.S.S.R. was given to the world on October 3 and 4, filling out two entire issues of *Pravda*. And on October 5 the Nineteenth Congress of the Communist Party of the U.S.S.R. opened. Though nobody but a handful could know it, its proceedings reflected the current impasse of Soviet politics. Paradoxically, Stalin's power, while still absolute, was no longer unlimited. He could dictate the format of the Congress and the contents of its resolutions, but he had not been able to do away with "placement," had not been able to find a way to break down his lieutenants' determination to forestall a purge in their ranks. As of old the Congress resounded with his name: every speaker paid homage to the greatest genius of mankind. "Comrade Stalin's works on problems of economics and linguistics mark a new stage in the development of Marxism. . . . [His] discoveries in the field of theory have world-historic importance."[37] But of what good was all that flattery in view of the palpable fact that he was a sick old man? As with Lenin at the Eleventh Congress in 1922, so now with Stalin, every delegate must have sensed an approach of the end. His hair, eyewitnesses reported, was sparse and completely white. He sat through Malenkov's keynote address—the report he had delivered at every Congress from 1924 through 1939. It had been one of the foundations on which he had built his absolute power. It was in these reports that he had crossed swords with and destroyed Trotsky, Zinoviev,

[37] From Malenkov's speech, cited in *Current Soviet Policies* (New York, 1953), p. 123.

Bukharin, and the others, reported on the triumphs of socialist construction, been the voice and incarnation of defiant, then victorious, Communism. And he had relished the ovation which would shake the room when the chairman announced: "To deliver the Political Report of the Central Committee: Comrade Stalin." "He would hardly open his mouth when all, jumping to their feet, would shout, 'Hurrah! Once more he will show us the way!' "[38] There were still ovations and eulogies, in greater profusion than ever, but these were cheers of propitiation, not exultation. Of all the attributes of absolute power he retained in full only one: he could no longer lead, he was still capable of sowing terror and destruction in the land.

Apart from his attendance at Malenkov's address, Stalin appeared at the Congress only a few times, never longer than for fifteen to twenty minutes.[39] The resolutions followed his wishes. Two of them, of minor importance, were still characteristic: the All-Union Communist Party (of the Bolsheviks) was renamed the Communist Party of the Soviet Union, and the parenthetical description was dropped. Also symbolic of Stalin's desire to attenuate links with the Leninist past was the renaming—as Presidium—the Politburo. "Lenin's Politburo" conjured up the ghosts of Trotsky, Zinoviev, and Bukharin. Those memories rankled.

The fact that Malenkov was entrusted with the Political Report of the Central Committee *seemingly* marked him as the chosen successor of the dictator, who in two months would turn seventy-three. But Stalin judged it injudicious not to let the old guard play at least a symbolic part in the proceedings. The Congress was opened by Molotov and concluded with a speech by Voroshilov, for the public a fitting homage for the closest and oldest "comrades in arms of Great Stalin." Though forced by the passage of years to yield a more active role to younger men, they still appeared revered and important as elder statesmen.

But before the Congress was adjourned, Stalin himself took the tribune. Like an aging star no longer capable of an extended part but who by delivering a few lines can steal the limelight from the principals, the dictator chose to remind the world that he was still the master. And it is undeniable that, as against the drab ritualistic formulas, boring data and statistics of other speeches, his few minutes' oration exuded a certain crude eloquence reminiscent of the younger Stalin. He chose to address himself to the delegates of the fraternal parties present at the Congress, to discourse on the world prospects of Communism. It was up to the Communists in foreign countries, he said, to raise the banner of freedom and independence trampled everywhere by the bourgeoisie,

---

[38] Tvardovsky, p. 11.

[39] This is according to Admiral N. G. Kuznetsov, a delegate at the Congress. *Neva*, No. 5 (Leningrad, 1965), p. 161.

"which sells the nations' rights and independence for dollars." And under this banner they would achieve power in their countries, free the world from imperialism and the specter of war. Unlike some other speakers he did not single out the Chinese Communists for special praise. He spoke warmly of the leaders of the Italian and French parties but did not mention the man in Peking, who in the world's eyes was already the most important Communist next to himself. But for all such undertones it was still a star performance. Years appeared to have receded, and for a moment one could believe that it was a fervent revolutionary and internationalist who spoke, prophesying the inevitable triumph of the cause.

Following the Congress the newly elected Central Committee met to select members of the highest Party organs, the Presidium and the Secretariat. The key to what was to happen in Soviet politics for several years thereafter undoubtedly lies in the events of this meeting of October 16, 1952. It is therefore particularly exasperating that we have been given but the merest hints of what transpired on this occasion. The official announcement listed members of the Presidium and the new Secretariat. The successor body to the Politburo was to be much larger. In place of the past pattern—ten to eleven full members and three to four alternates—the Presidium was to have twenty-five full and twelve alternate members. The Secretariat of the Central Committee was doubled in size, to ten people. Stalin's name headed both lists, the others' being listed in alphabetical order. Of the old members of the Politburo Stalin excluded Andreyev entirely and demoted Kosygin to an alternate. He did not exclude those of the old guard against whom he had nurtured grievances. ". . . Stalin, in his talk at the Plenum, characterized Vyacheslav Molotov and Anastas Mikoyan, and suggested that these old workers of our Party were guilty of some baseless charges. It is not excluded that had Stalin remained at the helm for another several months, Comrades Molotov and Mikoyan would probably not have delivered any speeches at this Congress."[40]

We know more or less how such "elections" were run. Members of the Central Committee assembled, the bigwigs sitting behind a table facing the "common" members in their chairs. Someone would propose a list of names composed by Stalin and his aides. The presiding officer, evidently never Stalin himself, maintained the fiction of a parliamentary procedure by asking if there were any other nominations, if someone objected to any of those proposed, etc. There was a chorused *"Nyet,"* and the list passed by acclamation. But on this occasion Stalin evidently chose to exercise his right to discussion. One may well imagine members of the Committee listening with fear and embarrassment to petulant

[40] Khrushchev at the Twentieth Congress, in Wolfe, p. 244.

and incoherent accusations. "Stalin gave the impression of being a sick man," a witness wrote.[41] But since Stalin did not actually propose to excise Molotov's and Mikoyan's names and since they did not withdraw their names themselves, the frightened assembly voted in the list as proposed.

At the same meeting Stalin offered his resignation as General Secretary. This title had not been employed by him since 1934, but officially he had it and very occasionally was referred to as such.[42] This time he definitely resigned it, as several Soviet sources confirmed after his death, describing him as General Secretary, 1922–52.[43]

For the majority of the roughly two hundred participants, the meeting of October 16 must have been a shock which shattered many of their ideas of what had been going on at the top. Did Stalin really wish to retire as the Party's chief officer? As dictator? Did he mean to destroy those who under him had ruled Russia for years? How did one explain this outburst against the old guard? The traumatic effect of the experience makes one eyewitness, Admiral Kuznetsov, commit a whopping mistake in relating the story: Stalin, he wrote, resigned at the session as Minister of Defense. But as we have seen, he had resigned from that office in 1947, and who should remember it better than the Minister of the Navy?

Who were the new additions to the Presidium? Most of them were not youngsters, but people who have been in the Party and state machinery for a long time. Thus the gray eminence of the purges, Matvie Shkiryatov, finally received a reward for services of long standing by being made a full member, while for similar deserts Vishinsky was raised to an alternate membership. Some were added to demonstrate continuity with the past: Otto Kuusinen, who miraculously survived his colleagues from the early apparatus of the Comintern, made the supreme body in his seventies. A number of technocrats and industrial managers were also advanced; these were people *relatively* free from the deadly intrigues and hatreds which had divided the old menbers of the Politburo. There were, finally, a few who had risen through the Party ranks: the new first secretary in Leningrad, Vassily Andrianov; Semyon Ignatiev, the current Minister of State Security; George Mikhailov, former leader of the Komsomol. These at least were Stalinists in the true sense of the word, men who had risen when he was already god.

But it must have been immediately clear to Stalin that there was one

[41] Kuznetsov, p. 161.

[42] E.g., *The Bolshevik* (Moscow), April 2, 1949.

[43] This is also alluded to in Alliluyeva, *Twenty Letters to a Friend*, p. 191. A quite recent Soviet source, *Lessons on the History of the Communist Party*, Part 2 (Moscow, 1969), asserts that he was General Secretary up to his death, but that is in line with the current official effort to obscure the story of Stalin's last years.

flaw: the new men had for the most part not been brought up by him the way he had nurtured a Yezhov or Malenkov in his private secretariat. They were bureaucrats to the core, their style was patient, behind-the-scenes intrigue. As beneficiaries of the Great Purge the newcomers could not be enthusiastic about another one: it might do to them what the horrors of 1936–39 did to the people whose jobs they inherited. That this was in fact their attitude has been demonstrated by their post-1953 careers. Demoted after Stalin's death, most of them adjusted to their humbler circumstances. Brezhnev, in 1952 an alternate Politburo member and Party Secretary, was cast down from the Olympus in March 1953 and began a slow ascent which only after eleven years has brought him to the very top. V. V. Kuznetsov, a full Presidium member who might conceivably have been groomed for Molotov's position,[44] became after Stalin's death Deputy Foreign Minister and remains as such to this day. Nicholas Patolichev, then close to the summit as one of the youngest alternate Presidium members, found a quiet niche as Minister of Foreign Trade. The newcomers, as Khrushchev later said, were indeed less experienced than the old members.[45] And to be sure, they were quite ready "to extol [Stalin] in all sorts of ways," but they would be reluctant accomplices to a new bloodbath or in the overthrow of people like Molotov and Beria.

The discovery that he had nurtured "vegetarians"—as the saying went in pre-1917 Russia about revolutionaries who balked at terror—must not have pleased Stalin. In the past he seldom chose to destroy by direct command. Others would divine his intentions, make the proper motion in the Politburo or Central Committee. Then there would be "proofs," confessions by those accused, and everyone would clamor for their heads. Now something had gone wrong with this blueprint.

He was in a hurry. Quite likely he really meant to lay down his Party office, the functions of which he could no longer fully discharge. But he would never do it if it meant turning over his powers to men who had waited all along for him to die or to become debilitated and who would destroy his legend. A few years hence another Communist despot faced a similar dilemma. At precisely the same age, seventy-three, Mao Tse-tung launched his "Cultural Revolution." Stalin employed more traditional methods for the same end.

Svetlana Alliluyeva visited her father on November 7 and then on his seventy-third birthday in December. She noticed changes. His usually gray, pale face was flushed. In retrospect, she believes it was a symptom

[44] The only Soviet leader with a prolonged exposure to the United States: he had been trained as a mechanic in a Ford plant.
[45] What he obviously meant to say is that they had had less experience of Stalin! As Party and managerial bureaucrats, the new men were at least as competent as the old bureaucrats.

of high blood pressure. But possibly it also reflected his internal agitation. He had stopped smoking, another sign that he felt his health to be failing.[46] To die now, he must have reflected, would have been the greatest political mistake of his career. He was sure there was a real conspiracy afoot. For the first time in many a year he had not taken a vacation in the south. He wanted to keep close to Moscow. The solidarity of the new Presidium must have confirmed his suspicions. He would strike first.

"Some time ago agencies of state security discovered a terrorist group of doctors who had made it their aim to cut short the lives of active public figures of the Soviet Union through wrecking methods of medical treatment." Thus began an official announcement on January 13 in *Pravda* and other newspapers. It went on to list the "murderer doctor." Among them was V. N. Vinogradov, until recently Stalin's personal physician. Their "wrecking methods" were said to have brought the premature death of Alexis Shcherbakov in 1945, of Andrei Zhdanov in 1948. And they were being unmasked as they administered similar treatment to a number of military figures: Marshals Vasilevsky and Konev, General Shtemenko, and others. Why this unprofessional behavior? The villainous doctors belonged to two groups: one "connected with the international Jewish bourgeois organization 'Joint,' established by American intelligence"; the other, including Vinogradov, composed of "old agents of British Intelligence." On January 20 it was revealed that Dr. Lydia Timashuk had received the Order of Lenin for first drawing attention to the suspicious methods of treatment employed by these villains.

Again, "murderer doctors"! It had become something of a tradition in Soviet Russia—and for a history buff like Stalin it must have recalled the fifteenth-century Ivan III, punishing by death Master Leon the Jew, his court physician, for allegedly causing the death of his son and heir at the instigation of the Grand Duke's second wife and some nobles. Within a month of Stalin's death the matter of the doctors was proclaimed a criminal hoax; they were fully rehabilitated and reinstalled in the Kremlin Medical Service. Dr. Timashuk had the Order of Lenin snatched from her bosom, although she continued at her job as a radiologist in the Kremlin Hospital.[47] The villain of the piece, Stalin's heirs announced, was Michael Ryumin, then Deputy Minister of Security and Chief Investigator. He had, for "*careerist* and adventurist purposes," falsified evidence and employed methods of investigation "forbidden by the Soviet law." After a secret trial in July 1954 Ryumin was shot.[48]

[46] Alliluyeva, *Twenty Letters to a Friend*, p. 193.
[47] This detail according to Medvedev, p. 494.
[48] *Pravda*, July 23, 1954. My italics.

The curtain was raised on what may perhaps have been intended as a new wave of terror on the scale of the 1930s. But the purges of that period were in their purpose prophylactic and educational. Stalin then liquidated those who *might* prove troublesome in case of war; he wanted the nation to absorb the lesson that opposition to or criticism of him was connected with treason. Now he really believed that he was faced with two conspiracies: a Zionist-Titoist-American intelligence network of agents which penetrated the Communist movement and hence *had* to have people in the interstices of the Soviet system; and, perhaps connected with it, a plot of his senior colleagues to curtail his powers.

On the second count there was some substance to his fears. The time was approaching when the senior figures of the Party might confront him in a body and urge that things could not go on this way, that supreme power must revert to the closed circle of the *old* Politburo, that the main offices of state, such as Foreign Affairs and Security, must go back to the experienced hands of Molotov and Beria, and so on. (That was, after all, what happened only a day after his death.)

The Doctors' Plot was Stalin's way of stealing the march on them. He himself instigated the "investigation" and kept in touch with its progress. When Minister of Security Ignatiev appeared squeamish about applying torture to the "murderer doctors," Stalin, according to Khrushchev, made him understand that his head might be forfeit.[49] The doctors' confessions were circulated among the Presidium members. Stalin must have sensed their sullen skepticism, for he taunted them: "You are blind. . . . What will happen without me? The country will perish because you do not know how to recognize enemies."[50]

This was his way of terrorizing his colleagues. In the past such methods never failed to bring results. How often were members of the Politburo on the point of coalescing and standing up against some measure of his when a trumped-up case would bring them to heel! We do not know whether this scenario was being repeated during those few frightful weeks in the beginning of 1953. But we do know that Stalin's fears were not feigned. Though ailing, he now refused to permit a doctor near himself. Vlasik, chief of his personal security since the Civil War, had been imprisoned. His confidential secretary, Poskrebyshev, was chased away and awaited a similar fate.

How widely he intended to cast the net of terror must remain a matter for speculation. Khrushchev suggests that he wanted to do in *all* the old members of the Politburo. But if he retained any of his political acumen, he must have known this would be impractical, perhaps

[49] The way Ignatiev was treated after Stalin's death suggests that unlike Ryumin he was an *unwilling* accomplice. He was eventually relegated to a minor provincial post.
[50] From Khrushchev's "secret speech," in Wolfe, p. 204.

impossible. He could frighten them all, demote most, kill only some. Beria must have ranked high as candidate for the last category. Obviously the security organs had been delinquent, if not worse, if they had not uncovered the monstrous conspiracy which had been going on since at least 1945, with the doctors planning to kill eminent military figures. Beria's relations with the army High Command had long been notoriously bad. What better reward and assurance of the generals' loyalty than to present them with the head of the intriguing scoundrel who had destroyed so many of their colleagues? That Beria would make a highly popular scapegoat was a conclusion Stalin's successors would echo in a few months' time.

Who would have schemed to have Shcherbakov and Zhdanov out of the way? Obviously, those who did not want Shcherbakov to become what Zhdanov already was, the second most important man in Russia— i.e., Malenkov and Molotov. And the Jewish angle had to be disturbing for people who, like Molotov, Voroshilov, and Andreyev, had Jewish wives.

A heavy pall of fear was cast over the whole country. There were ominous rumblings. Frol Kozlov, second secretary of the Leningrad Party, wrote in the January *Communist* an article hinting at another mass purge of the Party ranks. The Assistant Procurator-General of the Soviet Union evoked the most ominous memory of all: Stalin's speech at the February–March 1937 meeting of the Central Committee. He recalled how Stalin then warned against enemies who did not dare come out openly against Soviet power, but tried "to lull the vigilance of Soviet people by false assurances of . . . devotion to our cause." Once more there was the appeal to the common people to denounce bureaucrats "who commit arbitrary and illegal acts." But such warnings—in fact, incitements to a new wave of hysteria and denunciations—came from secondary figures. The oligarchs were silent, unlike in the 1930s when they chimed in with appeals for "vigilance" and for the "unmasking of the enemy." Were they preserving a united front, conveying to Stalin that he could not pick them off one by one, but would have to tackle them all? We do not know, but it is possible.

The last foreigner who is said to have seen Stalin was the Indian ambassador, K. P. S. Menon, who had an audience with him on February 18. His account—though Menon, who had no previous experience with him, did not realize it—makes it clear that the old Stalin who impressed and often charmed foreign visitors was no more. He was quite clearly preoccupied, and he kept doodling—something he had never done when entertaining an important visitor. He had not bothered to be adequately briefed, and revealed he did not know what languages were spoken in India, etc. At one point, Stalin told Menon that when a wolf attacks a Russian peasant, the peasant does not try to tame it but kills the animal. It was a remark that the awed ambassador took to have some deeper meaning.[51] Perhaps.

The stroke that felled Stalin occurred during the night of March 1–2. According to rumors which circulated in Moscow, he remained un-attended for several hours after his seizure, for the guards, who became disturbed when he failed to ask for his late-evening repast, did not dare to break open the locked iron-plated door that led to his bedroom. His daughter and son were summoned in the morning. Only when his condition was deemed hopeless, on March 4, did his colleagues com-municate news of his illness to the world. He was paralyzed on the right side, with a loss of speech and increasing difficulties in breathing. It was disingenuous to talk about "the *temporary* withdrawal of Comrade Stalin from the leadership of the Party and the state. . . ." He died at Kuntsevo the next evening.

There was one petty but significant lie in the announcement about Stalin's illness and death. The communiqué spoke of his being stricken in his "Moscow apartment," but he actually died in his suburban villa. There was an obvious reason behind the falsehood: his successors feared that a true statement about where he was at the time of the seizure would lead to rumors that in fact he had not been at the Kremlin for some time, and/or that the stroke had occurred while he was being kidnaped or incarcerated by the oligarchs. Crowds might surge on the Kremlin, demanding an accounting of what was being done to their father and protector.

And indeed the great illusion-maker would have been pleased by the public reaction to his death. Many, even some in concentration camps, wept when they heard the news. A man as intelligent and knowledge-able as Ilya Ehrenburg confesses that he "felt alarm: what would happen? I feared the worst."[52] For the last time he had fooled them, even more than might have been expected. ☆☆☆

66 WHAT can you put differently? What can you add? Such things did really happen on this our earth."[53] Some things will be added: as years pass, the archives will yield additional secrets. That is, assuming that Russia's present leaders, who believe that Khrushchev babbled too much, have not managed to destroy most of the evidence in their effort

[51] K. P. S. Menon, *The Flying Troika* (London, 1963), p. 29.
[52] Ilya Ehrenburg, *The Post-War Years, 1945–1954* (Cleveland and New York, 1967), p. 301.
[53] Tvardovsky, p. 9.

to preserve Stalin's image as that of neither beast nor god, but of "an outstanding Party leader who committed some mistakes." And many who might have told some interesting tales—Yezhov, Beria, Ryumin, Poskrebyshev—are not, alas, available for interviews.

But do we need any sensational revelations to understand Stalin? No, the explanation of his life is as banal as many of Stalin's own speeches: he was corrupted by absolute power. Absolute power turned a ruthless politician—but within the Soviet context not unusually ruthless—into a monstrous tyrant. And faith in the creed of Marxism-Leninism endowed him with a sense of his historic mission and enabled him to stifle any scruples and inhibitions in protecting that power. Dictatorship yielded to tyranny when the anxieties of middle age were added to the burden of power. And in the old man fear finally eroded both the politician and the diplomat: power was no longer an object of ambition or enjoyment; it was a desperate means of clinging to life. When power began to slip from his "relentless grip," he died.

"Great Lenin was not a god nor did he teach us to make gods."[54] But Lenin's legacy was "objective reality." The real world was to be seen through the prism of the "class struggle," the "capitalist contradictions in the countryside," the "capitalist encirclement." Stalin took the half-truths and half-myths of the dogma and turned them into palpable reality in the lives of millions.

When led to his execution, Assistant Commissar Livshitz, a victim of the Great Purge, kept repeating, "Why?" For more than twenty years now, this question has been asked by many in the Soviet Union and elsewhere. We can give an answer: Livshitz and countless others died and suffered for none of the usual reasons, and not even because of someone's criminality, as the term is usually understood. They died so that life should prove the truth of dogma. Life must not be allowed to appear a placid affair, with myriads pursuing their humdrum activities, with real treason and sabotage only extraordinary and rare occurrences. Life must be seen as a constant struggle between forces of light and darkness. To deny this struggle would have been to strip Communism of all its uplifting meaning, to make it a dry business of charts and administration, a philosophy that called for bureaucrats and experts, and not leaders and heroes.

Stalin—a restless, rebellious man—sensed this universal religious-existentialist craving in human nature because he felt it so acutely himself. And that is why he was able to build a system of terror and a structure of personal power unprecedented in modern history. The terror was necessary, not only to keep men obedient, but even more to make them believe. Without terror, who would have failed to notice the

[54] *Ibid.*, p. 11.

patent absurdity of Stalin's rule—the whole Soviet nation and many in foreign parts prostrating themselves before one man; platitudes being worshiped as sublime wisdom; so many people ready to accept a vision of the world in which a Witches' Sabbath of "traitors," "wreckers," and "murderer doctors" is continuous. Even those who recoiled in horror asked "Why?" when they should have said, "Not only is this evil, but it does not make any sense."

The man who contrived this world has been dead for more than twenty years. His reputation has been assailed, his body removed from the Mausoleum, where it rested next to Lenin's. But in spirit Soviet Russia of today is still much more Stalin's than Lenin's. It is only when the Soviet people are able to look at their recent past and recognize it for what it really was—tragic and heroic, certainly, but also and in many ways preposterous—that the spell will be lifted and the Stalin era will finally have ended.

Index

Index

Djugashvili, Catherine Geladze, 17–18, 20, 21, 31
Djugashvili, Jacob, 82, 83, 124, 211n, 548–49, 613–14
Djugashvili, Joseph. *See* Stalin, Joseph
Djugashvili, Vissarion, 17–18, 89n, 111n,
dogma, Communist, 13, 294, 303, 740
Dostoevsky, Fyodor, 286
Drax, Sir Reginald, 510
drunkenness, 67n, 149n, 207, 306, 307, 391, 436, 482, 484, 487, 532, 548, 636, 647, 665, 676–77
Dubrovinsky, Joseph, 109n, 122
Duclos, Jacques, 661
Duma, 74, 80, 82, 86, 115, 140; Second, 86, 90, 96, 144; Third, 96; Fourth, 118, 121, 439–40; Bolsheviks in, 90–91, 95, 102, 118, 125; government formed by, 130, 131; socialist faction, 144; JS on, 77; and war issue, 125. *See also under* elections
Dzerzhinsky, Felix, 141, 158, 164, 187, 189, 235, 395; death, 283n, 419; and political police, 175, 203, 228, 235, 443; JS and, 179, 221, 222, 279

East Germany, 624, 687, 693, 720
Economic Problems of Socialism in the U.S.S.R. (Stalin), 729–31
"Economism," 42–43
Eden, Anthony, 400, 571, 589, 619
education, 22–23, 389–91; Commissariat of, 441, 713; Moscow trials as, 409
Ehrenburg, Ilya, 31, 197, 436, 439, 484, 487, 533–34, 616, 647, 673n, 681–82, 739
Eikhe, R., 423, 461
Einstein, Albert, 105, 646, 648
Eisenhower, Dwight D., 595, 636
Eisenstein, Sergei, 73, 436, 648, 673
elections, 77–80, 165, 296; Communist Party, 286, 374n; Duma, 78–79, 86, 89, 96, 118, 121; soviets, 151, 462–63, 502; "Stalin Constitution" on, 403, 437; trade union, 206; U.S., 687–88, 728. *See also* Central Committee
"Empiriomonism," 102
Engels, Frederick, 72, 102, 193, 202, 265, 269, 363, 378, 645; JS on, 271–272, 310, 637
espionage, 473, 528–29, 534, 556; charges of, 466, 583, 682, 726, 736, 737; death penalty, 381, 564n; intraparty, 107, 321, 661, 666; in Moscow trials, 410, 417; in Red Army, alleged, 455
Estonia, 183, 506, 511, 512, 516
exile, administrative, 67, 99–100, 109, 111, 116n, 122, 123, 124, 257, 582; under JS, 273, 313, 391, 460, 675. *See also under* Lenin; Siberia; Stalin

factionalism, 87–88, 201, 228, 232, 268, 315

Fadeyev, Alexander, 6, 424n, 647
Fascism, 363, 376, 399, 401, 403, 404, 413, 558; diplomacy of, 525; in Spain, 420, 427, 467; U.S.S.R. and, 468, 518, 533–34
February Revolution, 16, 29, 55, 75, 126, 129–36, 156, 174
Fierlinger, Zdenek, 609
Finland, 62, 78, 86, 88, 96, 116, 141, 151, 166, 182, 183, 598, 632, 662; German invasion, 525, 527, 531; Soviet attack, 457, 519, 521–22, 668
Fish, Hamilton, 368
Five-Year Plans, 319; First, 293, 322–23, 324, 336, 337, 339, 342, 409, 421; Second, 353, 379, 617; Third, 617
food supply, 248, 298, 342; shortages, 139, 143, 151, 312, 314, 317, 336, 344–45, 405, 409
foreign aid, 196, 368, 561, 642, 655; to China, 696, 697, 729n
foreign investment, 265, 292
Forrestal, James, 641
Fotyeva, Lydia, 25, 219, 223
France, 127, 189, 250, 263, 272, 281, 336, 363, 376, 377, 382, 449, 522, 606; Communist Party, 264, 402, 425, 472, 517–18, 601, 648, 657–58, 660–661, 670, 686, 691, 733; fall, 518, 524; military mission to U.S.S.R., 510–11; treaties with, 364, 400, 404, 405, 406, 467, 600–601; in WWI, 163, 177, 479; in WWII, 399, 494, 496–98, 505–508, 513–23 *passim*, 560, 589
French Revolution, 271, 273, 392
Frinovsky, Michael, 489
Frumkin, Michael, 304, 312
Frunze, Michael, 247, 259–60, 449, 484

Gamarnik, Yan, 452, 453, 456
Gandhi, Mohandas K., 362
Gapon, George, 67–68, 72
Genet, Jean, 646
genocide, 347n, 551
Georgia, 19, 22–23, 27–28, 35, 39, 47, 68–71, 73, 74, 79, 170, 177, 194, 195, 220, 227, 526, 528, 716; Communist Party, 18, 220, 221; Menshevik faction, 55, 57–58, 63–64, 69, 70–71, 78, 79, 80, 88–89, 132, 177, 192, 193, 194, 195; Soviet rule, 214, 220–21, 222, 227, 631, 727; JS as native, 16, 17, 18–19, 338n, 487, 535, 679
Germany, 56, 60, 83, 125n, 127, 194, 202, 244, 258, 264, 265, 267, 277, 292, 302n, 352n, 382, 420, 426, 450, 467, 619; collaboration with, 377–78, 422, 423, 439, 449, 574; Communist Party, 225, 229, 264, 363, 377, 471, 686; invasion of U.S.S.R., 12, 166, 424n, 536–41, 551–61, 566–67, 572, 575; Lenin in, 139, 166; Nazi, 13, 317, 329, 363, 365, 373n, 376, 377, 378, 584; negotiations with, 507–508,

747

Index

Index

Kremlin Doctors' Plot, 684, 700, 724–725, 736–37
Krestinsky, Nikolai, 180, 478, 482n, 496
Kronstadt, mutiny at, 145, 148, 149n, 189, 228
Kropotkin, Prince Peter, 127
Krupskaya, Nadezhda, 118, 138n, 235, 316, 390; Lenin and, 54, 60n, 82, 218n, 219, 222, 232, 251–52, 267; in power struggle, 239, 251–53, 254, 267; JS and, 119, 219, 222–23, 269; Trotsky and, 245, 278
Krylov, Nicholas, 575
Kshesinskaya (ballerina), 133, 145
Kuibyshev, Valerian, 208, 309, 320, 391, 481, 483, 484
kulaks, 248–52, 258, 266, 354, 365, 433, 573; campaign against, 298–99, 322, 324–27, 329, 330, 332, 333, 343–44, 346, 408, 422, 474, 678, 685; NEP and, 263, 294; policy of JS, 295–96, 300; supporters of, 336–37; Trotsky and, 267, 271, 284, 292, 308
Kun, Béla, 472
Kuomintang, 274, 275–77, 279, 280, 469, 690, 692, 694, 722
Kurchatov, Igor, 625
Kurile Islands, 607, 628–29
Kurnatovsky, Victor, 39, 47
Kutuzov, M. I., 490, 557, 637, 692; Order of, 577
Kuusinen, Otto, 521, 522, 734
Kuznetsov, Alexis, 635, 706, 710, 712, 713, 726
Kuznetsov, Nicholas, 489, 519, 529, 540, 635, 702, 709, 732n, 734
Kuznetsov, V. V., 735

labor: convict, 418; exploitation, 249–50; forced, 11n, 322, 351–52, 391; nationalization, 309; turnover, 34
labor camps, 11n, 190, 351, 391, 426, 443, 445n, 518, 552, 731; numbers sent to, 460, 486, 487; sentencing to, 458, 583, 616, 679. See also jail institutes
labor movement, 34, 35, 97, 257, 267, 315; police agents in, 66–67, 72; U.S., 367. See also strikes; trade unions
Landau, Lev, 439, 443
land reform, 69, 80–81, 86, 143, 157, 248, 250n, 323n; Lenin on, 81, 138, 140, 291
Lange, Oscar, 591
Lashevich (Zinoviev associate), 266, 267, 280
Latsis, M., 174–75
Latvia, 91, 95, 120, 381, 382, 495, 506, 507, 511, 512, 516
Laval, Pierre, 401–402
League of Nations, 404, 581
"Left Oppositionism," 316, 348, 410, 418
Left Socialist Revolutionaries, 151, 155, 161, 166, 174, 230n, 470

"left-wing deviationism," 313, 334
Lend-Lease, 581, 621
Lenin, V. I., 21, 25, 29, 36, 37, 51–54, 60n, 125, 131, 173n, 196, 259, 265, 266, 740n; attempted assassination of, 174; authoritarianism, 160, 173–74, 217; and Brest-Litovsk treaty, 469; and capitalist visitors, 358; character, 159, 217; claims of infallibility, 237, 242; cult of, 10, 233, 238, 239, 393; death, 6, 232, 448, 484; as diplomat, 166, 184; disguises, 79, 152; and Duma, 78, 90; exile, 47, 88, 96, 124, 128, 131, 132, 133–34, 472; and expropriations, 93; followers, 101, 405, 407; funeral, 234–35; as German agent, alleged, 146, 166, 167, 472; harshness and insubordination of JS toward, 189, 190n, 213–14, 227, 435; hope for Communist Germany, 363; hypochondria, 260n; illness, 202, 205, 209, 210–11, 215, 221, 223; internationalist phase, 361; invocation of by JS, 315, 318, 319; invoked in military planning, 593; Krasin and, 59, 95, 179; last years, 197, 199, 213–219, 731; letter to JS, 222–23; and Marxist philosophy, 102–103; Mausoleum, 5, 6, 8, 9, 348, 409, 614; and Menshevik-Bolshevik split, 50–51, 54–55, 57, 88; on Molotov, 307n; Old Guard of, 285; posthumous jealousy of JS toward, 159, 704; opinions of JS on, 78, 100, 233, 637–38; opponents, 106–109, 198–99, 203, 205, 207, 208, 228, 230, 244, 247; as People's Commissar, 157; personal intervention by, 207; plot to kill, alleged, 481–82; and police, 87; and Polish offensive, 186, 187, 188–89; political genius, 178; in Politburo, 152; popularity, 209; "reminiscences" of JS on, 238; return from exile, 77, 138; as revolutionary leader, 139, 143, 161, 261–62, 279; in revolutionary underground, 146–47, 152, 672, 673; in Soviet historiography, 12, 13; and career of JS, 16–17, 39, 49, 71, 104–105, 111–12, 117–18, 124, 148, 170, 171, 187, 202; support of JS, 9, 103, 119, 183–84, 434; support of by JS, 80, 108, 139, 153, 181, 182, 200, 204–205; struggle with JS, 189, 190n, 213, 219-20, 231; succession to, 236; as ward of Politburo, 216–17, 395, 396, 635; writings, 29n, 41n, 104, 169, 271, 272, 275. See also Central Committee; Krupskaya; Leninism; Malinovsky, A.; Menshevik faction; Politburo; Testament; Trotsky
Leningrad, 172, 521, 656; Communist Party, 254, 255, 375, 380, 386, 505, 644–45, 710, 738; Kirov in, 379–80, 383; Military Council, 547–48; Molotov in, 256; naming, 138, 168; oppositionists in, 284–85, 375; purges,

Index

Index

Index